"The ministry of John MacArthur has had a worldwide impact. MacArthur and Mayhue clearly unfold the doctrines that are at the heart of this ministry, which has touched so many. Here we see a ministry built on truth, the truth of God's Word and the truth of the gospel. A wonderful resource for students, pastors, and professors."

Thomas R. Schreiner, James Buchanan Harrison Professor of New Testament Interpretation and Professor of Biblical Theology, The Southern Baptist Theological Seminary, Louisville, Kentucky

"This book comes from a lifetime of studying and from the garnered wisdom of centuries. In combining devotion to Scripture with commitment to biblical doctrine, it addresses a great contemporary need. Strong beliefs make strong churches. One does not have to agree with the esteemed authors on every subject to be thankful for a volume of rich and enduring importance."

Iain H. Murray, author, *Jonathan Edwards: A New Biography* and *Evangelical Holiness*; Founding Trustee, Banner of Truth Trust

"This new resource is a rich and compelling presentation of Christianity's theological foundations, providing readers with an accessible but compelling systematization of biblical truth. As the last vestiges of Christian influence erode in the West, rich theological resources like *Biblical Doctrine* will edify and strengthen the church as it faces stiff opposition from the world."

R. Albert Mohler Jr., President and Joseph Emerson Brown Professor of Christian Theology, The Southern Baptist Theological Seminary

"It is a delight to wholeheartedly recommend John MacArthur and Richard Mayhue's *Biblical Doctrine*. It will be celebrated for the clarity of its outline and description of the Bible's doctrines. It is just too good to miss."

Walter C. Kaiser Jr., President Emeritus and Colman M. Mockler Distinguished Professor Emeritus of Old Testament, Gordon-Conwell Theological Seminary

"The emphasis of John MacArthur's ministry has always been preaching—unleashing God's truth by preaching God's Word. All the while, his ministry has been undergirded by doctrine— doctrine drawn carefully, consistently from the Bible. His thousands of expository sermons stand as proof of his faithfulness to the work of the preacher; *Biblical Doctrine* stands as proof of faithfulness to the work of the theologian. May both be used to encourage a new generation of preacher-theologians to commit their lives to the high calling of teaching and equipping Christ's church."

Tim Challies, blogger, Challies.com

"Clarity ought to be an essential requirement of books on systematic theology. And this one offers just that! A comprehensive summary of all that a Christian needs to know—sounds like something every Christian should have available, doesn't it? And written by a name that epitomizes orthodoxy and truth—John MacArthur. Enough said. It speaks for itself."

Derek W. H. Thomas, Senior Minister, First Presbyterian Church, Columbia, South Carolina; Robert Strong Professor of Systematic and Pastoral Theology, Reformed Theological Seminary–Atlanta; Dean of Doctor of Ministry Program, Ligonier Academy

"This volume is the life achievement of almost fifty years of preaching in one pulpit by this world-class expositor, John MacArthur. He has stood, week after week, even decade after decade, plumbing the depths of the biblical text and connecting its truths together, leading to this well-constructed body of divinity. Here is the crown jewel from this brilliant pastor and author that will cause the truth of Scripture to shine even brighter before our eyes."

Steven J. Lawson, Director of Doctor of Ministry Program and Professor of Preaching, The Master's Seminary; President and Founder, OnePassion Ministries; author, *The Kind of Preaching God Blesses* and *The Heroic Boldness of Martin Luther*

"For decades John MacArthur has exemplified expository preaching, putting on full display the Word of God for the people of God. Now MacArthur, teaming up with Richard Mayhue and the Master's Seminary faculty, has written a systematic theology, demonstrating how his verse-by-verse exposition naturally blossoms into a robust, colorful theological mosaic. This book is the theological dessert at the end of an expository meal. Regardless of your theological heritage, I encourage every Christian to sit under the doctrinal teaching of MacArthur and Mayhue. Certainly, you will walk away saturated in Scripture, left in total awe after relishing the majesty and glory of our gracious God."

Matthew Barrett, Tutor of Systematic Theology and Church History, Oak Hill Theological College

"In addition to presenting orthodox theology common to historic Protestants, MacArthur and Mayhue defend an unusual combination of views that evangelicals debate, such as young-earth creationism, Calvinist soteriology, credobaptism, elder-rule polity, complementarianism, cessationism, and traditional dispensationalism (or what they call futuristic premillennialism). They argue in a clear and orderly way that is worth engaging even if you disagree."

Andrew David Naselli, Assistant Professor of New Testament and Biblical Theology, Bethlehem College & Seminary, Minneapolis, Minnesota

"As a professor of theology, I am able to recommend this single volume on systematic theology by MacArthur and Mayhue to my students and tell them with confidence that this is a book I can endorse from cover to cover. I especially appreciate the dispensational aspects of this work and the way the authors consistently and firmly ground the doctrines in the biblical text."

Kevin D. Zuber, Professor of Theology, Moody Bible Institute, Chicago, Illinois; contributor to *Evidence for the Rapture: A Biblical Case for Pretribulationism* and *The Moody Bible Commentary*

Biblical Doctrine

Biblical Doctrine

A Systematic Summary of Bible Truth

John MacArthur and Richard Mayhue

GENERAL EDITORS

WHEATON, ILLINOIS

Biblical Doctrine: A Systematic Summary of Bible Truth

Copyright © 2017 by John MacArthur and Richard Mayhue

Published by Crossway
        1300 Crescent Street
        Wheaton, Illinois 60187

Some material in the book is adapted from the following publications by permission of Thomas Nelson, www.thomasnelson.com: John MacArthur, *The MacArthur Bible Commentary: Unleashing God's Truth, One Verse at a Time*, copyright © 2005 (in chap. 4); John MacArthur, *The MacArthur Daily Bible: New King James Version*, copyright © 2003 (in chap. 5); John F. MacArthur Jr., *The Murder of Jesus: A Study of How Jesus Died*, copyright © 2004 (in chap. 4); John MacArthur, *Slave: The Hidden Truth about Your Identity in Christ*, copyright © 2010 (in chap. 7); John MacArthur, *The Vanishing Conscience: Drawing the Line in a No-Fault, Guilt-Free World*, copyright © 1994 (in chap. 6). Material throughout the volume that is adapted from John MacArthur, ed., *The MacArthur Study Bible: English Standard Version* (Wheaton, IL: Crossway, 2010), is drawn from charts and notes that originate with *The MacArthur Study Bible*, copyright © 1997 by Thomas Nelson, and is used by permission of Thomas Nelson.

Permission to use additional material adapted from other publications is noted in the footnotes throughout the volume.

Cover design: Tim Green

Cover image: Kovalto1, Shutterstock.com

First printing 2017

Printed in the United States of America

Unless otherwise indicated, Scripture quotations are from the ESV® Bible (The Holy Bible, English Standard Version®), copyright © 2001 by Crossway, a publishing ministry of Good News Publishers. Used by permission. All rights reserved.

Scripture quotations marked HCSB have been taken from *The Holman Christian Standard Bible*®. Copyright © 1999, 2000, 2002, 2003 by Holman Bible Publishers. Used by permission.

Scripture quotations marked KJV are from the *King James Version* of the Bible.

Scripture quotations marked NASB are from *The New American Standard Bible*®. Copyright © The Lockman Foundation 1960, 1962, 1963, 1968, 1971, 1972, 1973, 1975, 1977, 1995. Used by permission.

Scripture references marked NIV are taken from The Holy Bible, New International Version®, NIV®. Copyright © 1973, 1978, 1984, 2011 by Biblica, Inc.™ Used by permission. All rights reserved worldwide.

Scripture references marked NKJV are from *The New King James Version*. Copyright © 1982, Thomas Nelson, Inc. Used by permission.

Scripture references marked RSV are from the Revised Standard Version of the Bible, copyright ©1952 (2nd edition, 1971) by the Division of Christian Education of the National Council of the Churches of Christ in the United States of America. Used by permission. All rights reserved.

Hardcover ISBN: 978-1-4335-4591-7
ePub ISBN: 978-1-4335-4594-8
PDF ISBN: 978-1-4335-4592-4
Mobipocket ISBN: 978-1-4335-4593-1

Library of Congress Cataloging-in-Publication Data

Names: MacArthur, John, 1939– editor.
Title: Biblical doctrine : a systematic summary of Bible truth / John MacArthur and Richard Mayhue, general editors.
Description: Wheaton : Crossway, 2017. | Includes bibliographical references and index.
Identifiers: LCCN 2016011479 (print) | LCCN 2016015096 (ebook) | ISBN 9781433545917 (hc) | ISBN 9781433545948 (epub) | ISBN 9781433545924 (pdf) | ISBN 9781433545931 (mobi)
Subjects: LCSH: Theology, Doctrinal.
Classification: LCC BT75.3 .B53 2017 (print) | LCC BT75.3 (ebook) | DDC 230/.041—dc23
LC record available at https://lccn.loc.gov/2016011479

Crossway is a publishing ministry of Good News Publishers.

SH   31   30   29   28   27   26   25   24   23   22   21
17   16   15   14   13   12   11   10   9   8   7   6   5

To all the faithful graduates of the Master's Seminary
who are serving Christ around the globe.

"Praise to the Lord, the Almighty"[1]

Praise to the Lord, the Almighty, the King of creation!
O my soul, praise Him, for He is thy health and salvation!
All ye who hear,
Now to His temple draw near;
Join me in glad adoration!

Praise to the Lord, who o'er all things so wondrously reigneth,
Shelters thee under His wings, yea, so gently sustaineth!
Hast thou not seen
How thy desires all have been
Granted in what He ordaineth?

Praise to the Lord, who doth prosper thy work and defend thee;
Surely His goodness and mercy here daily attend thee.
Ponder anew
What the Almighty can do
If with His love He befriend thee.

Praise to the Lord! O let all that is in me adore Him!
All that hath life and breath, come now with praises before Him!
Let the "amen"
Sound from His people again;
Gladly forever adore Him! Amen.

~Joachim Neander (1650–1680)

---

1. All hymns quoted in this volume are in the public domain.

Contents

Analytical Outline

List of Hymns

List of Tables

Preface

Professor Eugene Merrill has admonished his students that a biblically derived theology is "an old man's game." He explains,

> By this I mean it presupposes so many other disciplines and so much accumulation of knowledge that few scholars are prepared to undertake the task unless they have invested long, hard years in preparation of its accomplishment.[1]

We concur with his sage advice and have waited until the "evening hours" of our own lives to undertake this theology volume.

The following qualities shape the overall design and formation of *Biblical Doctrine*:

1. *Biblical* in content with a view to the progress of scriptural revelation
2. *Exegetical* in methodology because the meaning of Scripture is extracted from texts in the Bible
3. *Systematic* in presentation by focusing on an orderly synthesis of all that Scripture teaches on each area of doctrine
4. *Comprehensive* in breadth by evenly covering the major elements of systematic theology
5. *Pastoral* in application with expository preaching and holy living in view
6. *Practical* in its affordability, portability, and utility

Five interpretive principles guided our explanation of biblical revelation and doctrine:[2]

1. *The literal principle.* Scripture should be understood in its literal, natural, and normal sense. While the Bible does contain figures of speech and symbols, they are intended to convey literal truth. In general, however, the Bible speaks in literal terms and must be allowed to speak for itself.
2. *The historical principle.* A passage should be interpreted in its historical context. What the author intended and what the text meant to its first audience must

---

1. Eugene H. Merrill, *Everlasting Dominion: A Theology of the Old Testament* (Nashville: Broadman, 2006), xv.
2. The first four principles are drawn from John MacArthur, ed., *The MacArthur Study Bible: English Standard Version* (Wheaton, IL: Crossway, 2010), xxx. Charts and notes from *The MacArthur Study Bible: English Standard Version* originate with *The MacArthur Study Bible*, copyright © 1997 by Thomas Nelson. Used by permission of Thomas Nelson. www.thomasnelson.com.

be taken into account. In this way, a proper, contextual understanding of the original meaning of Scripture can be grasped and articulated.

3. *The grammatical principle.* This task requires an understanding of the basic grammatical structure of each sentence in the original languages. To whom do the pronouns refer? What is the tense of the main verb? By asking simple questions like these, the meaning of the text becomes clearer.

4. *The synthetic principle.* This principle, the *analogia scriptura*, means that Scripture is to be its own interpreter.[3] It assumes that the Bible does not contradict itself. Thus, if an understanding of a passage conflicts with a truth taught elsewhere in the Scriptures, that interpretation cannot be correct. Scripture must be compared with Scripture to discover its accurate and full meaning.

5. *The clarity principle.* God intended Scripture to be understood. However, not every portion of the Bible is equally clear. Therefore, clearer portions should be employed to interpret the less clear.

While many would label us *fundamentalists*, this term can be historically and pejoratively misleading. For almost four decades, we have periodically considered what one word would best describe us. *Futurists*, *normalists*, and *sovereigntists* have been considered but set aside because none of these adequately capture the one, most essential element of our theology. While not a perfect term, we have chosen *biblicists*, because at the core of our convictions lies an unshakable trust in God's inerrant and infallible Bible, rightly interpreted.

This volume is marked by the following noteworthy distinctives:[4]

1. A presuppositional approach to Scripture that affirms (1) the eternal existence of almighty God and (2) his progressive, written revelation collected in the sixty-six-book canon of Scripture, which is inerrant and infallible in the autographs
2. An affirmation of recent creationism, that is, a young earth and a global flood
3. An emphasis on covenants that are biblically derived, not theologically constructed
4. A soteriology that reflects God's sovereignty in the redemption of sinners
5. A belief in the cessation of all miraculous sign gifts at the completion of the biblical canon, which is concurrent with the end of the apostolic era
6. A biblically based understanding of the New Testament church
7. A complementarian approach to the roles of men and women in the home and in the church
8. A futuristic premillennial understanding of eschatology according to God's sovereign plan for the whole world, including Israel

Additionally, a substantial reservoir of bibliographic references will enable readers to expand their studies beyond this volume.

Biblical Doctrine's design has multiple audiences in mind:

---

3. R. C. Sproul, "Biblical Interpretation and the Analogy of Faith," in *Inerrancy and Common Sense*, ed. Roger R. Nicole and J. Ramsey Michaels (Grand Rapids, MI: Baker, 1980), 119–35.

4. *Biblical Doctrine* contains a distinct combination of features. These hallmarks generally follow in the footsteps of notable men like Allan A. MacRae (1902–1997), James Montgomery Boice (1938–2000), and S. Lewis Johnson (1915–2004).

1. Seminary, college, and Bible institute instructors
2. Seminary, college, and Bible institute students
3. National and international preachers[5]
4. Local church teachers
5. Lay people who want to understand Scripture in its entirety

All theologies should begin with biblical content arranged systematically that then leads to Christians being motivated to live holy lives of obedience to God's Word for the glory of God (1 Cor. 10:31; Col. 4:17; 1 Pet. 4:11). To this end, *Biblical Doctrine* goes forth with our hope that it will

> extend one's biblical knowledge, which will . . .
> enable one's sound understanding of doctrine, which will . . .
> enrich one's divine wisdom, which will . . .
> expand one's Christlike obedience, which will . . .
> elevate one's holy worship.[6]

The value of this volume will be enhanced by the complementary use of (1) the *MacArthur Study Bible* (ESV, NASB, NIV, and NKJV versions), (2) the *MacArthur Topical Bible*, and (3) the *MacArthur New Testament Commentary* series. A mini-library consisting of these four study tools will basically equip one to be a student of Scripture for a lifetime (2 Tim. 2:15).

A work of this magnitude comes about only as a result of significant involvement by many people. We greatly appreciate the vision and encouragement for *Biblical Doctrine* from Crossway, especially Dr. Lane Dennis (president), Dr. Justin Taylor (executive vice president of book publishing), Dave DeWit (vice president of book publishing), Dr. David Barshinger (editor, book division), and Jill Carter (editorial administrator). Our thanks go to the Master's University and Seminary board members who generously encouraged and prayed for this project. Our Master's Seminary colleagues Dr. Bill Barrick, Dr. Nathan Busenitz, Dr. Jim Mook, Dr. Bryan Murphy, Dr. Michael Vlach, and Professor Michael Riccardi supported us by producing drafts of several sections. Special thanks go to Jeremy Smith for his consultation. We express deep gratitude to Michael Riccardi and Nathan Busenitz for their comprehensive final edit of the entire volume. Janice Osborne cheerfully prepared innumerable drafts up to and including the final one presented to the publisher.

We offer this material with the prayer that

> the God of our Lord Jesus Christ, the Father of glory, may give you the Spirit of wisdom and of revelation in the knowledge of him, having the eyes of your hearts enlightened, that you may know what is the hope to which he has called

---

5. R. Albert Mohler Jr., "The Pastor as Theologian," in *A Theology for the Church*, ed. Daniel L. Akin (Nashville: B&H Academic, 2007), 927–34; John Murray, "Calvin as Theologian and Expositor," in *The Collected Writings of John Murray* (Edinburgh: Banner of Truth, 1976), 1:305–11.

6. "The goal of theology is the worship of God. The posture of theology is on one's knees. The mode of theology is repentance." Sinclair B. Ferguson, quoted in James Montgomery Boice and Philip Graham Ryken, *The Doctrines of Grace* (Wheaton, IL: Crossway, 2002), 179.

you, what are the riches of his glorious inheritance in the saints, and what is the immeasurable greatness of his power toward us who believe, according to the working of his great might. (Eph. 1:17–19)

John MacArthur, DD, LittD
Pastor, Grace Community Church
President, The Master's University and Seminary

Richard Mayhue, ThD
Executive Vice President, Dean,
and Research Professor of Theology Emeritus
The Master's Seminary

Abbreviations

Standard Abbreviations

AD	*anno Domini*, Latin for "in the year of our Lord"
BC	before Christ
ca.	about, approximately
cf.	compare
chap.	chapter
e.g.	*exempli gratia*, Latin for "for example"
esp.	especially
Gk.	Greek
Heb.	Hebrew
i.e.	*id est*, Latin for "that is"
Lat.	Latin
lit.	literally
p.	page
v., vv.	verse(s)

Resource Abbreviations

BECNT	Baker Exegetical Commentary on the New Testament
BETS	*Bulletin of the Evangelical Theological Society*
BSac	*Bibliotheca Sacra*
CTR	*Criswell Theological Review*
EEC	Evangelical Exegetical Commentary
ICC	International Critical Commentary
JETS	*Journal of the Evangelical Theological Society*
JTS	*Journal of Theological Studies*
MNTC	MacArthur New Testament Commentary
MSJ	*The Master's Seminary Journal*
NAC	New American Commentary
NICNT	New International Commentary on the New Testament
NICOT	New International Commentary on the Old Testament
NIGTC	New International Greek Testament Commentary
NTC	New Testament Commentary
PNTC	Pillar New Testament Commentary
RevExp	*Review and Expositor*
SNTSMS	Society for New Testament Studies Monograph Series
TJ	*Trinity Journal*
WTJ	*Westminster Theological Journal*

Bible Book Abbreviations

The Old Testament		The New Testament	
Gen.	Genesis	Matt.	Matthew
Ex.	Exodus	Mark	Mark
Lev.	Leviticus	Luke	Luke
Num.	Numbers	John	John
Deut.	Deuteronomy	Acts	Acts
Josh.	Joshua	Rom.	Romans
Judg.	Judges	1 Cor.	1 Corinthians
Ruth	Ruth	2 Cor.	2 Corinthians
1 Sam.	1 Samuel	Gal.	Galatians
2 Sam.	2 Samuel	Eph.	Ephesians
1 Kings	1 Kings	Phil.	Philippians
2 Kings	2 Kings	Col.	Colossians
1 Chron.	1 Chronicles	1 Thess.	1 Thessalonians
2 Chron.	2 Chronicles	2 Thess.	2 Thessalonians
Ezra	Ezra	1 Tim.	1 Timothy
Neh.	Nehemiah	2 Tim.	2 Timothy
Est.	Esther	Titus	Titus
Job	Job	Philem.	Philemon
Ps., Pss.	Psalm, Psalms	Heb.	Hebrews
Prov.	Proverbs	James	James
Eccles.	Ecclesiastes	1 Pet.	1 Peter
Song	Song of Solomon	2 Pet.	2 Peter
Isa.	Isaiah	1 John	1 John
Jer.	Jeremiah	2 John	2 John
Lam.	Lamentations	3 John	3 John
Ezek.	Ezekiel	Jude	Jude
Dan.	Daniel	Rev.	Revelation
Hos.	Hosea		
Joel	Joel		
Amos	Amos		
Obad.	Obadiah		
Jonah	Jonah		
Mic.	Micah		
Nah.	Nahum		
Hab.	Habakkuk		
Zeph.	Zephaniah		
Hag.	Haggai		
Zech.	Zechariah		
Mal.	Malachi		

"Amazing Grace"

Amazing grace! How sweet the sound
That saved a wretch like me!
I once was lost but now am found;
Was blind, but now I see.

'Twas grace that taught my heart to fear,
And grace my fears relieved.
How precious did that grace appear
The hour I first believed.

The Lord has promised good to me;
His Word my hope secures.
He will my shield and portion be
As long as life endures.

Thro' many dangers, toils and snares
I have already come.
'Tis grace hath brought me safe thus far,
And grace will lead me home.

When we've been there ten thousand years,
Bright shining as the sun,
We've no less days to sing God's praise
Than when we'd first begun.

~John Newton (1725–1807)
stanza 5, John P. Rees (1828–1900)

1

Introduction

Prolegomena

Major Subjects Covered in Chapter 1

What Is Theology?

Why Study Theology?

What Are the Various Major Kinds of Theology?

What Is Systematic Theology?

What Are the Categories of Systematic Theology?

What Is the Relationship between Exegetical, Biblical, and Systematic Theology?

What Are the Benefits and Limitations of Systematic Theology?

What Is the Relationship of Systematic Theology to Doctrine?

What Is the Overarching and Unifying Theme of Scripture?

What Are the Major Motifs of Scripture?

How Does Systematic Theology Relate to One's Worldview?

How Does Systematic Theology Relate to One's Mind?

How Does Systematic Theology Relate to One's Personal Life?

How Does Systematic Theology Relate to One's Ministry?

The term *prolegomena* originated from the combination of two Greek words, *pro*, meaning "before," and *legō*, meaning "to say," which together convey the general sense of "to say beforehand or "to say in advance." A prolegomena chapter serves as a prologue or a preliminary discussion that introduces and defines the central content of the work that follows. These prefatory comments include assumptions, definitions, methodology, and purposes, thereby providing a context for understanding the subsequent content. Here the prolegomena discussion is organized by giving answers to a series of significant questions that will prepare the reader for the ensuing material, which constitutes the main body of *Biblical Doctrine*.

What Is Theology?

Theology—from the Greek *theos*, "god," and *logia*, "word"—is not a uniquely Christian word. The Greek verb *theologeō* refers to the act of speaking about a god, while the noun *theologos* refers to a person who engages in *theologeō*, that is, a *theologian*. The adjective *theologikos* describes something *theological*, while the noun *theologia* means "a word about god"—literally, *theology*. These words were used in pagan religious contexts centuries before the New Testament. None of these four words are found in the New Testament or the Septuagint. The earliest known Christian use of one of these terms is a reference to the apostle John as a *theologos* early in the second century AD.

Christian theology is the study of the divine revelation in the Bible. It has God as its perpetual centerpiece, God's Word as its source, and godliness as its aim. As Alva McClain puts it,

> Out of God all things come—He is the origin. Through God all things exist—He is the sustainer of all things. Unto God—back to God—He is the goal. There is the circle of eternity: *out, through, back*.[1]

David Wells has crafted a notable working definition of Christian theology:

> Theology is the sustained effort to know the character, will, and acts of the triune God as he has disclosed and interpreted these for his people in Scripture . . . in order that we might know him, learn to think our thoughts after him, live our lives in his world on his terms, and by thought and action project his truth into our own time and culture.[2]

The apostle John died in about AD 98. With his writing of Revelation, the canon of Scripture was completed and closed. It did not take long for succeeding generations to begin writing about scriptural truth. Some of the more significant authors and their volumes include the following:

- Unknown author, *The Didache* (ca. 110)
- Irenaeus (ca. 120–202), *Proof of the Apostolic Preaching*
- Clement of Alexandria (ca. 150–ca. 215), *Stromata*
- Origen (ca. 184–ca. 254), *On First Principles*
- Gregory of Nazianzus (ca. 330–ca. 389), *Five Theological Orations*
- Augustine (354–430), *Enchiridion*
- John of Damascus (ca. 675–ca. 749), *An Exact Exposition of the Orthodox Faith*

---

1. Alva J. McClain, *Romans: The Gospel of God's Grace* (Chicago: Moody Press, 1973), 204.
2. David Wells, "The Theologian's Craft," in *Doing Theology in Today's World: Essays in Honor of Kenneth S. Kantzer*, ed. John D. Woodbridge and Thomas Edward McComisky (Grand Rapids, MI: Zondervan, 1991), 172.

- Peter Lombard (ca. 1095–ca. 1169), *Four Books of Sentences*
- Thomas Aquinas (1225–1274), *Summa Theologica*
- John Calvin (1509–1564), *Institutes of the Christian Religion*
- Thomas Watson (ca. 1620–1686), *A Body of Divinity*
- Francis Turretin (1623–1687), *Institutes of Elenctic Theology*
- John Gill (1697–1771), *A Body of Doctrinal Divinity*
- John Dick (1764–1833), *Lectures on Theology*

Prominent theologies from the nineteenth, twentieth, and twenty-first centuries are listed in the bibliography at the end of this chapter.

Why Study Theology?

Scottish pastor and theologian John Dick answered this penetrating query with seven profound responses. A better and more succinct answer would be difficult to come by:[3]

1. "To ascertain the character of God in its aspect towards us"
2. "To contemplate the display of his attributes in his works and dispensations"
3. "To discover his designs toward man in his original and his present state"
4. "To know this mighty Being, as far as he may be known, [which] is the noblest aim of the human understanding"
5. "To learn our duty to him, the means of enjoying his favor, the hopes which we are authorized to entertain, and the wonderful expedient by which our fallen race is restored to purity and happiness"
6. "To love him, the most worthy exercise of our affections"
7. "To serve him, the most honourable and delightful purpose to which we can devote our time and talents"

What Are the Various Major Kinds of Theology?

1. *Biblical theology*: The organization of Scripture thematically by biblical chronology or by biblical author with respect to the progressive revelation of the Bible (properly a component of systematic theology)
2. *Dogmatic theology*: The organization of Scripture with an emphasis on favored or selected church creeds
3. *Exegetical theology*: The methodical organization of Scripture by dealing exegetically with individual texts of the Bible (properly a component of both biblical and systematic theology)
4. *Historical theology*: The historical study of doctrinal developments after the apostolic era to the present time
5. *Natural theology*: The study of what can be known about God by human reason alone through the empirical study of the natural world
6. *Pastoral/practical theology*: The organization of Scripture with an emphasis on the personal application of doctrinal truth in the lives of the church and individual Christians

---

3. John Dick, *Lectures on Theology* (Cincinnati, OH: Applegate, 1856), 6.

7. *Systematic theology*: The organization of Scripture by a synthesis of scriptural teaching, summarized using major categories that encompass the entirety of God's written revelation (developed from exegetical and biblical theology)

What Is Systematic Theology?

The term *systematic* comes from the compound Greek word made up of *syn*, "together," and *histanai*, "to set up," meaning "to set up together" or "to systematize." As noted above, *theology* comes from the Greek word *theologia*, "a word about god," meaning "theology." Etymologically, *systematic theology* involves the orderly bringing together of words about God or a bringing together of theology in an organized fashion. Consider Charles Spurgeon's response to those who object to a systematic approach to theology:

> Systematic theology is to the Bible what science is to nature. To suppose that all the other works of God are orderly and systematic, and the greater the work the more perfect the system: and that the greatest of all His works, in which all His perfections are transcendently displayed, should have no plan or system, is altogether absurd.[4]

Systematic theology answers the question, what does the completed canon of Scripture teach about any one theme or topic? For example, what does the Bible teach from Genesis to Revelation about the deity of Jesus Christ? A basic definition of systematic theology, then, would be "the ordered exposition of Christian doctrines."[5]

A systematic theology must display (1) hermeneutical integrity, (2) doctrinal coherence, (3) ethical relevance, (4) worldview explicability, and (5) traditional continuity. Where these are present and operative, one will find a good systematizing that will be of value to the expositor. As he carefully examines every detail of the text in preparation to expound it, systematic theology allows him to also view the whole theological picture—one that has taken into account not only the studied conclusions from church history but also the progress of revelation culminating in the complete revelation of God.[6] (For a chronological overview of the progress of revelation, see the appendix).

One's understanding of systematic theology could be framed by the following observations from John Murray:

> When we properly weigh the proposition that the Scriptures are the deposit of special revelation, that they are the oracles of God, that in them God encounters and addresses us, discloses to us his incomprehensible majesty, summons us to the knowledge and fulfillment of his will, unveils to us the mystery of his counsel, and unfolds the purposes of his grace, then systematic theology, of all sciences and disciplines, is seen to be the most noble, not one of cold, impass[ive] reflection but one that stirs adoring wonder and claims the most consecrated exercise of all our powers. It is the most noble of all studies because its province is the whole

---

4. Charles Spurgeon, as quoted in Iain H. Murray, *The Forgotten Spurgeon* (London: Banner of Truth, 1973), 9.
5. James L. Garrett, *Systematic Theology: Biblical, Historical, and Evangelical* (Grand Rapids, MI: Eerdmans, 1990), 1:8.
6. This insight came from our colleague Trevor Craigen, retired Master's Seminary professor of theology.

counsel of God and seeks, as no other discipline, to set forth the riches of God's revelation in the orderly and embracive manner which is its peculiar method and function. All other departments of theological discipline contribute their findings to systematic theology and it brings all the wealth of knowledge derived from these disciplines to bear upon the more inclusive systemization which it undertakes.[7]

Systematic theology aims to expound in a comprehensive and thematically organized fashion the biblical doctrines focused on the persons of the triune God, their purposes, and their plans in relationship to the world and humanity. It begins with informing the intellect (knowing and understanding). The intellect shapes what we believe and love in our heart. Our will desires what we love and repudiates what we hate. Our actions then accord with what we want most. The mind shapes the affections, which shape the will, which directs the actions. Theology is not fully finished until it has warmed the heart (affections) and prompted the volition (will) to act in obedience to its content.[8]

What Are the Categories of Systematic Theology?

1. *Bibliology*: The doctrine of the inspiration, inerrancy, authority, and canonicity of the Bible (Gk. *biblion*, "book")
2. *Theology proper*: The doctrine of the existence and being of God, including the triunity of God (Gk. *theos*, "God")
3. *Christology*: The doctrine of the person and work of the Lord Jesus Christ (Gk. *christos*, "Christ")
4. *Pneumatology*: The doctrine of the person and work of the Holy Spirit (Gk. *pneuma*, "Spirit")
5. *Anthropology*: The doctrine of humanity (Gk. *anthrōpos*, "man")
6. *Hamartiology*: The doctrine of sin (Gk. *hamartia*, "sin")
7. *Soteriology*: The doctrine of salvation (Gk. *sōtēria*, "salvation")
8. *Angelology*: The doctrine of holy angels, Satan, and fallen angels (Gk. *angelos*, "angel")
9. *Ecclesiology*: The doctrine of the church, universal and local (Gk. *ekklēsia*, "assembly" or "church")
10. *Eschatology*: The doctrine concerning the entire scope of biblical predictive prophecy, especially end-time events, including the destination for both saved and unsaved people, heaven and hell (Gk. *eschatos*, "last things")

What Is the Relationship between Exegetical, Biblical, and Systematic Theology?[9]

All biblical theology is systematic in nature; all systematic theology is biblical in content; and both biblical and systematic theology are exegetical in the interpretive

---

7. John Murray, "Systematic Theology," in *The Collected Writings of John Murray* (Edinburgh: Banner of Truth, 1982), 4:4.
8. William Ames observed that theology should have as its end *eupraxia*, lit., "good practice." *The Marrow of Theology*, trans. and ed. John Dykstra Eusden (1629; repr., Grand Rapids, MI: Baker, 1997), 78.
9. The following resources represent some of the clearest definitions, distinctions, and dependencies of the three theological emphases under discussion: Richard B. Gaffin Jr., "Systematic Theology and Biblical Theology," *WTJ* 38, no. 3 (1976): 281–99; Eugene Merrill, *Everlasting Dominion: A Theology of the Old Testament* (Nashville: Broadman, 2006), 1–27; Murray, "Systematic Theology," 4:1–21; Roger Nicole, "The Relationship between Biblical Theology and Systematic Theology," in *Evangelical Roots: A Tribute to Wilbur Smith*, ed. Kenneth S. Kantzer (Nashville: Thomas Nelson, 1978), 185–93; and Charles Caldwell Ryrie, *Biblical Theology of the New Testament* (Chicago: Moody Press, 1959), 11–24.

process. Therefore, the key question is not which one is the best approach to theology but rather, how do the three interrelate with each other?

To use a construction metaphor,

- exegetical theology supplies the building material for the foundation and structure;
- biblical theology provides the foundational support for the structure; and
- systematic theology serves as the structure built on the foundation.

Exegetical theology involves the methodical organization of Scripture by dealing exegetically with the individual texts of the Bible. This is properly an initial component of both biblical and systematic theology. As a result, every word, sentence, and paragraph of Scripture is examined in detail.

Biblical theology is characterized by the organization of Scripture thematically by biblical chronology or biblical author with respect to the progressive revelation of the Bible. This is properly a component of systematic theology. It serves as a bridge from exegetical theology to systematic theology.

Systematic theology is the organization of Scripture by a synthesis of scriptural teaching, summarized by major categories that encompass the entirety of God's written revelation. Systematic theology develops out of exegetical and biblical theology and pulls all the teaching of Scripture together as a whole. Again, Murray is helpful in making sense of these connections:

> Hence exposition of the Scripture is basic to systematic theology. Its task is not simply the exposition of particular passages. That is the task of exegesis. Systematics must coordinate the teaching of particular passages and systematize this teaching under the appropriate topics. There is thus a synthesis that belongs to systematics that does not belong to exegesis as such. But to the extent to which systematic theology synthesizes the teaching of Scripture, and this is its main purpose, it is apparent how dependent it is upon the science of exegesis. It cannot coordinate and relate the teaching of particular passages without knowing what the teaching is. So exegesis is basic to its objective. This needs to be emphasized. Systematic theology has gravely suffered, indeed has deserted its vocation, when it has been divorced from meticulous attention to biblical exegesis. This is one reason why the charge mentioned above has so much to yield support to the indictment. Systematics becomes lifeless and fails in its mandate just to the extent to which it has become detached from exegesis. And the guarantee against a stereotyped dogmatics is that systematic theology be constantly enriched, deepened, and expanded by the treasures increasingly drawn from the Word of God. Exegesis keeps systematics not only in direct contact with the Word but it ever imparts to systematics the power which is derived from that Word. The Word is living and powerful.[10]

One other approach to theology should be added. Historical theology examines how exegetical and theological convictions developed over time. It takes into

---

10. Murray, "Systematic Theology," 4:17.

consideration the conclusions reached by prior generations of godly interpreters of Scripture.

What Are the Benefits and Limitations of Systematic Theology?

Benefits
Limitations

All Scripture, whether examined exegetically in particular texts or categorically within the full scope of the Bible, is spiritually profitable to accomplish at least four divine purposes (2 Tim. 3:16):

1. For establishing "teaching" or doctrine, that is, God's inspired self-disclosure about himself, his created world, and his redemptive plan to save and sanctify sinners
2. For confrontation or "reproof" of sin, whether in the form of false teaching or disobedient living
3. For "correction" of error in thinking and behaving so that the repentant one can be restored to the place of pleasing God
4. For "instruction" so that believers can be habitually trained to practice the righteousness of the Lord Jesus Christ—sinning less and obeying more

Scripture provides the only complete, wholly accurate, and trustworthy teaching about God, and it will sufficiently accomplish these four things for equipping "the man of God" (2 Tim. 3:17).

Benefits

Systematic theology can provide several benefits:

1. An unabridged collection of biblical truth
2. An orderly synthesis and summation of biblical doctrine
3. An imperative to take the gospel to the ends of the earth
4. A repository of truth for expositional preaching and teaching
5. A scriptural basis for Christian behavior in the church, the home, and the world
6. A defense of biblical doctrine against false teaching
7. A biblical response to ethical and social malpractice in the world

As James Leo Garrett Jr. puts it,

> Systematic theology is beneficial as an extension of the teaching function of the churches, for the orderly and integrated formulation of biblical truths, for the undergirding of the preaching of preachers and lay Christians, for the defense of gospel truth against error that has invaded the church, for the legitimation of the gospel before philosophy and culture, as the foundation for Christian personal and social ethics, and for more effective universal propagation of the gospel and interaction with adherents of non-Christian religions.[11]

---

11. James Leo Garrett Jr., "Why Systematic Theology?," *CTR* 3, no. 2 (1989): 281.

Limitations[12]

Systematic theology can be limited by the following factors:

1. The silence of the Bible on a particular topic (Deut. 29:29; John 20:30; 21:25)
2. A theologian's partial knowledge/understanding of the entire Bible (Luke 24:25–27, 32; 2 Pet. 3:16)
3. The inadequacy of human language (1 Cor. 2:13–14; 2 Cor. 12:4)
4. The finiteness of the human mind (Job 11:7–12; 38:1–39:30; Rom. 11:33–35)
5. The lack of spiritual discernment/growth (1 Cor. 3:1–3; Heb. 5:11–13)

What Is the Relationship of Systematic Theology to Doctrine?

Doctrine represents teaching that is considered authoritative. When Christ taught, the crowds were amazed at his authority (Matt. 7:28–29; Mark 1:22, 27; Luke 4:32). A church's "doctrinal" statement contains a body of teaching used as the standard of authoritative orthodoxy.

In the Old Testament, the Hebrew word *laqakh* means "what is received" or "accepted teaching" (Deut. 32:2; Job 11:4; Prov. 4:2; Isa. 29:24). It can be variously translated as "instruction," "learning," or "teaching."

In the New Testament, two Greek words are translated as "doctrine," "instruction," or "teaching": *didachē* (referring to the content of teaching) and *didaskalia* (referring to the activity of teaching). Paul used both words together in 2 Timothy 4:2–3 and Titus 1:9.

In Latin, *docere*, "to teach," *doctrina*, "what is being taught," and *doctor*, "the one who is teaching," all contribute to the meaning of the English word *doctrine*. The content may be informational (to be believed) or practical (to be lived out). It does not necessarily refer to categorized truth.

Biblically speaking, the word *doctrine* is a rather amorphous term that only takes shape in context. It refers to general teaching (systematized or not, true or false), such as the "teaching of Balaam" (Rev. 2:14) or "human teachings" (Col. 2:22), in contrast to biblical teaching such as Christ's teaching (Matt. 7:28) or Paul's teaching (2 Tim. 3:10).

Biblical doctrine, therefore, refers to the teaching of Scripture, whether it be proclamational, expositional, or categorical. That makes all Scripture "doctrinal," whether it be read, taught, preached, or systematized into theological categories. Systematic biblical doctrine (systematic theology) refers to a categorical summation of biblical teaching that follows normally employed themes or categories.

A survey of Scripture shows that all doctrine or teaching can generally be classified into one of two categories depending on its source:

- with regard to origin—from God the Creator (John 7:16; Acts 13:12) or from God's creation (Col. 2:22; 1 Tim. 4:1)
- with regard to truth content (2 Thess. 2:11–12)—true or false
- with regard to human source (1 Thess. 2:13)—biblical or unbiblical
- with regard to quality (1 Tim. 1:10; 6:3)—sound or unsound

---

12. This material is adapted from Augustus Hopkins Strong, *Systematic Theology: A Compendium and Commonplace-Book Designed for the Use of Theological Students* (Old Tappan, NJ: Fleming H. Revell, 1907), 34–36 (public domain).

- with regard to acceptability (1 Tim. 1:3; Heb. 13:9)—familiar or strange
- with regard to retention (Rev. 2:24)—to hold or not to hold
- with regard to benefit (1 Tim. 4:6)—good or bad
- with regard to value (2 Tim. 3:16)—profitable or unprofitable

The modern theological use of the term *doctrine* is too narrow, distorts the primary biblical use of the term, and can be misleading. It is far better in discussing *doctrine* to use the term in its broader sense of "teaching" (which certainly includes systematized truth but is not limited to this use) rather than to use *doctrine* in its secondary sense as though this were the only sense. The teaching of Scripture serves as the yardstick, gauge, standard, paradigm, pattern, measure, and plumb line by which all other teaching on any given subject is determined to be true or false, received or rejected, sound or unsound, orthodox or heretical.

Sound biblical doctrine has many implications for the life of Christ's church:

1. Sound doctrine exposes and confronts sin and false doctrine (1 Tim. 1:8–11, esp. 1:10; 4:1–6).
2. Sound doctrine marks a good servant of Christ Jesus (1 Tim. 4:6; see also 1 Tim. 4:13, 16; Titus 2:1).
3. Sound doctrine is rewarded with double honor for elders (1 Tim. 5:17).
4. Sound doctrine conforms to godliness (1 Tim. 6:3; Titus 2:10).
5. Sound doctrine is included in the apostolic example to follow (2 Tim. 3:10).
6. Sound doctrine is essential to equipping pastors (2 Tim. 3:16–17).
7. Sound doctrine is the continual mandate for preachers (2 Tim. 4:2–4).
8. Sound doctrine is a basic qualification for eldership (Titus 1:9).

Scripture teaches that there will always be opposition to sound doctrine, both by humans (Matt. 15:2–6; Mark 11:18; 1 Tim. 1:3, 10; 2 Tim. 4:3; Titus 1:9) and by Satan and demons (1 Tim. 4:1). The Bible outlines several antidotes/corrections to false doctrine:

1. Speaking the truth of sound doctrine in love (Eph. 4:15)
2. Teaching sound doctrine (1 Tim. 4:6; 2 Tim. 4:2)
3. Holding fast to sound doctrine (Titus 1:9; Rev. 2:24–25)
4. Refuting false doctrine (Titus 1:9)
5. Rejecting and turning away from teachers of false doctrine (Rom. 16:17; 2 John 9–10)

There is a direct, inseparable relationship between sound doctrine and saintly living, something Scripture teaches clearly and consistently (Rom. 15:4; 1 Tim. 4:16; 6:1, 3; 2 Tim. 3:10; Titus 2:1–4, 7–10). The reverse is also true—where there is false belief, there will be sinful behavior (Titus 1:16). In spite of Scripture's clear emphasis on both purity of doctrine and purity of life, a number of mistaken notions have arisen concerning the relationship between what a person believes and how a person should live. These wrong ideas include the following:

1. Right doctrine automatically leads to godliness.
2. It doesn't matter how a person lives so long as he or she has right doctrine.

3. Doctrine deadens, spiritually speaking.
4. There is no connection between what one believes and how one lives.
5. Christianity is life, not doctrine.
6. Doctrine is irrelevant.
7. Doctrine divides.
8. Doctrine drives people away.

In contrast to the negativity aimed at doctrine, the absence of sound doctrine and the presence of false doctrine will always lead to sinful behavior. Without sound doctrine, there is no scriptural basis to delineate right from wrong, no doctrinal authority to correct sin, and no biblical encouragement to motivate godly living.

On the other hand, the spiritual value of sound doctrine is incalculable:

1. Sound doctrine is spiritually profitable (2 Tim. 3:16–17).
2. Spiritual blessings are promised for obedience (Rev. 1:3; 22:7).
3. Sound doctrine guards against sin (e.g., Job, Joseph, Daniel, Christ).
4. Sound doctrine delineates between truth and error (2 Cor. 11:1–15; 2 Tim. 3:16–17).
5. Sound doctrine was central to Christ's ministry (Matt. 7:28–29; Mark 4:2; Luke 4:32).
6. Sound doctrine was central in the early church (Acts 2:42; 5:28; 13:12).
7. Sound doctrine was central to apostolic ministry (Paul: Acts 13:12; 17:19; Gal. 2:11–21; John: 2 John 9–10).
8. Martyrs gave their lives for sound doctrine (Christ: Mark 11:18; Stephen: Acts 7:54–60; James: Acts 12:2; Paul: 2 Tim. 4:1–8).
9. Christ and the apostles left a mandate to pass sound doctrine on to the next generation (Christ: Matt. 28:20; Paul: 2 Tim. 2:2).
10. Churches were commended for sound doctrine or condemned for lack of sound doctrine (Ephesus, commended: Rev. 2:2, 6; Pergamum and Thyatira, condemned: Rev. 2:14–15, 20).
11. Established sound doctrine anticipates and prepares for eras when sound doctrine is out of season (2 Tim. 4:3).
12. Sound doctrine protects the church from false teachers (Titus 1:9).
13. Sound doctrine provides true spiritual adornment for believers (Titus 2:10).
14. Sound biblical teaching and sound systematic doctrine are inseparably connected to "theology." Whether it be expositionally viewed in a text of Scripture or comprehensively categorized from all Scripture, biblical teaching cannot be disconnected from its identification with theology. Put another way, all biblical teaching is theological in nature, and all Christian theology is biblical in content.

What Is the Overarching and Unifying Theme of Scripture?[13]

The broad theme of *king/kingdom* (human and divine) appears throughout the Bible. With the exceptions of Leviticus, Ruth, and Joel, the Old Testament explicitly mentions this theme in thirty-six of its thirty-nine books. Except for Philippians, Titus,

---

13. Adapted from Richard L. Mayhue, "The Kingdom of God: An Introduction," *MSJ* 23, no. 2 (2012): 167–72. Used by permission of *MSJ*.

Philemon, and 1, 2, and 3 John, the New Testament directly mentions the subject in twenty-one of its twenty-seven books. All in all, fifty-seven of the sixty-six canonical books include the kingdom theme (86 percent).

The Hebrew words for "king," "kingdom," "reign," and "throne" appear over three thousand times in the Old Testament, while the Greek words for these terms appear 160 times in the New Testament. The first Old Testament mention occurs in Genesis 10:10 and the last in Malachi 1:14. The initial appearance in the New Testament comes in Matthew 1:6 and the last in Revelation 22:5.

The exact expression "kingdom of God" does not appear in the Old Testament. In the New Testament, Matthew alone uses the phrase "kingdom of heaven," but he uses it interchangeably with "kingdom of God" (Matt. 19:23–24). And where he uses "kingdom of heaven" in passages that parallel other Gospels, those Gospel writers use "kingdom of God" (cf. Matt. 13:11 with Luke 8:10), thus establishing the correspondence between these two phrases.

Jesus never precisely defined "kingdom of heaven/God" in the Gospels, although he often illustrated it (e.g., Matt. 13:19, 24, 44, 45, 47, 52). Surprisingly, no one ever asked Christ for a definition. It can be assumed that they at least thought they understood the basic idea from the Old Testament, even if their ideas were mistaken.

Most telling, perhaps, is the plethora of *King* titles given to Christ in the New Testament:

- "King of Israel" (John 1:49; 12:13)
- "King of the Jews" (John 18:39; 19:3, 19, 21)
- "King of kings" (1 Tim. 6:15; Rev. 17:14; 19:16)
- "King of the ages, immortal, invisible" (1 Tim. 1:17)
- "King of the nations" (Rev. 15:3)

His reign is said to be forever and ever (Rev. 11:15; 22:5).

A biblical study of God's kingdom would lead one to conclude that it is multi-faceted, multidimensional, multifocal, multifactorial, and multifarious. It certainly could not be considered monolithic in character.

The idea of God's kingdom encompasses every stage of biblical revelation. For instance,

- God is King of eternity (pre-Genesis 1, Revelation 21–22, post-Revelation 22)
- God is King of creation (Genesis 1–2)
- God is King of history (Genesis 1–Revelation 20)
- God is King of redemption (Genesis 3–Revelation 20)
- God is King of the earth (Genesis 1–Revelation 20)
- God is King of heaven (pre-Genesis 1, Genesis 1–Revelation 22, post-Revelation 22)

All *kingdom of God* passages can be summarized by recognizing several broad aspects. First is the *universal kingdom*, which includes the rule of God that has been, is, and forever will be over all that exists in time and space. Second is God's *mediatorial kingdom*, in which he rules on earth through divinely chosen human representatives. Third is the *spiritual or redemptive aspect of God's kingdom*, which uniquely deals with a person's salvation and personal relationship with God through Christ. When Scripture uses the word "kingdom" to refer to God's kingdom, it could point to any one aspect of the kingdom or several of its parts together. Careful interpretation in context will determine the particulars for a given biblical text.

With these ideas in mind, it is proposed that *God as King* and *the kingdom of God* should together be seriously considered as the grand, overarching theme of Scripture. A number of noble ideas have been considered in the past, such as the glory of God, redemption, grace, Christ, covenant, and promise. Each possibility explains a part of God's kingdom, but only *God's kingdom* explains the whole.

From before the beginning until after the end, from the beginning to the end, both in and beyond time and space, God appears as the ultimate King. God is central to and the core of all things eternal and temporal. The kingdom of God convincingly qualifies as the unifying theme of Scripture.

John Bright succinctly and eloquently captured this thinking as follows:

> Old Testament and New Testament thus stand together as the two acts of a single drama. Act I points to its conclusion in Act II, and without it the play is an incomplete, unsatisfying thing. But Act II must be read in the light of Act I, else its meaning will be missed. For the play is organically one. The Bible is one book. Had we to give that book a title, we might with justice call it "The Book of the Coming Kingdom of God." That is, indeed, its central theme everywhere.[14]

The authors of this volume would only edit Dr. Bright's brilliant summary by deleting one word, "Coming." For God's kingdom has been, is, and forevermore shall be.

The kingdom of God can be explained in this manner: The eternal triune God created a kingdom and two kingdom citizens (Adam and Eve) who were to have dominion over it. But an enemy deceived them, seduced them into breaking allegiance to the King, and caused them to rebel against their sovereign Creator. God intervened with consequential curses that exist to this day. Ever since, he has been redeeming sinful, rebellious people to be restored as qualified kingdom citizens, both now in a spiritual sense and later in a kingdom-on-earth sense. Finally, the enemy will be vanquished forever, as will sin. Thus, Revelation 21–22 describes the final and eternal expression of the kingdom of God, where the triune God will restore the kingdom to its original purity with the curse having been removed and the new heaven and the new earth becoming the everlasting abode of God and his people.

---

14. John Bright, *The Kingdom of God: The Biblical Concept and Its Meaning for the Church* (New York: Abingdon-Cokesbury, 1953), 197; see also 7, 244. See Alva J. McClain, *The Greatness of the Kingdom: An Inductive Study of the Kingdom of God* (Chicago: Moody Press, 1959), 4–53; George N. H. Peters, *The Theocratic Kingdom of Our Lord Jesus, the Christ, as Covenanted in the Old Testament and Presented in the New Testament* (1884; repr., Grand Rapids, MI: Kregel, 1978), 1:29–33; Erich Sauer, *From Eternity to Eternity: An Outline of the Divine Purposes* (1954; repr., Grand Rapids, MI: Eerdmans, 1994), 89.

What Are the Major Motifs of Scripture?[15]

The Revelation of the Character of God
The Revelation of Divine Judgment for Sin and Disobedience
The Revelation of Divine Blessing for Faith and Obedience
The Revelation of the Lord Savior and His Sacrifice for Sin
The Revelation of the Kingdom and Glory of the Lord Savior

The Bible is a collection of sixty-six books inspired by God. These documents are gathered into two Testaments, the Old (thirty-nine) and the New (twenty-seven). Prophets, priests, kings, and leaders from the nation of Israel wrote the Old Testament books in Hebrew (with some passages in Aramaic). The apostles and their associates wrote the New Testament books in Greek.

The Old Testament record starts with the creation of the universe and closes about four hundred years before the first coming of Jesus Christ. The flow of history through the Old Testament moves along the following lines:

1. Creation of the universe
2. Fall of man
3. Judgment flood over the earth
4. Abraham, Isaac, Jacob (Israel)—fathers of the chosen nation
5. The history of Israel
   a. Exile in Egypt (430 years)
   b. Exodus and wilderness wanderings (40 years)
   c. Conquest of Canaan (7 years)
   d. Era of the judges (350 years)
   e. United kingdom—Saul, David, Solomon (110 years)
   f. Divided kingdom—Judah and Israel (350 years)
   g. Exile in Babylon (70 years)
   h. Return and rebuilding of the land (140 years)

The details of this history are explained in the thirty-nine books, which can be divided into five categories:

1. The Law—5 (Genesis–Deuteronomy)
2. History—12 (Joshua–Esther)
3. Wisdom—5 (Job–Song of Solomon)
4. Major Prophets—5 (Isaiah–Daniel)
5. Minor Prophets—12 (Hosea–Malachi)

The completion of the Old Testament was followed by four hundred years of silence, during which time God did not speak through prophets or inspire any Scripture. That silence was broken by the arrival of John the Baptist announcing that the promised Savior had come. The New Testament records the rest of the story, from the birth of

---

15. This section is adapted from John MacArthur, ed., *The MacArthur Study Bible: English Standard Version* (Wheaton, IL: Crossway, 2010), xi–xv. Charts and notes from *The MacArthur Study Bible: English Standard Version* originate with *The MacArthur Study Bible*, copyright © 1997 by Thomas Nelson. Used by permission of Thomas Nelson. www.thomas nelson.com.

Christ to the culmination of all history and the final eternal state. So the two Testaments go from creation to consummation, eternity past to eternity future.

While the thirty-nine Old Testament books major on the history of Israel and the promise of the coming Savior, the twenty-seven New Testament books major on the person of Christ and the establishment of the church. The four Gospels give the record of his birth, life, death, resurrection, and ascension. Each of the four writers views the greatest and most important event of history, the coming of the God-man, Jesus Christ, from a different perspective. Matthew looks at him through the perspective of his kingdom, Mark through the perspective of his servanthood, Luke through the perspective of his humanness, and John through the perspective of his deity.

The book of Acts tells the story of the impact of the life, death, and resurrection of Jesus Christ, the Lord Savior—from his ascension, the consequent coming of the Holy Spirit, and the birth of the church through the early years of gospel preaching by the apostles and their associates. Acts records the establishment of the church in Judea, in Samaria, and into the Roman Empire.

The twenty-one Epistles were written to churches and individuals to explain the significance of the person and work of Jesus Christ, with its implications for life and witness until he returns.

The New Testament closes with Revelation, which starts by picturing the current church age and culminates with Christ's return to establish his earthly kingdom, bringing judgment on the ungodly and glory and blessing for believers. Following the millennial reign of the Lord Savior will be the last judgment, leading to the eternal state. All believers of all history enter the ultimate eternal glory prepared for them, and all the ungodly are consigned to hell to be punished forever.

To understand the Bible, it is essential to grasp the sweep of that history from creation to consummation. It is also crucial to keep in focus the unifying theme of Scripture. The one constant theme unfolding throughout the whole Bible is this: God for his own glory has chosen to create and gather to himself a group of people to be the subjects of his eternal kingdom, who will praise, honor, and serve him forever and through whom he will display his wisdom, power, mercy, grace, and glory. To gather his chosen ones, God must redeem them from sin. The Bible reveals God's plan for this redemption from its inception in eternity past to its completion in eternity future. Covenants, promises, and epochs are all secondary to the one continuous plan of redemption.

There is one God. The Bible has one divine Source. Scripture is one book. It has one plan of grace, recorded from initiation through execution to consummation. From predestination to glorification, the Bible is the story of God redeeming his chosen people for the praise of his glory.

As God's redemptive purposes and plan unfold in Scripture, five recurring motifs are constantly emphasized. Everything revealed on the pages of both the Old Testament and the New is associated with these five categories. Scripture is always teaching or illustrating (1) the character and attributes of God; (2) the tragedy of sin and disobedience to God's holy standard; (3) the blessedness of faith and obedience to God's standard; (4) the need for a Savior by whose righteousness and substitution sinners can be forgiven, declared just, and transformed to obey God's standard; and (5) the coming glorious end of redemptive history in the Lord Savior's earthly kingdom and the subsequent eternal reign and glory of God and Christ. While reading through the Bible, one should be able to relate each portion of Scripture to these dominant topics, recognizing that what is introduced in the Old Testament is also made clearer in the New Testament. Looking at these five categories separately gives an overview of the Bible.

The Revelation of the Character of God

Above all else, Scripture is God's self-revelation. He reveals himself as the sovereign God of the universe who has chosen to make man and to make himself known to man. In that self-revelation he has established his standard of absolute holiness. From Adam and Eve through Cain and Abel and to everyone before and after the law of Moses, the standard of righteousness has been established and is sustained in Scripture to the last page of the New Testament. Violation of it produces judgment, both temporal and eternal.

In the Old Testament, God revealed himself by the following means:

1. Creation (the heavens and the earth)
2. Creation of mankind, who was made in his image
3. Angels
4. Signs, wonders, and miracles
5. Visions
6. Spoken words by prophets and others
7. Written Scripture (Old Testament)

In the New Testament, God revealed himself again by the same means but more clearly and fully:

1. Creation (the heavens and the earth)
2. Incarnation of the God-man, Jesus Christ, who is the very image of God
3. Angels
4. Signs, wonders, and miracles
5. Visions
6. Spoken words by Christ, apostles, and prophets
7. Written Scripture (New Testament)

The Revelation of Divine Judgment for Sin and Disobedience

Scripture repeatedly deals with the matter of man's sin, which leads to divine judgment. Account after account in Scripture demonstrates the deadly effects in time and eternity of violating God's standard. There are 1,189 chapters in the Bible. Only four of them do not involve a fallen world: the first two and the last two—before the fall and after the creation of the new heaven and new earth. The rest chronicle sin's tragedy and God's redemptive grace in Christ Jesus.

In the Old Testament, God showed the disaster of sin—starting with Adam and Eve and carrying on to Cain and Abel, the patriarchs, Moses and Israel, the kings, the priests, some prophets, and the Gentile nations. Throughout the Old Testament is the relentless record of continual devastation produced by sin and disobedience to God's law.

In the New Testament, the tragedy of sin becomes clearer. The teaching of Jesus and the apostles begins and ends with a call to repentance. King Herod, the Jewish leaders, and the nation of Israel—along with Pilate, Rome, and the rest of the world— all reject the Lord Savior, spurn the truth of God, and thus condemn themselves. The chronicle of sin continues unabated to the end of the age and the return of Christ in judgment. New Testament disobedience is even more flagrant than Old Testament disobedience because it involves the rejection of the Lord Savior Jesus Christ in the brighter light of New Testament revelation.

The Revelation of Divine Blessing for Faith and Obedience

Scripture repeatedly promises wonderful rewards in time and eternity that come to people who trust God and seek to obey him. In the Old Testament, God showed the blessedness of repentance from sin, faith in himself, and obedience to his Word—from Abel, through the patriarchs, to the remnant in Israel, and even on to the Gentiles who believed (such as the people of Nineveh).

God's will, his moral law, and his standard for man were always made known. To those who faced their inability to keep God's standard, who recognized their sin, who confessed their impotence to please God by their own works, and who asked him for forgiveness and grace—to those came merciful redemption and blessing for time and eternity.

In the New Testament, God again showed the full blessedness of redemption from sin for repentant people. There were those who responded to the preaching of repentance by John the Baptist. Others repented at the preaching of Jesus. Still others from Israel obeyed the gospel through the apostles' preaching. And finally, many Gentiles all over the Roman Empire believed the gospel. To all those and to all who will believe through-out all history, God promises blessing, both in this world and in the world to come.

The Revelation of the Lord Savior and His Sacrifice for Sin

This is the heart of both the Old Testament, which Jesus said spoke of him in type and prophecy, and the New Testament, which gives the biblical record of his coming. The promise of blessing is dependent on grace and mercy given to the sinner. Mercy means that sin is not held against the sinner. Such forgiveness depends on a payment of sin's penalty to satisfy holy justice, which demands a substitute—one to die in the sinner's place. God's chosen substitute—the only one who qualified—was Jesus. Salvation is always by the same gracious means, whether during Old Testament or New Testament times. When any sinner comes to God in repentant faith, acknowledging that he has no power to save himself from the deserved judgment of divine wrath, believing in Christ, and pleading for mercy, God's promise of forgiveness is granted. God then declares him righteous because the sacrifice and obedience of Christ is credited to his account. In the Old Testament, God justified sinners that same way, in anticipation of Christ's atoning work. There is, therefore, a continuity of grace and salvation through all redemptive history. Various covenants, promises, and epochs do not alter that fundamental continuity, nor does the discontinuity between the Old Testament witness-nation, Israel, and the New Testament witness-people, the church. A fundamental continuity is centered on the cross, which was no interruption in the plan of God but is the very thing to which all else points.

Throughout the Old Testament, the Savior-sacrifice is promised. In Genesis, he is the seed of the woman who will destroy Satan. In Zechariah, he is the "pierced" one to whom Israel turns and by whom God opens the fountain of forgiveness to all who mourn over their sin (Zech. 12:10). He is the very one symbolized in the sacrificial system of the Mosaic law. He is the suffering substitute of whom the prophets speak. Throughout the Old Testament, he is the Messiah who would die for the transgressions of his people; from beginning to end, the Old Testament presents the theme of the Lord Savior as a sacrifice for sin. It is solely because of his perfect sacrifice for sin that God graciously forgives repentant believers.

In the New Testament, the Lord Savior came and actually provided the promised sacrifice for sin on the cross. Having fulfilled all righteousness by his perfect life, he fulfilled justice by his death. Thus God himself atoned for sin, at a cost too great for the human mind to fathom. Now he graciously supplies all the merit necessary for his people to be the objects of his favor. That is what Scripture means when it speaks of salvation by grace.

The Revelation of the Kingdom and Glory of the Lord Savior

This crucial component of Scripture brings the whole story to its God-ordained consummation. Redemptive history is controlled by God so as to culminate in his eternal glory. Redemptive history will end with the same precision and exactness with which it began. The truths of eschatology are neither vague nor unclear—nor are they unimportant. As in any book, how the story ends is both compelling and critically important—and so it is with the Bible. Scripture notes several very specific features of the end planned by God.

In the Old Testament, there is repeated mention of an earthly kingdom ruled by the Messiah, the Lord Savior, who will come to reign. Associated with that kingdom will be the salvation of Israel, the salvation of Gentiles, the renewal of the earth from the effects of the curse, and the bodily resurrection of God's people who have died. Finally, the Old Testament predicts that God will create a new heaven and new earth—which will be the eternal state of the godly—and a final hell for the ungodly.

The New Testament clarifies and expands these features. The King is rejected and executed, but he promises to come back in glory, bringing judgment, resurrection, and his kingdom for all who believe. Innumerable Gentiles from every nation will be included among the redeemed. Israel will be saved and grafted back into the root of blessing, from which she has been temporarily excised. Israel's promised kingdom will be enjoyed with the Lord Savior reigning on the throne in the renewed earth, exercising power over the whole world, and receiving due honor and worship. Following that kingdom will come the dissolution of the renewed but still sin-stained creation and the subsequent creation of a new heaven and new earth—which will be the eternal state, separate forever from the ungodly in hell.

How Does Systematic Theology Relate to One's Worldview?[16]

What is a worldview? A worldview comprises one's collection of presuppositions, convictions, and values from which a person tries to understand and make sense out of the world and life. As Ronald Nash puts it, "A world-view is a conceptual scheme by which we consciously or unconsciously place or fit everything we believe and by which we interpret and judge reality."[17] Similarly, Gary Phillips and William Brown explain, "A worldview is, first of all, *an explanation and interpretation of the world* and second, *an application of this view to life.*"[18]

How does one form a worldview? Where does one begin? Every worldview starts with *presuppositions*—beliefs that one presumes to be true without supporting evidence from other sources or systems. Making sense of reality, in part or in whole, requires that one adopt an interpretive stance, since there is no "neutral" thought in the universe. This becomes the foundation on which one builds.

What are the presuppositions of a Christian worldview that is solidly rooted and grounded in Scripture? Carl F. H. Henry, an important Christian thinker in the last half of the twentieth century, answers the question very simply by saying that "evangelical theology dares harbor one and only one presupposition: the living and personal God intelligibly known in his revelation."[19] This one major presupposition, which underlies a proper Christian worldview, breaks down into two parts. First, God exists eternally as the personal, transcendent, triune Creator. Second, God has revealed his character, purposes, and will in the infallible and inerrant pages of his special revelation, the Bible.

What is the Christian worldview? The following definition is offered as a working model:

> The Christian worldview sees and understands God the Creator and his creation—that is, man and the world—primarily through the lens of God's special revelation, the holy Scriptures, and secondarily through God's natural revelation in creation as interpreted by human reason and reconciled by and with Scripture,

16. This section is adapted from Richard L. Mayhue, "Introduction," in *Think Biblically: Recovering a Christian Worldview*, ed. John MacArthur (Wheaton, IL: Crossway, 2003), 13–16. Used by permission of Crossway, a publishing ministry of Good News Publishers, Wheaton, IL 60187, www.crossway.org.

17. Ronald H. Nash, *Faith and Reason: Searching for a Rational Faith* (Grand Rapids, MI: Zondervan, 1988), 24.

18. W. Gary Phillips and William E. Brown, *Making Sense of Your World from a Biblical Viewpoint* (Chicago: Moody Press, 1991), 29.

19. Carl F. H. Henry, *God, Revelation, and Authority*, vol. 1, *God Who Speaks and Shows: Preliminary Considerations* (Waco, TX: Word, 1976), 212.

for the purpose of believing and behaving in accord with God's will and, thereby, glorifying God with one's mind and life, both now and in eternity.

What are some of the benefits of embracing the Christian worldview? A biblical worldview provides compelling answers to the most crucial of life's questions:

1. How did the world and all that is in it come into being?
2. By what standard can I determine whether a knowledge claim is true or false?
3. How does/should the world function?
4. What is the nature of a human being?
5. What is one's personal purpose of existence?
6. How should one live?
7. Is there any personal hope for the future?
8. What happens to a person at and after death?
9. Why is it possible to know anything at all?
10. How does one determine what is right and wrong?
11. What is the meaning of human history?
12. What does the future hold?

Christians in the twenty-first century face the same basic questions about this world and life that confronted the earliest humans in Genesis. They also had to sift through various worldviews to answer the above questions. This has been true throughout history. Consider what faced Joseph (Genesis 37–50) and Moses (Exodus 2–14) in Egypt, or Elijah when he encountered Jezebel and her pagan prophets (1 Kings 17–19), or Daniel in Babylon (Daniel 1–6), or Nehemiah in Persia (Nehemiah 1–2), or Paul in Athens (Acts 17). They discerned the difference between truth and error, right and wrong, because they placed their faith in the living God and his revealed Word.

What essentially distinguishes the Christian worldview from other worldviews? At the heart of the matter, a Christian worldview contrasts with competing worldviews in that it (1) recognizes the God of the Bible as the unique source of all truth, and (2) relates all truth back to an understanding of God and his purposes for this life and the next.

Are there any common misperceptions about the Christian worldview, especially among Christians? There are at least two mistaken notions. The first is that a Christian view of the world and life will differ on all points from other worldviews. While this is not always true (e.g., all worldviews accept the law of gravity), the Christian worldview will differ and be unique on the most important points, especially as they relate to the character of God, the nature and value of Scripture, and the exclusivity of Jesus Christ as Savior and Lord. The second misperception is that the Bible contains all that we need to know in every sense. Common sense should put an end to this misdirected thought; for example, Scripture does not give instructions for how to change the oil in one's car. However, it is true that the Bible alone contains all that Christians need to know about their spiritual life and godliness through a knowledge of the one true God, which is the highest and most important level of knowledge (2 Pet. 1:2–4).

How and in what life contexts does a Christian worldview prove to be necessary? First, in the world of *scholarship* the Christian worldview is offered not as one of many equals or possibilities but as the one true view of life whose single source of truth and reality is the Creator God. Thus, it serves as a bright light reflecting the glory of God in the midst of intellectual darkness.

Second, a Christian worldview must be used as an essential tool in *evangelism* to answer the questions and objections of the unbeliever. However, it must be clearly understood that in the final analysis, it is the gospel that has the power to bring an individual to salvation (Rom. 1:16–17).

Finally, a Christian worldview is foundational in the realm of *discipleship* to inform and mature a true believer in Christ with regard to the implications and ramifications of one's Christian faith. It provides a framework by which one (1) can understand the world and all of its reality from God's perspective and (2) can order one's life according to God's will.

What should be the ultimate goal of embracing the Christian worldview? Why is the Christian worldview worth recovering? Jeremiah passes along God's direct answer:

> Thus says the LORD: "Let not the wise man boast in his wisdom, let not the mighty man boast in his might, let not the rich man boast in his riches, but let him who boasts boast in this, that he understands and knows me, that I am the LORD who practices steadfast love, justice, and righteousness in the earth. For in these things I delight, declares the LORD." (Jer. 9:23–24)

Man's chief end is to know and glorify God. Yet the knowledge of God is impossible apart from a Christian worldview.

Where do systematic theology and one's worldview intersect? First, both are erected on the same shared presupposition with its two parts: (1) the personal existence of the eternal God and (2) his self-revelation in Scripture. Second, a Christian worldview is dependent on systematic theology to know and understand God's truth, for systematic theology is nothing other than organizing all that God has revealed for the purpose of rightly knowing and living unto him. Third, a Christian worldview is dependent on systematic theology to know and embrace God's worldview as revealed in Scripture, for it is only as we think Christianly that we learn to think God's own thoughts after him. Finally, systematic theology is dependent on a Christian worldview in order to consistently and properly apply the truth of Scripture for living according to the will of God for God's glory.

How Does Systematic Theology Relate to One's Mind?[20]

The Redeemed Mind
The Renewed Mind
The Illuminated Mind
The Christlike Mind
The Tested Mind
The Profitable Mind
The Balanced Mind

---

20. This section is adapted from Mayhue, "Cultivating a Biblical Mind-Set," in MacArthur, *Think Biblically*, 42–53. Used by permission of Crossway.

Systematic theology is entirely about God's mind as found in Scripture. It is not about what humans think independently apart from the Bible. The necessary characteristics of the Christian's mind are discussed next because they qualify one to learn and teach Christian theology, whose source is Scripture and whose centerpiece is the triune God.

The Redeemed Mind

As a result of salvation, the mind of a newly redeemed person knows and comprehends the glory of God (2 Cor. 4:6). Whereas this person was previously blinded by Satan (2 Cor. 4:4), he or she now possesses "the helmet of salvation" (Eph. 6:17) to protect the mind against the "schemes" (a mind-related term in the Greek, Eph. 6:11) of Satan. No longer is this one left vulnerable against the Devil as before salvation. This new person (2 Cor. 5:17) now has a knowledge of God and his will that he or she previously lacked (1 John 5:18–20).

The Renewed Mind

When a person enters into a personal relationship with Jesus Christ, this one becomes a new creation (2 Cor. 5:17) who sings "a new song" (Ps. 98:1). The mind acquires a new way to think and a capacity to put off old, sinful ways of thinking. Unquestionably, God is in the business of mind renewal for Christians (Rom. 12:2; Eph. 4:23; Col. 3:10).

The Bible says to "set your minds on things that are above, not on things that are on earth" (Col. 3:2). Paul put this concept in military terms: "We destroy arguments and every lofty opinion raised against the knowledge of God, and take every thought captive to obey Christ" (2 Cor. 10:5). How do we do this? Scripture reveals the mind of God (1 Cor. 2:16)—not all of his mind, to be sure, but all that God wisely determined to reveal to us. To think like God, one must think like Scripture. That's why Paul encouraged the Colossians to let the Word of Christ dwell within them richly (Col. 3:16).

Harry Blamires, an Englishman with extraordinary understanding about the Christian mind, puts this quite well:

> To think christianly is to think in terms of Revelation. For the secularist, God and theology are the playthings of the mind. For the Christian, God is real, and Christian theology describes His truth revealed to us. For the secular mind, religion is essentially a matter of theory: for the Christian mind, Christianity is a matter of acts and facts. The acts and facts which are the basis of our faith are recorded in the Bible.[21]

At salvation, Christians are given a regenerated mental ability to comprehend spiritual truth. After salvation, Christians need to readjust their thinking chiefly by mind renewal, using the Bible as the means to do so. The ultimate goal is to have a full knowledge of God and his will (Eph. 1:17–18; Col. 1:9–10).

---

21. Harry Blamires, *The Christian Mind: How Should a Christian Think?* (1963; repr., Ann Arbor, MI: Servant Books, 1978), 110–11.

The Illuminated Mind

The Bible says that believers need God's help to understand God's Word (1 Cor. 2:12–13). Consequently, the Spirit of God enlightens the minds of believers, so that they might comprehend, embrace, and obey the truths revealed in Scripture. Theologians call this *illumination*.

A great prayer to offer as one studies Scripture is, "Open my eyes, that I may behold wondrous things out of your law" (Ps. 119:18). It acknowledges an indispensible need for God's light in Scripture. So do texts like Psalm 119:33–34, "Teach me, O Lord, the way of your statutes; and I will keep it to the end. Give me understanding, that I may keep your law and observe it with my whole heart" (see also Ps. 119:102).

God wants Christians to know and understand and obey. So he gives them the help that they need through his Holy Spirit. Believers, like the men to whom Jesus spoke on the road to Emmaus, require God's assistance: "Then he opened their minds to understand the Scriptures" (Luke 24:45). God's ministry of illumination by which he gives light on the meaning of the Bible is affirmed in texts such as Psalm 119:130; Ephesians 1:18–19; and 1 John 2:27.

The truth about God illuminating Scripture for Christians should greatly encourage the believer. While it does not eliminate the need for gifted men to teach (Eph. 4:11–12; 2 Tim. 4:2) or the hard labor of serious Bible study (2 Tim. 2:15), it does promise that there is no need to be enslaved to church dogma or to be led astray by false teachers. Primary dependence for learning Scripture needs to be on the author of Scripture—God himself.

The Christlike Mind

When one thinks like God wants him or her to think and acts like God wants him or her to act, then one will receive God's blessing for obedience (Rev. 1:3). Spiritually, the Christian will be that obedient child, that pure bride, and that healthy sheep in Christ's flock who experiences the greatest intimacy with God.

It is brazen idolatry to reject the mind of God in Scripture and worship at the altar of one's own independent thinking. A believer's greatest intimacy with the Lord occurs when the Lord's thoughts prevail and one's behavior then models that of Christ.

Christians should be altogether glad to embrace the certain and true mind of God the Father (Rom. 11:34), God the Son (1 Cor. 2:16), and God the Spirit (Rom. 8:27). In contrast to Peter, who was tempted by Satan to set his mind on the things of man, believers are to set their minds on the things of God (Matt. 16:23; Col. 3:2). This has to do not so much with different categories or disciplines of thought but rather with the way things are viewed from a divine perspective. Christians should stand in awe of God's mind, as did the apostle Paul (Rom. 11:33–36).

God's view is the only true view that accurately corresponds to all reality. God's mind sets the standard for which believers are to strive but which they will never fully achieve. Put another way, man's thoughts will never exceed, equal, or even come close to God's. Over 2,500 years ago, the prophet Isaiah said this very thing (Isa. 55:8–9).

The ultimate pattern of Christian-mindedness is the Lord Jesus Christ. Paul declares, "But we have the mind of Christ" (1 Cor. 2:16). How can this be? We have it with the Bible, which is God's sufficient, special revelation (2 Tim. 3:16–17; 2 Pet. 1:3). In Philippians 2:5, Paul instructs, "Have this mind among yourselves, which is yours in Christ Jesus." The apostle is specifically pointing to Christ's mindset of sacrifice for God's glory (Phil. 2:7) and submission to God's will (Phil. 2:8). By following Christ's model, Christians can train their minds to become more like Christ's.

The Tested Mind

The Christian mind should be a repository of God's revealed truth. It should not quake, waver, compromise, or bend in the face of opposing ideas or seemingly superior arguments (2 Tim. 1:7). Truth originates not with humans but with God. Therefore, Christians should be the champions of truth in a world filled with lies that are deceivingly disguised as and falsely declared to be the truth.

It was God who invited the nation of Israel, saying, "Come now, let us reason together" (Isa. 1:18). The subject matter to be considered was repentance from sin and salvation (Isa. 1:16–20). By application, the same invitation is extended to every person alive. But it will not be without Satan's roadblocks.

To be forewarned is to be forearmed. While a commitment to think Christianly honors Christ, it is not without opposition. Satan would have believers think contrary to God's Word and then act disobediently to God's will.

Remember that before one becomes a Christian, his or her mind is blinded by the Devil: "The god of this world has blinded the minds of the unbelievers, to keep them from seeing the light of the gospel of the glory of Christ, who is the image of God" (2 Cor. 4:4). Even after salvation, Satan continues his intellectual rampage. Thus Paul had great concern for the Corinthian church: "But I am afraid that as the serpent deceived Eve by his cunning, your thoughts will be led astray from a sincere and pure devotion to Christ" (2 Cor. 11:3). Eve had allowed Satan to do some thinking for her. Then she did some of her own thinking independent of God. When her conclusions differed from God's, she chose to act on her conclusions rather than on God's commands, which is sin (Gen. 3:1–7).

Satan aims his fiery darts (Eph. 6:16) at the minds of believers (2 Cor. 11:3), making their thought life the battlefield for spiritual conquest. Scriptural accounts abound of those who succumbed, like Eve (Genesis 3) and Peter (Matt. 16:13–23). Others walked away from the fray as victors, like Job (Job 1:1–2:10) and Christ (Matt. 4:1–11). When Christians fall, it is most likely that they have forgotten to wear the helmet of salvation or to wield the sword of truth (Eph. 6:17).

In warning believers about life's ongoing, never-ending battle with Satan, Paul on two occasions tells about the schemes or designs of the Devil. He uses two different Greek words, but both relate to the mind (2 Cor. 2:11; Eph. 6:11). Since no one is immune from these attacks, the Christian really does need to heed Peter's strong encouragement: "Therefore, preparing your minds for action, and being sober-minded, set your hope fully on the grace that will be brought to you at the revelation of Jesus Christ" (1 Pet. 1:13; see 3:15).

So far, this discussion has focused on a preventive or defensive military posture regarding the mind. The majority of Scripture deals with personal protection. However, Paul also addresses how to go on the intellectual offensive (2 Cor. 10:4–5). These offensive "weapons" (10:4) certainly feature the Word of God wielded by a Christian's mind in the context of worldview warfare. In this context of mind battle, the "strongholds" (10:4) are "arguments" (10:5) and "every lofty opinion raised against the knowledge of God" (10:5). In other words, any philosophy, worldview, apologetic, or other kind of teaching that undermines, minimizes, contradicts, or tries to eliminate the Christian worldview or any part of it is to be met head-on with an aggressive, offensive battle plan. God's intended end is the destruction ("destroy" is used twice in 10:4–5) of that which does not correspond to Scripture's clear teaching about God and his created world.

In the historical context of 2 Corinthians, Paul opposed any teaching on any subject that had come into the church and did not correspond to his apostolic instruction. Whether an unbeliever or a believer was responsible, whether the idea came from scholars or the uneducated, whether the teaching found wide acceptance or not, all thoughts or opinions that were not *for* the knowledge of God were to be considered *against* the knowledge of God. Therefore, they were to be targeted for intellectual battle and ultimate elimination. Thus, in today's context, all intellectual activities (e.g., reading, listening to the radio, viewing television and movies, studying in formal academia, engaging in casual conversations) must always be pursued using the filtering lens of a Christian theological worldview to determine whether they are allied with the truth of Scripture or are enemies of which to be wary.

The Profitable Mind

Psalm 119 provides detailed insight into a Christian's new relation to the Bible, which reveals the mind of Christ. First, a believer will develop a great love for and tremendous delight in the Scriptures (119:47–48). Second, a believer in Christ will have a strong desire to know God's Word as the best way to know God (119:16, 93, 176). Third, knowing God will then lead to a Christian obeying him (119:44–45).

MEDITATION

To hear something once is not enough for most people. To briefly ponder something profound does not allow sufficient time to grasp and fully understand its significance. This proves to be most true with God's mind in Scripture. Psalm 119 testifies to the importance and blessing of lingering long over God's Word.

The idea of meditating sometimes lends itself to misunderstanding. Meditation involves prolonged thought or pondering. The American figure of speech for meditating is "chewing" on a thought. Some have also likened it to the rumination process of the cow's four-stomach digestive system. A vivid picture comes from a coffee percolator. The water goes up a small tube and drains down through the coffee grounds. After enough cycles, the flavor of the coffee beans has been transferred to the water, which is then called coffee. So it is that Christians need to cycle their thoughts through the grounds of God's Word until they start to think like God and then act godly.

Scripture commands believers to meditate on three areas:

1. God (Pss. 27:4; 63:6)
2. God's Word (Josh. 1:8; Ps. 1:2)
3. God's works (Pss. 143:5; 145:5)

All 176 verses of Psalm 119 extol the virtue of living out the mind of God. Meditation is mentioned at least seven times as the habit of one who loves God and desires a closer intimacy with him: "O how I love your law! It is my meditation all the day. . . . My eyes are awake before the watches of the night, that I may meditate on your promise" (119:97, 148; see also 119:15, 23, 27, 48, 78, 99). In contrast, an aspect of Eve's sin can be attributed to her failure to adequately meditate on God's clear and sufficient word (Gen. 2:16–17).

Meditating on God's Word will purify the mind of old thoughts that are not of God and reinforce new thoughts from Scripture. It also puts a protective shield around the mind to block and reject incoming thoughts that contradict God. That is the scriptural process of renewing the mind.

THINK ON THESE THINGS

Someone has suggested that the mind is the taproot of the soul. That being so, one needs to carefully and nutritionally feed his or her soul by sinking one's taproot deep into God's mind in Scripture. One may ask, "What food will feed my soul?" Paul's menu for the mind includes thought entrées that are (1) "true," (2) "honorable," (3) "just," (4) "pure," (5) "lovely," (6) "commendable," (7) "excellen[t]," and (8) "worthy of praise" (Phil. 4:8). In meditating on God's Word and thinking on these things, Christians will avoid setting their minds on earthly things (Phil. 3:19) and prevent being double-minded (James 1:6–8).

The Balanced Mind

Are divine revelation and human reason like oil and water—do they never mix? Christians have sometimes reached two erroneous extremes in dealing with divine revelation and human reason. On one end of the spectrum is *anti-intellectualism*, which basically concludes that if a subject matter is not discussed in the Bible, then it is not worthy of serious study or thought. This unbiblical approach to learning and thinking leads to cultural and intellectual withdrawal. At the opposite extreme is *hyper-intellectualism*, which embraces natural revelation at a higher level of value and credibility than God's special revelation in Scripture; when the two are in conflict, natural revelation is the preferred source of truth. This unbiblical approach results in scriptural withdrawal.

Both errors must be rejected. The believer must appropriate knowledge from both special and general revelation. However, the creation and our faculties of reason and deduction by which we study the creation (i.e., general revelation) are fallen, fallible, and corrupted by sin. Scripture, on the other hand, is infallible and inerrant and therefore must take precedence over general revelation. Where the Bible speaks to a discipline, its truth is superior. Where the Bible does not speak, God has given us the whole world of creation to explore for knowledge—but with the caveat that man's ability to draw conclusions from nature is not infallible like God's Word. This is especially true of thinkers who continually reject their need for Christ's salvation. This does not necessarily mean that their facts are wrong or even that their basic ideas are in error. However, it does guarantee that their worldview is not in accord with God's perspective, and therefore, their conclusions ought to be subjected to a critical evaluation according to Scripture.

Unmistakably, from the perspective of a Christian worldview, believers are to engage their own minds and the minds of others to the best of their ability and as opportunity allows. However, several wise cautions are in order:

1. Becoming a scholar and trying to change the way one's generation thinks is secondary to becoming a Christian and changing the way one personally thinks about Christ.
2. Formal education in a range of disciplines is secondary to gospel education—namely, obeying the Great Commission (Matt. 28:18–20) and taking the gospel to the ends of the earth, to every creature.
3. General revelation *points* to a higher power, while special revelation *personally introduces* this higher power as the triune God of Scripture, who created the world and all that is in it (see Isaiah 40–48, where Yahweh reminds Israel of this critical truth) and who provided the only Redeemer in the Lord Jesus Christ.
4. To know about the truth is not nearly as important as personally and redemptively being in fellowship with the Truth, Jesus Christ (John 14:6), who is the only source of eternal life.
5. The New Testament church was not mandated to intellectualize their world, nor was this their practice. Rather, they "gospelized" it by proclaiming the saving grace of Jesus Christ to all without distinction, from key political leaders like King Agrippa (Acts 25:23–26:32) to lowly imprisoned slaves like Onesimus (Philem. 10).
6. To moralize, politicize, or intellectualize society without first seeing spiritual conversion is to guarantee only a brief and generally inconsistent change that is shallow, not deep; temporary, not lasting; and ultimately damning, not saving.

It bears repeating that both special and general revelation are necessary for cultivating a biblical mind-set. However, the study of special revelation is the priority, followed in the second place by learning from natural revelation. Solomon, the wisest man who ever lived (1 Kings 3:12; 4:29–34), wrote the same advice almost three thousand years ago. His are the most authoritative statements on the subject of the mind and knowledge, since they are Scripture (Prov. 1:7; 9:10; see also 1 Cor. 1:20–21).

The alpha and omega of Christian theology is a *knowledge of God* (2 Cor. 2:14; 4:6; Eph. 1:17; Col. 1:10; 2 Pet. 1:2–3, 8; 3:18) and a *knowledge of the truth* (1 Tim. 2:4; 2 Tim. 2:25; Titus 1:1). Above all, at the very center of a Christian worldview is the Lord Jesus Christ, "in whom are hidden all the treasures of wisdom and knowledge" (Col. 2:3). Nothing can be fully understood if God is not known first.

How Does Systematic Theology Relate to One's Personal Life?[22]

Intimacy and Maturity
Holiness
Sanctification

Godliness, Christlikeness, and Christian spirituality all describe a Christian becoming more like God. The most powerful way to effect this change is by letting the Word of God dwell in one richly (Col. 3:16). When one embraces Scripture without reservation, it will energetically work God's will in the believer's life (1 Thess. 2:13). The process could be basically defined as follows:

> Christian spirituality involves growing to be like God in character and conduct by personally submitting to the transforming work of God's Word and God's Spirit.

Intimacy and Maturity

There is no better way to saturate one's mind with Scripture than by sitting under expository preaching and studying systematic theology—both will enhance one's spiritual maturity. The author of Hebrews rejoiced that Jewish Christians had taken well to the intimacy of a child (Heb. 5:12–13) but deplored their lack of advancement to the maturity of meat. So he exhorted, "Therefore let us leave the elementary doctrine of Christ and go on to maturity" (Heb. 6:1). Paul wrote to the Corinthians with similar disappointment (1 Cor. 3:1–3).

Intimacy deals fundamentally with one's personal relationship with the Father, Son, and Holy Spirit in godwardness. Maturity is the result of intimacy reflecting God's abiding, growing presence in Christians in regard to godliness (John 15:1–11). Just as a baby or young child, although not yet mature, can enjoy intimacy with a parent, so should a new Christian with the freshly found Savior. This intimacy fuels the maturing process, whereby a child grows into parental likeness.

---

22. For more on this topic, see Benjamin B. Warfield, "The Religious Life of Theological Students," in *Selected Shorter Writings of Benjamin B. Warfield*, ed. John E. Meeter (Nutley, NJ: Presbyterian and Reformed, 1970), 1:411–25.

Intimacy without maturity results in spiritually infantile behavior instead of spiritually adult responses. In contrast, maturity without intimacy results in a stale, joyless Christianity that can easily deteriorate into legalism and sometimes even a major fall into sin. However, Scripture teaches that when intimacy and maturity complement and feed off one another, the result is a strong, vibrant Christian life. Genuine spirituality, then, must be marked by both intimacy and maturity.

Scripture is essential for growing in spiritual maturity. Jesus, Paul, and James each directly communicated God's clear and frequent pressing demand for spiritual development in the true believer, providing key words for understanding spiritual maturity. We are to be perfect (Matt. 5:48), to be built up to mature manhood (Eph. 4:11–13), to be presented mature in Christ (Col. 1:28), complete and equipped for every good work (2 Tim. 3:16–17), and lacking in nothing (James 1:2–4).

The quickest way to grasp the essence of maturity is to read about the obedience of such people as Abel, Noah, Abraham, Sarah, Isaac, Jacob, and Joseph in Genesis. But one should not quit there. Sixty-five more books of the Bible contain additional stirring accounts of spiritual maturity. This canonical "hall of faith" serves as the ultimate example of God's affirmation of intimate faith and mature faithfulness.

Hebrews 11 chronicles spiritual maturity at its best. But notice that an exhortation immediately follows Hebrews 11, calling for the same kind of maturity in those who received the letter (12:1–3). That exhortation is accompanied by a warning about the Father's discipline of those who persist in immaturity (12:4–11). Imperfect earthly parenthood is but a reflection of God's flawlessly consistent response to those who by faith in the Lord Jesus Christ have been born again into God's family (John 1:12–13).

A saint of old, Epaphras, prayed that the Christians at Colossae would stand perfect and fully assured in all the will of God (Col. 4:12). May God, in similar fashion, commend these compelling biblical truths about spiritual maturity to one's stewardship of worship and obedience for his great glory.

Holiness

Christians have been saved to be holy and to live holy lives (1 Pet. 1:14–16). What does it mean to be holy? Both the Hebrew and Greek words for "to be holy" (which appear about two thousand times in Scripture) basically mean "to be set aside for something special." Thus, God is holy in that he sets himself apart from creation, humanity, and all pagan gods by the fact of his deity and sinlessness. That's why the angels sing of God, "Holy, holy, holy" (Isa. 6:3; Rev. 4:8), and why Scripture declares him to be holy (Ps. 99:9; Isa. 43:15).

Thus, the idea of holiness takes on a spiritual meaning among the people of God based on the holy character of God. For instance, the high priest of God had inscribed across his headpiece "Holy to the Lord" (Ex. 39:30). The high priest was especially set apart by God to intercede on behalf of a sinful nation to a holy God for the forgiveness of their transgressions.

Holiness embodies the very essence of Christianity. The holy Savior has saved sinners to be a holy people (1 Pet. 2:4–10). That's why one of the most common biblical names for a believer is *saint*, which simply and wonderfully means "saved and set apart" (Rom. 1:7; 1 Cor. 1:2).

When one considers that a holy God saves, it is no surprise to learn that he gives his Holy Spirit to every believer at salvation. A primary purpose of this gift is to equip believers with the power to live a holy life (1 Thess. 4:7–8; 1 John 3:24; 4:13).

So God wants Christians to share his holiness (Heb. 12:10) and to present themselves as slaves of righteousness, which will result in holiness (Rom. 6:19): "Since we have these promises, beloved, let us cleanse ourselves from every defilement of body and spirit, bringing holiness to completion in the fear of God" (2 Cor. 7:1). Thus the author of Hebrews writes, "Strive for peace with everyone, and for the holiness without which no one will see the Lord" (Heb. 12:14). Holiness is the core of a Christian's experience.

Spiritual maturity springs out of holiness. Scottish theologian John Brown boils holiness down to a definition that we can all understand and pursue:

> Holiness does not consist in mystic speculations, enthusiastic fervours, or un-commanded austerities; it consists in thinking as God thinks, and willing as God wills. God's mind and will are to be known from his word; and, so far as I really understand and believe God's word, God's mind becomes my mind, God's will becomes my will, and according to the measure of my faith, I become holy.[23]

Sanctification[24]

Closely connected with holiness is *sanctification*. In many New Testament uses, the word means "salvation" (Acts 20:32; 1 Cor. 1:2). Sanctification, or being set apart in salvation, should result in believers being set apart for Christian living.

Sanctification not only includes the immediate act and fact of salvation but also involves a progressive or growing experience of greater holiness and less sinfulness. It expresses God's will and fulfills the purpose of God's salvation call (1 Thess. 4:3–7). Sanctification includes one's responsibility to participate in continuing what God's Spirit began in salvation (2 Tim. 2:21; Rev. 22:11).

Christians are constantly exhorted to pursue in their Christian experience what God has declared to be true of them in salvation. Believers are also promised that what is not now complete, God will ultimately finish in glory (Phil. 2:12–13; 1 Thess. 5:23). These passages express one of the great paradoxes of Scripture: Christians are to become what they already are and one day will be. Such certainty of the Christian's future is captured in texts like these:

> For everyone who calls on the name of the Lord will be saved. (Rom. 10:13)

> For the word of the cross is folly to those who are perishing, but to us who are being saved it is the power of God. (1 Cor. 1:18)

---

23. John Brown, *Expository Discourses on the First Epistle of Peter* (Edinburgh: William Oliphant, 1866), 1:117.
24. For a more detailed discussion of sanctification, see "Sanctification" in chap. 7 (p. 631).

Besides this you know the time, that the hour has come for you to wake from sleep. For salvation is nearer to us now than when we first believed. (Rom. 13:11)

Sanctification involves the spiritual process that is pictured by a body growing into adulthood (Heb. 5:11–14) or a tree bearing fruit (Ps. 1:3). Growth is not always easy or uniform; however, it should be the direction of a true Christian's life.

Several obstacles face the believer in this lifelong pursuit. Christians need to know about them and stay on guard to avoid them or to correct them if they become a part of one's thinking:

1. One may think more highly of self than one ought and not pursue holiness as one should (Rom. 12:3).
2. One may presume upon salvation and assume that since one is saved, holy living is optional (Rom. 6:1–2).
3. One may have been erroneously taught about the nature of Christian living and so neglect the lordship of Christ (1 Pet. 3:15).
4. One may lack the zeal or energy to make holiness a priority (2 Cor. 7:1).
5. One may think that he or she is saved but not truly be so and then try to live a holy life in the power of the flesh (Matt. 13:5–7, 20–22).

Nature teaches that growth is normal and to be expected; conversely, a lack of growth should sound an alarm that something is seriously wrong. Scripture teaches this principle too in a spiritual sense. Frequently, Acts reports that the early church grew and expanded (see 2:41; 4:4; 5:14; 6:7; 9:31, 35, 42; 11:21; 14:1, 21; 16:5; 17:12). God also has expectations for individual growth in the Christian's life. These exhortations of Scripture need to be taken seriously (1 Pet. 2:2; 2 Pet. 3:18).

The chief agents for this growth are God's Word (John 17:17; 1 Pet. 2:2) and God's Spirit (Eph. 5:15–21). When growth occurs, one can quickly acknowledge God as the cause (1 Cor. 3:6–7; Col. 2:19). The Holy Spirit plays a prominent role in providing a true believer with the assurance of salvation. His assurance connects directly with growth (Rom. 8:16–17; 1 John 3:24).

Having formerly been spiritually dead but now made alive to God, the believer can check his vital signs to substantiate the fact that he is indeed alive, because he walks in the works that God has prepared (Eph. 2:1–10). In order to check one's spiritual health, here are some of the most important vital signs of a true Christian:

1. Christian fruit (John 15:8)
2. Love for God's people (John 13:35)
3. Concern for personal holiness (1 Pet. 1:13–21)
4. Love for God's Word (1 Pet. 2:2–3)
5. A desire to obey (John 14:15, 21, 23)
6. A sense of intimacy with God (Rom. 8:14–17)
7. Perseverance (Phil. 1:27–28)
8. Fellowship with God's people (Heb. 10:24–25)
9. A desire to glorify God (Matt. 5:13–16)
10. Witness to Christ's personal reality (1 Pet. 3:15)

As a result of testing their spiritual vital signs, Christians are not to linger or remain at the childhood level but are to grow up in all things. As this individual maturity or growth occurs, it extends to the building up and growth of the corporate body of Christ (Eph. 4:14–16).

Spirituality involves God's Spirit taking God's Word and maturing God's people through the ministry of God's servants for the spiritual growth of individual believers, which results in the growth of Christ's body. This is the ultimate goal of systematic theology—to increasingly think and then act in accord with God's will as one matures in the Christian faith.

How Does Systematic Theology Relate to One's Ministry?

The noted theologian Benjamin Warfield gave the following answer to this vital question:

> If such be the value and use of doctrine, the systematic theologian is preeminently a preacher of the gospel; and the end of his work is obviously not merely the logical arrangement of the truths which come under his hand, but the moving of men, through their power, to love God with all their hearts and their neighbors as themselves; to choose their portion with the Saviour of their souls; to find and hold Him precious; and to recognize and yield to the sweet influences of the Holy Spirit whom He has sent. With such truth as this he will not dare to deal in a cold and merely scientific spirit, but will justly and necessarily permit its preciousness and its practical destination to determine the spirit in which he handles it, and to awaken the reverential love with which alone he should investigate its reciprocal relations. For this he needs to be suffused at all times with a sense of the unspeakable worth of the revelation which lies before him as the source of his material, and with the personal bearings of its separate truths on his own heart and life; he needs to have had and to be having a full, rich, and deep religious experience of the great doctrines with which he deals; he needs to be living close to his God, to be resting always on the bosom of his Redeemer, to be filled at all times with the manifest influences of the Holy Spirit. The student of systematic theology needs a very sensitive religious nature, a most thoroughly consecrated heart, and an outpouring of the Holy Ghost upon him, such as will fill him with that spiritual discernment, without which all native intellect is in vain. He needs to be not merely a student, not merely a thinker, not merely a systematizer, not merely a teacher—he needs to be like the beloved disciple himself in the highest, truest, and holiest sense, a divine.[25]

---

25. Benjamin B. Warfield, "The Idea of Systematic Theology," in *The Works of Benjamin B. Warfield*, vol. 9, *Studies in Theology* (1933; repr., Grand Rapids, MI: Baker, 2003), 86–87.

Prayer[26]

Eternal God and heavenly Father,
    we echo the psalmist: Praise the Lord!
We have not put our trust in human leaders, in mortal beings;
    in them there is no salvation.
But we have put our trust in You, the Lord our God.
    Creator of heaven and earth.
You are forever faithful. One day You will bring perfect justice
    throughout the earth.

In the meantime, You provide for all the needs of Your people.
We thank You that You have filled the hungry, liberated captives,
    given sight to the blind, raised up those who are bowed down,
    and comforted those who are oppressed.
Indeed, how blessed is he whose help is the God of Jacob,
    whose hope is in the Lord his God!
We thank You that You love perfectly and everlastingly
    those who are covered with Your righteousness.
We worship You, Lord, as the Maker and Sustainer of all things.
We give thanks to You, O God; we glorify You for Your wondrous deeds!

As blessed as we are to be under the cover of Your grace, however,
    we must confess that we have sinned. We have broken Your law,
    which is written in our hearts as well as in the Scriptures.
We have disregarded the voice of conscience and spurned
    the clear direction of Your Spirit. Worse yet, we have at times
    refused the clear commands of Your holy Word.
Yet You daily show us grace and longsuffering
    and in Christ we are forgiven.
Purge our lives of sin
    cleanse our souls from guilt,
    deliver us from earthly affections,
    guide our feet away from the path of evil,
    and make us walk in the way of righteousness,
        for the sake of Your holy Name.
May we pursue the beauty of Your holiness
    and the security of the hope You have set before us.
May we never lose our firm assurance in a salvation that is forever.

Thank You for equipping us with suitable spiritual armor to protect us
    against the wiles of the evil one.
Thank You for such a great High Priest,
    who intercedes for us always.
Thank You for Your Word,

---

26. This prayer is reproduced verbatim from John MacArthur, *At the Throne of Grace: A Book of Prayers* (Eugene, OR: Harvest House, 2011), 48–50. The closing prayers for each chapter of this volume are taken from *At the Throne of Grace*. Copyright © 2011 by John MacArthur. Published by Harvest House Publishers, Eugene, Oregon 97402, www.harvesthouse publishers.com. Used by permission of Harvest House.

which guides and teaches us.
Graciously empower us to bind it upon our hearts,
 and thus to set our minds on You.
We long to understand Your truths and to observe how You operate
 so we can see blessing in every trial and joy in every sorrow.

Fill our hearts with gratitude and praise,
 and may we see Your design in everything!
Cause us, Lord, to proclaim Your Gospel to all who will hear—
 and may we gain a better hearing because both our doctrine
 and our practice manifest the glory of Christ in His saving work.
In every condition of life
  whether we struggle or prosper,
   suffer or rejoice,
 may we know that in Your hands all these
  things are being worked together
 for our good and Your eternal glory.
We are privileged to be called Your children, and we pour out our hearts
 in prayer to You, loving Father.
In the name of Your Son we pray. Amen.

"All People That on Earth Do Dwell"

All people that on earth do dwell,
Sing to the Lord with cheerful voice.
Him serve with fear, His praise forth tell,
Come ye before Him and rejoice.

The Lord, ye know, is God indeed;
Without our aid He did us make;
We are His flock; He doth us feed,
And for His sheep He doth us take.

O enter then His gates with praise,
Approach with joy His courts unto;
Praise, laud, and bless His Name always,
For it is seemly so to do.

For why? The Lord our God is good,
His mercy is forever sure;
His truth at all times firmly stood,
And shall from age to age endure.

To Father, Son, and Holy Ghost,
The God whom heav'n and earth adore,
From earth and from the angel host
Be praise and glory evermore.

~William Kethe (unknown–1594)

Bibliography

Primary Systematic Theologies

Bancroft, Emery H. *Christian Theology: Systematic and Biblical.* 2nd ed. Grand Rapids, MI: Zondervan, 1976. 13–20.

Buswell, James Oliver, Jr. *A Systematic Theology of the Christian Religion.* 2 vols. Grand Rapids, MI: Zondervan, 1962–1963. 1:13–26.

Culver, Robert Duncan. *Systematic Theology: Biblical and Historical.* Fearn, Ross-shire, Scotland: Mentor, 2005. 2–11.

Erickson, Millard J. *Christian Theology.* Grand Rapids, MI: Baker, 1986. 15–149.

*Grudem, Wayne. *Systematic Theology: An Introduction to Biblical Doctrine.* Grand Rapids, MI: Zondervan, 1994. 21–43.

Hodge, Charles. *Systematic Theology.* 3 vols. 1871–1873. Reprint, Grand Rapids, MI: Eerdmans, 1975. 1:1–150.

Lewis, Gordon R., and Bruce A. Demarest. *Integrative Theology.* 3 vols. Grand Rapids, MI: Zondervan, 1987–1994. 1:7–58.

Reymond, Robert L. *A New Systematic Theology of the Christian Faith.* Nashville: Thomas Nelson, 1998. xxv–xxxvi.

Shedd, William G. T. *Dogmatic Theology.* 3 vols. 1889. Reprint, Minneapolis: Klock & Klock, 1979. 1:3–58; 3:1–25.

Strong, August Hopkins. *Systematic Theology: A Compendium Designed for the Use of Theological Students.* Rev. ed. New York: Revell, 1907. 1–51.

Thiessen, Henry Clarence. *Introductory Lectures in Systematic Theology.* Grand Rapids, MI: Eerdmans, 1949. 23–46.

Turretin, Francis. *Institutes of Elenctic Theology.* 3 vols. Edited by James T. Dennison Jr. Translated by George Musgrove Giger. 1679–1685. Reprint, Phillipsburg, NJ: P&R, 1992–1997. 1:1–54.

*Denotes most helpful.

Specific Works

*Carson, D. A. "The Role of Exegesis in Systematic Theology." In *Doing Theology in Today's World: Essays in Honor of Kenneth S. Kantzer*, edited by John D. Woodbridge and Thomas Edward McComisky, 39–76. Grand Rapids, MI: Zondervan, 1991.

Gaffin, Richard B., Jr. "Systematic Theology and Biblical Theology." *Westminster Theological Journal* 38, no. 3 (1976): 281–99.

Garrett, James Leo, Jr. "Why Systematic Theology?" *Criswell Theological Review* 3, no. 2 (1989): 259–81.

Holmes, Arthur F. *Contours of a World View.* Grand Rapids, MI: Eerdmans, 1983.

Macleod, Donald. "Preaching and Systematic Theology." In *The Preacher and Preaching: Reviving the Art*, edited by Samuel T. Logan Jr., 246–72. Phillipsburg, NJ: P&R, 2011.

*McCune, Rolland. *A Systematic Theology of Biblical Christianity.* Vol. 1, *Prolegomena and the Doctrines of Scripture, God, and Angels.* Detroit, MI: Detroit Baptist Theological Seminary, 2009.

*Murray, John. "Systematic Theology." In *Collected Writings of John Murray*, 4:1–21. Edinburgh: Banner of Truth, 1982.

Phillips, W. Gary, and William E. Brown. *Making Sense of Your World from a Biblical Viewpoint*. Chicago: Moody Press, 1991.

Warfield, Benjamin B. "The Indispensibleness of Systematic Theology to the Preacher." In *Selected Shorter Writings of Benjamin B. Warfield*, edited by John E. Meeter, 2:280–88. Nutley, NJ: Presbyterian and Reformed, 1973.

Wells, David F. *No Place for Truth: Or, Whatever Happened to Evangelical Theology?* Grand Rapids, MI: Eerdmans, 1993.

*Denotes most helpful.

"Holy Bible, Book Divine"

Holy Bible, book divine,
Precious treasure, thou art mine;
Mine to tell me whence I came;
Mine to teach me what I am.

Mine to chide me when I rove;
Mine to show a Savior's love;
Mine thou art to guide and guard;
Mine to punish or reward.

Mine to comfort in distress;
Suff'ring in this wilderness;
Mine to show, by living faith,
Man can triumph over death.

Mine to tell of joys to come,
And the rebel sinner's doom:
O thou Holy Book divine,
Precious treasure, thou art mine. Amen.

~John Burton (1773–1822)

2

God's Word

Bibliology

Major Subjects Covered in Chapter 2

Inspiration of Scripture

Authority of Scripture

Inerrancy of Scripture

Preservation of Scripture

Teaching and Preaching of Scripture

Obligation to Scripture

The doctrine of Scripture is absolutely fundamental and essential because it identifies the only true source for all Christian truth.[1] Scripture repeatedly claims to be the Word of God. The prophets appealed to it as the foundation for God's promises and judgments. Christ and his apostles based the whole of Christian doctrine on the Scriptures. Over 2,500 times in the Old Testament alone the Bible asserts that God spoke what is written within its pages (Isa. 1:2). From the beginning (Gen. 1:3) to the end (Mal. 4:3) and continually throughout, this is what the Old Testament claims.

The phrase "the word of God" occurs over forty times in the New Testament. It is equated with the Old Testament (Mark 7:13). It was what Jesus preached (Luke 5:1). It was the message the apostles taught (Acts 4:31; 6:2). It was the word the Samaritans received (Acts 8:14) as given by the apostles (Acts 8:25). It was the

---

1. This introduction is adapted from John MacArthur, ed., *The MacArthur Study Bible: English Standard Version* (Wheaton, IL: Crossway, 2010), xvii–xviii. Charts and notes from *The MacArthur Study Bible: English Standard Version* originate with *The MacArthur Study Bible*, copyright © 1997 by Thomas Nelson. Used by permission of Thomas Nelson. www.thomasnelson.com.

message the Gentiles received as preached by Peter (Acts 11:1). It was the word Paul preached on his first missionary journey (Acts 13:5, 7, 44, 48–49; 15:35–36), his second missionary journey (Acts 16:32; 17:13; 18:11), and his third missionary journey (Acts 19:10). It was the focus of Luke in the book of Acts, who recounted its wide and rapid spread (Acts 6:7; 12:24; 19:20). Paul was also careful to tell the Corinthians that he spoke the word as it was given from God, that it had not been adulterated, and that it was a manifestation of the truth (2 Cor. 2:17; 4:2). And Paul acknowledged it as the source of his preaching (Col. 1:25; 1 Thess. 2:13).

Psalms 19 and 119 and Proverbs 30:5–6 make powerful statements about God's Word, setting it apart from any other religious writing or instruction in the history of mankind. These passages make the case for the Bible being called "sacred" (2 Tim. 3:15) and "holy" (Rom. 1:2).

The Bible claims ultimate spiritual authority in doctrine, reproof, correction, and instruction in righteousness because it represents the inspired Word of almighty God (2 Tim. 3:16–17). Scripture asserts its spiritual sufficiency, so much that it claims exclusivity for its teaching (see Isa. 55:11; 2 Pet. 1:3–4).

God's Word declares that it is inerrant (Pss. 12:6; 119:140; Prov. 30:5; John 10:35) and infallible (2 Tim. 3:16–17). In other words, since it is absolutely true, it is therefore totally trustworthy. All these qualities are dependent on the fact that Scripture is God-given (2 Tim. 3:16; 2 Pet. 1:20–21), which guarantees its quality at the source and at its original writing.

In Scripture, the person of God and the Word of God are everywhere interrelated, so much so that whatever is true about the character of God is true about the nature of God's Word. God is true, impeccable, and reliable; therefore, so is his Word. What a person thinks about God's Word in reality reflects what a person thinks about God.

The Bible possesses many important and unique characteristics that set it apart from and immeasurably beyond any literature written by mankind. Seven of its most significant features portray it as (1) active (1 Thess. 2:13; Heb. 4:12); (2) certain (Isa. 55:10–11; Luke 16:17); (3) powerful (Rom. 1:16–17; 1 Cor. 1:18); (4) living (John 6:63; Heb. 4:12; 1 Pet. 1:23); (5) cleansing (Eph. 5:26); (6) nourishing (1 Pet. 2:2); and (7) sanctifying (John 17:17–19). Table 2.1 outlines the various symbols that Scripture uses to represent a variety of spiritual truths concerning God's Word.

Inspiration of Scripture

Revelation and Inspiration
Definition of Inspiration
Preparation for Inspiration
Proofs of Inspiration

God initiated the disclosure and revelation of himself to mankind (Heb. 1:1).[2] The vehicles varied; sometimes it was through the created order and at other times

---

2. These following two paragraphs are adapted from MacArthur, *MacArthur Study Bible: English Standard Version*, xviii–xix. Used by permission of Thomas Nelson.

Table 2.1 Symbols for the Bible*

Symbol	Reality	Texts
Jesus Christ	Personification of the Word	John 1:1; Rev. 19:13
Valuable metals	Incalculable worth	Silver: Ps. 12:6 Gold: Pss. 19:10; 119:127
Seed	Source of new life	Matt. 13:10–23; James 1:18; 1 Pet. 1:23
Water	Cleansing from sin	Eph. 5:25–27; Rev. 21:6; 22:17
Mirror	Self-examination	James 1:22–25
Food	Nourishment for the soul	Milk: 1 Cor. 3:2; 1 Pet. 2:1–3 Bread: Deut. 8:3; Matt. 4:4 Meat: 1 Cor. 3:2; Heb. 5:12–14 Honey: Ps. 19:10
Clothing	A life dressed in truth	Titus 2:10; 1 Pet. 3:1–5
Lamp	Light for direction	Ps. 119:105; Prov. 6:23; 2 Pet. 1:19
Sword	Spiritual weapon	Outwardly: Eph. 6:17 Inwardly: Heb. 4:12
Plumb line	Benchmark of spiritual reality	Amos 7:8
Hammer	Powerful judgment	Jer. 23:29
Fire	Painful judgment	Jer. 5:14; 20:9; 23:29

* Adapted from MacArthur, *MacArthur Study Bible: English Standard Version*, 873. Used by permission of Thomas Nelson.

through visions/dreams or speaking prophets (Heb. 1:1–3). However, the most thorough and understandable self-disclosures were through the written propositions of Scripture (1 Cor. 2:6–16). The written Word of God is unique in that it is the only revelation of God that clearly declares man's sinfulness and God's provision of the Savior.

The revelation of God was captured in the writings of Scripture by means of *inspiration*, which has more to do with the process by which God revealed himself than the fact of his self-revelation. Second Timothy 3:16 makes this claim when it states, "All Scripture is breathed out by God." Peter explains the process: "No prophecy of Scripture comes from someone's own interpretation. For no prophecy was ever produced by the will of man, but men spoke from God as they were carried along by the Holy Spirit" (2 Pet. 1:20–21). By this means, the Word of God was protected from human error in its original record by the ministry of the Holy Spirit (cf. Deut. 18:18; Matt. 1:22). Zechariah describes the process of inspiration most clearly, casting Scripture as "the law and the words that the LORD of hosts had sent by his Spirit through the former prophets" (Zech. 7:12). This ministry of the Spirit extended to both the part (the words) and the whole in the original writings.

Revelation and Inspiration

By definition and as it relates to revelation, the finite creature and the infinite Creator differ fundamentally. God enjoys infinite and perfect knowledge, while mankind possesses a finite and imperfect knowledge. Indeed, mankind cannot fully know what creation reveals apart from Scripture. Revelation involves God (the Creator) conveying truth about himself to humanity. According to Scripture, this revelation comes in two forms: general revelation (Ps. 19:1–6) and special revelation (Ps. 19:7–14).

GENERAL REVELATION[3]

General revelation is God's witness of himself through the creation to his creatures. David explains it this way: "The heavens declare the glory of God, and the sky above proclaims his handiwork" (Ps. 19:1). When a person looks up at the sky, the universe itself attests to the fact that it has a Creator—and that he is awesome. The term "glory" literally speaks of God's weightiness or significance, and that is precisely what looking up at the sky in the day or night reveals. The One who created this universe must be truly amazing and powerful to bring all this into existence. Creation's witness to the Creator is continuous. As David writes, "Day to day pours out speech, and night to night reveals knowledge" (Ps. 19:2). While it is a limited witness because it is nonverbal, it is nevertheless universally accessible to all:

> There is no speech, nor are there words,
>   whose voice is not heard;
> Their voice goes out through all the earth,
>   and their words to the end of the world.
>   (Ps. 19:3–4; cf. Acts 14:17; 17:23–31; Rom. 1:18–25; 10:18)

The types of things that can be discerned from general revelation include an appreciation of God's wisdom and power. The more a person examines either the vastness of space or the finest particles in his molecular structure, the more he is compelled to recognize with wonder and amazement the true greatness of the Creator. It is not unlike looking at a fine painting and appreciating the artist's genius by admiring everything from the choice of colors to the angle of the brush strokes. Similarly, one can observe countless brush strokes and color choices in creation. The vastness of the ocean, the unfathomable depth of the sea, and the sound and force of each wave as it strikes the shore—all these things and many more speak to the power of God. At the same time, the way the hydrologic cycle works to water the earth and preserve life attests to the goodness of its Creator. That rain falls on the fields of those who love and worship God as well as those who do not reveals the love God has for all his creatures (Matt. 5:45). For believers, God's providential care in working all things to their good can also be included in the category of his general revelation (Rom. 8:28)—though the doctrine of

---

3. For a more thorough discussion of general revelation, see Richard Mayhue, "Is Nature the 67th Book of the Bible?," in *Coming to Grips with Genesis: Biblical Authority and the Age of the Earth,* ed. Terry Mortenson and Thane H. Ury (Green Forest, AR: Master Books, 2008), 105–29.

providence is derived from promises given in special revelation. All these things and many more attest to the greatness of the Creator.

Another form of general revelation complements what can be observed in creation with that which can be observed in man himself: the inherent knowledge of right and wrong and the work of the conscience, which accuses sinners so that they stand condemned before their Creator and Judge. As Paul put it, "For when Gentiles, who do not have the law, by nature do what the law requires, they are a law to themselves, even though they do not have the law. They show that the work of the law is written on their hearts, while their conscience also bears witness, and their conflicting thoughts accuse or even excuse them" (Rom. 2:14–15). Creation not only attests to the infinite power and wisdom of its Creator but also works together with the innate understanding that God has placed within man to bring about an awareness of sin and judgment. Solomon affirms that man knows there is more to life than this physical existence. As he explains, God has placed an awareness of eternity within man's heart (Eccles. 3:11). Everyone begins with an internal comprehension of the fact that though man is finite, there is more to his existence than just this temporal reality.

While general revelation conveys a great deal about the power, wisdom, goodness, righteousness, and majesty of the Creator, it is limited to what can be observed by sinful man. The ultimate end of general revelation is that it leaves people without excuse for failing to recognize the nature of their Creator. But it conveys nothing regarding the way by which a fallen human being might gain access to or secure reconciliation with his Creator to escape judgment. That is why God deemed it necessary to also reveal himself directly through special revelation. He did it so that fallen humans would know (1) the fullness of God, (2) how to be redeemed from God's wrath toward sinners, and (3) how to live and please God.

Several concluding observations can be made from the Bible about general revelation:

1. The breadth of content includes only the knowledge of God, not all knowledge unqualified.
2. The time span is all time, not just more recent times.
3. The witness is to all people, not just to some with scientific training.
4. The acquisition is made by human sight and sense, not with scientific equipment or technique.
5. The whole corpus of general revelation was available immediately after creation; it did not accumulate with the passing of time and the progressive collection of knowledge.

Therefore, the purpose of general revelation in nature as defined by Scripture should not be broadened or expanded any further than the special revelation of Scripture allows. To do so, would be to do the unthinkable—add to the Scripture without divine authorization. No one can be saved by general revelation (Rom. 10:5–17; 1 Cor. 1:18–2:5).

SPECIAL REVELATION

God uses special revelation when he reveals himself directly and in greater detail. God has done this through (1) direct acts, (2) dreams and visions, (3) Christ's incarnation, and (4) Scripture. God has revealed himself by direct acts at various times and in varied ways throughout redemptive history (Heb. 1:1). He spoke directly with Adam in the garden of Eden (Gen. 2:16–17; 3:9, 11). He addressed the nation of Israel audibly at Sinai (Deut. 5:4). He spoke to Moses personally and confirmed his witness by many powerful signs and wonders (Deut. 34:10–12). God did miracles at key points in redemptive history to confirm his witnesses (Exodus 3–14), including the Father's vocal confirmation of the Son on three separate occasions (Matt. 3:17; 17:5; John 12:28).

God also revealed himself directly through dreams and visions. He gave Isaiah a vision of the Son of God in his full preincarnate glory (Isa. 6:1–4). Daniel was given multiple revelatory experiences, including one in direct response to his prayer for the nation of Israel (Dan. 9:20–21). The apostle John saw a vision of the resurrected Lord Jesus Christ in full glory on the island of Patmos (Rev. 1:10–16). In each case, God revealed himself to a human prophet in order to give him special revelation.

The ultimate manifestation of special revelation is the incarnation of the Son. The Creator God took on himself the limitations of human flesh and dwelt among his creatures (John 1:1–5, 14). While he was not generally recognized for who he truly was (John 1:10–11), he nevertheless revealed the fullness of God's person to men (John 14:9–10). Jesus is described as the "image of the invisible God" (Col. 1:15) and as the "exact representation of His nature" (Heb. 1:3 NASB). Jesus was a perfect revelation of God to men. He was the exact representation of who God is and what he is like.

An equally authoritative form of special revelation is the Bible. While the incarnate Word is an exact embodiment of the divine Creator, Scripture is likewise a special and divine revelation from God to men (Heb. 1:1). It is a fixed written testimony from the Creator to his creatures. It was composed over a period of more than fifteen hundred years by forty different human authors. But what was composed was more than the words of men. It was the inspired words of God himself. Its superiority to general revelation is attested by David (Ps. 19:7–11). The Scriptures reveal to man the mind of God, the ways of God, the righteousness of God, and the means by which man might please God. It is superior to general revelation because it is specific and verbal. It is a written revelation from God through his apostles and prophets (Deut. 8:3; Matt. 4:4) and is thereby a lasting and forever-settled witness to an unchanging God (2 Sam. 22:31; Ps. 18:30; Prov. 30:5–6; Jer. 26:2).

To fully grasp the qualitative and functional differences between general revelation and special revelation, one need only consider the following three contrasts between the two. First, the agents of general revelation in nature will perish (Isa. 40:8; Matt. 24:35; Mark 13:31; Luke 21:33; 1 Pet. 1:24; 2 Pet. 3:10), but the Word of special revelation will not pass away, because it is forever (Ps. 119:89; Isa. 40:8;

Table 2.2 General and Special Revelation in Scripture

General Revelation in Scripture	Special Revelation in Scripture
Only condemns	Condemns and redeems
Harmonizes with special revelation but provides no new material	Not only enhances and explains in detail the content of general revelation but also goes significantly beyond that explanation
In its perceived message needs to be confirmed by Scripture	Is self-authenticating and self-confirming in its claim to be God's Word
Needs to be interpreted in light of special revelation	Needs no other revelation to be interpreted since it interprets itself
Is never equated with Scripture by Scripture	Has no peer

Matt. 24:35; Mark 13:31; Luke 21:33; 1 Pet. 1:25). Second, the means of general revelation in nature was cursed and is in bondage to corruption (Gen. 3:1–24; Rom. 8:19–23). It is therefore not the perfect world God originally created (Gen. 1:31). However, the Word of special revelation is inspired by God and thus always perfect and holy (Pss. 19:7–9; 119:140; 2 Tim. 3:16; Rom. 7:12). Third, the scope of general revelation in nature is severely limited compared to the multidimensional expanse of special revelation in Scripture. To enlarge and clarify this line of thinking, additional differences are listed in table 2.2.

Definition of Inspiration

VIEWS OF INSPIRATION

Scholars have proposed numerous theories for explaining the divine process of inspiration. We will summarize the main views here.

Dictation Theory of Inspiration.[4] This view suggests that God gave the human authors of the Bible the precise words to write. The process of inspiration simply involved them penning these words verbatim. The human author was merely an instrument God used like a pen to compose his words on the page. Scripture certainly includes instances of divine dictation, such as God's instructions to Moses in recording the law on Mount Sinai (Ex. 34:27), to Jeremiah addressing the nation in Jerusalem (Jer. 30:2), and to John on the island of Patmos addressing the seven churches in Asia Minor (Rev. 2:1, 8, 12, 18; 3:1, 7, 14). In each of these cases, God gave the exact words to the human authors by way of dictation. Inspiration in these cases did, in fact, involve writing God's revelation word for word.

However, if the entire Bible were composed by means of divine dictation, we would expect one style and one consistent vocabulary throughout. It would be a record void of the individuality of the human authors' language and style. But just the opposite is observed in the texts of Scripture (Deut. 3:23–25; Rom. 9:1–3). The

---

4. This section and the next are adapted from John MacArthur, *Why Believe the Bible?*, Baker Books ed. (Grand Rapids, MI: Baker, 2015), 40, 43–44, copyright © 2015 by Baker Books, a division of Baker Publishing Group. Used by permission.

key argument against mechanical dictation is that every book of the Bible exhibits clear evidence of the writer's personality. Every book has a different character and way of expressing itself. Every author has a different style. God could have exclusively used dictation and given the truth that way. In fact, he really did not have to use men at all. But the writing in the Bible features variations in style. It displays variations in language and vocabulary. From author to author, their distinct personalities shine through. One can even feel the human authors' emotions as they pour out God's Word on paper.

Still, the question remains, how could the Bible be the words of men like Peter and Paul and at the same time be God's words as well? Part of the answer to this complex question is simply because God had made Peter and Paul and the other writers of Scripture into the men that he wanted them to be by forming their very personalities. He controlled their heredity and their environments. He controlled their lives, all the while giving them freedom of choice and will. And when these men were exactly what he wanted them to be, he directed and controlled their free and willing choice of words so that they wrote down the very words of God.

God made them into the kind of men whom he could use to express his truth, and then God literally selected the words out of their lives and their personalities, vocabularies, and emotions. The words were their words, but in reality their lives had been so framed by God that they were God's words. So it is possible to say that Paul wrote the book of Romans and to also say that God wrote it and to be right on both counts.

Partial or Conceptual Theory of Inspiration. Some theologians, preachers, and other biblical scholars teach conceptual inspiration. In other words, they say that God never gave the writers of the Bible the exact words they would write; rather, God gave them general ideas or impressions, and they put these down in their own words. For example, he planted the concept of love in Paul's mind, and one day Paul sat down and penned 1 Corinthians 13.

This view of inspiration claims that God suggested a general trend of revelation, but men were left free to say what they wanted, which is why (in the opinion of those who take this position) the Bible contains so many mistakes. This view is a denial of verbal inspiration. It denies that God inspired the very words of Scripture. The conceptual view of inspiration has been popular with neoorthodox theologians, who believe that the Bible contains the Word of God but is not the Word of God.

In this theory, God inspired the ideas within the authors but did not give them these concepts in actual words. Said another way, God conveyed his truth to the writers, but inspiration itself applies not to the words but only to the doctrine conveyed through their writings. This approach allows God to be true in what he conveyed to the human authors, while at the same time leaving room for inadequacies in what was actually written. In this view, God either accommodated himself to the limitations of the human writers or left it to them to convey his truth in their own words, explaining why what the human authors wrote is not necessarily factually accurate.

However, the Scriptures repeatedly make claims to be fully truthful (Ps. 119:43, 160; 2 Tim. 2:15). Jesus himself affirms that God's Word is truth (John 17:17). Furthermore, the Bible never speaks of Scripture's authority and message as limited to merely the concepts or the ideas generally conveyed by the words on the page. On the contrary, God expresses great concern for his Word and forbids any tampering with his commandments (Deut. 4:2; 12:32). Scripture confirms inspiration at the word level when it says, "Every word of God proves true; he is a shield to those who take refuge in him. Do not add to his words, lest he rebuke you and you be found a liar" (Prov. 30:5–6). This concern is expressed just as seriously in the final book of the Bible as it is in the Law of Moses (Rev. 22:18–19). A similar injunction in Jeremiah (26:1–2) makes this divine restriction a notable element in all four major sections of written revelation: the Law, the Prophets, the Writings, and the New Testament. God repeats it in every major section, making it emphatic and clear: God's concern is not just that the concepts are true but also that the words themselves are truly inspired. Divine inspiration occurred at the word level.

Natural Theory of Inspiration. Those who hold to this view argue that the biblical authors found inspiration for their writing of Scripture not from God but from within themselves. In the same way that gifted composers, artists, architects, and authors have been inspired in their great masterpieces, the biblical writers were moved naturally in the writing of Scripture. They were men who gained amazing spiritual insight through their exceptional sensitivity and giftedness. As a result, their writings were of an inspired quality.

The obvious objection to this view is that while it acknowledges the human authorship of Scripture, it negates or ignores the biblical claim of divine authorship (2 Tim. 3:16; 2 Pet. 1:20–21). This view exalts the human authors of the Bible but denies that God really had anything to do with its authorship. According to this view, God did not write the Bible. Smart and spiritual men did.

Another fatal flaw for this view is that smart, religious men would not write a book that condemns them all. Such men would not write a book that provided salvation only from above. Such men seek to provide their own salvation. All other religions promote the deadly lie that man contributes to salvation by works of morality, charity, or ritual. They do not want to trust solely in the perfect sacrifice made by God's Son. As a final note, even the noblest of men could never conceive of a personality like Jesus Christ. Even the most gifted minds could not fabricate a character who would surpass any human being who ever lived in wisdom, purity, love, righteousness, and perfection.

The Biblical View: Verbal, Plenary Inspiration. God through his Spirit inspired every word penned by the human authors in each of the sixty-six books of the Bible in the original documents (i.e., the autographs). Inspiration describes the process of divine causation behind the authorship of Scripture. It refers to the direct act of God on the human author that resulted in the creation of perfectly written revelation. It conveys the mysterious work of the Holy Spirit whereby he used the individual personality, language, style, and historical context of each writer to produce divinely authoritative writings. These works were truly the product of both the human author and the Holy Spirit. This fits the word Paul used in 2 Timothy 3:16 (*theopneustos*). This Greek word itself carries the sense of "God breathing out" the Scriptures through the biblical writers. "All Scripture is breathed out by God" (ESV) may even be the most accurate way to translate 2 Timothy 3:16. What is most important here is to recognize that the biblical claim of inspiration is one of divine superintendence. God produced the Scriptures by influencing the human author's own thoughts. This resulted in divinely authoritative and inerrant words written in the autographs.

THE PROCESS OF INSPIRATION

The actual processes by which the books of the Bible were composed are many and varied. Moses wrote the Pentateuch under the direct supervision of God. At times, God gave him the specific words to write (Ex. 34:27); in other cases, he included his own thoughts (Deut. 3:23–26). David wrote many psalms, which were collected into the book of Psalms. Some were the result of specific events in his life (Psalms 32; 51), while others were drawn from his general life experiences (Psalm 23). Some writers researched their subject prior to writing. Solomon searched out and collected many proverbs (Eccles. 12:9), and then he and others compiled them into what is now the book of Proverbs (Prov. 1:1; 10:1; 25:1).

Matthew and John wrote their Gospels on the basis of their personal experiences with Jesus. Luke was not an eyewitness of the events recorded in his Gospel. He investigated everything thoroughly before writing it out carefully and in order (Luke 1:1–4). This almost certainly included interviewing many of the apostles and other eyewitnesses. Some biblical writers were given special revelation through a dream or vision that resulted in the composition of Scripture. The apostle John received a vision of the risen Lord Jesus while he was in exile on the island of Patmos and was then instructed to write to the seven churches what he was told and what he saw (Rev. 1:9–11).

Even the writing process itself was sometimes unique to the authors and the books they composed. Jeremiah dictated the words God gave him to his scribe, Baruch, who did the actual writing (Jer. 36:32). Paul frequently used an amanuensis (i.e., a scribe or secretary of sorts) to write his letters as he dictated them. This is why in several cases Paul ends his letters with a note written in his own hand—to certify that the letter is from him (1 Cor. 16:21; Col. 4:18; 2 Thess. 3:17). His letter to the saints at Rome even includes a greeting from Tertius, who penned it for Paul (Rom. 16:22). On a couple of occasions, Paul wrote the entire letter in his own hand (Gal. 6:11; Philem. 19). Through all these many and varied features of composition, God the Holy Spirit was superintending every word of Scripture.

Peter best defines the inspiration process in 2 Peter 1. In the context of his own imminent martyrdom, he first speaks of the need to hold fast to the truth (2 Pet. 1:12–14). Prior to warning of false teachers, he affirms the reliability of Scripture because it is the product not merely of the human writers but of the Holy Spirit through them. He begins his explanation by referring to his own experience as a witness of Christ's transfiguration (Mark 9:1–13; 2 Pet. 1:18). On this basis he says, "And we have the prophetic word more fully confirmed, to which you will do well to pay attention as to a lamp shining in a dark place, until the day dawns and the morning star rises in your hearts" (2 Pet. 1:19). The "word of prophecy" is clearly a reference to Scripture given the way it is expanded in verse 20. The phrase "more fully confirmed" can be understood in two possible ways: confirmatively or comparatively. If taken in a confirmative sense (as a predicative), then it means that the word is even more reliable because of the firsthand experiences Peter and other writers have had. These kinds of signs make "the prophetic word" even more certain and believable. A better choice would be to take this in a comparative sense (as an attributive). While an experience like the one Peter had on the Mount of Transfiguration is an amazing witness to Christ, an even more reliable witness for God is his "prophetic word"—that is, Scripture. The reason is because of the means by which it was composed.

The "prophetic word" (Scripture) is more complete, more permanent, and more authoritative than experience.[5] More specifically, the Word of God is a more reliable revelation of the teachings about the person, atonement, and second coming of Christ than even the genuine firsthand experiences of the apostles themselves.

Peter describes the process of composition this way: "knowing this first of all, that no prophecy of Scripture comes from someone's own interpretation. For no prophecy was ever produced by the will of man, but men spoke from God as they were carried along by the Holy Spirit" (2 Pet. 1:20–21). The phrase "prophecy of Scripture" identifies "the prophetic word" definitively as the biblical text. The idea of "someone's own interpretation" means that what the biblical authors wrote was not just their own opinions, ideas, or personal interpretations of the events they saw or messages they penned. What they wrote was not "produced by the will of man." In other words, human initiative was not behind the creation of the biblical books. Rather, Peter affirms very directly that when the human authors wrote, it was God speaking through them. This is similar to David's testimony: "The Spirit of the LORD speaks by me; his word is on my tongue" (2 Sam. 23:2). It was a miraculous process that directly involved the personal attention and directed power of the Holy Spirit. The expression "carried along" is the same as that used in Acts to describe a ship being moved along by the wind (Acts 27:15, 17). In the writing of Scripture, it was the prophet communicating God's Word through his pen. It was also the Spirit moving continually to convey God's Word through the prophet. In the end result, that which was written was fully the words of the human authors in their language and style and from their personal perspectives, but it was under the direct superintendence of God by his Spirit producing on the page the very words of God. The ultimate product is

---

5. This paragraph is adapted from MacArthur, *MacArthur Study Bible: English Standard Version*, 1904. Used by permission of Thomas Nelson.

the divine, inspired, inerrant, and authoritative words of God on every page of all sixty-six books of the Bible.

AN EXPLANATION OF INSPIRATION

One of the most significant texts in the entire New Testament regarding the inspiration of Scripture is 2 Timothy 3:16, where Paul affirms both a claim to the inspiration of God primarily in the writings of the Old Testament (and by extension to the New Testament) and an inerrant view of Scripture. Yet because of the significance of this text, almost every word in Paul's statement has been attacked by skeptics. A few specific decisions determine the entirety of one's interpretation of this verse.

The first is the expression "all Scripture." In the original, the feminine singular adjective "all" together with the feminine singular noun "Scripture" can be taken several ways. There can be little doubt that the term translated "Scripture" is actually referring to Scripture. However, interpreters debate the extent of this meaning. Is it a reference to a particular passage of Scripture, as some insist, or is it a reference to the Scripture as a whole, as others affirm? The first view has the advantage of the absence of the definite article to support its case in both instances. If this is the correct view, then Paul is emphasizing the usefulness of "all the individual passages that make up the whole." However, the second view seems the better option. It is true that "all" usually means "every" when joined to a noun without the article, but this is not an absolute rule. A noun can be definite without the article. This is almost certainly the case here. The word "Scripture" (Gk. *graphē*) is used on at least two other occasions (Rom. 1:2; 16:26) in a definite way—even without the article. The usage of this word throughout the New Testament seems to confirm that Scripture is used collectively as a proper name for the entirety of the Bible. These considerations make "all Scripture" the preferred view. As a result, Paul's testimony in this passage is first of all one that concerns the totality of Scripture. Nevertheless, even if the alternative view is embraced, there is little actual difference in emphasizing the "totality" or the "individual parts" as inspired. The point that Paul is unmistakably making is that the whole and the parts of Scripture, without exception, are inspired of God.

The second significant issue to be resolved is probably the most crucial to this discussion. It centers on defining the biblical *hapax legomenon* commonly translated "inspired by God" (*theopneustos*), and in particular its meaning in relationship to "all Scripture." The term itself is a compound word, which is best rendered "breathed out by God." The idea of *inspiration* actually comes, as is well attested, from the Vulgate's rendering of *inspirata* (Latin for "inspiration"). The word, then, signifies the divine act in the process of writing the biblical text.

Beyond the definition of the term itself, the argument moves to the relationship of the term to the preceding phrase, "all Scripture." Some see "God-breathed" as an attributive adjective. If this is the case (and it is syntactically possible), then the expression is "all God-breathed Scripture." This reading, however, implies that some passages of Scripture are not inspired. The correct view is to recognize the structure as a predicative adjective. In this case, the expression reads, like most modern English translations, "all Scripture is God-breathed." This rendering is supported by the slightly better syntactical evidence in favor of this view, contextual arguments, and many similar biblical claims. Therefore, from Paul's own testimony to Timothy, all Scripture is God-breathed. As a result, it can be absolutely affirmed that it is profitable to the man of God. Its divine authorship makes it profitable. By extension, then, this same divine authorship demands inerrancy and infallibility. To conclude otherwise is to compromise the integrity of the God who is attributed with the authorship of it—and not just of some parts of Scripture but the whole of it.

Regarding the extent of the expression "all Scripture," one need look only to Paul's first letter to Timothy, where he writes, "For the Scripture says, 'YOU SHALL NOT MUZZLE THE OX WHILE HE IS THRESHING,' and 'The laborer is worthy of his wages'" (1 Tim. 5:18 NASB). Paul quotes from both the Law of Moses (Deut. 25:4) and the Gospel of Luke (Luke 10:7), and he attributes the title of Scripture to both. While the main emphasis of the 1 Timothy text is not inspiration, it cannot be missed that Paul uses the term "Scripture" to describe both the Old Testament and Luke's writing. The implication that one readily draws, then, is that Paul's statement that "all Scripture is God-breathed" applies the quality of divine authorship to Luke's writings on an equal level with the Old Testament. This is completely in line with Peter's description of the process of inspiration and the preauthentication Jesus gave of the New Testament.

OBJECTIONS TO INSPIRATION

It is true that God used fallible men to record Scripture. But at the same time, God produced infallible and inerrant words through them. As a person can draw a straight line with a crooked stick, God produced an inerrant Bible through imperfect men. The most obvious and direct parallel is the incarnation. Scripture records the miraculous conception of the sinless Son of God in the womb of Mary (Matt. 1:18–25; Luke 1:26–38). Mary was a sinner just like every other descendant of Adam, and yet God used her to bring Jesus to earth. The use of fallible and sinful instrumentality in no way limited God's ability to bring the sinless Savior into the world (2 Cor. 5:21). Jesus was fully Mary's son (Matt. 1:25) and fully God's Son (John 1:14)—yet untainted by Mary's sin nature. In the same way, God used human means to compose the Scriptures without compromising the integrity of the revelation.

This is true even though he used various kinds of human effort in the writing process. Whether Moses wrote the very words God told him to write (Ex. 24:4; Lev. 1:1; 4:1; 6:1, 8, 24; Num. 1:1; 2:1) or wrote prophetically from his own experiences, it was all under divine inspiration (Deut. 31:24–29). Luke wrote his two-volume work based on his personal research (Luke 1:1–4; Acts 1:1–3). Matthew and John wrote based on their firsthand experiences and their Spirit-inspired recollection of what was said and done (John 14:26). Paul, at times, authoritatively communicated his own reasoning into the composition of Scripture (1 Cor. 7:25; 14:37). God used human means to compose his inerrant Word. But the Bible is not merely the product of fallible men; it is at one and the same time the very words of the infallible Holy Spirit (1 Thess. 2:13; 2 Tim. 3:16; 2 Pet. 1:20–21).

Preparation for Inspiration

Behind the composition of the sixty-six books of the Bible was a divine superintendence that providentially orchestrated every aspect of its creation. This encompassed everything from the occasion of the writing to the unique personal makeup and experiences of the individual authors themselves. As we consider these factors, we will gain a full appreciation of the magnitude of divine power and wisdom displayed in Scripture.

PREPARATION OF THE WRITINGS

The preparation for the authorship of every book of the Bible obviously includes the historical context in which it was written. Many of these contexts are easily identifiable. The Pentateuch was written by Moses in the immediate context of the exodus and the beginnings of the conquest of the Promised Land. The Psalms were written frequently from the immediate life contexts of the human authors or as an expression of worship derived from some act(s) God did for his people. Ecclesiastes gives an inspired accounting of the spiritual lessons learned by Solomon throughout his life. The prophetic books are laced with historical references that identify the contexts in which they were written and the specific immediate and future issues that they addressed.

A survey of the New Testament books reveals the same. The Gospel of Luke is the only one of the four that specifically identifies its author. Nevertheless, all four clearly present the person and work of Jesus as a demonstration that he is the Christ. They also direct the reader to the conclusion that salvation is available through faith in him and his work on the cross. Luke alone indicates that he writes not as an eyewitness personally but on the basis of careful research that he has done to compose his two-volume work (Luke 1:1–4; Acts 1:1–3). Nevertheless, it is clear, based on the content in all four Gospels, that they are derived from the same historical events.

Every New Testament epistle stems from a specific historical context that prompted the human author to write it. Romans was written by Paul as an introduction of himself and his gospel ministry to the saints in Rome—in part because he sought their future assistance on his way to Spain (Rom. 1:11–13; 15:22–25). Paul wrote both Corinthian epistles as a result of numerous issues that surfaced within the church at Corinth. The Pastorals (1 and 2 Timothy and Titus) were addressed to ministry companions of Paul. Each was written from a distinct life and ministry situation, and all three letters give specific instructions related to the handling of affairs in the ministries of Ephesus and Crete. Even the book of Revelation was written from the context of John's exile (Revelation 1) and the historical contexts immediately present in the mid-AD 90s in the seven churches addressed by Christ (Revelation 2–3).

Each of these historical settings was used by God to provide the context from which his divinely inspired Word was penned. The providential arrangement of all the persons, problems, praises, personalities, cultures, governments, and social and secular challenges—and all the rest—collectively work together to provide the divinely intended context from which each book of the Bible was written.

PREPARATION OF THE WRITERS

Beyond orchestrating the events of history, which set the context for the writing of the biblical books, God also prepared the authors themselves. As an illustration of this, consider the book of Psalms. They are some of the most emotional, inspirational, and worshipful portions of the Bible. They vividly describe everything from exclamations of praise to desperate pleas for deliverance. They are explicitly and implicitly written out of many and varied historical contexts. Some are written from tragic or life-threatening circumstances. Others were penned specifically to set the proper attitude for God's people as they ascended to Jerusalem to participate in worship. All of them are laced with real human emotion and thought, rising from real-life experiences.

A great many of the psalms were penned by David—the sweet psalmist of Israel. So when he says that the Spirit of the Lord spoke by him and that God's own word was on his tongue when he penned his psalms, it reveals that the process of inspiration involved more than simply giving him the words to write (2 Sam. 23:2). They were, in fact, the very words of God that were on David's tongue and were produced by David's pen when he wrote. At the same time, these words were the product of God's Spirit through the human instrument, David. God used that instrument with all the elements of his personality, language, experiences, feelings, emotions, and style.

So, for instance, in Psalm 23, David's own words are being articulated. When he describes the loving care of the Lord as his Shepherd in the opening verses as the One who "makes me lie down in green pastures," both David's own faith and God's inspired words are being expressed at the same time (Ps. 23:2). When David switches to the second person and addresses God directly, saying, "I will fear no evil, for you are with me" (Ps. 23:4), these are still David's own words, yet they are also the words of God's Spirit producing this inspired scripture. The process of inspiration at no point in time violates the personality, language, or style of the human author. Indeed, it includes all these elements as well as the immediate historical context in which the text was written. God prepared the human authors to be used as his instruments for the composition of his own Word.

God providentially prepared each human author to be the precise instrument he needed to be in order to pen the book (or books) he wrote. It begins with God's creation of man in his image. This provided man the innate ability to think and communicate with God in a way that makes divine revelation possible and comprehensible. God can communicate with man because he made man in such a way as to facilitate verbal interaction and rational thought. This preparation extended to each author's ancestry and life experiences—immediate and remote.

God's providence extended to a writer's remote ancestors. The personal heritage of many biblical writers is frequently evident in the texts of Scripture. It is probable that every biblical writer with the exception of Luke was a Jew. Some were of priestly descent. Others had royal ancestry. All were chosen for their divinely ordained ministries long before their entrance into the world (Jer. 1:5; Gal. 1:15). This shows that God's selection of the human authors was no last-minute emergency. God guided even all of the prophets' ancestors to be exactly who he wanted them to be. He did this so he could convey his inspired Word through their unique heritages.

This providential preparation brought each writer a unique perspective that included almost every area of life. Each writer was conditioned by factors related to his place and time. Each had a distinctive heredity, environment, education, and upbringing, as well as distinctive interests, experiences, and even personal relationships. Every writer had his own unique vocabulary and style of writing influenced by all these varied factors.

Beyond these contextual experiences is the direct work of God. He was providentially preparing and preserving the biblical writers to become his people and his prophets through the normal course of life. God provided the material necessities of life for the prophet so that he could live and grow to maturity. He preserved each of them from any disqualifying evil prior to their calling. He restrained those who might have otherwise destroyed them. In his perfect time, he called them to the ministry he had ordained for them. And he did all this after having orchestrated each of the circumstances of their individual lives to draw them to himself. God worked all things together for their good, even their penning of inspired Scripture (Rom. 8:28), so that he could use them for that very purpose. Warfield expressed it accurately, explaining that God's preparation of the human authors was "physical, intellectual, spiritual, which must have attended them throughout their whole lives, and, indeed, must have had its beginning in their remote ancestors, and the effect of which was to bring the right men to the right places at the right times, with the right endowments, impulses, acquirements, to write just the books which were designed for them."[6]

An excellent example of this entire process is Moses and the authoring of the Pentateuch. Moses was born of the tribe of Levi to parents in bondage in Egypt. However, it was the edict of Pharaoh himself prior to Moses's birth that led to his unique upbringing and education. In order to preserve Moses's life as an infant, his mother was forced to subtly deliver him into the hands of Pharaoh's daughter to be raised as her son. This turn of events resulted in Moses receiving the highest and finest training Egypt had to offer for the first forty years of his life (Acts 7:22). Yet he also knew his own ancestry. He observed firsthand the suffering and injustice that Pharaoh brought on his people. This compelled him to take matters into his own hands, but Moses's efforts ended in his flight from Egypt, which in turn led him to spend his next forty years as a shepherd (Exodus 1–2).

It is at this point that God's preparation of Moses becomes apparent. In Exodus 3,

---

6. Benjamin B. Warfield, *The Inspiration and Authority of the Bible* (Louisville: SBTS Press, 2014), 155.

God appeared to Moses in a burning bush. He called on Moses to be the instrument by which he would deliver his people from bondage in Egypt. However, Moses himself was humbled to the point that he was unconvinced that he was the man for the job. The first eighty years of Moses's life had indeed taught him one thing: he was not able to do this work in his own strength. God fully prepared him for his calling. However, Moses did not deliver God's people from bondage; God did. Yet he used a human instrument that had been fully prepared for this task over eighty years. The next forty years of Moses's life and ministry are recounted in the books of Exodus, Leviticus, Numbers, and Deuteronomy. They are a record of divine accomplishment through human instrumentality. God was never dependent on Moses to accomplish his intentions, which is clearly evidenced by God banning Moses from entering the Promised Land because of his sin (Num. 27:12–14). God did not need Moses to fulfill his good purposes; he was, however, completely able to use a fallible and even sinful human prophet to accomplish that perfect plan.

The same holds true for Moses's authorship of the Pentateuch. The extensive formal education and training Moses received as a result of growing up in Pharaoh's house is readily apparent in the authorship of the Torah. The five books of the Law are formally composed as detailed legal documents and historical records. It is possible that Moses composed Genesis partially on the basis of records to which he would have had access during his studies in Egypt. It is also possible that Moses's training included exposure to other ancient Near Eastern treaties and legal codes that to some degree influenced his composition of the judicial sections of the Law. At the same time, Moses had a recurrent experience of direct access to God during the time when he wrote the Pentateuch. As a result, he did not ultimately depend on external sources. The first five books of the Bible are the work of God and Moses at one and the same time. The emotions Moses relates show them to be very much his words (e.g., Deut. 1:37; 3:23–26), yet those words also flawlessly convey through the pen of Moses the very words of God.

The evidences of this dual authorship are manifold and readily apparent throughout the Bible. Scripture clearly highlights the uniqueness of each author. Moses was educated in Egypt. Paul received rabbinic training on the highest level as a student of Gamaliel (Acts 22:3) and was even versed in the Greek philosophies of the Stoics and Epicureans. Luke was a physician (Col. 4:14). David was a shepherd, soldier, and king. Solomon was raised a prince and lived as a king. Daniel was trained as a statesman. Peter and John were fishermen. Matthew was a tax collector. James and Jude were the sons of a carpenter. Each writer had a unique heritage, upbringing, and background. Each is a composite of the life experiences God providentially took him through. And all these factors worked together to shape these men into the very instruments God intended them to be in order to produce divinely authoritative writings. This uniqueness is evidenced in every book of the Bible. For example, each of the four Gospels contains similar accounts and content, yet each reflects the unique perspective and content choices of its author—under the superintending influence of the Holy Spirit. There are no contradictions between the human and divine authors.[7]

All these unique social, cultural, historical, emotional, experiential, educational, and practical distinctives are reflected in the language and style of each human author's work. At the same time, a consistent divine influence overshadows the books of Scripture, indicating that in the penning of these sixty-six books God used human prophets to compose his own divinely authoritative writings. These preparatory elements to inspiration necessarily affirm that Scripture is a completely providential and miraculous work, an inerrant written revelation produced by God.

Proofs of Inspiration

OLD TESTAMENT PROOFS OF INSPIRATION

The nature of inspiration requires that the process of verifying the Bible's inspiration be equally divine. These self-attesting proofs are manifold throughout the Scriptures.

The Old Testament Is Identified as the Words of God. The Scripture affirms thousands of times that its words are the very words of God. Numerous times the text specifically states, "God said" (e.g., Ex. 17:14; 19:3, 6–7; 20:1; 24:4; 34:27). Ezra called the Old Testament "the words of the God of Israel" (Ezra 9:4; cf. 10:3). In the 176 verses of Psalm 119, twenty-four times it calls Scripture the "word(s) of the LORD," and 175 times it exalts the Word of God using several different synonyms. The prophets identified even their written messages as the word of the Lord with statements like "hear the word(s) of the LORD" (1 Kings 22:19; 2 Kings 20:16) and similar expressions. From beginning to end, the Old Testament claims in its entirety to be the Word of God. Most theologians refer to this characteristic of all Scripture (i.e., every word) as *plenary inspiration*.

The Old Testament Records Direct Speech by God. The opening Genesis narrative affirms that God created by direct verbal statements. He simply expressed his will for something to exist, and it came into being from nothing (Gen. 1:3, 6, 9, 11, 14, 20, 24). There are divine directives that authoritatively convey God's expectations of his creatures (Gen. 1:26, 28–29; 2:16–17). There are divine judgments rendered that record God's evaluation of acts committed by his creatures and reveal the consequences that will follow (Gen. 3:13–19). There are also a number of conversations recorded in the Old Testament between God and select individuals. God called Abram from the land of Ur and spoke directly to him on multiple occasions about the details of the covenant he made with him (Gen. 12:1–3; 15:1–21). The call of Moses is a detailed account of the conversation God had with him explaining his role in delivering Israel from bondage in Egypt (Ex. 3:1–4:23). Immediately following the death of Moses, God spoke directly with Joshua, instructing him about his role in conquering the Promised Land (Josh. 1:8–9). The Old Testament records many direct statements or

---

7. See John MacArthur, *One Perfect Life: The Complete Story of the Lord Jesus* (Nashville: Thomas Nelson, 2012), 13–15.

conversations God had with his prophets (1 Kings 14:5). Some of these revelations are verbal (1 Sam. 3:21). Others are in visions or dreams (1 Kings 3:5). All are a record of divine speech.

The Old Testament Records Prophetic Speech from God. Beginning with Moses (Ex. 3:15), God's prophets were recognized as authoritative messengers from God speaking directly on his behalf. Their authority was such that what they said on God's behalf was viewed as God himself speaking. Moses was told to go directly to Pharaoh and address him on God's behalf by saying, "Thus says the LORD" (Ex. 4:22). That pattern is followed throughout the Old Testament by God's prophets (see Joshua, Josh. 7:13; 24:2, 27; Gideon, Judg. 6:7–18; Samuel, 1 Sam. 2:27; 10:18; 15:2; Nathan, 2 Sam. 12:7, 11; and many others, 1 Kings 11:31; 12:24; 13:1–2; 13:21; 14:3–7). When a prophet speaks for God, the typical decree formula used is "thus says the LORD," and it can even include the prophet speaking for God in the first person (e.g., 1 Kings 20:13). The standard concluding formula is "declares the LORD," coupled with the repeated use of first-person statements to demonstrate that what the prophet said, God was saying through him (Ezek. 20:1–45).

In the same way that God gave Moses the very words he wanted spoken or written, he enabled other prophets to speak on his behalf (Ex. 4:11–12). David recognized that God was speaking through him when he said, "The Spirit of the LORD speaks by me; his word is on my tongue" (2 Sam. 23:2). It was the very fact that prophets spoke directly for God that necessitated God giving instructions on how to distinguish between true and false prophets (Deut. 12:32; 13:1–5; 18:15–22).

The Old Testament Records Dictated Speech from God. There are several accounts in the Old Testament that were written down as God's own words at his instruction (Ex. 34:27). At the end of his life, Moses was commanded to write down in the final book of the Law all the words that the Lord had commanded him (Deut. 31:24–26). At other times, God simply instructed him to write down what happened (Ex. 17:14). Both forms are equally authoritative and divinely inspired in their composition. In the case of Jeremiah, he was instructed to write all the words God spoke to him (Jer. 30:1–4). When David penned his psalms, he knew it was God speaking through him, yet the Davidic psalms are clearly the result of David's own thoughts, words, and emotions. Regardless of the actual process of composition, what was written was considered to be God's own words conveyed through his human prophet. What the prophet wrote, God revealed.

NEW TESTAMENT PROOFS OF INSPIRATION

The New Testament gives a clear and consistent witness to the inspiration of the Old Testament, whose writings are thought of as God's speech. Matthew says that the words penned by Isaiah regarding the Messiah were spoken by God through the prophet (Isa. 7:14; Matt. 1:22–23). A comparison with his additional citations shows that, from Matthew's perspective, what the prophets wrote was equivalent to God speaking (see Matt. 2:15, 17–18; 4:14–16). This divine inspiration of David by the Spirit carries down to the individual word level (Ps. 110:1; Matt. 22:44–45; cf. Acts 2:29–31). Even the minor details cited in the Old Testament prophetic texts are seen as fulfilled in Christ (Mic. 5:2; Matt. 2:5).

Historical narratives in the Old Testament are universally treated as factual accounts by New Testament writers, including both major miraculous events (the destruction of Sodom and Gomorrah, 2 Pet. 2:6; Jude 7; and the global flood, Heb. 11:7; 1 Pet. 3:20; 2 Pet. 2:5), and minor details (David eating the showbread, Matt. 12:3–4). Stephen's speech recorded in Acts 7 demonstrates a clear affirmation of the historicity of the Old Testament Scriptures from Abram to that day. Jesus based the entirety of the case for his work of redemption on the testimony of the Old Testament from the Law of Moses to the Prophets and Psalms (Luke 24:25–27, 44–47). The universal practice of the New Testament writers follows precisely this practice from the record of their preaching in Acts to the inspired texts they wrote that make up the New Testament. Based on the practices of Jesus (recorded in the Gospels), the preaching of the apostles (recorded in Acts), and the writings of the New Testament (in the Epistles), there can be no doubt that for Christ and his apostles, the thirty-nine books of the (modern-day English) Old Testament were (1) inspired by God and (2) the full extent of the Scriptures up to that time.

The New Testament also gives a clear witness to itself as the Word of God. It presents several accounts of direct speech from God, including God attesting audibly to Christ at his baptism (Matt. 3:16–17; Luke 3:22) and the transfiguration (Matt. 17:5–7; Mark 9:7; Luke 9:35). John records God's affirmation of his Son's faithfulness in a public setting even though most were unable to discern it as more than thunder or an angel speaking to him (John 12:27–30). Luke recounts the direct speech of the risen Lord Jesus to Saul on the road to Damascus (Acts 9:3–7). While his companions did not see the Lord, they did hear the voice. Immediately after this, he records the way the Lord spoke to Ananias in a vision instructing him how to receive Saul as a disciple (Acts 9:10–16). Jesus also appears in a glorious vision to John and through him addresses the seven churches in Asia Minor, giving John specific commendations and condemnations directly related to each individual church (Revelation 1–3). Additionally, the New Testament equates Jesus's words even before his ascension with God's words (Luke 5:1; John 3:34; 6:63, 68). This same authority and enablement was granted on special occasions to the apostles (Acts 4:29–31)—so much so that Paul declares that Christ is speaking through him when he addresses the churches (2 Cor. 13:2–3).

CHRIST'S VIEW OF THE SCRIPTURES

For a Christian, there can be no better witness to a correct understanding of the character, nature, and authority of Scripture than Christ himself. His view must be the believer's view. As one works through the many references Jesus makes to Scripture, a clear perspective emerges. Jesus used Scripture in all matters of doctrine and practice. He based his own identity and mission on it. He defined it personally as truth. All this confirms that Jesus understood the Scriptures to be the inspired, inerrant, authoritative Word of God in both Testaments. It can be shown from Scripture that Jesus (1) affirmed the Old Testament as Scripture (by affirming its authority, inspiration, and historicity) and (2) preauthenticated the New Testament as Scripture.

Jesus Affirmed the Authority of the Old Testament. In his every use of the Scriptures, Jesus declared the authority and veracity of the Old Testament.

Jesus appealed to the authority of the Old Testament against Satan (Matt. 4:1–11; Luke 4:1–13). When challenged to turn stones into bread, Jesus responded by saying, "Man shall not live on bread alone," quoting from Deuteronomy 8:3. When Satan referenced Psalm 91 and the promise of divine preservation for the one who trusts in God, Jesus answered with the command from Deuteronomy 6:16 not to put God to the test. In the end, Jesus dismissed Satan, saying, "Be gone, Satan! For it is written, 'You shall worship the Lord your God and him only shall you serve'" (Matt. 4:10, quoting Deut. 6:13; 10:20). In each case, Jesus's appeal to the Old Testament is presented as the final word on the subject because it is the authoritative Word of God.

Jesus appealed to the authority of the Old Testament to resolve all matters of faith and practice. When his disciples were charged with breaking the Sabbath, Jesus referred to principles derived from the Mosaic law, quoting from 1 Samuel 21:6 as the biblical justification for their actions (Matt. 12:1–8). When asked about divorce, Jesus responded by saying, "Have you not read?" and then appealed to both Genesis 2:23–24 and Deuteronomy 24:1–4 in giving his answer (Matt. 19:3–9). In both cases, he used the Scripture not only to affirm the principle in question but also to confirm the divine authority inherent in the Old Testament text itself. When Jesus cleansed the temple for the second time at the end of his earthly ministry (Matt. 21:12–13), he built a composite argument from two Old Testament passages to justify his actions and condemn the nation (Isa. 56:7; Jer. 7:11). Jesus so repeatedly cited the Old Testament using expressions like "Have you not read?" that he thereby affirmed not only his agreement with it but also his recognition of its divine authority. In all these cases (and many more), Jesus never once corrected either a factual error or a practical instruction; Jesus viewed the Old Testament as the factually accurate and divinely authoritative Word of God.

Jesus appealed to the authority of the Old Testament to testify to his identity. When the religious leaders challenged his act of healing on the Sabbath, he claimed equality with God (John 5:17–18). He then brought forth several proofs of his claims. He began by mentioning the witness of John the Baptist (5:33–35) but moved beyond it in this context because it was not in itself a divine witness. He then provided three divine witnesses to his person: (1) the testimony of his works (5:36); (2) the testimony of his heavenly Father (5:37–38); and (3) the testimony of the Old Testament Scriptures, specifically the books of Moses (5:39–47). In this way, Jesus said that what Moses wrote is equal to what God has said. It is just as much a divine witness as the words of God spoken audibly from heaven or the miraculous acts of

God done on earth. In fact, at the conclusion of Jesus's teaching about the rich man and Lazarus, he defined the testimony of the Old Testament as superior testimony to that of miracles—even the miracle of resurrection (Luke 16:27–31).

Jesus personally submitted to the authority of the Old Testament. In the Sermon on the Mount, he stated that he had come not to abolish the Law or the Prophets (i.e., the Old Testament Scriptures) but to fulfill them (Matt. 5:17). He went on to say that any violation of the Scriptures or instructing of others to do likewise would have eternal consequences (Matt. 5:18–19). Jesus even went so far as to define the Golden Rule as the essential point of the Scriptures (Matt. 7:12). When he finished speaking, those who heard recognized that his instruction was different from the scribes. He taught as one having authority (Matt. 7:28–29). Jesus spoke with the divine authority inherent in his person as God in human flesh, and at the same time, he consistently confirmed and conformed to the authority of the Scriptures. Even in his own witness to his identity, he submitted himself to the principles and mandates in the Old Testament Scriptures. So in John 5:31 he said, "If I alone bear witness about myself, my testimony is not true." Jesus was not denying the veracity of his own testimony (see John 8:14–20) but was submitting to the Old Testament call for two or three witnesses (Deut. 17:6; 19:15).

Jesus maintained the same view of the Old Testament Scriptures before and after his resurrection. Luke records two occasions in which Jesus met with his disciples immediately after the resurrection. The first was with two disciples on the road that leads from Jerusalem to Emmaus (Luke 24:13–35). The second was back in Jerusalem in a room where many of the disciples had gathered (Luke 24:36–47). In both cases, Jesus demonstrated the same convictions about both the authority of the Scriptures and the necessity of their fulfillment. On the first occasion, he confirmed the necessity of all the things written in the Old Testament concerning himself coming to pass—just as they did in his death, burial, and resurrection (Luke 24:26–27). On the second, he declared not only this but also that his followers' future ministry of bearing witness to him and his work was also based on the Old Testament Scriptures (Luke 24:44–47). Jesus's view of the Old Testament, its inspiration, inerrancy, and authority has not changed as a result of his glorification. This very fact goes a long way toward refuting the errant theories of accommodation.

Jesus Affirmed the Inspiration of the Old Testament. In Jesus's view, the authority of the Old Testament rested on its nature as the inspired Word of God.

Jesus affirmed the divine and human authorship of the Bible. He repeatedly recognized the men who wrote the Old Testament. He spoke directly of Moses (John 5:45–47), David (Luke 20:42), Isaiah (Matt. 13:14), and even Daniel (Matt. 24:15–16) as authors of the texts he referenced. At the same time, he attributed their writings not only to them solely but also to the work of the Holy Spirit as the divine author. Jesus identified both David and the Holy Spirit as the author of Psalm 110 (Mark 12:36). He interchangeably referred to portions of the Old Testament as the words of God and the work of human writers like Moses and Isaiah (Matt. 15:1–11). When the whole of Christ's use of the Old Testament is compared, it is clear that there is no difference in his perspective between "God says," "the Scripture says," or "David himself, in the Holy Spirit, says." By citing both the human and divine authors of Scripture, Jesus confirmed what David said himself—"The Spirit of the LORD speaks by me; his word is on my tongue" (2 Sam. 23:2).

Jesus affirmed the veracity of the Bible. The Old Testament itself contains more than 3,800 direct claims that what is written consists of the actual words of God. It also makes several universal claims concerning its truthfulness (Pss. 19:7, 9; 119:43, 160; 138:2; Prov. 30:5). The test given to identify a false prophet was directly tied to the truthfulness of his claims and whether his words were in complete conformity with the existing content of Scripture (Deut. 13:1–5; 18:20–22). So if what a prophet said failed to come true, he was a false prophet. If the miracle he foretold occurred but his words were contrary to Scripture, he was still to be rejected as a false prophet. According to the Old Testament, what the Scriptures say is true and of absolute lasting integrity and authority.

Jesus's testimony to the truthfulness of the Old Testament is identical to the Old Testament's own testimony. He considered the Scripture to be God's very words and commandments. As such, it was to be recognized as fully authoritative (Matt. 15:3–9). His rebuke of the scribes and Pharisees in this same passage aligns with the testimony of the Old Testament, which identified those who denied this belief as false—hence Jesus's labeling of them as "blind guides" (Matt. 15:14).

By saying, "Your word is truth" (John 17:17), Jesus personally identified Scripture as objective truth. This is perfectly in keeping with the testimony of Psalm 119:160, for the testimonies of both the Lord and the Old Testament are in perfect agreement. This absolute integrity, coupled with the appeal to the authority of the Old Testament by both Jesus and the New Testament writers alike, supports the fact that Jesus considered the Old Testament the inspired Word of God. As such, he considered it to be not just truthful but truth itself. He called God's Word "truth" (John 17:17). He treated every Old Testament testimony as a statement of fact. This included even the most miraculous events. Jesus treated the Old Testament as the true and truthful Word of God.

Jesus affirmed the verbal and plenary inspiration of the Bible. As mentioned above, the terms *verbal* and *plenary* refer, respectively, to *every word* and to *all the words* of Scripture. So a belief in verbal and plenary inspiration speaks of an assent to the fact that every single word in Scripture and the whole of it are inspired by God. That Jesus held to this view is evidenced in two ways. First, he quoted from or alluded to many of the books of the Old Testament in numerous ways and contexts. He quoted from all five books of Moses and the works of additional prophets. He made at least eight direct references to the Psalms. He mentioned in some way every major division of the Hebrew Bible (the Law, the Prophets, and the Writings). Even after his resurrection, he referred to the whole of the Old Testament as a divinely inspired and authoritative testimony to his own life and ministry (Luke 24:27). Second, Jesus based arguments of no less significance than the defense of his deity on individual words, phrases, and letters in the Old Testament text. This use of the Old Testament by the Lord demonstrates his affirmation of the divine, verbal inspiration of the Scripture.

Jesus says in Matthew 5:17–18 that not one letter or even the stroke of a pen that distinguishes between letters shall pass away until all the Scripture is fulfilled. Surely, no higher view of the finest details of Scripture could be expressed than this. There are more examples worth observing.

At the Feast of Dedication, Jesus asserted his deity by claiming equality with the Father (John 10:22–30). The Jews responded by picking up stones to hurl at him because of his perceived blasphemous statement. In John 10:34–35, Jesus defended his claim by directing his opponents' attention to what would seem to be an obscure phrase in Psalm 82:6. The weight of his argument is based on a single word in the text: "gods." He says, "Is it not written in your Law, 'I said, you are gods'? If he called them gods to whom the word of God came—and Scripture cannot be broken—do you say of him whom the Father consecrated and sent into the world, 'You are blaspheming,' because I said, 'I am the Son of God'?" (John 10:34–36). Christ used three different terms in these two verses to describe Psalm 82. He referred to it as "Law," "the word of God," and "the Scripture." The synonymous terminology demonstrates an affirmation of the plenary inspiration of the text. When he said, "Scripture cannot be broken" (John 10:35), he was declaring its seamless unity, echoing Matthew 5:18, "For truly, I say to you, until heaven and earth pass away, not an iota, not a dot, will pass from the Law until all is accomplished." In this case Jesus based his whole point on a single word: "gods." If God can use that word to describe unjust judges who will be condemned by him, can he not also use it for his eternal Son? Jesus Christ presented an argument for his deity from this one word in the Old Testament, showing that Jesus viewed the inerrancy of the smallest details of the Old Testament to be of serious significance.

When challenged by the Sadducees on the subject of the resurrection of the dead, Jesus based the whole of his rebuttal on the tense of a verb (Matt. 22:32). The Sadducees came to Jesus in an attempt to stump him by presenting an extreme case on a fine point of the Old Testament law having to do with the obligation of a brother to marry the widowed and childless wife of a brother. Their question was even more ridiculous than their illustration, for they asked whose wife she would be in the resurrection. But Jesus responded not only by affirming the authority and veracity of God's commandment through Moses but also by identifying that their error was their failure to understand Scripture. He said, "And as for the resurrection of the dead, have you not read what was said to you by God: 'I am the God of Abraham, and the God of Isaac, and the God of Jacob'? He is not God of the dead, but of the living" (Matt. 22:31–32). He meant that those patriarchs are alive, since even after their death God declares, "I am" their God, not "I was" their God. Again, the expression "Have you not read?" is an appeal to the authority of the Exodus 3:6 passage he quotes. Moreover, the argument here is for a doctrine no less significant than the resurrection—and it is based on the sense derived from the implied copula (or linking verb) of the nominal clause in the Hebrew text. "I AM" is a literal and exact understanding of the Hebrew construction.

Finally, Jesus silenced the last of his critics when he responded to the Pharisees by asking a question on the proper understanding of one word in Psalm 110:1. Matthew describes it this way:

> Now while the Pharisees were gathered together, Jesus asked them a question, saying, "What do you think about the Christ? Whose son is he?" They said to him, "The son of David." He said to them, "How is it then that David, in the Spirit, calls him Lord, saying, 'The Lord said to my Lord, "Sit at my right hand, until I put your enemies under your feet"'? If then David calls him Lord, how is he his son?" (Matt. 22:41–45)

Jesus makes a profound theological statement in this text regarding his deity. He was born as a son in David's line, which means that the only way David can call his son "Lord" is if his son is also superior to him. His son can only be superior if he is also God. Jesus based the entirety of his argument on the word "Lord." David can call his son "Lord" because his son by human birth is none other than the Lord, the incarnate Son of God. Again, a single word serves as a key part of the basis for a doctrine as significant as the deity of Christ.

Jesus attested to the verbal inspiration of the Old Testament when he rebuked the Pharisees on a different occasion with these words: "But it is easier for heaven and earth to pass away than for one dot of the Law to become void" (Luke 16:17). While the point here is that Scripture will be fulfilled to the letter, that does not negate the fact that it is correspondingly essential for it to be accurate and reliable down to the letter. This is similarly reflected in the Sermon on the Mount, in which Jesus said that every letter is perfectly preserved in heaven and will come to pass (Matt. 5:17–18). Not only did Jesus view the smallest portion of the text as inspired, he also considered every letter to be essential. He claimed that even the smallest part is eternal. The implications for historicity are massive. If Jesus attested to this degree of accuracy, reliability, and integrity in the Old Testament, then the Bible must be regarded as inspired, inerrant, and eternally true—down to the last word. In the end, Jesus's use of the Old Testament demonstrates an absolute confidence in the verbal and plenary inspiration of the Scriptures—in the whole, in its parts, and including every letter.

Jesus affirmed the necessity of the fulfillment of Scripture. He repeatedly attested to the necessity of fulfilling personally all that the Old Testament Scriptures said about him and his ministry (Matt. 26:31; Mark 9:12–13; 14:27, 49; Luke 20:17; 24:25–27, 44–46; John 5:39; 12:14; 13:18; 17:12). In the context of his betrayal, he cited Zechariah 13:7, stating that his own disciples would all fall away because Scripture said that this would happen (Matt. 26:31). This citation met with great objections by the disciples. Yet Jesus still affirmed the necessity of it because every Scripture would be fulfilled. Even as he hung on the cross, Jesus deliberately fulfilled the Scriptures to the letter (John 19:28–30). John goes so far as to state that during his life the disciples failed to notice how Scripture was being fulfilled. However, after Christ had risen, he and the rest of the apostles remembered what was written in the Old Testament and saw how Jesus had done exactly what the Scriptures said that he would (John 12:14–16). Jesus believed that every word of Scripture had to be fulfilled. That is precisely what the apostles testified concerning what took place in the life and ministry of Jesus Christ.

Jesus Affirmed the Historicity of the Old Testament. In addition to affirming the authority and inspiration of the Old Testament, Jesus declared his confidence in the veracity of the historical accounts contained within it.

Jesus affirmed the historicity of persons in the Old Testament. In every reference he made to the people mentioned in the Old Testament, Jesus treated them as real persons. When discussing the topic of divorce, Jesus confirmed the historical facts not only of the creation account but also of Adam and Eve. Furthermore, he built his case for the doctrine of marriage on the historic veracity of Genesis (Matt. 19:4–5). He demonstrated a firm confidence in the factuality of the Genesis 4 narrative, including not only Abel's existence but also his murder (Matt. 23:35). He affirmed the factuality of the historical records of numerous Old Testament persons, including Abraham, Isaac, and Jacob (Matt. 8:11; 22:32; Luke 13:28; John 8:56); Lot and his wife (Luke 17:28, 32); Moses (John 3:14; 5:45; 7:19); David (Matt. 12:3; 22:43–45); Solomon (Matt. 6:29; Luke 11:31); the queen of Sheba (Matt. 12:42; Luke 11:31); Elijah and the widow in Sidon (Luke 4:25–26); Elisha and Naaman (Luke 4:27); Jonah (Matt. 12:39–41; Luke 11:29–32); Zechariah (Matt. 23:35; Luke 11:51); and Daniel (Matt. 24:15). Jesus spoke of all these individuals as real historical persons, treating the details the Scriptures record about them as historical facts. From Adam and Noah to Jonah and Daniel, Jesus attested without hesitation to the historicity not just of the persons themselves but also of the events concerning them recorded throughout the Old Testament. That Jesus commonly referred to these individuals to make an important doctrinal point clearly shows that he accepted the historical accuracy of these texts.

Jesus affirmed the historicity of places and events in the Old Testament. Jesus referred to the Old Testament accounts frequently in his teachings. He used these references at times to prove a point. At other times, he used them as illustrations or confirmations of his teaching. In every case, he spoke of them as real places and real events. Remarkably, he commonly cited those accounts most characterized by miraculous events. He attested to the destruction of Sodom and Gomorrah by God as recorded in Genesis 19 (Matt. 11:20–24). He confirmed Jonah's days inside the great fish (Matt. 12:40) and Nineveh's repentance (Luke 11:30–32). He affirmed a literal, global flood in the days of Noah (Matt. 24:38–39). He was convinced that God supernaturally provided manna from heaven for Israel when they wandered in the wilderness for forty years (John 6:49). Jesus did not refer to these events simply in passing; he used these very narratives to lay the foundation for doctrines as eternally significant as his resurrection. For example, he related the factuality of his resurrection to the historical veracity of Jonah 1:17 and its account of Jonah's time in the great fish (Matt. 12:38–42). Jesus taught that the Scripture was not only inspired by God but also, as a necessary corollary, historically accurate.

Jesus affirmed the historicity of even the authorship of the Old Testament. On a number of occasions, Jesus cited the human author of Old Testament books by name. This demonstrates his confidence in the historicity of the human authorship of these works, thereby defying later higher-critical claims to the contrary. For example, Christ attributed the authorship of the Pentateuch to Moses (Matt. 8:4; Mark 12:26; John 5:45–46), even positing in John 5 that the writings of Moses testified to himself—Jesus directly linked his claims about himself to the Mosaic authorship of the Pentateuch. In addition, Jesus affirmed that David wrote Psalm 110 (Matt. 22:43–44), that Isaiah wrote the book of Isaiah (Matt. 13:14–15), and that Daniel wrote the book of Daniel (Matt. 24:15). Based on his use of the Old Testament, Christ clearly considered it to be a historically accurate record composed by divinely inspired men who produced divinely authoritative writings.

Jesus Preauthenticated the New Testament as Scripture. Whereas Jesus affirmed the authority, inspiration, and historicity of the Old Testament that had already been received, he preauthenticated the writings that would be written and collected after his ascension to make up the New Testament.

Jesus claimed that his words were the Father's words. Christ himself repeatedly declared that when he spoke, his words were the very words the Father had given him to speak. He set his words on an equal plane with both the spoken words of God and the Scriptures themselves. On that basis, it can be said that the apostolic record of his words is a divinely authoritative message from God. As Jesus put it,

> "I have much to say about you and much to judge, but he who sent me is true, and I declare to the world what I have heard from him." They did not understand that he had been speaking to them about the Father. So Jesus said to them, "When you have lifted up the Son of Man, then you will know that I am he, and that I do nothing on my own authority, but speak just as the Father taught me." (John 8:26–28)

According to Jesus, his crucifixion would prove the veracity of both his personal identity as the Son of Man and the divine source of his message to the world (cf. John 12:49–50).

In the upper room, Jesus informed his disciples that his words were part of the works of the Father and that they not only revealed the Father to men but also verified the unity of the Father and Son to them: "Do you not believe that I am in the Father and the Father is in me? The words that I say to you I do not speak on my own authority, but the Father who dwells in me does his works" (John 14:10). Finally, according to Christ's prayer on the night on which he was betrayed, it was the disciples' reception of his words from the Father that distinguished the eleven from both Judas and the rest of the unbelieving world. Jesus prayed, "Now they know that everything that you have given me is from you. For I have given them the words that you gave me, and they have received them and have come to know in truth that I came from you; and they have believed that you sent me" (John 17:7–8). Clearly, the words that Jesus gave to his disciples originated in God the Father, who granted the eleven an understanding of the true nature and mission of Jesus Christ (see John 17:14, 17).

Jesus was a prophet "like unto" Moses but far greater than Moses. God spoke to Moses face-to-face and revealed himself to him (Ex. 33:11; Deut. 34:10). Jesus Christ is the incarnate Word, and as such is himself the revelation of God. His words were the Father's words directly. Seeing Jesus was seeing the Father. But Jesus promised more to his disciples than just their memories of the divine revelation that he was and that he had given to them; he promised that they would be granted additional revelation by the Holy Spirit.

Jesus promised the apostles additional revelation. From the time of Peter's confession (Matt. 16:16), Jesus prepared his disciples for his departure. In the final hours of his life on earth, he gathered his disciples into the upper room to prepare them for the crucifixion. He had told them about it on many prior occasions—yet without their comprehension. Even on the final night, his disciples failed to either grasp or accept his testimony concerning the events that were about to transpire (John 13:12–38). Nevertheless, he proceeded to prepare them for their future ministry by making three significant promises.

First, he promised them that the Spirit would help them accurately recall his words: "But the Helper, the Holy Spirit, whom the Father will send in my name, he will teach you all things and bring to your remembrance all that I have said to you" (John 14:26). The Holy Spirit of God would grant a special twofold blessing to the eleven: (1) He would teach them all things. The implication from the context seems to be that he would instruct them concerning the things that Jesus himself had taught them, so that they would come to an understanding of them. (2) He would remind them accurately of all that Jesus said. This is the promise of a flawless remembrance of Jesus's words for these eleven men. As such, this is a preauthentication of the veracity and inspiration of the Gospels of Matthew, Mark (based on Peter's testimony), and John.

Second, Jesus promised that they would testify concerning him and that their testimony would come by way of the inspiration of the Holy Spirit: "But when the Helper comes, whom I will send to you from the Father, the Spirit of truth, who proceeds from the Father, he will bear witness about me. And you also will bear witness, because you have been with me from the beginning" (John 15:26–27). Two observations pertinent to this discussion emerge from this text: (1) The disciples' testimony concerning Christ would be based both on their eyewitness account of Christ and on revelation from the Spirit of truth. The significance of the dual aspect of this testimony is that though it would be a testimony to the Lord Jesus Christ and a testimony from the Holy Spirit, it would still bear the marks of their own eyewitness experience. (2) It would be a truthful testimony. Jesus specifically emphasized the truthfulness of this testimony by describing the Helper in this context as the "Spirit of truth." Therefore, though the testimony of the eleven would be their own testimony, it would also be the inspired testimony of the Holy Spirit of truth.

Third, Jesus promised them that they would receive additional revelation beyond what he had personally entrusted to them. As he stated to his disciples in the upper room,

> I still have many things to say to you, but you cannot bear them now. When the Spirit of truth comes, he will guide you into all the truth, for he will not speak on his own authority, but whatever he hears he will speak, and he will declare to you the things that are to come. He will glorify me, for he will take what is mine and declare it to you. All that the Father has is mine; therefore I said that he will take what is mine and declare it to you. (John 16:12–14)

There are three key observations to make from this text. First, Jesus indicated that he personally had more revelation to give them but was prevented from dispensing it because of their inability to receive it at that time. Surely, this includes the whole New Testament—even the book of Revelation, since he refers to "things that are to come" in verse 13. Second, he again says that the source of this revelation will be the Spirit of truth. The emphasis on *truth* cannot be missed. By preauthenticating the New Testament, Jesus showed that it would be characterized by the same truthfulness that characterizes the One who would inspire it. Finally, like the Old Testament, the New Testament will glorify the Son. Jesus viewed the Old Testament as a flawless revelation of himself and his work even after his resurrection. The New Testament would glorify the person and work of the Son in a way greater than the Old Testament Scriptures. It would be an equally authoritative, inspired, and inerrant revelation from God but would complete the divine message of Scripture. It would be, as the Old Testament was, the word of the Trinity (John 16:14–15). So Jesus preauthenticated the New Testament as the verbal, plenary, divinely inspired, and authoritative Word of God.

Jesus gave additional revelation personally. The New Testament has one other testimony concerning Jesus Christ that is relevant to this discussion. The Apocalypse or Revelation of Jesus Christ is so titled because it is the writing of the apostle John concerning the revelation he received directly from Christ himself near the end of the first century. Though this is certainly the testimony of John under the inspiration of the Holy Spirit concerning the things that are to come (i.e., directly in line with the promise of John 16:13), it is no less the testimony of Jesus himself (John 16:12, 14–15).

Jesus had more to say personally to his disciples, and it seems very reasonable to conclude that he viewed his personal message to John in the last book of the New Testament as a portion of the additional revelation he promised. This can be seen from Revelation 1:10–18 where John identifies the source of this revelation as the One who was dead and is now living, which can only be the Lord Jesus himself. That means the revelation included the rest of the book that he gave to John: his personal message to each of the seven churches (Revelation 2–3) and the additional revelation concerning the future outpouring of God's wrath (Revelation 4–18), the culmination of redemptive history in the second coming (Revelation 19), the establishment of the millennial kingdom (Revelation 20), and the final establishment of the new heavens and the new earth (Revelation 21–22).

The New Testament Writers Affirmed Christ's View. The testimony of the New Testament writers to their own writings affirms Jesus's preauthentication of the New Testament. This is readily apparent when one examines both what they said about the Old Testament and how they used it. A few key texts will likewise demonstrate that they considered their writings to be Scripture, in complete keeping with Jesus's preauthentication.

The New Testament writers recognized the authority of the Old Testament. Paul founded his gospel on the Old Testament Scriptures. He wrote to the saints in Corinth saying, "I delivered to you as of first importance what I also received: that Christ died for our sins in accordance with the Scriptures, that he was buried, that he was raised on the third day in accordance with the Scriptures" (1 Cor. 15:3–4). The Scripture Paul refers to is the Old Testament. In this way, he asserts that the life, death, and resurrection of Christ were a fulfillment of the Old Testament Scriptures. What the Old Testament says is to be taken as revelation from God. This is further supported by Luke's assessment of the Bereans. He described them as "more noble" than the Thessalonians because they too received the Word with eagerness when Paul preached it to them. However, they also checked what he preached to them against the Old Testament Scriptures daily to verify that what he told them matched the teachings of the Old Testament (Acts 17:10–11). This is especially relevant to this discussion about the New Testament, since Paul praised the Thessalonians for receiving his message for what it really was—the Word of God (1 Thess. 2:13). This shows that the New Testament writers recognized the authority of the Old Testament as the Word of God and that they believed that their message was equally from God and in conformity with the Old Testament Scriptures.

The New Testament writers recognized the Old Testament as the Word of God. Paul described the Old Testament as "the oracles of God" (Rom. 3:2), a phrase that identifies the Scriptures as messages directly from God. The apostles themselves declared that the Old Testament had to be fulfilled in all points (Acts 1:16; 2:15–16; 3:18; 4:8–12), and all the New Testament writers consistently followed this practice. The Gospels and Epistles include numerous Old Testament citations as the basis for the gospel. Beyond this, the biblical authors repeatedly referred to the teachings of Jesus or the Old Testament Scriptures, establishing them as grounds for New Testament doctrines or practices and demonstrating that they affirmed a view of the Old Testament and its authority that was consistent with the view of Jesus.

Every writer of the New Testament demonstrated a reverence for the Old Testament Scriptures. At times, they quoted from the Old Testament, saying, "Scripture says." At other times, they attributed what the Scriptures said to God. This lack of distinction makes it clear that the New Testament writers saw no real distinction between what God says and what Scripture says. Those two ideas were essentially synonymous. So when the New Testament writers say, "Scripture says," it is equally appropriate to understand them as saying, "God says," no matter who the human author was. For example, in Romans 9:17, Paul describes God's message to Pharaoh as Scripture speaking. The actual text of Exodus 9:16, though, makes it evident that God himself spoke. *God says*, *the Scripture says*, or *a biblical writer says* are all equivalent to *God says*.

The New Testament writers recognized their own writings as Scripture. Matthew, Peter, and John were all eyewitnesses of the risen Lord Jesus. They were included among Christ's chosen apostles from the beginning. Their writings give an inspired account of the life and ministry of Jesus Christ, and they frequently base their testimony on citations or references to the Old Testament Scriptures. While these Gospels omit any direct claims to inspiration, Christ's preauthentication promises, coupled with his selection of these men as apostles, attest to their authority. In fact, it was the apostolic office and the gift of prophecy that conveyed divine authority to New Testament writers and apostles, much as was the case with Old Testament prophets. Paul, for example, confirmed that his preaching was from God (1 Thess. 2:13), and he also declared his own writings to be the commands of God. He adamantly admonished the Corinthians, saying, "If anyone thinks that he is a prophet, or spiritual, he should acknowledge that the things I am writing to you are a command of the Lord. If anyone does not recognize this, he is not recognized" (1 Cor. 14:37–38). It was not simply Paul who declared his letters authoritative; Peter also recognized Paul's letters as inspired Scripture when he wrote, "And count the patience of our Lord as salvation, just as our beloved brother Paul also wrote to you according to the wisdom given him, as he does in all his letters when he speaks in them of these matters. There are some things in them that are hard to understand, which the ignorant and unstable twist to their own destruction, as they do the other Scriptures" (2 Pet. 3:15–16). Peter not only identified Paul's letters as inspired of God but also asserted that the New Testament would be composed by more than just the original apostles.

What about the New Testament writers who were not apostles? Some New Testament prophets (believers who had the gift of prophecy) only spoke, but others wrote Scripture. Just as some apostles did not write Scripture, so some prophets did not as well. As Paul explains, the mystery of the gospel "has now been revealed to his holy apostles and prophets by the Spirit" (Eph. 3:5). Luke says that there were prophets in Jerusalem who went down to Antioch, such as Agabus, who foretold by the Spirit the famine that was about to take place (Acts 11:27–28). That the famine came true shows that the gift of prophecy was active. Acts 13:1 identifies the leadership of the church as prophets and teachers and included in its list Barnabas, Simeon, Lucius, Manaen, and Saul (i.e., the apostle Paul). While the text is unclear on whether all of them or only select individuals among them had the gift of prophecy, it was a plurality.

Paul also equated Luke's writings with Scripture when he wrote, "For the Scripture says, 'You shall not muzzle an ox when it treads out the grain,' and, 'The laborer deserves his wages'" (1 Tim. 5:18). Paul here attributes the title of Scripture to both Deuteronomy (by quoting Deut. 25:4) and Luke's Gospel (by quoting Luke 10:7). While the main emphasis of the text is not inspiration, it cannot be missed that Paul uses the term "Scripture" to speak of both the Old Testament and Luke's writing. The clear implication is that Paul's statement applies the quality of divine authorship to Luke's writings on an equal level with the Old Testament. This is completely in line with Jesus's preauthentication of the New Testament. It merely expands it to include a nonapostolic writer, much like Peter expanded it with Paul.

Along with Paul and Luke can be added Mark, James, the author of Hebrews, and Jude to the list of nonapostolic, inspired New Testament writers. Each of these men was associated very closely with Christ and his apostles. Mark was a companion of Paul on his early journeys (Acts 12:25; 13:5). While Mark's failure resulted in the breakup of Paul and Barnabas (Acts 15:37–39), Paul himself attested to Mark's later maturity and spiritual progress (2 Tim. 4:11). Mark's Gospel was closely affiliated with the preaching of Peter, but its composition was the result of the inspiration of the Holy Spirit through the gift of prophecy. The same can be said of the epistles of James and Jude. James was recognized as a pillar in the early church (Gal. 2:9), and he was the chief spokesman for the church in Jerusalem during the council in Acts 15. He and Jude were both half brothers of Jesus writing Scripture under the inspiration of the Holy Spirit by way of the gift of prophecy. The same holds true for the author of Hebrews. Though the identity of this author remains unknown, the gift of prophecy through the Holy Spirit was the means by which it was composed. The twenty-seven books of the New Testament self-attest to the fact of their inspiration.

Authority of Scripture

Secondary Sources
Primary Source

The doctrine of authority boils down to one primary question: How does one become convinced that the Bible really is the Word of God?[8] Or, how does a person become certain that Scripture is the truth of God conveyed through the process of inspiration and that it thereby has the right to exercise authority over one's life?

The rightful idea of authority has always been a battleground. At the start of the twenty-first century, illegitimate forms and expressions of authority range from the illegal and abusive exercise of authoritarianism or totalitarianism to the individual authority that emerges from a postmodern mindset of selfishness.

The appropriate approach to this discussion commences with a working definition of *authority* in general, especially legitimate authority exercised in a proper fashion. A representative dictionary definition proffers that authority is the "power or right to enforce obedience; moral or legal supremacy; right to command or give a final

---

8. This introduction is adapted from Richard L. Mayhue, "The Authority of Scripture," *MSJ* 15, no. 2 (2004): 228–29. Used by permission of *MSJ*.

decision."[9] The New Testament noun most commonly translated "authority" (102 times)—*exousia*—carries a similar definition: "power exercised by rulers or others in high position by virtue of their office."[10]

Secular worldviews offer many approaches to authority, such as the following:

- *Oligarchical*: authority exercised by a powerful few
- *Democratic*: authority exercised by the people
- *Hereditary*: authority exercised by those in a particular family
- *Despotic*: authority exercised by one or more in an evil fashion
- *Personal*: authority exercised by one person

However, in a biblical worldview, original and ultimate authority resides with God and God alone. God did not inherit his authority—there was no one to bequeath it to him. God did not receive his authority—there was no one to bestow it on him. God's authority did not come by way of an election—there was no one to vote for him. God did not seize his authority—there was no one from whom to steal it. God did not earn his authority—it was already his.

God's authority becomes obvious and unquestionable when one considers three facts. First, God created the heavens, the earth, and all that exists therein (Genesis 1–2). Second, God owns the earth, all it contains, and those who dwell on it (Ps. 24:1). Third, in the end God will consume it all, just as he declared, "But the day of the Lord will come like a thief, and then the heavens will pass away with a roar, and the heavenly bodies will be burned up and dissolved, and the earth and the works that are done on it will be exposed" (2 Pet. 3:10).

To understand and accept God's authority is as simple as accepting the fact of God himself. Romans says this best: "Let every person be subject to the governing authorities. For there is no authority except from God, and those that exist have been instituted by God" (Rom. 13:1). This *locus classicus* lays out clearly the source of all authority and articulates the principle of *divine delegation* (see Job 34:13; John 19:11).

Numerous statements in the Old Testament explicitly testify to God's authority. For example, Psalm 62:11 asserts that "power belongs to God," and 2 Chronicles 20:6 reads, "O LORD, God of our fathers, are you not God in heaven? You rule over all the kingdoms of the nations. In your hand are power and might, so that none is able to withstand you."

The New Testament attributes the same authority to the Lord Jesus, who declared after his resurrection that "all authority in heaven and on earth has been given to me" (Matt. 28:18). Paul affirmed that in the end, "at the name of Jesus every knee should bow, in heaven and on earth and under the earth" (Phil. 2:10). Jude wrote it this way: "To the only God, our Savior, through Jesus Christ our Lord, be glory, majesty, dominion, and authority, before all time and now and forever. Amen" (Jude 25).

---

9. *The New Shorter Oxford Dictionary*, 4th ed. (Oxford: Oxford University Press, 1993), s.v. "authority."

10. Walter Bauer, *A Greek-English Lexicon of the New Testament and Other Early Christian Literature*, rev. and ed. Frederick W. Danker, 3rd ed., based on the previous English editions by W. F. Arndt, F. W. Gingrich, and F. W. Danker (Chicago: University of Chicago Press, 2000), 353.

Secondary Sources

Throughout church history people have argued that a number of sources establish the authority of Scripture. Among the most prominent are (1) rational evidences, (2) church authority, and (3) the Bible's existential impact on the reader. As each of these is discussed briefly, it will become apparent that none satisfactorily makes the case for the authority of Scripture.

RATIONAL EVIDENCES

Rational evidences include conclusions that can be drawn by making observations of the text of Scripture and the facts of history. Archaeological evidences provide one significant example. The Bible makes many historical references to people, places, and events, and a significant number of these are verifiable by tangible evidence. Archaeologists have uncovered everything from the city of Jericho (with some evidence that the walls fell flat) to the Tel Dan stela (which mentions King David by name). These discoveries include artifacts that confirm the existence of historical persons and the occurrence of historical events mentioned in the Scriptures. Throughout the last several centuries, most of the charges of the Bible's historical inaccuracies have been refuted through these kinds of findings. In addition, not one historical event or person in the Bible has been proven false. Even apparent inconsistencies have been answered in a way that confirms the historical veracity of the Scriptures.

Another rational argument entails the fulfillment of prophecy. Isaiah 53 alone gives abundant evidence that God revealed details related to the crucifixion that only he could know. This text was written approximately seven hundred years prior to the birth of Christ. Isaiah 44:28 also makes reference to Cyrus the king of Persia by name and even goes so far as to declare that he will be the one to give the order for rebuilding the temple in Jerusalem. This text was written more than one hundred years prior to the destruction of the temple. Daniel records the rise and fall of every major empire from Persia to Rome in such a way that it can only be explained by a divinely authoritative revelation from God to men (Daniel 7–8). Add to this the manifold prophecies of the Old Testament fulfilled throughout the course of redemptive history, and the case becomes insurmountable in favor of Scripture's inspiration and authority. These and other similar rational arguments can be used to affirm logically that Scripture is the authoritative Word of God.

CHURCH AUTHORITY

A second potential source of authority for Scripture is the church's authority. This includes the declarations made by church councils, early church fathers, and significant ecclesiastical bodies. The Roman Catholic Church is founded on this principle. In their view, the Bible is the Word of God because the Roman church has decreed it to be. The primary problem with this argument is this: Who authorized the church to make this kind of declaration? What is the source of the church's authority? If the Scriptures are the basis for the church's supreme authority (see Eph. 2:20), then such authority is invalidated because it rests on circular reasoning. If supreme authority relies on some other source, like apostolic succession, then proof of such authority must be given, but in the case of the Roman Catholic Church, there is no true evidence for apostolic succession. The church can affirm the authority of Scripture, but it cannot be the ultimate witness to it.

EXISTENTIAL IMPACT

A third argument for the authority of Scripture is its existential impact on the life of a believer. This idea includes the tangible impact on a believer's life that always accompanies genuine saving faith. It has also been used in liberal circles to speak of the Scriptures as not being the Word but becoming the Word when it has an existential impact on a reader. In either case, this amounts to basing one's conviction that the Bible is the Word of God on the practical or emotional effect that its content has on the individual's life.

The problem with all these arguments is that they are all subjective. They leave it up to the individual to determine whether or not the Bible is truly from God on the basis of his or her own evaluative standards. While these approaches do provide supporting evidence for Scripture as God's Word, they are inadequate as the primary or ultimate proof. That proof must be the testimony of Scripture itself.

Primary Source

The matter of authority is addressed frequently throughout Scripture. The descriptions of God and the titles applied to him demonstrate his absolute authority over his creation. He is identified from the beginning as the Creator of all things (Gen. 1:1). The titles Lord (Deut. 10:17) and God Almighty (Gen. 17:1) demonstrate his authority and power over all things. The nature of God expressed by his attributes equally affirms his authority. The Bible attests to God as the eternal, immortal, and only God (1 Tim. 1:17). He is described as omniscient (Ps. 139:1–6), omnipotent (Ps. 135:5; Jer. 32:17), omnipresent (Ps. 139:7–12), and righteous (Ps. 92:15). His wisdom is unsearchable (Rom. 11:33–36). His sovereignty is over all his creation (Gen. 1:1; Pss. 89:11; 90:2), now and forever (Psalm 104; 1 Cor. 15:24–28). This authority is conveyed to man through God's Word and is an unalterably authoritative message (Deut. 4:1–2; Prov. 30:5–6; Rev. 22:18–19).

THE TESTIMONY OF THE HOLY SPIRIT

Given the nature of God and his Word, he alone is qualified to establish and attest to Scripture's divine authority. This is precisely what he does through the internal testimony of the Holy Spirit to a believer. According to the Bible, the Holy Spirit works through the Scriptures to confirm its reliability, giving the believer a certainty that it is the Word of God. Authority is derived from a spiritual ministry of the Holy Spirit—not a subjective determination by the believer.

How does the internal testimony of the Spirit operate? It begins with the objective statements made by the Scriptures themselves. The Bible is a presuppositional declaration from God to man. Even the Bible's first verse begins with a statement of fact: "In the beginning, God created" (Gen. 1:1). Scripture makes no attempt to prove its truthfulness to the reader. It offers no lists of reasoned arguments as evidence. God's Word simply presents the truth as truth, while both expecting and demanding the reader to accept it as such. This is not to say that there are no evidences corroborating what the Bible says as true. Scripture presents a great many historical, geographical, scientific, prophetic, and even experiential facts that can be confirmed. What is more, a testimony composed by more than forty writers over a period of fifteen hundred years that consistently gives the same message throughout, without contradiction or provable error, is a compelling basis from which to derive confidence in what it says.

However, man in his depravity will always fundamentally rebel against God's Word as the truth expressing God's right to exercise absolute authority over him. As Paul attests in his writings, this rebellion is natural since man is born spiritually dead in his sin (Eph. 2:1; Rom. 3:10–18; cf. Ps. 51:5), darkened in his understanding (Eph. 4:18), unable to submit to the law of God from the heart (Rom. 8:7), and unwilling to accept the things of God because they can only be appraised spiritually (1 Cor. 2:14). Only regeneration can come to the gracious rescue. When the Holy Spirit regenerates a lost sinner, he or she is "made alive" in a spiritual sense (John 3:3; Eph. 2:4–5). Along with this newness of life comes illumination—i.e., an enablement from the Holy Spirit to discern that the Scriptures are, in fact, the Word of God (1 John 2:20, 27).[11] Jesus himself affirmed that the Bible is true (John 17:17). He also declared that a confident conviction of this fact is dependent on a heart that is willing to submit to God's will (John 7:17). This requires a new heart that only God's Spirit can provide (John 3:5–8).

The internal testimony of the Holy Spirit illuminates the believer so that he knows that the Scriptures are the Word of God. The biblical basis for this clarity is derived from two sources.[12] First, the words of Scripture are self-attesting because they claim to be from God (2 Tim. 3:16; 2 Pet. 1:20–21). Second, the Holy Spirit's dynamic power applies the truth of Scripture, resulting in a confident assurance in the Word itself (1 Cor. 2:4–16). This ministry of the Spirit is actuated through the reading and proclamation of Scripture (Rom. 10:14, 17). That does not mean that all who hear or read believe (Rom. 10:14–21), but it does mean that those who believe do so because of the convicting and illuminating work of the Holy Spirit.

THE CLARITY AND SUFFICIENCY OF SCRIPTURE

Illumination is not a work of the Spirit by which the Scriptures come alive in some subjective way to each believer. It does not provide new special revelation to the in-

---

11. An additional discussion of Scripture's illumination and interpretation is presented in chap. 5, "God the Holy Spirit," in the section "Instruction, Illumination, and Affirmation" (p. 389).

12. For an extended discussion of the biblical, theological, and historical basis for the doctrine of Scripture's clarity, see Larry D. Pettegrew, "The Perspicuity of Scripture," *MSJ* 15, no. 2 (2004): 209–25.

dividual believer over and above what the text itself says. It also does not guarantee that every word is immediately understood. This is where the clarity (or perspicuity) of Scripture enters the discussion. The Bible does clearly articulate God's truth. It is not a collection of mysterious writings or sayings that require some revelatory key to unlock their true spiritual meaning. The Bible accurately reveals and clearly communicates God's message. Nevertheless, readers still need to study to ensure that they understand the Word correctly (2 Tim. 2:15). Even the biblical writers had to study to discern the meaning of Scripture (Dan. 10:12; 1 Pet. 1:10–12). There are mysteries that are not fully revealed in Scripture (Deut. 29:29). While the overall message is clear, God has not revealed in his Word everything related to his mind and plans for redemptive history. What the illuminating work of the Spirit does provide is (1) a receptivity to the authority of God's Word, (2) a conviction that it is the truthful Word of God, and (3) a capacity aided by the Holy Spirit to discern the true meaning of the Word of God.

The Bible also attests to its sufficiency (Ps. 19:7–11).[13] It is a light to one's path (Ps. 119:105). It is more reliable than even the most amazing spiritual experiences (2 Pet. 1:19–20). It is able to lead a person to saving faith (2 Tim. 3:15). It instructs the religious elite as well as the common believer (Deut. 6:4; Mark 12:37; Phil. 1:1). It was given by God to parents to instruct their children (Deut. 6:6–7) and is able to bring even a child to saving faith (2 Tim. 3:14–15). Paul wrote that all Scripture is given by inspiration and that it is useful for teaching, reproof, correction, and training in righteousness (2 Tim. 3:16–17).

A closer look at each of these four features reveals the full sufficiency of Scripture to equip a believer in living out the Christian life. The first term, "teaching," means that the Bible instructs the believer in how to live, in what to believe, and in what God expects of him or her. It is related to content and doctrine. This concept fits with Jesus's injunction in the Great Commission that new disciples be taught to observe all he commanded (Matt. 28:18–20). The Scriptures instruct God's people in how to live in obedience to him.

The second term, "reproof," shows the Scripture's purpose of admonishment. It has to do with pointing out where a person has erred or departed from what God requires. Scripture is able to judge the heart when a believer has deviated in doctrine or practice from the faith once for all delivered to the saints (Heb. 4:12). The next term, "correction," is the companion to reproof. The Bible not only shows a person where he is wrong, it also identifies the corrected attitude, belief, or behavior that he should put on in its place (Eph. 4:20–24).

Finally, "training in righteousness" indicates that the Bible shows how to put its teachings into practice on a daily basis with illustrations and examples (Eph. 4:25–32). Between the Scriptures and the indwelling Holy Spirit, the believer needs no additional revelation to be informed on how to live the Christian life. Pastors and

---

13. For an extended exposition of Ps. 19:7–14, see John MacArthur, "The Sufficiency of Scripture," *MSJ* 15, no. 2 (2004): 165–74.

teachers (Eph. 4:11–12) are supplied to assist in the process of spiritual growth unto maturity, but even their ministries are founded on and informed by the all-sufficient Word of God (2 Pet. 1:2–3; cf. 1 Pet. 5:2–3).

GOD'S AUTHORITATIVE IMPRINT ON SCRIPTURE[14]

This truth principle can be fleshed out in a syllogistic fashion with the following argument:

1. Known truths:
   a. Scripture claims to be the Word of God.
   b. God is authoritative.
2. Conclusion: Scripture is authoritative.

Both the ontological basis (God is) and the epistemological basis (God speaks only truth) of the Bible's authority are established in Scripture (Gen. 1:1; Ps. 119:142, 151, 160). Thus, the very nature of God and the veracity of God's Word are determined not inductively by human reason but deductively from the testimony of Scripture (cf. Ps. 119:89; Isa. 40:8).

The objection is often raised, "If the Scriptures were penned by men, there is the highest likelihood of error in the writings!" This is countered with the following observations:

1. Human participation in the process of biblical inscripturation is not denied.
2. The idea of formal dictation is not required, although it occurred at times.
3. The background of the human writer is not eliminated.
4. The power, purposes, and workings of God the Father through God the Holy Spirit are not limited.
5. There is a perfect balance between divine initiation and human participation in the writing of the Scripture's autographa (or original manuscripts).

However, when all is said and done, Scripture is first and foremost "the Word of God," not the "word of men" (Ps. 19:7; 1 Thess. 2:13).

Since the origin of Scripture can ultimately be explained by divine inspiration (Zech. 7:12; 2 Tim. 3:14–17; 2 Pet. 1:20–21), as defined above, the authority of Scripture is directly derived from the authority of God. Those who do not acknowledge God's authority in Scripture are condemned (Jer. 8:8–9; Mark 7:1–13). On the other hand, those who rightfully honor and submit to God's authority in Scripture are commended (Neh. 8:5–6; Rev. 3:8).

Thus, the man of God—that is, God's herald—is to "preach the word" (2 Tim. 4:2). This declaration places the authority not with the preacher but rather with God (see 2 Tim. 3:16–17). Paul admonishes Titus to speak the Word of God with all authority (Gk. *epitagēs*, i.e., like the authority of a military commander), such that no one is exempt from obedience—not even the proclaimer himself (Titus 2:15).

---

14. This section is adapted from Richard L. Mayhue, "The Authority of Scripture," *MSJ* 15, no. 2 (2004): 232–34. Used by permission of *MSJ*.

The outworking of God's authority in Scripture can be summarized by a series of negative (what it is not) and positive (what it is) statements:

1. It is *not* derived authority bestowed by humans; rather, it is the *original* authority of God.
2. It does *not* change with the times, the culture, the nation, or the ethnic background; rather, it is the *unalterable* authority of God.
3. It is *not* one authority among many possible spiritual authorities; rather, it is the *exclusive* spiritual authority of God.
4. It is *not* an authority that can be successfully challenged or rightfully overthrown; rather, it is the *permanent* authority of God.
5. It is *not* a relativistic or subordinate authority; rather, it is the *ultimate* authority of God.
6. It is *not* merely a suggestive authority; rather, it is the *obligatory* authority of God.
7. It is *not* a benign authority in its outcome; rather, it is the *consequential* authority of God.

Inerrancy of Scripture

Accommodation and Inerrancy
Infallibility and Inerrancy
Jesus and Inerrancy
Explanation of Inerrancy

The inerrancy of Scripture is a doctrine that unbelievers have challenged primarily since the Enlightenment period (ca. AD 1650–1815). It is directly related to the doctrine of inspiration and the absolute veracity of the Word of God. There is no less at stake in this issue than the truthfulness and trustworthiness of God—his very character and nature.

Accommodation and Inerrancy

The ontological distinction between God the Creator and man the creature necessitates man's dependence on God for revelation. Man is epistemologically dependent on God. What man knows about God is only what God reveals to him. The Creator personally initiated the revelation of himself to his creatures. While general revelation discloses observable truths about the Creator, special revelation conveys, in language, truths about God that cannot be discerned merely by observing the creation. Some argue that human language necessarily forces God to accommodate himself to fallible means of communication. However, language is not a human invention. It is a divinely created means of personal communication between God and man, as well as between man and man. As such, there is no sense in which the process of communication through verbal and written forms is inadequate to accurately convey the truth of God to man. Even the confusion of the languages came about by a divine act (Gen. 11:1–9). Special revelation given through the process of inspiration is a fully accurate, truthful, sufficient, and reliable communication from God the Creator to man the creature. God used human agents to produce divinely authoritative writings by means of his Holy Spirit.

Historically, accommodation referred to God communicating with Scripture using symbols and expressions that were meaningful to man. These included cultural forms, figures of speech, anthropomorphic expressions, and the like. The Reformers saw accommodation as God's gracious use of multiple symbols in communicating with mankind. However, errantists have more recently redefined accommodation as God being forced to include error in the composition of Scripture because he used fallible human authors and language. Such advocates of error state that since God used finite human writers who were sinners to write his Word, the text is therefore liable to all the errors finite, sinful human beings commit. They even go so far as to say that the use of these human means of composition makes errors inevitable in the process. They conclude that the Bible is true in matters of faith and practice because these are at a general-principle level. However, they maintain that there can be (and are) factual errors throughout the Bible due to the fallible human instrumentality God used in the composition of the text.

The following responses to the modern errantist view demonstrate the fallibility of its argumentation. First, it confuses finiteness with sin and error. Humanness is not destroyed if God superintended the writing of Scripture through inspiration to protect it from all errors. Men do sin, make mistakes, and err on countless occasions throughout their lives. However, they do not sin or err on every occasion. It is possible for a fallible human being to write a sentence without erring. On the one hand, God's superintendence of Scripture did not compromise the humanness of the authors. On the other hand, the process of inspiration included God's work of safeguarding the human writers so that they did not err when they were writing his Word—word after word, sentence after sentence.

Second, the unanimous witness of Scripture affirms its total veracity. It claims repeatedly to be truthful (Ps. 119:43, 160; John 17:17; 2 Cor. 6:7; Col. 1:5; 2 Tim. 2:15; James 1:18). It is identified directly with both the human writers and God who inspired it. The direct calls by God to leave it unaltered demonstrate that what is written is precisely what God intended to say (Deut. 4:2; 12:32; Prov. 30:5–6; Rev. 22:18–19). God was in no way limited in his ability to convey absolute truth in every word simply because he used fallible human writers. Inspiration by means of the Spirit's direct involvement facilitated the origination of God's inerrant Word (2 Pet. 1:20–21).

Finally, the errantist view of accommodation is inconsistent with itself. How can one be sure that God can rightly convey to man spiritual truths concerning matters of faith and practice if he cannot guarantee that the facts of history are rightly recorded? If one affirms that the Bible is free from error in leading man to a right knowledge of God in salvation, then what prevents him from equally affirming the truthfulness of the rest? If God is able to keep the writers free from error at all, such as in writing spiritual truths, then there are no reasonable grounds to conclude that he was unable to secure a factual account of scientific and historical records.

Infallibility and Inerrancy[15]

DEFINITIONS OF INERRANCY AND INFALLIBILITY

Inerrancy means literally "without error." When applied to Scripture, it means that the Bible is without error in the original copies. It is therefore free, when properly interpreted, from affirming anything that is untrue or contrary to fact.

The term *infallibility* has historically been largely synonymous with an evangelical view of inerrancy. Infallibility means unable to mislead or fail in accomplishing the divinely intended purpose. Article 11 of the Chicago Statement on Biblical Inerrancy (1978) relates it this way: "We affirm that Scripture, having been given by divine inspiration, is infallible, so that, far from misleading us, it is true and reliable in all the matters it addresses."

Historically, inerrancy and infallibility have been inseparably linked. However, dating back to the early 1960s, *infallibility* became a term used in a new way by those who believe in *limited inerrancy*. They commandeered it to mean that the Bible is infallible in that it teaches no false or misleading doctrine related to faith and practice. However, in their view, that does not mean Scripture has to be factually accurate in all its words. The primary motivation behind the alteration in definition was tied to an effort to deny inerrancy yet maintain an identification with those of an orthodox faith. But biblically speaking, it is not orthodox to affirm infallibility apart from inerrancy. Denial of inerrancy is motivated by an unwillingness to accept all that Scripture declares. Deniers seek to excuse sin and to affirm unbiblical behavior by such efforts.

THE BIBLICAL BASIS FOR INERRANCY

Paul's direct claim for Scripture is that it is inspired by God (2 Tim. 3:16). It is the product of God's own work through the human authors by means of his Spirit (2 Pet. 1:20–21). Since these written words are the words of the God of truth, they must be without error. Inspiration deals with the means by which the text was composed, but it also directly implies that it is the work of God. As such, the final product is attributed to him. Regardless of the involvement of human agency in the composition process, the integrity of the divine author is at stake in the doctrine of inerrancy. Prior to the higher-critical assaults on the doctrine of Scripture in the nineteenth century, the fact of inspiration necessarily led to the affirmation that the written words of the God who is truth were entirely truthful and without error in the original autographs. This matches the position Jesus himself affirmed (John 17:17).

The Bible's view of its own authority attests to the fact of inerrancy. The recurrent declarations of "thus says the Lord" create an atmosphere in which inerrancy is assumed throughout the Old Testament. The New Testament writers universally assume the absolute truthfulness of the Old Testament. Following a pattern established by Jesus, they base their doctrine on the literal verbiage of the biblical texts

---

15. The seminal article on this theme is Paul D. Feinberg, "Infallibility and Inerrancy," *TJ* 6, no. 2 (1977): 120–32.

they quote (e.g., Paul's reference to "offspring," not "offsprings," in Gal. 3:16). More significantly, they base their faith in the truthfulness of the Old Testament on the character of the triune God. For Paul, the Father is the "God who never lies" (Titus 1:2). In John's Gospel, the Son is not only the way and the life but also the truth (John 14:6). Likewise, the Holy Spirit is the Spirit of truth (John 14:17; 15:26; 16:13; 1 John 5:6). John also records Jesus's affirmation that God's "word is truth" (John 17:17). This language coincides directly with the Old Testament witness that God's Word is truth and that it is fixed forever in heaven (Ps. 119:89, 160)—a testimony to the fact that it is not just a temporal earthly testimony from God but an eternal and heavenly one. If God is the author of Scripture, as the text claims, how can there be errors in what it affirms? If there are errors in what it says, how can God be the God of truth? Furthermore, if this is an eternal and lasting word, as Scripture attests, then how can the God of truth allow falsehood to be conveyed by it? There is nothing less at stake in the doctrine of inerrancy than the character and integrity of God himself. Since God is true, so is his revelation in Scripture.

Jesus and Inerrancy

That Jesus believed in an inerrant Bible has already been shown in the earlier section "Proofs of Inspiration" (p. 86). However, as a further demonstration, we can note that Jesus never challenged the accuracy or veracity of a single Old Testament passage. In fact, he never even broached the subject of an errant Scripture because the integrity of the text was always assumed and repeatedly affirmed. Christ never once indicated the slightest need to correct any statement in the Old Testament. Rather, he affirmed its truthfulness to the smallest details (Matt. 5:18; John 10:35). It is also worth pointing out that of all the questions people asked Jesus, no one asked if the Old Testament was inspired. No one asked if it contained any errors. From his disciples and numerous common folk to a host of adversaries, not one person questioned the inspiration and inerrancy of Scripture. Furthermore, Scripture gives no evidence to support the view that Jesus believed or taught merely conceptual inspiration. There is no evidence that Jesus believed that Scripture contained error in even the slightest way. Though an argument from silence is generally not the strongest argument, in this case the silence is deafening. If Jesus knew of error (even minor factual discrepancies) in the text, it is hard to imagine why he nowhere addressed this subject, especially with his disciples, that he might prepare them for such doctrinal difficulty.

It is equally inexplicable why Jesus never addressed this subject with his opponents. Throughout his ministry, Jesus never accommodated himself to his enemies. He challenged errant behavior and doctrine. He made a deliberate practice of confronting false rabbinic doctrines and practices at every opportunity. Yet Jesus never once challenged the veracity of Scripture. He only addressed the Jews' ignorance and mishandling of it. The Sermon on the Mount was a full-scale confrontation with those who had misrepresented or misunderstood the law of God (Matthew 5–7). Nevertheless, throughout this discourse Jesus corrected only the *misinterpretation* of Scripture. He never once even hinted at the possibility that biblical integrity may be in doubt—and the Gospel accounts make it clear that Jesus never hesitated to confront error. He made a practice of addressing even the most controversial issues with either his disciples or the religious leaders of the day. It is therefore unreasonable to conclude that Jesus would have accommodated himself to either his enemies or even his disciples over this issue. There is no convincing argument that can be brought forward to explain why Jesus would have neglected to address the issue if Scripture contained errors.

Explanation of Inerrancy

INERRANCY CANNOT BE PROVEN SCIENTIFICALLY

The doctrine of inerrancy is a natural companion to the doctrine of inspiration. It is also a reasonable and necessary conclusion based on the character of God and the truth claims of Scripture. In many instances, it can be confirmed even by external, empirical evidences. As such, inerrancy is a doctrine that is biblically and theologically presumed.

However, it is not possible to fully demonstrate the doctrine in every case with scientific data. This is simply because some things are not reproducible for scrutiny today. The creation and flood events cannot be repeated. And yet there was one impeccably reliable eyewitness—God—who wrote an inerrant account. Archaeological evidence does not exist to confirm every historical fact asserted in the Bible. Ultimately, in all cases, the miraculous events recorded in Scripture can be attested only by the eyewitness accounts given by the biblical writers themselves.

At the same time, it is equally true that there is no way to disprove the biblical record. Every historical challenge leveled against the veracity of Scripture has been proven false. In many cases, external witnesses have confirmed not only the biblical account in general but also the factual details themselves. In other cases, a harmonization or similar interpretive solution has adequately confirmed the accuracy of the biblical account. What is more, the evidences for scriptural veracity and factual accuracy go way beyond external confirmations. The fulfillment of Scripture alone attests to the truthfulness and trustworthiness of the biblical record. The truth claims of Scripture, the doctrine of inspiration, and the use of the Old Testament by New Testament writers all confirm a universal acceptance of the total truthfulness and reliability of the biblical text. Furthermore, the doctrine of inspiration demands the acceptance of the scriptural account over any external, human record based on the fact that it is God's Word.

INERRANCY APPLIES TO THE AUTOGRAPHS

Every book of the Bible was originally composed under the inspiration of the Holy Spirit by a human author. These original works—called *autographs*—were completely without error as the result of divine inspiration. None of these original manuscripts are in existence today. Instead, copies were made and soon thereafter copies of copies. These copies and multitudes of translations have been passed down through the centuries. The doctrines of transmission and preservation will be discussed later in this chapter, but here we must point out that the copying process had the obvious potential for introducing errors into the text. For this reason, the doctrine of inerrancy is restricted to the autographs themselves.

Unlike the autographs, copies are subject to errors due to fallible human involvement since the Scripture never speaks of the Holy Spirit superintending the work of copyists. Add to this the fact that no original manuscripts remain by which the copies may be confirmed, and it may seem that the doctrine of inerrancy is null and void. This could be even further extrapolated to include the process of translation. Since translations (like copies) are not produced by means of inspiration, they too are subject to error. How can one rely on Scripture if it is not the original text composed by the divinely inspired author?

God has not chosen to extend the miracle of inspiration to the copying and translation processes. But God providentially preserves copies and translations to the extent that they accurately reproduce the content of the original autographs. As will be discussed below, the evidence available today enables textual scholars to hold the confidence that Scripture translations today possess more than 99 percent of the original autographs.[16] Translations can be easily checked against a critical text to confirm how accurately they render the biblical autographs. As such, copies and translations can be said to accurately reflect the inerrant Word originally penned by the divinely inspired authors. The copying process superintended by God preserves the doctrine of inerrancy. A translation can still be called the Word of God as long as it accurately reflects the content of the original autographs.

INERRANCY ALLOWS FOR ORDINARY LANGUAGE

The doctrine of inerrancy does not mean that the normal laws of language are excluded. The Bible makes frequent use of estimates (1 Chron. 5:21; Isa. 37:36), and such round numbers are not factual errors. Scientifically imprecise statements do not equate to error; they are simply part of the way we normally use language. The same holds true in statements related to distance. Furthermore, inerrancy does not demand the use of technical or scientific language. The biblical authors did not intend to give scientific descriptions or explanations in their narrative accounts. In fact, in many cases the technical language of their day would have been wrong. But the way it is stated in Scripture matches with perceived reality—even though it is conveyed in normal language. A perfect example is Job 26:7, where God is said to hang the earth on nothing. This is not a scientific description. But it is completely accurate, factually speaking. Phenomenological language is also no violation of inerrancy. Joshua prayed for the "sun to stand still," and the following verse affirms that

---

16. Wayne Grudem, *Systematic Theology: An Introduction to Biblical Doctrine* (Grand Rapids, MI: Zondervan, 1994), 96. For an excellent introduction to the subject of textual criticism for both the Old and New Testament texts, see Paul D. Wegner, *A Student's Guide to Textual Criticism of the Bible: Its History, Methods and Results* (Downers Grove, IL: IVP Academic, 2006).

"the sun stood still, and the moon stopped, until the nation took vengeance on their enemies" (Josh. 10:12–13). This geocentric description in no way violates inerrancy. This is a completely truthful statement from an earthly perspective. Language allows for truth to be conveyed from the perspective of the writer or speaker.

Inerrancy allows for the use of the full range of language. This includes free quotations from the Old Testament by New Testament writers. The oldest Greek manuscripts did not contain punctuation marks. This makes identifying the precise quotations by the writers difficult at times. Since the Old Testament was written in Hebrew, the New Testament biblical writers had to use either an existing translation or produce their own. Furthermore, many times it is obvious that the author did not intend to give a word-for-word quotation but simply enough of a reference to the original that the reader would recognize it. This is a common practice even in contemporary writing or preaching. A loose quotation still accurately conveys the sense in the referenced text. None of these practices are violations of the integrity of the biblical text. In such cases, it is better to describe the New Testament use of the Old Testament as allusions rather than quotations because the writers clearly are not attempting to repeat them verbatim. Since the reader knows or has access to the Old Testament original, free citations of the Old Testament in the New do not deceive the reader or compromise the integrity of the text.

Inerrancy does not require perfect grammar in every case, nor exact wording (*ipsissima verba*) or even exhaustive detail. A statement can be grammatically unconventional and still be understandable and truthful. Many times syntactical and lexical choices merely reflect the style and skill of the human authors. The accounts they wrote are truthful even when they did not record every historical detail. In the case of parallel accounts in both Testaments, the human writers naturally made choices to maintain the focus of their narratives that necessarily resulted in the inclusion and exclusion of certain details from each account. The truth includes the sum of all accounts. None of these factors negate the factuality of the written Word.

The Bible is the inerrant, infallible Word of God. It is the result of divine inspiration, which produced divinely authoritative and factual accounts that are truthful in what they record. This doctrine applies directly to the original autographs and indirectly to the texts and translations of today.

Preservation of Scripture
    Explanation of Preservation
    Canonicity and Preservation
    Textual Criticism and Preservation

How can one be sure that the revealed and inspired written Word of God, which the early church recognized as canonical, has been handed down to this day without any loss of material?[17] Furthermore, since one of the Devil's prime concerns is to

---

17. This introduction is adapted from MacArthur, *MacArthur Study Bible: English Standard Version*, xx. Used by permission of Thomas Nelson.

undermine the Bible, have the Scriptures survived this relentless onslaught? In the beginning, Satan denied God's word to Eve (Gen. 3:4). He later attempted to distort the Scripture in his wilderness encounter with Christ (Matt. 4:6–7). Through King Jehoiakim, he even attempted to literally destroy the physical Scriptures (Jer. 36:23). The battle for the Bible rages, but God's Word has and will continue to outlast its archenemy and all other enemies.

God anticipated man's, Satan's, and demons' malice toward the Scripture by making divine promises to preserve his Word. The very continued existence of Scripture is guaranteed in Isaiah 40:8, "The grass withers, the flower fades, but the word of our God will stand forever" (cf. 1 Pet. 1:24–25). This even means that no inspired Scripture has been lost in the past that still awaits rediscovery.

The actual content of Scripture will be perpetuated, both on earth (Isa. 59:21) and in heaven (Ps. 119:89). Thus, the purposes of God, as published in the sacred writings, will never be thwarted, even in the least detail (cf. Matt. 5:18; 24:35; Mark 13:31; Luke 16:17).

Explanation of Preservation

DEFINITION OF PRESERVATION

Preservation as a doctrine refers to the acts of God whereby he has preserved through the centuries the written record of his special revelation for his people. It begins with the specific instructions he gave to his people to preserve it. It also includes the providential way in which God has kept his Word by the diligent efforts of human agents through the millennia. It began when it was originally written, and it has continued through time as it has been gathered into the collections of canonical writings extant today.

The Westminster Confession (AD 1646) describes the doctrine of preservation this way: "The Old Testament in Hebrew . . . and the New Testament in Greek . . . , being immediately inspired by God, and by his singular care and providence kept pure in all ages, are therefore authentical; so as in all controversies of religion, the Church is finally to appeal unto them" (1.8). In other words, God both inspired the writers during the composition of the text and has worked providentially through the centuries to preserve those writings. On this basis, these texts are authoritative and in their original languages can be appealed to as the final word on all matters of faith and practice.

The real question is, does the Bible itself affirm this doctrine? If it does, is that preservation miraculous or providential? Does it promise preservation in one manuscript or in a set of manuscripts or in a Greek or Hebrew edition? What place do versions (i.e., translations of the Bible into other languages) play in the process? What impact do the means of preservation have on canonization?

BIBLICAL TEACHING ON PRESERVATION

Do the Scriptures say anything concerning their own preservation through the processes of transmission (from one generation to the next) and translation (from one language to another)? An examination of what the Bible says does indicate that God has promised to preserve his Word forever in heaven (Ps. 119:89, 160). This brings both understanding and confidence to one's trust in God's preservation of the Scriptures themselves. The scriptural promises are for a divinely providential rather than a miraculous preservation of the text on earth.

The Case for Perfect, Eternal Preservation. The Bible makes a direct promise regarding the preservation of God's Word in heaven. Psalm 119:89 states, "Forever, O Lord, your word is firmly fixed in the heavens." In the original the term "firmly fixed" means literally to be established or set in place in a lasting way. This is similar to a pillar that is permanently placed within a building when constructed. So God's Word is forever fixed. But the key here is that the verse says that God's Word is fixed in heaven, not on earth. This indicates that God has a permanent and perfect record of his inspired written revelation to man, but he has kept that record in heaven. The psalmist goes on to say, "Long have I known from your testimonies that you have founded them forever" (Ps. 119:152). Again, God's Word is fixed, unchanging, and everlasting, but the perfectly preserved form of that Word is in heaven. Isaiah contrasts the transitory nature of man with the eternally enduring perfection of God's Word when he writes, "The grass withers, the flower fades, but the word of our God will stand forever" (Isa. 40:8). God's Word is eternal, but this text gives no direct indication that this eternality includes a promise of a perfectly preserved copy of it here on earth. Peter also refers directly to this verse and says, "This word is the good news that was preached to you" (1 Pet. 1:25). This statement equates the New Testament gospel message with the Old Testament as the Word of God. It also makes its eternal preservation a certainty by implication. But God still makes no direct promise in Scripture that he will preserve his Word here on earth in a flawless copy or an inspired edition beyond the original autographs themselves.

Scripture also affirms not just the certainty of the preservation of God's Word but also the fulfillment of it. Jesus speaks of the lasting nature of God's Word this way: "For truly, I say to you, until heaven and earth pass away, not an iota, not a dot, will pass from the Law until all is accomplished" (Matt. 5:18). There are two significant points to be made here. The first relates to the terms "iota" and "dot." The iota refers to the *yodh*, which is the smallest letter in the Hebrew alphabet. The dot is actually the word for "a hook," which here describes even the smallest stroke of a pen that would distinguish one letter from another. This could be compared to the hooked line on the *R* that distinguishes it from a *P* in the English alphabet. The point Jesus is making is clear: what God has said, he means. Nothing will prevent God from accomplishing any of it—down to the smallest point.

This text is often cited as proof that God has promised to preserve his written Word here on earth. However, a close examination of the text shows that Christ's point is not that it is necessarily preserved in print here but that all of it will be accomplished or come to pass. Still, this statement seems to inherently imply that God will preserve his written revelation. How can it be a witness to mankind if it is not preserved in print so that man can read it before, during, and after it has come to pass? Nevertheless, the promise is about fulfillment, not preservation. Jesus goes on to make the same statement about his own words when he says, "Heaven and earth will pass away, but my words will not pass away" (Matt. 24:35). Again, the implication is clear: when Jesus speaks, it is as lasting and eternally sure and binding as when God speaks. Contextually, though, Jesus was speaking about the fulfillment of all that he said concerning the events that would take place in that generation and in the coming age. It was not a promise directly related to the record of his words or of the teachings in the New Testament.

So the Bible affirms that God has promised to fulfill every word and every promise given in Scripture. It also confirms that God will preserve his Word forever, unchanged, in heaven. But there is no direct statement or guarantee of an absolutely flawless preservation of a copy or copies of his Word here on earth. That does not mean that he has not preserved it in a completely reliable way. It means that he has chosen to preserve the earthly record of his revelation in a providential way through diligent human efforts. Because thousands of Old Testament and New Testament manuscripts have been recovered and carefully compared, the best Christian scholars have concluded that the original biblical text has been essentially recovered and reconstituted.[18] So God's Word has been preserved perfectly in heaven and faithfully on earth.

The Call for Diligent Earthly Preservation. In the heavenly realm, God has promised to preserve his Word flawlessly forever. In the earthly realm, he has providentially preserved it through his people, who have the responsibility to protect and transmit it. This is evidenced first of all from the repeated commands God gave to his people not to add or take away anything from his Word (Deut. 4:2; 12:32; Prov. 30:6; Jer. 26:2; Rev. 22:18–19). These repeated charges make it clear that what God said through the pens of the human authors was exactly what he wanted to say. His people were accountable not only to obey it all but also to preserve it to the letter. When these statements are coupled with Jesus's words in Matthew 5:18, it is obvious that the final standard by which everyone will be measured is the originally inspired autographs. As such, it is essential that God's people exercise extreme care in copying, translating, and producing his Word, not to mention diligence in interpreting it. God has fixed his Word in heaven, but he leads believers in the responsibility to retain and secure its integrity here.

The best evidence that God has retained his Word flawlessly in heaven while entrusting the preservation of the earthly record to his people is found in the Scripture itself. In Exodus it says that when God finished speaking, he gave Moses "the two tablets of the testimony, tablets of stone, written with the finger of God" (Ex. 31:18). So God personally wrote this portion of Scripture in stone and gave it to Moses. But when Moses came down from Mount Sinai with the tablets in hand, he saw the sin

---

18. Wegner, *A Student's Guide*, 301.

of the people and in anger smashed the tablets (Ex. 32:19). God actually allowed Moses to destroy the only copy of those commandments—even before the people had seen or heard them. There was, at this point and for a brief time thereafter, no earthly copy of these commandments. Nevertheless, God was able to restore fully and verbatim what was lost through the actions of a man. He instructed Moses to cut out two tablets like the first ones and come up to Mount Sinai. Then, over the next forty days, he had Moses write out on those tablets the same commandments that he had originally given (Ex. 34:1–2, 27–28). God does entrust the care of his Word to his people.

He is also able to restore it to the letter if it is lost. The most extensive example of both God's willingness to allow his Word to be destroyed and his ability to restore it is in Jeremiah 36. It was the fourth year of Jehoiakim's reign as king over Judah. God told Jeremiah to take a scroll and pen his word as a message to be given to the king calling him to repentance. The text says, "Then Jeremiah called Baruch the son of Neriah, and Baruch wrote on a scroll at the dictation of Jeremiah all the words of the LORD that he had spoken to him" (36:4). Baruch then delivered that scroll to the officials, who took it to the king. When a servant read it to the king, his response to God's call to repent was clear: "As Jehudi read three or four columns, the king would cut them off with a knife and throw them into the fire in the fire pot, until the entire scroll was consumed in the fire that was in the fire pot" (36:23). This scroll was the first edition of the book of Jeremiah. God again allowed a man to destroy his Word. In this case, it was not anger over sin (as in the case of Moses) but an outwardly rebellious rejection of God's Word! That the Word of God was not destroyed is evidenced by the next event. God again restored it verbatim:

> Now after the king had burned the scroll with the words that Baruch wrote at Jeremiah's dictation, the word of the LORD came to Jeremiah: "Take another scroll and write on it all the former words that were in the first scroll, which Jehoiakim the king of Judah has burned." . . . Then Jeremiah took another scroll and gave it to Baruch the scribe, the son of Neriah, who wrote on it at the dictation of Jeremiah all the words of the scroll that Jehoiakim king of Judah had burned in the fire. And many similar words were added to them. (36:27–28, 32)

The book of Jeremiah found in today's Bible is the original text destroyed by the king along with God's additional revelations and judgments, which include the record of Jehoiakim's rejection and destruction of the original text. God's Word is settled in heaven, and he is able to recall it and inspire a prophet to write it accurately again.

While it is true that God has acted directly at times to restore portions of his Word that have been lost or destroyed on earth, he has also withheld it as a judgment. He allowed the temple priests to misplace the book of the Law for more than fifty years (2 Kings 22:8–10; 2 Chron. 34:14–16). For more than a generation God's people were without his Word because of their unfaithfulness. Yet even though a generation was ignorant of God's Word, he still held them accountable for it. God punished the nation for the wickedness committed during the time of their carelessness.

Coming at this point from a different angle, the exception proves the rule. For example, at least two words are missing from every extant copy of Samuel dating back at least two thousand years (see 1 Sam. 13:1). The significance of these omissions is minimal. The two words that are missing are numbers related to Saul's age at the time he became king and to the number of years he reigned as king. It is a fairly simple exercise to do the math and discern a limited number of potential readings that make sense of the text. Nevertheless, this missing portion of text alone proves that the earthly preservation of Scripture is not a perpetual, miraculous act of God. He has instead entrusted his people with the responsibility to retain his Word through diligent human efforts. The Old and New Testament scribal practices demonstrate precisely this kind of careful scrutiny and care of the extant copies and the copying process.

If God has not flawlessly preserved his Word on earth—and has instead left it up to the efforts of men—are the copies still considered Scripture? The Bible considers copies of the Scriptures to be the Word of God. For example, God gave instructions to Moses concerning the practices that were to be followed by the future kings of Israel:

> And when [the king] sits on the throne of his kingdom, he shall write for himself in a book a copy of this law, approved by the Levitical priests. And it shall be with him, and he shall read in it all the days of his life, that he may learn to fear the LORD his God by keeping all the words of this law and these statutes, and doing them, that his heart may not be lifted up above his brothers, and that he may not turn aside from the commandment, either to the right hand or to the left, so that he may continue long in his kingdom, he and his children, in Israel. (Deut. 17:18–20)

Two key points can be derived from this passage. First, the king's copying was to be done under the watchful eye of the priests, which indicates that the copies were to be done with extreme care and painstaking precision. The king was instructed to make as exact a copy as possible, which was then certified by the priests as accurate. God expects his people to be zealous in preserving his Word—even in the copying process. Second, the copy was to be obeyed with promises for obedience equal to following the instructions of the original itself. In this way, God tethered the copies of Scripture to the autographs of Scripture. A copy of the Word of God is the Word of God insofar as it matches the original.

As stated, the work of preserving the text of Scripture is a providential act, not a miraculous one. Even though God has at times acted directly to restore a portion of his Word that was destroyed, that has not proven to be his standard practice. Instead, he has placed the burden of responsibility to recognize, preserve, and transmit his Word on his faithful people. Thus, preservation involves two distinct elements—canonicity and textual criticism.

Canonicity and Preservation[19]

The Bible is actually one book from one divine author, though it was written over a period of fifteen hundred years through the pens of over forty men. Beginning with the creation account of Genesis 1–2, written by Moses around 1405 BC, and extending to the account of eternity future in Revelation 21–22, written by the apostle John around AD 95, God progressively revealed himself and his purposes in the inspired Scriptures.

All this raises a significant question: How can one know which supposed sacred writings were to be included in the canon of Scripture and which ones were to be excluded? Over the centuries, three widely recognized principles were used to validate the writings that constituted divine, inspired revelation. First, the writing had to have been authored by a recognized prophet or apostle or by someone associated with one, as in the case of the books of Mark, Luke, Hebrews, James, and Jude. Second, the writing could not disagree with or contradict any previous Scripture. Third, the church had to display a general consensus that a writing was an inspired book. Thus, when various councils met in church history to consider the canon, they held no official vote for the canonicity of a book but rather recognized universally—after the fact—that it was written by God and belonged in the Bible.

With regard to the Old Testament, by the time of Christ the entire Old Testament had been written and acknowledged by the Jewish community. The last book, Malachi, had been completed about 430 BC. Not only did the Old Testament canon of Christ's day conform to the Old Testament in Protestant Bibles today, but it did not contain the uninspired Apocrypha, that group of fourteen extrabiblical writings that were written after Malachi and attached to the Old Testament in the Greek translation of the Hebrew Old Testament called the Septuagint (ca. 200–150 BC). Though rejected, these spurious writings are included in some versions of the Bible. However, not one passage from the Apocrypha is cited by a New Testament writer, nor did Jesus affirm any of it when he recognized the Old Testament canon of his era (cf. Luke 24:27, 44).

By Christ's time, the Old Testament canon had been divided into two lists of twenty-two or twenty-four books respectively, each of which contained the same material as the thirty-nine books of our modern Protestant versions. In the twenty-two-book canon, some books were considered as one—for example, the Book of the Twelve (incorporating the twelve so-called Minor Prophets), Jeremiah and Lamentations, Judges and Ruth, and 1 and 2 Samuel.

The same three key tests of canonicity that applied to the Old Testament were also applied to the New Testament. In the case of Mark and Luke-Acts, the nonapostolic authors were considered to be, in effect, the penmen for Peter and Paul, respectively. James and Jude were written by Christ's own half brothers. While Hebrews is the only New Testament book whose authorship is unknown for certain, its content is

---

19. This section is adapted from MacArthur, *MacArthur Study Bible: English Standard Version*, xix–xx. Used by permission of Thomas Nelson.

so in line with both the Old and New Testaments that the early church concluded that it must have been written by an apostolic associate. Since circa AD 350–400, the twenty-seven books of the New Testament have been universally accepted as inspired by God.

DEFINITION OF CANONICITY

Canonicity refers to the church's recognition and acceptance of the books of Scripture as God's inspired Word. The term itself comes from the Greek word *kanōn*, which originally meant a "reed" or a "rod." Since a rod was frequently used as a measuring stick, the word began to convey the idea of a "standard" or "rule." The word *kanōn* is used four times in the New Testament, always in a metaphorical sense. Paul employs it three times in 2 Corinthians 10 (vv. 13, 15–16) to refer to a geographical boundary. In Galatians 6:16, he uses it to refer to a moral standard or rule for believers to live by. All this illustrates that by the end of the apostolic age, the term was predominantly understood as a word that referred metaphorically to a rule, a measure, a boundary, or a standard.

It was not until the middle of the fourth century AD that the term was used to speak of the authoritative collection of books recognized as the product of divine inspiration. In fact, Athanasius (295–373) first applied the term *canon* to Scripture in the *Decrees of the Council of Nicaea*, published shortly after AD 350. In these writings, he referred to *The Shepherd of Hermas* as not being part of the canon. Shortly thereafter, the Council of Laodicea used the terms "canonical" and "noncanonical" to refer to individual books either as accepted as part of the Bible or rejected as not inspired by God. It is in this sense that the term has been understood in reference to the Scriptures.

There are two primary ways in which the canon has historically been defined. The traditional view of Roman Catholicism holds that the Bible is an authoritative collection of writings. That is, the Bible contains the books that the church has collected and authoritatively determined and affirmed as Scripture. According to this view, the church decides which books belong in the Bible.

The biblical view understands that the canon is a collection of divinely authoritative writings. It is not the church (or the people of God) that determines which books are inspired by God and are thereby Scripture. The writings themselves are vested with the authority of God on the basis of divine inspiration. They are the Word of God because they were written under the Spirit's inspiration. The people of God (the church for the New Testament, Israel for the Old Testament) merely recognize the authority present within those writings. Canonicity is based on the fact of inspiration, not the process or agency that did the collecting.

NEED FOR THE CANON

Beginning with the composition of the Torah, there is a clear, divine injunction to recognize and preserve the written revelation of God. By the time of Christ, the thirty-nine books of the Old Testament (perhaps actually comprising twenty-two in Hebrew, with some books such as 1 and 2 Samuel combined in one scroll) were universally recognized as Scripture. The need for a New Testament canon on par with the Old Testament is also apparent. The apostles were Christ's formal and authorized representatives (Luke 24:44–49; John 20:19–23; Acts 1:4–8, 15–26; 2:42). As they began to pass from the scene (whether through death or martyrdom), it became increasingly necessary to preserve their teachings. Even the apostles were concerned about this issue (1 Cor. 11:2; 2 Thess. 2:15). Preserving the written testimony of the apostles became ever more significant as the first century neared its end. This providential process of preservation began with individual churches copying, collecting, and sharing these writings. Later, the church at large formally recognized the inspired twenty-seven books of the New Testament as Scripture. This process of recognition did not establish the canon but did formally affirm what was already established based on inspiration.

The Old Testament Canon. The Old Testament was written over a period of about one thousand years. The Pentateuch was completed by Moses just prior to his death in 1405 BC, with the exception of Deuteronomy 34:5–12, which chronicles Moses's death, possibly written by Joshua. These first five books were unhesitatingly accepted by Joshua and the elders of Israel as the divinely authoritative Word of God and were placed into the ark (Deut. 31:24–26). The Old Testament canon was functionally established by Ezra in the fifth century BC following the return from captivity. It is generally recognized that the Old Testament canon was established by a three-principle evaluation. First, the book was written through the process of inspiration itself—usually affirmed by the author himself (2 Sam. 23:1–2; Isa. 1:1; Jer. 1:1–2). Second, the prophet's contemporaries frequently recognized the work (Ex. 24:3; Josh. 1:8; Jer. 26:18; Dan. 9:2). Third, the prophet's contemporaries determined to preserve the book as part of God's Word (Deut. 31:26; 1 Sam. 10:25; Prov. 25:1; 2 Kings 23:24; Dan. 9:2). In addition to these basic considerations, Jewish leaders compared any new revelation with the existing Scriptures as required by God's law (Deut. 12:32; 13:1–5).

By the time of Christ, a universally accepted and fixed collection of books was recognized as the canonical Old Testament. These books coincide with the thirty-nine books contained in the Protestant Old Testament; Israel never accepted the Apocrypha as canonical. The testimonies of Jesus and the apostles demonstrate their absolute acceptance of the Hebrew canon as Scripture. Jesus quotes from each of the major sections of the Old Testament—including Moses and the Pentateuch (Matt. 4:1–11; John 3:14; 5:45–47), David in the Psalms (Luke 20:41–44), and Isaiah (Matt. 13:13–15) and Jonah (Matt. 12:39–40) from the Prophets. He affirms each as part of God's authoritative Scripture by basing both doctrine and practice on what it says. The testimony of the apostles mirrors that of Jesus. They quote from the Old Testament in their preaching (Acts 2:17–21, 25–28, 31, 34–35; 3:22, 25; 4:25–26). They frequently build their case for the gospel in the New Testament from Old Testament citations (Matt. 1:22–23; 4:14–16; 8:17; 12:17–21; 13:35; 21:4–5; John 12:38–41;

19:24; Rom. 1:16–17; 3:9–20; 4:1–12; 9:6–13, 15–17, 25–26, 27–29, 33). Even Paul's evangelistic practice of going first to the Jews in the synagogues and reasoning from the Old Testament Scriptures attests to their unreserved acceptance of the Jewish canon (Acts 17:2–3).

One noticeable distinction between the Hebrew Old Testament and modern Bibles in English and other languages is the arrangement of the books. Jesus and the New Testament writers generally acknowledged a two- or threefold arrangement of the Old Testament books—the Law and the Prophets or the Law, the Prophets, and the Writings (Luke 24:44). It would seem that Jesus recognized an arrangement of the Old Testament books that began with Genesis and ended with Chronicles, largely based on his reference (Luke 11:50–51) to the blood of the prophets from Abel (Gen. 4:1–16) to Zechariah (2 Chron. 24:20–22). This order is much like that found in the definitive edition of the Hebrew Old Testament, drawn from the Masoretic text. While the arrangement in the English Bible is derived primarily from the Vulgate and secondarily from the Septuagint, the English Bible's differences with the Hebrew Old Testament in no way alter the fact that it contains the same specific books that are recognized as canonical in the Hebrew Bible—the order is secondary.

The New Testament Canon. The New Testament was written over a period of fifty years. It consists of twenty-seven books composed by eight or nine different human authors and includes four Gospels, the book of Acts (the companion volume to Luke's Gospel), twenty-one Epistles, and the book of Revelation. The first written was the epistle of James in AD 45. The last was Revelation, penned by John in about AD 95. Prior to these New Testament books, the church had no authoritative writings apart from the Old Testament, which Jesus and the apostles recognized as the Word of God. The New Testament books were recognized as equally divinely inspired and authoritative as the Old Testament at the time they were written. Peter attested to Paul's letters as being Scripture (2 Pet. 3:14–16). Paul quoted from Deuteronomy and Luke, affirming both as Scripture (1 Tim. 5:18). John testified that he wrote Revelation at the direct insistence of Christ himself as a revelation from God to his church (Rev. 1:11, 19; 4:1; 22:8–13). The New Testament books were added to Scripture at the point of inspiration and original authorship. They were canonical at the time of writing—not when the church accepted them as such. There was, however, a process over time whereby the twenty-seven books of the New Testament were individually and collectively recognized as Scripture by God's people. This process of canonization for the New Testament included three historical stages: circulation, collection, and recognition.

The period of circulation. The early church recognized the thirty-nine books of the Old Testament as Scripture as a settled truth. The divine authority of these books was unquestioned. This commitment was demonstrated through the consistent practice of Christ and his apostles quoting from the Old Testament and identifying it as the very Word of God. At the time when the New Testament books were originally written, the churches that initially received them recognized them as Scripture, and soon afterward those churches began to read these texts side by side with the Old

Testament Scriptures in their assemblies (1 Thess. 5:27; 1 Tim. 4:13; Rev. 1:3). The practices of copying and sharing these texts with other churches accompanied the recognition of these books as Scripture, just as some books even called for such practices (Col. 4:16). This early circulation and collection process resulted in a largely church-wide awareness of most of the twenty-seven books of the New Testament by the early second century AD. However, the beginnings of this process involved primarily the circulation of these texts on an individual basis.

The period of collection. The corporate worship services of the early church followed the patterns established by the synagogue. This included the public reading of Scripture and expositions or homilies (sermons) often derived from those texts (Luke 4:16–21; Acts 17:2–3; 1 Tim. 4:13). Over time, churches copied, circulated, and collected more and more New Testament books so they could be read and included in the worship services. By the second century AD, these collections began to secure an increasingly universal acceptance among the churches, which resulted in the sharing of these texts more frequently as collections than as individual books.

The mid-second century saw the first significant church controversy over the identification of the canon itself. The second-century heretic Marcion (ca. AD 85–160) published his own formal list of what he considered to be authoritative New Testament writings. His canon included a shortened form of Luke's Gospel, and ten of Paul's epistles (excluding the Pastorals). Perhaps more than any other event, it was this act on the part of a heretic that compelled the orthodox church to begin to formally answer the question, which books belong in the New Testament canon?

The first significant response of the orthodox churches is reflected in the Muratorian Fragment. It is sometimes referred to as the Muratorian Canon (ca. 170) because it lists both the New Testament books that are to be accepted as authoritative and other books that should be excluded. This document very likely reflects a formal response to Marcion. While the condition of the document itself renders it incomplete as an absolute witness to the books that were accepted, it does identify twenty-one or twenty-two of the twenty-seven books in the New Testament today. Those missing include Hebrews, James, and 1 and 2 Peter. The epistles of John are included, but it is unclear if they are referred to as a single epistle or if one or more are excluded. Regardless of the missing content of this document, it is clear that controversy and practical considerations compelled the early church fathers to come to a consensus in identifying which New Testament books were divinely authoritative and belonged alongside the Old Testament canon.

The period of recognition. The beginning of the fourth century AD brought with it both an end to the persecution of the church and the establishment of Christianity as the state religion. This period concluded nearly three centuries of sporadic and concentrated efforts to stamp out the church throughout the Roman Empire. In the most recent persecution, Diocletian (AD 245–311) called for the deliberate burning of countless sacred Christian works, including copies of the New Testament Scriptures as a result of his edict in AD 303. When Constantine (AD 272–337) became emperor, he not only legalized Christianity in AD 313 but also commissioned Eusebius (ca. AD 260–ca. 340) to oversee the production of fifty copies of the New Testament. It was this decree that immediately elevated the issue of formally recognizing the specific books that make up the New Testament canon.

Eusebius, having personally experienced much of the persecution under Diocletian, became perhaps the most significant early church historian. He records in his history not only much related to the historical events themselves but also a great deal about the challenges in recognizing the New Testament canon. Eusebius divided the early church writings into three categories: the acknowledged books, the disputed books, and the heretical books. As the categories suggest, his list begins by identifying those books universally accepted as canonical (i.e., divinely authoritative). These are all the books whose authenticity is undisputed. The normal standard included the issue of divinely sanctioned authorship—that is, it was written by an apostle or one who possessed a derived apostolic authority (e.g., Luke). Of the twenty-seven books in the New Testament, Eusebius's list included all but James, 2 Peter, 2 and 3 John, and Jude in the acknowledged books. He also listed Revelation as possibly questionable due primarily to a lack of circulation among the Eastern churches. In the end, all twenty-seven books of the New Testament were included.

The finalization of the formal process of recognizing the New Testament canon was to a large degree completed by Athanasius (AD 295–373). In his Festal Letter of AD 365, he defined the extent of the New Testament canon as the twenty-seven books of our New Testament today. He also strictly forbade the use of any others as canonical—including the *Didache* and *The Shepherd of Hermas* (both of which were debated). These decisions were later ratified by the Council of Hippo in AD 393. Since that time, there has been throughout orthodox Christianity a universal acceptance of the twenty-seven books of the New Testament as canonical.

CRITERIA FOR CANONICITY

As mentioned, the canonicity of all sixty-six books of the Bible was established at the point of inspired authorship. Only God the Holy Spirit can testify to the authority of his Word. This is the reality of the self-witness of Scripture. From a Christian perspective, recognition of the Old Testament canon was settled by Jesus and the apostles' acceptance of the thirty-nine books of the Hebrew canon. For the New Testament, though early believers were living by the truths of the inspired books for centuries, the historical recognition took some time. However, that does not suggest that there was no canon. It only means that a consensus regarding the limits of the collection had to triumph over other suggestions and options.

The external criteria for accepting any book as canonical included the original essential qualifications of (1) apostolic or prophetic authorship evidencing inspiration, (2) consistent doctrinal agreement with existing Scripture, and (3) a universal acceptance by the people of God.

Human authorial credentials are a valid criterion for canonicity. God produced his Word through the agency of divinely authenticated human writers. In the Old Testament, these writers frequently authenticated their message by performing miraculous signs or making prophetic declarations that validated their divine calling. In the New Testament, God produced his Word through the agency or authority of an already authenticated apostle (1 Cor. 14:37–38; Gal. 1:9; 1 Thess. 2:13).

Second, God made it clear from the beginning that any future revelation was to be examined in light of existing Scripture before it was accepted as authentic (Deut. 13:1–5). God has consistently revealed himself throughout the canonical books so that all are in agreement with each other and the whole (Acts 17:11). Coupled with this, God directly limited both canons when he announced the close of each. To close the Old Testament canon, God announced that the next prophet would be the Elijah who was to come (Mal. 4:4–6). In the case of the New Testament, Jesus definitively declared the close of the canon to John (Rev. 22:18–19). So with the passing of the last apostle came the passing of any additional revelation until the Lord returns.

Third, the evidences of inspiration can be divided into two categories: (1) it must be true and truthful in what it says, and (2) there should be evidence in the very reading of the Word that it is able both to convey truth and to convict the human heart of sin (Heb. 4:12). Beyond this, God's Word should be able to persuade his people corporately to recognize and affirm the authenticity of any given book. Since God's Spirit inspired the writer to produce a divinely authoritative writing, that same Spirit has attested to it in the hearts of God's people.

In the end, only God is able to bear adequate witness to himself and to what he has inspired (John 5:33–47; Heb. 6:13). God's Word attests to itself. It is essential that God's people learn to discern for themselves from the pages of Scripture how to recognize God's inspired works. As it relates to both the Old and New Testament canons, there is stunning, definitive, and unanimous affirmation that the sixty-six books of the Protestant Bible, and no others, are inspired by God.

COMPLETION OF CANONICITY[20]

How does the church today know that God will not amend the current Bible with a sixty-seventh inspired book? In other words, is the canon closed?

Scripture texts warn that no one should delete from or add to Scripture (Deut. 4:2; 12:32; Prov. 30:6). Realizing that additional canonical books actually came after these words of warning, one can only conclude that while these admonitions permitted no deletions whatsoever, they did, in fact, allow for authorized, inspired writings to be added in order to complete the canon protected by these passages.

Several significant observations, when taken together, have convinced the church over the centuries that the canon of Scripture is actually closed, never to be reopened. First, the book of Revelation is unique to the Scripture in that it describes with unparalleled detail the end-time events that precede eternity future. As Genesis began

---

20. This section is adapted from MacArthur, *MacArthur Study Bible: English Standard Version*, xxi–xxii. Used by permission of Thomas Nelson.

Scripture by bridging the gap from eternity past to this present space-time existence with the only detailed creation account (Genesis 1–2), so Revelation transitions out of space and time into eternity future (Revelation 20–22). Genesis and Revelation, by their contents, are the perfectly matched bookends of Scripture.

Second, just as there was prophetic silence after Malachi completed the Old Testament canon, so there has been a parallel silence since John delivered the book of Revelation. This leads to the conclusion that the New Testament canon was closed then as well.

Third, since there have not been, nor are there now, any authorized prophets or apostles in either the Old Testament or New Testament sense, there are not any potential authors of more inspired, canonical writings. God's Word, "once for all delivered to the saints," is never to be added to but is to be earnestly contended for (Jude 3).

Fourth, of the four biblical exhortations not to tamper with Scripture, only the one in Revelation 22:18–19 contains warnings of severe divine judgment for disobedience. Further, Revelation is the only book of the New Testament to end with this kind of admonition and was the last New Testament book to be written. Therefore, these facts strongly suggest that Revelation was the last book of the canon and that the Bible is complete; to either add or delete would bring God's severe displeasure.

Finally, the early church, those closest in time to the apostles, believed that Revelation concluded God's inspired writings, the Scriptures. So based on solid biblical reasoning, we can conclude that the canon is and will remain closed. There will be no sixty-seventh book of the Bible.

Textual Criticism and Preservation[21]

Since the Bible has frequently been translated into multiple languages and distributed throughout the world, how can one be sure that error has not crept in, even if unintentionally? It is certainly true that as Christianity spread, people desired to have the Bible in their own languages, which required translations from the original Hebrew and Aramaic languages of the Old Testament and the Greek of the New Testament. Not only did the work of translators provide an opportunity for error, but publication also afforded continual possibilities of error since copies were made by hand until the printing press arrived circa AD 1450.

Through the centuries, the practitioners of textual criticism, a precise manuscript science, have discovered, preserved, catalogued, evaluated, and published an amazing array of biblical copies from both the Old and New Testaments. In fact, the number of existing biblical manuscripts dramatically outdistances the existing fragments of any other ancient literary work. By comparing text with text, the textual critic can confidently determine what the original prophetic/apostolic writing contained.

Although existing copies of the main, ancient Hebrew text (Masoretic) date back only to the tenth century AD, two other important lines of textual evidence bolster

---

21. This section is adapted from MacArthur, *MacArthur Study Bible: English Standard Version*, xx–xxi. Used by permission of Thomas Nelson.

the confidence of textual critics that they have reclaimed the originals.[22] First, we can compare the tenth-century AD Masoretic text to the Septuagint, the Greek version translated circa 200–150 BC, with the oldest existing manuscripts dating back to circa AD 325. There is, in general, an amazing consistency between the two, which speaks of the accuracy in copying the Hebrew text for centuries. Second, the discovery of the Dead Sea Scrolls in 1947–1956 (manuscripts that are dated ca. 200–100 BC) proved to be monumentally important. After comparing the earlier Hebrew texts with the later ones, only a few slight variants were discovered, none of which changed the meaning of any passage. While some argue for the development of a plurality of authoritative texts for the Old Testament because of periodic significant differences between the Septuagint and the Masoretic text, it appears far more likely that a single authoritative, early Masoretic text base was maintained by scribes following the Babylonian exile. While variants are evidenced in the Dead Sea Scrolls and various versions, the extant records show a consistent conformity to the Masoretic text. Even though the Old Testament had been translated and copied for centuries, the latest version (the Masoretic text) is readily recognized as an authentic and authoritative representation of the original autographs.

The New Testament findings are even more decisive because a much larger amount of material is available for study. There are over five thousand extant Greek New Testament manuscripts that range in size from the whole New Testament to scraps of papyri that contain as little as a part of a single verse. A few fragments date to within twenty-five to fifty years of the original writing. New Testament textual scholars have generally concluded (1) that over 99 percent of the original writings have been reclaimed, and (2) that of the remaining potentially alternate readings, there are no variants substantially affecting any Christian doctrine. It has even been asserted that if every possible variant were accepted, the message of each chapter of the Bible that would be affected would read essentially the same.

With this wealth of biblical manuscript evidence in the original languages and with the disciplined activity of textual critics to establish with almost perfect accuracy the content of the autographs, many errors that have been introduced or perpetuated by the thousands of translations over the centuries can be identified and corrected by comparing the translation or copy with the reassembled original. By this providential means, God has fulfilled his promise to preserve the Scriptures.

EXPLANATION OF TEXTUAL CRITICISM

While Protestants universally agree about the identification of the books of the Bible themselves, some issues related to content still demand attention. This is due to the fact that none of the original works of the biblical authors have survived to this day. The only way the biblical books were preserved and passed down was by hand copying them until about AD 1450, when printing presses began mass producing the Bible. This hand-copying process necessarily introduced scribal errors into the

---

22. Wegner, *A Student's Guide*, 298–301.

biblical text, which explains some of the issues related to the wording of individual passages and even some of the more significant controversial textual problems (e.g., Mark 16:9–20; John 7:53–8:11).

At this point, the process of textual criticism comes to help. Textual criticism is best defined as the careful examination of the existing ancient copies of Scripture in order to determine the purest copies of the original text. The process itself is a science, but fundamental valuation decisions factor into the equation when choosing one reading over another, and these involve human judgment. The basic process begins with a careful examination of every existing, reliable copy of the biblical text in question. The textual critic considers various alternate readings and identifies the reading that has the strongest textual evidence to be the original penned by the biblical author. If more than one reading has strong evidence for it, the secondary ones are listed as marginal readings (often in a column note or a footnote in most Bibles). Typical textual-critical weighting factors include the oldest reading, the shortest reading, the most widely attested reading geographically, and the reading that best explains the variant(s). When these factors are taken together, the textual critic can make an educated decision in order to affirm the reading that most likely reflects what the biblical author originally wrote.

The process of textual criticism involves issues of varying levels of complexity between the two Testaments. There is a massive amount of textual evidence for the New Testament. As noted, some Greek manuscripts date back to within a generation of the actual writing of the text. This evidence also covers a broad geographic area and is confirmed over the full time frame from about AD 100 to about 1450, when the first printing presses began to publish complete collections of the Greek New Testament. By way of comparison, the Old Testament was written over a period of about a thousand years from 1400 to 400 BC. There are far fewer existing witnesses to the Old Testament text than to the New Testament text. Much of the textual evidence is more than a thousand years removed from the original writing. Even the reliability of some of the oldest witnesses (like the Qumran scrolls) is debated. These factors collectively contribute to a greater reliance on versional evidence for the Old Testament text.

Nevertheless, when all the textual evidence for both Testaments is evaluated, most scholars affirm that the Bible is essentially in agreement word-for-word with the original from Genesis through Revelation.[23] Even beyond this, when all the variants are examined, most of them are readily identifiable and easily resolvable. They include things as obvious and insignificant as spelling errors, incidental omission of words, transposition of words or letters within a word, and the like. Still other variants are obviously a copyist's explanatory insertions or deliberate alterations for various reasons. When these added considerations are taken into account, the Bible can be shown to be reliable as a faithfully preserved copy of what the original authors wrote. For that which remains, there are no significant readings in doubt, and none alter or even bring into doubt any biblical doctrine. God has inspired the writing of his Word. He has also providentially preserved it through the process of human copying.

---

23. Wegner, *A Student's Guide*, 301.

If the Bible really is God's Word, then why are there are no original manuscripts of any of the sixty-six books of the Bible in existence today? Would not a quick look at the original letter Paul wrote to the saints at Rome or at the actual scrolls on which Moses penned the book of Genesis immediately resolve any questions as to what the Bible originally said? Why are there no preserved original autographs of any of the books of the Bible? The primary reason for this is that parchment, vellum, and other materials do not readily hold up over thousands of years. Add to this the normal wear and tear that comes with repeated usage, neglect, transportation, natural disasters, and even deliberate destruction in times of persecution, and it is easy to see why none of the originals remain. However, a divine motivation may also stand behind the loss of all the original autographs. It eliminates the possibility for hyper-reverence and cultlike veneration to be given to the documents themselves instead of to the God who inspired them. This human tendency compelled Hezekiah to destroy the bronze serpent because people began worshiping it instead of the God who used it (2 Kings 18:4).

BIBLE TRANSLATIONS

As discussed above, God providentially tethered the copies of Scripture to the autographs of Scripture. A copy of the Scriptures in the original language is the Word of God insofar as it matches the original. In the same way, a version (i.e., a translation) can be considered the Word of God insofar as it matches the meaning of the Word expressed in the original language. That is why there must be just as much care (if not more) given to the translation process. What a translation conveys in a different language must match as nearly as possible the meaning expressed in the original. If the copying process is expected to be exact (and that is just the process of copying word-for-word what the original says), how much more does God expect of those who are rendering it in a different language?

This is why great care should be exercised in choosing a Bible version. Readability is important in choosing a version. God intends his people to understand what he says and what he means by what he has said. At the same time, if a version poorly translates or errantly represents what God's Word says in the original language, it misleads God's people. God will not change his standards to match men's errors. Thus, the more literal a translation is and the more precisely it conveys what the original languages say, the more reliable it is as a witness to God's people. A good translation of the Scriptures into any language is the Word of God as it accurately reflects the meaning conveyed in the original language. Formal, word-for-word translations are best. But there is no evidence, biblically or historically, demonstrating that God miraculously endowed a translation with inspiration in itself. A translation is a derived witness to God's Word. It is not a correction or an updated version of the original.

Ancient translations can also play a key role in helping to confirm a correct reading in an original-language manuscript. This is because the ancient versions record what the translator understood as the sense conveyed by the original-language text in front of him. Since these versions were written in some cases many centuries before the oldest original-language records that are still extant, they were translated from texts that are older than those that exist today. As such, they can be useful in confirming a preferred alternate reading.

The most significant ancient versions are the Greek Septuagint, the Latin Vulgate, and the Syriac Peshitta. The Septuagint is the most noteworthy of these because it is a Greek translation of the Old Testament that the church fathers frequently cited. At times, it may even be cited in the New Testament itself. It dates back about two centuries prior to the birth of Christ. The Vulgate began as a revision of the Old Latin by Jerome. It dates back to the time of the early church fathers at the beginning of the fifth century AD. Its most significant feature is that much of the Old Testament was based on the examination of Hebrew texts (rather than a Greek version). As such, it may in some cases read more closely to the original than the Septuagint. The Peshitta is a translation of the Bible into Syriac. It is the first and oldest version of the entire Bible (Old Testament ca. AD 150 and New Testament ca. AD 425). The amazing thing about these versions is that they all agree essentially (in most cases, nearly verbatim) with the overall witness of the copies of the original-language manuscripts extant today. Even where variants occur, more than 90 percent of them are insignificant or easily resolvable (including issues such as spelling and word order). God has indeed providentially preserved his Word through the diligent efforts of his people.

God intended his Word to abide forever (preservation).[24] Therefore, his written, propositional self-disclosure (revelation) was protected from error in its original writing (inspiration) and collected in the sixty-six books of the Old and New Testaments (canonicity).

Through the centuries, thousands of copies and translations have been made (transmission) that did introduce some errors. However, because an abundance of ancient Old and New Testament manuscripts remain today, the exacting science of textual criticism has been able to reclaim the content of the original writings (revelation and inspiration) to an extreme degree.[25]

The sacred book that Christians today read, study, obey, and preach deserves to unreservedly be called the Bible or the Word of God since its author is God and it bears the qualities of total truth and complete trustworthiness, all of which characterize its divine source.

Teaching and Preaching of Scripture

Teaching
Preaching

Isolating scriptural doctrine from Christian ministry cannot be sustained biblically. J. Gresham Machen labeled this kind of thinking "the modern hostility to doctrine."[26] Christianity resists being separated from doctrine because the Christian movement

24. The following three paragraphs are adapted from MacArthur, *MacArthur Study Bible: English Standard Version*, xxi. Used by permission of Thomas Nelson.
25. Wegner, *A Student's Guide*, 301.
26. J. Gresham Machen, *Christianity and Liberalism* (Grand Rapids, MI: Eerdmans, 1923), 18.

is a way of life founded on a biblical message. That conviction is reflected in Paul telling Timothy to watch both his life and doctrine closely (1 Tim. 4:16).

Teaching[27]

Christ lamented about his day, as Isaiah did in his (29:13), that "this people honors me with their lips, but their heart is far from me; in vain do they worship me, teaching as doctrines the commandments of men" (Matt. 15:8–9). Strange teaching of every kind tickled the ears of first-century people who were carried away from the truth because they could not endure sound doctrine (Eph. 4:14; 2 Tim. 4:3–4; Heb. 13:9).

Christians must seriously revisit Pilate's inquiry, "What is truth?" (John 18:38), and embrace once again Christ's answer to his disciples that God's Word is truth (John 17:17). If truth is the goal, then Scripture is the source. Reflect on Moses's words later quoted by Jesus in fighting off Satan's wilderness temptations: "Man does not live by bread alone, but man lives by every word that comes from the mouth of the Lord" (Deut. 8:3; cf. Matt. 4:4). Biblical truth is the essence of life.

Biblically speaking, Christian teaching is scriptural truth. Two Greek New Testament words are most often translated "doctrine," "teaching," or "instruction"—*didachē* and *didaskalia*. Comparing their combined fifty-one appearances affirms that Christian doctrine refers to Scripture, whether read, explained, or even theologically systematized.

Perhaps the modern avoidance of doctrine lies partially in the fact that *doctrine* has been understood too narrowly, like a doctrinal statement or theological essay, rather than more broadly in the scriptural sense of biblical content. However, the Scriptures never envisioned doctrine referring to ivory-tower musings about theological speculation or minutiae.

Scripture always refers to "sound doctrine" in relationship to Christian doctrine that finds its ultimate source in God, while all other doctrine is either of man (Col. 2:22) or demons (1 Tim. 4:1). Christian doctrine is sound—all other "doctrine" is unsound (1 Tim. 1:10; 6:3). Christian doctrine is good, and thus profitable, while all other is bad and valueless (1 Tim. 4:6; 2 Tim. 3:16).

Since Christian teaching is all about biblical truth and biblical truth is all about God's Word, Christians must therefore affirm a high view of Scripture and doctrine. But with equal importance, they must also make Scripture the basis for translating sound Christian doctrine into godly living, "so that in everything they may adorn the doctrine of God our Savior" (Titus 2:10). Simply put, Christian doctrine serves as the constitution of godly living. Just as the skeleton is to the body or oxygen is to breathing, doctrine proves indispensable to Christianity. Without Christian doctrine, believers would be stripped of truth in living out the faith.

The New Testament Epistles overflow with exhortations to make "sound doctrine" the very heart of the Christian faith and ministry. Christians are reminded by Paul (1) to be a good minister of Christ Jesus, brought up in the truths of the faith and of

---

27. This section is adapted from Richard L. Mayhue, "Editorial," *MSJ* 13, no. 1 (2002): 1–4. Used by permission of *MSJ*.

good teaching (1 Tim. 4:6); (2) to keep as the pattern of sound teaching what was heard from him (2 Tim. 1:13); (3) to preach the Word (2 Tim. 4:2); (4) to hold firmly to the trustworthy message while encouraging others by sound doctrine (Titus 1:9); and (5) to teach what is in accord with sound doctrine (Titus 2:1). It is disconcerting to imagine where the gospel would be if Paul had not publicly confronted Peter over faulty doctrine (Gal. 2:11–21).

Christ's ministry (Matt. 7:28–29), the apostles' ministry (Acts 5:29), and the early church's ministry (Acts 2:42) all revolved around sound doctrine. In effect, to minimize or question the value of doctrine belittles Christ, the apostles, and the early church, not to mention countless Christian martyrs like John the Baptist (Mark 6:21–29) and William Tyndale (1494–1536). Why would anyone not fully embrace sound doctrine when it possesses such a glorious legacy, provides eternal value (2 Tim. 3:16), and promises God's blessing for obedience (Josh. 1:8; Rev. 1:3)?

Consider what would happen if the church forsook the standard of sound doctrine. On what basis would false teachers be rejected (Rom. 16:17; 2 John 9–10) or false doctrine be refuted (Titus 1:9)? How would believers know what was true and worth holding on to (1 Tim. 3:9; Rev. 2:24)? How would Christians distinguish between right and wrong? How would sin be confronted and corrected?

This kind of spiritual disaster must be prevented at all costs. Modern Christians, like their spiritual ancestors, must contend earnestly for the faith "once for all delivered to the saints" (Jude 3). Historically, indifference to Christian doctrine has produced heretics, but attention to doctrine has crowned heroes. So rather than getting beyond doctrine, the church urgently needs to get back to doctrine.

No approach to doctrine other than taking it seriously makes sense of Christ's command for his disciples to teach obedience to all that he commanded them (Matt. 28:20). Consider the many examples given in the New Testament:

1. Paul's ministry of proclaiming the whole will of God to the Ephesian elders (Acts 20:27)
2. The angel's command for the apostles to speak "all the words of this Life" (Acts 5:20)
3. Paul's mandate for Timothy to pass the apostolic teachings on to the next generation (2 Tim. 2:2)
4. Christ's commendation to the Ephesian church for taking doctrine seriously (Rev. 2:2, 6)

Previous Christian generations have labored faithfully, suffered, and died to pass sound, biblical doctrine on to today's believers. Nothing less than perpetuating it untarnished will be honoring to Christ and worthy of Christians' spiritual forefathers.

It is thus our prayer that the utilitarian approach to Christianity has run its unsatisfactory course and that those temporarily sidetracked would now return to their heritage of scriptural truth: Christian doctrine. Only by wholeheartedly embracing this commitment will believers protect their biblical legacy from being squandered in an era that is not inclined to endure sound doctrine.

Preaching[28]

Sound doctrine demands both exacting exposition and powerful preaching. So this discussion begins with five logically sequential postulates based on biblical truth that introduce and undergird three subsequent propositions:

1. God is (Gen. 1:1; Psalms 14; 53; Heb. 11:6).
2. God is true (Ex. 34:6; Num. 23:19; Deut. 32:4; Pss. 25:10; 31:5 [NASB]; Isa. 65:16; Jer. 10:10; John 14:6; 17:3; Titus 1:2; Heb. 6:18; 1 John 5:20–21).
3. God speaks in harmony with his nature (Num. 23:19; 1 Sam. 15:29; Rom. 3:4; 2 Tim. 2:13; Titus 1:2; Heb. 6:18).
4. God speaks only truth (Pss. 31:5 [NASB]; 119:43, 142, 151, 160; Prov. 30:5; Isa. 65:16; John 17:17; James 1:18).
5. God spoke his true Word as consistent with his true nature to be communicated to people (a self-evident truth illustrated in 2 Tim. 3:16–17; Heb. 1:1).

Therefore, consider the following propositions:

1. God gave his true Word to be communicated entirely as he gave it; that is, the whole counsel of God is to be preached (Matt. 28:20; Acts 5:20; 20:27). Correspondingly, every portion of the Word of God needs to be considered in the light of its whole.
2. God gave his true Word to be communicated exactly as he gave it. It is to be dispensed precisely as it was delivered without altering the message (Deut. 4:2; 12:32; Jer. 26:2).
3. Only the exegetical process that yields expository proclamation will accomplish propositions 1 and 2.

These propositions can be substantiated by answers to a series of questions that should channel one's thinking from the headwaters of God's revelation to its intended destination. First, why preach? Because that is what God commanded (2 Tim. 4:2). Preaching is also exactly what the apostles did in personally obeying God (Acts 5:27–32; 6:4). Second, what should be preached? The Word of God, that is, Scripture alone and Scripture in total (1 Tim. 4:13; 2 Tim. 4:2). Third, who should preach? Holy men of God (Luke 1:70; Acts 3:21; Eph. 3:5; 2 Pet. 1:21; Rev. 18:20; 22:6). Only after God had purified Isaiah's lips was he ordained to preach for God (Isa. 6:6–13).

Moving beyond these fundamentals, what is the preacher's responsibility? The preacher needs to realize that God's Word is not the preacher's word. He is to recognize himself as a messenger, not an originator (1 Thess. 2:13). He is a sower, not the source (Matt. 13:3, 19). He is a herald, not the authority (1 Tim. 2:7). He is a steward, not the owner (Col. 1:25). He is the guide, not the author (Acts 8:31). He is the server of spiritual food, not the chef (John 21:15, 17).

The preacher needs to reckon that Scripture is *the Word of God*. When he is committed to this awesome truth and responsibility, as J. I. Packer puts it,

---

28. This section is adapted from John MacArthur, "The Mandate of Biblical Inerrancy: Expository Preaching," *MSJ* 1, no. 1 (1990): 3–15. Used by permission of *MSJ*.

his aim . . . will be to stand under Scripture, not over it, and to allow it, so to speak, to talk through him, delivering what is not so much his message as its. In our preaching, that is what should always be happening. In his obituary of the great German conductor, Otto Klemperer, Neville Cardus spoke of the way in which Klemperer "set the music in motion," maintaining throughout a deliberately anonymous, self-effacing style in order that the musical notes might articulate themselves in their own integrity through him. So it must be in preaching; Scripture itself must do all the talking, and the preacher's task is simply to "set the Bible in motion."[29]

As it was with Christ and the apostles, so it is with preachers today: they are to deliver Scripture in such a way that they can say, "Thus says the Lord." Their responsibility is to deliver it as it was originally given and intended.

How did the preacher's message begin? It began as a true word from God and was given as truth because God's purpose was to transmit truth. It was ordered by God as truth and was delivered by God's Spirit in cooperation with holy men who received it as exactly the pure quality that God intended (2 Pet. 1:20–21). It was received as *Scriptura inerrantis* by the prophets and apostles, that is, without wandering from Scripture's original formulation in the mind of God. The term *inerrancy*, then, expresses the quality with which the writers of the canon received the text called Scripture.

How is God's message to continue in its original, true state? Since God's message is true and is to be delivered as received, what interpretive processes necessitated by changes of language, culture, and time can be applied without compromising its purity when preached today? The answer is that only an exegetical approach is acceptable for accurate exposition, for biblical preaching.

So pulling this all together in a practical way, what are the final steps in preaching? First, the preacher must use the true text. Christians are indebted to those select scholars who labor tediously in the field of textual criticism. Their studies recover the original text of Scripture from the large volume of extant manuscript copies that are flawed in places by textual variants. This is the starting point. Without the text as God gave it, the preacher would be helpless to deliver it as God intended.

Next, having begun with the true text, the preacher needs to interpret the text accurately. This involves the science of *hermeneutics*. Proper hermeneutics are the interpretive rules applied by exegesis in order to find the single meaning God intended to convey in the text. By employing the hermeneutical principles of literal, grammatical-historical interpretation, the student can understand this meaning. *Exegesis* can be defined as the skillful application of sound hermeneutical principles to the biblical text in the original languages with a view to discerning and declaring the author's intended meaning to both the immediate and subsequent audiences. In tandem, hermeneutics and exegesis focus on the biblical text to determine what it said and what it originally

---

29. James I. Packer, "Preaching as Biblical Interpretation," in *Inerrancy and Common Sense*, ed. Roger R. Nicole and J. Ramsey Michaels (Grand Rapids, MI: Baker, 1980), 203.

meant. Thus, exegesis in its broadest sense will include various disciplines of literary context, historical studies, grammatical analysis, and historical, biblical, and systematic theology. Proper exegesis will inform the student of what the text says and what the text means, guiding him to discern the proper personal implications of it.

Finally, based on the flow of this thinking, expository preaching is really exegetical preaching. As a result of this exegetical process, which begins with a commitment to inerrancy, the expositor is equipped with a true message, with true intent, and with true application. It gives his preaching perspective historically, theologically, contextually, literarily, synoptically, and culturally. His message is God's intended message.

The expositor's task, then, is to preach the mind of God as he finds it in the inerrant Word of God. He understands it through the disciplines of hermeneutics and exegesis. He declares it expositionally as the message that God spoke and commissioned him to deliver.

Inerrancy demands exegetical preparation and expository proclamation. Only such an approach preserves God's Word entirely, guarding the treasure of revelation and declaring its meaning exactly as he intended it to be proclaimed. Expository preaching is the essential result of the exegetical process and of inerrancy. It is mandated to preserve the purity of God's originally given inerrant Word and to proclaim the whole counsel of God's redemptive truth (Acts 5:20; 20:27).

Obligation to Scripture

Receive
Pray
Feed
Obey
Honor
Study
Preach/Teach
Compel
Disciple
Tremble

Throughout his New Testament writings, the apostle John summarized a Christian's obligation to obey the Scriptures. He made it clear that walking in the ways of the Word was not optional.

First, Christ said that if one loves him, that person will keep his commandments (John 14:15, 21, 23). On the other hand, the one who does not love him will not keep his words (John 14:24). A Christian's obedience to the Bible *demonstrates* one's love for Christ and the genuineness of one's salvation.

Second, John clearly stated that a Christian's duty is to walk in the same manner as Christ walked (1 John 2:6). God *demands* obedience to his Word.

Third, John broadly *defined* love in unmistakable terms: "This is love, that we walk according to his commandments" (2 John 6).

Fourth, John experienced great *delight* in watching and hearing of Christians obeying God's Word: "I have no greater joy than to hear that my children are walking in the truth" (3 John 4).

Finally, John announced the ultimate *distinction* of an obedient Christian—the Savior's blessing (Rev. 1:3). Now, to be more specific, Scripture provides a profile comprising at least ten exemplary characteristics of what John envisioned.

Receive

When Paul preached in Thessalonica, the people not only received his word but also accepted it. They did not reject it; rather, they embraced what he proclaimed as the Word of God, not of man:

> And we also thank God constantly for this, that when you received the word of God, which you heard from us, you accepted it not as the word of men but as what it really is, the word of God, which is at work in you believers. (1 Thess. 2:13)

Pray

The psalmist understood that God was the ultimate author of the Scriptures and that it would thus be most appropriate to solicit his aid in understanding it:

> Open my eyes, that I may behold
> wondrous things out of your law. (Ps. 119:18; see Acts 6:4)

Feed

The Bible figuratively describes Scripture as milk (1 Pet. 2:2), bread (Deut. 8:3; Matt. 4:4), meat (1 Cor. 3:2), and honey (Ps. 19:10) to nourish the soul. Job testified to the effectiveness of the spiritual menu:

> I have not departed from the commandment of his lips;
> I have treasured the words of his mouth more than my portion of food. (Job 23:12; see Jer. 15:16)

Obey

Caleb proved to be special (in contrast to the disobedient nation) because of his totally obedient response to God's commands:

> None of the men who have seen my glory and my signs that I did in Egypt and in the wilderness, and yet have put me to the test these ten times and have not obeyed my voice, shall see the land that I swore to give to their fathers. And none of those who despised me shall see it. But my servant Caleb, because he has a different spirit and has followed me fully, I will bring into the land into which he went, and his descendants shall possess it. (Num. 14:22–24)

Honor

The Jews who had returned to the land after seventy years of captivity in Babylon gladly honored God and his Word:

And Ezra opened the book in the sight of all the people, for he was above all the people, and as he opened it all the people stood. And Ezra blessed the LORD, the great God, and all the people answered, "Amen, Amen," lifting up their hands. And they bowed their heads and worshiped the LORD with their faces to the ground. (Neh. 8:5–6)

Study

Ezra understood that he had to study God's Word. But before he could speak, it was imperative that he first obey what he learned. This principle proves true for both the preacher and the congregation:

For Ezra had set his heart to study the Law of the Lord, and to do it and to teach his statutes and rules in Israel. (Ezra 7:10)

Preach/Teach

Everywhere Jesus went he taught and preached God's precious Word:

And he went throughout all Galilee, teaching in their synagogues and proclaiming the gospel of the kingdom and healing every disease and every affliction among the people. (Matt. 4:23; see 2 Tim. 4:2)

Compel

Apollos did not preach solely to dispense information. He passionately proclaimed the truth in order to convince his hearers and convert them to the way of God's truth:

Now a Jew named Apollos, a native of Alexandria, came to Ephesus. He was an eloquent man, competent in the Scriptures. He had been instructed in the way of the Lord. And being fervent in spirit, he spoke and taught accurately the things concerning Jesus, though he knew only the baptism of John. He began to speak boldly in the synagogue, but when Priscilla and Aquila heard him, they took him aside and explained to him the way of God more accurately. And when he wished to cross to Achaia, the brothers encouraged him and wrote to the disciples to welcome him. When he arrived, he greatly helped those who through grace had believed, for he powerfully refuted the Jews in public, showing by the Scriptures that the Christ was Jesus. (Acts 18:24–28)

Disciple

Paul understood the continuing and cumulative effect of multiplication; so he heartily commended it to Timothy, the third of five generations up to that time (Christ, Paul, Timothy, faithful men, and others):

And what you have heard from me in the presence of many witnesses entrust to faithful men who will be able to teach others also. (2 Tim. 2:2)

Tremble

Isaiah exemplified a humble believer who took God and his Word very seriously (see Isa. 6:1–13):

But this is the one to whom I will look:
> he who is humble and contrite in spirit
> and trembles at my word. (Isa. 66:2)

Prayer[30]

Father, may our lives and our fellowship be marked by
> works of faith, labors of love, and steadfastness of hope.
By Your grace, we are holy people, beloved and chosen by You,
> and when the gospel came to us,
> it came not only in word but also in power,
> in the Holy Spirit, and with full conviction.
Not that we are sufficient in ourselves
> to claim anything as coming from us,
> but our sufficiency is from You.
You are the One who accomplished our salvation,
> turning us from worldly things we once idolized
> to serve You, the living and true God.
You are the One who awakened us to receive Your Word—
> not as the word of men but for what it really is:
> the Word of God, which performs its perfect work
> in all who believe.

So our salvation comes solely from You.
You sent Your Son to die for our sake
> while we were still sworn enemies of righteousness.
You graciously removed the scales from our eyes and drew us to faith.
Open our eyes to see more of Your truth;
> open our hearts to believe it more earnestly;
> and open our mouths to declare it more faithfully.

May we be imitators of our Lord Jesus Christ
> and godly examples to one another.
Help us grow into fully maturity and Christlikeness.
We know that the necessary nourishment
> for that kind of growth is found only in Your Word.
We cannot thrive by bread alone,
> but by every word that proceeds out of Your mouth.

May we therefore search the Scriptures
> diligently and with singleness of heart,
> for in them we know we have eternal life.
They point us to Christ.
They unveil His glory.

---

30. This prayer is reproduced verbatim from John MacArthur, *At the Throne of Grace: A Book of Prayers* (Eugene, OR: Harvest House, 2011), 192–93. Used by permission of Harvest House.

They reflect His holy character.
From them we learn of His suffering, death, resurrection, ascension,
    intercession, and glorious return.
By them You speak to us from heaven.
In them we hear the voice of the Spirit speaking plainly.

Give us attentive hearts.
Cause us to hear Your truth with all humility and obedience.
Open our eyes to see with clarity,
    and open our ears to hear with understanding.
May we heed every line with fear and trembling—
    not only the instructions, but also the reproofs;
    not only the promises, but also the threats.

We bless You that Your holy Word has been translated
    into our own language to show us the way of life.
May we never take that privilege for granted.
May we never neglect
    the rich counsel available to us on those pages.
May we drink deeply of its truth
    and feed our famished souls with its nourishment.

And may our hearts, like the hearts of those on the road to Emmaus,
    burn within us as You teach us.
We pray in Jesus' name. Amen.

"How Firm a Foundation"

How firm a foundation, ye saints of the Lord,
Is laid for your faith in His excellent Word!
What more can He say than to you He hath said,
To you who for refuge to Jesus have fled?

Fear not! I am with thee; O be not dismayed,
For I am thy God, and will still give thee aid;
I'll strengthen thee, help thee, and cause thee to stand,
Upheld by My righteous, omnipotent hand.

When through fiery trials thy pathway shall lie,
My grace, all sufficient, shall be thy supply:
The flame shall not hurt thee; I only design
Thy dross to consume and thy gold to refine.

The soul that on Jesus hath leaned for repose
I will not, I will not desert to its foes;
That soul, though all hell should endeavor to shake,
I'll never, no never, no never forsake!

~author unknown[31]

---

31. The earliest known occurrence of this hymn comes from John Rippon's (1751–1836) *A Selection of Hymns* (1787).

Bibliography

Primary Systematic Theologies

Bancroft, Emery H. *Christian Theology: Systematic and Biblical*. 2nd ed. Grand Rapids, MI: Zondervan, 1976. 21–58.

Buswell, James Oliver, Jr. *A Systematic Theology of the Christian Religion*. 2 vols. Grand Rapids, MI: Zondervan, 1962–1963. 1:183–220.

Erickson, Millard J. *Christian Theology*. Grand Rapids, MI: Baker, 1986. 153–259.

*Grudem, Wayne. *Systematic Theology: An Introduction to Biblical Doctrine*. Grand Rapids, MI: Zondervan, 1994. 47–138.

Hodge, Charles. *Systematic Theology*. 3 vols. 1871–1873. Reprint, Grand Rapids, MI: Eerdmans, 1975. 1:151–88.

Lewis, Gordon R., and Bruce A. Demarest. *Integrative Theology*. 3 vols. Grand Rapids, MI: Zondervan, 1987–1994. 1:61–171.

Reymond, Robert L. *A New Systematic Theology of the Christian Faith*. Nashville: Thomas Nelson, 1998. 3–126.

Shedd, William G. T. *Dogmatic Theology*. 3 vols. 1889. Reprint, Minneapolis: Klock & Klock, 1979. 1:61–147.

Strong, August Hopkins. *Systematic Theology: A Compendium Designed for the Use of Theological Students*. Rev. ed. New York: Revell, 1907. 111–242.

*Swindoll, Charles R., and Roy B. Zuck, eds. *Understanding Christian Theology*. Nashville: Thomas Nelson, 2003. 1–134.

Thiessen, Henry Clarence. *Introductory Lectures in Systematic Theology*. Grand Rapids, MI: Eerdmans, 1949. 78–115.

Turretin, Francis. *Institutes of Elenctic Theology*. 3 vols. Edited by James T. Dennison Jr. Translated by George Musgrove Giger. 1679–1685. Reprint, Phillipsburg, NJ: P&R, 1992–1997. 1:55–167.

*Denotes most helpful.

Specific Works

*Allison, Gregg R. "The Doctrine of the Word of God." In *Historical Theology: An Introduction to Christian Doctrine*, 35–184. Grand Rapids, MI: Zondervan, 2011.

*Barrick, William D. "Ancient Manuscripts and Biblical Exposition." *The Master's Seminary Journal* 9, no. 1 (1998): 25–38.

Boice, James Montgomery, ed. *The Foundation of Biblical Authority*. Grand Rapids, MI: Zondervan, 1978.

Bruce, F. F. *The Canon of Scripture*. Downers Grove, IL: InterVarsity Press, 1988.

Carson, D. A. *Collected Writings on Scripture*. Compiled by Andrew David Naselli. Wheaton, IL: Crossway, 2010.

Frame, John M. *The Doctrine of the Word of God*. A Theology of Lordship 4. Phillipsburg, NJ: P&R, 2010.

*Geisler, Norman L., ed. *Inerrancy*. Grand Rapids, MI: Zondervan, 1980.

Geisler, Norman L., and William E. Nix. *A General Introduction to the Bible*. Chicago: Moody Press, 1986.

Grier, James M., Jr. "The Apologetical Value of the Self-Witness of Scripture." *Grace Theological Journal* 1, no. 1 (1980): 71–76.

*Harris, R. Laird. *Inspiration and Canonicity of the Scriptures*. Rev. ed. Greenville, SC: Attic, 1995.

Henry, Carl F. H. *God, Revelation, and Authority*. 6 vols. Waco, TX: Word, 1976–1983.

*Kaiser, Walter C., Jr. *Recovering the Unity of the Bible: One Continuous Story, Plan, and Purpose*. Grand Rapids, MI: Zondervan, 2009.

*Lightner, Robert P. *A Biblical Case for Total Inerrancy: How Jesus Viewed the Old Testament*. Grand Rapids, MI: Kregel, 1998.

Lillback, Peter A., and Richard B. Gaffin Jr., eds. *Thy Word Is Still Truth: Essential Writings on the Doctrine of Scripture from the Reformation to Today*. Phillipsburg, NJ: P&R, 2013.

*MacArthur, John, ed. *The Scripture Cannot Be Broken: Twentieth Century Writings on the Doctrine of Inerrancy*. Wheaton, IL: Crossway, 2015.

Mayhue, Richard L. "The Authority of Scripture." *The Master's Seminary Journal* 15, no. 2 (2004): 227–36.

Metzger, Bruce M. *The Canon of the New Testament: Its Origin, Development, and Significance*. Oxford: Clarendon, 1997.

*———. *The Text of the New Testament: Its Transmission, Corruption, and Restoration*. 3rd ed. New York: Oxford University Press, 1992.

Packer, J. I. *"Fundamentalism" and the Word of God: Some Evangelical Principles*. Grand Rapids, MI: Eerdmans, 1958.

———. "The Necessity of the Revealed Word." In *The Bible: The Living Word of Revelation*, edited by Merrill C. Tenney, 31–49. Grand Rapids, MI: Zondervan, 1968.

Radmacher, Earl D., and Robert D. Preus, eds. *Hermeneutics, Inerrancy, and the Bible*. Grand Rapids, MI: Zondervan, 1984.

Thomas, Robert L. *How to Choose a Bible Version*. Rev. ed. Fearn, Ross-Shire, Scotland: Mentor, 2005.

*Warfield, Benjamin B. *The Inspiration and Authority of the Bible*. Edited by Samuel G. Craig. Philadelphia: Presbyterian and Reformed, 1948.

Weeks, Noel. *The Sufficiency of Scripture*. Edinburgh: Banner of Truth, 1988.

*Wenham, John. *Christ and the Bible*. 3rd ed. Eugene, OR: Wipf & Stock, 2009.

Woodbridge, John D. *Biblical Authority: A Critique of the Rogers-McKim Proposal*. Grand Rapids, MI: Zondervan, 1982.

*Young, E. J. *Thy Word Is Truth: Some Thoughts on the Biblical Doctrine of Inspiration*. Grand Rapids, MI: Eerdmans, 1957.

*Denotes most helpful.

"Immortal, Invisible, God Only Wise"

Immortal, invisible, God only wise,
In light inaccessible hid from our eyes,
Most blessed, most glorious, the Ancient of Days,
Almighty, victorious—Thy great Name we praise.

Unresting, unhasting, and silent as light,
Nor wanting, nor wasting, Thou rulest in might;
Thy justice, like mountains, high soaring above
Thy clouds, which are fountains of goodness and love.

To all, life Thou givest—to both great and small;
In all life Thou livest—the true life of all.
Thy wisdom so boundless, Thy mercy so free,
Eternal Thy goodness for naught changeth Thee.

Great Father of glory, pure Father of light,
Thine angels adore Thee, all veiling their sight;
All praise we would render—O help us to see
'Tis only the splendor of light hideth Thee! Amen.

~Walter Chalmers Smith (1824–1908)

3

God the Father

Theology Proper

Major Subjects Covered in Chapter 3

The Existence of God

The Names of God

The Attributes (Perfections) of God

The Trinity

The Decree of God

Creation

Divine Miracles

Divine Providence

The Problem of Evil and Theodicy

Glorifying God

Having established that the Bible is the inspired, inerrant foundation for human knowledge about God and all things in their relation to God, our discussion moves next to the doctrine of God. This section will set forth the Bible's teaching about God's existence, attributes (perfections), triunity, and works in decreeing, creating, and ruling over all things outside himself.

The Existence of God

Scriptural Assertions
The Knowability and Incomprehensibility of God
Assessment of "Natural Proofs"

"In the beginning, God . . ." (Gen. 1:1). The Bible does not begin with a rationalistic argument for the existence of God but rather assumes that he exists, that he existed before the beginning of all things outside himself, and that there is only one God. Theology proper, as with all other areas of systematic theology, is properly derived from God's own testimony in his inspired, inerrant Word, the Bible. One's concept of God does not come "from below," from human reasoning about the universe, because human reason is finite in its components and operations, corrupted by indwelling sin, and therefore never able of itself to derive an accurate understanding about God, who is infinite and holy. Proof for God's existence must come, first and foremost, from God's testimony about himself. He has provided irrefutable proofs for his existence in the Bible.

Scriptural Assertions

This volume does not seek to prove the existence of God from human reasoning but rather presupposes that the God of the Bible exists and endeavors to set forth what the Bible teaches about God. The only reliable proof of the existence of the true God consists of statements from and about him in his inspired Word. God must not be excluded from testifying about himself. Quite the contrary, his testimony, given by his own inspiration, must be accepted as unique and perfectly reliable. Scripture alone is inspired, or "breathed out by God" (Gk. *theopneustos*, 2 Tim. 3:16), so one must first look to the Bible alone for evidence that is pure and that transcends the limitations of human intellectual finiteness and corruption. Other evidences of God's existence—for example, those in the created realm (Rom. 1:19–20)—must be evaluated and accepted only as they align with the Bible's statements about God.

Scripture asserts the existence of "the only true God" (John 17:3). The Bible begins with the foundational presupposition that God existed "in the beginning" (Gen. 1:1). So every statement from the Bible about God's nature and actions is proof from him of his existence.

PROOF FROM THE REDEMPTIVE REQUIREMENT
TO BELIEVE THAT GOD EXISTS

For example, the Bible requires that everyone who wants to be properly related to God must first believe that he exists: "Whoever would draw near to God must believe that he exists" (Heb. 11:6). To do otherwise makes one a fool. Scripture calls those who in their heart and thinking do not believe that God exists "fools" and "wicked":

> The fool says in his heart,
>   "There is no God." (Pss. 14:1; 53:1)

> In the pride of his face the wicked does not seek him;
>   all his thoughts are, "There is no God." (Ps. 10:4)

PROOF FROM THE ASSERTION THAT GOD IS ETERNAL

The Bible repeatedly states that God is eternal. God is without beginning, without ending, and without succession of moments in his experience and knowledge of himself and of all reality outside himself. In the Bible, God is called "the eternal God" (Deut. 33:27). Psalm 90:2 says that God existed eternally in the present before the world was created: "Before the mountains were brought forth, or ever you had formed the earth and the world, from everlasting to everlasting you are God." In Isaiah 41:4, God declares, "I, the LORD, the first, and with the last; I am he." Isaiah adds, "Thus says the LORD, the King of Israel and his Redeemer, the LORD of hosts: 'I am the first and I am the last; besides me there is no god'" (Isa. 44:6). And Isaiah 57:15 affirms that God "inhabits eternity."

PROOF FROM THE ASSERTION OF GOD'S SELF-EXISTENCE

A final proof of God's existence is his statements that he "is," without dependence on anything else for his life. God told Moses by what name Israel was to know him: "God said to Moses, 'I AM WHO I AM.' And he said, 'Say this to the people of Israel, "I AM has sent me to you"'" (Ex. 3:14). God is. So he depends on nothing for his existence. This inference from God's covenantal name is reflected in the apostle Paul's words: "For from him and through him and to him are all things" (Rom. 11:36), and, "The God who made the world and everything in it, being Lord of heaven and earth, does not live in temples made by man, nor is he served by human hands, as though he needed anything, since he himself gives to all mankind life and breath and everything" (Acts 17:24–25).

One could go on to multiply biblical proofs of God's existence from all the scriptural statements about God's being and works. However, these suffice to show that God affirms his existence in the statements of the Bible as the primary, foundational, and foremost proofs by which people must believe that he does exist.

The Knowability and Incomprehensibility of God

Because God has revealed the fact of his existence in Scripture, he has given humans statements by which they can have at least some knowledge of him. The Bible makes God knowable to humans, to the extent that the content of the Bible reveals truth about him. Scripture teaches that man may know God truly, yet not exhaustively. In the classical terminology, God is truly knowable but not exhaustively comprehensible.

GOD'S SUFFICIENT KNOWABILITY

The Bible affirms that God can be known, even known in a personal relationship of friendship. He walked with Adam and Eve in the garden of Eden (Gen. 3:8). He appeared to Moses in the burning bush (Ex. 3:3–4). He gave his law to Moses on Mount Sinai (Exodus 19). In ancient Israel, God made himself present in the tabernacle and in the temple on the mercy seat on top of the ark of the covenant (1 Sam. 4:4; 1 Kings 8:10–11). Jesus said that God can be personally known (John 17:3).

Jesus himself is the incarnation of God (Col. 2:9). The New Testament reveals that God indwells the church (1 Cor. 3:16), dwells within believers (John 14:23), and is the friend of believers (James 2:23).

GOD'S INCOMPREHENSIBILITY

Though God can be known truly, Scripture also reveals that God is not comprehensively or exhaustively knowable to humans in any aspect of his being or actions. Humans are limited to time and space and in Adam are corrupted by indwelling sin (Rom. 7:15–23), which has made them rebellious toward God and has darkened their understanding of God's revelation in the Bible and in nature (2 Cor. 4:3–4; Eph. 4:17–19). God is eternal and holy, transcending time and space, infinitely omniscient, and absolutely morally pure. God alone is great. Man was created as a different and inferior order of being. Even in his originally created state, humanity could not know God exhaustively, but after the fall of Adam, even the knowledge humans *can* have of God is corrupted by sin.

The Bible unmistakably testifies to the fact that God cannot be fully known by humans, even apart from the darkening factor of their internal sinful corruption. Man cannot see God and live (Ex. 33:20; Lev. 16:2). God "dwells in unapproachable light, whom no one has ever seen or can see" (1 Tim. 6:16; see John 1:18; 6:46). The spiritual form of God's essence is not revealed (Deut. 4:12, 15). The depths of God are known only by God (1 Cor. 2:11).

Going a step further, God cannot be fully searched out. Psalm 145:3 says, "Great is the LORD, and greatly to be praised, and his greatness is unsearchable." The word "unsearchable" is a translation of the Hebrew *'en kheqer*, "without searching." The Hebrew root, *khaqar*, from which the noun for "searching" comes, is used in the Old Testament of "searching exhaustively." For example, the same phrase is found in Isaiah 40:28: "Have you not known? Have you not heard? The LORD is the everlasting God, the Creator of the ends of the earth. He does not faint or grow weary; his understanding is unsearchable." The same root word is used in its verbal form to speak of miners searching exhaustively in the earth for ore: "Man puts an end to darkness and searches out to the farthest limit the ore in gloom and deep darkness" (Job 28:3; cf. Job 11:7–8; 36:26). Compare other Old Testament expressions of God's incomprehensibility:

> These are but the outskirts of his ways,
> and how small a whisper do we hear of him! (Job 26:14)

> He does great things that we cannot comprehend. (Job 37:5)

Adding to the biblical affirmation of God's incomprehensibility is the fact that he has not revealed to us all that he is or all that he knows. Deuteronomy 29:29 says, "The secret things belong to the LORD our God, but the things that are revealed belong to us and to our children forever, that we may do all the words of this law." According to Revelation 10:4, John was commanded not to write something he had witnessed: "And when the seven thunders had sounded, I was about to write, but I heard a voice from heaven saying, 'Seal up what the seven thunders have said, and do not write it down.'"

Finally, God's incomprehensibility is seen in scriptural statements that God's thinking transcends man's intellectual capacity, process, and output. Psalm 139:6 says that God's knowledge "is too wonderful for me; it is high; I cannot attain it." Psalm 139:17–18 states that God's thoughts are "more than the sand" in number. Psalm 147:5 declares that God's "understanding is beyond measure." God contrasts the superiority of his thoughts with the inferiority of man's thoughts: "For as the heavens are higher than the earth, so are my ways higher than your ways and my thoughts than your thoughts" (Isa. 55:9). This incomprehensibility of God's intellect is what Paul proclaimed in his explosion of praise in Romans 11:33–34: "Oh, the depth of the riches and wisdom and knowledge of God! How unsearchable are his judgments and how inscrutable his ways! 'For who has known the mind of the Lord, or who has been his counselor?'"

When trying to search out God's nature, one finds that it is infinitely beyond what can be learned or reasoned. This holds true with respect to any aspect of God's nature. Grudem summarizes helpfully:

> It is not only true that we can never fully understand God; it is also true that *we can never fully understand any single thing about God*. His greatness (Ps. 145:3), his understanding (Ps. 147:5), his knowledge (Ps. 139:6), his riches, wisdom, judgments, and ways (Rom. 11:33) are *all* beyond our ability to understand fully. . . . Thus, we may know *something* about God's love, power, wisdom, and so forth. But we can never know his love completely or *exhaustively*. We can never know his power exhaustively. We can never know his wisdom exhaustively, and so forth. In order to know any single thing about God exhaustively we would need to know it as he himself knows it. That is, we would have to know it in its relationship to everything else about God and in its relationship to everything else about creation throughout eternity! We can only exclaim with David, "Such knowledge is too wonderful for me; it is high, I cannot attain it" (Ps. 139:6).[1]

Assessment of "Natural Proofs"

Theology proper seeks to ground the knowledge of God's existence in Scripture and to relegate all other evidence of God's existence to secondary status, subordinate to Scripture's assessment. Still, God has revealed himself by means other than Scripture. He has revealed himself nonverbally to all people through nature, conscience, and history. This is referred to as *general* or *natural* revelation, and the Bible strongly affirms it. But knowledge of natural revelation of God must never be considered independent of Scripture, because the Bible shows that, left to his own thinking, man will corrupt the revelation of God in nature. Even the Christian needs the guidance of Scripture to properly assess God's revelation of himself in nature. John Calvin (1509–1564)

---

1. Wayne Grudem, *Systematic Theology: An Introduction to Biblical Doctrine* (Grand Rapids, MI: Zondervan, 1994), 150.

graphically portrayed this last point, comparing the Scriptures to "spectacles" that give people a clear manifestation of the true God:

> Just as old or bleary-eyed men and those with weak vision, if you thrust before them a most beautiful volume, even if they recognize it to be some sort of writing, yet can scarcely construe two words, but with the aid of spectacles will begin to read distinctly; so Scripture, gathering up the otherwise confused knowledge of God in our minds, having dispersed our dullness, clearly shows us the true God.[2]

Therefore, the so-called "natural proofs" for the existence of God cannot be allowed to stand as products of human observation and reason apart from Scripture's assessment of them. When we look at these "natural proofs," we must discern whether they do indeed "prove" the God of the Bible. And then we need to discern whether they have any use.

INADEQUACY OF THE "NATURAL PROOFS"

Considered in and of themselves, the "natural proofs" for the existence of God do not prove the existence of the God of the Bible. In fact, they do not even prove the existence of any god. Christians should expect that these "proofs" fail to prove the true God because at least some of them were derived from pagan philosophers such as Plato (ca. 428–348 BC) and Aristotle (ca. 384–322 BC).

The Ontological Argument. The ontological argument for the existence of God states that God's existence is proved by man's thought that God exists as the perfect being. In other words, if man can think that God exists as a perfect being, then this God must exist, since for him not to exist would make him not a perfect being. It should be a caution to Christians that the Greek philosopher Plato held a form of this argument, though he concluded that it pointed to many personal "forms," not to a single God. Plato held that man's concepts of perfect things cannot be derived from things in this imperfect world, so these concepts derive from real things in the transcendent "world of forms."[3]

One should be warned by the fact that nonevangelical thinkers have also held

The classic Christian form of the ontological argument was put forth by Anselm of Canterbury (1033–1109) in his works *Monologion* and *Proslogion*. He argued that we can think of something absolutely perfect ("something than which nothing greater can be thought").[4] But if it does not exist, then it is not absolutely perfect since existence must be an aspect of perfection. In that case, we can think of something even greater—something that exists not only in our thoughts but also in reality. So Anselm concluded that an absolutely perfect thing must necessarily exist, and that is God.

One should be warned by the fact that nonevangelical thinkers have also held

---

2. John Calvin, *Institutes of the Christian Religion*, ed. John T. McNeill, trans. Ford Lewis Battles, Library of Christian Classics (1559; repr., Philadelphia: Westminster John Knox, 1960), 1.6.1.

3. John M. Frame, *Apologetics to the Glory of God: An Introduction* (Phillipsburg, NJ: P&R, 1994), 115–16; John M. Frame, *A History of Western Philosophy and Theology* (Phillipsburg, NJ: P&R, 2015), 63–70; Frederick Copleston, *A History of Philosophy* (London: Search Press, 1946), 1:163–206.

4. Anselm, *Proslogion*, 2, in Anselm of Canterbury, *The Major Works*, ed. Brian Davies and G. R. Evans, Oxford World's Classics (Oxford: Oxford University Press, 1998), 87.

a form of this argument, including René Descartes (1596–1650), Baruch Spinoza (1632–1677), Gottfried Wilhelm von Leibniz (1646–1716), George Hegel (1770–1831), and Charles Hartshorne (1897–2000). The ontological argument did not lead them to the God of the Bible.

The Cosmological Argument. Another "natural proof" is the argument from the created realm to an Ultimate Cause for it all. It was captured in Thomas Aquinas's (1225–1274) "first way," "second way," and "third way" of proving the existence of God. As Aquinas taught, there cannot be an infinite sequence of causes, so there must be an unmoved mover (the "first way"), a "first cause" (the "second way"), an original and absolutely necessary being sufficient to produce all created things (the "third way"). And that "first cause" is God.[5]

However, caution must be noted in that the Muslim philosopher Al-Ghazali (1058–1111) used a form of the cosmological argument to argue for the existence of Allah. And the cosmological argument was later held by the nonevangelical Enlightenment philosopher Gottfried Wilhelm von Leibniz.

The Teleological Argument. Another "natural proof" is the teleological argument, the argument from design. This argument (Aquinas's "fifth way") holds that the complex order, design, purpose, and intelligence in the universe is the result of the work of an intelligent, purposeful designer, who is God. This argument has also been held by non-Christians: Plato, Aristotle, and Immanuel Kant (1724–1804). Therefore, this argument also does not necessarily point people to the true God.

The Moral Argument. The moral argument proposes that the ethical phenomena in man (conscience, reward and punishment, moral values, and the fear of death and punishment) imply a moral being who created and maintains the moral order in the world. A form of the moral argument is visible in Aquinas's "fourth way," which argues from the gradation of beings to an ultimately perfect being, who is their cause. Aquinas believed that this ultimate being must be the cause of all the perfections that characterize other beings, whether goodness, truth, or something else. And this ultimate being "we call God." Note, though, that the Enlightenment philosopher Immanuel Kant also asserted a form of the moral argument, and he denied both the Trinity and the incarnation.

Other Arguments. Two other arguments merit brief mention. First, the "universality of religion" argument states that because most people in the world believe in some kind of personal power, and because most of these either worship a personal deity or deities or word their devotions in personal terms, then this universality of religion points to something in the nature of man. The most reasonable explanation for the origin of this aspect of human nature is that a higher power has made man as a religious being. Second, the "progress of humanity" argument contends that

---

5. Thomas Aquinas, *The Summa Theologica*, trans. Fathers of the English Dominican Province, ed. Kevin Knight, 2nd ed. (Kevin Knight, 2008), 1.2.3, http://www.newadvent.org/summa/1002.htm#article3.

the apparent progress in human civilization throughout history indicates that man is on the way to fulfilling the plan of a wise and omnipotent world ruler, who is God.

Response to the "Natural Proofs." All the "natural proofs" represent a theology based on man's reason and do not necessarily lead to the true God. These "natural proofs" are exercises in building theology "from below," of measuring God by human thinking. As hinted by the cautions above, these arguments do not necessarily point logically to the triune God of the Bible since many who have used them did not believe in the true God. By themselves, these "natural proofs" are not proofs of the existence of any god without first presupposing what a god is.

Here are some general criticisms of these so-called "proofs":

1. None of these arguments necessitate only one God, and none of them necessitate the God of the Bible. These arguments can point just as easily to multiple beings.
2. None of these arguments necessarily point to something that is perfectly good or unchangeable, since the world is marked by so much evil and change.
3. None of these arguments necessarily point to that which is perfect, since perfection might transcend what man can think, since human ideas exist necessarily only in man and since not all people have a common concept of perfection.
4. None of these arguments prove that an infinite sequence of causes is inherently impossible, and none of these arguments necessitate that any original cause or designer is a "god," unless one has first presupposed a definition of "god."

USEFULNESS OF THE "NATURAL PROOFS" AS SCRIPTURE ARGUMENTS

The above response concerning the inadequacy of the "natural proofs" for the existence of God should warn against seeing them as having inherent value as humanly derived evidences that God exists. As humanly crafted arguments, they are useless; they do not prove the triune God of Scripture. Still, they can be useful. When derived from the Bible, they are forms of biblical truth and can be used by the Holy Spirit to convict people of their truthfulness.

In considering the usefulness of these arguments for God's existence, one must first ask several questions:

1. Are any of these arguments true without imported presuppositions?
2. What presuppositions make each argument "work"?
3. Is their reasoning so cogent that one should expect any of these arguments to persuade an otherwise rational person? Does their reasoning necessitate that an otherwise rational person who rejects them is acting irrationally?
4. Can these arguments be useful in evangelical ministry? If so, how?

As "natural proofs"—that is, as arguments based on man's observation of and reasoning about nature—these "proofs" do not logically prove the existence of the true God. Louis Berkhof writes that "none of them can be said to carry absolute conviction."[6] Of course, this fact means not that the existence of God is contrary

---

6. Louis Berkhof, *Systematic Theology*, 4th ed. (Grand Rapids, MI: Eerdmans, 1941), 27.

to logic but rather that these arguments fail to demonstrate the existence of God in a compelling way to those who suppress the truth in unrighteousness (Rom. 1:18). Instead, they must be considered in concert with biblical presuppositions—namely, that the God of the Bible exists, that he is one, and that he is sovereignly powerful over all creation. While God has given sufficient evidence of his own existence in creation and conscience, the unregenerate suppress the truth of general revelation in unrighteousness (Rom. 1:18–21). Therefore, all people have within them the awareness that God exists, but in their depravity they suppress and corrupt the knowledge of God revealed in nature.

Because man's depravity is total, the curse of sin reaches even to man's mind, so that his thinking is futile, his understanding is darkened, and he walks in ignorance (Eph. 4:17–18). As a result, the natural man's faculty of reasoning is corrupted by sin. For this reason, believers cannot and should not rely merely upon the "natural proofs" as evidence for the existence of the true God.

In fact, a significantly more radical change must take place for sinful man to come to a true knowledge of the triune God of Scripture. As those whose minds have been blinded to the glory of God revealed in Christ (2 Cor. 4:4), unbelievers do not need more evidence, whether logical or empirical; rather, they need new eyes to properly evaluate the sufficient evidence they already have. They need to experience the miracle of regeneration, in which God quickens the unbelieving heart by shining into it the light of the knowledge of his glory (2 Cor. 4:6). This happens only by the proclamation of the gospel that Jesus Christ is Lord (2 Cor. 4:5).

In the final analysis, then, only the gift of saving faith, imparted by the Holy Spirit through the Word of God (Rom. 10:17; James 1:18; 1 Pet. 1:23–25), supplies the basis for the knowledge of God (Heb. 11:1, 6). As Berkhof observes concerning Christians, "Their conviction respecting the existence of God does not depend on them [the 'natural proofs'], but on a believing acceptance of God's self-revelation in Scripture."[7] Christians believe that God exists because God has shone the light of his self-authenticating glory into their hearts through the Word of God.[8]

Nevertheless, the "natural proofs" do serve valid ministry purposes—when they are seen not as humanly derived proofs but as God-given biblical summaries of natural revelation and testimonies to the existence of the God of the Bible. As Berkhof helpfully explains,

> They are important as interpretations of God's general revelation and as exhibiting the reasonableness of belief in a divine Being. Moreover, they can render some service in meeting the adversary. While they do not prove the existence of God beyond the possibility of doubt, so as to compel assent, they can be so construed as to establish a strong probability and thereby silence many unbelievers.[9]

7. Berkhof, *Systematic Theology*, 27. For an example of theologians who depend more on rationalistic apologetic arguments for the existence of God, see John Gill, *Body of Divinity* (1769–1770; repr., Atlanta, GA: Turner-Lassetter, 1950), 1–10.

8. For more on the self-authenticating glory of Scripture as the proper warrant for faith, see John Piper, *A Peculiar Glory: How the Christian Scriptures Reveal Their Complete Truthfulness* (Wheaton, IL: Crossway, 2016).

9. Berkhof, *Systematic Theology*, 28.

Bavinck adds, "But though they are weak as proofs, they are strong as testimonies. They do not force the mind of the unbeliever, but they are signs and testimonies which never fail to leave an impression on the soul of any person."[10] Therefore, the "natural proofs" can instruct and encourage the believer and silence the unbeliever but only when they are drawn from Scripture and so partake of the unity of Scripture. Only then will these arguments function as they are designed: a valid part of proclaiming the gospel as a testimony to the existence of God.

An important model of properly arguing for the existence of God is Paul's sermon to the Greek philosophers on Mars Hill (Acts 17). It is important to note, first, that Paul did not engage in dialogue but preached a sermon. He said, "For as I passed along and observed the objects of your worship, I found also an altar with this inscription, 'To the unknown god.' What therefore you worship as unknown, this I proclaim to you" (Acts 17:23). Paul preached to the philosophers. In so doing, he drew on the Old Testament theology of God and creation and applied it against the false beliefs of Epicureanism, Stoicism, and other philosophies about God, nature, purpose, death, and sin.

For example, Paul proclaimed that God is the transcendent, personal, sovereign Creator by his imperial power: God "made the world and everything in it, being Lord of heaven and earth" (Acts 17:24). This statement reflected Old Testament theology (cf. Gen. 1:1; Ex. 20:11; Isa. 42:5) and directly contradicted the Epicurean view that everything came about by the chance concourse of eternal atoms.[11] Paul's assertion also stood against the Stoic concept that everything in the world originated from a fatalistic, impersonal, rational principle (the *logos*).

Also, Paul confronted the Epicureans with the Old Testament truth that the personal, sovereign God exists independently of man-made buildings: God "does not live in temples made by man" (Acts 17:24). Paul did not deny that God could manifest his presence in earthly buildings such as the Old Testament tabernacle and temple, but rather, Paul denied that God needed physical buildings to live in. This statement was also Old Testament truth. In reflecting on the temple that God told Solomon to build, Solomon said to God, "But will God indeed dwell on the earth? Behold, heaven and the highest heaven cannot contain you; how much less this house that I have built!" (1 Kings 8:27). And later, Isaiah delivered a message from God: "Thus says the LORD: 'Heaven is my throne, and the earth is my footstool; what is the house that you would build for me, and what is the place of my rest?'" (Isa. 66:1). Paul's use of Old Testament theology opposed the Epicurean belief that the gods lived in temples made with human hands.

Paul similarly focused Old Testament theology against the Stoic and Epicurean beliefs about man's duty to serve the gods properly. The Stoics taught that man should live by impassively accepting and conforming to impersonal fate. They believed that one should live by the principle of *apatheia* (passionless indifference). The Epicureans

---

10. Herman Bavinck, *The Doctrine of God*, trans. William Hendriksen (1951; repr., Edinburgh: Banner of Truth, 2003), 79.
11. For a helpful summary of Epicurean and Stoic philosophy, see Carl F. H. Henry, *Christian Personal Ethics* (Grand Rapids, MI: Eerdmans, 1957), 33–36, 74.

taught that man should serve the gods by the principle of *atarxia* (mental pleasure), which, to them, was a lack of desire for any pleasure. The Stoics and the Epicureans had differing views about what service to the gods should look like, but both systems believed that the gods needed man's service. Paul did not deny that man should serve God, but he did deny that the true God needed man's service: "nor is he served by human hands, as though he needed anything" (Acts 17:25). Paul could have also shown that the Old Testament concept of duty to God was a matter of love for God (Deut. 6:4–25). Regardless, Paul clearly preached Old Testament theology. The true, sovereign God needs nothing from man:

> I will not accept a bull from your house or goats from your folds. For every beast of the forest is mine, the cattle on a thousand hills. I know all the birds of the hills, and all that moves in the field is mine. If I were hungry, I would not tell you, for the world and its fullness are mine. (Ps. 50:9–12)

Yet another example of Paul using Old Testament theology to challenge the false beliefs of the Epicureans and Stoics is Paul's preaching that God, as the personal, sovereign Creator, governs the life of man and the world by his providence. He provides to all people what they need to live: "He himself gives to all mankind life and breath and everything" (Acts 17:25). And God has given people their national life with its time and boundaries: "And he made from one man every nation of mankind to live on all the face of the earth, having determined allotted periods and the boundaries of their dwelling place" (Acts 17:26). This message opposed the Epicurean belief that life arose from the blind-chance concourse of atoms and that everything in history has occurred because of man exercising his free will in cooperation with an impersonal nature. And Paul's preaching was against the Stoic assertions that life was by the impersonal, fatalistic *logos* principle and that the nations and all things in history ultimately had no distinctions and resulted from impersonal fate. These teachings echoed Old Testament theology. God personally created all things and gave life to all living creatures (Isa. 42:5), and he foreordained the political existence and boundaries of the nations: "When the Most High gave to the nations their inheritance, when he divided mankind, he fixed the borders of the peoples according to the number of the sons of God" (Deut. 32:8).

In proclaiming the gospel based on an Old Testament theology of God and creation, Paul expressed (1) that God is the personal First Cause and designer of all creation, (2) that he is independent of the world but sovereign over it in directing his determined course for it, (3) that all life is from him and depends on him, (4) that he is the source and final Judge of morals, and (5) that he has provided a way for sinners to be spared final judgment through repenting of sin and idolatry. So Paul used aspects of the various "natural proofs," yet he derived these concepts not from human reason but from God's self-revelation in the Old Testament. Thus Paul used a quotation from the pagan Greek poet Epimenides (ca. sixth century BC) not as a source of truth but to illustrate to the Aereopagites that their own cultural icons knew the truth even if they denied it (Acts 17:28; cf. Titus 1:12). He proclaimed

God's revelation to refute the false theism of the Greek philosophers, demonstrating that the "natural proofs" for God's existence must not ultimately appeal to human perception or reason but to God's own self-revelation in Scripture.[12]

In summary, God exists. He exists as he is revealed by the Bible. The reason one must believe that he exists is because he said that he exists. His existence must not be accepted on the basis of human reason, because that is limited to time and space and has been corrupted by indwelling sin. God has sufficiently revealed himself in the Bible, but he has not revealed himself exhaustively. Man can know only what God has revealed in Scripture about his nature and works. But that is sufficient for people to know him in a personal, saving relationship. One way God has sufficiently and personally revealed himself to man is by describing himself in Scripture by several different names. It is to the names of God that we now turn.

The Names of God

Yahweh and Compounds
El and Compounds
Adon/Adonai: Lord
Tsur: Rock
Ab: Father

A person's name symbolizes all that one is and does. The meaning of a person's name is more than its "dictionary definition," which many people do not even know for their own names. Rather, the meaning of a person's name comprises that person's character, position, and actions within that person's context. So a person's name is unique to that person because that person invests his or her name with individual meaning.

In the Bible, especially in the Old Testament, a person's name was important because the lexical meaning of that name reflected, or was hoped to reflect, something about the person. To God and to the people of Israel, God's names were especially important because they revealed aspects of who he was in himself, in his actions within himself, and in relation to his creation. God's names represented him so much that how one treated God's name was equivalent to how one treated God (cf. Mal. 1:6–7, 11–14). It is little wonder that at the burning bush Moses anticipated how the Hebrews in Egypt would respond to his announcement that "the God of your fathers has sent me to you"; they would ask, "What is his name?" (Ex. 3:13). And it is not surprising that God regards his name as holy and carefully assesses people's attitudes toward his name. He has promised that in the future when he restores Israel, he will be "jealous" for his "holy name" (Ezek. 39:25).

The following discussion focuses on Old Testament names and titles of God. New Testament names and titles for God should be seen as continuing the Old Testament meanings, although progressively revealing more about their implications for God's actions in time.

---

12. For more on the legitimate apologetic implications of Acts 17:16–34, see Greg L. Bahnsen, *Always Ready: Directions for Defending the Faith*, ed. Robert R. Booth (Nacogdoches, TX: Covenant Media Foundation, 1996), 235–76.

Yahweh and Compounds

YAHWEH

The most common name for God in the Old Testament is Yahweh, which appears more than 6,800 times and is derived from the tetragrammaton (the four Hebrew consonants transliterated into English as "YHWH"). God revealed this name as "his name" and "my name forever" at the burning bush (Ex. 3:13–15). It speaks of God's eternal and unchanging nature. As can be seen in Exodus 3:15, the name Yahweh is what God intended by his response to Moses's question about God's name in 3:13. God responded by saying, "I AM WHO I AM" and "I AM" (Ex. 3:14), and then by identifying "LORD" (Yahweh) as "my name forever" (Ex. 3:15). Although this name of God was known before the time of the burning bush (e.g., Gen. 4:26; 5:29; 9:26; 14:22), according to Exodus 6:3, God told Moses concerning Abraham, Isaac, and Jacob, "By my name the LORD I did not make myself known to them." There is no contradiction between these Genesis passages and Exodus 6:3, because the verb for "known" most likely here refers to relational knowledge. When the patriarchs addressed God as Yahweh, they did not relate to God with the understanding that Yahweh was "his name." Another possible explanation of Exodus 6:3 is to understand "known" as referring to experiential knowledge, meaning that the patriarchs did not have "the full experience of that which lies in the name."[13]

After the Babylonian exile, the people of Israel came to refrain from saying the name of Yahweh, replacing it in pronunciation by the Hebrew name *adonai*, or by the Hebrew name *elohim* when Yahweh preceded or followed *adonai* in the written text as the name of God. This change in oral reading was likely due to reverence for it and to fear of blaspheming it. The translators of the Greek Septuagint and the writers of the New Testament (under the inspiration of the Holy Spirit) respected this Jewish tradition, writing the Greek word *kyrios* ("Lord") when quoting an Old Testament passage with the name Yahweh. When the Masoretes invented the system of vowel pointing for the Hebrew Bible, they followed Jewish tradition in pronouncing the name of Yahweh, pointing "YHWH" with the vowels of the name *adonai* (*a, o, a*). Though the name was written as "YHWH," it was to be pronounced as *adonai* ("Lord").

The Masoretic pointing of "YHWH" led Latin-writing Christians to transliterate the Masoretic writing of "YHWH" with its vowel markings as "Iehovah." Some have claimed that Petrus Galatinus (ca. 1460–ca. 1539) innovated this transliteration in 1518, but it appears in Latin Christian writings as early as the twelfth century AD. So the church of the Middle Ages came to combine the consonants of "YHWH" (transliterated as "IHVH") and the vowels of *adonai* to produce the name Iehovah. The Reformers embraced this transliteration, and William Tyndale also used it in some passages in his Old Testament translation (1530). Then the Authorized Version (or King James Version) of 1611 (cf. Ex. 6:3) and the English Revised Version of 1885 used "Jehovah" in a few passages, accepting the *J* in place of the *I*, and this

---

13. Gustav Friedrich Oehler, *Theology of the Old Testament*, 2nd ed. (1884; repr., n.c.: HardPress, 2012), 97.

was the usual translation of Yahweh in the American Standard Version of 1901. But most modern English versions have respected the tradition of not pronouncing the tetragrammaton by translating "YHWH" as "Lord," generally set in small caps to differentiate it from *adonai*.

The meaning of Yahweh is important for theology. Since it is derived from the Hebrew verb for being (*hayah*), especially against the backdrop of Exodus 3:14–15, the basic meaning of Yahweh is "he is" or "he will be." So the name indicates that God "is" and "wills to be." The name implies that he had no beginning, will have no ending, and is ever present. The name also implies that his being is derived from his own self-determination to be and to be what he is, so he is eternally who and what he is.

Since God revealed this name to Moses in a specific historical circumstance and because God acted as Yahweh in prior events and would act as Yahweh in future acts, his name would indicate the constancy of his being amid the changing conditions of his creation, especially those of his people. For example, as Yahweh, he had been and would be present as (1) the Revealer of himself and his will, (2) the Redeemer (Gen. 1:1–2:3 compared with Gen. 2:4–25; 9:26–27; Ex. 3:15–16; 6:26; Deut. 7:9; Ps. 19:1–6 compared with Ps. 19:7–14; Isa. 26:4), (3) the Eternal One (Isa. 41:4; 48:12), (4) the Life Giver (Gen. 2:4–25; Ezek. 37:13–14, 27), and (5) the supreme Judge of all creation (Ezek. 6:13–14; 7:27; 11:10; 12:16). Later, the perfections (attributes) of God will be specified, but one needs to know from the name Yahweh that God is eternal, simple, self-existent, and present at every event in time.

YAHWEH COMPOUNDS

In his Word, God reveals the relevance of his name Yahweh to humans, especially to his people, through the compounds of his name. They are revealed in connection with God's actions.

Yahweh-tsabaoth. God is "the Lord of hosts" or "armies." Because he "is" and "will be" who he is, God created, governs, and leads the angels as the "armies" of heaven (Ps. 24:10; Isa. 6:1–5; 9:7; Hag. 2:6–9; Zech. 4:6) and his people as his "armies" (Ex. 7:4; 12:41; 1 Sam. 17:45) to accomplish his purposes in his creation.

Yahweh-yireh. God is "the Lord" who "will provide" or "will see" (Gen. 22:14). Because he "is" and "will be" who he is, God will see and provide what is needed to fulfill his promise. In Genesis 22:14, Abraham remembered God by this name because God had provided a ram to sacrifice in place of Isaac.

Yahweh-rophe. God is "the Lord, your healer" (Ex. 15:26). Because he "is" and "will be" who he is, God will deliver his people to fulfill his will. In Exodus 15:22–26, Moses remembered that God sweetened the water at Marah so the people could drink and live. God's mercy, compassion, and loving-kindness are on display.

Yahweh-nissi. God is "The Lord Is My Banner" (Ex. 17:15). Because he "is" and "will be" who he is, God will be the "banner" or "standard" that will lead his people to victory over their enemies. In Exodus 17:15, Moses worshiped God as the One who gave his people victory over Amalek and would destroy Amalek utterly from the earth.

Yahweh-meqaddishkem. God is "the Lord" who sanctifies his people. Because he "is" and "will be" who he is, God will sanctify or set apart his people from sin and the surrounding nations to obey him. Keeping the Sabbaths holy or set apart would be a sign to the people that God makes them holy, set apart from the other nations, to belong to and serve him only (Ex. 31:13).

Yahweh-shalom. God is "The Lord Is Peace" (Judg. 6:24). Because he "is" and "will be" who he is, God, through the angel of the Lord, sent Gideon to "save Israel" from the Midianites (Judg. 6:14). The angel of the Lord gave Gideon a sign—that the angel's staff consumed Gideon's sacrifice with fire—to assure him that he was sending Gideon and would go with him to give him victory. The Hebrew word for "peace," *shalom*, means wholeness and well-being. Through Gideon, God would grant his people wholeness in freedom from enemies and well-being in the Promised Land.

Yahweh-roiy. God is "the Lord is my shepherd" (Ps. 23:1). Because he "is" and "will be" who he is, according to Psalm 23, God will provide everything his people need in this life, in death, and forever. He will guide and protect his people.

Yahweh-tsidkenu. God is "the Lord is our righteousness" (Jer. 23:6). Because he "is" and "will be" who he is, in the future God will establish the Messiah as the Davidic King, and "he shall reign as king and deal wisely, and shall execute justice and righteousness in the land" (Jer. 23:5). When this Davidic King will reign in righteousness "in the land," then "Judah will be saved, and Israel will dwell securely" (Jer. 23:5–6).

Yahweh-shammah. God is "The Lord Is There" (Ezek. 48:35). Because he "is" and "will be" who he is, God will restore Israel as a saved nation in the Promised Land and will establish a new temple in a renewed Jerusalem, which will be called by the name "The Lord Is There."

El and Compounds

EL, ELOAH, AND ELOHIM

As Hebrew names for the true God, *el*, *eloah*, and *elohim* indicate God as supreme power, strength, and might. When depicting the true God, *el* is used with the article (e.g., Gen. 31:13; 46:3; Pss. 68:20; 77:14) or with other modifiers. For example, he is called "the God of your father" (Gen. 49:25), "God my exceeding joy" (Ps. 43:4), "the God of heaven" (Ps. 136:26), "the faithful God" (Deut. 7:9), "the Everlasting God" (Gen. 21:33), and "the living God" (Josh. 3:10; Pss. 42:2; 84:2). God is characterized by full strength, and as such, he is living, eternal, and faithful and so gives joy to those who trust in him.

The name *elohim* is a plural of the root *el* (appearing more than two thousand times), and when referring to the true God, it is probably a plural of intensity,[14] indicating that God has such a vast fullness to his power that a plural name is appropriate to him. This is the name that appears from the beginning of the biblical revelation (Gen. 1:1) and is used in many passages interchangeably with the singular *el* and other singular names of God (e.g., Deut. 7:9; Josh. 24:19). Because the plural form *elohim* is used for a singular being, the plurality must refer to something other than multiple beings. This plural form does not prove that God is triune, but it certainly is compatible with later biblical revelation of the triunity of God (cf. Gen. 1:26; 3:22; 11:7).

EL/ELOHIM COMPOUNDS

As stated above, when used of the true God, the Hebrew name *el* is often used with modifiers other than an article, resulting in a compound name. Here are some examples of *el* appearing in compound names for God.

El Shaddai. Scholars have debated the linguistic root of *shaddai,* some holding that it is from the Hebrew root *shadah,* indicating God's sufficiency to provide. But the stronger case is that *shaddai* is from the Hebrew root *shadad,* referring to power. With respect to the true God, *shaddai* has been traditionally translated "almighty," referring to God's omnipotence. Nevertheless, being almighty, God provides (Gen. 17:1; 28:3–4; 35:11; 43:14; 48:3–4; 49:25). He also acts to protect (Ps. 91:1) and to chasten or destroy in judgment (Ruth 1:20–21; Job 5:17; 6:4; 21:20; Ps. 68:14; Isa. 13:6; Joel 1:15). The New Testament confirms that this Old Testament name refers to God as omnipotent, using the Greek word *pantokratōr* to refer to the Old Testament concept of God as *shaddai* (cf. 2 Cor. 6:18; Rev. 1:8; 4:8; 11:17; 15:3; 16:7, 14; 19:6, 15; 21:22).

El Elyon. Translated "God Most High," this title refers to the supreme sovereignty of God. *El elyon* is usually used in the Old Testament in relation to Gentiles and the enemies of God and his people (Gen. 14:18–22; Num. 24:16; Deut. 32:8; Pss. 91:1, 9; 92:1; 97:9; Dan. 3:26; 4:2, 17, 24–25, 34; 5:18, 21; 7:25). As such, God has supreme authority over heaven (Isa. 14:13–14; Dan. 4:35, 37) and earth (Deut. 32:8; 2 Sam. 22:14–15; Pss. 9:2–5; 21:7; 47:2–4; 57:2–3; 82:6–8; 83:16–18; 91:9–12; Dan. 5:18–21). As *el elyon,* God divides people into nations and establishes the borders of the nations (cf. Acts 17:26).

El/Elohey Olam. Because God is omnipotent, he is eternal. He is God eternal or "the Everlasting God" (Gen. 21:33). In Isaiah 40:28, the plural form of God's name is used (cf. Pss. 90:2; 93:2; 103:17).

El/Elohim Khayyim/Khay. God's essence is consummate power, so he *is* life in and of himself, and he is the source of life for all (created) living beings and exercises authority

---

14. Heinrich Friedrich Wilhelm Gesenius, *Gesenius' Hebrew Grammar,* ed. E. Kautzsch, rev. A. E. Cowley, 2nd ed. (1910; repr., Oxford, UK: Clarendon, 1976), 246.d.

over them. He is "the living God" (Deut. 5:26; Josh. 3:10; 1 Sam. 17:26, 36; 2 Kings 19:4, 16; Pss. 42:2; 84:2; Isa. 37:4, 17; Jer. 10:10; 23:36; Dan. 6:20, 26; Hos. 1:10).

Adon/Adonai: Lord

Although the tetragrammaton, YHWH, is often pointed with the vowels in *adonai* ("my Lord"), this Hebrew name/title for God (or its absolute form, *adon* ["Lord"]) also appears. Since this name/title is also applied to humans, the word in and of itself does not mean the most supreme sovereignty. Many times it does not indicate sovereignty at all but is simply a term of respect, similar to the English word *sir*. But in most usages, it is addressed by someone to a person who is superior in some sense: general recognition of superiority (Gen. 24:18; 32:5; 44:7; Ruth 2:13), master (Ex. 21:4–8), superintendent (Gen. 45:8–9; Ps. 105:21), owner (1 Kings 16:24), father (Gen. 31:35), husband (Gen. 18:12), king (Gen. 40:1; Judg. 3:25; 1 Sam. 22:12; Jer. 22:18; 34:5), prince (Gen. 23:6; 42:10), captain (2 Sam. 11:11), governor (Neh. 3:5), and prophet (1 Kings 18:7; 2 Kings 2:3; 4:16). When used of the true God, *adonai* indicates that he possesses supreme sovereignty and ultimate authority over all things external to himself.

Tsur: Rock

The Bible depicts God as "the Rock," comparing him to a physical rock in order to communicate his impregnable strength and thus his perfect reliability (Deut. 32:4, 15, 18, 30–31; 2 Sam. 22:3; 23:3; Pss. 18:2, 31, 46; 19:14; 28:1; 31:2–3; 42:9; 62:2, 6–7; 71:3; 78:35; 89:26; 92:15; 94:22; 95:1; 144:1; Isa. 17:10; 26:4; 30:29; 44:8; Hab. 1:12). The Hebrew word *tsur* depicts a cliff or quarry (Isa. 51:1). Sometimes Scripture uses a metaphor so frequently or in such defining assertions that the metaphor becomes a name or a title. For example, though "the Word" is not a frequent designation for Jesus, yet the very significant thesis statement of the Gospel of John calls him "the Word." Since this expression is employed in the same way "God" refers to the Father, it is legitimate to conclude that "the Word" is a name or title of Jesus. The same phenomenon may be at play with respect to the expression "the Rock" as an eternal name or title of God. Nevertheless, this description of God seems more than metaphorical in the Old Testament. According to the apostle Paul, this Rock that cared for Israel was the preincarnate Messiah, the "spiritual Rock that followed them" (1 Cor. 10:1–4). The "Rock" of the Old Testament, therefore, referred to both Yahweh and the preincarnate Lord Jesus.[15] Just as Paul explicitly stated that "the spiritual Rock that followed them . . . was Christ" (1 Cor. 10:4), so in various Old Testament passages, Yahweh, the God of Israel, is called "the Rock." For example, Deuteronomy 32:3–4 says,

> For I will proclaim the name of the LORD;
> ascribe greatness to our God!

---

15. Robert Duncan Culver, *Systematic Theology: Biblical and Historical* (Fearn, Ross-shire, Scotland: Mentor, 2005), 56.

> "The Rock, his work is perfect,
>   for all his ways are justice.
> A God of faithfulness and without iniquity,
>   just and upright is he."

Another example is found in Habakkuk 1:12:

> Are you not from everlasting,
>   O Lord my God, my Holy One?
>   We shall not die.
> O Lord, you have ordained them as a judgment,
>   and you, O Rock, have established them for reproof.

Because both God the Father and God the Son are equally divine in the Trinity, the names Yahweh and "the Rock" can and do apply to both the Father and the Son in the Bible.

Ab: Father

Since the New Testament applies the name "Father" to the first person of the Trinity, when the Old Testament depicts God as "father," this Hebrew description should be considered a name/title of God. God is the "father" of Israel in Deuteronomy 32:6 (cf. 32:18; see also Ps. 89:26; Isa. 63:16; 64:8; Jer. 3:4, 19). The theme of God as Father is expanded in the New Testament, which reveals that the first person of the Trinity is especially the Father of the second person of the Trinity, the Son of God (Matt. 7:21; 10:32–33; 11:26–27; 12:50; 15:13; 16:17; 18:10, 14, 19, 35; 25:34; 26:39, 42, 53; John 5:17; Rom. 15:6; 1 Cor. 15:24; 2 Cor. 1:3; 11:31; Eph. 1:3; Col. 1:3; 1 Pet. 1:3; Rev. 2:27; 3:5, 21), and is the Father of believers (Matt. 5:45, 48; 6:8–9, 14–15, 18, 26, 32; 10:20, 29; Rom. 1:7; 8:15; 1 Cor. 1:3; 8:6; 2 Cor. 1:2; 6:18; Gal. 1:3–4; 4:6; Eph. 1:2; 4:6; Phil. 1:2; 4:20; Col. 1:2; 1 Thess. 1:3; 3:11, 13; 2 Thess. 1:1–2; 2:16; Philem. 3; James 3:9; 1 Pet. 1:17).

Father is an eternal name, indicating that there was never a time when the first person was not the Father of the second person, his only begotten Son. As the unbegotten Father, the first person of the Trinity is the eternal Prime Mover in all his relationships and works.

The Attributes (Perfections) of God
　　Method of Identification
　　Relation to God's Essence
　　Classifications
　　The Incommunicable Perfections
　　The Communicable Perfections

In considering the names and titles of God, we have already noted many of God's attributes, or perfections (e.g., eternity, omnipotence). The following discussion considers them more fully in order to describe the indescribable (Isa. 40:28; Rom. 11:33) in basic terms that humans can understand.

The attributes of God are his characteristics, the various aspects of his essence or nature. The term *perfections*, derived from the Greek term *aretas* ("excellencies") in 1 Peter 2:9, works better than *attributes* because *perfections* specifies that the characteristics of God are each perfect and inherently characterize the God who is perfect. The term *attributes* does not inherently specify perfect characteristics and might hint that these originate in someone's concept of God rather than in God himself.

A general definition of *perfections* is as follows: God's perfections are the essential characteristics of his nature. Because these characteristics are necessary to his nature, all his attributes are absolutely perfect and thus rightly called perfections. Further, since these perfections are essential to God's nature, if any one of them were denied, God would no longer be God.

Method of Identification

SCRIPTURE: THE ONLY DIVINELY ASSURED METHOD

Since these perfections characterize God, they cannot be discovered and defined by man, especially in his depravity, for man by himself cannot know God completely. Rather, God must reveal himself for man to assuredly know anything about God, including his perfections. God has revealed himself in nature, but humanity corrupts that knowledge. Only the Bible gives accurate information about God and his perfections. Even this information is not exhaustive, but it is true because it is written in the inspired text of Scripture.

FAULTY METHODS

People have tried human-based methods of discovering God's perfections. Louis Berkhof outlines methods attempted in the Middle Ages and in modern times.[16]

Scholastic Methods. In the Middle Ages, Scholastic theologians sought to derive knowledge of the perfections of God from observations about the creation:

1. The way of causality (four of Aquinas's five ways): Looking at the natural and moral order of creation and inducing an all-powerful, absolutely moral First Cause and ruler of creation
2. The way of negation: Discerning the imperfections of creatures, denying those as characteristic of God, and ascribing to God that which is perfectly opposite to the imperfections of the creatures (e.g., independent, infinite, incorporeal)
3. The way of eminence: Ascribing to God the good characteristics of man except in the most eminent way, based on the assumption that man's more limited good characteristics have their origin in a perfect cause

Modern Methods. Modern theologians have tried their own ways to know the perfections of God from observations based on human reasoning:

---

16. Berkhof, *Systematic Theology*, 52–54.

1. The way of intuition: Starting with unreasoned certainties in personal experience and inducing God's characteristics from those experiences
2. The way of need: Starting with man's needs and inducing the characteristics of God from those needs, based on the assumption that God is absolutely sufficient and dependable to meet man's needs
3. The way of action: Perceiving God's characteristics from his actions in the natural order
4. The way of love (Albrecht Ritschl [1822–1899]): Starting with the assumption that God is love and inducing that God is personal, has sovereign will, is the omnipotent Creator, and is eternal

Problems of Faulty Methods. All the Scholastic and modern methods summarized above are inadequate, because rather than beginning with God's self-revelation in Scripture, they begin with their own ideas. In short, they practice "theology from below." They build their concept of God from human observation and reasoning, which are finite at best and blighted by sin at worst. Theology from below assumes that what is in man is also in God and makes man the standard of measuring God, suggesting that man can discover God without God's initiated help. These methods often rely on faulty human presuppositions about God, even while they might describe them with biblical terminology (regularly stressing God's immanence at the expense of his transcendence). When derived from Scripture and employed by believers whose minds have been redeemed by the work of Christ, these Scholastic methods may serve to confirm what Scripture teaches about God. But ultimately, Scripture alone is the sole infallible authority for discovering who God is and what he is like.

Relation to God's Essence

Before turning to define each of God's perfections, it is necessary to ask what relationship God's perfections have to his essence, or nature. Do God's attributes constitute the parts of God's essence? Are they distinct from God's essence or identical to it? Does one perfection stand out as that which defines all the others? We turn to explore these questions.

FAULTY CONCEPTS OF THE RELATION[17]

Perfections: Parts of or Distinct from God's Essence. Medieval realists asserted that God's perfections are parts of God's essence, since each has a distinct name, indicating corresponding distinct realities. A similar thought is that God's perfections are distinct from his essence. Herman Bavinck has noted several problems with these views:[18]

1. If righteousness, power, or love were only parts of God's essence, it could not be said that God was *fully* righteous, powerful, or loving but only partially so.

---

17. Charles Hodge, *Systematic Theology* (1871; repr., Grand Rapids, MI: Eerdmans, 1981), 1:369–73.
18. Bavinck, *Doctrine of God*, 120–24.

2. If righteousness, power, or love were only parts of God's essence, it could not be said that God was *absolutely* righteous, powerful, or loving but only relatively so.

3. God would then be mutable in his essence, since the various attributes that make up his nature would fluctuate. At times he would emphasize his justice, while at other times he might emphasize his love. He would not be perfectly and absolutely both loving and just at every moment in time.

Perfections: All the Same Thing. Medieval nominalists said that all the perfections are the same thing, since the names of the perfections are distinct only in names, not in corresponding realities. For example, these teachers would say that God's love *is* his justice, which *is* his power, which *is* his mercy, and so on. Some early Lutheran and Reformed theologians—and, in a pantheistic way, liberal theologians (e.g., Baruch Spinoza [1632–1677] and Friedrich Schleiermacher [1768–1834])—similarly maintained that because God is simple (uncompounded) and therefore cannot have any components, there can be no actual distinction between the perfections, nor between God's acts. The variety of the effects of God on a diverse array of creatures was said to be the basis for the diversity of the perfections. However, Bavinck has responded with several observations:[19]

1. God has revealed his names to man. Man did not invent these names, and these names do indicate his attributes.

2. God's essence is not an abstract reality devoid of properties, relations, and characteristics; rather, it is "absolute fulness of life" and "infinitely rich." So it cannot be "seen at a glance" but must be "revealed to us in this, then in another relation, now from this then from another angle."

3. There are real distinctions in "thought" between the various perfections of God, even though they are the one simple unity of God's essence.

4. The many names and attributes of God create an impression of his "all-transcending majesty."

One Central Perfection as God's Essence While Others Derived. Open theists hold that only love is God's essence and that all other attributes are derived from and subordinate to his love (after all, they say, God is not just loving, but he is love itself, 1 John 4:8). Open theists also believe that God has chosen not to know the future acts of humanity because such knowledge would determine people's actions, thereby overriding their free will. They further believe that God would never determine man's actions since to do so would compromise any genuine relationship with man; God would not be able to respond in love to man's free choice to love God. Open theism's view that love is God's one superior perfection is faulty for the following reasons:

1. Scripture says not only that God *is* love (1 John 4:8), but also that he *is* light (1 John 1:5), thereby emphasizing his holiness as much as his love (cf. Isa. 6:3; Rev. 4:8).

---

19. Bavinck, *Doctrine of God*, 127–32.

2. This view tends to make God's other perfections less necessary.
3. Historically—for example, among nineteenth-century liberals—this view has tended to diminish God's justice, resulting in a rejection of Christ's atonement as a substitutionary, forensic, and sacrificial punishment.

THE TRUE CONCEPT OF THE RELATION

God's essence is identical to his perfections. There is no essential distinction between God's essence and his perfections, and there is no essential difference between God's perfections to one another. Each perfection characterizes God's complete essence simply and eternally. That is to say, God is what he has. He does not merely possess love, justice, and goodness; he is love and justice, eternally, fully, and completely. God is eternally all-powerful, all-holy, and all-loving.

Rationale. If God's perfections were not identified with his essence but were rather conceived as parts or properties that compose God's essence, the simplicity of God would be undermined. Then the perfections themselves would be not divine but only parts that make up the divine. Yet this is out of accord with the teaching of Scripture. Also, Scripture never discusses God's essence (being) in the abstract but always in connection with his perfections. Even God's assertion of his self-existence in Exodus 3:14 is in the context of his personal visitation to remember his covenant and redeem his people from bondage. Further, such terms as "deity" (Col. 2:9–10), "divine nature" (Rom. 1:20; 2 Pet. 1:4), and "form of God" (Phil. 2:6) speak of God's essence in connection with his perfections, such as "authority" (Col. 2:10), "power" (Rom. 1:20), "glory" (2 Pet. 1:3), and "love" (Phil. 2:2). Scripture also mentions certain perfections with a verb of being, indicating that God is totally that perfection; for example, 1 John 4:8 and 16 state that "God is love," and 1 John 1:5 declares that "God is light," signifying his holiness. Scripture also specifies some perfections adjectivally (e.g., "the living God," "the eternal God," "the Holy One").

Ramifications. This understanding of God's perfections leads to several ramifications:
God is fully each of his perfections. Whatever God is, he is totally in his essence. If God is not fully and absolutely love, or fully and absolutely holy, or fully and absolutely good, then he is not fully and absolutely God. God's perfections must characterize him totally, eternally, and infinitely, because if they do not, God would be neither immutable nor simple. His nature would change with the passage of time, because he would have to switch from being "loving" one moment to "holy" the next. Neither could his essence be regarded as uncompounded and simple, since he would be only partly love, partly justice, partly mercy, and so on. No, God *is* what he *possesses*; he is all his perfections, fully and completely.

God's perfections qualify each other. Because God is each of his perfections in all his essence, then each of his perfections complements and qualifies each of his other perfections. For example, his justice is a holy justice, and his love is a righteous love.

God's perfections are active. Each of God's perfections is fully active in his essence. God is never passive or inactive in any aspect of his essence. If all of God's perfections are not continuously and completely active in his essence, God is not actively God in any aspect, because some aspect of his entire essence is not active and his other perfections are without a necessary divine complement and qualifier. Whatever God is, he must be perfectly active in his essence.

God's perfections should be studied in concert with one another. Since God is totally each of his perfections, one should not study a single perfection of God in isolation from all his other perfections. Each perfection should be studied as complemented and qualified by (i.e., integrated with) all the other perfections and vice versa. All of God's perfections should be studied as influencing each other.

God's perfections are reflexive. Another ramification of the total identity of God's perfections with his essence is that God's perfections are reflexive. That is, they are focused on him; each of the perfections is active toward God as their perfect object. What God is, he is to and for himself before his perfections are directed toward anything or anyone else.

Clarification. While God is eternally and infinitely and completely all his perfections, humans consciously focus on only one attribute in a moment of time in Scripture. This single focus is because God condescends to reveal himself in Scripture to finite people. But whenever he reveals himself in time as one of his perfections, he is still fully and actively all his perfections. So whenever God reveals a particular perfection in any event or statement of Scripture, he is emphasizing that perfection in that specific context, not excluding the other perfections.

Classifications

One other issue should be considered before specifically defining God's perfections. Throughout the years, theologians have sought to categorize the divine perfections. The Bible does not explicitly establish categories, so these are devised by theologians. That fact should caution the student of Scripture against uncritically accepting any categorization. Yet because various kinds of categories have been proposed in the history of theology, it is necessary to consider whether they have merit.

NEGATIVE AND POSITIVE

Following Scholasticism's three ways of knowing God (causality, negation, and eminence), this classification (negative and positive) is based on (1) negative perfections, or those that are the opposite of creature limitations (e.g., infinite, incorporeal), and (2) positive perfections, or those that are present in man but are characteristic of God in an infinitely perfect way (e.g., goodness, holiness, righteousness, justice).

The problem with these categories is that they overlap. When one makes a negative assertion about God, he has a positive concept in mind, even though he might not be able to articulate it. For example, to say that God is immutable (negative) entails that one consciously knows that God is constant and faithful (positive). The reverse is true as well. When one makes a positive assertion about God, he also implies a negative assertion. For example, to say that God is omnipresent (positive) is to say that he is infinite (negative; i.e., not finite) with respect to space.

NATURAL AND MORAL (GREATNESS AND GOODNESS; CONSTITUTION AND PERSONALITY)

Natural perfections are those belonging to God's constitution (e.g., self-existence, simplicity, infinity), whereas moral perfections are those belonging to his will and therefore make him a moral being (e.g., goodness, truth, love, holiness).

The problem with this classification is that moral attributes are just as much aspects of God's essence as natural attributes. Perfections of goodness are also perfections of God's greatness (Psalm 145), and perfections of personality are also perfections of God's constitution.

ABSOLUTE AND RELATIVE

The absolute perfections characterize God's essence considered in and of itself (e.g., self-existence, infinity, spirituality), whereas the relative perfections characterize God's essence considered in God's relation to his creation (e.g., omniscience, omnipresence).

The problem in this instance is that this classification assumes that man can know about God in his essence, but the truth is that all of God's perfections are relative, revealed in relation to his creation. Even the so-called relative perfections are absolute, because they are eternally active in the relationships between the members of the Trinity, in God's essential existence.

IMMANENT/INTRANSITIVE/QUIESCENT/BEING VERSUS EMANANT/TRANSITIVE/OPERATIVE/CAUSATIVE

In explaining this classification, it is important to first define the following terms:

immanent: existing or remaining within; inherent
emanant: originating within but producing external results
intransitive: not requiring a direct object to complete its action or meaning
quiescent: inactive

According to this classification, the former are perfections that function outside the divine essence but remain immanent in God (e.g., immensity, eternity, simplicity), whereas the latter are perfections that produce things external to God (e.g., omnipotence, goodness, justice).

Contrary to this classification, man cannot know any characteristic of God as it is in his essence but only as his character is revealed in his works. Further, the operative and causative perfections must also be immanent and intransitive in God; otherwise, God would need something outside himself to be complete. Also, no perfection of God can be inactive; otherwise, God would not be constantly and actively all his being/essence.

INCOMMUNICABLE AND COMMUNICABLE

The best categorization is that which distinguishes between incommunicable and communicable perfections. The incommunicable perfections are those characteristics unique to God (e.g., self-existence, simplicity, immensity), whereas the communicable perfections are those characteristics transferable in part to humans (e.g., goodness, righteousness, love).

A problem with the incommunicable versus communicable categorization is that since man cannot know God in his essence apart from his relations to his creation, it is impossible to know any characteristic of God apart from those relations. Even the incommunicable perfections are at least somewhat like human characteristics, or no one could understand anything about God's perfections. Also, God's communicable perfections are not completely like human characteristics, or God would not be greater than man in every characteristic.

For example, with respect to God's incommunicable perfection of immutability (unchangeableness), one can have a limited understanding because he or she knows what it is for another human to have consistent thoughts, principles, and behavior over a long period of time. But such an understanding is limited because no human knows what it is for someone to be without the ability to change in nature and character. Concerning the communicable perfection of love, people have a partial picture because they know what God has revealed in Scripture about his love in his relations to humans, but they do not know what God's love is for himself in the Trinity, nor do they know exhaustively what God's love is for people.

The incommunicable versus communicable classification is employed here for the following reasons:

1. A classification can be a useful tool in studying God's perfections, as it can help people focus on how God is unique compared to mankind.
2. This classification has endured throughout the years among theologians of various traditions.
3. This classification stresses both the transcendence and the immanence of God, denying both pantheism and deism.
4. This classification is most helpful if one does not strictly divide the two groups of perfections but sees the incommunicable attributes as qualifying the communicable attributes and vice versa.

CAUTIONS ABOUT ALL CLASSIFICATIONS

Even the incommunicable versus communicable classification is a human observation, so no classification should be accepted uncritically. All classifications must be accompanied by the following cautions.

Dividing God in Two. All classifications of God's perfections seem to divide God in two, leaving no harmony between the perfections and thus no apparent unity in God. This weakness can be overcome by seeing the first class of perfections (incommunicable) as qualifying the second class (communicable) and vice versa, "so that it can be said that God is one, absolute, unchangeable and infinite in His knowledge and wisdom, His goodness and love, His grace and mercy, His righteousness and holiness."[20]

Dividing Negatives from Positives. Every classification tends to separate negative descriptions of God from positive descriptions of him, even though when thinking about one, people have the other in mind. Bavinck explains,

> If they were completely incommunicable, they would also be absolutely unknowable. The very fact that we are able to name them proves that in one way or another they were revealed by God in creation. Hence, the negative attributes have a positive content: though we need the idea of time in order to obtain a conception of God's eternity, and that of space in order to form an idea of his omnipresence, and that of finite, changeable creatures in order to become aware of his infinitude and immutability; nevertheless, these negative attributes furnish us with a very important positive knowledge concerning God. Thus, even though we cannot comprehend eternity in any positive sense, nevertheless, to know that God is exalted above the limitations of time is very important.[21]

Describing God Essentially. All the classifications seem to imply that we can know God in his essence, considered apart from his relations to his creatures. But God cannot be known by people in this way. No person, other than Jesus Christ, can know any divine characteristic in its perfection. This weakness must be overcome by seeing even the first class of perfections as, at least in some way, being like human characteristics and being active in relation to creatures.

The Incommunicable Perfections

With these preliminary observations about the divine perfections and how to study them, we can now define them based on Scripture. In light of the fact that God's perfections are identical to his essence, and especially based on the implications of this fact, we must not consider these perfections without consciously thinking about how they actively integrate with (i.e., complement and qualify) each other. One must also remember that these perfections are directed first toward God before anything or anyone outside him. The following definitions of divine perfections are accompanied by biblical truths on which these definitions are based.[22]

INDEPENDENCE (ASEITY)

God is independent of all things. He is perfectly self-sufficient, not depending on anything outside himself for anything, and is therefore the eternal, foundational being, the source of life and sustenance for all other beings.

The following list presents scriptural evidence for God's aseity:

---

20. Berkhof, *Systematic Theology*, 56.
21. Bavinck, *Doctrine of God*, 139.
22. Due to space limitations, this treatment of God's perfections must be brief. For fuller treatments of the attributes of God, see Herman Bavinck, *Reformed Dogmatics*, vol. 2, *God and Creation*, ed. John Bolt, trans. John Vriend (Grand Rapids, MI: Baker Academic, 2004); Stephen Charnock, *The Existence and Attributes of God* (1853; repr., Grand Rapids, MI: Baker, 1996); Arthur W. Pink, *The Attributes of God* (Grand Rapids, MI: Baker, 2006).

1. As Yahweh, God is self-existent, having life in and of himself (Ex. 3:14; John 5:26).
2. God existed before all things, and through him alone all things exist (Ps. 90:2; 1 Cor. 8:6; Rev. 4:11).
3. God is Lord of all (Deut. 10:17; Josh. 3:13).
4. He depends on nothing; all things depend on him (Rom. 11:36).
5. He is the source of everything (Deut. 32:39; Isa. 45:5–7; 54:16; John 5:26; 1 Cor. 8:6).
6. He does as he wills (Ps. 115:3; Isa. 46:10–11; 64:8; Jer. 18:6; Dan. 4:35; Rom. 9:19–21; Eph. 1:5; Rev. 4:11).
7. His counsel is the basis of everything (Ps. 33:10–11; Prov. 19:21; Isa. 46:10; Matt. 11:25–26; Acts 2:23; 4:27–28; Eph. 1:5, 9, 11).
8. He does everything for his own sake (Josh. 7:9; 1 Sam. 12:22; Pss. 25:11; 31:3; 79:9; 106:8; 109:21; 143:11; Prov. 16:4; Isa. 48:9; Jer. 14:7, 21; Ezek. 20:9, 14, 22, 44; Dan. 9:19).
9. He needs nothing, being all-sufficient (Job 22:2–3; Acts 17:25).
10. He is the first and the last (Isa. 41:4; 44:6; 48:12; Rev. 1:8; 21:6; 22:13).
11. He is independent in his mind (Rom. 11:33–35), his will (Dan. 4:35; Rom. 9:19; Eph. 1:5; Rev. 4:11), his counsel (Ps. 33:11; Isa. 46:10), his love (Hos. 14:4), and his power (Ps. 115:3).

IMMUTABILITY

God's immutability is his perfect unchangeability in his essence, character, purpose, and promises.

Scriptural Evidence. The following list summarizes the biblical teaching about God's immutability:

1. He is eternally the same (Ps. 102:25–27).
2. He is the first and the last (Isa. 41:4; 43:10; 44:6; 48:12).
3. He is what he is (Ex. 3:14).
4. He is incorruptible, alone having immortality, always remaining the same (Rom. 1:23; 1 Tim. 1:17; 6:15–16; Heb. 1:11–12).
5. His thought, purpose, will, and decrees are unchangeable:
   a. He executes his threats and promises (Num. 23:19; 1 Sam. 15:29).
   b. He does not repent of his gifts and calling (Rom. 11:29).
   c. He does not cast off people with whom he has made a unilateral covenant (Rom. 11:1).
   d. He glorifies those whom he foreknows (Rom. 8:29–30).
   e. He perfects what he starts (Ps. 138:8; Phil. 1:6).
   f. His faithfulness never lessens (Lam. 3:22–23).
6. He does not change (Mal. 3:6; James 1:17).

Questions concerning God's Immutability. Tensions are apparent to people when they read passages asserting God's unchangeability alongside passages stating that God repents (Gen. 6:6; Ex. 32:12; 1 Sam. 15:11, 35; Jer. 18:10; Amos 7:3, 6; Jonah 3:9–10; 4:2), changes his purpose (Gen. 18:23–32; Ex. 32:10–14; Jonah 3:10), gets angry (Ex. 4:14; Num. 11:1, 10; Ps. 106:40; Zech. 10:3), turns from his anger (Ex. 32:14; Deut. 13:17; 2 Chron. 12:12; 30:8; Jer. 18:8, 10; 26:3), relates differently to the unbeliever than to the believer (Prov. 11:20; 12:22), is pure to the pure but opposes the wicked (Ps. 18:25–26), is incarnated in time (Gal. 4:4), indwells the church (1 Cor. 3:16–17; Eph. 2:19–22; Col. 1:27), rejects Israel (Rom. 11:15), receives the Gentiles after having rejected them for years (Acts 11:18; Rom. 11:11–15), is wrathful at one time and forgiving at another (Ex. 34:7; Num. 14:18; Psalm 78), and is close at one time and far off at another (Jer. 23:23).

To resolve this tension, many, such as open theists, have said that God really does change his mind, purposes, and promises in response to what humans do. They contend that one cannot justly harmonize God's "changes" in Scripture with the traditional doctrine that God is unchangeable. They claim that if sinners turn from sin and respond in faith and love toward God, he will turn from (repent of, change his mind about) the judgment he intended and give them blessing instead. Correspondingly, if they turn from trusting in him, he will revoke any promises of blessing. According to open theists, God does not know how people will respond to him, and he waits to see what they will do in each moment before he chooses his response to them.

There are many errors in open theism and other such false teachings that deny God's immutability, each of which is refuted by viewing God's immutability in proper biblical perspective. Immutability does not mean that God is static or inert, nor does it mean that he does not act distinctly in time or possess true affections. God is impassible—not in the sense that he is devoid of true feeling or has no affections but in the sense that his emotions are active and deliberate expressions of his holy dispositions, not (as is often the case with human emotions) involuntary passions by which he is driven.

A good way to understand God's apparent changes in Scripture is to consider that God reveals himself in his relations to people. They perceive only one aspect of God at a time. God never changes, but creatures do change, and they perceive God's perfections and actions according to their current state. Thus, God's actions do not imply a change of essence or purpose.

For example, the language of God "repenting" or "changing" in any way is anthropopathic language—figurative expressions that communicate to man on his level of understanding about changes of dispositions or actions. Thus, God's perceived "changes" are always in the context of his eternal omniscience and will, so they are never because God is surprised and has to adjust. They are done in harmony with his truth and faithfulness (see 1 Sam. 15:29). All his acts that might be perceived as changes are eternally foreknown and predetermined.

INFINITY

God's infinity describes his nature as perfectly transcending (existing and acting beyond) all limitations of time and space. God's infinitude with regard to time is called his eternity or omnitemporality, and his infinitude with regard to space is called his immensity or omnipresence.

ETERNITY

God perfectly transcends all limitations of time, so that he is without beginning, without ending, and without succession of moments in the experience of his being and in his consciousness of all other reality. In other words, in his experience of himself and all reality outside himself, God is not limited by the moments of time.

Scriptural Evidence. The following list presents scriptural evidence for God's eternity:

1. He is the first and the last at once (Isa. 41:4; Rev. 1:8).
2. He existed before creation (Gen. 1:1; John 1:1; 17:5, 24).
3. He will endure forever (Ps. 102:26–27).
4. He is God from everlasting to everlasting (Pss. 90:2; 93:2).
5. The number of his years cannot be discovered (Job 36:26).
6. One thousand years in his sight are as a day, due to his immediate experience of all time (Ps. 90:4; 2 Pet. 3:8).
7. He is God eternal (Isa. 40:28).
8. He inhabits eternity (Isa. 57:15).
9. He lives forever (Deut. 32:40; Rev. 10:6; 15:7).
10. He is incorruptible and immortal (Rom. 1:23; 1 Tim. 6:16).
11. He was, is, and is to come all at once (Ex. 3:14; Rev. 1:4, 8).
12. His purpose is eternal (Eph. 3:11).
13. He is the eternal King (1 Tim. 1:17).
14. He existed and acted "before the ages began" (2 Tim. 1:9; Titus 1:2).

God's Essence as "Timeless." An important issue concerning God's perfection of eternity is whether God exists only in the passing moments of time or also exists outside the succession of the moments of time. Is God "timeless," atemporal in his inner life, or is his existence temporal, only within the moments of time?

God is in time, since he interacts with his creation and his creatures from moment to moment. But God must transcend time, or he is limited by another entity: time. In other words, God's eternity means that he is distinct from time. Nevertheless, he is not completely separate from it; rather, he is present (immanent) in every moment, controlling every moment for his purposes and glory. The biblical statement "In the beginning, God created the heavens and the earth" (Gen. 1:1) indicates that God existed before "the beginning," which commenced "the first day" (Gen. 1:5). God existed before the first moment of "the first day" of all reality outside himself. Therefore, God's existence is outside the bounds of time. Indeed, since God began "the beginning" by his creating action, God created time and upholds its totality and each of its moments by his power. God is fully present with every moment of time, and he knows its entirety and its succession of moments. But God is never subject to time. Rather, he uses it as his servant to reveal his perfections.

In his essence, God exists in an eternal "present." He always is with "the first" of time and with "the last" of time (Isa. 41:4; cf. 44:6). God purposed to give saving grace to his elect people "before the ages" (2 Tim. 1:9; Titus 1:2), so he acted before the first moment of the ages. God self-consciously exists outside the moments of time.

God is not confined or conditioned by limits or lengths of time (see Ps. 90:1–4; 2 Pet. 3:8). God is both the beginning and the end and remains so after the beginning has ended and before the ending has begun. In his essence, he encompasses both the beginning and the end, and both are consciously experienced and "present" realities. And since the expression "the beginning and the end" (Rev. 21:6; 22:13) is probably a merism (a literary device expressing a complete set of items by mentioning only the items marking the opposite limits of the set), God controls every moment as consciously experienced, "present" realities. God *is*. And he *is* before time began, before the first moment of "the ages." God in his essence never begins to be. He never becomes.

Argument from God's omniscience. All of God's perfections are consistent with the assertion that God is without succession of moments in his experience of his being and of his consciousness of all other reality. For example, God is omniscient, or all-knowing, so his knowledge embraces all events as equally real. Therefore, since his perfections are his essence, in his experience of his essence in itself, there is no past, present, or future. Although God experiences the succession of time (both because he created that succession and because God the Son experiences it especially through the incarnation), and although his thought has logical structure (including premises and conclusions), yet his experience of succession does not control, confine, or condition his existence and life so that he exists only in the moments of time. Everything is perceived and experienced as an "eternal now."

Argument from God's immensity and omnipresence. God transcends all limitations of space. He exists outside physical space and yet exists with every point of space and experiences every point of space with his entire being. Therefore, he must exist outside the moments of time, or else he is confined to being present within space as it exists in only one moment of time.

Argument from God's immutability. Since God's essence cannot change, he must not be conditioned by changing time. If God exists in only each moment, he must begin to exist in each succeeding moment—a conclusion that contradicts his immutability.

Argument from God's independence. Since God's essence depends on nothing for its existence but rather is the fount of all existence, he cannot be dependent on the moments of time for his existence. For if God exists only moment to moment, he is dependent on the existence of each moment.

Argument from God's omnipotence. Since God has active power over all things, he must exercise power in the future and the past in order to be omnipotent. If he exists only in the current moment, he does not actually have power in past and future moments.

God's immensity, immutability, independence, omnipotence, omnipresence, and omniscience are compromised by the "successive moments" view. If God exists only from moment to moment, his existence actually ends in one moment and begins in the next. He also has no control over the change of moments but rather is conditioned by their changing. Furthermore, he does not transcend space and time since he is confined to the current moment and to acting in space only as it exists in the current moment. Finally, although he may still govern current events to move inflexibly toward the final consummation of his plan, he does not in the present actually control events in the future, since the future moments have not yet arrived. Thus, given the various considerations above, it is necessary to view God as existing both inside and outside time. The "successive" view falls far short of God's scriptural self-revelation.

IMMENSITY AND OMNIPRESENCE

God is perfectly present with himself, transcending all limitation of space, and yet present with every point of space with all that he is. Transcendance means that God is greater than and independent of the creation. Immensity refers to the fact that God transcends and fills all space. And omnipresence indicates that God is present with every point of space in his entire being.

Scriptural Evidence. Biblical evidence for God's immensity and omnipresence is visible in the following observations:

1. He is the Creator and possessor of all things (Gen. 14:19, 22; Deut. 10:14; Col. 1:16; Rev. 10:6).
2. Heaven and earth cannot contain him (1 Kings 8:27; 2 Chron. 2:6; Isa. 66:1; Acts 7:48–49).
3. He fills heaven and earth, so nothing is hidden from his presence, and he is both close and far off (Ps. 139:7–10; Jer. 23:23–24; Acts 17:27–28).
4. He manifests himself variously in various places:
   a. He dwells and has his throne in heaven (Deut. 26:15; 2 Sam. 22:7; 1 Kings 8:32; Pss. 11:4; 33:13; 115:3, 16; Isa. 63:15; Matt. 5:34; 6:9; John 14:2; Eph. 1:20; Heb. 1:3; Rev. 1:4–5).
   b. He descends from heaven (Gen. 3:8; 11:5, 7; 12:7; 15:1; 18:1; Ex. 3:7–8; 19:9, 11, 18, 20; Deut. 33:2; Judg. 5:4).
   c. He dwells in the midst of his people (Ex. 20:24; 25:8; 40:34–35; Deut. 12:11; 1 Sam. 4:4; 2 Sam. 6:2; 1 Kings 8:10–11; 2 Kings 19:15).
   d. He is far (relationally) from the wicked (Pss. 11:5; 50:16–21; 145:20).
   e. He is close (relationally) to the righteous (Pss. 11:7; 51:19; Isa. 57:15).
   f. Christ is the fullness of the Godhead bodily (Col. 2:9).
   g. God indwells the church (John 14:23; Rom. 8:9, 11; 1 Cor. 3:16; 6:19; Eph. 2:22; 3:17).

Specifics of Immensity and Omnipresence. God transcends space. He is inherently immense and omnipresent, regardless of the existence of time and matter—that is, he is always present with himself. He is also immense and omnipresent with relation to the creation. Space is an aspect of creation, so it is not part of God. These perfections mean that God is not diffused through space so that only part of him is in each place. Also, God is not bound to one place. God is fully present in every place, but he is also sustaining space by his immensity. His immensity does not mean he is separate from creation in a deistic sense, even though it does mean he is distinct from and greater than creation. God upholds the created order by being entirely present with every point of space. This is true, for example, in both heaven and hell (e.g., Rev. 14:9–10) and in the righteous and the wicked. Actually, it is better to say that God is *with* time and space, rather than being *in* time and space (against nineteenth-century liberalism's concept of God as only immanent). But both are correct, provided that one does not see God as *of* or bound by time.

UNITY: NUMERICAL ONENESS

God's unity is his perfect uniqueness of essence, so that neither is he more than one essence nor is there more than one divine essence.

The following list presents scriptural evidence for the unity of God:

1. God is only one essence (Deut. 6:4; Mark 12:29).
2. God is unique; there is only one God (Deut. 4:35; 32:39; Ps. 18:31; Isa. 40:18; 43:10–11; 44:6; 45:5).
3. Idols are vain and empty (Deut. 32:21; Ps. 96:5; Isa. 41:29; 44:9–20; Jer. 2:5, 11; 10:14–15; 16:18; 51:17–18; Dan. 5:23; Hab. 2:19).
4. In the New Testament, God's unity is revealed in Jesus Christ (John 17:3; Acts 17:24; Rom. 3:30; 1 Cor. 8:4–6; Eph. 4:5–6; 1 Tim. 2:5).

UNITY: SIMPLICITY

God's simplicity is his indivisibility, his perfect lack of composition. This means that each of and all his perfections *are* his essence.

Scriptural Evidence. This perfection is intended by statements that God is truth, righteousness, wisdom, spirit, light, life, love, and holiness (Jer. 10:10; 23:6; John 1:4–5, 9; 4:24; 14:6; 1 Cor. 1:30; 1 John 1:5; 4:8, 16). Such passages reveal God as the complete fullness of each respective quality.

Compatibility with the Doctrine of the Trinity. God's simplicity does not contradict the doctrine of the Trinity. God's essence is not composed of three persons. Rather, the uncompounded, undivided divine essence exists in each of the three persons. The various personal properties unique to each person are not things added to the divine essence but are only distinctions of personal subsistence and of relationship. In all the external works of the Trinity, each person acts without dividing the divine essence.

OMNISCIENCE[23]

God's omniscience is his perfect knowing of himself, all actual things outside himself, and all things that do not become reality in one eternal and simple (not

---

23. Some theologians, including Herman Bavinck, Louis Berkhof, Charles Hodge, and W. G. T. Shedd, classify omniscience as a communicable perfection.

having any parts but having distinctions) act (exertion of energy). One should note that this definition does not say that God knows things that are "possible," because in God's eternal mind and plan there are only actual things, not possible things. He does know what would have occurred if circumstances had been different, but since in his mind and plan they never would occur, they are not "possibilities." Only what is in God's plan is "possible," because only that could ever become reality in time.[24]

Scriptural Evidence. The following list shows the objects of God's knowledge from Scripture:

1. Himself as triune (Matt. 11:27; John 1:18; 10:15; 1 Cor. 2:10)
2. All things (2 Chron. 16:9; Isa. 40:13; Rom. 11:34; Heb. 4:13; 1 John 3:20)
3. All needs (Matt. 6:8, 32)
4. Even the smallest physical things (Matt. 10:30)
5. The heart of man (1 Kings 8:39; Ps. 7:9; Prov. 15:11; Jer. 11:20; 17:9–10; 20:12; Luke 16:15; Rom. 8:27; 1 Thess. 2:4; 1 John 3:20)
6. The thoughts and meditations of man (Ps. 139:2; Ezek. 11:5; 1 Cor. 3:20)
7. Man in the totality of his being and acts (Psalm 139)
8. Sheol and Abaddon (Prov. 15:11)
9. Man's sin and wickedness (Ps. 69:5; Jer. 16:17; 18:23; 32:19)
10. Things that are contingent from a human perspective (1 Sam. 23:10–13; 2 Kings 13:19; Ps. 81:12–16; Jer. 26:2–7; 38:17–20; Ezek. 3:4–6; Matt. 11:21)
11. People before they are conceived (Ps. 139:13–16; Jer. 1:5; Rom. 8:28–30; Rev. 13:8; 17:8)
12. Future things (Isa. 41:22–26; 42:8–9; 43:9–12; 44:6–8; 46:9–11)
13. The days and geographical limits ordained for each person (Pss. 31:15; 39:4–5; 139:7–16; Job 14:5; Acts 17:26)

The Eternal Priority of God's Knowledge. God's knowledge is eternal and *a priori* ("from the previous," i.e., proceeding from a known or assumed cause to a necessarily related effect), not *a posteriori* ("from the subsequent," i.e., from particulars to principles, from effects to causes). God's knowledge precedes all things outside God, never being derived from reality outside himself (Rom. 8:29; 1 Cor. 2:7; Eph. 1:4–5; 2 Tim. 1:9). God's knowledge is also perfect, never increasing (Isa. 40:13–14; Rom. 11:34). It is definite—clearly defined, precise, certain, sure, and comprehensive (Ps. 139:1–3; Heb. 4:13). And God's knowledge is eternally active, never passive, because God's essence is eternally active.

The Effects of God's Knowledge. Because God's knowledge is active, it produces effects. These are transitory in man's experience yet are an ever-present reality to God—"present" not in the sense of time, since he is without succession of moments, but in the sense of God consciously and eternally perceiving them. The major effects of God's knowledge in time include the creation of the physical realm (Pss. 104:24;

---

24. Here we reject all forms of middle knowledge, whether the classic Molinist conception or the so-called "compatibilistic" reformulation. See below on "The Nature of God's Knowledge" (p. 176).

136:5); the formation of the church (Eph. 3:10); all of God's actions in time, including the application of salvation (Rom. 11:33); and worship from man (Job 11:7–9; Ps. 139:17–18; Rom. 11:33).

The Nature of God's Knowledge. There are two aspects of God's knowledge. God's *natural knowledge* is his self-conscious knowledge of himself. His *free knowledge* is his knowledge of (1) all things that become actual in time by his free, sovereign will based on his decree, (2) all things that do not become reality, and (3) how he is manifested and not manifested by all things outside himself.

It is necessary to distinguish between God's natural knowledge and his free knowledge. To fail to do so would lead to pantheism, since it would make God's knowledge of himself contingent upon his knowledge of creation. However, God is able to know himself perfectly, independent of his creation.

Nevertheless, his natural and free knowledge must not be so sharply separated so as to make his decree arbitrary. God did not arbitrarily select some of his ideas to make actual things; rather, his natural knowledge resulted in his free knowledge; that is to say, God's perfect knowledge of himself includes his knowledge of how to reveal himself to creatures unto his greatest glory. Guided by this principle to glorify himself to the utmost, God's natural knowledge issues in his eternal and exhaustive decree, whereby he foreordains whatsoever comes to pass. Because God is who he is, he does what he does.

People can know God through his free knowledge as it is manifested in the created order. But people cannot know God through his natural knowledge, since this knowing would involve knowing God as God knows himself. Man can, to a limited extent, possess God's free knowledge, but God's possession of his free knowledge is perfect, since his knowledge is infinite.

God's knowledge is also archetypal. It is the original pattern for all things outside himself.[25] God knows the universe in its eternal idea, logically prior to its finite existence in time and space. God's knowledge is from himself, independent of any outside source, and so prior to all things outside himself.

The knowledge God has is intuitive, inherent, and immediate, not resulting from observing and reasoning in successive moments of time. At the same time, it does have logical structure. God's knowledge refers to his activity, not merely to content, and it is simple and simultaneous in its exertion. He knows everything totally at once, not one thing only before he knows another thing. Yet he also knows the differences and order existing between all things.

God's knowledge is comprehensive and completely conscious. Man's knowledge is partial and mostly unconscious. God's knowledge is "pure act," never passive (knowledge based on learning) like man's, but rather is eternally willed by him. And it is immediate, not deistic. That is, God is not removed from the things he knows. He always has direct, immediate perception of all that he knows.

---

25. Berkhof, *Systematic Theology*, 66.

God's Foreknowledge in the New Testament. From the history of the Greek verb *proginōskō* (the word behind the New Testament concept of God's foreknowledge) and the biblical evidence of God's omniscience, theologians extend the concept of foreknowledge to cover his intimate and intentional knowledge of all things before they become actual in time and space. As proof of this more general foreknowledge, one could point to predictive prophecy (e.g., Isa. 41:22–26; 42:9; 43:9–12; 44:7; 46:10).

However, when used to depict God's foreknowledge, the verb *proginōskō* and the noun *prognōsis* are used of God's perfectly purposed relational knowledge of everyone who is in his redemptive plan before they exist in time and space. Understood in this way, especially from the New Testament, God's foreknowledge is soteriological. God foreknew elect Israelites as his covenant people (Rom. 11:2); Jesus Christ as crucified and resurrected (Acts 2:23–24; 1 Pet. 1:18–20); and all Christians as predestined, chosen, called, believing, sanctified, justified, and glorified (Rom. 8:29; 1 Pet. 1:2). God's foreknowledge is not passive, dependent on foresight of what humans would do. Rather, it is eternally purposed by God. Paul asserted that God "foreknew" (Gk. *proginōskō*) only those whom he also "predestined," "called," "justified," and "glorified" (Rom. 8:29–30). It is important to note that in Romans 8:28, these people were "called according to his purpose." In this context, God's foreknowing is divinely purposed, foreknowing only those who would be effectually called in time to saving faith in Christ. When the New Testament speaks of *God* foreknowing, the object is always people rather than facts, and these people are always objects of his redemption.[26]

OMNIPOTENCE[27]

God's omnipotence describes his ability to do anything consistent with his nature.

Scriptural Evidence. Biblical evidence for God's omnipotence is visible in the following observations:

1. God's names and titles display his power: *el, elohim* (God), *el shaddai* ("God Almighty"), *adonai*, Yahweh, *Yahweh-tsabaoth* ("LORD of hosts"), "the Mighty One of Israel" (Isa. 1:24), "King of kings and Lord of lords" (1 Tim. 6:15; Rev. 19:16), "the Lord Almighty" (2 Cor. 6:18; cf. Rev. 1:8; 4:8; 11:17), and "the blessed and only Sovereign" (1 Tim. 6:15).
2. Nothing is too hard for God; nothing is impossible (Gen. 18:14; Job 42:2; Jer. 32:27; Zech. 8:6; Matt. 3:9; 19:26; 26:53; Luke 1:37; 18:27; Eph. 3:20).
3. God does whatever he pleases (Ps. 115:3; Isa. 14:24, 27; 46:10; 55:11; Dan. 4:35).

---

26. Two passages may be brought as objections to this claim. In Acts 26:5, the Greek verb *proginōskō* is used of the Jews having known Paul in the past. In 2 Peter 3:17, the verb is applied to people knowing factual content. Some have argued from these passages that God's foreknowledge is only an intellectual, factual knowledge about someone or something prior to a later point in time. But Acts 26:5 and 2 Peter 3:17 speak only of *human* knowledge of another human, whereas the passages above consider *God's* knowledge of humans in his redemptive plan. Also, Acts 26:5 may involve more than prescience, possibly implying relational knowledge—the Jewish leaders did, in fact, know young Saul of Tarsus well. For more on God's foreknowledge as it relates to election and salvation, see "The Basis of Election" in chap. 7 (p. 497).

27. Some theologians, including Herman Bavinck, Louis Berkhof, Charles Hodge, and W. G. T. Shedd, classify omnipotence as a communicable perfection.

4. God's works reveal his omnipotence (Psalms 8; 18; 19; 24; 29; 33; 104): creation (Genesis 1; Ps. 8:3; Isa. 42:5; 44:24; 45:12, 18; 48:13; Zech. 12:1; Rom. 1:20), providence (Heb. 1:3), and redemption (Rom. 1:16; 1 Cor. 1:24).

5. Power belongs to God (Pss. 62:11; 96:7; Rev. 4:11; 5:12; 7:12; 19:1).

What God Cannot Do. There are things that Scripture says God is unable to do because they would contradict his character or revealed will: repent (like a man) or lie (Num. 23:19; 1 Sam. 15:29; Heb. 6:18); deny himself (2 Tim. 2:13); be tempted (so that he succumbs) (James 1:13); or change in his essence, purposes, or promises (James 1:17; Mal. 3:6).

Correct Distinctions in God's Power. While recognizing distinctions in God's power, one must distinguish between faulty and biblical ways of describing them.

Faulty distinction. In the history of thought, many have contended that God has absolute power in the sense that he is able to do anything, including sinning, suffering, dying, changing himself into a stone or animal, changing bread into the body of Christ, making contradictory things, changing the past, and making the true false or the false true. Others have said that God can do only what he wills (ordinate power).

Biblical distinction. Scripture reveals that God in his power is (technically) able to do more than what actually occurs but that his power operates within the context of his will and all his other perfections (Gen. 18:14; Jer. 32:27; Zech. 8:6; Matt. 3:9; 19:26; 26:53; Luke 1:37; 18:27; Eph. 3:20). So the correct distinction in God's power is that he has a theoretically absolute power to do more than what he actually does but not anything inconsistent with his essence. The only real divine power is God's "ordinate power," that is, his ability to do everything that he has decreed he will do. Since God's decree is the result of all his perfections, then he would only do what he has decreed he will do. Therefore, his ability is confined to what he eternally wills to do.

PERFECTION[28]

The perfection of God speaks not only of his moral perfection—that is, that he is perfectly holy, just, and good—but also that God is the sum total of all conceivable perfections.

The following list presents scriptural evidence for God's perfection:

1. God's greatness in its totality is beyond human discovery (Ps. 145:3; Isa. 40:28).
2. God's mercy toward those who fear him is greater than man's perception (Ps. 103:11).
3. God's work is perfect in that his acts are perfectly truthful and just (Deut. 32:4).
4. God's way is perfect, so his Word is perfectly true (2 Sam. 22:31).
5. God is morally perfect (Matt. 5:48).

---

28. Some theologians, including Herman Bavinck, Louis Berkhof, Charles Hodge, and W. G. T. Shedd, classify perfection as a communicable perfection.

Herman Bavinck helpfully illustrates what it means for God to be perfect: "A creature is perfect . . . in its kind and in its creaturely finite way, when the idea that is its norm is fully realized in it. Similarly, God is perfect inasmuch as the idea of God fully corresponds to his being and nature."[29] God is absolutely perfect, disturbed by nothing within himself and encumbered by nothing outside himself. He is perfectly self-sufficient. Bavinck later summarizes that God is "the sum of all conceivable perfections, the highest perfection in person, infinitely far removed from all defects and limitations."[30] Because of his absolute perfection and self-sufficiency, God is the happiest being that can be conceived. Thus, the doctrine of divine perfection implies the doctrine of divine blessedness (see "Blessedness" [p. 188]).

The Communicable Perfections

SPIRITUALITY AND INVISIBILITY

God's spirituality and invisibility describe his perfect lack of material in the divine essence, so that his essence cannot be perceived by the physical senses.

Scriptural Evidence. The following list summarizes the biblical teaching about God's spirituality and invisibility:

1. God is eternal (Ps. 90:1–2), omnipresent (Ps. 139:7–12), and invisible (Rom. 1:20; Col. 1:15–16; 1 Tim. 1:17; Heb. 11:27; see also Ex. 33:20).
2. Though God has an essential form (Phil. 2:6), his form is not seen (Deut. 4:12, 15; John 1:18; 5:37; 6:46; 1 Tim. 6:16; 1 John 4:12, 20) because it is not physical.
3. God is present in his creation in a spiritual manner (Gen. 2:7; Job 33:4; Pss. 33:5–6; 104:30; 139:7).
4. Jesus Christ said that God is spirit (John 4:24).

What about the Hope of Seeing God? The invisibility of God seems to contradict the hope that believers have of seeing God after the resurrection (Job 19:26; Ps. 17:15; Matt. 5:8; 1 John 3:2; Rev. 22:4). Past Christians have called this sight "the beatific vision." How is it that humans, even after receiving their resurrection bodies, will "see" God's "face"? The answer should take into account that, even in their resurrection bodies, people will still be human and therefore will still have finite form and capacities. Yet in heaven and in the eternal state, believers will not have any corruption caused by indwelling sin, so they will have a greater perception of God, because their spiritual vision will be greater. The statements about seeing God and his face in the future should be interpreted as relating to a comparatively greater spiritual vision of God's revelation of himself, not as a physical vision of his essence. In the eternal state, the believer's spiritual perception of God will reach beyond what physical senses can see. (On this, see John 14:7–9, where Jesus describes how one can see God in a mediated way without seeing every aspect of him; cf. 1 John 3:2.)

---

29. Bavinck, *Reformed Dogmatics*, 2:250.
30. Bavinck, *Reformed Dogmatics*, 2:250.

In Scripture, God's "face" (e.g., Matt. 18:10) is an anthropomorphism for God's external mediation of his presence. God's "face" is not his essence.[31]

WISDOM

God's wisdom is his perfect knowledge of how to act skillfully so that he will accomplish all his good pleasure—to glorify himself. This definition is based on the Hebrew word for "wisdom," *hokmah*, which can mean "skill."

The scriptural evidence for this attribute is visible in that God created by his wisdom (Job 9:4; 37–38; Pss. 19:1–7; 104:1–34; Prov. 8:22–31; Isa. 40:28; Jer. 10:12) and that God redeems by his wisdom (Deut. 4:6–8; Rom. 11:25–33 [esp. 11:33]; 16:25–27 [esp. 16:27]; 1 Cor. 2:6–13; Eph. 3:10–11; Rev. 5:12). God is the very source of wisdom itself (Prov. 2:6; 9:10; James 1:5). Moreover, he is omnisapient, meaning that he is all-wise (Job 12:13; Ps. 147:5; Isa. 40:28; Rom. 11:33; 16:27).

TRUTH AND FAITHFULNESS

God's truth and faithfulness are the perfect correspondence of God's nature with what God should be, with the reliability of his words and deeds, and with the accuracy of his knowledge, thoughts, and words.

The following list presents scriptural evidence for this attribute:

1. He is the only real God; thus, he is true, in contrast to the false gods (Deut. 32:21; Pss. 96:5; 97:7; 115:4–8; Isa. 44:9–10; John 14:6; 17:3; 1 John 5:20).
2. He cannot lie or repent like a man, that is, in such a way that his word is untrue (Num. 23:19; 1 Sam. 15:29).
3. He is the God of *khesed* (Heb. for "loyal love") and truth (2 Sam. 2:6; 15:20; Ps. 40:11).
4. All of God's words are true and faithful (2 Sam. 7:28; Pss. 19:9; 25:10; 33:4; 111:7; 119:86, 142, 151; Dan. 4:37; John 17:17; Eph. 1:13).
5. God is abounding in truth (Ex. 34:6 NASB).
6. God's faithfulness extends to the clouds (Ps. 36:5).
7. God is a rock of refuge, because of his dependable firmness (Deut. 32:4, 15, 18, 30, 37; Pss. 18:2–3; 31:6; 36:5; 43:2–3; 54:7; 57:3; 71:22; 96:13; 143:1; 146:6; Isa. 26:4).
8. God keeps his covenants (Deut. 4:31; 7:9; Neh. 1:5; Ps. 40:11; Dan. 9:4).
9. God is faithful to give a full salvation (1 Cor. 1:9; 10:13; 1 Thess. 5:24; 2 Thess. 3:3; Heb. 10:23; 11:11; 1 John 1:9).
10. All of God's promises in Christ are responded to by "Yes" and "Amen" (2 Cor. 1:18–20).

God is true metaphysically. He is what God should be. He is not like the false gods, which are vanities and lies (Pss. 96:5; 97:7; 115:4–8; Isa. 44:9–10).

God is true ethically. His revelation of himself is perfectly reliable (Ex. 34:6; Num. 23:19; Deut. 32:4; Pss. 25:10; 31:6; Jer. 10:8, 10; John 14:6; 17:3; Rom. 3:4; Titus

---

31. For more on the object of the beatific vision with consideration to God's invisibility, see Michael Riccardi, "Seeking His Face: A Biblical and Theological Study of the Face of God" (master's thesis, The Master's Seminary, 2015).

1:2; Heb. 6:18; 1 John 5:20–21). This means that God is absolutely faithful (Deut. 7:9; Ps. 89:33; Isa. 49:7; Lam. 3:22–23; 1 Cor. 1:9; 2 Tim. 2:13; Heb. 6:17–18; 10:23).

God is true logically. He knows everything as it really is.

GOODNESS

God's goodness is that he is the perfect sum, source, and standard (for himself and his creatures) of that which is wholesome (conducive to well-being), virtuous, beneficial, and beautiful.

Scriptural Evidence. The goodness of God is visible in the following evidence from the Bible:

1. There is no one good except God (Matt. 5:48; Mark 10:18; Luke 18:19).
2. All creatures are called to praise his goodness (1 Chron. 16:34; 2 Chron. 5:13; Pss. 106:1; 107:1; 118:1; 136:1; Jer. 33:11).
3. People are urged to trust in the Lord and discover that he is good (Ps. 34:8).

Explanation of God's Goodness. God is *the* absolute good (Mark 10:18; Luke 18:19). As such he cannot be pleased with anything short of absolute perfection. Hence, in an ultimate sense he can be pleased with only himself. Consequently, when he loves his creatures, he loves them with a chief regard to himself.[32] He is absolutely perfect good.

God is the source of all his creatures' blessings (James 1:17). He is the highest good (Lat. *summum bonum*) for his creatures—the proper goal of all who strive for true goodness.

LOVE

God's perfect love is his determination to give of himself to himself and to others, and is his affection for himself and his people. This definition affirms that God has affections or emotions, but once again, it is necessary to note that God's affections are not passions by which he is driven but active principles by which God expresses his holy dispositions. God is not unfeeling or incapable of compassion; however, it is a subbiblical understanding of God's affections that conceives of God as being surprised by emotional fluctuations.

The following list presents the biblical testimony concerning God's love:

1. The Old Testament testifies abundantly to God's love (Deut. 4:37; 7:8, 13; 10:15; 23:5; 2 Chron. 2:11; Isa. 43:4; 48:14; 63:9; Jer. 31:3; Hos. 11:1, 4; 14:4; Zeph. 3:17; Mal. 1:2).
2. God loves not only people (Deut. 4:37; 7:8, 13; 23:5; Pss. 78:68; 146:8; Prov. 3:12; 2 Chron. 2:11; Jer. 31:3; Mal. 1:2) but also virtues (as imaged in people), like justice and righteousness (Pss. 11:7; 33:5; 37:28; 45:7).
3. God's love is ultimately between the three persons of the Trinity (John 3:35; 5:20; 10:17; 14:31; 15:9; 17:24, 26). That this love includes affection is seen

---

32. See "The Ultimate Purpose of Salvation," in chap. 7 (p. 486).

by the use of the Greek verb *phileō* for the love that the Father has for the Son (John 5:20).

4. God's love is manifested in Christ's sacrifice for sin (John 15:13), for the world and the church (John 3:16; Rom. 5:7–8; 8:37; 1 John 4:9–10), and for individuals (John 14:23; 16:27; 17:23; Rom. 9:13; Gal. 2:20). In John 16:27, God the Father's love for believers includes affection, as attested by the use of the verb *phileō* for the Father's love.

5. God's essence is love (1 John 4:8, 16).

GRACE

God's grace describes God as perfectly bestowing favor on those who cannot merit it because they have forsaken it and are under the sentence of divine condemnation. Grace is simply "favor" (Heb. *khen*; Gk. *charis*), so in itself it does not include any basis in merit or lack of merit. God always favors himself before anything or anyone else.

The following list summarizes the biblical teaching on the grace of God:

1. Its object is mainly God's people (Gen. 6:8; Ex. 33:12, 17; 34:9; Prov. 3:34).
2. Israel was chosen and blessed by God due only to God's grace (Ex. 15:13, 16; 19:4; 34:6–7; Deut. 4:37; 7:7–8; 8:14, 17–18; 9:5, 27; 33:3; Isa. 35:10; 43:1, 15, 21; 54:5; 63:9; Jer. 3:4, 19; 31:9, 20; Ezek. 16:60–63; Hos. 8:14; 11:1).
3. God's grace is abundant (Ex. 34:6; 2 Chron. 30:9; Neh. 9:17; Pss. 86:15; 103:8; 111:4; 116:5; Jonah 4:2; Joel 2:13; Zech. 12:10).
4. In the New Testament, God's grace is especially his free, unmerited favor toward sinners in giving them salvation from sin (Rom. 3:24; 5:15; 6:23; Eph. 1:6–7; 2:5, 7–8; 2 Thess. 2:16; Titus 3:7; 1 Pet. 5:10). This is special, effectual, saving grace, in distinction to common grace, which is God's general care for his creation. And it is favor given by God's sovereign will without any consideration of merit or lack of merit. God always gives grace because he wills to do so.
5. God's grace is manifested in Jesus Christ (John 1:14; 1 Pet. 1:13).
6. God's gifts of spiritual and earthly blessings are called "grace" (Rom. 6:1; 12:6–8; Eph. 4:7–12; Phil. 1:2; Col. 1:2; James 4:6).
7. God's grace is unmerited; it does not allow for works of merit (John 1:17; Rom. 4:4, 16; 6:14, 23; 11:5–6; Gal. 5:3–4; Eph. 2:7–9).

MERCY

God's mercy describes him as perfectly having deep compassion for creatures (people), such that he demonstrates benevolent goodness to those in a pitiable or miserable condition, even though they do not deserve it. This definition is partly based on the words used in the original text of the Bible for "mercy" (Heb. *rakhamim*; Gk. *eleos*, *oiktirmos*). As with grace, this perfection does not consider the merit or lack of merit of the people to whom God gives mercy.

The following list presents scriptural evidence for the mercy of God:

1. It is a perfection or attribute of God (Ex. 34:6; Deut. 4:31; 2 Chron. 30:9; Pss. 86:15; 103:8; 111:4; 112:4; 145:8).

2. It is manifold (Ex. 20:6; Deut. 5:10; 2 Sam. 24:14; Neh. 9:19; Pss. 51:1–2; 57:10; 86:5; Dan. 9:9, 18).
3. It does not fail (Lam. 3:22).
4. It is an aspect of God's paternal affection and care (Ps. 103:13).
5. It is given to sinners after divine chastening (Isa. 14:1; 49:13–18; 54:8; 55:7; 60:10; Jer. 12:15; 30:18; 31:20; Hos. 2:21–23; Mic. 7:19).
6. God is called the "Father of mercies" (2 Cor. 1:3).
7. God showed his mercy in Christ (Luke 1:50–54).
8. Christ showed the mercy of God in his life on earth and as the Great High Priest in heaven (Matt. 9:36; 14:14; 20:34; Heb. 2:17).
9. God gives mercy by providing salvation in all its aspects, including sustenance in the Christian life and final salvation at Christ's return (Rom. 9:23; 11:30; 1 Cor. 7:25; 2 Cor. 4:1; Eph. 2:4; Phil. 2:27; 1 Tim. 1:2, 13, 16; 2 Tim. 1:2, 16, 18; Heb. 4:16; 1 Pet. 1:3; 2:10; 2 John 3; Jude 2, 21).

LONGSUFFERING

God's longsuffering speaks of his being perfectly placid in himself and toward sinners in spite of their continual disobedience and disregard for his warnings. God does not "lose his temper" but rather acts calmly with proper affection according to his eternal sovereign plan. Tranquility implies not that God lacks affections but rather that God's affections do not overwhelm him or cause him to act against his nature.

Scriptural evidence for God's longsuffering is visible in the following observations:

1. God is patient with those deserving divine punishment (Ex. 34:6; Num. 14:18; Neh. 9:17; Pss. 86:15; 103:8–9; 145:8; Jer. 15:15; Joel 2:13; Jonah 4:2; Nah. 1:3).
2. God was longsuffering before the time of Christ (Rom. 3:25; 1 Pet. 3:20).
3. God's longsuffering is shown to sinners now, especially through Jesus Christ (Rom. 2:4; 9:22–23; 1 Tim. 1:16; 2 Pet. 3:9, 15).
4. God is patient in not immediately responding to cries for justified vengeance (Rev. 6:9–11).

HOLINESS

God's holiness is his inherent and absolute greatness, in which he is perfectly distinct above everything outside himself and is absolutely morally separate from sin. This definition is centered on the concept of separation, which is signified by the Hebrew and Greek words for "holy" (Heb. *qadosh*; Gk. *hosios, hagios*). There are two aspects of God's holiness in the evidence found in Scripture:

Majestic Holiness. This speaks to the fact that God is inherently great and resists all compromises of his character and therefore is transcendently distinct from all his creatures in infinite majesty. He is majestically unique. This sense of God's holiness qualifies all his other attributes, and all these qualify his holiness. This transcendent distinction is asserted by both the Old Testament (Ex. 15:11; 1 Sam. 2:2; 2 Chron. 30:27; Pss. 5:7; 22:3; 48:1; 71:22; 89:18; 97:12; 98:1; 99:3, 5, 9; 103:1; 105:3;

145:21; Prov. 30:3; Isa. 5:16; 6:3; 10:20; 29:23; 43:14–15; 49:7; 54:5; 57:15; Jer. 51:5; Hos. 11:9; Hab. 1:12) and the New Testament (Mark 1:24; Luke 1:49; 4:34; John 17:11; Rev. 4:8; 6:10; 15:4).

Ethical, Moral Holiness. Since God is inherently great and therefore transcendently distinct from everything outside himself, he is most certainly separate from sin, being morally and ethically perfect, abhorring sin and demanding purity in his moral creatures (Lev. 11:44; 19:2; 20:26; 22:32; Josh. 24:19; Job 34:10; Pss. 5:5; 7:11; Isa. 1:12–17; Ezek. 39:7; Amos 2:7; 5:21–23; Hab. 1:13; Zech. 8:17; 1 Pet. 1:15–16).

RIGHTEOUSNESS (JUSTICE)

God's righteousness is his perfect absolute justice in and toward himself, his prevention of any violation of the justice of his character, and his revelation of himself in acts of justice. Both the Old Testament Hebrew term (*tsedeqah*) and the New Testament Greek term (*dikaiosynē*) for "righteousness" carry the sense of conformity to a standard.

Categorization and Scriptural Evidence. The Bible describes two kinds of justice:

Rectoral justice. This is God's rectitude (from the Lat. *rectus*, "straight") as the moral Ruler, Lawgiver, and Judge of the world—imposing law with promises of reward and punishment (Deut. 4:8; 2 Sam. 23:3; Pss. 9:4; 99:4; 119:7, 62, 75, 106; Isa. 33:22; Luke 1:6; Rom. 1:32; 2:26; 7:12; 8:4; 9:31; James 4:12).

Distributive justice. This aspect of God's righteousness is his rectitude in the execution of law, in distributing reward and punishment (1 Kings 8:32; 2 Chron. 6:23; Ps. 7:11; Isa. 3:10–11; 11:4; 16:5; 31:1; Rom. 2:6; 2 Tim. 4:8; 1 Pet. 1:17). Two categories within God's distributive justice are his retributive justice and his remunerative justice. Retributive justice is God's inflicting of punishment for disobeying his law (2 Chron. 12:6; Ezra 9:15; Neh. 9:26–30; Ps. 129:4; Isa. 5:15–16; Jer. 11:20; Ezek. 28:22; 36:23; 38:16–23; 39:27; 43:8; Dan. 9:14; Hos. 10:2; Zeph. 3:5; Rom. 1:32; 2:9; 12:19; 2 Thess. 1:8; Rev. 15:3; 16:5, 7; 19:2, 11). Remunerative justice is God's distributing of rewards for obeying his law (Deut. 7:9, 12–13; 2 Chron. 6:14–15; Ps. 58:11; Mic. 7:20; Matt. 25:21, 34; Rom. 2:7; Heb. 11:26). God is not required to give rewards for obedience, since man is required to obey God. But he graciously gives them (Job 41:11; Luke 17:10; 1 Cor. 4:7).

God's Holiness and Righteousness in Salvation. A holy and righteous God demands holiness and righteousness of people who would be rightly related to him (Lev. 11:44; Ps. 29:2; 1 Pet. 1:15–16). God stands in absolute, essential opposition to sin, so he must judge and punish sin. In the salvation of sinners, the holiness and righteousness of God are revealed, because in salvation God effectively judges sin and imputes righteousness to people so that he can accept them as holy without compromising his essential holiness and righteousness.

God manifested his holiness and righteousness in his past salvation of Israel and will do so in his future salvation of his people. For example, in Ezekiel 39:21–29, God judges and restores Israel in order to maintain and manifest his holiness. Many passages similarly show that God manifests his holiness and righteousness by separating from, judging, and saving Israel (holiness: Lev. 20:26; Pss. 98:1; 99:9; 105:3; 106:47; 108:7; 111:9; Isa. 10:20; 12:6; 41:14, 20; 43:3, 14; 45:11; 47:4; 49:7; 52:10; 55:5; Ezek. 36:21–23; Hos. 11:9; righteousness: Neh. 9:8; Pss. 72:2; 85:13; 116:5; Isa. 45:21–25; Jer. 33:15; Mal. 4:2). God's holiness and righteousness are especially manifested in salvation through the Lord Jesus Christ (Rom. 3:21–22, 24, 26, 30; 4:6, 25; 5:1, 9; 8:30, 33; 1 Cor. 6:11; Gal. 2:16–17; 3:24).

JEALOUSY

God's jealousy is his zealous protectiveness of all that belongs to him (himself, his name, his glory, his people, his sole right to receive worship and ultimate obedience, his land, and his city).

The jealousy of God is visible in the following teachings from Scripture:

1. God's name is "Jealous" (Ex. 34:14).
2. God is jealous to be the only God worshiped and served (Ex. 20:5; Deut. 4:24; 5:9; 6:15; 29:18–20; 32:16, 21; 1 Kings 14:22; Pss. 78:58–59; 79:1–7; 1 Cor. 10:22).
3. God is jealous to be served as the holy God (Josh. 24:19; James 4:5).
4. God jealously chastens his sinning people (Ps. 79:1–7; Ezek. 16:42; 23:25).
5. God restores his people by his jealousy (2 Kings 19:31; Isa. 37:32; 63:15).
6. God is jealous for his holy name and glory (Ezek. 39:25).
7. God by his jealousy will establish the Messiah's Davidic kingdom (Isa. 9:6–7).
8. God jealously takes vengeance on his enemies (Isa. 42:13; 59:16–20; Ezek. 5:13; 36:5; 38:19; Nah. 1:2; Zeph. 3:8).
9. God is jealous for the land of Canaan and Jerusalem (Ezek. 36:5–38; Zech. 1:14).

WILL

God's will is his perfect determination and sovereign ordination of all things, pertaining both to himself (including his decrees and actions) and to his creation (including the events of history and the thoughts and actions of people), all unto the magnification of his utmost glory.

Scriptural Evidence. Everything depends on the will of God:[33]

1. Creation and preservation (Ps. 135:6; Jer. 18:6; Rev. 4:11)
2. Government (Prov. 21:1; Dan. 4:17, 25, 32, 35)
3. Election and reprobation (Rom. 9:15–16, 18; Eph. 1:11–12)
4. Suffering of Christ (Luke 22:42; Acts 2:23; 4:27–28)
5. Regeneration (John 1:13; James 1:18)

---

33. Berkhof, *Systematic Theology*, 76.

6. Sanctification (Phil. 2:13)
7. Sufferings of believers (1 Pet. 3:17)
8. Man's life and destiny (Isa. 45:9; Acts 18:21; Rom. 15:32; James 4:15)
9. The smallest things (Matt. 10:29)

God's will is sovereignly independent of everything outside himself:[34]

1. He acts according to his own pleasure (Ps. 115:3; Prov. 21:1; Dan. 4:35).
2. He does not give account to anyone (Job 33:13; Isa. 46:10; Matt. 20:15; Rom. 9:19–20).
3. He is pictured as the potter, his creatures as clay (Job 10:9; 33:6; Isa. 29:16; 64:8; Jer. 18:1–10; Rom. 9:19–24).
4. The nations are "less than nothing" before him (Isa. 40:15–17).
5. No one can prevent him from doing as he pleases (Job 9:2–13; 11:10; Isa. 10:15; Dan. 4:35).
6. He shows mercy or hardens solely according to his will (Rom. 9:15–18).
7. The Holy Spirit divides spiritual gifts as he wills (1 Cor. 12:11).
8. Man does not have the right to demand that God express his will in particular ways (Matt. 20:13–16; Rom. 9:20–21).

Question. Does the Bible's teaching present a problem with apparent contradictions within the will of God?[35]

1. God wills what man should do (Matt. 7:21; 12:50; John 4:34; 7:17; Rom. 12:2), but God also wills what man does (Ps. 115:3; Dan. 4:17, 25, 32, 35; Rom. 9:18–19; Eph. 1:5, 9, 11; Rev. 4:11). At times it seems that God's will for man conflicts with his will in his own actions. For instance, he wills man to obey, but he hardens man in disobedience and unbelief (Ex. 4:21; 7:3–5; Rom. 9:17–19).
2. God wills that Abraham sacrifice his son, and then God prevents Abraham from slaying his son (Gen. 22:1–14).
3. God wills that Hezekiah die, but then extends his life fifteen years (2 Kings 20:1–11; Isa. 38:1, 5).
4. God wills that the righteous not be condemned, but Jesus was delivered up for crucifixion by the determined purpose and foreknowledge of God—and God held Israel responsible for the murder of the Messiah (Acts 2:23; 3:18; 4:27–28).
5. God hates sin, not willing that it exist, according to his precepts, but nevertheless ordaining that it exist and controlling it by his meticulous providence (Ex. 4:21; Josh. 11:20; 1 Sam. 2:25; 2 Sam. 16:10; Habakkuk 1; Acts 2:23; 4:27–28; Rom. 1:24, 26, 28; 2 Thess. 2:11). He even ordained Adam and Eve to disobey in the garden and Satan to afflict Job (Job 42:11; cf. Eph. 1:11).
6. God wills the salvation of everyone in one sense (Ezek. 18:23, 32; 33:11) but in another sense wills that some have saving mercy and that some be hardened.

The solution to these apparent contradictions is found in the distinction between two aspects of God's will: his decretive and preceptive will.

---

34. Bavinck, *Doctrine of God*, 228–29.
35. Bavinck, *Doctrine of God*, 236.

Decretive will. Some have called this God's "secret will," and yet while its full extent is hidden, aspects of it are revealed (e.g., predictive prophecy).

This is God's good pleasure, his eternal, unchangeable counsel or decree in which he has foreordained all things. God's decretive will characterizes all of God's essence, so it is eternal, immutable, independent, and omnipotent (Pss. 33:11; 115:3; Isa. 36:10; Dan. 4:25, 35; Matt. 11:25–26; Rom. 9:18; Eph. 1:4; Rev. 4:11). This does not mean that he is the immediate or efficient cause of all things but that all things exist or occur by his eternal sovereign decree. God's decretive will makes everything certain, but he does not coerce his creatures to do anything. He ordains the free choices of men. As the Westminster Confession (3.1) states, "God from all eternity, did, by the most wise and holy counsel of His own will, freely, and unchangeably ordain whatsoever comes to pass; yet so, as thereby neither is God the author of sin, nor is violence offered to the will of the creatures; nor is the liberty or contingency of second causes taken away, but rather established."

Thus, sin is in God's overall plan. He does not condone his creatures' disobedience, nor is he the immediate or efficient cause of sin (James 1:13). He does not delight in the existence of sin in itself, but he ordains it by his decree in order to accomplish the most wise and holy end of bringing ultimate glory to himself (Rom. 5:20–21; 9:17–24).

One should bear in mind two cautions about God's decretive will. First, whenever God's decretive will includes sin, that sin is certain to occur, but it will be initiated by the volition of the sinner. And second, God's meticulous providence includes him upholding the various natural processes and even crafting (without compromising his holiness) the circumstances of an individual's decision to sin.[36]

Preceptive will. This consists of God's precepts in the law and in the gospel for man's conduct (Matt. 7:21; 12:50; John 7:17; Rom. 12:2; 1 Thess. 4:3–8; 5:18; Heb. 13:21; 1 John 2:17). It is often called God's "revealed" or "signified" will. At times the decretive will and the preceptive will coincide, but often as part of his decretive will, God ordains that the creature disobey his preceptive will. God reveals his preceptive will by means of Scripture's commands, prohibitions, warnings, chastenings, and judgments. God's preceptive will is God's will only in a prescriptive sense. His decretive will is the perfection that results in actual occurrences. The preceptive will reveals not what God will do but what he demands of people.

God has included sin in his plan, forbidding man to sin yet using sin as a means of bringing the greatest amount of glory to himself (Gen. 50:20; Acts 2:23). In both his decretive will and his preceptive will, God does not take pleasure in sin, nor does he absolutely determine to save all people (e.g., Ezek. 33:11 should be classed under God's preceptive will). God's decretive will is executed by means of his preceptive will.

God's decretive will and preceptive will must be held in tension. To deny his preceptive will is to commit injustice against God's holiness and to ignore the gravity of

---

36. For more on the relationship between God's decretive will and the problem of evil, see "The Decree of God and the Problem of Evil" (p. 491) and "The Justification of God" (p. 509), both in chap. 7.

sin, but to deny God's decretive will is to deny his omniscience, wisdom, omnipotence, and sovereignty.[37]

BLESSEDNESS

God's blessedness speaks of God as being perfectly delighted with himself. This definition reflects the Greek word *makarios*, which has the meaning of happiness due to a sense of great privilege. These words are represented by the Latin *beatus*, which is the word from which we derive the English words *beatify*, *beatitude*, and *blessed*. Since God is absolutely perfect, sovereign, and unhindered in all his purposes and works to glorify his name, he is supremely happy—the happiest being conceivable. (For more on this theme, see "Perfection" above [p. 178].)

The scriptural evidence is visible in 1 Timothy, which describes God as "the blessed God" (1 Tim. 1:11) and "the blessed and only Sovereign" (1 Tim. 6:15).

GLORY

God's glory refers to the consummate beauty of the totality of his perfections. It is his supreme significance and splendor. This definition reflects the Hebrew words for "glory," *kabod*, *hod*, and *hadar*. The word *kabod* has the sense of "weight" and, in figurative extension, "significance." The words *hod* and *hadar* have the sense of "splendor." The Greek word for "glory," *doxa*, also has the primary meaning of "splendor" or "brightness."

As for scriptural evidence, most passages referring to God's glory speak of his manifested glory. Such manifestation is sourced in the glory of God's essence (Eph. 3:16; Phil. 4:19; Rev. 15:8). God manifested his glory to creation (1 Chron. 16:26–29; Pss. 29:3; 96:6; 104:1–5; 111:4; 113:4) and to Israel (Ex. 16:7, 10; 24:16; 33:18–23; Lev. 9:6, 23; Num. 14:10; 16:19; Deut. 5:24). God's glory filled the tabernacle and the temple (Ex. 29:43; 40:34; 1 Kings 8:11). God's "splendor" was given to Israel (Ezek. 16:14). In heaven, God's manifested glory was associated with God's holiness (Isa. 6:3). On earth, God's glory was seen as a cloud (1 Kings 8:10–11; Isa. 6:4) and a consuming fire (Ex. 24:17; Lev. 9:24). God later manifested his glory in Christ (John 1:14; 2 Cor. 4:4–6) and in the church (Rom. 15:7; 2 Cor. 3:18; Eph. 5:27).

In summary, God's perfections constitute his essence, or character, which far transcends all created things in greatness. God's essence is one indivisible whole, so that each and all of his perfections actively characterize God's entire being. God's perfections must be thought of as always actively present together and mutually influencing each other without any hierarchy, even when they are not all mentioned in a given passage of Scripture. God in his essential nature is truly beyond human understanding, and the only appropriate responses to studying even the fringes of his ways (cf. Job 26:14) are awe-filled reverence, worship, adoration, trust, and service.

---

37. For more on these two aspects of the divine will, see John Piper, "Are There Two Wills in God?," in *Still Sovereign: Contemporary Perspectives on Election, Foreknowledge, and Grace*, ed. Thomas R. Schreiner and Bruce A. Ware (Grand Rapids, MI: Baker, 2000), 107–31.

The Trinity[38]

Explanation
Old Testament Indications
New Testament Evidence
Early History of Theological Development

The sense of God's incomprehensibility is only heightened when the student of Scripture considers the reality that God is eternally triune. The classic Christian doctrine of the Trinity is well summarized by what is known as the Athanasian Creed. Though it bears his name, Athanasius (AD 295–373) did not write it; rather, it seems to have been penned in the fifth or sixth century AD at the earliest. The key defining statements are captured in this phrase: "We worship one God in Trinity, and Trinity in Unity; neither confounding the Persons: nor dividing the Substance."[39] The doctrine of the Trinity, simply put, is that God is absolutely and eternally one essence subsisting in three distinct and ordered persons without division and without replication of the essence.

Since the Trinity cannot be comprehended by the human mind, the doctrine of the Trinity must be defined with negative statements (often called "apophatic theology," or "negative theology"). For example, the phrase "without division and without replication of the essence," used above, is an expression of negative theology. Such phrases and assertions are needed to place proper boundaries on the positive statements, such as the one made above that "God is absolutely and eternally one essence subsisting in three distinct and ordered persons." This positive statement needs boundaries to prevent people from thinking that the three persons each have either a third of the divine essence (partialism) or a full divine essence that is distinct from the full but identical essences of the other two persons (tritheism). If the essence were divided among the three persons, none of the persons would be divine. And if the essence were replicated in the three persons, the result would be three gods.

Though various historical heresies and contemporary cult groups accuse the Trinity of being an illogical doctrine derived from human philosophy, the triunity of God is neither of those things, because it is first and foremost a biblical doctrine. While it may be ultimately incomprehensible, it is not contrary to reason and logic but can be rationally explained, supported, and understood through biblical revelation. Berkhof elaborates:

> The doctrine of the Trinity is very decidedly a doctrine of revelation. It is true that human reason may suggest some thoughts to substantiate the doctrine, and that men have sometimes on purely philosophical grounds abandoned the idea of a bare unity in God, and introduced the idea of living movement and self-distinction. And it is also true that Christian experience would seem to demand some such construction of the doctrine of God. At the same time it is a doctrine which we would not have known, nor have been able to maintain with any

38. For a supplementary discussion of the triunity of God, refer to "Deity and Triunity" in chap. 5, "God the Holy Spirit" (p. 341).

39. Philip Schaff, *The Creeds of Christendom*, vol. 2, *The Greek and Latin Creeds* (New York: Harper and Row, 1877), 66.

degree of confidence, on the basis of experience alone, and which is brought to our knowledge only by God's special self-revelation. Therefore it is of the utmost importance that we gather the Scriptural proofs for it.[40]

Explanation

ONE SIMPLE GOD

There is only one God, and he consists of one simple (uncompounded, indivisible) essence (Deut. 6:4; Mark 12:29; John 17:3; James 2:19; see "Unity: Numerical Oneness" and "Unity: Simplicity" above [p. 174]).

THREE PERSONS

The one God exists eternally as three distinct persons (also known as *subsistences* and *hypostases*). The following passages reveal that there are three divine persons: Matthew 3:16–17; 4:1; John 1:18; 3:16; 5:20–22; 14:26; 15:26; 16:13–15. The distinctions between the persons is further specified by the following ancient illustration, variously referred to as "The Shield of the Trinity" or "The Shield of the Faith" (the earliest attestation dates to the early thirteenth century AD).[41]

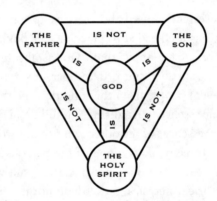

1. The Father is God.
2. The Son is God.
3. The Holy Spirit is God.
4. The Father is not the Son.
5. The Father is not the Holy Spirit.
6. The Son is not the Holy Spirit.

ESSENTIAL COEQUALITY

Each person of the Trinity (also known as the Godhead) possesses the entire simple (undivided) essence of God. This fact means that the three persons, though distinct from one another, are coequal in every perfection of the divine essence. They are *es-*

---

40. Berkhof, *Systematic Theology*, 85.
41. The "Shield of the Trinity" (or "Shield of the Faith") has appeared in various forms since the early thirteenth century. For a brief explanation of this illustration and another example of it, see Frederick Roth Webber and Ralph Adams Cram, *Church Symbolism: An Explanation of the More Important Symbols of the Old and New Testament, the Primitive, the Mediaeval and the Modern Church*, 2nd ed. (1938; repr., Whitefish, MT: Kessinger, 2010), 44–46.

sentially coequal. That is, with respect to the essence of God, the three persons are equal to each other. Another way to say this is that the three persons are ontologically (with respect to their being or essence) equal to each other.

PERSONAL DISTINCTIONS

Because each of the three persons of the Trinity equally possess the full, undivided divine essence and are thus equally God, the question arises as to how these persons may be distinguished from one another. The best answer is to turn to Scripture itself and note that the most common way the persons of the Trinity are spoken of are as "Father," "Son," and "Holy Spirit." These designations, also called the modes of subsistence,[42] reveal the personal properties that distinguish each member of the Trinity from the others.

By calling the first person of the Trinity "Father" (Lat. *pater*), Scripture intends to attribute the personal property of *paternity* to him with respect to the Son. By calling the second person of the Trinity "Son" (Lat. *filius*), Scripture intends to attribute the personal property of *filiation*, or sonship, to him with respect to the Father. By calling the third person of the Trinity "Spirit" (Lat. *spiritum*), Scripture intends to attribute the personal property of *spiration*, or procession, to him with respect to the Father and the Son. By virtue of his paternity, the Father is unbegotten but eternally begets (or "generates," Gk. *gennaō*) the Son. By virtue of his filiation, the Son is begotten, or eternally generated, by the Father. By virtue of his spiration, the Spirit eternally proceeds from both the Father and the Son. These concepts are best summarized by the Athanasian Creed:

> The Father is made of none; neither created, nor begotten.
> The Son is of the Father alone; not made, nor created; but begotten.
> The Holy Ghost is of the Father and of the Son; neither made, nor created, nor begotten; but proceeding.
> So there is one Father, not three Fathers; one Son, not three Sons; one Holy Ghost, not three Holy Ghosts.[43]

These distinct modes of relationship establish a definite order (Lat. *taxis*) within the Trinity, so that it is proper to say (with respect to their relationship only, not with respect to their essence, glory, or majesty) that the Father is first, the Son is second, and the Spirit is third.

These acts of eternal generation and eternal procession are sometimes called the *opera ad intra*, or the internal works, of the Trinity. That is, they are eternal acts within the inner life of the Trinity, which establish the modes of personal subsistence of each member of the Godhead. They differ from the *opera ad extra*, or the external works, which produce effects outside God's essence, that is, on the creation. Scripture ascribes God's various works in the economy of redemption to a particular member of the Trinity. The Father is particularly singled out as the Creator (1 Pet. 4:19); the

---

42. The use of the phrase "modes of subsistence" should not be confused with the error of Modalistic Monarchianism (or Modalism), which is rightly rejected as a heresy. See the discussion on Modalism under "Early History of Theological Development" (p. 208).
43. Schaff, *Creeds of Christendom*, 2:67–68. For more on eternal generation and eternal procession, see "Three Persons with Divine Relations: Eternal Generation and Eternal Procession" (p. 206).

Son is distinguished as the Redeemer and Mediator (Rom. 3:24; Eph. 1:7; 1 Tim. 2:5); and the Spirit is identified as the agent of sanctification (2 Thess. 2:13; 1 Pet. 1:2).[44] The external works of the Trinity in the economy of redemption therefore reflect the order established by the internal works of eternal generation and procession within the divine life. The Father sends the Son in the economy of redemption because he begets the Son eternally. The Spirit is sent by the Father and Son *ad extra* because he eternally proceeds from them *ad intra*.

Nevertheless, in all these works, all three persons of the Trinity work inseparably together (cf. John 14:10). Though one person or another may be emphasized in a particular work, no one person does any work exclusive of the other two persons, for, as the classic dictum states, "the external works of the Trinity are undivided" (*opera Trinitatis ad extra indivisa sunt*). Note, for example, the following passages, which ascribe the works outlined above to the other persons of the Trinity:

1. Creation and preservation
   a. Through the Son (John 1:3, 10; Col. 1:16–17; 1 Cor. 8:6; Heb. 1:2–3, 10)
   b. Through the Spirit (Gen. 1:2; Job 26:13; 32:8; 33:4; 34:14–15; Ps. 104:30)
2. Redemption
   a. Through the Father (1 Chron. 17:21; Isa. 63:16; Gal. 4:4–5)
   b. Through the Spirit (Heb. 9:14; Rom. 8:11)
3. Sanctification
   a. Through the Father (John 17:17; 1 Thess. 5:23)
   b. Through the Son (1 Cor. 1:30; Eph. 5:25–27)

A Mystery. The Trinity is a mystery in two senses. It is a mystery in the biblical sense in that it is a truth that was hidden until revealed. But it is also a mystery in that, in its essence, it is suprarational, ultimately beyond human comprehension. It is only partly intelligible to man, because God has revealed it in Scripture and in Jesus Christ. But it has no analogy in human experience, and its core elements (three coequal persons, each possessing the complete, simple divine essence, and each eternally relating to the other two without ontological subordination) transcend man's reason.

Consequently, the doctrine must be accepted by faith, based on how the Godhead is revealed in Scripture. And it must be articulated in such a way that the essence of God is not divided and that the distinctions and the coequality of being between the three persons are not compromised. The doctrine of the Trinity needs both positive and negative theology.

Illustrations. The Trinity has no perfect analogies in human experience. Theologians have attempted to find a perfect illustration of the Trinity, but all these attempts have either divided the essence, compromised the distinction between the three persons, or

---

44. Another way of stating this is that the *plan* of redemption is attributed to the Father, the *accomplishment* of redemption is attributed to the Son, and the *application* of redemption is attributed to the Spirit. Still another alternative is to say that in the economy of redemption, all things are *from* the Father, *through* the Son, and *in* the Spirit.

lost sight of God's *personal* essence. Nothing in the creation is exactly like the Trinity. What follows is a synthesis of these illustrations along with their weaknesses:[45]

1. Illustrations from inanimate nature:
   a. Water of the fountain, creek, and river
   b. Rising mist, cloud, and rain
   c. Rain, snow, and ice
   d. Root, trunk, and branches of a tree
   Weakness: The whole essence is not present but is divided or distributed.

2. Illustrations from man's life and mind:
   a. Psychological unity of memory, affections, and will (Augustine's analogy)
   b. Logical unity of thesis, antithesis, and synthesis (Hegel's analogy)
   c. Metaphysical unity of subject, object, and subject-object (Shedd's analogy)
   Weakness: These lack any unity of the three.

3. Illustration from love: Necessitates subject, object, and union of the two
   Weakness: Two persons (concretes) and a relationship (abstract) make up this triad, rather than three persons in the divine essence. Also, love is not a substance that is commonly possessed but a quality.

No illustration can fully communicate the Trinity, because the Trinity is God and always transcends the created order in essence, persons, and relationships. But as long as teachers make clear that every analogy will be to some extent inadequate, it may still be profitable to use these improper illustrations to explain why and how they fall short as adequate representations of the Trinity. By understanding that the Trinity is *not* like the three states of H_2O (ice, water, vapor), the student learns to reject modalism. By learning that the Trinity is not like the three leaves of a single clover, he eschews partialism. By grasping that the Trinity is not like the light and heat emanating from the sun, he disclaims Arianism.

Old Testament Indications

THE PLURAL NAME *ELOHIM*

The Hebrew divine name *elohim*, being a plural form, allows for a plurality in God. But the plural form does not necessitate this plurality, because there are reasons for using a plural other than indicating more than one entity (e.g., to show honor, or to denote intensity). Looking back from the clarity of the New Testament revelation, one can see *elohim* as at least a divine preparation for the later more complete revelation of God as triune.

OTHER PLURAL TITLES FOR GOD

In Ecclesiastes 12:1, "your Creator" translates a plural Hebrew participle, and in Isaiah 54:5, "your Maker" also translates a plural Hebrew participle. Again, because

---

45. Webber and Cram, *Church Symbolism*, 90. See also Grudem's comments on the inadequacies of all analogies in *Systematic Theology*, 240–41.

plurals have various possible uses in Hebrew, these titles do not prove that God is more than one person, although they are compatible with and prepare for the clearer New Testament revelation of the Trinity.

GOD SPEAKING OF HIMSELF AS PLURAL

Further possible Old Testament evidence of God being more than one person is found in passages where God speaks of himself using other plural forms. In Genesis 1:26, God says, "Let us make man in our image." The English verb with the plural pronoun translates a Hebrew first-person plural verb. God is speaking of himself and does not include the angels, because verse 27 says that "God created man in his own image." Another Hebrew first-person plural verb refers to God speaking of himself in Genesis 11:7: "Come, let us go down and there confuse their language." God is responding to man's decision to erect the tower of Babel as an act of rebellion against the divine command to disperse themselves over the earth. There is no indication in Genesis 11 of anyone else but God in heaven.

In Genesis 3:22, God uses a plural pronoun to refer to himself: "Behold, the man has become like one of us." In keeping with the Genesis 1:26 statement, Genesis 3:22 also refers only to God. Another plural pronoun is applied by God to himself in Isaiah 6:8, where God speaks so Isaiah can hear him: "Whom shall I send, and who will go for us?" Here the first-person singular Hebrew verb for God's sending is followed by a plural pronoun referring to God.

These passages show God speaking of himself as both singular and plural. As with the name *elohim*, these plurals could be plurals of intensity. But the progressive clarity of the New Testament concerning the Trinity argues more that these plurals, considered in combination with singular verbs and pronouns for God, constitute God's assertions that he is one and yet plural.

MORE THAN ONE PERSON AS "GOD"

Yet stronger Old Testament evidence that God is more than one person comes in passages in which more than one person is called "God" or "Lord." In Psalm 45:6–7, the Messiah is referred to as "God" (*elohim*) and is enthroned, having been anointed by "God" (*elohim*):

> Your throne, O God, is forever and ever.
>> The scepter of your kingdom is a scepter of uprightness;
>> you have loved righteousness and hated wickedness.
> Therefore God, your God, has anointed you
>> with the oil of gladness beyond your companions.

In Hebrews 1:8–9, by inspiration of the Holy Spirit, the author of Hebrews foretells that "God" will say the words of Psalm 45:6–7 to "the Son," who will be enthroned as "God" by "God."

Even more important is Psalm 110:1: "The LORD says to my Lord: 'Sit at my right hand, until I make your enemies your footstool.'" In this messianic psalm—the Old Testament text most frequently quoted and alluded to in the New Testament—Yahweh speaks to the Messiah as "my Lord" (Heb. *adonai*). By inspiration, the New Testament writers identify Jesus as the "Lord" to whom the "Lᴏʀᴅ" speaks. Jesus himself implicitly asserted to the Pharisees that in this psalm David called the Messiah "Lord" (Matt. 22:41–45; Mark 12:35–37; Luke 20:41–44). Jesus was claiming to be divine, and David addressed him as such. In Acts 2:32–36, Peter said that Psalm 110:1 was fulfilled by the exaltation of Jesus after his resurrection.

The importance of these passages for Trinitarianism is that in the New Testament God the Holy Spirit asserted that Psalms 45:6–7 and 110:1 did reveal that there are at least two divine persons, and one of these is "the Son," who is both *elohim* and *adonai*.

YAHWEH'S SON

There are a few Old Testament passages that say that God has a "son." Psalm 2:2, 6–7 predicts that God's "Anointed" will be enthroned "on Zion" on the basis of God's decree stating, "You are my Son; today I have begotten you." So this "King" will be enthroned as God's "Son" because of a decree naming him as God's "Son." Although in the Old Testament, Psalm 2:6–7 does not in and of itself assert that the one designated "my Son" is God's eternal, divine Son, the Spirit-inspired New Testament applies this passage to Jesus as the eternal, divine Son (Heb. 1:1–3).

"ONE" IN DEUTERONOMY 6:4

The Shema in Deuteronomy 6:4 states, "Hear, O Israel: The Lᴏʀᴅ our God, the Lᴏʀᴅ is one." This Jewish creed, concerning Yahweh as the one true God and as only "one," itself allows for a plurality in God as one. The word "one" in Deuteronomy 6:4 translates the Hebrew adjective *ekhad*, which affirms God's unity but can allow for plurality in that unity. This word is also used in Genesis 2:24 of the "one flesh" of the husband and the wife in marriage. It is true that in other uses of *ekhad*, a compound unity is not meant. But if Deuteronomy 6:4 had been intended to assert that God is only one person, another Hebrew word would certainly have been used, namely, *yakhid*, which has the sense of "only, solitary" (see Ps. 68:6). Deuteronomy 6:4 is an affirmation of monotheism, not Unitarianism. It does not contradict the doctrine of the Trinity (see 1 Cor. 8:6) and even allows for God to be more than one person.

THE ANGEL OF YAHWEH (ANGEL OF GOD)[46]

The Old Testament reveals this person as a divine person whom some passages refer to as Yahweh and God, and other passages depict as speaking to Yahweh. So the Old Testament presents the angel of Yahweh as Yahweh and yet also distinct from Yahweh.

Proofs that the angel of Yahweh was divine include the following:

---

46. For a more extensive discussion regarding the angel of the Lord, see "Angel of the Lord" in chap. 8, "Angels" (p. 719).

1. His name was used interchangeably with God's name (Gen. 16:7, 13; 21:17, 19–20; 22:11, 14; 31:11, 13; 48:15–16; Ex. 3:2, 4; Judg. 6:11, 14, 16, 20–21, 23; 13:3, 22–23).
2. When the angel of Yahweh made promises, God made them (Gen. 16:10; 22:15–17; cf. 12:2; 13:16).
3. Yahweh's name was in the angel of Yahweh (Ex. 23:20–21).
4. People offered sacrifices to the angel of Yahweh (Gen. 22:11–13; Judg. 6:21; 13:16, 19–22).
5. As the predicted angel ("messenger") of the covenant, he would be "the Lord" (Heb. *adon*, Mal. 3:1).
6. People who saw the angel of Yahweh identified him by name as divine (Gen. 16:11–13; Judg. 6:22–23; 13:21–22).
7. The angel of Yahweh could forgive sins (Ex. 23:21; Zech. 3:3–4).
8. The angel of Yahweh claimed to be "God" (Gen. 31:11, 13; Ex. 3:2–6).

What is especially important for Trinitarianism is that the Old Testament shows that the angel of Yahweh was called Yahweh and God but was also distinct from Yahweh:

1. Yahweh sent the angel of Yahweh (Ex. 23:20–23; 32:34; Num. 20:16).
2. The angel of Yahweh and Yahweh spoke to each other (Zech. 1:12–13).

The point of this section is that the Old Testament revelation of the angel of Yahweh is evidence that the Old Testament includes the truth that there is more than one person in the Godhead. It is little wonder that in light of the New Testament's clearer revelation concerning the triunity of God, many theologians in church history (e.g., Justin Martyr, Irenaeus, Tertullian, Clement of Alexandria, Origen, Cyprian, Hilary of Poitiers, Basil of Caesarea, and John Calvin) have identified the Old Testament angel of Yahweh as the preincarnate Jesus Christ. They saw the Old Testament passages on the angel of Yahweh not as contradicting but as supporting the doctrine of the Trinity.

THE HOLY SPIRIT AS DIVINE

The Old Testament also speaks of the Holy Spirit as divine. Old Testament passages assert that the Holy Spirit has divine perfections. According to Isaiah 11:2, the Spirit is the source of divine wisdom, power, and knowledge, and Psalm 139:7 teaches that the Spirit is omnipresent. The Old Testament also depicts the Spirit as involved in the original act of creation and in the work of preserving what God has created (Gen. 1:2; Job 26:13; 34:14–15; Pss. 33:6; 104:30). The Spirit of God even restrains sin (Gen. 6:3; Isa. 63:10). Whatever the Holy Spirit is in Old Testament revelation, he is personal and divine. It might be argued that one cannot build a doctrine of the Spirit as a distinct, divine person from such Old Testament passages, and that such passages are no more than poetic representations of God's presence. However, the Old Testament does not stand alone; the New Testament complements it with fuller revelation of the doctrine of the Trinity, including that the Holy Spirit is a distinct, divine person in the Godhead. Also, it should be noted that Jesus's Jewish contemporaries, especially his disciples, seemed to understand that the Holy Spirit is a distinct, divine person (cf. Matt. 1:20; 3:11; Luke 1:15, 35; 11:13; 12:10; John 14:26; 20:22). Clearly, they either drew this concept from the Old Testament or at least saw it as fully consistent with it.

THE WORD OF GOD

Another Old Testament aspect that prepares the way for the New Testament's clearer revelation of the doctrine of the Trinity is the concept of God's "word" (Heb. *dabar*). The New Testament revelation of the Son of God as the divine "word" is supported and foreshadowed by the following Old Testament truths:

1. God created by means of his word (Gen. 1:3, 6, 9, 11, 14, 20, 22, 24; Pss. 33:6, 9; 104:7; 147:18; 148:8).
2. God extends providential care by means of his word (Deut. 8:3; Pss. 106:9; 147:15–18).
3. God saves by means of his word: by his word, God gives life (Deut. 32:47; Ps. 119:25), guides (Ps. 119:105), chastens (Isa. 9:8), and will save the nation of Israel and restore the people to their land (Isa. 55:10–13).
4. God's word has God's power: God's word breaks and cuts (Isa. 9:8–10), consumes like fire (Jer. 5:14), destroys like a hammer (Jer. 23:29), accomplishes God's purpose (Isa. 55:11), and heals (Ps. 107:20).

OTHER OLD TESTAMENT INDICATIONS

There are at least three other Old Testament facets that serve as preparations for the New Testament doctrine of the Trinity.

Divine Wisdom. The Old Testament revelation of God's wisdom is compatible with the New Testament teaching that God's wisdom is a distinct, divine person, namely Christ. Thus, 1 Corinthians 1:24 calls Christ "the wisdom of God" (cf. 1 Cor. 1:30). In the Old Testament, God's wisdom is his means of creating all things (Prov. 3:19). In Proverbs 8:22–36, God's wisdom is poetically personified as God's possession and as his means of giving life, instruction, and grace. Thus, passages like Proverbs 8 and Job 28:12–28 depict God's wisdom as a distinct entity. Perhaps these passages describe wisdom as a person through poetic personification and therefore do not literally depict wisdom as a person. But the later apostolic revelation of Christ as "the wisdom of God" led many church fathers to see these passages as describing the preincarnate second person of the Trinity.

Three Distinct, Divine Entities. There are a few passages in Isaiah in which three distinct entities act. Isaiah 61:1–2 prophetically portrays the Messiah ("me") saying,

> The Spirit of the Lord GOD is upon me,
>   because the LORD has anointed me
> to bring good news to the poor;
>   he has sent me to bind up the brokenhearted,

> to proclaim liberty to the captives,
>> and the opening of the prison to those who are bound;
> to proclaim the year of the LORD's favor,
>> and the day of vengeance of our God;
>> to comfort all who mourn.

This passage contains "the LORD" (Yahweh), "the Spirit of the Lord," and the speaker, who is the Messiah. The NKJV editors are correct in seeing the Messiah's comments as starting in verse 1 and continuing through verse 9, which means that it is the Messiah who in verse 8 says, "I the LORD love justice." In other words, the Messiah is sent by Yahweh and calls himself Yahweh. There are at least two divine persons in this passage, and because "the Spirit" is named, this context advances the preparation for the New Testament doctrine of the Trinity.

Another passage to consider is Isaiah 63:7–10:

> I will recount the steadfast love of the LORD,
>> the praises of the LORD,
> according to all that the LORD has granted us,
>> and the great goodness to the house of Israel
> that he has granted them according to his compassion,
>> according to the abundance of his steadfast love.
> For he said, "Surely they are my people,
>> children who will not deal falsely."
>> And he became their Savior.
> In all their affliction he was afflicted,
>> and the angel of his presence saved them;
> in his love and in his pity he redeemed them;
>> he lifted them up and carried them all the days of old.
> But they rebelled and grieved his Holy Spirit;
> therefore he turned to be their enemy,
>> and himself fought against them.

Here, "the LORD" (Yahweh), "his Holy Spirit," and "the angel of his presence" are mentioned. It seems best to see the latter as the angel of Yahweh discussed earlier. If that is so, then there are at least two divine persons in this context. And the Holy Spirit is here a person, because he is "grieved." As such, the Holy Spirit is also divine, since it was the people's grieving of him through rebellion that resulted in divine retribution. This passage moves further toward the full New Testament doctrine of the Trinity.

One more Old Testament passage that may specify three divine persons is Isaiah 48:12, 16:

> "Listen to me, O Jacob,
>> and Israel, whom I called!
> I am he; I am the first,
>> and I am the last. . . .

"Draw near to me, hear this:
> from the beginning I have not spoken in secret,
> from the time it came to be I have been there."
And now the Lord GOD has sent me, and his Spirit.

There are at least two divine entities in this passage: "the Lord GOD" and "his Spirit" (Isa. 48:16). The personhood of the Spirit cannot be pressed immediately in this context, but when combined with Isaiah 63:7–10, it is clear that the Spirit is a divine person. But it is not absolutely clear if a third divine entity is depicted in Isaiah 48:12, 16. The English translations are divided over whether the speaker of verse 12, who is divine ("I am he; I am the first, and I am the last"), continues to speak to the end of verse 16. The NASB and NKJV hold that such is the case, which is the preferred view. In this translation, the Messiah is speaking; he is the "I am" and has been "sent" by "the Lord GOD" and "his Spirit." In such a construction, the speaker and "the Lord GOD" are both divine persons, and "the Spirit" must also be divine, since the Spirit is seen by these translations as combining with "the Lord GOD" in sending the Messiah.[47]

Emphasis on the Number Three. Finally, the Old Testament places an emphasis on the number three in various ways. These might have been divinely intended to prepare for the more explicit New Testament doctrine of the Trinity. Some of these emphases are threefold formulae, such as the seraphim praising Yahweh on his throne in heaven as "holy, holy, holy" (Isa. 6:3). Another example is the threefold Aaronic benediction in Numbers 6:24–27:

The LORD bless you and keep you;
the LORD make his face to shine upon you and be gracious to you;
the LORD lift up his countenance upon you and give you peace.

Peter Toon notes that the ancient church saw this threefold blessing as indicating the three persons of the Trinity, especially because the apostles were commanded to baptize in the "name" (singular) of the Trinity (Matt. 28:19). In Numbers 6:27, Yahweh said that this threefold blessing would be putting Yahweh's "name" on the people of Israel.[48]

Yet another threefold construction is Jacob's threefold blessing of Joseph and his sons in Genesis 48:15–16:

And he blessed Joseph and said,

> The God before whom my fathers Abraham and Isaac walked,
>> the God who has been my shepherd all my life long to this day,
> the angel who has redeemed me from all evil, bless the boys;

---

47. However, the ESV, HCSB, NIV, and RSV end the quotation marks before the last statement of verse 16. So the words "And now the Lord GOD has sent me, and his Spirit" are Isaiah's words concerning himself as a prophet. In this construction, the speaker of verse 12 is "the Lord GOD," and he has sent Isaiah as a prophet. Additionally, these translations probably do not understand that the Spirit has also sent Isaiah but rather that "the Lord GOD" has sent Isaiah and the Spirit. So at least in this passage in these translations, it would not be as clear that the Spirit is a divine person, although the Spirit would at least be a distinct entity.

48. Peter Toon, *Our Triune God: A Biblical Portrayal of the Trinity* (Wheaton, IL: Victor, 1996), 102.

> and in them let my name be carried on, and the name of my fathers
>> Abraham and Isaac;
> and let them grow into a multitude in the midst of the earth.

In light of the previous discussion of the angel of Yahweh, it is well to note that Jacob says that "the angel" redeemed Jacob and would join with "God" in blessing Joseph's sons. Since Jacob's prayer had in view that only God could "bless" the boys, it is best to understand that "the angel" must be a distinct, divine person to bless jointly with God the Father.

Other emphases on the number three can be seen in the following passages: Genesis 15:9; 30:36; 40:10, 16; Exodus 3:18; 19:11; 23:14; Leviticus 19:23; Numbers 19:12; 22:23–41; 31:19; Jeremiah 7:4 ("the temple of the LORD" three times). Perhaps the use of three in ceremonial worship was meant to testify to Israel's God being three yet one.

In light of the New Testament, the above aspects of the Old Testament progressively prepare for the New Testament's clearer revelation of God as triune. Benjamin B. Warfield made a helpful elaboration of how the Old Testament more than prepared for the more complete New Testament revelation of the Trinity:

> The upshot of it all is that it is very generally felt that, somehow, in the Old Testament development of the idea of God there is a suggestion that the Deity is not a simple monad, and that thus a preparation is made for the revelation of the Trinity yet to come. It would seem clear that we must recognize in the Old Testament doctrine of the relation of God to His revelation by the creative Word and the Spirit, at least the germ of the distinctions in the Godhead afterward fully made known in the Christian revelation. And we can scarcely stop there. After all is said, in the light of the later revelation, the Trinitarian interpretation remains the most natural one of the phenomena which the older writers frankly interpreted as intimations of the Trinity; especially of those connected with the descriptions of the Angel of Jehovah no doubt, but also even of such a form of expression as meets us in the "Let us make man in our image" of Gen. i. 26—for surely verse 27: "And God created man in his own image," does not encourage us to take the preceding verse as announcing that man was to be created in the image of the angels. This is not an illegitimate reading of the New Testament ideas back into the text of the Old Testament; it is only reading the text of the Old Testament under the illumination of the New Testament revelation. . . . The mystery of the Trinity is not revealed in the Old Testament; but the mystery of the Trinity underlies the Old Testament revelation, and here and there almost comes into view. Thus the Old Testament revelation of God is not corrected by the fuller revelation which follows it, but only perfected, extended and enlarged.[49]

New Testament Evidence

The New Testament is essential for a clear presentation of the doctrine of the Trinity. As discussed above, various Old Testament passages allow and even indicate that

---

49. Benjamin Breckinridge Warfield, "The Biblical Doctrine of the Trinity," in *Biblical and Theological Studies*, ed. Samuel G. Craig (1952; repr., Philadelphia: Presbyterian and Reformed, 1968), 30–31.

there is more than one divine person in God even though there is only one God. But the Old Testament assertions do not reveal enough details for believers to derive an explicitly Trinitarian doctrine of God. Such conclusive evidence is revealed in the New Testament. The church's doctrine of the Trinity appeals to the Old Testament for inspired evidence, but it has always been based primarily on the progress of the whole of God's revelation.

ONLY ONE GOD

As shown previously in the section on the divine perfection of unity (p. 174), the Bible asserts that God is numerically only one. In the New Testament, Jesus repeats Deuteronomy 6:4 in Mark 12:29: "The Lord our God, the Lord is one." In John 17:3, Jesus calls God the Father "the only true God." Other passages also affirm monotheism: "God is one" (Rom. 3:30; James 2:19); "there is no God but one" (1 Cor. 8:4); and "there is one God" (1 Tim. 2:5). In Romans 3:30; 1 Corinthians 8:4; and 1 Timothy 2:5, "God" is God the Father, the first person of the Trinity, but as demonstrated below, the New Testament sometimes refers to God the Father as "God" to emphasize that he is God while depicting that the other two persons of the Trinity are also divine. The New Testament articulates that there is only one God but also refers to each of the three persons of the Trinity—the Father, the Son, and the Holy Spirit—as equally divine in names, nature, prerogatives, and works.

MORE THAN ONE PERSON ASSOCIATED WITH GOD

In some passages, the speaker or writer associates two persons with God. In John 5:17–18, Jesus claimed that he had the same authority to work on the Sabbath as "my Father." Because of this statement, the Jewish religious leaders sought all the more to kill Jesus, because in their minds he had broken the Sabbath and "was even calling God his own Father, making himself equal with God" (John 5:18). In John 10:30, Jesus said, "I and the Father are one." Because of that statement, the Jewish leaders picked up stones to stone him, accusing him of blasphemy, because by saying he was one with the Father, they believed that he was deifying himself: "You, being a man, make yourself God" (John 10:33). Jesus also said that he has everything that the Father has (John 16:15; 17:10). God the Father and Jesus Christ worked together in creating all things (1 Cor. 8:6), grace and peace come to believers from both God the Father and the Lord Jesus (1 Cor. 1:3; Eph. 1:2), and believers will reign on the earth with Christ for one thousand years as priests of both God the Father and Christ (Rev. 20:6).

Other passages associate all three persons of the Trinity with God. The Scriptures name the three persons equally and divinely in the following activities:

1. Eternally planning for and providing salvation to people (Eph. 1:3–14; 2:13–18; 1 Pet. 1:2)
2. Testifying to Jesus as the Son of God and the means of eternal life (1 John 5:1–12)

3. Publicly recognizing Jesus as the Savior of Israel (John 1:29–34)
4. Being present with and revealing truth to Jesus's disciples (John 14:9–10, 26; 15:26; 16:7–15)
5. Giving faith, hope, and love in the hearts of believers (Col. 1:3–8)
6. Redeeming, justifying, and residing in believers (Gal. 3:11–14)
7. Bestowing spiritual gifts (1 Cor. 12:4–6)
8. Unifying the church (Eph. 4:4–6)
9. Continuing to bless believers (2 Cor. 13:14)
10. Securing believers in Christ (2 Cor. 1:20–22)

In the context of the New Testament, only God can provide what the Father, the Son, and the Holy Spirit are revealed as providing for the eternal salvation of believers in Christ.

THREE PERSONS DECLARED TO BE GOD

The Father Is God. The New Testament specifies that each of the three persons of the Trinity are "God." The name God (Gk. *theos*) combines with the name Father in many passages (e.g., John 6:27; Rom. 15:6; 1 Cor. 8:6; 15:24; Eph. 4:6; James 3:9). And as Murray Harris has demonstrated, when the name *theos* appears in the New Testament by itself in reference to the true God, it usually designates the first person of the Trinity, God the Father (e.g., James 1:5; 1 Pet. 3:18).[50]

Jesus Is God. The New Testament also explicitly declares that Jesus is God. Jesus's words claim that he is divine. He says that he is the Son of God (Matt. 26:63–64; Mark 14:61–62; Luke 22:67–71). He claims that he is the "I am" (Gk. *ego eimi*), thus bearing the Old Testament divine name of Yahweh. Many of these "I am" statements are connected with metaphors, such as "I am the bread of life" (John 6:35, 48), "I am the light of the world" (John 8:12), "I am the door" (John 10:9), "I am the good shepherd" (John 10:11, 14), and "I am the resurrection and the life" (John 11:25). But many of these statements are absolute, without any quali-fiers (e.g., Mark 14:62; John 8:24, 28, 58; 13:19; 18:5–8). The absolute usage in John 13:19 occurs in the context of Jesus predicting that one of the disciples will betray him. He tells his disciples that he makes this statement so that "when it does take place you may believe that I am he." The Greek words behind the En-glish translation are taken from the Septuagint translation of Isaiah 43:10, which states, "in order that you may know and believe and understand that I am." This statement appears in the larger context of Isaiah 40–48, in which God proves that he is the only true God, because only he can predict the future. So Jesus is saying that when his prediction that one of the disciples will betray him is fulfilled, it will prove that he is God.

Jesus also claims that the Father sent him, and so he came from heaven and had divine authority to do the works of the Father (John 3:13; 5:26–37; 6:31–58; 8:42;

50. Murray J. Harris, *Jesus as God: The New Testament Use of* Theos *in Reference to Jesus* (Grand Rapids, MI: Baker, 1992), 21–50.

16:28–30). And Jesus says that he has a special relationship with "my Father" that no one else has (e.g., Matt. 7:21; 10:32–33; 11:25–27; Luke 22:29; 24:49; John 2:16; 5:19–23; 8:36–38; 10:29–30, 36–38; 14:2–3, 11–12, 23; 15:8–10, 15; 16:10, 26–28; 17:1–26; 20:17).

John the Baptist says that Jesus is "the Lord" (John 1:15, 23, 30) and "the Son of God" (John 1:34). God the Father calls Jesus "my beloved Son" (Matt. 3:16–17; 17:5). Angels announce that Jesus is "the Son of God" (Luke 1:31–35) and "the Lord" (Luke 2:11)—in the latter passage, "Lord" is a divine name because it is a divine name in the near context (Luke 2:9, 15). In Matthew 14:33, the disciples worship Jesus as "the Son of God." Peter confesses that Jesus is "the Son of the living God" (Matt. 16:16), and Thomas confesses that the risen Jesus is "my Lord and my God" (John 20:27–29). Before Jesus's birth, he is called "Lord" by Elizabeth (Luke 1:43) and Zechariah (Luke 1:76). A centurion at the crucifixion affirms, "Truly this man was the Son of God!" (Mark 15:39).

Under the inspiration of the Holy Spirit, the New Testament writers say that Jesus is divine. Matthew says that Jesus is "God with us" (Matt. 1:23). Luke quotes Peter referring to Jesus as "Lord" in fulfillment of Psalm 110:1 (Acts 2:34–36) and also quotes Paul implying Jesus's divinity by discussing "the church of God, which he obtained with his own blood" (Acts 20:28). Paul refers to Christ with the words "who is over all, the eternally blessed God" (Rom. 9:5 NKJV). Romans 10:9 and 1 Corinthians 12:3 say that the saving confession is "Jesus is Lord." In Romans 14:8–9, Paul states that Christ is "Lord"—indeed, that he is "Lord both of the dead and of the living." According to Paul, Jesus Christ is "the Lord of glory" (1 Cor. 2:8), and he is the "one Lord, Jesus Christ, through whom are all things and through whom we exist" (1 Cor. 8:6). Paul proclaims that Jesus existed "in the form of God" but "emptied himself, by taking the form of a servant" (Phil. 2:6–7). Paul goes on to say that Jesus humbled himself by becoming obedient to the point of death on the cross, that God the Father has "highly exalted" Jesus, and that one day all people will confess that "Jesus Christ is Lord" (Phil. 2:11). In Colossians 2:9, Paul asserts that in Jesus "the whole fullness of deity dwells bodily."

A number of passages by the apostles name Jesus as "God" using a Greek grammatical construction for which grammarian Granville Sharp (1735–1813) articulated a rule (which now bears his name) and specified its relevance for the divine identity of Jesus Christ in the New Testament. The rule states that if the Greek conjunction *kai* joins two singular "nouns or participles" of personal description and of the same case, and if the Greek article *ho* precedes the first noun or participle but not the second, then "the latter . . . denotes a farther description" of the person described by the first noun or participle.[51] Classic examples of the Granville Sharp construction are Titus 2:13 ("our great God and Savior Jesus Christ"), 2 Peter 1:1 ("our God and Savior Jesus Christ"), and 2 Peter 2:20 ("the Lord and Savior Jesus Christ," NASB).

---

51. Granville Sharp, *Remarks on the Uses of the Definitive Article in the Greek Text of the New Testament* (Philadelphia: B. B. Hopkins, 1807), 3.

According to Sharp, the construction in these passages means that Jesus is not only "Savior" but also "God" and "Lord."

Yet another way in which the apostles identify Jesus as God is by referring to Jesus with Old Testament passages that refer to Yahweh. In John 12:36–41, by inspiration of the Holy Spirit, John quoted Isaiah 53:1 and Isaiah 6:10 as reasons why the Jews "did not believe in" Jesus even though "he had done so many signs before them" (John 12:37). John says that this unbelief fulfills the two Old Testament passages he quoted. John concludes in John 12:41 that "Isaiah said these things because he saw his glory and spoke of him." The antecedent of "his" and "him" in this verse is the "he" of verse 37, which refers to "Jesus" in verse 36. Thus, John identifies Jesus as the "Lord" (Heb. *adonai*) of Isaiah 6:1, whom Isaiah saw "sitting upon a throne," and the "LORD [Yahweh] of hosts" of Isaiah 6:3, whose "glory" fills "the whole earth." So Jesus is the "Lord" and "LORD" of Isaiah 6:1–3.

Other New Testament passages also refer to Jesus by using Old Testament passages referring to Yahweh. Acts 2:21 and Romans 10:13 quote Joel 2:32 to indicate that the phrase "calls on the name of the Lord" (Yahweh in Joel 2:32) means believing and confessing that Jesus is Lord. Hebrews 1:10–12 asserts that God "says" the words of Psalm 102:25–27 "to the Son" (Heb. 1:8), thus indicating that Jesus is the "God" (Heb. *el*) and the "LORD" (Yahweh) of Psalm 102. And Ephesians 4:7–8 uses the words of Psalm 68:18 to express that when Christ ascended, he gave gifts to his church. But the Old Testament passage refers to *God* ascending to his "mount" (Ps. 68:16) and "receiving gifts" (Ps. 68:18). So in citing Ephesians 4:7–8, Paul means that Christ was divine in his ascension and was authorized to distribute gifts to the church.

The Holy Spirit Is God. The New Testament also identifies the Holy Spirit as divine. His titles associate him with the other persons of the Trinity: "Spirit of God" (Matt. 3:16); "Spirit of the Lord" (Luke 4:18); "Spirit of your Father" (Matt. 10:20); "my Spirit" (Acts 2:17–18); "Spirit of Christ" (Rom. 8:9); "the Lord, the Spirit" (2 Cor. 3:17–18 NASB).

There are other even more explicit assertions that the Holy Spirit is God. In Acts 5:3–4, 9, Peter says that in lying to the Holy Spirit, Ananias and Sapphira had "not lied to man but to God." In 2 Corinthians 3:17–18, Paul declares, "The Lord is the Spirit," and refers to the Spirit as "the Lord, the Spirit" (NASB). Paul also says in 1 Corinthians 3:16 that "God's Spirit" indwells the church, because the church is "God's temple." And in Ephesians 2:22, Paul states that it is "by the Spirit" that the church is "being built together into a dwelling place for God."

Furthermore, the New Testament claims that the Holy Spirit spoke the words of Old Testament passages, words that those passages declare come directly from God. In Acts 28:25–27, Paul says that the Holy Spirit spoke "through Isaiah" the words of Isaiah 6:9–10, even though in Isaiah 6, it was "the voice of the Lord" who said these words (Isa. 6:8). The same correspondence between words of New Testament passages and Old Testament passages is visible in the following couplets: Hebrews 3:7–11 with Psalm 95:7–11; Hebrews 10:15–17 with Jeremiah 31:31–34.

THREE PERSONS WITH DIVINE PERFECTIONS

The New Testament depicts each person of the Trinity as having characteristics that are divine perfections. These characteristics are divine because the New Testament asserts them to be standards by which characteristics of other beings are measured. God the Father is powerful (Matt. 19:26), omnipresent (Matt. 6:4, 6), omniscient (Matt. 6:4, 6, 8; Luke 16:15), true (John 3:33), righteous (John 17:25; cf. Acts 10:34), and living (Matt. 26:63; John 5:26; 6:57).

God the Son, incarnate as Jesus Christ, is eternal (John 1:1; 8:58; 17:5; Rev. 1:8; 21:6; 22:13), omniscient (John 1:47–48; 2:24–25; 16:30; 21:17; Rev. 2:23), omnipresent (Matt. 18:20; 28:20; John 1:48–50), omnipotent (Matt. 8:26–27; 9:25; 21:19; 28:18; Mark 5:11–15; Luke 4:38–41; 7:14–15; John 2:11; 5:36; 10:25, 38; 11:43–44; Heb. 1:3; Rev. 1:8), immutable (Heb. 1:10–12; 13:8), loving (Eph. 5:2), holy (Luke 1:35; John 8:46; Heb. 7:26–27; 1 John 3:5), life (1 John 1:2; 5:20), and truth (John 14:6).

God the Holy Spirit is eternal (Heb. 9:14), holy (Eph. 4:30), omniscient (John 14:26; 16:12–13; 1 Cor. 2:10–11), omnipotent (Luke 1:35, 37; 1 Cor. 12:11; Rom. 15:19), glory (1 Pet. 4:14), life (Rom. 8:2), truth (John 14:17; 15:26; 16:13; 1 John 4:6), and grace (Heb. 10:29).

THREE PERSONS WITH DIVINE PREROGATIVES

According to the New Testament, each person of the Trinity has divine prerogatives. These are divine because the Bible ascribes them as if they are rights that no other beings have. God the Father has the right to receive worship (John 4:23; James 3:9), give commands (John 14:31), forgive sin (Matt. 6:14), and judge (John 5:30). God the Son has the right to receive worship (Matt. 14:33; 28:9; John 20:28; Heb. 1:6), give commands (John 15:12, 14), forgive sin (Mark 2:8–12), judge (Matt. 25:31–32; John 5:22; Acts 10:42; 17:31; Rom. 14:10–11; 2 Cor. 5:10; 2 Tim. 4:1; 1 Pet. 4:1, 5; Rev. 19:11–15; 22:12–13), and be the object of faith (John 1:12; 20:31). God the Holy Spirit has the right to receive worship (Eph. 4:30; 1 Thess. 5:19; Heb. 10:29),[52] know the deep things of God (1 Cor. 2:10), give commands (Acts 8:29; 10:19–20), and bestow gifts (1 Cor. 12:4, 7–8, 11).

THREE PERSONS PERFORMING DIVINE ACTIONS

The New Testament specifies that each person of the Trinity performs divine acts. These are divine because the New Testament asserts that they determine all other reality. God the Father creates (1 Cor. 8:6), sustains life (Matt. 6:26), reveals truth (Matt. 16:17; Heb. 1:1–2), raises the dead (Rom. 6:4), and judges (Matt. 15:13; Acts 17:31). God the Son creates (John 1:3, 10; 1 Cor. 8:6; Eph. 3:9; Col. 1:16; Heb. 1:2), sustains all things (Col. 1:17; Heb. 1:3), reveals truth (John 16:12–13), raises

---

52. None of the three passages listed here positively affirms that the Holy Spirit has the prerogative to be worshiped as God. Rather, they state that people should not "grieve," "quench," or "outrage" the Holy Spirit. These negative expressions, however, should be inferred as positively commanding people to do the opposite of these actions—that is, to obey, honor, and worship the Holy Spirit.

the dead (John 5:28–29; 10:17–18), and judges (John 5:22, 27; Acts 10:42; 2 Tim. 4:1). God the Holy Spirit creates (Gen. 1:2; Job 26:13; Ps. 33:6), reveals truth and inspires its writing (John 16:13; 1 Cor. 2:12–13; 2 Pet. 1:21), raises the dead (Rom. 8:11), regenerates (John 3:5–6; Titus 3:5), indwells (2 Tim. 1:14), secures by sealing (Eph. 1:13–14), gives God's love (Rom. 5:5), and guides (Rom. 8:14).

THREE PERSONS WITH DIVINE RELATIONS: ETERNAL GENERATION AND ETERNAL PROCESSION

As mentioned previously, there are eternal relations between the persons of the Trinity: the Father, the Son of God, and the Spirit of God. The Father eternally begets the Son and eternally spirates[53] the Holy Spirit. The Son is eternally begotten of the Father and eternally spirates the Holy Spirit. The Spirit eternally proceeds from the Father and the Son.

The eternal generation of the Son and the eternal procession of the Spirit are two of the most misunderstood doctrines of classic Trinitarianism, because there are no suitable analogies in the human realm that can be used to explain or illustrate the terminology. Although Scripture expressly speaks of the Father's begetting the Son (Ps. 2:7) and the Spirit's proceeding from the Father (John 15:26), the Bible gives no clear and complete explanation of what those expressions mean. Indeed, begetting and breathing are creaturely activities, so the language alone is clearly inadequate to express the full wonder and glory of the inner relationships within the eternal, immutable, ineffable Godhead. The words must therefore be understood (as best we can) in light of everything Scripture says about the Father, the Son, and the Holy Spirit. (This section is to be read in concert with the earlier section "Personal Distinctions" [p. 191]).

At first glance, *eternal generation* seems oxymoronic. In normal human discourse, the words *generate* and *beget* speak of bringing someone or something into existence. In the human realm, begetting occurs only once, at a definite point in time. To pair the idea with the adjective *eternal* is to change it in the most radical way. And it is absolutely vital to understand and affirm the difference between the begetting of a human child and the eternal generation of the Son of God. When we say Christ is eternally begotten of the Father, we are not talking about his beginning, for Scripture plainly says, "He was in the beginning with God. All things were made through him, and without him was not any thing made that was made" (John 1:2–3). There never was a time when the Son did not exist. He is "the Alpha and the Omega, the first and the last, the beginning and the end" (Rev. 22:13).

How, then, can Christ be eternally begotten of the Father? The answer is surprisingly simple. When terms like *begetting* or *generation* are used to speak of the heavenly Father's relation to his Son (e.g., Ps. 2:7; cf. Acts 13:33; Heb. 1:5; 5:5), what those words describe is not his beginning (for he had none) but the establishment from all eternity of the filial relationship between the first and second persons of the Trinity.

---

53. This is a unique word used by theologians to speak of the means by which the Holy Spirit "proceeds from the Father" (John 15:26). The term comes from the Latin *spirare*, "to breathe."

The expression thus describes the eternal, necessary, and self-differentiating act of God the Father by which he generates the personal subsistence of the Son and thereby communicates to the Son the entire divine essence (cf. John 5:26).[54]

This relationship is unique; it is the very thing that distinguishes the Son from the Father and the Spirit. In other words, the Spirit is not begotten; his mode of subsistence is *procession*. Similar to eternal generation, the procession of the Spirit from the Father and the Son describes the eternal, necessary, and self-differentiating act of the Father and the Son by which they spirate the personal subsistence of the Spirit and thereby communicate to him the entire divine essence.[55] Scripture does not explicitly define the difference between generation and procession, but the terminology befits the names Son and Spirit. *Begetting* has the connotation of filiation (i.e., that which is proper to sonship), and *procession* is a suitable expression to pair with the concepts of spirit or breath. Clearly, the distinction between *begetting* and *proceeding* is purposeful and important, even if we cannot fully explain how the two modes of subsistence differ from one another.[56]

It is well known that the Eastern church split from the Western church over the question of whether the Holy Spirit proceeds from the Father only or from the Father *and the Son* (Lat. *filioque*). In John 15:26, Jesus says, "The Spirit of truth . . . proceeds from the Father." And in John 20:22, in one of his early postresurrection appearances to the disciples, it states that "he breathed on them and said to them, 'Receive the Holy Spirit'"—symbolizing the very idea suggested by the language used to speak of the Spirit's procession. So we affirm—with the rest of the Western church—that the Holy Spirit proceeds from the Father and the Son. The Athanasian Creed (*Quicunque Vult*) states the relations within the Godhead in the most succinct language possible: "The Father is made of none; neither created, nor begotten. The Son is of the Father alone; not made, nor created; but begotten. The Holy Ghost is of the Father and of the Son; neither made, nor created, nor begotten; but proceeding."[57]

As mentioned earlier, these *opera ad intra* establish a definite order (Lat. *taxis*) within the Trinity, so that it is proper to say (with respect to their relationship only, not with respect to their essence, glory, or majesty) that the Father is first, the Son is second, and the Spirit is third. The *ad intra* works of eternal generation and procession become the ground for the order reflected in the *ad extra* works in the economy of redemption. The Son submits to the Father in the economy of redemption (cf. John 5:30; 6:38) because he was eternally generated by the Father.[58] The

---

54. Berkhof, *Systematic Theology*, 94.

55. Berkhof, *Systematic Theology*, 97.

56. John Owen aptly asked, perhaps echoing Acts 8:33 (cf. Isa. 53:8 in the Septuagint), "Who can declare the generation of the Son, the procession of the Spirit, or the difference of the one from the other?" *On Temptation and the Mortification of Sin in Believers* (Philadelphia: Presbyterian Board of Publication, 1880), 268.

57. Schaff, *Creeds of Christendom*, 2:67–68.

58. This is in contrast to the teaching of some who say that the *ad extra* submission of the Son to the Father is rooted in a kind of eternal functional subordination (*ad intra*) of the Son to the Father. There cannot be eternal relations of authority and submission between the Father and the Son (*ad intra*) without undermining the doctrine of divine simplicity, for the concept of submission entails the subjection of one person's will to another person's will. However, since the faculty of will is a predicate of nature, and since the divine nature (or essence) is single and undivided among the three persons of the

Spirit is sent by the Father and the Son (cf. John 14:26; 15:26) because he eternally proceeds from the Father and the Son. Yet none of this implies a rank or hierarchy of *essence* within the Trinity, for each person fully possesses the undivided divine essence. The Athanasian Creed likewise sums up the clear teaching of Scripture in a remarkable economy of words: "And in this Trinity none is afore, or after another; none is greater, or less than another. But the whole three Persons are coeternal, and coequal. So that in all things, as aforesaid: the Unity in Trinity, and the Trinity in Unity, is to be worshiped."[59]

Early History of Theological Development[60]

As a conclusion to the study of the Trinity, it is important to briefly observe how the doctrine of the Trinity was (1) observed in Scripture and (2) articulated by the ancient church. The word *Trinity* and other technical terms (e.g., *person, essence*) in the traditional orthodox doctrine of the Trinity are not found in Scripture yet are based on biblical verbiage. The doctrine of the Trinity was formally articulated by the Councils of Nicaea (AD 325) and Constantinople (AD 381), but these councils did not invent the doctrine; rather, they set forth a dogma (official proclamation) to counter prevailing heresies. In post–New Testament church history, the affirmation of the doctrine goes back to the expressions of the early apostolic fathers (ca. AD 90–150). These men—such as Clement of Rome (fl. ca. 88–99), Polycarp (ca. 69–155), and Ignatius (ca. 50–ca. 110)—affirmed the deity of the Father, the Son, and the Holy Spirit without speculating about their relations with each other. During this period, the church began to experience Roman persecution, and some of the apostolic fathers died as martyrs. The church also began to deal with the Gnostic heresy.

The next period of the ancient church (AD 150–300) witnessed increasing Roman persecution and fresh heresies, in addition to the spread of Gnosticism. Gnosticism was monistic and dualistic, denying real distinctions in reality and treating matter and flesh as inherently evil, not created by God, who was protected from matter by a series of emanations. Gnostics denied the incarnation of Christ since they believed that God would never join with matter nor come to earth, and they produced their own spurious books, including false gospels.

Other heresies from this period included various forms of Monarchianism (an early Unitarianism). Dynamic (Adoptionistic) Monarchianism taught that the Father alone is God and that Jesus was just a man who was indwelt by an impersonal divine force (the Logos) either at his birth, his baptism, or his resurrection. He had a

---

Trinity, there can be no submission or subjection from eternity. The incarnate Son is able to submit to the Father because, now possessing a fully human nature, he possesses a human will in addition to his divine will (cf. Luke 22:42; 1 Cor. 15:28).

59. Schaff, *Creeds of Christendom*, 2:68.

60. This historical summary is based on Gregg R. Allison, *Historical Theology: An Introduction to Christian Doctrine* (Grand Rapids, MI: Zondervan, 2011), 231–43; Louis Berkhof, *The History of Christian Doctrines* (1937; repr., Grand Rapids, MI: Baker, 1975), 83–92; John D. Hannah, *Our Legacy: The History of Christian Doctrine* (Colorado Springs: NavPress, 2001), 71–86; and Robert Letham, *The Holy Trinity: In Scripture, History, Theology, and Worship* (Phillipsburg, NJ: P&R, 2004), 89–220.

delegated divinity through this indwelling divine power, and his divinity was limited to this power only and featured no divine essence.

Modalistic Monarchianism (Modalism, Sabellianism, and Patripassianism) taught that the Father and the Son are one and the same. God is called Father or Son according to the figure of the times. Born of a virgin, he is called Son; to those who believed in him, he revealed that he was the Father. The one God was metamorphosed in external form according to the need of the moment. In other words, there is only one God who presents himself in various forms (Father, Son, or Spirit) as he wishes. In this heresy, these forms are modes of manifestation, not modes of being.

Church leaders in this period—such as Justin Martyr (ca. 100–165), Irenaeus (ca. 120–202), Tertullian (ca. 160–ca. 220), Clement of Alexandria (ca. 150–ca. 215), and Origen (ca. 184–ca. 254)—began to write more extensively as apologists and theologians to counter the false charges that pagans leveled against Christians and to oppose Gnosticism and Monarchianism. These men greatly advanced the orthodox explanation of Trinitarian doctrine. Irenaeus wrote five books against Gnosticism. His writings were more detailed concerning the relations of the Father, the Son, and the Holy Spirit. Tertullian coined the Latin word *trinitas* for the Godhead and the Latin word *persona* for the persons. Origen affirmed the eternal deity of the Son and identified the three persons by the Greek word *hypostasis* and the one essence by the Greek word *ousia*. All the apologists affirmed the divine essence and distinct personhood of each member of the Trinity.

One problem that occurred as the apologists wrote about the Trinity was a growing ontological subordinationism. Justin, Irenaeus, and Tertullian started to write about the generation of the Son as if it were an eternal production. Origen went even further, saying that the Son was a "secondary God," inferior to the Father.

Origen's thinking about the Father and the Son helped pave the way for the teachings of Arius (250–336) in Alexandria to gain some acceptance—even though Arius subordinated the Son in ways that Origen never did. Arius taught that Jesus was only a man into whom the Logos came. The Logos, the Son, was the highest and first creation of God. So the Son was not God but a creature.

Theological contemplation and explanation advanced in the next period (300–600) as peace finally came to the church, making it possible for the church to deal with the Arian heresy, as well as other Christological heresies. The Roman persecutions climaxed with an empire-wide persecution under Emperor Diocletian in the early fourth century. The persecutions ended under Emperor Constantine, who had a zeal for promoting the church. With the end of persecutions also came the advance of Arianism and doctrinal division in the church. In 325, Constantine called the first ecumenical council, the Council of Nicaea, to restore unity. Through the influence of Athanasius, secretary and future successor to Alexander, the bishop of Alexandria, the council issued a creed affirming that the Son is "very God of very God" and "of one substance" (*homoousios*) with the Father. However, there were many factions at the council, including Arians, and each had its own interpretation of the Greek word *homoousios*. For the next fifty years, semantic and theological conflict continued. The Macedonian heresy, derived from Arianism, argued that the Holy Spirit was also a created being. Gradually the Alexandrian view of the relationships of the Father, the Son, and the Holy Spirit prevailed as Greek and Latin churchmen discussed and agreed on common Trinitarian language. At the Council of Constantinople (381), the Nicene formula was reasserted and expanded. The majority knew that it was affirming the full and equal deity of both the Son and the Spirit as evidenced by the fact that this council specified that the Holy Spirit is "the Lord and Giver of life" and is to be "worshiped and glorified" equally with the Father and the Son.

In subsequent years, orthodox churches assumed the viewpoint of Nicaea and Constantinople, accepting the doctrine of these councils because it reflected what they already believed. Between 399 and 419, Augustine of Hippo wrote an extensive volume on the Trinity to further explain and defend orthodox Trinitarianism in the Latin-speaking churches. The Western churches made one formal change to the Creed of Constantinople at the Synod of Toledo in 589. The Latin word *filioque* ("and the Son") was added at the end of the expression that the Holy Spirit "proceeds from the Father" to indicate that the Holy Spirit also proceeds from the Son. The Greek-speaking Eastern churches resisted this revision to the creed because they believed that it changed the creed without the approval of the whole church and put the Son on the same plane as the Father as a "cause" of the Trinity. The Western churches instituted the change in the Niceno-Constantinopolitan Creed because they wanted to emphasize (against Arianism) the eternal, divine equality of the Son with the Father. The disagreement over this change was a major factor leading to the permanent division of the Eastern church from the Western church in 1054.

What is important to understand is that in the midst of the imperial and ecclesiastical politics of 300–500, the basic motivation behind the church leaders' aim to more clearly explain the doctrine of the Trinity was that they interpret Scripture correctly. Testifying to the influence of Scripture is the fact that the Greek wording of the Nicene Creed was based on the Greek language of 1 Corinthians 8:6, which was the focus of much conflict between the Arian and orthodox bishops. The explanation of the doctrine of the Trinity developed ultimately because these theologians disagreed over the meaning of the Bible. Later on, the major Reformers reaffirmed the wording of what has become known as the Niceno-Constantinopolitan Creed. The Reformation became a revival of belief in the Bible and of the study of it in the original languages. The Reformers would never have affirmed the Niceno-Constantinopolitan Trinitarian doctrine unless they believed that it agreed with Scripture, a sentiment captured in this statement by Martin Luther (1483–1546): "Scripture thus clearly proves that there are three Persons and one God. For I would believe neither the writings of Augustine nor the teachers of the Church unless the New and Old Testaments would clearly show this doctrine of the Trinity."[61]

---

61. Martin Luther, *D. Martin Luthers Werke: Kritische Gesamtausgabe* (Weimar, Germany:, H. Böhlau, 1883), 39II:305, quoted in Paul Althaus, *The Theology of Martin Luther*, trans. Robert C. Schultz (Philadelphia: Fortress, 1966), 199n1.

The Decree of God
Characteristics
Answering Objections

God's decree is his eternal plan, whereby, according to his decretive will and for his glory, he foreordained everything that comes to pass.[62]

Characteristics

The following list features the major characteristics of the decree of God:[63]

1. Single: "the counsel of his will" (Eph. 1:11)
2. Comprehensive: "works all things" (Eph. 1:11), including the ordination of the good actions of people (Eph. 2:10) as well as sinful acts (Prov. 16:4; Acts 2:23; 4:27–28), events that are contingent from a human perspective (Gen. 45:8; 50:20; Prov. 16:33), the means and ends of acts (Ps. 119:89–91; Eph. 1:4; 2 Thess. 2:13), and the length (Job 14:5; Ps. 39:4) and place of a person's life (Acts 17:26)[64]
3. Unconditional and not based on outside influences: "according to the counsel of his will" (Eph. 1:11; see also Acts 2:23; Rom. 8:29–30; Eph. 2:8; 1 Pet. 1:2)
4. Eternal: "who saved us and called us to a holy calling, not because of our works but because of his own purpose and grace, which he gave us in Christ Jesus before the ages began" (2 Tim. 1:9; see also Eph. 1:4)
5. Effectual: "declaring the end from the beginning and from ancient times things not yet done, saying, 'My counsel shall stand, and I will accomplish all my purpose'" (Isa. 46:10; see also Ps. 33:11; Prov. 19:21)
6. Immutable: "he is unchangeable, and who can turn him back?" (Job 23:13–14; see also Ps. 33:11; Isa. 14:24; 46:10; Acts 2:23)
7. Ordaining sin and controlling its effects: "God gave them up . . ." (Rom. 1:24, 26, 28; see also Pss. 78:29; 106:15; Acts 14:16; 17:30; Rom. 3:25)
8. Purpose of the decree: to manifest and bring praise to God's glory (Rom. 11:33–36; Eph. 1:6, 12, 14; Rev. 4:11)

Answering Objections

OBJECTION 1: THE DECREE OF GOD IS CONTRARY TO THE FREE MORAL AGENCY OF MAN

Response: Agents may properly be said to be free so long as their acts are uncoerced. People are free to act within the confines of their nature. Since all men are fallen in Adam, their nature is corrupted by sin, and they are therefore not free to choose righteousness. Nevertheless, they still freely make their moral choices according to their thinking and desires. Those choices arise from a fallen human nature, which is fundamentally opposed to obeying God. So people act freely in their sin and are not coerced by God to act against their nature. God's decree extends to the uncoerced choices of agents free to act within the bounds of their nature (cf., e.g., Gen. 50:19–20; Acts 2:23; 4:27–28).

62. For further discussion of God's decree, see "The Decree of God" in chap. 7 (p. 489).
63. Larry D. Pettegrew, "The Doctrine of God," unpublished notes (Sun Valley, CA: The Master's Seminary, n.d.), 169–71.
64. Berkhof, *Systematic Theology*, 105.

OBJECTION 2: THE DECREE OF GOD
DISCOURAGES HUMAN GOOD WORKS

Response: The decree is not addressed to men "as a rule of action" and cannot be such a rule because the content of the decree is not known until after events have occurred. But God has ordained a rule of life and belief in the Bible, so that man has the guidance available to do righteous deeds. Again, man is free in the decree to do according to his thoughts and desires, and God does not coercively prevent him from doing good. Also, God's decree includes free human choices that are determined by God to bring about his ordained ends:

> Since the decree establishes an interrelation between means and ends, and ends are decreed only as the result of means, they encourage effort instead of discouraging it. Firm belief in the fact that, according to the divine decrees, success will be the reward of toil, is an inducement to courageous and persevering efforts.[65]

In the Bible, there is "a theological distinction between certainty and compulsion" (see Acts 2:23).[66] Just because God has decreed an event, thereby rendering it certain, does not mean that he coerces people to go against their thoughts and desires. As long as there is no coercion in conditions inclining a person to act in a certain way, a human action may be determined by God and be certain to occur, and yet the person may remain free to do as he or she pleases.[67]

OBJECTION 3: THE DECREE OF GOD IS FATALISM

Response: Fatalism is impersonal, is unintelligent, and has no intended ultimate end. In contrast, God's sovereign determination of his decree is the personal act of the God who is perfect wisdom, omniscience, justice, love, and grace. Further, one of the ends of the decree is people being saved from sin and living forever in eternal blessedness. Fatalism allows for no free acts, casting humanity as impersonally coerced by cosmic forces. But the decree of God includes no moral coercion. Fatalism also has no distinction between right and wrong, no moral meaning in the universe. But the decree of God is based on his eternal, perfect righteousness and results in believers living in unsullied moral goodness forever.

OBJECTION 4: THE DECREE OF GOD MAKES GOD
THE CHARGEABLE CAUSE OF SIN

Response: It must be admitted that sin is a part of God's eternal plan, for he works *all* things according the counsel of his will (Eph. 1:11). This includes the greatest sin

---

65. Berkhof, *Systematic Theology*, 107.
66. Pettegrew, "Doctrine of God," 172.
67. Here we affirm the compatabilistic freedom of inclination and reject the libertarian freedom of indifference. For more on compatibilism, see "Compatibilistic Theodicy" below (p. 225). For more on the distinction between the freedom of inclination and the freedom of indifference, see Bruce A. Ware, *God's Greater Glory: The Exalted God of Scripture and the Christian Faith* (Wheaton, IL: Crossway, 2004), 61–95. We note our disagreement with Ware's conception of "compatibilist middle knowledge" elsewhere in this volume but find his discussion of the difference between compatibilist and libertarian freedom to be helpful.

in human history: the murder of the Son of God (cf. Acts 2:22–23; 4:27–28). God did not merely permit the crucifixion; he purposefully and wisely ordained it unto his honor and glory. Similarly, he did not merely allow Joseph's brothers to sell him into slavery in Egypt but *meant* their sinful action for his most wise and holy ends (Gen. 45:5–8; 50:20).

Nevertheless, while God ordains the evil choices of free moral agents, he does not thereby incur blame or wickedness, because he does not directly or efficiently cause any evil. He brings about the evil actions of man through secondary causation according to their own wicked desires. God is absolutely sovereign, and man is entirely responsible for his actions.[68]

Creation[69]

Divine Creation
Fiat Creationism

God's creation is defined as his work by his Word and for his glory in creating the universe out of nothing so that its original condition was without spiritual or physical corruption. The purpose of this discussion is not to set forth apologetic arguments for creationism but to summarize the biblical doctrine of God's work of creation and to set forth the fiat creationist model as the proper interpretation of the biblical creation narrative.

Divine Creation

The following features summarize the main biblical assertions regarding the divine creation of the universe.

THE BEGINNING OF THE UNIVERSE AND TIME

The universe had a beginning, and that beginning began with the first moment of time (Gen. 1:1; Matt. 19:4, 8; Mark 10:6; John 1:1–2; 17:5; Heb. 1:10). Since God created "in the beginning," the beginning must also include time. God began to create in the first moment of time, the beginning of the first day (Gen. 1:5). Genesis 1:1 evidences that God exists outside time and that he is its Creator.

CREATION WAS RAPID AND OUT OF NOTHING

God created the universe in six literal twenty-four-hour days, and he created it by his Word *ex nihilo* ("out of nothing") (Gen. 1:1; Pss. 33:6, 9; 148:5; Isa. 45:18; John 1:3; Acts 4:24; 14:15; 17:24–25; Rom. 4:17; Col. 1:16; Heb. 11:3; Rev. 4:11; 10:6). God created the first physical energy and matter because none existed when he began his creation acts. God is the only cause of the beginning of the universe.

---

68. For further development, see "The Problem of Evil and Theodicy" below (p. 221) and "The Decree of God and the Problem of Evil" in chap. 7 (p. 491).

69 For a supplementary discussion of creation, consult chap. 6, "Man and Sin."

THE UNIVERSE IS DISTINCT FROM AND DEPENDENT ON GOD

The universe was created by God, is distinct from him, yet is dependent on him (Job 12:10; Pss. 104:30; 139:7–10; Isa. 42:5; Jer. 23:24; Acts 17:24–28; Eph. 4:6; Col. 1:15–17; Heb. 1:3). God is greater than what he created.

THE UNIVERSE WAS CREATED BY THE TRIUNE GOD

The God who created the universe is the triune God revealed in the Bible. God the Father initiated the divine work of creation and governed it (1 Cor. 8:6). In submission to the Father as his means, God the Son created the universe (John 1:3; 1 Cor. 8:6; Col. 1:15–17; Heb. 1:10). And the Holy Spirit also participated in the divine work of creating the universe (Gen. 1:2; Job 26:13; 33:4; Ps. 104:30; Isa. 40:12–13). This work was not distributed; rather, each person of the Trinity acted in concert with the other two persons. God the Father is seen as the source; God the Son is seen as the Mediator of the acts of creation; and the Holy Spirit is seen as the agent of these acts. Each person worked fully and in concert with one another in the creation acts.

GOD'S CREATION WAS A FREE ACT

God acted freely in creating (Eph. 1:11; Rev. 4:11). The creation is not necessary to the essence of God. Even the decree of God is not essential to God but is rather a necessary eternal product of God's essence. The creation is dependent on the sovereign decree of God, so the creation is not in itself a necessity for God to be God. But creation is a necessary result of the integration of all that God is (his perfections/essence).

MAN WAS CREATED DIRECTLY, CLIMACTICALLY, AND SPECIALLY

God created Adam and Eve directly and specially as the climax of the divine work of creation (Gen. 2:7, 21–23). Adam was created first "of dust from the ground," and then Eve was formed by God from one of his ribs. They were individual people and were created on the sixth and final day of creation, the culmination of God's work of creation. God created man not from other beings over eons of time but from the ground on the literal sixth day of creation. God created man not from dead animals but directly from the dust of the ground in the image of God (Gen. 1:27). And when God formed Eve out of Adam, they were the first marriage partners and the pattern for all marriages (Gen. 2:24).

MAN WAS CREATED TO RULE THE EARTH

God created Adam and Eve and gave them a command to rule the earth (Gen. 1:27–31). They were God's servants to govern the earth for him.

ALL CREATURES WERE TO REPRODUCE "ACCORDING TO THEIR KINDS"

God created each creature to produce "according to its kind" (Gen. 1:11, 12, 21, 24, 25). As a result, there would be inviolable boundaries in each kind's genetic nature.

ALL THINGS WERE CREATED MATURE

God created all things mature, with the appearance of age. Living things were created ready to reproduce, including plant life (Gen. 1:12), animals (Gen. 1:20–25), and humans (Gen. 1:26–30). Adam and Eve were created ready to be given dominion over the world. Indeed, the entire universe was created with all systems in mature operation. For example, the stars were created with their light already reaching the earth (Gen. 1:14–19).

THE UNIVERSE WAS CREATED "VERY GOOD"

God created completely and perfectly; the universe was "very good" by his standard of perfection for creation (Gen. 1:31). At this point, there was no corruption or death. Evolution of the world is ruled out by this assertion since evolution requires decay and death.

CREATION WAS TO GLORIFY GOD

God created to manifest his glory (Isa. 43:7; 60:21; 61:3; Ezek. 36:21–22; 39:7; Luke 2:14; Rom. 9:17; 11:36; 1 Cor. 15:28; Eph. 1:5–6, 9, 12, 14; 3:9–10; Col. 1:16).[70] God would not have purposed an ultimate end other than himself since he is superior to everything outside himself. Only having his own glory as his primary purpose would preserve God's independence and sovereignty. Furthermore, no other ultimate purpose would encompass all things, and any lesser purpose would be subject to failure since creatures are finite.

Fiat Creationism

The explanation of creation that best fits the biblical doctrine of divine creation is *fiat creationism*, which contends that God created the universe by fiat (or decree). This view asserts and argues that God created everything in six literal twenty-four-hour days and that he created man as special and distinct from all other creatures in the image of God. That God created directly by his Word is explicitly stated in Scripture (Gen. 1:1–31; 2:7; Ex. 20:11; 31:17; Pss. 33:6; 148:1–6; John 1:3; Col. 1:16; Heb. 1:2; 11:3; Rev. 4:11).

Essential components of fiat creationism include the following tenets:

1. Creation was complete and immediate by the fiat (decree) of the personal, omniscient, omnipotent designer in six literal days.
   a. The primary use of the Hebrew word *yom* ("day") is of a literal twenty-four-hour day, used in this way over 1,900 times out of more than 2,200 Old Testament occurrences.
   b. The Hebrew word *yom* refers to a literal twenty-four-hour day when qualified by a cardinal or ordinal number, as in Genesis 1. There the ordinal numbers are also accompanied by the article, which means literal days are definitely in view.

---

70. Berkhof, *Systematic Theology*, 136.

    c. "Evening" and "morning" normally define a twenty-four-hour day.

    d. The order of creation's six days followed by one day of rest is the basis for the Sabbath law (Ex. 20:8–11; 31:15–17).

2. Creation was intelligently purposeful. Everything was intentionally planned and created by God to achieve his specific goals.

3. Genesis 1:1 summarizes God's acts of creation, while the remainder of the chapter rehearses the details. Genesis 1:1 asserts the entire creation process; 1:2 describes the first stage of creation as "without form and void"; and 1:3–31 unfolds God's subsequent stages of fashioning the original creation.

4. Living organisms were created whole and in well-defined "kinds," which have an inbred adaptability to environmental changes, an adaptability within themselves that does not transcend the bounds of the "kind."

5. Man and woman were created by God as the climax of creation. They were created whole and separately from the rest of creation in the image of God to have dominion over the world (Gen. 1:26–30; 2:7, 18–25; Ps. 8:3–8; Matt. 19:4–5; Luke 3:38; Rom. 5:12–14; 1 Cor. 15:45–49; 2 Cor. 11:3; 1 Tim. 2:12–14; Jude 14). The human body was created from the dust of the ground, but the soul/spirit was created directly by God's immediate act. Man has both material and immaterial aspects.

6. Creation was followed by processes of conservation.

7. The earth is relatively young—perhaps less than ten thousand years old.

8. There is a net decrease in complexity in the created order as time advances.

9. Geologic history is marked by postcreation global catastrophism. The Bible indicates a worldwide flood, which created atmospheric, topographical, and geological upheaval (Genesis 6–8). It involved waters in the sky descending in torrents, waters on and under the earth rising to cover the entire earth up to the height of the highest mountains now on earth, and a breaking apart of the land.

Divine Miracles[71]

The Bible defines a miracle using various words that describe the "effect spectrum" of a miracle. Four different Hebrew words in the Old Testament reveal the various shades of a miracle:

1. *Pele'* has the basic idea of "wonder" (Ex. 15:11; Ps. 77:11).

2. *'Ot* indicates a "sign" that establishes a certainty that was not previously present (Ex. 4:8–9; Num. 14:22; Deut. 4:34).

3. *Geburah* means "strength" or "might" (Pss. 145:4, 11–12; 150:2).

4. *Mophet* basically means "wonder," "sign," or "portent." It is used frequently in conjunction with *'ot*, as in Deuteronomy 4:34; 6:22; Nehemiah 9:10.

The New Testament uses four Greek words that correspond exactly to the Old Testament Hebrew terms:

---

71. This discussion of divine miracles is adapted from Richard Mayhue, *The Healing Promise: Is It Always God's Will to Heal?* (Fearn, Ross-shire, Scotland: Mentor, 1997), 164–73. Used by permission of Christian Focus. For more on the temporary nature and revelatory function of miracles, see "Temporary Gifts (Revelatory/Confirmatory)" in chap. 5, "God the Holy Spirit" (p. 381).

1. *Teras* ("wonder") describes the miracle that startles or imposes. Its extraordinary character indicates the marvel or wonder that the miracle inspires. *Teras* does not occur alone in the New Testament but is always accompanied by *semeion* ("sign"). It forms the Greek counterpart to *mophet* and *pele'* (see Deut. 4:34 in the Septuagint). Christ illustrates the usage in Acts 2:22, as do the apostles in Hebrews 2:4.
2. *Semeion* ("sign") leads a person to something beyond the miracle. It is valuable not for what it is but rather for what it points to. It is the Greek counterpart of *'ot* (see Num. 14:22 in the Septuagint).
3. *Dynamis* ("power" or "miracle") pictures the power behind the act and points to a new and higher power. It corresponds to its Hebrew equivalent, *geburah* (see Ps. 144:4 in the Septuagint).
4. *Ergon* ("work") is used by Jesus in the Gospels to describe distinctive works that no one else did (see John 15:24).

These various elements constitute a biblical miracle. By integrating each descriptive aspect, a miracle from God may be defined as follows:

an observable phenomenon delivered powerfully by God directly or through an authorized agent (*dynamis*), whose extraordinary character captures the immediate attention of the viewer (*teras*), points to something beyond the phenomenon (*semeion*), and is a distinctive work whose source can be attributed to no one else but God (*ergon*).

Boiled down to its core meaning, a miracle can be described as God suspending natural laws and personally reaching into life to rearrange people and their circumstances according to his will.

The outline below describes the various works of God. By using these definitions, some semantic confusion can be avoided.

   I. God's originating works of creation
  II. God's continuing works of providence
     A. Supernatural/miraculous/immediate
       1. Without human agency
       2. With human agency
     B. Natural/unmiraculous/mediate
       1. Explicable/known laws
       2. Inexplicable/unknown laws

All the above works involve God's divine participation at some level. With regard to healing, for example, any physical recovery can be called *divine healing*, but not all healing can be termed *miraculous*.

Miracles, according to the biblical definition, preclude the necessity of secondary means and are not limited by the laws of nature. They involve God's supernatural intervention. Jesus's miracles were never limited; they were never doubted; they were performed in public; they were abundant and instant. Anything that would claim the title *miracle* today should also possess those qualities. Unfortunately, the contemporary church tends to trivialize the idea of miracles by labeling anything out of the ordinary as *miraculous*.

Also, miracles do not automatically produce spirituality in those who witness them. The Israelites, set free from Egyptian slavery by miracles, very quickly degenerated into idol worshipers (Exodus 32), even though the marvelous miracles of God were fresh in their minds. Elijah performed spectacular miracles from God, yet the believing remnant of Israel became so small (seven thousand people) that Elijah thought he was fighting the battle alone (1 Kings 19). After Jesus fed the five thousand and spoke of the miracle's significance, many of his disciples withdrew and would no longer walk with him (John 6:66).

Just the opposite happens today. While first-century witnesses to Christ's authentic miracles walked away from them and from him (John 9:13–22), twenty-first-century Christians seem to be curiously drawn to experiences that are not even worthy to be compared with Christ's miracles.

Divine Providence

Scope
Caution concerning "Laws of Nature"
Divine Preservation of the Universe
Divine Concurrence in All Events
Divine Governance of All Things to Preordained Ends

Divine providence is God's preserving his creation, operating in every event in the world, and directing the things in the universe to his appointed end for them.

Scope

God's providence encompasses the following: the universe as a whole (Ps. 103:19; Dan. 4:35; Eph. 1:11), the physical realm (Job 37:1–13; Pss. 104:14; 135:6; Matt. 5:45), the animals (Ps. 104:21, 28; Matt. 6:26; 10:29), the nations (Job 12:23; Pss. 22:28; 66:7; Acts 17:26), man's birth and life (1 Sam. 1:19–20; Ps. 139:16; Isa. 45:5; Gal. 1:15–16), man's successes and failures (Ps. 75:6–7; Luke 1:52), things apparently accidental or unimportant (Prov. 16:33; Matt. 10:30), protection of his people (Pss. 4:8; 5:12; 63:8; 121:3; Rom. 8:28), provision for his people (Gen. 22:8, 14; Deut. 8:3; Phil. 4:19), answering prayers (1 Sam. 1:9–19; 2 Chron. 33:13; Ps. 65:2; Matt. 7:7; Luke 18:7–8), and judging the wicked (Pss. 7:12–13; 11:6).[72]

An important distinction in studying God's providence is between his general providence and his special/specific providence. God's general providence involves his control of the whole universe (Ps. 103:19; Dan. 2:31–45; Eph. 1:11). His special/specific providence encompasses his control of the details of the universe, including the details of history (Acts 2:23) and the details in the lives of individual people,

---

72. Philip Schaff, *History of the Christian Church* (Grand Rapids, MI: Associated Publishers & Authors, n.d.), 3:168. See also John M. Frame, *Systematic Theology: An Introduction to Christian Belief* (Phillipsburg, NJ: P&R, 2013), 146–70. Frame lists the following under God's universal control: the natural world, human history, individual human life, human decisions, sins, faith, and salvation.

especially the elect (Eph. 1:3–12). Some, such as open theists, are willing to concede that God has general providence but deny that he has specific providence in the lives of people. However, Romans 8:28–30 and Ephesians 1:1–12 show that God's control does extend to the lives of people, particularly his elect.

Caution concerning "Laws of Nature"

Before looking at the major components of God's works of providence, it is important to note that the "laws of nature" are not rules that God is bound to follow. Rather, the laws of nature are what people have perceived to be the normal principles and processes of the universe. Since the Enlightenment of the seventeenth and eighteenth centuries, many have denied the possibility of miracles because miracles violate the laws of nature. In response to such arguments, Scripture teaches that God is the Creator, ruler, and sustainer of nature. The laws of nature are the normal ways in which he upholds the universe. However, these laws are under God's sovereign control, so he has the right and the power to suspend them in working miracles. Since God is a God of order, his operation of the universe has regularity. But the laws of nature should not be regarded as independent of God and closing the universe to his interference. Rather, they should be viewed as the personal means that God ordained to normally operate the universe. And the laws of nature should not be seen as inviolate when producing the same effects in all conditions. Rather, they should be viewed as God's normal way of producing effects in the universe, although God often uses them in differing combinations, resulting in various effects. Thus, one "law" usually does not function by itself; rather, God employs multiple circumstances, combining different "laws" as he sees fit.

Divine Preservation of the Universe[73]

The first major aspect of God's providence is his preservation of the universe. This preservation is the triune God's ever-active work through God the Son in maintaining the things he created with all the characteristics and dynamics he gave them.

God the Son ever "upholds [Gk. *pherō*, 'actively carries'] the universe by the word of his power" (Heb. 1:3). In Christ, "all things hold together [Gk. *synistēmi*, 'stand together']" (Col. 1:17). The apostle Paul said that in God we "live and move and have our being" (Acts 17:28). And Peter said that "the heavens and earth that now exist are stored up for fire, being kept until the day of judgment and destruction of the ungodly" (2 Pet. 3:7). God revealed that he sustains the breath of people and animals, and if he would "gather to himself his spirit and his breath, all flesh would perish together, and man would return to dust" (Job 34:14–15). And when God takes away the breath of animals, "they die and return to their dust" (Ps. 104:29).

God preserves all things according to their own properties as long as he wills them to exist. God preserves what he created; he does not create new atoms, molecules, and

---

73. Grudem, *Systematic Theology*, 316–17. See also Frame, *Systematic Theology*, 174.

energy. God preserves the dynamics of nature in relative stability and predictability, so that science and technology are possible. But God always retains the sovereign right to suspend or end the normal processes of nature. In the future, he will give his people resurrection bodies that will never die, and the current processes of death and decay will no longer exist. The "laws of nature" will be different in the eternal state (Rev. 21:1–22:5).

Divine Concurrence in All Events[74]

The second major aspect of God's providence is his concurrence in all events. God's concurrence is his operation with created things, causing them (whether acting directly or ordaining them through secondary causes), through their properties, to act.

Examples in Scripture abound. Joseph said that God, not his brothers, sent him to Egypt (Gen. 45:5–8). The Lord (Yahweh) said that he would be with Moses's mouth to enable him to speak for God (Ex. 4:11–12). The Lord promised to deliver the enemies to Joshua and the people of Israel—the Israelites still had to attack, but the Lord gave them a great victory (Josh. 11:6). God turns a king's heart to do as God wills (Prov. 21:1), and the Lord turned the heart of the king of Assyria to help the people in building the temple (Ezra 6:22). The Lord gave the people of Israel the ability to acquire wealth (Deut. 8:18). God works in believers "to will and to work for his good pleasure" (Phil. 2:13). God has ordered evil acts, such as when he moved Shimei to curse David (2 Sam. 16:11). He used Assyria to chastise his people (Isa. 10:5). He "put" a lying spirit in the mouths of Ahab's prophets (1 Kings 22:23).

God's concurrence in all events does not implicate him in sin. Men sin according to God's predetermination in his decree but by secondary causes, so God does not directly and effectively cause the acts of sin (Gen. 45:5–8; 50:19–20; Ex. 10:1, 20; 2 Sam. 16:10–11; Isa. 10:5–7; Acts 2:23; 4:27–28). Also, God often restrains sin (Job 1:12; 2:6) or turns an evil act so it has good effects (Gen. 50:20; Ps. 76:10; Acts 3:13).

God's use of second causes (indirect causes) helps explain his concurrence in events. The dynamics of nature do not function by themselves, but God provides their energy in every act (contra deism). Second causes are real, not identical to God's power, or else there is no concurrence of the First Cause (God) with second causes (created things). God does more than simply give the energy to second causes to do something; he directs the actions of second causes to his intended end. In this way, God, not man, is in control. Of course, God can also work by direct causation if he so chooses.

This concurrence is not a cooperative synergism, which would involve partial participation by both God and man. Rather, both are entirely engaged in causing this action. God's will is ultimately behind the act, and he provides energy. But man as the second cause initiates the action in time, in response to God's direct causation or in response to man's own desires as stimulated by circumstances. The concur-

---

74. Berkhof, *Systematic Theology*, 171–75; Frame, *Systematic Theology*, 180–82; Grudem, *Systematic Theology*, 317–22. Grudem argues that God causes the following to act: inanimate creation, animals, seemingly "random" events, affairs of nations, and all aspects of individuals' lives.

rence is initiated by God, and he has the priority in the action, or else man would be independently sovereign in his actions. God's concurrence is logically prior to human action and predetermines everything outside God. The arrangement is never that man initiates an act and that God joins in after the initiation. God provides not energy in general but actual energy to do specific acts in his decree.

God's concurrence is also simultaneous. Man never works independently of God in anything. God always accompanies man with his (God's) effectual will, yet without coercing man to violate his nature in any act. There is a simultaneous working, and the act is the product of both causes (God and man), though in different ways. As Berkhof describes it, "This divine activity accompanies the action of man at every point, but without robbing man in any way of his freedom. The action remains the free act of man, an act for which he is held responsible."[75]

Divine Governance of All Things to Preordained Ends

The third major aspect of God's providence in and over the universe is his divine *governance* of all things. This governance involves God's continual active rule over all things so that, through them, he will accomplish his ultimate purpose of glorifying himself.

God governs as King of the universe.[76] The Bible's main theme is the glorious reign of the triune God, so its central point is the kingdom of God over all creation. God ever retains and exercises sovereign rule in and over all matters in the universe. God is King as well as Father (Matt. 11:25; Acts 17:24; 1 Tim. 1:17; 6:15; Rev. 1:6; 19:6).

God adapts his governance to the nature of the creatures. He ordinarily governs the physical realm by his laws of nature and the mind through the properties of the mind. God mediately governs humans in their moral choices by "moral influences, such as circumstances, motives, instruction, persuasion, and example," and also through direct divine operation by the Holy Spirit in their inner nature.[77]

God's governance extends over all his works—past, present, and future (Pss. 22:28–29; 103:17–19; Dan. 4:34–35; 1 Tim. 6:15). It is detailed, even over the smallest things (Matt. 10:29–31), over things that might commonly be ascribed to chance (Prov. 16:33), and over good and evil acts of men (Phil. 2:13; Acts 14:16). God is the King of Israel who will save and restore his people (Isa. 33:22), and he is King over all nations, having ultimate authority over all the earth (Psalm 47).

The Problem of Evil and Theodicy

Biblical Theodicy
A Biblical Perspective on Evil
Compatibilistic Theodicy
Theodicy in Evangelism

---

75. Berkhof, *Systematic Theology*, 173.
76. For an expanded discussion of God's kingship, see "What Is the Overarching and Unifying Theme of Scripture?" in chap. 1, "Introduction" (p. 42), and see chap. 10, "The Future."
77. Berkhof, *Systematic Theology*, 176. See also Frame, *Systematic Theology*, 172–74; Grudem, *Systematic Theology*, 331–32.

One of the most persistent arguments against the existence of God is based on the existence of physical and moral evil in the world. The question that many unbelievers voice is, if God is real, perfectly good, and omnipotent, how can evil exist? John Frame details the classic "problem of evil" as follows:

> Premise 1: If God were all-powerful, he would be able to prevent evil.
> Premise 2: If God were all-good, he would desire to prevent evil.
> Conclusion: So, if God were both all-powerful and all-good, there would be no evil.
> Premise 3: But there is evil.
> Conclusion: Therefore, there is no all-powerful, all-good God.[78]

The problem of evil has in view both physical evil (e.g., catastrophes, illness, pain, death) and moral evil (sin).

The Christian response to the problem of evil is called theodicy, which comes from the Greek words *theos* and *dikē*. These words combined mean "judicial hearing of God" (for *dikē*, see 2 Thess. 1:9; Jude 7), or the "justification of God." Theodicy involves a vindication of God's justice against the charge that the presence of evil in creation shows him to be unjust, impotent, both, or nonexistent. Theodicy declares that God is all-powerful and all-good even though this might not seem to be the case since evil exists in the creation.

Biblical Theodicy

The only proper theodicy comes from the Bible. When God is the One being charged before the court of human opinion, the Word of God provides a sufficient defense. God provides his own theodicy as he is revealed in his Word. John Frame has set forth principles of establishing God and his Word as the theodicy that is the legitimate response to the problem of evil.[79]

Scripture never assumes that God must explain his actions but rather asserts that he has the right to be trusted. In the Genesis 3 account of the beginning of moral and physical evil, God does not explain the origin of evil in Satan or how Adam and Eve could sin in a perfect world. Adam implied that God was at fault, but God did not defend himself and instead condemned Adam. In the Genesis 22 account of the sacrifice of Isaac, God does not explain how his command to sacrifice Isaac harmonizes with his goodness. According to Exodus 33:19, God will not submit to man's judgment but will show grace and mercy to whomever he wills without needing to explain his actions.

In Job 38–41, after Job's friends have blamed him for being the cause of his suffering, and after Job has expressed his desire to appeal to God, God asks the questions, asserting that man is incapable of understanding God's workings in distributing good and evil. God never explains why Job had to suffer. And the book of Job never explains why Job had to suffer as a response to Satan's charges. Job wanted to ques-

---

78. John M. Frame, *Apologetics to the Glory of God: An Introduction* (Phillipsburg, NJ: P&R, 1994), 150.
79. Frame, *Apologetics to the Glory of God*, 171–90. The next sections largely synthesize Frame's principles of how true biblical theodicy is established.

tion God but was questioned by God. In Ezekiel 18:25–30, God does not defend himself against Israel's charge of injustice but rather condemns Israel for injustice.

In the parable of the laborers in the vineyard in Matthew 20:1–16, the master does not defend himself against the charge of unfairly distributing payment but reverses the charge on the accusers. Divine sovereignty is thus asserted. The master presents his word as reliable. Proper perspective shows the generosity of the master, not any unfairness.

Similarly, in Romans 3:4–6, Paul does not ask questions about God's fairness but rather rebukes such questions by asserting God's rights as the sovereign Lord. In Romans 9:15–20, Paul affirms God's sovereign right to do as he pleases; to question God is disrespectful "back talk." According to Paul, man is disobedient in complaining against God. God is not obligated to explain his actions so as to satisfy human intellect with respect to the problem of evil. God's sovereignty must always be reaffirmed. God's Word is absolutely reliable, and Scripture is clear: God is holy, not unjust.

A Biblical Perspective on Evil

A proper biblical theodicy recognizes God's right to do as he pleases, to not explain himself, to condemn sinners for the evil in the world, and to call sinners to accept him as the remedy for evil. God is just and good because justice and goodness are his very nature. God vindicates his justice by helping people see history from his perspective.

First, God gives perspective on the past. God has always vindicated himself by bringing periods of suffering to an end by an act of grace. He provided Moses to end four hundred years of bondage. And even Moses had to wait forty years for his commission. The wilderness journey was a period of waiting that culminated in entering the Promised Land. Even the journey had periods of waiting for water and food, all ended by God's gracious preservation. The alternation between waiting periods and divine visitations continued in the cycles of bondage and deliverance under the judges and in the divided kingdom. The entire Old Testament period was a period of waiting for fulfillment of the Abrahamic covenant. In the Old Testament period, the length of time involved a dialectic between justice and mercy, which posed a question about the consistency of God's justice and mercy. Justice was predicted, but God also promised to fulfill his promises. Yet this fact raised the question of how God's justice and mercy could be reconciled and harmonized without compromising one or both. God's justice caused questions about his mercy and his mercy about his justice.

Jesus solved the Old Testament problem of evil by harmonizing divine justice and mercy. By his atoning death, he *is* the divine theodicy, vindicating both divine justice and mercy at the cross (Rom. 3:26; 5:8–9, 20–21). Grace reigns through righteousness, which is revealed by the gospel of grace (Rom. 1:17). And so through grace God moves us to praise his righteousness. Many Old Testament saints suffered more severely than any contemporary believers, and yet they died before seeing God's conquest of evil through Christ's cross. They had to trust that God would one day vindicate himself. How much more should new covenant believers trust God to vindicate his justice at Christ's return according to his faithful promises.

Second, God gives perspective on the present. Scripture shows us that God has always used and is now presently using evil to fulfill his purposes for good. The solution of the problem of evil must be theocentric, not anthropocentric. It must not have as its aim to make man happier or freer but to glorify God. The greater-good defense is valid only if the greater good is seen as that which glorifies God more fully than a lesser good. Man's happiness comes only through God-glorifying ways: obedience, self-denial, and suffering while anticipating final glory. When God's greater good of divine glorification is accomplished, believers and all creation (excluding unbelievers) will have their own greater good (Rom. 8:28).

While not giving exhaustive explanations of all evil and while calling for patience in the midst of adversities, Scripture shows some ways in which God uses evil to further his purposes: to display divine grace and justice (Rom. 3:26; 5:8, 20–21; 9:17); to judge evil in the present and future (Matt. 23:35; John 5:14); to redeem through Christ's sufferings (1 Pet. 3:18); to expand gospel witness through the suffering of Christ's people (Col. 1:24); to shock unbelievers, get their attention, and call for a change of heart (Zech. 13:7–9; Luke 13:1–5; John 9); to discipline believers (Heb. 12:3–17); and to vindicate God (Rom. 3:26).

God assures that he always has a purpose for the glory of himself and the good of his people in every event (Rom. 8:28). All the evidence of God using evil for good should encourage his people to trust in faith that currently unexplained evils are divinely purposed for good.

Third, God gives perspective on the future. Scripture promises that God will be finally vindicated and believers fully delivered from evil. In the future, suffering will end in glory for believers, and prosperity will end in judgment for the wicked (Psalm 73; Isaiah 40; Matthew 25; Luke 1:46–55). When God seems unjust in the present, one needs to wait for God's glory and judgment (Hab. 2:2–3) and remember his past acts (Hab. 3:1–18). In the future consummation, no one will doubt God's justice and mercy. Not that he will give a final, exhaustive theoretical theodicy, but when he is revealed to all in the second advent of Christ, all doubts will be transformed into ashamed silence or reverential praise. And when Christ reigns in perfect righteousness, there will be no more problem of evil. If one believes in the final divine vindication, one needs only to trust now that the problem of evil is solved in the mind and sovereign counsel of God. So Scripture responds to the problem of evil not with philosophical reasoning but with divine reassurance of final divine vindication. All Christians should follow this pattern in articulating a theodicy to the world in the present.

Finally, Scripture provides proper perspective by serving as the means by which God gives a new heart to believers. Through the Word of God, the Spirit saves and transforms doubt to faith, humbling people of their prideful autonomy and leading them to give thanks for God's mercy. Through his Word, God gives a new heart by which one sees Christ, believes, and praises (1 Cor. 2:12–13). The change of values given with the new heart lifts one's eyes past the evils of this life to the God who will finally end evil and is even now using it for his purpose. This new perspective is the Christian's theodicy.

Compatibilistic Theodicy

Compatibilism holds that, when properly defined, human free will and divine determinism are complementary ideas; that is, it is possible to accept both without being logically inconsistent. Compatibilism contends that one's will is free within the boundaries of one's nature. Unregenerated human will is free only within the limitations of human finiteness and depravity. Since depraved human nature cannot obey God, fallen humans are free only to sin. Fallen humans sin freely in that they want to sin, doing so without coercion. A biblical theodicy accords with a compatibilistic view of human freedom.[80] A biblical theodicy assumes not that man in his fallenness has the ability to obey God but rather that fallen humans in their corrupted nature choose only what serves their own pleasure and power. The following biblical principles explain how all this can be true:

1. God predetermines all events (Eph. 1:11).
2. The fall resulted in physical difficulties and catastrophes (Isa. 45:7; Rom. 8:20–22).
3. God predetermines sin but makes man accountable for his sin (Acts 2:23; 4:27–28; 14:16).
4. God hardens sinners in sin (Rom. 9:18).
5. God never tempts people to sin (James 1:13).
6. God is never blamed in Scripture for sin or portrayed as enjoying the sin he permits (Ps. 5:4).
7. God never coerces man to sin but ordains that man sin freely and thus be culpable (James 1:14–15).
8. God controls people's sin, working mysteriously through secondary causes (2 Sam. 24:1, 10; 1 Chron. 21:1).
9. God is glorified in his justice when he causes calamities and judges sin (Isa. 45:5–7; Ezek. 28:22; John 9:2–5).
10. God has graciously provided salvation from sin for those who believe in Christ (Rom. 3:24–26).

Theodicy in Evangelism

As Christians engage with unbelievers, they must not think that they can vindicate God by principles outside the Word of God. Rather, they should express God's inspired written theodicy by articulating its principles. These biblical principles can be illustrated by personal accounts, but the principles should be the ground of the conversation. To base theodicy on extrabiblical principles fails to present God as he has ordained in Scripture.

The Bible, being God's theodicy, vindicates all his perfections by what he has

---

80. Pettegrew, "Doctrine of God," 214–17.

revealed about what he has done in the past, is doing in the present, and will do in the future. As one presents God's theodicy, one must not fall into the trap of pandering to what unsaved man thinks is best for his happiness but must seek to call people from sinful self-centeredness to humble, submissive repentance from sin and faith in the true God through Jesus Christ. One must not allow unsaved man to establish human well-being according to human desires, making human thinking the standard for divine justice and mercy.

Glorifying God[81]

> God Directed
> Christian Directed
> Unbeliever Directed

God's glory dominates Scripture. Some have suggested that *glory* is the Bible's unifying theme. That the word appears over four hundred times in Scripture supports this possibility. Since God's glory is complete, though, how can Christians possibly add anything to it? Why does Scripture command believers to give him glory? As 2 Corinthians 3:18 explains, "And we all, with unveiled face, beholding the glory of the Lord, are being transformed into the same image from one degree of glory to another. For this comes from the Lord who is the Spirit."

By analogy God is to Christians as the sun is to the moon. As the sun is the exclusive source of light, so God is the sole source of glory; as the moon reflects light, so believers reflect God's glory. Because God's image in man was fractured by the fall, sinful humans refract God's glory more than they reflect it back to him. But once believers begin to be transformed into the same image at the moment of salvation, they reflect more than they refract. Thus, God's glory is more and more returned to him just as he transmitted it to his beloved ones. That's how Christians can give to God something that he alone possesses and shares with no one (Isa. 42:8; 48:11).

What can one do to glorify God? Three distinct realms can be identified and explored. The glorifying activities of a believer appear under three categories: activities that are (1) God directed, (2) Christian directed, and (3) unbeliever directed.

God Directed

Being God by definition includes being glorious. Many titles reflect God's glory:

1. "The Lord of glory" (1 Cor. 2:8)
2. "The Majestic Glory" (2 Pet. 1:17)
3. "The King of glory" (Ps. 24:7–10)
4. "The Spirit of glory" (1 Pet. 4:14)

Most of God's glory reflected back to him by Christians comes through acts of personal devotion and adoration that are God directed. Listed below are twenty

---

81. This section is adapted from Richard Mayhue, *Seeking God: The Pathway of True Spirituality* (2000; repr., Nashville: Lifeway, 2015), 228–33. Used by permission of the author.

activities of personal worship that glorify God, beginning with those that are God directed and then moving to those that are Christian directed and unbeliever directed.

1. Living with purpose: "So, whether you eat or drink, or whatever you do, do all to the glory of God" (1 Cor. 10:31). The famous eighteenth-century American preacher Jonathan Edwards (1703–1758) applied this thinking to his life by resolving, "That I will do whatsoever I think to be most to God's glory."[82] He framed the picture of life in all respects within God's glory. In imitating this aim, believers can be an answer to Paul's prayer for the Philippians (Phil. 1:9–11).

2. Confessing sins: "Then Joshua said to Achan, 'My son, give glory to the LORD God of Israel and give praise to him. And tell me now what you have done; do not hide it from me'" (Josh. 7:19). To continue in sin is an affront to God's holiness (Rev. 16:9), but to confess one's sins acknowledges God's holiness and brings him glory.

3. Praying expectantly: "Whatever you ask in my name, this I will do, that the Father may be glorified in the Son" (John 14:13). Prayers in Christ's name bring the Father glory. It would be wise to begin praying with Moses's petition, "Please show me your glory" (Ex. 33:18).

4. Living purely: "Flee from sexual immorality. Every other sin a person commits is outside the body, but the sexually immoral person sins against his own body. Or do you not know that your body is a temple of the Holy Spirit within you, whom you have from God? You are not your own, for you were bought with a price. So glorify God in your body" (1 Cor. 6:18–20). It glorifies God to live in the light of his holy character.

5. Submitting to Christ: "Therefore God has highly exalted him and bestowed on him the name that is above every name, so that at the name of Jesus every knee should bow, in heaven and on earth and under the earth, and every tongue confess that Jesus Christ is Lord, to the glory of God the Father" (Phil. 2:9–11).

6. Praising God: "For it is all for your sake, so that as grace extends to more and more people it may increase thanksgiving, to the glory of God" (2 Cor. 4:15). The Samaritan healed of leprosy glorified God with praise, as did the angels at Christ's birth (Luke 2:14; 17:11–19). The mouths of Christians should be filled with the Lord's praise and glory all day long (Ps. 71:8).

7. Obeying God: "By their approval of this service, they will glorify God because of your submission that comes from your confession of the gospel of Christ, and the generosity of your contribution for them and for all others" (2 Cor. 9:13).

8. Growing in faith: "No unbelief made him waver concerning the promise of God, but he grew strong in his faith as he gave glory to God, fully convinced that God was able to do what he had promised" (Rom. 4:20–21).

9. Suffering for Christ's sake: "But let none of you suffer as a murderer or a thief or an evildoer or as a meddler. Yet if anyone suffers as a Christian, let him not be ashamed, but let him glorify God in that name" (1 Pet. 4:15–16). Peter knew of

---

82. Jonathan Edwards, "Resolutions," in *The Works of Jonathan Edwards*, vol. 16, *Letters and Personal Writings*, ed. George S. Claghorn (New Haven, CT: Yale University Press, 1998), 753.

what he wrote, for years earlier Christ had told him by what kind of death he would glorify God (John 21:19).

10. Rejoicing in God: "Glory in his holy name; let the hearts of those who seek the LORD rejoice!" (1 Chron. 16:10).

11. Worshiping God: "All nations you have made shall come and worship before you, O Lord; and shall glorify your name" (Ps. 86:9).

12. Bearing spiritual fruit: "By this my Father is glorified, that you bear much fruit and so prove to be my disciples" (John 15:8).

Christian Directed

The Christian life begins by being right with God, but it does not end there. From the upward direction, we now turn inward to ways that believers can glorify God in the church and among themselves.

13. Proclaiming God's Word: "Finally, brothers, pray for us that the word of the Lord may speed ahead and be honored" (2 Thess. 3:1).

14. Serving God's people: "As each has received a gift, use it to serve one another, as good stewards of God's varied grace: whoever speaks, as one who speaks oracles of God; whoever serves, as one who serves by the strength that God supplies—in order that in everything God may be glorified through Jesus Christ. To him belong glory and dominion forever and ever. Amen" (1 Pet. 4:10–11).

15. Purifying Christ's church: "So that he might present the church to himself in splendor, without spot or wrinkle or any such thing, that she might be holy and without blemish" (Eph. 5:27).

16. Giving sacrificially: "By their approval of this service, they will glorify God because of your submission that comes from your confession of the gospel of Christ, and the generosity of your contribution for them and for all others" (2 Cor. 9:13).

17. Unifying believers: "The glory that you have given me I have given to them, that they may be one even as we are one" (John 17:22). As Christ accepted us, so we are to accept one another, to God's glory (Rom. 15:7).

Unbeliever Directed

First up, then in, and now out. That completes the cycle. Someone may ask, which of these three is most important? All are equally important, but the order in which one glorifies God is crucial. First, one must be fixed on him before ministering to one another. Then, unless one is right in the body of Christ, one can never hope to reach out to the lost with the gospel of Christ.

18. Proclaiming salvation to the lost: "His glory is great through your salvation; splendor and majesty you bestow on him" (Ps. 21:5). The language of "to the praise of his glory" dominates Paul's comments on salvation (Eph. 1:6, 12, 14). And so, the glorification of God characterized the salvation of Paul (Gal. 1:23–24) and Cornelius

(Acts 11:18). Since all have fallen short of God's glory (Rom. 3:23), then to be saved is to have that glory restored.

19. Shining Christ's light: "Let your light shine before others, so that they may see your good works and give glory to your Father who is in heaven" (Matt. 5:16).

20. Spreading God's gospel: "For it is all for your sake, so that as grace extends to more and more people it may increase thanksgiving, to the glory of God" (2 Cor. 4:15). This proved to be Paul's experience on his first missionary journey. When the Gentiles heard the gospel, they rejoiced, glorified God, and believed (Acts 13:48).

Ichabod, which means "no glory" in Hebrew, would be the worst thing imaginable for a believer (1 Sam. 4:21). For God's glory to be absent from a believer or the church is unthinkable. The glory of God needs to be a Christian's consuming quest.

Let the beatitude of the psalmist and the doxology of Paul be practiced now and forevermore:

> Blessed be the LORD, the God of Israel, who alone does wondrous things. Blessed be his glorious name forever; may the whole earth be filled with his glory! Amen and Amen. (Ps. 72:18–19)

> To our God and Father be glory forever and ever. Amen. (Phil. 4:20)

———

Prayer[83]

O Father, the heavens speak clearly of Your incomprehensible glory,
    and their expanse declares repeatedly the work of Your hands:
    "Day to day pours forth speech, and night to night reveals knowledge"
    of You, our awesome Creator—
        and this is speech that everyone can understand.
The sun moves under Your direction in a vast circuit.
Your glory is on display throughout our solar system and beyond,
    from one end of the heavens to the other.
We are in awe of Your incomprehensible power.

And yet even more wonderful to us than Your glorious creation
    is the revelation of Yourself in Scripture:
        Your law, testimony, precepts, commandments, and judgments,
        all of which are perfect, sure, right, pure, clean, and true.
Your Word converts the soul, makes us wise,
    brings us joy, enlightens us,
    and ponders righteousness in us.
    We therefore desire Your Word more than
        gold, finding it sweeter than honey.

83. This prayer is reproduced verbatim from John MacArthur, *At the Throne of Grace: A Book of Prayers* (Eugene, OR: Harvest House, 2011), 52–54. Used by permission of Harvest House.

Precious heavenly Father, all our delight is in You.
The deepest longing of our hearts is to see and to celebrate Your glory.
We will not be truly satisfied
    until we behold Your face in righteousness.
That is why we now pour out our love and worship to You in prayer.
    We trust in Your promises,
    rejoice in Your faithfulness,
    glory in Your goodness,
    hope in Your Word,
    believe in Your Son,
    and rest in Your grace.

Thank You for enabling us to rest in full assurance.
We know that past, present, and future are all in Your care.
We joyfully confess that Your plan is best,
    Your commandments are just,
    Your wisdom is flawless,
    Your power is supreme,
    and all Your ways are perfect.
You are full of lovingkindness, merciful, holy, upright, and gracious—
    the fountain of all that is truly good.
We yield to You as our King and our Redeemer,
    asking that Your will be done in us.

Give us hearts that trust without sighing or complaining
    about what Your providence brings into our lives.
Shower us with mercy and grace, as You always do,
    and may we live in constant gratitude.
Whenever we sin and act in a rebellious way,
    help us to recognize our folly quickly and repent.
Then take away our mournful sorrow and
    emblazon our hearts with gladness.
    Fill our hearts with holy songs of praise.
    Restore us that we might be beacons of Your grace.
We come to worship You, Father, relying on Your forgiveness and power
    that we might enter Your presence
    and be welcomed as true worshipers.
We come in the name of our Savior. Amen.

"Praise, My Soul, the King of Heaven"

Praise, my soul, the King of Heaven,
To His feet your tribute bring.
Ransomed, healed, restored, forgiven,
Evermore His praises sing.
Alleluia! Alleluia!
Praise the everlasting King!

Praise Him for His grace and favor
To our fathers in distress;

Praise Him, still the same as ever,
Slow to chide, and swift to bless.
Alleluia! Alleluia!
Glorious in His faithfulness!

Frail as summer's flow'r we flourish;
Blows the wind and it is gone.
But, while mortals rise and perish,
God endures unchanging on.
Alleluia! Alleluia!
Praise the high Eternal One!

Angels in the height, adore Him;
You behold Him face to face.
Saints triumphant, bow before Him,
Gathered in from every race.
Alleluia! Alleluia!
Praise with us the God of grace!

~Henry F. Lyte (1793–1847)

Bibliography

Primary Systematic Theologies

Bancroft, Emery H. *Christian Theology: Systematic and Biblical*. 2nd ed. Grand Rapids, MI: Zondervan, 1976. 59–94.

*Berkhof, Louis. *Systematic Theology*. 4th ed. Grand Rapids, MI: Eerdmans, 1939. 19–178.

Buswell, James Oliver, Jr. *A Systematic Theology of the Christian Religion*. 2 vols. Grand Rapids, MI: Zondervan, 1962–1963. 1:27–182.

Culver, Robert Duncan. *Systematic Theology: Biblical and Historical*. Fearn, Ross-shire, Scotland: Mentor, 2005. 12–225.

Dabney, Robert Lewis. *Systematic Theology*. 1871. Reprint, Edinburgh: Banner of Truth, 1985. 5–193.

Erickson, Millard J. *Christian Theology*. Grand Rapids, MI: Baker, 1986. 263–432.

*Grudem, Wayne. *Systematic Theology: An Introduction to Biblical Doctrine*. Grand Rapids, MI: Zondervan, 1994. 141–396.

Hodge, Charles. *Systematic Theology*. 3 vols. 1871–1873. Reprint, Grand Rapids, MI: Eerdmans, 1975. 1:189–482, 535–636.

Lewis, Gordon R., and Bruce A. Demarest. *Integrative Theology*. 3 vols. Grand Rapids, MI: Zondervan, 1987–1994. 1:177–335.

Reymond, Robert L. *A New Systematic Theology of the Christian Faith*. Nashville: Thomas Nelson, 1998. 129–414.

Shedd, William G. T. *Dogmatic Theology*. 3 vols. 1889. Reprint, Minneapolis: Klock & Klock, 1979. 1:151–546; 3:89–248.

Strong, August Hopkins. *Systematic Theology: A Compendium Designed for the Use of Theological Students*. Rev. ed. New York: Revell, 1907. 52–110; 243–443.

Swindoll, Charles R., and Roy B. Zuck, eds. *Understanding Christian Theology*. Nashville: Thomas Nelson, 2003. 137–287.

*Thiessen, Henry Clarence. *Introductory Lectures in Systematic Theology*. Grand Rapids, MI: Eerdmans, 1949. 51–75, 119–88.

Turretin, Francis. *Institutes of Elenctic Theology*. 3 vols. Edited by James T. Dennison Jr. Translated by George Musgrove Giger. 1679–1685. Reprint, Phillipsburg, NJ: P&R, 1992–1997. 1:169–538.

*Denotes most helpful.

Specific Works

*Allison, Gregg R. *Historical Theology: An Introduction to Christian Doctrine*. Grand Rapids, MI: Zondervan, 2011.

Ames, William. *The Marrow of Theology*. Translated by John Dykstra Eusden. 3rd ed. 1629. Reprint, Grand Rapids, MI: Baker, 1997.

*Bavinck, Herman. *The Doctrine of God*. Translated by William Hendriksen. 1951. Reprint, Edinburgh: Banner of Truth, 2003.

Beilby, James K., and Paul R. Eddy, eds. *Divine Foreknowledge: Four Views*. Downers Grove, IL: InterVarsity Press, 2001.

Berkhof, Louis. *The History of Christian Doctrines*. 1937. Reprint, Grand Rapids, MI: Baker, 1975.

Bray, Gerald. *God Is Love: A Biblical and Systematic Theology*. Wheaton, IL: Crossway, 2012.

*Calvin, John. *Institutes of the Christian Religion*. Edited by John T. McNeill. Translated by Ford Lewis Battles. 2 vols. Library of Christian Classics. 1559. Reprint, Louisville: Westminster John Knox, 1960.

Carson, D. A. *The Gagging of God: Christianity Confronts Pluralism*. Grand Rapids, MI: Zondervan, 1996.

Charnock, Stephen. *Discourses upon the Existence and Attributes of God*. 2 vols. 1853. Reprint, Grand Rapids, MI: Baker, 1979.

Feinberg, John S. *The Many Faces of Evil: Theological Systems and the Problems of Evil*. Rev. ed. Wheaton, IL: Crossway, 2004.

———. *No One Like Him: The Doctrine of God*. Foundations of Evangelical Theology. Wheaton, IL: Crossway, 2001.

*Frame, John M. *Apologetics to the Glory of God: An Introduction*. Phillipsburg, NJ: P&R, 1994.

———. *The Doctrine of God*. A Theology of Lordship. Phillipsburg, NJ: P&R, 2002.

———. *Systematic Theology: An Introduction to Christian Belief*. Phillipsburg, NJ: P&R, 2013.

Ganssle, Gregory E., ed. *God and Time: Four Views*. Downers Grove, IL: InterVarsity Press, 2001.

Geisler, Norman L. *Creating God in the Image of Man?* Minneapolis: Bethany House, 1997.

*Hannah, John D. *Our Legacy: The History of Christian Doctrine*. Colorado Springs: NavPress, 2001.

Harris, Murray J. *Jesus as God: The New Testament Use of Theos in Reference to Jesus*. Grand Rapids, MI: Baker, 1992.

Helm, Paul. *The Providence of God*. Contours of Christian Theology. Downers Grove, IL: InterVarsity Press, 1994.

Huffman, Douglas S., and Eric L. Johnson. *God under Fire: Modern Scholarship Reinvents God*. Grand Rapids, MI: Zondervan, 2002.

*Letham, Robert. *The Holy Trinity: In Scripture, History, Theology, and Worship*. Phillipsburg, NJ: P&R, 2004.

*MacArthur, John. *The Battle for the Beginning: Creation, Evolution, and the Bible*. Rev. ed. Nashville: Thomas Nelson, 2005.

Packer, J. I. *Knowing God*. Downers Grove, IL: InterVarsity Press, 1973.

Pink, Arthur W. *The Attributes of God*. 1920. Reprint, Grand Rapids, MI: Guardian, 1975.

Piper, John, Justin Taylor, and Paul Kjoss Helseth, eds. *Beyond the Bounds: Open Theism and the Undermining of Biblical Christianity*. Wheaton, IL: Crossway, 2003.

Sexton, Jason S., ed. *Two Views on the Doctrine of the Trinity*. Counterpoint: Bible and Theology. Grand Rapids, MI: Zondervan, 2014.

Toon, Peter. *Our Triune God: A Biblical Portrayal of the Trinity*. Wheaton, IL: Victor, 1996.

*Tozer, A. W. *The Knowledge of the Holy: The Attributes of God: Their Meaning in the Christian Life*. New York: Harper & Brothers, 1961.

Ware, Bruce A. *God's Lesser Glory: The Diminished God of Open Theism*. Wheaton, IL: Crossway, 2000.

———. *Perspectives on the Doctrine of God: 4 Views*. Nashville: B&H Academic, 2008.

Warfield, Benjamin Breckinridge. *Biblical and Theological Studies*. Edited by Samuel G. Craig. 1952. Reprint, Philadelphia: Presbyterian and Reformed, 1968.

*Denotes most helpful.

"All Hail the Power of Jesus' Name"

All hail the pow'r of Jesus' Name!
Let angels prostrate fall;
Bring forth the royal diadem,
And crown Him Lord of all;
Bring forth the royal diadem,
And crown Him Lord of all!

Ye chosen seed of Israel's race,
Ye ransomed from the fall,
Hail Him Who saves you by His grace,
And crown Him Lord of all;
Hail Him Who saves you by His grace,
And crown Him Lord of all!

Let every kindred, every tribe,
On this terrestrial ball,
To Him all majesty ascribe,
And crown Him Lord of all;
To Him all majesty ascribe,
And crown Him Lord of all!

O that with yonder sacred throng
We at His feet may fall!
We'll join the everlasting song,
And crown Him Lord of all;
We'll join the everlasting song,
And crown Him Lord of all!

~Edward Perronet (1726–1792)
adapted by John Rippon (1751–1836)

4

God the Son

Christology

Major Subjects Covered in Chapter 4

Preincarnate Christ

Incarnate Christ

Glorified Christ

The biblical witness concerning the Lord and Savior Jesus Christ is woven like a scarlet thread throughout the entirety of the written Word of God. As the second person of the Godhead, the Savior's person and work constitute the central testimony of all Scripture: "Worship God. For the testimony of Jesus is the spirit of prophecy" (Rev. 19:10).

Preincarnate Christ

Eternity Past
Eternal Son of God
Old Testament Appearances
Old Testament Activities
Old Testament Prophecies

Scripture speaks of both the deity and the humanity of Christ. The person of Christ is fully divine and fully human, a tenet that the early church defended time and time again. Only a fully biblical description can provide an accurate revelation of the existence of the Son of God from eternity past to eternity future. A chronological arrangement of the second person's existence must begin with eternity past.

Eternity Past

TRIUNITY

Throughout the Old and New Testaments, the writers make reference to distinctions between the persons in the Godhead. Father, Son, and Holy Spirit appear as distinct persons with individual operations.[1] In addition, the biblical writers ascribe divine attributes to those persons. Based on biblical evidence, the unprejudiced mind cannot doubt the existence of a plurality of persons in the Godhead without impugning the clarity, the inerrancy, and the inspiration of the Scriptures. Any accurate discussion of the Trinity must begin and end with what the Bible declares.

The revelation John received from God described the second person as being "with God" (John 1:1), a phrase that indicates a distinctly separate identity. In addition, only a distinct person of the Godhead can receive the love of another person of the Godhead (John 17:24). Their distinct identities also appear in the submission of the Son of God to the Father in the economy of redemption (Phil. 2:6–7; Heb. 10:5–7; see "Old Testament Appearances" [p. 240]). They also communicate with each other and about one another: "My Father, if it be possible, let this cup pass from me; nevertheless, not as I will, but as you will" (Matt. 26:39). The Trinitarian baptismal formulation indicates coequality among the three persons of the Trinity: "Go therefore and make disciples of all nations, baptizing them in the name of the Father and of the Son and of the Holy Spirit" (Matt. 28:19).

In affirming this biblical testimony about the triunity of God, William G. T. Shedd identified twelve actions and relations demonstrating that one person in the Godhead may do or experience something personally which is received by another person of the Godhead:

> One divine Person loves another, John 3:35; dwells in another, John 14:10, 11; suffers from another, Zech. 13:7; knows another, Matt. 11:27; addresses another, Heb. 1:8; is the way to another, John 14:6; speaks of another, Luke 3:22; glorifies another, John 17:5; confers with another, Gen. 1:26, 11:7; plans with another, Isa. 9:6; sends another, Gen. 16:7, John 14:26; rewards another, Phil. 2:5–11; Heb. 2:9.[2]

PREEXISTENCE

What kind of existence did Christ have prior to his incarnation? In other words, what was the state of his preexistence in his deity alone before he took on humanity? The second person of the Trinity resided in heaven and came to earth from heaven at the moment of the miraculous conception of his human nature in the womb of the Virgin Mary (Matt. 1:18–25; Luke 1:26–38). He was sent by the first person of the Trinity (God the Father) as a result of God's love for mankind: "For God so loved the world, that he gave his only Son, that whoever believes in him should not perish but have eternal life. For God did not send his Son into the world to condemn the

---

1. This paragraph is adapted from William D. Barrick, "Inspiration and the Trinity," *MSJ* 24, no. 2 (2013): 185–86. Used by permission of *MSJ*.
2. William G. T. Shedd, *Dogmatic Theology* (1889; repr., Minneapolis: Klock & Klock, 1979), 1:279.

world, but in order that the world might be saved through him" (John 3:16–17). The Son came down from heaven (John 3:31) when the Father sent him (John 6:38; 17:3; 1 John 4:9). The arrival of the Son on earth at the incarnation demonstrates that his prior existence was in heaven.

The second person of the Godhead existed before the creation of the universe. Indeed, the Bible identifies him as the Creator: "All things were made through him, and without him was not any thing made that was made" (John 1:3; see 1:10; 1 Cor. 8:6; Col. 1:16–17; Heb. 1:2, 10). The Creator of all things must exist prior to his act of creation—before the existence of all created things. Thus, the Scriptures testify to the fact that he possessed divine glory "before the world existed" (John 17:5). In that preincarnate existence within the Godhead, the second person of the Trinity experienced the first person's love (John 17:24). The persons of the Godhead exercised this divine, communicable attribute among themselves throughout eternity past.

The second person of the Godhead is eternal in his nature and existence. The clearest biblical statement appears in John 1:1: "In the beginning was the Word, and the Word was with God, and the Word was God." Lest the reader think that "the beginning" relates merely to the commencement of creation, the writer of the epistle to the Hebrews clearly contrasts the temporary, finite existence of the creation with the permanent, eternal existence of the Creator, the Son of God himself: "You, Lord, laid the foundation of the earth in the beginning, and the heavens are the work of your hands; they will perish, but you remain; they will all wear out like a garment, like a robe you will roll them up, like a garment they will be changed. But you are the same, and your years will have no end" (Heb. 1:10–12; see Ps. 102:25–27). The Old Testament describes his existence as "from of old, from ancient days" (Mic. 5:2). Isaiah ascribes the titles "Mighty God" and "Everlasting Father" to him and indicates that the incarnation of the God-man consisted of not only the birth of a child but also the giving of a son (Isa. 9:6). Christ has always existed as the Son of God but became a child only at the moment of his miraculous conception.

Eternal Son of God[3]

The eternal existence of the second person raises a question regarding the relationship he had within the Godhead. As the second person of the Trinity (or "the Word," as John 1:1 speaks of him), he existed from eternity past. But did he always in eternity past exist as *Son*? Two major views have arisen: eternal sonship and incarnational sonship.

Hebrews 1:5, at first glance, appears to speak of the Father's begetting the Son as an event that takes place at a point in time: "You are my Son, *today* I have begotten you" and "I *will be* to him a father, and he *shall be* to me a son." That verse presents some very difficult concepts. *Begetting* normally speaks of a person's origin.

---

3. This section is adapted from John MacArthur's 1999 revision of his earlier position on the sonship issue, articulated most clearly in MacArthur, "Reexamining the Eternal Sonship of Christ," *Journal for Biblical Manhood and Womanhood* 6, no. 1 (2001): 21–23. Used by permission of the *Journal for Biblical Manhood and Womanhood*.

Moreover, sons are generally subordinate to their fathers. Therefore, the text appears to speak of something incompatible with an eternal Father-Son relationship, which demands that perfect equality and eternality must exist among the persons of the Trinity. The incarnational sonship line of reasoning concludes that *sonship* indicates the place of voluntary submission to which Christ condescended at his incarnation (see John 5:18; Phil. 2:5–8).

The eternal sonship view rests on the observation that the title *Son of God*, when applied to Christ in Scripture, seems to always speak of his essential deity and absolute equality with God, not his voluntary subordination. The Jewish leaders of Jesus's time understood this. John 5:18 says that they sought the death penalty against Jesus, charging him with blasphemy "because not only was he breaking the Sabbath, but he was even calling God his own Father, making himself equal with God." In that culture, a dignitary's adult son was deemed equal in stature and privilege with his father. The same deference demanded by a king was afforded to his adult son. The son was, after all, of the very same essence as his father, heir to all the father's rights and privileges—and therefore equal in every significant regard. So when Jesus was called "Son of God," it was understood categorically by all as a title of deity, declaring him equal with God and (more significantly) of the same essence as the Father. That is precisely why the Jewish leaders regarded the title *Son of God* the ultimate high blasphemy.

If Jesus's sonship signifies his deity and absolute equality with the Father, it cannot be a title that pertains only to his incarnation. In fact, the main gist of what is meant by sonship (and certainly this would include Jesus's divine essence) must pertain to the eternal attributes of Christ, not merely the humanity he assumed.

The begetting spoken of in Psalm 2 and Hebrews 1 is not an event that takes place in time. Even though, at first glance, Scripture seems to employ terminology with temporal overtones ("today I have begotten you"), the context of Psalm 2:7 surely refers to the eternal "decree" of God. It is reasonable to conclude that the begetting Psalm 2 speaks of is also something that pertains to eternity rather than to a point in time. The temporal language should therefore be understood as figurative, not literal.

Orthodox theologians since the First Council of Constantinople (381) have recognized this, and when dealing with the sonship of Christ, they employ the term *eternal generation*—which is an admittedly difficult expression. In Spurgeon's words, it is "a term that does not convey to us any great meaning; it simply covers up our ignorance."[4] Yet the concept itself is biblical. Scripture refers to Christ as "the only Son from the Father" (John 1:14; see 1:18; 3:16, 18). The Greek word translated "the only Son" (ESV; "only begotten," KJV, NASB) is *monogenēs*. The thrust of its meaning has to do with Christ's utter uniqueness. Literally, it may be rendered "one of a kind"—and yet it also clearly signifies that he is of the very same essence as the Father. Therefore, while *monogenēs* does not explicitly imply generation, it neverthe-

---

4. Charles H. Spurgeon, "Blessing for Blessing" (sermon 2266), in *The Metropolitan Tabernacle Pulpit* (London: Passmore & Alabaster, 1892), 38:352.

less coheres with the biblical concept (cf. Ps. 2:7; John 5:26), for it is precisely his eternal generation that makes Christ the unique Son of the Father.

To say that Christ is "begotten" is itself a difficult concept. Within the realm of creation, the term *begotten* speaks of the origin of one's offspring. The begetting of a son denotes his conception—the point at which he comes into being. Some thus assume that "only begotten" refers to the conception of the human Jesus in the womb of the Virgin Mary. Yet Matthew 1:20 attributes the conception of the incarnate Christ to the Holy Spirit, not to God the Father. The begetting referred to in Psalm 2:7 and John 1:14 clearly refers to something more than the conception of Christ's humanity in Mary's womb.

Indeed, there is another, more vital, significance to the idea of *begetting* than merely the origin of one's offspring. In the design of God, each creature begets offspring "according to its kind" (Gen. 1:11–12, 21–25). The offspring bear the exact likeness of the parent. The fact that a son is generated by the father guarantees that the son shares the same nature as the father. Christ in his deity, however, is not a created being (John 1:1–3). He had no beginning but is as timeless as God himself. Therefore, the "begetting" mentioned in Psalm 2 and its cross-references has nothing to do with the origin of either his deity or his humanity. But it has everything to do with him sharing the same essence as the Father. Expressions like "eternal generation," "only begotten Son," and others pertaining to the filiation of Christ must all be understood as underscoring the absolute oneness of essence between Father and Son. In other words, such expressions aren't intended to evoke the idea of procreation; they are meant to convey the truth about the essential oneness shared by the members of the Trinity.

An incarnational view of Christ's sonship assumes that Scripture employs father-son terminology anthropomorphically—accommodating unfathomable heavenly truths to our finite minds by casting them in human terms. But human father-son relationships are merely earthly pictures of an infinitely greater heavenly reality. In the eternal sonship view, the one true, archetypal father-son relationship exists eternally within the Trinity. All others are simply earthly replicas, imperfect because they are bound up in mankind's finiteness yet illustrating a vital eternal reality.

If Christ's sonship is all about his deity, someone will wonder why this sonship applies only to the second person of the Godhead and not to the third. After all, theologians do not refer to the Holy Spirit as God's Son. Yet the Spirit is also of the same essence as the Father. The full, undiluted, undivided essence of God belongs alike to Father, Son, and Holy Spirit. God is but one essence, yet he exists in three persons. The three persons are coequal, but they are still distinct persons. The chief characteristics that distinguish the persons are wrapped up in the properties suggested by the names Father, Son, and Holy Spirit. Theologians have labeled these properties paternity, filiation, and spiration. That such distinctions are vital to our understanding of the Trinity is clear from Scripture. How to explain them fully remains something of a mystery. In fact, many aspects of these truths may remain forever inscrutable, but this basic understanding of the eternal relationships within the Trinity nonetheless represents the best consensus of Christian understanding over the centuries of church history. The doctrines of Christ's eternal sonship and eternal generation ought therefore to be affirmed, even while acknowledging them as mysteries into which we cannot expect to pry too deeply.[5]

Incarnational sonship viewpoints normally present a case based on either divine declarations concerning the Son at his birth (Mark 1:1; Luke 1:32, 35), his baptism (Matt. 3:17), or his transfiguration (Matt. 17:5), or on the apostolic declaration concerning his resurrection (Acts 13:30–33; Rom. 1:4). In light of the arguments presented above against incarnational sonship, the divine declarations at his baptism and transfiguration merely express the Father's approval and endorsement, not the initial appointment of the second person of the Godhead to the position and role of Son. The reference in Luke 1:35, when taken in light of Luke 3:38, could be the identification of Jesus as the second Adam.[6] The texts mentioning his sonship in the context of or in association with his resurrection do not state that his resurrection "made" him the Son of God. Rather, the resurrection revealed in a powerful fashion that he was the Son of God, not a mere man, and was evidence proving his sonship, rather than installing him as Son. As Schreiner aptly notes, "It is crucial to recall that the one who is exalted as Son of God in power was already the Son."[7] The endorsements at his baptism and transfiguration support such a conclusion, since those occasions preceded Jesus's resurrection but emphatically declare his sonship. What, then, was the purpose of the Father's approving endorsements?

> In calling Jesus His beloved Son, the Father declared not only a relationship of divine nature but a relationship of divine love. They had a relationship of mutual love, commitment, and identification in every way.
>
> In saying, "with whom I am well-pleased," the Father declared His approval with everything the Son was, said, and did. Everything about Jesus was in perfect accord with the Father's will and plan.[8]

Old Testament Appearances[9]

One of the primary occasions of the phenomenon referred to as a *theophany* ("an appearance of God") involves the presence of God at Mount Sinai (Exodus 19). Other instances of divine manifestation arise with the ministry of "the angel of the LORD [Yahweh]" in passages like the following:

1. Genesis 16:7–13: In this passage the narrator (Moses, not Hagar) identifies the messenger of Yahweh as Yahweh: "So she called the name of the LORD who spoke to her" (16:13).

---

5. For further discussion on the eternal generation of the Son, see "Personal Distinctions" in chap. 3 (p. 191).
6. Darrell L. Bock, *Luke 1:1–9:50*, BECNT 3A (Grand Rapids, MI: Baker, 1994), 123.
7. Thomas R. Schreiner, *Romans*, BECNT 6 (Grand Rapids, MI: Baker, 1998), 42.
8. John MacArthur, *Matthew 16–23*, MNTC (Chicago: Moody Press, 1988), 68.
9. This section is adapted from William D. Barrick, "Inspiration and the Trinity," *MSJ* 24, no. 2 (2013): 182–84. Used by permission of *MSJ*.

2. Exodus 3:2–4: Later in history, the messenger of Yahweh appears to Moses in a burning bush at Mount Horeb in the Sinai Desert. The narrator (again, Moses) declares that "God called to him out of the bush" (3:4).

3. Judges 6:11–23: The writer of the book of Judges (not Gideon or the messenger of Yahweh) reports that "the LORD turned to him and said . . ." (6:14).

Such appearances seem to possess one significant feature: all of them, as James Borland puts it, "reveal, at least in a partial manner, something about [God] Himself, or His will, to the recipient."[10] Should we identify the divine person in such appearances as the preincarnate Son of God (i.e., a christophany)? Borland defines these appearances as "those unsought, intermittent and temporary, visible and audible manifestations of God the Son in human form, by which God communicated something to certain conscious human beings on earth prior to the birth of Jesus Christ."[11] When the biblical account associates "the angel of the LORD" with a theophany, "messenger" might provide a better translation than "angel," because this title denotes the function or office of the individual, not his nature. In addition, the Scripture speaks of him as actually being God. He bears the name "LORD," he speaks as God, and he displays divine attributes and authority. Most significantly, however, he receives worship (Matt. 2:2, 11; 14:33; 28:9, 17). Given what John 1:18 says about the Son—that "no one has ever seen God; the only God, who is at the Father's side, he has made him known"—the appearances of God in the Old Testament must have been the Son, not the Father. The phrase "made him known" in Greek (*exēgeomai*) is the word from which we derive the verb *exegete* and its cognate noun, *exegesis*. Literally, the Son of God "exegeted" the Father to mankind.[12]

Old Testament Activities

The works of the second person of the Godhead in the Old Testament include creation, providence, revelation, and judgment. These are acts of deity and demonstrate that he is God. Jesus's works in the New Testament (e.g., resurrection) parallel the works attributed to him in the Old Testament and add significantly to those works.

CREATION

Obviously, this work of the second person of the Godhead takes place in his preincarnate state. Old Testament references to the Creator or Maker do not distinguish the divine person doing the creating from other persons of the Godhead. The New Testament, however, emphatically makes that very distinction:

> All things were made through him, and without him was not any thing made that was made. (John 1:3)

---

10. James A. Borland, *Christ in the Old Testament: Old Testament Appearances of Christ in Human Form*, rev. ed. (Fearn, Ross-shire, Scotland: Mentor, 1999), 24.
11. Borland, *Christ in the Old Testament*, 17.
12. For a more thorough discussion regarding the "angel of the LORD," see "Angel of the Lord" (p. 719) in chap. 8, "Angels."

He was in the world, and the world was made through him, yet the world did not know him. (John 1:10)

For by him all things were created, in heaven and on earth, visible and invisible, whether thrones or dominions or rulers or authorities—all things were created through him and for him. (Col. 1:16)

But in these last days he has spoken to us by his Son, whom he appointed the heir of all things, through whom also he created the world. (Heb. 1:2)

You, Lord, laid the foundation of the earth in the beginning, and the heavens are the work of your hands. (Heb. 1:10)

The Son's title "the Word" (John 1:1) affirms that God created all things by his spoken word—he spoke all things into existence (see the repetition of "God said" in Gen. 1:3, 6, 9, 11, 14, 20, 24, and the direct declarations in Ps. 33:6 in the Old Testament and Heb. 11:3 in the New Testament). Although all three persons of the Godhead participated in some way in creation, the Scripture identifies the Son of God as speaking everything into existence.

PROVIDENCE

Providence involves the care of God over all his creation. It includes the outworking of all his decrees in order that he might ultimately be glorified in all that he has done—that is, in the execution of his programs of kingdom and redemption in all their details. Since the Trinity acted together to create man in the image of God ("Let us make man in our image, after our likeness," Gen. 1:26), the Son of God, the preincarnate Christ, participated in initiating the kingdom program. When mankind rebelled against God after the flood, again the Trinity (including the Son) intervened in world history to direct the outcome (dividing mankind's language and scattering them on the surface of the earth) and to ensure that the divine program in the world would continue to unfold under the direction of all three persons of the Godhead (Gen. 11:7).

The Son of God, as Messiah, acts personally and directly to intervene in world history to establish the kingdom of God on earth (see Dan. 2:31–46; Matt. 23:37–25:46; Rev. 11:15). Christ was involved in the rejection of unbelieving Israel and the establishment of the church—and will yet be involved in the salvation of Israel (Rom. 11:13–36). Christ also works to redeem people and to establish them in every good work (2 Thessalonians 2). In addition, Christ has continually upheld the creation, sustaining and directing it in its role related to God's kingdom program (Heb. 1:3)—more than just preserving all things as in Col. 1:17. And he governed the outworking of God's program among mankind.

One significant aspect of the providence of God relates to his goodness. In the Old Testament, God's goodness emerges in the actions of one who appears to be the second person of the Godhead. Psalm 23 speaks of Yahweh as shepherd—one who cares for and provides. His goodness pursues his people all the days of their lives (Ps. 23:6). Jesus identified himself as that shepherd (John 10:11, "the good shepherd"). Acts 14:17 similarly describes God's goodness in showing that he "did good by giving you rains from heaven and fruitful seasons, satisfying your hearts with food and gladness." Throughout all ages, the work of saving mankind from their sins was the work of the Son of God, whose goodness appeared in that very action of providing for forgiveness of sins:

> But when the goodness and loving kindness of God our Savior appeared, he saved us, not because of works done by us in righteousness, but according to his own mercy, by the washing of regeneration and renewal of the Holy Spirit, whom he poured out on us richly through Jesus Christ our Savior, so that being justified by his grace we might become heirs according to the hope of eternal life. (Titus 3:4–7)

REVELATION[13]

The term *inspiration* identifies the work of God in giving written revelation to mankind. The key biblical text regarding inspiration is 2 Timothy 3:16: "All Scripture is breathed out [inspired] by God and profitable . . ." The phrase "breathed out by God" is but one word in Greek, and that word is an adjective modifying "Scripture." In fact, the next adjective ("profitable") also modifies "Scripture." Biblically speaking, Scripture, not the writers, possesses the quality of being "inspired" or "God-breathed"—just as "profitable" is also a quality of Scripture, not the writers. The point of the word for "God-breathed" is that the Scriptures owe their "origin and contents to the divine breath, the Spirit of God."[14] Thus, Paul by the superintending work of the Spirit of God writes to Timothy that inspiration relates directly to inscripturation (the writing of Scripture).

Each divine person of the Godhead was involved as both the author and the subject of the Scriptures. The second person of the Godhead fulfilled a vital role in the production of the Bible. Old Testament writers speak often of the appearance of God in some manifestation to his people for the purpose of delivering them, leading them, or communicating with them (see "Old Testament Appearances" [p. 240]). These theophanies reveal something about God or his will to those who witness the appearance. Since these events consist of appearances by the Son of God, they reveal the role of the second person of the Godhead in giving revelation leading to the production of Scripture. Jesus himself confirms that the Father sent his word by his messenger:

> For I have not spoken on my own authority, but the Father who sent me has himself given me a commandment—what to say and what to speak. (John 12:49)

> Do you not believe that I am in the Father and the Father is in me? The words that I say to you I do not speak on my own authority, but the Father who dwells in me does his works. (John 14:10)

---

13. This section is adapted from William D. Barrick, "Inspiration and the Trinity," *MSJ* 24, no. 2 (2013): 180–85. Used by permission of *MSJ*.

14. William Hendriksen, *Exposition of the Pastoral Epistles*, NTC (Grand Rapids, MI: Baker, 1957), 302.

I have manifested your name to the people whom you gave me out of the world. Yours they were, and you gave them to me, and they have kept your word. Now they know that everything that you have given me is from you. For I have given them the words that you gave me, and they have received them and have come to know in truth that I came from you; and they have believed that you sent me. (John 17:6–8)

I have given them your word, and the world has hated them because they are not of the world, just as I am not of the world. (John 17:14)

The Son of God appears in both the Old Testament and the New as one speaking to God's people. Thus the Bible reveals that the divine spokesman is the Son of God himself, the very One whom the apostle John describes as "the Word" in the opening to his Gospel: "In the beginning was the Word, and the Word was with God, and the Word was God" (John 1:1). The God who speaks is the second person of the Godhead, the preincarnate Christ—the same One who spoke the universe and all it contains into existence in Genesis 1 (see John 1:2–3, 10). When God imparted revelation to the prophets, the Son of God was often personally present.

Genesis 15:1–16 records how "the word of the LORD" appeared to Abram (15:1). He even brought Abram outside his tent to personally show him the stars (15:5). Then the Lord appeared as a "smoking fire pot and a flaming torch" (15:17) passing between the pieces of the sacrifices which Abram had prepared. The similarity of the smoke and the torch to the pillar of cloud by day and the pillar of fire by night during the exodus of Israel from Egypt is significant, especially in this context, which contains the prophecy about God bringing Israel back up out of Egypt (15:13–14). These personal appearances of a person of the Godhead testify to the role of the "angel of the LORD," the preincarnate Christ in a theophany. Moses's encounter with God in the burning bush at Mount Sinai (Ex. 3:1–12) provides yet another occasion when "the angel of the LORD" (Ex. 3:2; see Acts 7:30, 35) gave revelation by means of his personal presence. Other such incidents are reported in Judges 6:11–18; Isaiah 6 (see John 12:41); and Jeremiah 1:4–10.

The Spirit also plays a key role in the prophets' recording of that revelation. Therefore, the Father sends his messenger (the preincarnate Son) to his people with the divine message, and the Holy Spirit superintends the inscripturation of that message. While this Trinitarian involvement in inspiration seems to faithfully represent core functions for each person, there yet remain some areas of revelation and inscripturation in which their functions overlap. For example, David says, "The Spirit of the LORD speaks by me; his word is on my tongue" (2 Sam. 23:2).

JUDGMENT

The Son of God, as the Son of Man (a messianic title from Dan. 7:13), will judge the wicked and the righteous: "When he comes in his glory, and all the angels with him, then he will sit on his glorious throne. . . . Then he will say to those on his left, 'Depart from me, you cursed, into the eternal fire prepared for the devil and his angels'" (Matt. 25:31, 41). John's Gospel explains the appointment of the Son of God as the Judge of all: "The Father judges no one, but has given all judgment to the Son, that all may honor the Son, just as they honor the Father" (John 5:22–23). Authority to bring judgment rests on the fact that he is the Son of Man (John 5:27). Who better than the one person of the Godhead who is truly human and who has experienced life as a man in a fallen world and remained blameless, without sin? The Son of God came into this world in order to be the Son of Man and to execute judgment (John 9:39). Thus Peter declares that Jesus had commanded his disciples "to preach to the people and to testify that he is the one appointed by God to be judge of the living and the dead" (Acts 10:42). The apostle Paul confirms Jesus's appointment as the Judge by stating, "According to my gospel, God judges the secrets of men by Christ Jesus" (Rom. 2:16).

On the other hand, Jesus says that, in his first coming, he did not judge those who do not obey his words, because he "did not come to judge the world but to save the world" (John 12:47). However, "on the last day," at his second coming, the words of Jesus will judge those who reject him and do not give heed to his words. Jesus did not speak on his own authority; the Father commanded Jesus what to speak (John 12:49). Because he is one with the Father, his judgment is always just (John 5:30) and righteous. Therefore the Father "commands all people everywhere to repent, because he has fixed a day on which he will judge the world in righteousness by a man whom he has appointed; and of this he has given assurance to all by raising him from the dead" (Acts 17:30–31). He who is the Word of God speaks all things into existence and also pronounces judgment—he is Lord at the first as Creator, then Lord as Savior, and Lord at the end as Judge.

Besides judging the unrighteous, Jesus will also sit in an evaluative judgment of believers for the purpose of rewarding them: "For we must all appear before the judgment seat of Christ, so that each one may receive what is due for what he has done in the body, whether good or evil" (2 Cor. 5:10). Elsewhere, Paul speaks of himself standing at Christ's judgment: "Henceforth there is laid up for me the crown of righteousness, which the Lord, the righteous judge, will award to me on that Day, and not only to me but also to all who have loved his appearing" (2 Tim. 4:8).

Old Testament Prophecies

One very good reason to search the Old Testament for prophecies concerning Christ is that Jesus himself declared that the Prophets had spoken about him: "You search the Scriptures because you think that in them you have eternal life; and it is they that bear witness about me" (John 5:39). After his crucifixion and resurrection, Jesus expounded from the Scriptures ("Moses and all the Prophets," Luke 24:27) concerning himself, saying, "These are my words that I spoke to you while I was still with you, that everything written about me in the Law of Moses and the Prophets and the Psalms must be fulfilled" (Luke 24:44). This is the only time in Scripture that the Psalms are included with the Law and the Prophets with reference to the Messiah. Table 4.1 identifies what psalms Jesus might have included in the instruction he gave on the road to Emmaus.

Table 4.1 Christ in the Psalms (Luke 24:44) *

Psalms	New Testament Quote	Significance
2:1–12	Acts 4:25–26; 13:33; Heb. 1:5; 5:5	Incarnation, crucifixion, resurrection
8:3–8	1 Cor. 15:27–28; Eph. 1:22; Heb. 2:5–10	Creation
16:8–11	Acts 2:24–31; 13:35–37	Death, resurrection
22:1–31	Matt. 27:35–46; John 19:23–24; Heb. 2:12; 5:5	Incarnation, crucifixion, resurrection
40:6–8	Heb. 10:5–9	Incarnation
41:9	John 13:18, 21	Betrayal
45:6–7	Heb. 1:8–9	Deity
68:18	Eph. 4:8	Ascension, enthronement
69:20–21, 25	Matt. 27:34, 48; Acts 1:15–20	Betrayal, crucifixion
72:6–17	—	Millennial kingship
78:1–2, 15	Matt. 13:35; 1 Cor. 10:4	Theophany, earthly teaching ministry
89:3–37	Acts 2:30	Millennial kingship
102:25–27	Heb. 1:10–12	Creation, eternality
109:6–19	Acts 1:15–20	Betrayal
110:1–7	Matt. 22:43–45; Acts. 2:33–35; Heb. 1:13; 5:6–10; 6:20; 7:24	Deity, ascension, heavenly priesthood, millennial kingship
118:22–23	Matt. 21:42; Mark 12:10–11; Luke 20:17; Acts 4:8–12; 1 Pet. 2:7	Rejection as Savior
132:12–18	Acts 2:30	Millennial kingship

* Reproduced from John MacArthur, ed., *The MacArthur Study Bible: English Standard Version* (Wheaton, IL: Crossway, 2010), 835. Charts and notes from *The MacArthur Study Bible: English Standard Version* originate with *The MacArthur Study Bible*, copyright © 1997 by Thomas Nelson. Used by permission of Thomas Nelson. www.thomasnelson.com.

The Jews themselves read the Hebrew Bible in such a way that many came to understand its prophecies as direct predictions of the coming Messiah. After Philip had been called to service as a disciple of Jesus (John 1:43), he sought Nathanael in order to tell him that Jesus of Nazareth was truly the one about whom Moses and the prophets had written (John 1:45). That said, it is necessary to inject at this point the recognition of a dangerous trend to read the Lord Jesus Christ into every Old Testament text. This practice ignores the true prophecies, rejects the essential hermeneutic of authorial intent, kills authentic exegesis and exposition, and makes meaningless the Old Testament to its original Jewish readers. Such is not a spiritual approach but rather an attack on the divine meaning of the Old Testament.

So what are the Old Testament prophecies concerning Christ? What did the Old Testament reveal concerning Jesus's coming and his work? Table 4.2 presents 120 of those Old Testament prophecies. A study of the Old Testament prophecies would constitute a large volume all on its own.[15] Nevertheless, a few key examples will suffice for the purposes of this volume.

---

15. For example, see Ernst Wilhelm Hengstenberg, *Christology of the Old Testament and a Commentary on the Messianic Predictions*, Kregel Reprint Library (1847; repr., Grand Rapids, MI: Kregel, 1970).

Table 4.2 Messianic Prophecies of the Old Testament*

Prophecy	Old Testament References	New Testament Fulfillment
Seed of the woman	Gen. 3:15	Gal. 4:4; Heb. 2:14
Through Noah's sons	Gen. 9:27	Luke 3:36
Seed of Abraham	Gen. 12:3	Matt. 1:1; Gal. 3:8, 16
Blessing through Abraham	Gen. 12:3; 28:14	Gal. 3:8, 16; Heb. 6:14
Seed of Isaac	Gen. 17:19; 21:12	Rom. 9:7; Heb. 11:18
Blessing to nations	Gen. 18:18; 22:18; 26:4	Gal. 3:8
Of the tribe of Judah	Gen. 49:10	Rev. 5:5
No bone broken	Ex. 12:46	John 19:36
Blessing to firstborn son	Ex. 13:2	Luke 2:23
No bone broken	Num. 9:12	John 19:36
Serpent in wilderness	Num. 21:8–9	John 3:14–15
A star out of Jacob	Num. 24:17–19	Matt. 2:2; Luke 1:33, 78; Rev. 22:16
King of kings, Lord of lords	Deut. 10:17	1 Tim. 6:15; Rev. 17:14; 19:16
As a prophet	Deut. 18:15, 18–19	John 6:14; 7:40; Acts 3:22–23
Cursed on the tree	Deut. 21:23	Gal. 3:13
The throne of David established forever	2 Sam. 7:12–13, 16, 25–26; 1 Chron. 17:11–14, 23–27; 2 Chron. 21:7	Matt. 19:28; 25:31; Mark 12:37; Luke 1:32; Acts 2:30; 13:22–23; Rom. 1:3; 2 Tim. 2:8; Heb. 1:5, 8; 8:1; 12:2; Rev. 22:1
A promised Redeemer	Job 19:25–27	John 5:28–29; Gal. 4:4–5; Eph. 1:7, 11, 14
Declared to be the Son of God	Ps. 2:1–12	Matt. 3:17; Mark 1:11; Acts 4:25–26; 13:33; Heb. 1:5; 5:5; Rev. 2:26–27; 19:15–16
His resurrection	Ps. 16:8–10	Acts 2:27; 13:35; 26:23
Mocked and insulted	Ps. 22:7–8	Matt. 27:39–43, 45–49
Hands and feet pierced	Ps. 22:16	Matt. 27:31, 35–36
Soldiers cast lots for coat	Ps. 22:18	Mark 15:20, 24–25; Luke 23:34; John 19:23–24
Accused by false witnesses	Ps. 27:12	Matt. 26:59–60; Mark 14:57–58
He commits his spirit	Ps. 31:5	Luke 23:46
No bone broken	Ps. 34:20	John 19:36
Accused by false witnesses	Ps. 35:11	Matt. 26:59–61; Mark 14:57–58
Hated without reason	Ps. 35:19	John 15:24–25
Friends stand afar off	Ps. 38:11	Matt. 27:55; Mark 15:40; Luke 23:49
Came to do the Father's will	Ps. 40:6–8	Heb. 10:5–9
Betrayed by a friend	Ps. 41:9	Matt. 26:47–50; Mark 14:17–21; Luke 22:21–23; John 13:18–19
Known for righteousness	Ps. 45:6–7	Heb. 1:8–9
His resurrection	Ps. 49:15	Mark 16:6
Betrayed by a friend	Ps. 55:12–14	John 13:18

Prophecy	Old Testament References	New Testament Fulfillment
His ascension	Ps. 68:18	Eph. 4:8
Hated without reason	Ps. 69:4	John 15:25
Stung by reproaches	Ps. 69:9	Rom. 15:3
Given gall and vinegar	Ps. 69:21	Matt. 27:34, 48; Mark 15:23; Luke 23:36; John 19:29
Exalted by God	Ps. 72:1–19	Matt. 2:2; Phil. 2:9–11; Hebrews 1–8
He speaks in parables	Ps. 78:2	Matt. 13:34–35
Seed of David exalted	Ps. 89:3–4, 19, 27–29, 35–37	Luke 1:32; Acts 2:30; 13:23; Rom. 1:3; 2 Tim. 2:8
Son of Man comes in glory	Ps. 102:16	Luke 21:27; Rev. 12:5–10
Remains the same	Ps. 102:24–27	Heb. 1:10–12
Prays for his enemies	Ps. 109:4	Luke 23:34
Another to succeed Judas	Ps. 109:7–8	Acts 1:16–26
A priest like Melchizedek	Ps. 110:1–7	Matt. 22:41–45; 26:64; Mark 12:35–37; 16:19; Acts 7:56; Eph. 1:20; Heb. 1:13; 2:8; 5:6; 6:20; 7:21; 8:1; 10:11–13; 12:2
The chief cornerstone	Ps. 118:22–23	Matt. 21:42; Mark 12:10–11; Luke 20:17; John 1:11; Acts 4:11; Eph. 2:20; 1 Pet. 2:4
The King comes in the name of the Lord	Ps. 118:26	Matt. 21:9; 23:39; Mark 11:9; Luke 13:35; 19:38; John 12:13
David's seed to reign	Ps. 132:11; see 2 Sam. 7:12–13, 16, 25–26, 29	Matt. 1:1
Declared to be the Son of God	Prov. 30:4	Matt. 3:17; Mark 14:61–62; Luke 1:35; John 3:13; 9:35–38; Rom. 1:2–4; 2 Pet. 1:17
Repentance for the nations	Isa. 2:2–4	Luke 24:47
Hearts are hardened	Isa. 6:9–10	Matt. 13:14–15; John 12:39–40; Acts 28:25–27
Born of a virgin	Isa. 7:14	Matt. 1:22–23
God with us	Isa. 7:14	Matt. 1:23
A rock of offense	Isa. 8:14–15	Rom. 9:33; 1 Pet. 2:8
Light out of darkness	Isa. 9:1–2	Matt. 4:14–16; Luke 2:32
Full of wisdom and power	Isa. 11:1–10	Luke 2:52; 1 Cor. 1:30
Reigning on the throne of David	Isa. 16:4–5	Luke 1:31–33
The key of David	Isa. 22:21–25	Rev. 3:7
Death swallowed up in victory	Isa. 25:8	1 Cor. 15:54
A stone in Zion	Isa. 28:16	Rom. 9:33; 1 Pet. 2:6
The deaf hear, the blind see	Isa. 29:18	Matt. 11:5; John 9:39
Healing for the needy	Isa. 35:5–6	Matt. 9:30; 11:5; 12:22; 20:34; 21:14; Mark 7:30; John 5:9
Make ready the way of the Lord	Isa. 40:3–5	Matt. 3:3; Mark 1:3; Luke 3:4–5; John 1:23

Prophecy	Old Testament References	New Testament Fulfillment
The Shepherd dies for his sheep	Isa. 40:11	John 10:11; Heb. 13:20; 1 Pet. 2:24–25
The meek servant	Isa. 42:1–6	Matt. 12:17–21
A light to the Gentiles	Isa. 49:6	Luke 2:32; Acts 13:47; 2 Cor. 6:2
Scourged and spat on	Isa. 50:6	Matt. 26:67; 27:26, 30; Mark 14:65; 15:15, 19; Luke 22:63–65; John 19:1
Rejected by his people	Isa. 52:13–53:12	Matt. 27:1–2; Luke 23:1–25
His word not believed	Isa. 53:1	John 12:37–38
Suffered vicariously	Isa. 53:4–5, 11–12	Matt. 8:17; John 11:49–52; Acts 10:43; 13:38–39; Rom. 5:18–19; 1 Cor. 15:3; Eph. 1:7; 1 Pet. 2:24; 1 John 1:7
Silent when accused	Isa. 53:7	Matt. 27:12–14; Mark 15:3–4; Acts 8:28–35; 1 Pet. 2:23
No deceit in his words	Isa. 53:9	1 Pet. 2:22
Buried with the rich	Isa. 53:9	Matt. 27:57–60
Crucified with transgressors	Isa. 53:12	Matt. 27:38; Mark 15:27[-28]; Luke 23:32–34, 39–41; John 19:18
Leader and commander	Isa. 55:4	Acts 5:31; Rev. 1:5
Calling of those who are not Israel	Isa. 55:5	John 10:16; Rom. 9:25–26
Deliverer out of Zion	Isa. 59:20–21	Rom. 11:26–27
Nations walk in the light	Isa. 60:1–3	Luke 2:32
Anointed by the Spirit	Isa. 61:1	Luke 4:18; Acts 10:38
Anointed to preach liberty	Isa. 61:1–2	Luke 4:17–19
Called by a new name	Isa. 62:1–4, 12	Rev. 2:17; 3:12
A vesture dipped in blood	Isa. 63:1–3	Rev. 19:13
The elect shall inherit	Isa. 65:9	Rom. 11:5, 7
New heavens and a new earth	Isa. 65:17–25	2 Pet. 3:13; Rev. 21:1
The Lord our righteousness	Jer. 23:5–6	1 Cor. 1:30; Phil. 3:9
Born a King	Jer. 30:9	John 18:37; Rev. 1:5
Massacre of infants	Jer. 31:15	Matt. 2:17–18
Conceived by the Holy Spirit	Jer. 31:22	Matt. 1:20; Luke 1:35
A new covenant	Jer. 31:31–34	Matt. 26:27–29; Mark 14:22–24; Luke 22:15–20; 1 Cor. 11:25; Heb. 8:8–12; 10:15–17; 12:24; 13:20
A spiritual house	Jer. 33:15–17	John 2:19–21; Eph. 2:20–21; 1 Pet. 2:5
A tree planted by God	Ezek. 17:22–24	Matt. 13:31–32
The humble exalted	Ezek. 21:26–27	Luke 1:52
The good Shepherd	Ezek. 34:23–24	John 10:11
Stone cut without hands	Dan. 2:34–35	Acts 4:10–12
His kingdom triumphant	Dan. 2:44–45	Luke 1:33; 1 Cor. 15:24; Rev. 11:15

Prophecy	Old Testament References	New Testament Fulfillment
The Son of Man coming on the clouds in glory	Dan. 7:13–14	Matt. 24:30; 25:31; 26:64; Mark 14:61–62; Acts 1:9–11; Rev. 1:7
Kingdom for the saints	Dan. 7:27	Luke 1:33; 1 Cor. 15:24; Rev. 11:15
Time of his death	Dan. 9:24–27	Matt. 24:15–21; Luke 3:1
Israel restored	Hos. 3:5	Rom. 11:25–27
Flight into Egypt	Hos. 11:1	Matt. 2:15
Promise of the Spirit	Joel 2:28–32	Acts 2:17–21; Rom. 15:13
The sun darkened	Amos 8:9	Matt. 24:29; Acts 2:20; Rev. 6:12
Restoration of the tabernacle	Amos 9:11–12	Acts 15:16–18
Israel regathered	Mic. 2:12–13	John 10:14, 26
The kingdom established	Mic. 4:1–8	Luke 1:33
Born in Bethlehem	Mic. 5:2	Matt. 2:1; Luke 2:4, 10–11
Earth filled with the knowledge of the glory of the Lord	Hab. 2:14	Rev. 21:23–26
The Lamb on the throne	Zech. 2:10–13	Rev. 5:13; 21:24; 22:1–5
A holy priesthood	Zech. 3:8	1 Pet. 2:5
A heavenly High Priest	Zech. 6:12–13	Heb. 4:14; 8:1–2
The King comes	Zech. 9:9	Matt. 21:5
Triumphal entry	Zech. 9:9	Matt. 21:4–5; Mark 11:9–10; Luke 19:38; John 12:13–15
Sold for pieces of silver	Zech. 11:12–13	Matt. 26:14–15
Money buys potter's field	Zech. 11:12–13	Matt. 27:9–10
Piercing of his body	Zech. 12:10	John 19:34, 37
Shepherd smitten, sheep scattered	Zech. 13:7	Matt. 26:31; John 16:32
Preceded by a forerunner	Mal. 3:1	Matt. 11:10; Mark 1:2; Luke 7:27
Our sins purged	Mal. 3:3	Heb. 1:3
The light of the world	Mal. 4:2–3	Luke 1:78; John 1:9; 12:46; 2 Pet. 1:19; Rev. 2:28; 22:16
The coming of Elijah	Mal. 4:5–6	Matt. 11:14; 17:10–12

* This chart has been reproduced with minor revisions from Ralph P. Martin, "Messiah," in *Holman Illustrated Bible Dictionary*, rev. ed., ed. Chad Brand et al. (Nashville: Holman Bible, 2003), 1112–14. Used by permission of Holman Bible.

THE MESSIAH IS THE SEED OF THE WOMAN (GEN. 3:15)

God's verdict regarding the serpent was not completed with the curse of crawling on its belly in Genesis 3:14. He continued, "I will put enmity between you and the woman, and between your offspring [lit., seed] and her offspring" (Gen. 3:15). The physical, bodily effects of the curse were one thing. Alienation to some other living thing was yet another. The serpent would not only crawl on its belly all its life, it would also enter into a kind of warfare with Eve and her offspring. This warfare would last beyond that one serpent's lifetime. It would involve its own offspring.

What is meant by "your offspring [seed]"? Some have suggested that it is a figure of speech referring to evil men. They believe that Genesis 3:15 depicts a conflict between good men and evil men. Others, however, believe that the meaning is broader than that. They believe that a kingdom of evil exists over which Satan rules. He was the one who empowered the serpent and who was ultimately responsible for what happened. The New Testament confirms such an interpretation in Romans 16:20, "The God of peace will soon crush Satan under your feet," and in Revelation 12:9, "And the great dragon was thrown down, that ancient serpent, who is called the devil and Satan, the deceiver of the whole world."

This interpretation affirms that God intended the offspring of the woman in a broader sense as well. It refers to a kingdom of good over which some descendant of the woman will ultimately become the ruler. That future individual will finally defeat Satan and put an end to the conflict between the two kingdoms: "He shall bruise your head, and you shall bruise his heel'" (Gen. 3:15). As in the case of Jesus addressing Satan through Peter in Matthew 16:23, God addressed Satan through the serpent. Satan will strike at the heel of the woman's offspring. The attack will result in harm but not defeat. The woman's offspring, however, will do more than attack Satan—he will crush his head. The crushing of the head symbolizes total defeat. The New Testament writers understood that the offspring of the woman is the Messiah (see Matt. 1:23; Gal. 4:4; 1 Tim. 2:15; Heb. 2:14; 1 John 3:8). Such an interpretation makes this verse the first messianic prophecy in Scripture.

The rest of Scripture echoes Genesis 3:15 with its two protagonists of the *head* and the *heel* (Ps. 22:16; Luke 24:39–40; Rev. 13:3). A recovered skeleton of at least one first-century crucifixion provides evidence that the Roman executioners placed the nails so that the victim could not tear free. The feet were nailed through the structure of the foot below the ankle in a place that could be identified as closely related to the heel—either nailing each foot to one side of the vertical beam or twisting the lower body sideways to nail both feet with one nail.[16]

The serpent (Satan's representative) deceived Eve. Therefore, a woman will be the mother of the ultimate victor over Satan. In the midst of God's pronouncement of punishment on the serpent, Moses pens a note of hope, a glimpse of God's mercy and grace. An end to the conflict of the ages that started at the fall of man will come. Thus, some Bible scholars have called Genesis 3:15 the *protoevangelium* ("the first gospel"), because it is the earliest prophecy promising a future deliverer.

THE MESSIAH IS THE SON OF GOD (PSALM 2)

Many Bible scholars treat Psalm 2 as merely a reference to one of the Davidic kings, not as a messianic prophecy. However, the New Testament treats the psalm as prophetic and messianic, citing it eighteen times (seven times in the Gospels, five times

---

16. See Peter Connolly, *Living in the Time of Jesus of Nazareth: From Herod the Great to Masada* (Bnei Brak, Israel: Steimatzky, 1983), 51; Matti Friedman, "In a Stone Box, the Only Trace of Crucifixion," *The Times of Israel*, March 26, 2012, http://www.timesofisrael.com/in-a-stone-box-a-rare-trace-of-crucifixion/.

in Revelation, three times in Hebrews, twice in Acts, and once in Philippians). Verses 1–3 reveal a worldwide rebellion against the Lord and their king, God's anointed. In verses 4–6, he confirms his chosen king over the nations, and in verses 7–9, God confirms that his king is also his Son. Then he invites the world to contemplate his Son and to render full obedience to him (2:10–12). No historical king of Judah in the Davidic line ever fulfilled the elements of this psalm. The psalmist depicts God's Son as exercising universal dominion and judgment. Indeed, God demands that world leaders render to his Son spiritual service and fear by their submission to him. Spiritual blessing accrues to those who "take refuge in" God's Son—something never promised for submitting to a human king. The similarity of the individual and his actions in Psalm 2 and Isaiah 9:6 indicates that they are identical individuals.

TRINITARIAN REFERENCES TO MESSIAH

A number of passages in the book of Isaiah identify three distinct, divine persons:

- Isaiah 42:1: "I," "my servant," and "my Spirit"
- Isaiah 48:16: "the Lord God," "I," and "his Spirit"
- Isaiah 61:1: "the Lord," "me," and "the Spirit of the Lord God"
- Isaiah 63:7–10: "the Lord," "the angel of his presence," and "his Holy Spirit"

In these texts the Lord's servant will be sent by the Lord, and the Lord will empower him with his Spirit. Jesus confirms that Isaiah 61:1 speaks of him as the Lord's servant (Luke 4:17–21). Such specificity regarding distinct persons of the Godhead can be traced back to much earlier Old Testament references to multiple divine persons. The following are but a brief sampling of such references:

- Genesis 1:1–2: God and the Spirit of God
- Genesis 19:24: two persons named Yahweh ("the Lord"), one in heaven and one on the earth (see 18:17, 22–33)
- Joshua 5:13–15: "the commander of the Lord's army" and "the Lord" himself

THE MESSIAH IS THE MEDIATOR BETWEEN GOD AND MAN (JOB 33:23–28)

The apostle Paul's identification of Jesus as the God-man serving as the Mediator between God and mankind (1 Tim. 2:5) agrees with what the oldest book in the Old Testament had previously revealed. Job admitted that God was so just or righteous that a person could not be just in his presence (Job 9:2). The question was not how an individual could be justified but how one could have the quality of being just. People are sinners before a holy God. They can have no dealings with their just and holy God. There is only one way a person can communicate effectively with God—by means of a mediator. Job faced a hopeless future unless someone would intervene on his behalf (Job 33:24–28). He was destined for "the pit." Death would eventually take him, and then he would need to appear before the holy God. Already, in Job 19:25, Job had expressed his conviction that his Redeemer lived and would stand on the earth in the latter days. Who is this and how does he qualify as Job's Redeemer?

Job's Redeemer-Mediator must be both God and man (Job 9:32–33; 16:21). According to Job 33:23, that individual is an "angel" ("messenger"), a "mediator," and "one of a thousand" (meaning "one of a kind," like the New Testament's use of *monogenēs*, "only begotten," in texts like John 1:14, 18; 3:16; 1 John 4:9). This individual is able to declare what is right (Job 33:33) and to deliver Job from the pit by means of the "ransom" that this Mediator possesses (Job 33:24). The rest of the picture regarding this Redeemer-Mediator in the book of Job includes the following descriptions:

1. Being the faithful witness in heaven (Job 16:19; see Rev. 1:5)
2. Possessing a record on high (Job 16:19; see Heb. 9:12, 24)
3. Being Redeemer (Job 19:25; 33:24, 28; see Gen. 48:16; Gal. 3:8–22)
4. Being a Mediator (Job 33:23; see 1 Tim. 2:5–6)
5. Being the unique One (Job 33:23; see John 3:16)
6. Being the One who cleanses from sin (Job 9:30–31; see 1 John 1:5–2:2)
7. Being the healer (Job 33:25; see James 5:16; 1 Pet. 2:24)
8. Being the song giver (Job 33:27; see Eph. 5:18–19; Col. 3:16)

THE MESSIAH IS PROPHET, PRIEST, AND KING

The promise of the prophetic office of the Messiah appears first in Deuteronomy 18 in the revelation concerning a prophet "greater than Moses" (Deut. 18:15–22). Prophets like Moses (and other prophets who followed him from Joshua to Malachi) fulfilled a mediatorial office. The people of Israel could not approach or bear the Lord's glorious presence. His spoken revelation also transcended their ability to properly preserve, propagate, and obey what the Lord demanded of them. Deuteronomy 5:23–27 describes this state of affairs in regard to the divine presence and the divine word. Israel needed a mediator who could act on their behalf by communicating with God and by transmitting his words to them. This mediatorial ministry continued to be necessary for subsequent generations with whom God established his covenants.

Revelation and covenant enforcement require a divine representative, a great Prophet. In Acts 3:22–23, the apostle Peter declared that the Messiah fulfilled the prophecy of Deuteronomy 18:15–22. Stephen affirmed the same fulfillment and associated the great prophet with the theophany at the burning bush (Acts 7:35–38; see Ex. 3:2). First-century Jews understood Moses's prophecy as a reference to their Messiah (John 1:21, 25), and the people of Jerusalem recognized Jesus as a prophet (Matt. 21:11; see Luke 7:16; 24:19). Jesus himself identified his own prophetic office when he stated that he must die in Jerusalem, "for it cannot be that a prophet should perish away from Jerusalem" (Luke 13:33).

In the future, that prophet, the high priesthood, and the kingship over God's people will be combined in *one* person. The Old Testament announced that this person would also bear the title "the Branch" (Isa. 4:2; 11:1; Jer. 23:5–6; 33:14–22; Zech. 3:8; 6:12). Zechariah 6:12–13 specifically revealed that this Messiah-Priest-

Table 4.3 "The Branch" in View of the Gospels

The Messianic Title	The Gospels
"David, a righteous Branch, a king" (Jer. 23:5; 33:15)	The Gospel of Matthew: kingly aspect
"My servant the Branch" (Zech. 3:8)	The Gospel of Mark: servant aspect
"The man, whose name is Branch" (Zech. 6:12)	The Gospel of Luke: human aspect
"The Branch of Yahweh" (Isa. 4:2)	The Gospel of John: divine aspect

King would build the temple about which Haggai had prophesied (Hag. 2:1–9). Table 4.3 presents Walter C. Kaiser's compilation of these Old Testament references to "the Branch" in comparison to the individual emphases of the four New Testament Gospels.[17]

Of course, the future High Priest is the Lord Jesus Christ himself. Hebrews 5:5–6 says, "So also Christ did not exalt himself to be made a high priest, but was appointed by him who said to him, 'You are my Son, today I have begotten you'; as he says also in another place, 'You are a priest forever, after the order of Melchizedek.'" Then, in Hebrews 7:14, the writer points out that David and his descendants are of the tribe of Judah: "For it is evident that our Lord was descended from Judah, and in connection with that tribe Moses said nothing about priests." Jesus's high priesthood is greater than any priesthood Israel ever experienced, and his kingship is forever (see Psalm 110). The Messiah is divine, the great Priest-King to come.

Thus, the messianic kingship and priesthood move through biblical revelation and Israel's history until they converge in the Messiah in Zechariah's prophecies. Jesus sacrificed his own blood in a priestly manner and propitiated the wrath of almighty God, which had been stirred up by the sins of his people. Then Jesus rose triumphantly from the grave to sit down on an eternal throne, from which he rules the entire universe evermore and invites everyone to come and bow the knee in faith and submission to him as the great Priest-King. The identification of Jesus's present enthronement has a great bearing on an accurate understanding of his present and his future interventions in this planet's affairs. Jesus today does not sit on the throne of David that was promised to the greater Son of David in 2 Samuel 7:13–16 (cf. Rev. 3:21). Today, Jesus is King over the universal kingdom of God. In the future he will return to sit the throne of David (Matt. 25:31) and reign for one thousand years as the Davidic King over what has been variously termed "the messianic kingdom," "the intermediate kingdom," and "the millennial kingdom" (Rev. 20:1–6). The Old and New Testaments reveal the differences between these two distinct reigns (eternal vs. one thousand years), which have distinct roles (heavenly king vs. earthly king) and distinct purposes (fulfilling the kingdom program of God from creation onward vs. fulfilling the covenants with Israel).[18]

---

17. Walter C. Kaiser Jr. and Tiberius Rata, *Jeremiah and Lamentations*, EEC (Bellingham, WA: Lexham, forthcoming). Used by permission of Lexham Press.

18. Alva J. McClain's *The Greatness of the Kingdom: An Inductive Study of the Kingdom of God* (Chicago: Moody Press, 1968) makes these arguments more cogently and exhaustively than any other volume of Christian theology. See also Paul N. Benware, *Understanding End Times Prophecy: A Comprehensive Approach* (Chicago: Moody Press, 1995), 135–45, 279–89.

Incarnate Christ

Incarnation

DEITY

Jesus was the God-man—truly and fully God as well as truly and fully human. In his incarnation he manifested outwardly his internal divine essence (Gk. *morphē*, "form," Phil. 2:6). Christ possessed the divine glory (John 17:5; see Isa. 42:8). Thus, the writer of Hebrews most emphatically proclaims that Christ was the exact representation of the Deity: "He is the radiance of the glory of God and the exact imprint of his nature, and he upholds the universe by the word of his power" (Heb. 1:3; see Col. 1:15). As God, he is the worthy recipient of worship: "And again, when he brings the firstborn into the world, he says, 'Let all God's angels worship him'" (Heb. 1:6; see Matt. 2:2; 14:33; Phil. 2:10–11). Doxologies in the New Testament even ascribe glory to Christ in a fashion reminiscent of the Old Testament doxology in 1 Chronicles 29:10–11:

> Blessed are you, O LORD, the God of Israel our father, forever and ever. Yours, O LORD, is the greatness and the power and the glory and the victory and the majesty, for all that is in the heavens and in the earth is yours. Yours is the kingdom, O LORD, and you are exalted as head above all. (1 Chron. 29:10–11)

> Now may the God of peace who brought again from the dead our Lord Jesus, the great shepherd of the sheep, by the blood of the eternal covenant, equip you with everything good that you may do his will, working in us that which is pleasing in his sight, through Jesus Christ, to whom be glory forever and ever. Amen. (Heb. 13:20–21)

> . . . that in everything God may be glorified through Jesus Christ. To him belong glory and dominion forever and ever. Amen. (1 Pet. 4:11)

> But grow in the grace and knowledge of our Lord and Savior Jesus Christ. To him be the glory both now and to the day of eternity. Amen. (2 Pet. 3:18)

> Worthy are you, our Lord and God, to receive glory and honor and power, for you created all things, and by your will they existed and were created. (Rev. 4:11)

> Worthy are you to take the scroll and to open its seals, for you were slain, and by your blood you ransomed people for God from every tribe and language and people and nation, and you have made them a kingdom and priests to our God, and they shall reign on the earth. (Rev. 5:9–10)

In other words, Christ ought to be worshiped with worship equal to the worship given to the God of the Old Testament. The second person of the Trinity was not only "with God" at creation, he was himself God (John 1:1–3). By creating the universe, the second person accomplished a work that only God could accomplish (note that the Hebrew word *bara'*, "create," only takes God as its subject).

Prayer to Jesus Christ constitutes yet another evidence for his deity. Jesus instructed his disciples to pray to him (John 14:14; 15:16; 16:23–24). Acts 1:24–25 records that the disciples prayed to Christ for guidance in choosing a replacement for Judas Iscariot. Stephen voiced two prayerful requests to Jesus: "Lord Jesus, receive my spirit," and "Lord, do not hold this sin against them" (Acts 7:59–60). In Damascus, Ananias instructed Saul to be baptized and to call on the name of Jesus (Acts 22:16). The apostle Paul later wrote that "everyone who calls on the name of the Lord will be saved" (Rom. 10:13; see 1 Cor. 1:2). Paul also appealed to Christ to remove the "messenger of Satan" from him (2 Cor. 12:7–8). Indeed, the New Testament closes with a prayer to Christ: "Come, Lord Jesus!" (Rev. 22:20).

Worship includes more than just prayer; it also involves praise. Ephesians 5:18–20 addresses the matter of speaking to "one another in psalms and hymns and spiritual songs, singing and making melody to the Lord with your heart" (Eph. 5:19). The context distinguishes "God the Father" from "our Lord Jesus Christ" (Eph. 5:20; see also 5:21), making Christ the primary referent of "Lord." The song of praise in Revelation 5:9–10 also focuses on the Lord Jesus, who paid the ransom price by his own blood. Two biblical hymns in the early church voice praise to Jesus for who he is and what he has accomplished: Philippians 2:6–11 and 1 Timothy 3:16. These creedal hymns concentrate on the doctrine of Christology. Even the Old Testament contains Christological hymns, in the form of messianic psalms like Psalms 2; 22; 24; 45; 72; and 110. Thus, even pre-Christian Jews sang praise to and about the Messiah in the ancient Psalter, the hymnbook of Israel.

One core concept associated with the believer's recognition of deity consists of what the Scripture terms "the fear of the Lord" (2 Chron. 19:9; Ps. 111:10; see Deut. 6:2; 8:6; 10:12). Jesus Christ is also the object of such fear (Col. 3:22–24; see Eph. 5:21, "out of reverence for Christ"; NASB: "in the fear of Christ"), and that godly fear forms a key section of "the song of the Lamb" (Rev. 15:3):

> Who will not fear, O Lord,
> and glorify your name?
> For you alone are holy.
> All the nations will come
> and worship you,
> for your righteous acts have been revealed. (Rev. 15:4)

The second person of the Godhead also fully exhibits and exercises all the divine characteristics and attributes of God. Table 4.4 provides examples of Jesus Christ's extensive likeness to God.

According to the New Testament writers, Jesus is "the image of the invisible God" (Col. 1:15; see 2 Cor. 4:4; Heb. 1:3). Therefore, anyone who saw Christ could be said to have seen the Father (John 12:45; 14:7–10). In other words, the attributes and characteristics of the Father reside also in the person of his Son.

Table 4.4 Jesus's Divine Likeness

Divine Characteristics or Attributes	Biblical References
Eternality	Mic. 5:2; John 1:1; 8:58; Col. 1:17
Glory	Matt. 16:27; 24:30; Luke 9:32; John 17:5
Grace	John 1:14, 16–17; Romans 1:7; 16:20
Holiness	Luke 4:34; John 6:69; Heb. 7:26
Immutability	Heb. 1:10–12 (cf. Ps. 102:25–27); 13:8
Life	John 1:4; 5:21; 11:25; 14:6; Acts 3:15; Rev. 1:18
Love	Mark 10:21; John 11:3, 5; 14:21, 31; 15:9–11
Mercy	Mark 5:19; 1 Tim. 1:2; Heb. 2:17
Omnipotence	1 Cor. 1:23–24; Heb. 1:2–3
Omnipresence	Matt. 18:20; Eph. 4:10
Omniscience	John 1:47–49; 21:17; Acts 1:24; 1 Cor. 4:5
Righteousness	Acts 3:14; 7:52; 22:14; 2 Pet. 1:1
Self-existence (aseity)	John 1:1–3; Col. 1:16–17; Rev. 1:8, 17–18
Sovereignty	Eph. 1:21; Col. 2:10; 1 Pet. 3:22
Truth	John 1:14, 17; 14:6; Eph. 4:21

The Bible mentions many different titles for the Son of God. However, many on James Large's list,[19] which claims to identify 280 titles and symbols of Christ in the Bible, are mere symbols and are sometimes subjective, typological, or figurative (e.g., Aaron as a human picture of high priestly functions fulfilled in Christ, or "portion" as a reference to the believer inheriting Christ). For the purpose of a Christology, a more theological listing might be divided by a more careful selection of names referring to Jesus's deity and names referring to his humanity. Therefore, titles most likely related to his deity are listed here, while titles appropriately associated with his humanity will be listed under that discussion below (p. 263).

- "Commander of the Lord's army" (Josh. 5:14–15)
- "Wonderful" (Judg. 13:18)
- "The Lord of hosts [or the armies]" (Ps. 24:10; Isa. 6:3, 5 with John 12:41; Isa. 24:23; James 5:4)
- "The Lord," or *adonai* (Ps. 110:1 with Matt. 22:41–45; Rom. 10:9–10; Phil. 2:9–11)
- "Wisdom" / "Wisdom of God" (Proverbs 8; Luke 11:49; 1 Cor. 1:24)
- "Immanuel," or "God with us" (Isa. 7:14; Matt. 1:23)
- "Everlasting Father" (Isa. 9:6)
- "Mighty God" (Isa. 9:6)
- "Wonderful Counselor" (Isa. 9:6)
- "the Lord," or Yahweh (Isa. 40:3 with Mark 1:3; Joel 2:32 with Rom. 10:13)

19. James Large, *Concise Names of Christ* (1888; repr., Chattanooga, TN: AMG, 2009). See also David F. Wells, *The Person of Christ: A Biblical and Historical Analysis of the Incarnation*, Foundations for Faith (Westchester, IL: Crossway, 1984), 67–81.

- "Creator" (of Israel, Isa. 43:15; of souls, 1 Pet. 4:19; and of all things, with this title implied, John 1:3; Col. 1:16; Heb. 1:2)
- "The arm of the Lord" (Isa. 53:1)
- "The breaker" (Mic. 2:13 NASB)
- "The angel [messenger] of the Lord" (see Zech. 1:11–21, where 1:20 identifies the angel as Yahweh while 1:12–13 shows him praying to Yahweh as a distinct person)
- "The bridegroom" (Matt. 9:15)
- "The Son of God" (Mark 1:1; John 3:18; 5:25; Rom. 1:4; Eph. 4:13; Rev. 2:18)
- "The Holy One" (Mark 1:24; John 6:69; Acts 3:14; Rev. 3:7)
- "Son of the Most High" (Luke 1:32)
- "The Word" (John 1:1)
- "The only begotten" (*monogenēs* = unique one; John 1:14, 18; 3:16, 18; 1 John 4:9 NASB)
- "I am" (John 6:35; 8:12; 10:7, 11; 11:25; 14:6; 15:1; cf. "I am," Ex. 3:13–14)
- "The shepherd" (John 10:14; 1 Pet. 2:25; 5:4; see Ps. 23:1)
- "The life" (John 14:6)
- "The truth" (John 14:6)
- "The way" (John 14:6)
- "God" (John 20:28; Rom. 9:5)
- "The Author of life" (Acts 3:15)
- "The power of God" (1 Cor. 1:24)
- "The Lord of glory" (1 Cor. 2:8)
- "The head of the church" (Eph. 4:15; 5:23)
- "The blessed and only Sovereign" (1 Tim. 6:15)
- "King of kings" (1 Tim. 6:15; Rev. 17:14; 19:16; see Dan. 4:37)
- "Lord of lords" (1 Tim. 6:15; Rev. 17:14; 19:16)
- "Savior" (Titus 2:13; 2 Pet. 1:1)
- "The founder of their salvation" (Heb. 2:10)
- "The source of eternal salvation" (Heb. 5:9)
- "The founder and perfecter of our faith" (Heb. 12:2)
- "The Almighty" (Rev. 1:8)
- "The Alpha and the Omega" (Rev. 1:8)
- "The Lord God" (Rev. 1:8)
- "The first and the last" (Rev. 1:17; 2:8)
- "The true one" (Rev. 3:7)
- "Faithful and True" (Rev. 19:11)
- "The beginning and the end" (Rev. 21:6)

KENOSIS[20]

In his incarnation, Christ voluntarily yielded the independent exercise of his divine attributes to the will of his heavenly Father. The biblical basis for this fact is found in Philippians 2:5–7:

---

20. Portions of this section are adapted from John MacArthur, *Philippians*, MNTC (Chicago: Moody Press, 2001), 122–28 (used by permission of Moody Publishers), and from Mike Riccardi, "On the Incarnation: Avoiding Heresy and Pursuing Humility," *The Cripplegate* (blog), June 7, 2013, http://thecripplegate.com/on-the-incarnation-avoiding-heresy-and-pursuing-humility/ (used by permission of the author).

> Have this mind among yourselves, which is yours in Christ Jesus, who, though he was in the form of God, did not count equality with God a thing to be grasped, but emptied himself, by taking the form of a servant, being born in the likeness of men.

Drawing from the Greek word for "emptied himself," *kenoō*, theologians have chosen to refer to this concept as the "kenosis" or "emptying." The apostle Paul refers to a voluntary act involving the incarnation whereby the Son of God took on himself the form of a slave (Gk. *doulos*). The clause "though he was in the form of God" (Phil. 2:6) speaks about Christ's preexistent state, as well as about his humiliation.

The declaration that Christ "was in the form [Gk. *morphē*] of God" (Phil. 2:6) must be understood as a reference to the reality of Christ's deity, just as "taking the form [*morphē*] of a slave" (Phil. 2:7, author's trans.) speaks about the reality of his slavery. "Form" (*morphē*) does not mean that Christ became a slave only in appearance, nor that he was God merely in external appearance. Paul does not use the usual Greek word for "being" here. Instead, the apostle employs another term that stresses the essence of a person's nature—his continuous state or condition. He also uses the Greek word for "form" that specifically denotes the essential, unchanging character of something—what it is in and of itself. The mind of Christ "is revealed in two sublime self-renunciatory acts, the one described as a *kenōsis*, the other as a *tapeinōsis*. In the former He 'emptied himself,' stooping from God to humanity; in the latter He 'humbled himself,' stooping from humanity to death."[21]

Of what did the preincarnate Son empty himself at his incarnation? That question has been answered in several unfortunate ways by what has come to be known as kenotic theology. Named for the "emptying" spoken of in the *kenōsis*, kenotic theologians have misunderstood this concept and have indicated that Christ emptied himself of some aspect of his deity during his incarnation. In some forms, this erroneous teaching claims that Christ retained what they call his essential attributes of deity (e.g., holiness, grace) but surrendered what they call his relative attributes (e.g., omniscience, immutability).

However, it is by definition impossible for the eternal, immutable God to cease to exist as God. This fact concerning the Lord Jesus is confirmed throughout the New Testament. Even in his state of humiliation, the Lord Jesus could say, "I and the Father are one" (John 10:30). Far from a metaphorical expression of unity in purpose or plan, this was a metaphysical statement of the Son's shared essence with the Father. The Jews clearly understood this, for their reaction was to stone Jesus for blasphemy: "You, being a man, make yourself God" (John 10:33). Even as man, he could legitimately claim that to see him was to see the Father (John 14:9), declare that he had authority over all flesh (John 17:2), and receive worship from his disciples (John 20:28). On the Mount of Transfiguration, the incarnate Son's deity was revealed visibly, as he peeled back the veil of his humanity, as it were, and allowed the expression of his own divine essence to shine forth (Matt. 17:2; see

---

21. Alva J. McClain, "The Doctrine of the Kenosis in Philippians 2:5–8," *MSJ* 9, no. 1 (1998): 90.

"Transfiguration" [p. 276]). It is plain, then, that the Son did not empty himself of his deity or his divine attributes in his incarnation.

The question remains, then, of what did he empty himself? Yet this question itself seems to misunderstand Paul's language in Philippians 2. While the verb *kenoō* does mean "to empty," it is used exclusively in a metaphorical sense in the New Testament. It never means "to pour out," as if Jesus were pouring his divine attributes out of himself. If that were Paul's intent, he would have used the word *ekcheō* (e.g., Luke 22:20; John 2:15; Titus 3:6). Instead, *kenoō* means "to make void," "to nullify," or "to make of no effect." Paul employs the term in this sense in Romans 4:14, where he says, "For if those who are of the Law are heirs, faith is made void [*kekenōtai*] and the promise is nullified" (NASB). Yet one does not ask, of what has faith been emptied? Rather, Paul intends to say that if righteousness could come by the law, faith would be nullified—it would come to naught. Similarly, it is the wrong question to ask, of what did Christ empty himself? Christ himself is the object of this emptying; he nullified *himself*. As the King James Version translates it, he "made himself of no reputation" (Phil. 2:7).

The rest of the verse tells how Christ nullified himself in his incarnation: "by taking the form of a servant, being born in the likeness of men" (Phil. 2:7). Christ made himself of no reputation precisely by taking on a human nature. He emptied himself not by pouring out portions of his deity but by adding to himself full and true humanity. His was an emptying by addition, not by subtraction. If he actually surrendered or gave up his divine attributes, then it might suggest that he ceased to be God—but that would result in something at odds with how the Bible identifies him as being fully and truly God (see "Deity" [p. 255]). Yet even in taking on human nature, the Son of God fully possessed his divine nature, attributes, and prerogatives.

What, then, was his humiliation? For the sake of becoming a merciful and faithful high priest, he had to be made like his brothers in every respect (Heb. 2:17). Therefore, while the Son of God fully possessed his divine nature, attributes, and prerogatives, he did not fully express them. They were veiled. At times he did express them, such as when he read people's minds (Matt. 9:4) and worked divine miracles (e.g., Luke 5:3–10). But the Master willingly submitted himself to the life of a slave (Phil. 2:7; cf. 2 Cor. 8:9). He surrendered the preincarnate glories from which he came. He left the worship of saints and angels to be despised and rejected by men (Isa. 53:3), submitting himself to misunderstanding, denials, unbelief, false accusations, and every sort of reviling and persecution. As God the Son, he had every right to exercise his divine prerogatives at will. Yet as the suffering servant of Yahweh, he surrendered himself to the will of the Father in everything (John 5:19, 30). Thus, while he knew Nathanael without having met him (John 1:47) and indeed knew all men (John 2:25), in the humility of his incarnation he did not know the hour of his return (Matt. 24:36). His internal divine glory was still present, though temporarily veiled by him being in the form of a servant. Although he was truly human, he also remained fully divine.

No conceptualization of the kenosis can be consistent with Scripture if that concept makes it impossible for Christ to assert "equality with God" (Phil. 2:6). Though equal with God, the Son of God submitted voluntarily to humanity and death as One who fully possessed the sovereign, free, holy, and loving will to be limited by his choice to obey the Father for the purpose of the program of redemption and the glory of the Godhead.

VIRGIN BIRTH

The announcement of the victorious "offspring" (or seed) of the woman in Genesis 3:15 implies that this individual will not be the offspring of a man (see Gal. 4:4). Thus, the very first messianic prophecy directs attention to the woman, unlike the genealogy of Genesis 5, which lists only fathers. By omitting any relationship to Adam, God suggests that the promised offspring will not partake of Adam's sin. As the first Adam was fathered by God (see Luke 3:38, "Adam, the son of God"), so the second Adam, Jesus Christ, was fathered by God, not by a human male (Matt. 1:18–20). Matthew emphasizes this juxtaposition of the first Adam with the second Adam in the way he introduces his Gospel: "The book of the genealogy of Jesus Christ . . ." (Matt. 1:1). This is the same phraseology found only elsewhere in Genesis 5:1: "This is the book of the generations [or, genealogy] of Adam." In striking fashion, this phraseology introduces

1. a new book of revelation—the Gospel of Matthew as the opening book of the New Testament;
2. a new message—the good news concerning Jesus the Messiah and Savior who is "God with us" (Immanuel; Matt. 1:1, 23);
3. a new creation—a male child born to a virgin (Matt. 1:18–23); and
4. a new beginning—a new *genesis* (the Greek word for "birth" in Matt. 1:18).

In the reign of King Ahaz, king of Judah, the prophet Isaiah received a revelation from God to pass on to the king: "Therefore the Lord himself will give you a sign. Behold, the virgin shall conceive and bear a son, and shall call his name Immanuel" (Isa. 7:14). According to Matthew 1:22–23, that prophecy was fulfilled at the miraculous conception of Jesus in the womb of the Virgin Mary. Some object to this interpretation, insisting on the identification of the "virgin" as Isaiah's wife or another young woman of that time. However, the context itself indicates the accuracy of God's own New Testament commentary:

1. In the immediate context, Isaiah 1–12 prophesies divine judgment against Israel and eventual peace, which the Messiah will bring on the nation and the whole world.
2. Isaiah does not provide any specific contemporary fulfillment—he leaves the "virgin" unidentified.
3. Since Ahaz refuses to ask for a sign for himself and his time (Isa. 7:10–12), God announces a sign for the "house of David," one not limited to Ahaz or his time (Isa. 7:13–14).

4. The word "virgin" (Heb. *'almah*) refers to a young woman who has not had intimate relations with a man (see Gen. 24:43; Ex. 2:8; Song 1:3). The suggestion that *betulah* is the correct Hebrew word for "virgin" seems to be contradicted by the use of the term in Genesis 24:16, which adds "whom no man had known" (Gen. 24:16) in order to make *betulah* ("maiden") refer to a virgin. The term *'almah* requires no such qualification. The Septuagint, the ancient Jewish translation of the Old Testament into Greek, translates the Hebrew term with *parthenos*, the same word appearing in the New Testament at Matthew 1:23.

What is significant about the doctrine of the virgin conception and birth of Jesus? First of all, the integrity of the Gospel record concerning Jesus rests heavily on the truth of the virgin birth. If Matthew and Luke are undependable in their accounts of Mary's pregnancy occurring without male human involvement, then their entire histories of Jesus become suspect. Scientists might claim that a virgin conception is impossible, but the Gospel evidence remains authentic and credible in the light of the consistent testimony of the New Testament writers concerning the sinless human nature of Jesus. In other words, falsehood regarding the biblical claim to the virgin birth severely compromises the inerrancy and infallibility of Scripture. In addition, since Scripture's ultimate author is God himself, that compromise constitutes an attack on the truthfulness and trustworthiness of God.

Second, the virgin birth allows for the preexistence of the divine person and nature. The eternal Son of God existed before the miraculous conception in Mary's womb. The normal human process of conception would have produced a second person, not just a human body and nature. Jesus, as the God-man, is but one person with two natures. Isaiah said it so well: "For to us a child is born, to us a son is given" (Isa. 9:6). The Son of God already existed—as a divine person. An addition of a second personhood to Jesus would necessitate the existence of four persons in the Godhead, rather than preserving the three. And that fourth person, though a sinless human being, would be inferior to the other three persons by the finitude of his humanity. Jesus's humanity is not eternal—it had a beginning. (See "Humanity" [p. 263] for further discussion of the union of both divine and human natures in the person of Jesus.)

Third, without a virgin conception of Jesus, there can be no guarantee of his sinlessness. The descendants of Adam are sinners because Adam sinned; the descendants of Adam die (Rom. 3:23; 5:12–19; 6:23; see Ps. 51:5). Death can occur before an infant knows the difference between right and wrong and before that little one is even capable of understanding the gospel of salvation through Jesus Christ. Infant death necessitates the doctrine of original sin, for there is no death apart from sin. The sinless Jesus can only experience the death of his human body by God placing on him all of the elect's sin and guilt (2 Cor. 5:21).

Fourth, the elimination of the virgin birth would jeopardize the entirety of Jesus's life and ministry and the attendant doctrines. These include his being both truly God and truly man, his sinless life, his miraculous deeds, his truth-filled teaching, his voluntary sacrifice as a substitute for sinners, his bodily resurrection, his bodily ascension, and his future return. If any single doctrine within the biblical teaching concerning Jesus failed, it would lead one to question everything concerning him in the New Testament record.

Lastly, the virgin conception/birth of Jesus ought to be part of the Christian's confession of faith. Jesus's birth gave him a body of flesh. The spirit of antichrist denies that Jesus came in flesh (1 John 4:1–3; 2 John 7). The believer's confession states that Jesus took on himself flesh and blood (Heb. 2:14) in order to put away sin (1 John 3:5). That confession appears in the first line of the early Christian hymn cited by Paul in 1 Timothy 3:16: "He was manifested in the flesh."

HUMANITY

The Bible mentions many different titles for Jesus in his humanity. Titles related to his deity are listed above (see under "Deity" [p. 255]). The names provide insight into the person of Jesus, the work of Jesus, and the way that people identify him and relate to him.

- The "offspring" or seed of the woman (Gen. 3:15; Gal. 4:4)
- "Shiloh" (Gen. 49:10 ESV mg.)
- "Redeemer" (Job 19:25–27; Gal. 3:13)
- "Messiah" or "Anointed" (Heb.) and "Christ" (Gk.) (Ps. 2:2; John 1:41; 4:25; Acts 18:28)
- "The branch" (Isa. 4:2; Jer. 23:5; 33:15; Zech. 3:8; 6:12)
- "Servant" (Isa. 52:13; Acts 4:27)
- "The desire of all nations" (Hag. 2:7 KJV)
- "The sun of righteousness" (Mal. 4:2)
- "Jesus" (Matt. 1:21)
- "A Nazarene" (Matt. 2:23)
- "Son of David" (Matt. 12:23; 21:9; Mark 12:35–37; Rom. 1:1–4)
- "Son of Man" (Mark 2:10; John 12:34; Acts 7:56; Rev. 1:13; see Dan. 7:13)
- "Chosen One" (Luke 9:35; cf. Matt. 12:18; 1 Pet. 1:20)
- "The Lamb of God" / "the Lamb" (John 1:29; Rev. 5:6, 8, 12, 13)
- "Teacher" (John 3:2)
- "Helper" (John 14:16, by implication)
- "Jesus Christ" (Acts 2:38; 3:6)
- "Leader" (Acts 5:31)
- "The firstborn," or preeminent one (Rom. 8:29; Col. 1:15; Heb. 1:6)
- "The last Adam" (1 Cor. 15:45–49; cf. Rom. 5:14; 1 Cor. 15:21–22)
- "The cornerstone" (Eph. 2:20; 1 Pet. 2:4)
- "Mediator" (1 Tim. 2:5–6)
- "Brother" (Heb. 2:11–12, by implication)
- "Apostle" (Heb. 3:1)
- "High priest" (Heb. 3:1)
- "Lawgiver and judge" (James 4:12; see Matt. 28:18)
- "The morning star" (2 Pet. 1:19)
- "Advocate" (1 John 2:1)

- "The faithful witness" (Rev. 1:5; 3:14)
- "The Amen" (Rev. 3:14)
- "The beginning of God's creation" (Rev. 3:14)
- "The Lion of the tribe of Judah" (Rev. 5:5)
- "The Root of David" (Rev. 5:5)
- "The bright morning star" (Rev. 22:16)

The Hypostatic Union. In AD 325, the Council of Nicaea affirmed Scripture's revelation of Jesus being truly God. Then in AD 451, the Council of Chalcedon agreed that Jesus was at the same time human and divine, involving a "hypostatic union" of the two natures without confusion, without change, without division, and without separation.[22] The Apostles' Creed (fifth century AD) thus states, "I believe in . . . Jesus Christ, his only Son, our Lord, who was conceived by the Holy Ghost, born of the Virgin Mary." In other words, the hypostatic union consists of the two natures of Christ in one theanthropic (God-man) person. This union maintains Christ's deity undiminished and his humanity unexalted.

The hypostatic union is distinct from the virgin birth and from the incarnation. The incarnation refers to the whole concept of God manifesting himself in human flesh. The virgin birth constituted the means by which the incarnation was accomplished. As Charles Feinberg once explained, "The hypostatic union is that which was effected and brought into being by the incarnation."[23] The hypostatic union differs from theophanies in that there were multiple, temporary theophanies, while the existence of two natures in Christ since his incarnation is eternal. He is now and forever the God-man.

While the human nature that the Son of God received in his incarnation allows him to experience humanity, he does not exist as two persons. He is but one person with two natures—the divine and the human. Christ's deity effects the individualization (involving character and personality) of his human nature. God the Father prepared Christ's physical human body (Heb. 10:5–7; see Ps. 40:6–8) for the incarnation so that the Son of God might do the will of the Father. Each nature possesses its own will. In John 17:24, Christ's divine will appears in his Trinitarian relationship to the Father before the foundation of the world. But in the garden of Gethsemane, Jesus conforms his human will to the Father's will (Matt. 26:39). This duality within the one person can be seen also in the early youth of Jesus when he astounded the teachers in the temple with his wisdom and knowledge of the Scriptures as he spoke from his divine

---

22. It is useful to reproduce the entirety of the Chalcedonian definition of the hypostatic union: "We, then, following the holy Fathers, all with one consent, teach men to confess one and the same Son, our Lord Jesus Christ, the same perfect in Godhead and also perfect in manhood; truly God and truly man, of a reasonable [rational] soul and body; consubstantial [coessential] with the Father according to the Godhead, and consubstantial with us according to the Manhood; in all things like unto us, without sin; begotten before all ages of the Father according to the Godhead, and in these latter days, for us and for our salvation, born of the Virgin Mary, the Mother of God, according to the Manhood; one and the same Christ, Son, Lord, Only-begotten, to be acknowledged in two natures, inconfusedly, unchangeably, indivisibly, inseparably; the distinction of natures being by no means taken away by the union, but rather the property of each nature being preserved, and concurring in one Person and one Subsistence, not parted or divided into two persons, but one and the same Son, and only begotten, God the Word, the Lord Jesus Christ, as the prophets from the beginning [have declared] concerning him, and the Lord Jesus Christ himself has taught us, and the Creed of the holy Fathers has handed down to us." Philip Schaff, *The Creeds of Christendom*, vol. 2, *The Greek and Latin Creeds* (New York: Harper and Row, 1877), 62–63.

23. Charles Lee Feinberg, "The Hypostatic Union," *BSac* 92, no. 367 (1935): 262.

nature but then submitted his human will to his parents' wishes (Luke 2:47, 51–52). This was a matter not of dueling personalities but of two distinct yet perfect natures.

Humanness involves undergoing, not just encountering, what mankind commonly experiences. From the start of his incarnate life until the end of his earthly journey, Jesus experienced birth (Matt. 2:1), growth (Luke 2:40), exhaustion (John 4:6), sleep (Mark 4:38), hunger (Matt. 4:2; 21:18), thirst (John 4:7; 19:28), anger (Mark 3:5), sorrow (Matt. 26:37), weeping (Luke 19:41; John 11:35), compassion (Matt. 9:36), love (Mark 10:21; John 11:3, 5, 36), joy (Luke 10:21; John 15:11), temptation (Matt. 4:1; Heb. 4:15), prayer (Matt. 14:23; Heb. 5:7), suffering (Matt. 16:21; Luke 22:44; Heb. 2:18), and death (Mark 15:37–39; Luke 23:44–46; John 12:24, 33; Rom. 5:6, 8; Phil. 2:8). He also experienced first what all humans will eventually experience: resurrection (Matt. 17:9; John 2:22; 21:14; Acts 3:15; 1 Cor. 15:20). Jesus was, indeed, truly and completely human—as well as truly and completely God (see "Deity" [p. 255] above).

The writer of the epistle to the Hebrews has most succinctly and beautifully written of the necessity for Christ's humanity and the great blessing accruing to mankind from his humanity: "Therefore he had to be made like his brothers in every respect, so that he might become a merciful and faithful high priest in the service of God, to make propitiation for the sins of the people. For because he himself has suffered when tempted, he is able to help those who are being tempted" (Heb. 2:17–18). He is "Jesus of Nazareth, a man attested to you by God" (Acts 2:22). He is the "one mediator between God and men, the man Christ Jesus" (1 Tim. 2:5). Yes, "Behold, the man!" (John 19:5).

About this marvelous mystery of the hypostatic union of the two natures of Christ, John Walvoord observes that "while the attributes of one nature are never attributed to the other, the attributes of both natures are properly attributed to His person."[24] This fact requires that readers of Scripture rightly discern the so-called communication of properties (Lat. *communicatio idiomatum*) in the biblical record in order to rightly understand who Jesus is and what he has accomplished. That is, whatever can be said of one of Christ's natures can be rightly said of Christ as a whole person. For example, Paul's comment in Acts 20:28 does not mean that the divine nature has blood, for God is spirit (cf. John 4:24). But because "blood" is a property of Christ's human nature and "God" is a property of his divine nature, Paul can say of Jesus that God purchased the church with his own blood. The properties of both natures may be predicated of the one person of Christ. Walvoord helpfully provides seven classifications, summarized below, by which to distinguish between biblical references to the natures and person of Christ:[25]

1. Biblical references to Christ's whole person, in which both natures are essential:

> For to us a child is born,
>   to us a son is given;
> and the government shall be upon his shoulder,

---

24. John F. Walvoord, *Jesus Christ Our Lord* (Chicago: Moody Press, 1969), 116.
25. Walvoord, *Jesus Christ Our Lord*, 117–18.

and his name shall be called
Wonderful Counselor, Mighty God,
    Everlasting Father, Prince of Peace.
Of the increase of his government and of peace
    there will be no end,
on the throne of David and over his kingdom,
    to establish it and to uphold it
with justice and with righteousness
    from this time forth and forevermore.
The zeal of the Lord of hosts will do this. (Isa. 9:6–7)

She will bear a son, and you shall call his name Jesus, for he will save his people from their sins. (Matt. 1:21)

Since then we have a great high priest who has passed through the heavens, Jesus, the Son of God, let us hold fast our confession. (Heb. 4:14)

2. References to the whole person, but the attributes are true of his deity:

But Jesus on his part did not entrust himself to them, because he knew all people and needed no one to bear witness about man, for he himself knew what was in man. (John 2:24–25)

No one has ascended into heaven except he who descended from heaven, the Son of Man. (John 3:13)

But Jesus answered them, "My Father is working until now, and I am working." (John 5:17)

3. References to the whole person, but the attributes are true of his humanity:

Then Jesus was led up by the Spirit into the wilderness to be tempted by the devil. And after fasting forty days and forty nights, he was hungry. (Matt. 4:1–2)

And she gave birth to her firstborn son and wrapped him in swaddling cloths and laid him in a manger, because there was no place for them in the inn. (Luke 2:7)

And the child grew and became strong, filled with wisdom. And the favor of God was upon him. (Luke 2:40)

Jacob's well was there; so Jesus, wearied as he was from his journey, was sitting beside the well. It was about the sixth hour. (John 4:6)

4. Apparent contradiction in references describing the whole person according to an attribute of his divine nature but predicated of his human nature:

Pay careful attention to yourselves and to all the flock, in which the Holy Spirit has made you overseers, to care for the church of God [divine attribute], which he obtained with his own blood [human attribute]. (Acts 20:28)

When I saw him, I fell at his feet as though dead. But he laid his right hand on me, saying, "Fear not, I am the first and the last, and the living one [divine attribute]. I died [human attribute], and behold I am alive forevermore, and I have the keys of Death and Hades." (Rev. 1:17–18)

5. Apparent contradiction in references describing the whole person according to an attribute of his human nature but predicated of his deity:

Then what if you were to see the Son of Man [human attribute] ascending to where he was before [divine attribute]? (John 6:62)

To them belong the patriarchs, and from their race, according to the flesh [human attribute], is the Christ, who is God over all [divine attribute], blessed forever. Amen. (Rom. 9:5)

6. References describing the whole person according to his deity but predicated of both natures:

And he said to him, "Truly, I say to you, today you will be with me in Paradise." (Luke 23:43)

Jesus then took the loaves, and when he had given thanks, he distributed them to those who were seated. So also the fish, as much as they wanted. (John 6:11)

But Jesus, knowing in himself that his disciples were grumbling about this, said to them, "Do you take offense at this?" (John 6:61)

For you have died, and your life is hidden with Christ in God. When Christ who is your life appears, then you also will appear with him in glory. (Col. 3:3–4)

7. References describing the whole person according to his humanity but predicated of both natures:

And about the ninth hour Jesus cried out with a loud voice, saying, "Eli, Eli, lema sabachthani?" that is, "My God, my God, why have you forsaken me?" (Matt. 27:46; God cannot leave or abandon God. In his whole person Jesus is on the cross, yet the Father temporarily abandons him according to his humanity. As the God-man, Jesus dies with respect to his humanity, for the divine nature cannot die.)

And he has given him authority to execute judgment, because he is the Son of Man. (John 5:27)

Thus, a biblical theology of the person and natures of Christ must rest on a careful reading of the Scriptures coupled with a recognition of our limited understanding. The discerning reader will pay close attention to each detail of the biblical text so as to rightly interpret it regarding the theological understanding of who Jesus Christ is and what he has done, is doing, and will do.

Christ's Limited Knowledge. Mark 13:32 presents readers with an issue regarding Christ's self-limited knowledge: "But concerning that day or that hour, no one knows, not even the angels in heaven, nor the Son, but only the Father." Jesus spoke these words during the time of his incarnation (also referred to as his humiliation). After his ressurection, Acts 1:6–7 seems to indicate that Jesus knew the time of the restoration of the kingdom to Israel but would not reveal it at that time to his disciples. The limitation of Christ's knowledge on the time of the restoration does not mean that his declarations concerning the historicity of Old Testament events or the Mosaic authorship of the Pentateuch should also be reconsidered. After all, he fully trusted the Old Testament as God's Word, and his humanity could have derived all such information directly from the Scriptures. Nevertheless, even during the incarnation, as God the Son, Jesus remained omniscient (cf. John 16:30). His limited knowledge in this instance is a result of his voluntary surrender of the independent use of his divine attributes (see "Kenosis" [p. 258]).

ERRONEOUS VIEWS

Erroneous concepts of Jesus arise out of a careless and undiscerning reading of the Bible. Therefore, through such carelessness, compounded by man's fallen nature and the enmity of unbelievers, the person of Christ has come under attack from the very start. In the early church, error concerning the nature and person of Christ arose even in the first century and challenged the Christological orthodoxy of Bible believers. As with counterfeit currency, the best strategy for identifying falsehood comes through a focus on the truth. Studying what the Scriptures say about Jesus Christ exposes the error of those who seek to deny biblical truths or to offer up a counterfeit Christ. A brief consideration of the major Christological heresies merits attention (table 4.5 [p. 272] presents a summary of these heresies).

Ebionism. One of the earliest errors to infect the church insisted on the humanity of Christ to the exclusion of his deity because its proponents denied the preexistence of Christ—a view influenced by first-century Jewish teachings. This heresy became known as Ebionism. Jesus, to the Ebionites, was a great man, a prophet of God, one who was endowed with the Spirit of God and exalted to kingship after his death. Some of the Ebionites accepted Jesus's miraculous conception, but others rejected it.

By the fifth century this viewpoint had left the church. Some adherents probably returned to Judaism, while others capitulated to the biblical viewpoint (or perhaps to another erroneous view popular at the time) and remained in the church. Although the church left this view behind, the Islamic view of Jesus is essentially that of Ebionism, as Heick observes: "The religious syncretism evident in this movement was of great historical significance in that it contributed to the origin and rise of Mohammedanism as the third great monotheistic religion of the world."[26]

---

26. Otto W. Heick, *A History of Christian Thought* (Philadelphia: Fortress, 1965), 1:67.

Gnosticism. As a movement with roots preceding the New Testament church, Gnosticism gradually assimilated Christian elements. It consisted of a second-century eclectic cult combining Greek philosophy, Persian dualism, Judaistic thought, elements of oriental mystery religions, and Christianity. Gnosticism's main tenet echoed Plato's concept of matter being evil and spirit being good. Its proponents believed that a series of emanations had come from God. These emanations were termed *eons*, and each one became progressively more matter and less spirit—thus, more evil and less good. Since the Yahweh of the Old Testament was the creator of all things (just another eon), Gnosticism labeled him *Demiurge*. The Demiurge was a heavenly being who was subordinate to another, greater eon, the Supreme Being. As the creator and the controller of the physical world, the Demiurge was depicted by the Gnostics as antagonistic to that which is spiritual. In Gnostic thought, Christ was either a phantom seeming to appear in a body (see "Docetism" below), or an eon that united with Jesus sometime between his baptism and death on the cross. The Gnostic concept of salvation consisted of a special *gnosis* (or knowledge) given through Christ to only the elite through an intellectual process.

Adoptionism/Modalism. Some in the early church accepted a view holding that God adopted (thus the term *Adoptionism*) the man Jesus as his son at some point following his birth—either at his baptism or his resurrection. Artemon was often associated with this heresy, but little is known about him. Paul of Samosata (third century AD) and Theodotus the Cobbler (fl. ca. AD 190) propagated the viewpoint of the Adoptionists. The Adoptionists can be considered one of the Monarchianist groups, those who denied the Trinity and referred to one God as one ruler or monarch. Monarchianism emphasized the oneness of God—a Unitarian view. Proponents understood the three persons of the Godhead to be merely three different modes of the one God's existence and work. Since they did not believe the Father and the Son to be distinct persons, they spoke of Patripassianism—the notion that God the Father died on the cross of Calvary. Sabellius became an advocate of the Modalist movement in the early third century, and though he was excommunicated in AD 217, the movement arising out of his leadership became known as Sabellianism.

Docetism. The Docetists derive their name from the Greek term *dokeō*, meaning "seem" or "appear." This group took the opposite extreme of the Adoptionists and insisted on the deity of Christ while rejecting his humanity. To the Docetists, material existence is inherently evil—the view proposed by Plato. Therefore, it was impossible for the pure and holy Son of God to take on himself sinful flesh. They believed that the Son of God appeared on earth as an illusion, a kind of theophany. Jesus had no human body and could not suffer or die a real death. Valentinus (fl. ca. AD 136–ca. 165) became a leading personality in this heretical movement. Irenaeus (ca. AD 120–202) opposed Valentinus, writing a five-volume work against the errors of the Docetists. Marcion (ca. AD 85–ca. 160) was another famous member of the Docetist sect, and Tertullian (ca. AD 160–ca. 220) took up the pen to do battle with

Marcion's teachings (AD 207–208). The church father Ignatius (ca. AD 50–ca. 110), bishop of Antioch, insisted on the use of "really" and "truly" as descriptions of the divine and human natures of Christ in contradistinction to the Docetists' use of "apparently" to refer to Christ's humanity.

Arianism. The next heresy to assail the person and work of Christ arose out of the teachings of Arius (AD 250–336), an elder in the church at Alexandria, Egypt. He and his followers assumed that the Son's temporary submission to the will of the Father in the program of redemption involved an eternal inequality between the Father and the Son. Arians viewed Christ as merely a created being, although he was the first and most supreme of all creatures. Christ was not of the *same* substance as God but of a *similar* substance. Thus, they placed Christ in a realm somewhere between God and man as a creature to be worshiped because of the authority God had delegated to him.

The Councils of Nicaea (AD 325) and Constantinople (AD 381) responded to this heresy. The debate centered on the presence or absence of an *iota* ("i") in a single Greek word: *homoiousia* ("similar substance") or *homoousia* ("same substance"). The difference boiled down to whether or not Christ was truly God, and the council declared its conviction from Scripture that Christ was truly and completely God and man. Athanasius (AD 295–373), who later became bishop of Alexandria, rose in defense of the biblical testimony concerning the true deity of Jesus Christ. The councils resulted in the affirmation that Christ was "God of God, Light of Light, very God of very God, begotten, not made, being of one substance with the Father."

Apollinarianism. The next error to arise in the early church affirmed the true deity of Christ but denied his full humanity. The Apollinarians—named for Apollinaris (ca. AD 315–ca. 392), bishop of Laodicea—believed that Christ possessed a real body and an immortal sensitive soul, but they denied to him a truly human mind (or rational soul). In fact, they believed that Christ was God masquerading in human flesh. Therefore, they attributed all the human weaknesses of Jesus to his deity—such things as ignorance, suffering, obedience, and worship. In reality, Apollinaris had also been infected by the dualism of Plato, who taught that the spirit is good but the body is bad. Apollinaris held that Christ, if God, could not have a human will.

The Council of Constantinople condemned Apollinarian teachings as heretical in AD 381, and the Council of Chalcedon did likewise in AD 451. Those in the early church who responded to Apollinaris pointed out that he could not explain the struggle between the divine will and the human will of Jesus in a text like Luke 22:42. Also, since sin affects the body, will, and mind, a complete redemptive work by Jesus required that his mind be involved in redeeming the believer's mind. Certainly, imagining a truly human being without a mind would be inconceivable.

Nestorianism. A significant division occurred in the early church due to the false teachings of Nestorius of Constantinople (ca. AD 381–ca. 451). He attributed a dual personality to Christ—two persons and two natures, rather than one person and two natures. Nestorius correctly understood that Mary did not conceive the divine nature of Christ, yet he, in effect, proposed that Jesus was a deified man. He compared Jesus's relationship to the Father as basically the same as a believer's relationship to Christ.

Some historians argue that Nestorius received a bad reputation from those who misunderstood his view that the impassibility of the Logos and the full humanity of Jesus must be preserved. Even Martin Luther defended Nestorius against the charge that he taught that Christ should be divided into two persons or hypostases.[27] Nichols explains that Nestorius "so stressed the humanity and divinity of Christ that he veered very near to saying that the two natures are so distinct in Christ that Christ is a divided person, a human person and divine person, that Christ is two 'he's' and not merely two natures."[28] After his condemnation in the councils held at both Ephesus (AD 431) and Chalcedon (AD 451), Nestorius insisted that he had been misunderstood and that he had always adhered to Christ existing in two natures and one person. Thus, Nestorius might not have adhered to the erroneous doctrinal system that became known as Nestorianism. Yet he might have overemphasized Christ's two natures in such a fashion as to downplay Christ's unity in one person, thereby rightly drawing fire from Cyril, bishop of Alexandria, as well as the rebuke of the Councils of Ephesus and Chalcedon. It is clear that believers were demanding precise doctrines regarding the Lord Jesus Christ.

Eutychianism. The view of Apollinarianism led to another controversy called Monophysitism (belief in "one nature") or Eutychianism, referring to its originator, Eutyches of Constantinople (ca. AD 378–ca. 454). Eutyches held that the deity and humanity of Christ were devoid of distinction—the two were fused together into a third nature that was neither God nor man but something in between. Since Jesus possessed only one life, one mind, and one will, he must have possessed a single nature in a single person. The variation of Eutychianism that focused on the one will became known as Monotheletism. The Council of Chalcedon condemned Eutychianism in AD 451, and the Third Council of Constantinople condemned Monotheletism in AD 680.

BAPTISM[29]

God chose the prophesied forerunner of the Messiah to baptize Jesus in the water of the Jordan River (Mark 1:1–10; John 1:19–31; Acts 19:4). The purpose in the baptism was to reveal the personal presence of the Messiah in fulfillment of the Old Testament prophecies. John the Baptizer associated that revelation of the Messiah with Christ's identification as "the Lamb of God, who takes away the sin of the world" (John 1:29). Since John's father was a priest (Luke 1:5), John was the "God-appointed and God-provided priest and prophet" who baptized Jesus.[30]

---

27. Heick, *A History of Christian Thought*, 1:180.

28. Stephen J. Nichols, *For Us and for Our Salvation: The Doctrine of Christ in the Early Church* (Wheaton, IL: Crossway, 2007), 105.

29. Adapted from MacArthur, *MacArthur Study Bible: English Standard Version*, 1364. Used by permission of Thomas Nelson.

30. Lewis Sperry Chafer, *Systematic Theology* (1948; repr., Dallas, TX: Dallas Seminary Press, 1969), 5:59.

Table 4.5 Early Church Councils*

Council	Date	Issue
Nicaea	AD 325	Defended the deity of Christ; opposed Arianism
Constantinople I	AD 381	Defended the deity of Christ; opposed Arianism and Apollinarianism
Ephesus	AD 431	Defended the two natures of Christ; opposed Nestorianism
Chalcedon	AD 451	Defended the two natures of Christ; opposed Apollinarianism, Nestorianism, and Eutychianism/Monophysitism
Constantinople II	AD 553	Defended the two natures of Christ; opposed Eutychianism/Monophysitism
Constantinople III	AD 680–681	Defended the two natures of Christ; opposed Monotheletism
Nicaea II	AD 787	Defended the use of icons

* Adapted from the chart in Nichols, *For Us and for Our Salvation*, 56. Used by permission of Crossway, a publishing ministry of Good News Publishers, Wheaton, IL 60187, www.crossway.org.

Why was Jesus baptized? According to Jesus's own explanation, "It is fitting for us to fulfill all righteousness" (Matt. 3:15). By submitting to John's baptism, Christ obeyed the will of God and identified himself with sinners. He would ultimately bear their sins so that his perfect righteousness might be imputed to them (2 Cor. 5:21). This act of obedience in baptism exemplified a necessary part of the righteous life he lived to be imputed to believers. This first public event of Jesus's ministry possessed depth of meaning:

1. It prefigured the significance of Christian baptism.
2. It marked his first public identification with those whose sins he would bear (Isa. 53:11; 1 Pet. 3:18).
3. It publicly affirmed his messiahship by testimony directly from heaven (Matt. 3:17, which combined the messianic language of Ps. 2:7 and Isa. 42:1).[31]

TEMPTATION

After John baptized Jesus (Matt. 3:13–17), the Holy Spirit led Jesus into the wilderness, where he was tempted by Satan (Matt. 4:1–11). The Holy Spirit played a significant role in Jesus's life and ministry. The Spirit was the agent of Jesus's conception in Mary's womb (Matt. 1:20); he anointed and empowered Jesus in his ministry (Matt. 12:28; Luke 4:18–19; see Isa. 61:1); and he was also the active agent in Jesus's resurrection (Rom. 8:11). The Spirit's involvement in leading Jesus into the situation with Satan demonstrates that this testing accorded with God's sovereign purpose in the program of redemption.

Satan's temptations attacked Jesus in his humanity, since God himself (and therefore Jesus's divine nature) "cannot be tempted with evil" (James 1:13). In fact, God never acts even as the agent tempting anyone to evil. However, he does use demons,

---

31. For more on the significance of Jesus's baptism, see "The Obedience of Christ" in chap. 7 (p. 519).

Satan, and men to tempt when it fits his sovereign purposes (Job 1–2; Luke 22:31–32; 2 Cor. 12:7–10). In accord with the categories listed in 1 John 2:16, Satan tempted Jesus with hunger as one of "the desires of the flesh" (Matt. 4:2–3; 1 John 2:16), with putting God to the test as an exhibition of "the pride of life" (Matt. 4:5–6; 1 John 2:16), and with the possession of the kingdoms of the world and all their glory to fulfill "the desires of the eyes" (Matt. 4:8–9; 1 John 2:16). Through this specific time of testing as throughout his earthly life, Jesus was tempted "in every respect . . . as we are, yet without sin" (Heb. 4:15). Jesus was able to be tempted but was unable to sin.

Over the years some have asked, was Christ able to sin in thought or deed? Two main answers to this question have been represented by two Latin phrases.[32] The Latin phrase describing Jesus's impeccability is *non posse peccare* ("not able to sin"). That concept contrasts with *posse non peccare* ("able not to sin"), which implies that Jesus could have sinned but kept himself from doing so. To be clear, *peccability* and *impeccability* are not synonyms for *sinfulness* and *sinlessness*. The former does not presuppose a sin nature. Both views admit that Jesus did not sin (1 John 3:5).

The peccability position asserts that Christ could have sinned even though he did not. This is by far the minority view among theologians today. Arguments include the following:

1. *The full humanity of Christ*: If Christ in his incarnation assumed full humanity with all its attributes, he must have had the ability to sin, since by itself, unfallen human nature is capable of sinning, as the fall of Adam and Eve shows (Gen. 3:1–6).
2. *Christ's ability to be tempted*: Christ was tempted in all points as others are (Heb. 4:15). He endured numerous temptations throughout his life (Matt. 4:1–11), and the ability to be tempted implies the ability to sin. This argument is the one peccability advocates appeal to most often.
3. *The free will of Christ*: That Christ had, as Adam did before the fall, a free will implies peccability.

Peccability advocates see much at stake in this debate, preeminently the reality of Christ's humanity, his temptation, and a truly sympathetic priesthood. They assert that all the above are compromised if Christ had no ability to sin.

The Scripture, however, argues for the impeccability of Christ. The impeccability position asserts that Christ was unable to sin. This is by far the majority view within the evangelicalism of past and present. Arguments for this viewpoint include the following:

1. *The deity of Christ*: Since Christ is God and since God cannot sin (James 1:13), it follows that Christ could not sin either. Since "the wages of sin is death" (Rom. 6:23), God would have to die if he sinned—but God cannot die and, by implication, cannot sin.

---

32. The following brief discussion of the two views is adapted from Michael McGhee Canham, "*Potuit Non Peccare* or *Non Potuit Peccare*: Evangelicals, Hermeneutics, and the Impeccability Debate," *MSJ* 11, no. 1 (2000): 93–114. Used by permission of *MSJ*.

2. *The decrees of God*: Since God had decreed the plan of redemption to be accomplished by Jesus Christ, it follows that Christ could not have sinned, for had he sinned, the plan of redemption would have failed.

3. *The divine attributes of Christ*: Some impeccability advocates argue from the *immutability* of Christ (see Heb. 13:8). The reasoning is that if Christ could have sinned while he was on earth, then he could sin now. Since he cannot sin now, and since he is immutable, it follows that he could not sin while on earth. Other attributes appealed to include Christ's omnipotence (the ability to sin implies weakness, but Christ had no weakness) and omniscience (John 5:25). Someone might contend that arguments from the attributes of Christ's deity are indecisive for the peccability question because in the kenosis Christ voluntarily yielded the independent exercise of his divine attributes to the will of his heavenly Father (see "Kenosis" [p. 258]). Thus, while impeccability may be implied by each of these divine attributes standing alone, Christ always exercised these in subordination to his Father's will. And the Father would never direct the Son to restrict his divine attributes in order to make it possible for Christ to violate the Father's will.

4. *The Trinitarian relationship of Christ*: Being "full of the Holy Spirit" (Luke 4:1), Jesus could not fail the testing. The Holy Spirit could not fail in what he had been sent to do for Jesus.

Even though Jesus could not sin, the temptations he faced were genuine—their reality did not depend on his ability to respond. Indeed, since he never yielded to them, he endured their full force. Thus, temptation for Jesus was more real and more powerful than for any other human being. A comparison of Adam's temptation and Jesus's temptation reveals great differences and makes Jesus's victory all the more remarkable:

1. Adam faced temptation in the best of settings, the garden of Eden; Jesus faced temptation in a stark environment, the wilderness of Judea.

2. Adam lived in the perfection of the prefall world; Jesus lived in a deeply corrupt and sinful fallen world.

3. Adam gave in to the first temptation he faced; Jesus faced repeated temptations throughout his earthly life and ministry (Heb. 4:15) but never yielded.

4. Adam entered his time of temptation adequately fed in a delightful garden filled with fruit and fresh water; Jesus was weakened by forty days of fasting before his temptation in the wilderness.

5. The consequences of Adam's fall to temptation were lethal to the entire human race; the consequences of Jesus's triumph over temptation allowed him to complete the program of redemption successfully.

DEPENDENCE ON THE HOLY SPIRIT

The account of Jesus's temptation raises the matter of Jesus's relationship to and dependence on the Holy Spirit. Several Old Testament prophecies foretold that the Messiah would depend on the Holy Spirit:

And the Spirit of the LORD shall rest upon him,
the Spirit of wisdom and understanding,

the Spirit of counsel and might,
    the Spirit of knowledge and the fear of the LORD.
And his delight shall be in the fear of the LORD. (Isa. 11:2–3)

Behold my servant, whom I uphold,
    my chosen, in whom my soul delights;
I have put my Spirit upon him;
    he will bring forth justice to the nations. (Isa. 42:1)

The Spirit of the Lord GOD is upon me,
    because the LORD has anointed me
to bring good news to the poor;
    he has sent me to bind up the brokenhearted,
to proclaim liberty to the captives,
    and the opening of the prison to those who are bound;
to proclaim the year of the LORD's favor,
    and the day of vengeance of our God;
    to comfort all who mourn;
to grant to those who mourn in Zion—
    to give them a beautiful headdress instead of ashes,
the oil of gladness instead of mourning,
    the garment of praise instead of a faint spirit;
that they may be called oaks of righteousness,
    the planting of the LORD, that he may be glorified. (Isa. 61:1–3)

Christ's dependence on the Holy Spirit can be witnessed in his conception (Matt. 1:20), his baptism (Matt. 3:16–17), and his temptation in the wilderness (Matt. 4:1). John writes that Christ "utters the words of God, for he gives the Spirit without measure" (John 3:34). Indeed, Christ relied on the Spirit for power in his ministry (Luke 4:14) and especially in his preaching (Luke 4:17–22, fulfilling Isa. 61:1–2; Matt. 12:15–21, fulfilling Isa. 42:1–3). Christ "through the Spirit" gave commandments to his chosen apostles (Acts 1:2), and he "cast out demons by the Spirit of God" (Matt. 12:28 NASB). When Jesus healed, he did so by the power of the Spirit (Acts 10:38).

At the end of his earthly sojourn, Jesus offered himself as a sacrifice on the cross through the Spirit: "How much more will the blood of Christ, who through the eternal Spirit offered himself without blemish to God, purify our conscience from dead works to serve the living God" (Heb. 9:14). The Holy Spirit enabled Jesus to endure the hours of trial before and during the crucifixion—the inner agonies of Gethsemane, the humiliation before Pilate and Herod, the scourging and crown of thorns, the road to Golgotha, and the crucifixion. The Spirit preserved Jesus physically and otherwise, helping him maintain his purpose to offer himself on the cross as the substitutionary sacrifice for sinners in submission to the will of the Father. Christ's decision, though enabled by the Spirit, was still his own to make: "For this reason the Father loves me, because I lay down my life that I may take it up again. No one takes it from me, but I lay it down of my own accord. I have authority to lay it down, and I have authority to take it up again. This charge I have received from my Father" (John 10:17–18).

In Christ's resurrection from the dead, all three persons of the Godhead played a role. The Father and the Spirit were involved: "If the Spirit of him who raised Jesus from the dead dwells in you, he who raised Christ Jesus from the dead will also give life to your mortal bodies through his Spirit who dwells in you" (Rom. 8:11). And the passage cited above (John 10:17–18; see also 2:19–22) demonstrates the Son's involvement in his own resurrection.

From conception through resurrection, and, by inference, even through glorification, Jesus was sustained by the Holy Spirit. This admits to no weakness, but in Christ's state of submission to the Father (especially in his incarnation), the Spirit enabled his human nature to fully accomplish redemption and all other aspects of his mission on earth. Such condescension was confirmed when the Jewish leaders determined that Jesus was Satanic, yet he accused them not of blaspheming him but of speaking against the Holy Spirit (Matt. 12:30–32).

TRANSFIGURATION

Before Jesus began the series of events that would lead to his crucifixion, death, burial, resurrection, and ascension into heaven, he wanted to assure his disciples that he would return and establish his kingdom. The event known as Jesus's transfiguration gave the disciples that assurance. The kingdom focus of Jesus's ministry had reached a turning point marked by Matthew 16:21: "From that time Jesus began to show his disciples that he must go to Jerusalem and suffer many things from the elders and chief priests and scribes, and be killed, and on the third day be raised." Jesus underwent the transfiguration not primarily to prove his deity, reveal his heavenly glory, or prophesy of his coming death and resurrection. Rather, he intended it to give a preview of the glory he would display upon his return to establish his kingdom. He introduced that truth himself in Matthew 16:28: "Truly, I say to you, there are some standing here who will not taste death until they see the Son of Man coming in his kingdom." Peter later spoke of the transfiguration when he wrote,

> For we did not follow cleverly devised myths when we made known to you the power and coming of our Lord Jesus Christ, but we were eyewitnesses of his majesty. For when he received honor and glory from God the Father, and the voice was borne to him by the Majestic Glory, "This is my beloved Son, with whom I am well pleased," we ourselves heard this very voice borne from heaven, for we were with him on the holy mountain. (2 Pet. 1:16–18)

The brilliant light of Christ's countenance on the mountain ("his face shone like the sun, and his clothes became white as light," Matt. 17:2) portended the glory of "the Son of Man coming on the clouds of heaven with power and great glory" (Matt. 24:30). The apostle John described a similar vision of Christ's glory in Revelation 1:14–16:

The hairs of his head were white, like white wool, like snow. His eyes were like a flame of fire, his feet were like burnished bronze, refined in a furnace, and his voice was like the roar of many waters. In his right hand he held seven stars, from his mouth came a sharp two-edged sword, and his face was like the sun shining in full strength.

This vision bears marked similarities to the description of King Jesus in Revelation 19:11–16 as he comes in judgment:

Then I saw heaven opened, and behold, a white horse! The one sitting on it is called Faithful and True, and in righteousness he judges and makes war. His eyes are like a flame of fire, and on his head are many diadems, and he has a name written that no one knows but himself. He is clothed in a robe dipped in blood, and the name by which he is called is The Word of God. And the armies of heaven, arrayed in fine linen, white and pure, were following him on white horses. From his mouth comes a sharp sword with which to strike down the nations, and he will rule them with a rod of iron. He will tread the winepress of the fury of the wrath of God the Almighty. On his robe and on his thigh he has a name written, King of kings and Lord of lords.

The glory of God is most fully and clearly manifested in the Lord Jesus Christ (Heb. 1:1–3). Thus, the apostle Paul called him "the Lord of glory" (1 Cor. 2:8) and in 2 Corinthians 4:3–6 stated,

And even if our gospel is veiled, it is veiled to those who are perishing. In their case the god of this world has blinded the minds of the unbelievers, to keep them from seeing the light of the gospel of the glory of Christ, who is the image of God. For what we proclaim is not ourselves, but Jesus Christ as Lord, with ourselves as your servants for Jesus' sake. For God, who said, "Let light shine out of darkness," has shone in our hearts to give the light of the knowledge of the glory of God in the face of Jesus Christ.

The transfiguration event most powerfully and dramatically demonstrated that Jesus was the true glory of God, though veiled while he walked in flesh on this earth. The two comings of Christ, the first in humility robed in flesh and the second in glory robed in light, are the two great themes of biblical prophecy.

The two companions of Jesus in his transfiguration, Moses and Elijah (Matt. 17:3), might be symbolic of two categories of those saints who enter the kingdom—those who have died and those who have not died but are transformed at the rapture. However, a more certain identification of their significance comes from the vision in Zechariah 4. In that vision, the golden lampstand (menorah) and the two olive trees provide assurance to Zerubbabel that he will receive divine enablement for the task of rebuilding the temple. God also reveals that he will supply his Spirit and endless power (Zech. 4:6), even unto the future glory of Messiah's kingdom and temple. The two olive trees "are the two anointed ones who stand by the Lord of the whole earth" (Zech. 4:14). At the transfiguration, Jesus is the Lord of all the earth, and Moses and Elijah are the anointed ones alongside him. John later identifies these same two olive trees as the two witnesses prophesying for 1,260 days in the tribulation period (Rev. 11:3–4). The miracles they perform (Rev. 11:5–6) appear to confirm that they might be Moses and Elijah:

> While it is impossible to be dogmatic about the identity of these two witnesses, several observations suggest they might be Moses and Elijah: 1) like Moses, they strike the earth with plagues, and like Elijah, they have the power to keep it from raining; 2) Jewish tradition expected both Moses (cf. Deut. 18:15–18) and Elijah (cf. Mal. 4:5–6) to return in the future (cf. John 1:21); 3) both Moses and Elijah were present at the transfiguration, the preview of Christ's second coming; 4) both Moses and Elijah used supernatural means to provoke repentance; 5) Elijah was taken up alive in to heaven, and God buried Moses' body where it would never be found; and 6) the length of the drought the two witnesses bring (three and one-half years; cf. Rev. 11:3) is the same as that brought by Elijah (James 5:17).[33]

Teachings

Jesus's teachings reveal the fact that he was a master teacher and a master storyteller who possessed knowledge and wisdom beyond any other person. In every setting and with every hearer, Jesus displayed a mastery of communication. Because every person learns differently, he employed a variety of methods. A. B. Bruce speaks of the challenge facing Jesus in teaching just his twelve disciples:

> The humble fishermen of Galilee had much to learn before they could satisfy these high requirements; so much, that the time of their apprenticeship for their apostolic work, even reckoning it from the very commencement of Christ's ministry, seems all too short. They were indeed godly men, who had already shown the sincerity of their piety by forsaking all for their Master's sake. But at the time of their call they were exceedingly ignorant, narrow-minded, superstitious, full of Jewish prejudices, misconceptions, and animosities. They had much to unlearn of what was bad, as well as much to learn of what was good, and they were slow both to learn and to unlearn. Old beliefs already in possession of their minds made the communication of new religious ideas a difficult task. Men of good honest heart, the soil of their spiritual nature was fitted to produce an abundant harvest; but it was stiff, and needed much laborious tillage before it would yield its fruit.[34]

The fact that Jesus trained them and that they spearheaded postresurrection gospel preaching and wrote two of the four Gospels (Matthew and John), a number of the New Testament Epistles (1 and 2 Peter and 1, 2, and 3 John), and the book of Revelation demonstrates their successful preparation by the Master. Peter might also have influenced the author of the Gospel of Mark, thus extending his involvement, though indirectly, in the writing of the New Testament.

---

33. MacArthur, *MacArthur Study Bible: English Standard Version*, 1955.

34. Alexander Balmain Bruce, *The Training of the Twelve; Or, Passages out of the Gospels, Exhibiting the Twelve Disciples of Jesus under Discipline for the Apostleship*, 4th ed. (New York: A. C. Armstrong and Son, 1889), 14.

JESUS AS MASTER TEACHER

The Gospels reveal a number of significant details about Jesus as a master teacher. The following are a sampling of observations that can be made from the biblical text:[35]

1. Jesus was not a paid "professional" teacher: "But you are not to be called rabbi, for you have one teacher" (Matt. 23:8).
2. Jesus chose his pupils (even one who would betray him): "I am not speaking of all of you; I know whom I have chosen. But the Scripture will be fulfilled, 'He who ate my bread has lifted his heel against me'" (John 13:18).
3. Jesus was not restricted to a specific location or single setting; he taught in the temple (Matt. 21:12–13), in the synagogue (Mark 1:21), on a mountain (Matt. 5:1), in fishermen's boats (Luke 5:1–11), at a wedding (John 2:1–11), at a funeral (Luke 7:11–17), at a well (John 4:1–26), and in many other settings.
4. Jesus possessed a unique authority: "He was teaching them as one who had authority, and not as their scribes" (Matt. 7:29).
5. Jesus's curriculum was his own, though directed by the Father: "I do nothing on my own authority, but speak just as the Father taught me" (John 8:28).
6. Jesus understood his students:
   a. He knew their capacities fully and accurately: "Are you the teacher of Israel and yet you do not understand these things?" (John 3:10), and "I still have many things to say to you, but you cannot bear them now" (John 16:12).
   b. He used repetition effectively, teaching multiple kingdom parables that repeat the same lessons in Matthew 13 or repeating references to the Holy Spirit as the "Helper" (John 14:16, 26; 15:26; 16:7).
   c. He encouraged earnest students, instructing some privately concerning parables (Matt. 13:36–43) and giving special attention to Peter, John, and James at his transfiguration (Luke 9:28–36) and in the garden of Gethsemane (Matt. 26:37–38).
   d. He ensured a right attitude toward himself, such as in his teaching of the Samaritan woman in John 4:1–26.
   e. He established and maintained right relationships between his pupils: "This is my commandment, that you love one another as I have loved you. Greater love has no one than this, that someone lay down his life for his friends" (John 15:12–13).
7. Jesus's personal qualities and abilities maintained class control:
   a. He had an extraordinary ability to maintain the pupils' interest and attention: "The great throng heard him gladly" (Mark 12:37); and, "After three days they found him in the temple, sitting among the teachers, listening to them and asking them questions. And all who heard him were amazed at his understanding and his answers" (Luke 2:46–47).
   b. He possessed great patience, self-control, and self-discipline, as in his silence before his accusers, mockers, and persecutors (Matt. 26:63; 27:11–14; Luke 23:9).

---

35. The following summarizes almost the entire content of Clifford A. Wilson, *Jesus the Teacher* (Melbourne: Hill of Content, 1974), with a few examples omitted from his discussions.

c.   He maintained a dignified attitude: "Then Jesus came from Galilee to the Jordan to John, to be baptized by him. John would have prevented him, saying, 'I need to be baptized by you, and do you come to me?' But Jesus answered him, 'Let it be so now, for thus it is fitting for us to fulfill all righteousness.' Then he consented" (Matt. 3:13–15).

d.   He had a supernatural ability to lead: "Then Jesus told them plainly, 'Lazarus has died, and for your sake I am glad that I was not there, so that you may believe. But let us go to him.' So Thomas, called the Twin, said to his fellow disciples, 'Let us also go, that we may die with him'" (John 11:14–16).

e.   He corrected wrong thinking, as when he explained to his disciples that they had failed to recognize a food greater than physical sustenance (John 4:31–38).

f.   He used an effective look at Peter when that disciple uttered his third denial of association with Christ (Luke 22:61).

g.   He could level a stern rebuke when necessary: "But he turned and said to Peter, 'Get behind me, Satan! You are a hindrance to me. For you are not setting your mind on the things of God, but on the things of man'" (Matt. 16:23).

h.   He warned of consequences: "For I tell you, unless your righteousness exceeds that of the scribes and Pharisees, you will never enter the kingdom of heaven" (Matt. 5:20).

i.   He exemplified bold living based on biblical conviction, as when he cleared the money changers from the temple (Matt. 21:12–13) and as when he sent Judas out from among the disciples (John 13:27–30).

8.   Jesus used a variety of literary and communicative devices in his teaching:

a.   He used different types of linguistic devices and styles for effective communication, including symbolism (Matt. 5:13), synonymous parallelism (Matt. 12:30), antithetic parallelism (Matt. 10:39), metaphor (Matt. 15:26), hyperbole (Matt. 5:29–30), parable (Matthew 13), and proverb (Luke 4:23). Additional linguistic devices appear in the original language (Greek) that make Jesus's teachings unforgettable. Assonance and alliteration are one of the linguistic devices that cannot always be reproduced in translation. Matthew 7:2 provides just one example: "For with the judgment you pronounce you will be judged, and with the measure you use it will be measured to you." In the Greek, memorable climactic triplets embed the statements in the minds of Jesus's audience: *en hō gar krimati krinete krithēsesthe, kai en hō metrō metreite metrēthēsetai humin.*

b.   He employed visual aids: "And he told them a parable: 'Look at the fig tree, and all the trees. As soon as they come out in leaf, you see for yourselves and know that the summer is already near'" (Luke 21:29–30).

c.   He utilized novelty, as when he sent someone to find a coin in a fish's mouth by which he and one other might pay their temple tax (Matt. 17:24–27).

d.   He turned his pupils' surroundings into visual aids: "Do you not say, 'There are yet four months, then comes the harvest'? Look, I tell you, lift up your eyes, and see that the fields are white for harvest" (John 4:35).

    e. He used miracles as visual aids, as in his withering up the fig tree in Matthew 21:18–22.

    f. Jesus himself served as a visual aid: "Come to me, all who labor and are heavy laden, and I will give you rest. Take my yoke upon you, and learn from me, for I am gentle and lowly in heart, and you will find rest for your souls. For my yoke is easy, and my burden is light" (Matt. 11:28–30).

  9. Jesus employed questions as a teaching method:

    a. His questions were a point of contact: "Jesus said to her, 'Woman, why are you weeping? Whom are you seeking?'" (John 20:15).

    b. His questions aroused interest and guided thought: "Which is easier, to say, 'Your sins are forgiven you,' or to say, 'Rise and walk'?" (Luke 5:23).

    c. He probed with examination questions: "He said to them, 'But who do you say that I am?'" (Matt. 16:15).

    d. He used questions asked by his pupils: "Then Peter came up and said to him, 'Lord, how often will my brother sin against me, and I forgive him? As many as seven times?'" (Matt. 18:21).

Jesus was indeed the Prophet greater than Moses (Deut. 18:15–22; John 1:17; Heb. 3:3), the prophetic Teacher (Isa. 30:20; Matt. 26:18; John 13:13), and the wise Shepherd who was greater than Solomon (Eccles. 12:11; Matt. 12:42). These three depictions of the teaching ministry of the Messiah arise out of each of the three major sections of the Hebrew Bible: the Law, the Prophets, and the Writings. Jesus indeed fulfills that which the Old Testament announced concerning the Messiah—not just as Prophet, Priest, and King (see "Old Testament Prophecies" [p. 245]) but as Teacher.

JESUS'S PARABLES

The ancient Jews commonly used parables as a form of teaching. A parable consists of what could be a long analogy but is cast in the form of an ingeniously simple and often brief story taken from everyday life. Jesus excelled in the use of parables. His parables "epitomize the plain, powerful profundity of His message and His teaching style."[36] That said, a number of interpreters misunderstand and misrepresent the method and meaning of Jesus's parables.

First, Jesus did not speak in parables solely to make his teaching accessible to the multitudes.[37] Early in his ministry, Jesus employed many graphic analogies (see Matt. 5:13–16) whose meaning was fairly clear in the context of his teaching. Parables required more explanation (see Matt. 13:36), and Jesus employed them to obscure the truth from unbelievers as a judgment while at the same time making it clearer to his disciples (Matt. 13:11–12). At one point in his Galilean ministry, he began

36. John MacArthur, *Parables: The Mysteries of God's Kingdom Revealed through the Stories Jesus Told* (Nashville: Thomas Nelson, 2015), xiii.

37. This paragraph is adapted from MacArthur, *MacArthur Study Bible: English Standard Version*, 1382. Used by permission of Thomas Nelson.

Table 4.6 The Parables of Jesus*

Parable	Matthew	Mark	Luke
1. The lamp under a basket	5:14–16	4:21–22	8:16–17; 11:33–36
2. A wise man builds on rock and a foolish man builds on sand	7:24–27		6:47–49
3. Unshrunk (new) cloth on an old garment	9:16	2:21	5:36
4. New wine in old wineskins	9:17	2:22	5:37–38
5. The sower	13:3–23	4:2–20	8:4–15
6. The weeds	13:24–30		
7. The mustard seed	13:31–32	4:30–32	13:18–19
8. The leaven	13:33		13:20–21
9. The hidden treasure	13:44		
10. The pearl of great price	13:45–46		
11. The net	13:47–50		
12. The lost sheep	18:12–14		15:3–7
13. The unforgiving servant	18:23–35		
14. The laborers in the vineyard	20:1–16		
15. The two sons	21:28–32		
16. The wicked tenants	21:33–45	12:1–12	20:9–19
17. The wedding feast	22:2–14		
18. The fig tree	24:32–44	13:28–32	21:29–33
19. The wise and foolish virgins	25:1–13		
20. The talents	25:14–30		
21. The growing seed		4:26–29	
22. The master on a journey		13:33–37	
23. The moneylender and two debtors			7:41–43
24. The good Samaritan			10:30–37
25. A friend in need			11:5–13
26. The rich fool			12:16–21
27. The watchful servants			12:35–40
28. The faithful servant and the evil servant			12:42–48
29. The barren fig tree			13:6–9
30. The great banquet			14:16–24
31. Building a tower and a king making war			14:25–33
32. The lost coin			15:8–10
33. The lost son			15:11–32
34. The dishonest manager			16:1–13
35. The rich man and Lazarus			16:19–31

Parable	Matthew	Mark	Luke
36. The unworthy servants			17:7–10
37. The persistent widow			18:1–8
38. The Pharisee and the tax collector			18:9–14
39. The ten minas			19:11–27

* Adapted from MacArthur, *MacArthur Study Bible: English Standard Version*, 1383. Used by permission of Thomas Nelson.

speaking to the multitudes only in parables (Matt. 13:34). Jesus's veiling the truth from unbelievers acted as both judgment and mercy. It was judgment because it kept them in the darkness that they loved (see John 3:19), but it was mercy because they had already rejected the light, so any exposure to more truth would only have increased their eternal condemnation.

Second, Jesus used parables not because they proved to be a better method of teaching than didactic discourses or sermonic exhortation. Actually, the four Gospels record more discourses (at least forty-five[38]) than parables (thirty-nine, according to table 4.6).

Jesus employed a variety of methods to present propositional truth. He taught no allegorical stories with hidden, complex meanings. The interpretation of Jesus's parables should look for their main, uncomplicated point. The lesser elements within the parable's telling should not be taken as possessing some symbolic or spiritual meaning. When a parable's symbolism tends to be more complex, Jesus usually explains the symbolism for his hearers, so that they will not miss his main point.[39]

MARKS OF JESUS'S TEACHING

A look at the teaching ministry of Jesus uncovers its significant characteristics:[40]

1. *Originality*: Jesus's teaching was more than an echo of the Old Testament prophets and wise men. He said things that Moses and the prophets had not said—at least not with the clarity with which he spoke them. Six times in the Sermon on the Mount Jesus said, "You have heard that it was said. . . . But I say to you . . ." (Matt. 5:21–22, 27–28, 31–32, 33–34, 38–39, 43–44).
2. *Simplicity*: His teachings were simple, because he used the common language and spoke in the context of everyday living. His teaching was direct and to the point: "When you fast, do not look gloomy like the hypocrites, for they disfigure their faces that their fasting may be seen by others" (Matt. 6:16).
3. *Profundity*: Jesus's wisdom astounded and amazed his listeners (Matt. 13:54; Mark 6:2; Luke 2:47). His wisdom surpassed that of the Old Testament sages. No wonder he said of himself, "Wisdom is justified by all her children" (Luke 7:35), and, "Something greater than Solomon is here" (Matt. 12:42).

---

38. See the chart in W. Graham Scroggie, *A Guide to the Gospels* (Old Tappan, NJ: Revell, n.d.), 556–57.
39. MacArthur, *Parables*, chaps. 1–3.
40. This list is adapted from W. Graham Scroggie, *The Unfolding Drama of Redemption: The Bible as a Whole* (1953–1970; repr., Grand Rapids, MI: Kregel, 1994), 2:143–46 (public domain).

4. *Imagery*: Some of the sources for the images Jesus used in his teaching include natural phenomena (lightning, earthquake, storms, light, sunsets), animals (oxen, sheep, dogs, wolves, birds, serpents), plants (wild flowers, thorns, seeds), agriculture (farming, olive trees, vineyards, fig trees, wheat), commerce (tailors, fishermen, merchants, builders), and familiar social settings (weddings, hospitality, feasts, raising children, family bedtime). Jesus was a keen observer of human life together with all its challenges, pains, and joys.

5. *Practicality*: The emphasis in both parables and discourses falls on doing something: "So it is lawful to do good on the Sabbath" (Matt. 12:12); "For you always have the poor with you, and whenever you want, you can do good for them" (Mark 14:7); "My mother and my brothers are those who hear the word of God and do it" (Luke 8:21); "Do this in remembrance of me" (Luke 22:19); and, "Whoever believes in me will also do the works that I do" (John 14:12).

6. *Authority*: When Jesus taught, he taught with authority, not with guessing or with attempts to be right: "He was teaching them as one who had authority, and not as their scribes" (Matt. 7:29). When Jesus cast out demons, he wielded his divine authority and the people recognized it: "They questioned among themselves, saying, 'What is this? A new teaching with authority! He commands even the unclean spirits, and they obey him'" (Mark 1:27). As Jesus taught in the synagogue in Capernaum, the people "were astonished at his teaching, for his word possessed authority" (Luke 4:32).

7. *Finality*: In some ways this aspect of the Lord's teaching relates to his authority. The outcomes he foretells are inescapable and certain: "The one who rejects me and does not receive my words has a judge; the word that I have spoken will judge him on the last day" (John 12:48).

As a master teacher Jesus handled tough questions, showed compassion and understanding for his students, silenced critics and disrupters, and pointed his hearers again and again to divine revelation. He communicated with the educated and the uneducated, the rich and the poor, the elite and the outcasts, the young and the old. He was the incarnation of the divine Teacher: "And though the Lord give you the bread of adversity and the water of affliction, yet your Teacher will not hide himself anymore, but your eyes shall see your Teacher" (Isa. 30:20).

Miracles

Jesus proved his deity and his role as Messiah by means of the many miracles he performed during his earthly ministry (Matt. 11:4–5). A miracle consists of an act of God's power by which he intervenes in the physical world in suspension and contradiction to natural law. In other words, a miracle is a supernatural event within the realm of the natural world. The prophets and the apostles also wrought miracles, but they did so by a power outside themselves (Ex. 14:13; Josh. 3:5; Acts 3:12). Jesus's miracles came about through his inherent power (John 10:25, 37–38; 15:24). Although the Gospels record only thirty-seven miracles, listed in table 4.7, those represent the explosion of his divine power (Matt. 4:23–24; John 20:30–31).

Table 4.7 *The Miracles of Jesus**

Miracle	Matthew	Mark	Luke	John
1. Cleansing a leper	8:2–4	1:40–45	5:12–14	
2. Healing a centurion's servant (of paralysis)	8:5–13		7:1–10	
3. Healing Peter's mother-in-law	8:14–15	1:30–31	4:38–39	
4. Healing the sick at evening	8:16	1:32–34	4:40	
5. Stilling the storm	8:23–27	4:35–41	8:22–25	
6. Demons entering a herd of swine	8:28–34	5:1–20	8:26–39	
7. Healing a paralytic	9:2–7	2:3–12	5:18–26	
8. Raising the ruler's daughter	9:18–19, 23–25	5:22–24, 35–43	8:41–42, 49–56	
9. Healing the hemorrhaging woman	9:20–22	5:25–34	8:43–48	
10. Healing two blind men	9:27–31			
11. Curing a demon-possessed, mute man	9:32–33			
12. Healing a man's withered hand	12:9–14	3:1–6	6:6–11	
13. Curing a demon-possessed, blind, and mute man	12:22		11:14	
14. Feeding the five thousand	14:13–21	6:30–44	9:10–17	6:1–15
15. Walking on the sea	14:22–33	6:45–52		6:16–21
16. Healing the Canaanite woman's daughter	15:22–28	7:25–30		
17. Feeding the four thousand	15:32–39	8:1–10		
18. Healing the boy with the demon	17:14–20	9:14–29	9:37–43	
19. Two-drachma tax in the fish's mouth	17:24–27			
20. Healing two blind men	20:29–34	10:46–52	18:35–43	
21. Withering the fig tree	21:18–19	11:12–14, 20–25		
22. Casting out an unclean spirit		1:23–28	4:33–37	
23. Healing a deaf-mute		7:31–37		
24. Healing a blind man at Bethsaida		8:22–26		
25. Escape from the hostile multitude			4:28–30	
26. Catch of fish			5:1–11	
27. Raising of a widow's son at Nain			7:11–17	
28. Healing the afflicted, bent woman			13:10–17	
29. Healing the man with dropsy			14:1–6	
30. Cleansing the ten lepers			17:11–19	
31. Restoring a servant's ear			22:50–51	
32. Turning water into wine				2:1–11
33. Healing the royal official's son (of fever)				4:46–54

Miracle	Matthew	Mark	Luke	John
34. Healing an afflicted man at Bethesda				5:1–9
35. Healing the man born blind				9:1–7
36. Raising of Lazarus				11:1–44
37. Second catch of fish				21:1–8

* Adapted from MacArthur, *MacArthur Study Bible: English Standard Version*, 1423. Used by permission of Thomas Nelson.

The miracles that Jesus produced sometimes resulted in belief (John 2:11; 9:30–33; 11:45) or created a willingness in Jesus's hearers to listen to his teachings (Mark 12:37; Luke 5:15). The vast majority, however, rejected Jesus despite his miracles. Miracles do not necessarily convince people to believe in the Lord or in his gospel message (Matt. 13:58; Luke 16:31; John 2:23–25; 12:37; 15:24). Those who rejected (and who now also reject) his miracles will be severely judged (Matt. 10:1–15; Luke 10:1–15).

Jesus Christ's miracles demonstrate his deity, his supernatural origin, his power as Creator, and his authority as the sovereign Lord of all creation. His ministry confronted the antisupernatural worldview of his day and equally confronts the present world with the blindness of selling out to the uniformitarian naturalism of secular scientists. "It is impossible to remove the supernatural elements from Jesus's life and work, as anti-supernaturalist critics have attempted to do. The historical Jesus of Nazareth and the divine Christ are inseparably linked, for they are one and the same person. Jesus was and is the God-man."[41]

The wedding at Cana became the occasion for the first and most memorable example of the miracle-working power that Jesus displayed during his ministry (John 2:1–11). Jesus commanded the servants to fill large stone waterpots (John 2:7), so they filled them to their brims. The large amount of water (120–180 gallons) would provide an abundance of wine for the rest of the wedding celebration. Jesus's transformation of the water into wine was instantaneous—the servants immediately distributed it to the guests. The miracle consisted of creating out of nonliving water a wine that could only come from the fruit of living grapevines. The normal process of fermentation, or aging, took place instantaneously. Jesus demonstrated that he was the same Creator who instantly created mature living things out of nonliving earth during the six days of creation (Gen. 1:1–31). Denial of instantaneous creation in Genesis 1 must, to be consistent, likewise deny the miracle by which Jesus created the wine at Cana. Rejecting his miracle at Cana results in rejecting Jesus as the God-man and as the Redeemer.

Arrest and Trials

What significance do Jesus's arrest and trials have for the biblical doctrine of Christ? Do such considerations belong more properly to a study of the historical life of Jesus

---

41. John MacArthur, *John 1–11*, MNTC (Chicago: Moody Press, 2006), 76.

Christ? The apostle Paul reminds Timothy that "all Scripture is breathed out by God and profitable for teaching, for reproof, for correction, and for training in righteousness, that the man of God may be complete, equipped for every good work" (2 Tim. 3:16–17). Therefore, the biblical accounts of the arrest and trials of Jesus cannot be mere historical data but are explicit proof of his messiahship.

JESUS'S ARREST

The prophetic depiction of the Messiah being accused and led away to judgment implied something like an arrest (Isa. 53:8), and he himself announced his arrest beforehand (Matt. 17:22; 20:18). Such fulfillment of prior revelation demonstrates the authenticity of Jesus's claims to be the Messiah. His arrest also pits fallen mankind (the descendants of the first Adam) against the blameless, sinless second Adam (Rom. 5:17–19). Above all, the arrest reveals the perfect plan of God and the willing obedience of Christ to that plan, no matter the consequences for him personally (Matt. 26:39; Acts 2:23).

The trials of Jesus highlight his sinless perfection, his perfect obedience, and the strident injustice that prevailed from the merely human viewpoint as compared to the severe mercy of God from the divine viewpoint. Prior to his trials, the Jewish leaders had already hatched a conspiracy to "arrest Jesus by stealth and kill him" (Matt. 26:4). The religious leaders had been stung by Jesus's accusations of hypocrisy (Matt. 21:45; 23:1–36) and desired to do away with him, to assassinate him. Their fear of the people, among whom Jesus was very popular, prevented them from pursuing a public assassination (Matt. 21:46). The leaders were so convinced that Jesus was a false prophet and a blasphemer that they willingly accepted the responsibility for his death (Matt. 27:25).

If the Jews alone were responsible for Jesus's death, that guilt would not apply to all people. Therefore, it was necessary for Gentiles to also be involved in his execution, so that all might be held accountable. As Boice and Ryken point out, "An Idumean king named Herod handed Jesus over to the Romans. A Roman governor named Pontius Pilate ordered Jesus to be crucified. Roman soldiers carried out Pilate's orders, nailing Jesus to a wooden cross and hanging him up to die. The Jews brought Jesus to trial, but in the end the Gentiles killed him."[42] The biblical testimony appears in the prayer of the believers awaiting the release of Peter and John from jail: "For truly in this city there were gathered together against your holy servant Jesus, whom you anointed, both Herod and Pontius Pilate, along with the Gentiles and the peoples of Israel" (Acts 4:27).

The divine side of the arrest, trials, and crucifixion of Jesus also appears in that same prayer, which states that these people were gathered "to do whatever your hand and your plan had predestined to take place" (Acts 4:28). As Isaiah prophesied, "Yet it was the will of the LORD to crush him" (Isa. 53:10). Indeed, all was according to the precreation plan of the omniscient God:

---

42. James Montgomery Boice and Philip Graham Ryken, *Jesus on Trial* (Wheaton, IL: Crossway, 2002), 26.

. . . knowing that you were ransomed from the futile ways inherited from your forefathers, not with perishable things such as silver or gold, but with the precious blood of Christ, like that of a lamb without blemish or spot. He was foreknown before the foundation of the world but was made manifest in the last times for the sake of you who through him are believers in God, who raised him from the dead and gave him glory, so that your faith and hope are in God. (1 Pet. 1:18–21)

God has no "plan B"—everything is still operating by his one and only plan for his redemption and kingdom.

Besides "knowing all that would happen to him" (John 18:4), Jesus at the time of his arrest provided additional external evidence of his deity. He asked whom the band of soldiers and officers of the chief priest sought, and they responded, "Jesus of Nazareth" (John 18:3–5). As soon as he identified himself saying, "I am he," "they drew back and fell to the ground" (John 18:5–6). Why did they react in such a fashion? It is not unreasonable to suppose that their drawing back might be due to their fear of Jesus given his reputation as a miracle worker. But why would they all fall to the ground? The power of his word and of his presence may very well have been due to the way in which he said, "I am he." "He" is not in the Greek. Jesus's revelatory self-declaration was simply "I am," the same title of deity disclosed to Moses at the burning bush in Exodus 3:14. This is the final such self-declaration spoken by Jesus during his earthly ministry (see "The 'I Am' Statements" below for a list of all these declarations in the Gospel of John; similar statements occur only three times in the other Gospels: Matt. 22:32; Mark 6:50; 14:62). The power of Jesus's spoken word caused the soldiers and officers to fall to the ground before him. Even his betrayer, Judas, fell.

The "I Am" Statements*

Twenty-three times we find our Lord's meaningful "I am" (*egō eimi*) in the Greek text of this Gospel (John 4:26; 6:20, 35, 41, 48, 51; 8:12, 18, 24, 28, 58; 10:7, 9, 11, 14; 11:25; 13:19; 14:6; 15:1, 5; 18:5, 6, 8). In several of these, he joins his "I am" with seven tremendous metaphors that are expressive of his saving relationship toward the world:

"I am the bread of life" (John 6:35, 41, 48, 51).
"I am the light of the world" (John 8:12).
"I am the door of the sheep" (John 10:7, 9).
"I am the good shepherd" (John 10:11, 14).
"I am the resurrection and the life" (John 11:25).
"I am the way, the truth, and the life" (John 14:6).
"I am the true vine" (John 15:1, 5).

* Reproduced from MacArthur, *MacArthur Study Bible: English Standard Version*, 1550. Used by permission of Thomas Nelson.

As if that were insufficient to prove that Jesus is truly God, an additional incident drove the point home. When Peter drew his sword and sliced off the ear of Malchus, the servant of the high priest (John 18:10), Jesus miraculously reattached it to Malchus's head (Luke 22:51). In addition to that physical miracle of healing, Jesus said, "Do you think that I cannot appeal to my Father, and he will at once send me more than twelve legions of angels? But how then should the Scriptures be fulfilled, that it must be so?" (Matt. 26:53–54). God himself had foreordained the very minutest details of how Jesus would die (Acts 2:23; 4:27–28). Therefore, dying was Christ's consummate act of submission to the Father's will. In all this, Jesus himself was in absolute control (see John 10:17–18). These events at his arrest display his divine sovereignty and purposeful fulfillment of the Old Testament prophecies concerning him.

JESUS'S TRIALS

The Sanhedrin. As is clear in the Gospel accounts of Jesus's trials,

> he was tried in two general phases: first, before the religious authorities (the Jewish Sanhedrin), and second, before the secular political authorities (Rome, represented by governor Pontius Pilate). Each of these phases had three parts: preliminary interrogation, formal arraignment, and formal sentencing. None of the gospel writers provide a comprehensive account of all the details and stages of these trials. A complete picture requires the material from all four gospels being combined.[43]

During the period between the Old Testament and the New, Jewish authorities established the Great Sanhedrin in Jerusalem as the highest court in Israel.[44] They patterned it after the council of elders Moses convened in Numbers 11:16: "Then the LORD said to Moses, 'Gather for me seventy men of the elders of Israel, whom you know to be the elders of the people and officers over them, and bring them to the tent of meeting, and let them take their stand there with you.'" Those seventy men plus Moses formed a council of seventy-one elders whose job it was to govern the Israelites in the wilderness.

Since Moses's council of elders served as the pattern for the Sanhedrin, that council also numbered seventy-one members—comprising twenty-four chief priests (the heads of the twenty-four priestly divisions; see 1 Chron. 24:4) and forty-six more elders chosen from among the scribes, Pharisees, and Sadducees. The high priest acted as both the overseer and a voting member of the Sanhedrin, bringing the number to seventy-one. (The odd number ensured that decisions could be reached by majority vote.)

By Jesus's time, the Sanhedrin had become a corrupt and politically motivated body. Men could buy an appointment to the council with political favors and sometimes even with money. Favoritism and partisanship ran rife, and political expediency

---

43. John MacArthur, *One Perfect Life: The Complete Story of the Lord Jesus* (Nashville: Thomas Nelson, 2012), 437na.
44. The following description of the Great Sanhedrin and its trial system is adapted from John MacArthur, *The Murder of Jesus: A Study of How Jesus Died* (Nashville: Thomas Nelson, 2004), 102–5. Used by permission of Thomas Nelson. www.thomasnelson.com.

often determined who rose to power or fell from it within the Sanhedrin. Rome exercised ultimate control over the high priesthood, because Rome could appoint or depose the high priest. Both the high priest and the ruling priests of the temple were all Sadducees, who openly denied the supernatural elements of the Old Testament. Due to political tensions seething between the various factions of the Sanhedrin, the citizens of Israel, Rome, and Herod, the Sanhedrin often made decisions that were politically motivated. In fact, aside from their obvious religious animosity to the teaching of Christ, sheer political expediency was the motive for conspiring to carry out the arrest and crucifixion of Christ and to placate the Romans (see John 11:47–53).

Principles of Justice. Despite ubiquitous corruption, the rules of evidence and principles of impartiality that had been established under Moses still governed the justice system. Those rules required two credible witnesses in order to establish guilt. The accused was entitled to a public trial and a defense, including the right to call witnesses and present evidence. To deter anyone from bringing false testimony against an accused person, Moses's law established the principle of a penalty for false witness equivalent to the penalty for a guilty defendant (Deut. 19:16–19). Therefore, if someone testified falsely against a person accused of a capital crime, the false witness himself could be given the death penalty.

Rabbinical tradition had added another restriction on death-penalty cases. The council had to observe a full day of fasting between the passing of sentence and the execution of the criminal. That requirement not only prevented hasty trials and executions but also kept capital cases off the docket during the feasts. After the obligatory day of fasting, council members were polled again to see if they had changed their opinions. Guilty verdicts could thus be overturned, but innocent verdicts could not be rescinded.

All such principles were established to ensure that trials were both fair and merciful. To maintain fairness, the council could try cases only where an outside party had brought the charges. If council members had brought charges against the accused, the entire council was disqualified from trying the case. All witnesses had to give precise, consistent testimony as to the date, time, and location of the event under question. Women, children, slaves, and the mentally incompetent were not permitted to testify. Persons of questionable character were also disqualified from being witnesses. The council had to presume the accused to be innocent until they reached an official guilty verdict. Criminal trials were not to be convened at night, and if a trial was already underway when nighttime fell, court was to be recessed until the following day.

Nearly all these regulations were openly flouted in the trial of Christ. His trial was unjust and illegal by virtually every principle of jurisprudence known at the time. Caiaphas the high priest and the Sanhedrin turned their council into a kangaroo court with the predetermined purpose of killing Jesus. The trial they imposed on him was one extended act of deliberate injustice, the greatest miscarriage of justice

Table 4.8 The Trials of Jesus*

Trials	Scripture Passages	Theological Focus
RELIGIOUS TRIALS		
Before Annas—a preliminary hearing about Jesus's disciples and his teaching	John 18:12–14, 19–23	General teaching
Before Caiaphas and the Sanhedrin—the first formal hearing, finding Jesus guilty of blasphemy and deserving of death	Matt. 26:57–27:2 (see also Mark 14:53–15:1; Luke 22:54–23:1; John 18:24)	Jesus's deity
CIVIL TRIALS		
Before Pontius Pilate, the Roman governor—wherein the Jews charge Jesus with sedition rather than blasphemy but Pilate declares him innocent	John 18:28–38 (see also Matt. 27:2, 11–14; Mark 15:1–5; Luke 23:1–5)	Jesus's humanity and kingship
Before Herod Antipas, the tetrarch of Galilee—wherein Herod apparently concludes, as Pilate did, that Jesus was innocent of the charge of sedition	Luke 23:6–12	Jesus's humanity and deity
Before Pontius Pilate, the Roman governor—wherein Pilate capitulates to the Jews and condemns Jesus to die	John 18:39–19:16 (see also Matt. 27:15–26; Mark 15:6–15; Luke 23:13–25)	

* Adapted from John MacArthur, *The MacArthur Bible Commentary: Unleashing God's Truth, One Verse at a Time* (Nashville: Thomas Nelson, 2005), 1330. Copyright © 2005 by John MacArthur. Used by permission of Thomas Nelson. www.thomasnelson.com.

in the history of the world. The various trials of Jesus that led to his execution are summarized in table 4.8 and expounded in what follows.

The Religious Trials. Jesus was taken first to Annas before whom he would face his first legal trial (John 18:12–14). Annas, the father-in-law of Caiaphas, had previously functioned as high priest ca. AD 6–15 (until Pilate's predecessor removed him from his priestly office). He continued to exercise great influence over the office even after his tenure, most likely because the Jews still regarded him as the true high priest and also because five of his sons and his son-in-law Caiaphas each held the position at different times. The trial under Annas consisted of a preliminary examination (John 18:12–14, 19–23), probably to give time for the Sanhedrin to be hastily gathered. Annas questioned Jesus about his disciples and his teaching. Jesus responded by pointing out that Annas needed witnesses to establish just cause for making a case against him. One of the officers standing nearby struck Jesus for rebuking Annas. When Jesus indicated that everyone knew he was right about the need for witnesses, no one responded because his Jewish opponents had no intention of providing a fair trial (John 11:47–57). Annas remanded him over to Caiaphas and the Sanhedrin (John 18:24).

A session before the Sanhedrin then followed, with Caiaphas chairing the formal council (Matt. 26:57–27:2). The Roman prefect, Valerius Gratus, had appointed Caiaphas as high priest ca. AD 18. Caiaphas remained in office until AD 36 when, along with Pontius Pilate, he was removed by the Romans. He took a leading part in this first formal trial and condemnation of Jesus. In the residence of Caiaphas, the chief priests (who were mostly Sadducees) and the Pharisees had assembled "in order to arrest Jesus by stealth and kill him" (Matt. 26:3–4). Now they gathered to put him on trial. Although they had sought out many false witnesses, those witnesses failed to agree in any substantial fashion that would justify continuing the trial. Jesus maintained his silence since the witnesses obviously had nothing substantive to offer against him—he saw no need for defense against such a weak showing. Finally, Caiaphas asked him to declare whether he was indeed "the Christ, the Son of God" (Matt. 26:63). Jesus affirmed the identification, appealing to Psalm 110:1 and Daniel 7:13, which he would fulfill. With that, Caiaphas tore his clothes and declared Jesus guilty of blasphemy, and the council voiced its conclusion by calling for his execution. Strictly speaking, Jesus's words did not constitute blasphemy or any defiant irreverence for God—he spoke truth concerning his deity. Then those around him began to spit on Jesus and strike him, asking him to exercise his alleged deity by frivolously identifying those who had struck him secretly. Jesus, however, never glibly used the powers of his deity and never employed them to prevent his suffering and death when the time had come (though he had exercised them to prevent his premature demise, as at Nazareth, Luke 4:28–30).

The Civil Trials. The religious trials were over. The third trial took place before the Roman governor, Pontius Pilate, opening the civil phase of Jesus's trials (John 18:28–38). When Pilate asked the Jewish authorities by what charge Jesus might be tried by him, they did not mention blasphemy. They indicated that they had no authority to execute him, because they were under Roman law on capital crimes. Then they deliberately lied by accusing Jesus of telling people not to pay taxes to Caesar (Luke 23:2; see 20:20–25) and of claiming himself to be king—in other words, charges of sedition, not blasphemy. Pilate focused on the second of the charges and asked Jesus if he was "King of the Jews" (John 18:33). Jesus responded by saying that his kingdom was "not of this world" (John 18:36). He thereby laid out the fact that the Messiah's kingdom originated not with the efforts of human beings but with the Son of Man himself forcefully and decisively conquering sin in the lives of his people. At his second coming he would conquer the evil world system and establish the temporary earthly form of his kingdom. For the time being, however, his kingdom presented no physical or political threat to either Israel or Rome.

Jesus did not deny that he was king but indicated a higher purpose for his coming: "to bear witness of the truth" (John 18:37). To a Jew, Jesus's statement about his coming "into the world" would have been understood as another claim to deity. But Pilate was a Roman, not a Jew, so he missed this finer detail. Pilate pressed on with a question concerning the truth about which Jesus had spoken. If Jesus answered that question, the Gospels do not reveal it. Perhaps Pilate did not wait for an answer, since his mind had already been made up: he found no guilt in Jesus worthy of death (John 18:38). The Jews renewed their accusations and their call for Jesus's death, but Jesus maintained his silence, to Pilate's amazement (Matt. 27:12–14). Jesus may have remained silent in fulfillment of prophecy (Isa. 42:1–2; 53:7) or because Pilate had declared him innocent (Luke 23:4; John 18:38)—or both.

Jesus's fourth trial continued in the political realm with his appearance before Herod Antipas (Luke 23:6–12).[45] Despite the Jewish leaders' desperate attempts to accuse Jesus, Pilate was satisfied that he was no insurrectionist. However, the ferocity of the people made him afraid to exonerate Jesus. He was relieved to hear that Jesus was a Galilean, because that gave him an excuse to send him to Herod (Luke 23:5–6). Herod Antipas was one of the Jewish rulers appointed by Rome over four districts of Israel. Antipas was the tetrarch over Galilee, Jesus's home. Herod had come to Jerusalem for the feasts, and Pilate seized the opportunity to free himself from a political dilemma by sending Jesus to his rival.

No one was more curious or more eager to lay eyes on Jesus than Herod Antipas, a member of the Herodian dynasty. He had killed John the Baptist a year or two earlier (Matt. 14:1–12). Jesus's ministry covered the entire region of Galilee, but Scripture never mentions that he ever visited Tiberias, Herod Antipas's capital. It may be that Jesus was deliberately keeping his distance from Herod. There were rumors that Herod was also seeking to kill Jesus. While it is clear that Jesus was not intimidated by Herod, he knew that he must die in Jerusalem so that the Scriptures might be fulfilled (Luke 13:31–33).

How different Christ must have looked from the strong, prophetic miracle worker Herod expected to see! His face was already badly bruised and swollen from the abuse he had taken. Spittle and blood were drying in his matted hair. Tired and physically weakened from a sleepless night, he stood before Herod, bound and under guard like a common criminal. Herod beheld Jesus in his full humanity, which veiled Jesus's deity from his spiritually blind eyes. Jesus refused to perform any miracle for Herod that might reveal that Jesus was more than a man. Herod "questioned him at some length, but he made no answer" (Luke 23:9). The Sanhedrin was still dogging Christ, standing nearby and vehemently shouting denunciations and accusations at him (Luke 23:10). But Jesus refused to utter even so much as a word (see Matt. 27:14)—never allowing himself to rail at his accusers or say anything in self-defense (1 Pet. 2:23).

Only before Herod, though, did he remain in utter and complete silence. Why might this be? In the first place, Herod had no legitimate jurisdiction in Jerusalem. If Herod intended to impose any sentence in this case, Jesus would first have needed to be taken back to Galilee and put on trial there. So Jesus had no legal obligation to answer him anyway. But there may have been another reason Jesus kept silent. Herod's treatment of Jesus's forerunner, John the Baptist, made clear where he stood regarding the truth of Christ. For Jesus to answer him would have been like giving what is holy to the dogs or casting pearls before swine. Herod was already poised

---

45. The following description of Jesus's appearance before Herod Antipas is adapted from MacArthur, *Murder of Jesus*, 176–78. Used by permission of Thomas Nelson. www.thomasnelson.com.

to turn and tear Christ in pieces (see Matt. 7:6). Silence was the only appropriate response under such circumstances.

After a short time, Herod grew tired of questioning Jesus and decided to make sport of him: "And Herod with his soldiers treated him with contempt and mocked him. Then, arraying him in splendid clothing, he sent him back to Pilate" (Luke 23:11). Luke adds a historical footnote: "And Herod and Pilate became friends with each other that very day, for before this they had been at enmity with each other" (Luke 23:12). It was an unholy alliance, a friendship based on the one thing they had in common: their cowardly and contemptuous treatment of Christ. Both Herod and Pilate knew that Christ posed no immediate threat to their political interests. His appearance and his demeanor spoke for themselves. How could such an apparently passive, serene, fragile man—whose claim to fame was as a teacher and a healer—pose any political threat to anyone? It was as clear to Herod as it had been to Pilate that the Sanhedrin's charges were fabricated and ill-motivated. But Herod happily joined in the game. He clothed Jesus in a gorgeous robe, and then he and his security forces subjected him to mockery in front of the growing crowd of onlookers.

Herod Antipas returned Jesus to Pilate for the final trial (Matt. 27:15–26; Mark 15:6–15; Luke 23:13–25; John 18:39–19:16). Pilate announced that both Herod and he had found Jesus innocent of any of the Jewish charges of sedition (Luke 23:13–16). The Roman governor proceeded to seek a way to release Jesus by offering to make him the freed prisoner customarily released on the Passover, but the Jews would not allow it, calling instead for Barabbas to be released (Matt. 27:18–22). Pilate asked the Jews, "Why, what evil has he done?" (Matt. 27:23), but they insisted on Jesus's crucifixion. Washing his hands to symbolize his guiltlessness, Pilate announced that the Jews themselves were guilty of this innocent man's blood (Matt. 27:24). Pilate's final act in this drama was to release Barabbas, have Jesus flogged, and deliver him over to the Roman executioners for crucifixion (Matt. 27:26). Severe injustice perpetrated against the blameless and sinless character of Christ, the Son of Man, made all the participants in the trial guilty.

JESUS'S EXECUTION[46]

Suffering Prior to Crucifixion. The Roman soldiers had no idea whom they were tormenting. As far as they were concerned, they were simply crucifying another criminal under orders from Pilate, their commander-in-chief. Pilate's orders were to scourge and crucify Jesus, but the cruel mockery they heaped on him revealed their own wickedness. As they led Jesus back to the Praetorium, they deliberately made a spectacle of him for the amusement of the taunting crowd. The tumult drew the entire garrison of soldiers to watch.

The cohort (six hundred soldiers) was stationed at the Antonio Fortress (which overlooked the temple mount from the north). They were an elite unit, assigned to

46. The following description of Jesus's suffering and crucifixion is adapted from MacArthur, *Murder of Jesus*, 190–206. Used by permission of Thomas Nelson. www.thomasnelson.com.

serve the governor and to keep the peace that was so fragile in this most volatile region of the Roman Empire. Since Jews were exempt from military service, all these soldiers would have been Gentiles. They probably assumed that Jesus deserved whatever ridicule and torment they could heap on him. Condemned Roman prisoners were considered fair game for such abuse, as long as they were not killed before the sentence of crucifixion could be carried out.

Jesus had already been abused and beaten repeatedly, even before he was delivered to Pilate, so his face was undoubtedly swollen and bleeding already. After the scourging, his back would have been a mass of bleeding wounds and quivering muscles, and the robe they fashioned for him would have only added to the pain of those wounds. They stripped him of his garments apart from the robe they fashioned for him. The robe was likely made from an old tunic—probably a garment that had been discarded by one of the soldiers. Matthew says that the robe was scarlet (Matt. 27:28), but Mark and John call it "purple" (Mark 15:17; John 19:2)—suggesting that it was a badly faded tunic. It was probably the nearest thing to purple (signifying royalty) the soldiers could find.

Their aim was clearly to make a complete mockery of his claim that he was a king. To that end, they also fashioned a crown of thorns. Caesar wore a laurel wreath as a crown; thorns were a cruel corruption of that wreath. These were no doubt the longest, sharpest thorns that could be found. Many varieties of these grow in Jerusalem to this day—some with two-inch barbed quills that would penetrate deep into his head as the crown was pressed hard on him. The reed in his hand to represent a scepter was a further attempt to lampoon his royal claim.

Jesus's silence may have convinced them that he was merely a madman, and they showed their utter contempt for him by feigning the sort of veneration one would show to royalty, bowing at his feet but saying, "Hail, King of the Jews!" in jeering tones. Then, as the Jewish priests had done, they spat on him, and one of them took the reed from his hand and used it to strike him repeatedly on his head. The reed, though a flimsy scepter, would have been firm enough to inflict great pain on his already battered head. The apostle John records that they also beat him with their hands (John 19:3)—probably slapping with open hands while taunting him some more. But Jesus continually remained silent. "When he was reviled, he did not revile in return; when he suffered, he did not threaten, but continued entrusting himself to him who judges justly" (1 Pet. 2:23). Jesus knew these things were part of the Father's plan for him, so he suffered them all willingly and patiently. He endured the mocking, the flogging, the humiliation, and the shame:

> I gave my back to those who strike,
>   and my cheeks to those who pull out the beard;
> I hid not my face
>   from disgrace and spitting.
> But the Lord God helps me;
>   therefore I have not been disgraced;

therefore I have set my face like a flint,
    and I know that I shall not be put to shame. (Isa. 50:6–7)

"And when they had mocked him, they stripped him of the robe and put his own clothes on him and led him away to crucify him" (Matt. 27:31). Victims of crucifixion were usually made to wear a placard around the neck on which was written the crime for which they were condemned. It was part of the shame that was deliberately inflicted on victims of crucifixion (see Heb. 12:2; 13:13). They were led through the streets and made to walk in a public procession in order to maximize the humiliation of the spectacle. They were also forced to carry their own cross to the place of execution. A Roman cross large enough to crucify a grown man might weigh as much as two hundred pounds—an extremely heavy load to bear in any circumstances. But for someone in Jesus's severely weakened condition, it would have been virtually impossible to drag such a load from the Praetorium to the place of crucifixion outside the walls of Jerusalem. In fact, Matthew records that Jesus needed help bearing his cross: "As they went out, they found a man of Cyrene, Simon by name. They compelled this man to carry his cross" (Matt. 27:32).

Christ's last public message was given on the road to Calvary. Luke describes it:

> And there followed him a great multitude of the people and of women who were mourning and lamenting for him. But turning to them Jesus said, "Daughters of Jerusalem, do not weep for me, but weep for yourselves and for your children. For behold, the days are coming when they will say, 'Blessed are the barren and the wombs that never bore and the breasts that never nursed!' Then they will begin to say to the mountains, 'Fall on us,' and to the hills, 'Cover us.' For if they do these things when the wood is green, what will happen when it is dry?" (Luke 23:27–31)

Part of the message was a reference to Hosea 10:8: "They shall say to the mountains, 'Cover us,' and to the hills, 'Fall on us.'" It was a dire warning of disaster to come. Since in that culture childbearing was understood to be the highest blessing God could give a woman, only the worst kind of plague or disaster could ever cause anyone to say, "Blessed are the barren and the wombs that never bore and the breasts that never nursed!" (Luke 23:29).

The green tree represented a time of abundance and blessing, and the dry tree stood for bad times. Jesus was saying that if a tragedy like this could happen in good times, what would befall the nation in bad times? If the Romans crucified someone who they admitted was innocent, what would they do to the Jewish nation when they rebelled? Christ was referring to events that would happen less than a generation later, in AD 70, when the Roman army would lay siege to Jerusalem, utterly destroy the temple, and slaughter thousands upon thousands of Jewish people—multitudes of them by crucifixion. Christ had spoken before of the coming holocaust (see Luke 19:41–44). His awareness of that approaching catastrophe—and the knowledge that some of these same people and their children would suffer in it—still weighed heavily on his mind as he made his way to the cross.

In the Jewish mind, crucifixion was a particularly execrable way to die. It was similar to the hanging on a tree that Moses described in Deuteronomy 21:22–23: "And if a man has committed a crime punishable by death and he is put to death, and you hang him on a tree, his body shall not remain all night on the tree, but you shall bury him the same day, for a hanged man is cursed by God." The Mosaic law also required that all executions occur outside the city walls (Num. 15:35; see Heb. 13:12). The Romans had a slightly different concept. They made sure that all crucifixions took place near major thoroughfares in order to generate fear by making the condemned person a public example for all passersby. So Jesus's crucifixion took place outside the city but in a heavily trafficked location carefully selected to make him a public spectacle.

Matthew writes, "And when they came to a place called Golgotha (which means Place of a Skull), they offered him wine to drink, mixed with gall, but when he tasted it, he would not drink it" (Matt. 27:33–34). Mark 15:23 says that the bitter substance was myrrh, which acts as a mild narcotic. The soldiers may have offered it for its numbing effect just before they drove the nails through the flesh. Jesus spat it out, because he did not want his senses numbed. He had come to the cross to be a sin bearer, and he would feel the full effect of the sin he bore; he would endure the full measure of its pain. His heart was still steadfastly set on doing the will of the Father, and he would not anesthetize his senses before he had accomplished all his work.

The vinegar and gall fulfilled a messianic prophecy from Psalm 69:19–21:

> You know my reproach,
>> and my shame and my dishonor;
>> my foes are all known to you.
> Reproaches have broken my heart,
>> so that I am in despair.
> I looked for pity, but there was none,
>> and for comforters, but I found none.
> They gave me poison for food,
>> and for my thirst they gave me sour wine to drink.

Crucifixion. The intense shame of the crucifixion was accompanied by an equally intense physical pain, and yet even in that unparalleled suffering, Christ spoke forth words of truth and grace. We explore these matters below.

The prophecies concerning crucifixion. As previously discussed, the "head" and the "heel" of the two protagonists in Genesis 3:15 foreshadow important details regarding the conflict between Satan's offspring and the woman's offspring. The promise regarding the victorious offspring ("seed") of the woman involved his being wounded on the heel. Psalm 22:16 expands this image to include the hands, referring to wounds suffered in what appears to be an execution, wounds that fit the method of first-century Roman crucifixion: "They have pierced my hands and feet." The Greek Septuagint supports this translation nearly two hundred years before Christ. The Hebrew text might alternatively read, "Like a lion, my hands and my feet."

However, even that reading allows for wounds that a lion might have caused by biting or clawing—both actions might "pierce" hands and feet. Luke 24:39–40 confirms that Jesus's crucifixion left wounds in his hands and feet: "'See my hands and my feet, that it is I myself. Touch me, and see. For a spirit does not have flesh and bones as you see that I have.' And when he had said this, he showed them his hands and his feet." That Psalm 22:16 preserves a prophecy concerning the Messiah's execution becomes quite clear when repeated parallels occur between the events surrounding Jesus's crucifixion, as recorded in the Gospels, and the events described in Psalm 22. Table 4.9 identifies the parallels.

The method and effects of crucifixion. Crucifixion was a form of execution that the Romans had learned from the Persians, who developed a method of crucifying victims by impaling them on a pole, thus raising them high above the earth, where they were left to die. By the time of Christ, crucifixion had become the favorite method of execution throughout the Roman Empire, and especially in Judea, where it was regularly used to make a public example of rioters and insurrectionists.

The exact process used in Jesus's crucifixion is a matter of some conjecture. None of the Gospel accounts gives a detailed description of the method used on him. After Jesus's crucifixion Thomas had said to the other disciples, "Unless I see in his hands the mark of the nails, and place my finger into the mark of the nails, and place my hand into his side, I will never believe" (John 20:25). From his remark we know that Christ was nailed to the cross, rather than being lashed by leather thongs.

The nails had to be driven through the wrists (not the palms of the hands) because neither the tendons nor the bone structure in the hands could support the body's weight. Nails in the palms would simply tear the flesh between the bones.[47] Nails through the wrists would usually shatter carpal bones and tear the carpal ligaments, but the structure of the wrist was nonetheless strong enough to support the weight of the body. As the nail went into the wrist, it would usually cause severe damage to the sensorimotor median nerve, causing intense pain in both arms. Recovered skeletons of first-century crucifixions preserve evidence that the feet were nailed through the structure of the foot between the ankle bone and the heel bone. That coincides with the description in Genesis 3:15 of the woman's offspring sustaining a wound to the "heel."

After the victim was nailed in place, several soldiers would slowly elevate the top of the cross and carefully slide the foot into a deep posthole. The cross would drop with a jarring blow into the bottom of the hole, causing the full weight of the victim to be immediately borne by the nails in the wrists and feet. That would cause a bone-wrenching pain throughout the body, as major joints were suddenly twisted out of their natural position. That is probably what Christ prophetically referred to in Psalm 22, which reads, "I am poured out like water, and all my bones are out of joint" (22:14).

Death normally came from slow suffocation. The victim's body would hang

---

47. See Erich H. Kiehl, *The Passion of Our Lord* (Grand Rapids, MI: Baker, 1990), 126–31, for a description of a Roman crucifixion.

Table 4.9 The Chronology of Christ's Crucifixion*

Time	New Testament Scripture	Event	Psalm 22
9 a.m.	Luke 23:26	Jesus is led to Calvary.	
	Luke 23:33	Jesus is crucified.	Ps. 22:16
10 a.m.	Luke 23:34a	Jesus prays, "Father, forgive them."	
	Luke 23:34b	The soldiers divide up Jesus's clothes.	Ps. 22:18
	Matt. 27:39–43	People hurl "abuse at him, wagging their heads."	Ps. 22:6–8
	Luke 23:35	The chief priests and rulers mock, "He saved others . . ."	Ps. 22:12–13
	Luke 23:39	One criminal mocks, "Save yourself and us!"	
11 a.m.	Luke 23:40, 42	The other criminal pleads, "Jesus, remember me . . ."	
	Luke 23:43	Jesus assures the criminal, "Today you will be with me in Paradise."	
	John 19:26–27	Jesus says, "Woman, behold, your son!"	
Noon	Luke 23:44	Darkness covers the whole land for three hours.	
1 p.m.	Matt. 27:46	Jesus cries out, "My God, my God, why have you forsaken me?"	Ps. 22:1
	John 19:28	Jesus says, "I thirst."	Ps. 22:14–15
2 p.m.	John 19:30	Jesus declares, "It is finished."	Ps. 22:31
	Luke 23:46	Jesus prays, "Father, into your hands I commit my spirit!"	Ps. 22:19–21
3 p.m.	Matt. 27:51	An earthquake hits, and the temple curtain is torn in two.	
	Matt. 27:52	Tombs break open.	
	Matt. 27:54	A centurion exclaims, "Truly this was the Son of God."	
	Luke 23:48	A crowd witnesses Jesus's suffering and beats their breasts.	
	John 19:31–32	The soldiers break the two criminals' legs.	
	John 19:34	A soldier pierces Jesus's side with a spear.	
	Matt. 27:57–60	Jesus is buried.	Ps. 22:15
6 p.m.		The Sabbath begins.	

* Adapted from William D. Barrick, "Messianic Trilogy: Part One: Psalm 22—The Suffering Messiah," in *Psalms, Hymns, and Spiritual Songs: The Master Musician's Melodies* (unpublished class notes, Placerita Baptist Church, 2004), 5; available at http://drbarrick.org/files/studynotes/Psalms/Ps_022.pdf. Used by permission of the author.

in such a way that the diaphragm was severely constricted. In order to exhale, he would have to push up with the feet so that the diaphragm would have room to move. Ultimately, fatigue, intense pain, or muscle atrophy would render the victim unable to do this, and he would finally die from the lack of oxygen. Once strength or feeling in the legs was gone, the victim would be unable to push up in order to breathe, and death would occur quickly. That is why the Romans sometimes broke the legs below the knees, to hasten the process (see John 19:31).

The mockery by the members of the Sanhedrin was a desperate attempt to convince themselves and all other witnesses that Jesus was not Israel's Messiah. They believed that the Messiah could not be conquered. The fact that Jesus hung there dying so helplessly was proof, as far as they were concerned, that he was not who he claimed to be. So they reveled in their triumph, strutting and swaggering among the crowd of observers, announcing to everyone but to no one in particular, "He saved others; he cannot save himself. He is the King of Israel; let him come down now from the cross, and we will believe in him. He trusts in God; let God deliver him now, if he desires him. For he said, 'I am the Son of God'" (Matt. 27:42–43). If they had been the kind of spiritual leaders they were supposed to be, they would have noticed that their words were an almost verbatim fulfillment of the prophecy of Psalm 22:8.

These were the spiritual leaders in Israel. They had everything to do with religion but nothing to do with God. They therefore bore the greatest guilt of all who participated in the humiliation of Christ. Although they pretended to sit in Moses's seat (Matt. 23:2), they did not believe Moses (John 5:46). Although they claimed to be spokesmen for God, they were actually children of Satan (John 8:44).

As always, Jesus did not revile those who reviled him. Rather, his only words about his tormenters as he hung on the cross were a tender plea to God for mercy on their behalf (Luke 23:34). He had come to the cross willingly, knowingly, and in submissive obedience to God—to die for others' sins. Though the abuse and torture men heaped on him amounted to an agony beyond their ability to fathom, those were nothing compared to the wrath of God against the sin he bore on their behalf.

Jesus's seven last sayings on the cross. As Christ hung on Calvary's cross, he spoke seven times (see table 4.9 [p. 299]). His cries from the cross have struck a chord with believers throughout the ages. The last words uttered by a person before death have often held significance for their loved ones. Those from Christ's lips are unparalleled in their richness. The seven might be presented in the following fashion:[48]

1. A plea for forgiveness: "Father, forgive them, for they know not what they do" (Luke 23:34).
2. A promise of salvation: "Truly, I say to you, today you will be with me in Paradise" (Luke 23:43).
3. A provision for his mother: "Woman, behold, your son! . . . Behold, your mother!" (John 19:26–27).
4. A petition to the Father: "My God, my God, why have you forsaken me?" (Matt. 27:46).
5. A plea for relief: "I thirst" (John 19:28).
6. A proclamation of victory: "It is finished" (John 19:30).
7. A prayer of consummation: "Father, into your hands I commit my spirit!" (Luke 23:46).

---

48. MacArthur, *Murder of Jesus*, 209–24.

Jesus's seven sayings on the cross are weighted with deep theological significance that helps believers better understand his person, character, suffering, and redemptive work.

1. A plea for forgiveness: "Father, forgive them, for they know not what they do" (Luke 23:34).

Divine forgiveness consists of God forgoing his rightful retribution that sinners deserve for their sins committed against him. Jesus suffered pitiless violence at the hands of wicked men prior to and during his crucifixion. It was his right to demand their punishment for their crimes against him. However, Jesus willingly let go of that right and chose to forgive them unconditionally. He forgave them because, in his deity, he knew full well that they did not fully understand who he was and what they were doing.

As the God-man, Christ's forgiveness comes from a sympathetic and compassionate human nature combined with divine power, righteousness, holiness, mercy, and grace through his deity (see Ex. 34:6–7). This cry for pardon reveals the inexorable nature of God's sovereign plan to provide a Savior whose sacrifice would purchase the forgiveness that the blood of bulls and goats could never supply (Heb. 10:4; see Matt. 26:28; Heb. 9:22). Thus, Jesus's first words from the cross highlight what he came to accomplish: "redemption, the forgiveness of sins" (Col. 1:14), for those who would repent (Rom. 2:4).

2. A promise of salvation: "Truly, I say to you, today you will be with me in Paradise" (Luke 23:43).

The second saying from the cross came as a response to the heartfelt request of one of the criminals crucified alongside Jesus:

> One of the criminals who were hanged railed at him, saying, "Are you not the Christ? Save yourself and us!" But the other rebuked him, saying, "Do you not fear God, since you are under the same sentence of condemnation? And we indeed justly, for we are receiving the due reward of our deeds; but this man has done nothing wrong." And he said, "Jesus, remember me when you come into your kingdom." (Luke 23:39–42)

Again, as with the first saying, Jesus acted in his role as the God-man, exhibiting the attributes of both natures by means of his human sympathy and compassion and his divine omniscience. He knew that this man's words revealed a truly repentant heart smitten with his own sin and desiring the mercy and forgiveness of the Savior. The promise reveals Christ's deity in that only God can know the state of the heart and the ultimate destiny of any individual. The Gospel account indicates that Jesus died before the two criminals—when the executioners broke the legs of those two men, they found that Jesus had already expired (John 19:31–34). Therefore, Jesus made this promise to the repentant criminal, knowing that he would be in heaven first and would greet the man when he arrived. Jesus was numbered with the transgressors so that sinners like the thief might be numbered with the redeemed.

3. A provision for his mother: "Woman, behold, your son! . . . Behold, your mother!" (John 19:26–27).

One of the most poignant episodes occurring during Jesus's crucifixion finds Jesus addressing the mother who had given him his humanity (Isa. 49:1). Simeon's prophecy had come to its bitter fruition:

> And Simeon blessed them and said to Mary his mother, "Behold, this child is appointed for the fall and rising of many in Israel, and for a sign that is opposed (and a sword will pierce through your own soul also), so that thoughts from many hearts may be revealed." (Luke 2:34–35)

In Jesus's statement here, Mary's son gave all his attention to her and her need for care. To John, the disciple nearest to the heart of Jesus, the Savior committed the care of his most precious earthly relationship—his mother. In this the perfect man demonstrated his fulfillment of the command to honor one's parents (Ex. 20:12; Eph. 6:2–3). He left to his followers a superb example of what he meant by instructing them to set a priority on caring for parents before presenting their gifts to God:

> And why do you break the commandment of God for the sake of your tradition? For God commanded, "Honor your father and your mother," and, "Whoever reviles father or mother must surely die." But you say, "If anyone tells his father or his mother, 'What you would have gained from me is given to God,' he need not honor his father." So for the sake of your tradition you have made void the word of God. You hypocrites! (Matt. 15:3–7)

While Jesus gave his life completely as a sacrifice before his heavenly Father, he took pains to not make God's Word void by failing to properly honor his mother, which demanded caring for her in her later years. Before his sacrifice was completed, he had cared for his mother as he ought—a deed all the more urgent since the silence of Scripture concerning Joseph seems to indicate that he had already died and left Mary as a widow.

4. A petition to the Father: "My God, my God, why have you forsaken me?" (Matt. 27:46).

No man can fully fathom the significance of this cry from Jesus's lips. Herein lies the mystery of the hypostatic union (see "Humanity" [p. 263]). The presence of darkness (Matt. 27:45) symbolized both the loss of fellowship's light and the reality of abandonment.

The Father and the Son were not separated in their being or in their essence through this experience. The unity of the Trinity remained intact. The three-hour darkness occurred due to the wrath of the omnipresent Father who acted faithfully in his role to bring about the completion of Christ's perfect, substitutionary sacrifice.

Some interpreters of the Bible have concluded that Jesus was merely reciting the words of Psalm 22:1 at this point. However, given that Psalm 22 is an extended prophecy about the crucifixion, the psalm actually presents a prophetic anticipation of Jesus's heart cry as he bore the sins of the elect on the cross. Therefore, his statement should not be taken simply as a recitation of the psalm or a mere identification with the human sufferings of the psalmist.[49]

The physical pains of crucifixion were nothing compared to the wrath of the Father poured out on Jesus. In anticipation of this event, Jesus sweat as blood in the garden of Gethsemane (Luke 22:44). All of mankind's worst fears about the horrors of hell were realized by Jesus as he received the due penalty for the sins of all who would believe in him. In that period of darkness, in some incomprehensible way, the Father had abandoned him. "Though there was surely no interruption in the Father's love for Him *as a Son*, God nonetheless turned away from Him and forsook Him *as our Substitute*."[50]

This substitutionary aspect of Christ's death does not rest on his physical death alone. Christ had to bear the outpouring of God's unmitigated wrath against sin in order to satisfy justice completely. True substitutionary atonement therefore involved a painful sense of estrangement from the Father, expressed by Christ in his heartfelt petition in Matthew 27:46—"My God, my God, why have you forsaken me?" Although it was temporary, the agony Christ experienced in absorbing the Father's wrath was the full equivalent of hell.[51]

This is the suffering that Jesus anticipated in the garden of Gethsemane when he prayed, "Let this cup pass from me" (Matt. 26:39). The "cup" refers to the greatest of all suffering for the perfectly sinless God-man—the wrath of God poured out on him when he was made to be a sin offering. A cup is often the symbol of divine wrath against sin in the Old Testament (Isa. 51:17, 22; Jer. 25:15–17, 27–29; Lam. 4:21–22; Ezek. 23:31–34; Hab. 2:16). Christ would "bear the sins of many" (Heb. 9:28), and the fullness of divine wrath would fall on him (Isa. 53:10–11; 2 Cor. 5:21). This was the price of the sin he bore, which he paid in full. His cry of anguish in Matthew 27:46 reflected the extreme bitterness of the cup of wrath he was soon to receive.

Jesus's suffering thus included his temporary separation from the Father (pictured by the three hours of darkness on the cross) while experiencing the fullness of divine wrath prior to his physical death. The subsequent seventh saying on the cross, "Father, into your hands I commit my spirit!"' (Luke 23:46), demands this chronology, since it demonstrates the restoration of eternal fellowship because the temporary separation had ended. This sequence fits the experience of those for whom Jesus died—all are dead spiritually before they die physically. Christ first accomplished victory over

---

49. MacArthur, *Murder of Jesus*, 218.
50. MacArthur, *Murder of Jesus*, 221.
51. This is to be distinguished from the heretical doctrines of certain charismatic leaders who teach that Jesus actually became a sinner on the cross, or that he literally went to hell to undergo further punishment. Rather, as our substitute, Jesus bore the very punishment that was due to his people: the Father's wrath in all its fullness. While the wrath poured out on sinners in hell is eternal, Jesus, because of the dignity and worth of his person, could extinguish the infinite wrath of God in only three hours of suffering. In this sense, he bore the full weight of every curse and penalty our sins deserve.

spiritual death while still on the cross. Three days later he would be victorious over physical and eternal death when he rose from the dead.

5. A plea for relief: "I thirst" (John 19:28).

A single word in the Greek text, Jesus's fifth saying from the cross reveals the humanness of this experience—physical thirst arising out of intense exhaustion and physical agony. Yet this very concise saying reveals more than his humanity; it reveals his knowledge of the Scriptures and his determination to fulfill all that the Scriptures said about him. The psalmist had written, "For my thirst they gave me sour wine to drink" (Ps. 69:21). John made a point of saying that Jesus's statement was "to fulfill the Scripture" (John 19:28). And Jesus himself described thirst as a characteristic of the unrighteous in their experience after death (Luke 16:24). Again, apart from the existence of an eternal hell, the work of Christ on the cross cannot be fully understood and appreciated.

6. A proclamation of victory: "It is finished" (John 19:30).

The sixth saying of Jesus from the cross, like the previous saying, is but a single word in the Greek text: *Tetelestai!* His cry was triumphant and full of rich meaning since the Greek form implies that the state of completion would continue. Jesus did not refer to his earthly life as over; he meant that he had completed the work the Father had given him to accomplish. In fact, the statement in Psalm 22:31 is "He has done it"—also just one word in the Hebrew. Jesus celebrated the greatest triumph in the history of the universe, because his atoning work was finished. All the prophecies of the Scripture regarding the Messiah's redemptive work had been fulfilled, and God's justice was fully satisfied. Sin's ransom was paid in full; the wages of sin were settled forever for all of God's chosen throughout all history. All that remained for Christ to do was to die so that he might rise from the dead. Nothing can be added to the finished work of Christ for salvation.

7. A prayer of consummation: "Father, into your hands I commit my spirit!" (Luke 23:46).

Christ addressed his final statement from the cross to the Father, as he had in the first ("Father, forgive them, for they know not what they do," Luke 23:34) and the fourth ("My God, my God, why have you forsaken me?" Matt. 27:46). These three were prayers—the prayers of the Son of Man. In his humanity, Jesus lived as a man of prayer, and he died as a man of prayer (see Matt. 14:23; 19:13; 26:36–44; Heb. 5:7).

Christ died as no other man has ever died. In one sense, he was murdered by the hands of wicked men (Acts 2:23). In another sense, the Father sent him to the cross and put him to grief (Isa. 53:10). However, in still another sense, no one took Jesus's life. He himself gave it up willingly for those whom he loved selflessly and sacrificially:

For this reason the Father loves me, because I lay down my life that I may take it up again. No one takes it from me, but I lay it down of my own accord. I have authority to lay it down, and I have authority to take it up again. This charge I have received from my Father. (John 10:17–18)

When he breathed his last, there was no frantic struggle against his executioners. No witness observed any frenzied death throes. His final passage into death was a deliberate act of his own sovereign will. He "bowed his head and gave up his spirit" (John 19:30). Simply, quietly, submissively, he purposefully yielded up his life, in complete control of his dying.

Death and Atonement

The seven sayings on the cross present the death of Jesus as an experience that he purposefully and willingly entered. How he died is one thing; why he died is infinitely more important. The biblical fact is that his death was necessary, determined from before the foundation of the earth, and a necessity for the salvation of sinners.

CHRIST'S DEATH

Christian theology focuses on the saving work of Jesus Christ in his substitutionary death and his resurrection from the dead. These two truths form the gospel's core message regarding salvation. The apostle Paul wrote,

Now I would remind you, brothers, of the gospel I preached to you, which you received, in which you stand, and by which you are being saved, if you hold fast to the word I preached to you—unless you believed in vain.

For I delivered to you as of first importance what I also received: that Christ died for our sins in accordance with the Scriptures, that he was buried, that he was raised on the third day in accordance with the Scriptures, and that he appeared to Cephas, then to the twelve. (1 Cor. 15:1–5)

These two major elements of the gospel also appear in Paul's defense before Agrippa: "I stand here testifying to both small and great, saying nothing but what the prophets and Moses said would come to pass: that the Christ must suffer and that, by being the first to rise from the dead, he would proclaim light both to the people and to the Gentiles" (Acts 26:22–23).

The apostle Peter, speaking of "the salvation of your souls" (1 Pet. 1:9), outlined the same two-part work of Christ with regard to the gospel:

Concerning this salvation, the prophets who prophesied about the grace that was to be yours searched and inquired carefully, inquiring what person or time the Spirit of Christ in them was indicating when he predicted the sufferings of Christ and the subsequent glories. It was revealed to them that they were serving not themselves but you, in the things that have now been announced to you through those who preached the good news to you by the Holy Spirit sent from heaven, things into which angels long to look. (1 Pet. 1:10–12)

It should be noted that "inquiring what person or time" (1 Pet. 1:11) might also be understood as "inquiring what time or what character of time," making the unknown aspects of messianic fulfillment only the timing.[52] The prophets understood that they spoke about the Messiah. The Old Testament prophets revealed the person of the Messiah by means of a series of prophecies tying him to the line of Abraham (Gen. 12:3; see Gal. 3:8), the nation of Israel (Num. 24:17; see Matt. 2:2; Rev. 22:16), the tribe of Judah (Gen. 49:10; see Matt. 1:2–3; 2:6; Heb. 7:14), the clan of Ephrathah in the town of Bethlehem (Mic. 5:2; see Matt. 2:5–6; Luke 2:11), a virgin conception (Isa. 7:14; see Matt. 1:23), and a ministry to Galilee of the Gentiles (Isa. 9:1–2; see Matt. 4:12–16). Isaiah 53 provides a detailed prophecy of the Messiah's ministry, rejection, trial, death, resurrection, and exaltation.

CHRIST'S ATONEMENT

Old Testament Revelation about Sacrifice.[53] Penal substitution means that Christ gave himself to suffer and die by bearing the full penalty for sin in the place of all the sinners whom God saves. God prepared mankind for the atoning, substitutionary sacrifice of Christ by providing early instruction about sacrifice. The Old Testament presents twelve basic principles regarding animal sacrifices:

1. Only believers should offer Old Testament sacrifices—believers who should be indoctrinated and obedient (i.e., exhibiting right teaching and right behavior). Leviticus 1:2–3 and 2:1 speak of Israelite believers, while Leviticus 17:8 and 22:18, 25 speak of foreign believers (cf. Num. 15:14–16; Isa. 56:6–8).

2. Old Testament sacrifices should be the outward demonstration of a vital faith. Without faith the sacrifices are worthless (Heb. 11:4; see 1 Sam. 15:22–23; Ps. 51:15–19; Isa. 1:11–15; Mic. 6:6–8).

3. Old Testament sacrifices do not save from sin or forgive sins. Levitical sacrifices include no provision for removing or doing away with any individual's sinful nature. Animal sacrifices are insufficient to fully and finally atone for the sins of human beings—only a human life can fully atone for a human life (cf. Lev. 1:3 with Ps. 49:5–9; see Gal. 3:10–14; Heb. 10:1–18; 1 Pet. 1:18–19).

4. Old Testament sacrifices do not eliminate temporal punishment for sin, especially willful, defiant sin. Many sins require capital punishment—no animal sacrifice can avail for such sin (Lev. 24:10–23; Num. 15:30). Premeditated, deliberate sin requires the death of the sinner. Therefore, due to the pattern of voluntary, deliberate sin, each individual finds himself under sentence of death, and due to the universality of sin, death reigns, as evidenced by the genealogies recording those deaths (Gen. 5:5, 8, 11, 14, 17, 20, 27, 31). "Died" as a repetitive term provides the epitaph for person after person (see also Gen. 11:32; 23:2; 35:19; 50:26). This raises a fitting pair of questions: Is there really no sacrifice for deliberate sin? And is there no forgiveness for such deliberate rebellion?

---

52. Thomas R. Schreiner, *1, 2 Peter, Jude*, NAC 37 (Nashville: Broadman, 2003), 73–74.
53. This section is adapted from William D. Barrick, "Penal Substitution in the Old Testament," *MSJ* 20, no. 2 (2009): 2, 6–8. Used by permission of *MSJ*.

5. Old Testament sacrifices have as their chief object fellowship with God. They outwardly symbolize forgiveness for sins, which brought a measured reconciliation with the covenant-keeping God of Israel (Ex. 29:42–43; 30:36). According to John Oswalt,

> While temporal punishment for sin is serious and ought not to be dismissed, it is by no means as serious as spiritual punishment: alienation from God. This is what the entire sacrificial system is about: making it possible for sinful humans to have fellowship with a holy God. The sacrifices do not mitigate the temporal effects of sin, so what do they do? They deal with the spiritual effects of sin; they address the truths that the soul that sins shall die (not merely physically; Ezek. 18:4, 20), and that there is no forgiveness for sin apart from the shedding of blood (Lev. 17:11; Heb. 9:22).[54]

6. Old Testament sacrifices declare, emphasize, and magnify sin and its consequences (Rom. 3:19–20; 5:20; 7:5–11; Gal. 3:21–22).
7. Old Testament sacrifices declare, emphasize, and magnify God's holiness, righteousness, love, grace, mercy, and sovereignty (Ps. 119:62; Neh. 9:13; Matt. 23:23; Rom. 7:12). The combination of these two declarations concerning sin and the character of God expresses the dual function of sacrifice in the Old Testament. On the one hand, sin is essentially "theofugal"—it leads mankind *away from God*.[55] On the other hand, sacrifice, which by its bloodshed displays the terrible nature and consequences of sin, is theocentric, turning sinners' attention *to God*. They begin to see the effects of their sin on God. Their sin is enmity against God, alienating them from God and proving their rebellion against divine authority and character. Their sacrifices propitiate God's just wrath and reconcile them to God.
8. Old Testament sacrifices demonstrate that the Mosaic legislation offers the Old Testament believer no independent access to God (Heb. 9:8–10).
9. Old Testament sacrifices demonstrate that God's desire with regard to his people's offerings (giving) does not exceed their normal ability. The sacrificial objects (cattle, sheep, goats, doves; flour, oil, wine, and frankincense) are all immediately available to the individual Israelite. God does not require that his people bring something exotic or beyond their normal means. He does not require them to extend themselves to the point of either financial discomfort or disaster (see 1 Cor. 16:2; 2 Corinthians 8–9).
10. Old Testament sacrifices emphasize the ministry of the priesthood (Lev. 1:9; 2:8; 4:20; 6:6; Hebrews 5–10; 1 Pet. 2:5).
11. Old Testament sacrifices involve the recognition of God's covenant with his people (Lev. 2:13; Ps. 50:5, 16).
12. God commands Old Testament sacrifices in part to sustain the priesthood. The covenant community provides for those who minister (Lev. 7:34–35; Neh. 13:5; Mal. 3:8–10).

---

54. John N. Oswalt, *The Book of Isaiah: Chapters 40–66*, NICOT (Grand Rapids, MI: Eerdmans, 1998), 385.
55. Norman H. Snaith, *The Distinctive Ideas of the Old Testament* (New York: Schocken, 1964), 60.

In summary, these twelve principles provide evidence that sacrifices deal primarily with corporate worship. They are corporate in the sense that Old Testament believers bring offerings publicly to the sanctuary, where the priests participate in the accompanying rituals. Benefits from the sacrifices might be personal or individual, but there is no private sacrifice. The Passover lamb might appear to be private since it involves one household, but passersby can see the blood on the doorposts at the entrance to the home—and the lamb can be shared with a neighbor (Ex. 12:4). Old Testament sacrifices are confessional, because they demonstrate repentant faith in Yahweh and obedience to his statutes and laws. By offering sacrifices, the Old Testament believer identifies himself outwardly with the covenant God and his covenant people. That outward demonstration ought to be the result of true faith. However, when that initiating faith is absent, the sacrifice is worthless—an empty gesture, devoid of any spiritual value (i.e., a false confession). God hates false sacrifice and cannot accept it as true worship (see 1 Sam. 15:22; Ps. 50:7–15; Isa. 1:13–15).

With these principles in mind, the reader can consider how the Old Testament deals with penal substitutionary sacrifices. The ram provided by the "angel [messenger] of the LORD" as a substitute for Isaac in Genesis 22:1–14 illustrates the giving of a life as a substitute. Eugene Merrill offers an excellent treatment in his volume on Old Testament theology, where he states that Isaac's own death "was enacted through a substitute, an animal whose literal death provided full satisfaction to God's demands."[56]

Old Testament Revelation about Christ's Substitutionary Sacrifice.[57] The different sacrifices described and commanded in the book of Leviticus provided Israel with God's instruction regarding the nature of sacrifice and helped prepare them for the necessity of the Messiah's substitutionary sacrifice for sin. Table 4.10 identifies some of the lessons that God intended his people to learn from the sacrifices in the Old Testament. Table 4.11 compares Jesus Christ's own sacrifice to the sacrifices under the Mosaic legislation.

To understand the relationship of the Old Testament sacrificial system to the person of the Messiah, several key texts must be examined more closely. The most significant of these texts are Exodus 12 (the Passover festival), Leviticus 16 (the Day of Atonement), and, perhaps most important of all, Isaiah 52:13–53:12. The Passover and the Day of Atonement represent two of the chief religious festivals in Israel's calendar, all of which introduce concepts involved in the person and work of the Messiah (see table 4.12).

Exodus 12: The Passover. In concluding the plagues just prior to Israel's exodus from Egypt, God instituted the Passover observance in which the lamb of the Passover served as a substitutionary sacrifice for the Israelites' firstborn sons. In Exodus 12:3, the Lord instructs Moses concerning the sacrifice of the Passover lamb: "Every man

---

56. Eugene Merrill, *Everlasting Dominion: A Theology of the Old Testament* (Nashville: Broadman, 2006), 236.
57. This section, the charts excepted, is adapted from William D. Barrick, "Penal Substitution in the Old Testament," *MSJ* 20, no. 2 (2009): 8–21. Used by permission of *MSJ*.

Table 4.10 Christ in the Levitical Offerings*

Offering	Scripture Passages	Christ's Provision	Christ's Character
Burnt offering	Lev. 1:3–17; 6:8–13	Atonement	Christ's sinless nature
Grain offering	Lev. 2:1–16; 6:14–23	Dedication/consecration	Christ was wholly devoted to the Father's purposes
Peace offering	Lev. 3:1–17; 7:11–36	Reconciliation/fellowship	Christ was at peace with God
Sin offering	Lev. 4:1–5:13; 6:24–30	Propitiation	Christ's substitutionary death
Trespass offering	Lev. 5:14–6:7; 7:1–10	Repentance	Christ paid it all for redemption

* Adapted from MacArthur, *MacArthur Study Bible: English Standard Version*, 156. Used by permission of Thomas Nelson.

Table 4.11 Old Testament Sacrifices Compared to Christ's Sacrifice*

Leviticus	Scripture Passages	Hebrews
Old covenant (temporary)	Heb. 7:22; 8:6, 13; 10:20	New covenant (permanent)
Obsolete promises	Heb. 8:6–13	Better promises
A shadow	Heb. 8:5; 9:23–24; 10:1	The reality
Aaronic priesthood (many)	Heb. 6:19–7:25	Melchizedekian priesthood (one)
Sinful priesthood	Heb. 7:26–27; 9:7	Sinless priest
Limited-by-death priesthood	Heb. 7:16–17, 23–24	Forever priesthood
Daily sacrifices	Heb. 7:27; 9:12, 25–26; 10:9–10, 12	Once-for-all sacrifice
Animal sacrifices	Heb. 9:11–15, 26; 10:4–10, 19	Sacrifice of God's Son
Ongoing sacrifices	Heb. 10:11–14, 18	Sacrifices no longer needed
One-year atonement	Heb. 7:25; 9:12, 15; 10:1–4, 12	Eternal propitiation

* Reproduced from MacArthur, *MacArthur Study Bible: English Standard Version*, 158. Used by permission of Thomas Nelson.

Table 4.12 Christ Fulfills Israel's Feasts*

The Feasts (Leviticus 23)	Christ's Fulfillment
Passover (March/April)	Death of Christ (1 Cor. 5:7)
Unleavened bread (March/April)	Sinlessness of Christ (1 Cor. 5:8)
Firstfruits (March/April)	Resurrection of Christ (1 Cor. 15:23)
Pentecost (May/June)	Outpouring of the Spirit of Christ (Acts 1:5; 2:4)
Trumpets (September/October)	Israel's regathering by Christ (Matt. 24:31)
Atonement (September/October)	Substitutionary sacrifice by Christ (Rom. 11:26)
Booths (September/October)	Rest and reunion with Christ (Zech. 14:16–19)

* Reproduced from MacArthur, *MacArthur Study Bible: English Standard Version*, 186. Used by permission of Thomas Nelson.

shall take a lamb according to their fathers' houses, a lamb for a household." The phrase "for a household" might imply substitution. In fact, the sacrifice appears to forestall the penalty of death for those who are within the household—especially firstborn sons. Although the lamb signifies substitution, the text does not state that the blood atones for or expiates sin; it only protects and preserves the household from temporal judgment.

In Exodus 12:12, the Lord says that he will execute judgment as he passes through the land of Egypt. Israelites who follow the instructions and apply the blood of the slaughtered lamb to the doorposts of their houses will escape that judgment (Ex. 12:13, 23, 27). And the obedient Israelites do indeed escape death (Ex. 12:30). What have the Israelites done that would merit death? Why would they be subject to death and judgment like the Egyptians? Two texts help explain the matter. Exodus 12:12 indicates that the death of the firstborn of Egypt brought judgment against the gods of the Egyptians. Ezekiel 20:4–10 reveals that the Israelites worshiped idols while in Egypt (esp. 20:7–8), a reality Joshua 24:14 confirms: "Now therefore fear the LORD and serve him in sincerity and in faithfulness. Put away the gods that your fathers served beyond the River and in Egypt, and serve the LORD." Indeed, Israelite idolatry in Egypt causes the Lord to respond in wrath and to pour out judgment on them (Ezek. 20:8). Just like the Egyptians, the Israelites come under the sentence of death. What a surprise that proves to be to the Israelites, who are comfortable with the preceding sequence of nine plagues—as long as the Egyptians are the ones suffering. But the Israelites had sinned like the Egyptians, and therefore, in the tenth plague God reveals his people's sins as well as his provision for their salvation. Yahweh's judgments on the gods of Egypt prove that he alone can deliver one from sin's penalty of death. Psalm 49 teaches the same truth but focuses on mankind being unable to muster up such deliverance—only God can provide the "ransom" payment that he requires (Ps. 49:7–9, 15). As Merrill points out with reference to Psalm 49:14–15, "This glimpse into immortality, if not resurrection, marks a high point of Old Testament revelation with respect to the matter of the state of the righteous after death and in the hereafter."[58]

By providing the Passover sacrifice, the Lord graciously spares guilty Israelites by means of the sacrificial blood of animals and preserves his own holiness by fulfilling his promises to deliver his people out of Egypt (Ex. 12:12–13; see Lev. 22:32–33). According to Leon Morris, "The obvious symbolism is that a death has taken place, and this death substitutes for the death of the firstborn."[59] Bruce Waltke agrees, describing the Passover lamb as "both substitutionary and propitiatory. It *nullifies* God's wrath against sinful people because it *satisfies* God's holiness."[60] Once again it is evident that divine wrath on sinners relates to the penalty aspect of penal substitution. The New Testament confirms the substitutionary nature of the Passover

---

58. Merrill, *Everlasting Dominion*, 588.
59. Leon Morris, *The Apostolic Preaching of the Cross*, 3rd ed. (Grand Rapids, MI: Eerdmans, 1965), 117.
60. Bruce K. Waltke, *An Old Testament Theology: An Exegetical, Canonical, and Thematic Approach*, with Charles Yu (Grand Rapids, MI: Zondervan, 2007), 382.

sacrifice. In 1 Corinthians 5:7, Paul, at minimum, draws an analogy between the substitutionary nature of the Passover lamb and Christ's sacrificial death on the cross. Thus, it is no surprise to see that Jesus was crucified during Passover (Matt. 26:2).

Leviticus 16: The Day of Atonement. Merrill Unger presents the following overview of the first three books of the Torah: "Genesis is the book of beginnings, Exodus the book of redemption, and Leviticus the book of atonement and a holy walk. In Genesis we see man ruined; in Exodus, man redeemed; in Leviticus, man cleansed, worshiping and serving."[61] Leviticus speaks of more than just cleansing for sinners and preparation for worship. It describes how sinful persons might enter the presence of the holy God. Leviticus deals with mankind's spiritual relationship to God by means of sacrificial rituals that prefigure the atoning death of Christ. Some refer to Leviticus as the seedbed of New Testament theology. On the one hand, the holiness theme of Leviticus reveals the bad news that God's holiness cannot allow for sinful human beings to have access to him. On the other hand, however, Leviticus presents the good news that God provides a means for sinners to be accepted and to enter his presence through sacrifices.

Of all the sacrifices and festivals, the Day of Atonement exceeds all others in its significance to Israel's relationship to Yahweh. The historical setting of Leviticus is found in God's judgment on the priests Nadab and Abihu (Lev. 10:1–20)—a stark reminder of the holiness of God and its incompatibility with human sinfulness. Emphasis thus falls on the necessity of atonement even for the priests' sins. If the priests are defiled, they cannot mediate between the people and God. Without mediators, sinful Israelites cannot approach God's presence, and God's presence cannot continue to reside in their midst.

The "scapegoat" (Lev. 16:8–10) symbolizes the removal of sin from the presence of God's glory in the midst of his people (see Ps. 103:12; Mic. 7:19). "Scapegoat" (William Tyndale's translation of the Hebrew term *'azazel*) is not mentioned again in the Old Testament or the New Testament. On the Day of Atonement both the scapegoat and the other goat sufficed as a sin offering (Lev. 16:5). Some interpreters see an allusion to the scapegoat in Isaiah 53:6 and Hebrews 13:12.[62] *'Azazel* is most likely a general reference to the wilderness to which the goat was banished. Good arguments can be made for taking the Hebrew term as meaning "removal."[63] Whatever the meaning, it does not materially alter the essential nature of the ritual.

The description of laying hands on the head of the goat (Lev. 16:21–22) pictures the transfer of sins from Israel to the living goat. It serves as their substitute— condemned to die in the wilderness, isolated from Israel. The scapegoat carries away on it "all the iniquities" of the Israelites (Lev. 16:22). In addition, Leviticus 16:24, 29–34 indicates that the entire ritual provides atonement for the sins of the priests as well as the people. Snaith, discussing the views of Rabbi Ishmael, mentions that

---

61. Merrill F. Unger, *The New Unger's Bible Handbook*, rev. ed., rev. Gary N. Larson (Chicago: Moody Press, 1984), 85.
62. E.g., Mark F. Rooker, *Leviticus*, NAC 3A (Nashville: Broadman, 2000), 221, 226.
63. Allen P. Ross, *Holiness to the Lord: A Guide to the Exposition of the Book of Leviticus* (Grand Rapids, MI: Baker Academic, 2002), 319.

"in all cases of deliberate sin, the Day of Atonement at most combines with repentance to suspend punishment, but is never itself efficacious even for that, still less for atonement."[64] There is a certain sense in which Rabbi Ishmael is correct. Paul wrote that God displayed Jesus Christ "as a propitiation by his blood, to be received by faith. This was to show God's righteousness, because in his divine forbearance he had passed over former sins" (Rom. 3:25). The Day of Atonement anticipated the Messiah's propitiatory sacrifice by his blood. Thus, having planned it just that way (see Heb. 9:26; 1 Pet. 1:18–21; Rev. 13:8), God could suspend the penalty in light of its ultimate, full removal through Christ's perfect and complete atonement. Suspension of the temporal penalty applies equally to believer and unbeliever alike within Israel, because the "grace period" involves the temporary benefits of remote substitution, as compared to the permanent and full application of intimate substitution after Christ's death.

Does the ritual of the Day of Atonement indicate the penal aspect of substitution explicitly or implicitly? The Hebrew word for "ransom" (*koper*) represents the concept of "substitute" because it depicts that means by which evil or guilt is transferred and thereby eliminated. The term carries this meaning in the following situations:

- the law of census in which the ransom averts the penalty of plague when the law is violated (Ex. 30:12–16)
- laws regarding homicide in which death is the penalty for the crime (Num. 35:31–33; Deut. 21:1–9)
- the matter of the Levites guarding the sanctuary's sanctity to avert wrath, plague, and death on the congregation (Num. 1:53; 8:19; 18:22–23; compare these with the case of Phinehas in 25:11; Ps. 106:30–31)
- the inability of Babylon to ransom herself from divine judgment (Isa. 47:11; see Ps. 49:7–9)
- the atoning significance of the sacrifice's blood (Lev. 17:11)

Thus, the use of the term *koper* as "ransom" relates explicitly to both substitution and penalty.

The Day of Atonement stands as the central observance of the sacrificial system in the book of Leviticus. It emphasizes, more than any other Jewish observance, the holiness of God and the sinfulness of his people. For Israel the Day of Atonement provided symbolic cleansing or purification so that they might have access to the worship of Yahweh. Therefore, the Day of Atonement provides a symbol of the real atonement by the Lord Jesus Christ (Hebrews 8–10). The chief point of Hebrews (see Heb. 8:1) is in direct contrast to the chief point of the Mosaic law (see Heb. 9:8). In summary, the Day of Atonement temporally and temporarily *expiated* the nation's sins, *cleansed* the sanctuary from the pollution caused by those sins, and *removed* those sins from the community, so that God accepted their worship. This was not personal salvation, which was always by faith alone (Rom. 4:13).

Isaiah 52:13–53:12: The suffering servant's sacrifice. This is truly the first Gospel,

---

64. Snaith, *Distinctive Ideas*, 68.

followed by the other four in the New Testament. It reveals seven hundred years before his coming the life and work of the one true and perfect Sacrifice who actually took away sin. Isaiah first describes the sufferings of the servant of Yahweh whose griefs and sorrows are not his own. That fact identifies the servant's sufferings as substitutionary: "Surely he has borne our griefs and carried our sorrows" (Isa. 53:4). The substitutionary imagery of Isaiah 53:6—"The LORD has laid on him the iniquity of us all"—is drawn straight from Leviticus 16. The vicarious elements in Christ's sufferings in his death relate quite closely to the substitutionary elements in Isaiah 52:13–53:12. Second, the language of Isaiah 53 clearly includes the penal aspect (see 53:5, "pierced . . . crushed . . . chastisement . . . wounds"). Third, key New Testament references include an apparent echo of Isaiah 53, such as in Matthew 26:28: "For this is my blood of the covenant, which is poured out for many for the forgiveness of sins" (see also Rom. 8:3; Gal. 1:4; Heb. 5:3; 10:8, 18, 26; 13:11; 1 Pet. 3:18; 1 John 2:2; 4:10).

The servant of Yahweh voluntarily bore the penalty for the iniquities of "many." His sacrificial death did not occur by some sort of abuse or forced action. Rather, he purposefully decided, accepted, and submitted to his suffering. Isaiah 53:10 ("when his soul makes an offering for guilt") and 53:12 ("poured out his soul to death") make that same point regarding the servant's voluntary sacrifice. Eugene Merrill states that the prophet himself understood what he was writing:

> By reflection on his person and experience, it became clear to the prophet that this servant of the Lord was suffering vicariously for us, that is, for Israel and, by extension, for the whole world (vv. 4–6). . . . Most astounding of all, what he did was in compliance with the will of God who, through the servant's death and subsequent resurrection (thus implicitly in vv. 10b–11a), will justify sinners on the basis of the servant's substitutionary role (v. 11b). Then finally, in God's time, he will reign triumphant, having gained victory over sin and death (v. 12).[65]

Indeed, Yahweh's servant meets all the requirements for being a substitutionary sacrifice: (1) identification with condemned sinners ("for the transgression of my people," Isa. 53:8), (2) being blameless and without any stain or spot to mar his sacrifice ("no violence . . . no deceit," 53:9; "the righteous one," 53:11), and (3) being acceptable to Yahweh ("it was the will of the LORD to crush him," 53:10).

In the ritual of the Day of Atonement, the scapegoat could not be slaughtered as a sacrifice because it carried the sins of Israel, thereby making it unclean. If the servant of the Lord were a mere human being (the prophet himself or even the nation of Israel), the same problem would arise. This is one reason why sinful people cannot serve as the ransom or atonement price for anyone else (see Ps. 49:7–9). Such revealed truths make it necessary that Yahweh's servant in Isaiah 53 be someone who cannot be tainted even by carrying or bearing the sins of many—in other words, he must be a person of the Godhead. Christ's death corresponds to the ritual of the

---

65. Merrill, *Everlasting Dominion*, 514.

scapegoat, because Jesus (1) bore the people's sins (2 Cor. 5:21; see Gal. 3:13; Heb. 9:28; 1 Pet. 2:24), and (2) died outside the camp (Heb. 13:12; see Matt. 21:39; Luke 20:15; John 19:17).

It must also be noted that the phrase "by oppression and judgment" (or "justice," Isa. 53:8) refers to the judicial aspect of the penalty that the servant bore. Translations vary for the line "when his soul makes an offering for guilt" (53:10). The Lord's servant becomes a guilt offering, a sin-bearing sacrifice that imputes righteousness. Why does the prophet identify the sacrifice of Yahweh's servant as a guilt offering ('*asham*)? It could refer generally to any expiatory sacrifice. David Baron distinguishes between the guilt offering and the sin offering as follows: "While the sin offering looked to the sinful state of the offerer, the trespass offering was appointed to meet *actual transgressions*, the fruit of the sinful state. The sin offering set forth propitiation, the trespass offering set forth satisfaction."[66] Satisfaction refers to the fact that Christ paid for the elect every sin-debt owed to God. The guilt offering involves both unintentional sin (Lev. 5:15–19) and intentional sin (such as theft or fraud, Lev. 6:1–5; 19:20–22). Since most sacrifices deal only with unintentional sin, any ultimately efficacious atoning sacrifice must go beyond those sacrifices to provide expiation for intentional sins. This answers the earlier question regarding the availability of sacrifice for deliberate sin. Yes, the servant's perfect sacrifice takes care of deliberate sin and provides forgiveness for planned rebellion. In addition, the guilt offering, rather than purifying, sanctifies; it reconsecrates Israel as a holy nation, restoring the people to the land and to their God. The servant's perfect guilt offering meets these needs—needs unmet by the Levitical system.

Motyer summarizes verse 11 by pointing out six separate elements of the atoning work of Yahweh's servant:

> Isaiah 53:11 is one of the fullest statements of atonement theology ever penned. (i) The Servant knows the needs to be met and what must be done. (ii) As "that righteous one, my servant" he is both fully acceptable to the God our sins have offended and has been appointed by him to his task. (iii) As righteous, he is free from every contagion of our sin. (iv) He identified himself personally with our sin and need. (v) The emphatic pronoun "he" underlines his personal commitment to this role. (vi) He accomplishes the task fully. Negatively, in the bearing of iniquity; positively, in the provision of righteousness.[67]

Therefore, there should be no doubt that the servant's sacrifice was vicarious and substitutionary (penal substitution—bearing the penalty for sin). His was the one true and satisfactory sacrifice to God.

The New Testament writers rightly understood the plain intent of the prophet, finding every reason to take the text as directly messianic. Note the parallels between the servant passage in Isaiah and Mark 10:43–45 as one example: The suffering

---

66. David Baron, *The Servant of Jehovah: The Sufferings of the Messiah and the Glory That Should Follow* (1920; repr., Minneapolis: James Family, 1978), 121.

67. J. Alec Motyer, *The Prophecy of Isaiah: An Introduction and Commentary* (Downers Grove, IL: InterVarsity Press, 1993), 442.

servant of Yahweh (Isa. 52:13) is the "slave of all" (Mark 10:44; cf. Isa. 53:6, "of us all"), who is "great" (Mark 10:43) because he is "high and lifted up, and shall be exalted" (Isa. 52:13). As "slave," he gave himself (lit., "his soul") as a guilt offering (Isa. 53:10)—the direct equivalent of "to give his life [lit., soul] as a ransom" (Mark 10:45). The servant's guilt offering / ransom went above and beyond the penalty of sacrifice to cover intentional as well as unintentional sin in the place of "many" (Mark 10:45; Isa. 52:14–15; 53:12).

The atoning work of Christ accomplished salvation for the elect. Jesus Christ is Savior—"there is salvation in no one else, for there is no other name under heaven given among men by which we must be saved" (Acts 4:12; see 2 Tim. 1:10; Titus 2:13). His blood cleanses from sin (Heb. 13:12; 1 John 1:7). He is the Mediator of the new covenant (Heb. 12:24). As Savior, Christ gives life to believers in the present (2 Cor. 4:10; 2 Tim. 1:1) and is himself the pattern for the future resurrection of believers (2 Cor. 4:14; 1 Thess. 4:14). Christ, by his atoning work, is the Shepherd who makes it possible for believers to do good works (Heb. 13:20–21). He is the One in whom the church is placed and blessed (Eph. 2:13).

Resurrection and Ascension

Without the resurrection of Christ, his sacrificial death fails to provide the ground for salvation from sin (1 Cor. 15:13–19). Therefore, no consideration of the biblical teaching regarding the work of Christ can end with his atoning death.

OLD TESTAMENT REVELATION ABOUT CHRIST'S RESURRECTION

Since both Jesus and the New Testament writers declare that the significant facts concerning Christ had already been revealed through the prophets of the Old Testament (Luke 24:25–27, 44–47; Acts 2:25–32; 1 Cor. 15:3–4), it is important to consider the textual evidence to support their claim. Another factor that imposes a challenge in seeing Christ's resurrection in the Old Testament arises from the way that New Testament writers tend to refer to his resurrection obliquely, by speaking of his "glory." For example, Peter explains that the Old Testament prophets were "inquiring what person or time the Spirit of Christ in them was indicating when he predicted the sufferings of Christ and the subsequent glories" (1 Pet. 1:11). The display of Jesus's glory is most often associated with his second advent, not his resurrection. Without a resurrection from the dead, the crucified Christ cannot return in glory: "Was it not necessary that the Christ should suffer these things and enter into his glory?" (Luke 24:26; see also Matt. 16:27; 24:30; 25:31; Mark 10:37; Luke 9:26; John 17:5).

The apostle Paul correlates Jesus's resurrection with the divine glory—"just as Christ was raised from the dead by the glory of the Father" (Rom. 6:4)—which further explains the association of glory and resurrection in the minds of both prophets and apostles. In fact, he uses an analogy concerning glory in his treatise on resurrection in 1 Corinthians 15:40–41: "There are heavenly bodies and earthly bodies, but the glory of the heavenly is of one kind, and the glory of the earthly is of another. There is one glory of the sun, and another glory of the moon, and another glory of the stars; for star differs from star in glory." The resurrected body is "raised in glory" (1 Cor. 15:43), and the believer's resurrection shares that same glory: "When Christ who is your life appears, then you also will appear with him in glory" (Col. 3:4).

Therefore, when searching the Old Testament for references to the Messiah's resurrection, readers must pay proper attention to references to his glory. So Psalm 24 speaks of the Messiah in his role as "the King of glory" (24:7–10) when he comes to reign as king in Jerusalem. At that time, "the moon will be confounded and the sun ashamed, for the LORD of hosts reigns on Mount Zion and in Jerusalem and his glory will be before his elders" (Isa. 24:23).

According to Ezekiel, the glory of Yahweh departed from the temple and the city to rest briefly on the mountain east of the city: "The glory of the LORD went up from the midst of the city and stood on the mountain that is on the east side of the city" (Ezek. 11:23). At the time of the future millennial temple, the glory of Yahweh will reenter the temple from the same direction—from the east:

> And behold, the glory of the God of Israel was coming from the east. And the sound of his coming was like the sound of many waters, and the earth shone with his glory. And the vision I saw was just like the vision that I had seen when he came to destroy the city, and just like the vision that I had seen by the Chebar canal. And I fell on my face. As the glory of the LORD entered the temple by the gate facing east, the Spirit lifted me up and brought me into the inner court. (Ezek. 43:2–5)

Zechariah expounds on this prophecy by specifying the Mount of Olives as the site to the east of the city and the Messiah as the one with divine glory: "On that day his feet shall stand on the Mount of Olives that lies before Jerusalem on the east, and the Mount of Olives shall be split in two from east to west by a very wide valley, so that one half of the Mount shall move northward, and the other half southward" (Zech. 14:4). This coincides exactly with the statement that the angels delivered at the ascension of Jesus from the Mount of Olives following his resurrection from the dead: "'Men of Galilee, why do you stand looking into heaven? This Jesus, who was taken up from you into heaven, will come in the same way as you saw him go into heaven'" (Acts 1:11).

Several Old Testament references to the Messiah's resurrection appear in Job and the Psalter. The salient passage from Job reads as follows:

> For I know that my Redeemer lives,
>   and at the last he will stand upon the earth.
> And after my skin has been thus destroyed,
>   yet in my flesh I shall see God,
> whom I shall see for myself,
>   and my eyes shall behold, and not another. (Job 19:25–27)

Since Job speaks of seeing his Redeemer following his own death (implied by the destruction of his own flesh) and since he sees him standing on the earth, the implied time reference has to be after the second advent of the Messiah.

Another important text appears in Psalm 16:10:

> For you will not abandon my soul to Sheol,
>> or let your holy one see corruption.

Both Peter and Paul discuss this text later. In Acts 2:22–31, Peter says,

> Men of Israel, hear these words: Jesus of Nazareth, a man attested to you by God with mighty works and wonders and signs that God did through him in your midst, as you yourselves know—this Jesus, delivered up according to the definite plan and foreknowledge of God, you crucified and killed by the hands of lawless men. God raised him up, loosing the pangs of death, because it was not possible for him to be held by it. For David says concerning him,
>
>> "I saw the Lord always before me,
>>> for he is at my right hand that I may not be shaken;
>> therefore my heart was glad, and my tongue rejoiced;
>>> my flesh also will dwell in hope.
>> For you will not abandon my soul to Hades,
>>> or let your Holy One see corruption.
>> You have made known to me the paths of life;
>>> you will make me full of gladness with your presence."
>
> Brothers, I may say to you with confidence about the patriarch David that he both died and was buried, and his tomb is with us to this day. Being therefore a prophet, and knowing that God had sworn with an oath to him that he would set one of his descendants on his throne, he foresaw and spoke about the resurrection of the Christ, that he was not abandoned to Hades, nor did his flesh see corruption.

In treating Psalm 16:10, Paul similarly explains (Acts 13:34–37),

> And as for the fact that he raised him from the dead, no more to return to corruption, he has spoken in this way,
>
>> "I will give you the holy and sure blessings of David."
>
> Therefore he says also in another psalm,
>
>> "You will not let your Holy One see corruption."
>
> For David, after he had served the purpose of God in his own generation, fell asleep and was laid with his fathers and saw corruption, but he whom God raised up did not see corruption.

According to Paul, therefore, Christ's resurrection was prerequisite to his someday occupying David's throne on earth.

In addition, Peter cites Psalm 110:1 right after his exegesis of Psalm 16:10:

This Jesus God raised up, and of that we all are witnesses. Being therefore exalted at the right hand of God, and having received from the Father the promise of the Holy Spirit, he has poured out this that you yourselves are seeing and hearing. For David did not ascend into the heavens, but he himself says,

> "The Lord says to my Lord:
> 'Sit at my right hand,
>   until I make your enemies your footstool.'" (Acts 2:32–35)

In other words, the very fact that the Messiah takes his seat at the right hand of the Father proves that he has risen from the dead. His exaltation (equivalent to his glory) assumes that he is no longer in the grave. Since David is not sitting at the right hand of the Father, it is obvious to Peter that David was speaking not of himself but of his future descendant, the greater Son of David. Jesus already used Psalm 110:1 to reveal to the Pharisees that he was indeed the Lord (Matt. 22:41–46), so Peter is merely passing on what Jesus taught.

NEW TESTAMENT HISTORY OF CHRIST'S RESURRECTION

Jesus himself announced beforehand that he would rise from the dead:

> And as they were coming down the mountain, Jesus commanded them, "Tell no one the vision, until the Son of Man is raised from the dead." (Matt. 17:9)

> And taking the twelve, he said to them, "See, we are going up to Jerusalem, and everything that is written about the Son of Man by the prophets will be accomplished. For he will be delivered over to the Gentiles and will be mocked and shamefully treated and spit upon. And after flogging him, they will kill him, and on the third day he will rise." (Luke 18:31–33)

> Jesus answered them, "Destroy this temple, and in three days I will raise it up." The Jews then said, "It has taken forty-six years to build this temple, and will you raise it up in three days?" But he was speaking about the temple of his body. When therefore he was raised from the dead, his disciples remembered that he had said this, and they believed the Scripture and the word that Jesus had spoken. (John 2:19–22)

All four Gospel writers are unanimous in recording that Jesus rose from the dead on the first day of the week (Matt. 28:1–10; Mark 16:1–11; Luke 24:1–12; John 20:1–10). Table 4.13 displays Jesus's postresurrection appearances.

NEW TESTAMENT DOCTRINE OF CHRIST'S RESURRECTION

When Jesus rose from the dead, he experienced a bodily resurrection entailing his full humanity. His resurrection body allowed him to digest food: "And while they still disbelieved for joy and were marveling, he said to them, 'Have you anything here to eat?' They gave him a piece of broiled fish, and he took it and ate before them" (Luke 24:41–43; see Acts 10:41). Other human beings who were still in

Table 4.13 Christ's Post-Resurrection Appearances

Appearance	Matthew	Mark	Luke	John	Acts	1 Corin-thians
To Mary Magdalene at the tomb		16:9–11		20:11–18		
To the other women on the road	28:9–10		24:9–11			
To two disciples travel-ing to Emmaus		16:12–13	24:13–32			
To Peter			24:34			15:5a
To the ten assembled disciples			24:36–43	20:19–25		
To the eleven assem-bled disciples		16:14		20:26–31		15:5b
To the seven disciples fishing				21:1–23		
To the eleven disciples in Galilee	28:16–20	16:15–18				
To over five hundred people						15:6
To James, his brother						15:7a
To all the apostles			24:44–49		1:4–8	15:7b
To all the disciples at his ascension		16:19	24:50–53		1:4–11	
To Paul on the road to Damascus					9:1–6; 18:9–10; 22:6–11; 26:12–18	15:8
To Paul imprisoned in Jerusalem					23:11	

their mortal flesh could touch Jesus's body: "And behold, Jesus met them and said, 'Greetings!' And they came up and took hold of his feet and worshiped him" (Matt. 28:9; see Luke 24:38–40; John 20:17). The wounds of Jesus's crucifixion remained present and visible in his resurrected body, as witnessed by Thomas, the doubting disciple:

> So the other disciples told him, "We have seen the Lord." But he said to them, "Unless I see in his hands the mark of the nails, and place my finger into the mark of the nails, and place my hand into his side, I will never believe."
>
> Eight days later, his disciples were inside again, and Thomas was with them. Although the doors were locked, Jesus came and stood among them and said, "Peace be with you." Then he said to Thomas, "Put your finger here, and see my hands; and put out your hand, and place it in my side. Do not disbelieve, but believe." Thomas answered him, "My Lord and my God!" Jesus said to him, "Have you believed because you have seen me? Blessed are those who have not seen and yet have believed." (John 20:25–29)

Jesus will forever be fully God as well as fully man. He is the last Adam, the Head of the church, and the representative Head of all redeemed mankind. This fact of his continuing humanity is as significant for the accomplishment of redemption as is his continuing deity. Christ had to be man to represent believers in living a holy life on earth that could be imputed to believers and to be their sacrificial substitute on the cross. He also had to be their leader through death into resurrection.

Christ's resurrection achieved the following vast and glorious results:

1. The fulfillment of Old Testament prophecies (see "Old Testament Revelation about Christ's Resurrection" [p. 315])
2. The fulfillment of Jesus's own predictions (see "New Testament History of Christ's Resurrection" [p. 318])
3. Confirmation of the Son's deity (Rom. 1:4)
4. The exaltation of the Father, manifesting his perfections (Acts 2:23–24; Rom. 6:4)
5. The perfection of Jesus's obedience to his Father's will (John 10:17–18)
6. Proof that the Father accepted the atoning work of Christ in his sacrificial death on the cross (Rom. 4:25)
7. Provision of regeneration for the elect (1 Pet. 1:3)
8. Assurance that believers will not perish due to their sins (1 Cor. 15:17–18)
9. Securing the justification of believers and assurance that they will never be condemned by God (Rom. 8:1–11, 31–34)
10. Opening the way for Christ to send the Holy Spirit to indwell believers and form them into the church, the body of Christ (John 16:7)
11. Declaration of Christ as the Head of the church and ruler of creation (Eph. 1:19–23; Col. 1:15–19)
12. Establishment of God's pattern of power in spiritually raising believers from spiritual death in their trespasses (Eph. 1:19–20; 2:1–6)
13. Motivation for spiritual living, since believers are already seated with Christ in heaven and assured of being with him in glory (Eph. 2:5–6; Col. 3:1–4)
14. Rendering of mandatory, valid, and fruitful service for Christ (Rom. 7:4; 1 Cor. 15:14, 58)
15. Encouragement to establish the first day of the week for worshiping Christ and serving him in local assemblies (Matt. 28:1; John 20:19; Acts 20:7; 1 Cor. 16:2)
16. Establishment of an unshakable foundation for hope (confident expectation) for God to fulfill all his promises (Rom. 8:23–25; 1 Cor. 15:19–20; 1 Pet. 1:3)
17. The guarantee of a future resurrection life for all believers (John 5:26–29; 14:19; Rom. 4:25; 6:5–10; 1 Cor. 15:20, 23)
18. Confirmation of the future fulfillment of the Davidic covenant (Acts 2:29–36; 13:34–37)
19. The guarantee that Christ will judge the world (John 5:24–30; Acts 17:31)
20. The glorification and exaltation of the Son with the glory he once shared with the Father (John 17:5; Phil. 2:8–9; 1 Pet. 1:10–11, 20–21)

There exists no greater event in redemption history than the resurrection of Christ, because it completes and validates his sacrificial death and advances the program of the kingdom with an eternally living King. The resurrection must be believed in order for someone to experience salvation (Rom. 10:9–10).

THE RESURRECTED CHRIST'S ASCENSION

Scripture teaches that Christ ascended back into heaven to be seated at the right hand of his Father, and this teaching is essential because it is associated with the superiority of the Son of God:

> He is the radiance of the glory of God and the exact imprint of his nature, and he upholds the universe by the word of his power. After making purification for sins, he sat down at the right hand of the Majesty on high, having become as much superior to angels as the name he has inherited is more excellent than theirs.
> For to which of the angels did God ever say,
>
> > "You are my Son,
> >   today I have begotten you"?
>
> Or again,
>
> > "I will be to him a father,
> >   and he shall be to me a son"?
>
> And again, when he brings the firstborn into the world, he says,
>
> > "Let all God's angels worship him."
>
> Of the angels he says,
>
> > "He makes his angels winds,
> >   and his ministers a flame of fire."
>
> But of the Son he says,
>
> > "Your throne, O God, is forever and ever,
> >   the scepter of uprightness is the scepter of your kingdom.
> > You have loved righteousness and hated wickedness;
> > therefore God, your God, has anointed you
> >   with the oil of gladness beyond your companions." (Heb. 1:3–9)

The disciples had heard from Jesus that he was going to ascend to his Father:

> "A little while, and you will see me no longer; and again a little while, and you will see me." So some of his disciples said to one another, "What is this that he says to us, 'A little while, and you will not see me, and again a little while, and you will see me'; and, 'because I am going to the Father'?" (John 16:16–17; see 7:33–34; 8:21; 14:19, 28–29)

Jesus fulfilled his declarations, physically departing from the earth and ascending to heaven from the Mount of Olives (Acts 1:9–11). The Father received him into his glory (1 Tim. 3:16), and Christ is now seated on the throne of the Father (Rev. 3:21), at his right hand (Acts 5:31; Eph. 1:19–20), the throne of the universal and eternal kingdom of God (Mark 16:19; Acts 5:31; 7:55–56; Eph. 1:19–20). His session on the Father's throne testifies to the reality of his completed work of redemption (Heb. 10:12–13; 12:2).

Christ's ascension was confirmed by the visions of Stephen (Acts 7:55–56), Paul (Acts 9:3–5; 22:6–8; 26:13–15), and John (Rev. 4:1; 5:6). For Paul, Jesus's ascension left a lasting impression and was a key element in his salvation experience—the living, risen, ascended, heavenly Messiah spoke to him from heaven.

Glorified Christ[68]

> Heavenly Intercessor
> Rapture
> Judgment Seat
> Second Coming
> Millennial Reign
> Great White Throne Judgment
> Eternity Future

Heavenly Intercessor

Christ's present ministry in glory on behalf of his people occurs in his heavenly intercession on their behalf. He has ascended to the right hand of the Father, where he mediates as the believers' advocate and High Priest (Rom. 8:34; Heb. 7:25; 9:24; 1 John 2:1). There the Savior "is interceding for us" (Rom. 8:34), serving as the exalted High Priest for all believers: "Now the point in what we are saying is this: we have such a high priest, one who is seated at the right hand of the throne of the Majesty in heaven, a minister in the holy places, in the true tent that the Lord set up, not man" (Heb. 8:1–2). Thus, the hope of godly Job has been realized: "Even now, behold, my witness is in heaven, and he who testifies for me is on high" (Job 16:19). An exquisite example of his priestly intercession for his own is given in his prayer to the Father recorded in John 17.

Rapture

All the remaining aspects of the postresurrection ministry of Christ relate to his future work. His church awaits his call to the true church, which is his body, to come up to be with him. This has been called the "rapture" of the church, signifying a gathering of believers dead and alive into heaven. Paul's first letter to the Thessalonians describes the rapture:

> But we do not want you to be uninformed, brothers, about those who are asleep, that you may not grieve as others do who have no hope. For since we believe that Jesus died and rose again, even so, through Jesus, God will bring with him those who have fallen asleep. For this we declare to you by a word from the

---

68. For a more thorough discussion of these themes, see chap. 10, "The Future."

Lord, that we who are alive, who are left until the coming of the Lord, will not precede those who have fallen asleep. For the Lord himself will descend from heaven with a cry of command, with the voice of an archangel, and with the sound of the trumpet of God. And the dead in Christ will rise first. Then we who are alive, who are left, will be caught up [Gk. *harpazō*; Lat. *rapiemur*, from *raptus*] together with them in the clouds to meet the Lord in the air, and so we will always be with the Lord. Therefore encourage one another with these words. (1 Thess. 4:13–18)

As Jesus died and rose again, so too will those who have died in Christ (1 Cor. 15:51–58; 1 Thess. 4:14). There is no judgment connected to this event; it is for believers. This imminent, divine collection of believers into heaven is a signless event and is the next one on the redemptive schedule.

Those who are alive and those who have died will experience the Lord's gathering into heaven in glorified bodies. Apparently, the Thessalonians were informed fully about the judgment on the day of the Lord (1 Thess. 5:1–2) but not about the preceding event—the rapture of the church. Until Paul received it as God's revelation to him, the only prior allusion appeared in Jesus's teaching in John 14:1–3. Because Paul didn't know God's timing for this event, he lived and spoke as if it could happen in his lifetime. As with all early Christians, he believed that it was imminent (Rom. 13:11; 1 Cor. 6:14; 10:11; 16:22; Phil. 3:20–21; 1 Tim. 6:14; Titus 2:13).

The phrase "the Lord himself will descend" (1 Thess. 4:16) fulfills the pledge by Jesus in John 14:1–3. Until then, he remains in heaven (1 Thess. 1:10; Heb. 1:1–3). Believers who have died will rise first (1 Thess. 4:16; 1 Cor. 15:52). Those alive at the rapture will accompany those dead, who rise first, and all will "meet the Lord in the air" (1 Thess. 4:17).

Judgment Seat[69]

The Lord Jesus Christ is the One through whom God will judge all people (John 5:22–23). He will judge believers at what is called the judgment seat of Christ: "For we must all appear before the judgment seat of Christ, so that each one may receive what is due for what he has done in the body, whether good or evil" (2 Cor. 5:10). A comparison of this text with 1 Corinthians 3:10–15 indicates that the wood, hay, and straw are worthless rather than specifically sinful and so will not stand the test of eternal value. This describes the believer's deepest motivation and highest aim in pleasing God—the realization that every Christian is inevitably and ultimately accountable to him.

The term "judgment seat" metaphorically refers to the place where the Lord will sit to evaluate believers' lives for the purpose of giving them eternal rewards. The seat (*bēma*) was an elevated platform where victorious Greek athletes (for example, during the Olympics) went to receive their crowns. The term is also used in the New

---

69. This section is adapted from MacArthur, *MacArthur Study Bible: English Standard Version*, 1723. Used by permission of Thomas Nelson.

Testament to refer to the place of judging, as when Jesus stood before Pontius Pilate (Matt. 27:19; John 19:13), but Paul uses it with the athletic analogy. Corinth had such a platform where both athletic rewards and legal verdicts were dispensed (Acts 18:12–16), so the Corinthians understood Paul's reference. Christ will judge the actions that occur during the believer's time of earthly ministry. This does not include sins, since their penalty was paid in full at the cross (Eph. 1:7). Paul was referring to all those activities believers do during their lifetimes that relate to their eternal reward and praise from God. What Christians do for his glory in their temporal bodies will, in God's estimation, have an eternal impact.

Second Coming

The Greek term *parousia* (Matt. 24:3, 27, 37, 39; 2 Thess. 2:8; James 5:7–8) literally means "presence." In the New Testament, this term describes the visitation of important people. Thus the word points to a unique and distinct "coming." The New Testament writers use this term at times to designate the second coming of Christ (it is also used to refer to the rapture in 1 Thess. 2:19; 3:13; 4:15; 5:23). Another Greek noun, *apokalypsis* (1 Cor. 1:7; 2 Thess. 1:7; 1 Pet. 1:7, 13; 4:13), meaning "to uncover or unveil," also describes the revelation of Christ's second coming. This glorious return will reveal Christ as King over all.

Jesus will return to earth with divine power and glory to judge the living inhabitants of the earth (Matt. 24:30; 25:31–46; Luke 9:26; see Dan. 7:13; Titus 2:13; 2 Pet. 3:12; Jude 14; Rev. 1:7). The prophets of the Old Testament speak often of God's future judgment. One of the prophets, Zephaniah, explicitly portrays the judgment of God by presenting the Messiah as "a mighty one" who will bring salvation to the earth (Zeph. 3:17). Christ himself made allusions to Zephaniah (Zeph. 1:3 in Matt. 13:41; Zeph. 1:15 in Matt. 24:29), further connecting the prophecies of Zephaniah and the second coming of Christ.

The Father has already given all authority to the Son for the execution of judgment: "And he has given him authority to execute judgment, because he is the Son of Man" (John 5:27; see Matt. 25:31–32). With that assignment in mind, God provided his written revelation with a grand finale focusing on final judgment. What the final book of the Bible, the book of Revelation, reveals or unveils are the features of Jesus Christ's return in glory.

Millennial Reign[70]

Returning with his raptured and glorified church, Christ will establish his millennial kingdom on earth (Acts 1:9–11; 1 Thess. 4:13–18; Rev. 20:1–6). Six times Revelation 20 mentions Christ's kingdom that will last a thousand years. There is no reason not to take these references as a literal thousand-year period during which Jesus Christ will reign on the earth in fulfillment of both numerous Old Testament prophecies

---

70. This section is adapted from William D. Barrick, "The Kingdom of God in the Old Testament," *MSJ* 23, no. 2 (2012): 179–80, 184. Used by permission of *MSJ*.

(2 Sam. 7:12–16; Psalm 2; Isa. 11:6–12; 24:23; Amos 9:8–15; Mic. 4:1–8; Zech. 14:1–11) and Jesus's own teaching (Matt. 24:29–31, 36–44).

In the realm of society, Christ will abolish warfare and establish peace (Isa. 9:7; Mic. 4:3–4). Justice will prevail in every class and race of mankind (Ps. 72:4; Isa. 65:21–22), and God will reclaim social wastes (Ps. 72:16; Isa. 61:4). Christ will teach mankind to emphasize worthwhile relationships, as, for example, through his gentle treatment of the oppressed and hurting (Isa. 42:3) or his healing of relationships between parents and children (Mal. 4:6).

In the political venue, Christ will establish himself as the international absolute ruler (Ps. 2:8–10; Isa. 2:2–4) and will establish his world capital at Jerusalem (Jer. 3:17). In his kingdom, Christ will put an end to the nations' animosity toward Jews (Zech. 8:13, 23). As a reversal of the curse at Babel, language will cease to be a barrier to all human interaction and relationships (Isa. 19:18; Zeph. 3:9).

Ecclesiastically, Christ will rule as Priest-King over Israel and the world community (Ps. 110:4; Zech. 6:12–13). In the messianic kingdom, Israel will become the religious leader of the world (Ex. 19:6; Isa. 61:6, 9), and the world's religious capital will be Jerusalem (Zech. 14:16–17). As a result, the temple in Israel will be the focal point of worship (Ezekiel 40–48; Hag. 2:6–9).

The fall interrupted God's creation blessing and mandate for mankind. Because of his disobedience, Adam could no longer exercise his vice-regency in the way God had intended. Any exercise of that original dominion became and continues to be incomplete and imperfect. The psalmist refers to that high and lofty role in Psalm 8:3–9:

> When I look at your heavens, the work of your fingers,
>   the moon and the stars, which you have set in place,
> what is man that you are mindful of him,
>   and the son of man that you care for him?
>
> Yet you have made him a little lower than the heavenly beings
>   and crowned him with glory and honor.
> You have given him dominion over the works of your hands;
>   you have put all things under his feet,
> all sheep and oxen,
>   and also the beasts of the field,
> the birds of the heavens, and the fish of the sea,
>   whatever passes along the paths of the seas.
>
> O Lord, our Lord,
>   how majestic is your name in all the earth!

With these words the psalmist presents the ideal for mankind, not the current reality—the designed future of the Lord's kingdom rule, not the dismal past and present. Of course, Jesus Christ, as the ultimate "son of man" (Ps. 8:4), will fulfill mankind's role as the human race's only perfect representative. Hebrews 2:5–14 reveals that "we do not yet see everything in subjection" to Christ (2:8), because his mediatorial kingdom has not commenced. In the end, even the currently reigning prince of this world, Satan (John 12:31; Eph. 2:2), will come under Christ's reign and kingdom power. As long as Satan reigns as prince of this world, the kingdom of Christ has yet to be established. For that reason Jesus taught his disciples to pray, "Your kingdom come" (Matt. 6:10). "Amen. Come, Lord Jesus!" (Rev. 22:20).

Great White Throne Judgment

After the millennial kingdom, Christ will judge the unbelieving dead at the great white throne (Rev. 20:11–15). As the Mediator between God and people (1 Tim. 2:5); the Head of his body, the church (Eph. 1:22; 5:23; Col. 1:18); and the coming universal King who will reign on the throne of David (Isa. 9:6–7; Ezek. 37:24–28; Luke 1:31–33), Christ is the final Judge of all who fail to place their trust in him as Lord and Savior (Matt. 25:14–46; Acts 17:30–31).

Eternity Future

At the end of this world's history, God will gather believers together in the millennial kingdom, what Ephesians 1:10 calls "a plan for the fullness of time," meaning the completion of history (see Rev. 20:1–6). After that, God will gather everything to himself in the new heaven and new earth that he will create (Rev. 21:1–5). The new eternal state will be totally unified under Christ:

> For "God has put all things in subjection under his feet." But when it says, "all things are put in subjection," it is plain that he is excepted who put all things in subjection under him. When all things are subjected to him, then the Son himself will also be subjected to him who put all things in subjection under him, that God may be all in all. (1 Cor. 15:27–28)

The paradise of eternity is thus revealed as a magnificent kingdom where both heaven and earth unite in a glory that surpasses the limits of the human imagination and the boundaries of earthly dimensions. But the real glory of eternity future rests in the fact that all believers will reside in the presence of the Lord Jesus Christ. They shall fellowship with the Lord himself in heaven, a glorious communion with God in Christ, which is the perfection of happiness. As believers derive their grace from the Lamb, so they shall derive their glory from him as well. The man Christ Jesus will be the center of the divine glory in heaven, from whence it is diffused unto all the saints. The Scriptures express heaven's happiness as being with Christ: "Truly, I say to you, today you will be with me in Paradise" (Luke 23:43). This joy seems to be that which even Christ himself desires and will experience: "Father, I desire that they also, whom you have given me, may be with me where I am, to see my glory that you have given me because you loved me before the foundation of the world" (John 17:24). The apostle Paul, in speaking of the church's imminent rapture, summarizes the significance of the event by saying, "So we will always be with the Lord. Therefore encourage one another with these words" (1 Thess. 4:17–18).

Indeed, such communion with Christ seems to be the import of Scripture speaking jointly of God and the Lamb (the slain Savior) when revealing the happiness of the saints in heaven: "For the Lamb in the midst of the throne will be their shepherd, and he will guide them to springs of living water, and God will wipe away every tear from their eyes" (Rev. 7:17). Also, "Behold, the dwelling place of God is with man. He will dwell with them, and they will be his people, and God himself will be with them as their God. He will wipe away every tear from their eyes, and death shall be no more, neither shall there be mourning, nor crying, nor pain anymore, for the former things have passed away" (Rev. 21:3–4). The word translated "dwelling place" here is the same word sometimes translated "tabernacle" in signifying the flesh of Christ (John 1:14). Finally, the apostle John declares, "And I saw no temple in the city, for its temple is the Lord God the Almighty and the Lamb. And the city has no need of sun or moon to shine on it, for the glory of God gives it light, and its lamp is the Lamb" (Rev. 21:22–23).

Prayer[71]

Our gracious God, we thank You for our heavenly Advocate,
    Jesus Christ the righteous, whose death on the cross
        made propitiation for our sins—
        perfectly satisfying every demand of Your holy justice.
It is He who brought us
    out of guilt and into forgiveness,
    out of darkness into light,
    out of our rebellion and into Your love,
    out of death and into life.
He delivered us from this evil world, into Your glorious kingdom.
How we praise You for the wonder of Your love in Jesus Christ!
We thank You for sending Your Son, the Incarnate One,
    who was despised, rejected, beaten, mocked, and crucified—
        all in order to atone for our sin.

In Him Your love has outloved all other loves.
Your mercy extends beyond comprehension to sinners
    with complete and permanent forgiveness of our sins
    through faith in Jesus Christ.
We therefore long to love You with a love like Yours.
    We know that it is not possible, so with the apostle Peter
    we plead that You would know our hearts, knowing we truly love You
        in spite of what it often looks like.
Our hearts are too much like stone; we ask that
    You melt them with Your grace.

---

71. This prayer is reproduced verbatim from John MacArthur, *At the Throne of Grace: A Book of Prayers* (Eugene, OR: Harvest House, 2011), 20–22. Used by permission of Harvest House.

Our private lives are too often gated and locked as if we could shut You out
    and thereby do what we want.
Help us throw open the door and lose the key! May Your will rule our lives.

We worship You, Father, for Your great love and the gift of Jesus Christ,
    Your only-begotten Son, which is to say God the Son.
We praise You, Lord Jesus, for the wondrous gift of salvation
    You provided for us.
We adore You, blessed Spirit, for revealing to us the truth of the gospel
    and for making our hearts Your dwelling place.
Heavenly Father, in us may Your Son see the fruit
    of His soul's anguish and be glad.
Bring us away from all that we falsely trust,
    and teach us to rest only in Him.
Never let us be calloused to the astonishing greatness of the gift of salvation.
May we pursue sanctification—ever-increasing
    holiness—with all our might!

Lord Jesus, Master, Redeemer, Savior, take
    possession of every part of our lives—
    Yours by right through purchase.
        Sanctify every faculty.
        Fill our hearts with hope.
        May we flee the many temptations that relentlessly hound us
           and mortify the sins that continually plague us.
        May there be no hypocrisy in us.
        Help us trust You in the hour of distress.
        Protect us when evildoers pursue us.
        And deliver us from the evil of this present world.

Dear Father of lights, with whom there is no variation or shifting shadow,
    we confess that You alone are the giver of every good and perfect gift,
    and You have given us so many things,
    richly supplying us with things to enjoy.
And we are reminded by the passage [1 John 2:1–19] that
    the greatest gift of all is Your Son, Jesus Christ,
        who sacrificed His very life in order that
        we might be freed from sin's bondage.
Fill our hearts with gratitude, and may our lives
    reflect overflowing thankfulness
    so that all who see may honor You.
In the name of Jesus Christ we pray. Amen.

"O for a Thousand Tongues"

O for a thousand tongues to sing
My great Redeemer's praise,
The glories of my God and King,
The triumphs of His grace.

Jesus! The Name that charms our fears,
That bids our sorrows cease,
'Tis music in the sinner's ears,
'Tis life and health and peace.

He breaks the pow'r of cancelled sin,
He sets the prisoner free;
His blood can make the foulest clean;
His blood availed for me.

Hear Him, ye deaf; His praise, ye dumb,
Your loosened tongues employ;
Ye blind, behold your Savior come;
And leap, ye lame, for joy.

My gracious Master and my God,
Assist me to proclaim,
To spread thro' all the earth abroad,
The honors of Thy name.

~Charles Wesley (1707–1788)

Bibliography

Primary Systematic Theologies

Bancroft, Emery H. *Christian Theology: Systematic and Biblical.* 2nd ed. Grand Rapids, MI: Zondervan, 1976. 95–156.

Berkhof, Louis. *Systematic Theology.* 4th ed. Grand Rapids, MI: Eerdmans, 1939. 305–412.

Buswell, James Oliver, Jr. *A Systematic Theology of the Christian Religion.* 2 vols. Grand Rapids, MI: Zondervan, 1962–1963. 2:17–69.

Culver, Robert Duncan. *Systematic Theology: Biblical and Historical.* Fearn, Ross-shire, Scotland: Mentor, 2005. 419–638.

Dabney, Robert Lewis. *Systematic Theology.* 1871. Reprint, Edinburgh: Banner of Truth, 1985. 182–93, 500–553.

Erickson, Millard J. *Christian Theology.* Grand Rapids, MI: Baker, 1986. 661–841.

*Grudem, Wayne. *Systematic Theology: An Introduction to Biblical Doctrine.* Grand Rapids, MI: Zondervan, 1994. 529–633.

Hodge, Charles. *Systematic Theology.* 3 vols. 1871–1873. Reprint, Grand Rapids, MI: Eerdmans, 1975. 1:483–521; 2:378–638.

Lewis, Gordon R., and Bruce A. Demarest. *Integrative Theology.* 3 vols. Grand Rapids, MI: Zondervan, 1987–1994. 2:251–496.

Reymond, Robert L. *A New Systematic Theology of the Christian Faith.* Nashville: Thomas Nelson, 1998. 545–801.

*Shedd, William G. T. *Dogmatic Theology.* 3 vols. 1889. Reprint, Minneapolis: Klock & Klock, 1979. 2A:261–349; 3:378–400.

Strong, August Hopkins. *Systematic Theology: A Compendium Designed for the Use of Theological Students*. Rev. ed. New York: Revell, 1907. 669–776.

Swindoll, Charles R., and Roy B. Zuck, eds. *Understanding Christian Theology*. Nashville: Thomas Nelson, 2003. 291–387.

Thiessen, Henry Clarence. *Introductory Lectures in Systematic Theology*. Grand Rapids, MI: Eerdmans, 1949. 283–340.

Turretin, Francis. *Institutes of Elenctic Theology*. 3 vols. Edited by James T. Dennison Jr. Translated by George Musgrove Giger. 1679–1685. Reprint, Phillipsburg, NJ: P&R, 1992–1997. 1:282–302; 2:271–449.

*Denotes most helpful.

Specific Works

Banks, William L. *The Day Satan Met Jesus: The Temptation of Christ—Cast, Action and Effects of the Wilderness Drama*. Chicago: Moody Press, 1973.

Beilby, James K., and Paul R. Eddy, eds. *The Historical Jesus: Five Views*. Downers Grove, IL: IVP Academic, 2009.

*Berkouwer, G. C. *The Person of Christ*. Studies in Dogmatics. 1954. Reprint, Grand Rapids, MI: Eerdmans, 1975.

Boettner, Loraine. "The Person of Christ." In *Studies in Theology*, 140–351. 12th ed. N.p.: Presbyterian & Reformed, 1974.

*Boice, James Montgomery, and Philip Graham Ryken. *Jesus on Trial*. Wheaton, IL: Crossway, 2002.

*Borland, James A. *Christ in the Old Testament: Old Testament Appearances of Christ in Human Form*. Rev. ed. Fearn, Ross-shire, Scotland: Mentor, 1999.

*Bowman, Robert M., Jr., and J. Ed Komoszewski. *Putting Jesus in His Place: The Case for the Deity of Christ*. Grand Rapids, MI: Kregel, 2007.

Charnock, Stephen. *Christ Crucified: The Once-for-All Sacrifice*. 1830. Reprint, Fearn, Ross-shire, Scotland: Christian Focus, 2012.

*Feinberg, Charles Lee. *Is the Virgin Birth in the Old Testament?* Whittier, CA: Emeth, 1967.

Gaffin, Richard B., Jr. *The Centrality of the Resurrection: A Study in Paul's Soteriology*. Grand Rapids, MI: Baker, 1978.

Geisler, Norman L., and F. David Farnell, eds. *The Jesus Quest: The Danger from Within*. [Maitland, FL?]: Xulon, 2014.

*Gromacki, Robert Glenn. *The Virgin Birth: Doctrine of Deity*. Nashville: Thomas Nelson, 1974.

*Heick, Otto W. *A History of Christian Thought*. 2 vols. Philadelphia: Fortress, 1965.

*Hengstenberg, Ernst Wilhelm. *Christology of the Old Testament and a Commentary on the Messianic Predictions*. Kregel Reprint Library. 1847. Reprint, Grand Rapids, MI: Kregel, 1970.

Janowski, Bernd, and Peter Stuhlmacher, eds. *The Suffering Servant: Isaiah 53 in Jewish and Christian Sources*. Grand Rapids, MI: Eerdmans, 2004.

Kiehl, Erich H. *The Passion of Our Lord*. Grand Rapids, MI: Baker, 1990.

*Lawlor, George L. *When God Became Man*. Chicago: Moody Press, 1978.

MacArthur, John. *The Jesus You Can't Ignore: What You Must Learn from the Bold Confrontations of Christ*. Nashville: Thomas Nelson, 2008.

*———. *The Murder of Jesus: A Study of How Jesus Died*. Nashville: Word, 2000.

*———. *One Perfect Life: The Complete Story of the Lord Jesus*. Nashville: Thomas Nelson, 2012.

———. *Our Sufficiency in Christ*. Dallas: Word, 1991.

*———. *Parables: The Mysteries of God's Kingdom Revealed through the Stories Jesus Told*. Nashville: Thomas Nelson, 2015.

———. *The Upper Room: Jesus' Parting Promises for Troubled Hearts*. [The Woodlands, TX]: Kress Biblical Resources, 2014.

MacArthur, John, and Richard Mayhue. *Christ's Prophetic Plans: A Futuristic Premillennial Primer*. Chicago: Moody Publishers, 2012.

*McClain, Alva J. "The Doctrine of the Kenosis in Philippians 2:5–8." *The Master's Seminary Journal* 9, no. 1 (1998): 85–96.

*Nichols, Stephen J. *For Us and for Our Salvation: The Doctrine of Christ in the Early Church*. Wheaton, IL: Crossway, 2007.

*Pentecost, J. Dwight. *The Words and Works of Jesus Christ: A Study of the Life of Christ*. Grand Rapids, MI: Zondervan, 1981.

Rydelnik, Michael. *The Messianic Hope: Is the Hebrew Bible Really Messianic?* NAC Studies in Bible and Theology 9. Nashville: B&H Academic, 2010.

Ryrie, Charles Caldwell. *Biblical Theology of the New Testament*. 1959. Reprint, Chicago: Moody Press, 1973.

*Scroggie, W. Graham. *A Guide to the Gospels*. Old Tappan, NJ: Revell, n.d.

———. *The Unfolding Drama of Redemption: The Bible as a Whole*. 3 vols. 1953–1970. Reprint, Grand Rapids, MI: Zondervan, 1976.

Thomas, Robert L., and F. David Farnell, eds. *The Jesus Crisis: The Inroads of Historical Criticism into Evangelical Scholarship*. Grand Rapids, MI: Kregel, 1998.

*Walvoord, John F. *Jesus Christ Our Lord*. Chicago: Moody Press, 1969.

*Warfield, Benjamin B. *The Person and Work of Christ*. Edited by Samuel G. Craig. Philadelphia: Presbyterian & Reformed, 1950.

*Wells, David F. *The Person of Christ: A Biblical and Historical Analysis of the Incarnation*. Foundations for Faith. Westchester, IL: Crossway, 1984.

*Wilson, Clifford A. *Jesus the Teacher*. Melbourne: Hill of Content, 1974.

Wilson, William Riley. *The Execution of Jesus: A Judicial, Literary and Historical Investigation*. New York: Scribner, 1970.

*Denotes most helpful.

"Praise Ye the Triune God"

Praise ye the Father for His loving-kindness,
Tenderly cares He for His erring children.
Praise Him, ye angels, praise Him in the heavens,
Praise ye Jehovah!

Praise ye the Savior—great is His compassion;
Graciously cares He for His chosen people.
Young men and maidens, ye old men and children,
Praise ye the Savior!

Praise ye the Spirit, Comforter of Israel,
Sent of the Father and the Son to bless us;
Praise ye the Father, Son, and Holy Spirit—
Praise ye the Triune God!

~Elizabeth R. Charles (1828–1896)

5

God the Holy Spirit

Pneumatology

Major Subjects Covered in Chapter 5

Introduction to the Holy Spirit

Deity and Triunity

Salvation

Sanctification

Service

Creation

Scripture

Prophetic Ministry

This chapter introduces the Holy Spirit, the third person of the triune Godhead, who appears throughout Scripture from Genesis to Revelation.

Introduction to the Holy Spirit

Old Testament Survey
New Testament Survey
Holy Spirit Reality
Names and Titles
Holy Spirit Word Pictures
Holy Spirit Ministry to Christ
Holy Spirit Ministries
Sins against the Holy Spirit

Old Testament Survey

The Hebrew word *ruakh* appears 378 times in the Old Testament, while the identical Aramaic word occurs 11 times (in Daniel only). It primarily means "spirit" (1 Sam. 16:14), "wind" (Ex. 10:13), or "breath" (Gen. 6:17). Context almost always determines the intended reference, distinguishing, for example, between the Spirit of God (Gen. 6:3) and the spirit of man (Job 10:12) or between an attitude (Prov. 16:18) and the immaterial part of man (Ps. 31:5).

This word, *ruakh*, itself appears in all but seven (Leviticus, Ruth, Esther, Song of Solomon, Obadiah, Nahum, Zephaniah) of the thirty-nine Old Testament books (about 82 percent). However, it refers specifically to the Holy Spirit in only 79 of 378 appearances (21 percent) and in only twenty-one of the thirty-nine Old Testament books (51 percent), including Genesis, Exodus, Numbers, Deuteronomy, Judges, 1 Samuel, 2 Samuel, 1 Kings, 2 Kings, 1 Chronicles, 2 Chronicles, Nehemiah, Job, Psalms, Isaiah, Ezekiel, Joel, Micah, Haggai, Zechariah, and Malachi.

The Holy Spirit is referred to from the time of creation (Gen. 1:2) all the way to the last Old Testament book (Mal. 2:15). God's Spirit appears most frequently in Isaiah (15 times), Ezekiel (15 times), Numbers (7 times), Judges (7 times), 1 Samuel (7 times), and Psalms (5 times).

New Testament Survey

New Testament revelation about the Holy Spirit far exceeds that of the Old Testament. The Greek word *pneuma* occurs 379 times in the New Testament (almost the same as the Hebrew term *ruakh* in the Old Testament), yet it refers to the Holy Spirit on over 245 occasions (65 percent), triple the number of Old Testament occurrences. Of the combined Old Testament and New Testament references to the generic English translation "spirit," about 43 percent (324 of 757 occurrences) refer to the Holy Spirit.

Pneuma appears in twenty-five New Testament books (93 percent), being absent from only 2 and 3 John. It refers to the Holy Spirit in twenty-three books (85 percent)—Philemon, James, 2 John, and 3 John excepted.

The Holy Spirit appears throughout the New Testament from Matthew 1:18 to Revelation 21:10. The Holy Spirit is mentioned most frequently in Acts (56 times), Romans (28 times), and 1 Corinthians (22 times). One of the most dominant themes is that the Holy Spirit is a gift from God to every believer (Rom. 5:5; 2 Cor. 1:22; 5:5; Gal. 3:5; Eph. 1:13–14; 1 Thess. 4:8; 1 John 3:24; 4:13).

Holy Spirit Reality

Biblically speaking, there can be no doubt about the Holy Spirit's existence in that he is mentioned over 320 times. But is the Holy Spirit a person, like God the Father and God the Son? Personhood is not measured by physical elements such as body parts, flesh, blood, and bones. Rather, it is determined by the possession of three basic characteristics: (1) cognition/intellect, (2) volition/will, and (3) emotion/

affection.[1] The Bible provides more than sufficient evidence that the Holy Spirit possesses all three essentials of personhood. Thus, the Spirit can be classified as the third person of the triune Godhead.

COGNITION/INTELLECT

1. He counsels (Isa. 11:2).
2. He imparts wisdom (Isa. 11:2).
3. He inspired Scripture (Acts 1:16; Heb. 3:7; 10:15; 1 Pet. 1:11; 2 Pet. 1:21).
4. He intercedes (Rom. 8:26).
5. He knows (Isa. 11:2).
6. He possesses a mind (Rom. 8:27; 1 Cor. 2:10–13).
7. He reminds (John 14:26).
8. He provides truth (John 14:17, 26; 15:26; 16:13; 1 John 4:6).
9. He speaks (Acts 8:29; 10:19; 11:12; 13:2; 28:25; Rev. 2:7–3:22).
10. He teaches (Luke 12:12; John 14:26; 1 Cor. 2:13; Heb. 9:8).
11. He testifies (John 15:26; 1 John 5:7–8).

VOLITION/WILL

1. He contends with sinners (Gen. 6:3; Acts 7:51).
2. He directs (Acts 16:6–7).
3. He distributes spiritual gifts (1 Cor. 12:11; Heb. 2:4).
4. He regenerates (John 3:7–8; Titus 3:5).

AFFECTION/EMOTION

1. He experiences joy (1 Thess. 1:6).
2. He can be insulted (Heb. 10:29).
3. He grieves over sin (Isa. 63:10; Eph. 4:30).
4. He loves (Rom. 5:5; 15:30; Gal. 5:22).

Names and Titles

One of the chief evidences for the triunity of the Godhead involves the names used in relationship to the Holy Spirit. Some relate to the Father, some to the Son, while others are unique to the Holy Spirit. These are listed in the following four sections:

THE HOLY SPIRIT AND THE FATHER

"his Spirit" (Num. 11:29; Rom. 8:11)
"my Spirit" (Gen. 6:3)
"your Spirit" (Ps. 139:7)
"your Holy Spirit" (Ps. 51:11)
"the promise of the Father" (Acts 1:4)
"the Spirit of God" (Gen. 1:2; Matt. 3:16; 1 Cor. 2:11)

---

1. In using the language of "affection" and "emotion," we do not mean to imply that God's affections are involuntary passions by which he is driven, as is often the case with human emotions. As the Westminster Confession states, God is "without body, parts, or passions, immutable" (2.1). God is not driven by his emotions; rather, his affections are the sovereign and deliberate expressions of his holy dispositions. For more, see "Immutability" in chap. 3 (p. 169).

"the Spirit of our God" (1 Cor. 6:11)
"the Spirit of the living God" (2 Cor. 3:3)
"the Spirit of him" (Rom. 8:11)
"the Spirit of your Father" (Matt. 10:20)
"The Spirit of the LORD" (Judg. 3:10)
"The Spirit of the Lord" (Luke 4:18)
"the Spirit of the Lord GOD" (Isa. 61:1)
"the Lord who is the Spirit" (2 Cor. 3:18)

THE HOLY SPIRIT AND THE SON

"the Spirit of Jesus" (Acts 16:7)
"the Spirit of Christ" (Rom. 8:9; 1 Pet. 1:11)
"the Spirit of Jesus Christ" (Phil. 1:19)
"the Spirit of the Lord" (Acts 5:9; 8:39)
"the Spirit of his Son" (Gal. 4:6)

UNIQUE TO THE HOLY SPIRIT

"the Spirit" (Num. 11:17; Matt. 4:1)
"the eternal Spirit" (Heb. 9:14)
"your good Spirit" (Ps. 143:10)
"the Holy Spirit" (Matt. 1:18)
"one Spirit" (Eph. 4:4; cf. 4:6, "one God and Father," and 4:5, "one Lord")
"the seven Spirits" (Rev. 1:4; 3:1; 4:5; 5:6)

ATTRIBUTES OF THE HOLY SPIRIT

"the Spirit of counsel and might" (Isa. 11:2)
"the Spirit of faith" (2 Cor. 4:13)
"the Spirit of glory" (1 Pet. 4:14)
"the Spirit of grace" (Heb. 10:29; cf. Zech. 12:10)
"the Spirit of holiness" (Rom. 1:4)
"the Spirit of knowledge and the fear of the LORD" (Isa. 11:2)
"the Spirit of life" (Rom. 8:2)
"the promised Holy Spirit" (Eph. 1:13)
"the Spirit of truth" (John 14:17; 15:26; 16:13; 1 John 4:6; cf. 1 John 5:6)
"the Spirit of wisdom and of revelation in the knowledge of him" (Eph. 1:17)
"the Spirit of wisdom and understanding" (Isa. 11:2)
"the Helper" (John 14:26; 15:26; 16:7)

Holy Spirit Word Pictures

The Bible uses eight word pictures that clearly and explicitly connect the Holy Spirit with the illustration in a metaphorical sense. Some of the emblems can appear elsewhere in Scripture without necessarily referring to the Holy Spirit, such as fire, which can also symbolize judgment (Matt. 25:41; 1 Cor. 3:13). These metaphors come from the natural world (dove, fire, oil, water, and wind), the legal world (pledge and seal), and the domestic world (clothing).

Table 5.1 Holy Spirit Word Pictures

Clothing	Empowerment/enablement by the Holy Spirit
Dove	Righteousness of the Holy Spirit
Fire	Visible presence of the Holy Spirit
Oil	Anointing with the Holy Spirit
Pledge	Guarantee with the Holy Spirit
Seal	Ownership of and security with the Holy Spirit
Water	Salvation, enablement, and induction by the Holy Spirit
Wind	Salvation and invisible empowerment by the Holy Spirit

The contexts of these emblems show that they can represent the Holy Spirit's ministry to Christ (dove and oil), to the apostles (clothing, fire, oil, water, and wind), and to believers (oil, pledge, seal, water, and wind). All five pictures connected with the apostles refer to various elements occurring on the day of Pentecost. Symbols for Christ and for believers relate to baptism and salvation respectively. Oil involves all three subjects (Christ, apostles, and believers); water and wind relate to both apostles and believers; the remaining five images apply to only one subject or group.

Interestingly, very few of the pictures appear clearly in the Old Testament (only water and wind), while all eight are found in the New Testament. They show up in the Gospels (clothing, dove, water, and wind), Acts (fire, oil, water, and wind), the Pauline epistles (oil, pledge, and seal), the Petrine epistles (wind), and the Johannine epistles (oil). The pictures and the realities they represent are summarized in table 5.1.

CLOTHING (LUKE 24:49)

The Son instructed the disciples that the Father would send "the promise" (the Spirit; see John 14:16–17) so that they could be "clothed" (Gk. *endyō*) with "power from on high" (Luke 24:49). This was anticipated (Acts 1:4–5) and fulfilled (Acts 2:1–4), just as Christ said. The disciples were all powerfully enabled by the Holy Spirit to accomplish Christ's purposes (Acts 2:4). This word picture involves God sovereignly clothing humans, not humans clothing themselves (cf. Col. 3:12–14). This explains how the apostles did what they could not do before as a result of Pentecost.

DOVE (MATT. 3:16; MARK 1:10; LUKE 3:22; JOHN 1:32)

What does the dove (Gk. *peristera*) represent about the reality of the Holy Spirit? The dove is innocent and blameless (Gk. *akeraios*, Matt. 10:16). In Romans 16:19 and Philippians 2:15, believers are described with the same Greek word (*akeraios*) to show that they are "innocent as to what is evil" and "children of God without blemish," respectively. That is why in the Old Testament sacrificial system a dove could be offered by the poor, who could not afford a lamb, as an acceptable burnt offering to cover for sin (Lev. 1:14; 5:7; Luke 2:22–24). In Scripture, a dove represents righteousness.

How does *righteousness* relate to the Holy Spirit and Christ's baptism? The context of Christ's baptism focuses particularly on righteousness. The Son identified his ministry as one of fulfilling all righteousness (Matt. 3:15). Therefore, the Spirit (pictured by the dove, which represented righteousness) inaugurated Christ's ministry of righteousness (Matt. 3:16). As a result, the Father authenticated Christ as the righteous Son (Matt. 3:17) with the Spirit's testimony.

FIRE (ACTS 2:3)

The presence of God is prominently pictured by fire (Ex. 3:2–6; 13:21; Lev. 9:24; Acts 7:30–33). The use of fire in Acts 2:3 occurs on the day of Pentecost and most appropriately portrays the visible presence of the Holy Spirit. Paul must have had this imagery in mind when decades later he urged the Thessalonians to avoid quenching the Spirit with sin (1 Thess. 5:19).

OIL (2 COR. 1:21; 1 JOHN 2:20, 27)

Anointing with oil in the Old and New Testaments symbolizes appointment to an important position. Old Testament priests were anointed to the priesthood (Ex. 40:12–15). David was anointed by Samuel to be king of Israel (1 Sam. 16:13). New Testament disciples were anointed to be apostles (2 Cor. 1:21).

In like manner, Christ—which means "anointed one" in Hebrew (*meshiakh*) and Greek (*christos*)—was anointed with the Holy Spirit (Acts 4:27; 10:38) for ministry, which most likely occurred at the time of his baptism. Believers, called a royal priesthood (1 Pet. 2:9), are anointed with the Holy Spirit so they can know the truth about Christ (1 John 2:20, 27). Paul was anointed with the Holy Spirit for his apostleship (2 Cor. 1:21–22).

So it had to be with the apostles on the day of Pentecost. By inference, what happened to Paul (2 Cor. 1:21) also occurred to the disciples when they were anointed with the Holy Spirit for their apostleship, which is pictured in Acts 2:1–4.

PLEDGE (2 COR. 1:22; 5:5; EPH. 1:14)

In three New Testament texts (2 Cor. 1:22; 5:5; Eph. 1:14), the Holy Spirit is said to be given to every believer as a guarantee (Gk. *arrabōn*) of his or her full salvation, which would not be completely fulfilled until the resurrection. This term could be described with many synonyms such as *down payment*, *earnest*, or *pledge*, ensuring that a promise made and begun would unquestionably be fulfilled completely in the future. The indwelling Holy Spirit is God's pledge that what he began when a person first believed in Christ for eternal life will eventually result in eternal life (Phil. 1:6).

SEAL (2 COR. 1:22; EPH. 1:13; 4:30)

The Father set his seal on the Son (John 6:27). God set his seal on the apostles (2 Cor. 1:22). The Lord set his seal on believers (Eph. 1:13; 4:30). The seal that God placed on all believers (Gk. *sphragizō*) is the Holy Spirit. This redemptive seal marks out the ownership of believers by God, who redeemed them out of the domain of darkness and put them into Christ's kingdom of light (Col. 1:13). The seal indicates that believers look to God for their spiritual security in this life and the next (see "Salvation" [p. 349] for an expansion of this discussion).

WATER (JOHN 7:38-39; ACTS 1:5; 2:33; 1 COR. 12:13 [2X]; TITUS 3:5-6)

The Holy Spirit is pictured as (1) life-giving water, that is, salvation (John 7:38–39; 1 Cor. 12:13b; Titus 3:5–6); (2) life-enabling water, that is, empowerment (Acts 1:5; 2:33); and (3) life-sustaining water, that is, induction (1 Cor. 12:13a).

Using the word picture of water, Christ looked forward (Acts 1:5) and Peter looked backward (Acts 2:33) to the powerful enablement of the disciples with the Holy Spirit on the day of Pentecost. The disciples were "baptized" (Acts 1:5), and the Father "poured out" the promise of the Holy Spirit (Acts 2:33).

Paul spoke salvifically of the Holy Spirit as water when it is consumed in 1 Corinthians 12:13b (see John 4:14). Christ spoke about the Holy Spirit being rivers of living water (John 7:38–39; cf. Ezek. 36:25–27). Paul pictured the Holy Spirit as water being poured out for the washing of regeneration (Titus 3:5–6). At the time of Christ's millennial kingdom, God will pour out his Spirit redemptively on the house of Israel (Isa. 32:15; 44:3; Ezek. 39:29; Joel 2:28–29).

Christ baptizes believers with the Holy Spirit at the moment of salvation, ushering them into the church (1 Cor. 12:13a). Like salvation and empowerment, this induction into the body of Christ is permanent and therefore irreversible.

WIND (JOHN 3:8; ACTS 2:2; 2 PET. 1:21)

The Greek word *pneuma* can be translated "spirit" (Matt. 5:3), "Spirit" (Matt. 1:18), "wind" (John 3:8), or "breath" (Rev. 13:15), as context determines. In John 3:8, Jesus likened the phenomenon of wind to the work of God's Spirit in salvation in that it is invisible, unexpected, unpredictable, yet always powerfully accomplishing its end (cf. Ezek. 37:9–14).

Luke pictured the sound of the coming of the Holy Spirit on Pentecost as that of a mighty rushing wind (Acts 2:2). It could only be heard, not seen, and it created a powerful effect that culminated in Peter's remarkable preaching that day. The invisible Spirit empowered an undeniable and unforgettable beginning to the church of Jesus Christ.

Peter described the writing of Scripture using wind as an emblem of the Holy Spirit's work of inspiration (2 Pet. 1:21). As wind carries along a ship at sea, so the Holy Spirit carried along the apostles in writing the Bible. Ships are "dead in the water" without the propelling power of the wind, and likewise, Scripture writers were impotent to write the Word of God without the attendant power of the Holy Spirit.

Holy Spirit Ministry to Christ

The Holy Spirit ministered to Christ in many ways:

1. Prophesying his ministries (Isa. 11:1–2; 42:1–4; 61:1–3; Zech. 12:10)
2. Implementing his virgin conception and birth (Matt. 1:18, 20; Luke 1:34–35)

3. Descending on him in baptism (Matt. 3:13–17; Mark 1:9–11; Luke 3:21–22; John 1:29–34)
4. Anointing him to preach (Matt. 12:15–21; Luke 4:17–21)
5. Empowering him (Matt. 12:28; Luke 4:14–15; 11:20; Acts 10:38)
6. Filling him (Luke 4:1–2; John 3:34)
7. Leading him (Matt. 4:1; Mark 1:12; Luke 4:1, 14; Acts 1:2)
8. Rejoicing with him (Luke 10:21)
9. Aiding him in offering himself for crucifixion (Heb. 9:14)
10. Raising him from the dead (Rom. 1:4; 8:11)

Holy Spirit Ministries

This basic summary of Holy Spirit ministries demonstrates what Christ meant when he told the disciples that it was advantageous for the Son to depart so that he could send the Holy Spirit (John 16:7):

1. He adopts (Rom. 8:15).
2. He baptizes (1 Cor. 12:13).
3. He bears witness (Acts 5:32; Rom. 8:16; 9:1; 1 John 5:6–8).
4. He calls to ministry (Acts 13:2–4).
5. He convicts (John 16:8–11).
6. He empowers (Ex. 31:1–3; Judg. 13:25; Acts 1:8).
7. He fills (Luke 4:1; Acts 2:4; Eph. 5:18).
8. He guarantees (2 Cor. 1:22; 5:5; Eph. 1:14).
9. He guards (2 Tim. 1:14).
10. He helps (John 14:16, 26; 15:26; 16:7; 2 Tim. 1:14).
11. He illuminates (1 Cor. 2:10–13).
12. He indwells (Rom. 8:9–11; 1 Cor. 3:16; 6:19).
13. He intercedes (Rom. 8:26–27; Eph. 6:18; Jude 20; see 1 John 5:14–15).
14. He leads (Ps. 143:10; Matt. 4:1; Mark 1:12; Luke 4:1; Acts 20:22–23; Rom. 8:14).
15. He produces fruit (Gal. 5:22–23).
16. He provides spiritual character (Gal. 5:16, 18, 25).
17. He regenerates (John 3:5–6, 8; Titus 3:5).
18. He reminds (John 14:26).
19. He restrains/convicts of sin (Gen. 6:3; Acts 7:51; 2 Thess. 2:6–7).
20. He resurrects (Rom. 1:4; 8:11).
21. He reveals truth (2 Sam. 23:2; Neh. 9:30; Zech. 7:12; John 14:17; 1 Cor. 2:10; Eph. 3:5).
22. He sanctifies (Rom. 15:16; 1 Cor. 6:11; 2 Thess. 2:13; 1 Pet. 1:2).
23. He seals (2 Cor. 1:22; Eph. 1:13–14; 4:30).
24. He selects overseers (Acts 20:28).
25. He sends (Acts 13:4).
26. He strengthens (Eph. 3:16).
27. He teaches (John 14:26; Acts 15:28; 1 John 2:20, 27).

The Holy Spirit is also the source of the following realities:

1. Fellowship (2 Cor. 13:14; Phil. 2:1)
2. Liberty (2 Cor. 3:17–18)
3. Life and peace (Rom. 8:6)
4. Power (Rom. 15:13; 1 Cor. 2:4; Eph. 3:16)
5. Spiritual gifts (1 Cor. 12:4–11)
6. Truth (John 14:17; 15:26; 1 John 5:6)
7. Unity (Eph. 2:18; 4:3–4)
8. Wisdom (Isa. 11:2)
9. Worship (Phil. 3:3)

Sins against the Holy Spirit

It is not fully clear how the will of man opposes the will of God. However, it is a fact, as illustrated by many passages in Scripture.

Believers oppose God's will in the following actions against the Holy Spirit:

1. Grieving him (Eph. 4:30)
2. Lying to him (Acts 5:3)
3. Neglecting him (Gal. 3:3–6; 5:17)
4. Quenching him (1 Thess. 5:19)
5. Testing him (Acts 5:9)

Unbelievers oppose God's will in the following actions against the Holy Spirit:

1. Blaspheming him (Matt. 12:31; Mark 3:29; Luke 12:10)
2. Grieving him (Isa. 63:10)
3. Insulting/provoking him (Heb. 3:10; 10:29)
4. Rebelling against / resisting him (Gen. 6:3 [NASB]; Neh. 9:30; Isa. 30:1; 63:10; Acts 7:51; Gal. 5:17)
5. Testing him (Ps. 78:41; Heb. 3:8–9)

Both believers and unbelievers can sin against the Holy Spirit in the following ways:

1. Grieving him (Isa. 63:10; Eph. 4:30)
2. Testing him (Ps. 78:41; Acts 5:9; Heb. 3:8–9)

Deity and Triunity[2]

Deity
Triunity

The deity and triunity of the Holy Spirit have occasionally been called into question but not frequently. When this has occurred, it is because the content of Scripture has been disregarded, either due to human logic wrongly supplanting God's impeccable revelation in the Bible or due to plain, unvarnished unbelief. What follows unfolds significant evidence supporting the Holy Spirit's deity and the triunity of the Godhead.

---

2. For a more thorough discussion of deity and triunity, please refer to chap. 3, "God the Father," and chap. 4, "God the Son."

Deity

ATTRIBUTIONS

In Acts 5, Peter confronts Ananias, saying, "Why has Satan filled your heart to lie to the Holy Spirit?" (5:3). He then indicts Ananias: "You have not lied to man but to God" (5:4). In so doing, the apostle equates a lie to the Holy Spirit with a lie to God. Thus, he identifies the Holy Spirit as God.

The words of Yahweh in the Old Testament are at times attributed to the Holy Spirit in the New Testament. Thus, the Holy Spirit, like Yahweh, is God. Compare Psalm 95:8–11 with Hebrews 3:7–11; Isaiah 6:8–10 with Acts 28:25–27; and Jeremiah 31:33–34 with Hebrews 10:15–17.

Christians are said to serve as the temple of God (1 Cor. 3:16; 6:19) because the Holy Spirit is God and dwells in them individually (Rom. 8:9, 11; 2 Tim. 1:14). Just as God's glory dwelt within the Most Holy Place during Old Testament times, so God's Spirit now dwells in true believers.

God's work in forming the church, the body of Christ (1 Cor. 12:18, 24, 28), is also attributed to the Holy Spirit (1 Cor. 12:11). Because this is described as *God's* work, the deity of the Holy Spirit is thus confirmed again.

In one of the most unforgettable moments of Christ's ministry on earth, he said, "Whoever blasphemes against the Holy Spirit never has forgiveness, but is guilty of an eternal sin" (Mark 3:29; see Matt. 12:31–32; Luke 12:10). This passage again demonstrates the deity of the Holy Spirit, since only God can be blasphemed.[3]

APPELLATIONS

See "The Holy Spirit and the Father" and "The Holy Spirit and the Son" under "Names and Titles" (p. 335). For our purposes here, the Holy Spirit's names are related to both God the Father and God the Son since the Holy Spirit possesses the same divine essence as the Father and the Son.

ATTRIBUTES

The Holy Spirit possesses the perfections of God, that is, the incommunicable attributes of deity. These qualities are unique to God in kind and extent. Such divine characteristics certify that the Holy Spirit is indeed God:

1. Eternality (Heb. 9:14)
2. Glory (1 Pet. 4:14; cf. Isa. 42:8; 48:11)
3. Holiness (Ps. 51:11; Isa. 63:10–11; Matt. 1:18; Rom. 1:4)
4. Omnipotence (Gen. 1:1–2; Luke 1:35; Rom. 1:4)
5. Omnipresence (Ps. 139:7–10; cf. Jer. 23:24)
6. Omniscience (Isa. 40:13; 1 Cor. 2:10–11)
7. Truth (John 14:17; 15:26; 16:13)

---

3. For a discussion of the nature of the blasphemy of the Holy Spirit, see "The Blasphemy of the Holy Spirit and Apostasy" below (p. 351), and "The Unpardonable Sin" in chap. 6 (p. 469).

ACTIONS

Only God can be engaged in the following divine activities. Therefore, the Holy Spirit is God and works in perfect harmony and unity with God the Father and God the Son:

1. Creation (Gen. 1:2; Job 26:13; 33:4)
2. Help/comfort (John 14:16, 26; 15:26; 16:7)
3. Inspiration (2 Pet. 1:20–21)
4. Intercession (Rom. 8:26–27; cf. Eph. 6:18; Jude 20)
5. Miracles (Matt. 12:28; 1 Cor. 12:9, 11)
6. Regeneration (John 3:5–8; Titus 3:5)
7. Resurrection (Rom. 8:11)
8. Sanctification (2 Thess. 2:13; 1 Pet. 1:2)

ASSOCIATIONS

Several passages in Scripture clearly associate the Holy Spirit with deity:

1. Matthew 28:19: Jesus's baptismal instructions here unite Father, Son, and Spirit together as equal participants in the salvation of a believer, which baptism by immersion represents.
2. John 14:16, 26; 15:26; 16:7: In these passages, Jesus refers to the Spirit of truth, whom he will ask the Father to send as "another Helper." The Greek term for "another," *allos*, means "another of the same kind," that is, another member of the triune Godhead. Jesus does this so that the disciples will not be orphaned when Christ ascends to heaven (Acts 1:9). Four times in the Gospel of John (14:16, 26; 15:26 [2×]) Father, Son, and Holy Spirit are associated together as equals.
3. 1 Corinthians 2:10–13: This passage shows that the Father and Holy Spirit complement one another equally in the revelation, illumination, and interpretation of God's Word.
4. 2 Corinthians 13:14: All three members of the Godhead are mentioned and set on equal footing in this Pauline Trinitarian benediction.
5. Revelation 1:4–5: This Johannine Trinitarian invocation links the Father, the Spirit, and the Son together as coequals.

ATTACKS

The most serious historical heresies regarding the Holy Spirit fall into two categories: (1) the denial that the Holy Spirit was a person, and (2) the denial that the Holy Spirit was eternal God, which was consequently a denial of God's triunity.

Sabellianism. This blasphemous heresy dating to the late second or early third century proposed that there was one God in three manifestations, modes, names, or roles. It affirmed the one person of God but denied the personhood of Christ and the Holy Spirit, thus denying the triunity of God.

Sabellianism, also known as Modalism, taught that the Father is also the Son and also the Holy Spirit depending on what mode or role God is assuming at any one moment in time. It has also at times been called Monarchianism because it attempted to "protect the one God," albeit at the unacceptable expense of God's triunity. One version was even called Patripassianism ("the Father suffered") because, allegedly, when the Father assumed the mode/role of the Son, he was crucified. Some taught that this one God took on successive roles: first as the Father in creation, then as the Son in redemption, and ultimately as the Holy Spirit in regeneration and sanctification.

These false teachers sought to protect the doctrine of one God from the false accusation that they were teaching three gods, or polytheism. Unwittingly, this attempt to protect monotheism resulted in an equally egregious error of denying the persons of Christ and the Holy Spirit. In so doing, it rejected God's triunity. The true biblical doctrine of the triune Godhead affirms that there is one God (not three) in three persons (not one) who are coexistent, coeternal, and coequal. The erroneous view of Sabellianism continues in a modified form in the modern Unitarian movement.

Arianism. This early to mid-fourth-century heresy taught that the one God created Christ in eternity past, who in turn created the Holy Spirit. While this false teaching affirmed the personhood of both Christ and the Holy Spirit (unlike Sabellianism), it denied their deity and consequently God's triunity. Like Sabellianism, Arianism taught that the Godhead consisted of one person with the essence of deity. This false doctrine was confronted at the Council of Nicaea (AD 325) and the Council of Constantinople (AD 381).

Socinianism. This sixteenth-century aberration affirmed the personhood of Christ while denying his deity. It also denied the Holy Spirit's personhood and thus the Holy Spirit's deity and resultantly God's triunity. Various modern Unitarian movements affirm much of Socinianism.

Table 5.2 summarizes key elements of these three major historical attacks on the deity of the Holy Spirit and the triunity of God. Analyzing the chart results in the following summary statements:[4]

1. All three views affirmed the personhood of God the Father.
2. Only Sabellianism denied the personhood of Christ.
3. Only Arianism affirmed the personhood of the Holy Spirit.
4. All three views affirmed the deity of God the Father.
5. All three views denied the triunity of God.

Triunity[5]

God's triunity (Trinitarianism) stands unarguably as a *sine qua non*, or an indispensable fact, of Christianity. It has been, is, and forever will be an indisputable bedrock belief of the Christian faith.

---

4. For additional details, consult George Smeaton, *The Doctrine of the Holy Spirit*, 2nd ed. (1889; repr., Carlisle, PA: Banner of Truth, 1958); Henry Barclay Swete, *The Holy Spirit in the Ancient Church: A Study of the Christian Teaching in the Age of the Fathers* (1912; repr., Grand Rapids, MI: Baker, 1966); John F. Walvoord, *The Holy Spirit: A Comprehensive Study of the Person and Work of the Holy Spirit* (1954; repr., Grand Rapids, MI: Zondervan, 1991).

5. This section is adapted from Richard Mayhue, "Editorial: One God—Three Persons," *MSJ* 24, no. 2 (2013): 161–65. Used by permission of *MSJ*. For a more thorough discussion of the triunity of God, refer to chap. 3, "God the Father."

Table 5.2 Historical Attacks on the Trinity and the Holy Spirit

		Sabellianism*	Arianism	Socinianism
Person	Father	Affirmed	Affirmed	Affirmed
	Son	Denied	Affirmed	Affirmed
	Holy Spirit	Denied	Affirmed	Denied
Deity	Father	Affirmed	Affirmed	Affirmed
	Son	Affirmed	Denied	Denied
	Holy Spirit	Affirmed	Denied	Denied
Triunity		Denied	Denied	Denied

* To be clear, Sabellianism denied the deity of the *persons* of the Son and Spirit in that it denied their person-hood; at the same time, it affirmed their deity insofar as they were actually manifestations of God the Father.

The Master's Seminary doctrinal statement succinctly summarizes this precious truth thus: "We teach that there is but one living and true God (Deut. 6:4; Isa. 45:5–7; 1 Cor. 8:4), an infinite, all-knowing Spirit (John 4:24), perfect in all His attributes, one in essence, eternally existing in three Persons—Father, Son, and Holy Spirit (Matt. 28:19; 2 Cor. 13:14)—each equally deserving worship and obedience." So there is one God in three persons, who are distinct from one another yet inseparably one in essence and who are coexistent, coeternal, and coequal.

While God's trinity appears implicitly and explicitly throughout the Bible, no one text declares or explains the fullness associated with the incomprehensible triune God (Isa. 40:28). However, the plethora of evidence in both the Old and New Testaments, plus the writings of the early church, make this an overwhelmingly undeniable tenet of biblical orthodoxy.

Starting in the Old Testament, one immediately encounters Genesis 1:26 and 3:22 (cf. Gen. 11:5–7), where God uses the plural pronoun "us" in reference to himself:

> Then God said, "Let us make man in our image, after our likeness. And let them have dominion over the fish of the sea and over the birds of the heavens and over the livestock and over all the earth and over every creeping thing that creeps on the earth." (Gen. 1:26)

> Then the LORD God said, "Behold, the man has become like one of us in knowing good and evil. Now, lest he reach out his hand, and take also of the tree of life and eat, and live forever—" therefore the LORD God sent him out from the garden of Eden to work the ground from which he was taken. (Gen. 3:22–23)

The same use of "us" also appears in Isaiah 6:8: "And I heard the voice of the Lord saying, 'Whom shall I send, and who will go for us?' Then I said, 'Here I am! Send me.'"

But how can one be three? Deuteronomy 6:4 hints at the answer: "Hear, O Israel: The LORD our God, the LORD is one." The Hebrew word translated "one" here (*'ehad*), frequently communicates the idea of unity in diversity. For instance, see Genesis 1:5 (one day in two parts—evening and morning); Genesis 2:24 (one couple in two partners—male and female); Exodus 24:3 (one voice in many people);

Exodus 26:6 (one tabernacle in multiple parts); and Numbers 13:23 (one cluster in many grapes). So it is no surprise to see God revealing an allusion to one God in three persons in the last book of the Pentateuch.

With even greater specificity, Isaiah writes of three persons when referring to the one God of Israel: "the Lord God," "me" (i.e., Christ), and "his Spirit" (Isa. 48:16). Isaiah 61:1 similarly says, "The Spirit of the Lord God is upon me," that is, Christ, and in fact, Christ interpreted this text in just such a manner in Luke 4:18–19.

In the progress of God's written revelation, the New Testament evidence becomes more direct and frequent in showing that Father, Son, and Holy Spirit are of the same divine essence and are coequal, one God in three persons expressing unity in diversity. All three appear together in numerous New Testament texts:

> And when Jesus was baptized, immediately he went up from the water, and behold, the heavens were opened to him, and he saw the Spirit of God descending like a dove and coming to rest on him; and behold, a voice from heaven said, "This is my beloved Son, with whom I am well pleased." (Matt. 3:16–17)

> Go therefore and make disciples of all nations, baptizing them in the name of the Father and of the Son and of the Holy Spirit. (Matt. 28:19)

> And the angel answered her, "The Holy Spirit will come upon you, and the power of the Most High will overshadow you; therefore the child to be born will be called holy—the Son of God." (Luke 1:35)

> But when the Helper comes, whom I will send to you from the Father, the Spirit of truth, who proceeds from the Father, he will bear witness about me. (John 15:26; cf. 14:16, 26; 16:7–10, 14–15)

> If the Spirit of him who raised Jesus from the dead dwells in you, he who raised Christ Jesus from the dead will also give life to your mortal bodies through his Spirit who dwells in you. (Rom. 8:11)

> I appeal to you, brothers, by our Lord Jesus Christ and by the love of the Spirit, to strive together with me in your prayers to God on my behalf. (Rom. 15:30)

> The grace of the Lord Jesus Christ, and the love of God and the fellowship of the Holy Spirit be with you all. (2 Cor. 13:14)

> For if the blood of goats and bulls, and the sprinkling of defiled persons with the ashes of a heifer, sanctify for the purification of the flesh, how much more will the blood of Christ, who through the eternal Spirit offered himself without blemish to God, purify our conscience from dead works to serve the living God? (Heb. 9:13–14)

> By this you know the Spirit of God: every spirit that confesses that Jesus Christ has come in the flesh is from God. (1 John 4:2)

> But you, beloved, building yourselves up in your most holy faith and praying in the Holy Spirit, keep yourselves in the love of God, waiting for the mercy of our Lord Jesus Christ that leads to eternal life. (Jude 20–21)

The additional like-minded New Testament texts listed below eliminate any doubt as to the triunity of God, with the Holy Spirit being the third member:

Acts 2:33	Ephesians 2:19–22
Romans 5:5–6	Ephesians 3:16–19
Romans 8:3–4	Ephesians 4:4–6
Romans 8:8–9	Ephesians 5:18–20
Romans 8:15–17	Philippians 3:3
Romans 8:26–29	1 Thessalonians 1:3–5
Romans 15:16	2 Thessalonians 2:13–14
1 Corinthians 2:2–5	Titus 3:4–6
1 Corinthians 6:11	Hebrews 10:29–31
2 Corinthians 1:21–22	1 Peter 1:2
Galatians 3:1–5	1 Peter 4:14

The *magnum opus* of Trinitarian passages comes in Ephesians 1:3–14, which speaks of each person's involvement in the salvation of believers:

- God the Father: 1:3–6
- God the Son: 1:7–12
- God the Holy Spirit: 1:13–14

Actually, and not unexpectedly, the three members of the single Godhead appear by allusion or direct mention at the beginning and end of both the Old and New Testaments, from Genesis to Malachi and Matthew to Revelation, as illustrated in table 5.3.

As time passed beyond the completed canon of Scripture and the apostles, the early church fathers began to write about the Trinity in more detail. Note these three examples:

Irenaeus (ca. AD 120–202):
And this is the drawing-up of our faith, the foundation of the building, and the consolidation of a way of life. God, the Father, uncreated, beyond grasp, invisible, one God the maker of all; this is the *first and foremost article* of our faith. But the *second article* is the Word of God, the Son of God, Christ Jesus our Lord, who was shown forth by the prophets according to the design of their prophecy and according to the manner in which the Father disposed; and through Him were made all things whatsoever. He also, *in the end of times*, for the recapitulation of all things, is become a man among men, visible and tangible, in order to abolish death and bring to light life, and bring about the communion of God and man. And the *third article* is the Holy Spirit, through whom the prophets prophesied and the patriarchs were taught about God and the just were led in the path of justice, and who *in the end of times* has been poured forth in a new manner upon humanity over all the earth renewing man to God.[6]

---

6. Irenaeus, *Proof of the Apostolic Preaching*, trans. Joseph P. Smith, Ancient Christian Writers 16 (London: Longmans, Green, 1952), 50. Italics for numbered "articles" added for emphasis; italics for the phrase "in the end of times" original.

Table 5.3 Trinitarian References at Testament Bookends

Book	Passage	Allusion/Mention
Genesis	1:26	"us"
Malachi	2:15	Holy Spirit
	2:16	Father
	3:1-2	Christ
Matthew	1:18	Christ
	1:18	Holy Spirit
	1:22	Father
Revelation	22:17	Holy Spirit
	22:18-19	Father
	22:20-21	Christ

Gregory of Nazianzus (ca. AD 330–ca. 389):
The Son is not Father; . . . yet he is whatever the Father is. The Spirit is not Son. . . . Yet whatever the Son is, he is. The three are a single whole in their Godhead and the single whole is three in personalities.[7]

Augustine (AD 354–430):
Whatever . . . is spoken of God in respect to himself, is both spoken singly of each person, that is, of the Father, and the Son, and the Holy Spirit; and together of the Trinity itself, not plurally but in the singular.[8]

Not only were men writing as individuals, but also groups began to compose creedal statements. Several of the more important early ones include the following:

The Niceno-Constantinopolitan Creed (ca. AD 381):
We believe in one God the Father Almighty. . . . And in one Lord Jesus Christ, . . . very God of very God. . . . And in the Holy Ghost, . . . who with the Father and the Son together is worshiped and glorified.[9]

The (Pseudo) Athanasian Creed (ca. AD 375–525):
And the Catholic faith is this: That we worship one God in Trinity, and Trinity in Unity;
    Neither confounding the Persons: nor dividing the Substance [Essence].
    For there is one Person of the Father: another of the Son: and another of the Holy Ghost.
    But the Godhead of the Father, of the Son, and of the Holy Ghost, is all one: the Glory equal, the Majesty coeternal.[10]

---

7. St. Gregory of Nazianzus, *On God and Christ: The Five Theological Orations and Two Letters to Cledonius*, trans. Fredrick Williams and Lionel Wickham (Crestwood, NY: St. Vladimir's Seminary Press, 2002), 122–23.
8. Augustine, *On the Holy Trinity*, in *A Select Library of the Nicene and Post-Nicene Fathers of the Christian Church*, ed. Philip Schaff (New York: Charles Scribner's Sons, 1905), 3:92 (5.8.9).
9. Philip Schaff, *The Creeds of Christendom*, vol. 2, *The Greek and Latin Creeds* (New York: Harper & Brothers, 1889), 58–59.
10. Schaff, *The Creeds of Christendom*, 2:66.

Since the time of the Athanasian Creed, theologians have observed that at least seven lines of thought can be developed from the entire section (paragraphs 3–28):

1. The Father is God.
2. The Son is God.
3. The Holy Spirit is God.
4. The Father is not the Son.
5. The Father is not the Holy Spirit.
6. The Son is not the Holy Spirit.
7. There is exactly one God.[11]

These seven truths, when summarized, teach that there is one living and true God, one in essence and eternally existing in three persons—Father, Son, and Holy Spirit. There can be no other conclusion reached, biblically or logically.

Salvation

    Regeneration
    Baptism
    Sealing

Though mankind was created in the image of God, perfectly suited for fellowship with him, as a result of Adam's sin the entire human race is born in sin, alienated from God, and subject to his judgment. As an overflow of his grace, the Triune God purposed to save a remnant of his creation through the atoning work of God the Son. Scripture teaches, however, that the saving benefits purchased by Christ's cross are applied to believers through the work of the Holy Spirit. In this section, we outline his work with respect to salvation.[12]

Regeneration

The first step in the Spirit's application of salvation is regeneration. Fundamental to understanding regeneration are the realities of spiritual death and life. Every human being who has ever lived has suffered from spiritual deadness (Rom. 3:23; Eph. 2:1, 5). Will they ever live again, and if so, how will that happen? God the Father, God the Son, and God the Holy Spirit give new spiritual life to those who were previously dead in their sins (Rom. 8:2, 6, 10–11). Regeneration directly addresses this gracious act of God.

WORD PICTURES

Scripture pictures regeneration using four different images: (1) spiritual birth, (2) spiritual cleansing, (3) spiritual creation, and (4) spiritual resurrection.

---

11. John S. Feinberg, *No One Like Him: The Doctrine of God*, Foundations of Evangelical Theology (Wheaton, IL: Crossway, 2001), 438.

12. For more on the doctrine of salvation, particularly with respect to the Holy Spirit's work of regeneration, see chap. 7, "Salvation," especially "The Internal Call: Regeneration" (p. 576).

Spiritual Birth (Titus 3:5). The Greek word normally translated "regeneration" (*palingenesia*) appears only twice in the New Testament (Matt. 19:28; Titus 3:5). Matthew uses it to refer to the millennium as a regenerated world, but in Titus it refers to salvation. A combination of two words, *palingenesia* literally means "born again" (see Gal. 4:29). The same idea appears in 1 Peter in the Greek term *anagennaō*, which also literally means "born again" (1 Pet. 1:3, 23) and has been translated so. When speaking to Nicodemus, Jesus told him, "You must be born again," using two Greek words that literally mean "born from above" and that refer to spiritual rebirth by God who dwells above (John 3:3, 7; see James 1:17). John's first epistle repeatedly refers to being born of God (1 John 2:29; 3:9; 4:7; 5:1, 4, 18). In the act of regeneration, the Holy Spirit has brought conviction of sin, righteousness, and judgment (John 16:8–11), and he provides assurance of salvation afterward by bearing witness to the believer of its reality (Rom. 8:16; 1 John 3:24).

Spiritual Cleansing (Titus 3:5). Paul twice uses the Greek word *loutron* to refer to those who are filthy with sin (Isa. 64:6) being washed clean by regeneration (Eph. 5:26; Titus 3:5). After Paul recounts the many heinous sins of the Corinthians (1 Cor. 6:9–10), he uses the Greek word *apolouō* to describe their being washed, which he associates with the sanctification of salvation and justification (1 Cor. 6:11).

Spiritual Creation (Titus 3:5). In Titus 3:5, Paul uses the Greek word *anakainōsis*, which literally means "new again" and is translated "renewal." This is a compound word using *kainos*, which means "new in quality," in contrast to *neos*, which means "new in time." Paul employed both words for "new" in his epistles. When emphasizing newness in quality of life, he chose *kainos* to describe God's redemptive creation (2 Cor. 5:17; Gal. 6:15; Eph. 4:24); when intending the newness in time of spiritual life renewal, he turned to *neos* (Col. 3:10). Because of regeneration in the sense of spiritual renewal, Christians have a new nature (2 Cor. 5:17) with new spiritual capacities (Rom. 6:18, 20; 1 Cor. 12:3). The regenerated, renewed believer has been graced with a condition even better than what Adam originally had before his fall into sin and his experience of God's curse. Adam was innocent, but the regenerated believer is declared righteous—the Holy Spirit's spiritual re-creation, alive to God.

Spiritual Resurrection (John 6:63). Both Paul (2 Cor. 3:6) and John (John 6:63) declare that the Spirit gives life. Elsewhere, Scripture states that God gives life (John 5:21; Rom. 4:17; 6:13; Eph. 2:5; Col. 2:13). John reveals that Christ gives life (John 5:21). Obviously, a coordinated Trinitarian effort is involved in bringing spiritual life to those who would otherwise be spiritually dead. Thus Scripture portrays regeneration as a spiritual resurrection.

THE OLD TESTAMENT

Were Old Testament believers regenerated, or did regeneration begin at Pentecost? The answer is definitively that both Old Testament and New Testament believers experienced regeneration.

Two different lines of reasoning reveal the same affirmative conclusion. First, since only those who are "born again"—that is, regenerated—can be in the kingdom of God (John 3:3, 5, 7), and second, since Old Testament believers were salvifically in the kingdom of God, Old Testament saints were necessarily regenerated. Approaching it from a different angle, since it is impossible for a believer to be justified by God without being regenerated, and since Old Testament believers were justified (Rom. 4:1–12; see Ps. 32:1–2), then Old Testament saints were regenerated.

TRINITARIAN INVOLVEMENT

All three members of the Godhead were involved in some aspect of regeneration, since Scripture says that all three give life:

1. God the Father (John 1:13; 2 Cor. 5:17–19; Eph. 2:4–6; Col. 2:13; James 1:18; 1 Pet. 1:3; 1 John 5:11)
2. God the Son (John 1:12; 5:21)
3. God the Holy Spirit (John 3:3, 5–7; 6:63; Titus 3:5)

This is why Jesus gave the baptismal formula, ". . . baptizing them in the name of the Father and of the Son and of the Holy Spirit" (Matt. 28:19). This statement recognizes each member of the Godhead because of their individual and combined involvements in regeneration.

THE HOLY SPIRIT AND GOD'S WORD

Salvation comes only by God's will, not by human will (John 1:13; Eph. 2:8–10; James 1:18). While all three members of the Godhead make unique contributions to the effort of regeneration, Scripture emphasizes that it is by the complementary interaction of God's Spirit (John 3:3, 5–7; Gal. 3:2–3, 14; 1 Thess. 1:5; Titus 3:5) with God's Word (Rom. 1:16; 1 Thess. 1:5; 2:13; 1 Pet. 1:23) that regeneration takes place.

Therefore, regeneration involves the triune God's instantaneous impartation of eternal spiritual life to people who were formerly spiritually dead but have embraced Christ by faith because of God's grace. This act of efficacious grace is effected entirely, without human aid, by the Holy Spirit through the Word of God. This creation of new life results in believers being new creations with a new nature, new abilities, new desires, new relationships, and new responsibilities—forever.

THE BLASPHEMY OF THE HOLY SPIRIT AND APOSTASY

Despite the glory of the Spirit's work in salvation, Scripture identifies two instances in which people decisively exclude themselves from the Spirit's regenerating work. First, there are those who commit the unpardonable or unforgiveable sin, the blasphemy of the Holy Spirit (Matt. 12:31–32; Mark 3:28–30; Luke 12:10). Jesus taught about this as the Pharisees repeatedly confronted him and charged him with breaking the Sabbath. Jesus explained that his compassion for his hungry disciples (Matt. 12:1–7) and for a man with a withered hand (Matt. 12:9–13) were examples of the true fulfillment of God's law. Not only this but also the claim to be Lord of the Sabbath (Matt. 12:8), along with the divine healings (Matt. 12:13) and exorcisms (Matt. 12:22), undeniably demonstrated that Jesus was the divine Messiah (Matt. 12:23). Unable to deny his power, the Pharisees sought to sway the crowds by insisting that Jesus worked his miracles by the power of Satan rather than the power of God. Jesus noted the absurdity (Matt. 12:25–26) and hypocrisy of such an accusation (Matt. 12:27). They had no good reason to suppose Jesus's miracles were demonic; they simply did not want to accept his divine authority.

In this context, Jesus identified the Pharisees' accusations as blasphemy against the Holy Spirit (Matt. 12:31), for it was by the Spirit that he performed these works. Such blasphemy is unforgiveable (Matt. 12:32). Though the Pharisees had received the clearest revelation of Jesus's authority, their hearts were so hardened that they refused to accept what they knew to be true, and levied a slanderous charge in a malicious attempt to silence him. As a result, Jesus declared them to be past the point of repentance and forgiveness. It is this hardened, determined, willful rejection and unbelief—even in the face of the most undeniable evidence—that characterizes the unpardonable sin. In sum, one commits the unforgiveable sin by witnessing the acts of the Spirit of God in Jesus and, because of a hard heart of unbelief, attributing those acts to Satan.

Second, Scripture also identifies those people who counterfeit their profession of faith in Christ—outwardly and temporarily giving the appearance of being truly regenerated by the Spirit, only to eventually fall away and abandon the faith (e.g., Heb. 2:1–3; 3:7–13; 6:4–6; 2 Pet. 2:20). This is *apostasy*, a term that means "to fall away." Professing Christians who identify themselves with Christ and then subsequently renounce him prove themselves to have never truly been converted, demonstrating by their going out from the fellowship of the faith that they were never really in Christ (cf. 1 John 2:19). Peter wrote that for these spiritual impostors, their last state becomes worse than the first, and that it would have been better for them not to have known the way of righteousness than to have known and then turned away (2 Pet. 2:20–21). This is because it is impossible for someone who has truly abandoned the faith in the light of full revelation to be renewed again unto repentance (Heb. 6:4–6). Similar to the blasphemy of the Holy Spirit, apostasy consists of a hard-hearted, resolute rejection of Christ and of regarding as false the truth of God, from which there is a point of no return, so to speak. Though that point may only be knowable to God, there is a kind of rejection that excludes the possibility of repentance.

Often the sensitive consciences of genuine believers trouble them as to whether they may have sinned so severely as to have committed the unpardonable sin or apostatized. However, both of these egregious acts involve a hardness of heart and a severe hatred for the Savior. These are not the marks of those who love Christ such that they are fearful of falling away from him. Sinning believers must continue to turn from sin and trust in the sufficiency of Christ's life, death, and resurrection to save them from God's wrath. For those who do, Christ has promised to never leave his own (Matt. 28:20; Heb. 13:5) or let them be snatched away from him (John 10:28–29). God promises to finish his work of salvation (Phil. 1:6), so that nothing can separate true believers from God's love in Christ (Rom. 8:38–39). Fearful believers ought to examine themselves, repent of sin, look to Christ alone for righteousness, rejoice in the sufficiency of his saving love, and follow after him with renewed strength.

Baptism

After God's Spirit regenerates those who were previously dead in their sins (Eph. 2:1–3) so that they inherit eternal life, at least six significant spiritual enhancements involving the Spirit occur simultaneously:

1. Christ *baptizes* the believer with the Spirit into the body of Christ (1 Cor. 12:13).
2. The Father *seals* the believer with the Holy Spirit as a show of ownership and a guarantee of one's salvation (Eph. 1:13).
3. The Spirit *indwells* the believer (1 Cor. 3:16).
4. The Spirit *fills/controls* the believer (Eph. 5:18).
5. The Spirit *produces* spiritual fruit in the believer's life (Gal. 5:22–23).
6. The Spirit *gifts* the believer for service in the church (1 Cor. 12:4).

These features will be discussed consecutively in this section and in the "Sanctification" (p. 359) and "Service" (p. 379) sections below. All six occur concurrently with salvation, but each is treated individually in Scripture.

The most appropriate time to commence Christ's promised coming of the Spirit (John 14:16–17; Acts 1:4–5) was Pentecost (fifty days after Passover, in May or June), which celebrated the Jewish Feast of Weeks (Ex. 34:22), also known as the Feast of the Harvest (Ex. 23:16). As the Jews celebrated the firstfruits of the physical harvest (Lev. 23:15–17), the new covenant era for the church inaugurated the firstfruits of the Holy Spirit's (Acts 2:1–4; see Rom. 8:23) salvation harvest (see John 4:35 for the imagery). The Spirit now ministers under the authority of the new covenant, not the old (Rom. 7:6; 2 Cor. 3:2–11; Heb. 8:6–7, 13; 9:15; 10:1).

SCRIPTURAL CONSIDERATIONS

The *expectation* of Spirit baptism appears in all four Gospels and in Acts 1. The *experience* of Spirit baptism began in Acts 2, as recalled in Acts 11. The *explanation* of Spirit baptism came later, in 1 Corinthians 12.

Expectation. Matthew 3:11–12; Mark 1:8; Luke 3:16–17; and John 1:32–34 all report John the Baptist's reference to Christ baptizing with the Holy Spirit. The Greek preposition *en* should be translated "in" or "with" since these renderings have been used earlier in the obvious sense of "by means of" with reference to water.[13] As one is immersed (*baptizō*) "in," "with," or "by means of" water, so is one baptized "in," "with," or "by means of" the Holy Spirit.

Three different baptisms appear in these texts: (1) water baptism, signifying previous repentance; (2) Spirit baptism, signifying salvation and entrance into the universal church, the body of Christ (1 Cor. 12:13); and (3) fire baptism, pointing to the judgment of unbelievers (Matt. 3:12; 25:41; Luke 3:16; John 15:6; Rev. 20:14–15).

In Matthew, Mark, and Luke, this event occurs before Christ's baptism (ca. spring AD 26), while John refers to another occasion after Christ's baptism (ca. fall AD 26). More than three years later, Christ gave the disciples last-minute instructions regarding Spirit baptism (Acts 1:4–5). As he prepared to ascend to heaven from the Mount of Olives in the spring of AD 30, the Lord reminded them of what John the Baptist had previously said and indicated that the initial fulfillment would be just days away as they waited in Jerusalem (Acts 1:4–5).

Experience. Ten days later, on Pentecost, John's and Christ's previous pronouncements came to pass (Acts 2:1–21). How can this conclusion be drawn since Luke did not explicitly record it as such? About six years later (ca. AD 36), when Peter visited the Roman centurion Cornelius's house in Caesarea (Acts 11:13–18), he preached the gospel to this Gentile household. They were saved and received the Holy Spirit. Peter recalled (1) that it was like the day of Pentecost in Acts 2, and (2) that it was similar to the words of Christ's expectation in Acts 1:5. Thus, he concluded that what occurred on Pentecost was then happening to Cornelius's family. Later, at the Jerusalem Council (ca. AD 49), Peter confirmed and repeated what he had previously said thirteen years earlier in Caesarea (Acts 15:6–11).

Explanation. The historical narratives in the Gospels and Acts recount the facts of the *expectation* and the *experience* of Spirit baptism, but they do not provide any *explanation* as to its meaning or significance. However, Paul wrote to the Corinthian church (ca. AD 55) and explained the resultant reality of Spirit baptism: "For in [with] one Spirit we were all baptized into one body—Jews or Greeks, slave or free—and all were made to drink of one Spirit" (1 Cor. 12:13).

To make further sense of the unique aspects of Spirit baptism, table 5.4 shows the parallel pattern of six essential factors for three baptismal scenarios. To sum it up, Spirit baptism occurs when Jesus Christ, Lord of his church, from Pentecost on, by the Spirit, places Christians into his body, the church, at the moment a person puts faith in Christ as Savior and Lord. By Christ's doing so, Christians are immersed into and participate in the universal body of Christ by the Savior's sovereign will.

The book of Acts presents some scenarios that, when compared with this explanation, raise a few questions.[14] Jesus had told his disciples to preach the gospel in Jerusalem, in Judea, in Samaria, and to the end of the earth (Acts 1:8). The apostles

---

13. Daniel B. Wallace, *Greek Grammar Beyond the Basics: An Exegetical Syntax of the New Testament* (Grand Rapids, MI: Zondervan, 1996), 374.

14. The following three paragraphs are adapted from John MacArthur, *The MacArthur Daily Bible: New King James Version* (Nashville: Thomas Nelson, 2003), 608. Used by permission of Thomas Nelson. www.thomasnelson.com.

Table 5.4 Comparing Three Baptismal Scenarios

	Baptism of Repentance	Local Church Baptism	Spirit Baptism
The baptizer	John the Baptist	Pastor	Christ
The means	Water	Water	Holy Spirit
The baptized	Repentant person before Pentecost	Believer from Pentecost forward	Believer from Pentecost forward
The condition	Repentance	Faith in Christ	Faith in Christ
The mode	Immersion in water	Immersion in water	Immersion in the Holy Spirit
The results	Recognized as an Old Testament believer	Obedience to Christ's command in the local church	Entrance into the universal body of Christ

obeyed, and the milestones of this expansion are recounted in Acts 2; 8; 10–11; and 19. As they proceeded from Jerusalem to Ephesus, from Jew to Gentile, each progression was marked by special circumstances.

Acts describes the arrival of the Holy Spirit in his role as the promised Helper (John 14:16) as a startling audiovisual event (Acts 2:1–13), which was partially and selectively repeated (Acts 8:14–19; 10:44–48; 19:1–7). These repetitions were special cases in which believers were reported to have received or been filled with the Holy Spirit. Each of these cases lacked the sound of a rushing mighty wind and the tongues as of fire that were present in the original event (Acts 2:1–13); however, the people spoke in tongues that they did not know but that others recognized. These events should not be taken as the basis for teaching that believers today should expect the same tongues-evidence to accompany the filling of the Holy Spirit. Even in Acts itself, genuine conversions did not necessarily lead to such extraordinary phenomena accompanying the filling by the Holy Spirit. For example, a crowd of three thousand people believed and were baptized on the same day of Pentecost that started so dramatically (Acts 2:41), yet Scripture makes no mention of tongues in their case.

So why in some cases did tongues accompany the confirmation of faith? That this actually occurred likely demonstrated that believers were being drawn from very different groups into the church. Each new group received a special welcome from the Holy Spirit. Thus, Samaritans (Acts 8:14–19), Gentiles (Acts 10:44–48), and believers from the old covenant (Acts 19:1–7) were added to the church, and the unity of the church was established. To demonstrate that unity, it was imperative to have some replication in each instance of what had occurred at Pentecost with the believing Jews, such as the presence of the apostles and the coming of the Spirit, manifestly indicated through speaking in the languages of Pentecost. Table 5.5 summarizes the details of these four special cases.

Over a period of about two decades, the gospel spread from Jerusalem to Ephesus, to Jews and Gentiles. These four significant steps represent the expansion of the church, which was marked by Spirit baptism with speaking in tongues used as a sign

Table 5.5 Four Special Cases of Conversion

Location	Jerusalem/Judea	Samaria	Caesarea	Ephesus
Text	Acts 2:1–21	Acts 8:14–24	Acts 10:1–11:18	Acts 19:1–7
Time	Day of Pentecost, ca. AD 30	ca. AD 31–32	ca. AD 36	ca. AD 52
People	Jews	Samaritans	Gentiles	Disciples of John the Baptist
Holy Spirit	Baptized and filled with the Holy Spirit	Received the Holy Spirit	Received the Holy Spirit	Received the Holy Spirit
Sign	Spoke in tongues as a sign to the Jews	None recorded	Spoke in tongues as a sign to the Jews	Spoke in tongues and prophesied as a sign to the Jews
Circumstances	Tarrying together	Laying on hands	Peter preaching	Laying on hands

to authenticate the genuineness of God's gospel outreach. Some have concluded that these four historical cameos represented the norm back then, which continues to the present. However, the Epistles as a whole give the very different sense that these were actually extraordinary moments not to be repeated.

Which approach is correct? Two classic, standard rules of biblical interpretation, when objectively and consistently applied to Acts and the Epistles, yield the answer:

1. Employ Scripture, not personal experience, to determine doctrinal truth.
2. Use teaching (didactic) sections of Scripture, not historical (narrative) portions, to determine what is prescriptive rather than what is merely descriptive—what is exceptional compared to what should be considered normative.

The application of these principles leads one to believe that the experiences outlined in Acts 2; 8; 10–11; and 19 were exceptions to the norm, given in order to historically validate and illustrate the spread of the gospel during the unique period of transition from God-fearing Judaism to new covenant Christianity as chronicled in the book of Acts. They have not been the normative expectation and experiences of gospel ministry through the subsequent centuries up to the present time.[15]

There are four other New Testament texts that speak of baptism in such a vague way that commentators hold significantly divergent opinions. A few brief observations are in order:

1. Romans 6:3: "baptized into Christ." This passage addresses a Christian's union "with Christ"; therefore, it would not refer to water baptism.
2. Galatians 3:27: "baptized into Christ." This text teaches the same truth as Romans 6:3. The Greek preposition *eis*, not *en*, is used, meaning "an inseparable union with and total submission to."

---

15. See Walter C. Kaiser Jr., "The Baptism in the Holy Spirit as the Promise of the Father: A Reformed Perspective," in *Perspectives on Spirit Baptism: Five Views*, ed. Chad Owen Brand (Nashville: Broadman, 2004), 15–37.

3. Ephesians 4:5: "one baptism." Very possibly this text refers to water baptism "in Christ." It seems that this applies without exception to every Christian.
4. Colossians 2:12: "buried with him in baptism." This language is quite similar to Romans 6:3–4, and Paul therefore most likely means a Christian's union "with Christ."

In the highest likelihood, all four of these Pauline statements refer to a Christian's union "with Christ."

SUMMATION BY CONTRASTS

In order to be clear about what Spirit baptism is and is not, the following list provides a series of contrasting positive and negative statements:

1. Spirit baptism is a gracious gift from God; it is not something to be sought after, agonized over, or prayed for.
2. Spirit baptism is exclusively associated with regeneration/salvation; it is not normative for it to be associated with the temporary sign gift of tongues or with other miraculous gifts limited to the apostolic era.
3. Spirit baptism is a permanent, one-time event; it is not a reversible or recurring event.
4. Spirit baptism is evidence of one's salvation; it is not by itself the measure of one's spiritual maturity.
5. Spirit baptism is an initial blessing and an enduring result of salvation; it is not a second work of grace or second blessing.
6. Spirit baptism is inseparably linked to salvation; it is not detached from or subsequent to salvation.
7. Spirit baptism is sovereignly initiated by Christ; it is not obtained by any act of a believer.
8. Spirit baptism is assumed by the New Testament to be the Christ-provided experience of every believer; it is never commanded of believers to acquire or retain it.
9. Spirit baptism is experienced by every Christian from Pentecost to the present time; it was not an experience of either Old Testament or Gospel-era believers.
10. Spirit baptism includes every believer; it is not limited to the spiritually mature.
11. Spirit baptism freely grants entrance into the universal body of Christ; it is not based on subsequent individual spiritual achievement.
12. Spirit baptism is distinct from, though associated with, indwelling and filling; it is not to be equated with either one.

Holy Spirit baptism is a positional act, taking place in the life of every Christian concurrently with regeneration. The texts in Acts that refer to a postconversion baptism of the Spirit are associated with the transitional nature of the period described in Acts. First Corinthians 12:13 records the normative doctrine of Spirit baptism, stating that it results in a new position in the body of Christ for all Christians at the moment of faith in Christ. It can be inferred from the fleshly nature of the Corinthian Christians, to whom Paul wrote this passage, that it does not necessarily have any influence on subsequent holiness. The church, the spiritual body of Christ, is formed as believers are immersed by Christ in the Spirit and united with all other Christians beginning with Pentecost. Holy Spirit baptism is not an experience to seek but rather a salvation reality for which to thank God.

Sealing

God's own Spirit comes to regenerate, indwell, and secure a believer's salvation at the moment one repents of sin and believes by faith in the death, burial, and resurrection of Jesus Christ. The Spirit of promise (Eph. 1:13) is given by God as his guarantee of a believer's future inheritance in glory.

Paul developed this theme of *sealing* using two Greek words: *sphragizō*, "to seal," and *arrabōn*, "a pledge" (2 Cor. 1:21–22; 5:5 [AD 55–56]; Eph. 1:13–14; 4:30 [AD 60–62]). Both of these terms originated with a secular sense, but Paul later appropriated them as spiritual word pictures to describe a significant salvation ministry involving the Holy Spirit. *Sphragizō*, or "sealing," pictured an ancient practice of placing soft wax on one's correspondence or property, which was then stamped with a unique mark that unmistakably identified the owner or originator. It symbolized security, protection, ownership, authority, and authenticity. *Arrabōn*, or "guarantee," was a financial down payment or deposit given in good faith that the remaining payment(s) would be forthcoming to complete a business transaction. It communicated the idea of a pledge to promote certainty and assurance.

In the context of salvation, the seal points to God's ownership of the believer, who has been bought with a price—the blood of God's Son Jesus Christ (1 Cor. 6:19–20). God seals the believer (2 Cor. 1:22; 5:5) with the Holy Spirit much as he earlier sealed Christ (John 6:27). Thus, the Holy Spirit is the actual seal (2 Cor. 1:22) that authenticates a Christian as a child of God.

All true believers receive the seal of the Holy Spirit because of their salvation (Rom. 8:9). Just as one is saved by grace through faith in Christ, one is also sealed by God with the Holy Spirit because of his grace. Believers are never instructed to seek sealing or to work for it. It is always assumed that they are sealed because of their salvation. Instead, Christians are warned not to grieve the Holy Spirit, by whom they have been sealed by God (Eph. 4:30).

The immediate purpose of the seal is to identify those who will one day receive the full and final benefit of salvation, namely, resurrection (Rom. 8:20–23). That is why Romans 8:23 speaks of a believer's present life as having "the firstfruits of the Spirit," since there is much more to come on the future day's resurrection and redemption of the believer's body (2 Cor. 5:4–5; Eph. 1:14; 4:30). The immediate sealing is current but temporary because it foretells of the ultimate outcome, which is yet future and permanent. As a believer sealed by God with the Holy Spirit, one's salvation is granted by the authority of God and authenticated by the possession of God's own Spirit. Because they are owned by God, Christians are spiritually secure and protected by his omnipotent and invincible spiritual resources.

The Spirit is not only God's seal on believers but also God's guarantee (2 Cor. 1:22; 5:5; Eph. 1:14) that he will ultimately fulfill his promise of eternal life with a resurrected and glorified body. The Spirit is God's pledge, down payment, and deposit that certifies with impeccable assurance the certainty that what God began he will also complete (Phil. 1:6). This is why Paul referred to the Spirit as "the promised Holy Spirit, who is the guarantee of our inheritance until we acquire possession of it, to the praise of his glory" (Eph. 1:13–14). The Spirit is the immediate guarantee of receiving the ultimate promise of God (see John 10:28–29; Rom. 8:31–39)—eternal life.

Sanctification[16]

Introduction
Indwelling
Filling
Fruit

Introduction[17]

The New Testament employs a variety of terms to refer to believers in the Lord Jesus Christ. Most frequently used in contemporary terminology is the term "Christian" (Gk. *Christianos*). However, this name appears in Scripture on only three occasions (Acts 11:26; 26:28; 1 Pet. 4:16). The originally intended connotation (positive or negative) remains uncertain; however, it applies only to those who have believed in and followed the way of Christ Jesus.

A favorite term in the Gospels and Acts was "disciple" (Gk. *mathētēs*), which appears over 250 times, most often used of those who followed Christ. From its connection to "Christians" in Acts 11:26, it can be concluded that the use of "disciple" preceded that of "Christian" and, more important, defined a Christian as an authentic disciple of Christ.

Throughout the New Testament, spiritual family imagery of the *new birth* is suggested by the frequent use of "brother" (Gk. *adelphos*) and the rare appearance of "sister" (Gk. *adelphē*, Philem. 2; 2 John 13) in reference to a spiritual relationship in Christ. Another striking expression is "slave" (Gk. *doulos*) in contrast to Christ as "Lord" (Gk. *kyrios*).

Each of the above five terms seems rather appropriate and obvious. However, one additional reference to a believer is not—"saint" (Gk. *hagios*). It is the most surprising, the most intriguing, and the least deserved. Used sparsely in the Gospels and Acts, "saint" is the preferred terminology in the Epistles and Revelation.

Why are Christians, disciples, brothers, sisters, and slaves called "saints" or "holy ones"? They were not holy before salvation; they are not holy during their lives on earth, as God alone is holy; and they will not be without sin until after death in

---

16. For a more thorough discussion of sanctification, refer to chap. 7, "Salvation."
17. This section is adapted from Richard L. Mayhue, "Sanctification: The Biblical Basics," *MSJ* 21, no. 2 (2010): 143–57. Used by permission of *MSJ*.

heaven. But Scripture clearly, frequently, and emphatically declares believers to be "saints" or "sanctified ones."

The concept of being holy or sanctified serves as bookends in the canon: "So God blessed the seventh day and made it holy" (Gen. 2:3); "Let . . . the righteous still do right, and the holy still be holy" (Rev. 22:11). More to the point, God commanded Moses, "You shall be holy, for I the LORD your God am holy" (Lev. 19:2), and Peter repeated the mandate, "But as he who called you is holy, you also be holy in all your conduct, since it is written, 'You shall be holy, for I am holy'" (1 Pet. 1:15–16). This idea of being "separated out," "devoted to," or "holy" permeates all Scripture—both the Old Testament and the New. While not limited to the work of the Holy Spirit, sanctification is often directly associated with the Holy Spirit (Rom. 8:23; 1 Cor. 6:11; 1 Thess. 4:7–8; 2 Thess. 2:13; Titus 3:5; 1 Pet. 1:2).

Why "saint"? It is the one name of the six designations mentioned previously that focuses on God's attribute of holiness (cf. Isa. 6:1–8) and his design that all true believers in Christ increasingly demonstrate and emulate this quality as their mark of Christian authenticity (cf. Heb. 12:10). The Spirit of holiness (Rom. 1:4), elsewhere referred to as the Holy Spirit (Ps. 51:11; Isa. 63:11; Matt. 1:18; Jude 20), personifies this preeminent attribute. By focusing on this title for believers, the discussion that follows will explore the salvific implications of sanctification and holiness as they appear in such familiar biblical texts as the following:

You therefore must be perfect, as your heavenly Father is perfect. (Matt. 5:48)

And we know that for those who love God all things work together for good, for those who are called according to his purpose. For those whom he foreknew he also predestined to be conformed to the image of his Son, in order that he might be the firstborn among many brothers. And those whom he predestined he also called, and those whom he called he also justified, and those whom he justified he also glorified. (Rom. 8:28–30)

And I am sure of this, that he who began a good work in you will bring it to completion at the day of Jesus Christ. (Phil. 1:6)

Beloved, we are God's children now, and what we will be has not yet appeared; but we know that when he appears we shall be like him, because we shall see him as he is. And everyone who thus hopes in him purifies himself as he is pure. (1 John 3:2–3)

Now to him who is able to keep you from stumbling and to present you blameless before the presence of his glory with great joy, to the only God, our Savior, through Jesus Christ our Lord, be glory, majesty, dominion, and authority, before all time and now and forever. Amen. (Jude 24–25)

Three distinct word groups in the New Testament synonymously describe salvation in terms of that which is past, present, and future. Table 5.6 illustrates this

Table 5.6 Word Groups Describing Salvation

	Completion/ Perfection (Gk. *teleioō, teleios*)	Salvation (Gk. *sōzō, sōtēria, sōtērion*)	Sanctification (Gk. *hagiazō, hagiasmos, hagios*)
Past	"For by a single offering he has *perfected* for all time those who are being *sanctified.*" (Heb. 10:14)	"He *saved* us, not because of works done by us in righteousness, but according to his own mercy, by the washing of regeneration and renewal of the Holy Spirit." (Titus 3:5)	"And such were some of you. But you were washed, you were *sanctified*, you were justified in the name of the Lord Jesus Christ and by the Spirit of our God." (1 Cor. 6:11)
Present	"Since we have these promises, beloved, let us cleanse ourselves from every defilement of body and spirit, bringing holiness to *completion* in the fear of God." (2 Cor. 7:1)	"Therefore, my beloved, as you have always obeyed, so now, not only as in my presence but much more in my absence, work out your own *salvation* with fear and trembling." (Phil. 2:12)	"For this is the will of God, your *sanctification*: that you abstain from sexual immorality; that each one of you know how to control his own body in holiness and honor.... For God has not called us for impurity, but in holiness." (1 Thess. 4:3-4, 7)
Future	"But you have come ... to God, the judge of all, and to the spirits of the righteous made *perfect.*" (Heb. 12:22-23)	"Besides this you know the time, that the hour has come for you to wake from sleep. For *salvation* is nearer to us now than when we first believed." (Rom. 13:11)	"Now may the God of peace himself *sanctify* you completely, and may your whole spirit and soul and body be kept blameless at the coming of our Lord Jesus Christ." (1 Thess. 5:23)

pattern with representative passages from Scripture, and the data there can best be summarized with these ten observations:

1. "Salvation," "sanctification," and "completion"/"perfection" can be used synonymously in Scripture as word groups with significant salvific importance.
2. Salvation is part of sanctification in its broadest sense, and sanctification is part of salvation in its fullest sense.
3. Therefore, salvation and sanctification are inseparable. You cannot have one without the other.
4. Each of these three word groups can describe the past, the present, or the future.
5. Each of these three word groups can describe inauguration, continuation, or culmination in the context of redemption.
6. Each of these three word groups can describe the part or the whole of salvation.
7. Unless one accepts this biblical tension, erroneous conclusions will most certainly be reached in developing soteriology.
8. A person is said by Scripture to already be what a person is actually becoming.
9. A person is commanded in the Bible to now be what one cannot completely be until eternity.
10. The key to maintaining clarity in the midst of possible interpretive confusion is to correctly identify the individual parts in each biblical text.

These introductory thoughts deal with sanctification in its several parts and as a whole to provide a context for what follows. By design, the subsequent discussion

Table 5.7 Aspects of Sanctification

Primary divine agents	FATHER	SON	HOLY SPIRIT
	"For God has not called us for impurity, but in *holiness*." (1 Thess. 4:7)	"To the church of God that is in Corinth, to those *sanctified* in Christ Jesus, called to be saints together with all those who in every place call upon the name of our Lord Jesus Christ, both their Lord and ours . . ." (1 Cor. 1:2)	"But we ought always to give thanks to God for you, brothers beloved by the Lord, because God chose you as the firstfruits to be saved, through *sanctification* by the Spirit and belief in the truth." (2 Thess. 2:13)
Time sequence	PAST	PRESENT	FUTURE
	"And now I commend you to God and to the word of his grace, which is able to build you up and to give you the inheritance among all those who are *sanctified*." (Acts 20:32)	". . . that each one of you know how to control his own body in *holiness* and honor . . ." (1 Thess. 4:4)	". . . so that he may establish your hearts blameless in *holiness* before our God and Father, at the coming of our Lord Jesus with all his saints." (1 Thess. 3:13)
Primary means	GOSPEL	GLORY/SCRIPTURE	RESURRECTION
	". . . that he might *sanctify* her, having cleansed her by the washing of water with the word . . ." (Eph. 5:26)	"And we all, . . . *beholding the glory* of the Lord, are being *transformed* into the same image from one degree of glory to another." (2 Cor. 3:18) "*Sanctify* them in the truth; your word is truth." (John 17:17)	"And not only the creation, but we ourselves, who have the firstfruits of the Spirit, groan inwardly as we wait eagerly for adoption as sons, the *redemption* of our bodies." (Rom. 8:23)
Effects	INAUGURATION	CONTINUATION	CULMINATION
	"And by that will we have been *sanctified* through the offering of the body of Jesus Christ once for all." (Heb. 10:10)	"Since we have these promises, beloved, let us cleanse ourselves from every defilement of body and spirit, bringing *holiness* to completion in the fear of God." (2 Cor. 7:1)	"Let the evildoer still do evil, and the filthy still be filthy, and the righteous still do right, and the *holy* still be *holy*." (Rev. 22:11)
Primary results	POSITION	PROGRESSION	PERFECTION
	". . . to open their eyes, so that they may turn from darkness to light and from the power of Satan to God, that they may receive forgiveness of sins and a place among those who are *sanctified* by faith in me." (Acts 26:18)	"But now that you have been set free from sin and have become slaves of God, the fruit you get leads to *sanctification* and its end, eternal life." (Rom. 6:22)	". . . so that he may establish your hearts *blameless in holiness* before our God and Father, at the coming of our Lord Jesus with all his saints." (1 Thess. 3:13)

Personal outcomes	JUSTIFICATION	SANCTIFICATION	GLORIFICATION
	"And such were some of you. But you were washed, you were *sanctified*, you were justified in the name of the Lord Jesus Christ and by the Spirit of our God." (1 Cor. 6:11)	"For this is the will of God, your *sanctification*: that you abstain from sexual immorality." (1 Thess. 4:3)	"And we know that for those who love God all things work together for good, for those who are called according to his purpose. For those whom he foreknew he also predestined to be conformed to the image of his Son, in order that he might be the firstborn among many brothers. And those whom he predestined he also called, and those whom he called he also justified, and those whom he justified he also *glorified*." (Rom. 8:28–30)
Spiritual realities	FORENSIC DECLARATION	OBEDIENT SUBMISSION	SUPERNATURAL COMPLETION
	"For by a single offering he has perfected for all time those who are being *sanctified*." (Heb. 10:14)	"I am speaking in human terms, because of your natural limitations. For just as you once presented your members as slaves to impurity and to lawlessness leading to more lawlessness, so now present your members as slaves to righteousness leading to *sanctification*." (Rom. 6:19)	"Now may the God of peace himself *sanctify* you completely, and may your whole spirit and soul and body be kept blameless at the coming of our Lord Jesus Christ." (1 Thess. 5:23)

will focus primarily on *progressive sanctification*, namely, that which occurs in a Christian's life following salvation. Without moving to progressive sanctification too hastily, though, table 5.7 introduces several aspects of sanctification to highlight its complexity.

Though one might be tempted to think this discussion of sanctification impractical, just the opposite is true. *Systematic* theology yields God's plan for *spiritual* theology. Christian doctrine translates into Christian living. In a very real sense, all theology and all Christian living can be discussed, developed, and discerned by studying and applying what the Bible says about sanctification.

The following lists allow Scripture to speak for itself concerning the three time perspectives of sanctification—positional, progressive, and perfective.

INAUGURATION: POSITIONAL (DEFINITIVE) SANCTIFICATION

And now I commend you to God and to the word of his grace, which is able to build you up and to give you the inheritance among all those who are *sanctified*. (Acts 20:32)

. . . to open their eyes, so that they may turn from darkness to light and from the power of Satan to God, that they may receive forgiveness of sins and a place among those who are *sanctified* by faith in me. (Acts 26:18)

To the church of God that is in Corinth, to those *sanctified* in Christ Jesus, called to be saints together with all those who in every place call upon the name of our Lord Jesus Christ, both their Lord and ours . . . (1 Cor. 1:2)

And because of him you are in Christ Jesus, who became to us wisdom from God, righteousness and *sanctification* and redemption. (1 Cor. 1:30)

And such were some of you. But you were washed, you were *sanctified*, you were justified in the name of the Lord Jesus Christ and by the Spirit of our God. (1 Cor. 6:11)

. . . that he might *sanctify* her, having cleansed her by the washing of water with the word . . . (Eph. 5:26)

But we ought always to give thanks to God for you, brothers beloved by the Lord, because God chose you as the firstfruits to be saved, through *sanctification* by the Spirit and belief in the truth. (2 Thess. 2:13)

And by that will we have been *sanctified* through the offering of the body of Jesus Christ once for all. (Heb. 10:10)

. . . according to the foreknowledge of God the Father, in the *sanctification* of the Spirit, for obedience to Jesus Christ and for sprinkling with his blood: May grace and peace be multiplied to you. (1 Pet. 1:2)

CONTINUATION: PROGRESSIVE SANCTIFICATION

Sanctify them in the truth; your word is truth. (John 17:17)

I am speaking in human terms, because of your natural limitations. For just as you once presented your members as slaves to impurity and to lawlessness leading to more lawlessness, so now present your members as slaves to righteousness leading to *sanctification*. (Rom. 6:19)

But now that you have been set free from sin and have become slaves of God, the fruit you get leads to *sanctification* and its end, eternal life. (Rom. 6:22)

And we all, with unveiled face, *beholding the glory* of the Lord, are being *transformed* into the same image from one degree of glory to another. (2 Cor. 3:18)

Since we have these promises, beloved, let us cleanse ourselves from every defilement of body and spirit, bringing *holiness* to completion in the fear of God. (2 Cor. 7:1)

For this is the will of God, your *sanctification*: that you abstain from sexual immorality. (1 Thess. 4:3)

. . . that each one of you know how to control his own body in *holiness* and honor . . . (1 Thess. 4:4)

For God has not called us for impurity, but in *holiness*. Therefore whoever disregards this, disregards not man but God, who gives his Holy Spirit to you. (1 Thess. 4:7–8)

Therefore, if anyone cleanses himself from what is dishonorable, he will be a vessel for honorable use, set apart as *holy*, useful to the master of the house, ready for every good work. (2 Tim. 2:21)

CULMINATION: PERFECTED SANCTIFICATION

. . . so that he may establish your hearts blameless in *holiness* before our God and Father, at the coming of our Lord Jesus with all his saints. (1 Thess. 3:13)

Now may the God of peace himself *sanctify* you completely, and may your whole spirit and soul and body be kept blameless at the coming of our Lord Jesus Christ. (1 Thess. 5:23)

The following eight descriptions summarize the essentials of what sanctification is as taught in Scripture:

1. A salvific work inaugurated by God and in which all three members of the Godhead participate
2. A salvific work that is continued by God in this life unto completion in heaven
3. A salvific work that cannot be separated from justification or glorification[18]
4. A salvific work of God that is empowered by God's Word and God's Spirit
5. A salvific work of God that, once begun, cannot be lost, stopped, or undone
6. A salvific work of God that prompts a holy response of biblical obedience to the work of the Holy Spirit from those who are genuine saints
7. A salvific work of God that does not eradicate sin from the believer until glorification
8. A salvific work that provides confident hope in this life because of a certain eternal hope for the next life

Indwelling

One encounters two extreme conclusions when studying the Holy Spirit. First, a radical continuity supposes that whatever the Holy Spirit did in the New Testament

---

18. J. C. Ryle explains, "In what, then, are justification and sanctification alike: a. Both proceed originally from the free grace of God. It is of His gift alone that believers are justified or sanctified at all. b. Both are part of that great work of salvation which Christ, in the eternal covenant, has undertaken on behalf of His people. Christ is the fountain of life, from which pardon and holiness both flow. The root of each is Christ. c. Both are to be found in the same persons. Those who are justified are always sanctified, and those who are sanctified are always justified. God has joined them together, and they cannot be put asunder. d. Both begin at the same time. The moment a person begins to be a justified person, he also begins to be a sanctified person. He may not feel it, but it is a fact. e. Both are alike necessary to salvation. No one ever reached heaven without a renewed heart as well as forgiveness, without the Spirit's grace as well as the blood of Christ, without a meetness for eternal glory as well as a title. The one is just as necessary as the other." *Holiness* (1879; repr. Old Tappan, NJ: Revell, n.d.), 30.

was also surely done in the Old Testament. In contrast, a radical discontinuity avers that whatever the Holy Spirit did in the New Testament was essentially different from anything done in the Old Testament. These extreme conclusions follow the same pattern as another set of polar-opposite extremes: the idea that the Holy Spirit was essentially dormant in the Old Testament but hyperactive in the New Testament versus the idea that the Holy Spirit was equally and identically active in both Testaments.

Polarized positions are particularly common when discussing the indwelling ministry of the Holy Spirit. While it is accurate to state that the Holy Spirit indwelt believers in both Testaments, that is essentially where the agreement ends. Christian scholars differ here. One side promotes indwelling in the Old Testament as being the same as in the New Testament.[19] The other side supports the view that the Spirit's indwelling ministry, which began at Pentecost in Acts 2, differed significantly from the Old Testament.[20]

Before the issue can be adequately understood, a look at what the Old Testament and the New Testament say about indwelling is in order. After the evidence has been gathered, then a sound conclusion may be reached.

OLD TESTAMENT

On at least four occasions, several Old Testament believers are said to have been indwelt by the Holy Spirit. First, Joshua is described as "a man in whom is the Spirit" (Num. 27:18) because of the future leadership role that he will play as Moses's successor. Second, Scripture reveals that the Spirit entered into Ezekiel in preparation for him to confront the exceedingly rebellious nation of Israel (Ezek. 2:2; 3:24). Interestingly, this appears to have happened on two separate occasions, which means that the Holy Spirit departed after the first indwelling and returned for the second—thus, the first was not a permanent indwelling. Third, the New Testament comments on an Old Testament time of prophetic activity when the Spirit of Christ was actively indwelling the prophets (1 Pet. 1:10–11). The phrase "Spirit of Christ" refers to the Holy Spirit (Acts 16:7; Rom. 8:9; Gal. 4:6; Phil. 1:19), as does the phrase "Spirit of God" in Romans 8:9, where the two are used interchangeably.

It has been claimed that Joseph and Daniel were also indwelt (Gen. 41:38; Dan. 4:8–9, 18; 5:11–14; 6:3). However, this testimony came from several pagan rulers (Pharaoh, Nebuchadnezzar, Belshazzar's queen, Belshazzar, and Darius) who knew nothing about God's Holy Spirit and thus are not qualified to be expert witnesses. To their credit, however, they were trying to explain the extraordinary ministries of these two special men of God. Whether Joseph and Daniel were indwelt cannot be determined in these instances.

There are several additional Old Testament texts that speak about God putting his Spirit within the heart of the nation of Israel (Ezek. 11:19; 36:26–27; 37:14). This divine promise will be fulfilled in the millennial reign of Christ after his second advent.

19. Leon J. Wood, *The Holy Spirit in the Old Testament* (Grand Rapids, MI: Zondervan, 1976), 69–70.
20. James M. Hamilton Jr., *God's Indwelling Presence: The Holy Spirit in the Old and New Testaments* (Nashville: B&H Academic, 2006).

Table 5.8 Cases of Holy Spirit Empowerment

Person	Scripture Reference
Bezalel	Ex. 31:3; 35:30–31
Moses	Num. 11:17
Seventy elders	Num. 11:25
Balaam	Num. 24:2
Joshua	Deut. 34:9
Othniel	Judg. 3:10
Gideon	Judg. 6:34
Jephthah	Judg. 11:29
Samson	Judg. 14:6, 19; 15:14
Saul	1 Sam. 10:10; 11:6; 19:23
David	1 Sam. 16:13
Messengers of Saul	1 Sam. 19:20
Amasai	1 Chron. 12:18
Azariah	2 Chron. 15:1
Jahaziel	2 Chron. 20:14
Zechariah	2 Chron. 24:20
Isaiah	Isa. 61:1
Ezekiel	Ezek. 3:24; 11:5

On far more numerous occasions than indwelling, the Old Testament speaks of the Holy Spirit coming "upon" particular leaders of Israel as an act of empowerment. This was also the language used of Simeon, who held Christ as an infant in the temple (Luke 2:25–35). This language, which precludes indwelling, appears in the Old Testament from Exodus to Joel (see table 5.8).

The Spirit also on rare occasions physically relocated people (1 Kings 18:12; 2 Kings 2:16; Ezek. 3:12, 14; 8:3; 11:1, 24; 37:1; 43:5). This also occurred in the post-Pentecost era with Philip and John (Acts 8:39–40; Rev. 21:10).

The major characteristics of indwelling in the Old Testament can be summarized as follows:

1. Infrequent
2. Involving selected leaders in Israel only
3. Temporary
4. An empowerment for service

NEW TESTAMENT

The closely related Greek terms *oikeō*, *enoikeō*, and *katoikētērion* describe the Holy Spirit "dwelling within" true believers. Without the indwelling Holy Spirit, a person is not a true believer (Rom. 8:9; Jude 19). The six key passages discussing the Spirit's indwelling believers include Romans 8:9, 11; 1 Corinthians 3:16; 6:19; Ephesians

2:22; and 2 Timothy 1:14. Taken in context, every use but one refers to believers as individuals. Ephesians 2:22, however, seems to speak of indwelling both in an individual sense and in a collective sense, referring to the body of Christ, the church. God dwelt in a physical temple in Old Testament Jerusalem; the Spirit of God dwells individually in each member of the New Testament body as well as collectively in them altogether.

The major characteristics of indwelling in the New Testament can be summarized as follows:

1. Always at salvation
2. Inclusive of all believers individually
3. Permanent
4. Cohesive in the collective sense of the universal church
5. An empowerment for holy living and fruitful service

By comparing the qualities of Old Testament indwelling with the hallmarks of New Testament indwelling, one can observe some very distinct contrasts. This then raises the question, were Old Testament and Gospel believers indwelt by the Holy Spirit in the same manner as believers at Pentecost (Acts 2) and beyond?

OLD AND NEW TESTAMENT BELIEVERS INDWELT IDENTICALLY?

The Spirit's work in the Old Testament was not exactly the same as what the New Testament presents. Pentecost marked the beginning of certain distinctive differences. When one examines the Spirit's coming at Pentecost and beyond, it does not mean that the Spirit was absent from the scene before then. However, the situation was significantly different in that the Spirit took up permanent residency in believers at Pentecost.

For the following reasons, it seems certain that Old Testament believers were not indwelt by the Holy Spirit in the same manner as believers at Pentecost and beyond:

1. The seriously differing major characteristics mentioned above show a dramatic contrast between Old Testament and New Testament indwelling.
2. While all Old Testament believers, like New Testament believers, were regenerated by the power of God's Spirit, nowhere does Scripture teach that indwelling was a necessary component of salvation in the Old Testament.
3. In John 7:39, Jesus explicitly said that the Holy Spirit had not yet been given in the sense of Spirit baptism, Spirit indwelling, and Spirit filling for all believers.
4. In John 14:17, Christ said of the Holy Spirit, "He dwells with you and will be in you." The Greek verb *menō*, here translated "dwells," would be more appropriately rendered "abides," since neither *oikeō*, *enoikeō*, nor *katoikētērion* is used. Furthermore, while the future tense of the verb "to be" has a textual variant in the present tense, the manuscript evidence is far superior in supporting the future tense. Thus, Christ was teaching about a future indwelling (post-Pentecost) that was different from the abiding Jesus was describing to his disciples at that time.

5. In John 13–17, Jesus told the apostles to expect something significant to occur, because when he departed, the Holy Spirit would be sent in his place. The old covenant was being replaced by the new covenant (Hebrews 8). Indwelling of the Holy Spirit would be a part of the new.

6. There would be no need for Scripture to speak explicitly of the few indwellings in the Old Testament if all Old Testament saints had been indwelt.

7. First Samuel 16:14 records that the Holy Spirit departed from Saul, and in Psalm 51:11, David prays that God would not take the Holy Spirit from him. These passages make the best sense if they are understood to speak of Holy Spirit empowerment and not salvation since indwelling would have been irreversible otherwise.

8. New Testament indwelling refers not only to individuals but also corporately to the church. Since the church did not begin until Pentecost, the Old Testament would have had no indwelling like that in the New Testament.

9. Second Corinthians 6:16, quoting Exodus 29:45 and Leviticus 26:12, records God saying, "I will make my dwelling among them and walk among them." None of these three texts state that God by his Spirit will dwell "in" them either nationally or individually but rather that he will dwell "among" them externally.

Filling

The Holy Spirit's filling ministry occurred in both the Old and New Testaments. If one were reading the Scriptures from Genesis to Revelation, references to the Spirit's filling would be encountered first in Exodus 31:3 and last in Colossians 1:9. Three periods will be used to discuss variations of emphasis and manifestation: (1) pre-Pentecost (Genesis to John, ca. 1440 BC–AD 30), (2) Pentecost (Acts 1–2, AD 30), and (3) post-Pentecost (Acts 3 until the rapture, AD 30 until the rapture). Being filled produced the effects of Spirit-enhanced capabilities or Spirit-produced character.

The Hebrew word *male'* (Gk. *empimplēmi* [Septuagint]) is used in the Old Testament. The New Testament employs three Greek terms that are different but very similar in meaning: (1) *pimplēmi*, (2) *plērēs*, and (3) *plēroō*. All these words carry the basic idea of domination or total control. When describing the work of the Holy Spirit, they convey the general idea of divine sovereignty as the cause and human submission as the effect.

PRE-PENTECOST

Old Testament. The pre-Pentecost era can be split into two broad periods. The first encompasses the Old Testament, which describes a handful of Spirit fillings.

Occasions. Five mentions of "filling" occurred during (1) the building of the tabernacle (ca. 1444 BC), (2) the leadership of Joshua (ca. 1405 BC), (3) the building of Solomon's temple (ca. 966 BC), and (4) the ministry of Micah (ca. 700 BC). They specifically include the following:

1. Bezalel was (explicitly) equipped by the Holy Spirit to construct the tabernacle and its contents (Ex. 31:2–3).

2. Bezalel and Oholiab were (explicitly) equipped by the Holy Spirit with special artistic skills to work on the contents of the tabernacle (Ex. 35:31–35).
3. Joshua was (implicitly) equipped by the Holy Spirit with wisdom to lead Israel as the successor to Moses (Deut. 34:9).
4. Hiram was (implicitly) equipped by the Holy Spirit to help Solomon build the original temple in Israel (1 Kings 7:14, 40, 45).
5. Micah was (implicitly) equipped by the Holy Spirit to function as a confrontational prophet (Micah 3:8; see Zech. 4:6).

Observations. The occasions of filling in the Old Testament were noticeably infrequent, although it is possible that the Spirit filled others without Scripture mentioning such occasions. Old Testament filling involved only the Holy Spirit equipping or enabling selected leaders to carry out God's plans at special times in Israel's history. None of the filling events involved Spirit-produced character. In terms of cause and effect, Holy Spirit filling seems very much like these other Old Testament descriptions: "the Spirit rested on them" (Num. 11:26), God "put his Spirit on them" (Num. 11:29), and "the Spirit of God came upon him" (Num. 24:2).

Gospels. The second period prior to Pentecost is the time of Jesus's ministry, which also featured only a few instances of Spirit filling.

Occasions. "Filling" is mentioned explicitly only four times in the Gospels—all by Luke. These and two implicit fillings occurred during an approximately thirty-year span of time, involving four different people:

1. John the Baptist was (explicitly) "filled" from the time of his conception (Luke 1:15).
2. Elizabeth was (explicitly) "filled" during the time she carried John (Luke 1:41).
3. Zechariah was (explicitly) "filled" in order to prophesy (Luke 1:67).
4. Jesus was (implicitly) "filled" as a child (Luke 2:40).
5. Christ was (explicitly) "filled" at the outset of his adult ministry (Luke 4:1; see Luke 3:22).
6. Very possibly, Christ (implicitly) caused a filling when he breathed on the disciples, saying, "Receive the Holy Spirit" (John 20:22). This act can be understood as Christ's pledge that the Holy Spirit would be coming at Pentecost, just as he promised (John 14:26–27; Acts 1:4; 2:4).

Observations. As with the Old Testament, filling in the Gospels involved only selected individuals for very unique, not-to-be-repeated ministries. The fillings involved Spirit enablement. From the first Old Testament mention of "filling" until the final Gospel mention—the entire pre-Pentecost period, lasting about 1,475 years—only nine individuals (not including the eleven disciples) are cited as having been filled by the Holy Spirit. Spirit fillings prior to Pentecost were rare, limited, and very exceptional.

PENTECOST

Occasion. Acts 1–2 records the transition from a primary focus on the nation of Israel to a primary focus on the church. This transition took place on the day of Pentecost, after Christ's resurrection and ascension to heaven (Acts 1:1–11). The eleven (later joined by Matthias, Acts 1:13, 15–26), close family members (Acts 1:14), and the remainder of believers (Acts 1:15) gathered in Jerusalem to wait and pray for what Christ promised in the upper room (John 13–17) and in Acts 1:4–5 regarding the imminent ministry of the Holy Spirit.

When the day of Pentecost arrived, so did the Holy Spirit (Acts 2:1–4). All 120 believers were baptized by Christ with the Holy Spirit into the church (see "Baptism" [p. 353]; 1 Cor. 12:13) and were filled with the Holy Spirit (Acts 2:3–4). All 120 were Spirit-enabled to speak other existing languages that they did not previously know (Acts 2:4–12). Additionally, they all were filled by the Holy Spirit in the sense of Spirit-produced character, which would be explained later by Paul (Eph. 5:18–21).

Observations. Selective, special Spirit enablement continued, as had been the historical pattern in the Old Testament and the Gospels. On Pentecost, filling became the experience of all Christians, not just a few selected individuals for significantly special occasions. A new dimension involving Spirit-produced character for all Christians also commenced on Pentecost (Eph. 5:18–21).

POST-PENTECOST

The Holy Spirit continued to enable select individuals and several select groups of people for ministry, up to and including the first missionary journey (Acts 11:24; 13:9, 52). It can be assumed that the Holy Spirit continued to produce godly character in all Christians as begun at Pentecost and explained by Ephesians 5:18–21.

Until ca. AD 48. The period from Pentecost through Paul's first missionary journey gives further illustrations of Spirit filling in the church age. Scripture records eight occasions of Holy Spirit enablement from AD 30 to 48:

1. Peter preached in his native tongue, as he had in Acts 2:14–40 (Acts 4:8).
2. Christians spoke God's Word with boldness in their native tongues (Acts 4:31).
3. Seven men were chosen to assist the apostles (Acts 6:3, 5).
4. Stephen preached fearlessly (Acts 7:55; see 6:10).
5. Paul was filled shortly after his conversion (Acts 9:17).
6. Barnabas ministered at Antioch (Acts 11:24).
7. Paul rebuked Elymas the magician (Acts 13:9–11).
8. Paul, Barnabas, and their disciples ministered on the first missionary journey (Acts 13:52).

AD 48 and Beyond. From Acts 14 through Revelation 22 and beyond (at least until the rapture of the church), there are no mentions of "filling" that relate to enablement or equipping as had been the case in the Old Testament, the Gospels, Pentecost, and the period after Pentecost through the first missionary journey. It is thus assumed that the "filling" described in Ephesians 5:18–21 prevailed as the exclusive form of filling beginning with the second missionary journey, which commenced in Acts 14.

Ephesians 5:18–21.[21] Paul wrote, "And do not get drunk with wine, for that is debauchery, but be filled with the Spirit" (5:18). Since the apostle began by explaining what being filled is *not*, it would be good to begin this discussion in like manner.

First, being filled with the Holy Spirit is not a dramatic, esoteric experience of suddenly being energized and spiritualized into a permanent state of advanced godliness by a second act of blessing subsequent to salvation. Nor is it some temporary effect that results in ecstatic speech or visions.

Second, being filled with the Spirit is not a notion at the other extreme—stoically trying to do what God wants us to do, with the Holy Spirit's blessing, in our own power. It is not merely a human act that has God's approval.

Third, being filled is not the same as possessing or being indwelt by the Holy Spirit, because he indwells every believer at the moment of salvation. Paul states in Romans 8:9, "Anyone who does not have the Spirit of Christ does not belong to him." Unlike believers before Pentecost, on whom the Holy Spirit would come temporarily (Judg. 13:25; 16:20; 1 Sam. 16:14; Ps. 51:11), all Christians are indwelt permanently by the Spirit.

Fourth, being filled with the Spirit does not describe a process of receiving him progressively by degrees. Every Christian not only possesses the Holy Spirit but also possesses him in his fullness. God does not parcel out the Spirit, as if he could somehow be divided into various parts.

Fifth, it is also clear from 1 Corinthians 12:13 that the filling with the Spirit is not the same as the baptism of the Spirit because every believer has been baptized with and has received the Spirit. Although its results are experienced and enjoyed, baptism by and reception of the Spirit are not realities one can feel and are certainly not experiences reserved only for specially blessed believers. Spirit baptism is a spiritual reality that occurs in every believer the moment one becomes a Christian and is placed by Christ into his body by the Holy Spirit, who then takes up residence in that life. Filling can be interrupted by personal sin.

Paul did not accuse the Corinthians of being immature and sinful because they did not yet have the Holy Spirit or had not yet been baptized into the church, and then exhort them to seek the Spirit in order to remedy the situation (1 Cor. 1:1–8). Rather, he reminded them that each one of them already possessed the Holy Spirit (1 Cor. 12:7, 11). They were sinning not because of the Holy Spirit's absence but in spite of the Holy Spirit's presence. Even when a Christian sins, one is still indwelt by the Holy Spirit, and it is that very fact that makes one's sin even worse. When a Christian grieves the Spirit (Eph. 4:30) or quenches the Spirit (1 Thess. 5:19), one grieves or quenches the Spirit who resides within.

Finally, being filled with the Spirit is not the same as being sealed or secured by him. That is an accomplished fact (Eph. 1:13). Nowhere are believers commanded

---

21. This section is adapted from John MacArthur, *Ephesians*, MNTC (Chicago: Moody Press, 1986), 247–48. Used by permission of Moody Publishers.

or exhorted to be indwelt, baptized, or sealed by the Holy Spirit. The *only* command is to be filled.

On the other hand, Paul uses the term "fill" in regard to salvation in Philippians 1:11 ("fruit of righteousness"; see also James 3:18). He also employs "fill" to explain sanctification here in Ephesians 5:18–21 (see Col. 1:9–10). Ephesians 1:23 and 3:19 are echoes of 5:18, while Romans 15:13–14 and Colossians 3:12–4:6 parallel the larger context in Ephesians 5:15–6:9. Paul's focus assumes the Ephesians' salvation, and in 5:18–21 he explains their responsibility in the sanctification process as being filled with the Spirit.

Command. Unlike all previous mentions of Spirit "filling," in Ephesians 5:18 Paul commands believers to *continue* being filled or controlled by the Holy Spirit. He employs an imperative to insist that they continuously submit to the Holy Spirit's control because it is God's will (Eph. 5:17).

Humans have two choices—be filled by the flesh in unbelief (Rom. 1:29–32; see Acts 13:10, 45; 19:28–29) or be filled by the Holy Spirit in salvation and sanctification (Eph. 5:18). Being filled authenticates one's genuine salvation by allowing God's will to prevail in obedience to Scripture's teaching and the Holy Spirit's direction.

Conditions. How can a Christian comply with God's will? By not grieving the Holy Spirit (Eph. 4:30) or quenching the Holy Spirit (1 Thess. 5:19) with such sinful habits as being drunk with wine (Eph. 5:18) or lying to the Holy Spirit, like Ananias and Sapphira did (Acts 5:3, 9).

On the other hand, Christians need to walk wisely (Eph. 5:15). Elsewhere Paul admonishes believers to walk by and live in the Spirit (Gal. 5:16, 25). God's Word applied by God's Spirit energizes or empowers the Christian to do so. In Colossians 3:16, Paul urges that the Word of Christ dwell in Christians richly. Not surprisingly, the cause of Scripture produces the effect of being filled with the Spirit (cf. Col. 3:12–4:6 with Eph. 5:15–6:9).

Confirmations. The chief characteristic of one's salvation and subsequent sanctification is an ongoing, habitual, growing obedience to God's Word that is empowered by the indwelling Holy Spirit, who controls the lifestyle of a true Christian. Ephesians 5:19–6:9 illustrates some primary particulars.

First, evidence of the Spirit's filling includes the nature of one's conversations (Eph. 5:19). They are to be outward, toward one another. They are to be inward, from the heart. And they are to be upward, to the Lord.

Second, one's continuously grateful response to the Lord regardless of the circumstances proves the Spirit's filling ministry (Eph. 5:20; see 1 Thess. 5:18). This reaction is to be manifested always in all events of life.

Third, the Spirit's ministry in the life of a Christian strongly influences one's humble relationship with others. This includes Christians with other Christians (Eph. 5:21), wives with husbands (Eph. 5:22–24), husbands with wives (Eph. 5:25–33), children with parents (Eph. 6:1–3), parents with children (Eph. 6:4), employees with employers (Eph. 6:5–8), and employers with employees (Eph. 6:9).

All the representative indicators in Ephesians 5–6 are expanded on in other New Testament texts such as 1 Corinthians 13:4–7; Galatians 5:22–23; and 2 Peter 1:5–11. It is the believer's obligation to be filled with the Holy Spirit individually, corporately, continuously, normally, submissively, willingly, and obediently.

Fruit

Isaiah prophesied that the Spirit of the Lord would enable God the Son with the fruit (Isa. 11:1) of wisdom and understanding, counsel and strength, knowledge and the fear of the Lord, righteousness and faithfulness (Isa. 11:2, 5). This ministry will take place during the Messiah's fulfillment of the Davidic covenant (2 Sam. 7:12–16) at the time of his millennial reign on earth (Isa. 11:6–16).

John the Baptist urged those claiming to be believers to bring forth good fruit in their lives appropriate to—that is, authenticating—their repentance (Matt. 3:8–10; Luke 3:8–9). According to Christ, a tree's inherent character is made known outwardly by the kind of fruit that it produces (Matt. 7:16–20; 12:33; Luke 6:43–44). The Psalmist concurred (Ps. 1:3–6).

In John 15, Christ contrasted a branch that bears no fruit (John 15:2, 6; see Matt. 13:18–22) with one that does bear fruit (John 15:2, 5; see Matt. 13:23). The one who bears fruit will be pruned to bear more fruit (John 15:2) and eventually much fruit (John 15:5). Paul spoke of this as the fruit of righteousness (Phil. 1:11), as did James (James 3:18). The fruitless branch will eventually be set aside as useless and burned (John 15:6).

Paul wrote extensively about the work of the Spirit in Galatians. He first discussed the Holy Spirit's work of salvation (Gal. 3:2–3, 5, 15; 4:6, 29; 5:5) and then followed with the Holy Spirit's work of sanctification (Gal. 5:16–18, 22–25). There he contrasted the spoils of the flesh (Gal. 5:19–21) with the fruit of the Spirit (Gal. 5:22–23). Later, in Ephesians, he similarly spoke of the unfruitful deeds of the darkness (Eph. 5:3–7, 11) compared to the fruit of the light (Eph. 5:8–9).

All in all, as these varied passages from Scripture illustrate, Spirit-produced fruit can be defined as Christian thinking and living in obedience to Scripture that honors God. It can be classified using six categories:

1. Fruit of attitudes (Gal. 5:22–23; Eph. 5:9)
2. Fruit of actions (Col. 1:10; Titus 3:8, 14)
3. Fruit of worship (Heb. 13:15)
4. Fruit of gospel telling (Rom. 1:13; Col. 1:5–6)
5. Fruit of truth telling (Eph. 5:9; 1 John 4:2)
6. Fruit of abundant giving (Rom. 15:26–28; 2 Cor. 9:6–8, 13; Phil. 4:17)

THE FRUIT OF THE SPIRIT

The Galatians were urged to "walk by the Spirit" (Gal. 5:16, 25), to be "led by the Spirit" (Gal. 5:18), to bear "the fruit of the Spirit" (Gal. 5:22–23), and in so doing to "live by the Spirit" (Gal. 5:25). This saintly lifestyle, commended by Paul and inaugurated at salvation, which brings the indwelling presence of the Holy Spirit (1 Cor. 3:16; 6:19), should then evidence being "filled with the Spirit" (Eph. 5:18). Paul concluded Galatians with the same thought (Gal. 6:7–16).

Fruit (Gk. *karpos*) in Galatians 5:22 is singular, not plural, in that true believers can manifest all these elements simultaneously. Paul later described this sanctifying work as "the fruit of righteousness" (Phil. 1:11). So the nine representative qualities (Gal. 5:23, "such things") refer to the whole work of the Spirit's sanctifying labor in the life of one who has been justified, that is, declared righteous by faith in the Lord Jesus Christ. This picture is similar in kind to the fifteen facets of the diamond called "love" in 1 Corinthians 13:4–7, the qualities of an elder (1 Tim. 3:1–7; Titus 1:6–9), and the qualities commended to and commanded of believers in Christ (Col. 3:12–17; 2 Pet. 1:5–11).

During the upper room meal the night before his crucifixion, Christ said, "By this all people will know that you are my disciples, if you have love for one another" (John 13:35; see 15:8). Not surprisingly, Paul begins his discussion of spiritual fruit with the characteristic of love.

Love. Christ's substitutionary death provided the ultimate example of love (Gk. *agapē*). He said, "Greater love has no one than this, that someone lay down his life for his friends" (John 15:13). Paul called for this supreme love to be characteristic of a husband's love for his wife: "Husbands, love your wives, as Christ loved the church and gave himself up for her" (Eph. 5:25). First Corinthians 13:8 promises that "love never fails" (NASB).

Thus, love is a communicable, divine attribute that is central to the Father's character (1 John 4:8), put on display by Christ at the cross, and enabled in believers by the Holy Spirit. Love can be defined broadly as the conscious, sacrificial, and volitional commitment to the welfare of another person, in obedience to God's Word (2 John 6), regardless of that person's response or what one does or does not receive from him or her, or what love costs one to give. This love of Christians toward other Christians (Col. 1:8), as might be expected, is the most often commended "one-another" response in the New Testament.

Joy.[22] Joy (Gk. *chara*) is a happiness based on unchanging divine promises and eternal spiritual realities. It is the sense of well-being experienced by one who knows that all is well between oneself and the Lord (1 Pet. 1:8). Joy is not the result of favorable circumstances but occurs even when those circumstances are the most painful and severe (John 16:20–22; 1 Thess. 1:6). Joy is a gift from God, and as such, believers are not to manufacture it but to delight in the blessings they already possess (Phil. 4:4).

Produced by the Holy Spirit (Rom. 14:17), joy is appropriate both in the good times (3 John 4) and in the times of testing (James 1:2–4). Joy is a deep, abiding inner

22. This section is adapted from John MacArthur, ed., *The MacArthur Study Bible: English Standard Version* (Wheaton, IL: Crossway, 2010), 1751. Charts and notes from *The MacArthur Study Bible: English Standard Version* originate with *The MacArthur Study Bible*, copyright © 1997 by Thomas Nelson. Used by permission of Thomas Nelson. www.thomasnelson.com.

thankfulness to God for his goodness that is not diminished or interrupted when less-than-desirable circumstances intrude on one's life.

Peace.[23] Peace (Gk. *eirēnē*) results in an ordered, settled, and undisturbed response to whatever life brings one's way. Peace produced by the Holy Spirit is beyond human understanding (Phil. 4:6), an inner calm that results from confidence in one's saving relationship with Christ. The verb form of the Greek term denotes binding together and is reflected in the expression "having it all together." Like joy, peace is not determined by one's circumstances (John 14:27; Rom. 8:28; Phil. 4:7, 9). Peace during the storms of life involves a heartfelt tranquility and trust that are anchored in the overwhelming consciousness that one's life is in the hands of the sovereignly powerful God.

Patience. Patience (Gk. *makrothymia*) involves self-restraint that does not retaliate reactively. It endures injuries inflicted by others without the need for revenge and willingly accepts irritating or painful situations. *Longsuffering* captures the essential sense in one word.

Paul displayed his own patience in ministry to the Corinthians, attributing his longsuffering to the Holy Spirit (2 Cor. 6:1–10, esp. 6:6). James extolled patience in times of suffering for the faith (James 5:7–11). Peter reminded his readers of God's patience before their salvation (1 Pet. 3:20; 2 Pet. 3:15). Patience is an element of love (1 Cor. 13:4) and, in the end, is to be demonstrated toward everyone (Eph. 4:2; 1 Thess. 5:14).

Kindness. Kindness (Gk. *chrēstotēs*) is expressed as a tender, gentle concern for others that actively seeks out ways to serve them. The Father (Rom. 2:4; Titus 3:4) and the Son (Matt. 11:30) displayed kindness in the act of salvation. Believers are to be kind toward one another (Eph. 4:32; Col. 3:12) and are to commend themselves to others through kindness (2 Cor. 6:6).

Goodness. Goodness (Gk. *agathōsynē*) exhibits an actively determined capacity to deal with people in the best interest of God's glory, even when confrontation and correction are required. Goodness is associated with the "fruit of the light" (Eph. 5:9). The Greek word for "goodness" appears nowhere in Greek literature except in the Bible, where in the Septuagint translation of the Old Testament, "goodness" is said to be an attribute of God (Neh. 9:25).

Faithfulness. Faithfulness (Gk. *pistis*) is an inner commitment that consistently expresses itself as an outward loyalty that remains true to one's spiritual convictions. The eleventh chapter of Hebrews recounts the faith and faithfulness of notable Old Testament saints. God exemplifies faithfulness in his own divine character (Rom. 3:3). And the saints in Daniel's seventieth week are urged to be faithful in the face of possible martyrdom (Rev. 13:10; 14:12).

---

23. This section is adapted from MacArthur, *The MacArthur Study Bible: English Standard Version*, 1751. Used by permission of Thomas Nelson.

Gentleness. Gentleness (Gk. *prautēs*), sometimes translated "meekness," basically pictures controlled strength expressed by a humble heart. In its ancient secular sense, the Greek term meant a gentle breeze or a tamed beast, that is, strength used for good, not evil. Paul characterized Christ in this manner (2 Cor. 10:1; see Matt. 11:29). And Christ taught, "Blessed are the meek, for they shall inherit the earth" (Matt. 5:5). Gentleness describes three attitudes: (1) submission to the will of God (Col. 3:12); (2) teachability (James 1:21); and (3) consideration of others (Eph. 4:2).

Self-Control. Self-control (Gk. *enkrateia*), which literally means "in strength," refers to an inward restraint of appetites and passions resulting in a spiritual mastery that submits consistently to the greater cause of God's will, not man's. This is a commended quality of godliness (2 Pet. 1:6), one with which Paul described the discipline of a winning athlete (1 Cor. 9:25). To the church in Crete pastored by Titus, Paul listed this consistently practiced quality as an identifiable trait of an elder (Titus 1:8).

Table 5.9 summarizes the Bible's teaching on Spirit-produced fruit in terms of New Testament exhortations to fruitfulness and New Testament examples of Christlike fruit. At least six significant conclusions can be drawn from Paul's discussion about the fruit of the Spirit:

1. This teaching is addressed to all true believers as basic to their Christian life (2 Tim. 3:16–17).
2. These qualities are commanded in the context of the charge to "walk by the Spirit" (Gal. 5:16, 25).
3. These Spirit-enabled qualities represent communicable attributes of God that are authenticating marks of Christian godliness (Gal. 5:22–23).
4. Because "fruit" is singular, not plural, Paul intended it to be understood as one fruit with multiple characteristics, all of which should be reflected at any given time.
5. These fruitful traits (Gal. 5:22–23) certify the authenticity of a genuine Christian in contrast to the spoils of the flesh (Gal. 5:13, 16–17, 19–21), which condemn unbelievers (Gal. 5:21).
6. While the law was completely against the deeds of the flesh, there is no law against the work of the Holy Spirit (Gal. 5:23). This fruit represents true spiritual freedom for one who has been freed from the law (Gal. 5:18) and now lives in the new covenant era.

THE SPOILS OF THE FLESH

Paul preceded his discussion of "fruit" with a contrasting discussion about the "flesh" (Gal. 5:19–21). In context, he listed attitudes and actions that could be accounted for only by the unredeemed flesh of unbelievers, not by the Spirit's sanctifying work in Christians. They cover the categories of sexual, spiritual, attitudinal, and relational sin (cf. Rom. 1:24–32; 1 Cor. 6:9–10).

The apostle spelled out fifteen specific examples to illustrate his point. The list was intended to be not exhaustive but representative. He also took an illustrative

Table 5.9 Christlike Fruit*

The Fruit	Exhortations to Christians	Examples of Christlikeness
Love	Matt. 22:34–40 John 13:34 1 Cor. 16:14 Eph. 5:2 Col. 3:14 1 John 4:7	John 10:11–18; 13:1; 15:9–10, 13 Eph. 5:2
Joy	Rom. 12:12, 15 Phil. 3:1; 4:4 James 1:2 1 Pet. 4:13	John 15:11; 17:13 Heb. 12:2
Peace	2 Cor. 13:11 Eph. 4:3 Phil. 4:7–8 Col. 3:15 2 Tim. 2:22 1 Pet. 3:11	John 14:27; 16:33; 20:19, 21
Patience	Eph. 4:2 Col. 3:12 1 Thess. 5:14 2 Tim. 4:2	1 Tim. 1:16 2 Pet. 3:15
Kindness	Col. 3:12 2 Tim. 2:24	Matt. 11:30 Titus 3:4
Goodness	Rom. 12:9, 21 Gal. 6:10 Eph. 4:28	Luke 18:18–19 John 7:12
Faithfulness	Rev. 2:10	Rev. 1:5
Gentleness	Gal. 6:1 Eph. 4:2 Col. 3:12 1 Tim. 6:11	Matt. 11:29
Self-control	2 Pet. 1:5–6	Isa. 53:7 1 Pet. 2:23

* This chart is adapted from two charts in Keith H. Essex, "Sanctification: The Biblically Identifiable Fruit," *MSJ* 21, no. 2 (2010): 210–11. Used by permission of *MSJ*.

approach elsewhere, in both positive and negative contexts, by using the phrase "such things" (Rom. 1:32; 2:2; Gal. 5:21, 23).

Paul emphasized not an occasional sin but rather the habitual, willful practice of many sins, indicating an ongoing ungodly lifestyle. He concluded (Rom. 1:32) that these kinds of people deserve to die, by which he meant the second death of Revelation 20:11–15. In Galatians 5, Paul reasoned in the same manner that "those who do such things will not inherit the kingdom of God" (Gal. 5:21; see also Matt. 5:20; John 3:5; 1 Cor. 6:10; Eph. 5:5).

In summary, the New Testament uses the imagery of fruit with two variations to contrast Christians with non-Christians, who lack the Holy Spirit's work of sanctification. First, the lack of fruit identifies an unbeliever, while abundant fruit authenticates a true believer (Matt. 13:18–23; esp. 13:23; John 15:2–6). Second, believers bear good fruit, while unbelievers produce rotten fruit (Matt. 7:16–20; 12:33; Luke 6:43–44; Gal. 5:19–23).

Service

Overview of Gifts
Temporary Gifts (Revelatory/Confirmatory)
Permanent Gifts (Speaking/Serving)
Important Questions

In the Old Testament, only a few select people were empowered by the Holy Spirit for spiritual service. However, in the New Testament, every believer is gifted to serve in the body of Christ, the church.

Several New Testament Greek words help to explain how this works. First, *charis* (Rom. 12:6; 1 Pet. 4:10), normally translated "grace," indicates undeserved/unearned favor. It is the basis for the term *charisma* (Rom. 11:29; 12:6; 1 Cor. 1:7; 12:4, 9, 28, 30–31; Eph. 4:7; 1 Pet. 4:10), which means "grace gift." Both words are used together in Romans 12:6 and 1 Peter 4:10 to provide the fullest sense of spiritual giftedness in the church. Second, *pneumatikos*, used in 1 Corinthians 12:1 and 14:1 in the context of gifts, adds the dimension of being *spiritual* as opposed to being *natural* (see *psychikos* in 1 Cor. 2:14–15; 15:46). In other words, these are gifts associated with the Holy Spirit that have a spiritual nature and that are given for a spiritual purpose. Finally, *merismos* (Heb. 2:4) conveys the idea that the originator and distributor of these gifts is God, not humans.

New Testament spiritual gifts have a Trinitarian involvement. God the Father has planned for and appointed the gifts (1 Cor. 12:18, 28). God the Son has provided these gifts (Eph. 4:7–8, 11). God the Holy Spirit indwells and empowers people with spiritual gifts (1 Cor. 12:11). All three persons of the Godhead are involved (1 Cor. 12:4–6).

Overview of Gifts

At least seven gift lists can be found in the New Testament. No two lists are identical; thus, they are representative, not exhaustive (see table 5.10). They are located in 1 Corinthians 12–13 (AD 55), Romans 12 (AD 56), Ephesians 4 (ca. AD 61), and 1 Peter 4 (ca. AD 64).

While the lists primarily discuss gifts given by the Holy Spirit, several speak to both gifts and to gifted offices. Apostles, prophets, and teachers are included with gifts in 1 Corinthians 12:28–30. In contrast, Ephesians 4:11 exclusively lists apostles, prophets, evangelists, and shepherds/teachers.

The following observations constitute some of the most important descriptions and conclusions from God's revelation concerning spiritual gifts:

1. Salvation is a *charisma* gift, that is, an undeserved gift by God's grace (Rom. 6:23; Eph. 2:8; Titus 2:11).
2. The Holy Spirit is also a *charisma* gift, that is, an undeserved gift by God's grace (Rom. 5:5; 1 Thess. 4:8; 1 John 3:24; 4:13; also see Acts 2:38; 10:45; Heb. 6:4).

Table 5.10 Spiritual Gifts

1 Corinthians 12:8-10	1 Corinthians 12:28-30	1 Corinthians 13:1-3	1 Corinthians 13:8-9	Romans 12:6-8	Ephesians 4:11	1 Peter 4:10-11
Utterance of wisdom	Apostles	Tongues	Prophecy	Prophecy	Apostles	Speaking
Utterance of knowledge	Prophets	Prophecy	Tongues	Service	Prophets	Serving
Faith	Teachers	Knowledge	Knowledge	Teaching	Evangelists	
Gifts of healing	Miracles	Faith		Exhorting	Shepherds / teachers	
Working of miracles	Gifts of healing	Giving		Generous contributions (giving)		
Prophecy	Helping			Leading		
Distinguishing between spirits	Administering			Mercy		
Various kinds of tongues	Various kinds of tongues					
Interpretation of tongues	Interpretation of tongues					

3. Like Spirit baptism, spiritual gifts accompany salvation.
4. God's will, not human will, determines individual giftedness (1 Cor. 12:11, 18, 24; Heb. 2:4).
5. Spiritual gifts are permanent and irrevocable (Rom. 11:29).
6. Spiritual gifts received with salvation should be distinguished from natural talents possessed from physical birth (1 Cor. 12:11). However, the Holy Spirit can certainly use both kinds of giftedness for his own divine purposes.
7. Spiritual giftedness alone does not necessarily make a Christian spiritual, as demonstrated by the Corinthian church (1 Cor. 14:20). Spiritual character is the highest priority (Col. 1:28).
8. All Christians are gifted without exception (1 Cor. 12:7, 11; Eph. 4:7; 1 Pet. 4:10) and can have more than one gift, resulting in a unique gift combination.
9. The Holy Spirit produces a variety of gifts (1 Cor. 12:4), which Christians employ in a variety of ministries (1 Cor. 12:5–6) with a variety of outcomes (1 Cor. 12:6).
10. Individual giftedness enhances the corporate good (1 Cor. 12:7) through Christians serving one another (1 Pet. 4:10).
11. Gifts are to be exercised in love (1 Cor. 13:8, 13), because without love, the practice of giftedness is useless (1 Cor. 13:1–3).
12. Gifts differ according to God's grace given (Rom. 12:6; Eph. 4:7) and are to be ministered by Christians as good stewards of God's grace (1 Pet. 4:10).
13. Scripture commands Christians to exercise their gifts (Rom. 12:6; Eph. 4:11–14) as a human responsibility and obligation.

14. The primary purpose of permanent gifts is for the edification of the church (1 Cor. 14:4–5, 12, 17, 26; see Eph. 4:12–13).
15. The fruitful exercise of one's giftedness brings God glory (1 Pet. 4:11).

Temporary Gifts (Revelatory/Confirmatory)[24]

The following discussion addresses both temporary gifts that ceased with the apostolic age[25] and permanent gifts that continue to the end of the church age. The seven gift lists record temporary and permanent gifts in three ways. First, two lists emphasize temporary gifts (1 Cor. 12:8–10; 13:8–9). Second, two lists focus on permanent gifts (Rom. 12:6–8; 1 Pet. 4:10–11). Finally, three lists recount a mix of temporary and permanent gifts (1 Cor. 12:28–30; 13:1–3; Eph. 4:11). We will begin with temporary gifts, which served both revelatory and confirmatory purposes in authenticating God's special messengers and the inauguration of the new covenant era.

Three New Testament statements speak directly about divinely initiated miracles involving temporary gifts done through people. First, consider Peter's inspired commentary on the purpose of Jesus's miracles in Acts 2:22: "Men of Israel, hear these words: Jesus of Nazareth, a man attested to you by God with mighty works and wonders and signs that God did through him in your midst, as you yourselves know . . ." Here Peter essentially echoed Christ, who asserted that his works certified his claims to deity and messiahship. Jesus's miracles attested undeniably to the truth of his claim to be the God-man (John 11:47–48). They distinguished Christ, who had impeccable miraculous credentials, as the true Messiah in contrast to all the false christs throughout history.

Second, Paul made a direct statement about miracles in relationship to the apostles in 2 Corinthians 12:12. He noted emphatically that the marks (*sēmeia*) of an apostle were signs, wonders, and miracles. God used those supernatural phenomena to authenticate the apostolic messenger and thus validate his message (Acts 2:43; 5:12; Rom. 15:19; Heb. 2:1–4). Much the same method was used by God to authenticate the Old Testament prophets—God fulfilled the prophets' message and performed miracles through them (see Deut. 13:1–5; 18:21–22). Miracles distinguished between true and false prophets and apostles.

Third, the author of Hebrews argued that God used miracles to authenticate the salvation message. Hebrews 2:3–4 states that God bore witness to true salvation through the apostles by miracles.

These passages from Acts, 2 Corinthians, and Hebrews teach that God's primary purpose for the miracles he worked through men with temporary giftedness was *to authenticate his messengers as bearing a true revelation from God*. This was true of both temporary revelatory gifts and temporary confirmatory gifts.

---

24. Much of the following discussion of miracles and temporary gifts is adapted from Richard Mayhue, *The Healing Promise: Is It Always God's Will to Heal?* (Fearn, Ross-shire, Scotland: Mentor, 1997), 167–72. Used by permission of Christian Focus.

25. For a more thorough discussion concerning specific temporary gifts and their cessation, refer to chap. 9, "The Church." Also consult the articles in two *Master's Seminary Journal* issues devoted to cessationism and the revelatory gifts: *MSJ* 14, no. 2 (2003): 143–327, and *MSJ* 25, no. 2 (2014): 17–93.

THE BIBLICAL PATTERN OF AUTHENTICATING MIRACLES

There are many illustrations of this major kind of purpose in the Old Testament. In Exodus 3 and 4, God finally convinced Moses that he should represent him in Egypt. To every one of Moses's objections God responded with a supernatural sign that would authenticate Moses's commission. In Exodus 4:30–31, the signs were performed, and the Jews believed. After one sign and three plagues, the magicians of Pharaoh believed (Ex. 8:18–19). After ten plagues and the Red Sea incident, it can be assumed that Pharaoh believed (Ex. 14:26–30), and the Jews' faith was rekindled (Ex. 14:31).

After feeding Elijah with her last morsels, the widow of Zarephath saw her food replenished supernaturally (1 Kings 17:8–16). At the death of her son, she doubted (1 Kings 17:17–18), but when her son was brought back to life supernaturally, she believed (1 Kings 17:24). Elijah had been attested as authentic by a miracle from God. This happened again on Mount Carmel when, at the command of Elijah, fire came from heaven and made believers of the people in the midst of rampant unbelief and gross idolatry (1 Kings 18:30–40). Naaman was convinced of Elisha's credibility after being healed of leprosy (2 Kings 5:14–15). Nebuchadnezzar knew Daniel's reliability after he correctly reviewed and interpreted the king's dream (Dan. 2:46–47).

Clearly, God used miracles through men to authenticate his messengers. The miracles were never used merely for display, for frivolity, or to exalt the messenger.

A review of biblical history reveals three major periods during which God performed miracles through men. Such miracles through human agents did occur in other eras but only rarely by comparison. These three major periods include the following:

1. The ministries of Moses and Joshua, ca. 1450–1390 BC
2. The ministries of Elijah and Elisha, ca. 860–800 BC
3. The ministries of Christ and his apostles, ca. AD 30–60

Still, even in those periods, miracles were not the norm for all of God's servants. Speaking of John the Baptist, the Lord said, "I tell you, among those born of women none is greater than John. Yet the one who is least in the kingdom of God is greater than he" (Luke 7:28). Yet John the apostle writes of the Baptizer, "John did no sign, but everything that John said about this man was true" (John 10:41). Later John's message was vindicated by Christ's miracles. So the stature of a man of God was primarily evidenced not by sign miracles but by the truthfulness of the message.

CAUTION FROM EXTRABIBLICAL HISTORY

Reports of miracles are not limited to biblical history or even Christianity. In fact, if the mere number of alleged miracles were used to measure the authenticity of a religion, true Christianity would be eclipsed by false religion. The fact that alleged miracles happen outside the Christian faith should cause Christians to be wary of those who claim to do the miraculous.

The history of alleged miracles within the sphere of Christianity since AD 100 is abundant in the area of healing. Noted theologian Benjamin Warfield observed,

> There is little or no evidence at all for miracle-working during the first fifty years of the postapostolic church; it is slight and unimportant for the next fifty years; it grows more abundant during the next century (the third); and it becomes abundant and precise only in the fourth century, to increase still further in the fifth and beyond. Thus, if the evidence is worth anything at all, instead of a regularly progressing decrease, there was a steadily growing increase of miracle-working from the beginning on.[26]

However, do the character and quality of reported postapostolic miracles match those recorded in Scripture? The eminent church historian Philip Schaff offers these weighty considerations against those miracles:[27]

1. They are of "a much lower moral tone" and "far exceed" biblical miracles "in outward pomp."
2. They do not serve "to confirm the Christian faith in general."
3. "The further they are removed from the apostolic age, the more numerous they are."
4. The church fathers did not truthfully report all there was to know about the alleged miracles.
5. The church fathers admitted that there were "extensive frauds."
6. "The Nicene miracles met with doubt and contradiction even among contemporaries."
7. The church fathers contradicted themselves by teaching that miracles no longer took place and then reporting the occurrence of actual miracles.

Christians need to heed history's warnings regardless of their own position on miracles done through human agents. Satan will do all that he can to mislead and deceive Christians along the dead-end path of alleged miracles (2 Cor. 11:13–15). Those on the path will one day approach Jesus with claims of having done miracles in his name, but to them he will respond, "I never knew you; depart from me, you workers of lawlessness" (Matt. 7:23).

THE CESSATION OF REVELATORY AND CONFIRMATORY GIFTS

Have miracles and temporary gifts through men really continued beyond the apostolic age? Scripture teaches that miracles served to authenticate the messenger of God and ultimately God's message. However, when the book of Revelation was recorded by John, the canon of the New Testament and the total revelation of Scripture from God was completed. After AD 95, God had no reason to perform miracles through men because he was no longer revealing truth that needed to be authenticated; the

---

26. Benjamin B. Warfield, *Counterfeit Miracles* (1918; repr. Edinburgh: Banner of Truth, 1972), 10.
27. Philip Schaff, *History of the Christian Church* (Grand Rapids, MI: Associated Publishers & Authors, n.d.), 3:191–92.

canon closed with the completion of Revelation. Therefore, God's work of miracles and temporary gifts through men ceased.

There is no single, explicitly clear biblical statement that specifies whether miracles through men and temporary gifts ceased with the apostles or continued, but if one consults the whole counsel of God, one will find the answer. Here are some New Testament indicators that the age of miracles through men and temporary gifts indeed ceased with the apostolic age.

Acts 2:22; Romans 15:18–19; 2 Corinthians 12:12; and Hebrews 2:4 indicate that God gave sign miracles in order to authenticate the messenger of God. With the completion of the canon, those signs no longer served their God-intended purpose.

Following the historical progress of the apostles who wrote about miraculous gifts, miracles diminished in scope as time moved onward.[28] In Acts 19:11–12 (AD 52); 1 Corinthians (AD 55); and Romans (AD 56), the writers report extraordinary miracles that were taking place. Later epistles indicate that those phenomena were waning. Paul did not heal Epaphroditus (Phil. 2:27, AD 60). Paul prescribed wine for Timothy's stomach ailment (1 Tim. 5:23, AD 62–64) instead of recommending that Timothy submit himself to someone who could heal. Trophimus was left sick by Paul at Miletus (2 Tim. 4:20, AD 66–67).

James, writing around AD 45–49, exhorted believers who were seriously ill to call for the elders to anoint them and pray over them rather than to call for someone who had the ability to heal. In the seven letters to the seven churches (Revelation 2–3, AD 95), no mention is made of miraculous sign gifts. These epistles were Christ's last and final scriptural words to his church.

The Scriptures teach that miracles through human agents served a very specific purpose. That purpose focused on authenticating the prophets and apostles of God as certified messengers with a sure word from heaven (Acts 2:22; 2 Cor. 12:12; Heb. 2:1–4). When the canon of Scripture closed with John's Revelation, there no longer existed a divine reason for performing miracles through men. Therefore, such miracles ceased along with temporary gifts.

The following nine temporary, miraculous gifts/offices served revelatory or confirmatory purposes and ceased at the completion of the apostolic era because their purposes had been accomplished:

1. Apostle (1 Cor. 12:28; Eph. 4:11): Men directly commissioned by the risen Christ and sent out to found and establish the church
2. Distinguishing between spirits (1 Cor. 12:10): The divine enablement to discern true from false statements made by people who deceptively claimed that their words were prophetic revelations from God
3. Healing (1 Cor. 12:9, 28, 30): The divine enablement to restore the sick to immediate health without a necessary faith response by the one(s) being healed
4. Miracles (1 Cor. 12:28): The divine enablement to perform works of power that contravene or exacerbate the normal processes of nature

---

28. The following three paragraphs are adapted from Richard L. Mayhue, "The Gifts of Healing," *MSJ* 25, no. 2 (2014): 21–22. Used by permission of *MSJ*.

5. Prophecy (1 Cor. 12:10; Eph. 4:11): The divine enablement of receiving and communicating direct verbal revelation from God to man
6. Tongues (1 Cor. 12:10, 28; 13:1): The divine enablement to speak in a real, human language that had not been previously learned
7. Interpretation of tongues (1 Cor. 12:10, 30; see 14:26–28): The divine enablement to interpret the words of one speaking in tongues
8. Utterance of knowledge (1 Cor. 12:8; 13:2, 8): The divine enablement to communicate a direct word of insight from the Lord to guide the local church in understanding a prophecy (deemed a revelatory gift because it is linked with prophecy in 13:8)
9. Utterance of wisdom (1 Cor. 12:8): The divine enablement to give a direct word from the Lord to skillfully guide the local church in a specific decision (deemed a revelatory gift because it is connected with the word of knowledge, which is linked to prophecy in 13:8)

Permanent Gifts (Speaking/Serving)

The following eleven permanent, ministering gifts/offices involve speaking and serving purposes that have continued beyond the apostolic era to this present time:

1. Evangelist (Eph. 4:11): The divine enablement to effectively explain, exhort, and apply the gospel to the unsaved
2. Exhorting (Rom. 12:8): The divine enablement to effectively incite practical holiness in heart and action through encouragement, comfort, admonishment, and entreaty
3. Faith (1 Cor. 12:9; 13:2): The divine enablement to trust God in all details of his work even when the outcome seems uncertain. This gift produces stellar assurance that God will accomplish his purposes.
4. Giving (Rom. 12:8; 1 Cor. 13:3): The divine enablement to generously, joyfully, and sacrificially give earthly possessions to the Lord for the work of the ministry
5. Helping/serving (Rom. 12:7; 1 Cor. 12:28): The divine enablement to sacrificially and submissively help meet the needs of other Christians
6. Leading/administrating (Rom. 12:8; 1 Cor. 12:28): The divine enablement to zealously govern Christians toward the goal of accomplishing the will of God
7. Mercy (Rom. 12:8): The divine enablement to cheerfully detect, empathize with, and assist in meeting the physical, emotional, and spiritual needs of other people
8. Prophecy/preaching (Rom. 12:6): The nonrevelatory, divine enablement to forthtell, that is, to proclaim the Scriptures
9. Shepherd/teacher (Eph. 4:11): The divine enablement to shepherd Christians by leading, providing, feeding, protecting, and otherwise caring for them
10. Spiritual discernment (1 Cor. 12:10): The divine enablement to identify forms of doctrinal error and religious deception. This represents the permanent, ministry aspect of the gift. As "the father of lies" (John 8:44), Satan continually seeks to counterfeit the true work of God by disguising himself as an angel of light (cf. 2 Cor. 11:14), working primarily through false teachers, who dispense the "doctrines of demons" (1 Tim. 4:1 NASB). There are those in the church today who have been given a significant ability to identify falsehood by comparing it to biblical truth.

11. Teaching (Rom. 12:7; 1 Cor. 12:28): The divine enablement to clearly interpret, explain, and apply the Scriptures to Christians

Important Questions

What follows are five of the most frequently asked questions about spiritual giftedness accompanied by their scripturally based answers.

Question 1. Do Christians receive only one gift?
    Answer: Most likely, each Christian has a unique blend of several gifts, not just one exclusive gift.

Question 2: What do Christians need to know about spiritual giftedness?
    Answer:
- Salvation is a *charisma*, that is, a free gift (Rom. 6:23).
- God's Holy Spirit is a gift as a part of salvation (Rom. 5:5; 1 Thess. 4:8; 1 John 3:24; 4:13).
- Every believer has received a spiritual gift—spiritual in source and nature (1 Cor. 1:7; 7:7; 1 Pet. 4:10).
- God's will, not man's, is the basis for who gets what gift (1 Cor. 12:11, 18).
- Spiritual gifts are diverse (1 Cor. 12:12–27), since of the several gift lists in the New Testament, no two are the same (Rom. 12:6–8; 1 Cor. 12:8–10, 28–30; 13:1–3, 8; cf. 1 Cor. 7:7).
- In the qualities desired for church leaders and mature believers, spiritual gifts are not emphasized (Gal. 5:22–23; 1 Tim. 3:1–7; Titus 1:5–9; cf. 1 Cor. 13:4–7).
- The kind of spiritual gifts people are given do not necessarily indicate their level of spirituality.

Question 3. How can Christians identify spiritual giftedness?
    Answer:
- Believing that God uniquely gifts individuals, one should focus more on one multifaceted gift than on multiple gifts (1 Pet. 4:10).
- One clear indicator is that a believer is able to maximize a particular ministry with minimum effort.
- Spiritual gifts will be used most effectively in the context of the local church, where, sooner or later, other Christians will recognize and comment on one's spiritual giftedness.
- Personal inclinations and observations of others will lead one to fruitful ministry.

Question 4. What should Christians do with spiritual giftedness?
    Answer: They should use their gifts to build up the church (1 Cor. 14:12) and serve one another (1 Cor. 12:7; 1 Pet. 4:10).

Question 5. What errors should Christians avoid in exercising spiritual giftedness?
    Answer:
- Self-edification rather than the edification of others (1 Pet. 4:10)
- Self-exercise rather than being Spirit exercised (1 Pet. 4:11)
- Self-exaltation rather than using one's gift for God's glory (1 Pet. 4:11)

Creation[29]

Very little is written in Scripture about the Holy Spirit and creation. Yet the Holy Spirit's participation appears in the very first chapter of the Bible, exactly where one would expect to find it. When God said, "Let us make man in our image, after our likeness," he used the plural pronoun three times (Gen. 1:26). Here the Scriptures undeniably imply that God the Father, God the Son, and God the Holy Spirit were all three involved in creation. Genesis 1:2 actually describes one aspect of the Holy Spirit's contribution.

Looking elsewhere in Scripture, commentators have connected the Holy Spirit with creation in two passages in Job (a book penned possibly earlier than Genesis). However, understood in context, neither Job 26:13 nor Job 33:4 appear to refer to original creation. Also, two verses in the Psalms (Pss. 33:6; 104:30) have sometimes been linked to the creation account in Genesis 1–2. Nevertheless, in context, the Hebrew term *ruakh* in these passages would be better translated "breath," which means these texts do not likely refer to creation.

One must ask, how many biblical references does it take to establish a teaching as true? Actually, it takes only one, clearly and correctly interpreted, to establish the truth. In this case, Genesis 1:2 and 1:26 are more than sufficient to establish the irrefutable truth that God the Holy Spirit joined God the Father and God the Son in creating the heavens and the earth (Gen. 1:1).

Scripture[30]

> Revelation and Inspiration
> Instruction, Illumination, and Affirmation
> Utilization

The Spirit of truth (John 14:17, 26; 15:26; 16:7, 13; 1 John 4:6; 5:7) has been actively engaged in every aspect of mediating God's Word, as illustrated below:

God Giving	Believers Receiving
Revelation	Salvation
Inspiration	Sanctification
	Instruction
	Illumination
	Affirmation
	Utilization

Christ taught his disciples that God's Spirit was the Paraclete, the divine friend who would do whatever was necessary to forward the best interest of God through the apostles. Since Christ had discipled these men to bear witness of him and lead

---

29. For a more thorough discussion of creation, refer to "Creation" in chap. 3, "God the Father" (p. 213).
30. For a more thorough discussion of Scripture, refer to chap. 2, "God's Word."

others to a knowledge of the truth, then in Christ's absence, the Paraclete would come alongside the apostles to equip and exhort them to continue teaching what Christ had taught (John 14:16, 26), to help the disciples bear witness of Christ (John 15:26–27), and to help the disciples convict the world with their message of truth (John 16:7–11). In all four of these passages in John's Gospel, the Greek term *paraklētos* is best translated "Helper." In every instance, as the immediate contexts of these verses show, John's emphasis is on the Paraclete helping the disciples specifically to *know* and *remember* and *preach* the truth about Christ. The first five chapters of Acts further confirm that the Paraclete came and helped the disciples to know the truth and to declare it with power (Acts 1:8; 2:4, 33; 4:8, 31; 5:32).

This work of the Spirit with the apostles lays the foundation of the Holy Spirit's ministry with relation to Scripture. Paul spoke of this aspect of the Spirit's ministry in 1 Corinthians 2:10–16, addressing the Spirit's work of revelation and inspiration (2:10–11), instruction (2:12–13), and illumination, affirmation, and utilization (2:14–16).

Revelation and Inspiration

The term *revelation* generally refers to the divine disclosure, whether by general or special means, of what was previously unknowable to humans (1 Cor. 2:10–11). Inspiration applies only to the written Word of God, whereby the Holy Spirit protects God's revelation through human writers from error in order to provide a completely true and trustworthy writing, down to the very words used (2 Tim. 3:16–17). Peter further explained inspiration by stating that the prophecy of Scripture was made not by an act of human will but rather by men who were directed by the Holy Spirit (2 Pet. 1:20–21). John was in the Spirit (Rev. 1:10) when he received inspired revelation from the seven spirits (Rev. 1:4), an idiom that refers to the Holy Spirit using the number of perfection (seven), which speaks of the Spirit's fullness (see Rev. 4:5; 5:6).

The Holy Spirit's role in revelation finds confirmation from many who spoke on behalf of God:

Prophets, during and after the exodus (Neh. 9:20, 30; Isa. 63:11, 14; Hag. 2:5)
David (2 Sam. 23:2)
Ezekiel (Ezek. 3:24, 27)
Micah (Mic. 3:8)
Zechariah (Zech. 7:12)
Simeon (Luke 2:26)
Christ's disciples (Matt. 10:20; Mark 13:11; Luke 12:12)
Agabus (Acts 11:28)
Paul (1 Cor. 2:10)
Peter (1 Pet. 1:10–12)

Similar testimony from others confirms that the Holy Spirit gave aid not only in revelation but also in inspiration:

Isaiah (Isa. 59:21)
John (John 16:13; Rev. 1:4, 10)
Paul (Eph. 3:5)

At times, the biblical writers speak specifically of scriptural texts that were both revealed and inspired by the Holy Spirit:

Matthew (Matt. 22:43; Mark 12:36, citing Ps. 110:1)
Luke (Acts 1:16, 20, citing Pss. 41:9; 69:25; 109:8)
Luke (Acts 4:25–26, citing Ps. 2:1–2)
Luke (Acts 28:25–27, citing Isa. 6:9–10)
Paul (1 Tim. 4:1, possibly citing Matt. 7:15; 24:24)
Author of Hebrews (Heb. 3:7–11, citing Ps. 95:7–11)
Author of Hebrews (Heb. 9:1–8, citing Exodus 25–26)
Author of Hebrews (Heb. 10:15–17, citing Jer. 31:33–34)
John (Rev. 2:7, 11, 17, 29; 3:6, 13, 22; 14:13, general examples)

Instruction, Illumination, and Affirmation

Nehemiah wrote, "You gave your good Spirit to instruct them" (Neh. 9:20). Paul testified, "We impart this in words not taught by human wisdom but taught by the Spirit" (1 Cor. 2:13). John encouraged his readers, "You have no need that anyone should teach you. But as his anointing [see 'the Holy One,' 1 John 2:20] teaches you about everything . . ." (1 John 2:27; see also 1 Cor. 2:14–16). Paul prayed for the Ephesians that "the God of our Lord Jesus Christ, the Father of glory, may give you the Spirit of wisdom and of revelation in the knowledge of him, having the eyes of your hearts enlightened, that you may know . . ." (Eph. 1:17–18).

Of all the chapters in the Bible, Psalm 119 most frequently mentions the human need for divine instruction. On nine occasions, the psalmist urgently asks, "Teach me your statutes" (Ps. 119:12, 26, 33, 64, 66, 68, 108, 124, 135). It can be assumed that he looked to the Holy Spirit for instruction. What Christ did for the disciples in opening their minds to understand the Scripture (Luke 24:45), the Holy Spirit does for Christians.

Illumination can refer either to one's salvation (2 Cor. 4:4, 6; see Acts 26:18; Heb. 6:4) or to a believer's need for greater understanding of or enlightenment regarding the Bible. The psalmist who prayed for the Holy Spirit to teach also asked for illumination: "Open my eyes that I may behold wondrous things out of your law" (Ps. 119:18; see also 119:27, 34, 73, 125, 144, 169; Eph. 1:18). Then he testified to the benefit of illumination: "The unfolding of your words gives light; it imparts understanding to the simple" (Ps. 119:130).

While Holy Spirit illumination is indispensably helpful, there are certain things that it is not and certain things that it cannot do. These limitations remind believers not to expect what Scripture does not promise:

1. Illumination does not function outside God's Word (Ps. 119:18; Luke 24:45).
2. Illumination does not guarantee that every Christian will agree doctrinally, because the human element can cause false doctrine (Gal. 2:11–21).

3. Illumination does not mean that everything about God is knowable (Deut. 29:29).
4. Illumination does not render the need for human teachers unnecessary (Eph. 4:11; 1 Tim. 3:2; 2 Tim. 4:2).
5. Illumination is not a substitute for dedicated, personal Bible study (2 Tim. 2:15).
6. Illumination is not a one-time experience (2 Tim. 2:15).

In addition to instructing and illuminating the Christian, the Holy Spirit also bears witness to the believer that Scripture is truthful and trustworthy. At least three New Testament texts speak to this aspect of the Spirit's ministry in regard to God's Word (Acts 5:32; Heb. 10:15; 1 John 5:6). By far the most stellar and unimpeachable witness to the Bible is the Spirit of Truth (John 14:17).

Utilization

Not only is the Holy Spirit involved in the delivery and teaching aspects of Scripture (1 Cor. 2:4–5; 1 Thess. 1:5), but he also empowers believers in their obedience. The very similar outcomes from letting the word of Christ dwell in a believer (Col. 3:16–17) and from letting the Holy Spirit control the believer's life (Eph. 5:18–20) illustrate that, in addition to the intellectual side of knowing Scripture, the Holy Spirit is equally involved in energizing the volition of believers in obeying Scripture.

The Spirit also provides Christians with and helps them employ spiritual weaponry in battling the spiritual darkness of Satan and demons. A vital part of the Christian's armament is "the sword of the Spirit, which is the word of God" (Eph. 6:17). So whether it involves walking in the way of Christ or fighting for the glory of Christ, the inseparable connection of the Holy Spirit with Scripture propels the believer onward to victory.

Prophetic Ministry[31]

Regeneration
Resurrection
Daniel's Seventieth Week
The Millennium
Eternity Future

Relatively speaking, Scripture says very little about the Spirit's role in prophetic matters. What follows is a summary of what is written.

Regeneration

People of all kinds will be converted during Daniel's seventieth week (Rev. 6:9–11; 7:9–17; 14:6) and Christ's millennial kingdom (Isa. 25:9; 44:2–5; Jer. 24:6–7; Ezek. 36:25–31). From Adam and Eve to the last person who is saved, everyone

---

31. For a more thorough discussion of prophecy, see chap. 10, "The Future."

will have been made alive spiritually by the regenerating work of the Holy Spirit (John 3:1–15).[32]

Resurrection

It is by the power of the Holy Spirit that every believer, from the first (1 Thess. 4:13–18) to the last (Rev. 20:5–6), will be resurrected from the grave (Rom. 1:4; 8:11, 23).

Daniel's Seventieth Week

Christ recited Isaiah 61:1–2a in the synagogue at Nazareth, claiming that he was fulfilling what he read at that time. He will later fulfill Isaiah 61:2b–3 at his second coming. In both cases, the Holy Spirit is the One who empowers him (see Luke 4:17–21).

The Holy Spirit will execute God's will in the judgment of the nations (Isa. 34:8–16, esp. 34:16). God's work at that time will be empowered by the Holy Spirit (Zech. 4:3–6; cf. 4:11–14; Rev. 11:3–4).

A restrainer is spoken of in 2 Thessalonians 2:6. Numerous suggestions have been made as to the identity of the restrainer: (1) the Roman Empire, (2) human government, (3) the Jewish state, (4) gospel preaching, (5) the binding of Satan, (6) angels, (7) the providence of God, (8) some prophetic person like Elijah or Paul, (9) the church, or (10) the Holy Spirit.

The lawless one mentioned in this passage is empowered by Satan (2 Thess. 2:9; see Rev. 13:2, 4), so the question is, who or what is powerful enough to severely restrain Satan's influence over thousands of years? In reviewing the alternatives, the Holy Spirit seems most likely. Early in Scripture, the Holy Spirit exercised that kind of ministry (Gen. 6:3), and there is no reason to believe that he has relinquished it (see John 16:8–11; Acts 7:51). Only God has the power to effectively control Satan and his delegated evil (cf. Jude 9, where Michael the archangel defers to God in a conflict with Satan). How the Holy Spirit restrains is not mentioned, although it could possibly be through a combination of means such as human government (Rom. 13:1–7) and true believers, that is, the church.

The Millennium

Isaiah wrote of Christ's millennial reign and the restoration of Israel to the promised Davidic kingdom (Isa. 11:2–16; see 2 Sam. 7:10–17). During that time, when Christ rules, the Holy Spirit will enable him (Isa. 11:2). Isaiah described the overall purpose of Christ's millennial ministry (Isa. 42:1–4).

About the nation of Israel, the Bible makes three kinds of general references to the Holy Spirit. First, God will "pour out" his Spirit on the nation (Isa. 32:15; 44:3; Ezek. 39:29; Joel 2:28–29; Zech. 12:10). Second, God promises to put his Spirit "within them" (Ezek. 11:19; 36:26–27; 37:14). Third, God says that his Spirit will

---

32. For a more thorough discussion of regeneration, see "The Internal Call: Regeneration" in chap. 7 (p. 576).

be "upon them" (Isa. 59:21). As such, the Spirit will gather Israel back to the land at the God-chosen time in the future (Isa. 34:16).

Eternity Future

Scripture does not specifically mention the Holy Spirit in relation to eternity future. However, the deity of the Spirit and the triunity of God ensure that God the Holy Spirit will continue to work in perfect harmony with God the Father and God the Son forever.

———————

Prayer[33]

Our great heavenly Father,
    blessed Son, and eternal Spirit,
    we come to worship You—God in three Persons,
        one in essence,
        perfect in every way,
        the only true God.
Our hearts are filled with gratitude for the redemption our heavenly Father
    has furnished for us in Christ the Son
    and applied to us by the Holy Spirit.
Undeserving though we are, You have welcomed us
    into Your everlasting Kingdom,
    so that we might be partakers of Your unspeakable glory.

Again, Father, we thank You that in the fullness of Your grace,
    You have loved us and sent Your only begotten Son to redeem us.

Lord Jesus, though existing eternally in the form of God,
    You did not count that as something to be clung to.
You humbled Yourself, took on the form of a servant,
    and were made in the likeness of men.
As a man You became a servant, being obedient to the Father's will—
    even unto death on the cross.
That one sacrifice atoned for our sins forever
    and provided us with a covering such as we needed—
    the spotless garment of Your perfect righteousness.

Holy Spirit, You too have loved us everlastingly,
    and now You make Your permanent abode in our hearts,
        letting your life and power flow through us,
        producing abundant fruit and conforming
            us to the image of Christ.

———————

33. This prayer is reproduced verbatim from John MacArthur, *At the Throne of Grace: A Book of Prayers* (Eugene, OR: Harvest House, 2011), 55–57. Used by permission of Harvest House.

O God—one God yet three Persons—we praise You and thank You
for mercy so undeserved and for grace beyond measure.
Your lovingkindness is inexhaustible;
Your mercies endure forever;
Your faithfulness extends to all generations;
Your glory is seen in all Your works;
and Your steadfast love is our song.

We come to You, the triune God,
enthroned in our lives,
presiding over the universe,
and we humbly ask for You to strengthen us where we are weak,
beginning with our acts of worship.
You who spoke the universe into existence with but a word
are the One who has shone in our hearts
to give the Light of the knowledge of the glory of God
in the face of Christ.
How we thank You again for commanding salvation on our behalf!

Lord, we come before You in prayer to bring You our praise.
Set our lives in order before You,
and renew our commitment to love and obedience,
usefulness and faithfulness.
Be honored through our lives, we pray,
in the name of Christ. Amen.

"Come, Thou Almighty King"

Come, Thou Almighty King,
Help us Thy name to sing,
Help us to praise.
Father all-glorious,
O'er all victorious,
Come, and reign over us,
Ancient of Days.

Come, Thou Incarnate Word,
Gird on Thy mighty sword;
Our prayer attend.
Come, and Thy people bless,
And give Thy word success.
Spirit of holiness,
On us descend.

Come, Holy Comforter,
Thy sacred witness bear
In this glad hour.
Thou, who Almighty art,
Now rule in ev'ry heart

And ne'er from us depart,
Spirit of pow'r.

To Thee, great One in Three,
Eternal praises be,
Hence evermore;
Thy sov'reign majesty
May we in glory see,
And to eternity
Love and adore. Amen.

~author unknown

Bibliography

Primary Systematic Theologies

*Bancroft, Emery H. *Christian Theology: Systematic and Biblical*. 2nd ed. Grand Rapids, MI: Zondervan, 1976. 157–82.

Berkhof, Louis. *Systematic Theology*. 4th ed. Grand Rapids, MI: Eerdmans, 1939. 82–99; 423–31.

Dabney, Robert Lewis. *Systematic Theology*. 1871. Reprint, Edinburgh: Banner of Truth, 1985. 193–201.

Erickson, Millard J. *Christian Theology*. Grand Rapids, MI: Baker, 1986. 845–83.

Grudem, Wayne. *Systematic Theology: An Introduction to Biblical Doctrine*. Grand Rapids, MI: Zondervan, 1994. 634–53.

Hodge, Charles. *Systematic Theology*. 3 vols. 1871–1873. Reprint, Grand Rapids, MI: Eerdmans, 1975. 1:522–34.

Strong, August Hopkins. *Systematic Theology: A Compendium Designed for the Use of Theological Students*. Rev. ed. New York: Revell, 1907. 304–52.

*Swindoll, Charles R., and Roy B. Zuck, eds. *Understanding Christian Theology*. Nashville: Thomas Nelson, 2003. 389–536.

Thiessen, Henry Clarence. *Introductory Lectures in Systematic Theology*. Grand Rapids, MI: Eerdmans, 1949. 144–46.

Turretin, Francis. *Institutes of Elenctic Theology*. 3 vols. Edited by James T. Dennison Jr. Translated by George Musgrove Giger. 1679–1685. Reprint, Phillipsburg, NJ: P&R, 1992–1997. 1:302–10.

*Denotes most helpful.

Specific Works

Bickersteth, Edward Henry. *The Holy Spirit: His Person and Work*. 1869. Reprint, Grand Rapids, MI: Kregel, 1976.

*Biederwolf, William Edward. *Study of the Holy Spirit*. 1903. Reprint, Grand Rapids, MI: Kregel, 1985.

Carson, D. A. *Showing the Spirit: A Theological Exposition of 1 Corinthians 12–14.* Grand Rapids, MI: Baker, 1987.

Cole, Graham A. *He Who Gives Life: The Doctrine of the Holy Spirit.* Foundations of Evangelical Theology. Wheaton, IL: Crossway, 2007.

*Cumming, James Elder. *Through the Eternal Spirit: A Bible Study on the Holy Ghost.* New York: Revell, 1896.

Firth, David G., and Paul D. Wegner. *Presence, Power, and Promise: The Role of the Spirit of God in the Old Testament.* Downers Grove, IL: IVP Academic, 2011.

*Hamilton, James M., Jr. *God's Indwelling Presence: The Holy Spirit in the Old and New Testaments.* Nashville: B&H Academic, 2006.

*MacArthur, John. *The Silent Shepherd: The Care, Comfort, and Correction of the Holy Spirit.* 2nd ed. Colorado Springs: Cook, 2012.

Owen, John. *The Holy Spirit: His Gifts and Power.* Abridged edition. Edited by George Burder. 1792. Reprint, Grand Rapids, MI: Kregel, 1954. Owen's full work, *Pneumatologia,* first published in 1674.

*Pache, René. *The Person and Work of the Holy Spirit.* Translated by J. D. Emerson. Chicago: Moody Press, 1979.

Smeaton, George. *The Doctrine of the Holy Spirit.* 2nd ed. 1889. Reprint, Carlisle, PA: Banner of Truth, 1958.

Swete, Henry Barclay. *The Holy Spirit in the Ancient Church: A Study of the Christian Teaching in the Age of the Fathers.* 1912. Reprint, Grand Rapids, MI: Baker, 1966.

———. *The Holy Spirit in the New Testament: A Study of Primitive Christian Teaching.* 1910. Reprint, Grand Rapids, MI: Baker, 1964.

Thomas, Robert L. *Understanding Spiritual Gifts: A Verse-by-Verse Study of 1 Corinthians 12–14.* 2nd ed. Grand Rapids, MI: Kregel, 1999.

*Thomas, W. H. Griffith. *The Holy Spirit.* 1913. Reprint, Grand Rapids, MI: Kregel, 1986.

*Walvoord, John F. *The Holy Spirit: A Comprehensive Study of the Person and Work of the Holy Spirit.* 1954. Reprint, Grand Rapids, MI: Zondervan, 1991.

Wood, Leon J. *The Holy Spirit in the Old Testament.* 1976. Reprint, Eugene, OR: Wipf & Stock, 1998.

*Denotes most helpful.

Charismatic/Pentecostal Issues

*Chantry, Walter J. *Signs of the Apostles: Observations on Pentecostalism Old and New.* 2nd ed. Edinburgh: Banner of Truth, 1976.

Edgar, Thomas R. *Satisfied by the Promise of the Spirit: Affirming the Fullness of God's Provision for Spiritual Living.* Grand Rapids, MI: Kregel, 1996.

Frost, Henry W. *Miraculous Healing: A Personal Testimony and Biblical Study.* 1931. Reprint, London: Evangelical Press, 1972.

Gaffin, Richard B., Jr. *Perspectives on Pentecost: Studies in New Testament Teaching on the Gifts of the Holy Spirit.* Phillipsburg, NJ: P&R, 1979.

Gromacki, Robert G. *The Modern Tongues Movement.* Rev. ed. Phillipsburg, NJ: P&R, 1972.

Grudem, Wayne A., ed. *Are Miraculous Gifts for Today? Four Views.* Counterpoints. Grand Rapids, MI: Zondervan, 1996.

Hanegraaff, Hank. *Christianity in Crisis: 21st Century.* Nashville: Thomas Nelson, 2009.

Horton, Michael. *The Agony of Deceit.* Chicago: Moody Press, 1990.

Kole, André, and Al Janssen. *Miracles or Magic?* Eugene, OR: Harvest House, 1987.

*MacArthur, John F., Jr. *Charismatic Chaos.* Grand Rapids, MI: Zondervan, 1992.

*———. *Strange Fire: The Danger of Offending the Holy Spirit with Counterfeit Worship.* Nashville: Thomas Nelson, 2013.

Masters, Peter. *The Healing Epidemic.* London: Wakeman, 1988.

*Mayhue, Richard L. *The Biblical Pattern for Divine Healing.* 1979. Reprint, Winona Lake, IN: BMH, 2001.

*———. *The Healing Promise: Is It Always God's Will to Heal?* Fearn, Ross-shire, Scotland: Mentor, 1997.

McConnell, D. R. *A Different Gospel: A Historical and Biblical Analysis of the Modern Faith Movement.* Peabody, MA: Hendrickson, 1988.

Moriarty, Michael G. *The New Charismatics: A Concerned Voice Responds to Dangerous New Trends.* Grand Rapids, MI: Zondervan, 1992.

Napier, John. *Charismatic Challenge: Four Key Questions.* Homebush West, Australia: Anzea, 1991.

Nolen, William A. *Healing: A Doctor in Search of a Miracle.* Greenwich, CT: Fawcett, 1976.

*Smith, Charles R. *Tongues in Biblical Perspective: A Summary of Biblical Conclusions concerning Tongues.* 2nd ed. Winona Lake, IN: BMH, 1973.

Tada, Joni Eareckson. *A Place of Healing: Wrestling with the Mysteries of Suffering, Pain, and God's Sovereignty.* Colorado Springs: Cook, 2010.

Torrey, R. A. *Divine Healing: Does God Perform Miracles Today?* 1924. Reprint, Grand Rapids, MI: Baker, 1974.

*Warfield, Benjamin B. *Counterfeit Miracles.* 1918. Reprint, Edinburgh: Banner of Truth, 1972.

*Denotes most helpful.

"I Sing the Mighty Power of God"

I sing the mighty pow'r of God
That made the mountains rise,
That spread the flowing seas abroad,
And built the lofty skies.
I sing the wisdom that ordained
The sun to rule the day;
The moon shines full at His command,
And all the stars obey.

I sing the goodness of the Lord,
That filled the earth with food;
He formed the creatures with His word,
And then pronounced them good.
Lord, how Thy wonders are displayed
Where'er I turn my eye:
If I survey the ground I tread,
Or gaze upon the sky!

There's not a plant or flow'r below,
But makes Thy glories known;
And clouds arise, and tempests blow
By order from Thy throne;
While all that borrows life from Thee
Is ever in Thy care,
And ev'rywhere that man can be,
Thou, God, art present there.

~Isaac Watts (1674–1748)

6

Man and Sin

Anthropology and Hamartiology

Major Subjects Covered in Chapter 6

MAN	SIN
Introduction to Man	Introduction to Sin
Created in God's Image	Consequences of the Fall
The Human Constitution	Sin Issues
Origin of the Soul	Biblical Theology of Sin
Gender	
Personhood	
Man and Society	
Biblical Theology of Man	

MAN

Introduction to Man

Importance of Anthropology
Sudden Creationism
Adam as a Historical Person

Importance of Anthropology

There is an old saying, "Beware of the barrenness of a busy life." Life is often hectic, and most people rarely contemplate what is most important. But few matters are as significant as considering who we are and why we exist. King David was a busy man, but as he looked to the heavens and saw the moon and stars, he thought deeply and asked, "What is man that you [God] are mindful of him, and the son of man that you care for him?" (Ps. 8:4). Against the backdrop of God's wonderful creation, man seemed small and insignificant. David's question is one that all should contemplate.

The psalmist's question, "What is man?" relates to the doctrine of anthropology. The Greek term *anthrōpos* means "man" or "humanity." So anthropology is the study of humankind. But anthropology must be pursued from the proper standpoint. Secular universities and schools offer courses on anthropology, but they do so from a man-centered perspective. By excluding God from the discussion, they miss who man really is and how he fits in this world. To properly understand man, one must do so from a God-centered perspective.

Why is anthropology so important? First, anthropology is a topic where the student studies himself. What could be more personal and practical? Anthropology answers ultimate questions like, who am I? Why am I here? Why am I able to reason and feel? What is my purpose in life? Where am I headed?

Second, created last on the sixth day of creation week, man is the high point of God's creation. As Louis Berkhof notes, "Man is represented as standing at the apex of all the created orders. He is crowned as king of the lower creation, and is given dominion over all the inferior creatures."[1] With the doctrine of man we learn that man is unique. This helps inform man's role in the created order.

Third, anthropology helps us understand our relationship to God. Since man is a creature in God's image, we learn how he is supposed to act and relate to God. Those concerned with the biblical doctrine of man can learn what God thinks of and expects from them.

Fourth, a biblical anthropology helps address specific issues like abortion, euthanasia, homosexuality, transgenderism, and environmentalism. Much of the world today is confused and acts sinfully in regard to these issues since the world operates from a faulty view of God and man. But an anthropology from God's perspective instructs us truthfully on these and other issues. A biblical anthropology guides us in applying a Christian worldview to critical matters facing our world.

Fifth, a biblical view of man refutes false philosophies. Secular naturalism asserts that there is no God and that the universe is only material. Man is just an accidental collection of molecules that randomly evolved from lower life forms with no intentional design. Since man is here by chance, nothing he does has real value or eternal significance. He is just a higher form of animal. Humanity itself will one day expire, being snuffed out of existence.

Some philosophies of the last century emphasized certain aspects of mankind. Communism stressed that man is primarily an economic being driven by material needs. It alleged that history is the inevitable progression of man from slavery to feudalism to capitalism and then to the highest ideal of communism, where there will be no private property and where the state will own all. Sigmund Freud (1856–1939) asserted that

---

1. Louis Berkhof, *Systematic Theology*, 4th ed. (1939; repr., Grand Rapids, MI: Eerdmans, 1991), 183.

man is primarily a sexual being with his behavior stemming from sexual motivation. Postmodernism has taught that people are products of their social settings and that no transcendent moral realities exist. Supposed "truths" are mental constructs, meaningful only to people within certain cultures. Grand stories or metanarratives that help people understand their place in a bigger story are viewed with scorn.

Eastern religions like Hinduism and Buddhism have claimed that man's destiny is a spiritual or mystical union with an impersonal force such as Brahman. Like a drop of water placed in the ocean, man's goal is to lose personhood, feelings, and desires in order to achieve impersonal union with the divine, whatever that may be.

But all false views of man are refuted by a biblical anthropology that reveals man to be a direct creation of a personal God who designed man with dignity and purpose to serve God. To know what to do, we must know who we are. This is the benefit of a Scripture-based doctrine of man.

Since humanity consists of both male and female, is it appropriate to use the term *man* to refer to humanity? The Hebrew term translated "man" in the Bible, *'adam*, is used for both mankind in general and man as a male distinct from a woman. The universal sense of *'adam* is found in Genesis 1:27 and 5:1–2:

> So God created man [*'adam*] in his own image,
> > in the image of God he created him;
> > male and female he created them. (Gen. 1:27)

> This is the book of the generations of Adam [*'adam*]. When God created man [*'adam*], he made him in the likeness of God. Male and female he created them, and he blessed them and named them Man [*'adam*] when they were created. (Gen. 5:1–2)

In both passages *'adam* (or "man") includes male and female. Yet *'adam* (or "man") is also used of the male as distinct from the female, as the following two examples reveal:

> And the rib that the Lord God had taken from the man [*'adam*] he made into a woman and brought her to the man [*'adam*]. (Gen. 2:22)

> And the man [*'adam*] and his wife were both naked and were not ashamed. (Gen. 2:25)

So there is scriptural support for using *man* for mankind. Some think that using *man* reflects a negative bias against women and that therefore only terms like *humanity* or *humankind* should be used. These terms certainly can be used to describe humanity, but *man* has long been an appropriate term for humanity and should not be avoided. The use of *man* for all humanity is also consistent with the concept of male headship in the family and male leadership in the church. In both 1 Corinthians 11:2–16 and 1 Timothy 2:8–15, Paul used creation truths to emphasize functional distinctions between men and women in the church. This chapter will use terms like *humanity*, *humankind*, and *persons* to refer to mankind in general, but *man* in its broader meaning is also appropriate and will be used.[2]

Sudden Creationism[3]

The origin of the physical universe has emerged as one of the most significant biblical battlegrounds in the twenty-first century. Secular and Christian communities both debate the veracity of the creation accounts in Genesis 1–2. Even many Christians seriously question the biblical record and strongly prefer scientific conclusions over the testimony of Scripture. Today, only a minority of theologians hold to *sudden creationism*, the view that the creative process described in Genesis 1 occurred in six literal and consecutive days. Many assert that the universe is millions or even billions of years old and that a long interval existed between the origin of the earth and the first human beings.

A full discussion of the various creation views is beyond the purpose of this chapter, but the position presented here is sudden creationism.[4] This is the view of Scripture and the context for understanding the creation of man on day six. Key truths, including the greatness and power of God, are lost when one abandons the plain sense of Genesis 1 and 2 that the earth was created directly by God in six literal days.

The creation of the universe was not a long process, nor was the creation of man. The power and glory of God were manifested in a sudden creation, which included both earth and man. Specific statements about God's power in creation occur throughout Scripture:

> You are the Lord, you alone. You have made heaven, the heaven of heavens, with all their host, the earth and all that is on it, the seas and all that is in them; and you preserve all of them; and the host of heaven worships you. (Neh. 9:6)

> Thus says the Lord, your Redeemer,
>   who formed you from the womb:
> "I am the Lord, who made all things,
>   who alone stretched out the heavens,
>   who spread out the earth by myself." (Isa. 44:24)

> Ah, Lord God! It is you who have made the heavens and the earth by your great power and by your outstretched arm! Nothing is too hard for you. (Jer. 32:17)

> Men, why are you doing these things? We also are men, of like nature with you, and we bring you good news, that you should turn from these vain things to a living God, who made the heaven and the earth and the sea and all that is in them. (Acts 14:15)

---

2. See Wayne Grudem, *Systematic Theology: An Introduction to Biblical Doctrine* (Grand Rapids, MI: Zondervan, 1994), 439–40.

3. This section is adapted from Richard Mayhue, "Editorial: Scripture on Creation," *MSJ* 23, no. 1 (2012): 1–6. Used by permission of *MSJ*.

4. For more on this view, see "Creation" in chap. 3, "God the Father" (p. 213).

You, Lord, laid the foundation of the earth in the beginning, and the heavens are the work of your hands. (Heb. 1:10)

Worthy are you, our Lord and God,
> to receive glory and honor and power,
for you created all things,
> and by your will they existed and were created. (Rev. 4:11)

In addition to these strong affirmations that God created the universe, the Bible also makes definitive assertions concerning the nature of the creation. To illustrate how the fourth commandment of Sabbath rest should be celebrated, God, through Moses, referred to creation as the model:

Remember the Sabbath day, to keep it holy. Six days you shall labor, and do all your work, but the seventh day is a Sabbath to the LORD your God. On it you shall not do any work, you, or your son, or your daughter, your male servant, or your female servant, or your livestock, or the sojourner who is within your gates. For in six days the LORD made heaven and earth, the sea, and all that is in them, and rested on the seventh day. Therefore the LORD blessed the Sabbath day and made it holy. (Ex. 20:8–11)

Man is to labor for six days because God made the heaven and the earth in six days. Since the days of work were measured in twenty-four-hour segments, the periods for creation that served as the prototype also had to be of equal duration. The same logic also applies to the seventh day of rest. Unless days of equal length were intended, the illustration would be meaningless.

The writer of Hebrews addressed how the world came to exist: "By faith we understand that the universe was created by the word of God, so that what is seen was not made out of things that are visible" (Heb. 11:3). God spoke the universe into existence (Ps. 33:6, 9). He did not use preexisting matter (Rom. 4:17). Nor is matter eternal. Creation was *ex nihilo*—the material and spiritual creation came into being from nothing.

The majesty of creation reflects God's power, glory, and dominion: "The heavens declare the glory of God, and the sky above proclaims his handiwork" (Ps. 19:1). No mechanistic process of evolution could point to the greatness and power of God. Only sudden creationism testifies to God's power from the start. Paul declared, "For [God's] invisible attributes, namely, his eternal power and divine nature, have been clearly perceived, ever since the creation of the world, in the things that have been made. So they are without excuse" (Rom. 1:20).

A sudden, divine act of creation is supported by the truth that man was created in the image of God (Gen. 1:26). Humans could not have evolved into the image of God, because there is no time gap between man's creation and man being made in the likeness of God. Thus Genesis 5:1 records, "This is the book of the generations of Adam. When God created man, he made him in the likeness of God." God, in a moment of time, created man in his image. Evolutionary process cannot account for man's unique nature or for the fact that mankind was infected by sin. God sent his Son to redeem mankind, not the multitudes of other life forms.

Evidence for sudden creationism is also found with Jesus Christ. Jesus was directly involved in creation himself: "All things were made through him [Jesus], and without him was not any thing made that was made" (John 1:3). Also, "For by him all things were created, in heaven and on earth, visible and invisible, whether thrones or dominions or rulers or authorities—all things were created through him and for him" (Col. 1:16). Most alternative explanations of creation require a significant interval between the creation of matter and the origin of man. Yet Jesus said, "But from the beginning of creation, 'God made them male and female'" (Mark 10:6). Jesus claimed that man was a part of the creation from the beginning and not a subsequent development.

Jesus's creative miracles also speak to this issue. Jesus created wine out of water (John 2:1–11), and twice he created food to feed thousands (Matt. 14:13–21; 15:34–39). These miracles occurred immediately, apart from any process or passing of time.

Evidence for sudden creationism can also be gleaned by looking at the coming glorification of believers. In a moment God will resurrect and glorify the bodies of his people (Dan. 12:2; John 5:29; Rom. 8:23; 1 Cor. 15:51; 1 Thess. 4:16–17). They will be instantly re-created from the dust of the earth. This is like a repeat of the creation of Adam, only this time, not just one body will be re-created but millions. Since multitudes will be given re-created bodies in the resurrection, how easy must it have been for God to create just Adam and Eve in the beginning?

In addition, what God will do to this earth at the end of its existence is evidence for sudden creationism. In a rapid exertion of divine power, God will destroy the present cursed earth and universe in a fiery atomic implosion. In its place he will create a "new heavens and a new earth" (2 Pet. 3:10–13). The new will not evolve from the old. In a rapid exertion of divine power, God will quickly and powerfully destroy and create, ushering in the final age. If he will suddenly create the new universe out of nothing, it is reasonable to hold that God initiated the present one in the same manner.

Genesis 1–2 also contains support for God creating the earth in a short period of time. First, the term translated "day" (Heb. *yom*) in Genesis 1 refers to either the period of light within a twenty-four-hour cycle or the entire period of both darkness and light (twenty-four hours). The one exception is Genesis 2:4, where "day" refers to the entire period of creation.

Second, the Hebrew word for "day" (*yom*) when accompanied by a numerical adjective such as "third" or "fourth" (i.e., an ordinal) is never used figuratively. It is always a twenty-four-hour period. In addition, the Hebrew plural for "day" is never used figuratively in the Old Testament outside a creation context (e.g., Ex. 20:9).

Third, the terms "evening" and "morning" in Genesis 1 are never used figuratively in the Old Testament. They always describe a twenty-four-hour day. God defines "day" in Genesis 1:5 as a period of light and then darkness. After creating light (Gen. 1:3) and causing a spatial separation between the darkness and the light with respect to earth (Gen. 1:5), God established the cycle of light and darkness as a principle measurement of time—one day (Gen. 1:5). This cycle is one full earth rotation or a twenty-four-hour day.

Together these points show that God created the earth and everything in it in six consecutive twenty-four-hour days. The human species did not evolve from lower life forms but was created by divine fiat through the exertion of God's divine will from lifeless dust (Gen. 2:7; 3:19; Eccles. 3:20; 12:7). Further, the female did not evolve from the male but was personally and immediately fashioned by God (Gen. 2:21–23; 1 Cor. 11:8, 12). When woman (which would constitute a mutation in any other system of origins) came from man, there were no major time gaps to allow for her to "develop." Because male and female came into being in a close time sequence, this demands God's creative power as proposed by the sudden creationism model.

As a capstone point, the New Testament witness to Genesis 1–2 confirms the testimony from the Old Testament. The New Testament directly quotes or alludes to Genesis 1–2 more than thirty times. In each instance, the New Testament writers understood the Genesis text in a normal, nonsymbolic, and nonfigurative sense (e.g., Matt. 19:4; Rom. 5:12; 1 Cor. 15:38; 2 Cor. 4:6; Col. 3:10; 1 Tim. 2:13; 2 Pet. 3:5).[5]

Adam as a Historical Person

Another issue of debate concerns whether or not Adam in Genesis was a real person. The church has historically affirmed that Adam was a historical man, yet with the acceptance of evolutionary science, some now claim that this is not the case. Those who believe that the earth is millions or billions of years old will not accept that God fully formed the human Adam a few days after creating the universe. However, Genesis presents Adam as a real historical man, not the result of eons of evolution.

The simplest and most natural interpretation of Genesis 1 declares that God created the specific person Adam on the sixth day of creation. Genesis 2 then offers more detail on the creation of Adam and Eve. Adam's connection with other historical persons supports the claim that he was indeed a specific person. Adam is the father of Cain, Abel, and Seth (Gen. 4:1–2, 25; 5:1–3). Adam is also said to have had conjugal relations with his wife Eve to bear Cain and Seth, and Genesis 5:3 further states that Adam fathered Seth at age 130. These details cannot be legitimately identified as poetic or figurative language describing something other than reality.

The long list of Adam's descendants who lived and died until Noah in Genesis 5 confirms that Adam is a specific historical person. So Genesis 5:1 explicitly declares, "This is the book of the generations of Adam." Adam is real, just like those who descended from him are actual persons. Not only is Adam's creation mentioned, so too is his death. Adam died at age 930 (Gen. 5:5).

The theology of seed in Genesis affirms a literal Adam. The Hebrew term for "seed," *zera*, is used six times in Genesis 1, all concerning vegetation. The presence

---

5. For a more thorough biblical defense of a young earth and of literal six-day creationism, see Terry Mortenson and Thane H. Ury, eds., *Coming to Grips with Genesis: Biblical Authority and the Age of the Earth* (Green Forest, AZ: Master Books, 2008).

of seed means each plant and tree will produce other vegetation after its kind. In Genesis 3:15, God promises that a coming "seed of the woman" (NASB) will eventually defeat the power behind the serpent (Satan). The rest of Genesis develops the seed theme as God unfolds his plans to save and restore mankind. Noah, Shem, Abraham, Isaac, and then Jacob are part of God's seed plan. They are the offspring of Adam, and just as they are real persons, so too is Adam, their ancestor. Also, one should not accept the historicity of Genesis 12–50—including Abraham, Isaac, and Jacob—and then disconnect this section historically from the persons in Genesis 1–11. The promised seed line of Genesis 3:15 and its relation to all of Genesis does not allow this separation.

The New Testament writers also affirm Adam as a historical figure. Jesus's genealogy in Luke includes Adam (3:38). This is consistent with 1 Chronicles 1:1, which also includes Adam in its genealogy. The apostle Paul clearly believed in a literal Adam. In Romans 5:12 and 14, Paul states, "Sin came into the world through one man [Adam]," and "death reigned from Adam to Moses, even over those whose sinning was not like the transgression of Adam." Paul treats Adam as a person, just as he treats Moses as a person. Further, in Romans 5:12–21, Paul makes several comparisons between Adam and Jesus, showing that both are literal heads of humanity who bring certain consequences for mankind. The man Adam brings death, guilt, and condemnation to all who are in him (i.e., all who possess human life, with the exception of the Lord Jesus), while the man Christ Jesus brings life, righteousness, and justification to all who are granted spiritual life through their faith-union with him. If Adam is not a person, then the comparison collapses, including Jesus's role as the One who represents mankind as Savior. Rejecting the historicity of Adam truly undermines the gospel itself.

In similar fashion, Paul contrasts Adam and Jesus several times in 1 Corinthians 15:

> For as in Adam all die, so also in Christ shall all be made alive. (1 Cor. 15:22)

> Thus it is written, "The first man Adam became a living being"; the last Adam became a life-giving spirit. (1 Cor. 15:45)

> The first man [Adam] was from the earth, a man of dust; the second man [Jesus] is from heaven. (1 Cor. 15:47)

> Just as we have borne the image of the man of dust, we shall also bear the image of the man of heaven. (1 Cor. 15:49)

Paul's point is that just as we humans bear the image of Adam, so with the coming glorification we will bear the image of Jesus. The comparison assumes that both Adam and Jesus are historical persons who represent humanity. Jesus as a person can only be a "last Adam" if Adam was also a real human being. Further, in 1 Timothy 2:13, Paul makes an argument for functional distinctions between men and women in the church because "Adam was formed first, then Eve." His point would make no sense if Adam were merely a symbolic figure.

The historicity of Adam is not a trivial matter. A literal Adam is foundational for understanding the origin and history of the human race, the nature of humanity, the origin of sin, the beginning of human and animal death, the need for salvation, the basis for historical events in Genesis, the reason for functional order within the church, and even the future existence of mankind.[6]

Created in God's Image

Man Created Directly by God
Man as Image of God (*Imago Dei*)
Jesus as Image of God
The Bible's Storyline and the Image of God

Man Created Directly by God

Man's existence is wholly a result of divine creation. Such recognition leads to a biblical anthropology that addresses three aspects of man's existence: (1) man's ontology or essence, (2) man's relationships, and (3) man's function.

Genesis 1:1 declares, "In the beginning, God created the heavens and the earth." God is the eternal transcendent cause of everything. In six literal twenty-four-hour days, God made all things material and immaterial (see Col. 1:16). Genesis 1 is structured to highlight the creation of man on day six. Being created last highlights man's significance. Also, for the first five days and the beginning of day six, the phrases "Let there be . . ." or "Let there . . ." are used to describe God's creative acts (Gen. 1:3, 6, 9, 11, 14, 20, 24). Yet with the creation of man, a different phrase is used: "Let us make man . . ." (Gen. 1:26). This shift stresses that man is unique within God's creation. In addition, the word "then" in Genesis 1:26—"*Then* God said, 'Let us make man . . .'"—marks the creation of man as special.

The purpose of man is also highlighted in Genesis 1–2. Only passing reference is made to the creation of the sun, moon, stars, plants, and living creatures in Genesis 1. Yet Genesis 2 is wholly devoted to the creation of mankind, including how the first man and woman were made. Also, various terms such as "make"/"made," "create," and "form" emphasize God's active involvement in the creation of man:

1. "Make"/"Made" (Heb. *'asah*)

Then God said, "Let us *make* man." (Gen. 1:26)

And God saw everything that he had *made*. (Gen. 1:31)

Then the Lord God said, "It is not good that the man should be alone; I will *make* him a helper fit for him." (Gen. 2:18)

This is the book of the generations of Adam. When God created man, he *made* him in the likeness of God. (Gen. 5:1)

---

6. For a further defense of the historicity of Adam, see William D. Barrick, "A Historical Adam: Young-Earth Creation View," in *Four Views on the Historical Adam*, ed. Matthew Barrett and Ardel B. Caneday, Counterpoints: Bible and Theology (Grand Rapids, MI: Zondervan, 2013), 197–227.

So the LORD said, "I will blot out man whom I have created from the face of the land, man and animals and creeping things and birds of the heavens, for I am sorry that I have *made* them." (Gen. 6:7)

2. "Create" (Heb. *bara'*)

So God *created* man in his own image,
  in the image of God he *created* him;
  male and female he *created* them. (Gen. 1:27)

This is the book of the generations of Adam. When God *created* man, he made him in the likeness of God. Male and female he *created* them, and he blessed them and named them Man when they were *created*. (Gen. 5:1–2)

3. "Formed" (Heb. *yatsar*)

Then the LORD God *formed* the man of dust from the ground. (Gen. 2:7)

And the LORD God planted a garden in Eden, in the east, and there he put the man whom he had *formed*. (Gen. 2:8)

God's direct creation of man is affirmed throughout Scripture. Psalm 100:3 states, "Know that the LORD, he is God! It is he who made us, and we are his." Jesus said, "Have you not read that he who created them from the beginning [i.e., God] made them male and female?" (Matt. 19:4). James referred to "people who are made in the likeness of God" (James 3:9).

Man's creation by God carries significant implications. First, humans do not exist in a vacuum. The precondition for man is God, and man can only be understood from the starting point of the Creator. While addressing pagan philosophers at Athens, Paul started with creation, namely, "the God who made the world and everything in it" (Acts 17:24). He then said that people only exist and function because of God: "In him we live and move and have our being" (Acts 17:28). The only reason we are alive is because God exists, created us, and sustains our lives. Some people try to imagine that there is no God, but in reality, there would be no act of imagining and no people to do the imagining if God did not exist. Something cannot come from nothing. No one times nothing does not equal everything. Persons do not come from the impersonal. To imagine no heaven and no God is to imagine nothing at all. God is the precondition for everything.

Second, direct creation means that man is not God. Man is neither divine nor the highest being in existence. A metaphysical or ontological gap exists between God and man. Man can never be God, nor should he seek to be God. The Mormon leader Lorenzo Snow stated, "As man now is, God once was; as God now is, man may be."[7] This is false. God was never man (Christ's incarnation as the God-man being the one unique exception), and man can never be God. Hosea 11:9 declares,

---

7. The Church of Jesus Christ of Latter-Day Saints, "The Grand Destiny of the Faithful," chap. 5 in *Teachings of Presidents of the Church: Lorenzo Snow*, accessed April 8, 2016, https://www.lds.org/manual/teachings-of-presidents-of -the-church-lorenzo-snow/chapter-5-the-grand-destiny-of-the-faithful?lang=eng.

"For I am God and not a man, the Holy One in your midst." Creatures will always be under the eternal Creator who made them.

Third, as a creature, man is obligated to submit to God. Man is not free to do whatever he desires, as if his actions have no consequences with God (cf. Eccles. 11:9). Everything man does must be viewed in light of God's will for him. According to Romans 1, the primary problem with fallen man is that he acts independently from his Creator. He does not give God glory, and he serves creatures rather than the Creator. Paul said that unbelieving people "exchanged the truth about God for a lie and worshiped and served the creature rather than the Creator" (Rom. 1:25).

To show that people cannot act independently of God, Jesus told the parable of the foolish rich man, who lived for himself only to find that God would hold him accountable that night: "But God said to him, 'Fool! This night your soul is required of you, and the things you have prepared, whose will they be?'" (Luke 12:20). People often act independently and convince themselves that they can live apart from and in defiance of God, but without repentance and saving faith they are accumulating wrath for themselves. Paul warns people not to take God's patience and kindness lightly (Rom. 2:4), since doing so means "you are storing up wrath for yourself on the day of wrath when God's righteous judgment will be revealed" (Rom. 2:5). Even with perfect conditions on the coming new earth, the people of God will serve God; they do not become God. Revelation 22:3 states, "The throne of God and of the Lamb will be in it [the New Jerusalem], and his servants will worship him." Even in the paradise of eternity, sinless human beings will joyfully serve and worship God.

Fourth, man has a unique role in God's creation. Genesis 1:26–28 reveals that man is called to multiply, to fill the earth, and to subdue it. The psalmist declared, "The heavens are the LORD's heavens, but the earth he has given to the children of man" (Ps. 115:16). Even in eternity, man will reign forever on the new earth (see Rev. 21:1; 22:5).

Fifth, man was created to give God glory. Isaiah 43:6–7 describes God calling his "sons" and "daughters" to come to him, "everyone who is called by my name, whom I created for my glory, whom I formed and made." Here God says that his people are created for his glory. Paul declares that Christians have been "predestined according to the purpose of him who works all things according to the counsel of his will" (Eph. 1:11). Everything man does should be for the glory of God (1 Cor. 10:31).

Man as Image of God (*Imago Dei*)

Understanding mankind involves grasping the fact that man is God's "image" and "likeness." As Beck and Demarest state, "The implications of human persons created in the image of God are immense for theology, psychology, ministry, and Christian living. Ramifications of the *imago* embrace issues of human dignity and value, personal and social ethics, relations between the sexes, the solidarity of the human family . . .

and racial justice."[8] Passages that explicitly refer to the "image" (Heb. *tselem*) or "likeness" (Heb. *demuth*) of God include the following:

> Then God said, "Let us make man in *our image*, after *our likeness*." (Gen. 1:26)

> God created man in *his own image*,
>   in the *image of God* he created him;
>   male and female he created them. (Gen. 1:27)

> This is the book of the generations of Adam. In the day when God created man, he made him in the *likeness of God*. Male and female he created them, and he blessed them and named them Man in the day when they were created. (Gen. 5:1–2)

> Whoever sheds the blood of man,
>   by man shall his blood be shed,
> for God made man in *his own image*. (Gen. 9:6)

> For a man ought not to cover his head, since he is the *image* and glory *of God*. (1 Cor. 11:7)

> With it [the tongue] we bless our Lord and Father, and with it we curse men, who have been made in the *likeness of God*. (James 3:9 NASB)

The Hebrew term for "image" signifies a "copy" but also carries the idea of "representation." In the ancient world, a king or ruler would place an image or idol of himself in his realm to symbolize his sovereignty there. When others saw the image, they knew who had control. Likewise, God's image bearers represent God in the world. But unlike lifeless statues, God's image bearers are alive. They should operate as God's representatives and mediators on the earth. Thus, "image" has implications for kingship. While God is *the* King, God created man as *a* king, a vice-regent and mediator over the creation on God's behalf.

Complementing this word, the Hebrew term for "likeness" (*demuth*) can refer to "pattern," "shape," or "form." It signifies something patterned after an original. Its use in Genesis 1:26 indicates that man is patterned after God; he is a son of God. This understanding is supported by Genesis 5:3, which reveals that Seth was a son in the "likeness" of his father, Adam. To join these two meanings together, we can conclude that because he is a son of God, man may function as God's representative.

IMPLICATIONS OF HUMANS BEING MADE IN GOD'S IMAGE

Though human beings are not divine, the fact that they are created in the "image" and "likeness" of God carries significant truths. First, the image of God is affirmed for all persons—male and female alike. Genesis 1:27 states, "So God created man in his own image, in the image of God he created him; male and female he created them." While distinct genders, both male and female are equal as persons and equal in value.

---

8. James R. Beck and Bruce Demarest, *The Human Person in Theology and Psychology: A Biblical Anthropology for the Twenty-First Century* (Grand Rapids, MI: Kregel, 2005), 131.

Second, even after the fall (see Genesis 3) all people still possess the image and likeness of God. This is affirmed in Genesis 5:1–3 for both male and female and for the offspring of Adam and Eve:

> This is the book of the generations of Adam. When God created man, he made him in the likeness of God. Male and female he created them, and he blessed them and named them Man when they were created. When Adam had lived 130 years, he fathered a son in his own likeness, after his image, and named him Seth.

Genesis 9:6 says that capital punishment is the appropriate penalty for murder since man is still the image of God: "Whoever sheds the blood of man, by man shall his blood be shed, for God made man in his own image." After the flood humans are still the image of God. Similarly, James 3:9 condemns cursing people since they are "made in the likeness of God." This also affirms that people after the fall still bear something of God's likeness. God's image bearers were certainly marred with the curse, but the image and likeness of God, though distorted, was not obliterated.

Third, the image of God explains mankind's need to live in relationship with others. The triune God is three persons in one: Father, Son, and Holy Spirit. This is the foundational definition of the essential nature of God. For all eternity, the members of the Trinity have enjoyed perfect, personal communion with one another. If God were simply a solitary, unipersonal being—like false gods—he could not be eternally loving, because prior to creation there would have been no one to love. But God is love, and that love was perfectly expressed in eternity past within the Trinity (John 5:20; 17:24, 26).

The love of God is also directed toward his creation. God loves the world (John 3:16) and especially his own children (John 13:1; 15:9; 16:27; 17:23, 26; Rom. 5:5), who are empowered by him to love their enemies (Matt. 5:42–48), fellow believers (John 13:34–35; 15:12–13), and God himself (John 14:21–24). Thus, man is designed in the image of God as a relational being, who is not only able to relate to other people and to God in a loving way but is also required to do so in order to experience fulfillment (Gen. 2:18, 22–24).

Fourth, the image of God is connected with man's task to "rule" and "subdue" the earth on God's behalf. Immediately after declaring that man is made in God's image and likeness, God says, "Let them have dominion over the fish of the sea and over the birds of the heavens and over the livestock and over all the earth and over every creeping thing that creeps on the earth" (Gen. 1:26). Then God says, "Be fruitful and multiply, and fill the earth, and subdue it; and rule over the fish of the sea and over the birds of the sky and over every living thing that moves on the earth" (Gen. 1:28, NASB). The Hebrew term for "rule," used twice in Genesis 1:26–28, is *radah* and means "have dominion," "rule," or "dominate."[9] Later, in Psalm 110:2, the term refers to the Messiah's future rule: "The LORD sends forth from Zion your mighty scepter. Rule [*radah*] in the midst of your enemies." Also, the Hebrew word

---

9. See Francis Brown, S. R. Driver, and Charles A. Briggs, *A Hebrew and English Lexicon of the Old Testament* (Oxford: Clarendon, 1962), 921.

translated "subdue" in Genesis 1:28 is *kabash*, which means "bring into bondage," even by forceful means. The term is used in 2 Samuel 8:11 concerning King David's subduing of nations.

Both "rule" and "subdue" are linked to kingly authority and show, as Eugene Merrill observes, that "man is created to reign in a manner that demonstrates his lordship, his domination (by force if necessary) over all creation."[10] This authority is seen in man's naming of the animals, a demonstration of dominion (see Gen. 2:19–20). Thus, there is a royal and kingly aspect to man being in the image of God.

This authority to rule over creation is not the sole possession of Adam and Eve. God says, "Let them have dominion" (Gen. 1:26). The plural "them" could refer specifically to Adam and Eve, but such a limitation is unlikely. Since Adam and Eve were to multiply and fill the earth, "them" probably includes all mankind coming from Adam. Mankind as a whole, through Adam, was given authority to rule and subdue God's creation.

Man's right to rule the creation is affirmed in Psalm 8:4–8:

> What is man that You take thought of him,
>   And the son of man that You care for him?
> Yet You have made him a little lower than God,
>   And You crown him with glory and majesty!
> You make him to rule over the works of Your hands;
>   You have put all things under his feet,
> All sheep and oxen,
>   And also the beasts of the field,
> The birds of the heavens and the fish of the sea,
>   Whatever passes through the paths of the seas. (NASB)

Hebrews 2:5–9 states that in "the world to come," mankind will rule over the earth. Humanity will do so through the ultimate man—Jesus the Messiah, who will also share his reign with those united to him (see 1 Cor. 15:27; Rev. 5:10). Man is God's image bearer who functions as a mediator-king on earth. God tasks man to manage the world as his representatives.

HOW IS MAN THE IMAGE OF GOD?

Three views have been offered in answer to the question of how exactly man is God's image: substantive, functional, and relational. First, the substantive view says that the image of God is inherently structural to man. It is a characteristic within the makeup of man. The image is part of man, not just something he does. Some have asserted that the image is the physical body of man or some physical characteristic like walking upright. Some say that the image is a psychological or spiritual quality, such as reason, memory, will, or moral capacity.

Second, the functional view asserts that the image of God is something humans

---

10. Eugene H. Merrill, "A Theology of the Pentateuch," in *A Biblical Theology of the Old Testament*, ed. Roy B. Zuck (Chicago: Moody Press, 1991), 15.

do. Since Genesis 1:26–28 links the image with ruling and subduing the earth, some believe that the image is man's dominion over creation. German Protestant theologian Hans Walter Wolff (1911–1993) stated, "It is precisely in his function as ruler that he [man] is God's image."[11]

Third, the relational view claims that relationship is the image of God. Summarizing this view, Millard Erickson writes, "Humans can be said to be in the image or to display the image [of God] when standing in a particular relationship, which indeed is the image."[12] This perspective was popular with neoorthodox and existential theologians. Support for the relational view is found in the way that the image of God is closely connected with man being created male and female (Gen. 1:27). Since the concept of relationship is central to man's connection with God and people, the image is viewed as man being in relationship.

So which position is correct? All three views are closely connected to the image of God, and truth can be gleaned from each of them. The best view, however, is that the image of God is substantive or structural to man. Function and relationship are the *consequences* of man being the image of God structurally. This view acknowledges the importance of function and relationship, yet it casts structure as the basis for accomplishing function and relationship. Since man is the image of God, he is able to exercise dominion and experience relationships. According to Genesis 1:26–28, man is made in God's image (Gen. 1:26a), and *then* he is tasked with ruling and subduing the earth and being in relationship (Gen. 1:26b–28).

What is this structure that makes man the image of God? It is best not to narrow the structure to any one characteristic or quality. The image permeates man's being. The structure probably consists of the complex qualities and attributes of man that make him human. This includes his physical and spiritual components. The image could also be linked to personhood and personality and to the powers to relate and operate. It could be connected with thinking and reasoning. Grudem may be closest when he says, "Every way in which man is like God is part of his being in the image and likeness of God."[13] All that makes one a human person is related to the image of God. The following characteristics help to further define man as an image bearer:

Ontologically, man is a living, personal, self-conscious, active being with personality. He is a complex unity of soul/spirit and body. While God is spirit (John 4:24) and grants a spirit to man, the bodily component of man is related to the image of God. Robert Culver notes, "There is something about the human body which is analogous to something in the Godhead. . . . It is apparent that while the human body, *per se*, is in no respect an image of the God of the Bible, all of man's physical nature was originally created to bear that image."[14]

Volitionally, man has a will and the ability to select between various choices. He

---

11. Hans Walter Wolff, *Anthropology of the Old Testament* (Philadelphia, PA: Fortress, 1974), 160–61.
12. Millard J. Erickson, *Christian Theology*, 2nd ed. (Grand Rapids, MI: Baker, 2006), 524.
13. Grudem, *Systematic Theology*, 444.
14. Robert Duncan Culver, *Systematic Theology: Biblical and Historical* (Fearn, Ross-shire, Scotland: Mentor, 2005), 251–52.

can discern right from wrong. This volitional aspect separates man from the animals and other creatures mentioned in Genesis 1–2.

Intellectually, man has a rational mind. He is aware of himself, his environment, others, and God. He can think critically and logically. He possesses memory, imagination, creativity, and language skills for communicating and understanding the thoughts of others.

Emotionally, a human experiences a wide range of emotions and feelings, such as fear, anger, guilt, anxiety, regret, shame, happiness, and joy. He can both laugh and cry. Also, human emotionality is complex, as people can experience two or more emotions almost simultaneously. For example, parents can feel sadness, pride, nervousness, and happiness when their daughter moves out of town for college.

Relationally, man is equipped to participate in relationships with God and with other people. Jesus said that the greatest commandments are to love God and to love others (Matt. 22:36–40). Only persons can give and receive love.

Functionally, man has what he needs to fill, rule, and subdue the earth on God's behalf for God's glory. Males and females have bodies able to reproduce and interact with a physical environment. Humanity possesses the ingenuity to implement a successful strategy for the earth.

While not God himself, man reflects the image and likeness of God in wonderful, complex, and mysterious ways.

Jesus as Image of God

The best way to understand the image of God is to look at the Lord Jesus, in whom it is perfectly revealed. Paul refers to Jesus as the "last Adam" (1 Cor. 15:45), connecting Jesus with humankind. He also says, "He [Jesus] is the image of the invisible God" (Col. 1:15). The Greek term for "image" is *eikōn* and compares to the Hebrew term for image, *tselem*. It conveys both "representation" and "manifestation." God is spirit and is thus invisible, but Jesus as the God-man is the image of the invisible God.

In addition, Hebrews 1:3 declares, "He [Jesus] is the radiance of the glory of God and the exact imprint of his nature." The Greek term for "imprint," *charaktēr*, refers to a "stamp" or "impress" made on a coin or stamp. So Jesus as the last Adam is the perfect imprint or stamp of God. When we look at Jesus, we see everything God intended for man. Jesus said, "Whoever has seen me has seen the Father" (John 14:9).

Jesus fully manifested the divine image in three connections: with God, with people, and with creation. In doing so, Jesus shows humanity how to manifest the image properly. First, Jesus manifested the foundational nature of the triune God by his relationship to the Holy Spirit and by his fellowship with the Father. He loved and perfectly obeyed the Father in the power of the Holy Spirit. Second, Jesus loved people. He loved those who hated him. And John 13:1 says of Jesus, "Having loved his own who were in the world, he loved them to the end." The phrase "to the end" translates the Greek phrase *eis telos*, meaning "infinitely" or "eternally" (cf. John 17:23). The greatest command for man is to love God and to love people (Matt. 22:36–40). Jesus exhibited perfect love for both. And third, Jesus displayed mastery over creation with his miracles and healings. When he walked on water, multiplied bread and fish, or calmed a storm, Jesus showed absolute control over nature, a dominion that will be fully manifested in his coming millennial kingdom on the earth (Isaiah 11; 35).

The Lord Jesus made God's image visible. God is calling and saving sinners to be conformed and transformed into the image of his Son. Paul says, "For those whom he [God] foreknew he also predestined to be conformed to the image of his Son" (Rom. 8:29). He also states, "And we all, with unveiled face, beholding the glory of the Lord, are being transformed into the same image from one degree of glory to another" (2 Cor. 3:18). God is at work in believers to make them more like his Son. Consequently, they increasingly evidence what the image of God is to be. Growing more like Christ in sanctification is manifesting the image of God. The image of God is not some mysterious, abstract doctrine. Jesus is the image of God in action and the model to follow.

When Christians are glorified at Jesus's return, the transformative process will be complete. As 1 John 3:2 says, "Beloved, we are God's children now, and what we will be has not yet appeared; but we know that when he appears we shall be like him, because we shall see him as he is." In discussing the coming resurrection, Paul declared, "Just as we have borne the image of the man of dust [Adam], we shall also bear the image of the man of heaven" (1 Cor. 15:49). Before Jesus comes, we are being transformed into Christ's image, but at his coming, in a moment, we will be like him.

The Bible's Storyline and the Image of God

The image of God relates to the Bible's storyline in the following ways:

Creation: Man, including both male and female, is created in the image of God. Like his Creator, man evidences both unity and diversity in a relationship of love. "Man" comprises both male and female, yet male and female are distinct in gender and have differing roles. At creation man functioned in proper relationships with God, other humans, and creation.

Fall: Man violated the Creator/creature distinction by acting autonomously and rebelling against God. The image of God became marred but not lost. Man's threefold relationships suffered: (1) in regard to God, man is spiritually dead; (2) in regard to humans, tension plagues men and women, and women must suffer pain in childbirth; (3) in regard to creation, the earth now works against man and frustrates him, and the earth will swallow up man in death.

Incarnation (Jesus Christ): Jesus, the God-man, is the perfect image of God. He manifests the image exactly by perfectly loving God, loving people, and exercising authority over nature. Those who belong to Jesus through saving faith become new creatures, and by their love they display the restored image of God, although imperfectly before the final resurrection. Sanctification is the process by which Christians are being conformed to the image of Christ, who himself is the perfect image of God.

Restoration: When Jesus returns, Christians will be glorified and made like Jesus. They will perfectly exhibit the image of God forever.

The Human Constitution

Body
Soul
Spirit
Heart
Conscience
Three Views of the Human Constitution

Various terms are used to refer to human persons in Scripture. Five of the more common terms include *body, soul, spirit, heart,* and *conscience.* It is helpful to examine each of these.

Body

Man's constitution includes a physical component. According to Genesis 2:7, "The LORD God formed the man of dust from the ground." A link exists between earth and man. Man comes from the ground. Just as the creation is material, God's image bearers possess a material element, often called a "body."

In the Old Testament, two primary Hebrew terms refer to "body." *Gewiyyah* occurs twelve times for a living body (Gen. 47:18; Neh. 9:37) or a dead carcass (1 Sam. 31:10, 12). *Basar,* often translated "flesh," occurs 266 times. It refers to (1) a blood relative (Gen. 29:14; 2 Sam. 5:1); (2) humanity collectively (Gen. 6:12–13; Job 34:15); (3) every living thing (Gen. 9:15–17); (4) the material substance of the body (Gen. 2:23; 17:14; Job 19:26); (5) the whole person (Lev. 17:11; Pss. 16:9; 63:1; Eccles. 4:5); and (6) the person as weak, dependent, and temporary (Gen. 6:3; 2 Chron. 32:8; Ps. 78:39; Isa. 40:6).

In the New Testament, the Greek word for "body" is *sōma.* It can refer to (1) the physical body (Mark 5:29; Rom. 8:11; Gal. 6:17; James 2:16); (2) the whole person (Rom. 12:1; Eph. 5:28; Phil. 1:20); and (3) the fallen, carnal nature (Rom. 6:6; 8:13; Phil. 3:21).

Genesis 1:31 states that everything God made was "very good." This includes the human body. The creation of the physical world is the context for the making of man. God gave man a physical body to rule a material world (Gen. 1:26, 28). The bodies of Christians are also the residence of the Holy Spirit. Paul asked, "Do you not know that your body is a temple of the Holy Spirit within you?" (1 Cor. 6:19). The body is so essential to being human that God will give people a resurrected body fit for their eternal dwelling (John 5:25–29; Rom. 8:23).

The goodness of the body has been rejected by many in history. Dualistic philosophical traditions connected with Plato convinced many that the human body—and in fact, all matter—is inferior. Socrates, for instance, believed that the human body was a prison for the soul. He longed for death so he could be released forever from his carnal frame. Gnosticism threatened Christianity with its overspiritualized and antimaterial views. Eastern religions like Hinduism and Buddhism teach that the human body and material realities are illusions (*maya*). Even many in Western societies today believe that heaven or the ultimate ideal is an eternal, bodiless existence.

The biblical view of the human body, however, starkly contrasts with these unbiblical philosophies. Adam's body at creation was sinless and deathless, but sin brought dramatic change to the human body. God promised death for sin, and with Adam's sin, his body experienced decay leading to death, passing its corruption to all human bodies. The current body is a "lowly body" (Phil. 3:21) and a "body of death" (Rom. 7:24). Bodily cravings and desires contribute to man's sinful state, and thus the body needs discipline (1 Cor. 9:27; 1 Tim. 4:8). It longs for redemption from corruption (Rom. 8:23). Although nonglorified bodies cannot enter God's eternal kingdom (1 Cor. 15:50), there is hope for the body. Jesus died and was raised bodily, and he is the firstfruits of the resurrection to life eternal and the guarantee that others will be raised bodily as well (1 Cor. 15:20–24).

Paul likened existence without the body to nakedness (2 Cor. 5:3). He longed for a glorified body whose source is heaven (2 Cor. 5:1–5). The church will experience resurrection of the body at the rapture (1 Thess. 4:13–18). This is a great hope for Christians who "await a Savior, the Lord Jesus Christ, who will transform our lowly body to be like his glorious body" (Phil. 3:20–21). Old Testament saints and martyred saints during the tribulation period will be resurrected at the time of Jesus's kingdom (Dan. 12:2; Rev. 20:4).

Bodily resurrection, though, is not just for believers. The wicked will be resurrected for eternal punishment (Dan. 12:2). Jesus said, "Do not marvel at this, for an hour is coming when all who are in the tombs will hear his voice and come out, those who have done good to the resurrection of life, and those who have done evil to the resurrection of judgment" (John 5:28–29). Just as righteous saints are raised, so too the wicked will rise and receive a body fit for punishment in the lake of fire (Rev. 20:11–15). In this present age, death brings a temporary separation between body and spirit (James 2:26), but with God's resurrection program, all people—believers and unbelievers—will possess a body fit either for eternal life on the new earth or for eternal separation from God in the lake of fire.

Soul

Another important aspect of man's nature is the *soul*. The Hebrew word for "soul," *nephesh*, occurs about 750 times in the Old Testament. In regard to humans, *nephesh* often refers to a person in his entirety as a living being. Genesis 2:7 states that after forming man from the dust of the ground, God "breathed into his nostrils the breath of life, and the man became a living creature [*nephesh*]." In Exodus 4:19, God told Moses, "Go back to Egypt, for all the men who were seeking your life [*nephesh*] are dead." Again, *nephesh* here is synonymous with being a person.

There are also places where *nephesh* carries the narrower sense of referring to only the immaterial part of a person. While giving birth to Benjamin, Rachel's soul left her body: "Her soul [*nephesh*] was departing (for she was dying)" (Gen. 35:18). In this example the soul is distinguished from the body since it leaves the body. Sometimes *nephesh* refers to the life principle that animates the body. Leviticus 17:11 declares, "For the life [*nephesh*] of the flesh is in the blood." It can also be linked with interior functions of the person, such as intellect, will, and emotions: "My soul [*nephesh*] continually remembers it [afflictions] and is bowed down within me" (Lam. 3:20).

The Greek New Testament word for "soul" is *psychē* and occurs around 110 times. It is translated as "soul," "life," and "I." This term denotes (1) the whole person (Acts 2:41; Rom. 13:1; 2 Cor. 12:15); (2) the essential being or seat of personal identity, often in relation to God and salvation (Matt. 10:28, 39; Luke 1:46; John 12:25); (3) the inner life of the body (Acts 20:10; Eph. 6:6); (4) the intellect (Acts 14:2; Phil. 1:27); (5) the will (Matt. 22:37; Eph. 6:6); (6) the emotions (Matt. 26:38; Mark 14:34); and (7) the moral and spiritual life (Heb. 6:19; 1 Pet. 1:22; 3 John 2).

At physical death, the soul survives and is immediately in God's presence. In the parable of the rich man, God told the foolish rich man, "This night your soul is required of you" (Luke 12:20). This rich man would die, but his soul would be in God's presence for an accounting. Similarly, in Revelation 6:9, saints killed on earth find their souls in heaven: "I saw under the altar the souls of those who had been slain for the word of God and for the witness they had borne" (Rev. 6:9). Thus, the soul returns to God at physical death.

Ultimately, all souls will be united with resurrected bodies. At Jesus's return to earth, the martyrs of Revelation 6:9–11 will be resurrected so they can reign in Jesus's kingdom on earth (Rev. 5:10). Revelation 20:4 states, "Also I saw the souls of those who had been beheaded for the testimony of Jesus and for the word of God, and those who had not worshiped the beast or its image and had not received its mark on their foreheads or their hands. They came to life and reigned with Christ for a thousand years." Souls in heaven will one day receive a physical, glorified body.

Spirit

The immaterial part of man is also referred to as "spirit." The Hebrew word for "spirit" is *ruakh* which occurs 378 times in the Old Testament. The term is used for wind (Gen. 8:1; Amos 4:13), physical breath (Job 9:18; Ps. 135:17), the Spirit of God (Pss. 51:11; 106:33; Isa. 42:1), and the life force of lower creatures (Gen. 6:17; Eccles. 3:19, 21).

In regard to human beings, *ruakh* refers to (1) the whole person (Ps. 31:5; Ezek. 21:7); (2) the vital power of life from God that animates the body (Gen. 2:7; Judg. 15:19; Job 27:3); (3) the inner life, including the seat of intellect (Gen. 41:8; Ezek. 20:32), spiritual understanding (Job 20:3; 32:8), wisdom (Ex. 28:3), will (Dan. 5:20), and emotions (1 Sam. 1:15; Prov. 15:13); and (4) the openness of the soul to God (Ps. 51:10; Isa. 26:9).[15]

---

15. See Beck and Demarest, *The Human Person*, 132.

The Greek term for "spirit" is *pneuma*. As with *ruakh*, the word *pneuma* can refer to various realities. In an anthropological sense, it connotes the life force that animates the body and departs at death (Matt. 27:50; Acts 7:59; James 2:26; Rev. 11:11). It refers to the self that interacts with God. *Pneuma* often refers to interaction with God and the spiritual realm (Rom. 1:9; 8:16; 1 Cor. 14:14; Rev. 21:10). And it is commonly used of the Holy Spirit (Gal. 5:18).

In sum, *ruakh* and *pneuma* are used in Scripture to refer to (1) wind or breath (Gen. 8:1; John 3:8), (2) an attitude or disposition (Matt. 5:3), (3) the Holy Spirit (Gen. 1:2; Matt. 1:18, 20), (4) angelic spirits (1 Sam. 16:14; Matt. 8:16; Luke 7:21), and (5) the human spirit (Gen. 41:8; Acts 17:16). The most common sense of *ruakh* in the Old Testament is "wind," while in the New Testament *pneuma* most often refers to the Holy Spirit. Concerning human beings, "spirit" often signifies the capacity of humans to be in relationship with God, and "spirit" is sometimes used interchangeably with "soul" (Ps. 31:5; Eccles. 12:7; Heb. 12:23; Luke 1:46–47).

Heart

The Bible says much about the heart—not the physical organ but the control center of a person and the seat for thoughts, attitudes, motivations, and actions. The Hebrew words for "heart" are *leb* (598 times) and *lebab* (252 times). In regard to humans, these two terms can refer to the whole person (Ps. 22:26) or to the core of the inner life (Ex. 7:3, 13; Ps. 9:1; Jer. 17:9). From the heart flow "the springs of life" (Prov. 4:23). Both good and evil thoughts stem from the heart (Gen. 6:5; 1 Kings 3:12; Job 8:10). Intentions come from the heart (Ex. 35:5; Dan. 5:20), as do emotions and passions (Deut. 19:6; 1 Sam. 1:8). Conscience is linked with the heart (1 Sam. 24:5; Job 27:6). Actions are from the heart. Isaiah 32:6 declares, "For the fool speaks folly, and his heart is busy with iniquity."

The Greek word for "heart" is *kardia*. It refers to the governing faculty of the person (Matt. 18:35; Rom. 6:17; 2 Cor. 5:12). Jesus reaffirmed the Old Testament teaching that all thoughts and deeds flow from the heart: "For out of the heart come evil thoughts, murders, adultery, sexual immorality, thefts, false witness, slanders" (Matt. 15:19). He also said, "The good man out of the good treasure of his heart brings forth what is good; and the evil man out of the evil treasure brings forth what is evil; for his mouth speaks from that which fills his heart" (Luke 6:45 NASB). The heart is also the source of the intellect: "But Jesus, knowing their thoughts, said, 'Why do you think evil in your hearts?'" (Matt. 9:4; cf. Acts 8:22).

All people are born with a dark and evil heart. God's evaluation of mankind at the global flood was this: "Every intention of the thoughts of his heart was only evil continually" (Gen. 6:5). God also said, "The intention of man's heart is evil from his youth" (Gen. 8:21). Jeremiah 17:9 similarly declared, "The heart is more deceitful than all else and is desperately sick: Who can understand it?" (NASB). Concerning unbelieving people, Paul observed, "Their foolish hearts were darkened" (Rom. 1:21).

God changes evil hearts by replacing them with new ones. In the new covenant passage of Ezekiel 36:26, God declared, "I will give you a new heart, and a new spirit I will put within you. And I will remove the heart of stone from your flesh and give you a heart of flesh." Also, Jeremiah 31:33 promised that God would write his law on those new hearts. Jesus himself declared, "Blessed are the pure in heart" (Matt. 5:8), and he also said, "But the seed in the good soil, these are the ones who have heard the word in an honest and good heart, and hold it fast, and bear fruit with perseverance" (Luke 8:15 NASB). Paul referred to "those who call on the Lord from a pure heart" (2 Tim. 2:22), while the writer of Hebrews proclaimed, "Let us draw near with a sincere heart in full assurance of faith, having our hearts sprinkled clean from an evil conscience" (Heb. 10:22 NASB). The Christian experiences a new heart that loves God, desires to obey him, is purified, and produces good fruit.

Conscience

God has created everyone with a conscience, the faculty of moral evaluation concerning right and wrong, good and evil. Connected with self-awareness and rational capacity, the conscience alerts a person concerning the morality of his or her actions. The conscience functions like a divine moral referee. Failure to heed the conscience often leads to guilt and shame.

Although the concept is clearly there, the Old Testament has no specific term for "conscience." For example, Solomon asked God for "an understanding mind" so he could "discern between good and evil" (1 Kings 3:9). Abigail told David that he should "have no cause of grief or pangs of conscience for having shed blood without cause" (1 Sam. 25:31).

The Greek term for "conscience" is *syneidēsis*, which occurs thirty times in the New Testament, with more than two-thirds of these occurrences found in Paul's writings. Romans 2:14–15 explains the conscience. There Paul said that Gentiles who lack access to the written Mosaic law still know what God requires of them. How? "They [Gentiles] show that the work of the law is written on their hearts, while their conscience also bears witness, and their conflicting thoughts accuse or even excuse them" (Rom. 2:15). As God's image bearers, all people are born with an innate knowledge of right and wrong based on God's law. The conscience reacts to behavior based on its compliance with that moral law or its violation of it. While asserting his love for fellow Jews, Paul declared, "I am speaking the truth in Christ—I am not lying; my conscience bears me witness in the Holy Spirit" (Rom. 9:1).

Lies and error can override the moral law that God has given each person and thus misinform the conscience. Sin can also blunt and sear the conscience. Both lead to dangerous and deadly situations. Paul stated, "To the pure, all things are pure, but to the defiled and unbelieving, nothing is pure; but both their minds and their consciences are defiled" (Titus 1:15). He also described "the insincerity of liars whose consciences are seared" (1 Tim. 4:2). The warning light of conscience should never be violated.

In 1984, an Avianca Airlines jet crashed in Spain.[16] The recovered black box of cockpit recorders revealed that several minutes before impact, the plane's automatic warning system repeatedly told the crew, "Pull up! Pull up!" The pilot, thinking that the system was malfunctioning, snapped, "Shut up, Gringo!" and switched the system off. Minutes later, the plane slammed into a mountain. Everyone on board died. This tragic story illustrates the catastrophic results of misinforming the conscience or ignoring its warnings.

Three Views of the Human Constitution

Generally speaking, man is described by several terms: *body, soul, spirit, heart,* and *conscience.* But how many actual components or elements does a person possess? One? Two? Three? More than three? The main views of the human constitution are considered below.

MONISM

Monism is the view that the human person is one element. Man is a unified self, not a combination of multiple parts. Secular materialism asserts that matter is the only substance in the universe. No God or spiritual entities exist. There is no soul or immaterial part to anyone. All mental and spiritual activities are chemical products of the brain. Man is a lump of thinking matter. At physical death, there is no immaterial part to survive. A lesser-held monistic view, idealism claims that all reality is composed merely of mind or ideas. George Berkeley (1685–1753) espoused the notion that ideas or perceptions are the only existing realities.

John A. T. Robinson, in his work *The Body: A Study in Pauline Theology* (1952), argued that there is no distinction between soul and body. Robinson claimed that the ancient Hebrews had a unitary view of the human person and that they lacked a word for "body" comparable to the Greek term *sōma*. Allegedly, the distinction between body and soul is a Greek idea foreign to Hebrew and biblical thought. With this perspective, body and soul are not contrasting realities; instead, they are interchangeable synonyms. The same is asserted for terms like "flesh" (Gk. *sarx*), "soul" (Gk. *psychē*), and "spirit" (Gk. *pneuma*). These are synonyms for the whole person. Thus, in this view the Bible does not teach a distinction between body and soul.

DICHOTOMISM

Dichotomism holds that man is a two-part being consisting of a body and an immaterial element called either "soul" or "spirit." No real distinction exists between the two terms, which are interchangeable. Dichotomism, then, affirms the human person as a combination of body and soul/spirit. This view differs from materialistic

---

16. This paragraph is adapted from John MacArthur, *The Vanishing Conscience: Drawing the Line in a No-Fault, Guilt-Free World* (Nashville: Thomas Nelson, 1994), 36. Used by permission of Thomas Nelson. www.thomasnelson.com.

monism, since dichotomism asserts that reality and humanity consist of more than matter; a spiritual element also exists. While a person has a physical body, the soul/spirit animates the body and survives physical death.

Christian dichotomists point to Genesis 2:7, where God's creation of man involved God forming man from the ground (material) and God breathing life into him (immaterial). Jesus also affirmed a distinction between body and soul in Matthew 10:28: "And do not fear those who kill the body but cannot kill the soul. Rather fear him who can destroy both soul and body in hell." Additionally, the Bible says that the immaterial element survives physical death. The souls of martyred saints appear in heaven in Revelation 6:9–11. Both the rich man and Lazarus exist after their deaths, according to Luke 16:19–31. And in the midst of being stoned, Stephen expected Jesus to receive his spirit (Acts 7:59).

TRICHOTOMISM

Trichotomism also affirms that man consists of multiple parts, but it holds that man is a three-part being comprising body, soul, and spirit. The term *trichotomy* comes from the combination of the Greek terms *tricha*, "three," and *temno*, "to cut." The first element of man is the body, which is the material part of a person. The second part is the soul, which is the psychological element of man and the part that enables interaction with people and the natural world. The soul is the basis of reason, emotion, personality, and social interaction. The third part is the spirit, which is usually identified as the religious element that perceives and responds to spiritual matters and to God. Whereas the soul is said to interact with horizontal areas related to man's experience with people and nature, the spirit interacts with vertical matters such as man's experience with God. The presence of spirit allegedly distinguishes humans from animals.

Two passages are often used to support trichotomism. First Thessalonians 5:23 states, "Now may the God of peace Himself sanctify you entirely; and may your spirit and soul and body be preserved complete, without blame at the coming of our Lord Jesus Christ" (NASB). Here all three components—"spirit," "soul," and "body"—are mentioned side by side. Hebrews 4:12 also mentions both soul and spirit: "For the word of God is living and active, sharper than any two-edged sword, piercing to the division of soul and of spirit."

Trichotomism was popular among the Alexandrian fathers of the early church, especially Clement of Alexandria (ca. 150–ca. 215) and Origen (ca. 184–ca. 254). This view went through a general decline until the nineteenth century, when it became more popular.

EVALUATION OF THE THREE VIEWS

Materialistic monism must be rejected since it denies the existence of God and all spiritual realities. Idealistic monism must also be rejected. Reality is not simply all mind or spirit or ideas. God created a physical universe with material creatures and declared them "very good" (Gen. 1:31). Furthermore, God did not create our senses to deceive us into thinking that we interact with a material world.

Christian forms of monism rightly assert that the human person is a unified self, but they fail to recognize diversity within the unity. The Bible affirms a distinction between body and soul (Matt. 10:28) and an immaterial part that survives physical death (Rev. 6:9–11). Paul expected physical death to place him in Jesus's presence (Phil. 1:23), and Jesus said that the repentant thief on the cross would be with him that day in paradise (Luke 23:43). The reality of an intermediate state refutes Christian variations of monism.

Both dichotomism and trichotomism correctly affirm that man consists of more than matter. The dividing issue centers on whether there exists a substantive distinction between soul and spirit. The biblical evidence indicates that there does not. "Soul" and "spirit" are used interchangeably in Scripture, and both terms indicate similar functions in relating with God, other people, and nature. So it is difficult to argue that they are distinct parts of a person. Some verses even place "soul" and "spirit" together in parallel form, showing that the same concept is in view:

> Therefore I will not restrain my mouth;
> > I will speak in the anguish of my spirit [*ruakh*];
> > I will complain in the bitterness of my soul [*nephesh*]. (Job 7:11)

> My soul [*nephesh*] yearns for you in the night;
> > my spirit [*ruakh*] within me earnestly seeks you. (Isa. 26:9)

> And Mary said,
> > "My soul [*psychē*] magnifies the Lord,
> > and my spirit [*pneuma*] rejoices in God my Savior." (Luke 1:46–47)

These passages demonstrate that "soul" and "spirit" in the Bible are interchangeable and address the same realities. In Isaiah 26:9 and Luke 1:46–47, the soul is even interacting with God, meaning that such activity is not restricted to the spirit.

The following two examples also reveal that "soul" and "spirit" refer to the same entity. First, Jesus expresses grief over his coming suffering:

> Now is my soul [*psychē*] troubled. And what shall I say? "Father, save me from this hour?" (John 12:27)

> After saying these things, Jesus was troubled in his spirit [*pneuma*]. (John 13:21)

Second, two passages describe saints in heaven:

> And to the assembly of the firstborn who are enrolled in heaven, and to God, the judge of all, and to the spirits [*pneuma*] of the righteous made perfect . . . (Heb. 12:23)

> When he opened the fifth seal, I saw under the altar the souls [*psychē*] of those who had been slain for the word of God. (Rev. 6:9)

But what about 1 Thessalonians 5:23 and Hebrews 4:12? Must these texts be seen to support trichotomism? No. Scripture gives the immaterial aspect of the person different terms, but not every designation means a distinguishable part. At times, terms can be piled up or combined for emphasis. In Luke 10:27, for example, Jesus mentions loving God with all one's "heart," "soul," "strength," and "mind." He uses four terms and does not even mention "spirit." So should we conclude that there are four or five or even more parts to the human person? No, the immaterial part of the person can be called "soul," "spirit," "heart," or "mind," and yet sometimes these designations can refer to the whole person. So these are overlapping concepts, not distinguishable parts. The dichotomism position, therefore, has the strongest scriptural support.

Yet is there a better designation than dichotomism? Since Scripture presents a person as a unified yet complex self, the designation "complex unity" is preferred.[17] The material (body) and immaterial (soul/spirit) function together in one person, embracing both unity and diversity. This complex unity is conditional, since death in a fallen world separates body and spirit (James 2:26). Yet this separation is temporary, since all people are headed for resurrection, a reunion of body and spirit in eternal forms. The concept of complex unity even parallels other realities. For example, there is one God, yet God is also plurality. God is Trinity—Father, Son, and Holy Spirit. Also, Jesus is one person, yet he is both God and man.

Man as a complex unity also covers all aspects of a person's physical and spiritual needs. While discussing the importance of saving faith, James mentions the importance of meeting physical needs: "If a brother or sister is poorly clothed and lacking in daily food, and one of you says to them, 'Go in peace, be warmed and filled,' without giving them the things needed for the body, what good is that?" (James 2:15–16). Also, God's salvation eventually brings restoration to the whole person. The Holy Spirit regenerates dead sinners, making them spiritually alive to God (Titus 3:5), yet Jesus will also redeem and glorify their bodies (Rom. 8:23; Phil. 3:20–21).

Origin of the Soul
    Preexistence
    Creationism
    Traducianism
    Evaluation of the Three Views

Personhood is the expression of an immaterial soul/spirit. But what is its origin? Is the soul created directly by God at conception, or is it passed down from one's parents through natural processes? There are three main views concerning the origin of the soul: preexistence, creationism, and traducianism.

Preexistence
Some, like the ancient Greeks, have believed that souls preexisted before conception. The early church theologian Origen (ca. 184–ca. 254) taught that God originally created

---

17. See Beck and Demarest, *The Human Person*, 137.

a fixed number of spirits, some of which were joined to material bodies and became humans. Islam also holds to a form of preexistence before birth. This view has no biblical support and has rightly been rejected by orthodox Christians—Origen excepted.

Creationism

Creationism teaches that each individual soul is created by God sometime between conception and birth rather than being transmitted from one's ancestors, as the body is. Scriptural support for this view is drawn from Genesis 2:7, which states that God created Adam's soul and joined it to his body. Likewise, Ecclesiastes 12:7 states that at death, "the spirit returns to God who gave it." Isaiah 42:5 describes God as Creator of heaven and earth, "who gives breath to the people on it and spirit to those who walk in it." Zechariah 12:1 says that God "formed the spirit of man within him." Also, God is "the Father of spirits" (Heb. 12:9). Considerable support for the creationist view can be found in church history; Jerome (ca. 340–420), Thomas Aquinas (1225–1274), and John Calvin (1509–1564) affirmed this view.

Traducianism

Traducianism says the soul is transmitted from parents to children by the natural procreation process, just as the body is. While God certainly is man's Creator and while Adam's body and soul were created directly by God, the constitution of all persons after Adam is passed on through God-ordained human procreation. Direct creation of each body and soul is not required. God uses the secondary means of human procreation. Traducianists argue that Adam cannot be used as support for creationism since Adam is unique as the first man and since his situation is not normative for his descendants. Genesis 5:3 states that Adam had a son in his own likeness and image, and this probably includes the soul. Adherents of the traducianist view in church history include Tertullian (ca. 160–ca. 220), Gregory of Nyssa (ca. 330–ca. 395), and Martin Luther (1483–1546).

Evaluation of the Three Views

The traducianist position seems best. An important weakness of creationism is that God's direct-creation acts are said to have ceased on the sixth day of creation. If creationism were true, then God would have been constantly involved in "out of nothing" creation acts since the sixth day of creation. But this notion goes against the fact that God rested from creating on the seventh day (Gen. 2:1–2).

Further, there is no scriptural evidence to conclude that while human bodies are created through natural means, souls are created directly by God. The creationist view introduces an unnecessary asymmetrical element into the origin of a human person. While it is true that several verses speak of God making a person's soul or spirit, that is also true for the body. David stated, "For you formed my inward parts; you knitted me together in my mother's womb. . . . My frame was not hidden from you, when I was being made in secret, intricately woven in the depths of the earth"

(Ps. 139:13, 15). These statements do not mean that the body is created directly by God apart from natural procreation. God is man's Creator, but God also ordained human procreation for the filling of the earth (Gen. 1:28). God uses natural means for procreation, yet he is the Ultimate Cause of the process. As a complex unity of body and soul/spirit, our entire being, including the soul, is a result of the God-ordained procreation process.

Gender

Gender Created by God
Gender and Marriage
Gender and Procreation
Homosexuality

Modern society is becoming increasingly confused on gender and gender roles. This is sad since gender is strategic to God's purposes for mankind and since God has clearly revealed his will on the matter. The foundational section for the creation and purpose of gender is found in Genesis 1–2. Other passages supplement the truths there.

Gender Created by God

God created gender and human sexuality. Genesis 1:27 states, "So God created man in his own image, in the image of God he created him; male and female he created them." Jesus repeated this truth: "Have you not read that he who created them from the beginning made them male and female" (Matt. 19:4). Gender is not vague, flexible, or personally determined by preference, nor does it occur by accident or through evolutionary process.

Genesis 2 adds detail to the creation of the first man and woman. Man was formed first from the dust of the ground, and then God breathed into him the breath of life. With this breath, "the man became a living creature" (Gen. 2:7). Later, God took a rib from the man and fashioned it into a woman (Gen. 2:21–22). Thus, the first man and woman were created directly by God as part of the "very good" creation (Gen. 1:31).

In addition to being created by God, the man and the woman were created differently. God formed man from dust, but God did not create the woman in the same way. God took a rib from Adam to make the woman (Gen. 2:22). So woman was made from man. Far from an incidental detail, this has significance for functional distinctions between men and women. When discussing order between men and women in the church, Paul highlighted this point by saying, "For man was not made from woman, but woman from man" (1 Cor. 11:8). In explaining why men are to do the teaching in the church, Paul declared, "For Adam was formed first, then Eve" (1 Tim. 2:13). The roles that men and women have in society, the family, and the church are grounded in the differences between men and women that God instituted at creation.

Gender is deeply embedded in human identity and is established at conception.

When a sperm carrying an X chromosome fertilizes the ovum, a girl is produced, while a Y chromosome brings a boy. When a child is born, often the first reaction is, "It's a boy!" or "It's a girl!" At birth, all recognize that gender exists. Parents do not choose the gender of their child or say that it does not matter. Neither do they have to wait to see if the boy will later become a girl or vice versa. Gender is defined permanently at conception and revealed at birth.

Both God's creation of gender and the biological reality of gender show that sexuality is objective. It is not subjective, as if it could be determined by the whims of individuals and societies. No person can legitimately claim that he or she is really another gender, nor can anyone truly change his or her gender. Gender confusion is addressed in Deuteronomy 22:5: "A woman shall not wear a man's garment, nor shall a man put on a woman's cloak, for whoever does these things is an abomination to the LORD your God." God commands women to present themselves as women, and men to present themselves as men. For a woman to dress like a man or vice versa is considered "an abomination," an extreme offense against God. This shows that God expects the person to live in accord with the gender God granted him or her at birth.

Sadly, transgenderism is becoming more acceptable in some societies. This occurs when a person identifies, dresses, or presents himself or herself contrary to his or her God-given biological gender. This includes transvestites or crossdressers. Still, in spite of what is true and obvious, gender is increasingly seen in modern culture as subjective. Supposedly, a male can declare himself a female or vice versa, and society must accommodate such a claim. Some even use medical technologies to attempt gender alteration. But gender confusion and tampering assault God's creative purposes for humanity. The Christian worldview affirms that gender and the biological structure of our bodies matter. They have a purpose granted by God. They are not the product of evolutionary accident with no moral implications but are gifts from God to be used for his purposes and glory. Since God made male and female, he is the starting point for defining gender. Deviating from God's plans for gender and sexuality is rebellion against God (see Rom. 1:24–27).

Gender and Marriage

Male and female were created for relationship, not isolation. As God evaluated the newly created male, he said, "It is not good that the man should be alone; I will make him a helper fit for him" (Gen. 2:18). So God would make a "helper" (Heb. *'ezer*) to assist Adam. The other creatures were wonderful, but they were not suitable for the man. Desire for human companionship is thus not faulty, as if it were a postfall development. Adam was not wrong for desiring human companionship, and it is not a challenge to man's relationship with God. God desired and designed humans for relationships.

When God made the woman from Adam's rib, he brought her before the man, and Adam then exclaimed,

> This at last is bone of my bones
>> and flesh of my flesh;
> she shall be called Woman,
>> because she was taken out of Man. (Gen. 2:23)

Adam immediately realized that the woman was the suitable companion for him. His incompleteness gave way to wholeness. This woman was like him. She was "bone of my bones" and "flesh of my flesh." Yet she was different. She was designed to complement him and bring fulfillment to his life. She brought femininity to complement his masculinity. He named her "Woman," because she came from man.

Genesis 2:24 then summarizes God's intent for man and woman: "Therefore a man shall leave his father and his mother and hold fast to his wife, and they shall become one flesh." The marriage relationship involves leaving father and mother to become "one flesh" in marriage. The term for "leave" (Heb. *'azab*) is forceful and means "abandon" or "forsake." Also, the word for "hold fast" (Heb. *dabaq*) means "strong personal attachment and devotion." It is later used to prescribe how Israel should show its commitment to God—"But you shall cling [*dabaq*] to the LORD your God" (Josh. 23:8). The result of this marital clinging is becoming "one flesh." This unity certainly involves the sexual union at the heart of the oneness, as well as the children who are one from two. Yet it goes beyond that so as to involve mutual dependence in all areas of life. Oneness and intimacy should permeate the relationship.

Marriage is a gracious and good institution from God. It is intended to be a blessing. First Peter 3:7 calls it "the grace of life." Proverbs 18:22 declares, "He who finds a wife finds a good thing and obtains favor from the LORD." In Matthew 19:4–6, Jesus reaffirms the one-flesh union of man and woman in marriage. Paul also says, "But because of the temptation to sexual immorality, each man should have his own wife and each woman her own husband" (1 Cor. 7:2). Ultimately, marriage points to Christ and the church: "Therefore a man shall leave his father and mother and hold fast to his wife, and the two shall become one flesh. This mystery is profound, and I am saying that it refers to Christ and the church" (Eph. 5:31–32). Marriage should illustrate the loving relationship of Christ and his church, with the husband loving his wife as Christ loves the church and the wife responding to her husband's loving leadership as the church responds to Christ (Eph. 5:22–33). Though marriage is subject to the curse after the fall of man, Christians under the control of the Holy Spirit should experience peaceful, productive, and fulfilled marriages. Believers must marry only other believers (1 Cor. 7:39; 2 Cor. 6:14).

Marriage has only one definition, and it is sanctioned by God: the union of one man and one woman (Gen. 2:23–24). Marriage is to be a public, formal, and officially recognized covenant between a man and a woman. Prolonged conjugal cohabitation does not establish and is not equivalent to marriage (John 4:18). Where a valid marriage has been established prior to faith in Christ, the couple should keep the covenant and remain married (1 Cor. 7:24).

Gender and Procreation

The man-woman relationship in marriage is designed for procreation. According to Genesis 1:28, God blessed the male and female and said, "Be fruitful and multiply and fill the earth." The God-designed biological structures of male and female produce children.

Mankind was to expand beyond the first man and woman and reproduce so that the earth would be filled with others bearing God's image. These children in turn were also expected to multiply and fill the earth. God would use procreation to save mankind and restore the creation after the fall. When Adam and Eve sinned, God told the power behind the serpent (Satan), "I will put enmity between you and the woman, and between your offspring and her offspring; he shall bruise your head, and you shall bruise his heel" (Gen. 3:15). The "offspring" of the woman would experience an ongoing battle that would culminate in a "he" who would give a fatal blow to the power behind the serpent. When Eve gave birth to her first son, Cain, she declared, "I have gotten a man with the help of the LORD" (Gen. 4:1). Some believe that this could be translated, "I have gotten a man—even the Lord." If so, Eve may have believed that her first son, Cain, was the deliverer God promised in Genesis 3:15. Later, Lamech thought his son Noah could be the promised deliverer: "When Lamech had lived 182 years, he fathered a son and called his name Noah, saying, 'Out of the ground that the LORD has cursed, this one shall bring us relief from our work and from the painful toil of our hands'" (Gen. 5:28–29). Both expectations of a deliverer went unfulfilled. Cain murdered his brother Abel. And Noah, while greatly used by God, was also a sinner and not qualified to be the promised Savior (Gen. 9:20–23). Eventually, Mary's son, Jesus, was born to be the promised "offspring," or "seed," who would restore all things (Acts 3:21; Gal. 3:16).

The procreation command given to Adam was repeated to Noah: "And God blessed Noah and his sons and said to them, 'Be fruitful and multiply and fill the earth'" (Gen. 9:1, 7). This mandate was necessary after the global flood, when all but eight persons perished. A major threat to multiplying and filling the earth, however, was the murder of fellow humans. So with the Noahic covenant, God sanctioned capital punishment for those who murder God's image bearers: "Whoever sheds the blood of man, by man shall his blood be shed, for God made man in his own image" (Gen. 9:6). God gave man the right to protect life by executing those who kill their fellow image bearers. This shows how valuable God considers human life to be.

After the fall, the curse on the woman meant giving birth would be painful. God told Eve, "I will surely multiply your pain in childbearing; in pain you shall bring forth children" (Gen. 3:16). Procreation, with all its blessings, is painful for the woman in a fallen world and is often filled with tragedy. Rachel died while giving birth to Benjamin (Gen. 35:16–18). Some children will die in the womb, and others will have their lives cut short by abortion. Some women who desire to have children will be barren (Gen. 30:1).

The dangers of giving birth will be removed during the Messiah's coming kingdom after Jesus's return. Isaiah prophesied of that time, stating, "No more shall there be in [that city] an infant who lives but a few days" (Isa. 65:20), and, "They shall not labor in vain or bear children for calamity, for they shall be the offspring of the blessed of the LORD, and their descendants with them" (Isa. 65:23). Jesus's millennial kingdom will reverse the painful and tragic consequences of the fall for women and children (Rev. 20:1–6). Since there will be no marriage in the eternal state after the millennium, there will also be no procreation (Matt. 22:30).

Homosexuality[18]

Satan and men continually attempt to pervert all that is good in God's creation, including gender and marriage. This corruption occurred quickly in Genesis. Once Adam and Eve sinned, they immediately became aware of their nakedness: "Then the eyes of both were opened, and they knew that they were naked. And they sewed fig leaves together and made themselves loincloths" (Gen. 3:7). Innocence was replaced with guilt and shame (Gen. 3:8–10). Even the holy gift of their physical, sexual relationship was polluted. Gone was its purity. Wicked and impure thoughts were introduced. By sewing fig leaves, the first couple attempted to cover their shame, and ever since, clothing has been a universal expression of human modesty.

Sexual perversion also spread quickly. Polygamy appears in Genesis 4:19. Demonic sexual perversion occurs in Genesis 6:2. Other deviations include lewdness (Gen. 9:22), adultery (or near adultery) (Gen. 12:15–19), fornication (Gen. 16:4), incest (Gen. 19:36), rape (Gen. 34:2), prostitution (Gen. 38:15), and sexual harassment (Gen. 39:7). Homosexuality appears on a large scale in Genesis 19.

Marriage is good and holy, but homosexuality is a perverse rebellion that threatens God's intent for marriage and family. God did not create men to engage in sexual acts with other men, nor women with women. In recent times homosexuality has reached a level of acceptability that is unparalleled in human history. Societies that once saw it as the deviation it is, now promote it as acceptable. When the twenty-first century dawned, no country had legalized homosexual marriage. But since then, several countries have done so, including the United States, which legalized same-sex marriage in 2015.

The Bible presents homosexuality as sin and explicitly states that practicing homosexuals will not inherit God's kingdom (1 Cor. 6:9–10). Homosexuality perverts God's design that marriage reflect Christ's relationship to his church: "Therefore a man shall leave his father and mother and hold fast to his wife, and the two shall become one flesh. This mystery is profound, and I am saying that it refers to Christ and the church" (Eph. 5:31–32). Marriage illustrates the relationship of the Lord Jesus to his church; the loving headship of a husband pictures the loving headship of Christ over his bride, and the joyful submission of a wife pictures the joyful submission of the church to her Lord. By tampering with the participants of marriage, homosexual activity or homosexual marriage distorts the gospel picture that God intended mar-

---

18. This section is adapted from John MacArthur, "God's Word on Homosexuality: The Truth about Sin and the Reality of Forgiveness," *MSJ* 19, no. 2 (2008): 153–74. Used by permission of *MSJ*.

riage to portray. It defies the will of the Creator, threatens what is good, and hurts those involved in this practice.

In Genesis 1:27, the Hebrew words for "male" and "female" are emphatic, giving the sense of "the one male and the one female." Only one man and one woman existed in the beginning, so that monogamous, heterosexual marriage could occur. This is God's paradigm for marriage. Based on this paradigm of one man and one woman established at creation, the rest of Scripture strictly forbids any sexual activity outside marriage—including all fornication (Acts 15:29; 1 Cor. 6:9; Heb. 13:4), adultery (Ex. 20:14; Lev. 20:10; Matt. 19:18), bestiality (Ex. 22:19; Lev. 18:23; 20:15–16; Deut. 27:21), and homosexuality (Lev. 18:22; 20:13; Rom. 1:26–27).

Homosexual unions cannot rightly be called "marriages," since they involve only one gender, possess no ability to procreate, and cannot provide the kind of sexual companionship God intended. Nor do they picture the relationship between Jesus and his church. Homosexuality is not another option for two consenting adults; it is an aberration of God's design for the procreation, pleasure, and preservation of the human race. In 1 Timothy 1:9–10, Paul denounced "immoral men and homosexuals" as those who are "lawless and rebellious" and act "contrary to sound teaching" (NASB). The Greek word he used for homosexuals, *arsenokoitais*, literally means "males in the marriage bed" and seems to have been drawn from the terminology of the Septuagint (Lev. 18:22; 20:13). This term itself underscores that homosexual acts deviate from God's norm for the marriage bed.

HOMOSEXUALITY IN GENESIS

God's opposition to homosexual behavior is illustrated in his response to the men at Sodom in Genesis 19. During an angelic rescue mission to save Lot, the inhabitants of Sodom demonstrated the appalling extent of their lust. A savage mob from every part of the city was consumed by immoral lust. Even after being blinded, they groped for the doorway (Gen. 19:10–11). Lot recognized their homosexual passions as inherently wicked (Gen. 19:7), and God destroyed them for their great iniquity (Gen. 18:20–33; 19:23–29).

Some say that the incident was simply a breach of ancient hospitality laws, but such an idea ignores the context. The mob did not want "to know" (Gen. 19:5) Lot's guests in a social way. Their intentions were entirely sexual, as evidenced by Lot's condemnation in verse 7, where he calls their actions "wicked." Also, Lot offered his daughters in verse 8, where the same verb "to know" is used. Though their violence deserved condemnation, their homosexual lust was particularly despicable to God, a point Jude 7 and 2 Peter 2:6–7 make certain. Thus, it is not merely violence or even homosexual rape being condemned. It is any homosexual act or lifestyle. Because the Sodomites were so perverse, the Lord destroyed the entire city with fire and brimstone. The term *sodomy*, coming from this incident, refers to homosexual behavior practiced by the Sodomites.

Both Jude 7 and 2 Peter 2:6 affirm that sexual perversion was the primary characteristic of the city and the main reason it was judged. Jude writes of "Sodom and Gomorrah and the cities around them" that they "indulged in gross immorality and went after strange flesh" (NASB). By using a word for "sexual immorality" (Gk. *ekporneuō*), Jude reveals that their homosexual behavior was especially despicable in the eyes of God. The "strange flesh" they pursued were Lot's angelic guests, whom the men of the city thought were male visitors (Gen. 19:5). Peter said that Sodom and Gomorrah were characterized by "the sensual conduct of the wicked" and were therefore "condemned . . . to extinction" (2 Pet. 2:6–7). Lot, though, was regarded as righteous because "he was tormenting his righteous soul over their lawless deeds that he saw and heard" (2 Pet. 2:8). Lot and his daughters were spared, while the people remaining in Sodom and the surrounding cities were destroyed.

Sodom establishes that depraved men cannot pursue sensuality and ungodliness and escape God's judgment (Matt. 25:41; Rom. 1:18; 2:5, 8; Eph. 5:6; 1 Thess. 2:16; 2 Thess. 1:8; Heb. 10:26–27; Rev. 6:17). Scripture refers back to Sodom and Gomorrah over twenty times as an illustration and warning concerning what will happen to those who live such ungodly lives (cf. Matt. 10:14–15; 11:23–24; Luke 17:28–32).

HOMOSEXUALITY AND THE MOSAIC CODE

The Mosaic legal code declares that homosexuality is detestable in the sight of God. Leviticus 18:22 states, "You [men] shall not lie with a male as with a woman; it is an abomination." And the consequences are equally clear: "For everyone who does any of these abominations, the persons who do them shall be cut off from among their people" (Lev. 18:29). The prohibition is also reiterated later in Leviticus: "If a man lies with a male as with a woman, both of them have committed an abomination; they shall surely be put to death; their blood is upon them" (Lev. 20:13).

Homosexuality is listed in Leviticus 18 and 20 in the context of other sexual sins and is treated as morally equal to adultery, incest, and bestiality. The fact that Christians are no longer under the Mosaic code does not mean that God's attitudes toward these sexual sins, including homosexuality, have changed. The New Testament reaffirms that homosexual activity is sin.

God's view of homosexual behavior is revealed in the word "abomination." The word occurs repeatedly in this context (Lev. 18:22, 26, 27, 29, 30; 20:13) and is also a term found frequently in the book of Deuteronomy (see Deut. 7:25; 12:31; 17:1, 4; 18:9–14; 27:15). Just as idolatry is a perpetual offense to God's moral character, so also is any perversion of God's design for marriage.

HOMOSEXUALITY AND ROMANS 1

The apostle Paul reiterates the prohibition against homosexuality in Romans 1:26–27:

> For this reason God gave them up to dishonorable passions. For their women exchanged natural relations for those that are contrary to nature; and the men likewise gave up natural relations with women and were consumed with passion

for one another, men committing shameless acts with men and receiving in themselves the due penalty for their error.

Both male homosexuality and lesbianism are in view in this passage. God's judgment falls on both because they involve unnatural acts. The word translated "relations" (Gk. *chrēsis*) was a common way to speak of sexual intercourse and in this context refers to homosexual acts. Such behavior stems from "degrading passions" driven by selfish lust, not love. They are a twisted expression of God's creative design. When man forsakes the author of nature, he inevitably forsakes the order of nature.

Marriage is a sacred institution, and any sexual activity with someone other than one's spouse is strictly forbidden by God (Gal. 5:19; Heb. 13:4). This includes not only fornication and adultery but any form of homosexuality, since these are contrary to the divine design established at creation.

Personhood

Beginning of Personhood
End of Human Life
Destiny at Death

Beginning of Personhood

Like the issue of gender, views of human personhood have also been distorted by modern society, which often denies personhood to those whom the Bible considers persons. According to the Bible, all human beings are persons who possess dignity because they are made in God's image. This includes the very young, the very old, and everyone in the middle.

When does personhood begin? Various views concerning the beginning of personhood have been offered. Only one is biblical. Personhood begins at conception.

Scientific fact demonstrates that human life begins at conception, when all twenty-three pairs of chromosomes are complete. The fertilized egg then contains a fixed genetic structure (DNA).[19] Between days twelve and twenty-eight, a heart begins to beat. Blood cells form at day seventeen, and eyes begin to form at day nineteen. Between weeks four and six, brain waves can be measured. At one month, the embryo looks like a distinct human person. Fingerprints exist at two months. The skeleton, circulatory system, and muscular system are complete by the eighth week. The manifestation of personhood appears rapidly after conception.

Yet not all associate human personhood with human biological life. Some speculate that personhood begins after conception but before birth, perhaps with the development of brainwaves or the viability of the fetus. In 1973, with its infamous *Roe v. Wade* decision, the Supreme Court of the United States declared that the concept of "person," as used in the United States Constitution, applies only at birth. As a result, millions of people in the womb have been killed because they are deemed "nonpersons." The bioethicist Michael Tooley even argued that personhood does not

---

19. Beck and Demarest, *The Human Person*, 43.

begin until self-consciousness, well after birth. In his work, *Abortion and Infanticide*, Tooley argued that full personhood is not achieved until about one year of age.[20]

The Bible refers to babies in the womb as persons, with no indication that any process must occur after conception before personhood begins. For example, when Isaac prayed that his barren wife, Rebekah, could bear children, we are told, "And the LORD granted his prayer, and Rebekah his wife conceived. The children struggled together within her" (Gen. 25:21–22). Here a close connection exists between "conceived" and "children." Job similarly connected conception with personhood when he declared, "Let the day perish on which I was born, and the night that said, 'A man is conceived'" (Job 3:3). So Job was a person, "a man," at his conception. Luke 1:41 likewise records, "And when Elizabeth heard the greeting of Mary, the baby leaped in her womb." Elizabeth then said, "For behold, when the sound of your greeting came to my ears, the baby in my womb leaped for joy" (Luke 1:44). The one in Elizabeth's womb (John the Baptist) is called a "baby" and expresses emotion—"joy." God also referred to Jeremiah as a person before his birth: "Before I formed you in the womb I knew you, and before you were born I consecrated you" (Jer. 1:5). Other passages refer to God's intimate knowledge of and involvement with people in the womb (e.g., Job 10:8–11; Ps. 139:13–16; Isa. 44:24).

In addition, Exodus 21:22–25 strongly shows that the unborn are to be considered persons:

> When men strive together and hit a pregnant woman, so that her children come out, but there is no harm, the one who hit her shall surely be fined, as the woman's husband shall impose on him, and he shall pay as the judges determine. But if there is harm, then you shall pay life for life, eye for eye, tooth for tooth, hand for hand, foot for foot, burn for burn, wound for wound, stripe for stripe.

This passage indicates that if a pregnant woman is hit by a man and the child within her is born alive without sustaining harm, the man who struck her must pay a fine. But if the child is harmed, then the law of retaliation must be enforced, including death if the child dies ("pay life for life"). The baby in the womb must be a person since the death penalty is required if the baby in the womb is killed. Any baby in the womb is a person and should be treated as a person.

Personhood is not a development; it is an event. It occurs at conception. Attempts to separate personhood from biological human life are unscientific, arbitrary, and dangerous. All that physically constitutes a person is made immediately at conception. Biological human life means that personhood exists. A human life is a person. Separating human life from personhood has resulted in the killing of persons in the womb through abortion and has even led to the murder of babies after birth. Beck and Demarest note that four conditions must exist for an act to be considered murder:

1. A person must be killed.
2. The person must be killed intentionally.

---

20. Michael Tooley, *Abortion and Infanticide* (Oxford: Clarendon, 1983), 424.

3. The victim must be innocent.
4. An unlawful or sinful motive must be involved in the killing.

They also rightly conclude, "Abortion as commonly practiced today satisfies these criteria."[21]

End of Human Life

In a fallen world, human death is the harsh and inevitable final reality. Death involves the separation of the spirit from the body (James 2:26). At physical death the body returns to the ground, where it decays. Except for those alive at the rapture who are taken to heaven without dying, and for the rare examples of Enoch and Elijah, death overcomes everyone. God told Adam that if he sinned, death would come (Gen. 2:17). Romans 5:12 states that "sin came into the world through one man [Adam], and death through sin." Genesis 5 functions much like a graveyard as it records the descendants of Adam who lived and then died. Solomon stated that there is "a time to be born, and a time to die" (Eccles. 3:1–2) and that one day "the silver cord" of life would be "snapped" and the body would return to the earth (Eccles. 12:6–7).

Death is "the king of terrors" (Job 18:14) and is used by Satan to cause fear and slavery (Heb. 2:15). Paul referred to death as an "enemy" that must be defeated (1 Cor. 15:26). Not only does death extinguish life, it leaves behind the carnage of grief. When Sarah died, Abraham wept and mourned for her (Gen. 23:2). When Jacob died, his son Joseph "fell on his father's face and wept over him and kissed him" (Gen. 50:1).

While death is often viewed as natural, death is an intrusion into God's creation. God created humans for life, not death. In his original state, man was not created to die, though death was nonetheless a possibility if he rebelled against his Creator. Jesus conquered death by his resurrection, and the fact that death will be finally removed in the coming eternal state (Rev. 21:4) demonstrates that death is not inherent to being human.

God holds sovereign control over life and death. First Samuel 2:6 states, "The LORD kills and brings to life; he brings down to Sheol and raises up." Job said, "In his [God's] hand is the life of every living thing and the breath of all mankind" (Job 12:10). In the future, death will be thrown into the lake of fire after the great white throne judgment, prior to the eternal state (Rev. 20:14).

The Bible links death with a person's final breath (Job 14:10). Genesis 25:8 says, "Abraham breathed his last and died." The same is said of Ishmael (Gen. 25:17). On the cross, "Jesus uttered a loud cry and breathed his last" (Mark 15:37).

The reality of personhood begins in the womb and extends to this final breath, the end of life. The Bible treats all humans through death as persons with dignity. Since being in God's image is structural to being human, there never comes a point when a person becomes anything less than a full person. This includes the elderly and the severely handicapped. Some argue that personhood exists only if someone

---

21. Beck and Demarest, *The Human Person*, 45.

can function in a certain capacity. But that makes personhood dependent on what a human does rather than on who he or she is. Understanding this point rules out the killing of people whom society might deem unworthy of living. A biblical understanding of human life places a barrier before the termination of a life simply because that person cannot "contribute to society," however that may be defined. From conception to last breath, all human beings are God's creations and should be treated as such.

Destiny at Death

What happens to a person at death? The stakes are high on this issue, impacting greatly how we should live in the present. There are several views.

CESSATION OF EXISTENCE

Those holding to a naturalistic worldview believe that death means the cessation of existence. Since naturalists believe that reality and humans consist only of matter, death of the body means a permanent end to one's existence. Since consciousness and thoughts are tied only to brain tissue, once the human body dies, all consciousness and thought totally cease. Nothing carries over to a next life. The body is buried or cremated, and that is the end. People live on only in the memories of those who knew them. And even these memories fade as those who knew them also die. In this view, the universe is headed for eventual extinction.

The ancient philosopher Epicurus (341–270 BC) is one who denied an afterlife. For him, because death is ceasing to exist, it should not be feared. No divine judgment awaits, and since death is the end of self-awareness, it is a nonissue. The atheist Richard Dawkins, who similarly asserts that death is nonexistence, argues that people should be satisfied that they lived at all. Knowing that they have lived, Dawkins says, indicates that they are the "lucky ones," who "won the lottery of birth against all odds."[22]

CONTINUATION OF THE SOUL ONLY

Some believe that people possess an immaterial soul that survives physical death to exist in another realm—whether in heaven or some soulish existence. The physical body, however, is temporary and will not be resurrected. Only the soul is immortal. The Greek philosopher Socrates (ca. 470–399 BC) believed that the body was a prison for the soul. He longed for physical death so his soul could be released from its carnal encasing and move to a greater spiritual existence. Plato (ca. 428–348 BC) also believed that the soul alone survived death. This view of the immortality of the soul has been promoted by some adherents of Protestant liberalism. Harry Emerson Fosdick (AD 1878–1969) said, "I believe in the persistence of personality through death, but I do not believe in the resurrection of the flesh."[23]

---

22. Richard Dawkins, *Unweaving the Rainbow: Science, Delusion, and the Appetite for Wonder* (New York: Houghton Mifflin, 1998).

23. Harry Emerson Fosdick, *The Modern Use of the Bible* (New York: Macmillan, 1924), 99.

ANNIHILATIONISM

Annihilationism teaches that only some people will cease to exist. Unlike the cessationist view, annihilationists affirm that believers will live forever, experiencing the resurrection of the body. The wicked, however, will at some point be snuffed out of existence. Advocates suggest that this could occur at physical death, at a coming judgment, or after a finite period of punishment in hell.

This view proposes an asymmetrical relationship in the destiny of the saved and the lost. The saved will be granted immortality and live forever, while the lost will cease to exist. Allegedly, passages that speak of "eternal" or "forever" punishment for the lost do not mean never-ending, conscious torment. It is only the consequences of being extinguished that last forever. Philip Edgcumbe Hughes (1915–1990) claimed, "Everlasting death is destruction without end . . . , the destruction of obliteration."[24] For Edward Fudge, the biblical language of a lake of fire is a symbol of "irreversible annihilation."[25]

Two supposed theological beliefs undergird the annihilation view. The first is that God's character is inconsistent with conscious, eternal punishment. Allegedly, God's love cannot be harmonized with such a destiny. The second is that immortality is not inherent to man's existence. Immortality is granted to those who trust in God, while it is refused to those who are lost. It is a reward for those who receive salvation but is withheld from those who do not.

SOUL SLEEP

The notion of soul sleep, or *psychopannychia*, asserts that physical death brings a temporary end to one's conscious existence until a subsequent day of resurrection. Just as a person can be in a deep sleep for many hours with no memory of the sleeping period, so too a gap in consciousness occurs between death and resurrection. This view denies an intermediate state of conscious existence after death and affirms that the souls of believers sleep rather than going immediately to heaven. Proponents claim scriptural support for soul sleep in Ecclesiastes 9:5, "For the living know that they will die, but the dead know nothing, and they have no more reward, for the memory of them is forgotten," and Daniel 12:2, "And many of those who sleep in the dust of the earth shall awake, some to everlasting life, and some to shame and everlasting contempt." Defenders of soul sleep include Jehovah's Witnesses, Seventh-Day Adventists, and Christadelphians.

REINCARNATION

Reincarnation, or the transmigration of the soul, asserts that at physical death the soul of a person inhabits another entity, such as a human or animal. Most often linked with the Eastern religion of Hinduism, reincarnation is the belief that all living things experience a cycle of births, deaths, and rebirths until they achieve an impersonal

---

24. Philip Edgcumbe Hughes, *The True Image: The Origin and Destiny of Man in Christ* (Grand Rapids, MI: Eerdmans, 1989), 405.

25. Edward W. Fudge, *The Fire That Consumes: A Biblical and Historical Study of Final Punishment* (Fallbrook, CA: Verdict, 1982), 117.

union with the highest reality. In Hinduism this highest reality is Brahman. Then the cycle of reincarnation ceases. Since union with the divine is very difficult, most experience reincarnation thousands of times and more. The law of karma allegedly governs the reincarnation process. Karma functions like a law of cause and effect that determines one's existence in the next life. If one acts properly, karmic debt can be released, and one can attain a higher form of existence. However, acting improperly increases karmic debt and lowers one's existence in the next life—perhaps even to a lowly creature like a worm.

Reincarnation is held by millions of Hindus, Buddhists, and Jains. Increasing religious pluralism has brought reincarnation to Western societies. Forms of reincarnation are found in neo-paganism, witchcraft, the occult, and New Age philosophies. The 2009 Pew Research Center poll "Many Americans Mix Multiple Faiths" revealed that 24 percent of Americans believe in reincarnation.[26]

ENTRY INTO AN INTERMEDIATE STATE AWAITING RESURRECTION

The traditional Christian view is that the soul/spirit lives in an intermediate state between death and bodily resurrection. While the human person is a complex unity of body and soul/spirit, death causes a temporary separation of body and soul. The body returns to the ground, while the soul resides in another realm. The soul of the believer resides with God in heaven, but the soul of the unbeliever is separated from God in hell. At the coming resurrection, the souls and bodies of all people will be united forever in the final heaven or hell.

EVALUATION OF VIEWS

The biblical evidence strongly sides with the view that souls enter into an intermediate state awaiting resurrection. The case against the other views is found mostly in the strong evidence for this understanding, which is based on three truths: (1) the human person possesses an immaterial soul; (2) an intermediate state exists; and (3) there is a coming resurrection.

That the human person possesses an immaterial soul was discussed in previous sections on the soul and the human constitution. In regard to the intermediate state, Paul said that being separated from the body meant being with the Lord (2 Cor. 5:8). He also said that departing to be with Christ was better than his current life on earth (Phil. 1:22–24). Moses and Elijah's presence at Jesus's transfiguration reveals their conscious existence beyond their earthly careers (Luke 9:30–31). Both the rich man and Lazarus existed after their deaths (Luke 16:19–31), and Jesus told the thief on the cross that he would be with him in paradise that day (Luke 23:43). Stephen also prayed that Jesus would receive his spirit while being stoned (Acts 7:59–60). These examples refute the perspectives of the cessation of existence, reincarnation, and soul sleep. Conscious life exists after physical death.

---

26. "Many Americans Mix Multiple Faiths," Pew Research Center, accessed July 14, 2016, http://www.pewforum.org /2009/12/09.

Multiple passages also teach a coming resurrection of the body. Job expressed hope in his bodily resurrection in connection with his Redeemer's presence on the earth: "For I know that my Redeemer lives, and at the last he will stand upon the earth. And after my skin has been thus destroyed, yet in my flesh I shall see God" (Job 19:25–26). Concerning the coming kingdom of God, Isaiah declared, "Your dead shall live; their bodies shall rise. You who dwell in the dust, awake and sing for joy! For your dew is a dew of light, and the earth will give birth to the dead" (Isa. 26:19). Daniel stated, "And many of those who sleep in the dust of the earth shall awake, some to everlasting life, and some to shame and everlasting contempt" (Dan. 12:2). Like Daniel, Jesus warned of the bodily resurrection of the righteous and wicked in John 5:28–29. Paul said that Christians look forward to "the redemption of our bodies" (Rom. 8:23) and that Jesus "will transform our lowly body to be like his glorious body" (Phil. 3:21). Additionally, Jesus is described as the firstfruits of the resurrection (1 Cor. 15:23); since Jesus was raised bodily from the grave, one historical resurrection has already happened.

The Bible's clear teaching on the coming bodily resurrection refutes the view that only the soul continues after death. Furthermore, this notion does not account for the goodness of the material realm in God's creation, including the body (Gen. 2:7). Rather, it holds man's destiny to be a purely spiritual existence and treats the body as an encumbrance gladly to be discarded.

The annihilation perspective denies the testimony of Scripture that the wicked will experience eternal, conscious torment. The Bible uses the language of "eternal fire" (Matt. 25:41) and says that the "smoke of their torment goes up forever and ever" (Rev. 14:11) and that "they have no rest, day or night" (Rev. 14:11). Having no rest indicates self-consciousness. Finally, Jesus set eternal life and eternal punishment side by side in Matthew 25:46: "And these [the wicked] will go away into eternal punishment, but the righteous into eternal life." As eternal life is unending for believers, so too will eternal punishment for the unbeliever be unending. The relationship between the two is symmetrical, not asymmetrical.

Man and Society

Ethnicity and Nations
Human Government
Human Culture

Ethnicity and Nations

An important but often neglected part of biblical anthropology concerns ethnicity and nations. Approximately 196 nations currently exist on the earth, consisting of thousands of ethnic groups. How do the various people groups fit into God's purposes?

Just as God is both unity (one God) and plurality (three persons), God's image bearers evidence unity and diversity. Humanity is unified since all humans are descendants of Adam, yet many ethnic groups and nations exist. Paul referred to both unity and diversity in mankind when he stated, "And he [God] made from one man [Adam] every nation of mankind to live on all the face of the earth" (Acts 17:26). People come from "one man" (unity), but this leads to "every nation" (diversity/plurality).

Adam, who transcends ethnic diversity and nations, was the head of the human race. God created Adam and Eve with the genetic ability to produce a multiplicity of races and various skin colors. God commanded man to multiply and fill the earth (Gen. 1:26–28). Later revelation makes clear that this multiplying and filling would involve differing people groups. Genesis 10–11 records various peoples stemming from Noah's three sons. Paul says that God "determined allotted periods and the boundaries of their [i.e., the nations'] dwelling place" (Acts 17:26).

After the global flood, Noah represented mankind as the one from whom diversity would again emerge. Noah's sons—Ham, Shem, and Japheth—became the heads of various peoples in the world. Genesis 9:19 states, "These three were the sons of Noah, and from these the people of the whole earth were dispersed." Often misunderstood, the curse on Canaan in Genesis 9:18–27 was a prediction of Israel's eventual victory over the Canaanite inhabitants of the Promised Land. It was not a curse on Noah's son Ham nor a prediction that dark-skinned descendants from Ham would be slaves of other groups.

The table of nations of Genesis 10–11 is central for understanding the importance of ethnic groups. It is also the backdrop for God's plan to use Abraham to bless all peoples (Gen. 11:27–12:3). The catalyst for diversity is the Tower of Babel event described in Genesis 11:1–9. Sinful people settled in the land of Shinar and built a tower to make a great name for themselves and stay located in one place (Gen. 11:4), rebelling against God's command to fill the earth (Gen. 9:1). God thwarted their plans by confusing their language. This was the origin of multiple languages, and it caused people to scatter over the earth.

Dispersion is connected with the spread of descendants from Noah's three sons. Genesis 10 records the descendants of Japheth (Gen. 10:2–5), the sons of Ham (Gen. 10:6–20), and finally the sons of Shem (Gen. 10:21–31). This genealogy of descendants from Noah's sons occurs before the account of the Tower of Babel in Genesis 11, indicating that the spread of people groups was not God's judgment but was part of God's plan from the beginning.

Eventually, the ethnic makeup of the Old Testament world reflected diversity. There were Asiatics (Israel and their Semitic cousins—Canaanites, Moabites, Edomites, Ammonites), black Africans (Cushites/Ethiopians), black-African Asiatics (Egyptians), and Indo-Europeans (Philistines, Hittites). The Old Testament focuses mostly on Israel, but God's call of Abraham (from the line of Shem) reveals God's intent for blessing the world. A "great nation," Israel, will come from Abraham. The purpose of Abraham and Israel is worldwide blessing: "In you all the families of the earth shall be blessed" (Gen. 12:3). God's later promise to Abraham in Genesis 22:18 stresses the broader concept of "nations" being blessed.

People units can vary, ranging from families and tribes to clans, larger groups, and nations. Israel itself went from Abraham to Abraham's family via Isaac and Jacob and then extended to a larger people group (Hebrews) and eventually to a nation (Israel). Revelation 5:9 promises that God's salvation will extend to "every tribe and language and people and nation."

From Genesis 12 to Malachi, the Old Testament emphasizes Israel, yet it also discusses blessings to other groups. Genesis 49:8–10 reveals that a leader from the tribe of Judah will be the one to whom the nations will give obedience. During the exodus from Egypt a "mixed multitude" journeyed with the people of Israel (Ex. 12:38), which probably consisted of both foreigners, including some Egyptians, and families that were a mixture of Egyptian and Hebrew peoples. Moses himself married a Cushite, an African woman from near Ethiopia (Num. 12:1).

Exodus 19:6 states that Israel was to be a kingdom of priests for God to the world. If Israel acted rightly, she would attract other nations to the God of Israel (Deut. 4:5–6). The Mosaic law mandated that the people of Israel treat foreigners well. They were not to abuse or oppress them (Ex. 22:21). Instead, they were to deal with foreigners like native Israelites: "You shall treat the stranger who sojourns with you as the native among you, and you shall love him as yourself, for you were strangers in the land of Egypt: I am the LORD your God" (Lev. 19:34).

Some Gentiles in the Old Testament believed in the God of Israel. Rahab the prostitute, a Canaanite woman, helped Israel and became an example of a Gentile with faith (Heb. 11:31). Ruth, a Moabite woman, expressed faith and became an ancestor of Jesus (Matt. 1:5). During Jonah's time the people of Nineveh repented and avoided God's wrath for a time.

Yet the Messiah needed to arrive for Gentiles to participate in Israel's covenants and promises as Gentiles, without converting to Judaism. Paul reminded Gentile believers, "Remember that you were at [one] time separated from Christ, alienated from the commonwealth of Israel and strangers to the covenants of promise, having no hope and without God in the world" (Eph. 2:11–12). Jesus's death and his new covenant break down the dividing barrier between Jews and Gentiles (Eph. 2:14–16).

Tragically, Israel in the Old Testament era did not obey God. Not only did Israel fail in being a testimony to other nations, she actually worshiped the gods of the nations. As a result, God made the people captives to Assyria and Babylon and then later to Medo-Persia, Greece, and Rome. Yet the prophets foretold a coming restoration of the kingdom to Israel, and they promised blessings to the nations. Isaiah predicted a day when God would establish international harmony from Jerusalem and when the nations would come to learn the law of God (Isa. 2:2–4). He taught that God would raise up an ultimate servant of the Lord, an ultimate Israelite, who would restore the nation Israel and bring blessings to the Gentiles (Isa. 49:1–6). Isaiah also foretold that foreigners would be included among God's people (Isaiah 56). And Amos said that the restoration of the Davidic kingdom in Israel would mean blessings for the nations of the world (Amos 9:11–15).

As the New Testament opens, Jesus is the One who will bless both Israel and Gentiles.

Thus Simeon prophesied that Jesus would be "a light for revelation to the Gentiles, and for glory to your people Israel" (Luke 2:31–32). The angel Gabriel told Mary that her son Jesus would reign from the throne of David over Israel forever (Luke 1:32–33), and when the Magi visited Jesus in Matthew 2:1–12, Gentiles worshiped Israel's King. In Matthew 8:5–13, Jesus praised the faith of a Roman centurion and said that Gentiles would participate in God's kingdom banquet before unbelieving Jewish leaders.

Early in his ministry, Jesus directed the message of the kingdom solely to Israel (Matt. 10:5–7), yet after Jesus's death and resurrection, the gospel was proclaimed to the entire world, with Jesus himself commanding his followers, "Go therefore and make disciples of all nations" (Matt. 28:19). On the day of his ascension, Jesus affirmed the expectation of a restored kingdom for national Israel yet proclaimed the necessity of taking the gospel to all people groups of the world (Acts 1:6–8). As the book of Acts records, the gospel spread from Jerusalem to Samaria to the broader Gentile world. The Jerusalem Council also testified that the resurrected Son of David brought messianic salvation to Gentiles as Gentiles (Acts 15:13–18), which meant that they did not need to be incorporated into Israel or keep the Mosaic law.

Reflecting these historical developments, the apostle Paul gave clear teaching in his epistles about ethnicity for the church. Thus, Galatians 3:28 explains that believers equally share salvation and spiritual blessings in Christ regardless of race, gender, or social status. Ephesians 2:11–3:6 says that believing Gentiles are coequal with believing Jews in the people of God and participate together in the covenants and promises mediated through Israel. Believing Gentiles do not become spiritual Jews; instead, Jews and Gentiles share common life together in the church. The unity among Jews and Gentiles is grounded in the death of Jesus and the removal of the Mosaic law (Eph. 2:13–16). And so Colossians 3:9–11 speaks of a renewal in Christ "in which there is no distinction between Greek and Jew, circumcised and uncircumcised, barbarian, Scythian, slave and freeman" (NASB). Salvation is equally accessible to all groups.

The last book of the Bible also describes universal blessings. Representatives of every tribe, tongue, people, and nation will be saved by Christ and will reign when the kingdom comes to the earth (Rev. 5:9–10). Revelation 7:4–9 reveals the salvation of both the tribes of Israel and people from all nations. Revelation 21:3 uses the Greek term *laoi* to refer to the "peoples" of God (ESV mg.), showing ethnic diversity on the new earth. Revelation 21:24, 26 testifies that nations with their kings will bring contributions to the New Jerusalem. And Revelation 22:2 says that the leaves of the tree of life maintain healing and harmony among the nations. Never again will ethnic or national hostility exist, only harmony.

A biblical theology of ethnicity and nations reveals the following truths and principles:

1. All people of every ethnicity are made in the image of God.
2. No people group is superior or inferior to any other.
3. Racism is a heinous sin in that it denies full personhood to certain people groups, thus violating the dignity of all God's image bearers.

4. Israel was chosen to be the nation through which God would restore fallen humanity and bring salvation and restoration to all the world.
5. Salvation is provided to all through the ultimate Israelite, Jesus the Messiah, who will restore the nation of Israel and bring blessings to the Gentiles through salvation.
6. The death of Christ and the establishment of the new covenant bring unity to all who identify with Jesus. True racial unity and harmony are found only in Jesus the Messiah, not simply in education, social reform, legislation, or any other man-centered attempts.
7. The church should evidence racial harmony and serve as an example to the world of God's intention.
8. When Jesus returns, he will rule the nations from Israel and will bless all the nations (Isa. 27:6; Rom. 11:12).
9. In the eternal state, nations and governmental leaders will exist in harmony.

Human Government

God is a God of order, not chaos. Human government is an institution created by God to provide social order in the world.

BIBLICAL PRINCIPLES OF HUMAN GOVERNMENT

The most extensive discussion on the purpose of government is found in Romans 13:1–7:

> Let every person be subject to the governing authorities. For there is no authority except from God, and those that exist have been instituted by God. Therefore whoever resists the authorities resists what God has appointed, and those who resist will incur judgment. For rulers are not a terror to good conduct, but to bad. Would you have no fear of the one who is in authority? Then do what is good, and you will receive his approval, for he is God's servant for your good. But if you do wrong, be afraid, for he does not bear the sword in vain. For he is the servant of God, an avenger who carries out God's wrath on the wrongdoer. Therefore one must be in subjection, not only to avoid God's wrath but also for the sake of conscience. For because of this you also pay taxes, for the authorities are ministers of God, attending to this very thing. Pay to all what is owed to them: taxes to whom taxes are owed, revenue to whom revenue is owed, respect to whom respect is owed, honor to whom honor is owed.

Peter expressed the same view of human government in 1 Peter 2:13–14:

> Be subject for the Lord's sake to every human institution, whether it be to the emperor as supreme, or to governors as sent by him to punish those who do evil and to praise those who do good.

Several truths come from these two passages.

1. God has appointed human government (Rom. 13:1–2) as his "servant" (Rom. 13:4). Government is part of God's common goodness to mankind.

2. Since God appointed government, resisting government is resisting God. Those who resist its authority will be judged (Rom. 13:2).

3. One purpose of government is "to punish those who do evil" (1 Pet. 2:14). Thus, the one in authority is "an avenger who carries out God's wrath on the wrongdoer" (Rom. 13:4). Government functions as God's mediator to curb evil.

4. Government has the right to carry out capital punishment: "He does not bear the sword in vain" (Rom. 13:4). When Pilate told Jesus that he had the authority to crucify him (John 19:10), Jesus did not dispute this, but he did inform Pilate that his authority came from God: "You would have no authority over me at all unless it had been given you from above" (John 19:11).

5. Another function of government is to approve and praise those who do good (Rom. 13:3; 1 Pet. 2:14). Peaceful, law-abiding citizens need not fear the authorities. Few governments will harm those who obey their laws; rather, they seek to honor them.

6. Government is a cause for "terror" to those who do bad things (Rom. 13:3). Those who break the law must be afraid of the consequent punishment. Even the most godless governments can deter criminal behavior.

7. All people, and especially Christians, are to be "subject" to human government (Rom. 13:1, 5; 1 Pet. 2:13). The word "subject" was used of a soldier's absolute obedience to his superior. The one exception arises if obeying a civil command means disobeying a command of God (Ex. 1:7; Dan. 3:16–18; 6:7, 10). In this case, "We must obey God rather than men" (Acts 5:29).

8. Obeying government eases one's conscience (Rom. 13:5).

9. People are to pay taxes and show respect to governing authorities (Rom. 13:7). Jesus affirmed taxation when he said, "Render to Caesar the things that are Caesar's" (Matt. 22:21).

HUMAN GOVERNMENT IN THE UNFOLDING STORY OF SCRIPTURE

While societies existed after creation, God established the power of government as a mediatorial institution after the flood. Cain murdered his brother Abel and feared personal retribution. "I shall be a fugitive and a wanderer on the earth, and whoever finds me will kill me," said Cain (Gen. 4:14). Yet God protected Cain by placing a mark on him that warned of vengeance for any who tried to kill him (Gen. 4:15). Lamech also killed a young man who struck him (Gen. 4:23–24). Cain and Lamech were murderers who feared retribution but not by a civil magistrate. Cain moved on to build a city east of Eden in the land of Nod and named it after his son Enoch (Gen. 4:16–17). This is the first city mentioned in the Bible.

The force and ultimate threat of government began after the flood, when God introduced capital punishment. He declared that he would "require a reckoning for the life of man" and that "whoever sheds the blood of man, by man shall his blood be shed, for God made man in his own image" (Gen. 9:5–6). Here God granted government the right to inflict capital punishment on those who murder a person made in God's image. This is not to be done in acts of personal vengeance but by an established government given the responsibility and right to punish wrongdoers.

An attempt at a centralized human government occurred in Genesis 11:1–9.

Those building the Tower of Babel in the land of Shinar wanted to make a name for themselves by remaining in one location in disobedience to God's command to fill the earth (Gen. 9:1). God viewed their proud plans as defying his will, so he confused them by miraculously introducing differing languages. The long list of ethnic groups in Genesis 10–11 was the result of the dispersion from Babel.

At the time of Israel's patriarchs, social interactions occurred on a smaller level through families and groups of families gathered into tribes. Later, the growing Hebrew people that descended from Abraham, Isaac, and Jacob were enslaved by the government of Egypt, the superpower of that time. After the exodus from Egypt, the Hebrew people became a kingdom themselves (Ex. 19:6), and the Mosaic covenant functioned as Israel's constitution. Under Joshua, land was given as the place where Israel would operate its government. Genesis 17:6 revealed God's intent for Israel to eventually have a king, and Saul became the first king of Israel. The next king, David, received the Davidic covenant, which promised an eternal kingdom over Israel and the world with an heir of David reigning forever (2 Sam. 7:12–19; Luke 1:32–33).

Israel, however, was characterized by disobedience, which led to captivity and dispersion. Israel's kingdom, both leaders and people, failed to run a righteous government. The kingdom reached its highpoint in 1 Kings 8–10 when God's presence filled the temple and when the Abrahamic promises of land, seed, and universal blessing seemed on their way to fulfillment. Even governments outside Israel were seeking the wisdom of Israel's king, Solomon (1 Kings 10:1–13, 23–25). But Solomon's idolatry (1 Kings 11) put the kingdom of Israel on a trajectory that led to the twelve tribes dividing into two kingdoms and eventually getting dispersed throughout the nations. Israel's government ended in failure, not only for the Hebrews but also for the world it was designed to bless. This monumental failure would be devastating but not terminal.

Human governments in a fallen world are always mixed with corruption and wickedness. Babylon, in particular, was a city that represented self-glory, pride, and opposition to God's purposes, both religiously and politically. The governments of Egypt and Assyria were godless, although God still used them as his instruments. While interpreting the statue dream of the Babylonian monarch Nebuchadnezzar, Daniel revealed that five successive governments—Babylon, Medo-Persia, Greece, Rome, and a coming revived Roman Empire—would rule the world until God's kingdom from heaven arrived dramatically and crushed these Gentile governments. Then the kingdom of God, centered in Israel, would be the preeminent global power on the earth (Daniel 2). Isaiah predicted that when God's kingdom would be established, even traditional enemies like Egypt and Assyria would become the people of God alongside Israel (Isa. 19:24–25).

Central to a righteous government is a righteous leader. Concerning the coming Messiah, Isaiah predicted, "The government shall be upon his shoulder. . . . Of the increase of his government and of peace there will be no end, on the throne of David and over his kingdom" (Isa. 9:6–7). In reference to this Davidic leader "from the stump of Jesse," Isaiah also said, "Righteousness shall be the belt of his waist" (Isa. 11:5), and, "With righteousness he shall judge the poor, and decide with equity for the meek of the earth" (Isa. 11:4).

When Jesus arrived, he was identified as the rightful descendant of Abraham and David who would rule over Israel (Matt. 1:1; Luke 1:32–33). Yet the people did not believe in him, and thus his kingdom reign over the nations awaits his second coming. At that future time he will come with his angels to judge the nations of the earth (Matt. 25:31–46) and establish his reign. The twelve apostles will then rule under him with the church over a restored nation of Israel (Matt. 19:28; Rev. 2:26–27; 5:10).

Yet shortly before Jesus's return, Satan will be exercising rule over the nations through the Antichrist whom he will empower (2 Thess. 2:3–12; Revelation 13), and the city of Babylon will function as his capital (Revelation 17–18). When Jesus returns, however, he will "strike down the nations, and he will rule them with a rod of iron" (Rev. 19:15).

Nations and governments will exist during Jesus's millennial kingdom, since Revelation 20:3 says that Satan will be removed from the earth at that time so "he might not deceive the nations any longer." This means that nations will exist in that era. Isaiah 2:2–4 reveals that the Lord will then make executive decisions on behalf of the nations and will establish international harmony. When the thousand-year reign of Jesus is nearing its end, Satan will be released from his prison and "will come out to deceive the nations" (Rev. 20:7–8). Those who join him from the nations will be destroyed by fire from heaven (Rev. 20:9–10).

Nations will also exist in the eternal state. Revelation 21:24, 26 refers to "nations" and "kings of the earth" that "bring their glory" into the New Jerusalem. The leaves of the tree of life will maintain harmony among these nations (Rev. 22:2), and these nations will reign over the new earth in the presence of God the Father and Jesus the Son (Rev. 22:1–5).

Human Culture

Human culture has roots in Genesis 1–2. The command for man to rule and subdue the earth and its creatures (Gen. 1:26, 28) is often referred to as "the cultural mandate" since man was to use his abilities and status as God's image bearer to control the creation on God's behalf. This included the land, vegetation, animals, birds, and aquatic creatures. In Genesis 2:15, God put Adam "in the garden of Eden to work it and keep it." Man was given an earthly vocation, and this created culture.

Culture includes works, art, music, education, and all areas where man interacts with his environment. God is the Creator of culture, and man is called to carry it out on God's behalf. The human ability to develop God-honoring culture was damaged by the fall in Genesis 3. Man came under a death sentence, and the environment and all its components were cursed. Mankind would labor hard, but the ground would work against him with thorns and thistles and would eventually consume him in death (Gen. 3:17–19).

Still, culture developed with the events of Genesis 4. Jabal, Enoch's descendant through Lamech, became the first cattle rancher or dweller with herds. He was "the father of those who dwell in tents and have livestock" (Gen. 4:20). Jabal's brother, Jubal, became the first to compose and play music. He "was the father of all those who play the lyre and pipe" (Gen. 4:21). Another son of Lamech, Tubal-cain, was the first to specialize in metals. He "was the forger of all instruments of bronze and iron" (Gen. 4:22).

Even with these cultural developments, the period before the global flood of Noah's day was characterized by dominating wickedness (Gen. 6:5). After the flood, the Noahic covenant promised stability in nature as the foundation for carrying out God's plans. This would have positive results for farming and agriculture: "While the earth remains, seedtime and harvest, cold and heat, summer and winter, day and night, shall not cease" (Gen. 8:22).

Noah focused on agriculture: "Noah began to be a man of the soil, and he planted a vineyard" (Gen. 9:20). Yet Noah's sinfulness was manifest when "he drank of the wine and became drunk and lay uncovered in his tent" (Gen. 9:21). Culture was also adapted for collective yet nefarious uses, such as in Genesis 11, when people gathered in the land of Shinar (modern-day Iraq) to build a tower into heaven:

> And they said to one another, "Come, let us make bricks, and burn them thoroughly." And they had brick for stone, and bitumen for mortar. Then they said, "Come, let us build ourselves a city and a tower with its top in the heavens, and let us make a name for ourselves, lest we be dispersed over the face of the whole earth." (Gen. 11:3–4)

The details of "brick for stone" and "bitumen for mortar" show cultural prowess in architecture, although here men used it to make a great name for themselves and stay located in one area against God's command to multiply (Gen. 9:1). God was so concerned about this rebellious act that he came down from heaven to thwart their plans by confusing their language and causing the people to scatter over the earth (Gen. 11:5–9). God continues to intervene in judgment to thwart man's cultural ingenuity if it opposes his purposes (cf. Rom. 1:18–32).

During the time of Israel's patriarchs, culture focused on pasturing flocks (Gen. 37:13–17). The people constructed temporary dwelling places in winter, and in spring they sought pastures for their flocks. Later, the Hebrew people intersected with Egypt, which had a sophisticated culture for its day. While imprisoned, Joseph interacted with Pharaoh's "chief cupbearer" and "chief baker" (Gen. 40:1–2). When placed in leadership in Egypt, Joseph helped the Egyptians gather grain for an upcoming drought (Gen. 41:53–57). As the Hebrew people became enslaved in Egypt, they were tasked with building "store cities" for Pharaoh (Ex. 1:11).

Moses was trained in the culture of Egypt (Acts 7:22), although his loyalty was with God's people—the Hebrews. When the Hebrews were freed from Egypt in the exodus, they plundered the wealth of the Egyptians (Ex. 12:36). The Mosaic covenant given at Sinai contained cultural instructions such as the building of the tabernacle, which would be at the center of Israel's worship life. Two gifted artisans, Bezalel and Oholiab, would head up this work, and Exodus 31:2–6 displays their great ability:

> See, I have called by name Bezalel the son of Uri, son of Hur, of the tribe of Judah, and I have filled him with the Spirit of God, with ability and intelligence, with knowledge and all craftsmanship, to devise artistic designs, to work in gold, silver, and bronze, in cutting stones for setting, and in carving wood, to work in every craft. And behold, I have appointed with him Oholiab, the son of Ahisamach, of the tribe of Dan. And I have given to all able men ability, that they may make all that I have commanded you.

Yet Israel's wicked use of culture manifested itself when the people constructed a golden calf to worship (Exodus 32). The contrast between Exodus 31 and 32 highlights culture in a fallen world. As God's image bearers, men are capable of great cultural works, yet apart from God's will, culture can be used for idolatry and wickedness.

Culture was prominent in the life of David. He was a gifted musician and psalmist. His example shows that musical instruments should be used to praise the Lord, including trumpets, tambourines, strings, pipes, and cymbals (Ps. 150:3–5). Solomon also invested much artistic effort and materials in building the glorious and beautiful First Temple (1 Kings 7–8). When the queen of Sheba saw Solomon's wisdom, the temple, the food on Solomon's table, the order of his servants, and their clothes, it took her breath away (1 Kings 10:4–5). She was overwhelmed by the beauty and order of Israel's culture during this high point of Israel's kingdom.

Unfortunately, both Solomon and the people of Israel become enamored with the idolatrous cultures of other nations. This would lead to divine judgment in the form of dispersion and enslavement. Babylon's conquest of Israel brought the destruction of the temple and the plundering of its gold and precious items (2 Kings 24:13). While in captivity, Daniel and three associates became an example of being educated in the ways of Babylonian culture without compromising their devotion to the God of the Bible. They refused to partake of the king's food or worship a golden statue (Daniel 1 and 3).

While railing against Israel's covenant disobedience, the prophets of Israel also foretold of a future restoration of Israel with cultural glory. Isaiah 60:5–7 depicts this flourishing time:

> Then you shall see and be radiant;
> > your heart shall thrill and exult,
> because the abundance of the sea shall be turned to you,
> > the wealth of the nations shall come to you.
> A multitude of camels shall cover you,
> > the young camels of Midian and Ephah;
> > all those from Sheba shall come.
> They shall bring gold and frankincense,
> > and shall bring good news, the praises of the LORD.
> All the flocks of Kedar shall be gathered to you;

the rams of Nebaioth shall minister to you;
they shall come up with acceptance on my altar,
and I will beautify my beautiful house.

Kingdom conditions would also include agriculture, architecture, and interaction with the animal kingdom, according to Isaiah 65:17–25.

When Jesus arrived, he proclaimed the nearness of the kingdom of God in all its dimensions (Matt. 4:17), yet both the leaders and people of Israel rejected him (Matthew 11–12). Nonetheless, Jesus's death atoned for sins and laid the basis for the reconciliation and restoration of Israel, all nations, and all things (Acts 3:21; Col. 1:20; Rev. 5:9–10). When Jesus comes again in glory, there will be a "new world." Those who left all to follow him will receive houses, family members, and lands in his kingdom (Matt. 19:28–29).

During the present era, Satan is the ruler of this evil world system (Eph. 2:2). He continues to steal, kill, and destroy (cf. John 8:44; 1 Pet. 5:8). The high point of his deception will come during the future tribulation period when the city of Babylon will commit religious, economic, and political rebellion (Revelation 17–18). That is Satan-inspired culture at its worst. Yet the final Babylon will come to a wretched end when the Lord Jesus returns. Satan will be removed from the earth (Rev. 20:1–3), and the nations will flourish under Christ's leadership (Isa. 2:2–4). Jesus's coming kingdom will include a restoration of culture (Isaiah 11; 35; 65–66). Even the eternal state will possess the best of human culture, as the nations and kings of the earth bring their "glory" into the New Jerusalem. This "glory" probably refers to the cultural contributions from the nations. All culture during this time will exist for the glory of God, and its headquarters will be the New Jerusalem, made of pure gold and precious jewels (Rev. 21:9–21).

In sum, God created culture. He made a diverse world and tasked man to rule and subdue it for his glory. There is no dichotomy between God and culture or man and culture. God expects man to successfully rule over his creation (Ps. 8:4–8), although the complete fulfillment of this expectation awaits Jesus's kingdom in the "world to come" (Heb. 2:5–8). Culture in this fallen world is infested with sin, so there must also be a purging with fire of all negative remnants of a fallen world, including fallen human culture (2 Pet. 3:8–13). On the new earth, culture will always point to the glory of God. Heaven's culture will do so with absolute holy perfection.

Biblical Theology of Man

The doctrine of man can be summarized as follows:

At the culmination of a literal six-day creation, God created man in two genders—male and female. Starting from the first man (Adam) and the first woman (Eve), mankind was mandated both to multiply and fill the earth and to rule and subdue the creation on God's behalf. These are man's primary responsibilities.

Man was created in the "image" and "likeness" of God, which means that he is like God in some ways and that he represents God on the earth. Man is both a king and a son. Yet at the same time, he is not God. Man is inherently tied to the earth and the created order, though he is the pinnacle of God's creation. Humanity is placed into three relationships: (1) with God, (2) with other humans, and (3) with creation. As God's image bearer, man is constituted to relate to all three effectively. Each human person is also a complex unity of body and soul/spirit. As a volitional and reasoning being, man is called to love God and to show his allegiance by obeying God.

Man, however, disobeyed God and failed the kingdom command to rule and subdue creation. He died spiritually, and the process of physical death began. His relationship with other humans suffered, as did his relationship to the earth, which began to work against him. Man was still the image of God, but this image was marred and distorted by sin. Man became totally corrupt in his being, and he could do nothing to save himself. Hope was not lost, though, as God initiated a plan to save mankind and reverse the curse through a coming seed of the woman. Humanity fell, but a coming specific man would be the Savior of the world. Adam and Eve and their descendants anticipated this coming Deliverer, though they did not know the timing of his arrival (see Gen. 4:1; 5:28–29). Man's right to rule the world was affirmed even after the fall (Ps. 8:4–8), although in this present age he is not ruling the earth successfully. That ability awaits the "world to come" (Heb. 2:5–8).

God raised up people, saved by grace through faith, to further his plan to save mankind and creation. These included covenant heads such as Noah, Abraham, Moses, and David. But each of these men was sinful and unable to be the Savior. Israel as a nation would be used to further God's purposes, although the nation too showed itself to be sinful. The same was true for the kings in the line of David, who were supposed to model obedience and righteousness in Israel yet also failed.

When Jesus arrived, he was the "last Adam" (1 Cor. 15:45), the Messiah, and the ultimate seed of the woman (Gal. 3:16). In other words, he was (and is) the ultimate man—God's man. He was the perfect image of God, who manifested God's intent for humanity. Jesus fulfilled God's plans for man. He was righteous and obedient. Relationally, Jesus loved God and loved people infinitely. Functionally, he showed his dominion over the earth by his miracles.

Jesus presented himself as King and his kingdom as near (Matt. 4:17). Yet the people did not receive him. With his death Jesus atoned for the sins of God's image bearers and laid the basis for the kingdom of God and the restoration of all things (Col. 1:20; Heb. 2:5–9; Rev. 5:9–10). Jesus ascended to heaven as the exalted Messiah and sat down at God's right hand in heaven, ruling his spiritual kingdom of salvation while awaiting his earthly rule from his Davidic throne at his second coming (Ps. 110:1–2; Matt. 25:31; Rev. 3:21).

Based on Christ's atoning work and the establishment of the new covenant at the cross, those who are united to Jesus receive salvation and are being conformed to the image of Christ, who is the perfect image of God. Sanctification is the process by which God's people in this age become more like Christ, increasingly manifesting what the image of God is supposed to be. Yet this world is still evil, and man's successful rule over the earth awaits Jesus's kingdom at his return. When Jesus returns to earth, he will bind Satan and remove his presence from the earth. Then, with those who belong to him, Christ will rule for a millennium over an earthly kingdom that fulfills the kingdom mandate of Genesis 1:26–28. Jesus will rule the nations (Psalm 2) and share his rule with his saints (Rev. 2:26–27; 3:21).

When Jesus fulfills man's destiny on the earth and finally and fully succeeds where the first Adam failed, his kingdom will transfer to the Father's kingdom in the eternal state (1 Cor. 15:24–28; Revelation 20–21). As a result of the work of the ultimate man, Jesus, the earth will have been successfully ruled and subdued, Satan will have been defeated, unbelievers will have been judged, and the curse will be forever removed. The saints of God will eternally enjoy a perfect relationship with God, other people, and the new creation. Man's task will be a success because of Jesus! The last verse describing activity on the new earth proclaims, "And they will reign forever and ever" (Rev. 22:5). What has been impossible for thousands of years will happen—the story ends well for redeemed humanity!

SIN

Introduction to Sin

Sin Defined
Sin's Relationship to Other Doctrines
Origin of Sin

The universal sinfulness of man is obvious and verifiable. Sin permeates every aspect of our existence. It impacts us individually and societally. It is deeply rooted within us and is manifested continually. Throughout history, societies have consistently acknowledged man's natural sinfulness. Since the Enlightenment, however, Western civilization has become increasingly antagonistic to the reality of sin, especially as it is defined biblically. There are four main reasons for this change.

First, modernity tends to view human beings as naturally good. Before the philosophical shifts of the eighteenth century, a general understanding of human depravity prevailed. The Protestant Reformation, for example, was connected with Martin Luther's angst over his own sinfulness. With the coming of the modern era, though, the traditional view of man's sinfulness began to wane, and man was viewed as inherently good. Human problems and suffering were linked with ignorance. In the false euphoria of the Enlightenment, many concluded from the advances in education, science, and technology that man was inherently good and that as he was educated, the world would get better. The twentieth century clearly obliterated that illusion, and man's depravity was put on display, as the world exploded with the largest scale of warfare and bloodshed in history—including two devastating world wars, the Holocaust, and the Cold War. The twenty-first century so far has also been rife with wars, unstable nations pursuing or possessing nuclear weapons, and increasing

Islamic terrorism. Global media have exponentially exposed human depravity at a level never before imagined. The education, science, and technology that brought great medical advances and comforts have at the same time devised weapons of mass destruction. Societies are increasingly opposed to God's standards, even redefining basic aspects of human identity such as gender and marriage. Contrary to the modern and postmodern mindsets, the reality of sin is alive and on full display.

Second, deterministic views of humanity have challenged the biblical understanding of sin. People are viewed primarily as products of their environment, social upbringing, or psychological drives or deprivations. Society has gone so far in accommodating its own depravity that it is reluctant to hold anyone morally culpable for almost any behavior. This accommodation is consistent with the view that man is basically a machine that does what he is preprogramed to do.

Third, with the rise of postmodernism, our society has shifted toward moral relativism. Today, right and wrong, good and evil, are not defined in absolute terms but are viewed subjectively. Individuals and societies, not God, are seen as having the authority to determine what is wrong. A strong majority of people now believe that truth and morals are flexible and subjective, not fixed. And they have no interest in what Scripture says.

Fourth, sin is an unpleasant subject. In our age of self-esteem and subjectivity, people do not like to think of themselves as evil. Millard Erickson notes, "To speak of humans as sinners is almost like screaming out a profanity or obscenity at a very formal, dignified, genteel meeting, or even in church. It is forbidden. This general attitude is almost a new type of legalism, the major prohibition of which is, 'You shall not speak anything negative.'"[27]

Sin Defined

Of the Bible's sixty-six books and 1,189 chapters, only two books and four chapters do not mention sin or sinners. Genesis 1–2 and Revelation 21–22 stand alone as unique chapters that rehearse the creation before sin and the new heaven and new earth, which will never be infected by sin. The rest of the Bible, from Genesis 3:1 to Revelation 20:15, abounds with the themes of human sin and the need for salvation. Sin is a major doctrine.

The study of sin is called *hamartiology*. This designation comes from the Greek word for "sin," *hamartia*. Several associated terms and concepts indicate that sin is a multifaceted and complex reality. In the Old Testament Hebrew, *khata'* is often translated "sinning" or "sinned" (Gen. 20:6; Ex. 10:16). The word is also linked with missing the mark (Judg. 20:16). Proverbs 19:2 states, "Whoever makes haste with his feet misses [*khata'*] his way." This term is closely related to the Greek noun *hamartia* ("sin") and its verb form *hamartanō*, meaning "miss the mark," "err," or "be mistaken." The verb form is found in Romans 3:23: "For all have sinned [*hamartanō*] and fall short of the glory of God."

---

27. Erickson, *Christian Theology*, 582.

Pasha' is another strong Hebrew term for sin in the Old Testament. The word means "to rebel," "to trespass," or "to betray." It is used of Israel's revolt against God in Isaiah 1:2: "But they have rebelled [*pasha'*] against me." Also, the Hebrew word *'abar* means "to transgress" or "to pass over." In a moral context it refers to transgressing a commandment or violating a covenant. Moses said, "Why then are you transgressing [*'abar*] the command of the LORD, when it will not succeed?" (Num. 14:41). In Judges 2:20, God was angry with Israel because "this people have transgressed [*'abar*] my covenant that I commanded their fathers and have not obeyed my voice."

Various Greek terms for "sin" exist in the New Testament. The word *adikia* means "unrighteousness" or "injustice" (Rom. 1:18). Paul referred to certain persons "who did not believe the truth but had pleasure in unrighteousness [*adikia*]" (2 Thess. 2:12). The term *planaō* emphasizes "wandering" or "straying" (2 Tim. 3:13; 2 Pet. 3:17). Sin is also *anomia*, which means "lawlessness," that is, rejecting God's law. First John 3:4 simply declares, "Sin is lawlessness."

Apeitheō carries the sense of being disobedient and willfully obstinate toward God's will (Rom. 11:31; John 3:36). *Asebeia* can be translated "ungodliness," "wickedness," or "impiety." Jude said, "In the last time there will be scoffers, following their own ungodly [*asebeia*] passions" (Jude 18). *Agnoia* refers to ignorance or the absence of understanding. Paul said that unbelievers were darkened in their understanding "because of the ignorance [*agnoia*] that is in them" (Eph. 4:18). *Parabasis* is a breaking of or deviation from God's law. Romans 2:23 states, "You who boast in the law dishonor God by breaking [*parabasis*] the law."

The above is not an exhaustive list, but together these representative biblical terms demonstrate the multidimensional nature of sin. Sin is clearly wrong in many ways. But is there a central or core element of sin? Various answers to this question have been offered. Augustine asserted that pride is the heart of sin, because it is the motive behind man's attempt to live his life in the power of self. Others have postulated that lack of *shalom*, or peace, is the core of sin, since it always brings disruption and pain. Selfishness and idolatry are other suggestions. Selfishness is loving oneself more than God. Idolatry is worshiping a creature instead of the Creator. The first commandment warns against idolatry—"I am the LORD your God. . . . You shall have no other gods before me" (Ex. 20:2–3). Certainly all the concepts surveyed above are components of the complexity of human depravity.

Sin must be understood from a theocentric or God-centered standpoint. At its core, sin is a violation of the Creator-creature relationship. Man only exists because God made him, and man is in every sense obligated to serve his Creator. Sin causes man to assume the role of God and to assert autonomy for himself apart from the Creator. The most all-encompassing view of sin's mainspring, therefore, is the demand for autonomy.

Because God is the Creator of everything, all creatures are obligated to obey him and to live according to his will. The falls of Satan and then Adam and Eve are tied to acting autonomously and disobediently seeking to be like God. Through a human king, Satan declared, "I will make myself like the Most High" (Isa. 14:14). Later, the Satan-inspired serpent told Eve, "When you eat of it [the tree of the knowledge of good and evil] your eyes will be opened, and you will be like God" (Gen. 3:5). Eve and then Adam, without regard for God's command, acted on this belief: "So when the woman saw that the tree was good for food, and that it was a delight to the eyes, and that the tree was to be desired to make one wise, she took of its fruit and ate, and she also gave some to her husband who was with her, and he ate" (Gen. 3:6).

In the cases of Satan and of Adam and Eve, they were not satisfied in obeying God. They were created to love God with all their being and to interpret the world from his perspective. But they did not desire to love God through obedience. Acting autonomously, they stepped out on their own in an effort to be like God. That wicked presumption is repeated with every sin. Instead of saying, "God's will be done," the sinner says, "My will be done." Sin, therefore, is acting autonomously and usurping the authority of God.

In his detailed treatise on the sinfulness of mankind in Romans 1–3, Paul explained how sinful creatures violated their relationship with the Creator: "They exchanged the truth about God for a lie and worshiped and served the creature rather than the Creator, who is blessed forever! Amen" (Rom. 1:25). Thus, idolatry occurs when persons exchange the worship of God for the worship of creatures. The peace and wholeness that only comes from worshiping the true God is forfeited when worship is instead directed toward creatures. By rejecting the Creator, the unbelieving heart seeks to satisfy itself with that which cannot bring lasting joy or true fulfillment— whether material possessions, success, admiration, immoral relationships, drugs, alcohol, gambling, or many other substitutes. Those who devote themselves to such things become enslaved to them (2 Pet. 2:19).

In the context of Romans 1, Paul said that foolish people with darkened hearts "exchanged the glory of the immortal God for images resembling mortal man and birds and animals and creeping things" (Rom. 1:23). He singled out homosexuality by both women and men: "For their women exchanged natural relations for those that are contrary to nature; and the men likewise gave up natural relations with women and were consumed with passion for one another, men committing shameless acts with men and receiving in themselves the due penalty for their error" (Rom. 1:26–27).

In light of these factors we offer this short definition of sin: *Sin is any lack of conformity to God's will in attitude, thought, or action, whether committed actively or passively. The center of all sin is autonomy, which is the replacing of God with self. Always closely associated with sin are its products—pride, selfishness, idolatry, and lack of peace (shalom).*

Sin's Relationship to Other Doctrines

DOCTRINE OF GOD

The doctrine of sin is inseparable from all other biblical doctrines. The doctrine of sin is linked to God since sin is primarily against God. Psalm 51:4 says, "Against you,

you only, have I sinned and done what is evil in your sight." In addition, only God can take the initiative to remove the enmity between man and God (2 Cor. 5:19).

DOCTRINE OF MAN

The doctrine of sin directly defines mankind as fallen and affects everyone since sin defines every life at birth; corrupts everyone's relationship with God, with other persons, and with creation; and brings all to death. Sin impacts our entire human constitution and existence, distorting every aspect of our being—body and soul. Sin also affects man's ability to fully rule and subdue the creation. Only a righteous man—Jesus—can succeed perfectly where Adam and mankind failed. Only the Son of Man can and will reverse the curse.

DOCTRINE OF SALVATION

The doctrine of sin obviously affects the doctrine of salvation since sinners need to be rescued but are unable to save themselves. Because they are profoundly and pervasively sinful, sinners are in need of salvation by grace. Without salvation by divine grace alone, man not only fails his God-intended relationships and functions but also is left to face the eternal wrath of God.

DOCTRINE OF CHRIST

The doctrine of sin relates to Jesus Christ since Jesus is the last Adam, the suffering servant, the Messiah, and the seed of the woman—the One who conquers sin and all its forms and effects, redeems believers, restores creation, and defeats Satan. Jesus does all this by atoning for the sins of his people. Without his perfect, substitutionary death, there would be no salvation from sin. And without his resurrection and exaltation as Lord of all, man would not be able to rule over creation as God promised and expects.

DOCTRINE OF ANGELS

Both Satan and the fallen angels sinned against God and were removed from his presence. No salvation is provided for Satan and the demons who followed him. While holy angels are ministering spirits who serve people inheriting salvation (Heb. 1:14), Satan and his evil spirits are deceivers who tempt mankind to disobey God. Satan and all fallen angels will be punished by being made to dwell forever in the lake of fire prepared for them.

DOCTRINE OF THE CHURCH

The church is the community of people saved from sin in this age. It is also God's global ambassador for proclaiming reconciliation to sinners. The church proclaims the gospel of the forgiveness of sins found in Jesus Christ. God's grace in Christians breaks the power of sin in their lives, and they are to experience victory over sin by obeying God's Word in the power of the Holy Spirit, which testifies to the power of God in salvation.

DOCTRINE OF ESCHATOLOGY

The fallen world is dominated by sin and its effects. But it is not as bad as it could be or will be, because a time is coming when the Holy Spirit will cease to restrain sin as he does presently. When that time occurs, the Antichrist figure will appear, being Satan's man who embodies lawlessness (cf. 2 Thess. 2:3–4; Rev. 13:1–10). Demons who have long been bound will be released from the pit and will come to earth to tempt and torment (Rev. 9:1–11). At his return to earth, Jesus will defeat the Antichrist and his followers (Rev. 19:19–21). Satan and his demons will be bound during the millennial period (Rev. 20:1–6) and will ultimately be thrown into the lake of fire (Rev. 20:10), and sin and its effects will be finally removed with the coming eternal state. In regard to the new earth, Revelation 21:4 states, "He will wipe away every tear from their eyes, and death shall be no more, neither shall there be mourning, nor crying, nor pain anymore, for the former things have passed away."

Origin of Sin

SATAN

The Bible lays the blame for the sin and death in the world on the first man, Adam (Rom. 5:12). Yet in Genesis 3 and its account of man's fall, a dark spiritual figure lurks with evil intentions. This creature tempted God's image bearers and cast doubt on what God had told them. He enticed them to interpret the world from his perspective, not God's. Though this creature was a literal serpent (Gen. 3:1), the force behind the snake was the fallen angel Lucifer, now known as Satan, which means "adversary."

Genesis does not describe Satan's fall, but the chief demon arrives in Genesis 3 as a fallen being fiercely opposed to God. The fall of Satan is probably being referred to in Ezekiel 28 and Isaiah 14. Both passages speak of human kings (of Tyre and Babylon), yet what is depicted goes far beyond any human monarch. Rather, both passages describe the first sin in the cosmos. Ezekiel 28:13 says, "You were in Eden, the garden of God." We are told that Satan was an "anointed guardian cherub . . . on the holy mountain of God" (Ezek. 28:14). The reference to "cherub" means that Satan was an angel in God's presence. Ezekiel 28:15 then states, "You were blameless in your ways from the day you were created, till unrighteousness was found in you." So Satan went from "blameless" to "unrighteousness." God is not the chargeable cause of unrighteousness. Unrighteousness was found in Satan; the blame lies with him. Isaiah 14:14 says that the desire to be like God ("the Most High") was the reason for this angelic worship leader's rebellion (Isa. 14:11–12).

ADAM AND EVE

The Serpent approached Eve with the lie that eating from the tree of the knowledge of good and evil would bring enlightenment and make her like God. Eve was seduced by the lie and ate first from the tree and then gave the fruit to Adam (Gen. 3:6). Still, Scripture places the primary responsibility for this act on Adam, since Adam, not Eve, was the representative head of humanity. Adam and Eve immediately became sinners and hid themselves out of fearful guilt. God called for Adam specifically: "But the LORD God called to the man and said to him, 'Where are you?'" (Gen. 3:9). Paul says that both Adam and Eve sinned, yet the key difference is that "Adam was not deceived, but the woman was deceived and became a transgressor" (1 Tim. 2:14). Romans 5:12 explicitly places the blame for the sin and death in the world on Adam, the representative head: "Sin came into the world through one man [Adam], and death through sin."

There are parallels between the first two rebellions. Satan and Adam both sinned after being created sinless and directly experiencing God's presence. Satan was in God's presence in heaven, while Adam walked with God in the garden of Eden (Gen. 3:8). Both were unsatisfied with their perfect conditions, rebelliously desiring to be like their Creator (Gen. 3:5). But rather than making them equal to God, their rebellion made them far less like God than they had already been and separated them from God.

Since God cannot be the author of sin and does not tempt anyone to sin (James 1:13), and since Lucifer, the angels who followed him, and Adam and Eve were all created sinless, the question arises as to where sin originated. Many believe that since God is all-powerful, the blame for sin must belong to him. This is false. Certainly, the origin of sin is a deep and dark mystery, but God is not the chargeable cause of sin. Because created persons sinned, the capacity for sin had to exist as a possibility within them. Sin occurred because Satan, Adam, and Eve chose to exercise their volition to disobey God rather than to love God. Consequently, as creatures, they cannot escape accountability to their Creator.

Sin does not surprise God. He is able to overcome sin and has even ordained it to most fully display his glory, but the blame for sin lies at the feet of the persons who choose to disobey. God's absolute sovereignty in no way undermines man's accountability.[28] This is true both for Satan and fallen angels and for Adam and Eve, who passed on their sinfulness to all their descendants.

Consequences of the Fall

Personal Consequences
The Fall's Impact on Relationships
Three Forms of Death
Transmission of Adam's Sin
Old Self and New Self
Total Depravity

Personal Consequences

Sin always disappoints and never satisfies. Adam and Eve were instantly faced with this reality. The aftermath of their sinful act reveals sin's consequences. Embracing the Serpent's lie, Adam and Eve expected to become like God, enlightened and fulfilled.

---

28. For more on how God's sovereignty over sin and evil does not make him the chargeable cause of either, see "The Decree of God and the Problem of Evil" (p. 491) and "The Justification of God" (p. 509), both in chap. 7.

Yet the opposite occurred. When Eve and then Adam ate of the forbidden tree, their eyes "were opened" but not in the way they expected (Gen. 3:7). They did not discover contentment and bliss. Instead, they experienced guilt and shame. They were immediately aware of their nakedness and sewed fig leaves together to cover their condition (Gen. 3:7). The purity and innocence of their prefall state ended. Everything suddenly changed. A Pandora's box of perversion and negative consequences was unleashed. They were entirely unlike God.

Satan promised Eve that eating from the tree would bring knowledge of good and evil (Gen. 3:5), and this came true in a way Eve would never have expected. Adam and Eve now knew evil experientially, along with its devastating consequences. In addition to shame came another consequence—fear. When the couple heard God walking in the garden, they "hid themselves from the presence of the LORD God among the trees of the garden" (Gen. 3:8). Adam said, "I was afraid" (Gen. 3:10). Sin causes fear and hiding from God. When Adam and Eve ate of the tree, they set God aside and focused on their desires. But acting autonomously did not mean escaping from God. Their holy Creator came looking for them, and for the first time, with sin on their minds, they were afraid.

Another result of sin was blame. When God confronted Adam, Adam appeared to blame Eve: "The woman whom you gave to be with me, she gave me fruit of the tree, and I ate" (Gen. 3:12). In reality, Adam blamed God when he said, "The woman whom *you* gave to be with me . . ." Then when God asked Eve what she had done, she blamed the animal, saying, "The serpent deceived me, and I ate" (Gen. 3:13). The universal default position among fallen persons is to blame someone else for their sin.

These personal consequences for sin are severe. Sin promises enlightenment and peace, but instead it brings shame, fear, and blame, as well as death (Gen. 2:17). And as the next section shows, the consequences reach far beyond even this.

The Fall's Impact on Relationships

The negative consequences for sin go beyond personal turmoil and despair. Man was created for relationships with God, with other people, and with the creation. All three connections were damaged by the fall of man.

GOD

First and most important, man's relationship with God was severed. Man became spiritually dead. (More on what spiritual death entails will be discussed below [p. 460].)

In addition, sin brings the wrath of God, which is God's righteous displeasure toward sin. Romans 1:18 says, "For the wrath of God is revealed from heaven against all ungodliness and unrighteousness of men, who by their unrighteousness suppress the truth" (cf. Col. 3:5–6). Ephesians 5:6 states, "The wrath of God comes upon the sons of disobedience." God's wrath hangs over all in rebellion against him and will be manifested in the future day of the Lord and the final judgment in the lake of fire

(Rev. 20:11–15). Paul said to the unrepentant, "You are storing up wrath for yourself on the day of wrath when God's righteous judgment will be revealed" (Rom. 2:5).

Sin also invites God's punishment. Because he is holy and righteous, God must punish sin. Jesus said that the wicked "will go away into eternal punishment" (Matt. 25:46). The seriousness of sin's penalty was demonstrated when the Son of God took upon himself the punishment for the sins of all of God's elect on the cross.

Sin creates enmity, a hostile situation between parties. Romans 5:10 says that before salvation in Christ, people are "enemies" of God. Unbelievers are "alienated from the life of God" (Eph. 4:18). Also, "the mind that is set on the flesh is hostile to God" (Rom. 8:7). The responsibility for the enmity lies solely with man.

PEOPLE

Next, sin disrupted all human relationships. First, God said that the woman would have increased pain in childbirth, so that even the procreation of another person would be difficult: "To the woman he said, 'I will surely multiply your pain in child-bearing; in pain you shall bring forth children'" (Gen. 3:16a).

Second, tension between man and woman in the basic and necessary union of marriage would also transpire. God told Eve, "Your desire shall be for your husband, and he shall rule over you" (Gen. 3:16b). While "desire" could refer to a physical desire for her husband, a desire to control is probably in view. Genesis 4:7, which has a parallel construction, uses "desire" in a controlling sense: "And if you [Cain] do not do well, sin is crouching at the door. Its desire is for you, but you must rule over it." So Genesis 3:16 predicts struggle and conflict within marriage, the most intimate love relationship.

Third, strife between persons in general society is promised and realized. Cain slew his brother Abel for jealous reasons (Gen. 4:8). Lamech killed a young man who struck him (Gen. 4:23). The history of mankind manifests continual hatred, strife, murders, and war.

CREATION

Man's sin negatively affected his relationship to the creation. Man's mandate to rule and subdue the earth and its creatures is not revoked (Ps. 8:4–8), but creation now works against man and frustrates his efforts. God told Adam, "Cursed is the ground because of you; in pain you shall eat of it all the days of your life" (Gen. 3:17). The cursed ground will lead to "pain" for man. Adam is also told, "Thorns and thistles it shall bring forth for you; and you shall eat the plants of the field. By the sweat of your face you shall eat bread" (Gen. 3:18–19a). So man's interaction with the earth will be difficult, and the earth will even consume him at death (Gen. 3:19b). God's expectation for a successful rule of man remains unfulfilled. Hebrews 2:5–8 reaffirms that God created man to rule creation but recognizes that "at present, we do not yet see everything in subjection to him" (Heb. 2:8). It will take the last Adam, Jesus

(1 Cor. 15:45), and those who believe in him, to successfully rule the earth (Rev. 5:10). This will occur when Jesus returns and establishes his millennial reign (Rev. 20:1–6).

In sum, not only will Adam and his descendants suffer and die as individuals, but also all his relationships will suffer. Only the Lord Jesus will be able to restore mankind's relationship to God, to one another, and to the creation. As the "last Adam" (1 Cor. 15:45), he will love God and people perfectly and will manifest absolute control over creation.

Three Forms of Death

The widespread and devastating results of sin can be summarized in one word—death. God told Adam, "But of the tree of the knowledge of good and evil you shall not eat, for in the day that you eat of it you shall surely die" (Gen. 2:17). Death is the penalty for disobedience. It is a complex concept involving (1) spiritual death, (2) physical death, and (3) eternal death.

SPIRITUAL DEATH

When Adam and Eve sinned, physical death did not occur immediately. Adam lived 930 years (Gen. 5:5). Spiritual death, however, happened instantly. Spiritual death is the state of spiritual alienation from God. As a result of Adam's sin, all living people are born spiritually dead (with the exception of the Lord Jesus Christ). Paul refers to spiritual death in Ephesians 2:1: "And you were dead in [your] trespasses and sins." In Ephesians 2:5, Paul says that unsaved people are "dead in [their] trespasses." For Adam and Eve, sin brought separation from God, banishment from his presence, and forfeiture of spiritual life (Gen. 2:23–24). All their descendants have likewise been born in a state of spiritual death. This deadness also renders a person unresponsive to spiritual truth (Rom. 8:7–8; 1 Cor. 2:14; 2 Cor. 4:4; Eph. 4:17–18). Only by the divine miracle of regeneration does God end spiritual death and re-create sinners, making them alive to himself (2 Cor. 4:6).

PHYSICAL DEATH

While God mercifully did not impose physical death on Adam and Eve immediately, the process of physical death started when they sinned. God told Adam, "By the sweat of your face you shall eat bread, till you return to the ground, for out of it you were taken; for you are dust, and to dust you shall return" (Gen. 3:19).

Adam was formed from dust, but here a tragic irony was introduced. Because of sin, he would return to dust and the ground would swallow him up in death. Physical death would happen since Adam and Eve were barred from the tree of life (Gen. 3:24).

Also, even before any human died, animal death occurred when God killed an animal to use its skin to clothe Adam and Eve (Gen. 3:21). Human death first occurred when the initial offspring of Adam and Eve—Cain—slew his brother Abel (Gen. 4:8). The list of Adam's descendants in Genesis 5 starkly reveals that death became the end of every human life, by repeating after every person listed, ". . . and he died" (Gen. 5:5, 8, 11, 14, 17, 20, 27, 31). Besides the past exceptions of Enoch and Elijah and the future exceptions of those who will be alive at the rapture (1 Thess. 4:13–18), physical death will consume all descendants of Adam. The writer of Hebrews declares, "It is appointed for man to die once, and after that comes judgment" (Heb. 9:27). Physical life became brief after the flood. Moses said, "The years of our life are seventy, or even by reason of strength eighty; yet their span is but toil and trouble; they are soon gone, and we fly away" (Ps. 90:10).

ETERNAL DEATH

Eternal death awaits those who physically die while being spiritually dead. Those who die in unbelief will face the lake of fire forever (Rev. 20:11–15). John refers to this as "the second death" (Rev. 20:6). While it does not cause people to cease to exist, eternal death is still a kind of death since it involves everlasting ruin, punishment for sins, and separation from God's presence to bless. Only those who are delivered by the gracious work of the Lord Jesus escape eternal death. Revelation 20:6 states, "Blessed and holy is the one who shares in the first resurrection! Over such the second death has no power."

Transmission of Adam's Sin

How does the first man's sin affect all born after him? Theologians often refer to this reality as *original sin*, from the Latin *peccatum originale*. In one sense, original sin refers to the first sin committed by Adam. But original sin also encompasses the sinful state and condition of all people because of their relationship to Adam, which is the reason people are depraved and tainted with sin from conception.

Several verses support the concept of original sin, including Psalm 51:5, "Behold, I was brought forth in iniquity, and in sin did my mother conceive me," and Ephesians 2:3, "We . . . were by nature children of wrath, like the rest of mankind." Also, Adam's sin is linked with man's sinfulness in Romans 5:12–21, the most detailed Scripture passage on this topic. This passage is also one of the most debated sections in Romans, since several views have been proffered regarding how Adam's sin impacts mankind.

Romans 5:12 states, "Therefore, just as sin came into the world through one man, and death through sin, and so death spread to all men because all sinned . . ." Four truths are asserted here. First, sin entered the world through "one man"—Adam. Second, sin brought death. Third, death spread to all people. Fourth, the reason death spread to all people is "because all sinned." It is this last point that is most disputed. Augustine used Latin translations of Romans 5:12 that interpreted the Greek phrase *eph hō* in the sense of *in quo* ("in whom"), translating the last part of the verse as "in whom [i.e., Adam] all sinned." Most translations today rightly opt instead for a causal sense: "because all sinned."

But how have "all sinned" in Adam? Is Paul referring to the fact that all people commit acts of sin? Or does "all sinned" somehow connect Adam's sin with all people being sinners? In Romans 5:18–19, Paul explains that "one trespass led to condemnation for all men" and that "by the one man's disobedience the many were made sinners." In Romans 5:15, he also states, "Many died through one man's trespass." Plus, the aorist tense for "sinned" (Gk. *hēmarton*) at the end of Romans 5:12 points to a specific historical event. So a direct connection exists between Adam's sin and the sinfulness of Adam's descendants. But what is this connection? Several answers have been offered.

UNEXPLAINED SOLIDARITY

One view is that Romans 5:12–21 reveals a vague solidarity between Adam and all people that is not explained. Some connection admittedly exists, but proponents of this opaque idea suggest that it cannot be known with certainty. We must be content with not knowing. This unexplained solidarity position appears to be the default for those unsatisfied with the other views mentioned below.

BAD EXAMPLE

Some hold that Adam's sin is a bad example left for all people. When people sin, they follow Adam's bad precedent. Humans are not actually guilty for Adam's sin, nor do they inherit a sinful nature from him. They rather choose to follow Adam's bad example. No direct transmission of sin exists between people and Adam. This Adam-as-bad-example view is historically linked with Pelagius (ca. 354–ca. 420), the British monk who rejected the doctrine that all humans possess a sin nature. He taught that people are able to obey God without divine grace. Thus, all people are like Adam when he was created, and all are free to obey or disobey God.

This bad-example view is flawed, since it does not adequately grasp the sinfulness of people after Adam's fall (Eph. 2:1, 5). It also does not do justice to the comparison between Adam and Christ in Romans 5:12–21. Further, if Adam is only a bad example, does this mean that Christ is only a good example and that we are left to save ourselves? Judging by Pelagius's reliance on the freedom of the human will for salvation, one has to answer affirmatively. His condemnation for heresy at the Council of Ephesus in 431 is therefore justified.

INHERITED SINFUL NATURE

The idea of an inherited sinful nature affirms that all people do receive a corrupt and sinful nature from Adam. Adam's offspring are conceived with a disposition that is bent toward sin. This understanding makes a real connection between Adam and the transmission of sinfulness. Adam actually passes on a corrupt nature to the human race. Yet Adam's guilt is not placed on others. So pollution or corruption from Adam is passed on naturally to a person, but the guilt for Adam's sin is not. Some who hold this view acknowledge that the inherited sinful nature is enough to render a person condemned by God as a sinner, but they maintain that such condemnation is not on account of Adam's guilt being imputed or reckoned to his descendants.

Variations of this perspective exist among Arminians, who have asserted that both Adam's guilt and corruption pass to all descendants of Adam but that prevenient grace removes the guilt and depravity coming from Adam. No one besides Adam is held responsible for what Adam did. A person only becomes responsible as a sinner when he chooses to sin.

This view has been criticized for not going far enough. While rightly affirming that all persons have a corrupt nature from Adam, it does not recognize that Adam's sin directly brings guilt to all people. Paul said, "One trespass led to *condemnation* for all men" (Rom. 5:18), an inherently legal term that establishes guilt. This verse teaches, therefore, that people receive more than just a corrupt nature, since Adam's trespass leads to condemnation. All humans are constituted sinners by his action (Rom. 5:19). Also, the Arminian concept of prevenient grace, which removes or neutralizes guilt from Adam, has no scriptural support.

REALISM

Also known as the Augustinian or seminal view, realism asserts that all humanity was physically present in Adam when he sinned. As the first man, Adam collectively represented human nature, of which Adam's descendants are all a part. And all were in Adam in seed form when he sinned. This means that Adam's descendants were in Adam's loins participating in his sin. And since everyone participated in Adam's sin, all people are morally guilty and condemned for doing so. Thus, both the corrupt nature and guilt are passed down naturally from Adam.

Support for the realism view is drawn from Hebrews 7:9–10: "One might even say that Levi himself, who receives tithes, paid tithes through Abraham, for he was still in the loins of his ancestor when Melchizedek met him." Levi was a great-grandson of Abraham, yet Levi paid tithes through his great-grandfather Abraham, since Levi was "still in the loins of his ancestor [Abraham] when Melchizedek met him." Here a distant descendant of Abraham is said to have actively paid tithes through Abraham. The action of Abraham was the action of Levi, and this could also be true for descendants of Adam, who sinned when Adam sinned.

The realism view affirms that the connection between Adam's sin and the sin of humanity is more than just a bad example from Adam or an inherited sin nature. Instead, all people actually participated in Adam's sin. So the guilt and condemnation are deserved because all actually sinned. Realism offers an explanation as to how all people can appropriately be guilty for Adam's sin. When Adam sinned, all sinned in him. If that is so, advocates say, no one can make the charge that "innocent" people are wrongly imputed with Adam's sin, since everyone actually participated in his transgression.

However, it does not fall to us to sit in judgment on the "appropriateness" of God's legal declarations. The supposition that it would be unjust to impute Adam's sin to man unless we had "actually participated" in Adam's transgression does violence to the parallel between Adam and Christ in Romans 5:12–21. No one questions the "appropriateness" of the forensic imputation of righteousness to sinners. We would not say that sinners are wrongly imputed with Christ's righteousness unless they actually participated, seminally, in his obedience.

And, of course, we did not. The union between Christ and his people is not a seminal union, for Christ fathered no physical children. Rather, it is a legal union. As our representative, Christ's obedience is counted—legally imputed or judicially reckoned—by God to be our obedience. For the parallel between the first and last Adam to hold together (Rom. 5:12–21; cf. 1 Cor. 15:45), Adam's sin must be transmitted in the same manner as Christ's righteousness is. Therefore, because Adam was the representative of all humanity, his disobedience is counted—legally imputed or judicially reckoned—by God to be the disobedience of all who were in him. Those who would charge that such imputation is wrong or inappropriate because not everyone actually participated in Adam's sin show their inconsistency when they do not make the same charge against the imputation of Christ's righteousness. The former draws objections because it is punishment, while the latter is excused because it is a gift. As John Murray explains,

> The analogy instituted in Romans 5:12–19 (cf. 1 Cor. 15:22) presents a formidable objection to the realist construction. It is admitted by the realist that there is no "realistic" union between Christ and the justified. . . . On realist premises, therefore, a radical disparity must be posited between the character of the union that exists between Adam and his posterity, on the one hand, and the union that exists between Christ and those who are his, on the other. . . . But there is no hint of that kind of discrepancy that would obtain if the distinction between the nature of the union in the two cases were as radical as realism must suppose. . . . [And] the case is not merely that there is no hint of this kind of difference; the sustained parallelism militates against any such supposition. . . . This sustained emphasis not only upon the one man Adam and the one man Christ but also upon the one trespass, and the one righteous act points to a basic identity in respect of *modus operandi*.[29]

REPRESENTATIVE HEADSHIP

The most acceptable position is that Adam's sin is imputed to all who were united to him as the representative of humanity. Adam's guilt is our guilt. While affirming that a corrupt nature is passed down from Adam, representative headship teaches that all people are condemned because of their direct relationship to Adam.

The representative-headship view (often called *federal headship*) asserts that the action of a representative is determinative for all members united to him. When Adam sinned, he represented all people; therefore, his sin is reckoned to his descendants.

An example of headship affecting others is found in Joshua 7 with Achan and his family. Israel's defeat at Ai was attributed to Achan, who disobeyed God by wrongly confiscating silver and gold for himself in his tent. While Achan alone committed this sinful action, his sons and daughters were stoned with him, bearing the punishment

---

29. John Murray, "The Imputation of Adam's Sin: Second Article," *WTJ* 19, no. 1 (1956): 36.

along with Achan for his deed (Josh. 7:24–25). In like manner, the guilt of Adam's sin is imputed or placed on the rest of the family of mankind.

Those who affirm the representative-headship view first appeal to the parallels made with Jesus in Romans 5:12–21 (discussed above under the realism view). Romans 5:18 says that Jesus's "one act of righteousness leads to justification and life for all men." Jesus's act of dying on the cross brings justification to sinners. Romans 5:19 adds, "For as by the one man's disobedience the many were made sinners, so by the one man's obedience the many will be made righteous." Jesus's obedience is imputed to others as their righteousness. The logic here suggests that if the justification and righteousness of the Lord Jesus is imputed to those in him, so too the guilt of Adam's sin has been imputed to those he represented. As already stated, the Adam-Christ parallel in Romans 5:12–21 is best explained by the idea of representation. Just as Christians are considered righteous because Christ's alien righteousness (i.e., righteousness that is external to the believer) is imputed to all who are Christ's, so too Adam's guilt is imputed to all his descendants, even though they did not personally sin when he did.

Adherents of this view also appeal to 1 Corinthians 15:22, which says, "For as in Adam all die, so also in Christ shall all be made alive." This verse shows that death and life are linked with Adam and Christ as two representatives of mankind. In addition, Romans 5:14 states that "death reigned from Adam to Moses, even over those whose sinning was not like the transgression of Adam." This verse explicitly teaches that Adam's offspring did not commit Adam's sin. So Adam relates to his offspring as their representative head, and thus the act of Adam is imputed to others, even though the others did not actually commit the sin that Adam did.

In sum, both men—Adam and Christ—are seen as representatives of humanity, and for both, the effects of their actions are placed on others. Adam is the representative of sinful humanity, and Jesus is the representative of righteous humanity. Significantly, while this view emphasizes imputation via headship with Adam, it also encompasses inherited corruption passed on from Adam to the whole of humanity.

The representative view was promoted by Johannes Cocceius (1603–1669) and became popular among many in the tradition of covenant theology, who connect this perspective with an alleged "covenant of works," in which Adam as the head of the human race was tasked with perfect obedience for the goal of obtaining eternal life. When Adam violated this so-called covenant of works, he failed on behalf of all mankind, so that his sin was counted as the failure of all his descendants. Nonetheless, not all covenantalists who affirm federal headship tie it to a covenant of works. For example, Anthony Hoekema declared, "Although . . . I rejected the doctrine of the covenant of works, this does not imply the rejection of direct imputation, as long as we maintain that Adam was indeed the head and representative of the human race."[30] Hoekema was right to reject a covenant of works as the orienting principle for federal headship, since Scripture makes no mention of a covenant of works.

Though historically referred to as *federal headship*, the label *representative*

---

30. Anthony A. Hoekema, *Created in God's Image* (Grand Rapids, MI: Eerdmans, 1994), 161n65.

headship is preferable since it better conveys the fact that both Adam and Christ act as the legal representatives for those who are reckoned to be in them. As explained above, this position makes the best sense out of the parallels between Adam and Christ articulated in Romans 5 and 1 Corinthians 15.

Some suggest that the representative-headship view is contrary to the strong scriptural testimony that children will not be held accountable for the sins of their fathers. For example, Deuteronomy 24:16 declares, "Fathers shall not be put to death because of their children, nor shall children be put to death because of their fathers. Each one shall be put to death for his own sin." Ezekiel 18:20 adds, "The soul who sins shall die. The son shall not suffer for the iniquity of the father, nor the father suffer for the iniquity of the son. The righteousness of the righteous shall be upon himself, and the wickedness of the wicked shall be upon himself." However, there is no real connection between the doctrine of original sin and these passages, which address the guilt and punishment for *personal* sin.

Old Self and New Self

The relationship of Adam and Jesus Christ to humanity is also connected to the concepts of "old self" and "new self," found twice in Paul's letters:

> . . . to put off your *old self*, which belongs to your former manner of life and is corrupt through deceitful desires, and to be renewed in the spirit of your minds, and to put on the *new self*, created after the likeness of God in true righteousness and holiness. (Eph. 4:22–24)

> Do not lie to one another, seeing that you have put off the *old self* with its practices and have put on the *new self*, which is being renewed in knowledge after the image of its creator. (Col. 3:9–10)

The Greek word for "self" in both passages is *anthropos* and refers to "man." Some justifiably translate these as "old man" and "new man."

Paul is making a contrast with significant implications. In Colossians 3:9–10, he reminds his Christian readers that the old self has been put off while the new self has been put on. This is a statement of fact, not a command. Christians are no longer the old self but are now the new self. This change occurred when they believed in Christ.

In regard to Ephesians 4:22–24, debate exists as to whether Paul is commanding his readers to put off the old self and put on the new self or whether he is stating a fact that Christians are already a new self, much like Colossians 3:9–10. Either way, Paul is emphasizing that in Christ a transformation has occurred. Christians have gone from being the old self to being the new self. And they are to live in light of this reality.

But what does Paul mean by "old self [man]" and "new self [man]," and how does this relate to the doctrines of man and sin? The old self is the unregenerate self, connected with Adam. It encompasses everything a person is in Adam before union with Christ. The new self is the regenerate self, united with Christ, who replaces the old man. When a person becomes a Christian, he puts on the new self and becomes a "new creation" in Christ (2 Cor. 5:17). He is no longer the old man. The unregenerate self in Adam is gone forever. The new self in Christ is reality. Yet since glorification of the body has not occurred and Christians still struggle with the flesh, believers must continually put aside fleshly desires. They must walk by the power of the Holy Spirit so they do "not gratify the desires of the flesh" (Gal. 5:16).

These paradigms of "old man" and "new man" are important distinctions contrasting humanity in Adam and humanity in Christ. One is either in Adam or in Christ; no other option exists. According to Romans 5:18–19, being in Adam means death, guilt, and condemnation. Being in Christ, however, means life, justification, and righteousness.

Total Depravity

The Bible teaches what has been called total (or pervasive) depravity to describe the corruption and pollution of sin passed down from Adam. Total depravity emphasizes the devastating impact of sin on the person and covers three related concepts: (1) the pollution and corruption of all aspects of a person; (2) the complete inability of a person to please God; and (3) universality, in that all are conceived and born as sinners. Together these show the abysmal state of unredeemed humanity, all of whom are both unable and unwilling to glorify God.

Total depravity does not mean that unsaved people always act as badly as possible. Nor does it mean that unsaved people cannot do relative acts of goodness. Unbelievers can do good things for society, their friends, and their family. They can stop a fight, give to charity, perform life-saving surgery. They can help a lost child find her parents. These acts have a relative goodness, which corresponds with what Jesus said: "If you then, who are evil, know how to give good gifts to your children . . ." (Matt. 7:11).

Concerning the first feature, sin is total or pervasive in that all components of a person are polluted by sin. Just as smoke from a fire permeates everything in a room, the whole person is corrupted by sin. No part of man escapes. This includes both the material and immaterial aspects of a person—body and soul. The body decays and is headed for physical death, and along the way, the body functions as an instrument for evil activity. The spiritual part of man is also fully corrupt. This includes all of man's thinking, reason, desires, and affections. Thus Paul concludes, "To the defiled and unbelieving, nothing is pure; but both their minds and their consciences are defiled" (Titus 1:15). Speaking of the godless, Paul refers to "the futility of their minds" (Eph. 4:17). The heart is also debased; so Jeremiah 17:9 says, "The heart is deceitful above all things, and desperately sick; who can understand it?" Jesus also teaches that it is from the heart that wicked deeds occur (Mark 7:21–23). On multiple occasions the Bible addresses both corrupt thinking and an evil heart. Paul said, "They are darkened in their understanding, alienated from the life of God because of the ignorance that is in them, due to their hardness of heart" (Eph. 4:18). Also, sinful mankind "became futile in their thinking, and their foolish hearts were darkened" (Rom. 1:21). John Calvin rightly stated, "We are so entirely controlled by the power of sin, that the whole mind, the whole heart, and all our actions are under its influence."[31]

Second, sin is total in that man is incapable of pleasing God on his own. Paul states, "For the mind that is set on the flesh is hostile to God, for it does not submit to God's law; indeed, it cannot. Those who are in the flesh cannot please God" (Rom. 8:7–8). And Jesus says, "Apart from me you can do nothing" (John 15:5).

Third, sin is universal in that all humans are sinners. First Kings 8:46 declares, "For there is no one who does not sin." And Psalm 14:3 states, "They have all turned aside; together they have become corrupt; there is none who does good, not even one." The entire section of Romans 1:18–3:20 is dedicated to showing that all people are sinners and unable to save themselves, concluding that "all have sinned and fall short of the glory of God" (Rom. 3:23).

Therefore, man's spiritual state is not one of relative neutrality, in which he is able to accept or reject God and his gospel. He is an active hater of God (Rom. 8:7) who cannot accept spiritual truth (1 Cor. 2:14). The total depravity of man demonstrates the absolute sovereignty of God in salvation. Man can do nothing. God must accomplish all as a gift of sovereign grace.

Sin Issues

Are Some Sins Worse Than Others?
The Unpardonable Sin
Sin Leading to Death
Are There Mortal and Venial Sins?
Sin and the Christian
The Coming Man of Sin
God and the Problem of Evil

Are Some Sins Worse Than Others?

Are all sins the same in God's eyes, or are some sins worse than others? All sins are the same in the sense that each renders a person guilty and worthy of God's wrath. The root of all sin is autonomy and replacement of God with self. However small a sin may seem, it is an assertion that the person is acting independently of God. Eating fruit from a tree in a garden, like Adam and Eve did, might not seem immoral and may seem minor compared to other crimes, but it was an act of iniquity that had grave consequences for the human race. Breaking any command is an assault against the divine Lawgiver. James declared, "For whoever keeps the whole law but fails in one point has become accountable for all of it. For he who said, 'Do not commit adultery,' also said, 'Do not murder.' If you do not commit adultery but do murder, you have become a transgressor of the law" (James 2:10–11). Grudem is correct that "in terms of our legal standing before God, any one sin, even what may seem to be a very small one, makes us legally guilty before God and therefore worthy

---

31. John Calvin, *Commentaries on the Epistle of Paul the Apostle to the Romans*, trans. John Owen, vol. 19 of *Calvin's Commentaries* (Edinburgh: Calvin Translation Society, 1849), 261.

of eternal punishment."[32] Even one sin against an infinitely holy God demands an infinite punishment.

At the same time, Scripture does speak of the reality that some sins are considered greater than others. When being shown abominations in the temple, Ezekiel was told, "You will see still greater abominations that they commit" (Ezek. 8:13). Here some abominations were "greater" than others. Jesus explained that those who delivered him to Pilate committed "the greater sin" (John 19:11). In Matthew 11:20–24, Jesus said that the Jewish cities that heard the kingdom message would fare worse on judgment day than the Gentile cities that did not. Greater knowledge brings greater responsibility. In Luke 12:47–48, Jesus taught that a servant who knew the Master's will but did not do it would be treated more harshly than one who did not know the Master's will. Also, James said that a stricter judgment awaits teachers: "Not many of you should become teachers, my brothers, for you know that we who teach will be judged with greater strictness" (James 3:1).

These two biblical realities are harmonized by considering that there is both a quantitative and a qualitative aspect to sin and punishment. All mankind is guilty of sinning against an infinitely holy God. Therefore, all who die without repenting and trusting in Christ face the same quantitatively eternal punishment for their sins. And yet, because God is strictly just, he will punish those who have committed qualitatively greater offenses with a qualitatively greater punishment. The character of their suffering will be exactly proportional to the crimes they've committed (e.g., 2 Pet. 2:17; Jude 13).

The Unpardonable Sin

Jesus says that there is a sin that will never be forgiven:

> Therefore I tell you, every sin and blasphemy will be forgiven people, but the blasphemy against the Spirit will not be forgiven. And whoever speaks a word against the Son of Man will be forgiven, but whoever speaks against the Holy Spirit will not be forgiven, either in this age or in the age to come. (Matt. 12:31–32)

What is this unforgivable or unpardonable sin? The context for Jesus's statement is his confrontations with the contentious Pharisees in Matthew 12. In 12:1–21, Jesus was accused of acting unlawfully on the Sabbath, and in answering the Pharisees, he declared that he had authority over the Sabbath because he was the Lord of the Sabbath (12:8). In 12:22–24, the Pharisees accused Jesus of casting out demons by the power of Satan. Jesus responded on several levels. First, he noted that if he cast out demons by Satan, then Satan would be working against himself. Not only did this strategy make no sense, it was also doomed to failure (12:25–26). Second, Jewish exorcists also cast out demons (12:27). So why did the Jewish leaders accept these exorcists but not Jesus? Third, the truth was that Jesus cast out demons by the power of the Holy Spirit to demonstrate that the kingdom had come upon the

---

32. Grudem, *Systematic Theology*, 501.

people (12:28). This was the correct significance of his miracles. Casting out demons by the Holy Spirit showed that God's kingdom was at work through the Messiah.

Jesus then spoke of the unforgivable sin (12:30–32), which involved blaspheming the Holy Spirit. This sin could not be forgiven either in the present age or in the coming age. This sin was more than making offhand, derogatory statements about Jesus or the Holy Spirit from a distance or from ignorance. It involved disparaging the clear works that the Holy Spirit was doing through the Son of God. *The unpardonable sin, therefore, is the willful and final rejection of the Holy Spirit who is working through Jesus, by attributing God's work in Christ to Satan.* For the hostile religious leaders in Matthew 12, this was a determined and final unbelief in the face of clear revelation. After seeing firsthand what the Lord had done and hearing his teaching, these leaders made the final conclusion that he was Satanic—exactly the opposite of the truth. Such terminal rejection could not be pardoned. Since the conditions necessary for committing the unpardonable sin were limited to Jesus's earthly ministry, the sin itself was restricted to the time period of his career on earth.

But is there any parallel to the unpardonable sin beyond Jesus's earthly ministry? The answer could be yes. The main issue with the unpardonable sin was hardened and willful unbelief in spite of the clear testimony of the Holy Spirit. Hebrews 6:4–6 refers to those who have "once been enlightened" and have been made "partakers of the Holy Spirit." Yet they are warned against falling away from the faith, since "it is impossible to renew them again to repentance." This passage refers to people who had great knowledge of the Holy Spirit. They saw the Spirit work miracles through the apostles (Heb. 2:3–4), but they stopped short of committing to Jesus. By persisting in unbelief, they were in danger of reaching a point of no return. Even today, it is possible for people to know the gospel and continually reject it. Such people are apostates who are beyond repentance and grace (Heb. 10:26–31).

The reality is that all who reject the Lord Jesus in this life, never embracing him in saving faith, cannot be pardoned, since forgiveness is only offered to those who believe in him. Though the unpardonable sin described in Matthew 12 involved final hardness of heart against Jesus when he was on earth, the unrepentant rejection of the Lord Jesus Christ is always a sin that remains unforgiven, since forgiveness is found only through repentant faith in Christ. Conversely, anyone who comes to Christ in true repentance and genuine faith will be forgiven (cf. John 6:37; Rom. 10:9).

Sin Leading to Death

In 1 John 5:16, the apostle mentions two types of sin concerning a fellow Christian ("brother"). First, he says that there is a sin that does not lead to death. And second, he speaks of a sin that does lead to death:

> If anyone sees his brother committing a sin not leading to death, he shall ask, and God will give him life—to those who commit sins that do not lead to death. There is sin that leads to death; I do not say that one should pray for that.

Of particular interest is the "sin that leads to death." What sin is this? One answer offered is that John is referring to a professing believer who demonstrates through habitual sin that he is not an authentic Christian (1 John 3:6). So the sin in question concerns an unbeliever's sin that leads to eternal death. Such a rejection of Jesus has the same consequence as that committed by the Jewish leaders who attributed Jesus's miracles to the power of Satan (Matt. 12:31–32). Apostasy is unforgivable. Praying for restoration in this case is futile because God has already set the rejecter's future (Heb. 6:6).

Another view is that the sin leading to death could refer to a true believer whose life, like that of some at Corinth (1 Cor. 11:29–30), brought shame to Christ, and thus God's discipline resulted in premature death. The Christian's sin is so serious that God takes the person's life. For example, Ananias and Sapphira died on the spot when they lied to the Holy Spirit in front of the church (Acts 5:1–11). Similarly, in 1 Corinthians 5:5, Paul mandated discipline for a sinning church member involved in immorality: "You are to deliver this man to Satan for the destruction of the flesh, so that his spirit may be saved in the day of the Lord." If a Christian is under church discipline, believers in the church should not pray for the consequences of such discipline to be removed until the sinner repents. With the goal that this person will repent, the church delivers him or her to Satan's realm. The sin that leads to death in 1 John 5:16, then, is not one particular sin but any sin that the Lord determines is serious enough for drastic chastisement.

Both of these views reflect biblical truth, and it is difficult to know with certainty which one John intended. In both cases, John concludes that prayer for those committing a sin leading to death will not end as one might anticipate because the prayer is not in accord with God's will (1 John 5:14–15).

Are There Mortal and Venial Sins?

The Roman Catholic Church promotes the concepts of mortal sins and venial sins. Allegedly, mortal sins result in the spiritual death of the soul. They are intentional and grave sins such as murder, adultery, and fornication. If a person dies with a mortal sin on his soul, he is lost forever. The remedy for a mortal sin is the sacrament of penance, which brings a person back into relationship with God. A venial sin is a lesser or forgivable sin that does not break fellowship with God or result in the soul being eternally separated from God. For example, while intentional slander is a mortal sin, a person who says something unkind in a moment without much reflection could be guilty of a venial sin.

The Bible does not affirm the Roman Catholic ideas of mortal and venial sins—or the sacramental, penitential context in which they are understood. All sins establish legal guilt, and without faith in Christ sinners are worthy of eternal separation from God. The two categories of mortal and venial sins operate within a faulty view of salvation, in which justification is viewed as a process during which a person can commit certain sins that remove him from a relationship with God, while other sins do not sever that fellowship. The biblical view is that at the moment of saving faith, the Christian is declared righteous because of the imputed righteousness of Christ (Rom. 4:3–5). All sins are forgiven so that nothing can separate the Christian from fellowship with God (Rom. 8:1, 38–39). Furthermore, the Roman Catholic idea of meritorious penance as necessary for the removal of a mortal sin is an error that strikes at the sufficiency of Jesus's atoning sacrifice for sin. Rather than looking to his own acts of penance, the Christian looks to Christ's sacrifice as the full payment for all his sin (Heb. 10:10–18).

Sin and the Christian

What is the effect of a Christian sinning? The Bible does not teach perfectionism in this life or before the resurrection, so Christians will sin. First John 1:8 states, "If we say we have no sin, we deceive ourselves, and the truth is not in us."[33] But when a person trusts in Christ, he receives both forgiveness of sins and Christ's righteousness. As a result, Paul declares, "There is therefore now no condemnation for those who are in Christ Jesus" (Rom. 8:1). Christ died for our sins (1 Cor. 15:3), so all sins—past, present, and future—are forgiven. God, who began a good work in us, will be faithful to complete what he started (Phil. 1:6). Sin will not remove a Christian from God's love; indeed, Paul says that nothing "will be able to separate us from the love of God in Christ Jesus our Lord" (Rom. 8:39).

However, while instances of personal sin cannot break the believer's *union* with Christ, they do have a negative impact on the believer's *communion* with Christ. When Christians sin, they grieve the Holy Spirit (Eph. 4:30). Sin also brings God's discipline. Jesus said, "Those whom I love, I reprove and discipline, so be zealous and repent" (Rev. 3:19). In addition, "For the Lord disciplines the one he loves, and chastises every son whom he receives" (Heb. 12:6). Christians should examine themselves for sin and be open to loving exhortation and rebuke from other believers (Gal. 6:1). Jesus instituted a church discipline process for dealing with sin in the life of a professing Christian (Matt. 18:15–20). Unrepentant sin should lead to expulsion from the church, so that the church maintains its purity (1 Cor. 5:13).

Sin in the life of a Christian is a serious matter. It harms one's spiritual growth and testimony for Christ. While Christians will never face judicial punishment for sins, they will stand before the judgment seat of Christ to give an account for their deeds done in the body, whether good or bad (2 Cor. 5:10). The dross will be burned away, and the eternal reward will reflect what remains (1 Cor. 3:12–15).

The Coming Man of Sin

Sin has a devastating and deadly impact on humanity's past and present. Will the future be any different? Before Christ's second coming, the Bible predicts a specific "man of sin," an ultimate Antichrist figure, who will be the consummate embodiment of sin and evil. During the coming day of the Lord, this person will be Satan's counterfeit

---

33. For more on the biblical refutation of the doctrine of perfectionism, see "Perfected Sanctification" in chap. 7 (p. 636).

to the Lord Jesus (2 Thess. 2:3–4). Jesus is the God-man who is the embodiment of righteousness and love. But Satan's man will be the opposite. Paul called him "the man of lawlessness" (2 Thess. 2:3).

The conditions surrounding this "man of lawlessness" are detailed in 2 Thessalonians 2. There Paul refuted the erroneous belief that the "day of the Lord" had already started. He revealed that two events would coincide with the coming of the day of the Lord, and since neither of them had occurred, the day of the Lord could not yet have arrived. The first event would be a massive rebellion in which a great apostasy against God would occur. The second would be the arrival of the man of sin who would oppose God and demand worship of himself:

> Let no one deceive you in any way. For that day will not come, unless the rebellion comes first, and the man of lawlessness is revealed, the son of destruction, who opposes and exalts himself against every so-called god or object of worship, so that he takes his seat in the temple of God, proclaiming himself to be God. (2 Thess. 2:3–4)

The word for "lawlessness" comes from the Greek term *anomia*, which means "against law" or "lawless." In this context it means "to be opposed to God's law and purposes." The coming man of lawlessness will embody flagrant rebellion against God and will be known as "the son of destruction" (2 Thess. 2:3). Earlier, Jesus said that Satan comes to "steal and kill and destroy" (John 10:10); so too will this representative of Satan.

The 2 Thessalonians passage goes on to describe the activity of this man of sin. He will oppose God and exalt himself against every object of worship, including the true God. He will demand that only he be worshiped (2 Thess. 2:4). He will also sit in God's temple in Jerusalem and declare himself to be God (see Dan. 9:27; Matt. 24:15). While the Holy Spirit currently restrains this wicked figure from appearing, he will "be revealed in his time," when the Spirit ceases to restrain him (2 Thess. 2:6). This does not mean that sin is not already in operation, because "the mystery of lawlessness is already at work" (2 Thess. 2:7). But when the restrainer is removed, "then the lawless one will be revealed" (2 Thess. 2:8). His work will encompass these activities: "The coming of the lawless one is by the activity of Satan with all power and false signs and wonders, and with all wicked deception for those who are perishing, because they refused to love the truth and so be saved" (2 Thess. 2:9–10). The eschatological man of lawlessness will do his work "by the activity of Satan." Just as Jesus did his miracles in the power of the Holy Spirit, this man will be empowered by Satan. He will come with "false signs and wonders" that further the "wicked deception" of lost people who are perishing.

The man of sin will have a short career: "And then the lawless one will be revealed, whom the Lord Jesus will kill with the breath of his mouth and bring to nothing by the appearance of his coming" (2 Thess. 2:8). Satan's man will be thrown into the lake of fire, and his reign of wickedness will be replaced by the kingdom of righteousness, ruled by the Lord Jesus Christ (Isaiah 11; Zechariah 4).

God and the Problem of Evil

The reality of evil and suffering is used by some as a reason for rejecting God. Allegedly, if God were all-good and all-powerful, then evil and suffering would not exist. But contrary to disproving God, the existence of evil and suffering can be adequately explained only from a Christian worldview rooted in the biblical perspective of creation and the fall. More on theodicy—the defense of God in light of the problem of evil—is found in chapter 3 ("The Problem of Evil and Theodicy," p. 221) and in chapter 7 ("The Decree of God and the Problem of Evil," p. 491; "The Justification of God," p. 509). But some comments are appropriate here in light of sin's role in producing evil and suffering.

One must remember that God is the sovereign King of the universe who does as he wills without needing to answer to man (Rom. 9:20). God is not on trial, and any apparent contradictions between God's existence and the reality of evil are simply that—apparent, not real. With this reality understood, several points can help one understand evil and suffering.

First, God created the world and called everything in it "very good" (Gen. 1:31). No sin or death existed during creation week. These were introduced later by Adam (Genesis 3; Rom. 5:12). God told Adam that eating from the tree of the knowledge of good and evil would bring death (Gen. 2:15–17), but Adam nevertheless willfully disobeyed his Creator, to whom he was accountable. The responsibility for sin lies at the feet of sinful man. God is not the chargeable cause of evil (cf. Rom. 3:5–6; 9:14).

Second, when Adam disobeyed God, Adam introduced both moral and natural evil into the world. By sinning against God, man brought hostility into human relationships and moral evil into creation. Sin also affected the natural order. Since man was the pinnacle of creation and was tasked with ruling and subduing the rest of creation, his sin impacted all nature. God cursed the ground because of man's sin, and thus, nature now works against man (Gen. 3:17). Paul says that creation was subjected to futility against its will (Rom. 8:20). So responsibility for the fallen world lies with man, not God.

But why doesn't God simply fix the world or intervene to stop tragedies and acts of evil? Part of the answer is that mankind is experiencing the consequences for sin. He is facing the mess he created. God made man his vice-regent, and man possessed everything he needed to rule the earth successfully. Yet when he sinned, God was not bound to shield man from the consequences of his rebellion.

Third, God has not left man alone to wallow and suffer without hope. He introduced a promise to restore creation and defeat the evil power behind the serpent (Gen. 3:15), a plan that ultimately culminates in Jesus Christ and will be fulfilled by his first and second comings. Also, God brings undeserved common goodness to mankind (Matt. 5:45). He restrains evil (2 Thess. 2:7), and he instituted the conscience to restrict sinner's freedom (Rom. 2:14–15) and human government to punish evildoers (Rom. 13:1–7). God himself also experienced the effects of a fallen world when Jesus became a "man of sorrows" (Isa. 53:3) who lived, suffered, and died on a cross as a sin bearer under divine wrath. Jesus's death and resurrection laid the foundation for the coming restoration of all things (Col. 1:20; Rev. 5:9–10). No one can rightly say that God is a detached observer to evil and suffering. Jesus left heaven and suffered as no person has ever suffered in order to deliver sinners from eternal suffering.

Finally, a judgment day is coming when God will make all things right. He will reward what is right and punish what is wrong. All the thoughts and actions of all people will be judged immediately. Paul noted that when Jesus comes, he "will bring to light the things now hidden in darkness and will disclose the purposes of the heart. Then each one will receive his commendation from God" (1 Cor. 4:5). The righteous, who have received salvation in Christ, will experience glory far beyond the sufferings of this life. Paul said, "For I consider that the sufferings of this present time are not worth comparing with the glory that is to be revealed to us" (Rom. 8:18). This truth gives eternal perspective to our temporal sufferings in this fallen world. A day is coming when all tears of sorrow will be removed and when death will be no more (Rev. 21:4). Believers will experience the joys of a new earth forever, and sin will forever cease. As Paul explained, "The sting of death is sin. . . . But thanks be to God, who gives us the victory through our Lord Jesus Christ" (1 Cor. 15:56–57). And all the children of God will be forever loved by God as he has always loved his eternal Son (John 17:24–26).

Biblical Theology of Sin

Many issues regarding sin have already been examined in this chapter, but it is important to conclude with a summary of the biblical doctrine of sin. Both angels and humans were created with volition and the ability to obey or sin against God. Satan committed the first sin in the cosmos by desiring and aspiring to elevate himself above God. One third of the angels, now known as demons, chose to follow him in his rebellion. The sin of Satan did not bring sin and death into the world, but Satan would tempt man to sin, which would lead to death.

God warned Adam that he would die if he disobeyed by eating from the tree of the knowledge of good and evil. God did not tempt Adam or force him to sin against his will, but he did present Adam with a choice to obey or disobey. In Genesis 3, a tempting serpent appeared, empowered by the already-fallen angel Satan. The serpent tempted Eve to sin by casting doubt on God's Word and telling her she could be like God if she ate from the forbidden tree. Eve and then Adam ate of the tree. This disobedient act of autonomy led to fear, shame, avoidance of God, and the blaming of another. Sin introduced death and the curse into the world.

Adam and Eve died spiritually, and their bodies became subject to decay and death. Conflict was also introduced into the man-woman relationship and into all other relationships, as shown when their firstborn son murdered their second son. In addition, the creation was cursed, and man's ability to fulfill his commission to rule the earth was turned to constant failure. Instead of governing a submissive and pliable earth, the ground fought back to frustrate man and consume him in death.

Sin makes man a failure both in his relationships and in his ability to function as ruler of the earth on God's behalf.

Genesis 3:15 offered the first promise of hope for cursed man. God predicted a coming seed of the woman who would reverse the curse and defeat the satanic power behind the serpent. Sin resulted in a struggle between the seed of the woman and the seed of the serpent, but Satan and his followers would one day be defeated by one person coming from Eve. Eve thought that her first son, Cain, could be the man who would deliver the human race (Gen. 4:1). But Cain was a killer himself. Noah's father, Lamech, believed that Noah could be the promised savior (Gen. 5:28–29). But while Noah was greatly used by God, he was sinful and could not qualify to be the promised deliverer of Genesis 3:15.

The genealogy of death in Genesis 5 revealed that all the descendants of Adam except for Enoch died. At the time of Noah, God's evaluation of man was that he was always wicked (Gen. 6:5, 11–13). God judged sinful mankind through the global flood, saving only Noah and his family and two of each animal (Genesis 7–8). With the Noahic covenant God promised not to destroy sinful man, so that God's kingdom and salvation plans could play out (Gen. 8:20–9:17). After the flood, man rebelled against God at the Tower of Babel. Sinful men gathered to make a name for themselves and remained located in one place, against God's mandate to cover the earth (Gen. 11:1–9), but God punished the human race by separating them linguistically.

The sequence of events in Genesis 1–11 revealed that sin remained mankind's primary problem. The global flood punished the world of sinners but could not remove sin since it dwelt in the hearts of men. The wait for a Deliverer and Savior from sin continued. The plan for defeating sin advanced when God chose Abraham and the great nation (Israel) to come from him. Together they were to be God's chosen means for blessing and saving the world (Gen. 12:2–3; 22:18). Abraham was a great man, yet he too was sinful and was unable to be the savior himself (Gen. 20:2). The people of Israel multiplied numerically, and after the exodus from Egypt, they received the Mosaic covenant and became a nation. The Passover event, in which the blood of a lamb protected the people from death, pictured the coming sacrifice of the one Deliverer, the Lord Jesus Christ (1 Cor. 5:7).

Israel was called to be a kingdom of priests to the nations, and Israel's obedience to God should have been a witness to the nations (Ex. 19:6; Deut. 4:5–6). Instead, Israel sinned egregiously against God in the worship of the golden calf and continued to violate the Mosaic covenant. Israel deteriorated greatly after Solomon's idolatry (1 Kings 11) and was on a trajectory for division and dispersion. Not only did the people of Israel fail, but also the kings in the line of David—who were supposed to model obedience to God—showed themselves to be sinful failures.

The prophets rebuked Israel for continually disobeying the Mosaic covenant and thus God himself. They predicted coming dispersions to the nations. But hope came as Isaiah foretold a future servant of Israel who would sacrificially atone for the sins of Israel and bring salvation to the Gentiles (Isa. 49:3–6; 52:13–53:12). The solution to man's sin problem was to be remedied by the righteous servant who would take on himself the guilt of others' sins. He would suffer divine judgment in their place (Isaiah 53).

This servant appeared at the opening of the New Testament in the person of Jesus, the Deliverer and sinless Savior. A descendant of Abraham and David, Jesus is both Messiah and King. And John the Baptist declared, "Behold, the Lamb of God, who takes away the sin of the world!" (John 1:29). John the Baptist and Jesus preached the same word: "Repent, for the kingdom of heaven is at hand" (Matt. 3:2; 4:17). This message showed that entrance into the Messiah's kingdom required repentance from sin. Jesus said that he came to give his life as a ransom for many (Mark 10:45), and with his death, Jesus atoned for the sins of his people as a sacrificial substitute (2 Cor. 5:21; 1 Pet. 2:24).

The apostle Paul revealed that all people, whether Jew or Gentile, are sinners and unable to save themselves (Rom. 1:18–3:20). Salvation from sin may be found and received but only through faith in Jesus and the righteousness he gives (Rom. 3:21–5:21). Jesus's suffering and the new covenant established by his death break the power of sin for all who are united with him (Rom. 6:1–8:17). Believers in the Lord Jesus are saved from sin and receive spiritual and eternal life. They are a new creation (2 Cor. 5:17). Yet the removal of death and of the effects of sin from the physical body awaits the return of the Savior and the resurrection (Rom. 8:23; 1 Cor. 15:20–24).

While Jesus conquered death at the cross, the final defeat of sin awaits the future. The coming day of the Lord will be a time when God judges and punishes sinners on the earth (Isa. 13:9, 11). An impending man of sin and lawlessness will appear in connection with the day of the Lord, and the Holy Spirit will cease his restraining ministry to allow this man of sin to be revealed and lawlessness to run its course (2 Thess. 2:1–12). Yet this man of sin, along with all who follow him, will be destroyed by Jesus when he returns to earth (Rev. 19:11–21).

The kingdom of the Lord Jesus will be positively characterized by righteousness and blessings to the nations. It will also be a rule with a rod of iron (Ps. 2:9), and all who disobey King Jesus will be punished (Isa. 65:20; Zech. 14:16–19). The millennial reign of the Messiah and his saints will be the fulfillment of the successful kingdom reign that God expected from Adam and humanity at creation (Gen. 1:26–28). After Jesus's thousand-year kingdom, one final rebellion will occur, as Satan is released from the Abyss to lead a last revolt against the Lord at Jerusalem. Remaining unbelievers will join this revolt but will all be instantly destroyed by fire from heaven (Rev. 20:7–10). Even with Satan's presence removed and perfect order set in place during the millennial kingdom, sinners' hearts will be corrupt, and when given the opportunity, those who reject Christ in that period will join in that final rebellion. Afterward, all unbelievers will be gathered for the great white throne judgment. Their judgment will be based on deeds, but since no deeds can save, they will all be sent to the lake of fire forever. Sin will never occur again, and the saints of God will reign forever in God's presence on the new earth (Rev. 22:3–5). Sin and its effects will be removed forever (Rev. 21:3–4). All will be glory, peace, joy, and love.

Prayer[34]

Father, thank You for the vital truth
    that Your Spirit transforms us.
We know that the transformed life is a fruit,
    not the cause, of our salvation.
You are the One who chose and drew us,
    and Christ is both the Author and Finisher of our faith.
His work is the sole ground and reason for our justification.
We're not saved because of any merit or goodness of our own,
    for we have none.

But we likewise know that when You give us a standing by faith in Christ,
    You completely transform us.
If anyone is in Christ, he is a new creature;
    the old things passed away; behold, new things have come.
Your Spirit gives us new hearts.
From the moment of our conversion, He indwells us,
    and through His living presence in our hearts,
        You are steadily conforming us to the image of Christ.

We understand, of course,
    that we will never attain sinless perfection in this life,
    because we won't fully be like Christ
        until we finally see Him face-to-face.
But when we sin, we know that we have an Advocate with the Father,
    Jesus Christ the righteous.
We thank You that He is pleading for us even now,
    seeking our welfare before Your throne
        with prayers that put our paltry prayers to shame.
Your Spirit likewise intercedes for us,
    with groaning that cannot be uttered.

More and more, Lord, we are conscious of our guilt,
    and ashamed of our sin.
Help us therefore to bless You more and more
    for Your steadfast love toward us.
Empower us more and more
    to serve You with faithfulness and joy.
Above all, make us more and more like Christ.

------

34. This prayer is reproduced verbatim from John MacArthur, *At the Throne of Grace: A Book of Prayers* (Eugene, OR: Harvest House, 2011), 160–62. Used by permission of Harvest House.

And remind us, Lord, that we are now slaves of righteousness
    rather than slaves of sin.
We come before You humbly,
    grateful for Your mercy and thankful for the transformation
        that has caused us to love and do the things that please You.

O God, our Creator and Lord,
    we delight in Your righteousness and wisdom.
We have been blessed by Your mercy and grace.
We rejoice in Your lovingkindness and compassion
    toward sinners like us.
Though we are totally unworthy of Your favor,
    You graciously saved us from the guilt and condemnation
        of our own sin.
Our judgment was rendered on Christ at Calvary,
    who put away our sins by the sacrifice of Himself,
    and You raised Him from the dead
        as affirmation of His great accomplishment.

Your mercy and grace were thus secured for us
    by Christ our Savior.
That is why we desire to honor Him through our service.
But may we never think of our own works as meritorious—
    or even as worthy supplements to His finished work.
We confess that our best service
    is altogether unprofitable,
    and when we have rendered our best obedience,
    we are still merely unworthy slaves
        who have done no more than that which we ought to do.

May we therefore forever rely only on Christ,
    trust in Him,
    honor Him,
    and serve Him faithfully but humbly.
We repudiate our sins and trust in Your ongoing cleansing and forgiveness.
Enable us to live in a way
    that draws others to the glories of Christ,
    in whose name we pray. Amen.

"Grace Greater than Our Sin"

Marvelous grace of our loving Lord,
Grace that exceeds our sin and our guilt,
Yonder on Calvary's mount outpoured,
There where the blood of the Lamb was spilt.

Refrain:
Grace, grace, God's grace,
Grace that will pardon and cleanse within!

Grace, grace, God's grace,
Grace that is greater than all our sin!

Sin and despair, like the sea waves cold,
Threaten the soul with infinite loss;
Grace that is greater, yes, grace untold,
Points to the refuge, the mighty cross.

Dark is the stain that we cannot hide—
What can avail to wash it away?
Look! There is flowing a crimson tide;
Whiter than snow you may be today.

Marvelous, infinite, matchless grace,
Freely bestowed on all who believe!
You that are longing to see His face,
Will you this moment His grace receive?

~Julia H. Johnston (1849–1919)

Bibliography
Primary Systematic Theologies: Man

Bancroft, Emery H. *Christian Theology: Systematic and Biblical*. 2nd ed. Grand Rapids, MI: Zondervan, 1976. 183–210.

Berkhof, Louis. *Systematic Theology*. 4th ed. Grand Rapids, MI: Eerdmans, 1939. 181–218.

Buswell, James Oliver, Jr. *A Systematic Theology of the Christian Religion*. 2 vols. Grand Rapids, MI: Zondervan, 1962–1963. 1:221–430.

Culver, Robert Duncan. *Systematic Theology: Biblical and Historical*. Fearn, Ross-shire, Scotland: Mentor, 2005. 227–335.

Dabney, Robert Lewis. *Systematic Theology*. 1871. Reprint, Edinburgh: Banner of Truth, 1985. 292–305.

Erickson, Millard J. *Christian Theology*. Grand Rapids, MI: Baker, 1986. 455–558.

*Grudem, Wayne. *Systematic Theology: An Introduction to Biblical Doctrine*. Grand Rapids, MI: Zondervan, 1994. 439–89.

Hodge, Charles. *Systematic Theology*. 3 vols. 1871–1873. Reprint, Grand Rapids, MI: Eerdmans, 1975. 2:3–122.

Lewis, Gordon R., and Bruce A. Demarest. *Integrative Theology*. 3 vols. Grand Rapids, MI: Zondervan, 1987–1994. 2:17–180.

Reymond, Robert L. *A New Systematic Theology of the Christian Faith*. Nashville: Thomas Nelson, 1998. 415–40.

*Shedd, William G. T. *Dogmatic Theology*. 3 vols. 1889. Reprint, Minneapolis: Klock & Klock, 1979. 2A:3–147; 3:249–331.

Strong, August Hopkins. *Systematic Theology: A Compendium Designed for the Use of Theological Students*. Rev. ed. New York: Revell, 1907. 465–532.

Swindoll, Charles R., and Roy B. Zuck, eds. *Understanding Christian Theology*. Nashville: Thomas Nelson, 2003. 641–722.

Thiessen, Henry Clarence. *Introductory Lectures in Systematic Theology*. Grand Rapids, MI: Eerdmans, 1949. 214–37.

Turretin, Francis. *Institutes of Elenctic Theology*. 3 vols. Edited by James T. Dennison Jr. Translated by George Musgrove Giger. 1679–1685. Reprint, Phillipsburg, NJ: P&R, 1992–1997. 1:569–89.

*Denotes most helpful.

Primary Systematic Theologies: Sin

Bancroft, Emery H. *Christian Theology: Systematic and Biblical*. 2nd ed. Grand Rapids, MI: Zondervan, 1976. 211–35.

Berkhof, Louis. *Systematic Theology*. 4th ed. Grand Rapids, MI: Eerdmans, 1939. 219–61.

Buswell, James Oliver, Jr. *A Systematic Theology of the Christian Religion*. 2 vols. Grand Rapids, MI: Zondervan, 1962–1963. 1:255–320.

Culver, Robert Duncan. *Systematic Theology: Biblical and Historical*. Fearn, Ross-shire, Scotland: Mentor, 2005. 337–417.

Dabney, Robert Lewis. *Systematic Theology*. 1871. Reprint, Edinburgh: Banner of Truth, 1985. 306–51.

*Erickson, Millard J. *Christian Theology*. Grand Rapids, MI: Baker, 1986. 561–658.

*Grudem, Wayne. *Systematic Theology: An Introduction to Biblical Doctrine*. Grand Rapids, MI: Zondervan, 1994. 490–514.

Hodge, Charles. *Systematic Theology*. 3 vols. 1871–1873. Reprint, Grand Rapids, MI: Eerdmans, 1975. 2:123–309.

Lewis, Gordon R., and Bruce A. Demarest. *Integrative Theology*. 3 vols. Grand Rapids, MI: Zondervan, 1987–1994. 2:183–245.

Reymond, Robert L. *A New Systematic Theology of the Christian Faith*. Nashville: Thomas Nelson, 1998. 440–58.

*Shedd, William G. T. *Dogmatic Theology*. 3 vols. 1889. Reprint, Minneapolis: Klock & Klock, 1979. 2A:148–257; 3:331–77.

Strong, August Hopkins. *Systematic Theology: A Compendium Designed for the Use of Theological Students*. Rev. ed. New York: Revell, 1907. 533–664.

Swindoll, Charles R., and Roy B. Zuck, eds. *Understanding Christian Theology*. Nashville: Thomas Nelson, 2003. 723–800.

Thiessen, Henry Clarence. *Introductory Lectures in Systematic Theology*. Grand Rapids, MI: Eerdmans, 1949. 238–72.

Turretin, Francis. *Institutes of Elenctic Theology*. 3 vols. Edited by James T. Dennison Jr. Translated by George Musgrove Giger. 1679–1685. Reprint, Phillipsburg, NJ: P&R, 1992–1997. 1:591–685.

*Denotes most helpful.

Specific Works

Barrick, William D. "A Historical Adam: Young-Earth Creation View." In *Four Views on the Historical Adam*, edited by Matthew Barrett and Ardel B. Caneday, 197–254. Grand Rapids, MI: Zondervan, 2013.

Berkouwer, G. C. *Man: The Image of God*. Grand Rapids, MI: Eerdmans, 1962.

———. *Sin*. Studies in Dogmatics 11. Grand Rapids, MI: Eerdmans, 1971.

Clark, Gordon H. *The Biblical Doctrine of Man*. Trinity Paper 7. Jefferson, MD: Trinity Foundation, 1984.

*Hoekema, Anthony A. *Created in God's Image*. Grand Rapids, MI: Eerdmans, 1994.

Hughes, Philip Edgcumbe. *The True Image: The Origin and Destiny of Man in Christ*. Grand Rapids, MI: Eerdmans, 1989.

Laidlaw, John. *The Biblical Doctrine of Man*. 1895. Reprint, Minneapolis: Klock & Klock, 1983.

*MacArthur, John. *The Battle for the Beginning: Creation, Evolution, and the Bible*. Rev. ed. Nashville: Thomas Nelson, 2005.

*———. *The Vanishing Conscience*. Dallas: Word, 1994.

Machen, J. Gresham. *The Christian View of Man*. 1937. Reprint, Edinburgh: Banner of Truth, 1984.

Mortenson, Terry, and Thane H. Ury, eds. *Coming to Grips with Genesis: Biblical Authority and the Age of the Earth*. Green Forest, AR: Master Books, 2008.

Pink, Arthur W. *Gleanings from the Scriptures: Man's Total Depravity*. Chicago: Moody Press, 1969.

Ramm, Bernard. *Offense to Reason: A Theology of Sin*. San Francisco: Harper & Row, 1985.

Whitcomb, John Clement. *The Early Earth: An Introduction to Biblical Creationism*. 3rd ed. Winona Lake, IN: BMH, 2010.

*Denotes most helpful.

Social Issues

*Clouse, Robert G., ed. *War: Four Christian Views*. Rev. ed. Downers Grove, IL: InterVarsity Press, 1991.

*DeYoung, Kevin. *What Does the Bible Really Teach about Homosexuality?* Wheaton, IL: Crossway, 2015.

*Feinberg, John S., and Paul D. Feinberg. *Ethics for a Brave New World*. 2nd ed. Wheaton, IL: Crossway, 2010.

Köstenberger, Andreas J. *God, Marriage, and Family: Rebuilding the Biblical Foundation*. With David W. Jones. 2nd ed. Wheaton, IL: Crossway, 2010.

*MacArthur, John. *Different by Design*. Colorado Springs: Victor, 1994.

*———. *The Divorce Dilemma: God's Last Word on Lasting Commitment*. Leominster, England: Day One, 2009.

*Murray, John. *Principles of Conduct: Aspects of Biblical Ethics*. Grand Rapids, MI: Eerdmans, 1957.

*Piper, John, and Wayne Grudem, eds. *Recovering Biblical Manhood and Womanhood: A Response to Evangelical Feminism*. Wheaton, IL: Crossway, 1991.

Strauch, Alexander. *Men and Women, Equal yet Different: A Brief Study of the Biblical Passages on Gender*. Littleton, CO: Lewis and Roth, 1999.

Young, Curt. *The Least of These: What Everyone Should Know about Abortion*. Chicago: Moody Press, 1983.

*Denotes most helpful.

"And Can It Be?"

And can it be that I should gain
An int'rest in the Savior's blood?
Died He for me, who caused His pain?
For me, who Him to death pursued?
Amazing love! How can it be,
That Thou, my God, shouldst die for me?

Refrain:
Amazing love! How can it be,
That Thou, my God, shouldst die for me?

He left His Father's throne above,
So free, so infinite His grace.
Emptied Himself of all but love,
And bled for Adam's helpless race.
'Tis mercy all, immense and free,
For, O my God, it found out me.

Long my imprisoned spirit lay
Fast bound in sin and nature's night.
Thine eye diffused a quick'ning ray,
I woke, the dungeon flamed with light.
My chains fell off; my heart was free.
I rose, went forth, and followed Thee.

No condemnation now I dread;
Jesus, and all in Him, is mine!
Alive in Him, my living Head,
And clothed in righteousness divine;
Bold I approach th'eternal throne
And claim the crown, thro' Christ, my own.

~Charles Wesley (1707–1788)

7

Salvation

Soteriology

```
Major Subjects Covered in Chapter 7
Introduction to Soteriology
The Plan of Redemption
The Accomplishment of Redemption
The Application of Redemption
```

Introduction to Soteriology

The Ultimate Purpose of Salvation
Common Grace

In coming to the doctrine of soteriology, the student of Scripture arrives at the pinnacle of Christian theology because the themes and topics addressed in the study of salvation run to the very heart of the gospel and to the center of redemptive history. As has been demonstrated in chapter 6, man was created in the image of God and was charged with ruling over creation as God's representative on earth. Yet man has utterly failed in that commission, having sinned against God in Adam's disobedience and fallen from the original state of blessed fellowship he experienced in the garden. As a result, all of Adam's descendants are conceived in sin and are born enemies of God. By nature, man is both relationally alienated from God and judicially accountable to him, both unable to enjoy the fellowship with God for which he was created and required to pay the penalty for breaking God's laws and belittling his glory—namely, death.

And yet God is a Savior who has acted in saving grace to redeem from sin and death those who would believe. His plan of redemption began in eternity past, as God the Father set his electing love on undeserving sinners, determining to rescue them from the fall and the deserved consequences of their disobedience. He appointed the Lord Jesus Christ, God the Son, to accomplish redemption on behalf of the elect by becoming man, by rendering perfect obedience to God as a man, and by dying as the substitute in the place of his people to pay the penalty for their sin. The Father and the Son have sent God the Holy Spirit to apply to the elect all the saving benefits that the Son purchased for his people. Thus, this chapter follows a Trinitarian form in which the Father's plan of redemption, the Son's accomplishment of redemption, and the Spirit's application of redemption are unfolded, each in their turn, shedding light on the following doctrines: election and reprobation, atonement, calling and regeneration, repentance and faith, union with Christ, justification, adoption, sanctification, the perseverance of the saints, and glorification.

The Ultimate Purpose of Salvation

Before addressing the doctrine of soteriology, it is necessary to consider that the driving purpose for which God saves his people is in accordance with his ultimate purpose for all things—namely, to bring glory and honor to himself. Because believers receive such immense blessings at the hand of God's saving grace, it is a common misconception to assume that God's chief regard in salvation is to sinners themselves. The privilege of being chosen by God for salvation on the basis of nothing in oneself; of being provided a substitute of such worthiness and honor as the Son of God himself; of receiving the gift of the new birth apart from any works of one's own; of being united to Christ, declared righteous apart from works, adopted into the family of God, and conformed into his image, progressively on earth and perfectly in heaven—the flood of gracious benefits that man enjoys in salvation tempts the student of Scripture to believe that God's saving love terminates ultimately on man. Scripture, however, reveals that salvation is not man centered but God centered. God saves sinners for "the praise of his glorious grace" (Eph. 1:6).

The Scriptures are replete with testimony of God's fundamental commitment to pursue the glory of his name. The Old Testament archetype of God's salvation is the redemption of Israel from slavery in Egypt. Speaking of this earthly pinnacle of God's saving deliverance, the psalmist comments, "Yet he saved them for his name's sake, that he might make known his mighty power" (Ps. 106:8). While God surely had compassion on the plight of his people and desired to see them freed from their yoke of bondage (cf. Ex. 2:23–25; 3:7–8, 16), and while he unmistakably desired to bring justice on Egypt for their cruel oppression (cf. Ex. 3:9; 6:1–9), nevertheless his ultimate concern in Israel's redemption was to honor his name (cf. Ex. 9:16; 14:4, 17–18). Later, as God promises the coming of his Spirit-filled servant to establish justice in the earth, to open blind eyes, and to free prisoners from darkness (Isa. 42:1–7), he proclaims, "I am Yahweh; that is my name. And my glory I will not give to another" (Isa. 42:8, author's trans.). This is as if to say, "I will not allow the honor and praise that belongs to my name to be given to anyone else. *I* am Yahweh, and therefore I will be praised." Similarly, in response to Israel's obstinacy, God declares, "For my name's sake I defer my anger, for the sake of my praise I restrain it for you, that I may not cut you off" (Isa. 48:9). Though Israel receives the mercy of God's wrath restrained, the Lord's ultimate motivation is to exalt his person. He emphasizes this purpose further in Isaiah 48:11: "For my own sake, for my own sake, I do it, for how should my name be profaned? My glory I will not give to another." The reader hears the logic that undergirds God's reasoning: he will act for his own sake, for it is unthinkable that he should not receive the glory of which he is worthy. Further, the God centeredness of salvation extends to God's decision not only to delay wrath but also to finally save from wrath. On the precipice of the Babylonian exile, God declares that he will eventually rescue and restore Israel, yet he explicitly denies that he will save them for their own sake:

> It is not for your sake, O house of Israel, that I am about to act, but for the sake of my holy name. . . . I will vindicate the holiness of my great name, which has been profaned among the nations, and which you have profaned among them. And the nations will know that I am the LORD . . . when through you I vindicate my holiness before their eyes. (Ezek. 36:22–23)

God has so attached his name to his people that their destruction would stain his reputation (cf. Ex. 32:7–14; Dan. 9:18–19). Therefore, he will deliver his people for his own glory. Most ultimately, the saving God wipes out transgressions for his own sake (Isa. 43:25); he forgives sins for the sake of his name (1 John 2:12).

There is no greater testimony to God's chief commitment to his glory in salvation than that stated in Paul's glorious hymn of praise to the Savior-God revealed in Ephesians 1. As he extols the divine Giver of every spiritual blessing, Paul declares that all aspects of man's salvation—the election by the Father (1:4–6), the redemption accomplished by the Son (1:7–12), and the sealing ministry of the Holy Spirit (1:13–14)—have been carried out "to the praise of the glory of His grace" (1:6 NASB), "to the praise of his glory" (1:12), "to the praise of his glory" (1:14). Though man is the recipient of God's great love in salvation (Rom. 5:8; Eph. 2:4), he is not the ultimate concern of God's saving grace. God himself and the glory of his name are uppermost in God's affections. Any view of salvation that exalts man as God's chief regard necessarily denigrates the glory of God.[1]

Common Grace

Another preliminary matter is the treatment of the doctrine of common grace. It is not, strictly speaking, soteriological, because common grace is not saving grace.[2] As

---

1. For more on God's chief commitment to his glory in all acts of creation, providence, and redemption, see Jonathan Edwards, *Dissertation on the End for Which God Created the World*, in *The Works of Jonathan Edwards*, ed. Edward Hickman (1834; repr., Carlisle, PA: Banner of Truth, 1974), 1:94–121. Edwards's treatise has been reprinted with a helpful introduction and explanatory notes in John Piper, *God's Passion for His Glory: Living the Vision of Jonathan Edwards* (Wheaton, IL: Crossway, 1998), 115–251.

2. This understanding of common grace is distinct from the Arminian conception of it, which views common grace as God giving all people without exception the ability to repent and believe the gospel. In that sense it is simply the beginning

an expression of the universal goodness and benevolence of God (Ps. 145:9), common grace is experienced by all people without exception, including those who will never receive salvation (cf. Pss. 33:5; 52:1; 107:8; 119:68). It stands in distinction to *special grace*, or *saving grace*, by which God rescues his elect from the penalty and power of sin (Eph. 2:5; Col. 1:13–14), regenerating and sanctifying them through the work of the Holy Spirit (2 Cor. 5:17; Titus 3:5). Common grace, then, does not impart forgiveness for sin, nor does it regenerate unbelieving hearts. Though it reveals truths about the Creator (Rom. 1:18–20) and brings conviction of wrongdoing (Rom. 2:15), it cannot lead to salvation on its own, apart from saving grace. For this reason, it could just as well have been treated in chapter 3, "God the Father," as an expression of God's attributes of grace and mercy. Nevertheless, because common grace is preparatory for the enjoyment of saving grace, it is treated here.

God's common grace provides the human race with at least three benefits. First, it temporarily restrains sin and militates against sin's damaging effects. Apart from divine grace, the full expression of humanity's fallen nature would be unleashed in society—with catastrophic results. Although sinners are totally depraved, meaning that sin affects every aspect of their being (Rom. 3:10–18, 23; cf. Jer. 17:9; Eph. 2:1; Titus 3:3), the full manifestation of that sinfulness is restrained through the conscience, which enables sinners to understand the difference between right and wrong (Rom. 2:15); the authority of parents, who teach and discipline children (Prov. 2:1–5; 3:1–2; 13:1–2, 24; 19:18); and the civil government, which maintains order in human society (Rom. 13:1–5).

Second, common grace enables unbelievers to enjoy beauty and goodness in this life (Ps. 50:2). Both the righteous and the unrighteous experience numerous physical blessings from God's hand (Ps. 104:14–15; Matt. 5:45; Acts 14:15–17; 17:25). Every breath taken, every morsel eaten, every earthly beauty, and every wholesome moment is only possible by God's gracious provision (cf. Job 12:10; Acts 17:28). He is the sole source of all goodness (Ps. 106:1; Mark 10:18; 1 Tim. 4:4; James 1:17). Consequently, all that is good and worthwhile comes from his benevolent hand. Though this world has been devastated by the curse of sin (Rom. 8:20–22), the common grace of God allows sinners to taste of his abundant loving-kindness (see Ps. 34:8).

Third, common grace affords sinners time to hear the gospel so that they might be motivated to repent. Though God could justly execute judgment against sinners instantly, he temporarily withholds the punishment they should receive (cf. Ezek. 18:4, 32; Rom. 6:23; 9:22–23; 1 Tim. 4:10). As the apostle Paul explained, "Do you presume on the riches of his kindness and forbearance and patience, not knowing that God's kindness is meant to lead you to repentance?" (Rom. 2:4; cf. 2 Pet. 2:5; 3:9, 15). Though sinners suppress the truth of the gospel in unrighteousness, the common grace of God makes their rejection of him inexcusable (Rom. 1:18–20).

---

of saving grace and is virtually synonymous with the Arminian doctrine of prevenient grace, which is said to overcome the effects of total depravity in all sinners, bringing them to a place of moral neutrality whereby they may on their own choose to accept or reject Christ. Yet the grace of God that extends to all people without exception is not salvific in any spiritual sense, for all the blessings of salvation are stored up in Christ, the Savior, alone (Eph. 1:3). Because unbelievers may never be said to be "in Christ" in any sense, they do not partake of any of the blessings of salvation.

While common grace expresses the goodness and kindness of God to all humanity, it is in the overflowing blessings of his special grace that God's character as Savior is fully displayed. The remainder of this chapter details the revelation and operation of God's sovereign, saving grace.

The Plan of Redemption

The Decree of God
The Decree of Election
The Decree of Reprobation
Conclusion

The outworking of God's saving grace on sinners begins long before any individual sinner experiences the benefits of that grace. Before the sinner's conversion and justification, before the Savior's substitutionary atonement, and even before the creation of the world itself, God's redemptive grace has its origin in eternity past in the sovereign counsel of the will of the triune God. As Paul wrote to Timothy, God saves his people according to his own eternal purpose, having lavished on them grace "in Christ before the ages began" (2 Tim. 1:9). In sovereign freedom, solely out of the overflow of his loving-kindness and grace, God set his love on particular individuals, chose them to be saved from sin and death, and purposed that they would be restored to a right relationship with him through the redemptive work of his Son applied by his Spirit. Therefore, both the Son's accomplishment of redemption and the Spirit's application of redemption are carried out according to the Father's eternal plan of redemption (Eph. 3:11).

The Decree of God

Because the decree of election is a subset of God's general decree (cf. 1 Cor. 2:7) by which he has infallibly determined all that comes to pass[3] and according to which he works all things (Eph. 1:11), it is necessary to briefly review the biblical teaching on God's decree, for whatever is true of his decree in general must be true of his decree to elect and save.[4] Scripture employs various terms to identify God's decree, including his eternal purpose (Eph. 3:11; cf. Isa. 46:10; Rom. 8:28; 9:11; Eph. 1:9; 2 Tim. 1:9; Heb. 6:17), his definite plan (Acts 2:23; 4:28), his counsel (Ps. 33:11; Isa. 5:19; 46:10), the counsel of his will (Eph. 1:11), the purpose of his will (Eph. 1:5), his good pleasure (Luke 12:32; Phil. 2:13), and his will (Rom. 9:19).

THE CHARACTER OF GOD'S DECREE[5]

A survey of these and other passages yields the key characteristics of God's decree. In the first place, Scripture presents God's decree as having been determined before the

---

3. As has been excellently described in the Westminster Confession of Faith, "God from all eternity, did, by the most wise and holy counsel of His own will, freely, and unchangeably ordain whatsoever comes to pass" (3.1).
4. For a summary of God's decree in the context of God's providence, see chap. 3, "God the Father."
5. This section is adapted from Mike Riccardi, "I Will Surely Tell of the Decree of the Lord," *The Cripplegate* (blog), August 28, 2015, http://thecripplegate.com/i-will-surely-tell-of-the-decree-of-the-lord/. Used by permission of the author.

creation of time, and thus it is said to be eternal. David praises God because all his days were ordained and written in God's book before any one of them came to pass (Ps. 139:16). Paul explains that the plan of saving the Gentiles was accomplished in accordance with God's eternal purpose (Eph. 3:11), a mystery that "God decreed before the ages" (1 Cor. 2:7). He also explicitly teaches that God chose to save his own "before the foundation of the world" (Eph. 1:4; cf. 2 Tim. 1:9), and thus Jesus can say that the kingdom has been prepared for the elect "from the foundation of the world" (Matt. 25:34). In Isaiah 46:10, Yahweh asserts that he will accomplish all his good pleasure and establish all things according to his purpose. Paul makes a similar statement in Ephesians 1:11 when he states that believers have been "predestined according to the purpose of him who works all things according to the counsel of his will." Thus, all of God's providential actions in time conform to a fixed purpose that precedes time.

Second, a significant implication of the eternality of God's decree is that it is necessarily unconditional. That is to say, because the eternal, self-existent triune God was the only entity present in eternity past (Isa. 43:10; 44:24), it is impossible that anything external to God moved him to decree one thing as opposed to another, for there *was* nothing external to him (Gen. 1:1; John 1:1–3). Thus, every decision which is part of God's decree was an uninfluenced, free decision in accordance with God's "good pleasure," or that which pleases him (Pss. 115:3; 135:6; Isa. 46:10; 48:14; Phil. 2:13). So far from his decree being contingent on the choices or actions of men, Scripture proclaims, "All the inhabitants of the earth are accounted as nothing, and he does according to *his* will among the host of heaven and among the inhabitants of the earth" (Dan. 4:35).

Third, God's decree is immutable and therefore efficacious. Just as nothing could influence God's sovereign decree from its inception in eternity past, so nothing in time can change his decree. No creature can alter what God has determined to bring to pass; rather, the psalmist declares that it is *God* who nullifies the *creature's* counsel, even frustrating the plans of peoples (Ps. 33:10). The subsequent verse cements that reality: "The counsel of the LORD stands forever, the plans of his heart to all generations" (Ps. 33:11). Nebuchadnezzar confesses that "none can stay his hand" or call him to account for his actions (Dan. 4:35); when God puts his hand to accomplish something, it cannot be reversed. In a similar fashion, God himself taunts the nations, asking, "For the LORD of hosts has purposed, and who will annul it? His hand is stretched out, and who will turn it back?" (Isa. 14:27). And after receiving what may be the most scathing, forceful rebuke in all Scripture, Job summarizes the immutability of God's decree: "I know that you can do all things, and that no purpose of yours can be thwarted" (Job 42:2). The plans of man often need to be revised because men lack either wisdom or the ability to carry out their plans. Yet God lacks neither the wisdom nor the power to bring his infinitely wise counsel to pass. His decree is immutable and therefore efficacious, for he says, "My counsel shall stand, and I will accomplish all my purpose. . . . I have spoken, and I will bring it to pass; I have purposed, and I will do it" (Isa. 46:10–11).

Finally, God's eternal, unconditional, immutable, and efficacious decree is also exhaustive. "God causes *all things* to work together" according to his purpose (Rom. 8:28 NASB) and works "*all things* according to the counsel of his will" (Eph. 1:11). The psalmist repeats that the Lord does *whatever* he pleases (Pss. 115:3; 135:6). God himself declares that he will accomplish *all* his "good pleasure" (Isa. 46:10 NASB).

Further, this exhaustiveness points not merely to a general control but also to God's specific and meticulous providential governance of all things. Scripture declares that God is the cause of various kinds of weather: snow, rain, ice, winds, and lightning all "turn around and around by his guidance, to accomplish all that he commands them on the face of the habitable world. Whether for correction or for his land or for love, he causes it to happen" (Job 37:12–13; cf. 37:6–12; Ps. 148:8). God causes the sun—which Jesus calls *his* sun—to shine both on the just and the unjust (Matt. 5:45), which in turn causes the grass to grow and brings forth produce from the earth (Ps. 104:14). He determines the lifespan of even the smallest of birds (Matt. 10:29) and provides food for the animals that roam his creation (Ps. 104:27; Matt. 6:26). He determines the boundaries of nations (Acts 17:26) and rules over them (Ps. 22:28), removing and setting up kings (Dan. 2:21) and even turning their hearts wherever he wishes (Prov. 21:1). That God turns their hearts indicates that he ordains even the desires and free choices of men, whether for good (Eph. 2:10) or for evil (Gen. 45:5–8; 50:20; 1 Sam. 2:25; 2 Sam. 24:1; Isa. 10:1–8; Acts 2:23; 4:27–28). Even seemingly random events are determined by God, for "the lot is cast into the lap, but its every decision is from the LORD" (Prov. 16:33). Neither do the events of the personal lives of men escape God's sovereign ordinance, for he supplies their every need (Phil. 4:19; James 1:17), determines the length of their lives (Job 14:5; Ps. 139:16), and even directs their individual steps (Prov. 16:9; Jer. 10:23). Perhaps the greatest summary statement of the exhaustiveness of God's decree comes in Paul's doxology in Romans 11:36: "For from him and through him and to him are *all* things."[6] Whether ends, means, contingencies, desires, choices, or even the good and evil actions of men, nothing escapes the providential governance of God's decree.

THE DECREE OF GOD AND THE PROBLEM OF EVIL[7]

A natural objection that arises to the doctrine of exhaustive sovereignty is that it seems to make God morally culpable for sin. However, while God is properly said to ordain—and thus to be the Ultimate Cause of—all things, he is never the proper chargeable cause of evil. Scripture distinguishes between the (1) Ultimate Cause of an action and (2) the proximate and efficient causes of an action, indicating that only the proximate and efficient causes are blameworthy for an evil action. In addition, Scripture also takes into account the motive for an evil action. While God ordains the evil choices of free moral agents, he does not coerce them; rather, they act according

---

6. For an excellent survey of God's work in providence, see Wayne Grudem, *Systematic Theology: An Introduction to Biblical Doctrine* (Grand Rapids, MI: Zondervan, 1994), 317–37.

7. This section is adapted from Mike Riccardi, "God and Evil: Why the Ultimate Cause Is Not the Chargeable Cause," *The Cripplegate* (blog), October 9, 2015, http://thecripplegate.com/god-and-evil-why-the-ultimate-cause-is-not-the-charge able-cause/. Used by permission of the author.

to their own freedom of inclination. Because God is never the efficient cause of evil and because he always ordains evil for good, he incurs no guilt.

This theodicy is substantiated by numerous passages in the Bible, such as God's role in sending Joseph into slavery (Gen. 45:5–8; 50:20), in sending Assyria to destroy Israel (Isa. 10:1–8), and in inciting David to take the census of Israel (2 Sam. 24:1; 1 Chron. 21:1). But the clearest example comes from the apostolic record of the greatest evil event in history: the murder of the Son of God. If God can be absolved of wrongdoing for ordaining the greatest evil, then there can be no objection to his justice in ordaining lesser evils.

For example, Herod, Pontius Pilate, the Gentiles, and the people of Israel were rightly to blame for the crucifixion of Christ (Acts 4:27). Indeed, Peter openly indicted the men of Israel for their crime (Acts 2:23, 36). And yet Peter also explicitly said that such evil was accomplished by God's decree, that is, "according to the definite plan and foreknowledge of God" (Acts 2:23). Indeed, Herod, Pilate, the Jews, and the Gentiles were gathered against Jesus "to do whatever [*God's*] hand and [*his*] plan had *predestined* to take place" (Acts 4:27–28).

It may be observed, first, that God is the *Ultimate* Cause of the crucifixion, having predestined every circumstance that led to its occurrence and thus rendering it certain. Second, the Jews were a *proximate* cause, having incited the Romans to crucify Christ. Third, Herod, Pilate, and other godless men were the *efficient* cause, because the crucifixion was carried out by Roman authority. The Jews were thus held accountable as a proximate cause, as Peter said to them, "*You* crucified and killed [Jesus] *by the hands of* lawless men" (Acts 2:23). That it was the Romans who actually nailed Jesus to a cross made the Jews no less culpable for that crime. And yet God, by whose hand all these things ultimately came about, is not the chargeable cause of any evil, because, while the perpetrators meant it for evil, God meant it for good. As Jonathan Edwards (1703–1758) explains,

> [It is consistent to say] that God has decreed every action of men, yea, every action that they do that is sinful, and every circumstance of those actions; [that] he determines that they shall be in every respect as they afterwards are; [that] he determines that there shall be such actions, and so obtains that they shall be so sinful as they are; and yet that God does not decree the actions that are sinful as sinful, but decrees [them] as good. . . . [B]y decreeing an action as sinful, I mean decreeing [it] for the sake of the sinfulness of the action. God decrees that it shall be sinful for the sake of the good that he causes to arise from the sinfulness thereof, whereas man decrees it for the sake of the evil that is in it.[8]

Thus, Herod, Pilate, Judas, and the Jews conspired to bring about the crucifixion because they wanted to be rid of this man who indicted them for their sin. But God ordained the evil of the cross *for the good* that it would bring, namely, the salvation of his people from their sin. Such an explanation may not satisfy every objection of

---

8. Jonathan Edwards, "The 'Miscellanies' no. 85," in *The "Miscellanies": Entry Nos. a–z, aa–zz, 1–500*, ed. Thomas A. Schafer, vol. 13 of *The Works of Jonathan Edwards* (New Haven, CT: Yale University Press, 1994), 250.

fallen man, but such is the theodicy that arises from Scripture itself. On that basis, it must be accepted that while God is the Ultimate Cause of all things, he is not the chargeable cause of evil.

THE DECREE OF GOD AND PREDESTINATION

Because God's decree is exhaustive, his sovereignty extends to the plan of redemption. Indeed, the doctrine of God's eternal and universal decree and the doctrine of predestination are not separate doctrines; the latter is a subset of the former. Therefore, that which characterizes God's decree to accomplish all things also characterizes his decree concerning the salvation and damnation of man. God's predestination of man is thus eternal, unconditional, immutable, and efficacious. The term *predestination* is often employed as a synonym for God's decree, since he predestines all things. However, it is also used more narrowly to summarize God's dealings with fallen man concerning salvation, and in that sense it has a twofold meaning: the doctrine of predestination concerns God's decision to elect some to salvation (election) and his decision to pass over others and punish them for their sins (reprobation). Such truth necessitates a discussion of election and reprobation in their turn.

The Decree of Election

The decree of election is the free and sovereign choice of God, made in eternity past, to set his love on certain individuals, and, on the basis of nothing in themselves but solely because of the good pleasure of his will, to choose them to be saved from sin and damnation and to inherit the blessings of eternal life through the mediatorial work of Christ.

THE BIBLICAL CONCEPT OF ELECTION

The doctrine of election is one of the most controversial doctrines in Christian theology. Misconceptions of the nature of God, an unbiblical conception of love, and fallen humanity's notions of fairness have caused many to balk at the idea that God unconditionally chooses some and not others to receive salvation. Because the sovereign freedom of God scandalizes the subversive human mind, some theologians have altogether denied the biblical teaching concerning election and predestination.

However, both the terminology and the concept of election are taught explicitly throughout Scripture. In Ephesians 1:4–5, Paul writes that the Father "*chose* [Gk. *eklegomai*] us in him [Christ] before the foundation of the world, that we should be holy and blameless before him. In love he *predestined* [Gk. *proorizō*] us for adoption as sons." In Romans 8:29–30, he says, "For those whom he [the Father] foreknew [Gk. *proginōskō*] he also *predestined* [Gk. *proorizō*] to be conformed to the image of his Son, in order that he might be the firstborn among many brothers. And those whom he *predestined* [Gk. *proorizō*] he also called." In the next chapter, Paul illustrates God's absolute freedom in salvation by pointing to his discriminating choice between the twins, Jacob and Esau:

> Though they were not yet born and had done nothing either good or bad—in order that God's *purpose of election* [Gk. *hē kat' eklogēn prothesis tou theou*, lit. "the according-to-election purpose of God"] might continue, not because of works but because of him who calls—she was told, "The older will serve the younger." As it is written, "Jacob I loved, but Esau I hated." (Rom. 9:11–13)

Perhaps the clearest statement on God's sovereign election in salvation comes in Paul's remarks to the Thessalonians: "God has *chosen* [Gk. *haireomai*] you from the beginning *for salvation* [*eis sōtērian*] through sanctification by the Spirit and faith in the truth" (2 Thess. 2:13 NASB).

In addition to these several references to God's sovereign, predestining choice, the New Testament also recognizes a category of individuals designated "the elect" (Gk. *hoi eklektoi*). They are the specific objects of God's saving choice. It is customary for the apostles to refer to all believers as "God's chosen ones" (Col. 3:12; cf. Titus 1:1) or "those who are elect" (1 Pet. 1:1; cf. 1 Thess. 1:4). It is for "God's elect" that Christ was delivered over to death; they are thereby justified and saved from all accusations and condemnation (Rom. 8:32–34). Because they are his own, God does not delay to "give justice to his elect, who cry to him day and night" (Luke 18:7). It is "for the sake of the elect" that the days of the great tribulation will be cut short (Matt. 24:22; Mark 13:20), that Christ may return with his angels and "gather his elect from the four winds" to himself (Matt. 24:31; Mark 13:27). And it is "for the sake of the elect" that the apostle Paul endures his many ministerial hardships, that those who have been chosen by God in eternity past may finally come to "obtain the salvation that is in Christ Jesus with eternal glory" (2 Tim. 2:9–10). The reader of Scripture simply cannot deny that the doctrine of election is a biblical teaching that permeates the pages of divine revelation.

THE CATEGORIES OF ELECTION

Scripture employs the terminology of election in several senses. First, God is said to choose, or elect, certain people either to an office or to perform a specific task of service. He chose people for leadership over the nation of Israel, as in the case of Moses (Num. 16:5–7) and Zerubbabel (Hag. 2:23). Scripture indicates that God chose those whom he pleased to the priestly ministry of Israel, both the tribe of Levi in general (Deut. 18:1–5; 21:5; 1 Chron. 15:2) and men individually (e.g., 1 Sam. 2:27–28). As with the office of priest, so also God elected his chosen ones to serve in the offices of king (Deut. 17:15; 1 Sam. 10:24; 1 Chron. 28:4–6; 29:1) and prophet (Jer. 1:10). The Father also, in a special manner, chose the Son for the task of accomplishing salvation for the elect (Isa. 42:1; Luke 9:35; 1 Pet. 1:20; 2:4, 6). Then, during his earthly ministry the Lord Jesus himself chose twelve of his disciples for the task of apostolic service and preaching (Mark 3:13–15; Luke 6:13; John 6:70; 13:18; 15:16, 19; Acts 1:2, 24).

Second, Scripture also speaks of corporate election—the choice of certain nations or groups to enjoy special privileges or perform unique services to God. This is never clearer than in the case of God's choice of Israel to be the recipient of his covenant love and blessings. As Moses declared the law of God to the second generation of Israelites preparing to enter the Promised Land, he insisted that their covenant relationship with Yahweh was rooted in his sovereign election:

> The Lord your God has chosen [Heb. *bakhar*] you to be a people for his treasured possession, out of all the peoples who are on the face of the earth. It was not because you were more in number than any other people that the Lord set his love [Heb. *khashaq*] on you and chose [Heb. *bakhar*] you, for you were the fewest of all peoples. (Deut. 7:6–7)

> Yet on your fathers did the Lord set His affection [Heb. *khashaq*] to love them, and He chose [Heb. *bakhar*] their descendants after them, even you above all peoples. (Deut. 10:15 NASB; cf. 4:37; 1 Kings 3:8; Isa. 41:8; 44:1; 45:4; Amos 3:2)

God set his electing love and affection on Israel to be his special possession among all the nations of the earth. He entered into covenant with them, and, as such, his choice of that nation is irrevocable. While the vast majority of the Jewish nation are presently enemies of the gospel and cut off from covenant blessing, nevertheless a time is coming when "all Israel will be saved" (Rom. 11:26), for "God has not rejected his people whom he foreknew [Gk. *proginōskō*]" (Rom. 11:2). "As regards *election* [Gk. *eklogē*]," Paul says, "they are beloved for the sake of their forefathers. For the gifts and the calling of God are irrevocable" (Rom. 11:28–29).

Finally, in addition to election unto service and corporate election, Scripture clearly teaches that God chooses certain individuals for salvation. Some theologians point to the several passages of Scripture that teach vocational election or corporate election in order to argue against the doctrine of unconditional individual election. However, such an argument is invalid. It is not disputed that Scripture employs the terminology of election in multiple senses, but the mere occurrence of one sense is not in itself an argument against the legitimacy of any other sense. Indeed, Scripture is replete with references to individual election to salvation. In the Old Testament, Nehemiah proclaimed that God chose Abram and entered into covenant with him (Neh. 9:7), which God himself declared from the beginning: "For I have chosen him, that he may command his children and his household after him to keep the way of the Lord by doing righteousness and justice, so that the Lord may bring to Abraham what he has promised him" (Gen. 18:19). He also chose Isaac over Ishmael (Gen. 17:19–21; 21:12; cf. Rom. 9:7–9) and Jacob over Esau (Rom. 9:10–13) to be children of the promise.

The New Testament is especially clear that God has chosen particular individuals for salvation. In the first place, it makes the relationship between election and salvation explicit. God's foreknowledge and predestination are intimately linked with the other aspects of the application of redemption, including the effectual call, justification, sanctification, and glorification (Rom. 8:29–30). Paul declares that the sphere of God's election is *in Christ* (Eph. 1:4), so that those who are recipients of

God's election are chosen in union with the Mediator of their salvation. Further, he indicates that the purpose of God's election is for those whom he has chosen to stand holy and blameless before him as adopted sons (Eph. 1:5), clearly linking election to soteriology. Luke narrates the conversion of the Gentiles in Pisidian Antioch by noting that "as many as were appointed [Gk. *tassō*] to eternal life believed" (Acts 13:48), an explicit affirmation that individuals believe because they are appointed to eternal life. Using similar language, Paul declared to the Thessalonians that God had "destined [them] . . . to obtain salvation [Gk. *etheto . . . eis peripoiēsin sōtērias*]" (1 Thess. 5:9). And he explicitly proclaimed to them, "God has chosen you from the beginning for salvation" (2 Thess. 2:13 NASB). In the case of the nation of Israel, though the majority had rejected the Messiah and were hardened, "the elect obtained" salvation by the grace of God (Rom. 11:7).

Since, then, there can be no question that election is intimately linked to salvation, opponents of this doctrine question the proper objects of election. That is, while they admit that election clearly concerns salvation, they contend that this election is corporate rather than individual. In other words, God does not choose specific persons to receive salvation but rather chooses to save a class or category of people who trust in Christ. Just as God chose the nation of Israel corporately in the Old Testament, so now in the new covenant era God elects the church as a corporate body. Thus, they say, when Paul declares that God "chose *us* in [Christ] before the foundation of the world" (Eph. 1:4), the "us" is plural and therefore refers to the church as a corporate body, not to individuals.[9]

Yet this is a tenuous claim, since the first-person plural pronoun was the only option that would not confuse Paul's intent. If he had used the first-person singular *me*, he would have communicated that God had chosen only him, which was certainly not his intent. Neither would he have used the second person singular *you*, for he was writing to all the saints (Gk. *toi hagioi*, Eph. 1:1) at Ephesus, not merely one individual. Further, if he had used the second person plural *you*, he could have been mistaken to mean that only the Ephesians were elect, which was also not his intent. The first-person plural *us* was the only option that would communicate that God had chosen each individual believer in Christ according to his sovereign pleasure. Thus, this isolated argument for corporate election on the basis of the plurality of the direct object in Ephesians 1:4 fails to overturn the clear teaching of Scripture.

Another argument for corporate election is built on Paul's statement that believers are chosen in Christ. Since Christ is God's archetypal elect one (Isa. 42:1; Luke 9:35; 1 Pet. 1:20; 2:4, 6), God has chosen only Christ as an individual; believers become part of the elect at the moment of faith by virtue of their union with Christ.[10] Several problems arise from this position. First, it fails to do justice to the fact that Paul says

9. William G. MacDonald, "The Biblical Doctrine of Election," in *The Grace of God, the Will of Man: A Case for Arminianism*, ed. Clark H. Pinnock (Grand Rapids, MI: Zondervan, 1989), 219–26.

10. Karl Barth, *Church Dogmatics*, trans. G. T. Thompson, G. W. Bromiley, et al., ed. G. W. Bromiley and T. F. Torrance, vol. 2, part 2 (Edinburgh: T&T Clark, 1957), 94–194; Markus Barth, *Ephesians 1–3: A New Translation with Introduction and Commentary*, Anchor Bible 34, ed. William Foxwell Albright and David Noel Freedman (Garden City, NY: Doubleday, 1974), 107–9.

that God "chose *us*" in Christ (Eph. 1:4); the direct object of God's electing is "us," not "him." Second, corporate election is foreign to the context, for each of the salvific blessings outlined in Ephesians 1:3–14 is received by individuals. In salvation, individuals receive spiritual blessings (1:3); individuals are made holy and blameless (1:4); individuals are adopted as sons and daughters of God (1:5); individuals receive freely bestowed grace (1:6); and individuals have been redeemed (1:7–8) and sealed with the Spirit (1:13). These final two blessings are unquestionably personal and individual; each individual believer, not merely an undefined group, has been ransomed by Christ and sealed with the Spirit. In the same way, individuals are the proper object of the spiritual blessing of election. Third, Paul elsewhere teaches that God chose foolish, weak, and base individuals—not merely an unnamed, faceless mass—in order that no individual may boast before him (1 Cor. 1:27–31). God did not elect Christ and leave humanity to unite themselves with Christ by faith. As Boettner says, such a scheme "makes the purposes of Almighty God to be conditioned by the precarious wills of apostate men and makes temporal events to be the cause of His eternal acts."[11] Yet Paul teaches that God chose us in Christ "before the foundation of the world" (Eph. 1:4), not at the moment of our faith. It is by *his* doing—not ours—that we are in Christ Jesus (1 Cor. 1:30).

Therefore, while it is indeed true that God has chosen his people to be a fellowship, the corporate body of the church is made up of individual members, whom God knows personally by name (Ex. 33:12, 17; Isa. 45:4). Jesus, as the Good Shepherd, insisted that he personally knew his sheep (John 10:14)—even those who had not yet existed (John 17:20–21)—who were given to him by the Father (John 10:29; cf. 6:37, 39, 44, 65; 17:2). He even said to the Father of his sheep, "Yours they were, and you gave them to me" (John 17:6). From all eternity, the Father has so chosen particular individuals that they are said to be his, and it is these precious sheep that he entrusts to the Shepherd. Election is so intimately personal that the names of those chosen by the Father have been written in the book of life from before the foundation of the world (Rev. 13:8; 17:8; 21:27). Clearly, God has chosen individuals for salvation.

THE BASIS OF ELECTION

In the above definition of election, it was stated that God's choice of certain individuals is made not on the basis of anything in those individuals themselves but solely because of the sovereign and good pleasure of God's will. This is to say that election is *unconditional*; God's choice of individuals for salvation is not predicated on any virtue or worthiness that God sees in those individuals. As Moses told the people of Israel, "It was not because you were more in number than any other people that the LORD set his love on you and chose you, for you were the fewest of all peoples" (Deut. 7:7). In other words, there was nothing in Israel that commended them to God as a ground for choosing them. Rather, he continued, "it is because the LORD

---

11. Lorraine Boettner, *The Reformed Doctrine of Predestination* (1932; repr., Phillipsburg, NJ: Presbyterian and Reformed, 1991), 101.

loves you and is keeping the oath that he swore to your fathers" (Deut. 7:8). Moses is nearly tautologous: God set his love on his people in election because he loves them. When the question is asked, why does God choose one person over another? the answer cannot be because that person did this or that but rather because God acted according to the sovereign freedom of his will (Eph. 1:5).

The Arminian Doctrine of Conditional Election. Arminian theologians reject the teaching of unconditional election. They contend that it would be unfair for God to save some and not others, all things being equal between them. Instead, on the basis of Paul's comment on God's foreknowledge in Romans 8:29, they posit that God has chosen those whom he will save because in eternity past he looked ahead into the future and foresaw who would believe in Christ and who would reject him. God is often pictured as "looking down the corridors of time" and discovering those who according to their own free will would believe in Christ—these he chose to save on the basis of their foreseen faith. Discovering that the rest would reject Christ, he decided not to save them on the basis of their lack of faith. For this reason, this view is often called the *foreseen faith* view, the *prescient* view, or the *simple foreknowledge* view of election. Thus, the Arminian conception of election rests the ultimate cause of salvation on man, not on God; election is simply God's ratification of the choices that he foresaw individuals would make.

There are several significant problems with the prescient view of election. In the first place, it posits that the events of reality are somehow disconnected from God himself. When God "looks into the future," it is said, he discovers what will happen independently of his sovereign decree and then makes decisions on the basis of what he learns by his so-called foreknowledge. Besides fundamentally undermining the omniscience of God, this position misunderstands that the events of the future take place precisely because God has decreed them to take place. As has been demonstrated above, God "works all things according to the counsel of his own will" (Eph. 1:11; cf. Pss. 115:3; 135:6; Isa. 46:10; Dan. 4:35). Thus, God does not form his decree because he knows the future; rather, he knows the future because he has decreed the future.[12]

Second, the prescient view of election also fundamentally misunderstands the nature of God's foreknowledge, especially as taught in Romans 8:29. To begin, this verse does not say that God foreknew facts concerning the actions or choices of his creatures; it says that God foreknew particular *persons* themselves: "For *those whom* he foreknew"—that is, "those who love God" and "who are called according to his

---

12. The knowledge of God that is "based" on his decree is his free knowledge, which has to be distinguished from his necessary knowledge. Berkhof provides a helpful summary: "There is in God . . . a necessary knowledge, including all possible causes and results. This knowledge furnishes the material for the decree; it is the perfect fountain out of which God drew the thoughts which He desired to objectify. Out of this knowledge of all things possible He chose, by an act of His perfect will, led by wise considerations, what He wanted to bring to realization, and thus formed His eternal purposes. The decree of God is, in turn, the foundation of His free knowledge or *scientia libera*. It is the knowledge of things as they are realized in the course of history. While the necessary knowledge of God logically precedes the decree, His free knowledge logically follows it. This must be maintained over against all those who believe in a conditional predestination (such as Semi-Pelagians and Arminians), since they make the pre-determinations of God dependent on His foreknowledge." Louis Berkhof, *Systematic Theology*, 4th ed. (1932; repr., Grand Rapids, MI: Eerdmans, 1996), 102.

purpose"—"he also predestined" (Rom. 8:28–29). If the foreknowledge spoken of in Romans 8:29 is, as the Arminian contends, to be equated simply with "knowing in advance" (i.e., simple foreknowledge), what sense could it make to speak of a subset of people within the larger set of those whom God has foreknown? If he is omniscient, he must have foreknown everybody, not just those whom he predestined to become conformed to the image of Christ. Yet if "those whom he foreknew" includes every individual in history without exception, one must commit himself to the doctrine of universal, final salvation. For Romans 8:29–30 teaches that those whom he foreknew he also predestined to become conformed to the image of Christ, and those whom he predestined he effectually called by his Spirit, and those whom he called he justified and glorified. The Arminian interpretation thus impales its advocates on the horns of a dilemma: to be consistent with their interpretation of foreknowledge, they must either (a) deny God's omniscience (i.e., affirm that he foreknew only those who are saved), or (b) embrace universal final salvation (i.e., affirm that all those he foreknew, which is to say everybody, will finally be justified and glorified). The Arminian rightly denies both of these conclusions, which do violence to Scripture, yet he does so at the cost of the consistency of the Arminian system.

In reality, the Greek verb *proginōskō* in Romans 8:29 speaks not of simple foreknowledge but of the knowledge that characterizes an intimate personal relationship. There are two other places in the New Testament in which *proginōskō* speaks of God's foreknowledge. In the first, the apostle Peter writes, "He [Christ] was foreknown before the foundation of the world but was made manifest in the last times for the sake of you" (1 Pet. 1:20). If foreknowledge means nothing more than God looking ahead to see what is going to happen, this verse is meaningless. To be consistent with the simple-foreknowledge definition, one would have to say that this verse means that God looked down the corridors of time, discovered that Christ would willingly lay down his life for sinners, and then on that basis decided to appoint him the Mediator between God and man. Instead, Peter's intent is to point to the intimate knowledge of personal relationship between the Father and the Son in the Trinitarian counsel of redemption. The other occurrence comes in Romans 11:2, where Paul employs the term with respect to Israel, saying, "God has not rejected his people whom he foreknew." Once again, we cannot conclude that Israel was the only people of whom God was aware; rather, Paul's point is to emphasize the intimate relationship between God and Israel founded on the covenants of promise.

This understanding of *proginōskō* is substantiated by its Old Testament Hebrew counterpart, *yada'*, which, though often used to speak of simple knowledge, many times carries the connotation of intimate, personal knowledge. Perhaps the most vivid illustration of this meaning is Scripture's use of *yada'* to refer to sexual relations between a man and a woman. The Genesis account records, "Now Adam knew [*yada'*] Eve his wife, and she conceived and bore Cain" (Gen. 4:1), and "Adam knew [*yada'*] his wife again, and she bore a son and called his name Seth" (Gen. 4:25; cf. 4:17; 19:5, 8; 24:16; 38:26; Judg. 11:39; 19:25; 21:11–12; 1 Sam. 1:19).

So personal and intimate is the knowledge connoted by *yada'* that it adequately describes the sexual union between a husband and a wife. No mere "simple knowledge" results in the conception of children! Further, as God contemplates hiding the destruction of Sodom from Abraham, he says, "For I have chosen [*yada'*] him, that he may command his children and his household after him to keep the way of the LORD by doing righteousness and justice, so that the LORD may bring to Abraham what he has promised him" (Gen. 18:19). The knowledge connoted by *yada'* so aptly describes God's personal, sovereign election that all the modern translations translate it as "chosen" (ESV, HCSB, NASB, NIV). A similar dynamic is at play in Amos 3:2, in which God tells Israel, "You only have I known [*yada'*] of all the families of the earth." Just as in Romans 11:2, this cannot mean that Israel was the only people group that God had known *about* but rather points to the intimate covenant relationship between God and Israel grounded in his sovereign choice of them (Deut. 7:6–8). In fact, several translations render *yada'* as "chosen" to adequately bring out the force of the verb (NASB, NIV).

Still further, as Moses pleads for God's presence to accompany Israel, God says to him, "This very thing that you have spoken I will do, for you have found favor in my sight, and I know [*yada'*] you by name" (Ex. 33:17; cf. 33:12). Here the concept of being known by name is parallel to having found favor in the sight of God. Of course, God knows every individual by name in the literal sense, because he is omniscient. But in this sense, God's knowing one by name is synonymous with his having graced him or her with his favor. A similar comment concludes the first psalm, where the psalmist declares, "The LORD knows [*yada'*] the way of the righteous, but the way of the wicked will perish" (Ps. 1:6). By virtue of his omniscience, God knows every man's way. Yet the psalmist's intent is to say that God graciously favors the righteous and protects his way from perishing. Finally, the connection between this intimate knowledge and love is drawn in the synonymous parallelism of Psalm 91:14, where God speaks of the believer: "*Because he has loved Me*, therefore I will deliver him; I will set him securely on high, *because he has known My name*" (NASB).

The term *yada'* is the Hebrew counterpart not only to *proginōskō* but also to its cognate *ginōskō*, which can have a similar meaning as well. To those who named Christ but never did the will of his Father, Jesus declares, "I never knew [*ginōskō*] you" (Matt. 7:23). In 1 Corinthians 8:3, Paul defines the believer and lover of God as one who is "known [*ginōskō*] by God" (cf. Gal. 4:9), and in 2 Timothy 2:19, he declares, "The Lord knows [*ginōskō*] those who are his" (cf. John 10:15, 27). If one accepts the Arminian concept of simple foreknowledge, the knowledge in these verses would be not the intimate knowledge of relationship but bare knowledge. However, that would make it impossible for Jesus to say, "I never knew you" (Matt. 7:23), because the Lord knows all men; he is omniscient (John 16:30; 21:17). Once again, the doctrine of simple foreknowledge is shown to do violence to the omniscience of God.

Therefore, the testimony of *proginōskō*, its close cognate *ginōskō*, and their Old Testament counterpart, *yada'*, confirms that the sense of God's knowledge used in

Romans 8:29 speaks not of a simple knowledge of facts but rather of an intimate, covenant relationship grounded in God's sovereign choice and marked by his favor and love. When Paul declares that God has *foreknown* individuals, he is indicating that God has determined to set his electing love and favor on them, setting them apart for an intimate, personal, saving relationship with him. To foreknow is to "forelove." In this sense, both the foreknowledge of Romans 8:29 and the predestination Paul brings up in the next phrase are simply synonyms for God's election. Predestination speaks of election from the perspective of God's sovereignty, while foreknowledge speaks of election from the perspective of his love. Thus, the Arminian doctrine of simple foreknowledge cannot be sustained from Romans 8:29, and without it there is no biblical support for the doctrine of conditional election based on foreseen faith.

God's Unconditional, Electing Love. Not only is there no biblical basis for conditional election, but also Scripture explicitly testifies to the contrary. In Ephesians 1:4, after identifying both the beneficiaries of election (i.e., every individual believer) and the sphere of election (i.e., union with Christ), Paul comments on the timing of election, namely, "before the foundation of the world." The Father's election was an eternal decree, predating creation and history. Just as the Father loved the Son "before the foundation of the world" (John 17:24) and foreknew the Son "before the foundation of the world" (1 Pet. 1:20), so were the elect loved and foreknown before the foundation of the world, by virtue of God's choosing them—this grace having been "granted us in Christ Jesus *from all eternity*" (2 Tim. 1:9 NASB). An important implication of this reality—indeed, Paul's point in discussing the timing of election—is to rule out personal merit as its ground. No temporal circumstances or personal characteristics influenced the Father's election of his people, for it was a decree made before time began.

Paul then goes on to explicitly state the basis of God's choice: "In love he predestined us to adoption as sons through Jesus Christ to himself, according to the good pleasure of his will [Gk. *kata tēn eudokian tou thelēmatos autou*]" (Eph. 1:4–5, author's trans.). The prepositional phrase "according to" (*kata* plus the accusative) indicates the standard or basis of an action.[13] Thus, Paul says that predestination is carried out according to the standard or on the basis of the good pleasure of God's will. Though either *eudokia* ("good pleasure") or *thelēma* ("will") would by themselves have adequately expressed Paul's intent, he employs both terms in synonymous repetition in order to emphasize God's absolute freedom in election. This delivers a fatal blow to the supposition that election was conditioned on faith—or on anything else the sinner might think or do. If the basis of God's choice was the foreseen faith or actions of those whom he chose, Paul would have had to write that God "predestined us . . . according to his foreknowledge of our faith." Yet he explicitly asserts that it was the good pleasure of *God's* will, not man's will, that was the ground of his

---

13. Walter Bauer, *A Greek-English Lexicon of the New Testament and Other Early Christian Literature*, rev. and ed. Frederick W. Danker, 3rd ed., based on the previous English editions by W. F. Arndt, F. W. Gingrich, and F. W. Danker (Chicago: University of Chicago Press, 2000), 404, 512.

choice. Quite simply, if election were conditioned on faith, as the Arminian contends, Paul has misspoken in Ephesians 1:5. On the contrary, similar to Moses's comments to Israel in Deuteronomy 7:6–8, the reason the Lord has set his love on his own is not because they commended themselves to him in any way but only because, in the exercise of his sovereign freedom, he determined to savingly love them.

Paul develops and illustrates this concept further in Romans 9:6–18. He recounts God's dealings with Isaac over Ishmael and Jacob over Esau to illustrate his sovereign freedom in choosing his own for salvation. While his choice of Isaac over Ishmael illustrates that he is a discriminating God, his choice of Jacob over Esau gives specific insight into the unconditional nature of election. Paul writes, "Though they were not yet born and had done nothing either good or bad—in order that God's purpose of election might continue, not because of works but because of him who calls—[Rebekah] was told, 'The older will serve the younger.' As it is written, 'Jacob I loved, but Esau I hated'" (Rom. 9:11–13). Just as Paul did when he stated that election occurred "before the foundation of the world" in Ephesians 1:4, so here he makes the point that God's choice predates Jacob and Esau precisely in order to rule out personal merit as the ground of his decision. At the point of God's choice, they had done nothing good or bad; none of Esau's evil actions prejudiced God against him, and none of Jacob's righteous actions prejudiced God in his favor. Rather, God chose Jacob over Esau "in order that God's purpose of election might continue" (Rom. 9:11)—again grounding God's choice in his own sovereign purpose.

Paul gets clearer as he continues. Adding an explicit negation, he goes on to say that God's election is "not because of works but because of him who calls" (Rom. 9:11). To the statement that God had chosen Jacob over Esau *before* they had done anything good or bad, some reply that, while that is true, God could still have based his choice on the foreseen *future* actions of Jacob and Esau. Here, however, Paul repudiates this notion. He states unequivocally that the choice was *not* because of works at all, in any sense. Rather, it was because of *him* who calls.

This statement is the undoing of conditional election based on foreseen faith. Throughout Paul's letters, he regularly contrasts works and faith:

> Then what becomes of our boasting? It is excluded. By what kind of law? By a law of *works*? No, but by the law of *faith*. For we hold that one is justified by *faith* apart from *works* of the law. (Rom. 3:27–28)

> What shall we say, then? That Gentiles who did not pursue righteousness have attained it, that is, a righteousness that is by faith; but that Israel who pursued a law that would lead to righteousness did not succeed in reaching that law. Why? Because they did not pursue it by *faith*, but as if it were based on *works*. (Rom. 9:30–32)

> Yet we know that a person is not justified by *works* of the law but through *faith* in Jesus Christ, so we also have believed in Christ Jesus, in order to be justified by *faith* in Christ and not by *works* of the law. (Gal. 2:16)

Did you receive the Spirit by *works* of the law or by hearing with *faith*? . . . Does he who supplies the Spirit to you and works miracles among you do so by *works* of the law, or by hearing with *faith*? (Gal. 3:2, 5)

Therefore, when one comes to his statement in Romans 9:11 and reads that election is "not because of works," it is natural to expect him to say, "but because of faith." If the Spirit desired to convey that the conditioning basis of election was faith, there was no better opportunity to reveal it than in this passage. Yet the apostle breaks from his consistent pattern of contrasting works and faith precisely because election is not based on faith. He declares rather that it is "not because of works but because of *him* who calls." Once again, the basis of God's electing choice is grounded in God himself, which is to say that election is based on the good pleasure of God's own will (cf. Eph. 1:5). While faith is a condition of justification, it is not a condition of election. Election is unconditional.[14]

Paul recognizes that when his doctrine confronts fallen human reasoning, the response will be to charge God with injustice (Rom. 9:14). This is significant because the Arminian doctrine of conditional election would never draw this objection. Who would accuse God of being unjust for choosing to save people on the basis of their foreseen acceptance or rejection of Jesus? Only the doctrine of God's unconditional choice of some and not others elicits accusations of injustice. But Paul does not let up. He quotes God's own declaration to Moses, "I will have mercy on whom I have mercy, and I will have compassion on whom I have compassion" (Rom. 9:15; cf. Ex. 33:19), and he concludes, "So then it [election] does not depend on the man who wills [Gk. *ou tou thelontos*] or the man who runs [Gk. *oude tou trechontos*], but on God who has mercy" (Rom. 9:16 NASB). This verse ought to be enough to end the controversy concerning salvation and man's will. Paul unequivocally denies that human will and human effort have anything to do with the basis of God's election to salvation. Neither faith born of human will nor works of love born of human effort constitute the ground of God's choice of his people. Rather, election depends on *God* who has mercy, once again an affirmation that the decisive basis for election is God's own sovereign will. Election is unconditional.

A final problem concerning the doctrine of conditional election is that it is unable to escape the charge of undermining the doctrine of salvation by grace alone (*sola gratia*). By grounding God's electing purpose in man's foreseen faith and not in God's sovereign will, the Arminian ultimately makes man the determinative cause of salvation and not God. On this view, what ultimately differentiates the saved person from the unsaved is not something God has done but something man has done. To Paul's question in 1 Corinthians 4:7, "For who makes you differ from another?" (NKJV), the Arminian, if he is to be consistent, must ultimately answer, "I make the difference. God chose me and not my neighbor because he foresaw that I would freely believe and my neighbor would not." In that case the believer has grounds for

---

14. John Piper, *The Justification of God: An Exegetical and Theological Study of Romans 9:1–23* (Grand Rapids, MI: Baker, 1983), 51–53.

boasting. Yet Paul replies that God has chosen the foolish, and the weak, and the base—not the wise, the strong, or the faithful—"so that no man may boast before God. But by *His* doing you are in Christ Jesus" (1 Cor. 1:29–30 NASB). Grudem summarizes helpfully:

> What *ultimately* makes the difference between those who believe and those who do not? If our answer is that it is ultimately based on something God does (namely, his sovereign election of those who would be saved), then we see that salvation at its most foundational level is based on *grace alone*. On the other hand, if we answer that the ultimate difference between those who are saved and those who are not is because of *something in man* (that is, a tendency or disposition to believe or not believe), then salvation ultimately depends on a combination of grace plus human ability.[15]

The Decree of Reprobation

The saving blessings that flow from God's sovereign election are not enjoyed by all who are made in his image. The Lord Jesus says that few will enter the narrow gate that leads to life but that many will travel the broad way to destruction (Matt. 7:13–14). He teaches that there will be sheep as well as goats—those who inherit eternal life and others who go away into eternal punishment (Matt. 25:46). Most succinctly, he declares that "many are called, but few are chosen" (Matt. 22:14). Thus, Scripture instructs that in his inscrutable wisdom, God has not chosen to save all men. His election is particular, not universal. Given this, we must inquire as to the destiny of those whom he has not chosen to save.

Because God's decree is exhaustive, the doctrine of predestination extends not only to his decision to elect some unto salvation but also to his decision not to elect others and thus to leave them to the destruction that their sins deserve. Just as God has determined the eternal destiny of those sinners who will eventually be saved, so also has he determined the destiny of those sinners who will eventually be lost. The former is the decree of election; the latter is the decree of reprobation.

THE STATEMENT OF THE DOCTRINE

The decree of reprobation is the free and sovereign choice of God, made in eternity past, to pass over certain individuals, choosing not to set his saving love on them but instead determining to punish them for their sins unto the magnification of his justice.[16]

The doctrine of reprobation is a difficult teaching to accept. It is not pleasant to contemplate the miseries of eternal suffering in and of themselves, let alone to consider that the God who is love and is by nature a Savior has sovereignly determined to consign sinners to such a wretched end. Because it so easily offends fallen man's sensibilities, many Christians who embrace the doctrine of election nevertheless reject the doctrine of reprobation altogether. That is also the case because the doctrine is

---

15. Grudem, *Systematic Theology*, 678. Italics original.
16. Berkhof, *Systematic Theology*, 118.

so easily and so often misunderstood. Because of that, it is necessary to state what precisely we do and do not believe concerning the doctrine of reprobation.

In the first place, reprobation is often wrongfully conflated with the doctrine of equal ultimacy. Equal ultimacy teaches that God's actions in election and reprobation are perfectly symmetrical, so that God is just as active in working unbelief in the heart of the reprobate as he is in working faith in the heart of the elect. It pictures God in eternity past contemplating all humanity as yet unfallen and morally neutral and arbitrarily deciding to work sin and unbelief in the reprobate in order to be justified in consigning them to eternal punishment. Though this is what many think of when they hear the terms *reprobation* or *double predestination*, it is a gross caricature of the biblical doctrine of reprobation that is utterly foreign to Scripture, repugnant to the love and justice of God, and an aberration of historic Calvinism that has been rejected throughout Reformed orthodoxy.[17]

Instead, Scripture teaches an unequal ultimacy with regard to election and reprobation—that is, while God does indeed decree both the salvation of some and the damnation of others, there is a necessary asymmetry in these decrees. Such an asymmetry is observed in Romans 9:22–23, for example, where Paul uses the active voice to speak of God's involvement in election ("vessels of mercy, which he has prepared beforehand for glory") and the passive voice to speak of his involvement in reprobation ("vessels of wrath prepared for destruction"). When God chose some and not others for salvation, he regarded them not as morally neutral but as already-fallen creatures. That is not to say that they were already created and fallen, for God's decree is eternal and thus pretemporal. Rather, from eternity, before anyone had been created, God conceived of or contemplated all people in light of their fall in Adam and thus as sinful creatures.[18] In the case of the elect, he actively intervenes—setting his love on them, determining to appoint Christ as their Savior and to send the Spirit to sovereignly quicken them from spiritual death unto new life in Christ. In the case of the nonelect, however, he does not intervene but simply passes them by, choosing to leave them in their state of sinfulness and then to punish them for their sin. While he is the efficient cause of the blessedness of the elect, he is not the efficient cause of the wretchedness of the nonelect; rather, he ordains them to destruction by means of

---

17. Sproul rightly notes that it has been identified with hyper-Calvinism, which he prefers to call "sub-Calvinism" or "anti-Calvinism." R. C. Sproul, *Chosen by God* (Wheaton, IL: Tyndale House, 1986), 142.

18. That is to say, the decrees of election and reprobation logically followed the decrees of creation and the fall. In this, we hold to an infralapsarian order of the decrees. Though God's decree is a single and timeless act within himself in eternity past, the limits of human thought and language constrain us to speak of several aspects or elements of his decree, which, though permitting no chronological order, nevertheless may be arranged in a logical order. Supralapsarianism (which means "above the fall") teaches that God's decrees of election and reprobation logically preceded his decrees to create and to ordain the fall. Infralapsarianism (which means "after the fall") teaches the opposite, namely, that election and reprobation were logically subsequent to God's decrees to create and to ordain the fall.

Infralapsarianism is preferable for several reasons. It seems inescapable that God would have had to logically determine to *create* men and women before he could determine to save or damn them. How could he choose persons whose existence he had not yet decreed? Similarly, it seems unavoidable that the decrees unto *salvation* and *punishment* necessarily presuppose that there is *sin* from which to be saved or for which to be punished. Thus, the decree of creation and the decree to ordain the fall of man must logically precede the decree to choose some to be saved from sin. Finally, when Paul speaks of God's decrees of election and reprobation, he pictures God as a potter fashioning vessels of wrath and vessels of mercy from the same lump of clay (Rom. 9:19–23). Because he calls the elect "vessels of *mercy*," it is right to infer that he contemplates the clay as a sinful lump, for one can be merciful only to vessels that are inherently undeserving of mercy.

For a helpful introduction to the doctrine of the order of the divine decrees, see Berkhof, *Systematic Theology*, 118–25; Boettner, *The Reformed Doctrine of Predestination*, 126–32.

secondary causes.[19] Thus, the elect receive mercy, for they are not punished as their sins deserve, but the nonelect receive justice, for they are rightly condemned as their sins deserve. On neither ground can God be charged with unrighteousness, because all are guilty and because he is not obligated to show grace to any.

Sometimes, in order to rightly distinguish reprobation from equal ultimacy, people make inaccurate statements concerning precisely how election and reprobation are unequal or asymmetrical. In particular, they often wrongly state that election is positive and unconditional while reprobation is negative and conditioned on man's sin. While such statements can be true depending on what one intends, they are confusing because they fail to distinguish between the two elements of the decree of reprobation: (1) the decision to pass over some, called *preterition*, and (2) the determination to condemn those passed over, called *precondemnation*. With respect to the positive-negative distinction, preterition is indeed a negative or passive action on God's part; God simply passes over man and leaves him in his state of sinfulness. Precondemnation, however, is a positive action in which God actively determines to visit judicial punishment on sin. The "vessels of wrath" are "prepared for destruction" (Rom. 9:22), destined to disobedience (1 Pet. 2:8), and "designated for this condemnation" (Jude 4).[20] With respect to the unconditional-conditional distinction, precondemnation is indeed conditional, for God assigns men to condemnation on the basis of their sin and guilt. Preterition, however, is unconditional. Sin cannot be the basis on which God passes over some men, for all men without exception are sinners. Like election, God's decision not to choose someone for salvation is based on nothing in that individual but rather is a sovereign act of God's good pleasure. Thus, preterition is passive and unconditional, while precondemnation is active and conditional. To say that election is positive while reprobation is negative is to fail to adequately emphasize the active nature of precondemnation. And to say that election is unconditional while reprobation is conditional is to fail to adequately emphasize the unconditional nature of preterition. Avoiding both of these imprecise statements will ensure an accurate understanding of the doctrine of reprobation.

THE VINDICATION OF THE DOCTRINE

Having understood what is and is not meant by reprobation, it is essential to prove the rightness of this doctrine from Scripture. Once again, it is acknowledged that reprobation is a difficult doctrine, one that Calvin himself called a *decretum horribile*, "a fearful decree."[21] Nevertheless, the doctrine of reprobation *is* taught in the Bible,

19. See "The Decree of God and the Problem of Evil" earlier in this chapter (p. 491), which explains why God, though the Ultimate Cause of all things, is not the chargeable cause of evil. See also Rom. 9:19–23, where Paul teaches that the reprobation of vessels of wrath displays the riches of God's glory to the vessels of mercy, which is a sufficiently good and loving motive even for reprobation.

20. Though these are passive verbs, they are what grammarians call "divine passives," indicating that God is the implied agent. See Daniel B. Wallace, *Greek Grammar Beyond the Basics: An Exegetical Syntax of the New Testament* (Grand Rapids, MI: Zondervan, 1996), 437–38. The authors use the passive voice precisely to illustrate the unequal ultimacy between election and reprobation—that God is not as active in reprobation as he is in election and that he is not the efficient cause of wickedness in the reprobate as he is the efficient cause of blessedness in the elect, instead bringing reprobation about through secondary causes. However, it would be a mistake to conclude from this that he is not the agent of this work in any sense.

21. John Calvin, *Institutes of the Christian Religion*, ed. John T. McNeill, trans. Ford Lewis Battles, Library of Christian Classics (1559; repr., Philadelphia: Westminster John Knox, 1960), 3.23.7. It is important to note, however, as Grudem

and we are therefore obliged to reverently submit our minds and our emotions to the infinite wisdom of God's revelation, trusting that what he says and does is right and just (Rom. 3:4).

In the first place, reprobation is a necessary implication of the biblical teaching concerning election. If God has chosen only some sinners unto salvation, he has necessarily not chosen to save others. The very existence of a category of persons called *elect* (Matt. 24:22; Luke 18:7; Rom. 8:33; 11:7; 2 Tim. 2:10; 1 Pet. 1:1) necessarily implies a category of persons who are *nonelect*. The decision not to choose is in itself a determinative choice. Thus, as Boettner rightly concludes,

> Those who hold the doctrine of Election but deny that of Reprobation can lay but little claim to consistency. To affirm the former while denying the latter makes the decree of predestination an illogical and lop-sided decree. The creed which states the former but denies the latter will resemble a wounded eagle attempting to fly with but one wing.[22]

Not only is reprobation implied in the biblical doctrine of election, it is also taught explicitly in the New Testament. In his first epistle, the apostle Peter speaks of unbelievers who "stumble because they disobey the word, as they were destined to do" (1 Pet. 2:8). Significantly, Peter does not merely say that their stumbling or disobedience was destined, though of course that is true. Rather, using a third-person plural verb (Gk. *etethēsan*), he says that these people themselves were destined to disobey and stumble. When one asks, by whom were they thus destined? the only reasonable answer is that they were destined by the only One who destines anything: God himself. Similarly, Jude speaks of the false teachers who troubled the church with their teaching that salvation by grace permits licentiousness and sensuality. He describes them as "certain people . . . who long ago were designated for this condemnation" (Jude 4). The Greek term translated "beforehand marked out" is *prographō*, which literally means "to write beforehand." Jude pictures God's reprobation of these false teachers as the writing of a script in eternity past that was to come to pass in time, the end of which is their condemnation. They are among those "whose name[s] ha[ve] not been written before the foundation of the world in the book of life of the Lamb" (Rev. 13:8; cf. 17:8; 20:15; 21:27).

The clearest portion of Scripture affirming the doctrine of reprobation is Romans 9, in which Paul discusses God's sovereign freedom in unconditional election. Just as God has loved Jacob (election), he has also hated Esau (reprobation) (9:13). Paul goes on to use God's dealings with Pharaoh to illustrate the truth that "he has mercy on whomever he wills, and he hardens whomever he wills" (9:18), and that he does so in order to demonstrate his power and proclaim his name throughout the earth

---

does, that "[Calvin's] Latin word *horribilis* does not mean 'hateful' but rather 'fearful, awe-inspiring.'" Grudem, *Systematic Theology*, 685n23.

22. Boettner, *The Reformed Doctrine of Predestination*, 105. He helpfully continues, "In the interests of a 'mild Calvinism' some have been inclined to give up the doctrine of Reprobation, and this term (in itself a very innocent term) has been the entering wedge for harmful attacks upon Calvinism pure and simple. 'Mild Calvinism' is synonymous with sickly Calvinism, and sickness, if not cured, is the beginning of the end."

(cf. 9:17, 22). Having taught, then, that God inviolably determines the destiny of both the saved and the lost without respect to human will, effort, or merit (cf. 9:11, 16), Paul anticipates this objection: "You will say to me then, 'Why does he still find fault? For who can resist his will?'" (9:19). If no one can resist God's sovereign will or decree, how can he justly hold people accountable for that which they are unable to do?[23] Paul answers those who would reproach God by reminding them that mere mortals are in no position to call God to account: "But who are you, O man, to answer back to God? Will what is molded say to its molder, 'Why have you made me like this?'" (9:20). Paul then continues with this analogy and pictures God as a potter, likening the election of some to fashioning a clay vessel for honorable use and likening the reprobation of others to fashioning another clay vessel for dishonorable use (9:21). In defending God's freedom to do what he wishes with what is his own (Matt. 20:15), Paul then goes on to describe the elect as "vessels of mercy, which he has prepared beforehand for glory" and the reprobate as "vessels of wrath prepared for destruction" (Rom. 9:22–23). These vessels could only have been "prepared" by the potter himself, and Paul clearly indicates that those whom he hardens (9:18) are those whom he has fitted for destruction.

While these passages are enough to vindicate the doctrine of reprobation, Scripture also speaks clearly concerning the means God employs to bring about the destruction he has decreed for the reprobate. Because Paul himself used God's dealings with Pharaoh to illustrate reprobation, it is appropriate to consider God's hardening of Pharaoh's heart as evidence of the means of reprobation (Ex. 4:21; 8:19; 9:7; 10:1; 11:10; 14:4, 8). The Lord's purpose was to display the glory of his redeeming power in the deliverance of Israel from slavery, and in order to do so, he hardened Pharaoh's heart on numerous occasions (cf. also Deut. 2:30; Josh. 11:20; 1 Sam. 2:25). In the same way, his purpose in reprobation is to justly punish the sins of those he has not chosen to save, hardening their hearts as the means to achieving that end. Paul explicitly teaches this idea in 2 Thessalonians 2:11–12: "Therefore God sends them a strong delusion, so that they may believe what is false, in order that all may be condemned who did not believe the truth but had pleasure in unrighteousness." Because God had decreed the condemnation of these unbelievers, he also ordained the means by which that condemnation would be brought about, in this case by purposefully deceiving them. Elsewhere he is said to have blinded the eyes and hardened the hearts of the unbelieving precisely so that they would not see, understand, and repent (John 12:37–40; cf. Isa. 6:9–10). Jesus's own response to this reality is to publicly thank the Father for hiding truth from the wise and understanding and yet for revealing it to little children, which he attributes to no other basis than the

---

23. It is necessary to consider that the Arminian doctrines of conditional election and libertarian free will can make no sense of this objection. It would be no mystery why God still finds fault with those he has not chosen if his choice was based ultimately on *their* choice. They posit that God's will is in fact resistible, the very thing that Paul assumes *not* to be the case as a matter of course. He asks rhetorically, "For who can resist his will?" indicating that the obvious response is, "No one!" The only way it could make any sense for Paul to raise this objection at this point in his argument is if (1) God commands men to repent and believe, (2) men lack the moral ability to do so, and (3) God still holds men accountable to repent and believe and will punish them for their failure to do so. In philosophical terms, Paul's objection only makes sense if "ought" does not imply "can"—that is, if responsibility does not necessarily imply moral ability.

good pleasure of the Father's will (Matt. 11:25–26). Thus it is plain that God has ordained both the ends and the means of reprobation.

THE JUSTIFICATION OF GOD[24]

As mentioned, the chief charge leveled against the doctrine of reprobation is that it is incompatible with the justice of God. Yet it must be remembered that God is not subject to fallen notions of fairness, nor will he be tried at the bar of human reason. To those who would bring such charges, Paul's rebuke is apropos: "But who are you, O man, to answer back to God?" (Rom. 9:20). All such accusations are born of the erroneous presumption that if God gives grace to any of his creatures, he must give grace to all. Boettner says, "Many people talk as if salvation were a matter of human birthright. And, forgetful of the fact that man had lost his supremely favorable chance in Adam, they inform us that God would be unjust if He did not give all guilty creatures an opportunity to be saved."[25] Yet it undermines the very nature of grace to suppose that it is *owed* to sinful human beings. Truly, the question concerning God's decree of predestination is not, why did God not choose *everybody*? but rather, how can it be that this supremely holy God would choose *anybody*? It is the marvel of marvels that the King of kings, whose glory is exalted above the heavens, should lift a finger to rescue even one of such vile traitors as the sons of Adam. Then to learn that this infinitely worthy King has purposed to redeem not one but countless multitudes at the cost of the life of his own dear Son bows the sinner's heart in humble wonder. For those with eyes to see, all the objections to these difficult doctrines are answered in the revelations of such glory.

And this is precisely the defense that Paul gives in Romans 9:22–23. The arrogant objector is rebuked severely and told to put his hand over his mouth. But to the submissive, inquiring worshiper for whom the furthest thing from his mind is to find fault with God, who simply wants to know his God and worship him for who he is, Paul gives another answer as to how God can still find fault with those who cannot resist his will. He says, "What if God, desiring to show his wrath and make known his power, has endured with much patience vessels of wrath prepared for destruction, in order to make known the riches of His glory for vessels of mercy, which he has prepared beforehand for glory?" God has ordained sin and evil—even the eternal punishment of the wicked—to display to the elect the full glories of his name. None has explained this better than Jonathan Edwards:

> 'Tis a proper and excellent thing for infinite glory to shine forth; and for the same reason, it is proper that the shining forth of God's glory should be complete; that is, that all parts of his glory should shine forth, that every beauty should be proportionably effulgent, that the beholder might have a proper notion of God. It was not proper that one glory should be exceedingly manifested and another not

---

24. This section is adapted from Mike Riccardi, "God and Evil: Why the Ultimate Cause Is Not the Chargeable Cause," *The Cripplegate* (blog), October 9, 2015, http://thecripplegate.com/god-and-evil-why-the-ultimate-cause-is-not-the-chargeable-cause/. Used by permission of the author.

25. Boettner, *The Reformed Doctrine of Predestination*, 116.

at all. . . . Thus 'tis necessary that God's awful majesty, his authority and dreadful greatness, and justice and holiness [should be manifested]; and this could not be except sin and punishment were decreed, or at least might be decreed. So that the glory shining forth would be very imperfect, both because these parts of divine glory would not shine forth as the others do, and [because] then the glory of his goodness and love and holiness would be faint without them; nay, they could scarcely shine forth at all.

If it were not right that God should decree and permit and punish sin, . . . [t]here could be no such thing as any manifestation of God's holiness in hatred of sin, or in showing any preference in his providence to godliness before it.

It would be no manifestation of God's grace or true goodness to be free from all sorts of evil, for it would be absolutely impossible that any should be any otherwise; and how much happiness soever he bestowed, his goodness would be nothing near so much prized and admired, and the sense of it not near so great. . . .

And as it [is] necessary that there should be evil, because the glory of God could not but be imperfect and incomplete without it, so it is necessary in order to the happiness of the creature, in order to the completeness of that communication of God for which he made the world; because the creature's happiness consists in the knowledge of God and the sense of his love, and if the knowledge of him be imperfect, the happiness must be proportionably imperfect.[26]

God has ordained whatsoever comes to pass—even the preparation of vessels of wrath unto destruction—in order that his people might enjoy the fullest display of his glory. Those who would reproach God for ordaining the destiny of the wicked for his own glory must remember that, far from a megalomaniacal narcissism, God's pursuit of his own glory is, as Edwards said, "in order to the happiness of the creature . . . because the creature's happiness consists in the knowledge of God." Our knowledge of God would be imperfect if we did not see the full expression of his attributes: grace, mercy, forgiveness, justice, righteousness, and the rest of the panoply of his perfections. And yet none of those attributes could be expressed fully if there was not sin to punish and to forgive or sinners to whom to be gracious or on whom to exercise justice. God is not less glorious but more glorious because he has ordained evil, and the more he magnifies his glory, the greater is his love to his people. Surely God cannot be charged with unrighteousness for doing that which amounts to the greatest benefit for those who are his.

Neither do the doctrines of election and reprobation undermine the reality that all are commanded to repent and believe the gospel. Those who suppose that God's sovereign choice is incompatible with man's responsibility to believe fail to do justice to the whole of God's revelation. Indeed, immediately following what is the most exalted teaching on divine sovereignty in Romans 9, Paul just as clearly teaches human responsibility in Romans 10. He declares that "everyone who calls on the name of the Lord will be saved" (10:13), mandates that preachers of the gospel be

---

26. Edwards, "The 'Miscellanies' no. 348," in *The "Miscellanies": Entry Nos. a–z, aa–zz, 1–500,* 419–21.

sent to call all to repentance (10:14–17), and pictures God's loving benevolence even to the obstinate by depicting him as one who stretches out his hands and calls them to salvation (10:21). Scripture never teaches that God's absolute sovereignty obviates the sinner's responsibility to turn from his sins and trust in Christ. Neither is the sinner exhorted to determine whether God has chosen him for salvation or not. The sinner's responsibility is not to discern the secret counsels of God's decree but rather to heed the clear commands of Scripture to repent and believe the gospel (Mark 1:15; Acts 17:30).

Conclusion

Paul concludes his treatment of the doctrines of election and reprobation by bowing in worship before the magnificence of this sovereign God: "Oh, the depth of the riches and wisdom and knowledge of God! How unsearchable are his judgments and how inscrutable his ways!" (Rom. 11:33). Meditating on these truths caused him in the opening verses of his letter to the Ephesians to erupt in praise of the God who "has blessed us in Christ with every spiritual blessing in the heavenly places, even as he chose us in him before the foundation of the world, that we should be holy and blameless before him" (Eph. 1:3–4). The same must be so for us who are the beneficiaries of such glorious grace. Above all else, the doctrines of sovereign election and reprobation should lead us to bow our minds in humble wonder of the God whose wisdom is inscrutable and whose grace is so bountiful as to save such wretched rebels as ourselves. We are graced with every spiritual blessing, not because of any commendable or redeemable quality in ourselves but because of the free and sovereign mercy of the God who delights to set his love on the undeserving. Such truth must evoke praise from the depths of our souls: "To him be glory forever. Amen" (Rom. 11:36).

And yet the lavish administration of God's grace did not stop with his choice of us in eternity past. God has not only planned our redemption but has also sent the Lord Jesus Christ to accomplish our redemption. It is to the accomplishment of redemption that we now turn.

The Accomplishment of Redemption

The Plan of Salvation and the Mission of the Son
The Cause of the Atonement
The Necessity of the Atonement
The Nature of the Atonement
Incomplete Theories of the Atonement
The Perfect Sufficiency of the Atonement
The Extent of the Atonement
Resurrection, Ascension, and Intercession

Practically all religions have some concept of *atonement*—a means by which reparations are made, sin is expiated, deity is satisfied, and reconciliation is achieved between the deity and the sinner. Man-made religions propose some means by which the sinner must make an acceptable atonement to earn merit that will compensate for or erase sin, removing guilt through good works, religious ritual, restitution, the payment of a penalty, the offering of a sacrifice, or some sort of self-abasement. The distinctive teaching of biblical Christianity is that God himself has made full atonement for sinners—and he accomplished this by the substitutionary sacrifice of his own Son on the cross. Sinners contribute nothing by way of merit or sacrifice to the atonement.

This doctrine is the foundation of the gospel itself. God is perfectly righteous, and therefore, by definition he cannot countenance a less-than-perfect righteousness in anyone who would have fellowship with him (Matt. 5:48; 1 John 1:5). Sinners by definition have already violated God's law and rebelled against him, and because sin has infected the very core of their being, they have no way to pay for sin or secure the righteousness needed to stand before him. They have no inclination or ability to submit to God's authority (Rom. 8:7–8) and are doomed to face the just punishment of the outpouring of God's righteous wrath (John 3:36; 2 Thess. 1:9). The divide between the sinner's depravity and God's unapproachable holiness is so vast, the sinner, even with his noblest efforts, has no hope of ever standing in a right relationship with a holy God. The only hope for salvation comes—as it must—from outside the sinner. It is found in God's own provision of full and free atonement for sin. That glorious provision satisfies justice and releases the grace of forgiveness.

In 1 Corinthians 15, the apostle Paul tells us that the very heart of the gospel is "that Christ died for our sins in accordance with the Scriptures, that he was buried, that he was raised on the third day in accordance with the Scriptures" (1 Cor. 15:3–4). As has been demonstrated in chapter 6, man's depravity has established the *need* for salvation. And as has been observed in the previous portion of the present chapter, the Father's unconditional election has formed the *plan* of salvation. But it is the atonement of God the Son that *accomplishes* that redemption in space and time. If we are going to be fundamentally committed to the gospel, we must devote ourselves to an accurate, robust, biblical understanding of the atonement.

The Plan of Salvation and the Mission of the Son

In the previous discussion, we examined the biblical teaching concerning the Father's plan of redemption—his intention to rescue his creatures from sin and death and to restore them to a right relationship with himself. That gracious plan materialized in God's decree of unconditional election—his free and sovereign decision to set his love on certain individuals and, on the basis of nothing in themselves but solely because of the good pleasure of his will, to choose them to receive his salvation. Yet in his wisdom, God did not decree that his salvation would be accomplished and applied to the sinner merely by this sovereign choice. Instead, the triune God devised an eternal plan in which man's salvation would be accomplished by the redemptive work of God the Son and in which the saving benefits secured by that redemptive work would be applied by God the Spirit. The second member of the Trinity would take on all the weakness and infirmity (yet not sin) of human nature and would secure for his people the righteousness, forgiveness, and cleansing that they could never obtain for themselves. He would live as a man in perfect obedience to the Father, die on the cross as a substitutionary sacrifice to atone for the sins of those whom the Father had chosen, and rise again in victory over sin and death, all in the power of the Holy Spirit. Redemption would be accomplished by the miraculous incarnation, vicarious life, penal-substitutionary death, and death-defeating resurrection of the God-man, the Lord Jesus Christ.

It is imperative for the student of Scripture to understand that the Son's mission to accomplish redemption is birthed out of this Trinitarian plan of salvation. The atonement wrought by the Son is inextricably rooted in the Father's purpose to save those whom he has chosen. Thus, in undertaking to pay for sin and provide righteousness, Christ was not "going rogue," haphazardly embarking on a mission of his own devising. He stated explicitly that he came to do not his own will but the will of the One who sent him (John 6:38). That is, he was acting strictly in accordance with a specific, agreed-upon plan, devised in the eternal councils of the Trinity.[27]

Several passages of Scripture testify to this pretemporal, determinate plan of salvation. In the first place, some passages identify the Son's atoning work as divinely predetermined. Paul speaks of it as the Father's "eternal purpose which He carried out in Christ Jesus our Lord" (Eph. 3:11 NASB). This verse clearly states that the work that Christ accomplished during his earthly mission was carried out according to a predetermined plan—according to the Father's purpose that was devised in eternity (see also Eph. 1:9, 11). Similarly, when Jesus predicted his betrayal at the Last Supper, he said, "For the Son of Man goes as it has been determined [Gk. *kata to hōrismenon*, lit. 'according to the determination']" (Luke 22:22). Though he would be betrayed by Judas, the death of the Messiah had been determined in eternity past. For this reason Jesus is said to be "foreknown before the foundation of the world" (1 Pet. 1:20) and the One in whom grace is granted from all eternity according to the "purpose" (Gk. *prothesis*) of God (2 Tim. 1:9). Indeed, the crucifixion itself is merely the execution of the eternal purpose of God, for Peter states that Jesus was "delivered up according to the definite plan [Gk. *tē hōrismenē boulē*] and foreknowledge of God" (Acts 2:23), and the entire church confesses to God that Herod, Pilate, the Gentiles, and Israel did only "whatever your hand and your plan had predestined [Gk. *proōrisen*] to take place" (Acts 4:27–28).

In addition to these general statements of predetermination, the mission of the Son is often spoken of as a matter of obedience to the Father's will, indicating that he had made his will known to the Son in a prior agreement. When Jesus speaks of

---

27. Many theologians refer to this in different ways. Some theologians simply call this God's eternal plan, purpose, or decree of salvation, after a popular Latin phrase, *pactum salutis*, which means "agreement of salvation." Others, however, speak of it as a covenant—whether the covenant of redemption or the covenant of creation. For two reasons, we contend that it is inaccurate to describe this pretemporal, intra-Trinitarian agreement as a covenant. First, in Scripture the word *covenant* is used to designate an agreement between two unequal parties: a sovereign lord and a vassal (or lesser person). Though there is a diversity of roles within the Godhead, the persons of the Trinity are nevertheless entirely equal. There is no lord-vassal relationship that characterizes a covenantal agreement. Second, Scripture seems to indicate that a covenant is instituted by blood (Heb. 9:16–18), which certainly does not describe the *pactum salutis*. Therefore, this intra-Trinitarian agreement is distinctly different from a biblical covenant. It is more accurate to see it as an aspect of God's eternal decree.

laying down his life as a sacrifice for sin, he says, "This commandment I received from My Father" (John 10:18 NASB). Elsewhere he speaks of offering himself as a sacrifice for sin, being ready to do the Father's will (Heb. 10:7). As he prays to the Father on the eve of his betrayal, he speaks of the eternal fellowship he enjoyed with the Father (John 17:5) and declares that he has accomplished the work the Father gave him to do (John 17:4), indicating that he has acted obediently in accordance with the Father's plan. Each of these instances shows that Jesus was acting in consistency with a prior directive from his Father. Thus Paul characterizes Jesus's redemptive work as a matter of obedience: "And being found in human form, he humbled himself by becoming obedient to the point of death, even death on a cross" (Phil. 2:8).

A third aspect of this eternal plan was the Father's promise to reward the Son once he completed his work. In a dialogue between the Father and the Son, the Son speaks of the Father's *decree*, in which he promised the Son, as a reward for his obedience, "the nations [as] your heritage, and the ends of the earth [as] your possession" (Ps. 2:7–8). In the prophecy of the suffering servant, Isaiah comments on the terms of this agreement with respect to obedience and reward:

> But the LORD was pleased
>   To crush Him, putting Him to grief;
>   If He would render Himself as a guilt offering,
>   He will see His offspring,
>   He will prolong His days,
>   And the good pleasure of the LORD will prosper in His hand.
> As a result of the anguish of His soul,
>   He will see it and be satisfied;
>   By His knowledge the Righteous One,
>   My Servant, will justify the many,
>   As He will bear their iniquities.
> Therefore, I will allot Him a portion with the great,
>   And He will divide the booty with the strong;
>   Because He poured out Himself to death,
>   And was numbered with the transgressors;
>   Yet He Himself bore the sin of many,
>   And interceded for the transgressors. (Isa. 53:10–12 NASB)

Thus, in this intra-Trinitarian council, the Father commissioned the Son to lay down his life for sinners as a sacrificial offering, and he promised him the reward of an inheritance of nations—populated with his spiritual offspring whom he would justify—and of the enjoyment of the Lord's prosperity. And immediately after Paul mentions Christ's obedience unto death, he states, "Therefore"—that is, for this reason—"God has highly exalted him and bestowed on him the name that is above every name" (Phil. 2:9). As a result of his obedience to this eternal divine commission, the Father rewards the Son with the exalted title "Lord," at which name every knee will bow and every tongue will confess that the One crucified as a slave has become the Master of all (Phil. 2:10–11).

Finally, perhaps the most significant aspect of the eternal plan of salvation is that the Father gives specific individuals to the Son on whose behalf he is to accomplish redemption. That is to say, the Father commissions the Son to be the representative and substitutionary sacrifice for a particular people—namely, all and only those whom the Father has chosen for salvation. Several comments from Jesus in the Gospel of John bear this out, as he speaks of the people whom the Father has given him:

> *All that the Father gives me* will come to me, and whoever comes to me I will never cast out. For I have come down from heaven, not to do my own will but the will of him who sent me. And this is the will of him who sent me, that I should lose nothing *of all that he has given me*, but raise it up on the last day. For this is the will of my Father, that everyone who looks on the Son and believes in him should have eternal life, and I will raise him up on the last day. (John 6:37–40)

> I am the good shepherd. I know my own and my own know me, just as the Father knows me and I know the Father; and I lay down my life for the sheep. . . . My Father, *who has given them to me*, is greater than all, and no one is able to snatch them out of the Father's hand. (John 10:14–15, 29)

> Father, the hour has come; glorify your Son that the Son may glorify you, since you have given him authority over all flesh, to give eternal life to *all whom you have given him*. And this is eternal life, that they know you the only true God, and Jesus Christ whom you have sent. . . . I have manifested your name to the people *whom you gave me* out of the world. *Yours they were, and you gave them to me*, and they have kept your word. . . . I am praying for them. I am not praying for the world but for *those whom you have given me, for they are yours*. . . . Father, I desire that they also, *whom you have given me*, may be with me where I am, to see my glory that you have given me because you loved me before the foundation of the world. (John 17:1–3, 6, 9, 24)

In these passages from the Gospel of John, Jesus declares that he has come to earth to accomplish not his own will but rather the will of his Father who sent him (6:38; 17:4). Thus, once again, Jesus affirms that his mission is connected to and driven by the Father's eternal purpose. In the context of this Trinitarian, eternal plan of salvation, Jesus states that the Father has given him a group of individuals on whose behalf he accomplishes his redemptive work. He calls them his own (10:14) and his sheep (10:15). As the Good Shepherd, Jesus will never lose these sheep (6:39), nor permit them to be snatched out of his hand (10:29). Because they are effectually drawn to Christ by the Father (6:44, 65), the sheep come to Christ (6:37), look on him in faith (6:40), know him intimately (10:14), receive eternal life from him (6:40; 10:28; 17:2), enjoy the unique benefit of his intercession that is denied to the world (17:9), eventually partake in the resurrection of the dead (6:40), and dwell with Jesus forever in admiration of his glory (17:24). And the Lord declares that when the Father commissioned the Son to accomplish redemption as a part of the eternal plan of salvation, he gave these particular individuals to the Son. They are the elect, those whom the Father chose for salvation (Eph. 1:4)—that is, those whom he foreknew, predestined, called, justified, and glorified in Christ (Rom. 8:29–30; cf. 8:33). Those he has chosen the Father gives to the Son to be his bride (Rev. 19:7; cf. John 3:29; Eph. 5:23–24), whom the Son would purify at the cost of his own life (Eph. 5:25–27; Titus 2:14), who would be presented to him in perfect holiness as a love gift from the Father to love, honor, worship, and serve him for all eternity (Rev. 21:2, 9; 22:17).

This eternal, intra-Trinitarian plan of salvation shapes and conditions every aspect of the Son's mission as he undertakes to accomplish redemption. The Father has purposed to save his own, and the means by which he will accomplish redemption for his own is to give them to the Son. Having entrusted them to his Son, he commissions the Son to be born as the God-man by the Holy Spirit (Matt. 1:18; Luke 1:35), to live a life of perfect obedience to the Father in the power of the Spirit (Matt. 3:15; Rom. 5:18–19), to lay down his life as a sacrifice for the sins of his people (John 10:14–15; Hebrews 9–10; Rev. 5:9), and to rise again as the firstfruits and guarantee of their resurrection (Rom. 4:25; 1 Cor. 15:22–23, 42–57). John Murray provides a helpful summary: "God was pleased to set his invincible and everlasting love upon a countless multitude and it is the determinate purpose of this love that the atonement secures."[28]

The Cause of the Atonement

What was the triune God's motivation for devising this plan of redemption? Often the concept of a penal-substitutionary atonement, in which the Son must die in the place of sinners to assuage the wrath of the Father, is reproached by foes and misunderstood by friends. To many, this view of the atonement pictures the Father as inherently angry and wrathful toward man and as won over only reluctantly by the loving sacrifice of the Son. However, this is precisely backward. The Father does not love his people strictly on the grounds that Jesus died for them; rather, Jesus died for his people because the Father loved them.[29] In this sense, then, the love of God is not the result of Christ's death but rather its cause, for it is because God so *loved* the world that he gave his only Son to be sacrificed on the cross (John 3:16). God himself *is* love (1 John 4:8), and the sending of the Son to be the propitiation for man's sins is the consequence, expression, and demonstration of God's love to his people (Rom. 5:8; 1 John 4:9–10). In other words, the plan of redemption is born out of the good pleasure of the Father's free and sovereign electing love (Eph. 1:4–5, 9). It is because the Lord "set his love on . . . and chose" his people (Deut. 7:7) that he has decreed to accomplish their redemption by the atoning work of Christ. The love of God is a cause and source of Christ's atonement.

In addition to his love, God's justice in a real sense also constrains Christ's atonement. Once the triune God had decreed in his love to reconcile to himself those he had chosen, it was necessary that he decree to accomplish this in a way that was

---

28. John Murray, *Redemption Accomplished and Applied* (Grand Rapids, MI: Eerdmans, 1955), 10.

29. John Stott wrote, "It cannot be emphasized too strongly that God's love is the source, not the consequence, of the atonement. . . . God does not love us because Christ died for us; Christ died for us because God loved us. If it is God's wrath which needed to be propitiated, it is God's love which did the propitiating." *The Cross of Christ* (Downers Grove, IL: InterVarsity Press, 1986), 174.

consistent with his justice.[30] Because of sin, mankind is guilty of breaking God's law, has incurred his righteous wrath, and is therefore alienated from him. Though God's love motivates him to save and forgive, man's sin cannot simply be overlooked. For God to reconcile such guilty sinners to himself, sin must be punished, the broken law must be satisfied, and God's wrath must be justly assuaged. All these objectives are met in the person and work of the Lord Jesus Christ, who fulfilled the law (Matt. 3:15; Rom. 5:18–19; Gal. 4:4–5), paid sin's penalty (1 Pet. 2:24), and extinguished God's wrath (Heb. 2:17) on behalf of the elect. As Paul says, the Father put the Son forward "as a propitiation by His blood, through faith, to demonstrate His righteousness" (Rom. 3:25 NKJV). God's wrath is satisfied by the cross, because on the cross Jesus bore in his own person the full exercise of the Father's righteous wrath against the sins of his people. Sin is not overlooked but punished in Christ, and therefore God "show[s] his righteousness at the present time, so that he might be just and the justifier of the one who has faith in Jesus" (Rom. 3:26).

Therefore, the love of God and the justice of God constitute the twofold cause of the atonement accomplished by the Son. It is his love that moves him to act savingly at all, and it is his justice that ensures he will accomplish salvation in a manner consistent with his holiness. Neither may be overlooked. Failure to emphasize the love of God as the motivation for salvation reduces the atonement to an impersonal transaction or, worse yet, an arbitrary display of vindictiveness and hatred. And yet failure to emphasize the justice of God as that which guides and constrains his love obscures the fullness of God's character and renders the significance of the cross unintelligible, for propitiation—the satisfaction of just wrath—is the pinnacle of God's expression of love (1 John 4:10). As has been aptly said, "If we blunt the sharp edges of the cross, we dull the glittering diamond of God's love."[31]

The Necessity of the Atonement

The freedom of God's good pleasure to save sinners has led many to raise the question of the necessity of Christ's atonement. In other words, was it possible for God to have accomplished salvation for his people in any other way, or was he bound to do so by the substitutionary death of his Son? Could God have simply exercised his inexhaustible power to destroy sin in another way? Could he, by virtue of his infinite authority, have declared his people saved simply by divine fiat? Or is there something inherent to the person and work of Christ that makes the cross not merely the only *actual* way of salvation but also the only *possible* way of salvation?[32] While students

---

30. The insufficiency of language and the limitation of our finite minds cause us to speak somewhat imprecisely with respect to logical succession in God's decree. As demonstrated in "The Plan of Redemption" (p. 489), God's decree is eternal and immutable and thus is a single, timeless act. Therefore, when we speak of God's decree to save as antecedent to his decree to save in a certain way, we are speaking only of logical, not chronological, succession.

31. Steve Jeffery, Michael Ovey, and Andrew Sach, *Pierced for Our Transgressions: Rediscovering the Glory of Penal Substitution* (Wheaton, IL: Crossway, 2007), 153. The context for the above quotation is as follows: "A penal substitutionary understanding of the cross helps us to understand God's love, and to appreciate its intensity and beauty. Scripture magnifies God's love by its refusal to diminish our plight as sinners deserving of God's wrath, and by its uncompromising portrayal of the cross as the place where Christ bore that punishment in the place of his people. If we blunt the sharp edges of the cross, we dull the glittering diamond of God's love."

32. This discussion of the necessity of the atonement is not the same as asking, can men be saved on some other basis than Christ's substitutionary death? Those who deny the absolute necessity of the atonement do not necessarily teach mul-

of Scripture have answered these questions in a number of ways, we may concern ourselves with just the two most popular views.

Several of the church fathers (e.g., Athanasius, Augustine), medieval theologians (e.g., Thomas Aquinas), and early Reformers (e.g., John Calvin) espoused what is known as the *hypothetical necessity* view of the atonement. This view teaches that, based on the sovereign freedom of the God for whom nothing is impossible, he could have chosen to save his people by a means other than the vicarious atonement of Christ. While he ultimately *has* decreed to save by the shedding of Christ's blood, there is nothing inherent in the nature of God or the nature of forgiveness that makes this absolutely necessary.

In contrast, an overwhelming majority of theologians (e.g., Irenaeus, Anselm, John Owen, Francis Turretin, Charles Hodge, A. A. Hodge, Louis Berkhof, John Murray) maintain what is called the *consequent absolute necessity* view of the atonement. This view acknowledges that it is not absolutely necessary for God to save anyone from sin at all—a fact illustrated by his immediate damnation of sinful angels, for whom no provision of salvation has ever been made (2 Pet. 2:4; cf. Heb. 2:16). As in the case of the fallen angels, God was entirely within his rights to abandon sinful humanity to misery and to vindicate his justice by consigning all to hell. In this sense, the atonement was not absolutely necessary; that God has graciously chosen to rescue anyone is a free act of the good pleasure of his will (Eph. 1:5). However, once God *had* determined to save man, the cross of Christ was, consequently, absolutely necessary. Murray explains, "In a word, while it was not inherently necessary for God to save, yet, since salvation had been purposed, it was necessary to secure this salvation through a satisfaction that could be rendered only through a substitutionary sacrifice and blood-bought redemption."[33]

Scripture clearly vindicates this latter view, as it often speaks of the necessity of Christ's cross. In Hebrews 2:10, the author declares that it was fitting—that is, that it was consistent with the nature of God, sin, and salvation—that the Father, in bringing many sons to glory, should make Christ perfect through sufferings. A few verses later, he adds that it was not only fitting but also necessary: Jesus "*had* to be made like his brothers in every respect, so that he might become a merciful and faithful high priest in the service of God, to make propitiation for the sins of the people" (Heb. 2:17). Man could not be saved by the Levitical sacrifices, "for it is impossible for the blood of bulls and goats to take away sins" (Heb. 10:4). Instead, "it was *necessary* for the copies of the heavenly things to be purified with these rites, but the heavenly things themselves with better sacrifices than these" (Heb. 9:23). Because of the standard of God's holiness, no one lacking perfect righteousness can have any fellowship with him (Matt. 5:48; 1 John 1:5). Yet man could not achieve his own righteousness by keeping the dictates of God's law, for no law had been given that was able to give life (Gal. 3:21). Instead, the law served only as our tutor to lead us to Christ, whose

---

tiple ways of salvation. Stipulating that the cross *is* necessary for salvation, proponents of this view simply ponder whether it was possible for God to decree that it should be otherwise.

33. Murray, *Redemption Accomplished and Applied*, 12.

righteousness is credited as a gift through faith in his atoning work (Gal. 3:22–27). Further, the Lord Jesus himself makes it plain that unless God had loved the world by sending his only Son to be lifted up as a sacrifice for sin, all humanity would have perished in their sins (John 3:14–16; cf. Num. 21:6–9).

Ultimately, the love and justice of God that cause the atonement are also the ground of its necessity. The Scriptures indicate that the substitutionary sacrifice of Christ to make propitiation on behalf of sinners is the supreme demonstration of God's love to man (Rom. 5:8; 1 John 3:16; 4:10). The magnitude of God's love is manifested by the extraordinary cost that he is willing to absorb in order to accomplish our rescue. Yet it is unthinkable that the Father would unleash the fullness of his righteous fury on his beloved Son, in whom he was well-pleased, unless it was absolutely necessary—unless this price was the only means of securing his desired end. Further, the justice and veracity of God himself require sin to be punished. God has declared that he "will by no means clear the guilty" (Ex. 34:7). God cannot lie (Heb. 6:18), and therefore the fullness of his righteous wrath must be poured out against sin. It is precisely through Christ's cross that God vindicates his righteousness, for man's sin is punished in his substitute (Rom. 3:25; Gal. 3:13). God's unwavering demand of justice required that salvation be accomplished by a propitiatory sacrifice, for in no other way could God be both "just and the justifier" of his people (Rom. 3:26).

As the people of God, we behold the special brilliance of the infinite glory and worth of Christ's atonement when we consider that not even almighty God himself could have accomplished our salvation in any other way. If anyone was to enjoy the saving grace and beneficent mercy of the God who saves, the cross of Christ was absolutely necessary.

The Nature of the Atonement

Scripture employs several themes to describe what Christ accomplished on the cross. The work of Christ was a work of substitutionary sacrifice, in which the Savior bore the penalty of sin in the place of sinners (1 Pet. 2:24); it is a work of propitiation, in which God's wrath against sin is fully satisfied and exhausted in the person of our substitute (Rom. 3:25); it is a work of reconciliation, in which the alienation between man and God is overcome and peace is made (Col. 1:20, 22); it is a work of redemption, in which those enslaved to sin are ransomed by the price of the Lamb's precious blood (1 Pet. 1:18–19); and it is a work of conquest, in which sin, death, and Satan are defeated by the power of a victorious Savior (Heb. 2:14–15). Each of these themes is worthy of study and will be the subject of this section's discussion.

THE OBEDIENCE OF CHRIST

However, there is a unifying principle in Scripture that encompasses the many facets of Christ's atonement: obedience.[34]

---

34. Calvin wrote, "Now someone asks, how has Christ abolished sin, banished the separation between us and God, and acquired righteousness to render God favorable and kindly toward us. To this we can in general reply that he has achieved this for us by the whole course of his obedience." *Institutes*, 2.16.5.

There are three senses in which obedience encapsulates the whole of the substitutionary work of Christ. First, Scripture characterizes Christ's work as obedience to the divine plan of salvation, which has been delineated above. The Father has sent the Son from heaven to earth to accomplish the divine mission of redemption, and the Son declares that he has "come down from heaven, not to do my own will but the will of him who sent me" (John 6:38; cf. 12:49). With reference to offering himself as a final sacrifice, the Messiah declares to the Father, "I have come to do your will" (Heb. 10:7, 9), for he always does the things that are pleasing to his Father (John 8:29). He freely and willingly lays down his life as a sacrifice for sin because, he says, "This commandment I received from My Father" (John 10:17–18 NASB), and "I do exactly as the Father commanded Me" (John 14:31 NASB). Thus, in Paul's hymn of praise concerning the incarnation and atonement of the Son of God, he describes Christ's work as his "becoming *obedient* to the point of death, even death on a cross" (Phil. 2:8). Christ's atoning work was a work of obedience to the Father.

Second, it was necessary for Christ to be obedient to all of the Father's commands in order for him to be a suitable substitutionary sacrifice for sinners. In the Levitical sacrificial system, it was imperative that any animal offered to the Lord be without blemish: "You shall not offer anything that has a blemish, for it will not be acceptable for you. . . . To be accepted it must be perfect; there shall be no blemish in it" (Lev. 22:20–21; cf. 1:3, 10; 3:1, 6; 22:18–25). The same was true of Israel's Passover lamb; if it was to be accepted as a suitable substitute, God stipulated, "Your lamb shall be without blemish" (Ex. 12:5). If the penalty for sinners was to be executed on a substitute, that substitute was required to be without any spot or defect. The same principle extends to Christ's atoning sacrifice, the fulfillment of the Levitical sacrifices (Heb. 9:23). Christ himself is our Passover Lamb (1 Cor. 5:7; cf. Isa. 53:7; John 1:29; Rev. 5:12), and therefore it is by his precious blood, "like that of a lamb without blemish or spot," that we are redeemed (1 Pet. 1:18–19). For Christ to have been a fitting substitute to bear the punishment for sin in the place of sinners, he himself had to be sinless—holy, innocent, undefiled, and separate from sinners (Heb. 7:26). For this reason, Scripture links the life of Christ, in which "he learned obedience through what he suffered" (Heb. 5:8), with his fitness to become "the source of eternal salvation to all who obey him" (Heb. 5:9). Of course, his learning obedience was not a process of putting off sin and increasing in practical righteousness, as it is for us. However, before his incarnation, Jesus never knew what it was to obey the Father in the infirmity of human flesh, with all the weaknesses and temptations that men and women face as they strive to obey God. But as he experienced the suffering of life in a fallen world, he learned to obey as a suffering man, just as we must. And "because he himself has suffered when tempted, he is able to help those who are being tempted" (Heb. 2:18; cf. 4:15). Having learned obedience through the sufferings that human life brought, he was prepared to be obedient in the sufferings that death would bring as well.

Finally, it was necessary for Christ to be obedient to the law of God in order to provide the righteousness that is the ground of justification. The perfect standard of God's righteousness expressed in his law consisted of two key aspects: prescriptive commands that required full obedience and penal sanctions for the breaking of those commands. Not only has sinful man failed to obey the positive demands of God's law, he has no way to pay the prescribed penalty for his disobedience, since the wages of sin is death (Rom. 6:23; cf. Titus 3:5). To be our Savior, therefore, Christ had to meet both necessities. By becoming obedient to death on a cross (Phil. 2:8), "Christ redeemed us from the curse of the law by becoming a curse for us" (Gal. 3:13; cf. Deut. 21:23)—that is, by bearing the fullness of divine wrath against himself. But if this was the end of our substitute's work, we could never be saved. In that case, the penal sanctions of the law would be met, and our guilt would be removed, but we would still lack the positive righteousness that the law required of us. We would be left in the state Adam was in before the fall—innocent but without the positive righteousness God required for fellowship with him (cf. Matt. 5:20, 48). Therefore, man stands in need of a substitute who will not only die obediently in our place to forgive sins but will also live obediently in our place to provide the righteousness that is credited to us through faith (Rom. 4:3–5; Phil. 3:9). For this reason, Paul contrasts the first Adam with Christ, the last Adam (1 Cor. 15:22, 45), saying, "For as by the one man's disobedience the many were made sinners, so by the one man's obedience the many will be made righteous" (Rom. 5:19; cf. Gal. 4:4–5). Adam's sin provides an actual, lived-out record of human disobedience, which, counted to be ours through our union with him, becomes the basis on which God justly constitutes all men guilty (Rom. 5:12). In the same way, Christ's vicarious obedience provides the actual, lived-out record of human righteousness, which, counted to be ours through our union with him, becomes the basis on which God justly constitutes guilty sinners righteous. Justified sinners are not righteous in themselves, but the record of Christ's perfect life is counted to be theirs through their union with him through faith: "Because of him [God] you are *in* Christ Jesus, who became to us . . . *righteousness*" (1 Cor. 1:30; cf. Rom. 10:4; 2 Cor. 5:21).

The Lord Jesus Christ did more than just die for our sins; he also lived to fulfill our righteousness. Jesus's interaction with John the Baptist at his baptism speaks to this fact. John the Baptist went into the region around the Jordan "proclaiming a baptism of repentance for the forgiveness of sins" (Matt. 3:11; Luke 3:3). Originally developed in the intertestamental period, that baptism was a ceremonial rite for Gentile converts to Judaism by which they confessed their uncleanness and need for spiritual cleansing. In John's day, Israel had so multiplied their wickedness—that is, they were in need of such cleansing—that ethnic Jews submitted themselves to proselyte baptism to signify their repentance.[35] People from Jerusalem, all Judea, and all

---

35. This baptism was "different from the Levitical washings, which consisted of washing the hands, feet, and head. The Essenes, a group of Jewish ascetics who lived on the northwest shore of the Dead Sea, practiced a type of ceremonial washing that more nearly resembled baptism. But both the Levitical and the Essene washings were repeated, those of the Essenes as much as several times a day or even hourly. They represented repeated purification for repeated sinning. John's washing, however, was one-time. The only one-time washing the Jews performed was for Gentiles, signifying their com-

throughout the region of the Jordan River came to confess their sins and be baptized (Matt. 3:5–6). So when Jesus came to his cousin to be baptized, John was rightly incredulous: "John would have prevented him, saying, 'I need to be baptized by you, and do you come to me?'" (Matt. 3:14). John knew that Jesus was the sinless Son of God (John 1:29; cf. Luke 1:41); why should he be asking for a baptism of repentance? Jesus's brief reply is full of significance: "Let it be so now, for thus it is fitting for us to fulfill all righteousness" (Matt. 3:15). Jesus had no need to undergo the rite of a proselyte baptism for repentance. He had no sins for which to repent. His inherent divine righteousness would have qualified him to be a righteous sacrifice; he would not have been any less fit to be the spotless Lamb of God had he not been baptized. He submitted himself to this baptism "to fulfill all righteousness"—not for his own sake but for the sake of his people who needed righteousness to be fulfilled on their behalf. From the beginning of his life, Jesus continued to amass a perfect record of human righteousness that would be imputed to sinners who would trust in him for salvation (Rom. 4:4–5). In this way, "by the one man's obedience the many will be made righteous" (Rom. 5:19).[36]

Thus, Scripture identifies both aspects of Christ's substitutionary work—namely, the payment for sin and the provision of righteousness—as having been accomplished by his obedience to the Father. By his obedience he fulfilled all righteousness, became a sympathetic high priest, demonstrated himself fit to be the perfect sacrifice for sinners, and submitted himself to that sacrificial death. As John Murray concludes, "It was by obedience he secured our salvation because it was by obedience he wrought the work that secured it."[37]

PENAL SUBSTITUTION

After the rubric of obedience to the Father, the most fundamental description one can ascribe to the atonement is that it is a work of penal substitution. That is to say, on the cross, Jesus suffered the penalty for the sins of his people (hence *penal*) as a substitute for them (hence *substitution*). When man sinned against God, his sin erected a legal and relational barrier between him and God. The divine law was broken; man thus incurred guilt and is required to pay the penalty of spiritual death. The holiness of God was offended, and thus God's wrath was aroused against sin. This leaves man alienated from God; broken fellowship and even hostility mark the relationship between God and man, who is in bondage to sin and death. If there is to be any redemption from sin and reconciliation to God, man's sin must be atoned for. And yet man's spiritual death and depravity leave him unable to pay the penalty

---

ing as outsiders into the true faith of Judaism. A Jew who submitted to such a rite demonstrated, in effect, that he was an outsider who sought entrance into the people of God—an amazing admission for a Jew. Members of God's chosen race, descendants of Abraham, heirs of the covenant of Moses, came to John to be baptized like a Gentile! That act symbolized before the world that they realized their national and racial descent, or even their calling as God's chosen and covenant people, could not save them. They had to repent, forsake sin, and trust in the Lord for salvation." John MacArthur, *Matthew 1–7*, MNTC (Chicago: Moody Press, 1985), 58.

36. For more on what is traditionally called the active obedience of Christ, see "The Ground of Justification: Imputed Righteousness" (p. 614).

37. Murray, *Redemption Accomplished and Applied*, 24.

for his sin. However, God in his love has appointed the Lord Jesus Christ to stand in the place of sinners to bear their sin, guilt, and punishment and thereby satisfy God's wrath on their behalf.

For this reason Isaiah characterizes the suffering servant as the one who "has borne our griefs and carried our sorrows" (Isa. 53:4), who "bore the sin of many" (Isa. 53:12). "The LORD has laid on him the iniquity of us all" (Isa. 53:6), and so "he shall bear their iniquities" (Isa. 53:11). Thus, when Jesus comes into the world, John the Baptist announces him as "the Lamb of God who takes away the sin of the world" (John 1:29)—that is, by taking sin on himself. The apostle Paul declares that "for our sake [the Father] made [Jesus] to *be* sin" (2 Cor. 5:21a), which cannot mean that the Father turned Jesus *into* sin in any ontological sense but rather that he made him to be sin in the same sense in which he makes us to become the righteousness of God (2 Cor. 5:21b): by imputation—that is, by counting our guilt to be his. The curse of the law that we were under was borne by Christ, who became a curse for us (Gal. 3:13). The apostle Peter says, "He himself bore our sins in his body on the tree, that we might die to sin and live to righteousness." Then, quoting Isaiah's account of the suffering servant, he adds, "By his wounds you have been healed" (1 Pet. 2:24; cf. Heb. 9:28). The Lord Jesus Christ bore the punishment of the sins of his people and thereby brought them blessing: "He was pierced for our transgressions; he was crushed for our iniquities; upon him was the chastisement that brought us peace" (Isa. 53:5).

In addition to these clear statements, the New Testament attaches the concept of penal substitution to the cross of Christ by using four Greek prepositions that all have a substitutionary force: *peri* ("for," "concerning"), *dia* ("because of," "for the sake of"), *anti* ("in place of," "instead of"), and *hyper* ("on behalf of"). First, Christ "suffered . . . for sins" (Gk. *peri hamartiōn*, 1 Pet. 3:18) and thus is "the propitiation for our sins" (Gk. *peri tōn hamartiōn hēmōn*, 1 John 2:2; 4:10). These texts teach that our sins demanded that we suffer under the wrath of God yet that Christ has done this in our place. Second, Jesus is said to have died "for your sake" (Gk. *di' hymas*, 2 Cor. 8:9; cf. 1 Cor. 8:11), another clear indicator of substitution.

Third, the preposition *anti* is perhaps the strongest indicator of substitution, literally signifying "in place of." This sense is clearest in Matthew 2:22, where it speaks of "Archelaus . . . reigning over Judea in place of [*anti*] his father Herod." Matthew 5:38 also uses *anti* to translate the *lex talionis*—"An eye for [*anti*] an eye and a tooth for [*anti*] a tooth"—which mandated that an offender be deprived of his eye or tooth in place of the eye or tooth of which he deprived someone else. Jesus uses this phrase with respect to his own death when he says, "For even the Son of Man came not to be served but to serve, and to give his life as a ransom for many" (Gk. *anti pollōn*, Matt. 20:28; Mark 10:45). That is to say, while sinners deserved to die because of their sin, Jesus laid down his life as the ransom price in the place of the lives of his people, so that they might go free.

Finally, while *anti* has the strongest connotations of substitution, *hyper* is a close second, meaning "on behalf of." It is also by far the most common preposition to signify the substitutionary relationship between Christ and his people. The body of Christ is "given for you" (Gk. *hyper hymōn*, Luke 22:19; cf. 1 Cor. 11:24) and "for the life of the world" (Gk. *hyper tēs tou kosmou zōēs*, John 6:51), and the blood of the new covenant is poured out "for many" (Gk. *hyper pollōn*, Mark 14:24) and "for you" (Gk. *hyper hymōn*, Luke 22:20). That is to say, Christ's body and blood are given as a substitutionary sacrifice on behalf of sinners so that they might avert wrath and punishment. As the Good Shepherd, Jesus lays down his life on behalf of the sheep (Gk. *hyper tōn probatōn*, John 10:11, 15; cf. 1 John 3:16), and he died on behalf of us, the ungodly (Gk. *hyper asebōn*, Rom. 5:6; *hyper hēmōn*, Rom. 5:8; 1 Thess. 5:10). He gave himself for his bride, the church (Eph. 5:25), which Paul describes both collectively (Eph. 5:2; Titus 2:14) and personally (Gal. 2:20). On our behalf (Gk. *hyper hēmōn*) he was made sin (2 Cor. 5:21), became a curse (Gal. 3:13), and tasted death (Heb. 2:9). The Righteous One suffered the penalty of sin on behalf of the unrighteous (Gk. *dikaios hyper adikōn*) so that he might reconcile those sinners to God (1 Pet. 3:18).

As the above passages show, there is no more well-attested doctrine in all the New Testament than the vicarious suffering of the Lord Jesus Christ on behalf of his people. Penal-substitutionary atonement is woven into the fabric of new covenant revelation from beginning to end, for it is the very heart of the gospel message. In free and willing obedience to his Father, the Lord Jesus Christ has stood in the stead of sinners, has died as a sacrifice for their sin and guilt, has propitiated the Father's wrath toward them, has reconciled them to the God for whom they were created, has redeemed them out of the bondage of sin and death, and has conquered the rule of sin and Satan in their lives. Each of those themes—sacrifice, propitiation, reconciliation, redemption, and conquest—is a different facet of Christ's substitutionary work and deserves further examination.

Sacrifice.[38] The New Testament explicitly identifies the death of Christ as a sacrifice for sins: "But as it is, he has appeared once for all at the end of the ages to put away sin by the sacrifice of himself" (Heb. 9:26). Such imagery draws from the history of Israel and the Old Testament's prescriptions for sacrificial worship to God. The book of Hebrews explicitly identifies Christ's atoning work as the antitype and fulfillment of the Levitical sacrifices instituted under the Mosaic covenant (Heb. 9:23). For this reason, to properly understand the significance of Christ's death as sacrifice, we must turn to the Levitical law.

The book of Leviticus begins immediately after the glory of God has filled the completed tabernacle (Ex. 40:34–38), symbolizing that the spiritual presence of the Lord is now dwelling in the midst of his people. In fact, the Hebrew term for "tabernacle," *mishkan*, means "dwelling place." Thus, the presence of God is a key theme in the book of Leviticus, as confirmed by the fifty-nine occurrences in

---

38. An extended discussion is located in the "Death and Atonement" section of chap. 4, "Christology" (p. 305).

the book of the phrase "before the Lord" (Heb. *liphne Yahweh*, lit., "to the face of Yahweh," signifying presence). Leviticus also teaches that this God who is present is fundamentally *holy*; the Hebrew word for "holy" and its cognates appear 150 times in the book's twenty-seven chapters, more frequently than in any other book. The question that Leviticus seeks to answer, then, is, how can the holy presence of God dwell in the midst of a sinful people? The answer to that question is that sinners are to make sacrifices to the Lord that will atone for their sin and render them acceptable in his presence: "He shall offer [his sacrifice] at the doorway of the tent of meeting, that he may be accepted before the LORD. He shall lay his hand on the head of the burnt offering, that it may be accepted for him to make atonement on his behalf" (Lev. 1:3–4 NASB).

While not every Levitical sacrifice is prescribed to atone for sin, the ceremonies of the Day of Atonement surely are. Once a year, the high priest of Israel was to enter the Most Holy Place in order to "[make] atonement for himself and for his house and for all the assembly of Israel" (Lev. 16:17; cf. 16:24, 32–34). Two goats were to be offered: one as a sacrifice and another as a scapegoat that bore the sins of the people and was banished from the presence of the Lord (Lev. 16:8–10). The blood of the sacrificial goat was to be sprinkled on the mercy seat, the covering of the ark of the covenant where atonement was made (Lev. 16:15–19). Because "the life of the flesh is in the blood, [God has] given it for you on the altar to make atonement for your souls, for it is the blood that makes atonement by the life" (Lev. 17:11). After this, the high priest was to deal with the scapegoat:

> And Aaron shall lay both his hands on the head of the live goat, and confess over it all the iniquities of the people of Israel, and all their transgressions, all their sins. And he shall put them on the head of the goat and send it away into the wilderness by the hand of a man who is in readiness. The goat shall bear all their iniquities on itself to a remote area, and he shall let the goat go free in the wilderness. (Lev. 16:21–22)

By laying his hands on the head of the scapegoat and confessing all of Israel's sins on it, the high priest was symbolizing that God had reckoned the sin and guilt of the people to be transferred to the goat. Instead of bearing their own iniquity (cf. Lev. 5:1, 17; 7:18; 17:16; 19:8; 20:17, 19; 22:16) and thus suffering the punishment of being banished from God's holy presence (i.e., "cut off from his people," cf. Lev. 7:20–27; 17:4, 9, 10, 14; 18:29; 19:8; 20:3–6, 17–18; 22:3; 23:29), the people of Israel had their sin imputed to a substitute. The innocent scapegoat bore the sin, guilt, and punishment of the people and was banished in their place. By sprinkling the sacrificial blood of one substitute on the mercy seat, and by virtue of the imputation of sin to a second substitute, the priests atoned for Israel's sins, and the people were released from punishment.

Another picture of Old Testament sacrifice—the only other one that rivals the Day of Atonement in significance for Israel—is the Passover sacrifice of Exodus 12. The manner in which God redeemed his people out of slavery in Egypt became a picture of how he would finally redeem his people out of slavery to sin and death. God had promised to kill every firstborn child and animal throughout all Egypt. Though Israel had been spared from the first nine plagues, they were not automatically exempted from the tenth, for they had fallen into idolatry and turned to worship the gods of Egypt (Ezek. 20:8). In order to be spared from his wrath, God required each family in Israel to kill an unblemished lamb and to put its blood on the doorposts of the house. He said, "The blood shall be a sign for you, on the houses where you are. And when I see the blood, I will pass over you, and no plague will befall you to destroy you, when I strike the land of Egypt" (Ex. 12:13). The Passover lamb died as a substitute in place of the firstborn children of Israel. The wrath of God was turned away by the blood of a spotless lamb. Israel was to "observe this rite as a statute for [them] and for [their] sons forever" (Ex. 12:24) to commemorate the Lord's forgiving their sins by substitutionary sacrifice (Ex. 12:27).

Both of the Levitical sacrifices as epitomized in the Day of Atonement and the rite of the Passover portray the sacrificial work of the Lord Jesus Christ. The Passover meal was the setting of Jesus's Last Supper with his disciples, wherein he instituted the new covenant, declaring that his body would be broken and his blood poured out for them (Matt. 26:17–29; Mark 14:12–25; Luke 22:7–20). In this way he declared that his death would be the fulfillment of the feast of the Passover: "Whereas the old Passover focused on the body and blood of a lamb, slain as a penal substitutionary sacrifice for the redemption of Israel, the Lord's Supper focuses on the body and blood of Christ, who gave himself as a penal substitutionary sacrifice for his people."[39] Jesus is "the Lamb of God, who takes away the sin of the world" (John 1:29; cf. 1:36). It is by "the precious blood of Christ, like that of a lamb without blemish or spot" that the people of God are redeemed (1 Pet. 1:18–19). Paul explicitly identifies Jesus as the fulfillment of the Passover when he says, "For Christ, our Passover lamb, has been sacrificed" (1 Cor. 5:7). Just as the blood of the slain lamb protected Israel from the execution of God's judgment, so also the blood of the slain Lamb, Jesus, protects his people from the Father's wrath against their sin.

Similarly, the New Testament identifies Jesus as the fulfillment of the Levitical priesthood and sacrificial system. While God allowed himself to be temporarily propitiated by Israel's sacrifices, that never changed the fact that those sacrifices "cannot perfect the conscience of the worshiper" (Heb. 9:9):

> For since the law has but a shadow of the good things to come instead of the true form of these realities, it can never, by the same sacrifices that are continually offered every year, make perfect those who draw near. . . . For it is impossible for the blood of bulls and goats to take away sins. (Heb. 10:1, 4)

Therefore, the author of Hebrews instructs us,

> But when Christ appeared as a high priest of the good things that have come, then through the greater and more perfect tent (not made with hands, that is, not

---

39. Jeffery, Ovey, and Sach, *Pierced for Our Transgressions*, 39.

of this creation) he entered once for all into the holy places, not by means of the blood of goats and calves but by means of his own blood, thus securing an eternal redemption. (Heb. 9:11–12)

The parallel imagery is astounding. Just as the high priest entered beyond the veil into the Most Holy Place, so also Christ is the Great High Priest (cf. Heb. 3:1; 4:15; 7:26; 8:1) who has entered beyond the veil of the heavenly tabernacle (which Scripture characterizes as his own flesh, Heb. 10:20), into the very presence of God himself. And while the high priest sprinkled the blood of the sacrificial goat on the mercy seat to make atonement, the Lord Jesus sprinkled his own blood (Heb. 9:21–22; 12:24; 1 Pet. 1:2), and inasmuch as his blood is infinitely more valuable than that of goats and calves, he thus secured an eternal redemption. He is therefore the fulfillment of both the high priest and the sacrifice; he is both offerer and offering, for "he offered himself without blemish to God" (Heb. 9:14; cf. Eph. 5:2; Heb. 7:27; 9:23, 26, 28; 10:10, 12, 14).

Not only is Jesus the fulfillment of both the high priest and the sacrifice, but he is also the fulfillment of the mercy seat itself. The high priest was commanded to sprinkle the blood on the mercy seat (Heb. *kapporet*; Gk. *hilastērion* [Septuagint]), where God's holy presence was uniquely manifested for fellowship with Israel (Ex. 25:22; 30:6). God himself warned that anyone who approached the mercy seat aside from the high priest on the Day of Atonement would die, "for," he said, "I will appear in the cloud over the mercy seat" (Lev. 16:2). And yet the apostle Paul declares that God displayed Jesus "as a propitiation [Gk. *hilastērion*] by his blood" (Rom. 3:25), using the very same Greek word for "propitiation" as is used for the word "mercy seat" in the Septuagint version of Exodus. Just as the mercy seat was the place where atonement was made and God's wrath against sin was averted, so now is Jesus the place where atonement is made and God's wrath against sin is averted. Jesus is the High Priest who offers the sacrifice, the sacrifice that is offered, and the mercy seat on which the sacrifice is offered.

Finally, Jesus perfectly fulfills the scapegoat as well. The imputation of sin from Israel to the scapegoat is epitomized by the Father laying on him the iniquity of us all (Isa. 53:6), reckoning him to be sin on our behalf (2 Cor. 5:21), so that he has borne our sins in his body on the tree (1 Pet. 2:24). As the midday sun was shrouded in darkness, the Father was, as it were, laying his hands on the head of the Son and confessing over him the sins of his people. As a result of bearing their sin, the Son was banished from the presence of the Father, leaving him to suffer outside the gate (Heb. 13:12) and to experience the terrifying abandonment of his Father (Matt. 27:46).[40] "Outside the camp," away from the presence of the Lord and of his people, was where the sacrifices were to be disposed of (Lev. 4:12, 21; 6:11; 8:17; 9:11; 16:27; cf.

---

40. This abandonment is the mystery of mysteries. Jesus's cry of dereliction is, as Albert Martin has preached, the utterance that eternity will never exegete for us. Yet we must note that this separation between the Father and the Son was a relational separation, not an ontological one. The Son could never be ontologically separated from the essence of the Trinity, for then the triune God would cease to be. Christ remained God; the Trinity remained unbroken and unchanged. Nevertheless, in a way our minds cannot fully comprehend, God the Father forsook God the Son as he laid upon Christ the iniquity of us all, abandoning him to bear his unleashed fury against the sins of his people.

Heb. 13:11); it was that lonely place where the leper was isolated to bear his shame (Lev. 13:46) and where the blasphemer was to be stoned (Lev. 24:14, 23). And it is to that place of shame and isolation that the Son of God was banished so that we might be welcomed into the holy presence of God.

Propitiation. Scripture represents Christ's death not merely as a sacrifice but as a *propitiatory* sacrifice. That is to say, by receiving the full exercise of the Father's wrath against the sins of his people, Christ satisfied God's righteous anger against sin and thus turned away his wrath from us who, had it not been for our substitute, were bound to suffer it for ourselves. The New Testament explicitly identifies Christ's work as a propitiation in four texts:

> [We] are justified by his grace as a gift, through the redemption that is in Christ Jesus, whom God put forward as a propitiation [Gk. *hilastērion*] by his blood, to be received by faith. (Rom. 3:24–25)

> Therefore he had to be made like his brothers in every respect, so that he might become a merciful and faithful high priest in the service of God, to make propitiation for [Gk. *eis to hilaskesthai*] the sins of the people. (Heb. 2:17)

> He is the propitiation [Gk. *hilasmos*] for our sins, and not for ours only but also for the sins of the whole world. (1 John 2:2)

> In this is love, not that we have loved God but that he loved us and sent his Son to be the propitiation [Gk. *hilasmos*] for our sins. (1 John 4:10)

While the Scripture is very straightforward in identifying Christ's work with the Greek term *hilasmos* (from the *hilaskomai* word group), some have insisted that "propitiation" is an improper translation of the word. Rather than speaking of a sacrifice that satisfies and turns away God's wrath, they have argued that it speaks of expiation, the cancellation or removal of sin.[41] Evangelical scholarship has offered very capable responses that vindicate the traditional understanding of the *hilaskomai* word group as signifying propitiation.[42] Though it is beyond our scope to engage that debate fully, there is nevertheless clear biblical justification for reading *hilaskomai* as a wrath-averting sacrifice.

The Greek *hilaskomai* word group also translates the Hebrew term *kaphar*, which has a range of meanings, including "to forgive" (e.g., Lev. 4:20, 26, 31; 19:22), "to cleanse" (e.g., Lev. 14:18–20, 29–31; 15:19–30; 16:16, 18–19, 30), and "to ransom" (e.g., Ex. 30:11–16; Num. 35:29–34).[43] Yet several key texts show that *kaphar* can also refer to propitiation, the concept of averting God's wrath. First, when Israel committed its first act of brazen idolatry with the golden calf, God responded in wrath, telling Moses, "Now therefore let me alone, that my wrath may burn hot

---

41. Most notably C. H. Dodd, "*Hilaskesthai*. Its Cognates, Derivatives, and Synonyms, in the Septuagint," *JTS* 32, no. 128 (1931): 352–60; reprinted in *The Bible and the Greeks* (London: Hodder & Stoughton, 1935).

42. See Leon Morris, *The Apostolic Preaching of the Cross*, 3rd ed. (Grand Rapids, MI: Eerdmans, 1965); Roger Nicole, "C. H. Dodd and the Doctrine of Propitiation," *WTJ* 17, no. 2 (1955): 117–57.

43. Jeffery, Ovey, and Sach, *Pierced for Our Transgressions*, 44–45.

against them and I may consume them, in order that I may make a great nation of you" (Ex. 32:10). The next day, Moses told the people of his intentions to intercede with God on their behalf. He said, "You have sinned a great sin. And now I will go up to the LORD; perhaps I can make atonement for [Heb. *kaphar*; Gk. *exilaskomai* (Septuagint)] your sin" (Ex. 32:30). Moses clearly understood the problem: God's wrath was kindled against the sin of his people. His instinctive solution was to seek to "make atonement" for their sin—that is, to seek to turn God's wrath away from his people. This clearly suggests that propitiation is a concept inherent to the biblical teaching on atonement and a meaning carried by the Hebrew term *kaphar*.

Second, in Numbers 25, Israel found herself in a similar morass of idolatry. The people had committed sexual immorality with Moabite women and had begun worshiping the gods of Moab. Here again, the Lord responded in wrath: "And the anger of the LORD was kindled against Israel" (Num. 25:3). He manifested it in the form of a plague that eventually claimed twenty-four thousand lives (cf. Num. 25:8–9), and he directed Moses to kill the leaders of Israel so that his wrath might be turned away (Num. 25:4). Just then, another Israelite brought a Midianite woman to his family's tent, apparently intending to follow in the sexual immorality of the rest of the people. Phinehas, one of the priests, was so incensed by such brazen rebellion that he "took a spear in his hand, and he went after the man of Israel into the chamber and pierced both of them, the man of Israel and the woman through her belly" (Num. 25:7–8). As a result of Phinehas's zeal, God's wrath was propitiated and the plague ended (Num. 25:8). The Lord praised Phinehas for his righteous indignation:

> Phinehas the son of Eleazar, son of Aaron the priest, *has turned back my wrath* from the people of Israel, in that he was jealous with my jealousy among them, so that I did not consume the people of Israel in my jealousy. Therefore say, "Behold, I give to him my covenant of peace, and it shall be to him and to his descendants after him the covenant of a perpetual priesthood, because he was jealous for his God and *made atonement for* [Heb. *kaphar*; Gk. *exilaskomai* (Septuagint)] the people of Israel." (Num. 25:11–13)

Here turning back God's wrath is synonymous with making atonement. This clearly indicates that propitiation is inherent in the concepts denoted by the Hebrew *kaphar* and the Greek *hilaskomai*.

A final example comes in Numbers 16, as Israel was grumbling against Moses in the wilderness in response to the death of Korah and his men. In response to the people's mutiny against Moses and Aaron, the Lord's wrath was kindled against Israel, again in the form of a plague, which eventually killed 14,700 people (cf. Num. 16:48–49). He directed Moses and Aaron, "Get away from the midst of this congregation, that I may consume them in a moment" (Num. 16:45). Moses told Aaron, "Take your censer, and put fire on it from off the altar and lay incense on it and carry it quickly to the congregation and make atonement for [Heb. *kaphar*; Gk. *exilaskomai* (Septuagint)] them, for *wrath* has gone out from the LORD; the plague has begun" (Num. 16:46). Aaron did as Moses said: "And he put on the incense and made atonement for [Heb. *kaphar*; Gk. *exilaskomai* (Septuagint)] the people. And he stood between the dead and the living, and the plague was stopped" (Num. 16:47–48). Once again, a clear parallelism emerges between making atonement and turning away God's wrath against sin as exercised in the form of a plague. While not every instance of *kaphar* may speak of propitiation, in certain instances this meaning is unmistakable.

Therefore, when the New Testament writers use the Greek *hilaskomai* word group—that is, the same word group used to translate the Hebrew *kaphar* in the Septuagint—it is reasonable to expect that it denotes propitiation just as it did in the Old Testament, especially given the contexts in which the term is used. For example, the first use of "propitiation" in the New Testament comes in Romans 3:25, after Paul has spent two chapters detailing how the wrath of God is kindled against the sin of all mankind—both Gentiles (Rom. 1:18–32) and Jews (Rom. 2:1–3:20). God has manifested this righteous anger by delivering the Gentiles over to "lusts" and "impurity," to "dishonorable passions," and to "a debased mind" (Rom. 1:24, 26, 28). To the Jews who have the law and who are yet unrepentant, Paul says, "You are storing up wrath for yourself on the day of wrath when God's righteous judgment will be revealed" (Rom. 2:5; cf. 2:8; 3:5). The thread of divine wrath has been so woven through this opening section of the letter that the reader almost expects to be confronted with how God will provide for its abatement. We see precisely that in Romans 3:21–26: God has put forward his Son, the Lord Jesus Christ, "as a propitiation by his blood, to be received by faith" (Rom. 3:25). God has satisfied his wrath against sin by the sprinkling of the blood of the spotless Lamb on the mercy seat of the heavenly altar (Heb. 9:11–15, 23–24). He has punished the sins of his people in a substitute, and thus his wrath has been turned away from them.[44]

Ultimately, any denial of a propitiatory component to Christ's atonement is a denial that God's wrath is aroused against sin or that it must be appeased for man to be granted salvation. Yet such a supposition does violence to the full breadth of biblical revelation. The small sample of texts that we have considered has demonstrated this point clearly. God's response to man's sin—whether idolatry, sexual immorality, or grumbling against his leaders—is to be righteously aroused in wrath. Then to read in such universal terms that "the wrath of God is revealed from heaven against all ungodliness and unrighteousness of men" (Rom. 1:18) is to remove all doubt. And since God is holy, he must exercise his wrath against sin. As Murray says, "Because he loves himself supremely he cannot suffer what belongs to the integrity of his character and glory to be compromised or curtailed. That is the reason for propitiation."[45]

---

44. A similar case can be made for the occurrence of the Greek term *hilasmos* in 1 John 2:2. Reymond writes, "In 1 John 2:1 the reference to Jesus as our Advocate before the Father when we sin, specifically in his character as the *Righteous One*, implies that the One before whom he pleads our cause—who represents the offended Triune Godhead—is displeased with us. Accordingly, the description of Jesus which immediately follows in 1 John 2:2 surely suggests that it is his advocacy before the Father specifically in his character as our *hilasmos*, which removes that divine displeasure." Robert L. Reymond, *A New Systematic Theology of the Christian Faith*, 2nd ed. (Nashville: Thomas Nelson, 2010), 638. Italics original. And while the contexts of Heb. 2:17 and 1 John 4:10 could permit either expiation or propitiation, these other instances show a precedent for reading the *hilaskomai* word group as denoting propitiation.

45. Murray, *Redemption Accomplished and Applied*, 32.

The significance of propitiation, then, is that it identifies Christ's work as a wrath-bearing sacrifice. Sin may not merely be overlooked; sin must ever and always be punished, whether in the sinner in hell or in Christ the substitute on the cross. God has not relaxed his justice, for he himself declares that he will by no means leave the guilty unpunished (Ex. 34:7). Every ounce of wrath that the elect sinner deserved—all the wrath that God would have exercised on the sinner in the eternal torments of hell—was poured out fully on our substitute in those three terrible hours on Calvary. Because of this, there is no longer any wrath left for Christ's people. God is propitious toward them, for their sin has been paid for.

Reconciliation. Man's sin has not only incurred guilt and aroused the wrath of God but has also effected an enmity and alienation between God and man. Such alienation is pictured throughout Scripture, most notably in the garden, where Adam and Eve's immediate instinct after sinning is to hide from God and avoid his fellowship (Gen. 3:8), from which fellowship they are driven out (Gen. 3:22–24). In Israel's history, God's separation from sinful man is powerfully illustrated by the threefold barrier of the tabernacle and temple: the outer court, accessible only to those bringing sacrifices; the Holy Place, accessible only to the priests offering sacrifices for the people; and the Most Holy Place, accessible only to the high priest on the Day of Atonement to make propitiation for the sins of the nation. This is a far cry from speaking with God face-to-face in the cool of the day (Gen. 3:8). The prophet Isaiah comments on the nature of the broken relationship when he says, "Your iniquities have made a separation between you and your God, and your sins have hidden his face from you so that he does not hear [your prayers]" (Isa. 59:2). God has become man's enemy (Gk. *echthros*, Rom. 5:10), and the mind of man is "hostile" (Gk. *echthra*) toward God (Rom. 8:7).

For this reason, Scripture also speaks of the atonement as a work of reconciliation, whereby the ground of the enmity between God and men—namely, the guilt of sin and the punishment of God's wrath—is removed and dealt with, thus accomplishing peace. The following key texts with highlighted Greek terms establish this theme:

> For if while we were enemies [*echthroi*] we were reconciled [*katēllagēmen*] to God by the death of his Son, much more, now that we are reconciled [*katallagentes*], shall we be saved by his life. More than that, we also rejoice in God through our Lord Jesus Christ, through whom we have now received reconciliation [*katallagēn*]. (Rom. 5:10–11)

> All this is from God, who through Christ reconciled [*katallaxantos*] us to himself and gave us the ministry of reconciliation [*katallagēs*]; that is, in Christ God was reconciling [*ēn . . . katallassōn*] the world to himself, not counting their trespasses against them, and entrusting to us the message of reconciliation [*katallagēs*]. (2 Cor. 5:18–19)

> . . . [that Christ] might reconcile [*apokatallaxē*] us both to God in one body through the cross, thereby killing the hostility [*tēn echthran*]. (Eph. 2:16)

> [God was pleased] through him to reconcile [*apokatallaxai*] to himself all things, whether on earth or in heaven, making peace by the blood of his cross.
> And you, who once were alienated [*apēllotriōmenous*] and hostile [*echthrous*] in mind, doing evil deeds, he has now reconciled [*apokatēllaxen*] in his body of flesh by his death, in order to present you holy and blameless and above reproach before him. (Col. 1:20–22)

Several characteristics of the doctrine of reconciliation emerge from these texts. First, reconciliation is a work of God, accomplished in the person of Christ through the efficacy of his blood (2 Cor. 5:18; Col. 1:20). Man does not effect this reconciliation by doing something to remove God's hostility toward his sin. Rather, sinners passively receive reconciliation as a gift through the work of Christ (Rom. 5:11). Second, Scripture presents reconciliation as a finished work accomplished by Christ's sacrifice. Each of the above passages indicates that reconciliation occurred in the past through the once-for-all death of Christ. Third, reconciliation is fundamentally forensic. This is demonstrated by the parallelism in Romans 5, where the phrase "we were reconciled to God by the death of his Son" is parallel to "we have now been justified by his blood" in the immediately preceding verse (Rom. 5:9–10). Since justification is forensic and is parallel with reconciliation, it is likely that reconciliation also ought to be understood in forensic terms. Paul removes all doubt in 2 Corinthians 5:19 when he explicitly identifies the work of reconciliation as God's "not counting [the world's] trespasses against them." "Counting" comes from the Greek word *logizomai*, the New Testament's most common term for "imputation" (e.g., Rom. 4:1–25). By imputing our sins to Christ our scapegoat, by exercising his wrath on him as our substitute, and by imputing his righteousness to us (2 Cor. 5:21), God has removed the ground of his enmity against us, namely, the guilt of sin. As propitiation is the removal of God's wrath against sinners, so reconciliation is the removal of God's enmity against sinners.

This means that, like sacrifice and propitiation, which speak of "things pertaining to God" (Heb. 2:17; 5:1 NASB), the biblical concept of reconciliation is primarily objective rather than subjective; that is, it has its fundamental effect in God and not man. The alienation between God and man is double edged. To be sure, man is hostile to God because his mind and heart are depraved, but God is also hostile to man because in his holiness he hates sin. When we consider (1) that the Bible pictures reconciliation as a forensic act decisively accomplished by God in Christ and (2) that elect sinners who have not yet come to faith remain hostile to God, it is apparent that reconciliation "does not refer to the putting away of the subjective enmity in the heart of the person said to be reconciled, but to the alienation on the part of the person to whom we are said to be reconciled."[46] Therefore, the mutual peace accomplished by the act of reconciliation is experienced as the result of reconciliation, when the regenerating work of the Holy Spirit overcomes man's hostility to God as the Spirit applies Christ's objective work to sinners, granting them the justifying faith by which

---

46. Murray, *Redemption Accomplished and Applied*, 38.

they have peace with God (Rom. 5:1). Because of Christ's atonement, sinners once separated from God may be restored to loving fellowship with him whom they were created to know and worship: "For Christ also suffered once for sins, the righteous for the unrighteous, that he might bring us to God" (1 Pet. 3:18).

Redemption. As sacrifice, Christ's atonement is suited to remove the guilt and penalty of sin. As propitiation, it is suited to remove the wrath incurred by sin. As reconciliation, it is suited to remove the alienation and enmity incited by sin. In addition, Christ's atonement is characterized as redemption, that by which man is redeemed from the bondage of sin and the law through the payment of Christ's shed blood as a ransom.

The most significant implication of characterizing Christ's atonement as redemption is that redemption language is fundamentally commercial. The Greek terms *agorazō* and *exagorazō* come from the noun *agora*, which means "marketplace" (Matt. 20:3; Luke 7:32; Acts 17:17). Thus, to redeem is to purchase out of the marketplace. *Lytroō*, another Greek word for "redemption," refers to purchasing by payment of a ransom (*lytron*). For example, when an Israelite had become so poor that he had to sell himself into slavery, God's law made provision for his family to redeem (Heb. *ga'al*; Gk. *lytroomai* [Septuagint]) him out of slavery by paying a price (Lev. 25:47–55). In a similar way, then, sinners have found themselves in bondage to sin (Rom. 6:6), and Christ has redeemed them by the ransom price of his life. He himself declares that he came "to give his life as a ransom [Gk. *lytron*] for many" (Matt. 20:28; Mark 10:45; cf. 1 Tim. 2:6). Jesus characterizes the mission of his incarnation as a work of ransom, of which his life was the ransom price that would be given "in the stead of" (Gk. *anti*) the many sinners whose freedom he bought. For this reason, Paul can exhort believers to glorify God in their body, for "you were bought [Gk. *agorazō*] with a price" (1 Cor. 6:20; cf. 7:23). The apostle Peter speaks similarly when he tells believers that they were "ransomed [Gk. *lytroō*; NASB: 'redeemed'] . . . not with perishable things such as silver or gold, but with the precious blood of Christ, like that of a lamb without blemish or spot" (1 Pet. 1:18–19). Here contrasted with silver and gold, the blood of Christ is explicitly identified as the price by which redemption is purchased. Thus, when the apostle John describes creatures in heaven worshiping the ascended Christ, he notes that they praise him for his atoning work: "Worthy are you . . . for you were slain, and by your blood you ransomed [Gk. *agorazō*; NASB: 'purchased'] people for God from every tribe and language and people and nation" (Rev. 5:9; cf. Acts 20:28). Christ's people—that is, those "who follow the Lamb wherever he goes"—are therefore called the "redeemed" (Rev. 14:3–4), the purchased ones, for they "have redemption through his blood" (Eph. 1:7; cf. Col. 1:14).

It is plain, then, that Christ has redeemed sinners out of slavery by paying the ransom price of his blood. Yet we must ask, to whom did he render this payment? One might expect that a ransom had to be paid to Satan, for he is the custodian of sin and death (Heb. 2:14–15), to which men are enslaved. For this reason, several church fathers conceived of the atonement as a ransom to Satan.[47] However, God the Son is not beholden to Satan that he should make payments to him; Satan himself is God's chief captive and thus is in no position to make demands on God. Instead, the ransom of Christ's blood was paid to God, whose holiness demanded a just payment for the penalty of sin. Here again is observed the fundamentally objective nature and "Godward" direction of the atonement: the blood of the Lamb was sprinkled on the mercy seat of the heavenly altar as a sacrifice, as a propitiation, and as a ransom for sinners.

However, redemption also has a "manward" direction, for while God is propitiated and reconciled, man is redeemed. In the first place, "Christ redeemed us from the curse of the law" (Gal. 3:13; cf. 4:4–5). The law of God has always brought with it promised blessings for obedience and promised curses for disobedience (see Deuteronomy 27–28). In fact, in the Galatians 3 passage, Paul quotes the promised curse for disobedience just a few verses earlier: "For all who rely on works of the law are under a curse; for it is written, 'Cursed be everyone who does not abide by all things written in the book of the Law, and do them'" (Gal. 3:10; cf. Deut. 27:26). For those who seek to attain righteousness by their works, the law requires perfect obedience (James 2:10). Because "all have sinned and fall short of the glory of God" (Rom. 3:23), all come under the curse of the law. It is from this curse of spiritual death and destruction that Christ has redeemed his people. He has done this by becoming a curse for us, that is, by bearing the penal sanctions of that curse in our place.

Second, Christ has redeemed us from sin. Sinners are enslaved by sin (John. 8:34; Rom. 6:6, 16–17; 2 Pet. 2:19), and therefore, "a death has taken place for redemption from . . . transgressions" (Heb. 9:15 HCSB). By his substitutionary death, Christ has redeemed his people from the guilt of sin by paying its penalty (cf. Rom. 6:23). Thus, by the redemption that comes through his blood we have forgiveness of sins (Matt. 26:28; Eph. 1:7; Col. 1:14). Yet Christ has also redeemed his people from the power of sin in the flesh. Having been redeemed from the enslaving power of sin, they have become "slaves of righteousness" (Rom. 6:18), and thus Paul concludes, "But now that you have been set free from sin and have become slaves of God, the fruit you get leads to sanctification and its end, eternal life" (Rom. 6:22). Redemption from sin's power, then, becomes the ground on which believers put off sin and put on righteousness (1 Pet. 1:17–19), for Christ "gave himself for us to redeem us from all lawlessness and to purify for himself a people for his own possession who are zealous for good works" (Titus 2:14).

Finally, several texts in Scripture speak of man's redemption in an eschatological sense, in which we are finally freed not only from the penalty and power of sin but even from its presence. In Romans 8:23, Paul comments on how believers "wait eagerly for adoption as sons, the redemption of our bodies." This is not to suggest that the redemption purchased on the cross is somehow inefficacious until the believer's

---

47. See "Incomplete Theories of the Atonement" (p. 536).

glorification but rather that Christ's perfectly efficacious redemption applied to the believer's soul at his justification will also finally be applied to the body at his glorification. In other words, the cross has secured the consummation of our salvation no less than its inauguration. For this reason, that final day is called "your redemption" (Luke 21:28) and "the day of redemption" (Eph. 4:30).

Conquest. While the redemption of his people did not consist in paying a ransom to Satan, the redemption Christ accomplished does affect Satan. In paying the penalty of sin and freeing his people from sin and death, Jesus also accomplished a victory of conquest over Satan and the rulers, authorities, cosmic powers, and "spiritual forces of evil in the heavenly places" (Eph. 6:12). Since "the whole world lies in the power of the evil one" (1 John 5:19), who is "the god of this world" (2 Cor. 4:4) and "the prince of the power of the air" (Eph. 2:2), overcoming the penalty and power of sin in the lives of his people is to triumph over Satan, to enter the "strong man's house and plunder his goods" (Matt. 12:29; cf. Luke 11:21–22). For this reason, as he nears the end of his earthly ministry, Jesus declared, "Now is the judgment of this world; now will the ruler of this world be cast out" (John 12:31), and then several days later he proclaimed, "The ruler of this world is judged" (John 16:11). That is, by his redemptive work on the cross, Christ dealt the decisive death blow to Satan and his kingdom of darkness, realizing—that is, inaugurating even if not yet consummating—the purpose for which he came into the world: "to destroy the works of the devil" (1 John 3:8). When he forgave us "all our trespasses, by canceling the record of debt that stood against us with its legal demands," setting it aside by "nailing it to the cross," he removed the ground of Satan's accusations against us (Col. 2:13–14). Therefore, Paul writes, "He disarmed the rulers and authorities and put them to open shame, by triumphing over them in him" (Col. 2:15). Through the paradoxical triumph of his death, he "destroy[ed] the one who has the power of death, that is, the devil, and deliver[ed] all those who through fear of death were subject to lifelong slavery" (Heb. 2:14–15). And on the third day, Jesus displayed his conquest over the power of sin and death by rising from the grave. It was impossible for him to be held in death's clutches (Acts 2:24), for, having defeated death, "the keys of Death and Hades" belong to him (Rev. 1:17–18).

Summary. Such, then, is the character of the penal-substitutionary atonement of Christ. The guilt of our sin demanded the penalty of death, and so the Lamb of God was slain as an expiatory sacrifice on our behalf. The wrath of God was kindled against our sin, and so Christ was set forth as a propitiation to bear that wrath in our place. The pollution of our sin alienated us from God and aroused his holy enmity against us, and so by atoning for sin Christ has reconciled God to man. Obedient to sin, man was in bondage to sin through the law that exposed sin in our lives, and so Christ has paid the ransom price of his precious blood to God the Father in order to redeem us from such slavery. In doing so, he has plundered Satan's house, conquering death and its captain by the exercise of his own power.

Incomplete Theories of the Atonement[48]

As has been demonstrated, the nature of the atonement concerns the very heart of the gospel of Christ. Because of this, misunderstanding the character of Christ's work can result in serious theological error and, in some cases, even heresy. Church history has provided examples of both, as there have been various views and theories put forward concerning what really happened on the cross. For this reason, it is important to know some of the major historical conceptions of the atonement and to evaluate each by Scripture.

THE RANSOM THEORY

First, proponents of the ransom, or classic, theory of the atonement argue that in the cosmic struggle between good and evil and between God and Satan, Satan had held humanity captive to sin. Therefore, in order to rescue humanity, God had to ransom them from the power of Satan by delivering Jesus over to him in exchange for the souls held captive. Proponents of the ransom theory often appeal to Jesus's statement that he came to give his life as a ransom for many (Matt. 20:28; Mark 10:45). A contemporary variation on the ransom theory has become known as the Christus Victor theory, which emphasizes Christ's atonement as accomplishing a victory over the cosmic forces of sin, death, evil, and Satan.

Though Christ did give his life as a ransom for many, and though his death did indeed disarm the powers of darkness (Col. 2:15), rendering powerless the Devil, who had the power of death (Heb. 2:14), this view of the atonement affords more power to Satan than he actually has. Satan has never been in any position to make demands of God. Further, it is the holiness of God, not any supposed sovereignty of Satan, that requires a just penalty to be paid for sin. Scripture makes it clear that Jesus paid the price of the cross in order to ransom sinners from the just punishment of God's holy wrath (Rom. 5:9). In the deepest sense, Jesus saved us from God, not merely the power of sin and Satan.

THE SATISFACTION THEORY

The satisfaction theory, championed chiefly by Anselm of Canterbury (1033–1109), supports the idea that Christ's death made a satisfaction to the Father for sin. However, taking a cue from the paradigm of feudalism that characterized society at that time, Anselm focused more on the notion of making satisfaction for God's wounded honor than on the appeasement of his righteous wrath.

It is certainly true that God's glory is belittled when his creatures commit sin. Indeed, sin is synonymous with failing to *honor* God by giving him thanks (Rom. 1:21) and with falling short of his *glory* (Rom. 3:23). Thus, any adequate theory of atonement will provide for the vindication of God's righteousness and the restoration

---

48. This section is adapted from Mike Riccardi, "Theories of the Atonement: What Happened on the Cross?," *The Cripplegate* (blog), June 26, 2015, http://thecripplegate.com/theories-of-the-atonement-what-happened-on-the-cross/. Used by permission of the author.

of his honor. However, Christ accomplished this vindication of righteousness in a particular way—namely, by becoming a substitute for sinners, vicariously enduring in his body the punishment that was justly due to his people (1 Pet. 2:24). By setting forth Jesus as a propitiation of holy wrath, God has displayed himself as both just *and* justifier of the one who has faith in Christ (Rom. 3:26).

THE MORAL-INFLUENCE THEORY

The moral-influence theory of the atonement regards Christ's work as little more than a beautiful example of sacrificial Christian love and behavior. Propounded first by Peter Abelard (1079–1142) and adapted later by the Socinians and subsequent liberal theologians, the moral-influence theory posits that Jesus's death accomplished nothing objective, for God required no penalty to be paid for sin. God was not wrathful against humanity, and because God is free, there was no absolute need for his justice to be satisfied. Instead, Christ's death was merely an example of how humanity should act. By the demonstration of such love, Christ's death was said to win over the hearts of impenitent sinners and thus woo them to live a moral life as Jesus did—hence the designation *moral influence*. Proponents have also stressed that the cross was a way for God to empathetically identify with his creatures by sharing in their sufferings.

While these are nice sentiments, and while it is certainly true that Jesus's sacrifice is the *exemplar* of Christian love and service (cf. John 15:12; Eph. 5:1–2; 1 Pet. 2:24; 1 John 3:16), to reduce the atonement to a *mere* example vitiates it of what makes it truly loving—namely, that Christ has objectively and sufficiently paid for our sins, appeased the holy wrath of a deeply offended God who was made our mortal enemy because of our sin (Rom. 5:10; 8:7–8), and thus removed our guilt and alienation. One cannot deny these central truths of sin and grace inherent in the atonement without fundamentally undermining the gospel of Jesus Christ.

THE GOVERNMENTAL THEORY

The governmental theory of the atonement was first advocated by Hugo Grotius (1583–1645), a student of Jacobus Arminius (1560–1609). The governmental theory downplays the notion that Christ actually paid a penalty corresponding to man's particular sins. Instead, Christ's death served as a token suffering for sins in general—demonstrating that a penalty must be paid when laws are broken but not actually paying a specific penalty imposed against specific infractions. In fact, proponents of the governmental theory hold that God's justice did not *demand* a payment for sin at all.[49] By accepting merely token suffering, God set aside or relaxed his law, since he is "liable to no law."[50] Nevertheless, he chose to punish Christ in order to maintain the moral order and government of the universe (hence the name). Christ's punishment

---

49. Thus, Grotius would have rejected both the *hypothetical necessity* and *consequent absolute necessity* views of the atonement presented above. Instead, he taught that the atonement was not necessary to God's saving purpose. See Berkhof, *Systematic Theology*, 368.

50. Hugo Grotius, *A Defense of the Catholic Faith concerning the Satisfaction of Christ against Faustus Socinus*, trans. Frank Hugh Foster (Andover, MA: Warren F. Draper, 1889), 100.

also acts as a deterrent against future sin, since it shows the fearful lengths to which God will go in order to uphold the moral government of the world.

This is another case of capturing a part of the picture but, by not reflecting the full breadth of scriptural testimony, failing to present a truly biblical conception of the atonement. Christ did, in fact, pay the penalty for specific sins (1 Cor. 15:3; Heb. 2:17). His sufferings were not merely a token example of God's antipathy toward evil, as if God were simply averse to evil in general but tolerates it on the whole. No, God's justice is meticulous; he has provided a fully sufficient payment for sin in Christ. Without particular payment for particular sins, God's absolute justice is not satisfied, and thus sinners have no hope of forgiveness.

THE BIBLICAL CENTER: PENAL SUBSTITUTION

Ultimately, the only conception of the atonement that does justice to the fullness of the Bible's revelation of the gospel is penal substitution. Each of the preceding views contains some truth. It is right to affirm that Christ's death and resurrection defeated death and ransomed sinners, yet we must qualify that that ransom was paid to God and not to Satan. It is right to affirm that Christ's death satisfied God's wounded honor, but we must hasten to add that it also satisfied God's righteous anger and justice by providing a sufficient payment for sin. Further, the cross is indeed a wonderful moral example of Christian behavior, but we fall woefully short if we fail to recognize that it is so much more than that. Finally, the atonement was indeed an instance of God's moral governance of the universe, yet it was more specific than Grotius and others stated it to be. Without the concept of penal substitution undergirding all these pictures of the atonement, we fail to do justice to the full-orbed biblical revelation of Jesus as the sin-bearing, wrath-propitiating substitute for sinners.[51]

In his death, the Lord Jesus Christ paid the penalty that our sins incurred by suffering vicariously as our substitute. The righteous wrath that our sins aroused in God was exercised fully on the suffering servant when the Father "laid on him the iniquity of us all" (Isa. 53:6). The Savior, our Passover Lamb (John 1:29; 1 Cor. 5:7; Rev. 5:12), who knew no sin, was made sin on our behalf (2 Cor. 5:21), becoming a curse for us (Gal. 3:13), and he thus extinguished the Father's wrath against our sin (Heb. 2:17). Because of this sufficient sacrifice and the provision of Christ's righteousness reckoned to be ours (Rom. 4:3–5; 5:18–19; cf. Matt. 3:15), our sins can be justly forgiven (Rom. 3:25–26), and we can be reconciled to God (Rom. 5:10). This is most fundamentally what the cross is about. It is not *merely* a demonstration of God's love or an example for Christian ethics—though it is those things (Rom. 5:8; 1 Pet. 2:21). At its core, the significance of the cross is that the innocent and righteous Son of God bore the sins of his people by being crushed under his Father's righteous wrath, bearing their punishment in their place and thus taking away their sin. If the

---

51. Jeffery, Ovey, and Sach write, "Of course the idea that Jesus died in the place of sinners, bearing the punishment of God's wrath due to them on account of their rebellion, is not the *only* thing the Bible teaches about the crucifixion. . . . The biblical portrayal of the atonement has many facets. Our task here is simply to show that penal substitution is one of them, and has such prominence that it cannot be sidelined." *Pierced for Our Transgressions*, 33–34.

wrath-bearing, substitutionary nature of the cross is denied—or even not properly emphasized—one fundamentally misunderstands the very gospel itself, which stands at the heart of the Christian faith.

The Perfect Sufficiency of the Atonement[52]

If there is one description to be applied to the nature of Christ's penal-substitutionary atonement, it is that it is a perfectly sufficient sacrifice. Several features establish its perfect sufficiency.

In the first place, it is an objective atonement. Those who have held to the sufficiency of the atonement have always had to defend this sound doctrine against the attacks of false teaching. Throughout the history of the church, the spirit of the age has always driven men to arrogantly exalt themselves to the position of being their own cosavior. It is the natural delusion of the sinful human heart that man himself has retained enough goodness to at least cooperate with the saving work of the Lord Jesus Christ—that sinners can and must partner with the Savior to effect their own atonement. Thence flow the polluted streams of all false religion, according to which man adds to Christ's work his own religious performance—the multiplication of good works and the repudiation of bad works—to secure his salvation. Liberal theology has not only embraced such idolatry but has canonized it as one of the few dogmas on which it stands: man is basically good, and to be accepted before God, he need only respond to the moral influence of Christ's death and imitate his example of self-sacrifice. By this, it is argued, even if never so explicitly, God will be pleased with us and will not count our sins against us.

However, the Lord Jesus fully possesses the very nature of God, who said, "I am the Lord, and besides me there is no savior" (Isa. 43:11), and "I am the Lord; that is my name; my glory I give to no other" (Isa. 42:8; cf. 48:11). The name of our Lord is Jealous (Ex. 34:14), and he will not share with others the glory that is due to him as the only Savior of man. The atonement that he effected is *objective*—a work accomplished independent of and apart from those who will eventually partake of its benefits. No cooperating work or response to grace adds to or energizes this ground of our salvation. To be sure, those who subjectively experience the benefits of the atonement must respond in repentance and faith, but such responses belong to the *application* of redemption—not its *accomplishment*—and are themselves purchased by the perfect work that Christ has wrought. "It is finished!" was the triumphant cry from the cross, not "It has begun." As with the Father's work of election, which depends "not of him who wills or runs" (Rom. 9:16 ESV mg.), and with the Spirit's work of application, in which he blows where he wishes (John 3:8), so it is with the Son's work of redemption. Salvation is of the Lord (Jonah 2:9), and therefore, it has been perfectly accomplished *by* him, two thousand years ago, external to those who will reap its divine blessings.[53]

---

52. This section follows John Murray's helpful presentation in *Redemption Accomplished and Applied*, 51–58.

53. Murray writes, "Christ has indeed given us an example that we should follow his steps. But it is never proposed that this emulation on our part is to extend to the work of expiation, propitiation, reconciliation, and redemption which

Second, the sufficiency of the atonement is established by its finality. It is a single, finished, unrepeatable work. The Roman Catholic Church teaches precisely the opposite, demeaning the sufficiency of Christ's work by proposing to repeat his sacrifice in the ceremony of the mass. In blasphemous candor, Catholic theologian Ludwig Ott wrote the following:

> In the Sacrifice of the Mass and in the Sacrifice of the Cross the Sacrificial Gift and the Primary Sacrificing Priest are identical; only the nature and the mode of the offering are different. . . . According to the Thomistic view, *in every Mass Christ also performs an actual immediate sacrificial activity*, which, however, must not be conceived as a totality of many successive acts but as one single uninterrupted sacrificial act of the Transfigured Christ. The purpose of this Sacrifice is the same in the Sacrifice of the Mass as in the Sacrifice of the Cross; primarily the glorification of God, secondarily *atonement*, thanksgiving, and appeal.[54]

Contrast this, however, with the incessant testimony of the book of Hebrews to the finality of Christ's sacrifice:

> For it was indeed fitting that we should have such a high priest, holy, innocent, unstained, separated from sinners, and exalted above the heavens. He has no need, like those high priests, to offer sacrifices daily, first for his own sins and then for those of the people, since he did this *once for all* when he offered up himself. For the law appoints men in their weakness as high priests, but the word of the oath, which came later than the law, appoints a Son who has been made perfect *forever*. (Heb. 7:26–28)

> But when Christ appeared as a high priest of the good things that have come, then through the greater and more perfect tent (not made with hands, that is, not of this creation) he entered *once for all* into the holy places, not by means of the blood of goats and calves but by means of his own blood, thus securing an *eternal* redemption. (Heb. 9:11–12)

> *Nor* was it to offer himself *repeatedly*, as the high priest enters the holy places every year with blood not his own, for then he would have had to suffer repeatedly since the foundation of the world. But as it is, he has appeared *once for all* at the end of the ages to put away sin by the sacrifice of himself. And just as it is appointed for man to die once, and after that comes judgment, so Christ, having been *offered once* to bear the sins of many, will appear a second time, not to deal with sin but to save those who are eagerly waiting for him. (Heb. 9:25–28)

---

he accomplished. . . . From whatever angle we look upon his sacrifice we find its uniqueness to be as inviolable as the uniqueness of his person, of his mission, and of his office. Who is God-man but he alone? Who is great high priest to offer such sacrifice but he alone? Who shed such vicarious blood but he alone? Who entered in once for all into the holy place, having obtained eternal redemption, but he alone?" *Redemption Accomplished and Applied*, 56.

54. Ludwig Ott, *Fundamentals of Catholic Dogma*, ed. James Canon Bastible, trans. Patrick Lynch, 4th ed. (Rockford, IL: TAN Books, 1974), 408, emphasis added. Here we stand on the research of Wayne Grudem, *Systematic Theology*, 578n16. Just as striking is the following statement from Roman Catholic priest John O'Brien: "When the priest pronounces the tremendous words of consecration, he reaches up into the heavens, brings Christ down from His throne, and places Him upon our altar to be offered up again as the Victim for the sins of man. . . . While the Blessed Virgin was the human agency by which Christ became incarnate a single time, the priest brings Christ down from heaven, and renders Him present on our altar as the eternal Victim for the sins of man—not once but a thousand times! The priest speaks and lo! Christ, the eternal and omnipotent God, bows His head in humble obedience to the priest's command." John A. O'Brien, *The Faith of Millions: The Credentials of the Catholic Religion*, rev. ed. (Huntington, IN: Our Sunday Visitor, 1974), 256.

And by that will we have been sanctified through the offering of the body of Jesus Christ *once for all*. And every priest stands daily at his service, offering repeatedly the same sacrifices, which can never take away sins. But when *Christ had offered for all time a single sacrifice for sins*, he *sat down* at the right hand of God, waiting from that time until his enemies should be made a footstool for his feet. For *by a single offering* he has perfected *for all time* those who are being sanctified. (Heb. 10:10–14)

These passages explicitly deny that Christ was to offer himself repeatedly (Heb. 9:25). To suggest such a thing is to impugn the character of Christ himself, for it was the *weakness* of the high priests—the fact that they themselves were sinful and could never bring a perfect sacrifice to atone for sins—that demanded their repeated offerings (Heb. 7:28). Yet there is no such weakness in our High Priest; he is the eternally perfect Son—holy, innocent, undefiled, and separate from sinners (Heb. 7:26).

Further, many pieces of holy furniture adorned the tabernacle and temple, such as the laver, the showbread, the lampstand, and the ark. Yet one piece of furniture that was nowhere to be found was a chair. The priest of Israel never sat down but stood constantly, because his work was never done. Sin was ever present, and thus sacrifice was ever necessary. But as different as the new covenant is from the old, so is our Great High Priest from the priests of Israel. For Christ entered the perfect tabernacle not made with hands (Heb. 9:11; cf. 8:2), offered a single sacrifice, and *sat down* (Heb. 10:12), for his offering was unlike their offering. He offered not the blood of bulls and goats, which can never take away sins (Heb. 10:4), but rather his own precious blood, by which he secured "an eternal redemption" (Heb. 9:12). And inasmuch as the Son of God himself is intrinsically worthy, his was a *better* sacrifice (Heb. 9:23; cf. 8:6), of such a character as to *perfect*—for all time—those for whom it was offered (Heb. 10:14). Can there be any greater violence done to these texts than to suggest that Christ's sacrifice has to be repeated? Such perverse doctrine drains the cross of its very saving power, for "where there is forgiveness of these [sins], there is no longer *any* offering for sin" (Heb. 10:18; cf. Rom. 6:10). If there remains an offering to be given, there has been no forgiveness of sins.

Finally, the sufficiency of the atonement is established by its efficacy. That is to say, by dying on the cross, Christ has *actually* saved his people. He came not to make salvation hypothetical, possible, or merely available but to actually "save his people from their sins" (Matt. 1:21). He came not to make men redeemable but to redeem them. He died not potentially but actually, and so he made not a provisional atonement but an actual one. As the Lord of glory prepared to yield up his spirit to the care of the Father, conscious that he had accomplished the work he came to do, he declared: "It is finished" (John 19:30). Redemption had been accomplished. Our High Priest had actually made purification for sins, and, his work completed, he sat down (Heb. 1:3). The Good Shepherd had actually taken away the sins of his sheep (1 John 3:5) by bearing them in his own body (1 Pet. 2:24). He had actually extinguished the full exercise of the Father's wrath (Rom. 3:25), having actually become a curse for us (Gal. 3:13) and thus exhaustively paying the full penalty for our sins. In so doing, he actually purchased the redemption of his people by the ransom price of his own blood (Acts 20:28; Rev. 5:9). Each of these passages is a statement of efficacious accomplishment. To artificially insert the concept of provision or potentiality into any of those texts is to force one's theology on the plain meaning of Scripture.

In fact, this element of efficacy has been inherent in the biblical conception of atonement from its beginning in the Levitical law. The Hebrew verb *kaphar* is the most common verb in the Old Testament for the concept "to make atonement," and more than half of its occurrences are in Leviticus. In many of these occurrences, the word appears without any modifying phrase (e.g., Lev. 16:32). However, in several cases the speaker comments on the atonement he has just prescribed, and every time he does so, he makes a statement of the atonement's efficacy:

> And the priest shall make atonement for them, and they shall be forgiven. (Lev. 4:20)

> The priest shall make atonement for him for his sin, and he shall be forgiven. (Lev. 4:26, 31, 35; 5:10, 13, 16, 18; 6:7; 19:22)

> And the priest shall make atonement for her, and she shall be clean. (Lev. 12:8)

> Thus the priest shall make atonement for him, and he shall be clean. (Lev. 14:20)

> So he shall make atonement for the house, and it shall be clean. (Lev. 14:53)

The repetition of the laws for sacrifice would have indelibly impressed on the mind of the faithful Israelite that when the priest made atonement, he actually atoned, and that atonement brought about its intended effect of the forgiveness of sins.[55] Thus, when the same Greek word group (*hilaskomai, hilasmos, hilastērion*) that was used to translate *kaphar* in the Septuagint appears in the New Testament to describe the atoning work of Messiah, the reader naturally understands that same efficacy to inhere in the concept of Christ's atonement. Jesus's death did not make sins forgivable; it accomplished forgiveness. His atonement was not hypothetical, potential, or provisional; it was an efficacious atonement.

None of this is to suggest that the elect were justified or granted saving faith and repentance at the time of Christ's death in the first century. Neither is it to suggest that anyone is saved apart from faith. To assume so is to confuse the accomplishment of redemption with its application. Rather, to speak of definite atonement and accomplished salvation is to say that Christ has endured all the punishment of, paid the full penalty for, and satisfied the whole of God's wrath against the sins of his people. It is to say that he has done everything necessary to completely secure the salvation of those for whom he died—to render certain and definite the application

---

55. Of course, this is not to say that sins were forgiven other than through the atonement of Christ, for all the old covenant sacrifices looked forward to and derived their efficacy from Christ's final sacrifice (Rom. 3:24–26; Heb. 9:11–10:18). Nevertheless, on the basis of the work of Christ, God graciously allowed himself to be temporarily propitiated by the sacrifices he prescribed to Israel.

of salvation's benefits to all those for whom Christ purchased them. It is, finally, to say that nothing can be added to Christ's work in order to invest it with power or efficacy but that because our substitute has actually borne the full penalty of sin's condemnation, "there is therefore now no condemnation for those who are in Christ Jesus" (Rom. 8:1).

The Extent of the Atonement

Having understood the glorious nature of Christ's atoning work, it is now necessary to answer the question of its extent. For whom did Christ die? On whose behalf did Christ offer himself as a penal-substitutionary sacrifice? For whom did he propitiate the wrath of his Father? Whom did Christ reconcile to God and redeem out of slavery to sin and Satan?[56]

At the very outset, it must be observed that this topic is not merely a theoretical quibble on which only doctrinaire theologians speculate for sport. Answers to the above questions are not the impractical and esoteric musings of ivory-tower academicians. This is an intensely practical discussion, for the nature of Christ's cross work runs to the very heart of the gospel; it is not very far from the center of the Christian faith to ask, for whom has Christ accomplished these things? While it is a shame that the question of the extent of the atonement has often been a topic of intense disagreement and disunity among otherwise like-minded believers, it is a greater shame that some, with little patience for disciplined theological debate, have regarded it as an unworthy discussion and have mocked those who insist on a position out of biblical conviction. If the Son of God has destroyed the power of sin and has purchased the redemption by which sinners may be freed from divine judgment, can there be any more important question to ask than, for whom has he done this? This is a question to which the student of Scripture must devote himself to answering biblically.

The answers given to this vital question typically fall into two general categories. The universalist school of thought answers that Christ has paid for the sins of every person who has ever lived without exception. This is often called *general, unlimited,* or *universal atonement.*[57] By contrast, *particularists* teach that Christ died as a

---

56. Two indispensible guides in this discussion are John Owen, *Salus Electorum, Sanguis Jesu: Or, The Death of Death in the Death of Christ,* in *The Works of John Owen,* vol. 10, *The Death of Christ,* ed. William H. Goold (1854–1855; repr., Edinburgh: Banner of Truth, 1967), 139–428 (originally published in 1648); and David Gibson and Jonathan Gibson, eds., *From Heaven He Came and Sought Her: Definite Atonement in Historical, Biblical, Theological, and Pastoral Perspective* (Wheaton, IL: Crossway, 2013).

57. Though *universalist* is a common designation for those who believe that all people without exception will finally be saved, that is not how it is intended here. In the discussion of the extent of the atonement, the term refers to those who believe that the atonement has a universal extent—i.e., that Christ died for all without exception—even though its application will be limited to the elect alone. This includes Arminians, Amyraldians, and hypothetical universalists. Trueman's comments are helpful in distinguishing these views in the context of the contemporary debate: "Hypothetical universalism refers to those positions which argue for a potentially general, unlimited, or universal atonement. . . . Arminianism refers to those schools of Christian thought that see the atonement as universal and the decisive factor in the atonement's individual efficacy as lying in the individual's noncoerced act of faith. Amyraldianism has become a trendy term for those who regard themselves as Calvinist or Reformed but who reject the traditional notion of limited atonement. In fact, Amyraldianism, technically speaking is a specific form of covenant theology that places the decree to appoint Christ as mediator logically prior to the decree of election; thus, Christ is appointed mediator for all, even though not all will benefit from it. The contemporary use of Amyraldian[ism] is thus in general a rather sloppy and inaccurate appropriation of the term. Most modern 'Amyraldians' are more likely hypothetical universalists: they believe simply that Christ died for all, even though God's election is restrictive and particular." Carl R. Trueman, "Definite Atonement View," in *Perspectives on the Extent of the Atonement: 3 Views,* ed. Andrew David Naselli and Mark A. Snoeberger (Nashville: B&H Academic, 2015), 21–22n4.

substitute for the elect alone—for only those particular individuals whom the Father chose in eternity past and gave to the Son. While this position has long been known as *limited atonement*—that Christ's atonement is limited to the elect—many proponents have found such a label to be easily misunderstood and have preferred *definite atonement* or *particular redemption*.[58] Throughout the discussion of soteriology in the present volume, particular redemption has been affirmed. In this section it will be defended from Scripture.

That discussing this topic too often generates more heat than light is owing to two primary factors. First, the precise question under consideration is often misunderstood. Asking the question, for whom did Christ die? is not asking, to whom should the gospel be preached? Both particularists and universalists readily acknowledge that the gospel ought to be proclaimed to all people without exception; Christ genuinely offers himself as Savior to anyone who would turn from his or her sins and trust in him for righteousness. Neither is it to ask, for the forgiveness of whose sins is Christ's work sufficient? Both sides agree that, had God chosen to save more sinners than he actually has, Christ would not have had to suffer any more than he did in order to save them. Nor is the question, who will finally be saved? Both stipulate that the benefits of Christ's salvation will be applied only to those who repent and believe in him. Thus, both particularists and universalists can subscribe to the popular dictum that the atonement is "sufficient for all, yet efficient for only the elect."[59] This is also not a dispute over whether any nonsaving benefits resulting from the atonement accrue to the nonelect. If God had not intended to save sinners through Christ's atonement, it is likely that he would have immediately visited justice on sinful man as he did the fallen angels (2 Pet. 2:4). Yet because God intended to save his people through Christ in the fullness of time, even those whom he will not ultimately save will have enjoyed the benefits of common grace, divine forbearance, and a temporary reprieve from divine judgment. Therefore, to avoid unnecessary confusion and contention, it ought to be acknowledged that one's position on the extent of the atonement does not necessarily affect one's answer to these other questions. Instead, the question is, in whose place did Christ stand as a substitutionary sacrifice when he bore the full fury of his Father's righteous wrath against sin? The answer is, only those who will never bear that wrath themselves, namely, the elect alone.

Another reason this discussion often leads to frustration relates to methodology. Too often, universalists cite a number of proof texts containing the words "all" or "world" and consider the matter closed, declaring the particularist interpretation a violation of the "plain reading" of the text. Yet such an approach fails to take into account the context of these isolated texts along with the rest of the teaching of

---

58. Hence we use the label *particularist* to refer to the traditional Reformed view of the extent of the atonement. This position has often been dubbed "five-point Calvinism," indicating that one believes in all five of the doctrines of grace, including the doctrine of limited atonement, which is the most disputed of the five.

59. Naselli insightfully writes, "It is not helpful to describe your position on the extent of the atonement if it does not meaningfully contrast with other positions. Specifically, it is not helpful when people define their position with the phrase 'sufficient for all, efficient for the elect.' . . . Arminians, hypothetical universalists, and Calvinists alike have used that elastic phrase to describe their positions; so using it to define one's position results in confusion rather than clarity and precision." Andrew David Naselli, "Conclusion," in *Perspectives on the Extent of the Atonement*, 219.

Scripture and thus demonstrates that what is often claimed to be the "plain reading" is nothing more than a superficial reading.

Numerous passages of Scripture contain universalistic language while they do not speak of every individual without exception. For example, Romans 5:18 says, "Therefore, as one trespass led to condemnation for all men, so one act of righteousness leads to justification and life for all men." The so-called "plain reading" of this text would seem to require that the two phrases "all men" be interpreted identically in both halves of the verse. Such a position, however, leads either to affirming the doctrine of universal salvation or to denying the doctrine of original sin. All without exception are condemned in Adam (Rom. 5:12), yet not all indiscriminately receive justification and life (Matt. 7:13, 22–23; Rev. 21:8). In Romans 5:12–21, Paul contrasts Adam and Christ as the two representative heads of humanity, which sheds light on his intent in 5:18. Just as Adam's actions affect all men who are in him, so also Christ's actions affect all those who are in him. Thus, considering the context can correct a superficial reading of an isolated passage of Scripture.

In other instances, universal language is simply a convention of common speech. When the Pharisees said of Jesus, "Look, the world has gone after him" (John 12:19), they did not mean that everyone alive on the earth at that time had begun to follow Christ. When Paul said, "All things are lawful for me" (1 Cor. 6:12; cf. 10:23), he did not mean that he was at liberty to do anything and everything without exception, for he acknowledged that he was not without law but was "under the law of Christ" (1 Cor. 9:21). Therefore, the presence of universal language should not automatically be read to mean "all without exception." Like anything else, universal language needs to be properly interpreted according to its context and in accordance with the entirety of biblical teaching.

Rather than volleying proof texts back and forth, it is essential to consider the clear teaching of Scripture concerning the *nature* of Christ's mission to accomplish redemption. The Bible's teaching on the nature of the atonement has significant bearing on the proper understanding of its extent. Several lines of scriptural evidence must be considered to support the particularist view of the atonement.

TRINITARIAN PARTICULARISM

The beginning of this chapter set forth the biblical teaching concerning the divine plan of salvation and its relationship to the Son's mission. It was demonstrated that the decision for the Son to take on human flesh and rescue sinners from death and judgment was made not unilaterally but in accordance with an agreed-upon Trinitarian plan. In perfect unity, the Father commissioned the Son to go in the power of the Holy Spirit in order to save sinners. The Father *sent* the Son for a specific purpose, to accomplish a particular mission. That is why Jesus continually described his ministry as doing the will of the Father who sent him, going so far as to say, "My *food* is to do the will of him who sent me and to accomplish his work" (John 4:34; cf. 6:38; 17:4; Heb. 10:7). When he spoke of his atoning death, he stated that he was thus commanded by his Father to lay down his life (John 10:17–18), and so the totality of his mission is rightly characterized as an act of obedience to the Father (Phil. 2:8). Whatever the Son intended to accomplish on his saving mission, it was precisely that purpose for which the Father had sent him. There is a perfect unity of purpose and intention in the saving will of the Father and the saving will of the Son.[60]

However, it is plain that the Father has not chosen everyone for salvation. Those on whom he set his electing love he also predestined, and those he predestined he also called effectually, and those whom he called he also declared righteous in Christ, and those whom he justified he also glorified (Rom. 8:29–30, 33; cf. Eph. 1:4–5). Since not everyone is justified and glorified, it follows that not everyone has been foreknown and predestined by the Father for salvation. There are "vessels of wrath" that were prepared for destruction and "vessels of mercy" that he prepared for glory (Rom. 9:22–23). The election of the Father is not universal. If the Father's election is particular and not universal, and if the Father and the Son are perfectly united in their saving will and purpose, it is impossible that the Son's atonement should be universal and not particular. As Reymond writes,

> It is unthinkable to believe that Christ would say: "I recognize, Father, that your election and your salvific intentions terminate upon only a portion of mankind, but because my love is more inclusive and expansive than yours, I am not satisfied to die only for those you have elected. I am going to die for everyone."[61]

Yet this is the unavoidable conclusion of those who deny particular redemption. Said another way, if the atonement is universal, then either election is also universal, or the Father and Son are at cross-purposes with one another. Yet Scripture has refuted both notions. The saving will of the Father is expressed in his particular election (that he has chosen some, not all, to be saved), and the Son has come to do the will of his Father who sent him.

What is that will? Jesus explicitly explained, "And this is the will of him who sent me, that I should lose nothing *of all that he has given me*, but raise it up on the last day" (John 6:39). There exists a group of chosen individuals whom the Father has given the Son, and it is on *their* behalf that he accomplishes his redemptive work. They are all those who will eventually come to him (John 6:37) and believe (John 6:40) because they have been effectually drawn by the Father (John 6:44, 55–65); they are the sheep for whom the Son lays down his life (John 10:14–15, 27) and to whom he gives eternal life (John 6:40; 10:28; 17:2). Christ says plainly, "Yours they were, [Father,] and you gave them to me" (John 17:6; cf. 17:9, 24), and he clearly distinguishes them from the rest of the world (John 17:9). These individuals who belonged to the Father before the foundation of the world can be none other than the elect whom he has chosen for salvation. It is therefore these, and these alone,

---

60. Trueman argues, helpfully, that such unity of will and purpose between the Father and the Son implies their consubstantiality: "Significantly, the *homoousian* means the interaction between Father and Son cannot be construed in any terms that would imply even the most mildly adversarial relationship"; such would be to "clearly tend toward tritheism." Trueman, "Definite Atonement View," 26.

61. Reymond, *Systematic Theology*, 678.

whom the Father gives to the Son, and thus it is these, and these alone, for whom the Son accomplishes redemption.

Therefore, it is not surprising to read of the many ways in which Scripture identifies a *particular* people as the beneficiaries of Christ's work on the cross. He has given his life as a ransom for *many* (Matt. 20:28; Mark 10:45; cf. Isa. 53:12; Matt. 26:28), not all. He is the Good Shepherd, who lays down his life for his *sheep* (John 10:11–15), not for the goats who are not his (cf. John 10:26). He is the lover of the brethren who lays down his life for his *friends* (John 15:13). He is the great Redeemer, who with his own blood purchased the *church* of God (Acts 20:28). He is the bridegroom of the *church* (Rev. 19:7; cf. John 3:29), whom he loved and for whom he gave himself up (Eph. 5:25). He was delivered over for the *elect* (Rom. 8:32–33), for whom he continues to intercede (Rom. 8:34; cf. John 17:9). And he is the sanctifier of "*a people for his own possession* who are zealous for good works" (Titus 2:14).

It is popular for universalists to respond that such particularistic language does not necessarily rule out universalism; that is, Christ may have died for his sheep, but it does not follow that he did not also die for the goats. Yet this defense of particular redemption is far more than merely marshaling a number of isolated particularistic proof texts; it is setting those texts in the context of the explicit unity between the saving will of the Father and the Son, which Scripture defines as particular and not universal. Further, there is evidence that at least some of these particularizing designations are necessarily exclusive. Paul identifies those for whom the Father gave up his Son as "God's elect" (Rom. 8:32–33)—a category that necessarily excludes those not chosen and that has already been established as not universal. Jesus declares that he lays down his life for his sheep (John 10:14–15), which are defined as those whom the Father has given him (John 10:29), thus making "sheep" simply another designation for the elect. Add to that Jesus's remark to the Pharisees, "But you do not believe because you are not among my sheep" (John 10:26). Given that Jesus says, "I lay down my life for the sheep," just moments before he declares to the Pharisees, "You are not among my sheep," it is legitimate to infer that he did not lay down his life for those Pharisees. Finally, when Paul makes Christ's sacrificial love for the church the pattern for the husband's love for his wife, he shuts us up to a particularistic understanding of Christ's love for his bride (Eph. 5:25–27). Clearly, husbands ought to love their wives in a way that is special and different from the way they love all others. If (1) Christ loved even the nonelect and gave himself up for them in precisely the same way he gave himself for his own bride, and if (2) husbands were called to love their wives after that pattern, then husbands are to love their wives in a way that is no different from the way they love other women. Surely that was not Paul's intent. Thus, it can be soundly inferred that Christ's dying love for his church is unique and distinguishing.

In summary, by virtue of their own unity of essence, the Father, Son, and Holy Spirit are perfectly united with respect to their saving will and purpose. Christ was sent by the authority of the Father and in the power of the Holy Spirit to save no more and no fewer people than the Father chose and the Spirit regenerates (cf. Eph.

1:3–14). The Father has elected some, not all; the Spirit regenerates some, not all. To suggest that Christ has atoned for all, not some, is to put the persons of the Trinity entirely at odds with one another; it is to be forced to say that the will of the Son is not the will of the Father and the Spirit. This not only threatens the consubstantiality of the persons of the Trinity, but it flatly contradicts Christ's own explicit statements that he had undertaken his saving mission precisely to do the will of his Father. As the Father has given to the Son a particular people out of the world, it is for these— his sheep, his own, the church—that Christ lays down his life. Unity in the Trinity demands a particular atonement.

EFFICACIOUS ATONEMENT

Perhaps the most common argument from those who hold to some form of an unlimited atonement is that Christ died for all without exception in a *provisional* sense. Christ died to *provide* salvation for all yet not to infallibly secure it for anyone in particular. He has died *potentially* for all, it is said, such that the potential exists for anyone to have the benefits of his sacrifice applied to him or her through repentance and faith. Very rarely is this provisional nature of the atonement argued based on the exegesis of Scripture; rather, it is presented as a theological construct to explain texts that speak of Christ's death in universalistic terms. The argument usually takes the following form:

1. Scripture speaks of the death of Christ in universalistic terms; thus, Christ died for all without exception.
2. Not everyone receives the saving benefits of Christ's death; some perish in hell.
3. Therefore, Christ died for all in only a provisional or potential sense; the atonement is granted its efficacy by the decision of the sinner to repent and believe.

The entirety of this argument depends on the unproven assumption in the first point, namely, that universalistic language must be interpreted to mean "all without exception." Yet that assumption does not follow. If it can be shown (1) that universalistic language taken in context can be properly interpreted to mean "all without distinction," and (2) that the whole of biblical teaching identifies atonement not as provisional but as inherently efficacious, the universalist's argument fails. The former will be addressed below.[62] The latter is taken up here.

The key to the universalist's argument is to cast Christ's atonement as intrinsically ineffectual. However, in the above treatment of the perfect sufficiency of the atonement, it was established from Scripture that the attribute of efficacy is inherent and essential to the biblical concept of atonement. To review, Scripture teaches that Christ has actually—not potentially, provisionally, or hypothetically, but actually—accomplished the salvation of his people by virtue of his work on the cross. It is nearly tautologous to say that when Scripture states that our substitute "bore our sins in his body on the tree" (1 Pet. 2:24), it means he *actually*, not potentially, bore our sins in his body on the tree. When Scripture says, "But he was pierced for our transgressions; he was crushed for our iniquities; upon him was the chastisement that brought us peace, and with his

---

62. See "Making Sense of Universalistic Texts" (p. 554).

wounds we are healed" (Isa. 53:5), it would be exegetically monstrous to conclude that he was only potentially pierced or potentially crushed—that his chastisement brought only a potential peace or that his wounds brought only potential healing. That would be to artificially inject the concept of *potentiality* into texts that speak of efficacious, objective accomplishment. No, Christ was *actually* pierced, crushed, chastised, and wounded, and therefore he accomplished actual peace and actual healing. Scripture does not say, "By his wounds, you were made healable." It does not say, "By his wounds, you were put into a state in which you *might* be healed if you fulfill certain conditions that activate the hypothetically universal scope of Christ's wounds."[63] The text simply says, "By his wounds you have been healed" (1 Pet. 2:24). That is, Christ's objective, substitutionary suffering and death actually accomplished the spiritual healing of those for whom he died—those who, because of the intrinsic worth and efficacy of Christ's sacrifice, "not only may be saved, but are saved, must be saved, and cannot by any possibility run the hazard of being anything but saved."[64]

Examples such as this one could be multiplied throughout the Scriptures. As has already been mentioned, beginning as early as the Levitical law, atonement has always been presented as inherently efficacious, always accomplishing its intended effect (cf. Lev. 4:20, 26, 31, 35; 5:10, 13, 16, 18; 6:7; 12:7–8; 14:20, 53; 19:22). Thus, when the New Testament applies the Old Testament terminology for atonement to the work of the Messiah, it is proper to regard Christ's atonement with the same inherent efficacy. And this is precisely how the New Testament writers portray it: Jesus actually expiated our sins (1 John 3:5), actually propitiated the Father's wrath against us (Rom. 3:25; Heb. 2:17–18), actually reconciled God to us (Col. 1:22), and actually purchased our redemption (Acts 20:28; Rev. 5:9). He came not to make salvation possible but to decisively save his people (Matt. 1:21). In his atoning work, Christ did not provide a hypothetical salvation but rather infallibly secured the salvation of those for whom he died by actually bearing their punishment. Packer writes poignantly,

> God's saving purpose in the death of his Son was [not] a mere ineffectual wish, depending for its fulfillment on man's willingness to believe, so that for all God could do Christ might have died and none been saved at all. . . . The Bible sees the cross as revealing God's power to save, not his impotence. Christ did not win a hypothetical salvation for hypothetical believers, a mere possibility of salvation for any who might possibly believe, but a real salvation for his own chosen people. His precious blood really does save us all; the intended effects of his self-offering do in fact follow, just because the cross was what it was. Its saving power does not depend on faith being added *to* it; its saving power is such that faith flows *from* it. The cross *secured* the full salvation of all for whom Christ died.[65]

---

63. Borrowing language from Trueman, "Definite Atonement View," 42.

64. Charles Spurgeon, "Particular Redemption," in *The New Park Street Pulpit* (London: Alabaster and Passmore, 1856), 4:135. As Motyer writes, "The theological implications are profound: the atonement *itself*, and not something outside of the atonement [e.g., the sinner's decision], is the cause for any conversion. The resources for conversion are found in the Servant's death; they flow from it. Thus, it is the atonement that activates conversion, not vice versa (cf. Titus 3:3–5)." J. Alec Motyer, "'Stricken for the Transgression of My People': The Atoning Work of Isaiah's Suffering Servant," in Gibson and Gibson, *From Heaven He Came and Sought Her*, 261–62.

65. J. I. Packer, "Saved by His Precious Blood: An Introduction to John Owen's *The Death of Death in the Death of Christ*," in J. I. Packer and Mark Dever, *In My Place Condemned He Stood: Celebrating the Glory of the Atonement*

Since, then, Christ's atonement is inherently efficacious, and since it is agreed that not all will finally be saved, the extent of the atonement must be limited. The only other option is to suggest that God demands the payment of sin's penalty first from Christ on the cross and then again from the unbelieving sinner in hell. But surely such double jeopardy is wholly inconsistent with the justice of God. In his memorable hymn "From Whence This Fear and Unbelief?," Augustus Toplady (1740–1778) captured this truth beautifully:

> If thou hast my discharge procured,
> And freely in my room endured
> The whole of wrath divine,
> Payment God cannot twice demand—
> First at my bleeding surety's hand,
> And then again at mine.

Scripture affirms that our "bleeding Surety" efficaciously endured "the whole of wrath divine" in the stead of those for whom he died. If there is wrath left to pour out on the unbelieving sinner, then that wrath was not satisfied by the substitutionary work of Christ. If there is a penalty left for the sinner to pay in hell, then that penalty was not paid by Christ on the cross. That leaves only two options: either (1) Christ's sacrifice was impotent and ineffective, or (2) Christ's powerful and efficacious sacrifice was accomplished for a specific number of persons. Since the former is blasphemous and explicitly contrary to Scripture, the student of God's Word is constrained to embrace the latter.

Since, then, Christ's atonement is by its very nature an efficacious substitution—that is, since he actually satisfied all of the Father's wrath against the sins of those for whom he died—one cannot affirm a universal atonement but at the same time deny universal salvation without emptying the atonement of its saving power. Again, Packer argues,

> Any who take this position must redefine substitution in imprecise terms, if indeed they do not drop the term altogether, for they are committing themselves to deny that Christ's vicarious sacrifice ensures anyone's salvation. . . . If we are going to affirm penal substitution for all without exception we must either infer universal salvation or else, to evade this inference, deny the saving efficacy of the substitution for anyone; and if we are going to affirm penal substitution as an effective saving act of God we must either infer universal salvation or else, to evade this inference, restrict the scope of the substitution, making it a substitution for some, not all.[66]

It becomes plain, then, that unless one believes in universal final salvation, *everyone* limits the atonement. The particularist limits its extent, while the universalist limits its efficacy. Yet an inefficacious atonement not only contradicts the biblical teaching

---

(Wheaton, IL: Crossway, 2007), 123, emphasis added. Murray also summarizes the point well: "It is to beggar the concept of redemption as an effective securement of release by price and by power to construe it as anything less than the effectual accomplishment which secures the salvation of those who are its objects. Christ did not come to put men in a redeemable position but to redeem to himself a people. We have the same result when we properly analyze the meaning of expiation, propitiation, and reconciliation. Christ did not come to make sins expiable. He came to expiate sins . . . (Heb. 1:3). Christ did not come to make God reconcilable. He reconciled us to God by his own blood." *Redemption Accomplished and Applied*, 63.

66. J. I. Packer, "What Did the Cross Achieve? The Logic of Penal Substitution," in *In My Place Condemned He Stood*, 90–91.

concerning the nature of the atonement (as outlined above), it also fundamentally undermines the gospel itself, for an inefficacious atonement is no atonement at all. An atonement that is inefficacious is an atonement that does not atone.

The implications of this way of thinking are disastrous. If Christ has provided the same "potential atonement" for everyone, then the decisive difference between the saved and the lost is not the omnipotent grace of the Savior but the depraved will of the sinner. Taken to its logical conclusion, it is to say that "Christ saves us with our help; and what that means, when one thinks it out, is this—that we save ourselves with Christ's help."[67] Yet this is neither the perfectly sufficient atonement nor the almighty saving gospel revealed in the pages of Scripture. So far from *undermining* the free offer of the gospel, as is so often charged, the doctrine of definite atonement *establishes* the free offer of the gospel.[68] A universal atonement can offer sinners nothing more than the *possibility* of salvation—merely the opportunity to be put into a savable condition. Indeed, what does it mean for the universalist to declare to sinners, "Christ died for you," when, according to him, those for whom Christ died may very well perish in hell? Without an efficacious substitution, what, if any, saving substance can be offered? Only a perfectly efficacious atonement offers an accomplished salvation to which nothing need be added, a gift to be received by faith alone.[69] Therefore, we must conclude with Spurgeon that the universalist may keep his ineffectual atonement:

> The Arminians say, Christ died for all men. Ask them what they mean by it. Did Christ die so as to secure the salvation of all men? They say, "No, certainly not." We ask them the next question—Did Christ die so as to secure the salvation of any man in particular? They say, "No." They are obliged to admit this if they are consistent. They say, "No; Christ has died so that any man may be saved if"—and then follow certain conditions of salvation. We say then, we will just go back to the old statement—Christ did not die so as beyond a doubt to secure the salvation of anybody, did He? You must say "No"; you are obliged to say so. . . . Now, who is it that limits the death of Christ? Why you. You say that Christ did not die so as infallibly to secure the salvation of anybody. We beg your pardon, when you say we limit Christ's death; we say, "No, my dear sir, it is you that do it." We say Christ so died that He infallibly secured the salvation of a multitude that no man can number, who through Christ's death not only may be saved, but are saved, must be saved, and cannot by any possibility run the hazard of being anything but saved. You are welcome to your atonement; you may keep it. We will never renounce ours for the sake of it.[70]

---

67. Packer, "Saved by His Precious Blood," 129.

68. For more on how particularism in election, in atonement, and in the application of redemption does not contradict a universal, *bona fide* offer of the gospel, see "The External Call: Gospel Proclamation" (p. 571).

69. Murray writes, "What is offered to men in the gospel? It is not the possibility of salvation, not simply the opportunity of salvation. What is offered is *salvation*. To be more specific, it is Christ himself in all the glory of his person and in all the perfection of his finished work who is offered. . . . But he could not be offered in this capacity or character if he had not secured salvation and accomplished redemption. He could not be offered as Saviour and as the one who embodies in himself salvation full and free if he had simply made the salvation of all men possible or merely had made provision for the salvation of all. It is the very doctrine that Christ procured and secured redemption that invests the free offer of the gospel with richness and power. It is that doctrine alone that allows for a presentation of Christ that will be worthy of the glory of his accomplishment and of his person." *Redemption Accomplished and Applied*, 65.

70. Spurgeon, "Particular Redemption," 4:135.

THE UNITY OF THE HIGH PRIESTLY WORK OF CHRIST

Scripture frequently speaks of Christ as the Great High Priest of his people (Heb. 2:17; 3:1; 4:14–15; 5:1, 5, 10; 6:19–20; 8:1–6; 9:11–12, 25), borrowing the conceptual framework of the Old Testament sacrificial system as a foundation for understanding Christ's work of atonement. Thus, except for where the New Testament explicitly contrasts Christ's priestly ministry with that of the Old Testament priests (e.g., Heb. 7:27), there is a basic continuity between them. The work of the Levitical priests thus sheds light on the extent of the atonement in the inseparable unity between the priest's work of sacrifice and his work of intercession.

On the Day of Atonement, the high priest was to slay one goat as a sacrifice for the sins of the people of Israel (Lev. 16:9). Yet the sacrificial death was not the end of the priest's work. After slaying the goat, he was required to "bring its blood inside the veil" into the Most Holy Place, and "sprinkl[e] it over the mercy seat and in front of the mercy seat" (Lev. 16:15; cf. 16:18–19). It is this twofold work—both the slaughter of the goat and the intercessory sprinkling of its blood—that accomplished atonement for Israel's sins. This was the case not only for the Day of Atonement but also for all the sacrifices that required the death of animals. The priest was first to slay the animal and then to "offer up the blood and sprinkle the blood around on the altar" (Lev. 1:5 NASB; cf. 1:11; 3:2, 8, 13; 4:6–7, 17–18, 25, 30, 34; 5:9; 7:2; 17:6). The observation we must make from these rituals is that the scope of the priest's sacrifice is identical to the scope of his intercession. It is not the case that the high priest would sacrifice the goat on behalf of everyone throughout the Gentile world and then sprinkle its blood only on behalf of Israel. No, the sacrifice and the intercession were two sides of the same atoning coin, both done on behalf of Israel alone.

The same principle applies to the unity of the twofold High Priestly ministry of Christ. The author of Hebrews depicts Christ as our Great High Priest who both offered himself as the perfect sacrifice and entered into the Most Holy Place to intercede for his people: "For Christ has entered, not into holy places made with hands, which are copies of the true things, but into heaven itself, now to appear in the presence of God on our behalf" (Heb. 9:24). In other words, Christ's sacrificial offering of himself is inextricably linked to his intercessory work on behalf of his people in the presence of God (Heb. 4:14–15; 7:25; 1 John 2:1). That is, Christ intercedes for everyone for whom he died, and he died for everyone for whom he intercedes.

That conclusion is also supported by Romans 8:29–39, where Paul discusses redemption from beginning to end—from the Father's election in eternity past (8:29–30), to the death and resurrection of Christ (8:32–34), through to the application of redemption to sinners both in justification (8:33) and in perseverance unto glorification (8:35–39). Of particular interest is Paul's comment in Romans 8:34, where he connects Christ's death and resurrection with his present intercession: "Christ Jesus is the one who died—more than that, who was raised—who is at the right hand of God, who indeed is interceding for us." The question is, to whom does the word "us" refer? The nearest antecedent is found in Romans 8:32: "He who did not spare his own Son but gave him up *for us all*, how will he not also with him graciously give *us* all things?" Thus, those for whom Christ presently intercedes are the ones for whom the Father gave Christ over to death.

Once again it is observed that Christ intercedes for everyone for whom he died and that he died for everyone for whom he intercedes. The key question is, does Christ intercede before the Father on behalf of all men without exception or on behalf of the elect alone? Surely it is the latter. Is Christ praying to the Father for the salvation and blessing of the nonelect, a request the Father, because he does not intend to save the nonelect, will refuse his Son? Are the persons of the Trinity so divided? Here again the doctrine of unlimited atonement would drive a wedge between the will of the Father and the will of the Son, which has disastrous implications for biblical Trinitarianism.[71] Further, Christ himself answers this question in the High Priestly Prayer of John 17. Here the Great High Priest is interceding before the Father on behalf of those for whom he will soon offer himself as a sacrifice, and he explicitly says, "I am praying for *them*. I am *not* praying for the world but for those whom you have given me, for they are yours" (John 17:9). Jesus offers his High Priestly intercession only to those whom the Father has given him (cf. John 6:37, 39, 44, 65; 10:29; 17:2, 6, 20, 24)—namely, the "elect" of Romans 8:33. Since the priestly work of sacrifice and intercession are inextricably linked, and since it is unthinkable that Christ would refuse to intercede for those for whom he shed his precious blood, we must conclude that the extent of the atonement—like the extent of Christ's intercession—is limited to the elect.

THE ARGUMENT OF ROMANS 8:29-39

Coming back to Romans 8, Paul's comments in this passage are themselves a biblical argument for particular redemption. He speaks explicitly of the extent of the atonement in 8:32 when he says that the Father did not spare his Son but gave him up "for us all." Who is the "us all" for whom Christ was given up to death? Paul answers this question in a number of ways. First, if we look for an antecedent to "for us all" (8:32), we find another "us" in 8:31, referring to those whom God is *for*. Continuing our search for an antecedent, we find that those whom God is for are those whom he foreknew, predestined, called, justified, and glorified (8:29–30). Moving forward, we learn that those for whom Christ was delivered over are those to whom God will graciously give all the saving benefits purchased by Christ's death, for "how will he not also with him graciously give us all things" (8:32)? Romans 8:33 then explicitly identifies these people as "God's elect" and those whom he justifies, and 8:34 identifies them as those for whom Christ intercedes. Finally, those for whom Christ died are those who can never be separated from the love of Christ (8:35–39).

Several conclusions should be drawn from these observations. First, since the nonelect do not receive all the saving benefits of God's grace as promised in Romans 8:32

---

71. Trueman insightfully observes, "Father and Son cannot have adversarial wills, for that would require them to be different gods; nor can the Father simply overrule the Son against his will, for that would require a situation where the Son is clearly subordinate to the Father—a species of Arianism." "Definite Atonement View," 47.

(particularly being rescued from eternal punishment), they are not part of the "us all" for whom Christ was delivered over. Second, since Paul identifies the "us all" for whom Christ was delivered over to be "God's elect" in 8:33, Christ was not delivered over for those who are nonelect. Third, since all for whom Christ was delivered over will also be the beneficiaries of his intercessory ministry at the Father's right hand, and since Christ does not intercede on behalf of the nonelect, they are not included in the "us all" for whom Christ was delivered over. Fourth, since all for whom Christ was delivered over can never be separated from the love of Christ, and since the nonelect will in fact be separated from the love of Christ in eternal punishment, they are not included in the "us all" for whom Christ was delivered over. The extent of Christ's atonement is once again shown to be necessarily limited to the elect.[72]

MAKING SENSE OF UNIVERSALISTIC TEXTS

The preceding positive arguments are sufficient to establish particular redemption as a biblical doctrine. However, the most common objection against limiting the extent of the atonement comes from several passages of Scripture that seem to explicitly contradict it by using universalistic language in relation to Christ's death: "For God so loved the *world*, that he gave his only Son" (John 3:16); Christ Jesus "gave himself as a ransom for *all*" (1 Tim. 2:6); and so on. Therefore, in order for the case for particular redemption to stand, these universalistic texts must be explained in a way that (1) harmonizes with the precepts of particular redemption and (2) is consistent with contextual, grammatical-historical interpretation. This section, then, will examine three categories of texts that are used to support a universal atonement, interpret them in their contexts, and demonstrate how none of them contradicts the doctrine of particular redemption but how they all complement and in some cases provide further supporting evidence for the doctrine.

Christ Died for "All." As was mentioned above, one of the most disappointing aspects of discussing the extent of the atonement occurs when universalists appeal to texts containing the word "all" and simply declare the unwarranted assumption that "all" must always mean "all people without exception." To be sure, there are instances where that is the case: all people without exception "have sinned and fall short of the glory of God" (Rom. 3:23; yet even here there is one exception—the Lord Jesus Christ). But as has been shown, in several passages of Scripture the word

---

72. Hypothetical universalists may respond by arguing to this effect: "Yes, Paul is speaking of those for whom Christ died in Romans 8:28–39, but he is not speaking of *all* for whom Christ died. Christ died for others too—namely, the non-elect; he simply does not mention them here." This line of reasoning fails for two reasons. First, it is virtually tautologous to claim that when Paul says Christ was delivered over for "us all," he is speaking of *all* for whom Christ was delivered over. If Paul intended to refer to only a subset of those for whom Christ died, it is unlikely that he would have added the universalistic "all" when he could have left it at "for us." Second, Paul's entire argument is meant to give encouragement and assurance to those who are beneficiaries of the atoning sacrifice of Christ. To do this, he enumerates the benefits that accrue to them by virtue of Christ's death. If not everyone for whom Christ died is guaranteed those benefits (such as never being separated from Christ's love), why would Paul make Christ's death the very basis of their consolation? It would be no comfort at all. The troubled saints could simply respond, "What does Christ's death have to do with my security? He died for everyone without exception, and millions are separated from Christ's love!" It is unquestionable that the "us all" in Rom. 8:32 refers to *everyone* for whom Christ was delivered over.

"all" simply cannot refer to all people without exception. To deny that is to make a liar out of Jesus (Matt. 10:22; John 18:20) and to commit oneself to the final salvation of all without exception (Rom. 5:18; 11:32). Paul himself necessarily limits universalistic language when he comments on Psalm 8:6 in 1 Corinthians 15:27: "But when it says, 'all things are put in subjection,' it is plain that he is excepted who put all things in subjection under him." That is, in this case, "all things" does not mean "all things without exception." Therefore, "all" is not a self-defining expression. While it may legitimately be understood to speak of every person who has ever lived (i.e., all without exception), it may also legitimately be understood to speak of all kinds of people throughout the world (i.e., all without distinction). The determining factor of the proper sense of "all" is not one's *a priori* assumptions but rather the context of the particular passage in which the word occurs. When those passages are subjected to the scrutiny of contextual exegesis, it becomes clear that none of them supports an unlimited atonement.

In John 12:32, Jesus declares, "And I, when I am lifted up from the earth [i.e., crucified; John 12:33; cf. 3:14], will draw all people to myself." Universalists teach that the phrase "all people" refers to all without exception, and they posit that this "drawing" refers to a universal grace that removes the effects of depravity for everyone, bringing all men into a state of neutrality by which they can accept or reject Christ. This is often called *prevenient grace*, signifying a grace that "comes before." It is worth noting that, in order to maintain what they believe is the plain meaning of "all people," universalists must distort beyond recognition the plain meaning of "draw," for Scripture nowhere speaks of an ineffectual prevenient grace but only of the effectual call of the sovereign and almighty God (John 6:37, 44, 65). Besides this, however, the context of John 12:32 favors interpreting "all people" as "all without distinction." A few verses earlier, in John 12:20–21, John reports that a number of Greeks were asking to see Jesus. In response to this, Jesus explains the certain necessity of his death (John 12:22–28) and then declares that by his death he will draw all men to himself—that is, not only his Jewish countrymen but even Gentiles like those who were searching for him.

Universalists also appeal to 2 Corinthians 5:14–15. There Paul writes, "For the love of Christ controls us, because we have concluded this: that one has died for all, therefore all have died; and he died for all, that those who live might no longer live for themselves but for him who for their sake died and was raised." Universalists claim that the phrase "one has died for all" indicates that Christ has died for all men without exception. Yet this interpretation is not without significant problems. Paul immediately follows that statement by saying, "Therefore,"—that is, on the basis of Christ's death for them—"all have died." That is, they have died in and with Christ (Rom. 6:8; Col. 2:20; 3:3), and thus they have died to themselves and now live for Christ (2 Cor. 5:15). Further, Christ not only died for his people but also was raised on their behalf (2 Cor. 5:15). If union with Christ in his death necessarily effects the spiritual death of those for whom he died, it must also be the case that union with

Christ in his resurrection necessarily effects their spiritual resurrection as well. Paul says this explicitly in Romans 6:5: "For if we have been united with him in a death like his, we shall certainly be united with him in a resurrection like his." However, unless one embraces universal final salvation, it simply cannot be said that all people without exception, including unbelievers, have died to themselves, have been raised to newness of life, and now live for Christ. Instead, Paul uses the language of corporate solidarity—that the One died for the many—to emphasize the union between Christ and his people. He has died *for* them, and they have died to sin and to self *in* him, so that they now live for his honor and glory.

The universal statement in Hebrews 2:9 ought to be handled similarly. Because Christ is said to have tasted death for everyone, universalists argue that the atonement is unlimited. However, several contextual considerations militate against such an interpretation. First, in the very next verse the author proclaims the efficacy of Jesus's death: by his sufferings he was bringing many sons to glory. This statement is inconsistent with an atonement that is universal in its extent but limited in its efficacy. He was not bringing many sons into a condition in which they might hypothetically avail themselves of glory; rather, by the efficacy of his sufferings apart from any response on their part, he was actually bringing them to glory. Second, those for whom he suffered are characterized as his "brothers" (Heb. 2:11–12); such an intimate, familial designation cannot properly be made of anyone but the elect. Third, the author characterizes the beneficiaries of Christ's death as the "children God has given" him (Heb. 2:13). The language of the Father giving a certain group of individuals to the Son is reminiscent of Jesus's High Priestly Prayer: "You [Father] have given him [the Son] authority over all flesh, to give eternal life to *all whom you have given him*" (John 17:2; cf. 6:37, 39; 10:29; 17:6, 9, 20, 24), namely, the elect. Finally, Hebrews 2:16 states that Jesus savingly "helps the offspring of Abraham." If all people without exception were the objects of Jesus's saving design, the reader would have expected to read that the Son helps the offspring of Adam. Yet the author of Hebrews restricts the Son's help to God's chosen people, the children of the promise. Therefore, the universalistic language of Hebrew 2:9 must be conditioned by the several particularistic comments in the immediate context and must thus be understood to emphasize the corporate solidarity between the One and the many for whom he has interceded.

Hypothetical universalists often have recourse to Colossians 1:20, which says that God was pleased "through [Jesus] to reconcile to himself all things, whether on earth or in heaven, making peace by the blood of his cross." "All things" is grammatically in the neuter gender and therefore most likely refers to the whole created order. Because such a reconciliation is accomplished by the blood of Christ's cross, hypothetical universalists argue retrospectively that Christ must have died in some sense for everyone. However, arguing on the basis of this text that Christ has in some sense atoned for the created order confuses the atonement with the results of the atonement. The creation is cursed (and thus is in need of reconciliation to God) not for its own sins but rather as a consequence of human sin (Gen. 3:17; Rom. 8:20). In the same way, then, "the creation itself will be set free from its bondage to corruption" (Rom. 8:21) as a consequence of human redemption. That is why Paul calls the creation's freedom "the freedom of the glory of the children of God" (Rom. 8:21). Therefore, Colossians 1:20 teaches not that Christ atoned for the sins of the created order but rather that the particular redemption Christ accomplished for men carries cosmic implications. The consequences of atonement should not be conflated with atonement itself. Thus, Colossians 1:20 provides no basis for universal atonement. Jonathan Gibson argues persuasively that

> [Paul's] focus is the eschatological impact of Christ's cross, not the substitutionary extent of it. To argue retrospectively from the eschatological effects of Christ's death back to a universal atonement is a false deduction. Indeed, the parallel passage, Romans 8:19–23, shows that what lies behind the *cosmic* renewal is not a universal provision made by Christ's atonement but a consummated redemption of a *particular* group of people—"the sons of God."[73]

Another text often marshaled in support of an unlimited atonement is 1 Timothy 2:3–6, which speaks of "God our Savior, who desires all people to be saved and to come to the knowledge of the truth. For there is one God, and there is one mediator between God and men, the man Christ Jesus, who gave himself as a ransom for all, which is the testimony given at the proper time." If God desires all people to be saved, and if Christ has given himself as a ransom for all, how can we deny a universal atonement? Again, this passage must be read in its context. When Paul wrote 1 Timothy, certain persons were teaching "different doctrine" (1:3), swerving from sound teaching and wandering into vain discussion (1:6). These false teachers had ambitions to be "teachers of the law" (1:7), and their speculation regarding genealogies (1:4) and forbidding of marriage and certain foods (4:1–3) indicates that their false doctrine consisted of an exclusive Jewish elitism.

Paul's universalistic statements throughout the letter (cf. 1 Tim. 2:2, 4, 6; 4:10) make perfect sense in light of the context of this elitist false teaching. He is not teaching that Christ died for all without exception but rather that, contrary to this false teaching, Christ died for all without distinction.[74] This conclusion is strengthened by the fact that he urges prayers to be made "for all people" (1 Tim. 2:1), by which he means not all people throughout the entire world (for such would be impossible) but rather all kinds of people: "for kings and all who are in high positions" (1 Tim. 2:2). Also, immediately after the passage in question, Paul speaks of his apostolic appointment as a teacher of the Gentiles (1 Tim. 2:7), indicating further that his intent is to speak of all without distinction (i.e., not just Jews but Gentiles also). Finally, it

---

73. Jonathan Gibson, "For Whom Did Christ Die? Particularism and Universalism in the Pauline Epistles," in Gibson and Gibson, *From Heaven He Came and Sought Her*, 310.

74. Even I. Howard Marshall, who held to an unlimited atonement, wrote, "This universalistic thrust is most probably a corrective response to an exclusive elitist understanding of salvation connected with the false teaching. . . . The context shows that the inclusion of Gentiles alongside Jews in salvation is the primary issue here." *A Critical and Exegetical Commentary on the Pastoral Epistles*, in collaboration with Philip H. Towner, ICC (Edinburgh: T&T Clark, 2006), 420, 427.

must be remembered that the ransom Jesus paid was not a potential ransom but an actual and efficacious one. If we accept the universalist interpretation of 1 Timothy 2:6, we must either (1) embrace universal final salvation or (2) denigrate the efficacy of the atonement. Instead, the particularist interpretation makes the best sense of the totality of the biblical data. Paul uses the word "all" to refer to all kinds of people in order to undermine a heretical Jewish elitism that had taken hold at Ephesus.

The same conclusion is warranted for Paul's statement in Titus 2:11. Given that Paul had been providing instruction concerning different classes of people—older men, older women, younger women, younger men, and slaves (Titus 2:2–6, 9–10)—the "all people" to whom grace has brought salvation refers to all people without distinction, not all people without exception. This interpretation is buttressed by another statement of the efficacy of the atonement in Titus 2:14, where Christ is said to have given himself to both redeem and purify a particular people for his own possession.

A passage that has been the subject of much discussion is 1 Timothy 4:10, where Paul describes God as "the Savior of all people, especially of those who believe." Universalists teach that Jesus is the Savior of all people in the sense that he died for all but that he is especially the Savior of believers because the benefits of salvation are applied only to them. However, it is worth noting that the Son is not the nearest antecedent to "Savior" in this passage; rather, it is God the Father, "the living God," who is in focus here. This verse is speaking not about the atonement of Christ in particular but about God's nature as a Savior. Paul is thus outlining two ways in which God's saving nature is expressed. He is the Savior of all men in a temporal sense; that is, though all men have sinned against him, incurred guilt, and will pay for their sins in hell, God has not immediately visited his justice on them as he did with the fallen angels (cf. Rom. 3:25; 2 Pet. 2:4). Even the reprobate enjoy a temporary stay of execution and thus experience the joys of life in a world infused with the common grace of God (Matt. 5:44–45). Yet God's saving nature is also expressed in a more profound way for those who are his own. He is the Savior of all men in a temporal sense but the Savior of the elect—that is, those who eventually come to saving faith—in an eternal sense.

Finally, though 2 Peter 3:9 does not explicitly speak of the atonement, universalists argue that it reveals a universal saving will in God that contradicts a particular redemption. Peter writes, "The Lord is not slow to fulfill his promise as some count slowness, but is patient toward you, not wishing that any should perish, but that all should reach repentance." Since God does not wish that any should perish but that all should repent, it is argued that God has done everything he can to provide salvation in the universal atonement of Christ and that now it remains to the sinner to appropriate salvation by repentant faith. However, it simply does not follow that since God in some sense takes no pleasure in the death of the wicked (Ezek. 18:31–32; 33:11), Christ has atoned for all without exception.

Two responses may be made to the universalist approach to this text. The first has to do with the complexity of the divine will. What does it mean for God to desire that all without exception should repent when he himself has expressed his saving will in choosing some, not all, for salvation? And what does it mean for the God who accomplishes all his good pleasure (Isa. 46:9–10; Pss. 115:3; 135:6; Eph. 1:11) and whose purpose can be thwarted by no one (Job 42:2) to desire the salvation of all when he does not exercise his sovereign will to finally bring all to salvation? Rather than denying God's absolute sovereignty, as the universalists do, it is right to observe a distinction in the way Scripture talks about God's will.[75] God's *decretive* will is his "good pleasure" that accords with his sovereign decree. Isaiah speaks of this aspect of God's will when he prophesies of the crucifixion of Christ, saying, "It was the will of the LORD to crush him" (Isa. 53:10). It is this sovereign, efficacious will that can never be thwarted and that always comes to pass. On the other hand, God's *preceptive* will is that aspect of his will that is expressed in the precepts, or commands, of Scripture. God issues to all people the command, or precept, to repent and believe in the gospel (Acts 17:30). Unlike his decretive will, God's preceptive will is thwarted any time someone disobeys any one of God's commands. Third, Scripture also sometimes speaks of God's will to describe God's disposition—what is pleasing to him or that in which he takes delight. We might call this his *optative* will.[76]

Which of these senses fits Peter's statement in 2 Peter 3:9? It cannot be his decretive will, for if God had decreed the repentance of all without exception, all without exception would repent. Yet universal final salvation is at odds with biblical teaching. Neither is it best to characterize this as a statement of his preceptive will, for that would be to say that God forbids that anyone should perish. In this sense, perishing would be against God's law, and he would have to punish people for perishing. It is best to understand this verse as expressing the optative will of God. Peter is describing the same truth about God that Ezekiel did when he recorded God's words: "I have no pleasure in the death of the wicked, but that the wicked turn from his way and live" (Ezek. 33:11). Even though God has not chosen all, and even though the Son has not atoned for all, God nevertheless sincerely desires the good of all his creatures. And though God does take pleasure in the exercise of his justice against sin and evil, he does not maliciously enjoy meting out punishment against his creatures. Thus, God wills the repentance of all people in this optative sense. However, because God is absolutely sovereign, and because not all people do in fact repent, God has not decreed that all should repent. Thus, God does not will the repentance of all people in this decretive sense. Though we may not understand the complexity of God's will, we may not redefine his sovereignty to accommodate our lack of understanding.[77]

Though this answer refutes the universalist interpretation of 2 Peter 3:9, and while

---

75. This is masterfully argued in John Piper, "Are There Two Wills in God?," in *Still Sovereign: Contemporary Perspectives on Election, Foreknowledge, and Grace*, ed. Thomas R. Schreiner and Bruce A. Ware (Grand Rapids, MI: Baker, 2000), 107–31.

76. *Optative* is a grammatical term that describes the mood of verbs expressing a wish or desire (e.g., 2 Thess. 3:16; 1 Pet. 1:2).

77. It should also be noted that the decretive and preceptive wills of God are not two distinct wills but rather two distinguishable aspects of the single will of God. Calvin helpfully explains, "God's will is one and simple in him," but it "appears manifold to us on account of our mental incapacity." Calvin, *Institutes*, 1.18.3.

it is true that God desires the repentance of all according to his optative will (cf. Ezek. 18:23, 32; 33:11), there is an even better way to understand Peter's comment. The recipients of Peter's letter and the immediate context of this passage must be taken into account. In this very verse, Peter addresses those to whom he is speaking, writing that the Lord is "patient toward *you*." When one considers that the "you" to whom he is speaking are the "beloved" of 2 Peter 3:8, "those who have obtained a faith of equal standing with ours, by the righteousness of our God and Savior, Jesus Christ" (2 Pet. 1:1), it must be acknowledged that Peter is addressing the people of God. The Lord Jesus delays his return because he is patient toward those who are his, those whom the Father has given him and for whom he has died but who have not yet come to faith. Thus, this passage does not speak of all people without exception, as the universalist claims, but is restricted by the context to the elect, consistent with a particularist view of the atonement.

Christ Died for the "World." Just as with the word "all," texts that speak of Jesus's death with respect to the "world" must also be interpreted according to their context. In the cases in which they are used to describe the extent of the atonement, they are properly interpreted to mean "all without distinction" rather than "all without exception."

Universalists often claim that John 3:16 decisively settles the matter of the extent of the atonement. Jesus says, "For God so loved the world, that he gave his only Son, that whoever believes in him should not perish but have eternal life." Universalists claim that, by giving his only Son over to a substitutionary and sacrificial death, God has expressed his love for the entire world, which they believe refers to every individual who will have ever lived on the earth. However, nothing in the passage demands that "world" be interpreted to mean "all without exception." In fact, there is good reason to understand it as "all without distinction." In particular, Jesus is discussing salvation with Nicodemus, "a man of the Pharisees . . . [and] a ruler of the Jews" (John 3:1). The Pharisees, like virtually all Israel in Jesus's day, regarded Gentiles as unclean and alienated from the covenant promises of God. As Jesus discusses salvation with this ruler of the Jews, he explains that God's love terminates not only on Israel but also on men and women throughout the whole world—Gentiles as well as Jews. Further, one must note Jesus's own particularism in this very verse. Christ has been given up so that whoever *believes* (Gk. *pas ho pisteuōn*, lit., "all the believing ones") should not perish but have eternal life. Jesus clearly limits the scope of his atoning death to those who will eventually believe in him for salvation.

The universalist alternative would create numerous problems. For instance, if Christ had been sent to atone for every individual without exception, would that not have included those sinners who had already died and were paying for their sins in hell? But for what reason? To give them an opportunity to repent? Yet such an opportunity had passed, for they had already been undergoing divine judgment (cf. Heb. 9:27). An even greater problem would be that, by saying that Christ atoned for people who will finally perish in hell, the universalist necessarily limits the efficacy of Christ's sacrifice. If Christ can atone for someone's sins and that person can still go to hell, then something other than Christ's atonement is ultimately responsible for salvation.

The same is the case for John the Baptist's declaration, "Behold, the Lamb of God, who takes away the sin of the world!" (John 1:29). If Christ takes away the sin of all without exception and yet some still perish in hell, what does it mean to say that their sin was taken away? At this point, the universalist must voice an unstated assumption: "takes away" has been redefined to mean "potentially takes away." Yet this is not what the text says. Again, the atonement Christ achieved was not merely an offer or a potential; he actually secured the salvation of those for whom he died. Thus, to avoid fundamentally undermining the nature of the atonement, one must interpret "world" to refer to Jews and Gentiles—all without distinction, not all without exception.[78]

Similar issues are at play in 1 John 2:2. John writes, "He is the propitiation for our sins, and not for ours only but also for the sins of the whole world." Here we have a statement of the nature of the atonement (propitiation), followed by a statement of the scope or extent of that work (the whole world). A superficial reading of the text at first seems to leave the reader in tension, because propitiation—that is, the actual satisfaction of God's wrath against sin—for all without exception would demand universal final salvation. Yet again, because Scripture teaches that not all will finally be saved (Matt. 7:13, 23; 25:31–46; 2 Thess. 1:9; Rev. 21:8), such an interpretation is untenable.

At this point there are two options. First, the universalist accepts the superficial interpretation of "whole world" to mean "all without exception" and therefore modifies the propitiatory *nature* of the atonement to mean "a potential propitiation." Such an interpretive move, however, militates against everything Scripture teaches concerning the efficacious nature of propitiation. There is no exegetical basis for such an interpretation. The second option is that of the particularist. The particularist interprets the nature of propitiation in accordance with the rest of biblical teaching and seeks a way to understand "whole world" that both avoids doing violence to the grammar, context, and authorial intent of 1 John 1–2 and averts the problematic implications of universalism. Such a way is available. It is to understand "the whole world" to refer to "all without distinction" rather than "all without exception." This option fits better lexically because it respects the Bible's uniform definition of *hilasmos* as the efficacious satisfaction of wrath. It also fits better contextually, for John is writing to churches being harassed by the false teaching of sinless perfectionism (1 John 1:6–10), likely linked to an incipient Gnosticism promising that the key to spiritual victory was found in a secret knowledge that only the Gnostics possessed. Thus, when John writes of the scope of the Savior's accomplishment, he repudiates all vestiges of exclusivism: Christ is not the propitiation for our sins only, whether Jews rather than Gentiles, Gnostics rather than other Christians, or believers in Asia

---

78. The same approach ought to be taken with John 6:33 and John 6:51.

Minor rather than believers throughout the rest of the world. No, he is the propitiation for the sins of God's people scattered throughout the entire world.

Such an interpretation is only confirmed by the syntactical parallel in John 11:49–52. There John reports Caiaphas's prophecy concerning the death of Christ—that one man would die for the people (John 11:50). John then comments: "He did not say this of his own accord, but being high priest that year he prophesied that Jesus would die for the nation, and not for the nation only, but also to gather into one the children of God who are scattered abroad" (John 11:51–52). Note the parallelism:

> John 11:51–52 – . . . that Jesus would die for the nation, and not for the nation only, but also to gather into one the children of God who are scattered abroad.

> 1 John 2:2 – He is the propitiation for our sins, and not for ours only but also for the sins of the whole world.

Thus, this other comment from John's pen would support interpreting "the whole world" in 1 John 2:2 to mean "all without distinction," namely, the children of God who are scattered abroad throughout the whole world (cf. John 10:16). Indeed, in Revelation 5:9, John also writes explicitly of Christ's particular atonement, which he describes as for all without distinction, for the saints sing, "Worthy are you to take the scroll and to open its seals, for you were slain, and by your blood you ransomed people for God from every tribe and language and people and nation." John does not say that the Lamb ransomed every tribe and language and people and nation, which would fit the universalist interpretation, but that he ransomed people *from* every tribe and language and people and nation—that is, not all without exception but all without distinction.

With regard to 1 John 2:2, then, the particularist interpretation of "the whole world" fits the language, context, and authorial intent of the passage, does not contradict any other passage of Scripture, parallels other passages John wrote, and avoids the undesirable interpretive conclusions of either universal final salvation or an inefficacious propitiation, one of which is unavoidable in the universalist interpretation. Thus, the particularist interpretation is both biblically and theologically preferable.

Finally, Paul's comment in 2 Corinthians 5:19 must be addressed. He writes, "In Christ God was reconciling the world to himself, not counting their trespasses against them, and entrusting to us the message of reconciliation." Again, the immediate context guides the interpreter to read "world" not as "all without exception" but "all without distinction throughout the whole world." Paul immediately defines God's action of reconciliation as "not counting their trespasses against them." The only people whose trespasses God does not count against them are those who receive the blessing of salvation (Rom. 4:6–8). Unless one is prepared to adopt universal final salvation, this must refer to the elect alone. The previous verse also confirms this reading, since "the world" in 2 Corinthians 5:19 is coextensive with the "us" of 5:18—that is, those of us whom God has reconciled to himself through Christ. Once again, universalistic language proves to complement a limited extent of the atonement.

Christ Died for Those Who Will Finally Perish. A final set of texts must be addressed. These texts suggest that those who are the objects of Christ's death may finally perish for their sins in hell. Paul seems to make the same point in two texts:

> For if your brother is grieved by what you eat, you are no longer walking in love. By what you eat, do not destroy [Gk. *apollye*] the one for whom Christ died. (Rom. 14:15)

> And so by your knowledge this weak person is destroyed [Gk. *apollytai*], the brother for whom Christ died. (1 Cor. 8:11)

Here Paul's concern is that a believer whose strong conscience allows him to enjoy the Christian liberty of eating meat sacrificed to idols may cause a weaker brother to stumble. In both cases, the weaker brother is described as one "for whom Christ died," and also in both cases, the weaker brother faces the prospect of being destroyed. For this concept of destruction, Paul employs the Greek term *apollymi*, which he often uses to describe perishing in eternal punishment (cf. Rom. 2:12; 1 Cor. 1:18; 15:18; 2 Cor. 2:15; 4:3; 2 Thess. 2:10).

Though this line of thinking would seem to offer a significant challenge, one must keep in mind that the authors of Scripture often "can refer to those who may finally perish as, for a time, visibly possessing all the descriptions of genuine believers."[79] Smeaton calls this "the judgment of charity."[80] That is, they represented themselves as truly belonging to the covenant community and thus were regarded and spoken of as true believers while they remained in the church. In this way, John speaks of Judas as one of Jesus's disciples (John 12:4); the author of Hebrews addresses his many warnings to the "brethren," though the church includes a mix of believers and unbelievers (e.g., Heb. 3:12–4:7); and Peter speaks of the false teachers as those whom the sovereign Lord bought (2 Pet. 2:1). However, their eventual departure from the covenant community demonstrates that they never truly belonged to Christ, for nothing can separate the true believer from the love of Christ (Rom. 8:35–39; cf. John 10:27–30; Phil. 1:6). Thus, while the abuse of Christian liberty has the potential to "grieve" (Rom. 14:15) and "wound the conscience" of (1 Cor. 8:12) the weaker brother, a true brother for whom Christ died will never finally be lost. If such a person does fall away from the faith, they reveal themselves to have never truly been a brother in the first place (1 John 2:19).

Related to this is Peter's comment concerning the false teachers in 2 Peter 2:1: "But false prophets also arose among the people, just as there will be false teachers among you, who will secretly bring in destructive heresies, even denying the Master who bought them, bringing upon themselves swift destruction." Here Peter indicates that the false teachers were "bought" or "redeemed" (Gk. *agorazō*) by the Master (Gk. *despotēs*) and yet will nevertheless face eternal destruction. Thus, universalists argue that Christ the Master died for all without exception, even purchasing the false

---

79. Gibson, "For Whom Did Christ Die?," 322.

80. George Smeaton, *The Apostles' Doctrine of the Atonement* (1870; repr., Carlisle, PA: Banner of Truth, 2009), 447.

teachers, but that because they are never truly saved, they will not finally partake of the saving benefits of Christ's death.

However, at least five considerations prompt us to reject this interpretation. First, in all but one instance in the New Testament (Jude 4), the word "Master" (Gk. *despotēs*) is used to indicate not the Son but the Father. Thus, Christ's redeeming work on the cross is likely not in view here. Second, Long explains,

> Of its thirty occurrences in the New Testament, *agorazō* is never used in a soteriological context (unless 2 Peter 2:1 is the exception) without the technical term "price" (*timēs*—a technical term for the blood of Christ) or its equivalent being stated or made explicit in the context (see 1 Cor. 6:20; 7:23; Rev. 5:9; 14:3, 4).[81]

That is, it is very likely that Peter is using *agorazō* in a nonsoteriological sense. Third, Peter is clearly alluding to Deuteronomy 32:6, which says, "Do you thus repay the LORD, O foolish and unwise people? Is not He your Father who has bought you? He has made you and established you" (NASB). The language of "denying the Master who bought them" serves to identify the false teachers of Peter's day with the false prophets of Israel. Fourth, it is likely that Peter is granting, for the sake of argument, the premise that the false teachers are true believers. In other words, as Schreiner says, "It *appeared as if* the Lord had purchased the false teachers with his blood [2 Pet. 2:1], though they actually did not truly belong to the Lord."[82] Peter is thus sarcastically saying, "These who claim to be redeemed deny by their deeds and their doctrine the Master whom they claim has bought them. They are no better than the false prophets of Israel." Fifth, if taken to its logical conclusion, the universalist interpretation denies not only an efficacious redemption—which Scripture explicitly affirms (Eph. 1:7; Col. 1:14)—but also the doctrine of the perseverance of the saints, that is, that one who is truly redeemed cannot be lost (John 10:27–30; Rom. 8:31–39; 1 John 2:19).

SUMMARY

In summary, though several texts of Scripture employ universalistic language with respect to the scope of Christ's death, not one text stands under exegetical scrutiny as support for an unlimited atonement. Rather, when interpreted in context, passages that refer to Christ's death for "all" and for "the world" are used to speak of all without distinction, not all without exception, and passages that might seem to indicate that those for whom Christ died can finally perish in their sins are shown to teach no such thing.

Because Scripture reveals (1) that the three persons of the Trinity are entirely united in their saving will and purpose, (2) that atonement is never potential or provisional but always actual and efficacious, (3) that Christ's High Priestly ministry of sacrifice is coextensive with his High Priestly ministry of intercession, (4) that several passages of Scripture speak of Christ's atoning work in particularistic terms, and (5) that no

---

81. Gary D. Long, *Definite Atonement* (Nutley, NJ: Presbyterian and Reformed, 1976), 72.
82. Thomas R. Schreiner, "'Problematic Texts' for Definite Atonement in the Pastoral and General Epistles," in Gibson and Gibson, *From Heaven He Came and Sought Her*, 390.

passage of Scripture teaches that Christ atoned for all without exception, therefore Scripture teaches that the extent of Christ's atonement is not universal but is limited to the elect alone.

Resurrection, Ascension, and Intercession

It is also necessary to mention that Christ's intercessory work was not exhausted at the cross. He was not only "delivered up for our trespasses"; he was also "raised for our justification" (Rom. 4:25). Further, he also ascended to the right hand of the Father to rule over all things (Eph. 1:20–23), in which place believers are said to be seated with him (Eph. 2:6). Because he ascended, he sent the Holy Spirit to permanently indwell every member of his church (John 14:17; 16:7) and to empower us for holiness and service. Further still, he presently intercedes for us at the right hand of the Father (Rom. 8:34; Heb. 7:25), praying for our greatest spiritual benefit, defending us against our Accuser, sanctifying our prayers, and ministering to us in our time of need (cf. Heb. 4:16).[83]

The culmination of our study of the accomplishment of redemption must be to worship the triune God for the work of the Son. Accurate theology must always issue in transcendent doxology. Satan has an excellent theology of the atonement; the demons believe and shudder (James 2:19). While Satan and the demons may be excellent students of the work of Christ, they are not beneficiaries of the Son's atonement. But we his people *are* beneficiaries. And so we conclude our study of the atonement of Christ with the song of the saints and angels in Revelation 5:9–13:

> Worthy are you to take the scroll
>   and to open its seals,
> for you were slain, and by your blood you ransomed people for God
>   from every tribe and language and people and nation,
> and you have made them a kingdom and priests to our God,
>   and they shall reign on the earth. . . .
>
> Worthy is the Lamb who was slain,
> to receive power and wealth and wisdom and might
> and honor and glory and blessing! . . .
>
> To him who sits on the throne and to the Lamb
> be blessing and honor and glory and might forever and ever!

The Application of Redemption

The Order of Salvation
The External Call: Gospel Proclamation
The Internal Call: Regeneration
Conversion
Union with Christ
Justification

---

83. For more on Christ's resurrection, ascension, and present intercession, see chap. 4, "God the Son."

Adoption
Sanctification
Perseverance
Glorification

One of the most significant characteristics of the saving work of the Lord Jesus Christ is that his work is sufficient and effective. The Son of God is no potential Savior. He did not merely "do his part" to secure the salvation of his people, only to leave the decisive determination up to them. Indeed, as he prayed to his Father on the eve of his betrayal and arrest, he declared that he had decisively accomplished the work that the Father had given him to do (John 17:4). On the cross, as he drank not only the jar of sour wine but the bitter cup of his Father's wrath, absorbing in his own person the full punishment for the sins of his people (2 Cor. 5:21; Gal. 3:13; 1 Pet. 2:24), he cried out victoriously, "It is finished!" (John 19:30). In that moment, the Savior of the world infallibly secured the salvation of his people once for all (Rom. 6:10; Heb. 7:27; 10:10). The Son's mission of redemption was fully accomplished.

Because of the sufficiency of Christ's atoning work, if a believer is asked when God saved him, there is a sense in which he ought to reply, "Two thousand years ago." And yet no one comes into this world saved. We are all brought forth in iniquity (Ps. 51:5), dead in our trespasses and sins (Eph. 2:1), by nature children of wrath (Eph. 2:3), and enemies of God (Rom. 5:10; 8:7–8). Though all the blessings of salvation were purchased once for all at the cross, the people of God do not enjoy the benefits of Christ's work until the Holy Spirit applies those blessings to individual believers—until they are born of the Spirit unto repentance and faith, are united to Christ, and are thereby justified, adopted, and set apart for a life of holiness and service to God. It is for this reason that we must distinguish between the accomplishment of redemption and the application of redemption.

In the wisdom of God, the Holy Spirit does not immediately, at conversion, apply to the believer all the fullness of the benefits secured by Christ's work. Instead, these blessings are imparted to us progressively, in stages. For example, sanctification is promised but progressive; we do not receive the spiritual blessing of glorification in the same moment that we are converted. Though we might have preferred to be immediately freed from the presence of sin the moment we believed, God has planned glorification to be the consummation of a lifelong journey of progressive sanctification. Further, even those aspects of salvation that are applied simultaneously are nevertheless to be properly distinguished from one another. For instance, although we are justified and adopted in the same moment (i.e., when we are granted saving faith), both justification and adoption are unique blessings. Collapsing one of them into the other robs each of its distinctive glory. Like a precious diamond, the glory of the application of redemption is multifaceted and is only fully comprehended as each individual facet contributes to the brilliance of the whole. Thus, the study of soteriology is concerned to explore the distinctiveness of each aspect of the application of redemption.

The Order of Salvation

Not only are these aspects of salvation distinct from one another, but they are also logically, and sometimes chronologically, related to one another. The *ordo salutis*, a Latin phrase that means "order of salvation," aims to define these logical and chronological relationships between the various stages of the application of redemption.[84]

Some have questioned whether it is proper even to attempt such a thing, since they contend that the Bible does not provide us with a detailed *ordo salutis*. However, while no text is devoted to explicitly spelling out the order of salvation, there is a significant scriptural basis for recognizing such an order. In some cases, the biblical definition of a particular doctrine insists on even a chronological order. For example, the doctrine of glorification describes the application of salvation unto its consummation, when Christ "will transform our lowly body to be like his glorious body" (Phil. 3:21). This is not a present reality for believers but a prospect that we await eagerly (Rom. 8:23; Phil. 3:20). When the Spirit says, "Now salvation is nearer than when we believed" (Rom. 13:11), this recognizes a definite order with respect to glorification; it is the last of the blessings of salvation to be applied to God's people. In other cases, the relationship of two or more of these aspects of salvation is explicitly defined in the text. An example of this comes in John 1:12, where John says, "But to all who did receive [Jesus], who believed in his name, he gave the right to become children of God." This text teaches that the legal right to become God's children—that is, to be given the grace of adoption—is conditioned on receiving and believing in Jesus. Thus, even if the grace of adoption is conferred at the precise moment one believes, faith is nevertheless *logically* prior to adoption. Similarly, numerous passages in Scripture testify that one is justified by faith (e.g., Rom. 3:28; 5:1), which is to say that faith is the instrumental cause of justification. Thus, faith must logically precede justification, just as it precedes adoption.

These few examples demonstrate clearly that the concept of an order of salvation is not foreign to the biblical text. Indeed, to suggest that glorification is anything but the last step in the application of redemption or to suggest that faith is given subsequent to justification would be to violate the plain sense of the above passages. Therefore, to speak of logical order or priority is not to unnaturally foist "human logic" on the text of Scripture. Instead, it is to read out of the text the divine logic and order that the Spirit of God himself has plainly revealed. This is the goal of a biblical *ordo salutis*.

THE *ORDO SALUTIS* AND ROMANS 8:29–30

The clearest single text that speaks to the order of salvation is Romans 8:29–30. There Paul writes, "For those whom he foreknew he also predestined to be conformed to

---

84. It is important to recognize this distinction between logical and chronological order. For example, when theologians posit that regeneration precedes faith in the *ordo salutis*, in most cases they are not suggesting that a gap of time separates the two, as if someone may be born again for several months and then later come to faith in Christ. Rather, they are saying that there is a causal relationship between the two, namely, that regeneration is the logical cause of faith. Though they are temporally simultaneous, occurring in the exact same moment, they are logically distinct. To say that regeneration precedes faith, then, is merely to say that one must be born again in order to believe, rather than that he must believe in order to be born again. This distinction between logical and chronological order must be kept in mind if one is to have any hope of understanding the *ordo salutis*.

the image of his Son, in order that he might be the firstborn among many brothers. And those whom he predestined he also called, and those whom he called he also justified, and those whom he justified he also glorified." As we examine this text, we will discover the beginnings of an *ordo salutis.*

First, it must be observed that the events of salvation outlined in this passage exceed the boundaries of merely the application of redemption, for the foreknowledge and predestination of the elect mentioned here reach back to the Father's eternal plan of redemption.[85] Nevertheless, they fit naturally into a definite order. Even the prefixes of both words—"fore-" and "pre-" (Gk. *pro-*)—speak of the fact that foreknowledge and predestination are antecedent to the later aspects of redemption. Their use elsewhere in Scripture also testifies to this order, as both terms appear with the phrase "before the foundation of the world" in other salvific contexts (Eph. 1:4–5; 1 Pet. 1:20). Thus, the eternal counsel of the Trinity, in which the Father set his electing love on those whom he meant to save, anchors all the saving activity that takes place in the accomplishment and application of redemption.

Second, Paul lists glorification last in this sequence. We have already demonstrated that glorification is the final feature in the application of redemption, as it describes the eradication of sin and infirmity from our present bodies, truly and consummately saving us from sin and all its effects (Rom. 8:19–25; 1 Cor. 15:50–57; Phil. 3:20–21). Therefore, no matter how any other elements of salvation relate to one another, it is certain that glorification must be last in the *ordo salutis.* Calling and justification must precede glorification.

What, then, is the relationship between calling and justification? In the first place, it is to be observed that the calling Paul has in view here is the effectual call of God that results in salvation (e.g., 1 Cor. 1:9, 24, 26; 2 Tim. 1:9; 2 Pet. 1:3, 10; cf. John 11:43–44),[86] rather than a general calling that may be rejected (e.g., Matt. 22:14; Acts 7:51). This is so because he says that all those who are thus called are also justified and glorified (Rom. 8:30). No one who hears this calling fails to receive the saving blessings of justification and glorification. Second, given that Paul lists foreknowledge and predestination first and glorification last, it is sound to conclude that he has a definite order in mind as he enumerates these various aspects of salvation. Thus, because he lists calling before justification, it is proper to understand that calling precedes justification. Therefore, the order of the application of redemption as presented in Romans 8:30 is effectual call, justification, and then glorification.

THE *ORDO SALUTIS* AND OTHER NEW TESTAMENT TEXTS

Romans 8:29–30 does not exhaustively treat every aspect of the application of redemption. There is no mention of regeneration, faith, or sanctification, among

---

85. For a more thorough development of the doctrines of foreknowledge and predestination and their place in the divine plan of redemption, see "The Decree of Election" (p. 493).

86. Though a full definition and discussion of *effectual call* awaits the treatment of the doctrine of calling, we may here define it as God calling the sinner out of his deadness and, by the creative power of that call, imparting spiritual life to him, enabling him to believe in Christ for salvation.

other saving benefits. To understand where these other doctrines fit in the order of salvation, we must examine the rest of the New Testament.[87]

In the first place, it may be easiest to place the gift of faith in the order of salvation, since Scripture is clear that faith is the condition of justification. Sinners are said to be justified "by faith" (Rom. 3:28; 5:1; Gal. 3:24), "through faith" (Gal. 2:16), and "on faith" (Phil. 3:9). A sinner will not be declared righteous in God's sight unless he believes, and it is only through the instrumentality of faith that he will lay hold of the righteousness of God in Christ. Thus, it is proper to place faith before justification, and because faith is itself the instrumental cause[88] of justification, nothing ought to come between them. Therefore, we may add faith to our *ordo salutis* as follows: effectual call, faith, justification, and then glorification.

Further, we must also consider that saving faith is always a repentant faith, for the faith that turns to Christ for salvation necessarily turns away from sin and self-righteousness (Acts 26:17–18; 1 Thess. 1:9). This is why the gospel is preached as a call to both repent and believe (Mark 1:14–15; Acts 20:21), for one cannot exist without the other. Repentance is so vital to saving faith that the apostle James says that to sever them is to kill faith, for faith without works (i.e., "fruits in keeping with repentance," Luke 3:8) is dead (James 2:17, 26). Such is no true and saving faith but is utterly useless (James 2:20). Further, faith and repentance are so intimately tied to one another that Scripture often speaks of one when both are implied. For example, when the men are convicted by Peter's sermon at Pentecost and ask him what they must do to be saved, Peter answers, "Repent and be baptized every one of you in the name of Jesus Christ for the forgiveness of your sins" (Acts 2:38). Yet when the Philippian jailer is similarly convicted and asks Paul and Silas the same question, they respond, "Believe in the Lord Jesus, and you will be saved" (Acts 16:31). Unless one is prepared to accept the absurd notion that Peter and Paul preached different gospels, it is plain that the repentance that saves is a believing repentance and that the faith that saves is a repentant faith (cf. Matt. 4:17; Luke 24:47; John 3:16; 20:31). Thus, repentance and faith are two sides of the same coin, and together they constitute conversion (cf. Acts 15:3). And because one must logically turn *from* something before he can turn *to* something else, repentance is placed before faith. Therefore, our order stands as follows: effectual call, conversion (repentance and faith), justification, and then glorification.

Significant disagreement surrounds the relationship between regeneration and faith, yet Scripture seems to clearly present faith as the consequence of the new birth. In the first place, because the natural man is dead in sin (Eph. 2:1–3) and thus unable to understand and accept the things of the Spirit of God (1 Cor. 2:14), he is absolutely incapable of faith until the Spirit quickens spiritual life in him. For this reason, Jesus says, "No one can come to me unless it is granted him by the Father" (John 6:65). Second, Jesus declares that the new birth is the prerequisite for seeing (John 3:3)

---

87. Again, a full definition and discussion of each of these doctrines awaits their treatment later in this chapter.
88. See Wallace, *Greek Grammar Beyond the Basics*, 431–35.

and entering (John 3:5) the kingdom of God. Seeing the kingdom is undoubtedly a figure of speech for exercising saving faith (cf. Heb. 11:1), and it cannot be disputed that one enters the kingdom at conversion (i.e., when the sinner repents and believes the gospel). It follows, then, that the new birth is logically prior to faith. Third, the apostle John says, "Everyone who believes that Jesus is the Christ has been born of God" (1 John 5:1). The verb tenses in this verse are significant. "Everyone who believes" (Gk. *Pas ho pisteuōn*) is a present participle, which describes present, continuous action. "Has been born of God" (Gk. *ek tou theou gegennētai*) translates a perfect indicative, which describes an action in the past whose results continue into the present. Thus, John declares that everyone who presently believes in Jesus *has been* born of God. The very same relationship (as evidenced by identical grammatical constructions) exists between the new birth and the practice of righteousness (1 John 2:29), love (1 John 4:7), and overcoming the world (1 John 5:4). Yet none of these precedes—and still less, causes—regeneration. Finally, there is good reason to believe that calling and regeneration speak of two aspects of the same reality, namely, the summons to spiritual life on the one hand and the impartation of spiritual life on the other.[89] If calling and regeneration can be thus identified with one another, it is understandable that when Paul speaks of calling in Romans 8:30, he does not need to include regeneration, for he conceives of them as one and the same act. Since it has already been demonstrated that faith is subsequent to calling, it is sound to conclude that while they are temporally simultaneous, regeneration logically precedes and gives birth to faith. Therefore, we may continue building our *ordo salutis*: effectual call / regeneration, conversion (repentance and faith), justification, and then glorification.

At this point the remaining aspects of the application of redemption are relatively easy to place. As with justification, believers are said to lay hold of the grace of adoption by faith (John 1:12; Gal. 3:26). This is good cause for considering justification and adoption to be contemporaneous blessings. However, it is proper that adoption should logically follow justification. Indeed, believers could not be justly given the legal rights of life in the family of God while they remained destitute of a right standing before him. God must first declare us righteous before welcoming us into the family of the One "whose name is Holy" (Isa. 57:15). Further, the faith by which we lay hold of justification and adoption is a faith that continuously works through love (Gal. 5:6). While regeneration, conversion, justification, and adoption all occur instantaneously, sanctification is a progressive process that takes place throughout the Christian life (2 Cor. 3:18). Thus, sanctification is subsequent to adoption but prior to glorification. The sanctification process is marked by the believer's persevering in faith (Matt. 24:13) and growing in the assurance of salvation (2 Pet. 1:10; 1 John 5:13).

---

89. In 2 Cor. 4:6, Paul compares the creation of the world by God's word (cf. Gen. 1:3; Ps. 33:6) to the regeneration of the sinner by God's word (cf. James 1:18; 1 Pet. 1:23, 25). When speaking of the creation of the world, we do not distinguish God's command to create from his act of creation. He literally spoke the universe into existence. We ought to take the same approach to the creation of spiritual life in the sinner. The call itself creates the life that it commands. Thus the effectual call ought to be identified with regeneration. For an excellent defense of this view, see appendix 3 of Matthew Barrett, *Reclaiming Monergism: The Case for Sovereign Grace in Effectual Calling and Regeneration* (Phillipsburg, NJ: P&R, 2013).

Therefore, based on the foregoing biblical analysis, we find Scripture to provide the following *ordo salutis*:

1. Foreknowledge / predestination / election (God's choice of some unto salvation)
2. Effectual call / regeneration (the new birth)
3. Conversion (repentance and faith)
4. Justification (declaration of right legal standing)
5. Adoption (placed into the family of God)
6. Sanctification (progressive growth in holiness)
7. Perseverance (remaining in Christ)
8. Glorification (receiving a resurrection body)

The first of these saving blessings is pretemporal and precedes even the application of redemption. Steps two through five all occur simultaneously at the time one becomes a Christian. Steps six and seven occur throughout the remainder of the Christian life. Finally, step eight completes the application of redemption at the return of Christ. We turn now to a more thorough discussion of these doctrines concerning the application of redemption.

The External Call: Gospel Proclamation

As mentioned previously, when Paul speaks of the doctrine of divine calling in Romans 8:30, he has in mind God's effectual call, or regeneration, whereby God sovereignly summons the sinner out of spiritual death and into spiritual life. In fact, when the New Testament Epistles speak of divine calling, in every case they are referring to this internal, effectual call. Certainly, the Gospels speak of another call, often termed the external call, the general call, or the gospel call. This refers to the verbal proclamation of the gospel by which all sinners are called to turn from their sin and trust in Christ for salvation (Matt. 22:14). In other words, there is a distinction between the call of God (the internal call) and the call of the preacher (the external call). The internal call is given only to the elect and always brings the sinner to salvation. By contrast, the external call is given to all people without distinction and is often rejected. Because of this, the external call does not properly belong to the *ordo salutis*, for the saving benefits of Christ's redemption are always and only effectually applied to the elect. Nevertheless, because the external call of the gospel is the means by which God issues the effectual call of regeneration, it is a requisite component in the study of the application of redemption.

THE NECESSITY OF THE EXTERNAL CALL

Romans 10:13 declares that the external call is essential for the sinner to be able to "call" on the Lord for salvation:

> For "everyone who calls on the name of the Lord will be saved."
> How then will they call on him in whom they have not believed? And how are they to believe in him of whom they have never heard? And how are they to

hear without someone preaching? And how are they to preach unless they are sent? As it is written, "How beautiful are the feet of those who preach the good news!" But they have not all obeyed the gospel. For Isaiah says, "Lord, who has believed what he has heard from us?" So faith comes from hearing, and hearing through the word of Christ. (Rom. 10:13–17)

This text clearly indicates that proclaiming the message of the gospel is absolutely imperative to people being saved. Sin has penetrated to the core of man's being, so that he is a sinner not only by choice but by nature (cf. Rom. 8:7; 1 Cor. 2:14; Eph. 2:3; 4:17–18). Because of this, God's revelation of himself in the natural world (Rom. 1:19–20) is sufficient to render all inexcusably guilty before God and to convict men of their sinfulness and the coming judgment both temporally (1:21–31) and eternally (1:32). The solution to the damning spiritual condition of mankind is not found, however, in natural revelation, nor by the sinner looking within himself or to his own resources. For salvation to come to anyone, the gospel message of the life, death, burial, and resurrection of the Son of God, sent from heaven to save sinners by grace through faith apart from works, must be proclaimed to them.

Hear what the Spirit of God says in 1 Corinthians 1:18–21:

For the word of the cross is folly to those who are perishing, but to us who are being saved it is the power of God. For it is written,

"I will destroy the wisdom of the wise,
    and the discernment of the discerning I will thwart."

Where is the one who is wise? Where is the scribe? Where is the debater of this age? Has not God made foolish the wisdom of the world? For since, in the wisdom of God, the world did not know God through wisdom, it pleased God through the folly of what we preach to save those who believe.

This is so because the word of truth is the means by which God brings about the new birth (James 1:18). As the apostle Peter declares, "You have been born again, not of perishable seed but of imperishable, through the living and abiding word of God" (1 Pet. 1:23). Two verses later he adds, "And this word is the good news that was preached to you" (1 Pet. 1:25). Thus, gospel preaching is a prerequisite for salvation, because it is by means of the message preached that sinners are awakened to new life. For this reason, the gospel is hailed as "the power of God for salvation" (Rom. 1:16–17; cf. 1 Cor. 1:18). It is by the foolishness of the message preached that God is pleased to save those who believe. Therefore, we must send preachers of the gospel.

THE ELEMENTS OF THE EXTERNAL CALL

In light of the fact that the external call of the gospel is essential to the salvation of sinners, it is imperative that we understand what truly constitutes that call. At least three elements must be communicated in the proclamation of the gospel. In the first place, the gospel preacher must explain the facts of God's holiness, man's sinfulness, and the work of Christ in accomplishing redemption. God is the Creator of all things (Ps. 24:1), and as his creature, man is accountable to God, his Judge. God is perfectly holy (Matt. 5:48); he is the essence of all that is good—so much so that he can have absolutely no fellowship with anyone who falls short of moral perfection (1 John 1:5; cf. James 2:10). And yet Scripture declares that all people have sinned against God by breaking his law and therefore fall short of the perfect standard of righteousness that is required for fellowship with him (Rom. 3:23). The verdict pronounced over the whole of mankind is, "None is righteous, no, not one" (Rom. 3:10), and the resulting sentence is death: "For the wages of sin is death" (Rom. 6:23). Because sin against an infinitely holy God demands an infinite punishment, this death is not merely physical or temporal but also spiritual and eternal. The just punishment for all sin is hell: conscious torment forever away from the saving presence of the Lord (Matt. 13:50; 25:46; 2 Thess. 1:9; Rev. 14:11).

It is into this miserable state of affairs that God steps forth in sovereign grace. While man was helpless under the weight of sin with no way to pay its penalty and escape its results (Rom. 5:6), God the Son became a man (1) to live the perfectly righteous life that the sons of Adam had failed to live and (2) to die a substitutionary death in the place of his people (Rom. 5:6, 8), absorbing in his own person the full penalty of the Father's wrath against their sin (Isa. 53:6; 2 Cor. 5:21; 1 Pet. 2:24). After dying in the stead of sinners, he was buried, and on the third day, he rose from the dead in triumph over sin and death (Rom. 4:25; 1 Cor. 15:4; Heb. 2:14–18) and ascended to the right hand of the Father in heaven (Eph. 1:20–23). Unless a preacher accurately explains man's predicament in sin and the incarnation, Christ's substitutionary atonement, and the resurrection of the Lord Jesus, the gospel has not been preached.

While believing these facts of the gospel is absolutely essential to salvation, that is not sufficient; indeed, even the demons believe true facts about God and his gospel (James 2:19). For a sinner to have a saving interest in Christ, he must respond to these facts by turning from sin and trusting in Christ for righteousness. Therefore, a second essential element of the external call is the preacher's earnest call for the sinner to repent and believe. The Lord Jesus himself modeled this kind of gospel preaching; Mark says that he came "proclaiming the gospel of God, and saying, 'The time is fulfilled, and the kingdom of God is at hand; repent and believe in the gospel'" (Mark 1:14–15). The apostolic gospel message is characterized as "repentance toward God" and "faith in our Lord Jesus Christ" (Acts 20:21; cf. 1 Thess. 1:9). That is to say, a biblical gospel presentation calls sinners to (1) acknowledge their sin and guilt before God (Luke 15:18), (2) abandon all hope of attaining forgiveness by good works (Heb. 6:1), (3) forsake their life ruled by sin and self (Isa. 55:7; Luke 9:23), and (4) put all their trust in the righteousness of Christ alone for being accepted by and reconciled to God (Rom. 10:4, 9; Phil. 3:4–9). Only by repentant faith may a sinner subjectively lay hold of the benefits objectively purchased by Christ. Further, because this is the sinner's only hope for life and salvation, this call to repent and believe is to be delivered with the utmost urgency. Preachers must not present Christ to the sinner in a cold and disinterested manner; rather, driven by the fear of the Lord (2 Cor. 5:11), they are to earnestly persuade and implore men to "be reconciled to God" (2 Cor. 5:20).

A third necessary element of the external call is the promise of forgiveness of sins and eternal life. As we call sinners to repentance and faith, we must present to them the incomparable blessings promised to those who are obedient to the gospel call. As with the other elements, we see examples of this element in the preaching of Jesus and the apostles. In John 3:16, Jesus promises that the one who believes in him will not perish but will have eternal life. In his Pentecost sermon, after Peter issued the call for repentance, he proclaimed to the Jews the promise of the forgiveness of sins (Acts 2:38; cf. 3:19). And Paul stated it explicitly in his sermon at Pisidian Antioch: "Let it be known to you therefore, brothers, that through this man forgiveness of sins is proclaimed to you, and by him everyone who believes is freed from everything from which you could not be freed by the law of Moses" (Acts 13:38–39). Ultimately, the greatest promise of the gospel is that sinners once alienated from God can be reconciled to a right relationship with him (Eph. 2:18; 1 Pet. 3:18). This reconciliation is so intimate that the sinner is given the right to become a child of God (John 1:12). Therefore, a God-centered gospel presentation will not only proclaim the magnificent promises of forgiveness and eternal life but will also declare that eternal life consists in the knowledge of and communion with the triune God (John 17:3) and will present him, the Giver, as the gospel's greatest gift.

THE CHARACTERISTICS OF THE EXTERNAL CALL

The external call to salvation as presented in the gospel is marked by several key characteristics. First, it is a general, or universal, call. That is, the good news of repentance and faith for the forgiveness of sins is to be proclaimed to all people without distinction. Whereas the internal call of regeneration is given only to the elect, the external call of the gospel is to be preached indiscriminately to elect and reprobate alike. Some desiring to exalt God's absolute sovereignty contradict this teaching by insisting that since God intends to save only the elect, his preachers ought to proclaim the gospel to them alone. However, not only is that impossible (for we have no means by which to distinguish the elect from the rest of humanity), it is patently contrary to Scripture. God represents himself as earnestly desiring that the wicked should repent (Ezek. 18:23, 32; 33:11; cf. 2 Cor. 5:20), and in accordance with that desire, he exuberantly calls all people to himself: "Come, everyone who thirsts, come to the waters; and he who has no money, come, buy and eat! Come, buy wine and milk without money and without price. . . . Incline your ear and come to me; hear, that your soul may live" (Isa. 55:1, 3). He entreats sinners to seek him, and is eager to have compassion on them and to forgive them (Isa. 55:6–7). Without discrimination he commands "all the ends of the earth" to turn to him and be saved (Isa. 45:22). The depth and breadth of divine compassion is also fully manifest in the

One who is the exact representation of the Father's nature. If it were the case that gospel preachers ought to limit the external call to the elect alone, surely we would find such an example in Jesus's ministry, for, unlike us, he knew full well who the elect were. And yet our Lord made no such discriminations but preached the gospel even to those who rejected him (Matt. 22:2–14; Luke 14:16–24), inviting everyone who was weary to find rest in him (Matt. 11:28–30). This universality is represented in the church's Great Commission to "make disciples of all nations" (Matt. 28:19; cf. Luke 24:47) and to "preach the gospel to every creature" (Mark 16:15 NKJV). Thus it is no surprise to see it modeled in apostolic preaching, as Paul declared to the philosophers on Mars Hill that God "commands all people everywhere to repent" (Acts 17:30). Indeed, the universality of the gospel call cannot be denied.

A second characteristic of the external call is that it is a sincere, bona fide offer. Some object that because God intends only to save those to whom he has chosen to grant repentance and faith, the universal call of the gospel cannot be genuine on God's part. This is nothing less than a blasphemous accusation from those who have exalted their own reasoning above God's revelation. As has been demonstrated, God truly does call all to repentance, and he represents himself as sincerely desiring the repentance of the wicked. He asks, "Have I any pleasure in the death of the wicked . . . and not rather that he should turn from his way and live?" (Ezek. 18:23; cf. 18:32; 33:11). Can anyone doubt the sincerity of the God who says, "Oh, that my people would listen to me, that Israel would walk in my ways!" (Ps. 81:13)? Indeed, he says of Israel, "All day long I have held out my hands to a disobedient and contrary people" (Rom. 10:21). While it may be difficult to understand how statements of compassion toward the nonelect can be reconciled with the doctrines of sovereign election and particular redemption, it is not an option to conclude that God does not mean what he says! As Berkhof comments,

> The external calling is a calling in good faith, a calling that is seriously meant. It is not an invitation coupled with the hope that it will not be accepted. When God calls the sinner to accept Christ by faith, He earnestly desires this; and when He promises those who repent and believe eternal life, His promise is dependable. This follows from the very nature, from the veracity, of God. It is blasphemous to think that God would be guilty of equivocation and deception, that He would say one thing and mean another, that He would earnestly plead with the sinner to repent and believe unto salvation, and at the same time not desire it in any sense of the word.[90]

The God who "has mercy on whomever he wills" and "hardens whomever he wills" (Rom. 9:18) is the God who takes no pleasure in the death of the wicked. To reason that the former is incompatible with the latter is not an option for the Bible-believing Christian. The offer of the salvation communicated in the external call of the gospel is conditioned on repentance and faith. For it to be a genuine, well-meant offer on God's part, he simply has to be sincerely disposed to provide the promised

---

90. Berkhof, *Systematic Theology*, 462.

blessings upon the satisfaction of the offer's conditions.[91] And this is precisely the case; if anyone repents and trusts in Christ, God *will* forgive and save him. However, such repentance and faith are impossible for the natural man (Rom. 8:7–8; 1 Cor. 2:14). Apart from regenerating grace, no man will ever repent and believe. Thus, in the case of the nonelect, the conditions of the offer will never be met. To suggest that God's offer is insincere—indeed, that he feigns sincerity!—because he does not provide the necessary grace to overcome man's depravity is to suppose that God is obligated to give grace to all. To such a notion the Lord himself responds, "Am I not allowed to do what I choose with what belongs to me?" (Matt. 20:15). The potter has the right over the clay "to make out of the same lump one vessel for honorable use and another for dishonorable use" (Rom. 9:21). God is not obligated to give grace to any man, let alone all men. The deficiency in the gospel call lies in man's depravity, not in any supposed parsimony in God's grace. To suggest such a thing approaches the highest strains of blasphemy.

Finally, a third characteristic of the external call is that, in and of itself, it is not efficacious. Unlike the effectual call in which man is summoned irresistibly to spiritual life (e.g., 1 Cor. 1:9; cf. John 6:44, 65) and is of necessity justified and eventually glorified (Rom. 8:30), the external call can be resisted. Jesus makes this distinction in his conclusion to the parable of the wedding banquet: "For many are called, but few are chosen" (Matt. 22:14). That is, many are invited to partake in the feast of the blessings of eternal life, yet because the Father has only chosen some and not all, few are effectually called. Therefore, many who are invited reject the external call. Any instance in which the gospel is preached and rejected is evidence for the inherent inefficacy of the external call (e.g., John 3:18; 6:64; 12:37; Acts 7:51; 17:32). It is for this very reason that the external call is insufficient for salvation.

The Internal Call: Regeneration

Because of the deficiencies of the external call, sinners stand in need of a sovereignly efficacious call, inherently powerful to overcome the effects of depravity and to bring them to repentance and saving faith. In his natural state, man is characterized by spiritual death (Eph. 2:1). By nature he is a spiritual corpse, entirely unresponsive to the spiritual truth proclaimed in the external call of the gospel. For this reason, the natural man will always reject the gospel, for the things of the Spirit of God "are folly to him, and he is not able to understand them because they are spiritually discerned" (1 Cor. 2:14). Sin has so pervaded man that all his faculties are corrupted by it. He is spiritually blind, for "the god of this world has blinded the minds of the unbelievers, to keep them from seeing the light of the gospel of the glory of Christ" (2 Cor. 4:4; cf. Rom. 1:21–22; Eph. 4:17–18). When the glory of Christ is presented in the gospel, the natural man does not see it, because the eyes of his heart have been blinded. He is also spiritually deaf; his ears are uncircumcised (Jer. 6:10), and

---

91. Nicole reasons, "The essential prerequisite for a sincere offer [is] simply this: that if the terms of the offer be observed, that which is offered be actually granted." Roger R. Nicole, "Covenant, Universal Call and Definite Atonement," *JETS* 38, no. 3 (1995): 403–12.

therefore, he cannot perceive the wisdom, grace, and truth announced in the gospel of grace (Isa. 6:9–10; Matt. 13:15; John 8:43). Still further, man's will and affections are entirely disordered, for, as the prophet Jeremiah testifies, "The heart is deceitful above all things, and desperately sick" (Jer. 17:9).[92] Indeed, the natural man is devoid of spiritual life, for Scripture says that his heart is a heart of stone (Ezek. 11:19; 36:26), cold and unresponsive to the meaning and glory of divinely revealed truth.

"But God, being rich in mercy, because of the great love with which he loved us, even when we were dead in our trespasses and sins, *made us alive* together with Christ" (Eph. 2:4–5). In the exercise of his sovereign pleasure, God issues an effectual call in the heart of the elect. He powerfully summons the sinner out of his spiritual death and blindness and, by virtue of the creative power of his word, imparts new spiritual life to him—giving him a new heart, along with eyes to see and ears to hear, and thus enabling him to repent and believe in Christ for salvation (Rom. 8:30; 1 Cor. 1:24; 2 Tim. 1:9; 1 Pet. 5:10; 2 Pet. 1:3). He effectually calls his people "out of darkness" and "into his marvelous light" (1 Pet. 2:9), "to himself" (Acts 2:39), into fellowship with his Son (1 Cor. 1:9) so that they belong to Christ (Rom. 1:6), and "into his own kingdom and glory" (1 Thess. 2:12). This is the divine miracle of regeneration, or the new birth.

THE AUTHOR OF REGENERATION

As is plain even from the above discussion, the author of this radical change of man's nature cannot be man himself but rather must be the Creator of all life, including eternal life—God alone. Some other aspects of the application of redemption require believers to participate actively. In conversion, for example, though repentance and faith are themselves sovereign gifts from God (Acts 11:18; Eph. 2:8), we ourselves must turn from sin and trust in Christ. Though God grants us faith, he does not believe the gospel for us. Similarly, though the Christian's growth in holiness is a sovereign work of the Spirit of God (Phil. 2:13; cf. 2 Cor. 3:18; Gal. 5:16–17, 22–23), we are called to avail ourselves of the means by which the Spirit sanctifies us, working out our salvation with fear and trembling (Phil. 2:12) and making every effort to supplement our faith with virtue (2 Pet. 1:5–8). The work of regeneration, however, is unlike these other aspects of the application of redemption. In regeneration, man is entirely passive; God is the sole active agent in bringing about the creative miracle of the new birth.

It is significant that Scripture uses the imagery of being born again to describe this work of regeneration (John 3:3–8; 1 Pet. 1:3, 23; 1 John 3:9). In the physical realm, a child makes absolutely no contribution to his conception or his birth. He is nonexistent and thus is entirely dependent on the will of his parents to be brought into being. In the same way, Jesus chooses this analogy to illustrate the reality that dead and depraved sinners cannot contribute to their rebirth unto spiritual life but

---

92. In the Hebrew language, the "heart" represents the controlling seat of one's emotions and spiritual life. It is a way of speaking of the will, desires, and emotions.

are entirely dependent on the sovereign will of God for regeneration. Jesus declared these things to Nicodemus, "a man of the Pharisees" and "a ruler of the Jews" who was described as "the teacher of Israel" (John 3:1, 10). He was a member of the strictest and most devout sect of Judaism, he sat on the governing body of the Sanhedrin, and as *the* teacher of Israel, he occupied a unique place of prominence in the religious system. It was to this man who had risen to the pinnacle of religious devotion that Jesus declared, "You must be born again" (John 3:7). And this is not limited to Nicodemus, for Jesus speaks of mankind in general when he says, "Truly, truly, I say to you, unless one is born again he cannot see the kingdom of God" (John 3:3). Sin has so infected and corrupted mankind that nothing less than the wholesale renovation of the soul is required for salvation. Rearranging your life, modifying your behavior, or multiplying religious performances will not suffice. Something is so drastically and irreversibly wrong with mankind that we must be born all over again. When Nicodemus asks how this can happen, Jesus does not give him a list of religious duties by which he can cooperate with God's grace. Instead, he points to the sovereign will of God and declares, "The wind blows where it wishes" (John 3:8). As John Murray observes, "The wind is not at our beck and call; neither is the regenerative operation of the Spirit."[93]

Aside from the imagery of the new birth, Scripture explicitly affirms that regeneration is an act of God alone. The apostle John declares that the children of God birthed in regeneration are born "not of blood nor of the will of the flesh nor of the will of man, but of God" (John 1:13). Man is not born again by blood, which is to say that the new birth is not passed down hereditarily through any bloodlines but is entirely supernatural. While the joining of the blood of a father and mother produces physical life, it can never produce spiritual life. One's heritage or ancestral lineage has no bearing on regeneration. Neither is the child of God born of the will of the flesh. He does not simply decide to be born again as an exercise of his will. No moral effort or religious activity can induce the new birth, for flesh can only give birth to flesh (John 3:6). Because the new birth is spiritual, it cannot come by the will of the flesh. Finally, John says that the child of God is not born of the will of man, which establishes that no man-made religion or sacramental system can produce regeneration.

Instead, the children of God are born *of God* (John 1:13). Scripture does not hesitate to employ the most active language with respect to God's role in regeneration. So far from depending on man's will, sinners are brought forth unto spiritual life by the exercise of *God's* will (James 1:18). While man was dead in his trespasses, utterly helpless to bring himself to life, "God . . . made us alive together with Christ" (Eph. 2:4–5; cf. Col. 2:13). According to the Father's great mercy, "he has caused us to be born again" (1 Pet. 1:3). Through the prophet Ezekiel, God promised a time when he would bring regeneration to his people:

> I will sprinkle clean water on you, and you shall be clean from all your unclean-nesses, and from all your idols I will cleanse you. And I will give you a new heart,

---

93. Murray, *Redemption Accomplished and Applied*, 99.

and a new spirit I will put within you. And I will remove the heart of stone from your flesh and give you a heart of flesh. And I will put my Spirit within you, and cause you to walk in my statutes and be careful to obey my rules. (Ezek. 36:25–27)

The monergistic[94] work of God in regeneration is unmistakable in this text. In just these three verses, God uses the phrase "I will" six times, insisting that this spiritual heart transplant is entirely his work. In the next chapter, God illustrates his own sovereignty and man's helplessness by picturing the future regeneration of Israel as his breathing life into a valley full of dry bones (Ezek. 37:1–11). While this is clearly a prophecy of the regeneration and salvation of the Jews before Christ's return, it assumes that God is the One who regenerates individuals—in Israel's case, a whole nation of them (Ezek. 37:11). Such is man's natural state of depravity; he is no more able to bring himself to life than a pile of dead and dry bones could bring themselves to life. Having illustrated his promise, God then declares, "Behold, I will open your graves and raise you from your graves. . . . And I will put my Spirit within you, and you shall live" (Ezek. 37:12, 14).

These passages in Ezekiel point to the Holy Spirit's role in regeneration. Many texts explicitly name the person of the Father as the agent of regeneration (James 1:18; 1 Pet. 1:3; cf. Rom. 8:30; 1 Cor. 1:9). However, Scripture also indicates that the Holy Spirit participates in this work. As Jesus discusses the new birth with Nicodemus, he says that the child of God is "born of the Spirit" (John 3:5, 6, 8). Later, he goes on to say that "it is the Spirit who gives life" (John 6:63), a concept that became a maxim of apostolic teaching (2 Cor. 3:6; cf. Rom. 8:2). The apostle Paul says that Christ saves us by "the washing of regeneration and renewal of the Holy Spirit" (Titus 3:5). We may conclude, therefore, that while the Father is the ultimate agent of regeneration, summoning us out of death and into life, the Holy Spirit is the efficient cause of regeneration, who carries out the will of the Father by giving us spiritual life.

THE NATURE OF REGENERATION

The Greek term for "regeneration" (*palingenesia*) appears only twice in the New Testament. First, in Matthew 19:28, Jesus tells his disciples, "Truly I say to you, in the new world [Gk. *en tē palingenesia*; lit., 'in the regeneration'] when the Son of Man will sit on his glorious throne, you who have followed me will also sit on twelve thrones, judging the twelve tribes of Israel." He uses the term "regeneration" to refer to the renovation of the creation that will begin in the millennial kingdom

---

94. *Monergism* is a word derived from the Greek *monos*, meaning "one," and *ergos*, meaning "work." It speaks of there being one agent at work. Theologians have employed this term to describe the view of regeneration argued for here, namely, that God is the sole agent at work in regeneration, while man is entirely passive. *Synergism*, on the other hand, speaks of "working together," and describes a view of regeneration in which man cooperates with God in regeneration. Wesleyan theologian and synergist John Miley wrote, "Regeneration is not an absolute work of the Spirit. . . . There are prerequisites which cannot be met without our own free agency. There must be an earnest turning of the soul to God, deep repentance for sin, and a true faith in Christ. Such are the requirements of our own agency. There is no regeneration for us without them." *Systematic Theology* (New York: Hunt & Eaton, 1892), 2:336. Such teaching is entirely contradictory to Scripture's emphasis on God's activity and man's helplessness with respect to regeneration. For a masterful defense of monergistic regeneration, see Matthew Barrett, *Salvation by Grace: The Case for Effectual Calling and Regeneration* (Phillipsburg, NJ: P&R, 2013).

and will come to consummation in the new heavens and the new earth. The second occurrence of "regeneration" in the New Testament comes in Titus 3:5: "He saved us, not because of works done by us in righteousness, but according to his own mercy, by the washing of regeneration [Gk. *palingenesia*] and renewal of the Holy Spirit." Here Paul uses the term to speak about man's salvation from sin and indicates that regeneration is characterized by both washing and renewal. This understanding of regeneration is similar to John 3:5, where Jesus says that the new birth consists in being "born of water and the Spirit," a reference to the prophecy in Ezekiel 36:25–26, which metaphorically describes regeneration as being sprinkled with clean water and being given a new heart. From the uses of the biblical term, then, we may conclude that regeneration speaks of a cleansing from sin and a creation of spiritual life. It is a purifying renovation.

At the most fundamental level, regeneration is the divine impartation of eternal spiritual life into the spiritually dead sinner. Scripture employs numerous pictures to illustrate God's effectual call of regeneration. As he did with the valley of the dry bones, God will, by the creative power of his word, speak spiritual life into the dead hearts of the Jews, breathing as it were the breath of divine life over the dry bones of their souls and making them alive. As Jesus stood at the tomb of his friend who had been dead four days, he cried out with a loud voice, "Lazarus, come out" (John 11:43). By this word, Jesus authoritatively summoned Lazarus out of death and into life, for "the man who had died came out" (John 11:44), stumbling from the tomb still wrapped in his grave clothes. So also does God command the spiritually lifeless corpse of the sinner to "come out" of his death and by that word effectually brings him to life. Perhaps most striking is the apostle Paul's comparison of regeneration to God's creation of the world. He says, "God, who said, 'Let light shine out of darkness,' has shone in our hearts to give the light of the knowledge of the glory of God in the face of Jesus Christ" (2 Cor. 4:6). In the beginning, God spoke the world into existence from nothing (Pss. 33:6; 148:5): "And God *said*, 'Let there be light,' and there was light" (Gen. 1:3), instantly "call[ing] into existence the things that do not exist" (Rom. 4:17). In regeneration, God unites the external call of gospel preaching with his sovereign, effectual call unto new life. Into darkened and dead hearts he speaks the command, "Let there be light," and instantaneously births in us the light of eternal spiritual life where it had not existed.[95]

This impartation of spiritual life is not limited to the immaterial part of man but is a fundamental re-creation of the whole person. Paul plainly states, "Therefore, if anyone is in Christ, he is a new creation. The old has passed away; behold, the new has come" (2 Cor. 5:17). It is not merely the sinner's spirit or soul that is a new creation, but he himself, as a whole person, is a new creation. Just as man's depravity is total—that is, just as sin has so pervaded man's nature as to leave no part of him

---

95. Thus, the effectual call of regeneration creates the very life that it commands. John Murray explains, "The summons is invested with the efficacy by which we are delivered to the destination intended—we are effectively ushered into the fellowship of Christ. There is something determinate about God's call; by his sovereign power and grace it cannot fail of accomplishment." *Redemption Accomplished and Applied*, 91.

untouched by sin's corruption—so also does regeneration reach to the totality of man. The natural man's mind is blinded (2 Cor. 4:4); he is darkened in understanding (Eph. 4:18) and thus unable to hear (John 8:43) or grasp spiritual truth (1 Cor. 2:14). His affections are entirely disordered, to the degree that he loves the darkness and hates the light (John 3:19–20), delighting in that which is objectively repulsive and being repulsed by that which is objectively delightful. So driven by his affections, his will obstinately refuses Christ and the glory of his gospel (John 5:40). Mentally, emotionally, and volitionally, man is captive to sin. Therefore, the renewal of man in regeneration is just as extensive as his depravity.

In regeneration, then, the Spirit opens the blind eyes of the mind (Acts 26:18; 2 Cor. 4:4, 6; Eph. 1:18), replacing, as it were, the mind of the flesh with the mind of the Spirit (Rom. 8:5–9)—indeed, with the mind of Christ himself (1 Cor. 2:16)—so that the regenerate man appraises all the things that he once could not understand (1 Cor. 2:15; cf. 1 John 2:20, 27). The Spirit removes the sinner's heart of stone and implants in him a heart of flesh capable of perceiving and loving spiritual truth (Ezek. 11:19; 36:26; cf. Deut. 30:6). The affections are thus renewed after the likeness of Christ so that the new man hates sin (Matt. 5:4), loves righteousness (Matt. 5:6; John 3:21), thirsts for the God whom he once abhorred (Pss. 27:4; 42:1–2), and loves and rejoices in the Christ whom he once regarded as foolish (1 Pet. 1:8; cf. 2 Cor. 5:16). With renewed affections, the sinner's will is finally freed from the bondage of sin unto the liberty of righteousness. He now wants what God wants (Ps. 40:8), for the Spirit of God is at work within him "both to will and to work for his good pleasure" (Phil. 2:13; cf. Ezek. 36:27). Once bound in sin and spiritual death, man's mind, heart, and will are now renewed unto life. Ferguson helpfully summarizes, "Regeneration is . . . as all-pervasive as depravity. . . . [W]hile the regenerate individual is not yet as holy as he or she might be, there is no part of life which remains uninfluenced by this renewing and cleansing work."[96] The regenerated sinner is truly a "new self, created after the likeness of God in true righteousness and holiness" (Eph. 4:24).

The picture of regeneration given in 2 Corinthians 4 is especially helpful in illustrating key truths about the nature of the new birth. In that passage, Paul describes the state of the natural man when he says, "The god of this world has blinded the minds of the unbelievers, to keep them from seeing the light of the gospel of the glory of Christ, who is the image of God" (2 Cor. 4:4). This is what Paul means when he describes unbelievers as "dead in the[ir] trespasses and sins" (Eph. 2:1; cf. Col. 2:13). He does not mean that they are motionless or stagnant; he means that they are devoid of the spiritual life that allows them to see the true value of the glory of Christ revealed in the gospel. The essence of spiritual death is spiritual blindness.[97] Man's spiritual perception is so disordered by sin that he has no taste for what is objectively delightful (i.e., the gospel of the glory of Christ) but is infatuated with

---

96. Sinclair B. Ferguson, *The Holy Spirit*, Contours of Christian Theology (Downers Grove, IL: InterVarsity Press, 1996), 122–23.
97. This is borne out by Scripture's frequent use of light as a metaphor for spiritual life and darkness as a metaphor for spiritual death and unbelief (John 12:46; Acts 26:18; Eph. 5:8; 1 Pet. 2:9). Further, Scripture also consistently parallels spiritual sight and spiritual life (John 6:40; Heb. 11:27; 1 John 3:6).

what is objectively repulsive and disgusting (i.e., sin and the glory of self). The unregenerate man pursues what is worthless because he is blind to its detriment, and he refuses what is most precious because he is blind to its value. Thus, when the objective beauty of Christ is held forth in the gospel message, the unregenerate man sees no glory in him, and therefore, left to himself, he will ever and always choose to reject the gospel.

What, then, is the remedy for such a miserable condition? There is no hope in man's enslaved will but only in the sovereign grace and life-giving power of God. Paul answers that the remedy for man's spiritual blindness is monergistic regeneration: "For God, who said, 'Let light shine out of darkness,' has shone in our hearts to give the light of the knowledge of the glory of God in the face of Jesus Christ" (2 Cor. 4:6). God shines the light of life into the blind heart. He gives us new spiritual eyes so that we finally see sin for what it is—in all its objective ugliness—and so finally see Christ for who he is—in all his objective beauty and glory. And when sinners finally have functioning spiritual eyes and the light necessary to see things as they actually are, they turn away in disgust from the filth of sin (repentance) and eagerly embrace the Christ whose glory they can at last see (faith).

It is for this reason that theologians speak of the regenerating grace of God as irresistible.[98] It is not that God's grace can never be resisted; God's common grace as expressed in the external call of the gospel is resisted all the time (Acts 7:51). Rather, it is that in the irresistible grace of regeneration, God overcomes man's natural resistance to the gospel by shining light into his heart and opening his eyes to the glory of Jesus. Irresistible grace, then, does not mean that man is coerced or forced into repentance and faith; his will is not violated. Rather, this grace *frees* man's will; it opens our eyes so we can accurately compare the glory of sin to the glory of Christ. The Westminster Confession explains,

> All those whom God hath predestinated unto life, and those only, He is pleased, in His appointed time, effectually to call, by His Word and Spirit, out of that state of sin and death, in which they are by nature to grace and salvation, by Jesus Christ; enlightening their minds spiritually and savingly to understand the things of God, taking away their heart of stone, and giving unto them an heart of flesh; renewing their wills, and, by His almighty power, determining them to that which is good, and effectually drawing them to Jesus Christ: *yet so, as they come most freely, being made willing by His grace.*[99]

It is impossible that anyone with restored spiritual sight through regeneration should see sin and Christ side by side and do anything but turn from sin and embrace Christ in saving faith. Thus, in regeneration man's will is not violated but transformed. In the final analysis, regenerating grace is irresistible because *Christ* is irresistible, for regenerating grace opens our spiritual eyes to his irresistibility.

---

98. *Irresistible grace* is the *I* in the acronym TULIP, which summarizes the doctrines of grace. The other letters stand for *total depravity*, *unconditional election*, *limited atonement*, and *perseverance of the saints*.

99. Philip Schaff, ed. *The Creeds of Christendom*, vol. 3, *The Evangelical Protestant Creeds* (1877; repr. Grand Rapids, MI: Baker, 1998), 624–25. Italics added.

THE MEANS OF REGENERATION[100]

As the Father is the ultimate agent of regeneration and the Spirit is the efficient cause of regeneration, Scripture identifies the word of God itself—specifically the gospel message—as the instrumental cause, or means, of regeneration. James highlights the roles of the Father and the word when he says, "Of his [i.e., the Father's] own will he brought us forth by the word of truth" (James 1:18). The Father's will is the ultimate cause of our new birth, but he has accomplished this miracle by means of the word of truth. Peter says that the children of God "have been born again, not of perishable seed but of imperishable, through the living and abiding word of God" (1 Pet. 1:23). Then, two verses later he identifies this living and abiding word as "the good news that was preached to you" (1 Pet. 1:25). Similarly, Paul says that God's effectual call unto regeneration is accomplished "through our gospel" (2 Thess. 2:14). Thus, it is by means of the preached gospel that the Spirit of God powerfully works to open the eyes of our hearts to the glory of Christ. To be clear, the external call is not efficacious in itself; though the preached gospel is the means of regeneration, it is not efficacious unless it is united with the Spirit's work in the internal call. Nevertheless, while the external call is insufficient for regeneration, it is absolutely necessary, for the external call of gospel preaching is the vehicle for the internal call of regeneration. For this reason Paul says, "So faith," which is the immediate result of regeneration, "comes from hearing, and hearing through the word of Christ" (Rom. 10:17), that is, the gospel message concerning Christ.

Since Scripture identifies the word of the gospel as the means of regeneration, any sacramental view of regeneration is discovered to be unbiblical. Roman Catholicism, Eastern Orthodoxy, and even some strains of Lutheranism and Anglicanism teach baptismal regeneration—that the grace of the new birth is mediated through the sacrament of baptism.[101] Proponents of baptismal regeneration often appeal to John 3:5, where Jesus says, "Truly, truly, I say to you, unless one is born of water and the Spirit, he cannot enter the kingdom of God." The reference to water, they argue, is a reference to Christian baptism.

However, there are a number of reasons why we ought not to understand "born of water" to refer to baptism. First, Jesus does not mention baptism anywhere in this interaction with Nicodemus. While it is tenuous to automatically assume that "water" refers to baptism in the first place, that teaching is only further undermined

---

100. Portions of this section are adapted from John MacArthur, *John 1–11*, MNTC (Chicago: Moody Press, 2006), 104–5. Used by permission of Moody Publishers.

101. The Catechism of the Catholic Church reads, "Baptism not only purifies from all sins, but also makes the neophyte 'a new creature,' an adopted son of God, who has become a 'partaker of the divine nature,' members of Christ and co-heirs with him, an the temple of the Holy Spirit." *Catechism of the Catholic Church*, 2nd ed. (Vatican City: Libreria Editrice Vaticana, 2000), 322 (§1265).

The Longer Catechism of the Eastern Church teaches, "Baptism is a Sacrament, in which a man . . . dies to the carnal life of sin, and is born again of the Holy Ghost." Philip Schaff, ed., "The Longer Catechism of the Eastern Church," in *The Creeds of Christendom*, 2:491.

Luther's Small Catechism explains, "Holy Baptism is the only means whereby infants, who, too, must be born again, can ordinarily be regenerated and brought to faith." *Luther's Small Catechism*, trans. Kleine Katechismus, rev. ed. (St. Louis, MO: Concordia, 1965), 172–73 (Q. 251b).

The Anglican Book of Common Prayer instructs, "We thank you, Father, for the water of Baptism. In it we are buried with Christ in his death. By it we share in his resurrection. Through it we are reborn by the Holy Spirit." *The (Online) Book of Common Prayer* (New York: The Church Hymnal Corporation, n.d.), 306, accessed May 3, 2016, http://www.bcponline.org/.

when one considers that the rest of the section makes no mention of baptism. Jesus speaks continually of the necessity of faith for salvation (John 3:15, 16, 18, 36) but says nothing about baptism. If baptism were the necessary instrument of being born again, it is difficult to explain why Jesus says nothing more about it as he discusses salvation. Second, such a sacramental understanding of baptism is out of accord with Jesus's statement in John 3:8 that, with respect to the new birth, the Spirit is like the wind that blows where it wishes. Such language pictures the sovereign freedom of the Spirit, an image that is incongruous with tying regeneration to a ritual, physical act of human will. Piper aptly observes that in that case "the wind would be confined by the sacrament."[102] Third, Jesus expects Nicodemus, the teacher of Israel, to understand his teaching on the new birth (John 3:10). However, Christian baptism did not yet exist at that time. It makes little sense to admonish Nicodemus for failing to understand a practice that had not yet been instituted.

Instead, one would expect Jesus to admonish Nicodemus for failing to understand Old Testament teaching on the subject, and in fact, that is the most likely explanation for his words. The Old Testament often employs the imagery of water and Spirit to symbolize spiritual cleansing and renewal, never baptism (cf. Num. 19:17–19; Isa. 4:4; 32:15; 44:3; 55:1; Joel 2:28–29; Zech. 13:1). In Ezekiel's prophecy of the new covenant, he famously speaks of both water and the Spirit in the context of regeneration:

> I will *sprinkle clean water* on you, and you shall be clean from all your uncleannesses, and from all your idols I will *cleanse* you. And I will give you a new heart, and a new spirit I will put within you. And I will remove the heart of stone from your flesh and give you a heart of flesh. *And I will put my Spirit within you*, and cause you to walk in my statutes and be careful to obey my rules. (Ezek. 36:25–27)

Surely this was the truth Jesus had in mind when he spoke of being born of water and the Spirit. He was declaring that regeneration was a truth revealed throughout the Old Testament (e.g., Deut. 30:6; Jer. 31:31–34; Ezek. 11:18–20) and thus a truth with which Nicodemus should have been familiar. Against this Old Testament backdrop, Christ's point was unmistakable: without the spiritual washing of the soul, a cleansing accomplished by the Holy Spirit (Titus 3:5) and solely by means of the word of the gospel (Eph. 5:26; 1 Pet. 1:23–25), no one can enter God's kingdom.[103] Given this proper understanding of John 3:5, the doctrine of baptismal regeneration is shown to be without biblical basis. The gospel itself is the sole instrument of the new birth.

THE RELATIONSHIP OF REGENERATION TO FAITH

One of the most common questions related to evangelical soteriology concerns the relationship between regeneration and faith. Which produces which? Does the sinner believe in Christ for salvation and, as a result of his faith, experience the new

---

102. John Piper, *Finally Alive: What Happens When We Are Born Again* (Fearn, Ross-shire, Scotland: Christian Focus, 2009), 39.

103. For a thorough examination of various interpretations for "born of water," see D. A. Carson, *The Gospel according to John*, PNTC (Grand Rapids, MI: Eerdmans, 1991), 191–96.

birth? Or, on the other hand, is the sinner born again unto saving faith? Which action induces the other? Does man's act of faith bring about the Spirit's work of regeneration, or does the Spirit's work of regeneration bring about man's act of faith? In numerous ways, Scripture answers in favor of the latter: regeneration is the cause, not the consequence, of saving faith.

At the outset, it is important to be reminded of the definition of regeneration that has been demonstrated from Scripture. Regeneration is the sovereign act of God, by the Holy Spirit and through the preached gospel, whereby he instantaneously imparts spiritual life to a sinner, bringing him out of spiritual death and into spiritual life. Many evangelicals who believe that faith precedes regeneration do not define the new birth in this way. Instead, they tend to confuse regeneration with the *results* of regeneration, viewing regeneration as virtually equivalent to sanctification—the ongoing process by which the sinner's nature is progressively "regenerated" more and more to reflect the image of Christ. If we were to define regeneration in that way, it would be inescapable to conclude that regeneration follows faith, for sanctification is a result of saving faith. However, Scripture counsels us against defining regeneration in terms of its results. Jesus asserts that regeneration itself is mysterious, unobserved, and uncontainable, like the wind that blows where it wishes (John 3:8). We may perceive the effects of the wind, such as hearing a loud gust or seeing the trees toss from side to side. Yet these results of the wind are not the wind itself. In the same way, the results of regeneration are not regeneration. While the believer's sanctification is linked organically with his new birth—in a sense, regeneration is sanctification begun, and sanctification is regeneration continued—nevertheless, this intimate relationship must not lead to a conflation of the two. The believer's continued progress in holiness is the *result* of regeneration, not an aspect of regeneration itself.

Another preliminary remark in this discussion is to observe that the distinction between regeneration and faith is to be defined not in terms of time but in terms of logical causality. Some synergists reject the notion that regeneration causes faith because they want to avoid saying that someone might be regenerated *without* saving faith. However, while some monergists have advocated that regeneration temporally precedes faith,[104] most have clarified that they are speaking of logical, not chronological, order. From a temporal perspective, regeneration and faith occur simultaneously; in the exact moment that man is born again, he repents and believes the gospel. Nevertheless, this simultaneity does not rule out causality. Though two events may occur at the same time, one may still cause the other. To illustrate this, consider the imagery Paul employs when he defines regeneration as the opening of the sinner's blinded spiritual eyes so that he sees the light of Christ's glory (2 Cor. 4:4, 6). Paul pictures regeneration as the opening of blind eyes and faith as the spiritual perception of Christ's glory (cf. John 3:3; Heb. 11:1). Now a man perceives light in

---

104. For example, Louis Berkhof argues for a passage of time between regeneration and faith in order to sustain his paedobaptism. This explains a baptized infant's status as a "covenant child" even before he exercises saving faith. Berkhof, *Systematic Theology*, 472. Scripture, however, makes no such provisions. See Matt Waymeyer, *A Biblical Critique of Infant Baptism* (The Woodlands, TX: Kress, 2008).

the very same moment that he opens his eyes; no time passes between the opening of his eyes and his perception of light. However, his perception of light is causally dependent on opening his eyes. Seeing does not cause him to open his eyes; his sight is the *consequence* of his eyes being opened. In the same way, though they occur in the exact same instant, the sinner's faith does not cause his regeneration; rather, the opening of the spiritual eyes in regeneration is the cause of the spiritual sight of faith.

Further, the Bible's teaching concerning the natural man's spiritual inability precludes any concept of synergism in regeneration. In his state of spiritual death (Eph. 2:1–3), man is incapable even of understanding the things of the Spirit, let alone receiving them (1 Cor. 2:14). The sinner's mind is so hostile to God that he is literally unable to submit to God's law (Rom. 8:7), and thus he cannot please God in any sense (Rom. 8:8), including the exercise of faith (Heb. 11:6). Man is blind to the value of God's glory revealed in Christ and is hopelessly enamored with sin, despite its worthlessness. To suggest that a sinner in such a state could, apart from the regenerating grace of the Holy Spirit, summon from within his own deadness the saving faith that God declares to be his sovereign gift (Eph. 2:8) is to wholly underestimate the miserable nature of man's depravity. As Murray explains, "Faith is a whole-souled act of loving trust and self-commitment."[105] But the natural man is utterly incapable of such a noble and spiritual act apart from the new birth. Indeed, Jesus tells Nicodemus, "Unless one is born again he cannot see the kingdom of God" (John 3:3). The sight of the kingdom of God can refer to nothing other than the spiritual sight of saving faith (Heb. 11:1, 27; cf. 2 Cor. 4:18), and Jesus says that such a sight is impossible apart from the new birth. Elsewhere he says, "No one can come to me unless the Father who sent me draws him" (John 6:44), and, "This is why I told you that no one can come to me unless it is granted him by the Father" (John 6:65). Coming to Jesus is a synonym for believing in Jesus—for it is this kind of coming that results in salvation (John 5:40)—and the "drawing" of John 6:44 is the gift spoken of in John 6:65, both referring to the effectual, irresistible call of God in regeneration. Therefore, Jesus is teaching that because of the sinner's depravity, no one can come to him in saving faith unless the Father grants the gift of being effectually drawn in regeneration.[106]

The apostle John also comments explicitly on the relationship between regeneration and faith in his first epistle. While John's intention is not to teach a theology lesson on the *ordo salutis* but rather to instruct the Asian churches about mutual love between believers, his comments nevertheless reveal his understanding of the relationship between regeneration and faith. In 1 John 5:1, he writes, "Everyone who believes [Gk. *Pas ho pisteuōn*, a present active participle] that Jesus is the Christ has been born of

---

105. Murray, *Redemption Accomplished and Applied*, 86.

106. Some synergists object that it is inconsistent to describe the Father's drawing as effectual, since drawing connotes persuasion rather than determination. They often argue that "drawing" does not mean "dragging." Interestingly, the Greek word *helkō*, translated "draws" in John 6:44, often refers to a decisive, effectual movement like dragging. Other New Testament occurrences of *helkō* refer to fishermen hauling in a fishing net (John 21:6, 11), a soldier drawing his sword from its sheath in the midst of battle (John 18:10), angry men dragging a foreigner before their court (Acts 16:19), and a mob dragging a traitor out of their city with the intent to kill him (Acts 21:30). Far from an ineffectual wooing, the Father's drawing in John 6:44 is the decisive, effectual calling of regeneration.

God [Gk. *ek tou theou gegennētai,* a perfect passive indicative], and everyone who loves the Father loves whoever has been born of him." The Greek present participle *ho pisteuōn* indicates present continuous action, while the perfect passive indicative *gegennētai* speaks of a past action whose results continue into the present time.[107] In other words, everyone who presently believes that Jesus is the Christ *has been* born of God. John thus represents faith as the consequence, not the cause, of the new birth.

This reading of the grammar of 1 John 5:1 is confirmed by examining a selection of grammatical parallels in the same letter. There are two other instances in which John employs a present active participle in concert with a perfect passive indicative to illustrate the relationship between the new birth and its concomitants:

> If you know that he is righteous, you may be sure that everyone who practices [Gk. *pas ho poiōn*] righteousness has been born of him [Gk. *ex autou gegennētai*]. (1 John 2:29)

> Beloved, let us love one another, for love is from God, and whoever loves [Gk. *pas ho agapōn*] has been born of God [Gk. *ek tou theou gegennētai*] and knows God. (1 John 4:7)

Both of these passages consist of precisely the same grammatical construction that appears in 1 John 5:1. In the first text, John teaches that a habitual pattern of practiced righteousness is an indication of the new birth. The causal relationship between the practice of righteousness and the new birth ought to be obvious. Surely man is not born again as a result of doing good works! Paul patently contradicts such a thought in Titus 3:5, where he explicitly opposes the new birth against salvation on the basis of righteous deeds. The relationship is plain: the impartation of new spiritual life in regeneration is the cause of an ongoing practice of good deeds (cf. Eph. 2:10). In the second text, John singles out a particular good work: everyone who loves has been born of God. Here again, the relationship between love and regeneration is evident: love does not cause the new birth but is the consequence of the new birth. To suggest otherwise fundamentally undermines the gospel of salvation by grace alone. Therefore, if we must conclude that practicing righteousness (1 John 2:29) and loving the brethren (1 John 4:7) are consequences, not causes, of regeneration, we cannot conclude otherwise than that faith is also a consequence of regeneration, since 1 John 2:29; 4:7; and 5:1 are grammatically identical.

One final text is worthy of consideration. In 1 John 5:4, John writes, "For everyone who has been born of God overcomes the world. And this is the victory that has overcome the world—our faith." Though the grammatical construction is not identical to the previous three passages discussed, it is nevertheless similar. Here John speaks of the new birth in the perfect tense ("everyone who has been born of God," Gk. *pan to gegennēmenon*) and a concomitant of the new birth in the present tense ("overcomes the world," Gk. *nika ton kosmon*). Again, the causal relationship between the two is clear: one does not overcome the world in order to be born again

---

107. Wallace, *Greek Grammar Beyond the Basics*, 573.

but rather overcomes the world as a consequence of being born again. In the next sentence, John identifies the victory (Gk. *nikē*) that overcomes (Gk. *nikēsasa*) the world: our faith. Once again, faith is identified as the consequence of the new birth.

Given the clarity of the biblical pictures of regeneration, the implications of man's total depravity, and the explicit comments of Jesus and the apostle John, the student of Scripture has to conclude that while regeneration and faith are experienced simultaneously, regeneration logically precedes faith and is its cause. Sinners do not believe in Christ in order to be born again but rather are born again unto believing.

THE RESULTS OF REGENERATION

It is clear from the above discussion that saving faith is the first and foremost result of regeneration. As the divine light shines into the sinner's heart, opening his spiritual eyes to the repulsiveness of sin and the loveliness of Christ (2 Cor. 4:6), the newborn soul turns away in disgust from sin and lays hold of Christ with the embrace of saving faith. However, the divine life birthed in the soul of man at regeneration does not lie stagnant after the moment of conversion. In God's bountiful grace, the Spirit continues to progressively strengthen that holy disposition born in regeneration throughout the believer's life. That is to say, after repentance and faith, the result of regeneration is sanctification. While a full discussion of sanctification awaits its respective treatment in the *ordo salutis*, it is worthwhile at this point to mention several aspects of sanctification that Scripture explicitly identifies as results of the new birth.

First, the regenerated believer necessarily makes a practice of righteousness, as the apostle John says, "Everyone who practices righteousness has been born of him" (1 John 2:29). The dominating tenor of the believer's life is one of increasing holiness (Rom. 6:4; Eph. 2:10; 4:24). To put it negatively, "No one born of God makes a practice of sinning, for God's seed abides in him, and he cannot keep on sinning because he has been born of God" (1 John 3:9). Just as a human birth results from an implanted seed that grows into new physical life, so also the "seed" of the divine life is implanted in the believer's heart through the Spirit's regenerating work (1 Pet. 1:23). His nature has been fundamentally changed from death in sin to life in Christ; the old has passed away and the new has come (2 Cor. 5:17), and he thus does not make a practice of sinning. This does not mean that the child of God has ceased entirely from sin at the moment of regeneration, for the principle of sin continues to dwell in our flesh (Rom. 7:14–25) and thus must be constantly put to death (Rom. 8:12–13). These texts do not speak of perfection but direction. The believer's life is characterized by gracious habits of putting away patterns of sin and putting on patterns of righteousness (Eph. 4:22–24). Those who profess to be saved but do not progress in cultivating patterns of life in obedience to Christ's commands can make no legitimate claim to being true children of God. Whatever they may say with their lips, their lives betray a heart that is still unregenerate. As the new birth is the work of the Spirit (John 3:5, 6, 8; 6:63; Titus 3:5; cf. Rom. 8:2; 2 Cor. 3:6), those who are born again necessarily bear the fruit of the Spirit and are increasingly characterized by love, joy, peace, patience, kindness, goodness, faithfulness, gentleness, and self-control (Gal. 5:22–23).

Second, the regenerate life is marked by overcoming the evil influences of this world system. The apostle John writes, "For everyone who has been born of God overcomes the world. And this is the victory that has overcome the world—our faith" (1 John 5:4). Earlier in his letter, John comments that the world is full of the lust of the flesh, the lust of the eyes, and the pride of life (1 John 2:15–17), all of which are tools of Satan, in whose power the whole world lies (1 John 5:19). He wields these tools as instruments of temptation in the lives of professing believers, earnestly desiring to cause shipwreck of faith and thus besmirch the name of Christ (1 Tim. 1:19; cf. James 2:17). Yet John declares that the regenerate child of God withstands the pressures and temptations of this "present evil age" (Gal. 1:4) and overcomes them through a persevering faith that walks in obedience to the Lord. He never finally and decisively yields to Satan's temptations, because "he who was born of God protects him, and the evil one does not touch him" (1 John 5:18). Believers need not ever live in fear of losing their salvation, for persevering faith is the heritage of those truly born from above.

The child of God obeys willingly and delightfully, for as John says in the immediately preceding verse, "His commandments are not burdensome" (1 John 5:3). Here is a great indication that the sovereign miracle of regeneration cannot be fabricated or imitated by sinful human hypocrisy. Self-righteous moralists may, by strong willpower, be able to bring their behavior into conformity with the external standards of God's Word (cf. Matt. 15:8), but they find such a task burdensome. They cannot exclaim with the psalmist, "O how I love your law!" (Ps. 119:97), and, "I delight to do your will, O my God; your law is within my heart" (Ps. 40:8). It requires a new heart, a new nature re-created in the likeness of God (Eph. 4:24), to delight in obedience. By God's grace, this is the birthright of every true child of God. The regenerated believer is not enslaved to do the duty he hates; rather, by virtue of the Spirit's work, his heart is liberated to love the law he is commanded to follow.

Third, the child of God experiences not only the love of God that issues in a lifestyle of willing obedience but also the love of his fellow believers that issues in a life of sacrificial service. John writes, "Beloved, let us love one another, for love is from God, and whoever loves has been born of God and knows God" (1 John 4:7). God himself is love (1 John 4:8, 16); it is his very nature. Those who are begotten of God share in his nature (2 Pet. 1:4) and therefore will reflect his nature by serving and benefitting others (1 John 3:16–18). Those who are truly born again manifest an evident love for the church, for the child of God loves the children of God (1 John 5:1) and is devoted to meeting the needs of his brothers and sisters in Christ.

Conversion

The preceding portion examined the first step in the application of redemption: God's effectual call of regeneration through the preaching of the gospel, in which he sovereignly imparts spiritual life to the sinner, changing his nature and bringing him from death to life. The very first act of the regenerated sinner's renewed nature is conversion (cf. Acts 15:3), the conscious decision to repent of sin and believe in Christ for salvation. Returning to Paul's illustration of spiritual awakening aids us in understanding conversion. As God shines the light of regeneration into the sinner's heart, he opens man's spiritual eyes so that he can see the bankruptcy of sin and the worthiness of Christ (Acts 26:18; 2 Cor. 4:6), who is perfectly suited to forgive our sins and provide the righteousness we need for eternal life. Finally furnished with the ability to perceive reality as it is, the newborn soul necessarily and immediately turns away in revulsion from sin and eagerly runs to embrace Christ. That turning from sin and unbelief is repentance, and the eager embrace of Christ as Savior from sin and as Lord over one's life is faith. Together, repentance and faith make up the single act of conversion.

It should be apparent that repentance and faith are intimately related and even inseparable from one another. They are truly two sides of the same coin. In the first place, their connection follows a simple logic: it is impossible for someone to turn away from something without turning toward something else. Conversely, one cannot turn toward something without turning away from whatever was previously occupying his attention. Further, it is impossible to look in two different directions at the same time. But the inseparability of repentance and faith is also a theological necessity. It is inconceivable that one who finally perceives sin and Christ as they actually are should pursue Christ without forsaking sin or should forsake sin without embracing Christ. Remember that regeneration is a spiritual heart transplant—a radical renewal of man's tastes, desires, and affections. To such a renewed heart, the beauty of Christ's glory is irresistibly compelling, and it outshines the false glories of sin just as the brilliance of the noonday sun renders the stars invisible. To suggest that one might embrace Christ without also decisively purposing to repudiate sin is to suggest that sin is more objectively desirable to the regenerated heart than Christ is. On the contrary, to the newly awakened sinner, Christ is an inestimably valuable treasure, and to gain him, one delightfully forsakes everything (Matt. 13:44–46; Phil. 3:8). Thus, the faith that saves is a repentant faith, just as the repentance that saves is a believing repentance.

For this reason, the gospel call to salvation is a summons to both repent and believe. According to Mark, the content of "the gospel of God" that the Lord Jesus proclaimed can be summarized as follows: "The time is fulfilled, and the kingdom of God is at hand; repent and believe in the gospel" (Mark 1:15). The apostles followed in the steps of their Lord, for in Paul's parting words to the elders at Miletus, he characterized his ministry as "testifying both to Jews and to Greeks of repentance toward God and of faith in our Lord Jesus Christ" (Acts 20:21). This was the commission Paul received from Christ himself, who, Paul recounted to Agrippa, sent him "to open [the Gentiles'] eyes, so that they may turn from darkness to light and from the power of Satan to God" (Acts 26:18). And it was this twofold conversion that was realized in the salvation experience of the Thessalonians who "turned to God from idols to serve the living and true God" (1 Thess. 1:9). In true conversion, there is always a turning *from* sin (repentance) and a simultaneous turning *to* God in Christ (faith). It is impossible that one should occur without the other.[108]

Nevertheless, as we examine what Scripture has to say about the nature of these two elements of conversion, we must discuss each in its turn. Though they are simultaneous actions, in each instance in which they are named together, the New Testament lists repentance first (Mark 1:15; Acts 19:4; 20:21; Heb. 6:1), indicating a logical priority. For this reason, we will treat repentance first and then faith.

REPENTANCE

To understand the fullness of the biblical concept of repentance, it is necessary to examine the various terms Scripture employs to describe it. First, the Hebrew term *nakham* is often used to communicate the emotional component of repentance. Its most basic meanings include "to be sorry or sorrowful," "to be grieved," and "to be regretful." Thought to be an onomatopoetic word, even the phonology of *nakham* communicates the idea of breathing deeply, or sighing, in sorrow or grief. For example, *nakham* describes a family mourning the death of a loved one (Gen. 37:35; 38:12). When the Lord brought judgment on the tribe of Benjamin for the wickedness done to the Levite's concubine (Judg. 19:1–30), the Israelites mourned [*nakham*] the loss of their countrymen (Judg. 21:6, 15). It is not difficult to see how mourning intersects with repentance when one considers that the Lord pronounced a blessing on those who mourn over their sin (Matt. 5:4). In addition to mourning, *nakham* expresses sorrow over sin, as in the case of Job, who declared from the ash heap, "Therefore I retract, and I repent [*nakham*] in dust and ashes" (Job 42:6). Such sorrow may also be accompanied by appropriate shame and humiliation (Jer. 31:19) and often leads to action, such as relenting of an evil course (Jer. 8:6). Thus, *nakham* teaches that the emotions have a place in repentance. Those who repent will be genuinely sorry and remorseful over their deeds and at times will experience such grief that they will demonstrate their sorrow in action.

The most common Old Testament Hebrew word for "repentance" is *shub*, whose most basic meaning is "to turn" or "to return." Hebrew scholars say that "better than any other verb it combines in itself the two requisites of repentance: to turn from evil and to turn to the good."[109] It describes biblical repentance as turning from sin (1 Kings 8:35), transgression (Isa. 59:20), and iniquity (Dan. 9:13) and as removing injustice from one's tent (Job 22:23). The repentance signified by *shub* includes forsaking a path of wickedness and amending one's deeds, turning from the plans of an evil heart (Jer. 18:11–12; 25:5; 26:3; 35:15). Such repentance involves repudiating all

---

108. Thus Berkhof writes, "True repentance never exists except in conjunction with faith, while, on the other hand, wherever there is true faith, there is also real repentance. The two are but different aspects of the same turning,—a turning away from sin in the direction of God. . . . The two cannot be separated; they are simply complementary parts of the same process." *Systematic Theology*, 487.

109. Victor P. Hamilton, "šub," in *Theological Wordbook of the Old Testament*, ed. R. Laird Harris, Gleason L. Archer Jr., and Bruce K. Waltke (Chicago: Moody Press, 1980), 2:909.

known sin and keeping the commands of God (Ezek. 18:21). Indeed, repentance and sin are mutually exclusive, for one's sinful deeds will not permit one to return [*shub*] to God (Hos. 5:4). Thus, repentance is not merely a turning *from* sin but also a turning *to* God. Repentant individuals are said to seek the Lord (Isa. 9:13) and his favor (Dan. 9:13), to tremble at his goodness and be enticed to be reconciled to him (Hos. 3:5), and to put away idolatrous worship and commit to worshiping God alone (Jer. 4:1–4; cf. 1 Sam. 7:3). Thus, repentance includes a change that results in obedience, requiring the sinner to "amend [his] ways and [his] deeds" (Jer. 18:11) and to keep the commandments of God's law (2 Kings 17:13; 23:25). Such repentant obedience is never merely external but rather comes from the heart (Deut. 30:2; 1 Kings 8:48; Jer. 3:10; Joel 2:12–13).

In the New Testament, the Greek term *metamelomai* represents the emotional component of repentance as denoted by *nakham*. It describes "regret" (2 Cor. 7:8; cf. 7:10–11) and "remorse" (Matt. 21:32; 27:3 NASB) for evil conduct. Similarly, the Greek term *epistrephō* and its cognates signify the same general concept of "turning" as the Hebrew *shub*. When speaking of repentance, it describes how one changes his life's direction—turning from sin and idolatry to worshiping and serving the true God (Acts 14:15; 1 Thess. 1:9). Such turning to the Lord is used synonymously with forsaking a hardened heart of unbelief and coming to God in faith for salvation (Matt. 13:15; Luke 1:16–17; Acts 3:19; 9:35; 11:21; 26:18, 20; 2 Cor. 3:16).

The most common New Testament Greek verb for repentance is *metanoeō* (noun, *metanoia*), which means "to change one's mind." It indicates first of all that repentance involves acknowledging one's sin. John the Baptist came "proclaiming a baptism of repentance [Gk. *metanoia*] for the forgiveness of sins" (Mark 1:4; Luke 3:3). If repentance is *for* the forgiveness of sins, those submitting to a baptism of repentance must have acknowledged that they were sinners in need of forgiveness. Indeed, Christ came to call sinners, not the righteous, to repentance (Luke 5:32). Such an acknowledgment also implies a fundamental change of attitude toward sin and a purpose to turn away from it. Such is the inescapable meaning of Peter's charge to Simon Magus (Acts 8:22) and Paul's charge to the Corinthians practicing impurity, sexual immorality, and sensuality (2 Cor. 12:21). Christ himself requires this when he intimately unites the command to repent with an exhortation to "do the works you did at first" (Rev. 2:5). Such obviously implies a change in attitude, resulting in a full change of course that issues in a changed life. Indeed, after acknowledging one's sin and deserved judgment and after altering one's course by turning from sins, the sinner is exhorted to "bear fruits in keeping with repentance" (Luke 3:8; cf. 3:10–14) and to be "performing deeds in keeping with . . . repentance" (Acts 26:20). Thus, the "change of mind" signified by *metanoeō* is not a mere intellectual alteration. The "mind" (Gk. *nous*) that is changed refers to the inner consciousness of the whole man and not merely to the mental faculties. Concerning *metanoeō*, Berkhof wisely observes,

While maintaining that the word denotes primarily a change of mind, we should not lose sight of the fact that its meaning is not limited to the intellectual, theoretical consciousness, but also includes the moral consciousness, the conscience. Both the mind and the conscience are defiled, Tit. 1:15, and when a person's *nous* is changed, he not only receives new knowledge, but the direction of his conscious life, its moral quality, is also changed.[110]

To summarize the above lexical analysis, biblical repentance is not a mere change of thinking, though it does involve an intellectual acknowledgment of sin and a change of attitude toward it. Neither is it merely shame or sorrow for sin, although genuine repentance always involves an element of remorse. True biblical repentance is also a redirection of the human will, a purposeful decision to forsake all unrighteousness and pursue righteousness instead. Thus, genuine repentance involves the mind, the heart, and the will.[111]

Intellectually, repentance begins with a recognition of sin. We must apprehend the truly wicked nature of sin and as a result humbly acknowledge that we are sinners who have broken God's law, have fallen short of his glory, and therefore stand guilty before him. To experience the intellectual aspect of repentance is to declare with Job, "I have uttered what I did not understand" (Job 42:3; cf. 42:6), and to confess as did David, "I have sinned against the LORD" (2 Sam. 12:13; cf. Ps. 51:3–4). It is to humbly confess one's need for grace and mercy and to ask for forgiveness (Ps. 51:1–2).

Emotionally, genuine repentance is marked by a sincere sorrow, remorse, and even mourning over one's sin (cf. Matt. 5:4). Old Testament saints would often act out their sorrowful repentance, by smiting their thigh (Jer. 31:19), sitting on an ash heap (Job 42:6), and donning sackcloth and ashes (Jonah 3:5–6; cf. Matt. 11:21). True, repentant sorrow is distinct from what Paul calls "worldly grief," which produces death (2 Cor. 7:10). Such was the case with Judas, who "felt remorse" (Matt. 27:3 NASB) for betraying Christ, even to the point of confessing, "I have sinned by betraying innocent blood" (Matt. 27:4). Yet his was a worldly grief that produced death, for "he went and hanged himself" (Matt. 27:5). Similarly, the rich young ruler went away sorrowful (Matt. 19:22), but he was not repentant, for he clung to the idol of his possessions rather than selling all he had to gain Christ (cf. Matt. 13:44). Nevertheless, while sorrow should not be equated strictly with repentance, it is a

---

110. Berkhof, *Systematic Theology*, 481. Goetzman likewise states, "The predominantly intellectual understanding of *metanoia* as a change of mind plays very little part in the NT. Rather the decision by the whole man to turn around is stressed. It is clear that we are concerned neither with a purely outward turning nor with a merely intellectual change of ideas." J. Goetzman, "Conversion," in *New International Dictionary of New Testament Theology*, ed. Colin Brown (Grand Rapids, MI: Zondervan, 1986), 1:358. Behm agrees: "It affects the whole man, first and basically the centre of personal life, then logically his conduct at all times and in all situations, his thoughts, words and acts (Mt. 12:33ff. par.; 23:26; Mk. 7:15 par.)." J. Behm, "*Metanoia*," in *Theological Dictionary of the New Testament*, ed. Gerhard Kittel, trans. Geoffrey W. Bromiley (Grand Rapids, MI: Eerdmans, 1967), 4:1002.

111. Vos writes, "Our Lord's idea of repentance is as profound and comprehensive as his conception of righteousness. Of the three words that are used in the Greek Gospels to describe the process, one emphasizes the emotional element of regret, sorrow over the past evil course of life, *metamélomai*; Matt. 21:29–32; a second expresses reversal of the entire mental attitude, *metanoéō*, Matt. 12:41; Luke 11:32; 15:7, 10; the third denotes a change in the direction of life, one goal being substituted for another, *epistréphomai*; Matt. 13:15 (and parallels); Luke 17:4; 22:32. Repentance is not limited to any single faculty of the mind: it engages the entire man, intellect, will and affections. . . . Again, in the new life which follows repentance the absolute supremacy of God is the controlling principle. He who repents turns away from the service of mammon and self to the service of God." Geerhardus Vos, *The Teaching of Jesus concerning the Kingdom of God and the Church* (1903; repr., Nutley, NJ: Presbyterian and Reformed, 1972), 92–93.

necessary component of it and is often a powerful impulse to genuinely turning away from sin. As Paul says, "Godly grief produces a repentance that leads to salvation without regret" (2 Cor. 7:10). Thus, true repentance will always include at least some element of contrition—not sorrow for getting caught, nor sadness because of the consequences, but a spirit broken by the sense of having sinned against God and a longing to be restored to fellowship with him (Ps. 51:12, 17).

Finally, repentance involves a change of direction, a transformation of the will. Far from being only a change of mind, repentance constitutes a determination to abandon stubborn disobedience and surrender the will to Christ. This is powerfully illustrated in the ministries of the Old Testament prophets, who characterized repentance in terms of the wicked forsaking his evil thoughts (Isa. 55:7), turning from his wickedness and practicing justice and righteousness (Ezek. 33:19), and turning from his wicked way (Jonah 3:10; cf. 2 Chron. 7:14). It is a resolute disowning of oneself and one's sinful way of life and an embrace of Christ for justifying and sanctifying righteousness. As such, genuine repentance will inevitably result in a change of behavior. It is important to note, though, that the behavior change itself is not repentance. The call to repentance is not a call to clean up one's life to fit oneself for salvation. That would turn repentance into a work of merit and would undermine the gospel of grace. Salvation is a sovereign gift of God's grace that the sinner apprehends by faith alone (Rom. 3:28; Eph. 2:8), precisely because it is impossible for sinners to satisfy the demands of God's righteousness by their deeds (Titus 3:5). But while repentance is not to be strictly defined as a change in behavior, a changed life *is* the fruit that genuine repentance will inevitably bear. Though sinners are not saved *by* good works, they are saved *for* good works (Eph. 2:10; Titus 2:14; 3:8).

Thus, in his ministry the apostle Paul proclaimed to Jews and Gentiles "that they should repent [Gk. *metanoeō*] and turn [Gk. *epistrephō*] to God, performing deeds in keeping with their repentance" (Acts 26:20). Similarly, John the Baptist demanded that those who professed to be repentant "bear fruits in keeping with repentance" (Luke 3:8). When his hearers asked what a repentant life looked like, he responded by saying that a man ought to stop being greedy and indifferent to his neighbor's suffering and should change his course by lending to him liberally (Luke 3:11). He called the tax collectors to turn from their extortion: "Collect no more than what you are authorized to do" (Luke 3:13). He answered that the soldiers must no longer extort by threats and false accusation but must be content with making an honest living (Luke 3:14). Both Paul and John the Baptist stood on the shoulders of the prophets, such as Isaiah, who identified the fruits of repentance for the corrupt nation of his day: "Wash yourselves; make yourselves clean; remove the evil of your deeds from before my eyes; cease to do evil, learn to do good; seek justice, correct oppression; bring justice to the fatherless, plead the widow's cause" (Isa. 1:16–17). One observes the progression in such a list: repentance begins internally with a cleansing, and then manifests itself in righteous attitudes and actions. In other words, there will be a sincere change in one's conduct. A person who has genuinely repented will stop doing evil and will begin to live righteously. Where there is no observable difference in conduct, there can be no confidence that repentance has taken place (Matt. 3:8; 1 John 2:3–6; 3:17).[112]

In summary, then, the Scriptures teach that repentance begins with the sinner's humble acknowledgment of his sin and need for forgiveness. Understanding the offensiveness of his sin before God produces great mourning, sorrow, and even shame and humiliation. His disgust with himself and his unrighteousness leads him to repudiate his wickedness and to decisively turn away from a life of sin. As he turns from his former way of life, he turns to trust and serve the God who is worthy of all worship. In Christ he finds forgiveness and is restored to fellowship with his Creator. Finally, he does not regard that forgiveness as the final step but lovingly, from the heart, purposes to live in obedience to the revealed will of God, empowered by the work of the Holy Spirit. The evidence of his inward repentance is thus manifested in his external deeds.

Repentance is an essential element of conversion and is therefore an indispensable element of the gospel message. Not only is repentance mentioned alongside faith in the proclamation of the gospel (Mark 1:15; Acts 20:21; Heb. 6:1), but also many passages in Scripture call for repentance alone to lay hold of salvation. This does not contradict the truth that faith is the sole instrument of justification but rather illustrates that the New Testament authors regarded the relationship between repentance and faith to be so intimate that the mention of the one implied the other—that one cannot turn from sin without turning to Christ in faith, and vice versa. Thus, while Mark records Jesus's first proclamation of the gospel as calling his hearers to "repent and believe the gospel" (Mark 1:15), Matthew records the same as Jesus's call to "repent, for the kingdom of heaven is at hand" (Matt. 4:17). Jesus would later characterize the objective of his ministry as calling sinners to repentance (Luke 5:32) and would demonstrate that truth by declaring, "Unless you repent, you will all likewise perish" (Luke 13:3, 5). In the only record of the Great Commission in which we are given Jesus's words concerning the content of the message the disciples are to preach, Jesus summarizes the gospel as the proclamation of "repentance for the forgiveness of sins" in his name (Luke 24:47 NASB). And the disciples were obedient to this commission. As the men of Israel listened to Peter's sermon on the day of Pentecost, they were seized with conviction and asked, "Brothers, what shall we do?" Peter responded by calling them to repentance: "Repent, and each of you be baptized in the name of Jesus Christ for the forgiveness of your sins" (Acts 2:38 NASB). In his sermon at Solomon's portico, he concluded with the same call: "Repent therefore, and turn back, that your sins may be blotted out" (Acts 3:19). As Paul preached the gospel to the Athenians on Mars Hill, the climax of his message was a call to repentance: "The times of ignorance God overlooked, but now he commands all people everywhere to repent" (Acts 17:30). Scripture is unmistakably clear: repentance is not an optional

---

112. John MacArthur, *The Gospel according to Jesus: What Is Authentic Faith?*, rev. ed. (Grand Rapids, MI: Zondervan, 2008), 180, 182.

element but is an essential component of the true gospel. Those who insist that it is possible to savingly trust in Christ without repenting of sin—to believe in Jesus as Savior but not submit to him as Lord—find themselves in direct contradiction to the gospel according to Jesus and the apostles.[113]

FAITH

Whereas repentance might be described as the negative aspect of conversion—that is, the act of turning away from sin—faith can be styled as the positive aspect, the soul's turn *to* God and trusting in the person and work of Christ to provide forgiveness, righteousness, and eternal life. As the miracle of the new birth banishes the blindness of spiritual death, the eyes of the sinner's re-created heart look on the glory of Jesus and delight to find in him an utterly sufficient Savior, perfectly suited to cleanse from sin, provide perfect righteousness, and satisfy the soul. Beholding the glory of God in the face of Christ (2 Cor. 4:6), the sinner embraces Jesus with all his heart, entrusting and committing himself to all that Christ is. Thus, saving faith is a fundamental commitment of the whole person to the whole Christ; with his mind, heart, and will, the believer embraces Jesus as Savior, Advocate, Provider, Sustainer, Counselor, and Lord God.

Thus, like repentance, its counterpart, saving faith consists of intellectual, emotional, and volitional elements: knowledge (Lat. *notitia*), assent (Lat. *assensus*), and trust (Lat. *fiducia*), respectively. The mind embraces knowledge, a recognition and understanding of the truth concerning the person and work of Christ. The heart gives assent, or the settled confidence and affirmation that Christ's salvation is suitable to one's spiritual need. The will responds with trust, the personal commitment to and appropriation of Christ as the only hope for eternal salvation.[114] Each of these components requires further elaboration.

Knowledge. The most basic element of faith is knowledge. Contemporary cultural thought, dominated by secular humanism, conceives of faith as the opposite of knowledge—that faith is what takes over when one does not have sufficient knowledge. It is not uncommon to hear someone say, "Well, I can't really *know*, but I just *believe* it." However, the biblical conception of faith is not an existential leap in the dark or a sentimental, wish-upon-a-star kind of hope. So far from being an alternative to knowledge, true faith is based on knowledge; it has its sure and solid foundation in the knowledge of divinely revealed truth.

Scripture testifies to this in a number of ways. First, the Bible often represents the knowledge of particular truths as the causal ground of faith. For example, faith

---

113. For a thorough discussion of the controversy over "Lordship salvation," as well as a thorough refutation of so-called "free grace" theology, see John MacArthur, *The Gospel according to Jesus*, and MacArthur, *The Gospel according to the Apostles: The Role of Works in the Life of Faith* (1993; repr., Nashville: Thomas Nelson, 2000). Especially helpful is the second chapter of the latter volume, "A Primer on the 'Lordship Salvation' Controversy," 5–20. For further analysis, see Robert Lescelius, *Lordship Salvation: Some Crucial Questions and Answers* (Asheville, NC: Revival Literature, 1992), and Richard P. Belcher, *A Layman's Guide to the Lordship Controversy* (Southbridge, MA: Crowne, 1990). A very brief, though helpful, overview is also found in Grudem, *Systematic Theology*, 715n5.

114. MacArthur, *The Gospel according to the Apostles*, 27.

in Christ for salvation is grounded on "knowing that a man is not justified by the works of the Law but through faith in Christ Jesus" (Gal. 2:16 NASB). It is *because we know* that works do not justify that we believe in Christ for salvation. Similarly, Paul grounds the believer's faith in his future resurrection on the knowledge of Christ's resurrection: "Now if we have died with Christ, we believe that we shall also live with Him, knowing [i.e., 'because we know'[115]] that Christ, having been raised from the dead, is never to die again" (Rom. 6:8–9 NASB; cf. 2 Cor. 4:13–14; 1 Pet. 5:9). These passages make plain that biblical faith and knowledge of the truth are not enemies but that the latter is the ground of the former. Scripture further testifies to this relationship between faith and knowledge by often employing the phrase "believe that . . ." followed by propositional truth claims that identify the content of saving faith.[116] One must believe that Jesus is God (John 8:24; 13:19, where Jesus applies the divine name "I Am" to himself; cf. Ex. 3:14) and is one with the Father (John 14:10–11), that he is the Messiah and Son of God (John 11:27; 20:31; 1 John 5:1, 5) who was sent from the Father (John 11:42; 16:27, 30; 17:8, 21), that he died for sins and rose from the grave (1 Thess. 4:14; cf. Rom. 10:9), that God exists and "rewards those who seek him" (Heb. 11:6), and that sinners are saved by grace through faith alone (Acts 15:11; cf. 15:9). The apostle Paul summarizes the matter when he declares that saving faith comes from hearing the gospel message concerning Christ (Rom. 10:17), so that it is impossible to believe without hearing that message (Rom. 10:14). Knowledge of the gospel message—namely, the divinely revealed facts of God's holiness, sin's penalty, Christ's identity, and what he has accomplished for sinners—is the very ground of saving faith. Clearly, then, true faith has objective substance. Believing is not a mindless leap in the dark or some ethereal kind of trust apart from knowledge. The truth of the gospel message as revealed in Christ and in Scripture provides a factual, historical, intellectual basis for our faith. Thus, we do not believe according to our subjective whims; we are to believe the truth (2 Thess. 2:11–12; cf. John 8:46; 1 Tim. 4:3). Faith that is not grounded in this objective, propositional truth is no faith at all.[117]

Assent. While knowing the facts is necessary to faith, it is not sufficient. It is entirely possible to know the truth without believing or embracing the truth. Many preachers, scholars, and theologians have intellectually grasped great truths of Scripture, such as the virgin birth of Christ and his bodily resurrection, and yet have rejected these doctrines as false. Also, many people understand the truths of the gospel—that man stands guilty before a holy God and will perish in his sins, that Christ has borne the punishment of his people by dying and rising in their place, and that the benefits of his work are to be received by faith apart from works—and yet fail to repent and trust in him themselves. For this reason, faith is said to have an emotional element as well as an intellectual element. Faith not only knows the truth but also assents

---

115. The participle *eidotes* (lit., "knowing") here bears a causal force: "because we know." See Wallace, *Greek Grammar Beyond the Basics*, 631.
116. Reymond, *Systematic Theology*, 727.
117. MacArthur, *The Gospel according to the Apostles*, 29–30.

to and wholeheartedly embraces the truth as it is revealed in Scripture. The truth is known and believed.

The writer of Hebrews speaks to this heartfelt assent as a component of faith when he defines faith as "the assurance of things hoped for, the conviction of things not seen" (Heb. 11:1). The word translated "assurance" is the Greek term *hypostasis*, made up of *stasis*, "to stand," and *hypo*, "under." It refers to a foundation, the ground on which something is built. The writer uses it here to describe faith as a supernatural certainty—a God-wrought conviction about the truth of the Bible's promises and the trustworthiness of Christ. The writer goes on to say that faith is the conviction of things not seen; that is, what cannot be seen with the physical eyes is unveiled for the spiritual eyes by faith. Hebrews 11:27 characterizes Moses's faith in precisely this way: "By faith he left Egypt, not being afraid of the anger of the king, for he endured as seeing him who is invisible." Moses's faith consisted of the resolute conviction that the riches of Christ's glory were more valuable than the treasures of Egypt (Heb. 11:24–26). He did not just intellectually apprehend that Christ was more precious; he was persuaded in the depths of his heart that it was true. It was Paul's resolute, faith-filled conviction of the sovereignty of Christ that fueled his endurance through the most intense suffering, for he said, "I know whom I have believed, and I am convinced that he is able to guard until that Day what has been entrusted to me" (2 Tim. 1:12).

With respect to conversion, then, the one who possesses saving faith wholeheartedly embraces the truth concerning his own sinfulness and Christ's suitableness to save him. When Bartimaeus heard that Jesus was passing by, his resolute conviction that the Son of David was perfectly suited to meet his need caused him to abandon propriety and cry out for Jesus to restore his sight. Jesus responded, "Go your way; your faith has made you well" (Mark 10:46–52). In the same way, the newly awakened believer becomes absolutely convinced that he is helpless to address the inevitable misery of his spiritual condition, and he looks on Christ with the certain conviction that Christ's sufficiency is the perfect answer to his spiritual bankruptcy. By this faith the sinner is made well.

Trust. There was something more to Moses's, Paul's, and Bartimaeus's faith than merely knowing and embracing the truth. James tells us that the demons know and believe the truth of monotheism (James 2:19). Nicodemus believed that Jesus was a teacher sent from God (John 3:2). Agrippa believed that the Old Testament spoke truth (Acts 26:27). Judas was convinced that Jesus was the Christ (Matt. 27:3–5). Yet none of these possessed saving faith. Faith begins with knowledge (*notitia*) and assent (*assensus*), but it does not stop until it reaches the will's utter reliance on Christ for one's personal salvation (*fiducia*). As Murray insightfully notes, "Faith is knowledge passing into conviction, and it is conviction passing into confidence. Faith cannot stop short of self-commitment to Christ, a transference of reliance upon ourselves and all human resources to reliance upon Christ alone for salvation.

It is a receiving and resting upon him."[118] That is to say, saving faith moves beyond "believing *that*" and arrives at "believing *in*"; it moves beyond mentally assenting to truth *about* Christ and arrives at personally trusting *in* Christ and depending *on* him for forgiveness of sins and reconciliation to God.

The apostle Paul narrates his own conversion story in Philippians 3. He characterizes the true Christian as one who puts no confidence in the flesh (Phil. 3:3), one who does not look within himself—to his inherited privileges or religious accomplishments—to acquire the righteousness that God requires. In his life as a Pharisee, he had indeed put full confidence in his flesh—in his heritage, social standing, religious ritualism, traditionalism, devotion, and sincerity, and even in the external observance of God's commands (Phil. 3:4–6). He trusted in these fleshly credentials to lift him up to reach the standard of God's righteousness. But that error disappeared after he met the risen Christ on the road to Damascus. As he said, "Whatever gain I had, I counted as loss for the sake of Christ" (Phil. 3:7). When God opened the eyes of Paul's heart in regeneration, all the self-righteousness that Paul counted on to be gain he came to regard as loss. He counted it all rubbish in order to "gain Christ, and be found in Him, not having my own righteousness, which is from the law, but that which is through faith in Christ, the righteousness which is from God by faith" (Phil. 3:8–9 NKJV). He had turned from depending on himself for righteousness to trusting in Christ alone for righteousness (cf. Rom. 10:4; 2 Cor. 5:21).

Not only does the one with saving faith trust in Christ for righteousness, he also receives Christ as treasure. Paul regarded knowing Jesus personally to be of such surpassing value that he was willing to lose everything in his life to gain him (Phil. 3:8). Jesus himself spoke of conversion as finding a treasure: "The kingdom of heaven is like treasure hidden in a field, which a man found and covered up. Then in his joy he goes and sells all that he has and buys that field" (Matt. 13:44; cf. 13:45–46). The man whose heart has been awakened in regeneration is like a man who stumbles on a priceless, buried treasure. And because of the surpassing value of the treasure that is Christ Jesus, the sinner willingly forsakes everything he has so he can lay hold of the Savior whom he regards as supremely precious (Luke 9:23; 14:26–33; cf. Matt. 10:37–39). These texts should caution the student of Scripture from conceiving of saving faith as that which merely uses Christ to escape punishment. Saving faith is preeminently an eager embrace of a *person*—a wholehearted, delightful reception of Christ for the fullness of who he is, namely, the source of all righteousness, life, and satisfaction for the newborn soul (Matt. 5:6; John 4:13–14; 6:35).

Finally, in this volitional aspect of faith, one not only trusts in Christ but also entrusts oneself *to* Christ, for believing in a person necessarily involves a personal commitment. The one who trusts Christ places himself in the custody of Christ for both life and death. The believer relies on the Lord's counsel, trusts in his goodness, and entrusts himself for time and eternity to his guardianship. Saving faith, then, is the sinner, in the whole of his being, embracing all of Christ. That is why Scripture

---

118. Murray, *Redemption Accomplished and Applied*, 111.

often uses such metaphors for faith as looking to him (John 3:14–15; cf. Num. 21:9), eating his flesh and drinking his blood (John 6:50–58; cf. 4:14), receiving him (John 1:12), and coming to him (Matt. 11:28; John 5:40; 6:35, 37, 44, 65; 7:37–38). One demonstrates his faith that bread satisfies hunger not merely by confessing, "Bread satisfies!" but by eating the bread. In the same way, one demonstrates his faith in Christ not merely by saying, "I believe!" but by coming to Christ, receiving all that he is, and entrusting to him all that the believer is. In summary, faith is leaning wholly on Christ—for redemption, for righteousness, for counsel, for fellowship, for sustenance, for direction, for succor, for his lordship, and for all in life that can truly satisfy.

This means that true, saving faith necessarily works itself out in loving obedience (cf. Gal. 5:6). The eleventh chapter of Hebrews is dedicated to illustrating this sole principle. After defining the nature of true faith in the opening verses, the author scans the whole of redemptive history to demonstrate that faith works. By faith Abel offered an acceptable sacrifice (Heb. 11:4); by faith Enoch walked with God and escaped death itself (11:5); by faith Noah built an ark (11:7); by faith Abraham obeyed (11:8), lived in a foreign land (11:9), and offered up Isaac to God (11:17–19); by faith Isaac and Jacob blessed their sons (11:20–21); by faith Joseph spoke of the exodus (11:22); by faith Moses's parents hid him from Pharaoh (11:23); by faith Moses rejected the passing pleasures of Egypt, embraced the reproach of Christ, and left without fear (11:24–27); by faith Moses kept the Passover (11:28); by faith Israel crossed the Red Sea (11:29) and conquered Jericho (11:30). Faith offers, walks, builds, blesses, hides, leaves, and conquers. In short, faith obeys. It compels one to act in accordance with the truth that one professes to believe. At conversion, saving faith does nothing but passively receive the provision of Christ. Yet true faith never remains passive; it immediately goes to work—not as a means of earning divine favor but as a consequence of having received the grace of God that works mightily within us (Col. 1:29). As we work out our salvation with fear and trembling, it is God who works in us, both to will and to work for his good pleasure (Phil. 2:12–13).[119]

GIFTS THAT KEEP ON GIVING

Two other features of repentance and faith must not go without mention. First, both repentance and faith are sovereign gifts of God himself. While it is true that repentant faith is held out to sinners as their responsibility and the condition for their justification, the corruption of their mind, affections, and will makes it impossible for them to truly repent and believe. It is only by the sovereign work of the Spirit in

---

119. MacArthur explains, "Does this mix faith and works, as some are fond of saying? Not at all. Let there be no confusion on this point. Faith is an *internal* reality with *external* consequences. When we say that faith encompasses obedience, we are speaking of the God-given *attitude* of obedience, not trying to make *works* a part of the definition of faith. God makes the believing heart an obedient heart; that is, a heart eager to obey. Faith itself is complete before one work of obedience ever issues forth. But make no mistake—real faith will always produce righteous works. Faith is the root; works are the fruit. Because God Himself is the vinedresser, fruit is guaranteed. That's why whenever Scripture gives examples of faith—as here in Hebrews 11—faith inevitably is seen as obedient, working, and active." MacArthur, *The Gospel according to the Apostles*, 34. For a more thorough discussion of the issues at play in the "Lordship salvation" controversy, see MacArthur, *The Gospel according to Jesus*, and MacArthur, *The Gospel according to the Apostles*.

regeneration, renewing man's heart and opening his spiritual eyes, that he is enabled to turn from sin and self and trust in Christ alone for righteousness.

For this reason, Scripture speaks of repentant faith not as a sovereign decision of the human will but as that which is supernaturally granted as a gift of God's grace.[120] In the case of repentance, Peter declared to the Sanhedrin that God accomplished Christ's death and resurrection in order "to give repentance to Israel and forgiveness of sins" (Acts 5:31). When Peter later testified to the Jews that the Spirit had fallen on the Gentiles, they concluded that God had given this gift to the Gentiles as well: "Then to the Gentiles also God has granted repentance that leads to life" (Acts 11:18). Similarly, Paul instructed Timothy to gently correct those who opposed him, in the hope that "God may perhaps grant them repentance leading to a knowledge of the truth" (2 Tim. 2:25).

Correspondingly, Scripture identifies faith as a gift of God's grace. Perhaps the most familiar passage on the subject is Ephesians 2:8–9, where Paul declares, "For by grace you have been saved through faith. And this is not your own doing; it is the gift of God, not a result of works, so that no one may boast." Here, Paul refers to the entirety of salvation as the gift of God, which necessarily includes the faith by which the sinner is justified.[121] Further, Luke characterizes Christians as "those who through grace had believed" (Acts 18:27); thus, faith comes only through God's grace and therefore is a gift. Paul explicitly teaches this idea in his letter to the Philippians when he tells them, "For to you it has been granted for Christ's sake, not only to believe in Him, but also to suffer for His sake" (Phil. 1:29 NASB). Along with suffering for the sake of the gospel, faith in Christ is granted as a gift from God.

As a divine gift, then, the repentant faith that saves could never be transient or temporary. It has an abiding quality that guarantees it will endure to the end, so that repentance and faith characterize the lifestyle of the true Christian. In the first of his "Ninety-Five Theses," Martin Luther (1483–1546) famously wrote, "When our Lord and Master Jesus Christ said, 'Repent,' he intended that the entire life of believers should be repentance."[122] Thus, when Peter asked Jesus how often he should forgive a brother who sins against him (Matt. 18:21), Jesus responded, "If your brother sins,

---

120. It is necessary to guard against a potential misunderstanding. The fact that repentance and faith are gifts of God does not imply that they are not also the acts of men. God does not repent from sin or believe in Christ *for* the believer, as Karl Barth taught (see G. C. Berkouwer, *Faith and Justification* [Grand Rapids, MI: Eerdmans, 1954], 172–75). Rather, God sovereignly awakens the sinner in regeneration so that he himself, in his personal consciousness and according to his renewed nature, necessarily turns from sin and trusts in Christ. God gives faith and man acts faith, but man's act is absolutely dependent on God's gift.

121. There is some disagreement on the proper referent of "this"; what exactly is not of man's doing but is the gift of God? While "faith" is its nearest antecedent, "this" appears in the neuter, and "faith" is a feminine noun. Normally, the gender of a pronoun agrees with its antecedent. Because that is not the case here, many conclude that the gift of God does not refer to faith. Neither then can it refer to "grace," which is also a feminine noun. Suggesting it refers to "you have been saved" faces the same problem, because it is a masculine participle. Some take it to be an adverbial phrase used emphatically, as in 3 John 5. Perhaps the best explanation is that the antecedent of "this" is the entire preceding phrase—"by grace you have been saved through faith." It is not unusual for the demonstrative pronoun to appear in the neuter when referring to multiple antecedents of varying genders. For example, in Phil. 1:28, Paul says, "This is a clear sign [Gk. *endeixis*, fem.] to them of their destruction [Gk. *apōleias*, fem.], but of your salvation [Gk. *sōterias*, fem.], and that [Gk. *touto*, neut.] from God." "That" refers to the sign of both the opponents' destruction and the believers' salvation. Paul views them as a unit and says that both are from God. Where it would have made sense to use the feminine, Paul uses the neuter to comment on the multiple antecedents at once. For more, see Wallace, *Greek Grammar Beyond the Basics*, 334–35, and Ernest Best, *A Critical and Exegetical Commentary on Ephesians*, ICC (Edinburgh: T&T Clark, 1998), 226.

122. Martin Luther, *Martin Luther's Ninety-Five Theses*, ed. Stephen J. Nichols (Phillipsburg, NJ: P&R, 2002), 23.

rebuke him, and if he repents, forgive him, and if he sins against you seven times in the day, and turns to you seven times, saying, 'I repent,' you must forgive him" (Luke 17:3–4). The principle is that one ought to repent as often as one sins. In his letters to the churches of Asia, Christ instructed believers (i.e., "those whom I love") at the church of Laodicea to "be zealous and repent" (Rev. 3:19), which shows that repentance is not just a one-time event at conversion but is expected even of true Christians. The Lord also taught his disciples to be in the habit of praying for forgiveness (Matt. 6:12), which necessarily requires ongoing repentance. The apostle John similarly states, "If we confess [Gk. *homologeō*] our sins, he is faithful and just to forgive us our sins and to cleanse us from all unrighteousness" (1 John 1:9). The present tense of *homologeō* indicates ongoing activity. Thus, believers show that they are the ones God has forgiven and cleansed because they are continually confessing their sins. In sum, though justification frees the believer from the penalty of sin, the presence of sin still remains in his unredeemed flesh. Therefore, because he continues to sin against God and others, he must continue to repent. In a believer's life, a spirit of repentance must be as indwelling as is his remaining sin.[123]

The same is true for faith.[124] The familiar words of Habakkuk 2:4, "The righteous shall live by his faith" (cf. Rom. 1:18; Gal. 3:11; Heb. 10:38), speak not of a momentary act of believing but of a living, enduring trust in God. Hebrews 3:14 emphasizes the permanence of genuine faith. Its very durability is proof of its reality: "We have come to share in Christ, if indeed we hold our original confidence firm to the end." The faith that God gives can never evaporate. And the work of salvation cannot ultimately be thwarted (1 Cor. 1:8; Phil. 1:6; Col. 1:22–23).[125] The apostle Paul summarizes the totality of the Christian life when he declares, "The life I now live in the flesh I live by faith in the Son of God, who loved me and gave himself for me" (Gal. 2:20; cf. Heb. 10:39). The Christian's life is to be distinguished by daily confession of, mourning over, and turning from sin, as well as a persevering faith in the person of Christ and the promises of God.

Union with Christ

One of the most precious truths in all Scripture is the doctrine of the believer's union with the Lord Jesus Christ. The concept of being united to Christ speaks of the most vital spiritual intimacy that one can imagine between the Lord and his people. While Christ relates to believers as Lord, Master, Savior, and Teacher, they are not merely associated with Christ as the object of his saving grace and love. It is not that Christians merely worship Jesus, obey him, or pray to him, though surely those privileges would be enough. Rather, they are so intimately identified with him and he with them that Scripture says they are united—he is in them and they are in him.

---

123. Christopher Jenkins explains, "At conversion, a sinner purposes to turn from sin generally conceived (i.e., as the dominant principle of life), and yet throughout the sanctified life, he also turns from specific sins as they occur." "What is Repentance? Settling the Debate," *Journal of Modern Ministry* 5, no. 2 (2008): 7–19, 21–28.

124. This paragraph is adapted from John MacArthur, "The Lordship Controversy," Grace to You, accessed April 14, 2016, http://www.gtycanada.org/Resources/Articles/A293.

125. MacArthur, *The Gospel according to Jesus*, 189.

The Lord and his people share a common spiritual life, such that the apostle Paul could say that our life is hidden with Christ in God (Col. 3:3), that Christ is himself our life (Col. 3:4), and that Christ lives in us (Gal. 2:20). United to his people in this way, Christ acts as their representative and substitute; that is, that which Christ has accomplished on behalf of his people God reckons to have counted for them, just as if they had done it themselves. Because of union with Christ, believers have been crucified with him (Gal. 2:20), have died with him (Rom. 6:8; Col. 2:20), have been buried with him (Rom. 6:3–4), have been raised with him (Eph. 2:5–6; Col. 3:1), and have even been enthroned in heaven with him (Eph. 2:6). He is thus the Mediator of all the benefits of salvation, for God our Father "has blessed us with every spiritual blessing in the heavenly places *in Christ*" (Eph. 1:3 NASB).

Such intimate spiritual union is unique to Christianity. In no other religion is the object of worship said to become the life of the worshiper. Muslims do not speak of being in Allah or in Muhammad; Buddhists never say that they are in Buddha. They may follow the teachings of their respective leaders, but Christians alone are said to be *in* Christ, united to him as their representative, substitute, and Mediator.

This concept of union with Christ is as pervasive as it is precious. Most commonly represented by the tiny preposition "in," the believer's union with Christ permeates the New Testament. Believers are often said to be "in Christ" (1 Cor. 1:30; 2 Cor. 5:17), "in the Lord" (Rom. 16:11), and "in him" (1 John 5:20). Similarly, Christ is also said to be in his people (Rom. 8:10; 2 Cor. 13:5; Eph. 3:17), a notion that Paul defines as the very "hope of glory" itself (Col. 1:27). Sometimes both of these aspects of union with Christ are presented in the same text, only further emphasizing the intimacy of the mutual indwelling of Christ and the believer (e.g., John 6:56; 15:4; 1 John 4:13). Clearly, the importance of the believer's union with Christ cannot be overstated.

UNION WITH CHRIST AND SOTERIOLOGY

How the doctrine of union with Christ relates to the rest of soteriology has long been a matter of discussion. That is because it is not merely another phase in the application of redemption, like regeneration, faith, or justification. Instead, union with Christ is the matrix out of which all other soteriological doctrines flow. Indeed, as Paul says in Ephesians 1:3, our union with Christ is the source of every spiritual blessing we receive—from the Father's election in eternity past, to the Son's redemptive life, death, burial, and resurrection, all the way to the glorification of the saints with Christ in heaven. For this reason, the great theologian John Murray called the believer's union with Christ "the central truth of the whole doctrine of salvation."[126] It is the unifying principle of all soteriology, spanning from eternity past to eternity future.

In the first place, the Father's election is rooted in Christ. Paul says, "[The Father] chose us in him [Christ] before the foundation of the world" (Eph. 1:4). He also tells us in 2 Timothy 1:9 that God gave us grace "in Christ Jesus before the ages began."

---

126. Murray, *Redemption Accomplished and Applied*, 161.

Though the Father's work of election occurred before we even existed, his choice to save his people is nevertheless in Christ. This means there was never a time when God contemplated his elect apart from their vital union to Christ.

Second, Scripture teaches that God reckoned the elect to be united with Christ throughout every act of the Son's accomplishment of redemption. It is in him we have redemption and forgiveness (Eph. 1:7; Col. 1:14). We are united to him in his perfect life of obedience. As he "fulfill[ed] all righteousness" (Matt. 3:15), so also those united to him are clothed in his righteousness (Gal. 3:27), that is, credited with his obedience (Rom. 5:19; cf. 1 Cor. 1:30; 15:22). This union was also the ground on which our sin could be justly imputed to Christ. The Father counts the elect to have lived Jesus's life because he counts Jesus to have lived our lives and thus punished him accordingly (2 Cor. 5:21; 1 Pet. 2:24). Thus we are said to have "died with Christ" (Rom. 6:8; Col. 2:20; cf. Col. 3:3; 2 Tim. 2:11), "our old self [having been] crucified with him" (Rom. 6:6). Not only this, but we were "buried with him" (Rom. 6:4; Col. 2:12), raised from the dead with him (Eph. 2:6; Col. 2:12; 3:1), and even "seated . . . with him in the heavenly places in Christ Jesus" (Eph. 2:6). His life is our life, his punishment our punishment, his death our death, his resurrection our resurrection, his righteousness our righteousness, his ascension and glorification our ascension and glorification. In summary, though we had not yet been born, God nevertheless counted his people to be in union with their Savior throughout the accomplishment of his redemptive work. Christ did not live, die, and rise again for a faceless, nameless group; redemption was remarkably personal, as the body was always reckoned to be united to the head (Eph. 5:23, 25).

Third, just as the plan and accomplishment of redemption occur in Christ, so too does the application of redemption. Believers are born again unto saving faith in union with Christ. Paul describes the believer's regeneration when he says that they have been "made . . . alive together with Christ" (Eph. 2:5) and are "created in Christ Jesus" (Eph. 2:10). If anyone is united to Christ, he is a new creation (2 Cor. 5:17), which is another way of saying that one is born again in union with Christ. This impartation of new spiritual life issues immediately in repentant faith, the instrument by which one subjectively appropriates all the spiritual blessings planned by the Father and purchased by the Son (Gal. 2:20). United to Christ by faith, believers lay hold of Christ's righteousness (Phil. 3:9), and so are justified in him (Gal. 2:17), for there is no condemnation for those who are in Christ Jesus (Rom. 8:1). Thus declared righteous in Christ, believers are adopted into the family of God through Christ (Eph. 1:5; cf. Gal. 3:26), and are sanctified in him for holiness and service to God (1 Cor. 1:2).

Union with Christ is also the source of the believer's progressive sanctification and perseverance. Christ is called our sanctification because it flows from him (1 Cor. 1:30). We bring forth the fruit of righteousness only as we stay connected to our vine (John 15:4–5). The members of the body grow into maturity as they receive the communication of life from their head (Eph. 4:15–16). Thus, believers "[died] to the

Law through the body of Christ," because it is only as they are "joined to another, to Him who was raised from the dead," that they might walk in his resurrection life and thereby "bear fruit for God" (Rom. 7:4 NASB; cf. 6:4–11). Increasing in holiness is impossible apart from union with Christ. Further, it is on the basis of this union that true believers always persevere until the end (John 10:27–28), for while they are in Christ nothing can separate them from the Father's love (Rom. 8:38–39). Indeed, not even death severs this union, for Christians who die are called the dead in Christ (1 Thess. 4:14, 16).

Finally, it is on the basis of union with Christ that believers will be raised from the dead. He is the firstfruits of our resurrection, as Paul comforts the Corinthians: "But in fact Christ has been raised from the dead, the firstfruits of those who have fallen asleep. For as by a man came death, by a man has come also the resurrection of the dead. For as in Adam all die, so also in Christ shall all be made alive" (1 Cor. 15:20–22). Paul reasons elsewhere, "For if we have been united with him in a death like his, we shall certainly be united with him in a resurrection like his" (Rom. 6:5; cf. 8:17).

It is plain, therefore, that the believer's union with Christ encompasses every step of salvation, from election in eternity past to glorification in eternity future. Those whom God has chosen, whom Christ has purchased, and to whom the Spirit gives life are never contemplated apart from their union with Christ. And yet this union is not actualized in the sinner's experience before his conversion, for the apostle Paul speaks of a time when believers were "separated from Christ, alienated from the commonwealth of Israel and strangers to the covenants of promise, having no hope and without God in the world" (Eph. 2:12). He continues, "But now in Christ Jesus you who once were far off have been brought near by the blood of Christ" (Eph. 2:13). That is to say, the sinner passes from separation to union with Christ when he becomes a partaker in the gospel purchased by Jesus's blood, the benefits of which he lays hold of by faith alone (Rom. 3:25; 4:24; Gal. 3:24). It is for this reason that we treat union with Christ at this point in discussing the application of redemption.

THE NATURE OF THE BELIEVER'S UNION

Having seen the significance and breadth of the believer's union with Christ, it is now appropriate to inquire into the nature of this union itself. What does it mean exactly that believers are united to Christ? Scripture answers by illustrating the intimacy of this union with a number of metaphors. By understanding these metaphors, we can reach sound, biblical conclusions concerning the nature of our union with Christ.

First, Scripture uses the picture of a building and its foundation. In Ephesians 2:19–22, Paul speaks of the church as God's household, a spiritual building laid on the foundation of the divine revelation communicated by the apostles and prophets. The cornerstone of that foundation is Christ himself (cf. 1 Pet. 2:5–7), and it is in him that "the whole structure, being joined together, grows into a holy temple in the Lord" (Eph. 2:21). The Greek term translated "joined together" speaks of the union of every component of this building. Just as every stone in a literal building is cut precisely to fit snugly, strongly, and beautifully with every other part and to rest perfectly on the foundation, so also does the unity and stability of the church depend on Christ, her foundation. It is only by being built on and permanently united to Christ, our cornerstone, that believers find their spiritual existence, support, and security to be well-founded.

Second, the believer's union with Christ is pictured as the union between the vine and its branches. Jesus taught, "As the branch cannot bear fruit by itself, unless it abides in the vine, neither can you, unless you abide in me. I am the vine; you are the branches. Whoever abides in me and I in him, he it is that bears much fruit, for apart from me you can do nothing" (John 15:4–5). Just as the branches depend on the vine for life, strength, and sustenance, so also does the believer depend on union with Christ for all spiritual nourishment and growth. Apart from Christ the vine, we the branches can bear no fruit; we are entirely useless, destitute of any spiritual vitality unless we remain connected to our vine.

Third, Scripture also uses the metaphor of marriage to portray the union between Christ and his church. The church is often pictured as Christ's bride (2 Cor. 11:2; Rev. 19:7; 21:9), and Christ as the husband and head of the church (Eph. 5:22–33). In Ephesians 5, Paul based all his instructions for the husband-wife relationship on the relationship between Christ and *his* bride. At the end of this discussion, Paul quoted from the first wedding sermon, Genesis 2:24, where God said, "Therefore a man shall leave his father and his mother and hold fast to his wife, and the two shall become one flesh" (Eph. 5:31). Then Paul added, "This mystery is profound; and I am saying that it refers to Christ and the church" (Eph. 5:32).

The metaphor of marriage has great significance for understanding the believer's union with Christ. First, it speaks to the intimacy of this union. The one-flesh union of husband and wife is the most private, personal, and intimate relationship among mankind, and its primary purpose is to be a picture of the union between Christ and the church. Second, it speaks to the organic nature of this union. The new life created via the one-flesh union of husband and wife portrays the mutuality and vitality of the church's union with her husband. Third, this figure illustrates the legality of this union. As marriage legally joins the husband to the wife, so also does the believer's union with Christ enable Christ to act as the legal representative in his stead (discussed further below). Finally, marriage illustrates the unbreakable bond that exists between Christ and the church. "To hold fast to" translates the Greek term *proskollaō*, which literally means "to be glued or cemented together." God's design for marriage is to be permanent (Mal. 2:16; Matt. 19:6), and it thus illustrates the permanence of the union between Christ and the church.

Fourth, perhaps the greatest metaphor given to illustrate union with Christ is the union of head and body (Rom. 12:5; 1 Cor. 12:12–13, 27; Eph. 1:22–23). Also pictured in the marriage text of Ephesians 5, Paul says, "Christ is the head of the church, his body" (Eph. 5:23). The one who nourishes and cherishes his own body loves *himself* (Eph. 5:28–30), because there is such an intimate union between the head and the body. Believers' bodies are members of Christ's own body, so much so that to unite oneself to a prostitute is to unite Christ to a prostitute (1 Cor. 6:15–16). Thus, what happens to the head happens to the body, and what happens to the body happens to the head.

This metaphor lays the groundwork for understanding the legal and representational nature of the believer's union with Christ, where Christ obeys (Rom. 5:18–19; cf. 1 Cor. 1:30), dies (Col. 2:20), rises (Col. 3:1), and ascends (Eph. 2:6) in their place, such that they are reckoned to have done all those things. Because this union is a legal union—that is, because Christ is the representative head of his people—there is no element of Christ's earthly life, death, burial, resurrection, and ascension in which the believer does not partake on account of being in him. Thus 1 Corinthians 15:22 says, "As in Adam all die, so also in Christ shall all be made alive." That is to say, all humanity was reckoned to be united with Adam as our representative, such that his disobedience counted as our disobedience and brought condemnation on us (Rom. 5:12, 18, 19). In the same way, all those in Christ are united to the last Adam (1 Cor. 15:45) as their representative, such that his obedience counts as our obedience and brings righteousness and the justification of life to all in him (Rom. 5:18, 19).

In summary, then, we can speak of at least five characteristics of the believer's union with Christ. First, it is an organic union. That is to say, Christ and believers form one body, of which he is the head and they are the members. Thus, what is true of the head is true of the body. Second, it is a legal union, fitting Christ to be the representative head of his people and fitting them to be the beneficiary of his substitutionary work of salvation. Third, it is a vital union, in which all spiritual life and vitality flows from the vine to the branches, such that the life of Christ becomes the dominating and animating principle of believers' lives (Gal. 2:20). Fourth, it may be called a spiritual union not only because spiritual life is communicated to and strengthened within the believer but also because this union has its source in and is mediated by the Holy Spirit (Rom. 8:9–10; 1 Cor. 12:13; John 14:17–18). Finally, it is a permanent union that can never be severed, as nothing can separate us from the love of God which is in—that is, which is ours in union with—Jesus Christ our Lord (Rom. 8:38–39).

ERRONEOUS CONCEPTIONS OF UNION WITH CHRIST

Some conceptions of union with Christ have missed the mark of the biblical picture. First, union with Christ is not merely speaking of the love and sympathy Jesus has for his own. It is not that believers are merely in touch with Jesus on a moral level as our teacher or friend. This was the error of the Socinians and the early Arminians. Such a conception falls short of the sharing of common spiritual life that is so vividly illustrated by the metaphors of the vine and the branches and of the head and the body. As mentioned above, Christians are not merely associated with Christ; our life is hidden in him, such that he himself is our life (Col. 3:3–4; Gal. 2:20).

On the other hand, other theologians make the opposite error by supposing that union with Christ speaks of the believer's union with his essence. This has become especially popular among certain Lutheran theologians who believe that man is divinized in justification.[127] However, it is impossible for any human being to become one with Christ in his essence, for that would remove all distinctions between the believer and the person of Christ. We do not become one with Christ in such a way that he is no longer himself nor we ourselves, any more than the union of husband and wife causes them to cease to be two persons. Such would destroy the distinct personhood of the Son and would effectively deify the believer, both of which are contrary to Scripture.

Still another error is sacramentalism—that union with Christ is mediated by participating in baptism or the Lord's Supper, as the Roman Catholic Church teaches. However, this is to undermine the very heart of the gospel, because it proposes that physical and tangible rituals are required for a believer to lay hold of a saving participation in Christ. Yet Scripture reserves this role for faith alone (Rom. 3:28; 4:3–5; Eph. 2:8–9; Phil. 3:9). Indeed, the ordinances of baptism and Communion presuppose that union with Christ already exists, as these are to be practiced only by believers. As A. H. Strong wrote, "Only faith receives and retains Christ; and faith is the act of the soul grasping what is purely invisible and supersensible: not the act of the body, submitting to Baptism or partaking of the Supper."[128]

IMPLICATIONS OF THE BELIEVER'S UNION WITH CHRIST

The foregoing study provides a number of implications with respect to the believer's union with Christ. First, since the Son is united to the Father and to the Spirit, believers, by their participation in Christ, are also made one with God the Father and God the Holy Spirit. Jesus thus prays for the unity of the church to reflect the unity he shares with his Father: ". . . just as you, Father, are in me, and I in you, that they also may be in us" (John 17:21). Thus, we are said to be in the Father (1 Thess. 1:1) and the Father in us (1 John 4:15). Similarly, believers are said to be in the Spirit (Rom. 8:9) and the Spirit in us (2 Tim. 1:14). In an unspeakable mystery, we who were once separated, alienated, and without God in the world are swept up into the divine life of the triune God himself (2 Pet. 1:4). This is great cause for worship.

Second, those who are one with Christ are also one with everyone else who is one with Christ. This speaks of the fundamental unity of all believers in Christ. It has become popular to speak of one's "personal relationship" with Jesus, but a more accurate expression would be that Christians have a *corporate* relationship with Christ, for we are united to all who are united to him. We are the unified members of his body (Rom. 12:5; 1 Cor. 12:26; Eph. 5:23), the living stones in the spiritual house built on Christ the foundation (Eph. 2:19–22; 1 Pet. 2:4–5). To suggest that one can

---

127. In doing this, they return to an essentially Eastern Orthodox conception of the doctrine of justification. For more, see Carl E. Braaten and Robert W. Jenson, eds., *Union With Christ: The New Finnish Interpretation of Luther* (Grand Rapids, MI: Eerdmans, 1998).

128. Augustus Hopkins Strong, *Systematic Theology* (1907; repr., Old Tappan, NJ: Fleming H. Revell, 1970), 800.

be united to Jesus apart from his church is to tear the head from the body. There is no union with Christ that does not issue in fellowship with his church (1 Cor. 1:9; cf. 1 John 1:3). Indeed, the unity of the Trinity is the ground of Jesus's prayer for the unity of the church (John 17:21). What a motivation for diligently pursuing the unity of the Spirit in the bond of peace among all believers (Eph. 4:3)!

Finally, we must grasp the significance that every spiritual benefit received in salvation comes only through Christ. As John Owen wrote, this union "is the cause of all other graces that we are made partakers of; they are all communicated unto us by virtue of our union with Christ. Hence is our adoption, our justification, our sanctification, our fruitfulness, our perseverance, our resurrection, our glory."[129] It is only as we share in Christ that we have a share in what is his. No spiritual blessing in all the world is found anywhere but in Jesus. Therefore, if we are to have an interest in Christ's blessings, we must have an interest in his person. The gifts are wrapped up only in the Giver.

Justification

In the previous section, we examined how the believer's union with Christ is the fountain out of which every spiritual blessing flows. The immediate result of that union is God's free gift of justification, by which he declares believers to be righteous because of their union with the Righteous One, the Lord Jesus. The application of redemption continues to unfold. In regeneration, God performs that divine operation in the sinner's soul whereby he births new spiritual life in him. In conversion, God grants the necessary gifts of repentance and faith by which we are united to Christ and lay hold of the blessings of salvation. Then, in justification, God legally declares that we are no longer deemed guilty under the divine law but are forgiven and counted righteous in God's sight.

In justification, God provides the answer to mankind's most basic theological and religious question: How can sinners come to be in a right relationship with the holy God of the universe? God is perfectly righteous (Matt. 5:48). He is light, says the apostle John, and in him is no darkness at all (1 John 1:5). That is, he is entirely holy, free from any moral defect or impurity. All mankind, on the other hand, has sinned against God and thus falls short of that holy standard (Rom. 3:23). By our sin, man has become the very darkness that has no fellowship with the God of light. All have broken his law and have thus incurred the penalty for their crimes: death and condemnation (Rom. 5:16; 6:23). If sinners are to have any good news at all, the consequences created by their breaking that law and being alienated from God must be overcome. But how can that be?

In every age of human history, religion has answered that we can get to heaven by being good people. The various religious systems of the world concoct lists of rituals and ceremonies that must be performed to achieve a measure of righteousness that might avail in the courtroom of God. However, the answer that Jesus himself gives

---

129. John Owen, *An Exposition of the Epistle to the Hebrews*, vol. 21 in *The Works of John Owen*, 150.

to this question was nothing short of shocking to his listeners: "For I tell you, unless your righteousness exceeds that of the scribes and Pharisees, you will never enter the kingdom of heaven" (Matt. 5:20). In Jesus's day, the scribes and Pharisees were the paragon of ceremonial righteousness in Israel. They were the religious elite; everyone in Jewish society would have expected the scribes and Pharisees to have attained the righteousness that God requires. And yet Jesus says that if man is to enter heaven, he needs a righteousness that surpasses even the most religiously devout people. In fact, he goes further than that just a few verses later when he says, "You therefore must be perfect, as your heavenly Father is perfect" (Matt. 5:48). If man is to be reconciled to God, he does not just need to be a good person; he needs to be a perfect person. He needs a perfect righteousness, for God himself is perfect and requires perfection.

At the very outset, then, it is necessary to understand that salvation is a matter of righteousness. People are condemned to eternal spiritual death because they lack the righteousness that a perfectly holy God possesses and requires for fellowship with him. And the only way sinners are ever reconciled to God is by being given the righteousness that belongs to God himself. That is why the thesis statement of the book of Romans—the most thorough treatment on justification in all Scripture—takes up this theme of righteousness. The gospel is "the power of God for salvation to everyone who believes" precisely because "in it the righteousness of God is revealed from faith for faith" (Rom. 1:16–17). The gospel saves because God gives his very own righteousness to man. The rest of the New Testament attests to this truth as well. Paul summarizes the essence of the gospel by casting it as "the righteousness of God through faith in Jesus Christ for all who believe" (Rom. 3:22; cf. 3:20–26). Israel's failure to attain salvation stemmed from their "being ignorant of the righteousness of God, and seeking to establish their own" (Rom. 10:3). Christ himself is described as "the end of the law for righteousness to everyone who believes" (Rom. 10:4). The explicit purpose for which the Father made the Son to be sin on the cross is "so that in [Christ] we might become the righteousness of God" (2 Cor. 5:21). Indeed, Jesus had to die precisely because the law could only condemn; it could never provide the righteousness that brings salvation and life (Gal. 2:21; 3:21–24). Speaking of his own conversion, Paul defines the nature of Christianity itself in terms of righteousness when he describes himself, like the true believer, as "not having my own righteousness, which is from the law, but that which is through faith in Christ, the righteousness which is from God by faith" (Phil. 3:9 NKJV).

Thus it is plain that the doctrine of justification flows from the very heart of the gospel and the soul of Christianity itself. It is, as Martin Luther said, the article by which the church stands or falls,[130] for it concerns the only way sinful man can be declared righteous in God's sight.[131] Man's answer is always to try to order his life

---

130. "Because if this article [i.e., justification] stands, the church stands; if this article collapses, the church collapses." Martin Luther, *D. Martin Luthers Werke: Kritische Gesamtausgabe* (Weimar, Germany: H. Böhlau, 1883–1993), 40:3.352.3.

131. To the English reader, the intimate relationship between "righteousness" and "justification" may not be as obvious as it would have been to a Greek reader. In the original language of the New Testament, the words "righteous," "righteousness," "justify," and "justification" all come from the same root word and appear in the following respective forms: *dikaios, dikaiosynē, dikaioō,* and *dikaiōsis* (and in Hebrew: *tsaddiq, tsedeq/tsedaqah, tsadoq/tsadeq*). To be justified, then, simply means to be declared righteous in the sight of God, as will be developed more fully below.

by some moral or ritualistic standard; if he does that successfully, he can contribute something to his salvation and thus achieve a righteousness acceptable to his god. Yet the Bible consistently denies that anyone can be justified by works. Rather, salvation is God's righteousness imputed to the believer by grace alone through faith alone in Christ alone:

> But now the righteousness of God has been manifested apart from the law, although the Law and the Prophets bear witness to it—the righteousness of God *through faith* in Jesus Christ for all who believe. For there is no distinction: for all have sinned and fall short of the glory of God, and are *justified by his grace as a gift*, through the redemption that is in Christ Jesus, whom God put forward as a propitiation by his blood, *to be received by faith*. This was to show God's righteousness, because in his divine forbearance he had passed over former sins. It was to show his righteousness at the present time, so that he might be just and *the justifier of the one who has faith in Jesus*. Then what becomes of our boasting? It is excluded. By what kind of law? By a law of works? No, but by the law of faith. For we hold that one is *justified by faith apart from works of the law*. (Rom. 3:21–28)

> Yet we know that a person is not justified by works of the law but *through faith in Jesus Christ*, so we also have believed in Christ Jesus, in order to be *justified by faith in Christ* and not by works of the law, because by works of the law no one will be justified. (Gal. 2:16)

> For if a law had been given that could give life, then righteousness would indeed be by the law. But the Scripture imprisoned everything under sin, so that the promise *by faith in Jesus Christ* might be given to *those who believe*. Now before faith came, we were held captive under the law, imprisoned until the coming faith would be revealed. So then, the law was our guardian until Christ came, in order that we might be *justified by faith*. But now that faith has come, we are no longer under a guardian, for in Christ Jesus you are all sons of God, *through faith*. (Gal. 3:21–26)

The distinction could not be clearer. In these passages, the apostle Paul is contrasting biblical Christianity with Judaism in particular, but what he says about Judaism can be applied to every other religious system in the world. There have only ever been two religions: the religion of human achievement, by which man works to contribute to his own righteousness, and the religion of divine accomplishment, whereby God accomplishes righteousness by the holy life and substitutionary death of the Son of God and then freely gives that righteousness as a gift through faith alone. The religion of human achievement encompasses every other religious system in the history of mankind—from the pursuit of nirvana in Buddhism, to the five pillars of Islam, to the sacraments and acts of penance of Roman Catholicism. Biblical Christianity is the lone religion of divine accomplishment. Because Christians are justified by faith alone, their standing before God is not in any way related to personal merit. Good works and practical holiness are not the grounds for acceptance with God.

God receives as righteous those who believe, not because of any good thing he sees in them—not even because of his own sanctifying work in their lives—but solely on the basis of Christ's righteousness, which is graciously reckoned to their account through faith alone. As Paul says, "To the one who does not work but believes in him who justifies the ungodly, his faith is counted as righteousness" (Rom. 4:5).[132]

Therefore, we may define justification as that instantaneous act of God whereby, as a gift of his grace, he imputes to a believing sinner the full and perfect righteousness of Christ through faith alone and legally declares him perfectly righteous in his sight, forgiving the sinner of all unrighteousness and thus delivering him from all condemnation.[133] We will unpack the elements of that definition throughout the rest of this section.

THE NATURE OF JUSTIFICATION: A LEGAL DECLARATION

Before examining any particular aspect of justification, we must be clear about what the Bible teaches concerning the nature of justification itself. Justification is a legal, or forensic, declaration of righteousness, not an actual impartation or infusion of righteousness. It describes what God *declares* about the believer, not what he *does to change* the believer. In fact, justification itself effects no actual change whatsoever in the sinner's nature or character.[134] It is an instantaneous change of one's status before God, not a gradual transformation that takes place within the one who is justified.[135]

Legal declarations like this are fairly common in everyday life. When a minister declares, "By the power vested in me, I now pronounce you husband and wife," there is an instant change in the legal status of the couple standing before him. Seconds before, the law regarded them as two distinct individuals. Yet on the basis of this pronouncement, their legal status before God and in society changes entirely. And while that declaration has profound and life-transforming implications, nothing about the couple's character or nature changes as a result of the minister's words. It is a legal declaration only. To take another example, when a jury foreman announces to the court that a defendant is not guilty, the legal status of the defendant changes instantly. Seconds before, the law regarded him as "the accused," innocent until proven guilty. But as a result of the foreman's verdict, he is not guilty in the eyes of the law. Yet the jury's verdict does not *make* the man not guilty; his own actions are the basis of his guilt or innocence. Neither does it declare his life free from any and all evil. The foreman's announcement simply declares the defendant's status before the law. In a similar way, the justification spoken of in Scripture is God's divine verdict of "not guilty—fully righteous" pronounced on the sinner. In the case of justification, it is not that the accused is innocent but that another has paid in full the penalty for his crimes.

---

132. MacArthur, *The Gospel according to the Apostles*, 69–70.
133. MacArthur, *The Gospel according to Jesus*, 196.
134. MacArthur, *The Gospel according to the Apostles*, 70.
135. MacArthur, *The Gospel according to Jesus*, 196.

Disagreement over the nature of justification was one of the key debates of the Protestant Reformation, and it still divides biblical Christianity and Roman Catholicism to this day. Roman Catholic theology teaches that justification is not merely forensic but transformative. In other words, according to Roman Catholic teaching, "to justify" does not mean "to *declare* righteous" but "to *make* righteous." Now, it is true that the saving grace of God is transformative; those who are declared righteous in conversion will be progressively made righteous throughout the course of their Christian lives. However, this progressive transformation defines the reality not of biblical justification but of sanctification. By failing to distinguish these two intimately related yet nevertheless distinct applications of redemption, Roman Catholicism collapses sanctification into justification. The inevitable consequence is that the believer's own imperfect righteousness replaces the perfect righteousness of Christ as the sole ground of justification. The result is "a righteousness of my own that comes from the law," which, as Paul says in Philippians 3:9, is not the saving righteousness of God. Because of this, failing to understand the nature of justification as a legal declaration and instead mischaracterizing it as a transformative process destroys the very foundation of the gospel.

Scripture itself testifies to this truth, for the biblical writers often use the terms for justification and righteousness in a way that must be declarative rather than transformative.[136] In the Old Testament, the *tsadeq* word group is often used in judicial contexts. Deuteronomy 25:1 is a clear example: "If there is a dispute between men and they go to court, and the judges decide their case, and they justify the righteous and condemn the wicked . . ." (NASB; see also Ex. 23:7; 1 Kings 8:31–32; Job 9:15; Isa. 43:9, 26; Jer. 12:1). As discussed above, judges do not *make* people righteous or wicked. They perform no transformative act that infuses righteousness or wickedness into the nature or character of a person. Instead, a judge merely declares a defendant to be righteous or guilty. Indeed, God pronounces woe on those "who justify the wicked for a bribe" (Isa. 5:23 NASB), for "he who justifies the wicked and he who condemns the righteous are both alike an abomination to the LORD" (Prov. 17:15). If justification were transformative, how could it be said that making a wicked person righteous is an abomination? Transforming the character of a wicked person and infusing him with righteousness would be a righteous act! Thus, a transformative understanding of justification violates the sense of these texts. To justify the wicked is not to make him righteous but to declare him righteous when he is not.

The New Testament presents further evidence supporting the declarative nature of justification. First, justification is shown to be declarative and not transforma-

---

136. This is not to say that Scripture never uses these terms in an ethical sense. In Ps. 11:7, Yahweh is said to love righteousness (Heb. *tsedaqoth*; Gk. *dikaiosynas* [Septuagint]), yet it is plain that this refers not to his love of a righteous status but of what is right—of righteous acts. Similarly, Paul's counsel to Timothy to "pursue righteousness" (Gk. *dikaiosynēn*, 1 Tim. 6:11) is an exhortation not to work for justification but to pursue practical righteousness—the sanctification without which no one will see the Lord (Heb. 12:14). However, as Schreiner notes, "The ethical use of the term in some contexts doesn't necessitate the conclusion that the term isn't forensic in other . . . texts." Thomas Schreiner, *Faith Alone: The Doctrine of Justification: What the Reformers Taught . . . and Why It Still Matters*, The Five Solas (Grand Rapids, MI: Zondervan, 2015), 158n1. The question is, in those key texts that describe the saving righteousness of God granted to sinners, does context support a forensic understanding of justification? We answer in the affirmative.

tive in those instances in which God is the one said to be justified. In Luke 7:29, we read, "When all the people heard this, and the tax collectors too, they declared God just" (Gk. *edikaiōsan ton theon*; KJV: "justified God"). If the sense of justification were transformative, this would be nothing short of blasphemy, for the notion that the people and the tax collectors could have effected a positive moral transformation in God is nonsense. The ESV properly brings out the sense in the translation, "declared . . . just." That is, God's righteousness was vindicated and demonstrated (cf. Rom. 3:26). Second, justification is often clearly contrasted with condemnation, and condemnation obviously speaks of a legal declaration. In Romans 8:33–34, we read, "Who shall bring any charge against God's elect? It is God who justifies. Who is to condemn?" (see also Rom. 5:18; 2 Cor. 3:9; cf. Job 9:20; Ps. 94:21; Prov. 17:15). God's justifying act is clearly contrasted with bringing a charge and condemning. But to condemn someone does not mean to make someone wicked; it means to render a verdict and declare that he is wicked. For the parallel between justification and condemnation to hold, we must also understand that justification does not mean to make righteous but to declare righteous.

Therefore, when we turn to texts that speak of God justifying the believer in a salvific sense (e.g., Rom. 3:20–28; 4:4–5; 5:1; Gal. 2:16; 3:11, 21–26; 5:4), we ought to understand them to be referring to God's instantaneous declaration that the sinner is in a right standing before him. These passages teach that God declares the believer to be righteous as a gift of his grace, which the believer receives by faith alone apart from works.

THE GROUND OF JUSTIFICATION: IMPUTED RIGHTEOUSNESS

But how is such a declaration by God just? Proverbs 17:15 says, "He who justifies the wicked . . . [is] an abomination to the LORD." All mankind is wicked. We are lawbreakers, deserving God's condemnation, "for all have sinned and fall short of the glory of God" (Rom. 3:23), and "the wages of sin is death" (Rom. 6:23). Indeed, Romans 4:5 explicitly says that God justifies the *ungodly*. How can God declare to be righteous those who are actually guilty, and not, as Proverbs 17:15 says, participate in something abominable? How can God be both "just and the justifier of the one who has faith in Jesus" (Rom. 3:26)? The answer to that question is the doctrine of imputation.[137] God's declarative act of justification is based on his constitutive act of imputation.[138] This is a twofold act; God imputes—that is, counts, credits, or

---

137. Schreiner offers a helpful summary of imputation: "We often find in Paul the expression that faith is credited or counted (*logizomai*) as righteousness (*dikaiosynē*, Rom 3:28; 4:3, 5, 9, 10, 11, 22, 23, 24; Gal 3:6). The word 'count' or 'credit' may be used in two different ways. Something may be counted to a person because it truly belongs to him. Thus, Phinehas's action was counted as righteous because it was righteous (Ps 106:31). But something can also be counted as true that is actually not the case. Jacob's wives were counted as outsiders by Laban even though they were actually his daughters (Gen 31:15)." The imputation of righteousness to the believer fits the latter category: "Sinners who aren't righteous are counted as righteous and considered as righteous, even though they are not righteous in themselves. They are counted to be something that is not theirs inherently." *Faith Alone*, 165.

138. Murray comments insightfully, "Justification is both declarative and a constitutive act of God's free grace. It is constitutive in order that it may be truly declarative. God must constitute the new relationship as well as declare it to be. The constitutive act consists in the imputation to us of the obedience and righteousness of Christ. The obedience of Christ must therefore be regarded as the ground of justification; it is the righteousness which God not only takes into account but reckons to our account when He justifies the ungodly." *Redemption Accomplished and Applied*, 124–25.

reckons—our sin to Christ and punishes him in our place, and he imputes Christ's righteousness to believers and grants them eternal life in him.

Forgiveness of Sins: The Imputation of Our Sin to Christ. First, God imputes our sin to Christ: "For our sake he [the Father] made him [Christ] to be sin who knew no sin" (2 Cor. 5:21). Now, in what sense did the Father "make" the Son "sin" on our behalf? In only one sense: the Father counted Jesus to have committed all the sins of all those who would ever repent and believe in him. He did not actually make Jesus a sinner; it would be blasphemous to suggest that the God-man was actually made a sinner, for God cannot sin. Instead, since justification is a legal declaration (as established in the previous section), the Father judicially reckoned Christ to have committed the sins of those for whom he was giving himself as a substitute. Just as the scapegoat bore the guilt of Israel when Aaron confessed the people's sins over its head (Lev. 16:21), so "the LORD has laid on him the iniquity of us all" (Isa. 53:6), such that Christ actually "bore our sins in his body on the tree" (1 Pet. 2:24; cf. Isa. 53:4–6). And just as the blood of the goat of the sin offering was sprinkled on the mercy seat (Gk. *hilastērion* [Septuagint]) to propitiate God's wrath (Lev. 16:15), so also was Christ "put forward as a propitiation [Gk. *hilastērion*] by his blood" (Rom. 3:25). Though innumerable sinners will escape divine punishment, no sin will ever go unpunished, for every sin of the elect has been reckoned to Christ and punished in him on the cross. In this way divine justice is satisfied. Sin has not merely been dismissed or swept under the rug; it has been justly punished in a substitute. This is the gospel through which God demonstrates his righteousness, "so that he might be just and the justifier of the one who has faith in Jesus" (Rom. 3:26).

Therefore, because the believer's sins have been imputed to and punished in Christ, they are not counted against him. As Paul quotes David's words from Psalm 32, "Blessed are those whose lawless deeds are forgiven, and whose sins are covered; blessed is the man against whom the Lord will not count [Gk. *logizomai*] his sin" (Rom. 4:7–8). Because they have been counted, or imputed, to Christ, the believer's sins are not imputed to (or counted against) him. They are forgiven and covered. Therefore, the justified believer faces no condemnation (Rom. 8:1, 33–34) but enjoys peace with God (Rom. 5:1) and the sure hope of eternal life (Rom. 8:30; Titus 3:7).

Provision of Righteousness: The Imputation of Christ's Righteousness to Us. But the forgiveness of sins does not exhaust God's work in justification. In fact, if the only benefit believers received in justification were the forgiveness of our sins, we could not be saved. The old Sunday school definition of justification—"just as if I'd never sinned"—is inadequate, because salvation is not merely a matter of sinlessness or innocence but is also a matter of righteousness (Matt. 5:20, 48). The law of God, which man broke, thereby incurring the death penalty (Rom. 6:23), carries both positive demands and penal sanctions. That is to say, God's law requires both (1) that his creatures perform certain duties suitable to his righteousness and (2) that they undergo a certain punishment if they fail to perform those duties. Man has failed to do both. We do not live lives of perfect righteousness, walking in obedience to God in all things, loving him with all our heart, soul, mind, and strength, and loving our neighbors as ourselves. Neither could we pay the penalty that our disobedience demands without perishing eternally in hell. Therefore, if we are to be saved, our substitute must not only pay our penalty by absorbing the wrath of God against our sin but must also obey all the positive demands of the law that were required of us. This twofold nature of Christ's substitutionary work is sometimes referred to as his *passive obedience* and *active obedience*. John Murray explains:

> The law of God has both penal sanctions and positive demands. It demands not only the full discharge of its precepts but also the infliction of penalty for all infractions and shortcomings. It is this twofold demand of the law of God which is taken into account when we speak of the active and passive obedience of Christ. Christ as the vicar of his people came under the curse and condemnation due to sin and he also fulfilled the law of God in all its positive requirements. In other words, he took care of the guilt of sin and perfectly fulfilled the demands of righteousness. He perfectly met both the penal and the preceptive requirements of God's law. The passive obedience refers to the former and the active obedience to the latter.[139]

Without the positive provision of righteousness, mere forgiveness would leave us in a state of innocence or moral neutrality, as Adam was before the fall—reckoned as never having sinned but as never having obeyed either.

For this reason, Scripture speaks of the justified sinner being counted righteous in addition to being forgiven. God's people testify to this in Isaiah 61:10: "I will greatly rejoice in the LORD; my soul shall exult in my God, for he has clothed me with the garments of salvation; he has covered me with the robe of righteousness, as a bridegroom decks himself like a priest with a beautiful headdress, and as a bride adorns herself with her jewels." In fact, salvation is described in terms of imputed righteousness as early as God's dealings with Abraham. Genesis 15:6 says that Abraham "believed the LORD, and he counted it to him as righteousness" (Gk. *elogisthē autō eis dikaiosynēn* [Septuagint]). The apostle Paul quotes this very verse in Romans 4:3 to substantiate his argument for justification on the basis of an imputed righteousness. He then comments, "Now to the one who works, his wages are not counted as a gift but as his due. And to the one who does not work but believes in him who justifies the ungodly, his faith is counted as righteousness" (Gk. *logizetai . . . eis dikaiosynēn*, Rom. 4:4–5).

In the next chapter, Paul identifies the righteousness that is imputed to believers to be Christ's own righteousness. In Romans 5:12–19, Paul compares and contrasts

---

139. Murray, *Redemption Accomplished and Applied*, 21–22. Some theologians object to the terminology of *active* and *passive obedience*, and it is granted that the language may be misleading. To call Christ's sufferings his *passive obedience* is not meant to imply that he was any less active in his obedience to the Father at that point in his ministry than any other. After all, no one took his life from him, but he willingly—one might even say, actively—laid it down of his own accord (John 10:17–18). He both *was* offered up (Heb. 9:28), in a passive sense, and offered up himself (Heb. 7:27), actively. Neither is this distinction designed to carve up aspects of Christ's redemptive work into totally exclusive categories. Murray continues, "It is our Lord's whole work of obedience in every phase and period that is described as active and passive." *Redemption Accomplished and Applied*, 21. The terminology is simply shorthand for adequately representing both aspects of Christ's obedience: the payment of a penalty and the provision of righteousness.

the two representative heads of humanity: (1) Adam and (2) Christ, the last Adam (1 Cor. 15:45). His argument climaxes in verses 18–19:

> Therefore, as through the one man's [Adam's] trespass there resulted condemnation to all men, so also through the one man's [Christ's] righteousness[140] there resulted justification of life to all men. For as through the one man's disobedience the many were constituted[141] sinners, so by the one man's obedience the many will be constituted righteous. (author's trans.)

Paul's main argument is as follows: Adam disobeyed God, and his disobedience was counted for condemnation to all who were in him. In the same way, Christ obeyed God, and his obedience was counted for righteousness to all who are in him. So far from a "legal fiction," both the imputation of sin and the imputation of righteousness have a basis in the actual, lived-out actions of Adam and Christ.[142]

With respect to justification, then, God not only satisfies the penal demands of the law by imputing our sin to Christ and punishing him in our place but also satisfies the positive demands of the law by imputing Christ's righteousness to us. Paul describes this great exchange in 2 Corinthians 5:21: "For our sake he made him to be sin who knew no sin, so that in him we might become the righteousness of God."[143] In justification, the perfect righteousness that God requires (Matt. 5:20, 48) is not worked in us in a transformative sense but is credited to us through our union with Christ, the Righteous One, who has fulfilled all righteousness on our behalf (Matt. 3:15; Gal. 3:27). Thus Paul says, "For the goal of the law is Christ for righteousness to everyone who believes" (Rom. 10:4, author's trans.). When we are "found in him," we do not have a righteousness of our own derived through commandment keeping; rather, we lay hold of the alien (i.e., belonging not to us but to another)

---

140. The ESV renders the Greek phrase *di' henos dikaiōmatos* of Rom. 5:18 as "one act of righteousness" because *dikaiōma* often refers to "a righteous deed" (e.g., Rom. 1:32; Rev. 19:8). However, *dikaiōma* can also be used in a comprehensive sense to speak of "the righteous requirement of the law," as in Rom. 8:4, or to "the declaration of righteousness," as in Rom. 5:16. Thus, it may be that Paul does not intend to isolate a particular righteous act in Christ's life (i.e., his obedience unto death, Phil. 2:8) but to speak of Christ's entire life of righteousness considered comprehensively as a whole. Nevertheless, even if one translates *dikaiōmatos* as "one act," it is difficult to identify even Christ's death as a single act of obedience. Piper incisively asks, "Were there not many acts of obedience in Jesus' final days and hours? Are we to think of the obedience of Gethsemane, or the obedience when the mob took Him away, or when He was interrogated, or the obedience when He was crowned with thorns, or the obedience when He was flogged, or the obedience when He was nailed to the cross, or the obedience when He spoke words of love to His enemies, or His obedience when He offered up His spirit to His Father?" John Piper, *Counted Righteous in Christ: Should We Abandon the Imputation of Christ's Righteousness?* (Wheaton, IL: Crossway, 2002), 112. Where do we draw the line? Especially since the more generic word "obedience" is used in the following verse, it seems best to understand *dikaiōmatos* to refer to Christ's entire life of obedience.

141. The ESV renders the Greek term *kathistēmi* as "made" in both instances in Rom. 5:19. Yet the word often unmistakably means "appoint." The apostles use this word to commission the church to appoint deacons (Acts 6:3); Paul uses it when he charges Titus to appoint elders (Titus 1:5); and it is the word used to describe the appointment of the high priest of Israel (Heb. 5:1; 7:28; 8:3). Therefore, one could translate Rom. 5:19, "through the one man's disobedience the many were *appointed* sinners," that is, legally established as sinners. Such an "appointment" is akin to, if not identical with, imputation. Cf. Piper, *Counted Righteous in Christ*, 108–9.

142. Piper helpfully observes, "It is significant that Paul does not say in Romans 5:19 that 'by the one man's disobedience the many were made' *guilty*. That is true. But it is important to see that what he actually says is: 'By the one man's disobedience the many were made *sinners* [ἁμαρτωλοι].' This is important because the imputation of Adam's sin is more than the imputation of a 'status.' We are counted as having *sinned* in Adam. Therefore, when Paul goes on to say, 'so by the one man's obedience the many will be made righteous,' he does not mean only that Christ's *status* was imputed to us. Rather, in Christ we are counted as having done all the righteousness that God requires. Imputation is not the conferring of a status without a ground of real imputed moral righteousness. It is the counting of an alien, real, moral, perfect righteousness, namely Christ's, as ours." John Piper, *The Future of Justification: A Response to N. T. Wright* (Wheaton, IL: Crossway, 2007), 170–71.

143. We "become" the righteousness of God in Christ in the same way in which Christ was "made" sin: by judicial reckoning, that is, by imputation (see "The Nature of Justification: A Legal Declaration" [p. 612]).

righteousness of God that comes through faith in Christ (Phil. 3:9).[144] By God's doing, we are united to Christ, "who became to us wisdom from God, *righteousness* and sanctification and redemption" (1 Cor. 1:30).

In summary, in Christ we have a substitute who has both paid our penalty *and* achieved our righteousness. Christ provided forgiveness by atoning for our sins on the cross. Just as our sins were reckoned to his account when he died on the cross, in the same manner his righteousness is counted as ours. His perfect righteousness is thus the ground on which we stand before God. Sinners are not justified because of some good thing in them; God can declare us righteous—he can justify the ungodly and yet remain just—because he graciously imputes to us the perfect righteousness of his own dear Son. Thus, the sole ground of justification is the righteousness of Christ counted to be ours as a gift by grace alone (cf. Rom. 3:24; Eph. 2:8–9; Titus 3:7).

THE MEANS OF JUSTIFICATION: FAITH ALONE

Christ's accomplishment of redemption—both in paying for sin and providing righteousness—occurred two thousand years ago, apart from any human influence. His work was objective, external to you and me. Therefore, the question that must be answered is, how can the objective work of Christ be applied to me personally? By what means can my sins be imputed to Christ and his righteousness be imputed to me? The answer Scripture consistently gives is that we are justified through faith alone apart from works. Faith unites us to Christ in his death and resurrection, so that his punishment counts for our punishment and his righteousness counts for our righteousness.

The clearest exposition of the doctrine of *sola fide*, "faith alone," comes in Paul's letters, especially the book of Romans. As Paul introduces the good news of salvation in Romans 3, he casts the gospel as the manifestation of "the righteousness of God through faith in Jesus Christ for all who believe" (3:22). He goes on to say that the gift of justification is "to be received by faith" (3:25) and that God is "the justifier of the one who has faith in Jesus" (3:26). He summarizes his argument in utter candor: "For we hold that one is justified by faith apart from works of the law" (3:28). After illustrating the truth of *sola fide* through the example of Abraham in Romans 4 (discussed below), he offers another summary of the gospel in Romans 5:1: "Therefore, since we have been justified by faith, we have peace with God through our Lord Jesus Christ." Taking up the matter again later in the epistle, he declares that saving righteousness comes by faith (9:30; 10:6), that Christ is righteousness to everyone who believes (10:4), and that "with the heart one believes and is justified" (10:10).

Paul also discusses this theme in his letter to the Galatians, where he says, "A

---

144. Some theologians object that because Paul uses the phrase, "the righteousness of God," he therefore does not refer to the obedience of Christ. But the righteousness imputed to believers is the righteousness of God *precisely because* it is the righteousness of Christ (cf. Rom. 1:17; 3:21–22; 10:3–4). As Murray argues, "It is the righteousness of the God-man, a righteousness which measures up to the requirements of our sinful and sin-cursed situation, a righteousness which meets all the demands of a complete and irrevocable justification, and a righteousness fulfilling all these demands because it is a righteousness of divine property and character, a righteousness undefiled and inviolable." *Redemption Accomplished and Applied*, 128.

person is not justified by works of the law but through faith in Jesus Christ, so we also have believed in Christ Jesus, in order to be justified by faith in Christ and not by works of the law, because by works of the law no one will be justified" (Gal. 2:16). Thus it is plain that one believes in order to be justified. In the next chapter, Paul denies that righteousness comes through law keeping:

> But the Scripture imprisoned everything under sin, so that the promise by faith in Jesus Christ might be given to those who believe.
> . . . So then, the law was our guardian until Christ came, in order that we might be justified by faith. . . . [F]or in Christ Jesus you are all sons of God, through faith. (Gal. 3:22, 24, 26)

Although Jesus never formally explained the doctrine of justification (as Paul does in Romans), the doctrine of *sola fide* underlies and permeates all his gospel preaching.[145] For example, in John 5:24, Jesus declared, "Whoever hears my word . . . has passed from death to life." Without undergoing any sacrament or ritual and without any waiting period or purgatory, the believer passes from death to life. The thief on the cross is the classic example. On the most meager evidence of his faith, Jesus told him, "Truly I say to you, today you will be with me in Paradise" (Luke 23:43). No sacrament or work was required for him to procure salvation. Furthermore, the many healings Jesus accomplished were physical evidence of his power to forgive sins (Matt. 9:5–6). When he healed, he frequently said, "Your faith has made you well" (Matt. 9:22; Mark 5:34; 10:52; Luke 8:48; 17:19; 18:42). All those healings were object lessons on the doctrine of justification by faith alone.

But the one occasion where Jesus actually declared someone "justified" provides the best insight into the way he taught the doctrine:

> He also told this parable to some who trusted in themselves that they were righteous, and treated others with contempt: "Two men went up into the temple to pray, one a Pharisee and the other a tax collector. The Pharisee, standing by himself, prayed thus: 'God, I thank you that I am not like other men, extortioners, unjust, adulterers, or even like this tax collector. I fast twice a week; I give tithes of all that I get.' But the tax collector, standing far off, would not even lift up his eyes to heaven, but beat his breast, saying, 'God, be merciful to me, a sinner!' I tell you, this man went down to his house *justified*, rather than the other. For everyone who exalts himself will be humbled, but the one who humbles himself will be exalted." (Luke 18:9–14)

Jesus's listeners "trusted in themselves that they were righteous" (Luke 18:9)—the very definition of self-righteousness—and so it was nothing short of shocking for him to place a detestable tax collector in a better spiritual position than a praying Pharisee. Without delving into abstract theology, Jesus clearly painted the picture: a sinner is declared righteous by faith alone.

---

145. The following three paragraphs are adapted from John MacArthur, "Jesus' Perspective on *Sola Fide*," *Grace to You*, accessed April 14, 2016, http://www.gty.org/resources/Articles/A192/Jesus-Perspective-on-Sola-Fide.

Note first that this tax collector's justification was an instantaneous reality. There was no process, no time lapse, and no fear of purgatory. Further, he "went down to his house justified" (Luke 18:14) not because of anything he had done but because of what had been done on his behalf. Notice also that the tax collector understood his own helplessness. He owed an impossible debt he knew he could not pay. All he could do was repent and plead for mercy. He knew that even his best works were sin, and so he did not offer to do anything for God. He simply pleaded for divine mercy. He was looking for God to do for him what he could not do for himself. That is the very nature of the penitence Jesus called for. Finally, note that this man went away justified without performing any works of penance, sacraments, or rituals. His justification was complete without any works whatsoever, because it was granted solely by means of faith. Everything necessary to atone for his sin and provide forgiveness had already been done on his behalf, and he looked outside himself to receive it as a gift. While the working Pharisee remained unjustified, the believing tax collector received full justification by faith alone.

Perhaps the clearest affirmation of justification by faith alone comes in Romans 4, as Paul turns to God's dealings with Abraham to illustrate that his gospel has ancient roots. In verse 3, he cites Genesis 15:6: "For what does the Scripture say? 'Abraham believed God, and it was counted to him as righteousness.'" God imputed righteousness to Abraham by means of Abraham's faith. His works had absolutely nothing to do with it, for Paul goes on to say, "Now to the one who works, his wages are not counted as a gift but as his due. And to the one who *does not work* but believes in him who justifies the ungodly, his faith is counted as righteousness" (Rom. 4:4–5). Here Paul explicitly negates the teaching that works constitute any part of the ground of justification. If we were to perform any good work for our salvation—whether baptism, church membership, Bible reading, prayer, or even faith—the righteousness that would result could never properly be called a gift. The worker earns wages. But the recipient of salvation is "justified by [God's] grace as a gift" (Rom. 3:24), and a gift can only be given apart from any work. The glorious consequence of this precious doctrine is that salvation is totally free. With an empty hand, the sinner lays hold of the righteousness of Christ through faith alone.

It is important to state that faith in Christ is not the *ground* of the believer's righteousness but merely the *means*, or instrument, through which we receive righteousness.[146] This is an important distinction, because many people mistakenly suppose that faith is the basis of our righteousness. Their hope for heaven rests on the fact that they had the good sense to believe the gospel. But such an understanding undermines the truth that we are saved by grace alone. Righteousness cannot be

---

146. Though Grudem acknowledges its shortcomings, his illustration of the difference between (1) *instrument* or *means* and (2) *ground* or *basis* is helpful: "One example from ordinary life might be seen in receiving a paycheck for work that has been done for an employer. The 'means' or 'instrument' that I use to get this paycheck is the act of reaching out my hand and taking an envelope from my mail box, then opening it and pulling out the check. But my employer does not pay me for doing any of those actions. The pay is entirely for the work that I did prior to that. Actually taking the check did not earn me one cent of the money I received—it was simply the *instrument* or *means* I used to take the paycheck into my possession. Similarly, faith is the *instrument* we use to receive justification from God, but it in itself gains us no merit with God." Grudem, *Systematic Theology*, 730n13. Italics original.

based on my faith without that righteousness becoming "a righteousness of my own" (Phil. 3:9). If saving righteousness is grounded on the sinner doing anything—even believing—it is no longer an alien righteousness given as a gift and therefore cannot be the righteousness of God required for salvation. In that case, faith would be made into a work, and "grace would no longer be grace" (Rom. 11:6). If we contribute to the basis of our righteousness in any way, then there is no good news, and we are all damned in our sins. God's holiness is so magnificently perfect—his standard so high and our depravity so pervasive—that all our righteousness must be a free gift of his sovereign grace, because we could never earn it. Thus, God declares sinners righteous not because their faith has earned them righteousness but because Christ has earned righteousness and because God has given sinners that gift by the means of faith.[147]

What is it about faith that makes it so suitable to be the instrument through which we receive justification? Paul gives us an answer in Romans 4:16, where he makes a comment that exposes the "inner logic" of salvation. He says, "For this reason, it [salvation] is by faith, in order that it may be in accordance with grace" (NASB). In other words, there is something inherent in the nature of faith that uniquely corresponds with the free gift of God's sovereign grace. Later in Romans, Paul says that if works have any part of salvation, "grace would no longer be grace" (Rom. 11:6). Rather than being the ground of our righteousness, faith is "something which looks out[side] of self, and receives the free gifts of Heaven as being what they are—pure undeserved favor. . . . Faith justifies, not in a way of merit, not on account of anything in itself, . . . but as uniting us to Christ."[148] So far from being the currency by which we purchase salvation from God, faith is uniquely suited to grace because it is nothing more than the outstretched arm and the empty hand that says, "I have nothing! I am bankrupt of any spiritual resources or ability! Lord, I receive your gift of salvation in Christ."

THE RESULT OF JUSTIFICATION: GOOD WORKS

Perhaps the most common objection to the doctrine of *sola fide* is the accusation that the apostle James explicitly contradicts it. James 2:24 says, "You see that a person is justified by works and not by faith alone." How can James's comment be reconciled with the doctrine of justification by faith alone? The answer is that James uses the word "justified" (Gk. *dikaioō*) in a different sense than Paul uses it in the above texts. In particular, James speaks of justification in the sense of "vindication" or "the demonstration of righteousness."

---

147. Warfield's famous remarks are worthy of wholehearted affirmation: "The *saving power* of faith resides . . . not in itself, but in the Almighty Saviour on whom it rests. It is never on account of its formal nature as a psychic act that faith is conceived in Scripture to be saving,—as if this frame of mind or attitude of heart were itself a virtue with claims on God for reward. . . . It is not faith that saves, but faith in Jesus Christ. . . . It is not, strictly speaking, even faith in Christ that saves, but Christ that saves through faith. The saving power resides exclusively, not in the act of faith or the attitude of faith or the nature of faith, but in the object of faith; . . . we could not more radically misconceive [the biblical concept of faith] than by transferring to faith even the smallest fraction of that saving energy which is attributed in the Scriptures solely to Christ himself." Benjamin Breckinridge Warfield, *The Works of Benjamin B. Warfield*, vol. 2, *Biblical Doctrines* (1932; repr., Grand Rapids, MI: Baker, 2000), 504.

148. Andrew Fuller, "Sermons and Sketches," in *The Complete Works of the Rev. Andrew Fuller* (Boston: Lincoln, Edmands, 1833), 2:285.

Scripture often uses the word "justification" in this sense. For example, when a lawyer purposed to test Jesus by asking him what he must do to gain eternal life, Jesus instructed him to love his neighbor as himself. Luke tells us that, in response, the lawyer "desir[ed] to justify himself, [and] said to Jesus, 'And who is my neighbor?'" (Luke 10:29). In saying this, the lawyer was not seeking a legal pronouncement of his righteousness; he was attempting to demonstrate to others that he was already righteous. In other words, he was seeking to vindicate his own righteousness. Similarly, we read in a confession of the early church that Christ "was manifested in the flesh" and "vindicated [Gk. *edikaiōthē*] by the Spirit" (1 Tim. 3:16). Certainly, the Lord Jesus stood in no need of forensic justification, of being legally declared righteous. Rather, this passage speaks of the Spirit's vindication of Christ by the many miracles he performed (Acts 2:22), as well as the ultimate vindication of the resurrection (Rom. 1:4). In the same way, James uses the term "justified" in the sense of "vindicated" or "demonstrated."

That he does so is borne out not only lexically but also contextually. In this passage, James is commenting on Abraham's sacrifice of Isaac according to God's commandment (James 2:21; cf. Gen. 22:1–14), an event that took place many years after it was declared that Abraham "believed in the LORD, and he counted it to him as righteousness" (Gen. 15:6). In contrast, when Paul desires to illustrate the truth of the imputation of righteousness through faith alone apart from works (Rom. 4:6), he chooses this earlier instance in Abraham's life before there was even any law for him to follow (Rom. 4:9–13). James, however, is not speaking of forensic justification and the imputation of righteousness. He is not speaking about good works that are the ground of our salvation. Rather, he is speaking about good works that are the necessary evidence of our salvation. Abraham's faith, which was credited to him as righteousness apart from anything he had done, was vindicated by his works. In other words, Abraham's works demonstrated that his faith was true faith and not dead faith (cf. James 2:17, 26). True faith is shown by its works (James 2:18), but those works are the evidence and result of our justification and initial sanctification, not the ground of our justification.

Far from refuting the doctrine of *sola fide* in favor of the legalists, James's argument actually provides a defense of the doctrine from the attack of the opposite error: antinomianism. This word comes from the prefix *anti-* and the Greek word *nomos*, which means "law." Antinomianism, then, speaks of those who are "against the law," specifically, in its theological sense, those who deny that sanctification is the necessary fruit of justification. Whereas legalism fails to distinguish between justification and sanctification, antinomianism severs the vital union between the two. Whereas legalism undermines the gospel by insisting that we must add our obedience to Christ's work in order to be justified, antinomianism perverts the gospel by subtracting from the efficacy of Christ's work, denying that those who receive Christ as Savior must also submit to him as Lord. James absolutely demolishes that proposition. He explains that the "faith" of professing Christians who fail to make progress in practical holiness, continuing to walk in patterns of unrighteousness, is no true and saving faith at all.

Theirs is a dead faith (James 2:17, 26), a demonic faith (James 2:19), and a useless faith (James 2:20) that marks them out as those who address Jesus as Lord but to whom he will chillingly declare, "I never knew you; depart from me, you workers of lawlessness" (Matt. 7:23).

In fact, John Calvin, the great Reformer and believer in *sola fide*, stood on the teaching of James 2 when he wrote, "It is therefore faith alone which justifies, and yet the faith which justifies is not alone."[149] In other words, salvation is not a result of good works (Eph. 2:9), but salvation does necessarily result in good works. This is the very purpose of our salvation: "For we are his workmanship, created in Christ Jesus *for good works*, which God prepared beforehand, that we should walk in them" (Eph. 2:10). Christ gave himself for us not only to forensically redeem us from all lawlessness but also to "purify for himself a people for his own possession who are zealous for good works" (Titus 2:14). Those who deny that good works are the necessary fruit of the justification received through faith alone make out the Lord Jesus Christ to be half a Savior—one who saves from sin's penalty but not its power. Yet Scripture teaches that we are united with Christ not only in his death but also in his resurrection, the necessary result of which is a holy life (Rom. 6:3–6; 2 Cor. 5:14–15). All true Christians have been "set free" from sin's bondage and have become "slaves to God," resulting in sanctification (Rom. 6:1–14, 22). Therefore, while it is faith alone that saves, the faith that saves is never alone but will always be accompanied by the fruit of righteousness (Phil. 1:11) wrought by the Holy Spirit in the life of the believer (Gal. 5:22–25; cf. John 15:8).[150]

CONCLUDING REMARKS REGARDING JUSTIFICATION

In summary, justification is that aspect of the application of redemption in which God legally declares the sinner to be righteous in his sight. The ground of this declaration is the righteousness of Christ that he accomplished in the sinner's stead by (1) dying to provide forgiveness of sin and (2) walking in perfect obedience to his Father in order to provide the righteousness required for fellowship with God. By grace alone, God imputes our sin to Christ so that he might truly bear our punishment, and he imputes Christ's righteousness to us so that we might stand before him in perfect holiness. This imputation is mediated through faith alone; it is received apart from any works on the sinner's part. The good works that necessarily follow justification are the evidence—not the ground—of true and saving faith.

The doctrine of justification runs straight to the very heart of the gospel. It offers the only hope of salvation to guilty sinners, who, apart from Christ, have no hope of a restored relationship with the holy God of the universe, yet who, in him, are clothed with the perfect righteousness of God's own beloved Son. The good news of the biblical gospel is that this blessing is offered freely to all who would receive

---

149. From Calvin's "Acts of the Council of Trent with the Antidote" (1547), quoted in Schreiner, *Faith Alone*, 62.

150. For a more detailed biblical case against antinomianism, especially as represented in the "No Lordship" doctrine of Zane Hodges and Charles Ryrie, see John MacArthur, *The Gospel according to Jesus*, and John MacArthur, *The Gospel according to the Apostles*.

it, apart from any works, through faith alone. The doctrine of justification is the very foundation of the gospel promise of John 3:16, that "God so loved the world, that he gave his only Son, that whoever believes in him should not perish but have eternal life," and of Romans 8:1, that "there is therefore now no condemnation for those who are in Christ Jesus."

Adoption

As the child of God meditates on the manifold spiritual blessings to be received in union with Christ, he cannot help but overflow in praise of God for his wisdom, kindness, and grace revealed in salvation. It is no wonder that, as Paul contemplates these spiritual blessings, he bursts into worship: "Blessed be the God and Father of our Lord Jesus Christ, who has blessed us in Christ with every spiritual blessing in the heavenly places" (Eph. 1:3). The Father has chosen us (Eph. 1:4), the Son has redeemed us (Eph. 1:7), and the Spirit has regenerated us (John 3:3–8; Eph. 1:13–14) and begotten divine spiritual life in us (John 6:63; cf. Ezek. 36:27; 37:14), giving us eyes to see the glory of Christ and the ruin of sin (2 Cor. 4:4, 6). As a result of that new birth, we experience conversion, having been given the gifts of repentance (Acts 11:17–18; 2 Tim. 2:25) and faith (Eph. 2:8). Through faith, we are intimately united to Christ, such that all that is his becomes ours. We are justified—forgiven of all our sin and the eternal punishment we rightfully deserve and credited with the full righteousness of Christ himself, such that we can stand confidently before our holy God. Blessed be God indeed!

While it may seem impossible to improve on such gifts as regeneration, conversion, union, and justification, the Word of God speaks of yet another spiritual blessing in the application of redemption: the Father's adoption of believers as his children.[151]

The concept of adoption is familiar to us because it remains common in today's world, and it is a rare case when the story of any particular adoption fails to warm the heart.[152] Eager to love and care for a child they have never met and who can do nothing to repay them, parents fill out stacks of paperwork, incur significant expenses, and often travel thousands of miles in order to welcome a little boy or girl into their family. After months and sometimes years of preparation, everything changes in a moment when the judge legally declares the child to be a member of his new family, with all the requisite rights and privileges. In many cases, if adopted children had remained in an orphanage or in the care of abusive and neglectful birth parents, the

---

151. The background for the New Testament concept of adoption comes from the practice of adoption in ancient Rome, conveniently outlined in John MacArthur, *Slave: The Hidden Truth about Your Identity in Christ* (Nashville: Thomas Nelson, 2010), 155–57: "The adoption process consisted of several specific legal procedures. The first step completely terminated the adopted child's social relationship and legal connection to his natural family. The second step made him a permanent member of his new family. Additionally, any previous financial obligations were eradicated, as if they had never existed. In order for the transaction to be legally formalized, the presence of seven reputable witnesses was required. If necessary, their testimony would refute any potential challenge to the adoption after the father had died. Once the adoption was complete, the new son or daughter was then completely under both the care and control of the new father. The previous father no longer had any authority over his former child. In Roman households, the authority of the *paterfamilias* ('father of the family') was final and absolute. And that authority extended to those adopted into the household, starting at the moment of their adoption."

152. This paragraph is adapted from MacArthur, *Slave*, 163–64. Used by permission of Thomas Nelson. www.thomas nelson.com.

outcome would likely have been tragic. But through the intervention of a compassionate benefactor, adopted children are welcomed into the loving home of a new family eager to provide protection, instruction, and the hope of a future.

The New Testament builds on this blessing of human adoption by using it as an analogy to describe God's fatherly love for us. We were spiritual orphans under the cruel oppression of sin and Satan. By nature, we were "children of wrath" (Eph. 2:3), "sons of disobedience" (Eph. 2:2; 5:6), and even children of the Devil himself (John 8:44). Our only home was this sin-cursed world that is fast passing away (1 John 2:17). Our only guardian was the avowed enemy of our souls (1 Pet. 5:8). Our only future was the terrifying expectation of hell's judgment (Heb. 10:27).

But God, eager to display the glory of his grace, intervened on our behalf:

> In love he predestined us for adoption as sons through Jesus Christ, according to the purpose of his will, to the praise of his glorious grace, with which he has blessed us in the Beloved. (Eph. 1:4–6)

> But when the fullness of time had come, God sent forth his Son, born of woman, born under the law, to redeem those who were under the law, so that we might receive adoption as sons. (Gal. 4:4–5)

The eternal Son of God himself traveled the infinite distance between heaven and earth, united the nature of God and the nature of man in his own person, and was forsaken by his Father so that we might be welcomed as sons. At great cost to himself, God took every legal measure to rescue us from sin and make us part of his family. As planned in eternity past, the Son purchased believers on Calvary, and they finally lay hold of the blessing of adoption at the time of conversion, "for," says the apostle Paul, "in Christ Jesus you are all sons of God, through faith" (Gal. 3:26; cf. John 1:12). In adoption, God legally places regenerated and justified sinners into his family, so that they become sons and daughters of God and thus enjoy all the rights and privileges of one who is a member of God's eternal family.

THE UNIQUE BLESSING OF ADOPTION

Though it has often been confused with regeneration or viewed as just another aspect of justification, the spiritual blessing of adoption is a unique privilege in God's economy of redemption. As Grudem observes, "We might initially think that we would become God's children by regeneration, since the imagery of being 'born again' in regeneration makes us think of children being born into a human family. But . . . the idea of *adoption* is opposite to the idea of being born into a family!"[153] Though they are intimately related, Scripture nevertheless distinguishes these two blessings with respect to the author, nature, and means of each. First, regeneration is a work of the Spirit (John 3:5–6, 8; 6:63), whereas adoption is an act of the Father (Eph. 1:5). Second, regeneration is transformative; it is a work in the heart of man that fundamentally transforms his nature (Ezek. 36:26–27; 2 Cor. 5:17). Adoption,

---

153. Grudem, *Systematic Theology*, 738.

on the other hand, is declarative; it does not change man's character. Rather, it is a fundamentally legal act in which God gives to those who receive Christ "the right"—that is, the legal authority[154]—"to become children of God" (John 1:12). Third, regeneration is said to be mediated by the Word of God (James 1:18; 1 Pet. 1:23–25), while the blessing of adoption is obtained through faith in Christ (John 1:12; Gal. 3:26). It is plain, therefore, that adoption is distinct from regeneration.

Further, adoption should not be viewed as just a subset of the work of justification. Though both justification and adoption are declarative acts mediated through faith, they are distinct blessings. Justification is the legal declaration that one is righteous with respect to the demands of God's law. Adoption, however, is the legal declaration by the divine Judge that the justified one has been made a member of the divine Judge's family.

It is an unspeakable blessing to be granted new spiritual life in regeneration. So also is it a remarkable privilege to be freed from the penalty of sin and declared righteous in Christ. If the bestowal of God's gifts stopped at regeneration and justification, no one would question his goodness or regard his grace as deficient. But the peculiar glory of adoption is in the superabundance of God's grace.[155] In an extravagant expression of love, God adopts believers into his family, so that we may relate to him not only as the Giver of spiritual life and the provider of legal righteousness but also as our loving and compassionate Father. For this reason, adoption has rightly been designated "the highest privilege that the gospel offers"[156] and "the apex of grace and privilege" that "staggers imagination because of its amazing condescension and love."[157] Indeed, as the apostle John considered the reality of the believer's adoption, he was compelled to let out yet another apostolic burst of praise: "See what great love the Father has lavished on us, that we should be called children of God!" (1 John 3:1 NIV). How great indeed!

CLARIFYING MISCONCEPTIONS OF ADOPTION

When speaking about sinful men becoming sons of God, it is necessary to distinguish between the Father's adopted sons and daughters, on the one hand, and his one and only Son, the Lord Jesus Christ, on the other. In one sense, we must not downplay the significance of the radical privileges of adoption. We are made partakers of the divine nature (2 Pet. 1:4), are indwelt by the Spirit of God himself (Rom. 8:14–16; Gal. 4:6), and are fellow heirs with Christ of eternal life (Rom. 8:17, 23; 1 Pet. 1:4). Believers have been so highly exalted that Christ is properly called our brother (Rom. 8:29; Heb. 2:17). Indeed, because Christ the sanctifier and we the sanctified have one Father, the Lord Jesus is unashamed to call us brothers (Heb. 2:11–12).

---

154. Leon Morris, *The Gospel according to John*, rev. ed., NICNT (Grand Rapids, MI: Eerdmans, 1995), 87. Also see John 5:27 and 19:11 for instances in which the same Greek phrase (*didōmi . . . exousia*) is used in unmistakably legal senses.

155. We must not think of adoption as a kind of second-class relationship, as some may perceive it in our day. Rather, in ancient times the adopted child was often the most wanted and honored, chosen in many cases because he was unique and desirable.

156. J. I. Packer, *Knowing God*, rev. ed. (Downers Grove, IL: InterVarsity Press, 1993), 206.

157. Murray, *Redemption Accomplished and Applied*, 134.

Our exalted position, however, does not eliminate the uniqueness of Christ's relationship to the Father as his eternal Son. The Lord himself clearly maintained this distinction when he instructed Mary to tell the disciples, "I am ascending to my Father and your Father, to my God and your God" (John 20:17). If the uniqueness of Jesus's sonship was not to be distinguished from ours, such a statement would be cumbersome and redundant; he could have simply said, ". . . to our Father and our God." But by distinguishing between "my Father" and "your Father," he emphasized that, though we relate to God as true sons and daughters, his position as Son was of a distinct and unique character. After all, he is *ton huion ton monogenē*—God's "only Son" (John 3:16). The Greek word *monogenēs* is derived from the terms *monos* ("only") and *genos* ("kind," "type"; e.g., Mark 9:29), and thus speaks of "one of a kind." In no sense, then, does our adoption as sons bring us into a union of essence with Christ so that we participate in the inner life of the Trinity, as some teach. We may become God's sons by adoption, but Christ is the Father's only eternal Son.

In the second place, the notion that believers *become* the children of God at the time of conversion deals the deathblow to the doctrine of the universal fatherhood of God—the liberal Protestant teaching that all human beings are God's children by default. It is true that Scripture sometimes speaks of God's fatherhood in universal terms. As Paul reasons with the philosophers on Mars Hill, he quotes the poet Aratus (ca. 315–ca. 245 BC), who said, "For we are indeed his offspring" (Acts 17:28), and then comments with approbation: "Being then God's offspring . . ." (Acts 17:29). However, the context of this statement clearly indicates that Paul was speaking of the reality that God is the Creator of all mankind and thus is the universal Father only in that sense. He is "the Father of spirits" (Heb. 12:9), who "gives to all mankind life and breath and everything" (Acts 17:25), and he "made from one man every nation of mankind" (Acts 17:26). Thus, "in him we live and move and have our being" (Acts 17:28). This may also be Malachi's intent when he rebukes the sinful priests of his day, asking, "Have we not all one Father? Has not one God created us?" (Mal. 2:10). However, given his reference to "the covenant of our fathers" at the end of the verse, it is more likely that he is referring to God's fatherhood of Israel as a covenant nation (Jer. 31:9; Hos. 11:1).

Nevertheless, the fact that God is the common Creator of all human beings does not mean that all are his children in the relational sense indicated by the doctrine of adoption. Jesus himself speaks most severely on this issue, noting that all unbelievers are children of Satan himself. He clearly distinguishes between his Father and the Pharisees' father (John 8:38), denies that God is their Father (John 8:42), and explicitly declares, "You are of your father the devil" (John 8:44). The apostle John comments on this distinction between the children of God and the children of the Devil, noting that the latter are those who do not practice righteousness (1 John 3:10). Scripture differentiates between the children of the flesh and the children of God (Rom. 9:8), the children of the slave woman and the children of the free woman (Gal. 4:22–31), and the children of light and the children of darkness (Eph. 5:8).

These passages militate against any understanding of the universal fatherhood of God. Indeed, rather than being sons of God, natural man is described as "the sons of disobedience" (Eph. 2:2; 5:6). So far from relating naturally to God as children, all fallen human beings are "by nature children of wrath" (Eph. 2:3). Unless something drastic happens—indeed, nothing less radical than being made alive from the dead (Eph. 2:4–5)—man in his natural condition will not know the blessings of a loving Father but rather will experience the wrath of a righteous Judge. It is only to those who receive Jesus and believe in his name that authority is given to become children of God (John 1:12), for all of God's adoptive children are "sons of God through faith in Christ Jesus" (Gal. 3:26 NASB) as a result of his work of redemption (Gal. 4:5).

Therefore, rather than an *essential* fatherhood of God or a universal *creative* fatherhood of God, these passages on adoption speak of the *redemptive* fatherhood of God, in which justified sinners become sons and daughters of the Father with all the rights and privileges that a member of his family enjoys.

THE PRIVILEGES OF ADOPTION

What, then, are those rights and privileges to be enjoyed by members of the family of God? In the first place, the chief blessing of our adoption is that the Holy Spirit himself takes up permanent residence in our hearts, freeing us from sin and fostering our fellowship with God. After speaking about the adoption accomplished by Christ's redemption, Paul adds, "Because you are sons, God has sent the Spirit of his Son into our hearts, crying, 'Abba! Father!' So you are no longer a slave, but a son" (Gal. 4:6–7). Elsewhere he speaks of believers having "received the Spirit of adoption as sons, by whom we cry, 'Abba! Father!' The Spirit himself bears witness with our spirit that we are children of God" (Rom. 8:15–16). Though we were enslaved to sin and idolatry (Gal. 4:8), the Spirit of adoption has liberated us from our slavery into "the freedom of the glory of the children of God" (Rom. 8:21; cf. 2 Cor. 3:17). We are no longer slaves of a master but permanent sons of our Father (John 8:35), and the Spirit himself bears witness in our hearts to assure us that this new relationship is genuine. So intimate is our bond with the God of the universe that the Spirit compels us to cry out to him with childlike affection, "Abba! Father!" An informal Aramaic term for "father," *Abba* signifies the most endearing tenderness and intimacy between a father and a son. Aside from these two passages, it occurs only one other time in the New Testament: on the lips of Jesus himself during the darkest hour of his earthly sojourn. In Gethsemane, as the Son poured out his heart to the Father, pleading that the cup of divine wrath be removed from him, he called to him as "Abba" (Mark 14:36). It is nothing short of staggering to think that we who were once alienated from God because of our sin (Eph. 4:18) have been given the privilege of crying out to the Father in the very same way that his beloved Son did. The glory of that thought is exceeded only by the reality that his cry of "Abba" was ignored so that ours would be heard.

Because we can relate to God as our Father, we share in the richness of his loving compassion, protection, provision, and beneficence. His disposition to us is as a father to his children, eager to display kindness and to act in our greatest interests. The psalmist tells us, "As a father shows compassion to his children, so the LORD shows compassion to those who fear him" (Ps. 103:13). That disposition to compassion is illustrated by the Lord himself, who asks,

> What father among you, if his son asks for a fish, will instead of a fish give him a serpent; or if he asks for an egg, will give him a scorpion? If you then, who are evil, know how to give good gifts to your children, how much more will the heavenly Father give the Holy Spirit to those who ask him! (Luke 11:11–13)

Not only will God give us his Spirit, but as the parallel passage puts it, God will also give us the "good things" for which we ask him (Matt. 7:11). Because of this, we have no need to become anxious about our daily necessities, for the Father is happy to provide these for us: "And do not seek what you are to eat and what you are to drink, nor be worried. For . . . your Father knows that you need them" (Luke 12:29–30). Immediately after these consolations from our Lord, he comforts us with the Father's beneficence in what may be the most tender words he ever spoke: "Fear not, little flock, for it is your Father's good pleasure to give you the kingdom" (Luke 12:32). God is not merely a distant, disinterested-though-generous benefactor. As a father delights to bless his children with an inheritance, it is his good pleasure—he eagerly delights—to make us sharers in the fullness of the kingdom itself.

Implied in this eagerness of God to bless his adopted children is the reality that we may approach the Lord of glory in prayer. As Jesus said, our Father is ready to give good gifts "to those who ask him" (Matt. 7:11; Luke 11:13), and he provides for the necessities of life as we seek first his kingdom (Luke 12:30–31), which is done preeminently through prayer. For this reason, when the Lord taught his disciples to pray to God, he instructed them to address him saying, "Our Father in heaven" (Matt. 6:9). What a privilege it is to approach the throne of grace with the confidence that the sovereign Lord is our heavenly Father, eager to hear our requests and bless us from his bounty!

Another privilege of our adoption as sons is the loving, fatherly discipline we receive from God. The author of Hebrews counsels us, "My son, do not regard lightly the discipline of the Lord, nor be weary when reproved by him. For the Lord disciplines the one he loves, and chastises every son whom he receives" (Heb. 12:5–6; cf. Prov. 3:11–12). When we depart from God's will and engage in sinful thoughts and actions, he will providentially order various hardships and afflictions in our lives to warn us of sin's consequences, to lead us to repentance, and to cultivate greater spiritual maturity in us (e.g., 2 Sam. 12:10–12; 1 Cor. 11:30). The author of Hebrews goes on to explain that when we experience this discipline, "God is treating [us] as sons. For what son is there whom his father does not discipline? If you are left without discipline, . . . then you are illegitimate children and not sons" (Heb. 12:7–8). Indeed, when God withdraws his discipline, it is the severest indication of his judgment, as he is giving people over to their sin and its consequences (Rom. 1:25–28). In the human realm, Scripture says that parents who withhold discipline from their children hate them (Prov. 13:24) and desire their death (Prov. 19:18). Thus, for God to discipline us as his children is sure testimony of his earnest love and sincere desire for our greatest benefit. As the author of Hebrews continues, "he disciplines us for our good, that we may share his holiness" (Heb. 12:10). Though in the moment "all discipline seems painful rather than pleasant, . . . later it yields the peaceful fruit of righteousness to those who have been trained by it" (Heb. 12:11). When we consider that there is a "holiness without which no one will see the Lord" (Heb. 12:14), we are compelled to treasure the loving discipline of our Father, for it fits us for fellowship with him. What a privilege that the God of the heavens has taken a personal interest in our spiritual welfare—not only to declare us righteous but also to work practical righteousness in us by his great grace!

Still another privilege of our adoption into God's family is the unity we enjoy with our brothers and sisters in Christ. The church is not merely a social club or a political organization knit together by common interests or shared hobbies. By virtue of the electing work of the Father, the redemptive work of the Son, and the regenerating work of the Spirit, we are objectively united to one another as members of the same family. No wonder the early believers addressed one another as brothers and sisters (e.g., Acts 1:15–16; Rom. 12:1; 16:14; Phil. 4:1; 1 Tim. 5:1–2; cf. Matt. 12:46–50). Now, a family is not merely a group of people with some shared interests and a subjective appreciation for one another. Instead, brothers and sisters are bound together by something much deeper—by the objective union that results from the love shared by their parents. And while brothers and sisters may not always relate to one another on the best terms, no amount of discord or conflict can break the objective bond that they share. The same is true within the family of God. Tensions and disagreements may arise between us and our brothers and sisters in Christ. But just as nothing can separate us from the loving union that we share with Christ individually (Rom. 8:38–39), neither can anything separate us from the union that we share with one another corporately. It is on the basis of this objective union that we pursue "the unity of the Spirit in the bond of peace" (Eph. 4:3). As long as Christians do that, we will never be alone. We will always belong to one another. Because of the adopting grace of our Father, we face life's darkest trials alongside our brothers and sisters as the family of God.

In addition to all these privileges that we enjoy in the present time, our adoption as children of God also guarantees us a share in the future inheritance of eternal life. Paul writes that if we are adopted children, we must also necessarily be heirs. We are no longer slaves but sons, "and if a son, then an heir through God" (Gal. 4:7)—indeed, "heirs of God and fellow heirs with Christ" (Rom. 8:17). In human relations, sons and daughters inherit the estate of their parents at the time of their passing. All that belonged to the parents is bequeathed to the children as they carry on the family legacy. In a similar way, though by nature we had no rightful claim to all the riches of the kingdom of God, by grace we have become God's adopted children and have thus become legal heirs of "an inheritance that is imperishable, undefiled, and unfading, kept in heaven" for us (1 Pet. 1:4). So genuine is our inheritance that we are described as fellow heirs with Christ (Rom. 8:17). Everything that Christ will receive by divine right as the natural Son of God, we will receive by divine grace as adoptive children of God.[158] Because Christ is God's Son, all that the Father has belongs to him. And because we are in Christ, everything that is Christ's is ours, "whether . . . the world or life or death or the present or the future" (1 Cor. 3:22–23)—all things belong to the children of God. The redeemed are sure to enjoy all the blessings of heaven in God's presence, for he promises that "he who overcomes will inherit these things, and I will be his God and he will be My son" (Rev. 21:7 NASB). Chief among these heavenly blessings is the promise of a glorified body after the likeness of Christ's resurrection body, free from all sin and infirmity (1 Cor. 15:23, 42–44; Phil. 3:20–21). While in this house we groan under the effects of sin's curse (2 Cor. 5:2), we look forward to the consummation of our adoption as sons and daughters of God, the redemption of our bodies (Rom. 8:23).

This glorification has, in a sense, begun in this present life in the form of progressive sanctification, yet another privilege of our adoption. Just as children imitate their father, so also are we exhorted to "be imitators of God, as beloved children" (Eph. 5:1). One of the richest blessings of God's grace in salvation is that he attaches his name to his people. He graciously pursues the welfare of his people with the same zeal with which he upholds the honor of his reputation, because they bear his name (cf. Josh. 7:9; 1 Sam. 12:22; Jer. 14:7, 9; Dan. 9:17–18). As children of God, we bear the "family name" of God, and as Isaiah says, his name is Holy (Isa. 57:15; cf. 1 Chron. 29:16; Ps. 33:21; Isa. 47:4; Luke 1:49). Thus the apostle Peter exhorts us, "As obedient children, do not be conformed to the passions of your former ignorance, but as he who called you is holy, you also be holy in all your conduct, since it is written, 'You shall be holy, for I am holy'" (1 Pet. 1:14–16). If we call on this holy One as Father, we ought to live lives that resemble his holiness (1 Pet. 1:17), conducting ourselves as "blameless and innocent, *children of God* without blemish in the midst of a crooked and twisted generation" (Phil. 2:15).

The conclusion to the study of the doctrine of adoption must be a call to holiness. God's promise to us is, "I will be a father to you, and you shall be sons and daughters to me" (2 Cor. 6:18). If we enjoy such an exalted position as children adopted into the family of God, enjoying all the rights and privileges as sons and daughters of the Almighty himself, we must respond as Paul instructs in the next verse: "Since we have these promises, beloved, let us cleanse ourselves from every defilement of body and spirit, bringing holiness to completion in the fear of God" (2 Cor. 7:1). Therefore, we now turn our attention to the doctrine of sanctification.

Sanctification[159]

Thus far in this study of the application of redemption, we have considered those benefits purchased by the work of Christ that the Spirit applies immediately to

---

158. John MacArthur, *Romans 1–8*, MNTC (Chicago: Moody Press, 1991), 445.
159. For an additional discussion of sanctification, see chap. 5, "The Holy Spirit."

believers at the inception of the Christian life. At regeneration, the sinner is made alive, granted repentance and faith, united to Christ, declared righteous on the basis of the imputed righteousness of Christ, and adopted into the family of God. However, the blessing of sanctification is a benefit of the application of redemption that, though it begins at regeneration, is applied throughout the entirety of the Christian's life. In sanctification, God, working especially by the Holy Spirit, separates the believer unto himself (cf. 1 Cor. 1:2) and makes him increasingly holy, progressively transforming him into the image of Christ (Rom. 8:29; 2 Cor. 3:18) by subduing the power of sin in his life and enabling him to bear the fruit of obedience in his life.[160]

THE RELATIONSHIP BETWEEN JUSTIFICATION AND SANCTIFICATION

Sanctification is intimately connected to justification, since both benefits are enjoyed by virtue of the believer's union with Christ. Nevertheless, sanctification is not to be confused with or collapsed into justification, as in Roman Catholic theology. Justification is the once-for-all judicial declaration of righteousness that defines man's legal standing before God. Sanctification, on the other hand, is a gradual, ongoing transformation of his nature. With respect to justification, Christ has secured forensic righteousness *for* the believer; in sanctification, the Spirit progressively works practical righteousness *in* the believer. Justification concerns the *imputation* of righteousness, whereas sanctification concerns the *impartation* of righteousness. To confuse the two is to fundamentally undermine the gospel.[161]

POSITIONAL (DEFINITIVE) SANCTIFICATION

Though sanctification is primarily understood to be a process in which the believer is conformed into the image of Christ (e.g., Scripture speaks of believers as "those who *are being* sanctified," Heb. 10:14), that process has a definite beginning at regeneration. The present-tense aspect of sanctification is often called progressive sanctification, whereas the past-tense aspect may be called either initial, positional, or definitive sanctification.

As discussed earlier, regeneration is not only the impartation of spiritual life but is also a definitive cleansing from sin.[162] That is why, in John 3:5, Jesus speaks of the new birth as being born of the *water* and the Spirit. In that passage he refers to Ezekiel's prophecy concerning regeneration, in which God promises not only to give his people a new heart and to cause his Spirit to indwell them but also to sprinkle clean water on them to purify them from their uncleanness (Ezek. 36:25–27). Mirroring Ezekiel's imagery, Paul designates regeneration as both a washing and a renewal (Titus 3:5). Thus, when the Spirit imparts spiritual life into the soul of the dead sin-

---

160. Berkhof's definition is a helpful complement: "Sanctification may be defined as *that gracious and continuous operation of the Holy Spirit, by which He delivers the justified sinner from the pollution of sin, renews his whole nature in the image of God, and enables him to perform good works.*" *Systematic Theology*, 532. Italics original.

161. For more on the relationship between justification and sanctification, see "The Nature of Justification: A Legal Declaration" (p. 612) and "The Result of Justification: Good Works" (p. 621).

162. See "The Nature of Regeneration" (p. 579) and the discussion of Ezek. 36:25–27 and John 3:5 in "The Means of Regeneration" (p. 583).

ner, opening his eyes to the filth of sin and the glory of Jesus (2 Cor. 4:4, 6), man's nature is sanctified—definitively transformed from spiritual death to spiritual life, such that Scripture calls him a new creation (2 Cor. 5:17). The holy disposition that is strengthened throughout the believer's progressive sanctification is that same holy disposition that is born in the believer at regeneration. In this sense, regeneration is the beginning of sanctification.

For this reason, the New Testament often employs the terminology of sanctification in the past tense, characterizing the Christian as one who has been initially sanctified by God. In his farewell address to the Ephesian elders at Miletus, Paul spoke of the inheritance they share "among all those who are sanctified" (Acts 20:32). In his defense before Agrippa, he recounted his conversion experience on the Damascus road, when Jesus had commissioned him to the Gentiles so "that they may receive forgiveness of sins and a place among those who are sanctified by faith in me" (Acts 26:18). That such a designation does not refer to some completed state of progressive sanctification is established by Paul's letter to the sinful Corinthian church members, whom he addressed as "those sanctified in Christ Jesus" (1 Cor. 1:2). The Corinthians were that motley crew of professing believers who were splitting up into factions (1 Cor. 1:11–13), whom Paul could only address as fleshly (1 Cor. 3:1), among whom there existed a kind of immorality not even named among the Gentiles (1 Cor. 5:1), who were suing one another before unbelieving judges (1 Cor. 6:1–7), who were defrauding the Lord's Table to satisfy their gluttony and drunkenness (1 Cor. 11:20–22), and who were abusing the gifts of the Holy Spirit (1 Corinthians 12–14). If to be sanctified meant to have reached a state of exalted practical holiness, that description could hardly be made of them! And yet Paul spoke of their definitive sanctification: "But you were washed, you were sanctified, you were justified in the name of the Lord Jesus Christ and by the Spirit of our God" (1 Cor. 6:11).[163] For this same reason, both the Old and New Testaments identify all of God's people as saints—literally, "the holy ones" (e.g., Pss. 16:3; 34:9; Dan. 7:18–27; Matt. 27:52; Acts 9:13, 32, 41; Rom. 1:7; 8:27; 1 Cor. 1:2; 2 Cor. 1:1; Eph. 1:1; 6:18; Phil. 1:1; Col. 1:2; Jude 3; Rev. 19:8). So far from identifying a spiritually elite people on the basis of their personal merits, as the Roman Catholic Church teaches, what makes a believer a saint is not his practical righteousness but his positional righteousness. All believers are saints because all believers have been set apart by a holy God and have been united to the holy Lord Jesus. This is precisely the concept of definitive sanctification.

The most significant reality in definitive sanctification is that, through union with Christ, the believer is set free from the dominion of sin. While justification and imputed righteousness grant the Christian freedom from sin's penalty, initial sanctification grants him freedom from sin's power. This is precisely Paul's point in Romans 6:1–7:6. There he states that believers have "died to sin" (6:2) by virtue of

---

163. Even the order of the three verbs indicates that, by using the Greek term *hagiazō*, Paul meant to refer to definitive sanctification, for if he intended to speak of progressive sanctification—which follows justification in the *ordo salutis*—it is unlikely that he would have placed "you were sanctified" before "you were justified." The order makes it clear that he is referring, first, to the washing of regeneration (cf. Titus 3:5), second, to definitive sanctification, and, third, to forensic justification.

their union with Christ in his death and resurrection (6:3–5) and that "our old self was crucified with [Christ] in order that the body of sin might be brought to nothing, so that we would no longer be enslaved to sin. For," Paul reasons, "one who has died has been set free from sin" (6:6–7). Because Christ died and was raised, sin and death no longer have dominion over him (6:9–10). Believers "were made to die to the Law through the body of Christ, so that [they] might be joined [i.e., united] to another" (7:4 NASB), and since the law to which they died "is binding on a person only as long as he lives" (7:1), they must "consider [them]selves dead to sin and alive to God in Christ Jesus" (6:11)—sin's legal right to rule over them is broken. For this reason Paul declares, "For sin will have no dominion over you, since you are not under law but under grace" (6:14), and "having been set free from sin, [believers] have become slaves of righteousness" (6:18). All this assures Christians that, though once hopelessly bound to the enslaving power of sin, they are now possessed of Christ's resurrection power to resist temptation, mortify sin, and pursue increasing holiness. To be sure, sin remains present in their flesh (7:14–25; 1 John 1:8), but its power has been defeated through the efficacy of Christ's death and the virtue of his resurrection.[164] Therefore, though the believer may struggle mightily with sin, he must never adopt a defeatist attitude in which he is resigned to accept the reality of sin in his life. To do so is to make peace with a dethroned enemy—to submit to sin's dominion that has nevertheless been conquered.

The Christian's freedom from the dominion of sin through union with Christ is the necessary foundation for all progress in progressive sanctification. Only because sin's reign has been overthrown is the believer exhorted to "let not sin therefore reign in your mortal body, to make you obey its passions. Do not present your members to sin as instruments for unrighteousness, but present yourselves to God as those who have been brought from death to life, and your members to God as instruments for righteousness" (Rom. 6:12–13). Believers can only obey these imperatives because union with Christ results in the indicative reality of freedom from sin. Indeed, it is the believer's contemplation of the end of sin's dominion ("*Consider* yourselves dead to sin," 6:11) that grounds the command to not let sin reign ("Let not sin *therefore* reign," 6:12). And then Paul repeats the gracious foundation of our battle against sin in Romans 6:14: "*For* sin will have no dominion over you." This indicative-imperative paradigm is the difference between truly biblical, distinctively Christian ethics and the moralism of legalistic religion or naturalistic philosophy. It is only because of what Christ has accomplished in his historical death and resurrection and only because we are united to him *in* his death and resurrection by the grace of God that the believer can make any progress in practical holiness. The believer can live a life of faithful obedience on the sole basis that he has really been crucified with Christ and that Christ now really lives in him (Gal. 2:20). Only because he is *already*

---

164. Murray, *Redemption Accomplished and Applied*, 143. He goes on to say, "Though sin still remains it does not have the mastery. There is a total difference between surviving sin and reigning sin. . . . It is one thing for sin to live in us: it is another for us to live in sin. It is one thing for the enemy to occupy the capital; it is another for his defeated hosts to harass the garrisons of the kingdom." *Redemption Accomplished and Applied*, 145.

chosen, holy, and beloved can the follower of Christ put on compassion, kindness, humility, meekness, and patience (Col. 3:12).

Therefore, any attempt at morally improving oneself apart from the working of God's supernatural grace bestowed through the believer's union with Christ is a man-made counterfeit of the work of sanctification that finds no favor with God and is ultimately ineffective (Rom. 8:8; 14:23; Heb. 11:6). The Christian pursues practical holiness not to enter a relationship with God or to earn his love; he pursues practical holiness because he has already entered a relationship with God by grace through faith in Christ and because he is already the recipient of God's love and favor in Christ. Worshiping Christ as the solid rock on which she stands, the church rightly sings, "He breaks the power of canceled sin; he sets the prisoner free."[165] The only kind of sin whose power is broken in the lives of people is *canceled* sin—sin that has already been punished in Christ's death and forgiven through faith. Thus it is necessary to fight sin in the strength and in the freedom of that gracious reality. Believers in Christ can be victorious over sin only because—and must be victorious over sin precisely because—Christ has conquered sin in them by virtue of his death and resurrection.

PROGRESSIVE SANCTIFICATION

As has already been implied, however, though the believer enjoys this decisive victory over the dominion of sin as a result of union with Christ, his heart and life are not totally purified. Though the penalty of sin is paid for and the power of sin is broken, the presence of sin still remains in the believer's flesh and therefore must continually be put to death. Thus, the sanctification that begins definitively at regeneration necessarily continues throughout the entirety of the Christian life. This continuous aspect of sanctification is called progressive sanctification.

The continual, progressive nature of sanctification is substantiated in the Bible's numerous calls to holiness in the present tense, indicating ongoing, continuous action. For example, Paul commands believers not to be conforming themselves to the world but to "be transformed [Gk. *metamorphousthe*, lit., 'be continually being transformed'] by the renewal of your mind" (Rom. 12:2). The author of Hebrews commands Christians to "strive for [Gk. *diōkete*, lit., 'be continually pursuing'] . . . the holiness without which no one will see the Lord" (Heb. 12:14). Putting to death the deeds of the body is the characteristic action of one who is indwelt by the Spirit of God (Rom. 8:13; cf. 8:9). Further, several passages explicitly assert the progressive nature of sanctification. Paul notes that his own sanctification is incomplete, so he continually presses on toward the goal of the heavenly prize (Phil. 3:12–14). Though the old self has been put off once and for all at conversion, yet the new self is continuously "being renewed [Gk. *anakainoumenon*] in knowledge after the image of its creator" (Col. 3:9–10). He prays that believers' love would "increase and abound" (1 Thess. 3:12) and "abound more and more" (Phil. 1:9). Peter charges

---

165. From the hymn by Charles Wesley, "O, for a Thousand Tongues to Sing" (1739).

believers to "grow up into salvation" (1 Pet. 2:2) and to "grow in the grace and knowledge of our Lord and Savior Jesus Christ" (2 Pet. 3:18)—the concept of growth indicating an ongoing process. And most clearly, Paul states that as believers behold the glory of Christ with the eyes of the heart, they are thereby "being transformed [Gk. *metamorphoumetha*] into the same image from one degree of glory to another [Gk. *apo doxēs eis doxan*, lit., 'from glory to glory']" (2 Cor. 3:18). Believers are not conformed to the image of Christ in an instant, but rather, they experience a progressive transformation into his image by degrees. Thus, the Holy Spirit's work in believers will cause them to increase in sanctification throughout their Christian lives.

PERFECTED SANCTIFICATION

Just as sanctification has a definitive beginning at regeneration and increases throughout one's life, it will also at some point be brought to completion—namely, at the end of the believer's life. Second Corinthians 3:18 outlines the directly proportional relationship in progressive sanctification between beholding the glory of Christ and being transformed into the image of his glory; to the degree that we behold his glory, to that degree are we sanctified. Because in this life we see him imperfectly, even if truly (1 Cor. 13:12), the perfection of our sanctification awaits the day when we will see him face-to-face. First John 3:2 explicitly shows that this directly proportional relationship continues until sanctification is perfected in glorification: "But we know that when he appears we shall be like him, *because* we shall see him as he is."

Yet for all who will have died in faith before the return of Christ, the perfection of sanctification comes in two stages: the soul is fully sanctified at death, while the body awaits its perfected sanctification at the second coming of Christ. When believers pass from this present life, their spirits are separated from their bodies (2 Cor. 5:8) and enter the presence of the Lord (Phil. 1:23). Thus the author of Hebrews speaks of the glorified citizens of heaven as "the spirits of the righteous made perfect" (Heb. 12:23). They are glorified in the sense that sanctification is complete, but it is specifically their spirits that experience this perfection, since their bodies undergo the corruption that is tied to sin and death. However, the Lord Jesus does not provide half a salvation. He has purchased the redemption not of men's souls alone but also of their bodies (Rom. 8:23). For this reason, says Paul, we eagerly wait for Christ's return from heaven, when he "will transform our lowly body to be like his glorious body, by the power that enables him even to subject all things to himself" (Phil. 3:20–21). The believer's perishable, inglorious, weak natural body will be raised from the dead and transformed into an imperishable, glorious, powerful spiritual body (1 Cor. 15:42–44; cf. 15:22–23). This is glorification, the final aspect of salvation.

Contrary to a number of notions throughout church history, sanctification can never be completed in this life. The doctrine of *perfectionism* holds that it is possible and necessary for the believer, in this present life, to attain a level of moral perfection. Several arguments used to substantiate this error must be refuted from the Bible.

First, it is argued that Scripture exhorts believers to holiness in language that sounds very absolute. Jesus commands his hearers, "You therefore must be perfect, as your heavenly Father is perfect" (Matt. 5:48), and Peter similarly cites the Levitical holiness code: "But as he who called you is holy, you also be holy in all your conduct, since it is written, 'You shall be holy, for I am holy'" (1 Pet. 1:15–16; cf. Lev. 11:44). If we are thus commanded, the perfectionists reason, we must have the ability to obey these commands.

However, this is nothing more than the unproven assumption that responsibility implies ability, that *ought* implies *can*—an assumption that Scripture explicitly contradicts. For example, Jesus proclaims the moral inability of humans when he says that "a healthy tree cannot bear bad fruit, nor can a diseased tree bear good fruit" (Matt. 7:18). However, he immediately follows up this statement by saying that the moral inability of the unbeliever (represented by the diseased tree) to produce good fruit does not absolve him of (1) his responsibility to do so and (2) the certain consequences of failing to do so: "Every tree that does not bear good fruit is cut down and thrown into the fire" (Matt. 7:19). Further, just because man is morally unable to repent and believe in Christ for salvation (Rom. 8:7–8; 1 Cor. 2:14) does not remove his responsibility to do so. All people everywhere are held responsible to repent and believe the gospel (Acts 17:30; cf. Mark 1:15)—the very thing Scripture elsewhere declares they are unable to do. Thus, the assumption that the existence of a command necessarily implies man's ability to obey is shown to be contradictory to Scripture.[166]

Perfectionists also appeal to passages such as 1 Thessalonians 5:23, in which Paul prays that God would sanctify the church entirely, and James 1:4, which speaks of endurance rendering a believer "perfect and complete, lacking in nothing" (cf. Col. 1:28; 2:10; 2 Tim. 3:17). Special recourse is made to statements by the apostle John in his first epistle, such as, "Whoever abides in Him does not sin. Whoever sins has neither seen Him nor known Him" (1 John 3:6 NKJV), and, "Whoever has been born of God does not sin, for His seed remains in him; and he cannot sin, because he has been born of God" (1 John 3:9 NKJV).

It is a misinterpretation to take these passages as referring to perfected sanctification. In 1 Thessalonians 5:23, complete sanctification refers to sanctification in the entirety of man's nature, which Paul mentions explicitly in the next phrase ("your whole spirit and soul and body"). He is praying that God would sustain their faith throughout their life and finally bring his sanctifying work to completion, perfecting both the spirit/soul and the body at the return of Christ (cf. Phil. 3:21). The passages that speak of believers being "perfect" (Gk. *teleios*) refer not to total sanctification but to spiritual maturity, as the word is often translated elsewhere (e.g., 1 Cor. 2:6; Heb. 5:14). And John's statements that no one who has been born of God and who abides in Christ sins are rightly understood when one properly translates the verb

---

166. For another example of how Scripture indicates that *ought* does not imply *can* as it relates to election and reprobation, see "The Vindication of the Doctrine" (p. 506). See also Bruce A. Ware, "Effectual Calling and Grace," in *Still Sovereign: Contemporary Perspectives on Election, Foreknowledge, and Grace*, ed. Thomas R. Schreiner and Bruce A. Ware (Grand Rapids, MI: Baker, 2000), 213–15.

tense of John's words. Rather than teaching that Christians never commit any acts of sin, John is teaching that no true believer continues in an unbroken lifestyle or pattern of sinning as he did in his unregenerate state. The ESV more accurately captures the continuous aspect of these verbs by translating 1 John 3:6 as, "No one who abides in him *keeps on* sinning [Gk. *hamartanei*]," and 3:9 as, "No one born of God *makes a practice* of sinning [Gk. *hamartian . . . poiei*]." Indeed, John's other comments from the same letter emphatically exclude any notion of sinless perfection in this life, for he tells us, "If we say we have no sin, we deceive ourselves, and the truth is not in us" (1 John 1:8). Those who believe themselves to have reached entire sanctification in this life have deceived themselves, "for," as Solomon says, "there is no one who does not sin" (1 Kings 8:46), and again, "Surely there is not a righteous man on earth who does good and never sins" (Eccles. 7:20). The concept of perfectionism is worthy of rhetorical derision, as seen in Proverbs 20:9: "Who can say, 'I have made my heart pure; I am clean from my sin'?" James comments that "we all stumble in many ways" (James 3:2), and as we daily commit sin, the Lord Jesus instructs us to daily pray for forgiveness (Matt. 6:11–12; cf. 1 John 1:9).

Far from thinking to attain spiritual perfection in this life, all believers ought to cry with Paul,

> *Not* that I have already obtained this or am already perfect, but I press on to make it my own, because Christ Jesus has made me his own. Brothers, I do not consider that I have made it my own. But one thing I do: forgetting what lies behind and straining forward to what lies ahead, I press on toward the goal for the prize of the upward call of God in Christ Jesus. (Phil. 3:12–14)

Then, in a display of apostolic irony, he adds the exhortation, "Let those of us who are mature [Gk. *teleios*] think this way, and if in anything you think otherwise, God will reveal that also to you" (Phil. 3:15). Those who are "perfect" (i.e., truly spiritually mature) are those who realize they are not perfect and who acknowledge the perennial need for exhausting one's efforts in the pursuit of personal holiness.

THE CHARACTER OF PROGRESSIVE SANCTIFICATION[167]

So much of the confusion over how to properly and successfully pursue sanctification comes from fundamentally misunderstanding the nature of sanctification. Followers of Christ, therefore, must understand the character of this holiness that they are commanded to pursue. While several passages of Scripture must be consulted to clarify this truth, two foundational texts stand out as especially pertinent:

> Therefore, my beloved, as you have always obeyed, so now, not only as in my presence but much more in my absence, work out your own salvation with fear and trembling, for it is God who works in you, both to will and to work for his good pleasure. (Phil. 2:12–13)

---

167. Much of this section is adapted from Michael Riccardi, *Sanctification: The Christian's Pursuit of God-Given Holiness* (Sun Valley, CA: Grace Books, 2015). Used by permission of Grace Books.

And we all, with unveiled face, beholding the glory of the Lord, are being transformed into the same image from one degree of glory to another. For this comes from the Lord who is the Spirit. (2 Cor. 3:18)

These and other texts establish several conclusions concerning the nature, author, means, and dynamics of progressive sanctification.

The Nature of Sanctification. In the first place, sanctification is fundamentally a supernatural work of God done in the inner nature of man. Paul declares that God is at work *in* believers that they may not only work for his good pleasure but even will for his good pleasure (Phil. 2:13). That is to say, God works for the believer to sanctify not merely his external actions but also his internal desires. Further, in 2 Corinthians 3:18, Paul speaks of sanctification as the believer's "being transformed" [Gk. *metamorphoumetha*] into the image of Christ, a term that describes an inward change in fundamental character.[168] Elsewhere, Paul indicates that such a transformation requires the renewal of one's mind (Rom. 12:2) and prays for believers to that end (Eph. 4:23), along with asking that they would be "strengthened with power through his Spirit in your inner being" (Eph. 3:16)—all of which testify to the fundamentally internal nature of sanctification. Commenting on Paul's exhortations for believers to be renewed in the spirit of their minds (Eph. 4:23), Charles Hodge rightly observes that

> sanctification . . . does not consist exclusively in a series of a new kind of acts. It is the making the tree good, in order that the fruit may be good. It involves an essential change of character. As regeneration is not an act of the subject of the work, but in the language of the Bible a new birth, a new creation, a quickening or communicating a new life, . . . so sanctification in its essential nature is not holy acts, but such a change in the state of the soul, that sinful acts become more infrequent, and holy acts more and more habitual and controlling.[169]

Therefore, believers should not conceive of holiness as the reformation of external behaviors, in which people bend their wills to perform duties for which they have no Godward motive; rather, believers must recognize that sanctification consists fundamentally in the miraculous inward transformation of the affections. To use Hodge's metaphor, it is not taking fruit and stapling it to the tree branch but is rather rooting the branch in the vine so that the fruit is borne by virtue of the believer's vital union with the Lord Jesus Christ. While the holy person certainly does what God

---

168. Bauer, *A Greek-English Lexicon*, 639. Even the etymology of the Greek term *metamorphoō* supports a fundamentally internal denotation. The root of *metamorphoō* is *morphē*, which, though it is often translated "form," refers not merely to "the external features by which something is recognized," but of those characteristics and qualities that are essential to it. Hence it means *that which truly characterizes a given reality*." Gordon Fee, *Paul's Letter to the Philippians*, NICNT (Grand Rapids, MI: Eerdmans, 1995), 204. For example, when Paul explains that Jesus existed in the *morphē* of God and then took the *morphē* of man (Phil. 2:6–7), he is saying not that Jesus had the outward appearance of God and man but that he was "in very nature" (NIV) both God and man. In the same way, *metamorphoō* describes an internal change.

169. Charles Hodge, *Systematic Theology* (1871–1873; repr., Grand Rapids, MI: Eerdmans, 1968), 3:226. Similarly, Dabney says, "Sanctification, in the gospel sense, means then, not only cleansing from guilt, though it presupposes this, nor only consecration, though it includes this, nor only reformation of morals and life, though it produces this; but, essentially the moral purification of the soul." R. L. Dabney, *Syllabus and Notes of the Course of Systematic and Polemic Theology*, 2nd ed. (St. Louis, MO: Presbyterian Publishing Company of St. Louis, 1878), 661.

commands, he does so because he loves God and loves what God loves. Sanctification is the spiritual transformation of the mind and the affections that in turn redirects the will and the actions.

The Author of Sanctification. Since sanctification is not fundamentally external but is rather an internal and supernatural work in the heart of man, its author must be God. Consistent with this understanding, Paul states that "it is *God* who works in you, both to will and to work for his good pleasure" (Phil. 2:13), and he elsewhere ascribes the entire work of sanctification to God (1 Thess. 5:23). The God of peace is entreated to equip his people that they might "do his will" and to work in them "that which is pleasing in his sight" (Heb. 13:20–21). For this reason, Scripture often employs the passive voice in key texts on sanctification, commanding believers not to transform themselves but to *be transformed* (e.g., Rom. 12:2; 2 Cor. 3:18). Thus, Berkhof concludes that sanctification "consists fundamentally and primarily in a *divine* operation in the soul."[170]

More specifically, Scripture identifies the Holy Spirit as the member of the Godhead who is the divine agent of sanctification. Peter speaks of "the sanctification of the Spirit" (1 Pet. 1:2). He is "the Spirit of holiness" (Rom. 1:4) who wages war directly against the desires of the flesh (Gal. 5:17), while those virtues that constitute a character of holiness and integrity are said to be the Spirit's fruit (Gal. 5:22–23). It is no surprise, then, that Paul says the believer's transformation into the image of Christ "comes from the Lord who is the Spirit" (2 Cor. 3:18).

The Means of Sanctification. However, while sanctification is properly said to be an internal work of the Spirit, it does not follow that the believer has nothing to do in this matter, since Scripture is replete with exhortations and imperatives for the believer to pursue holiness. Paul commands the church to "work out your own salvation with fear and trembling" precisely because God is at work within them (Phil. 2:12–13). So far from being an excuse not to work, God's sanctifying work in believers is the very ground of their efforts. Peter declares that, on the basis of the work of Christ, believers have been granted "all things that pertain to life and godliness," and have "escaped from the corruption that is in the world because of sinful desire" (2 Pet. 1:3–4). And he follows these precious indicatives with a rousing call to action: "For this very reason, make every effort to supplement your faith with virtue" (2 Pet. 1:5). As John Murray writes,

> God's working in us is not suspended because we work, nor our working suspended because God works. Neither is the relation strictly one of co-operation as if God did his part and we did ours so that the conjunction or coordination of both produced the required result. God works in us and we also work. But the relation is that *because* God works we work. All working out of salvation on our part is the effect of God's working in us.[171]

---

170. Berkhof, *Systematic Theology*, 532. Italics added.
171. Murray, *Redemption Accomplished and Applied*, 148–49.

Thus we are to "strive for . . . the holiness without which no one will see the Lord" (Heb. 12:14), to "put to death the deeds of the body" (Rom. 8:13), to "flee from sexual immorality" (1 Cor. 6:18), to "pursue righteousness" (2 Tim. 2:22), and even to "cleanse ourselves from every defilement of body and spirit, bringing holiness to completion in the fear of God" (2 Cor. 7:1).

Thus, while believers cannot directly effect the inner transformation of sanctification for their souls and while sanctification is properly said to be the Spirit's work, believers are not entirely passive in sanctification. Instead, the Holy Spirit effects his sanctifying transformation in the hearts of believers through the use of means that must be appropriated. The Scottish Puritan Henry Scougal provides an effective illustration:

> All the art and industry of man cannot form the smallest herb, or make a stalk of corn to grow in the field; it is the energy of nature, and the influences of heaven, which produce this effect; it is God "who causeth the grass to grow, and the herb for the service of man" (Ps. 104:14); and yet nobody will say that the labours of the [farmer] are useless or unnecessary.[172]

In other words, while it is true that God is the One who causes grass to grow and makes the land produce crops, only a foolish farmer passively waits for the land to yield its produce by divine fiat. Instead, he acknowledges that God brings forth fruits and vegetables from the earth by means of a farmer's labors—through the cultivation of the soil, the sowing of the seed, and the plant's exposure to sunlight and water. Similarly, in and of himself, the believer is just as powerless to effect holiness in his heart, for it is the work of God. Yet only a foolish person waits passively for his heart to spring forth in righteousness by divine fiat. Instead, the faithful Christian acknowledges that God brings forth the fruit of holiness by means of the believer's labors. Scripture's repeated calls to effort, action, and obedience are commands for believers to put themselves in the way of those channels of sanctifying grace that the Spirit employs to conform Christ's people into his image.

The means of sanctification include the following:

1. Reading and meditating on the Word of God (Pss. 1:2–3; 19:7–11; 119:105; John 17:17; Acts 20:32; 2 Tim. 3:16–17; Heb. 4:12; James 1:23–25)
2. Praying (Ps. 119:37; Luke 11:9; Phil. 4:6–7; Heb. 4:16; James 4:2; 1 John 1:9)
3. Fellowshiping with the saints in the context of the local church (Prov. 27:17; 1 Cor. 12:7; Eph. 4:11–16, 25; Heb. 3:12–13; 10:24–25)
4. Interpreting the experiences of God's providence according to Scripture (Rom. 8:28–29), especially the experience of trials (Ps. 119:71; Rom. 5:3–5; 8:17; Phil. 3:10–11; Heb. 12:10; James 1:2–4; 1 Pet. 1:3–7)
5. Keeping the commandments of God (John 15:10)

Sanctifying grace flows through all these channels, and thus it is the responsibility of Christians to put themselves in the way of these blessings. Though believers cannot

---

172. Henry Scougal, *The Life of God in the Soul of Man: Real Religion* (1677; repr., Fearn, Ross-shire, Scotland: Christian Focus, 2012), 78–79.

perform the divine operation of sanctification on their own souls, they must nevertheless pursue holiness by availing themselves of the means by which the Spirit of God accomplishes this divine operation.[173]

The Dynamics of Sanctification. The question of the dynamics of sanctification concerns how sanctification actually works. Why does reading and studying the Word of God sanctify? How is prayer a means of grace? Why does fellowship with other believers push the people of God to greater holiness? Once again, answers to these questions come in 2 Corinthians 3:18, where Scripture reveals a sixth means of sanctification that stands at the foundation of the rest, thus rendering them efficacious. Paul writes, "And we all, with unveiled face, *beholding* the glory of the Lord, are being transformed into the same image from one degree of glory to another. For this comes from the Lord who is the Spirit." Boiling that complex sentence down to a simpler form, it reads, "We all, beholding the glory of the Lord, are being transformed." As believers in Christ behold his glory as revealed in the Word with the eyes of their heart (Eph. 1:18), they are thereby progressively conformed into his image.

This theme of spiritual sight is not isolated to this single text but is established throughout the New Testament's teaching concerning sanctification. The author of Hebrews states that the Christian life is a race run with endurance as believers fix their eyes on Jesus, the founder and perfecter of faith (Heb. 12:1–2). Faith itself is spiritual sight that sees and believes the truth, "the assurance of things hoped for" and "the conviction of things not seen" (Heb. 11:1); that is, what cannot be seen with the physical eyes is unveiled by the spiritual eyes of faith. In this way, Moses's faith was strengthened to endure all manner of temptation by "looking to the reward" (11:26) and "seeing him who is invisible" (11:27). Paul encourages the Corinthians with the thought that the temporary affliction of this life is producing an eternal weight of glory for God's people, provided that they look with the eyes of faith at what is unseen: the spiritual truth that reveals the glory of the Savior (2 Cor. 4:17–18). And once again, the apostle John instructs us that our being perfected in the image of Christ will result from finally seeing him unhindered: "But we know that when he appears we shall be like him, *because* we shall see him as he is" (1 John 3:2).

The cumulative weight of these texts compels us to understand the spiritual sight that beholds the glory of Christ as the foundational means of sanctification. John Owen summarizes this biblical teaching:

> Let us live in the constant contemplation of the glory of Christ, and virtue will proceed from Him to repair all our decays, to renew a right spirit within us, and to cause us to abound in all duties of obedience. . . . It will fix the soul unto that object which is suited to give it delight, complacency, and satisfaction. . . . When the mind is filled with thoughts of Christ and his glory, when the soul thereon cleaves unto him with intense affections, they will cast out, or not give admittance unto, those causes of spiritual weakness and indisposition. . . . And nothing will

---

173. For further discussion of the means of grace, see "Means of Grace within the Church" in chap. 9 (p. 780).

so much excite and encourage our souls hereunto as a constant view of Christ and His glory.[174]

In other words, when the believer apprehends the glory of Christ with the eyes of faith, the sight of his beauty satisfies his soul in such a way that he does not go on seeking satisfaction in the false and fleeting pleasures of sin. Just as in regeneration, when the Spirit shone into sinners' hearts the light of the knowledge of God's glory in the face of Christ (2 Cor. 4:6), overcoming spiritual blindness by awakening souls to the filth of sin and the loveliness of Christ, so also does the Spirit work in progressive sanctification, strengthening that holy disposition created in regeneration. The spiritual apprehension of Christ's glory conforms believers' affections to the divine will, causing them to hate sin and love righteousness. Then, sanctified affections direct the will in such a way that it desires the righteousness it has come to love and repudiates the sin it has come to hate. Finally, the internal transformation is brought to fruition externally, as the sanctified will issues in holy living.

Therefore, as the believer avails himself of the various means by which he lays hold of the Spirit's sanctifying grace, he is to look with the eyes of faith to the transforming glory of Christ revealed through those means. The Word of God is a vehicle for the glory of God (Ex. 33:18; 34:5–7; 1 Sam. 3:1, 21). Prayer is the occasion for personal communion with God, in which the worshiper seeks God's face (2 Chron. 7:14; Pss. 24:6; 27:8; 105:4; Hos. 5:15) in order that he might behold his transforming beauty (Ps. 27:4). Fellowship in the local church is an opportunity to hear the Word preached skillfully, to sing songs of worship with sanctifying lyrics drawn from biblical truth, to pray corporately as the body of Christ, and to see the gospel pictured in the ordinances of baptism and communion. Besides this, to whatever degree Christians have been imperfectly conformed to the image of Christ (Rom. 8:29; 2 Cor. 3:18), to that degree they reflect the image of his glory to one another. Finally, obedience itself is the avenue for greater disclosure of the glory of Christ to the eyes of the heart (John 14:21). When confronted with temptations to sin, believers must reason with themselves, considering that sin never delivers the satisfaction it promises. They must consider that obedience brings fuller disclosures of the Savior, who is the source of all true pleasure and satisfaction. And out of a desire for the superior pleasure that is found in Christ, they must engage in (1) the work of mortification—putting to death the deeds of the body (Rom. 8:13), that is, laying aside the old self (Eph. 4:22) and the sin that so easily entangles (Heb. 12:1) and that clouds the sight of Christ's glory—and (2) the work of vivification—putting on the new self (Rom. 13:14; Eph. 4:24), that is, delightfully disciplining themselves to behold Christ in Scripture, prayer, fellowship, providence, and the obedience that brings deeper communion with him.

By fighting to behold the glory of Jesus by all the means of grace, the follower of Christ will be gradually transformed into his image from the inside out. He will therefore conduct himself in a manner worthy of the gospel (Phil. 1:27) and worthy

---

174. John Owen, *Meditations and Discourses on the Glory of Christ*, in *The Works of John Owen*, vol. 1, *The Glory of Christ*, 460–61.

of the Lord himself (Col. 1:10), working out his salvation with fear and trembling, just as Scripture commands (Phil. 2:12). As 2 Timothy 2:21 declares, "He will be a vessel for honorable use, set apart as holy, useful to the master of the house, ready for every good work."

Perseverance

A sincere (and often vexing) question among professing Christians concerns whether or not salvation in Christ is eternally secure. Do those who truly know Jesus Christ as Savior and Lord by faith persevere in that faith to the very end of their lives? Or is there a possibility that a genuine Christian could lose his salvation? Can those who genuinely trust Christ for salvation later abandon their faith and thus ultimately lose their eternal life? The unified teaching of the whole Scripture answers with an emphatic *no* to each of these questions. All those who are truly born of the Spirit and united to Christ by faith are kept secure in him by God's power and thus will persevere in faith until they go to be with Christ in death. This doctrine is often labeled the perseverance of the saints.[175]

THE PRESERVING POWER OF THE TRIUNE GOD

The eternal security of the true believer in Christ is ultimately founded on the preserving nature of the triune God. First, the believer's security is grounded in the unchanging love, infinite power, and saving will of the Father. Salvation began in eternity past, when God set his saving love on his elect and granted them grace in Christ Jesus (2 Tim. 1:9), appointing Christ to be their Mediator. Scripture describes this decree as the Father giving the elect to the Son (cf. John 6:37, 39; 10:29; 17:2, 6, 9, 24) and predestining them to become conformed to the Son's image (Rom. 8:29). It is impossible for those whom the Father has predestined to Christlikeness to fail to attain that end, for "those whom he predestined he also called, and those whom he called he also justified, and those whom he justified he also glorified" (Rom. 8:30). In these verses, Paul presents the events of redemption as an unbreakable chain of God's sovereign grace. The final consummation of the believer's salvation is so certain and sure that Paul can speak of the justified one as if he has already been glorified. All those whom God chose he also justified on the ground of the righteous work of the Son, and all those whom he justified he also glorified. It is impossible that one who has been united to Christ and granted his righteousness in justification will not be glorified as well. The Father will not fail to carry out the fullness of his electing purpose to its designed end. To this thought Paul adds that none for whom Christ died is subject to condemnation (Rom. 8:31–34; cf. 8:1). He declares that nothing in all creation shall separate true believers from the love of God in Christ:

> Shall tribulation, or distress, or persecution, or famine, or nakedness, or danger, or sword? . . . No, in all these things we are more than conquerors through him

---

175. For a fuller treatment of the believer's security and assurance, see John MacArthur, *Saved without a Doubt: Being Sure of Your Salvation*, 3rd ed. (Colorado Springs: David C. Cook, 2011).

who loved us. For I am sure that neither death nor life, nor angels nor rulers, nor things present nor things to come, nor powers, nor height nor depth, nor anything else in all creation, will be able to separate us from the love of God in Christ Jesus our Lord. (Rom. 8:35, 37–39)

The Lord Jesus makes this very point concerning the Father's saving will when he declares,

All that the Father gives me will come to me, and whoever comes to me I will never cast out. For I have come down from heaven, not to do my own will but the will of him who sent me. And this is the will of him who sent me, that I should lose nothing of all that he has given me, but raise it up on the last day. For this is the will of my Father, that everyone who looks on the Son and believes in him should have eternal life, and I will raise him up on the last day. (John 6:37–40)

The will of the Father is that Christ will lose *none* of those whom he has given him and that every elect believer will possess eternal life and will be raised to everlasting glory on the last day. And the Father's will cannot be overturned by anyone or anything (Job 42:2; Pss. 33:10–11; 115:3; Isa. 46:9–10; Dan. 4:35), for he is not only graciously disposed to his people but is also sovereignly powerful to accomplish his desired ends. As Jesus says, "I give [my sheep] eternal life, and they will never perish, and no one will snatch them out of my hand. My Father, who has given them to me, is greater than all, and no one is able to snatch them out of the Father's hand" (John 10:28–29). Using the strongest negative language available in the Greek language, Jesus emphatically declares that those who belong to Christ by faith "will never perish" (Gk. *ou mē apolōntai,* John 10:28) but will have eternal life (John 3:16). He grounds the eternal security of Christ's sheep in the sovereign power of the Father who holds them in his hand. The Father is so great and mighty that no one could snatch from his hand those whom he holds forever.

For this reason, Paul expresses his confidence that "he who began a good work in you will bring it to completion at the day of Jesus Christ" (Phil. 1:6). Quite simply, God finishes what he starts. Since it was the sovereign grace of the Father—not the free will of man—that *began* the work of salvation in the lives of sinners (cf. Acts 11:18; 16:14; Eph. 2:4–9; Phil. 1:29; James 1:18), so also will God exercise that same sovereign power to bring this great work to its completion. Believers can be confident that they will persevere by the preserving power of the Father.

Second, the believer's security is grounded in the merits of Christ's saving work and the efficacy of his present intercession. For this reason, Paul writes, "Who shall bring any charge against God's elect? It is God who justifies. Who is to condemn? Christ Jesus is the one who died—more than that, who was raised—who is at the right hand of God, who indeed is interceding for us" (Rom. 8:33–34). Christ's death, resurrection, and present intercession constitute the basis on which no charge against his people will ever stand. Because he has died, has risen, and is interceding before the Father, no one will separate us from his love (Rom. 8:35–39).

Just as the Father's predestining purpose fully achieves its desired end, so also the Son's redeeming work accomplishes its design with perfect efficacy. As the substitute for his people, the Son of God stood in the place of elect sinners on the cross and bore the fullness of divine punishment against their sins (1 Pet. 2:24). In doing so, he has fully propitiated the Father's wrath against his people (Rom. 3:25; Heb. 2:17; 1 John 2:2; 4:10), purchasing them out of the slave market of sin with the price of his own blood (Acts 20:28; Rev. 5:9). Not only this, but the Father has also certified, by raising Christ from the dead, that his death sufficiently atoned for sin. The resurrection was the great vindication and validation of Christ (1 Tim. 3:16), verifying that the Father had approved of his completed work and that there was no more penalty left to pay, no more wrath left to bear for those who are in him. To suggest, then, that sinners for whom Christ offered himself as a propitiation may yet suffer the eternal penalty of God's wrath is to demean the worth of his redemptive sacrifice and to contradict the Father's testimony in the resurrection. Further, through the Spirit's application of Christ's redemptive work, the sinner is credited with Christ's righteousness in justification. It is unthinkable that the Spirit would apply only a portion of those saving benefits purchased by Christ's redemption, so that a soul declared righteous on the basis of Christ's work should at some point be stripped of that righteousness to undergo the penalty of condemnation from which he had been redeemed. There is no condemnation for those who are united to Christ Jesus (Rom. 8:1; cf. Acts. 13:38–39).

Moreover, Christ not only has offered an infinitely worthy sacrifice on behalf of his people but also continuously intercedes for his people before the Father at the present time (Rom. 8:34). He prays particularly to ensure the eternal salvation of the elect, as Hebrews 7:25 says, "Consequently, he is able to save to the uttermost those who draw near to God through him, *since he always lives to make intercession for them.*" The writer is as emphatic as he can be: Jesus does not save his people in a manner in which that salvation can be forfeited or lost. No, he saves "to the uttermost" (Gk. *eis to panteles*)—perfectly, completely, and eternally—and he intercedes to ensure that salvation will not fail with an intercession that is always efficacious. When Satan had demanded to sift Peter like wheat, Jesus responded by assuring Peter, "But I have prayed for you that your faith may not fail" (Luke 22:31–32). Jesus's intercessory prayer is enough to ensure the preservation of Peter's salvation, for he continues, "And *when*"—not "if"—"you have turned again, strengthen your brothers" (Luke 22:32). All believers are the beneficiaries of their Great High Priest's perfectly efficacious intercession and thus are kept by the power of God (1 Pet. 1:5).

Third, the believer's security is grounded in the sealing ministry of the Holy Spirit. Paul writes, "In him you also, when you heard the word of truth, the gospel of your salvation, and believed in him, were sealed with the promised Holy Spirit, who is the guarantee of our inheritance until we acquire possession of it, to the praise of his glory" (Eph. 1:13–14; cf. 4:30). In Paul's day, affixing one's seal to something expressed the concepts of security, authentication, and ownership. God seals his people with the Holy Spirit himself, giving his own Spirit to personally indwell each believer as a pledge of the future inheritance of salvation (2 Cor. 1:22; 5:5). The Greek word translated "pledge" is *arrabōn*, a commercial term that refers to an earnest or down payment—a "first installment with a guarantee that the rest would follow."[176] Once again, God would not affix his seal of ownership to his people, causing the Holy Spirit himself to indwell them as a pledge of his earnest faithfulness to bring them to their promised inheritance, and yet fail to secure them so as to deliver fully on his promise for eternal life. As Grudem says, "All who have the Holy Spirit within them, all who are truly born again, have God's unchanging promise and guarantee that the inheritance of eternal life in heaven will certainly be theirs. God's own faithfulness is pledged to bring it about."[177]

THE PERSEVERING FAITH OF THE CHILD OF GOD

While all true believers are sovereignly preserved in their salvation by the almighty power of God, his sovereignty in no way eliminates their responsibility to persevere in faith throughout their lives. Just as God's sovereignty in conversion does not mitigate the responsibility to repent and believe (Rom. 9:14–18; cf. Rom. 10:11–21), and just as God's sovereignty in sanctification does not rule out the need for sustained effort in pursuing holiness (e.g., Phil. 2:12–13; 2 Pet. 1:3–5), so also God's sovereign preservation is not at odds with the necessity of the believer's perseverance. All true believers are "by God's power . . . being guarded through faith for a salvation ready to be revealed in the last time" (1 Pet. 1:5). God's power is the decisive preserving force, but his power keeps his people *through faith*—that is, through the continuing, persevering faith that works through love in every believer (Gal. 5:6).

Therefore, Scripture issues numerous calls to persevere in faith, indicating that failure to persevere will result in a failure to lay hold of final salvation. Jesus warns of the inevitable persecution his followers are bound to face in a world that is hostile to truth and righteousness. In the face of that hostility, he calls for endurance: "You will be hated by all for my name's sake. But the one who endures to the end will be saved" (Matt. 10:22). He speaks similarly of those believers alive in the tribulation: "And because lawlessness will be increased, the love of many will grow cold. But the one who endures to the end will be saved" (Matt. 24:12–13). Jesus exhorted the Jews who had made an outward profession of faith in him to demonstrate the genuineness of their faith by obedience: "If you abide in my word, you are truly my disciples" (John 8:31). Thus, those who do not abide in his Word are shown to be false disciples—or "false brothers" (2 Cor. 11:26; Gal. 2:4), who claim to belong to Jesus but fail to bring forth the necessary fruit that gives evidence of genuine conversion. Therefore, Paul seeks to give assurance to those for whom Christ has died yet suggests that some who claim to be among that number are not. He explains that Christ will "present you holy and blameless and above reproach before [the Father],

---

176. Harold W. Hoehner, *Ephesians: An Exegetical Commentary* (Grand Rapids, MI: Baker Academic, 2002), 241.
177. Grudem, *Systematic Theology*, 791.

if indeed you continue in the faith, stable and steadfast, not shifting from the hope of the gospel that you heard, which has been proclaimed in all creation under heaven" (Col. 1:22–23). Similarly, the author of Hebrews assures us that "we have come to share in Christ, *if indeed we hold our original confidence firm to the end*" (Heb. 3:14).

These passages clearly indicate that the professing believer must persevere in faith and obedience if he is to finally come to salvation. While some assure professing Christians that heaven is theirs no matter how they live after they profess faith—as is popular in forms of antinomianism, quietism, and so-called "free grace" theology— such conceptualizations of the preserving power of God stand in stark opposition to the teaching of Scripture.

An implication of this truth is that many people may give outward signs of devotion to Christ and his church who are inwardly not true Christians. Illustrated by the seed that fell on the rocky ground, some professing Christians seem to receive the Word of God joyfully. Yet they have no root, so when tribulation and persecution come, they fall away from Christ and abandon their profession of faith (Matt. 13:3–9, 18–23). Jesus warns that some who enthusiastically profess faith in Christ and even seem to exercise miraculous gifts of the Holy Spirit will come to the day of judgment expecting to inherit salvation but will instead be sent away to destruction:

> Not everyone who says to me, "Lord, Lord," will enter the kingdom of heaven, but the one who does the will of my Father who is in heaven. On that day many will say to me, "Lord, Lord, did we not prophesy in your name, and cast out demons in your name, and do many mighty works in your name?" And then will I declare to them, "I never knew you; depart from me, you workers of lawlessness." (Matt. 7:21–23)

Interestingly, Jesus does not say, "I knew you once, but you failed to persevere and fell away from the faith." Rather, he says, "I *never* knew you," indicating that those who make even the sincerest professions of faith but who fail to supplement their faith with the fruit of the Spirit (2 Pet. 1:5–10; Gal. 5:22–24) were never true Christians to begin with. This is significant, because many object to the doctrine of the perseverance of the saints on the basis of experiencing a friend or relative who professed faith in Christ but later fell away. Experience, in concert with several passages of Scripture that threaten final perdition for failing to persevere, suggests to them that true Christians may actually lose their salvation. However, Scripture teaches that those who fail to persevere to the end reveal that they were never true Christians to begin with. The apostle John writes, "They went out from us"—which is to say, certain people associated themselves with the church yet later departed—"but they were not of us; for if they had been of us, they would have continued with us. But they went out, that it might become plain that they all are not of us" (1 John 2:19).

Those who teach that Christians can lose their salvation also point to such passages as Hebrews 6:4–10 and 10:26–31, which on a superficial reading may seem to suggest that eternal life can be lost. Hebrews 6:4–10 declares,

> For it is impossible, in the case of those who have once been enlightened, who have tasted the heavenly gift, and have shared in the Holy Spirit, and have tasted the goodness of the word of God and the powers of the age to come, and then have fallen away, to restore them again to repentance, since they are crucifying once again the Son of God to their own harm and holding him up to contempt. For land that has drunk the rain that often falls on it, and produces a crop useful to those for whose sake it is cultivated, receives a blessing from God. But if it bears thorns and thistles, it is worthless and near to being cursed, and its end is to be burned. Though we speak in this way, yet in your case, beloved, we feel sure of better things—things that belong to salvation. For God is not unjust so as to overlook your work and the love that you have shown for his name in serving the saints, as you still do.

On closer examination, however, the writer of Hebrews is clearly contrasting at least two kinds of hearers of the same message of the gospel. The one group, illustrated in verse 7 as ripe ground, on which the rain of gospel seed falls, produces the fruit of eternal salvation. However, according to verse 8, a second group, presumably members of the same congregation, hears the exact same message, and yet in them the truth of the gospel produces worthless thorns and thistles destined to be burned. The writer is warning this second group of hearers that they are in danger of having never rightly responded to the gospel seed. This is why he says in verse 9, "Though we speak in this way [i.e., issuing these severe warnings in verse 8 to those who are in danger of rejecting the gospel], yet in your case, beloved [i.e., those in verse 7, who genuinely believe in Christ], we feel sure of better things—things that belong to salvation."

Thus, the key to interpreting this passage (as well as the other warning passages in Hebrews, such as 10:26–31) is to determine who is being warned and why. Those who respond positively to the gospel at first only to reject Christ later—even if they associate themselves with the people of God and attend to the external duties of religion—are not true believers who forfeited their salvation but are apostates who never exercised saving faith. In light of the full revelation of the truth, they abandoned the faith and renounced Christ in settled, callous unbelief. The writer of Hebrews declares, "It is impossible . . . to restore them again to repentance, since they are crucifying once again the Son of God to their own harm and holding him up to contempt" (Heb. 6:4–6). In light of the above scriptural testimony, it is impossible to apply such language to true believers who have been united to Christ by faith. Thus, these warning passages are just that: severe warnings to those in the midst of the assembly of professing Christians who, by their failure to persevere in faithful obedience to Christ, are in danger of apostasy and damnation.[178]

ASSURANCE OF SALVATION[179]

How, then, can one be assured that he is a true believer in Christ and will not one day fall away, revealing that he was never a true believer at all? Scripture calls those

---

178. For a further treatment of the warning passages in the book of Hebrews, see John MacArthur, *Hebrews*, MNTC (Chicago: Moody Press, 1983).

179. This section is adapted from MacArthur, *Saved without a Doubt: Being Sure of Your Salvation*, 67–91. Copyright © 2011 by John MacArthur. Used by permission of David C. Cook. Publisher permission required to reproduce. All rights reserved.

who profess faith in Christ to examine themselves. Paul urges the Corinthians, "Examine yourselves, to see whether you are in the faith. Test yourselves" (2 Cor. 13:5). Peter similarly exhorts the churches in his care, "Therefore, brothers, be all the more diligent to confirm your calling and election" (2 Pet. 1:10). The apostle John dedicated his entire first epistle to the subject, stating his theme at the end: "I write these things to you who believe in the name of the Son of God that you may know that you have eternal life" (1 John 5:13). The authors of Scripture clearly desired that believers be assured of their salvation by examining their lives for evidence of genuine spiritual life. Consider the following eleven lines of evidence—largely drawn from the tests outlined in 1 John—by which Christians can gain assurance that their faith and salvation are genuine.

Evidences from the Christian's Relationship with God. First, a true Christian enjoys fellowship with the Father and the Son through the Holy Spirit. At the beginning of his letter, John tells his readers that he is proclaiming the gospel to them in order that they might experience the same communion with God that he enjoys. He says, "That which we have seen and heard we proclaim also to you, so that you too may have fellowship with us; and indeed our fellowship is with the Father and with his Son Jesus Christ" (1 John 1:3). Indeed, the one who is born of God loves both the Father and the Son (1 John 5:1). Paul likewise describes salvation as being "called into the fellowship of [Christ]" (1 Cor. 1:9), and he characterizes his Christian life as living by faith in Jesus, who lives in him (Gal. 2:20). Salvation is to personally taste and see that the Lord is good (Ps. 34:8)—to walk with God, intimately knowing him as "the God of all comfort" (2 Cor. 1:3), "the God of all grace" (1 Pet. 5:10), and the God who supplies all our needs according to his riches in Christ (Phil. 4:19). He is the One to whom we draw near in times of trouble (Heb. 4:16), crying, "Abba! Father!" (Rom. 8:15). Those who regularly experience this communion with God in love, in joy, in prayer, and in the discovery of biblical truth can rejoice in the assurance that their faith is genuine.

A second evidence of genuine salvation is the ministry of the Holy Spirit in the heart. John writes, "By this we know that we abide in him and he in us, because he has given us of his Spirit" (1 John 4:13). When a sinner confesses that Jesus is the Son of God and Savior of the world and commits his life to him, it is the Spirit's doing. The Spirit also illumines the believer's mind to understand Scripture, as John says, "The anointing that you received from him abides in you, and . . . teaches you about everything" (1 John 2:27; cf. 1 Cor. 2:10, 12). The Spirit convicts, encourages, and brings joy to the true believer's heart as he studies the Bible. Further, the Spirit produces fruit in the true believer's life, such that his life is marked by "love, joy, peace, patience, kindness, goodness, faithfulness, gentleness, [and] self-control" (Gal. 5:22–23).

Third, Christians may gain assurance of salvation from answered prayer. John says, "And this is the confidence that we have toward him, that if we ask anything according to his will he hears us" (1 John 5:14; cf. 3:22). A true believer prays according to the will of God, asking for forgiveness and a clear conscience, for boldness to proclaim the gospel, and for contentment in times of difficulty. The hearts of God's people are strengthened and encouraged when their Father answers those prayers for his glory and their benefit.

Fourth, the true citizen of heaven eagerly longs for Christ's return (Phil. 3:20). The foundational characteristic of the true Christian is love for Christ (1 Cor. 16:22). That love causes him to eagerly await the day when he will see his Savior face-to-face and thus be perfectly conformed into his image (Phil. 3:21; 1 John 3:1–3). This is an indication of the presence of a new nature, which longs to be delivered from a body of sin to become like the perfect Christ. Such holy longings and affections are an indication of genuine salvation.

Evidences from the Christian's Spiritual Life and Growth. A fifth evidence of salvation is spiritual discernment. Those who are born again are able to discern between spiritual truth and error—to test the spirits to see whether they are from God (1 John 4:1–3). Adherents of false religious systems attempt to undermine the biblical truth concerning the person and work of Jesus Christ (2 Pet. 3:16), but God equips his children to recognize and reject false teachers and to cling to sound teaching (1 John 2:12–19; 4:5–6). While even the demons may believe sound doctrine and be destitute of saving faith (James 2:19), one will not enjoy true assurance without believing sound doctrine (1 Thess. 5:21; 1 Tim. 6:3–5; 2 Tim. 2:13–14).

Sixth, an acute awareness of the holiness of God and the guilt of one's sin always accompanies genuine salvation. John writes, "If we say we have no sin, we deceive ourselves, and the truth is not in us. If we confess our sins, he is faithful and just to forgive us our sins and to cleanse us from all unrighteousness. If we say we have not sinned, we make him a liar, and his word is not in us" (1 John 1:8–10). An identifying characteristic of unbelievers is that they do not regard themselves as sinners. They fail to recognize the absolute moral perfection of God—that he is light and that in him is no darkness at all (1 John 1:5). Failing to see themselves in the light, they do not recognize the extent to which they are polluted by the darkness of sin. True believers, however, have a keen sense of their sinfulness, and their lives are characterized by increasingly putting off sin and putting on righteousness. When they sin, they experience the godly sorrow of a cleansed conscience that leads them to repentance (2 Cor. 7:10), and they confess their sin and seek forgiveness in Christ. Paul's personal testimony in Romans 7:14–25 is an example of the believer's sensitivity and aversion to sin. Like the apostle, the true children of God sin in various ways but confess their sin and seek restoration to communion with God. The false Christian ignores and hides sin, but the genuine believer cries out with Paul: "Wretched man that I am! Who will deliver me from this body of death?" (Rom. 7:24). The child of God is wearied by the burden of sin and longs for restored fellowship with the Father through confession and repentance.

A seventh manifestation of genuine salvation is the decreasing pattern of sin in one's life. Not only is the child of God sensitive to his remaining sin, but by the grace of God and the power of the Spirit, he will also have progressive victory over those sins. John writes, "No one born of God makes a practice of sinning, for God's seed abides in him, and he cannot keep on sinning because he has been born of God" (1 John 3:9). Regardless of one's profession, unbroken patterns of sin mark the unregenerate (1 John 3:8), not the children of God. When the sinner is regenerated, the dominion of sin is broken and the Spirit births holy affections in the new convert. Indwelling sin remains, but the love of sin is broken. The true Christian is no longer enslaved to sin but is a slave to righteousness (Rom. 6:14–18).

Eighth, as patterns of sin decrease, patterns of obedience increase. John could not be clearer: "And by this we know that we have come to know him, if we keep his commandments" (1 John 2:3). The Greek word translated "keep" (*tēreō*) speaks of watchful, careful, thoughtful obedience—not just the hands but also the heart. True Christian obedience is a willing, habitual safeguarding of the Word both in letter and in spirit. A true believer obeys the commandments of Scripture (John 8:31), and patterns of sustained obedience produce confidence that one has a saving relationship with God.

Evidences from the Christian's Relationships with Other People. A ninth evidence of genuine salvation is a growing rejection of the worldliness that dominates human life. In 1 John 2:15, John writes about the true Christian's deepest affections, greatest desires, and ultimate goals, commanding us, "Do not love the world or the things in the world. If anyone loves the world, the love of the Father is not in him" (cf. James 4:4). "The world" speaks of the evil world system operated by Satan (cf. 2 Cor. 4:4; Eph. 2:2; 1 John 5:19), which encompasses false religion, errant philosophy, crime, immorality, materialism, and the like. While these things dominate the affections and will of all unbelievers, they disgust the true believer. It is true that Christians may sometimes be lured into worldly things, but such sin brings conviction, confession, and repentance. Though remaining sin is frustrating and discouraging, true believers can be grateful that sin is a reality they have been made to hate and no longer love (Rom. 7:15). New life in Christ nurtures love for God and the things of God. Thus, those examining themselves must ask whether they reject this evil world system, along with all its false ideologies, damning religions, godless lifestyles, and vain pursuits, and instead love God, his truth, and his people. Such affections are neither natural nor attractive to depraved humanity (John 3:19–20; 8:44) and therefore are evidence of the Spirit's grace at work in the heart.

Tenth, the genuine Christian not only rejects the world but is also rejected *by* the world. For this reason, John writes, "Do not be surprised, brothers, that the world hates you" (1 John 3:13). When God's people stand apart from the world—rejecting its sinful values and standing for righteousness—its evil is exposed. Because darkness hates the light (John 3:19–20), it reacts with animosity and hostility to those influences that expose it. In the preceding verse, John notes that Cain hated his brother and murdered him precisely because Abel's righteous behavior exposed Cain's wicked rebellion (1 John 3:12). God's people, then, will experience ostracism, rejection, and even persecution by the world because they belong to Christ, who also suffered for the sake of righteousness (Matt. 5:10–12; John 15:18–21; Phil. 1:29; 2 Tim. 3:12; 1 Pet. 4:12–14). Those searching for assurance must ask if they are readily accepted by the world or if, as those conformed to the image of Christ, they draw the same rejection that Christ himself drew from the enemies of righteousness (John 7:7).

Finally, antithetical to the hatred of and rejection by the evil world system is a true believer's love for fellow Christians. First John 3:10 says, "By this it is evident who are the children of God, and who are the children of the devil: whoever does not practice righteousness is not of God, nor is the one who does not love his brother" (cf. 1 John 2:9–11). Loving fellow Christians comes naturally to the believer. As Paul said to the Thessalonian church, "Now concerning brotherly love you have no need for anyone to write you, for you yourselves have been taught by God to love one another" (1 Thess. 4:9). Jesus went so far as to say that his disciples' love for one another would be the evidence before all people that they were his followers (John 13:35). Therefore, those who are cold, uncaring, and indifferent toward other believers betray a self-centeredness that is indicative of unbelief, but those who delight in the fellowship of their brothers and sisters in Christ and eagerly desire to meet the needs of the saints can be assured that they are of the truth (1 John 3:16–19).

Glorification

The final divine act in the application of redemption is glorification. Given its immense importance, it is critical at the outset to distinguish glorification from other eschatological events. It must not be confused with the intermediate state. For those who die in faith before the return of Christ, their souls immediately go to be with the Lord (Luke 23:43; 2 Cor. 5:8; Phil. 1:23). Because glorification involves both the body and the soul, it does not take place when a believer's soul enters the current intermediate heaven but rather at the second coming of Christ. Neither is glorification to be confused with the restoration of the earth. While it is a marvelous promise that the whole earth will be restored (Acts 3:21)—just as creation was cursed as a result of man's sin, so also will it be redeemed as a result of man's redemption (Rom. 8:20–21; cf. Isa. 65:17; 2 Pet. 3:7; Rev. 21:1)—these acts must not be conflated. Glorification refers to the final salvation of persons, not the redemption of inanimate objects. Finally, not all believers will be glorified at the same time. The dead in Christ and those alive at his coming will be glorified in the twinkling of an eye at his return (1 Cor. 15:23, 52; cf. 1 Thess. 4:16–17). Yet there will also be those who repent and turn to Christ during the time of the tribulation, while the saints are feasting with Christ at the marriage supper of the Lamb (Rev. 19:7–10). The tribulation saints will await their glorified bodies until the millennial reign of Christ (Rev. 20:4; cf. Isa. 26:19–20; Dan. 12:2). Those who die during the millennium may very well be instantly transformed at death into their eternal bodies and spirits.[180]

---

180. The rest of this treatment of glorification concerns the doctrine of the resurrection from a soteriological perspective. For further discussion of the resurrection in the context of eschatology, including the timing of the events, the effect on the physical creation, and the destiny of unbelievers, see chap. 10, "The Future."

Glorification is the radical transformation of both the body and the soul of believers, perfecting them in holiness, and thereby fitting them for eternal life on the new earth in perfect communion with the triune God. Murray helpfully describes glorification as "the complete and final redemption of the whole person, when in the integrity of body and spirit, the people of God will be conformed to the image of the risen, exalted, and glorified Redeemer, when the very body of their humiliation will be conformed to the body of Christ's glory" (cf. Phil. 3:21).[181]

THE CONSUMMATION OF SALVATION

The resurrection of the body is the consummation of our salvation, as the Spirit applies to completion the redemption that the Father planned and that Christ purchased. Romans 8:30 features glorification as the climax of redemption: "And those whom he predestined he also called, and those whom he called he also justified, and those whom he justified he also *glorified*." Those on whom the Father set his electing love he predestined for salvation, and these—whose redemption Christ purchased by dying in their place as a propitiation for their sins—enjoy the benefits of that redemption. In justification, they are freed from the penalty of sin, and in sanctification, they are freed from the power of sin. In glorification, they are finally freed from the very presence of sin in both body and soul.

Christ himself indicated that the salvific intentions of the triune God reached beyond man's soul even to the resurrection of the body, declaring,

> And this is the will of him who sent me, that I should lose nothing of all that he has given me, but *raise it up* on the last day. For this is the will of my Father, that everyone who looks on the Son and believes in him should have eternal life, and I will *raise him up* on the last day. (John 6:39–40; cf. 6:44, 54)

Glorification is also the fulfillment of Jesus's desire to see his church purified from all spot, wrinkle, or any such thing (cf. Eph. 5:27), dwelling with him for all eternity. Jesus explicitly prays for this in his High Priestly Prayer, saying, "Father, I desire that they also, whom you have given me, may be with me where I am, to see my glory that you have given me because you loved me before the foundation of the world" (John 17:24). Finally, glorification consummates the objective of salvation—namely, to glorify Christ by making him the firstborn among many brethren (Rom. 8:29). Because glorification is the consummation of sanctification, in which believers are perfectly conformed to the image of Christ, glorification especially magnifies Christ as the preeminent source of the beauty of holiness that is reflected in his perfected brethren.

Scripture regards the doctrine of glorification as absolutely essential to the Christian faith, so much so that if it were not true, the apostle Paul says that we, of all people, would be most to be pitied (1 Cor. 15:12–19). It was the hope of a glorified body that galvanized Paul to totally surrender his natural body to the mistreatment and

---

181. Murray, *Redemption Accomplished and Applied*, 175.

persecution that attended a life of gospel ministry. He said, "For we know that if the tent that is our earthly home is destroyed, we have a building from God, a house not made with hands, eternal in the heavens" (2 Cor. 5:1; cf. 4:14–18). The "sufferings of this present time are not worth comparing with the glory that is to be revealed to us," and so believers welcome the sufferings of Christ if it means that "we may also be glorified with him" (Rom. 8:17–18; cf. Phil. 3:10–11). Therefore, while life in a world and in a body that are both cursed by sin causes us to groan, that groaning is assuaged by the eager anticipation of "the redemption of our bodies" (Rom. 8:23).

Not only is the resurrection the eager anticipation of the New Testament Christian, it was also the great hope of the old covenant believer in Yahweh. When Job was abandoned by his brothers and acquaintances, his relatives and intimate friends, his wife and other members of his household, and his associates and those whom he loved (Job 19:13–19), he set his hope on fellowship with God on a new earth in a resurrection body: "For I know that my Redeemer lives, and at the last he will stand upon the earth. And after my skin has been thus destroyed, yet in my flesh I shall see God, whom I shall see for myself, and my eyes shall behold, and not another. My heart faints within me!" (Job 19:25–27). Job's confident hope was that *after* he had died and his body was destroyed by decay, he would nevertheless see God in his flesh. His Redeemer would vindicate him in the glory of a bodily resurrection in which he would enjoy perfect communion with God. As another example, at the end of Daniel's prophecy, he declared, "And many of those who sleep in the dust of the earth shall awake, some to everlasting life, and some to shame and everlasting contempt" (Dan. 12:2; cf. John 5:28–29; Rev. 20:4–6).

That the resurrection of the body unto glorification was taught in the Old Testament is evidenced by the New Testament's testimony that the Jews looked forward to a future resurrection. As Martha pled with Jesus to exercise his divine power with respect to the death of Lazarus, Jesus responded by telling her that he would rise again. Astutely, Martha replied, "I know that he will rise again in the resurrection on the last day" (John 11:24). As Paul stood trial before Felix, he declared that "a resurrection of both the just and the unjust" was "laid down by the Law and written in the Prophets" (Acts 24:14–15). And Hebrews 11:10 teaches that the Old Testament saints hoped to inherit a physical city that could only be made possible by bodily resurrection (cf. Heb. 11:16).[182]

Standing on that Old Testament foundation, the reader can view the New Testament Epistles' explicit teaching on the resurrection of the body as a welcome elaboration and development of the ancient and living hope of the people of God. Paul reveals that as the condemnation of Adam brought the whole human race guilt and corruption unto death, in the same way, union with the second Adam will cause all believers to overcome sin and death and to be made alive in him (1 Cor. 15:22, 45). This takes place "each in his own order: Christ the firstfruits, then at his coming

---

182. Similar to Paul's characterization of the resurrection body as spiritual, that the future city is "heavenly" does not mean it is immaterial, as if belonging to the intermediate heaven. Rather, it speaks of a city that is characterized by and in perfect harmony with the immediate dwelling place of God.

those who belong to Christ. Then comes the end" (1 Cor. 15:23–24). To the Thessalonians who were concerned that their deceased brothers and sisters would miss this glorious resurrection, Paul offered the comfort that

> through Jesus, God will bring with him those who have fallen asleep. For this we declare to you by a word from the Lord, that we who are alive, who are left until the coming of the Lord, will not precede those who have fallen asleep. For the Lord himself will descend from heaven with a cry of command, with the voice of an archangel, and with the sound of the trumpet of God. And the dead in Christ will rise first. Then we who are alive, who are left, will be caught up together with them in the clouds to meet the Lord in the air, and so we will always be with the Lord. (1 Thess. 4:14–17)

Indeed, the dead in Christ and those alive at his coming will be glorified in the twinkling of an eye at his return:

> Behold! I tell you a mystery. We shall not all sleep, but we shall all be changed, in a moment, in the twinkling of an eye, at the last trumpet. For the trumpet will sound, and the dead will be raised imperishable, and we shall be changed. For this perishable body must put on the imperishable, and this mortal body must put on immortality. (1 Cor. 15:51–53)

At that time, death itself—the very last enemy—will be destroyed (1 Cor. 15:26; cf. Acts 2:24; Heb. 2:14–15; Rev. 1:17–18), which will be cause for victorious celebration:

> When the perishable puts on the imperishable, and the mortal puts on immortality, then shall come to pass the saying that is written:
>
> > "Death is swallowed up in victory."
> > "O death, where is your victory?
> >   O death, where is your sting?"
>
> The sting of death is sin, and the power of sin is the law. But thanks be to God, who gives us the victory through our Lord Jesus Christ. (1 Cor. 15:54–57)

Clearly, Christianity is simply not Christianity without the resurrection. Glorification was promised in the Law and the Prophets and by Jesus and the apostles, and Paul wrote that without it, the Christian has no true hope (1 Cor. 15:16, 19). To deny this final work of God in the plan of salvation would be to deny the Christian message of peace and joy in final glory.

THE NATURE OF THE GLORIFIED BODY[183]

Not only does Paul identify glorification as the consummation of the Christian's hope of salvation, he also gives details as to the nature of the glorified body. While the natural body differs in numerous ways from the spiritual body, it must be noted

---

183. This section is adapted from Mike Riccardi, "The Heavenly Citizen's Prospect," *The Cripplegate* (blog), May 22, 2015, http://thecripplegate.com/the-heavenly-citizens-prospect/. Used by permission of the author.

that there is a fundamental continuity between them. That is to say, the body we inherit in glorification will not be an entirely new body but will be in some way the body we currently inhabit in this life. Scripture declares that God "will also give life to your mortal bodies through his Spirit who dwells in you" (Rom. 8:11). That is, he will not *replace* your current body; he will *renovate* it. Our bodies will be *changed*, not *exchanged* (1 Cor. 15:51). Paul says, "*This* perishable body [i.e., the body he inhabited during his life on earth] must put on the imperishable, and *this* mortal body must put on immortality" (1 Cor. 15:53). Further, since Christ himself is the firstfruits of the resurrection (1 Cor. 15:23), and since Scripture says that he will transform the bodies of believers "into conformity with the body of His glory" (Phil. 3:21 NASB), it is right to draw inferences about the nature of believers' glorified bodies by considering the nature of Christ's glorified body. And Christ rose in the very body in which he died, something that Thomas acknowledged when he placed his hands in the wounds that had been inflicted on Jesus's body during his crucifixion (John 20:27; cf. 20:20). Thus, whatever trauma the believer's body might experience as it succumbs to the curse of sin and death in this life, the omnipotent God will raise that body to perfection and unite it with the soul in the resurrection.

Nevertheless, while the resurrection body will have continuity with the natural body, the two bodies are significantly different from one another. In 1 Corinthians 15:42–44, Paul outlines four contrasts between the resurrection body and the current, natural body:

> So is it with the resurrection of the dead. What is sown is perishable; what is raised is imperishable. It is sown in dishonor; it is raised in glory. It is sown in weakness; it is raised in power. It is sown a natural body; it is raised a spiritual body. If there is a natural body, there is also a spiritual body.

Each of these four contrasts gives insight into the mystery of what the glorified body will entail.

First, the resurrection body will be imperishable. In this life, it is painfully obvious that our bodies are subject to infirmity and deterioration and will eventually succumb to the universal inevitability of death (Heb. 9:27). However, Paul teaches that our resurrection bodies will not be subject to the corruption and decay to which our present bodies are destined. They will not grow old or wear out, nor will they contract sickness or disease. Thus it is right to conclude that in the eternal state our bodies will not age, "but will have the characteristics of youthful but mature manhood or womanhood forever."[184]

Second, Paul says that the natural body is characterized by dishonor but that the resurrection body will be marked by glory. The body is not inherently dishonorable, but it has been dishonored by the curse of sin and is the instrument of man's sinful acts—the vehicle through which sinners dishonor God and gratify sinful desires (Rom. 6:13). The body that ought to be set apart and consecrated as the temple of

---

184. Grudem, *Systematic Theology*, 832.

the Holy Spirit (1 Cor. 6:19) is yielded to sin as an instrument of unrighteousness, which dishonors both God and the body. Even the most faithful believer will experience the ultimate dishonor of death, the body in a state of dishonor, imperfection, and incompleteness. However, that imperfect and dishonored body will one day be raised in glory. Throughout eternity, Christians' immortal bodies will also be pure and honorable bodies, perfectly suited to please, praise, and fully enjoy the Creator who made them and the Redeemer who restored them.

Third, the natural body is sown in weakness, but the glorified body is raised in power. It is only a matter of time before the reality of the physical limitations of our bodies confront us with what it is to be weak. If he lives long enough, even the strongest of the strong experiences the waning of his strength. Scripture even associates the flesh with moral weakness (Matt. 26:41). This will not be the case with the new bodies, for they will be raised in power. This is not necessarily to say that believers will possess superhuman strength, but glorified bodies will have "full and complete human power and strength," which God "intended human beings to have when he created them apart from sin. It will therefore be strength that is sufficient to do all that we desire to do in conformity with the will of God."[185]

Finally, Paul contrasts the "natural" body and the "spiritual" body. It is important to note that by "spiritual" Paul does not mean "immaterial," for the resurrection bodies of believers will be patterned after the resurrection body of Christ, who is the firstfruits of the material resurrection (1 Cor. 15:23). Again, Paul has said that Christ will transform the bodies of believers "into conformity with the body of His glory" (Phil. 3:21 NASB), and it is without question that Christ rose bodily from the grave. He himself declared that "a spirit does not have flesh and bones as you see that I have" (Luke 24:29), and he ate a piece of fish to prove his materiality, for disembodied spirits do not have stomachs and digestive tracts (Luke 24:36–43). No, Jesus was raised from the dead in his body, and so will believers be raised bodily. Instead, by calling the resurrection body "spiritual," Paul intends to teach that they will be entirely submitted to and in perfect harmony with the Holy Spirit. In the perfection of their sanctification, believers will have a heart undisturbed by the deceitful lusts of sin, truly godly ambitions and aspirations, and a physical body that is able to carry out those holy impulses without a moment's distraction or weariness, and therefore, they will be able to fully enjoy the bounties of the new creation God has created for his people. John Murray was right to observe that such a destiny "is the highest end conceivable for created beings, the highest end conceivable not only by men but also by God himself. God himself could not contemplate or determine a higher destiny for his creatures."[186]

We rejoice in the hope of the glory of God (Rom. 5:2) and bless the God and Father of our Lord Jesus Christ, because he, according to his great mercy, has caused us to be born again to this living hope of "an inheritance that is imperishable, unde-

185. Grudem, *Systematic Theology*, 832.
186. John Murray, "The Goal of Sanctification," in *The Collected Writings of John Murray* (Edinburgh: Banner of Truth, 1977), 2:316.

filed, and unfading, kept in heaven for [us], who by God's power are being guarded through faith for a salvation ready to be revealed in the last time" (1 Pet. 1:3–5).

In the face of so great a salvation, spanning from eternity past to eternity future, the only fitting conclusion is to add our voices to the heavenly chorus—that "great multitude that no one could number, from every nation, from all tribes and peoples and languages, standing before the throne and before the Lamb, clothed in white robes, with palm branches in their hands" (Rev. 7:9). We must cry out in worship along with them, "Salvation belongs to our God who sits on the throne, and to the Lamb!" (Rev. 7:10). Thanks be to God for his inexpressible gift!

———————

Prayer[187]

Our loving heavenly Father,
  You graciously gave Your Son as a sacrifice for our sins.
He obediently took our sins to the cross,
  where He bore unspeakable judgment on our behalf
    in accordance with Your perfect will.
You powerfully declared Him to be the true Son of God
  by raising Him from the dead.
And now through your precious Spirit
  You earnestly invite all who hunger and all who thirst
  to come (penitently yet boldly) and partake freely
    of the bread of heaven and the water of life—
    without money, and without price.

Those blessings are given freely to us;
  but they were not obtained without cost to You.
They cost You Your only begotten Son, and they cost Him His life.
He bore the curse incurred by our sin.
When the law thundered against us like Mount Sinai—
  threatening us with condemnation,
  pronouncing our doom,
  and consigning us to the darkness of hell—
    Christ silenced the law's claim against us
      by taking the condemnation upon Himself.
He paid, once for all, the awful price.
We could never have fully discharged that debt to Your justice,
  even if we suffered an eternity of torment in hell.

So we owe Him everything we are.
We were deeply stained,

---

187. This prayer is reproduced verbatim from John MacArthur, *At the Throne of Grace: A Book of Prayers* (Eugene, OR: Harvest House, 2011), 138–40. Used by permission of Harvest House.

guilty of countless sins (both careless and deliberate).
Our sins had cut us off from heaven,
    excluded us from the commonwealth of Israel,
      left us total strangers to the covenants of promise—
        without hope and without God in the world.
But then the blessed good news came to us.
The gospel declared to us the way of life.
Truly it is the power of God for salvation
    to everyone who believes.
Your Spirit graciously drew us into the household of faith
    and You adopted us into the family
      of Your redeemed children.

The human mind simply cannot fathom
    the magnitude of our debt to Your grace.
Nor is the human tongue capable of adequately expressing
    the fullness of our gratitude for so many undeserved mercies.

We know that there is no merit and no atoning value
    in our good works, our prayers,
      our tears, or our good intentions.
Only the atoning blood of Christ
    could ever make an appropriate satisfaction for our sins
      before You.
Therefore we were not redeemed with perishable things
    like silver or gold,
    but with that precious blood,
    shed by the spotless lamb of God.
This was the plan of salvation You ordained
    before the foundation of the world, for our sake.

When we ponder these truths carefully,
    we are astonished that You would save rebellious sinners.
Why should guilty evildoers like us
    be washed in the atoning blood of Your Son
      and clothed in His righteousness?
Why should we be allowed
    to radiate the bright glory that belongs only to You?
Why should we be advanced to such a high and eternal state?
Why would You choose us to adoption as Your children,
    even before the foundation of the world?
Such knowledge is too wonderful for us;
    it is high; we cannot attain it.

But we can thank You for Your kindness.
We can only do so in a feeble and inadequate way.
But in the name of Christ our Savior
    we offer what we can of our heartfelt gratitude.
Please receive our worship, loosen our tongues,

sanctify our lips, and enlarge our hearts
to worship you more fittingly than we are currently able.
And may our service be acceptable in Your sight. Amen.

"Our Great Savior"

Jesus! What a Friend for sinners!
Jesus! Lover of my soul;
Friends may fail me, foes assail me,
He, my Savior, makes me whole.

Refrain:
Hallelujah! What a Savior!
Hallelujah! What a Friend!
Saving, helping, keeping, loving,
He is with me to the end.

Jesus! What a Strength in weakness!
Let me hide myself in Him;
Tempted, tried, and sometimes failing,
He, my Strength, my vict'ry wins.

Jesus! What a Help in sorrow!
While the billows o'er me roll,
Even when my heart is breaking,
He, my Comfort, helps my soul.

Jesus! What a Guide and Keeper!
While the tempest still is high,
Storms about me, night o'ertakes me,
He, my Pilot, hears my cry.

Jesus! I do now receive Him,
More than all in Him I find,
He hath granted me forgiveness,
I am His, and He is mine.

~J. Wilbur Chapman (1859–1918)

Bibliography

Primary Systematic Theologies

Bancroft, Emery H. *Christian Theology: Systematic and Biblical.* 2nd ed. Grand Rapids, MI: Zondervan, 1976. 236–79.

*Berkhof, Louis. *Systematic Theology.* 4th ed. Grand Rapids, MI: Eerdmans, 1939. 415–549.

Buswell, James Oliver, Jr. *A Systematic Theology of the Christian Religion.* 2 vols. Grand Rapids, MI: Zondervan, 1962–1963. 2:70–215.

Culver, Robert Duncan. *Systematic Theology: Biblical and Historical*. Fearn, Ross-shire, Scotland: Mentor, 2005. 639–797.

Dabney, Robert Lewis. *Systematic Theology*. 1871. Reprint, Edinburgh: Banner of Truth, 1985. 553–713.

Erickson, Millard J. *Christian Theology*. Grand Rapids, MI: Baker, 1986. 887–1022.

*Grudem, Wayne. *Systematic Theology: An Introduction to Biblical Doctrine*. Grand Rapids, MI: Zondervan, 1994. 657–850.

Hodge, Charles. *Systematic Theology*. 3 vols. 1871–1873. Reprint, Grand Rapids, MI: Eerdmans, 1975. 2:313–53; 3:3–465.

Lewis, Gordon R., and Bruce A. Demarest. *Integrative Theology*. 3 vols. Grand Rapids, MI: Zondervan, 1987–1994. 3:17–236.

*Reymond, Robert L. *A New Systematic Theology of the Christian Faith*. Nashville: Thomas Nelson, 1998. 461–502.

Shedd, William G. T. *Dogmatic Theology*. 3 vols. 1889. Reprint, Minneapolis: Klock & Klock, 1979. 2B:353–587; 3:401–70.

Strong, August Hopkins. *Systematic Theology: A Compendium Designed for the Use of Theological Students*. Rev. ed. New York: Revell, 1907. 665–894.

Swindoll, Charles R., and Roy B. Zuck, eds. *Understanding Christian Theology*. Nashville: Thomas Nelson, 2003. 801–1075.

Thiessen, Henry Clarence. *Introductory Lectures in Systematic Theology*. Grand Rapids, MI: Eerdmans, 1949. 341–99.

Turretin, Francis. *Institutes of Elenctic Theology*. 3 vols. Edited by James T. Dennison Jr. Translated by George Musgrove Giger. 1679–1685. Reprint, Phillipsburg, NJ: P&R, 1992–1997. 2:501–724.

*Denotes most helpful.

Specific Works

*Barrett, Matthew. *Salvation by Grace: The Case for Effectual Calling and Regeneration*. Phillipsburg, NJ: P&R, 2013.

*Boettner, Lorraine. *The Reformed Doctrine of Predestination*. 1932. Reprint, Phillipsburg, NJ: Presbyterian and Reformed, 1981.

Calvin, John. *Institutes of the Christian Religion*. Edited by John T. McNeill. Translated by Ford Lewis Battles. 2 vols. Library of Christian Classics. 1559. Reprint, Louisville, KY: Westminster John Knox, 1960.

Gibson, David, and Jonathan Gibson, eds. *From Heaven He Came and Sought Her: Definite Atonement in Historical, Biblical, Theological, and Pastoral Perspective*. Wheaton, IL: Crossway, 2013.

Hoekema, Anthony A. *Saved by Grace*. Grand Rapids, MI: Eerdmans, 1989.

*Jeffery, Steve, Michael Ovey, and Andrew Sach. *Pierced for Our Transgressions: Rediscovering the Glory of Penal Substitution*. Wheaton, IL: Crossway, 2007.

MacArthur, John. *The Gospel according to Jesus: What Is Authentic Faith?* Rev. ed. Grand Rapids, MI: Zondervan, 2008.

———. *The Gospel according to the Apostles: The Role of Works in the Life of Faith*. Nashville: Thomas Nelson, 2000.

———. *Slave: The Hidden Truth about Your Identity in Christ*. Nashville: Thomas Nelson, 2010.

Morris, Leon. *The Apostolic Preaching of the Cross*. 3rd ed. Grand Rapids, MI: Eerdmans, 1965.

*Murray, John. *Redemption Accomplished and Applied*. 1955. Reprint. Grand Rapids, MI: Eerdmans, 2015.

Owen, John. *Salus Electorum, Sanguis Jesu: Or, The Death of Death in the Death of Christ*. In *The Works of John Owen*, edited by William H. Goold, 10:139–428. 1648. Reprint, Edinburgh: Banner of Truth, 1967.

Packer, J. I., and Mark Dever, *In My Place Condemned He Stood: Celebrating the Glory of the Atonement*. Wheaton, IL: Crossway, 2007.

Piper, John. *Counted Righteous in Christ: Should We Abandon the Imputation of Christ's Righteousness?* Wheaton, IL: Crossway, 2002.

———. *Finally Alive: What Happens When We Are Born Again*. Fearn, Ross-shire, Scotland: Christian Focus, 2009.

———. *The Future of Justification: A Response to N. T. Wright*. Wheaton, IL: Crossway, 2007.

Riccardi, Michael. *Sanctification: The Christian's Pursuit of God-Given Holiness*. Sun Valley, CA: Grace Books, 2015.

Schreiner, Thomas. *Faith Alone: The Doctrine of Justification: What the Reformers Taught . . . and Why It Still Matters*. The Five Solas. Grand Rapids, MI: Zondervan, 2015.

Schreiner, Thomas R., and Bruce A. Ware, eds. *Still Sovereign: Contemporary Perspectives on Election, Foreknowledge, and Grace*. Grand Rapids, MI: Baker, 2000.

Sproul, R. C. *Chosen by God*. Rev. ed. Carol Stream, IL: Tyndale House, 2010.

White, James R. *The God Who Justifies: A Comprehensive Study of the Doctrine of Justification*. Bloomington, MN: Bethany House, 2001.

*Denotes most helpful.

"Hark! The Herald Angels Sing"

Hark! the herald angels sing,
"Glory to the newborn King;
Peace on earth, and mercy mild,
God and sinners reconciled!"
Joyful, all ye nations, rise,
Join the triumph of the skies;
With th'angelic host proclaim,
"Christ is born in Bethlehem!"
Hark! the herald angels sing,
"Glory to the newborn King!"

Christ, by highest heav'n adored;
Christ, the everlasting Lord!
Late in time, behold Him come,
Offspring of the Virgin's womb:
Veiled in flesh the Godhead see;
Hail th'incarnate Deity,
Pleased as man with men to dwell,
Jesus, our Emmanuel.
Hark! the herald angels sing,
"Glory to the newborn King!"

Hail the heav'n-born Prince of Peace!
Hail the Son of Righteousness!
Light and life to all He brings,
Ris'n with healing in His wings.
Mild He lays His glory by,
Born that man no more may die,
Born to raise the sons of earth,
Born to give them second birth.
Hark! the herald angels sing,
"Glory to the newborn King!"

~Charles Wesley (1707–1788)

8

Angels

Angelology

<table>
<tr><td>

Major Subjects Covered in Chapter 8

Holy Angels

Satan

Demons

Angel of the Lord

Questions and Answers

</td></tr>
</table>

Theologies typically ignore or deal just briefly with angelology. However, the Bible contains a great amount of information on this subject. Therefore, this section attempts to capture all that Scripture reveals regarding angels—both those who are holy and those who are evil.

Holy Angels

Angels Introduction
Holy Angels' Reality
Holy Angels' Character
Holy Angels' History
Holy Angels' Population
Holy Angels' Residence
Holy Angels' Organization
Holy Angels' Power
Holy Angels' Ministries
Holy Angels' Destiny

Angels Introduction

The Old Testament Hebrew word *mal'akh* (213 occurrences) and the New Testament Greek word *angelos* (176 occurrences) can generally be translated "messenger," "envoy," or "ambassador" when referring to task or function (389 total occurrences in forty-two books). The messenger can be human in nature, such as the messengers of Jacob (Gen. 32:3, 6), the messengers of John the Baptist (Luke 7:24), the messengers of Christ (Luke 9:52), or pastors (Rev. 1:20; 2:1, 8, 12, 18; 3:1, 5, 7, 14). Frequently, the messenger is a nonhuman, supernatural, created being usually referred to as an "angel" (2 Chron. 32:21; Matt. 1:20, 24) or the "angel of the LORD" (Gen. 16:7). These Hebrew and Greek terms appear from Genesis 16:7 to Malachi 3:1 in the Old Testament and from Matthew 1:20 to Revelation 22:16 in the New Testament.

The context in which these words appear determine whether they refer to (1) humans, (2) holy angels, (3) Satan, (4) demons, or (5) the angel of the Lord. Refer to "Holy Angels' Character" (p. 668) for sixteen other names used of holy angels, to "Satan's Character" (p. 677) for twenty-eight additional names for Satan, to "Demons' Character" (p. 708) for seventeen more names identified with demons, and to "Angel of the Lord" (p. 719) for five other variations associated with the angel of the Lord.

OLD TESTAMENT

"Angel" appears 213 times in twenty-four of the thirty-nine Old Testament books. Most of the occurrences (157 times, or 74 percent) appear in the historical books (Genesis through Esther). The Prophets feature "angel" 41 times (19 percent), while the Poetical Books mention it only 15 times (7 percent).

The largest category of references speak of human messengers (100 times; 47 percent), with references to the angel of the Lord a close second (89 times; 42 percent). On only 24 occasions (11 percent) does "angel" refer to holy angels. Neither Satan nor demons are referred to as "angels" in the Old Testament.

The use of "angel" to refer to holy angels is scattered throughout the Old Testament:

1. The Historical Books: 7 times (29 percent) in Genesis, 1 Kings, and 2 Chronicles
2. The Poetical Books: 5 times (21 percent) in Job and Psalms
3. The Prophetic Books: 12 times (50 percent) in Zechariah 1:9–6:5

NEW TESTAMENT

"Angel" appears 176 times in eighteen of the twenty-seven New Testament books—all except Ephesians, Philippians, 1 Thessalonians, 2 Timothy, Titus, Philemon, 1 John, 2 John, and 3 John. Of these nine books, only Philippians, Titus, Philemon, 2 John, and 3 John make no mention of human messengers, holy angels, Satan, demons, or the angel of the Lord by name or title.

The term "angel" appears 55 times (31 percent) in the Gospels, with heavy emphasis in Matthew (20 occurrences) and Luke (26 occurrences). Acts has 21 occurrences (12 percent), while the Epistles refer to "angel[s]" 33 times (19 percent), with Hebrews (13 occurrences) being the most dominant. Revelation uses "angel[s]" more than any other New Testament section (67 occurrences; 38 percent), with appearances in nineteen of twenty-two chapters (chapters 4, 6, and 13 excepted). The books that use it most frequently, then, are Matthew, Luke, Acts, Hebrews, and Revelation, for a total of 147 occurrences, or 84 percent of its appearances in the New Testament.

Unlike the Old Testament, by far the greatest use of the Greek term for "angel" or "messenger" in the New Testament is to refer to holy angels (152 times; 86 percent). The remaining occurrences refer to humans (14 times; 8 percent), demons (6 times; 3.5 percent), Satan (2 times; 1 percent), and the angel of the Lord (2 times; 1 percent). When referring to humans, the term is used of three different groups: (1) church pastors (8 times), (2) human messengers (5 times), and (3) spies (once).

Holy Angels' Reality

In Christ's and Paul's days, the Sadducees (members of a very influential Jewish faction that included the high priest and believed that the Pentateuch alone was divinely inspired) denied the existence of angels because they wrongly believed that angels did not appear in the books of Moses (Acts 23:8). In fact, the undeniable existence of angels can be substantiated by the hundreds of references to them in Scripture from Genesis 3:24 (cherubim who guarded the garden of Eden) to Revelation 22:16 (Christ's angel who revealed so much to John).[1]

PERSONHOOD

Angels possess the three identifiable traits of personhood: intellect, emotions, and will. First, angels are wise beings (2 Sam. 14:20) who can converse (Matt. 28:5), sing (Job 38:7), and worship (Heb. 1:6). Second, they have the capacity for emotion. Angels are joyful over the repentance of sinners (Luke 15:10). They fear God in worship with awe, wonder, and respect (Heb. 1:6). They also find God preeminently praiseworthy (Ps. 148:2; Luke 2:13–14). Third, angels possess a will with which they choose to worship God (Heb. 1:6; Rev. 5:11). They also have a strong desire (Gk. *epithymeō*) to understand things related to salvation (1 Pet. 1:10–12).

PERSONAL QUALITIES

Angels are beings created by God (Neh. 9:6; Ps. 148:2–5; Col. 1:16), which is why they are called "sons of God" (Job 1:6; 2:1; 38:7). They are spirit beings ("ministering spirits," Heb. 1:14). Both Satan (a "lying spirit," 1 Kings 22:22–23) and demons ("evil spirits," Luke 7:21) are described as spirits. By Christ's definition, a *spirit* is immaterial, one without flesh and bones (Luke 24:39).

Angels were created morally pure and remain so in perpetuity, being called holy

---

1. See "Angels Introduction" (p. 666) for a detailed account of the biblical evidence concerning angels.

(Mark 8:38; Luke 9:26). Holy angels are elect angels (1 Tim. 5:21) who do not need redemption from a fallen state (Heb. 2:14–16). In contrast, Satan and the demons, who were created pure, subsequently defaulted, sinned, and became evil (Ezek. 28:15; Jude 6). There is no salvation for fallen angels (Matt. 25:41).

Not bound by physical space, angels are mobile to the extent that they are able to travel from heaven to earth and back to heaven again (Gen. 28:12; John 1:51). For example, angels traveled between heaven and earth to minister to Daniel (Dan. 9:20–23; 10:1–13, 20) and to Christ (John 1:51). And Jacob himself witnessed this angelic mobility (Gen. 28:12).

Angels may also be either visible or invisible. For example, they were visible in their visit to Sodom (Gen. 18:2; Heb. 13:2) and to Christ's tomb (John 20:11–12). They were invisible at first to Balaam (Num. 22:31) and to Elisha's servant (2 Kings 6:15–17).

As spirit beings, angels are without gender (Matt. 22:30; Mark 12:25; Luke 20:35–36) and cannot reproduce after their own kind. When they do appear in an angelophany, they look like men, never like women (Gen. 18:2; Dan. 10:16, 18; Mark 16:5).

Angels are multilingual. Scripture portrays them as speaking in whatever language the hearer of their message will understand. When Paul wrote about "tongues of angels" (1 Cor. 13:1), he most likely reasoned hypothetically since Scripture does not mention an angelic language elsewhere.

Angels are ageless and immortal in the future. Holy angels cannot die because they have not sinned (Luke 20:36). Fallen angels will not die but will be eternally punished in the lake of fire (Rev. 20:10).

Angels are messengers of God's truth (Rev. 1:1). Paul warned that if a spirit being claimed to be a holy angel from God but delivered a false gospel, it was actually a demon who was to be accursed (Gal. 1:8).

Holy Angels' Character

Angels are referred to in Scripture by names, titles, and functions. Seventeen appellations relate to God's "messengers." These references define who angels are and what they do.

1. *Angel*: See "Angels Introduction" (p. 666).
2. *Archangel* (Dan. 10:13; 1 Thess. 4:16; Jude 9): Michael is referred to in Daniel as "one of the chief princes," the Old Testament equivalent of "archangel." That he is one of them means that there are at least two, probably more. An unnamed archangel will shout at the rapture of the church (1 Thess. 4:16). Michael also contended with Satan over the body of Moses (Jude 9).
3. *Chariot(s)* (Ps. 68:17): This military language indicates that the number of angels cannot be calculated, much like in Revelation 5:11. The term "chariots" is used figuratively to portray angels carrying out military-like missions for God (2 Kings 2:11; 6:17). In Job 25:3, Bildad the Shuhite asks, "Is there any number to his [God's] armies?" (cf. Job 19:12). The implied answer is no!

4. *Cherubim* (Gen. 3:24; Ex. 25:18–22; 37:8; Ezek. 1:4–28; 10:1–20; 28:14, 16): This title expresses diligent service. Ezekiel wrote that Satan was originally a "guardian cherub" (Ezek. 28:14, 16). This would account for a cherub guarding the garden of Eden (Gen. 3:24) and the model of two cherubs on the mercy seat guarding the ark of the covenant (Ex. 25:18–22; 37:8; cf. Heb. 9:5). It is quite probable that the twelve angels at the twelve gates of the New Jerusalem are cherubim (Rev. 21:12). Ezekiel uses extreme figurative language to describe the living creatures in Ezekiel 1, which are later called cherubim in Ezekiel 10:15.

5. *Elohim* (Ps. 8:5; cf. Heb. 2:7): The Hebrew word *elohim* or "god(s)" is used here to refer to angels in the most basic sense of "superior ones," comparing angels to humans.

6. *Gabriel* (Dan. 8:16; 9:21; Luke 1:19, 26): Gabriel, which means "mighty one of God," appears only in Daniel and Luke. Gabriel came as God's messenger to give Daniel an understanding of his multiple visions. In similar fashion, Zechariah and Mary were given an understanding of God's intentions by Gabriel.

7. *Holy one(s)* (Deut. 33:2–3; Job 5:1; 15:15; Ps. 89:5, 7; Dan. 4:13, 17, 23; 8:13; Zech. 14:5; Jude 14): Angels who have not sinned are described as being holy. They delight in praising God, who is "holy, holy, holy" (Isa. 6:3; Rev. 4:8). The title "holy ones," or "saints," can also apply to humans (1 Thess. 3:13).

8. *Host(s)* (Deut. 4:19; Neh. 9:6; Ps. 33:6; Luke 2:13): This title pictures God as the military commander of an enormous host of soldiers ready to carry out the orders of their superior (cf. Matt. 26:53). Angels are the "hosts," and God is the "LORD of hosts" (1 Sam. 17:45; Ps. 89:8).

9. *Living creatures* (Rev. 4:6, 19:4): While the four living creatures of Ezekiel 1:5–14 are later identified as cherubim (Ezek. 10:20–22), the living creatures in Revelation 4:8 look and act more like seraphim (Isa. 6:1–4) in that they have six wings and are involved in noteworthy worship. The living creatures in Revelation are involved in worship (Rev. 4:6–11; 5:6–14; 7:11; 14:3; 19:4) and judgment (Rev. 6:1–7; 15:7).

10. *Men* (Gen. 18:2; Mark 16:5; Acts 1:10): While angels are essentially spirit in nature, they can appear at rare times in human form. When this occurs, they are always called men.

11. *Michael* (Dan. 10:13, 21; 12:1; Jude 9; Rev. 12:7): See "Archangel" above. Michael means "Who is like God?"

12. *Ministering spirit* (Pss. 103:21; 104:4; Heb. 1:14): Angels serve or minister by doing God's will (Ps. 103:21). Angels can be God's instrument for judgment (Ps. 104:4) or for blessing in serving the saints (Heb. 1:14).

13. *Morning stars* (Job 38:7): Satan is called "Day Star" (Isa. 14:12), and angels in general are called "stars of heaven" (Rev. 12:4).

14. *Prince(s)* (Dan. 10:13, 20, 21; 12:1): Michael is called "your prince" (Dan. 10:21) and the "great prince" (Dan. 12:1), referring to his ministry on behalf of Israel as "one of the chief princes" (Dan. 10:13). The term "prince" is also used of Satan's coconspirators (Dan. 10:20). See "Michael" above.

15. *Seraphim* (Isa. 6:2, 6): This kind of angel appears only in Isaiah 6. With a name meaning "burning ones," at least two seraphim (Isa. 6:3) were concerned with God's holiness. Some have thought that cherubim, living creatures, and

seraphim might be different versions of the same kind of angel.[2] See "Cherubim" and "Living creatures" above.

16. *Sons of God* (Job 1:6; 2:1; 38:7): It is natural to understand that the Creator of angels would be considered a father with sons. Elsewhere, similar language is used to describe angels as "sons of the mighty" (Pss. 29:1 NASB; 89:6 NASB). They are also called "mighty ones" (Ps. 103:20; Joel 3:11 NASB).

17. *Watchers* (Dan. 4:13, 17, 23): This term appears only in Daniel and seems somewhat vague. How these angelic "watchers" relate to God's omniscience is unclear.

Holy Angels' History

The Bible includes only twenty-six specific historical encounters with angels, ten in the Old Testament, sixteen in the New. This covers about 2,100 years from ca. 2015 BC to ca. AD 95. The appearances began with Abraham (Genesis 18) and continued until the time of John's prophetic visions in Revelation.

CREATION

God created all the angels (Neh. 9:6; Ps. 148:2–5; Col. 1:16). Job 38:7 states that the angels sang during the creation, indicating that they were created at the outset. Satan's fall (Ezek. 28:15) and the demons' rebellion (Rev. 12:4) would have occurred after Genesis 2 (the seventh day of creation) but before Genesis 3 (Eve's deception and Adam's disobedience). After the garden debacle, God placed cherubim at the east end of the garden to guard the way to the tree of life (Gen. 3:24).

OLD TESTAMENT

Ten specific Old Testament historical encounters occurred over about 1,500 years (ca. 2025–ca. 480 BC), from the time of Abraham (Genesis 18) to the days of Zechariah. These events involved patriarchs and prophets:

1. Genesis 18:1–19:22: Abraham, Lot, and Sodom (ca. 2025 BC)
2. Genesis 28:1–17: Jacob's dream (ca. 1950 BC)
3. Genesis 32:1–2: Jacob at Mahanaim (ca. 1950 BC)
4. 1 Kings 19:5: Elijah (ca. 860 BC)
5. Isaiah 6:1–4: Isaiah and the throne of God (ca. 740 BC)
6. Daniel 8:13–27: Daniel and Gabriel (ca. 551 BC)
7. Daniel 9:20–27: Daniel and Gabriel (ca. 538 BC)
8. Daniel 10:10–21: Daniel and an angel (ca. 536 BC)
9. Daniel 12:5–13: Daniel and angels (ca. 522 BC)
10. Zechariah 1:9–6:5 (twelve times): Zechariah and the angel who spoke to him (ca. 480 BC)

NEW TESTAMENT

At least sixteen specific New Testament historical encounters with angels occurred over about one hundred years (ca. 5 BC–ca. AD 95), from the time of Christ's birth

---

2. For a more detailed discussion of cherubim, living creatures, and seraphim, consult C. Fred Dickason, *Angels: Elect and Evil* (Chicago: Moody Press, 1975), 61–67.

to the days of John's prophetic visions in Revelation. (Most English versions of the Bible omit "an angel of the Lord . . . stirred the water" in John 5:4 because it is not included in the oldest and best New Testament manuscripts.) These events surrounded the Gospels, Acts, and Revelation:

1. Luke 1:8–23: Zechariah (ca. 5 BC)
2. Luke 1:26–38: Mary and Gabriel (ca. 5 BC)
3. Matthew 1:18–24: Joseph (ca. 5 BC)
4. Luke 2:8–20: Shepherds (ca. 5 BC)
5. Matthew 2:13–15: Joseph (ca. 5 BC)
6. Matthew 2:19–23: Joseph (ca. 4 BC)
7. Matthew 4:11: Jesus (ca. AD 27)
8. Luke 22:43: Jesus (ca. AD 30)
9. Matthew 28:1–10; Luke 24:1–12; John 20:11–18: Tomb encounters (ca. AD 30)
10. Acts 1:10–11: Apostles (ca. AD 30)
11. Acts 5:19: Apostles (ca. AD 31)
12. Acts 8:26: Philip (ca. AD 32)
13. Acts 10:3–8, 22; 11:13: Cornelius (ca. AD 36)
14. Acts 12:7–11: Peter (ca. AD 44)
15. Acts 27:23–26: Paul (ca. AD 58)
16. Revelation 1–22: John (ca. AD 95)

These documented visits do not negate the possibility of other encounters that the canonical text does not record. It does mean that these infrequent Old Testament and New Testament events would be representative of any other visits. Thus, they would be reserved for very significant events and limited to very important people of God.

END TIMES

Revelation 6–19 chronicles an overview of notable events that will unfold over the seven years of Daniel's seventieth week, especially the last three and one-half years. At the end of that time, Christ will come from heaven to earth with his angels in order to conquer the world and set up his one-thousand-year kingdom on earth (Matt. 13:39, 41, 49; 16:27; 24:31; 25:31; Mark 8:38; 2 Thess. 1:7).

Revelation 20 briefly explains Christ's millennial kingdom, including the angelic incarceration of Satan (20:1–3), Christ's reign (20:4–7), Satan's release at the end for eternal punishment (20:7–10), and the final judgment of all unbelievers at the great white throne judgment (20:11–15; cf. Luke 12:8–9). Revelation 21–22 provides a summary of the basics involved with the new heaven and new earth, New Jerusalem, and eternity future, including angels at the city gates (Rev. 21:12).

Holy Angels' Population

Unlike humans, angels neither procreate (Matt. 22:30) nor die. The angelic population was fixed at its creation (Neh. 9:6), leaving no need for a periodic census. Revelation 12:4 indicates that Satan lured one-third of the angelic population to defect and join his rebellion against God. These became evil angels. Two-thirds of the angels have remained faithful to God as elect angels (1 Tim. 5:21).

The Bible nowhere places an exact number on the quantity of angels. However, there are enough inexact descriptions of the angelic population to provide a general idea by considering these clues.

1. *1 Kings 22:19; 2 Chronicles 18:18*: Micaiah saw the Lord sitting on his throne with all the host of heaven standing around him. The word picture portrays a scene in which the angels of heaven seem to be as innumerable as the actual stars of heaven (Gen. 15:5; Job 38:7; Pss. 103:21; 148:2).

2. *2 Kings 19:35 (see Isa. 37:36)*: On one night, the angel of the Lord slew 185,000 Assyrian soldiers in Sennacherib's army, which caused the king to retreat in defeat. This kill ratio magnifies the strength of just one angel.

3. *Daniel 7:10*: In Daniel's vision of God's throne room, he saw thousands upon thousands and ten thousand upon ten thousand angels.

4. *Matthew 26:53*: Christ told the soldiers in the garden of Gethsemane that if he were to request it, God would send "more than twelve legions of angels to rescue him." That calculates as approximately six thousand soldiers per legion times twelve, equaling at least seventy-two thousand angels. Actually, the number would exceed this. The sense is that an overwhelmingly large army of angels could be dispatched instantly to overpower the more than six hundred or so soldiers in the Roman cohort and accompanying mob that showed up to arrest Christ.

5. *Luke 2:13*: In recounting the birth of Christ, Luke describes a "multitude" (Gk. *plēthos*) of the heavenly host suddenly appearing and singing a doxology appropriate to the moment. In Hebrews 11:12, this same Greek word is used to describe the numerical scope of all the stars in heaven, making the enormity of the angelic army begin to become more evident.

6. *Hebrews 12:22*: The writer of Hebrews describes the size of the angelic court in heaven as "innumerable." This is a translation of the Greek term *murias*, which literally means "ten thousand," a number beyond which the ancients did not conceive or count.

7. *Revelation 5:11*: The angelic scene in heaven is described as "numbering myriads of myriads and thousands of thousands," which meant, in other words, a number that far exceeds ten thousand times ten thousand (or one hundred million) and one thousand times one thousand (or one million). This is the most striking statement in Scripture that describes the number of holy angels as exceedingly incalculable (Deut. 33:2; Ps. 68:17; Dan. 7:10; Jude 14).

The population of holy angels is obviously twice that of evil angels. The number of them is not revealed, so it is beyond our understanding. Needless to say, there is no shortage of angels at God's disposal to carry out his will and to render appropriate worship and praise to their Creator.

Holy Angels' Residence

The term translated "heaven" in the Bible describes three different elevation levels above planet earth. First, in descending order, comes the "third heaven" or paradise, which is the heaven of God's presence (2 Cor. 12:2–3; cf. Ps. 123:1). It is referred to as (1) "the highest heaven" (1 Kings 8:27; Ps. 148:4), (2) the "heaven of heavens" (Deut. 10:14), (3) "his holy habitation in heaven" (2 Chron. 30:27), and (4) "far above all the heavens" (Eph. 4:10). Second is the stellar heaven of the sun, moon, and stars, termed the *second heaven* (Gen. 15:5; Ps. 8:3; Isa. 13:10; Heb. 4:14). Finally, there is the *first heaven*, or the earth's atmosphere (Gen. 8:2; Deut. 11:11; 1 Kings 8:35).

From creation (Job 38:4–7) through the end of Daniel's seventieth week, holy angels reside in the third heaven except when they depart on a temporary assignment to serve God elsewhere. This is true of the seraphim (Isa. 6:1–4), the four living creatures (Rev. 4:6–11; 5:8; 14:3), Gabriel (Luke 1:19), and unfallen angels in general (1 Kings 22:19; 2 Chron. 18:18; Dan. 7:10; Matt. 18:10; 22:30; 24:36; 28:2; Mark 12:25; 13:32; Luke 2:13, 15; 12:8; 15:10; John 1:51; Heb. 12:22; Rev. 5:11; 7:1–12; 20:1). Because they normally reside in the third heaven, all angels engage in worship (Heb. 1:6).

During Christ's millennial reign, those angels who come with him to conquer the earth will remain on earth to serve him (Matt. 25:31). Those angels who remain in heaven continue to worship God and serve his purposes there. Afterward, all angels will reside with God and all the redeemed in the new heaven and new earth (Rev. 20:1–22:21, esp. 21:12).

Holy Angels' Organization

Angels are organized into a powerful heavenly hierarchy to carry out their work. Words such as "angels," "authorities," "dominions," "powers," "rulers," and "thrones" can describe either holy or evil angelic hierarchies in Scripture. Romans 8:38; 1 Corinthians 15:24; Ephesians 2:2; 6:12; and Colossians 2:15 most likely refer to various ranks or levels among the evil angels, that is, the demon hierarchy. Ephesians 1:21; 3:10; Colossians 1:16; and 1 Peter 3:22 most likely refer to various ranks or levels in the holy angel hierarchy.

Scripture never elaborates on the specifics of these hierarchies to explain their order or function. Since Satan imitates and falsifies God's character and kingdom characteristics, it seems likely that there is an authoritative functional hierarchy for holy angels who worship God and a parallel counterfeit hierarchy for demons who give their allegiance to Satan.

Multiple descriptive titles are used of possibly several kinds of angels. See "Cherubim," "Living creatures," and "Seraphim" under "Holy Angels' Character" (p. 668). Only three angels are identified by name; see "Gabriel" and "Michael" under "Holy Angels' Character" above and "Satan" under "Satan's Character" (p. 677).

Holy Angels' Power

The power of angels appears in both the Old and New Testaments. In the Old Testament, angels caused blindness, rescued people, and destroyed cities (Gen. 19:1–26).

They struck down seventy thousand men of Israel (2 Sam. 24:10–17). Angels appear to be constantly at war with demons in the heavens (Dan. 10:13, 20–21).

In the New Testament, an angel moved the extremely large stone away from the entrance to Christ's tomb (Matt. 28:2; Mark 16:3–4) and released Peter from prison (Acts 12:7–11). Herod was struck with a fatal case of worms by an angel (Acts 12:20–23). Paul referred to angels as "mighty" (2 Thess. 1:7), and Peter called them "greater in might and power" than humans (2 Pet. 2:11).

In Revelation, angels will exercise power over nature (Rev. 7:1–3). Angels will execute the seven trumpet judgments (Rev. 8:2, 6) and the seven bowl judgments (Rev. 16:1–21). They will evict Satan and his angels permanently from heaven (Rev. 12:7–9). An angel will bind and incarcerate Satan for the duration of Christ's millennial kingdom (Rev. 20:1–3).

To summarize, angels are stronger than humans but not omnipotent like God (Ps. 103:20; 2 Pet. 2:11). Angels are greater than humans in knowledge but not omniscient like God (Matt. 24:36). Angels are swifter and more mobile than humans but not omnipresent like God (Dan. 9:21–23; 10:10, 14).

Holy Angels' Ministries

From the time of creation (Job 38:7) to the consummation (Rev. 21:12), angels have figured prominently in executing God's purposes. The following summaries highlight the ministries of angels to (1) God, (2) Christ, (3) Christians, (4) the church, (5) unbelievers, and (6) the nations.

GOD

Angels worship and praise God (Job 38:7; Ps. 148:2; Isa. 6:1–4; Rev. 4:6–11; 5:8–13; 7:11–12). They serve God (Ps. 103:20–21; Heb. 1:7). Angels congregate as the sons of God before God (Job 1:6; 2:1) in the "assembly of the holy ones" (Ps. 89:5) and in the "council of the holy ones" (Ps. 89:7).

These ministering servants also deliver messages for God. The Lord used angels to transmit his law to Moses (Acts 7:38, 53; Gal. 3:19; Heb. 2:2), and Gabriel took God's word to Daniel (Dan. 8:16; 9:21), Zechariah (Luke 1:19), and Mary (Luke 1:26). Angels frequently communicated to John in Revelation (Rev. 1:1–22:16).

Angels served as God's instrument of judgment on Sodom (Gen. 19:1, 12–13), and they will evict Satan and his angels at the midpoint of Daniel's seventieth week (Rev. 12:7–9). Angels will be directly involved in the trumpet judgment (Rev. 8:6–11:19) and bowl judgments on the world (Rev. 16:1–21) during Daniel's seventieth week.

CHRIST

Angels participated in announcing Christ's birth to Mary (Luke 1:26–38), Joseph (Matt. 1:18–23), and the shepherds (Luke 2:8–15). They protected Christ during his infancy (Matt. 2:13–15, 19–21).

Angels ministered to Christ from the beginning of his public ministry (Matt.

4:11) to the end of it (Luke 22:43), and they generally ministered to Christ during his ministry on earth (John 1:51; 1 Tim. 3:16). They helped people understand Christ's resurrection (Matt. 28:1–2, 6; Luke 24:5–8) and ascension (Acts 1:11). Hebrews 1–2 enumerates the reasons why angels minister to Christ with multiple comparisons to validate Christ's superiority to angels.

When Christ returns to earth at the rapture of the church, angels will also be active (1 Thess. 4:16). They will accompany Christ at his second advent (Matt. 25:31), gather in believers (Matt. 13:39–43; 24:31), and bring judgment on unbelievers (2 Thess. 1:7). An angel will bind and imprison Satan for the duration of Christ's millennial kingdom (Rev. 20:1–3).

CHRISTIANS

Angels minister generally to believers (Heb. 1:14), which includes rejoicing at a believer's salvation (Luke 15:10) and providing protection (Pss. 34:7; 35:5–6; 91:11–12; Matt. 18:10) as willed by God. Since the episode of the rich man and Lazarus (Luke 16:19–31) is most likely a parable, it should not be used with absolute certainty to argue that angels transport all believers to heaven at death (Luke 16:22).

THE CHURCH

Angels can be involved in the church with regard to (1) the leadership (1 Cor. 4:9), (2) women (1 Cor. 11:10), (3) the purity of pastors (1 Tim. 5:21), and (4) their own pursuit of understanding salvation (1 Pet. 1:12).

UNBELIEVERS

As Christ explains in one of his parables, angels will separate the "weeds" (unbelievers) from the "wheat" (believers) (Matt. 13:27–30, 36–43). An angel will preach the gospel to all the world during Daniel's seventieth week (Rev. 14:6–7). They will participate in Christ's second-coming judgment of unbelievers (Matt. 16:27; 2 Thess. 1:7).

THE NATIONS

Angels serve God's purposes for the nations in general (Dan. 10:13, 20) and for Israel in particular (Dan. 10:21; 12:1; Rev. 7:1–3). They will also specifically bring major judgment on all nations preceding Christ's second coming (Rev. 8:6–11:19; 16:1–21).

Holy Angels' Destiny

Holy angels will not face any judgment because they will never sin. This is in contrast to Satan and the demons, who will be judged (2 Pet. 2:4; Jude 6) and assigned to spend all eternity future in the lake of fire (Matt. 25:41; Rev. 20:10).

After the final, great white throne judgment (1 Cor. 15:24–28; Rev. 20:11–15), there will be a new heaven and new earth (Rev. 21:1). The dwelling of God will be with man in the holy city, the New Jerusalem (Rev. 21:2). Where God is, there also will his holy angels be, with twelve of them at the gates to the city (Rev. 21:12). God's redeemed people and God's angels will worship him in righteousness forevermore.

In the end, Eden will be revisited. God will look on all that he re-creates and find that it is very good—just as he did in the beginning (Gen. 1:31).

Satan

Satan's Reality

The fact of Satan's existence can be neither proven nor disproven by philosophical reasoning alone. Nevertheless, the incontrovertible existence of evil must have an actual perpetrator. Experiential claims by themselves cannot prove Satan's reality because they lack any objective standard by which the alleged experiences might be validated.

However, a reliable historical account of human history would serve to establish the factuality of Satan if the author were credible. Actually, one such book exists—the Bible, whose author is the God of creation, the originator of truth without error, and the Creator of Satan. Thus, the Bible is the Christian's only unimpeachable witness to the actual existence of Satan.

BASIC FACTS

The revelation of Satan's existence is found in only eight Old Testament books, yet it is completely consistent with the more frequent references in the New Testament. The Hebrew word for Satan basically means "adversary" or "one who opposes." Of the 27 Old Testament occurrences, 18 refer directly to Satan (once in 1 Chronicles 21; 14 times in Job 1–2; 3 times in Zechariah 3), while 9 refer to adversaries other than Satan. Additionally, 2 Corinthians 11:3 and Revelation 12:9; 20:2 testify to Satan's reality in Genesis 3, where he is disguised as a serpent. First Kings 22:21–22 and 2 Chronicles 18:20–21 refer to him as "a lying spirit." Isaiah 14 and Ezekiel 28 allude to Satan as the power behind the kings of Babylon and Tyre, respectively.

On the other hand, New Testament references abound. The terms translated "Satan" or "devil" refer to "the evil one" on 74 occasions. Every New Testament writer mentions him, and he appears in nineteen New Testament books (Galatians, Philippians, Colossians, Titus, Philemon, 2 Peter, 2 John, and 3 John excepted). An amazing 28 of 30 references in the Gospels involve either direct encounters with or mentions of Satan.

BASIC CHARACTERISTICS

Satan exhibits the three basic characteristics associated with personhood: intellect, emotion, and will. With his intellect, he tempted Christ (Matt. 4:1–11) and schemes against Christians (2 Cor. 2:11; Eph. 6:11; 1 Tim. 3:7; 2 Tim. 2:26). Emotionally, he exhibits pride (1 Tim. 3:6) and anger (Rev. 12:12, 17). The Devil also exercises his will against Christians (Luke 22:31; 2 Tim. 2:26).

Five additional personal qualities complete an elementary profile of this lying and murderous adversary. First, he is a created angel. According to Paul, God created all things (Col. 1:16), which includes angels. God's response to Job equates "morning stars" with "sons of God" (Job 38:4–7; cf. 1:6; 2:1), the first-created angelic ranks who sang and rejoiced over the remainder of creation. The evil power behind the King of Tyre is referred to as the "anointed guardian cherub" (Ezek. 28:14, 16) who was created (Ezek. 28:13, 15). Originally created as a chief angel at the level of Michael the archangel (Jude 9), Satan now rebelliously leads a band of evil angels (Matt. 25:41; Rev. 12:9). Although he is an angel of darkness, he disguises himself as an angel of light (2 Cor. 11:14).

Second, Satan is a spirit being (1 Kings 22:21–23; 2 Chron. 18:20–22; Eph. 2:2), although he appears at times like a physical person (Matt. 4:3–11), just like the holy angels (Mark 16:5). Whereas the writer of Hebrews refers to angels as "ministering spirits" (Heb. 1:14), Christ characterized demons as "unclean" (Luke 4:36) and "evil" (Luke 8:2) spirits. Such would also be true of the prince of demons.

Third, Satan possesses an extraordinary mobility. Both Job 1:7 and Job 2:2 portray Satan as "going to and fro on the earth," as does 1 Peter 5:8, which refers to Satan as one who "prowls around" the world. Fourth, Satan can function both in heaven (1 Kings 22:21–22; Job 1–2; Rev. 12:10) and on earth (Matt. 4:3–11). Finally, God will hold Satan morally responsible in the end for his treacherously evil deeds (Matt. 25:41; Rev. 20:10).

BASIC CONTRASTS

The theological understanding of Satan reflects a studied contrast with the Lord Jesus Christ (see table 8.1). This surprises no one, since Christ is the Creator and Satan a mere creature.

Satan's Character

Becoming acquainted with Satan requires a review of his various names and titles. Satan ("adversary") and Devil ("slanderer") are by far the most frequent terms used of Satan, but several others also warn of Satan's intentions and activities. The following twenty-nine attributions offer glimpses into his diabolical character:

1. *Abaddon* (Rev. 9:11): This transliterated Hebrew word is normally associated with death and destruction in the six Old Testament texts where it appears (Job 26:6; 28:22; 31:12; Ps. 88:11; Prov. 15:11; 27:20). Abaddon and its Greek counterpart, Apollyon, refer to Satan as the angelic king with

Table 8.1 *Satan and Christ Contrasted*

Satan	Christ
temporal	eternal
darkness	light
death	life
liar	truth
counterfeit	authentic
evil	righteous
enemy	friend
strong	strongest
imprisons	releases
accuses	advocates
imitates	originates

Satan	Christ
devious	honest
oppresses	relieves
slanders	intercedes
prideful	humble
enslaves	liberates
sinful	holy
destructive	constructive
thief	benefactor
hates	loves
debilitates	heals
murderer	Savior

dominion over demons in the bottomless pit in Revelation 9:1. See "Angel of the bottomless pit," "Apollyon," "Beelzebul," "Evil One," "God of this world," "King," "Prince of the power of the air," "Ruler of this world," and "Star" below.

2. *Accuser* (Zech. 3:1; Rev. 12:10): Satan acts as the prosecuting attorney in heaven before God, as the one accusing (Heb. *satan*; Gk. *katēgorōn*) the high priest of Israel, Joshua (Zech. 3:1), and Christians (Rev. 12:10) of being unworthy of God's grace in redemption and service. While some have identified the "accuser" in Psalm 109:6 as Satan, the context (109:4, 20, 28) seems to refer to David's human accusers.

3. *Adversary* (1 Pet. 5:8): Satan's adversarial role (Gk. *antidikos*) of opposing believers in Christ is portrayed as a ferocious, roaring lion stalking prey. See "Enemy" and "Satan" below.

4. *Angel of the bottomless pit* (Rev. 9:11): Much as Michael is the archangel of heaven (Rev. 12:7), so Satan is the "king" of the Abyss. There are demons on earth who do not want to go there (Luke 8:31). There are other demons in the Abyss who will be released by Satan for a short time (Rev. 9:1–2, 11). Some demons have been confined there for a considerable portion of human history and will not be released until the final judgment (2 Pet. 2:4; Jude 6), when they will be cast into the lake of fire with Satan and the rest. During Christ's millennial kingdom reign on earth, Satan will be imprisoned in the Abyss (Rev. 20:1–6). See "Abaddon" above and "Apollyon" below.

5. *Apollyon* (Rev. 9:11): This name represents the Greek parallel to the Hebrew Abaddon, best translated "destroyer." It appears only once in the New Testament. See "Abaddon" and "Angel of the bottomless pit" above and "Beelzebul," "King," and "Star" below.

6. *Beelzebul* (Matt. 12:24; Mark 3:22; Luke 11:15): Jewish leaders accused Christ of casting out demons by the power of the leader (Gk. *archōn*) of the demons, whose name meant "lord, prince" and who had originally been the pagan Philistine patron deity of the coastal city Ekron (2 Kings 1:2–3). After arguing that Satan would not oppose demons because that would be self-defeating,

Jesus acknowledged that while Satan was strong (Luke 11:21), he himself was far stronger (Luke 11:22) and would prevail. See "Abaddon" and "Apollyon" above and "Evil One," "God of this world," "King," "Prince of the power of the air," "Ruler of this world," and "Star" below.

7. *Belial* (2 Cor. 6:15): This transliterated Hebrew word appears twenty-seven times in the Old Testament (see Deut. 13:13; Judg. 19:22; 1 Sam. 2:12; 1 Kings 21:13; Prov. 6:12) and refers to vile, wicked, and worthless scoundrels and troublemakers. It is quite possible that Nahum 1:15 uses this word to refer to Satan. Certainly, Paul intended the term to portray Satan as the most vile, wicked, and worthless creature, without peer or superior.

8. *Devil* (see Matt. 4:1–Rev. 20:10): This word appears thirty-eight times in the New Testament, referring to Satan in thirty-four instances. It is the second-most-used term for Satan in the Bible. In the Septuagint, the ancient Greek translation of the Old Testament, Devil (*diabolos*) is used to refer to Satan in Job 1–2, where the Devil slanderously accuses Job of less-than-noble motives for serving God. He also slanders Joshua, the Jewish high priest (Zech. 3:1). The ultimate slander, however, is of God when Satan tells Eve that she will not die, even though God has said that death will be certain if she eats the fruit from the tree of the knowledge of good and evil (Gen. 2:17; 3:4). Satan slanders both God to man and man to God.

9. *Dragon* (Isa. 27:1; Rev. 12:3, 7, 9; 20:2): John employs the figure of an apocalyptic monster thirteen times in Revelation 12; 13; 16; and 20 to picture Satan. This word (Gk. *drakōn*) unmistakably refers to Satan since both Revelation 12:9 and 20:2 identify the "dragon" as "the serpent of old," "the devil," and "Satan." See "Leviathan" and "Serpent" below.

10. *Enemy* (Matt. 13:25, 28, 39; Luke 10:19): In the parable of the tares, Christ tells of the enemy (Gk. *echthros*), who planted darnel, a wheat-like weed, in the wheat field. Matthew 13:39 identifies the enemy as the Devil. See "Adversary" above and "Satan" below.

11. *Evil One* (Matt. 5:37; 6:13; 13:19, 38; John 17:15; Eph. 6:16; 2 Thess. 3:3; 1 John 2:13–14; 3:12; 5:18–19): Apart from Satan and Devil, the Evil One (Gk. *ponēros*) is the third-most-frequent appellation used. Evil stands in contrast to righteousness (Gk. *dikaiosynē*) since Satan stands in diametrical contrast to Christ. The whole world lies in the power of the Evil One (1 John 5:19). See "Abaddon," "Apollyon," and "Beelzebul" above and "God of this world," "King," "Prince of the power of the air," "Ruler of this world," and "Star" below.

12. *Father of lies* (John 8:44): Not only is Satan a perpetual liar, he is the originator of lies. The Devil, by deceiving Eve (Gen. 3:1–6; 2 Cor. 11:3; 1 Tim. 2:14) into disobedience, has in a sense fathered the entire human race, characterized by lies, sinful children who walk in the footsteps of their primogenitor (Rom. 3:10–11, 13). This family imagery continues in Acts 13:10, where Paul calls Elymas the sorcerer a "son of the devil," making crooked the straight paths of the Lord. John similarly identifies all who do not practice righteousness or love their brother as "children of the devil" (1 John 3:10). The "weeds" in Matthew 13:38 are branded "sons of the evil one," that is, false believers. The Antichrist is called "the son of destruction" (2 Thess. 2:3), with "destruction"

alluding to Satan as Abaddon (see above). The same is true of Judas (John 17:12). See "Liar" and "Lying spirit" below.

13. *God of this world* (2 Cor. 4:4): By God's sovereign ordinance, Satan is the superior power but not the deity (Gk. *theos*, as per Ps. 82:6 [Septuagint]; John 10:33–36) of this age (1 John 5:19). This title comes by virtue of his position, not his nature. It all began in Eden and will continue this way until the curse is reversed (Rev. 22:3). Satan is ultimately behind all false religions (Rev. 2:9; 3:9). See "Abaddon," "Apollyon," "Beelzebul," and "Evil One" above and "King," "Prince of the power of the air," "Ruler of this world," and "Star" below.

14. *King* (Rev. 9:11): In context, Satan is the king over demons, just as he is the "prince of the demons" in Matthew 12:24. See "Abaddon," "Apollyon," and "Beelzebul" above and "Star" below.

15. *Leviathan* (Isa. 27:1): See "Dragon" above and "Serpent" below.

16. *Liar* (John 8:44): Christ is the truth (John 14:6), and Satan is the prevaricator. All of Satan's messages and activities are built on global deceit (Rev. 12:9; 20:3, 8, 10). Satan is the "lying spirit" of 1 Kings 22:22–23 and 2 Chronicles 18:21–22. Elymas the magician was full of deceit and was thus called a "son of the devil" (Acts 13:10). This liar rules over deceitful spirits spreading the teaching of demons (1 Tim. 4:1). His first act of treason with humans was to deceive Eve (2 Cor. 11:3; 1 Tim. 2:14). He disguises himself as an angel of light (2 Cor. 11:14). From the beginning (Genesis 3) to the end (Revelation 20), Satan has opposed the truth of God with the lies and deceits of hell. See "Father of lies" above and "Lying spirit" below.

17. *Lucifer* (Isa. 14:12): Tradition, especially visible in the KJV/NKJV translations, has popularized this title. Literally, the Hebrew word (*helel*) is best translated as "light bearer" or "day star." It seems more likely that this description is used in reference to the king of Babylon than to Satan in this context. Isaiah compared the king to a morning star heralding a new day but quickly giving way to the glory of the sun.[3] See "Star" below.

18. *Lying spirit* (1 Kings 22:22–23; 2 Chron. 18:21–22): In keeping with Satan's propensity to lie (John 8:44), God used him and four hundred lying demons to deceive Israel's King Ahab to go into battle. As a result, Ahab was killed (1 Kings 22:37–38) according to God's promise (1 Kings 21:17–26). Satan was used by God for a "strong delusion" (2 Thess. 2:11). See "Father of lies" and "Liar" above.

19. *Murderer* (John 8:44): Jesus said, "He was a murderer from the beginning." As a result of Satan's lie to Eve, she ate of the tree, and God's promise in Genesis 2:17 was fulfilled: "For in the day that you eat of it you shall surely die." Satan had poisoned Eve's mind with lies so that she ate, and in eating, she immediately died—that is, she was spiritually separated from God. Later she would die physically, and apart from God's redemptive grace, she would finally and eternally die to God. All her offspring followed in her footsteps, including Cain, who was of the Evil One and murdered his brother (1 John 3:12).

20. *Prince of the demons* (Matt. 9:34; 12:24; Mark 3:22; Luke 11:15): See "Beelzebul" above.

---

3. See Robert L. Alden, "Lucifer, Who or What?," *BETS* 11, no. 1 (1968): 35–39.

21. *Prince of the power of the air* (Eph. 2:2): Satan rules over "the power" of demons, some of whom temporarily reside between God's heaven and the earth. Paul expanded on this concept, writing about "the spiritual forces of evil in the heavenly places" (Eph. 6:12). See "Abaddon," "Apollyon," "Beelzebul," "Evil One," "God of this world," and "King" above and "Ruler of this world" and "Star" below.

22. *Roaring lion* (1 Pet. 5:8): See "Adversary" above.

23. *Ruler of this world* (John 12:31; 14:30; 16:11): By God's sovereign ordinance, Satan is the spiritual prince (Gk. *archōn*) of this world (Gk. *kosmos*). The term "world" is used here in the sense of the global system that is hostile to God under Satan's dominion (1 John 5:19). This rulership began in Eden (Genesis 3) with evil results that will continue until the final judgment (Revelation 20). See "Abaddon," "Apollyon," "Beelzebul," "Evil One," "God of this world," "King," and "Prince of the power of the air" above and "Star" below.

24. *Satan* (Matt. 4:10–Rev. 20:7): This is the name used most often to refer to the Devil, appearing eighteen times in the Old Testament and thirty-six times in the New Testament. It basically means adversary, enemy, or opposition. From the time of Satan's spiritual/moral fall (Isa. 14:12–14) to his final judgment (Rev. 20:7–10), Satan has been the chief initiator, instigator, and perpetrator of evil aggression both against and within the purposes and plans of God. See "Adversary" and "Enemy" above.

25. *Serpent* (Gen. 3:1, 4, 13–14; Isa. 27:1; 2 Cor. 11:3; Rev. 12:9; 20:2): Although the names Satan, Devil, and Evil One are not used in Genesis 3, the imagery of the crafty serpent of old (Gen. 3:1) is unmistakably identified with the Devil or Satan on four later occasions. See "Dragon" and "Leviathan" above.

26. *Spirit* (1 Kings 22:21–23; 2 Chron. 18:20–22; Eph. 2:2): Satan is clearly marked as a "spirit" in contrast to a human being.

27. *Star* (Rev. 9:1, 11): All angels are created beings (Neh. 9:6; Ps. 148:2, 5; Col. 1:16). Angels are pictured as stars (Job 38:7) who were created early in the creation sequence and sang praises throughout the following days. Unholy angels, that is, demons (or stars of heaven), were pressed into service by Satan (Rev. 12:4). Revelation 9:1 portrays Satan as a "star fallen from heaven" and 9:11 identifies him as "king" over demons, "the angel of the bottomless pit," "Abaddon," and "Apollyon," (cf. Isa. 14:13). See "Abaddon," "Apollyon," "Beelzebul," "Evil One," "God of this world," "King," "Lucifer," "Prince of the power of the air," and "Ruler of this world" above.

28. *Strong man* (Matt. 12:29; Mark 3:27; Luke 11:21): While Jesus acknowledged that Satan was a "strong man" (Gk. *ischyros*), he asserted that he was stronger (Luke 11:22) and thus able to overpower the forces of evil that Satan ruled.

29. *Tempter* (Matt. 4:1, 3; Mark 1:13; Luke 4:2, 13; 1 Cor. 7:5; 10:13; 1 Thess. 3:5): See "Father of lies," "Liar," and "Lying spirit" above.

Satan's History

As we have seen, numerous biblical references to Satan, using a variety of names, titles, and descriptions, profile the Devil's activities from the beginning of time to the end, but Scripture recounts very few specific historical events involving him. These few moments portray Satan either opposing God or focused on imitating God with counterfeits.

OPPOSING GOD

These limited scriptural references do not mean that the Devil has been dormant during the past two millennia.[4] The few mentions are representative of a continued diabolical pattern involving the ever-active "ruler of this world" (John 12:31; 14:30; 16:11), who is constantly at work on earth during the present age. He not only "prowls around like a roaring lion, seeking someone to devour" (1 Pet. 5:8), but he is also involved in a host of other activities: he tells lies (John 8:44); he influences people to lie (Acts 5:3); he disguises himself as an angel of light (2 Cor. 11:13–15); he snatches the gospel from unbelieving hearts (Matt. 13:19; Mark 4:15; Luke 8:12); he holds unbelievers under his power (Eph. 2:2; 1 John 3:8–10; 5:19); he traps and deceives unbelievers, holding them captive to do his will (2 Tim. 2:26); he tempts believers to sin (1 Cor. 7:5; Eph. 4:27); he seeks to deceive the children of God (2 Cor. 11:3); he takes advantage of believers (2 Cor. 2:11); he seeks to destroy the faith of believers (Luke 22:31); he torments the servants of God (2 Cor. 12:7); he thwarts the progress of ministry (1 Thess. 2:18); and he wages war against the church (Eph. 6:11–17).

Much of Satan's work is covert. But when the Lord Jesus appeared, he drew demons out of their hiding places within people. Satan and his demonic minions were most intensely engaged during Christ's earthly ministry. Looking ahead, their maneuvering will reach a crescendo again during Daniel's seventieth week, especially the last half. The following summary highlights individual satanic incursions over time.

Old Testament. Of the eleven Old Testament events, four (36 percent) deal with Satan's creation, moral fall, deception of Eve, and the Edenic curse. Of the twenty-five total occasions in the whole Bible, these four in the Old Testament and six more in the New Testament refer to the beginning of time or the end of time (40 percent). The Old Testament events include the following:

1. Creation of Satan: beginning of creation (Neh. 9:6; Job 38:7; Ps. 148:2, 5; Ezek. 28:13, 15; Col. 1:16)
2. Moral fall of Satan: postcreation (Isa. 14:12–13; Rev. 12:4)
3. Deception of Eve: post–moral fall (Gen. 3:1–6; 2 Cor. 11:1–3; 1 Tim. 2:14; Rev. 12:9; 20:2)
4. Edenic curse: postdeception (Gen. 3:15; John 16:11; Rom. 16:20)
5. Accusing Job: ca. 2250 BC (Job 1–2)
6. Dispute with Michael: ca. 1405 BC (Jude 9)
7. Provocation of David: ca. 975 BC (1 Chron. 21:1)
8. Lying to Ahab: ca. 853 BC (1 Kings 22:1–40; 2 Chron. 18:1–34)
9. Influencing the king of Babylon: ca. 700–681 BC (Isa. 14:12–14)

---

4. This paragraph is adapted from Matt Waymeyer, "The Binding of Satan in Revelation 20," *MSJ* 26, no. 1 (2015): 21. Used by permission of *MSJ*.

10. Influencing the king of Tyre: ca. 590–570 BC (Ezek. 28:12–17)
11. Accusing the high priest: ca. 480–470 BC (Zech. 3:1–2)

Some have suggested that Psalm 82 relates to God's rebuke of Satan's or demons' rulership. It seems best, however, to understand this psalm as involving God's confrontation of earthly, human rulers because of (1) the nature of psalms; (2) the language being most naturally understood as human; and (3) Christ's use of Psalm 82:6 in John 10:34, which points to earthly human rulers, not spiritual beings.

New Testament. Of the fourteen New Testament events, five deal with Christ's life from birth to crucifixion, and six describe the end of time, together accounting for nearly 80 percent of the New Testament entries. The New Testament events include the following:

1. Birth of Christ: ca. 5–4 BC (Rev. 12:4)
2. Temptation of Christ: ca. AD 27–28 (Matt. 4:1–11; Mark 1:12–13; Luke 4:1–13)
3. Debilitating a woman: ca. AD 29–30 (Luke 13:16)
4. Sifting of Peter: ca. AD 30 (Luke 22:31)
5. Defection of Judas: ca. AD 30 (Luke 22:3; John 13:2, 27)
6. Influencing the lie of Ananias: ca. AD 31–32 (Acts 5:3)
7. Hindering Paul: ca. AD 51 (1 Thess. 2:18)
8. Inflicting Paul: ca. AD 55–56 (2 Cor. 12:7)
9. Final banishment from heaven: middle of Daniel's seventieth week (Rev. 12:7–13)
10. Empowering the Antichrist and the False Prophet: middle of Daniel's seventieth week (Rev. 13:2, 4)
11. Performing false signs: last half of Daniel's seventieth week (Rev. 16:13–14)
12. Millennial incarceration: Christ's millennial kingdom (Rev. 20:1–3)
13. Final battle: end of Christ's millennial kingdom (Rev. 20:7–9)
14. Final judgment: end of Christ's millennial kingdom (Isa. 27:1; Rev. 20:10)

IMITATING GOD

Satan operates as the unrivaled master of disguise (Gk. *metaschēmatizō*, 2 Cor. 11:13–15). He makes the bad appear good. He decorates sinful behavior to look righteous. His lies sound attractively better than the truth. He compellingly preaches the perversion that wrong is right and right is wrong. He remains the messenger of darkness while masquerading as an angel of light. He falsely gives a polished appearance of authenticity to all that is spiritually counterfeit.

The Devil substitutes the worldly things that give people instant pleasure for the holy things that bring God eternal glory. He camouflages his diabolical lies to be so appealing to people that they reject God's truth. He elevates thoughts about self to such a height that people then worship the creature rather than God the Creator (Rom. 1:25).

Satan mimics and imitates the holy things of God, while all along, his cheap substitutes continue as the abominable things of the prince of darkness. Preachers during the Reformation period called Satan "God's ape," who mimicked God by disguising the false to appear genuine, thus luring sinners to himself and away from God.[5]

The major counterfeits of Satan listed in Scripture include the following:

1. The Trinity, as (1) dragon/Satan (Rev. 13:4), (2) Beast/Antichrist (Rev. 13:4), and (3) the False Prophet (Rev. 13:11; see 16:13)
2. The kingdom, but actually the "domain of darkness"(Col. 1:13 NASB)
3. Angels (Matt. 25:41; 2 Cor. 11:14; 12:7; Rev. 12:7)
4. The throne (Rev. 2:13)
5. Churches (Rev. 2:9; 3:9)
6. Worship (Rom. 1:25; Rev. 13:4)
7. Workers (2 Cor. 11:13, 15)
8. Christs (Matt. 24:5, 24; Mark 13:22; 1 John 2:18, 22)
9. Prophets (Matt. 7:15; 24:11, 24; Mark 13:22; 2 Pet. 2:1)
10. Apostles (2 Cor. 11:13; Rev. 2:2)
11. Teachers (2 Pet. 2:1)
12. Believers (Matt. 13:38, 40; 2 Cor. 11:26; Gal. 2:4)
13. The gospel (Gal. 1:6–7)
14. Theology (1 Tim. 4:1)
15. Mysteries (2 Thess. 2:7; Rev. 2:24)
16. Miracles (Matt. 7:21–23; 2 Thess. 2:9; Rev. 16:13–14)
17. Communion (1 Cor. 10:20–21)

Satan's Power

Satan possesses the highest power of created beings, but his power does not begin to compare with God's, who is omnipotent (Jer. 32:17), omniscient (Ps. 139:1–6), omnipresent (Ps. 139:7–10), immutable (Ps. 102:27), sovereign (1 Chron. 29:11–12), eternal (Ps. 90:2), immortal (1 Tim. 1:17), great (Ps. 135:5), and self-existent (Isa. 44:6). Satan possesses none of these divine attributes, which belong uniquely to the Creator.

Satan's power can at least be equal to that of Michael the archangel (Dan. 10:13, 21; 12:1; Jude 9; Rev. 12:7). No human being possesses the supernatural power that belongs to Satan. He is powerful in heaven (1 Kings 22:19–23; 2 Chron. 18:18–22; Job 1–2; Zech. 3:1–5; Rev. 12:7) and on earth (Job 1:7; 1 Pet. 5:8).

Satan clearly strategizes (Gk. *noēma*, 2 Cor. 2:11; 11:3). He is a master tactician (Gk. *methodeia*, Eph. 6:11). And he excels at deceiving and entrapping (Gk. *planaō*, Rev. 12:9; 20:8; *pagis*, 1 Tim. 3:7; 2 Tim. 2:26).

Satan rules (Gk. *archōn*) this world's sinful system (John 12:31; 14:30; 16:11; Eph. 6:12; Rev. 13:2, 4–5, 7). He is also "the prince of the power of the air," that is, the ruler (Gk. *archōn*) over his demonic host (Matt. 25:41; Rev. 12:7, 9) who primarily dwell in the realm between earth and the third heaven. In heaven, Satan constantly

---

5. Thomas Watson, *A Body of Practical Divinity* (1692; repr., Aberdeen: George King and Robert King, 1838), 46.

accuses believers before God (Rev. 12:10). During the latter half of Daniel's seventieth week, Satan will lend his power to do false signs and wonders by the hands of the Antichrist (2 Thess. 2:9–10) and also by the False Prophet (Rev. 13:13–14) and demons (Rev. 16:13–14).

Satan has the power of death, but Christ has rendered him powerless for believers in Christ (Heb. 2:14). Satan has the power of deceit (2 Cor. 11:3, 14–15), but Christ has exposed him (2 Cor. 2:11) and destroyed the effect of his work (1 John 3:8). Satan has the power to imprison people (Rev. 2:10), but God's Word cannot be imprisoned (2 Tim. 2:9). Satan can dwell in a city (Rev. 2:13), but only God can dwell within a believer (1 John 4:4). Satan has the power of personal accusation and defamation (Rev. 12:10), but Christ is the believer's advocate at the right hand of God the Father (1 John 2:1), continually making intercession for those who believe (Rom. 8:33–34; Heb. 7:25). No power of Satan, regardless of how great, will separate a true believer from the love of God (Rom. 8:35–39). Satan is strong (Luke 11:21), but Christ is stronger (Luke 11:22).

God at times even limits Satan's power (Job 1:6–12; 2:1–6). Christ rejected his power and authority (Matt. 4:1–11). Christ healed those who were oppressed by the Devil (Acts 10:38). Paul was empowered to enlighten the minds of unbelievers so that they would turn "from the power of Satan to God" (Acts 26:18). Believers can overcome his power (James 4:7; 1 John 2:13–14). Ultimately, the Devil's power will be revoked permanently (1 Cor. 15:24; Rev. 12:9–10; 20:1–3, 7–10).

Satan's Schemes

Satan has sinned (1 John 3:8), deceived (2 Cor. 11:3), and murdered from the beginning (John 8:44). While God stood for light, life, and truth, Satan represented darkness, death, and deceit. Satan's *modus operandi* has been to deceive the entire world throughout all history, from the beginning with Adam and Eve (Gen. 3:1–24) to the end of time (Rev. 12:9; 20:3, 8).

Scripture uses three words to describe how Satan functions: (1) "snare" or "trap" (Gk. *pagis*), such as a hunter would use to capture and then kill an animal (1 Tim. 3:7; 2 Tim. 2:26); (2) "designs" or "strategies" (Gk. *noēma*), that is, the battle plan of a skilled military commander (2 Cor. 2:11); and (3) "schemes" or "specific tactics" (Gk. *methodeia*), which soldiers would execute in an actual battle (Eph. 6:11). Using lies and deceit, the Devil attempts to bring the world around to his perverted thinking and away from the pure truth of God.

Satan rules as the commanding general of the opposing army. He attempts daily to outwit or outthink believers in spiritual warfare. Deviousness colors Satan's character and conduct. He is a guerilla warrior who disguises himself as an angel of light (2 Cor. 11:14). To make the battle more difficult, Satan wages an invisible spiritual war using the most deceitfully clever tactics ever devised. He stands committed to spiritual espionage. He appears as a friend on the outside, but inside he remains the deceiving enemy. His lying statements, garnished with truth, are poison to the soul. His servants falsely present themselves as advocates of righteousness (2 Cor. 11:15).

While this all sounds daunting, even overwhelming, Paul writes to the Corinthians that we should "not be outwitted by Satan; for we are not ignorant of his designs" (2 Cor. 2:11). Exploring the schemes of the Devil helps prepare us to resist him.

SATAN'S TARGET[6]

Where does Satan aim his fiery darts (Eph. 6:16)? Paul gives a clear answer in 2 Corinthians 11:3: "But I am afraid that as the serpent deceived Eve by his cunning, your thoughts will be led astray from a sincere and pure devotion to Christ."

The Greek words translated "designs" in 2 Corinthians 2:11 and "schemes" in Ephesians 6:11 both refer to Satan's manipulation of the mind. Satan plays mind games with Christians. Human minds are Satan's chief target. The Christian's thought life becomes the battlefield for spiritual conquest. This truth is reinforced by the Bible's frequent statements on the importance of believers possessing spiritually strong minds (Matt. 22:37; Rom. 12:2; 2 Cor. 4:4; 10:5; Phil. 4:8; Col. 3:2; 1 Pet. 1:13).

Since Satan aims at the Christian's mind, what does he want to accomplish? Before answering this significant question, consider two scriptures:

For as he thinks within himself, so he is. (Prov. 23:7 NASB)

As in water face reflects face, so the heart of man reflects the man. (Prov. 27:19)

Who one is on the inside determines who one is on the outside. Thus, Satan attempts to corrupt minds so he can corrupt lives. *Satan's chief activity in the lives of Christians is to cause them to think contrary to God's Word and thus act disobediently to God's will.* The seventeenth-century Puritan preacher Thomas Watson put it this way: "This is Satan's master-piece . . . ; if he can but keep them from believing the truth, he is sure to keep them from obeying it."[7]

Every military leader devours intelligence reports on the enemy before he enters battle. The intelligence report on Satan is in the Bible. Therefore, ignorance of the enemy will never be a valid excuse for defeat. God has given Christians a decided edge in the contest with advance information on the enemy.

SATAN'S FIERY DARTS[8]

Satan will reach his goals by employing several well-chosen, unholy strategies in the Christian's life. Satan has four major objectives against the Christian. If he can accomplish one or more, he is moving toward his goals. It is important to understand these objectives, because Satan's attacks will fall under one or more of these four broad areas.

---

6. This section is adapted from Richard Mayhue, *Unmasking Satan: Understanding Satan's Battle Plan and Biblical Strategies for Fighting Back* (Grand Rapids, MI: Kregel, 2001), 20–22. Used by permission of Kregel Publications.
7. Watson, *A Body of Practical Divinity*, 287.
8. This section is adapted from Mayhue, *Unmasking Satan*, 22–24. Used by permission of Kregel Publications.

First, Satan will attempt to *distort or deny the truth of God's Word*. That's how Satan tripped up Peter in Matthew 16. Jesus had earlier called Satan's bluff, however, and the Devil failed in his attempt on Christ (Matt. 4:1–11). Satan will even deny unbelievers access to the Word of God, as illustrated by the seed falling on hard ground in Christ's parable of the sower (Matt. 13:3–4, 18–19).

Second, Satan will try to *discredit the testimony of God's people*. This strategy succeeded with Ananias and Sapphira (Acts 5:1–11). Satan has also tried it on Christian leaders (1 Tim. 3:7).

Next, by *depressing or destroying the believer's enthusiasm for God's work*, Satan will assault one's soul. The roaring lion of hell attempted this on both Paul (2 Cor. 12:7–10) and Peter (Luke 22:31–34).

Fourth, if Satan can *dilute the effectiveness of God's people*, he will be moving toward his goals. David (1 Chron. 21:1–8) knew the pain inflicted with this type of attack, as have new converts to the faith (1 Tim. 3:6).

For each strategy, Satan employs a variety of tactics or specific spiritual warfare techniques to achieve victory. The Bible identifies over twenty tactics in the historical narratives and teaching portions of Scripture. If believers think as God thinks and thwart the schemes of Satan, he will not take advantage of them. Victory is promised if Christians let the Word of God richly dwell within them (Col. 3:16).

The Bible exposes the devilish mindsets that Satan has attempted to foist on various people throughout time. Note carefully that they are all very much a part of current secular thinking. The tactics of Satan as revealed in the Bible are listed below and personalized, organized under the Devil's four major strategies. For each poisonous tactic designed to deceive, the antidote of God's truth is given.

The Adversary's First Strategy. Satan will attempt to *distort or deny the truth of God's Word.*

1. *Sensualism*: Attractiveness and desirability have replaced God's Word as my standard for determining God's best in my life (Gen. 3:1–6).
   God's Mind: 2 Timothy 3:16–17
2. *Sensationalism*: I believe that immediate success is more desirable than success in God's time (Matt. 4:1–11).
   God's Mind: 1 Corinthians 1:18–25
3. *Universalism*: Because we live together in the same world with the same kind of imperfections, we will live together in eternity (Matt. 13:24–30).
   God's Mind: John 1:12–13; 3:36; 5:24
4. *Rationalism*: I will substitute human reason for simple childlike faith anchored in the Word of God (Matt. 16:21–23).
   God's Mind: Isaiah 55:9
5. *Existentialism*: I am the master of my fate and the captain of my soul (2 Cor. 4:4).
   God's Mind: John 3:16–21
6. *Illusionism*: I believe that everything that appears or claims to be of God is of God without further investigation (2 Cor. 11:13–15).
   God's Mind: Deuteronomy 13:1–5; 1 John 4:1–4

7. *Ecumenism*: I believe that all sincere religions involve valid expressions of worshiping the true God (Rev. 2:9; 3:9).
   God's Mind: Acts 4:12
8. *Humanism*: I alone can defeat Satan without God's help (Jude 9).
   God's Mind: John 15:5

The Adversary's Second Strategy. Satan will try to *discredit the testimony of God's people.*

1. *Situationalism*: I believe that God's Word is flexible enough to bend when I judge that the situation demands it (Acts 5:1–11).
   God's Mind: Psalm 119:89
2. *Individualism*: My chief marriage responsibility is to satisfy myself, not my partner (1 Cor. 7:1–5).
   God's Mind: Ephesians 5:22–25
3. *Isolationism*: My reputation will have an effect on no one else but me (1 Tim. 3:7).
   God's Mind: 2 Samuel 12:14; 1 Timothy 6:1; Titus 2:5
4. *Hedonism*: Because God has removed my home responsibilities, I am free to satisfy myself while the church supports me (1 Tim. 5:14–15).
   God's Mind: 2 Thessalonians 3:10

The Adversary's Third Strategy. Satan will seek to *depress or destroy the believer's enthusiasm for God's work.*

1. *Materialism*: I prize material and physical blessings more highly than my spiritual relationship with Jesus Christ (Job 1:1–2:13).
   God's Mind: Matthew 6:33
2. *Defeatism*: Because I have failed, I am no longer useful in the King's service (Luke 22:31–34).
   God's Mind: Psalm 32:1–7
3. *Negativism*: My weakness prevents me from being effective for God (2 Cor. 12:7–10).
   God's Mind: Philippians 4:13
4. *Pessimism*: The difficult circumstances in my life cause me to doubt that I will ever accomplish anything significant for God (1 Thess. 2:17–3:2).
   God's Mind: Psalm 37:23–24

The Adversary's Fourth Strategy. Satan will aim to *dilute the effectiveness of God's people.*

1. *Egotism*: I will attribute what I am or what I will achieve to my own accomplishments rather than to God's activities in my life (1 Chron. 21:1; 1 Tim. 3:6).
   God's Mind: Jeremiah 9:24–25; 1 Peter 5:6
2. *Nominalism*: Because I am saved and my sins are forgiven, my present lifestyle is unimportant (Zech. 3:1–5).
   God's Mind: 1 John 2:1–6
3. *Cultism*: My salvation will be based on works rather than on faith in Jesus Christ (Luke 22:3–6).
   God's Mind: Ephesians 2:8–9

4. *Uniformitarianism*: My relationship with trespassing believers will remain the same despite their repentance and change of heart toward God (2 Cor. 2:5–11).
   God's Mind: Ephesians 4:32
5. *Assertivism*: It is healthy for me to vent my anger frequently for lengthy periods of time (Eph. 4:26–27).
   God's Mind: James 1:19–20

THE PROTOTYPICAL ASSAULT[9]

The most massive and far-reaching assault Satan ever launched was the initial one on Adam and Eve. Although it involved only two people, the episode affected the entire human race throughout all time, as everyone since then has been born dead in sin (Eph. 2:1–3). That is why Jesus referred to Satan as "the father of lies" and a murderer from the beginning (John 8:44). This was the mediate or indirect cause of all sin, which leads to the immediate or present course of contemporary sinful activity.

That greatest of all hoaxes with the most devastating effect on humanity is recorded in Genesis 3. Satan, the master of deceit, conned Eve into rejecting God's truthfulness and then acting independently of him. The first parents, Adam and Eve, were deceived by the Devil's trickery, and every person thereafter has suffered the consequences. The five aspects of that assault have constituted Satan's prototypical method for attacking humanity ever since.

Disguise. In Genesis 3:1, Satan arrived, craftily disguised as a serpent. The word "crafty" can be used positively or negatively. From the context here, it is used in a negative sense. The same word is used in Joshua 9:4 of the Gibeonites, crafty people, who tricked Joshua and the leadership of Israel. In the same way, Satan came disguised as a serpent to Eve.

Dialogue. Satan spoke to the woman. At first glance, it seemed like an innocent, religious discussion, but Satan was out to deceive. Satan in effect said, "Just one question, Eve. I want to make sure I have it right. Did God really say you shall not eat from any tree of the garden?" What she did not know was that she was doing battle with the greatest guerrilla fighter ever.

By the end of Genesis 3:1, Satan used three tactics on Eve that later proved fatal. First, he divided in order to conquer. He did not take Adam and Eve on as husband and wife. He singled out Eve, and he entered into an apparently innocent dialogue with her. This points to the high premium God places on the oneness of husband and wife, because they strengthen, encourage, edify, and build up one another.

Second, he surprised Eve with an unscheduled and obviously spectacular encounter. That is, he did something that was so surprising and unexpected that it threw her off balance. Eve at this moment was not practicing the presence of God, for had she been, she would surely have understood the danger.

---

9. This section is adapted from Richard Mayhue, *Bible Boot Camp: Spiritual Battles in the Bible and What They Can Teach You* (Fearn, Ross-shire, Scotland: Christian Focus, 2005), 44–53. Used by permission of Christian Focus.

Third, he made a seemingly innocent inquiry. He came with an apparent need to know what God had said. The Hebrew construction, though, suggests that the question he asked was not a research question but rather a question of ridicule. It might be better phrased, "Is it really true that God has said . . . ?" A modern-day paraphrase would be, "You've got to be kidding, Eve. God didn't *really* say you can't eat from any tree in the garden, did he?"

Doubt. This question is easy to answer because the answer is recorded in Genesis 2:16–17. God didn't say that they couldn't eat from any tree in the garden. As a matter of fact, God created a pristine environment for them to live in; everything was absolutely perfect. There was only one prohibition.

However, in her paraphrase of God's original words, Eve had begun in her own mind to question the certainty of death and judgment. One can see the masterful stroke of Satan, who planted a seed of doubt and watched Eve cultivate it. Soon, it became a blatant denial of the truthfulness, applicability, and trustworthiness of God.

Denial. In Genesis 3:4–5, Satan fed Eve five lies disguised by partial truth. The first lie claimed that Eve would not die. As the Hebrew text highlights, Satan very emphatically denied that eating from the forbidden tree would result in death. The truth of the matter is that when they ate, they did not die immediately in a physical sense. However, they did immediately die spiritually in their relationship with God. *Death* means separation. Adam and Eve thought only in the physical realm. Nonetheless, when they ate, they were spiritually separated from God by their sin. That spiritual death led them to their later physical death.

The second lie can be inferred from Genesis 3:4. Satan implied that if God said they would die but they did not, then God's word was unreliable. If it was unreliable, then there was no good reason to believe or live by it. With doubt rapidly translating into denial, Eve moved decisively to abandon the authority of God's word. In so doing, she changed the course not only of her life and her family but of the whole human race.

Then came the third lie: "For God knows that when you eat of it your eyes will be opened, and you will be like God, knowing good and evil" (Gen. 3:5). Most of what Satan said was true, but he left out one important fact. Adam and Eve were not unchangeably holy in nature like God. Rather, they were susceptible to sin if disobedience was a part of their life. They disobeyed and ate of the fruit. They sinned and God judged. They were cursed along with the Serpent and the world. Ever since then, all humanity has been cursed with sin. They and everyone else have known "good" and "evil" by experience. The ultimate intent of Satan's lie was to humanize God and deify man, to say that God can become like man and man can become like God. That lie still exists in many cults today.

The fourth lie also appears in Genesis 3:5. Satan tried to pry open the mind of Eve with the thought that God wished to jealously maintain his uniqueness, that he wanted to maintain his deity and not share it with anyone. Satan implied that this was bad, not good. Further, God was not really protecting man's sinlessness by his prohibition; rather, he was protecting his deity.

A final untruth has proven to be the lie among lies: "I, Satan, have your best interest at heart. Believe me, not God." That is the bottom line in this discussion. In all five lies, Satan has woven together an immense assault to pummel Eve with the thought that God's Word is untrue and unreliable and that, therefore, she ought to follow the desires of her own heart rather than the dictates of God's Word.

Deliberation. The scientific method did not surface in the nineteenth century. It did not originate with the industrial revolution. Rather, its roots go back to Genesis 3, when Eve concluded that the only way that she could decide whether God was right or wrong was to test him with her mind and senses. Autonomous empirical research originated with Eve in Eden.

Paul put it this way in Romans 1:25, speaking of those who would follow the path of Eve and then Adam: "They exchanged the truth about God for a lie and worshiped and served the creature rather than the Creator." By this time Eve had basically bought into the lies of Satan and believed that she now had a choice. Either she could choose to eat or she could choose to refrain. God's Word was no longer authoritative; it no longer dictated what was right and wrong in her life. God's Word was no longer binding, because all of a sudden, there were alternatives.

Genesis 3:6 describes Eve's mental process: "So when the woman saw that the tree was good for food, and that it was a delight to the eyes, and that the tree was to be desired to make one wise, she took of its fruit and ate, and she also gave some to her husband who was with her, and he ate." Here appears the "scientific method"— autonomous empirical research in its infancy. Eve decided that she would run tests on the tree to see whether God or Satan was right.

She subjected the tree to a trio of tests, the first being that of physical value. She observed the tree, and in observing she saw that it was good for food. It had nutritional value ("the desires of the flesh," 1 John 2:16).

Based on this positive response, she ran a second test. Eve discovered that it was a delight to the eyes ("the desires of the eyes," 1 John 2:16). Not only would it benefit her body nutritionally, but it had emotional or aesthetic value. It was pleasing. It did not give her a bad sensation. To put it in modern language, she felt good about looking at the tree.

Eve wasn't satisfied yet. She perhaps thought, "I'll take it one step further." With her third test, then, she looked and saw that the tree was desirable to make one wise. It had intellectual value. It would allow her to possess wisdom like God ("pride of life," 1 John 2:16).

In the midst of Eve's deliberation, she tested God. She saw that the tree really was good. It met her needs physically, aesthetically, and intellectually. That led to disobedience, for Eve rejected God's instructions and took from its fruit and ate (Gen. 3:6).

The battle in Genesis 3 was first for the mind and then for the soul. It was to cause Eve to think contrary to the Word of God. When she bought into wrong thinking, she bought into wrong motives, wrong responses, and wrong actions. She bought into the scheme of sensualism, the attempt to make attractiveness and desirability replace truth as the metrics for determining God's best in life. The implications of sensualism are incredibly important for a money-hungry, product-hungry, pleasure-seeking society.

Satan's battle is first for the mind. He lures people to think his thoughts and then, through doubt and denial, to put the Word of God aside and to test life with their own senses, even if the conclusions convolute the truth of God.

Death. "Then the eyes of both were opened, and they knew that they were naked. And they sewed fig leaves together and made themselves loincloths" (Gen. 3:7). Adam and Eve's minds were affected, and they suddenly perceived evil. They suddenly knew they were naked, and so they desired to cover up their nakedness. Before, when they were naked in the garden, all was pure, as Genesis 2:25 reports: "And the man and his wife were both naked and were not ashamed." But afterward they were naked and ashamed.

Guilt had entered the human race. "But the LORD God called to the man, and said to him, 'Where are you?'" (Gen. 3:9). God did not ask where they were because he did not know; he just wanted to alert Adam that he was there. "And he said, 'I heard the sound of you in the garden, and I was afraid, because I was naked, and I hid myself.' And God said, 'Who told you that you were naked? Have you eaten of the tree of which I commanded you not to eat?'" (Gen. 3:10–11). Evil had found them out. They were spiritually separated from God.

Conflict also arose between the man and woman. They began to blame each other: "The man said, 'The woman whom you gave to be with me, she gave me fruit of the tree, and I ate.' Then the LORD God said to the woman, 'What is this that you have done?'" (Gen. 3:12–13). Eve in effect responded, "It's not my fault, don't blame me, because the serpent deceived me and I ate." She experienced great guilt.

Sin's consequences stretch far beyond the one who sins. That is why the Word of God makes such a significant statement about holiness in the lives of believers (1 Pet. 1:14–16). The Word of God cites example after example of how sin committed by an individual or a couple can eventually affect whole nations.

Satan's Servant Role

Satan has well earned his title of "adversary." He has been the enemy of God ever since the garden incident. Usurping God's sovereign authority remains the Devil's chief objective. At times, it appears that "the god of this world" might overcome the God of creation and redemption. The history of his relentless opposition to God is chronicled from the snaring of Adam and Eve in the garden of Eden (Genesis 3) to the final assault on Christ's earthly kingdom (Revelation 20).

However, God's sovereignty has overruled and conquered the worst that Satan could execute. Thus, Paul wrote to the church in Rome that "all things work together for good" regarding true believers (Rom. 8:28) and then posed the question, "If God is for us, who can be against us?" (Rom. 8:31). The answer in Romans 8:32–39 unequivocally guarantees that there is no one, not even Satan!

As a matter of fact, even Satan's worst evil attacks will serve God's best righteous purposes. At the human level, Joseph told his less-than-loving brothers, "You meant evil against me, but God meant it for good" (Gen. 50:20). The brothers were actually God's servants. In the same way, Nebuchadnezzar, the pagan king of Babylon, carried out God's purposes (Jer. 25:9; 43:10), as did the Persian king Cyrus (Isa. 44:28; 45:1). These powerful monarchs served God. And on at least fourteen occasions mentioned in Scripture, so did Satan or his demons.

JUDGES 9

God sent an evil spirit between Abimelech and the leaders of Shechem. This divinely initiated act (Judg. 9:56–57) punished both sides for their idolatry and mass murder (9:1–22).

JOB 1–2

God gave Satan authority to touch all that Job had (possessions and family) but not Job himself (Job 1:12). Although Job lost his possessions and his children (1:13–19), he did not curse God. Rather, Job worshiped God. Then God granted Satan the authority to touch Job physically but not to kill him (2:6). Soon thereafter, Job suffered horribly (2:7–8). Although encouraged to do so by his wife, Job did not curse God or sin with his words (2:9–10). In both cases, Job honored God and proved wrong Satan's accusations that Job had a merely self-serving loyalty to God. In the end, God doubly blessed Job for his sincere and Satan-tested fidelity to God (42:10).

1 SAMUEL 16

After God's Spirit had departed from Saul (1 Sam. 16:14), on at least four occasions an evil or harmful spirit (demon) tormented Saul (16:14–16, 23; 18:10; 19:9). Only the harp playing of David brought Saul relief, thus causing him to love David greatly and to make him his armor bearer. As a result, at the appropriate time, David was in place to slay Goliath (17:26–49). Consequently, David found great favor with the people of Israel, especially Jonathan the son of Saul. All this then led to David becoming the king (2 Sam. 2:11; 5:4–5), which was God's plan all along, here aided by one or more of Satan's soldiers (Rev. 12:7).

1 KINGS 22 / 2 CHRONICLES 18[10]

These two texts occasion the challenge of identifying the "lying spirit" (1 Kings 22:21–23) in a way that best accounts for the reality of false prophecy in 1 Kings 22:6. Satan appropriately fits this "spirit." Demonic activity, superintended by God yet carried out by the agency of Satan, is the most probable and immediate dynamic behind this

---

10. This section is adapted from Richard L. Mayhue, "False Prophets and the Deceiving Spirit," *MSJ* 4, no. 2 (1993): 135–63. Used by permission of *MSJ*.

false prophecy. Some object that Satan is not omnipresent and could not affect all four hundred prophets simultaneously, but the answer to this objection centers on Satan's role as ruler over demons (Matt. 25:41). This relationship and the known activities of Satan provide the most theologically consistent explanation for identifying "the spirit" as Satan and the demons as Satan's workmen in the mouths of Ahab's false prophets.

Satan's influence on the four hundred prophets of Israel by the use of four hundred demons served God's purposes in at least two ways. First, it proved Micaiah to be the authentic prophet because his negative words came true concerning Ahab, in contrast to the uniformly positive message from the four hundred false prophets. Second, the defeat and death of Ahab fulfilled God's prophetic word from Elijah concerning Ahab's death (1 Kings 22:37–38; cf. 21:17–19).

1 CHRONICLES 21 / 2 SAMUEL 24

1 Chronicles 21:1 states, "Then Satan stood up against Israel and incited David to number Israel." David's latter years lacked the glory and successes of his youth. He sinned in his involvement with Uriah and Bathsheba (2 Samuel 11–12). Then came the conflict between Amnon and Absalom (2 Samuel 13), followed by Absalom's revolt and David's own eviction from the throne and capital city (2 Samuel 14–18). To top it all off, Sheba instituted a public slander campaign against the king (2 Samuel 20).

Even after all this, David believed that his success came more from his own ability than from God's faithfulness to keep his promises to Israel. David seems to have felt he could take greater confidence in the size of his army than in the power of his God, especially in light of the pressure from the people.

The king thus called Joab, his nephew and the general of David's army, and commanded him, "Go, number Israel, from Beersheba to Dan, and bring me a report that I may know their number" (1 Chron. 21:2). David yielded to the pressure of the situation, the push of the people, and Satan's relentless pounding. Joab responded to David's request, "May the Lord add to his people a hundred times as many as they are! Are they not, my lord the king, all of them my lord's servants? Why then should my lord require this? Why should it be a cause of guilt for Israel?" (1 Chron. 21:3). Joab strongly opposed the census, but the will of the king prevailed.

David bypassed two preventatives designed by God to avoid just such a disaster. First, David ran right past God's principle of seeking multiple counselors:

> Where there is no guidance, a people falls,
>   but in an abundance of counselors there is safety. (Prov. 11:14)

> For by wise guidance you can wage your war,
>   and in abundance of counselors there is victory. (Prov. 24:6)

Second, David failed to take God's counsel. Perhaps he penned these words himself: "The king is not saved by his great army; a warrior is not delivered by his great strength. The war horse is a false hope for salvation, and by its great might it cannot rescue" (Ps. 33:16–17). David sinfully put his trust in himself and his army, not in God, who had delivered him so many times before. This is where Satan won the victory, where egotism dominated David's thinking. God employed Satan (2 Sam. 24:1; cf. 1 Chron. 21:1) to test David's humility, and the king failed miserably.

ZECHARIAH 3

On several occasions, Satan has stood before God in the heavenly courts claiming that God's people are unworthy of the Lord. So he accused Job of sinful motives (Job 1:9–11; 2:4–5) and believers of being unworthy of salvation (Rev. 12:10–11). In Zechariah 3, he charged Israel with being unworthy to receive God's blessing.

The scene is invested with a judicial character. Satan stood at the right side, the place of accusation under the law (cf. Ps. 109:6), and he accused Joshua, the high priest who came back to the land in the first group of exiles with Zerubbabel (cf. Ezra 3:2; 5:2; Hag. 1:1). That Joshua was representative of the nation is evident from (1) the emphasis on the nation in these visions, (2) the fact that the rebuke in Zechariah 3:2 is based not on Joshua but on God's choice of Jerusalem, (3) the identification in Zechariah 3:8 of Joshua and his fellow priests as symbolic of future Israel, and (4) the reference to the land in Zechariah 3:9.

The malicious prosecuting adversary stood in the presence of the Lord to proclaim Israel's sins and their unworthiness of God's favor.[11] The situation was crucial: if Joshua was vindicated, Israel would be accepted; if Joshua was rejected, Israel would be rejected. The outcome would reveal the entire plan of God for the nation. Israel's hopes would either be destroyed or confirmed.

By using the phrase "filthy garments" (Zech. 3:3–4)—the most loathsome, vile term for filth, a reference to excrement—the prophet pictured the priesthood and the people's habitual condition of defilement (Isa. 4:4; 64:6). This became the basis of Satan's accusation that the nation was morally impure and unworthy of God's protection and blessing.

God responded that although he would keep his promise to justify Israel and reinstate the nation as his priestly people to serve in his house, keep his courts, and have complete access to his presence—all based on his sovereign, electing love and not by merit or works of man—that would not be fulfilled until Israel was faithful to the Lord. The promise awaited the fulfillment of Zechariah 12:10–13:1. The Lord used the occasion of Satan's accusations to declare that Israel had not forfeited the promises that God made to Abraham and David.

MATTHEW 4[12]

God himself is never the immediate agent of temptation (James 1:13), but here—as in the book of Job—God ordains and uses satanic tempting to serve his sovereign

---

11. This paragraph is adapted from John MacArthur, ed., *The MacArthur Study Bible: English Standard Version* (Wheaton, IL: Crossway, 2010), 1310–11. Charts and notes from *The MacArthur Study Bible: English Standard Version* originate with *The MacArthur Study Bible*, copyright © 1997 by Thomas Nelson. Used by permission of Thomas Nelson. www.thomasnelson.com.

12. This section is adapted from MacArthur, *MacArthur Study Bible: English Standard Version*, 1364–65. Used by permission of Thomas Nelson.

purposes. Christ was tempted in all points of human weakness (Heb. 4:15; 1 John 2:16): Satan tempted him with "the desires of the flesh" (1 John 2:16; cf. Matt. 4:2–3), "the desires of the eyes" (1 John 2:16; cf. Matt. 4:8–9), and the "pride of life" (1 John 2:16; cf. Matt. 4:5–6).

When Satan says, "If you are the Son of God . . ." (Matt. 4:3, 6), the conditional "if" carries the meaning of "since" in this context. There was no doubt in Satan's mind who Jesus was, but Satan's design was to get him to violate the plan of God and employ the divine power that he had set aside in his humiliation (cf. Phil. 2:7).

All three of Jesus's replies to the Devil were taken from Deuteronomy. The first one, from Deuteronomy 8:3, states that God allowed Israel to hunger, so that he might feed them with manna and teach them to trust him to provide for them. So the verse is directly applicable to Jesus's circumstances and a fitting reply to Satan's temptation that Jesus fulfill his desires of the flesh.

In the second case, Satan also quoted Scripture (Matt. 4:6; cf. Ps. 91:11–12)—but utterly twisted its meaning by employing a passage about trusting God to justify testing him. Christ replied (Matt. 4:7) with another verse from Israel's wilderness experience (Deut. 6:16)—recalling the experience at Massah, where the grumbling Israelites put the Lord to the test, angrily demanding that Moses produce water where there was none (Ex. 17:2–7).

Finally, Christ cited Deuteronomy 6:13–14, again relating to the Israelites' wilderness experiences. Christ, like them, was led into the wilderness to be tested (cf. Deut. 8:2). Unlike them, he withstood every aspect of that fierce test.

Satan's failure to tempt Christ into sin proved at least three essential truths concerning Christ's deity: Christ's impeccability, Christ's unswerving allegiance to the truth of God's Word, and Christ's superiority and authority over Satan.

LUKE 22

Satan demanded to sift Peter like wheat, and Christ granted his request (Luke 22:31). But Christ also prayed that Peter would recover, be spiritually strengthened by the experience, and be enabled to lead the disciples (22:32). While Peter could not imagine that he would ever fail Christ (22:33), Jesus stated emphatically that the disciple would shortly deny him three times (22:34).

After Peter denied Christ three times, he went out and wept bitterly (22:62). But a sense of God's love, mercy, and grace must have stirred Peter because several days later, he was back in the fellowship of the disciples. The eleven reassembled after Christ's crucifixion, and when the women reported Christ's resurrection (24:10–11) to them, Peter, along with John, raced to the tomb to see if this could be true (24:12). Peter had faced up to his fall and thus could rejoin the disciples. The disciples openly welcomed him back, not only because of his honest admission but also because they knew from Christ's words that Satan had set him up.

Peter was there when Christ appeared later that night as the disciples met behind locked doors (24:36–43). Peter could face the Savior because he had turned his back on his denial, admitted it, and returned as Christ had instructed him. Later on, Christ restored Peter to ministry. In the midst of a seaside breakfast, Jesus told Peter, "Feed my lambs. . . . Tend my sheep. . . . Feed my sheep" (John 21:15–17). The Master reaffirmed his trust in Peter and his ability to minister.

As Paul's thorn had two sides, one for Satan and another for God, so did Peter's sifting. He was now prepared to understand both Satan's fury, which nearly destroyed his ministry, and God's power, which sustained him in the battle. It is not surprising, then, that on the day of Pentecost, Peter fearlessly stepped out as God's chief spokesman. Peter stands as the dominant figure in establishing the church, as recorded in Acts 1–12.

JOHN 13

Satan served God in a most unusual and unexpected way in regard to Christ's death. Before the Passover meal, Satan entered Judas (Luke 22:3–6; cf. John 13:2), who began to scheme with the chief priests about how to betray him. During the supper, Satan again entered Judas, whom Christ then dispatched to quickly carry out his treacherous scheme (John 13:27). God used Satan to initiate the early morning events that led to Christ's death.

It is not surprising that Satan was involved, nor Judas. But this is the supreme example of God using Satan as his servant to be the catalyst for something that God had actually planned in eternity past. Amazingly, this case would result in believers being released from diabolical dominion in the kingdom of darkness:

> Men of Israel, hear these words: Jesus of Nazareth, a man attested to you by God with mighty works and wonders and signs that God did through him in your midst, as you yourselves know—this Jesus, delivered up according to the definite plan and foreknowledge of God, you crucified and killed by the hands of lawless men. God raised him up, loosing the pangs of death, because it was not possible for him to be held by it. (Acts 2:22–24)

ACTS 5

It is not shocking to read that "the father of lies" (John 8:44) filled the heart of Ananias to lie to the Holy Spirit (Acts 5:3). Ananias had an accomplice—his wife, Sapphira. As a result, they were killed by God in front of the Jerusalem assembly (Acts 5:5, 10).

Why was God so severe? Why is he not so harsh with unbelievers who lie? Peter wrote that judgment begins first with the household of God (1 Pet. 4:17). Paul later warned the Corinthians that because they profaned the Lord's Table, some were weak and sick, and a number had "died" by God's hand of judgment (1 Cor. 11:29–30). John drew attention to the sobering fact that sin can lead to physical death (1 John 5:16).

God used Satan to indelibly etch the consequences of lying to God onto the minds and memories of those present (Acts 5:11), those who heard (5:5, 11), and unbelievers in the city (5:13). A new heightened level of fearing God came on everyone there and on all who have read about the incident since. "It is a fearful thing to fall into the hands of the living God" (Heb. 10:31).

1 CORINTHIANS 5

The Corinthian church had tolerated a man's incestuous relationship with his step-mother (1 Cor. 5:5). Therefore, Paul delivered or handed over (Gk. *paradidōmi*; cf. Luke 24:20) this practitioner of extreme perversion to Satan—that is, the person was removed from the church (1 Cor. 5:13) to be treated as an unbeliever (cf. Matt. 18:17; 1 Cor. 5:11; 2 Thess. 3:14). The same is said of blasphemous Hymenaeus and Alexander (1 Tim. 1:20). Whether because of a perversion of holy behavior or of holy beliefs, Satan can serve God's purposes in the realm of church discipline when repentance remains absent. Both cases carry a sense of positive hope that these people will eventually put their faith in Christ.

2 CORINTHIANS 12

In 2 Corinthians 12:7, Paul described how his vision of the third heaven resulted in "a thorn . . . in the flesh, a messenger of Satan to harass me." On the one hand, God would use Satan's messenger to keep Paul from pride. On the other hand, the Devil would work to deflate Paul's faith with his sharpened thorn, which was actually a large, sharpened stake used to seriously injure or maim an enemy.

What is the thorn? Paul's thorn is most commonly identified as a physical problem, since it is "in the flesh." Malaria, epilepsy, headaches, or eye problems have all been suggested. However, following the Old Testament usage, several other possibilities strongly commend themselves. This figure of speech appears four times in the Old Testament (Num. 33:55; Josh. 23:13; Ezek. 28:24; Hos. 2:6). Three times it refers to people and once to life circumstances. As in Hosea 2:6, Paul's thorn could have been the adverse circumstances he experienced while serving the Lord (2 Cor. 11:23–28). But in view of the majority Old Testament use and the context in 2 Corinthians, Paul's thorn seems to be people who are "a thorn in the side" or "a pain in the neck," very possibly because they are demon-possessed false teachers and unbelievers. Alexander the coppersmith (2 Tim. 4:14), Hymaneaus with Philetus (2 Tim. 2:17–18), and Elymas (called by Paul a "son of the devil" in Acts 13:10) all qualify, as do the Corinthians themselves.

Satan meant the thorn for evil, yet God had ordained it and used it for good. Paul won both ways. It jolted him back to the reality best expressed by Peter: "Humble yourselves, therefore, under the mighty hand of God, so that at the proper time he may exalt you, casting all your anxieties upon him, because he cares for you" (1 Pet. 5:6–7).

Paul's suffering drove him to prayer (1 Cor. 12:8). As Jesus prayed three times in Gethsemane, so Paul prayed. He prayed that the thorn—whether physical circumstances or people—would be removed. He saw it as hindering his ministry and the Lord's cause. He needed a new dimension of understanding added by the Lord, who would use the satanic thorn for Paul's spiritual profit with new levels of personal humility and reliance on God.

2 THESSALONIANS 2

God says that a time will come when he will send "a strong delusion" (2 Thess. 2:11; literally "a working of deceit") by having the restrainer step aside (2:6–7) and by letting Satan's undiluted and unchecked lying have its sway over all the earth (2:9–12). Satan will temporarily experience a greater freedom to give the people exactly what they want to believe, a lie (John 8:44; Rom. 1:25; 1 John 2:21). The populace will not be restrained (2 Thess. 2:7) from believing Satan's ultimate deception—the lie that Antichrist is God and salvation is through him.

REVELATION 13

At the midpoint of Daniel's seventieth week (Rev. 13:5), the satanic trinity will be introduced. This trio of evil characters includes Satan (the dragon of 13:2–4; cf. 12:9; 20:2), the Antichrist (the beast of 13:1–10), and the False Prophet (the "another beast" of 13:11–17). Satan enables the Antichrist with his adversarial powers (13:2, 4).

Global deception will continue for forty-two months (13:5) until Christ's second coming (19:11–20:3) ends this diabolical dominion and King Jesus reigns for one thousand years (20:4–6). In all this, Satan functions as God's servant by setting up the occasion for the triumphant advent of Christ and the inauguration of his millennial kingdom on earth.

In summary,

> The Bible portrays Satan as an implacable enemy of God, whose designs on humanity are malicious; however, it does not represent Satan as God's equal or as one who acts independently of divine control. In the prologue of Job, the oldest text that speaks of . . . Satan . . . , he is clearly pictured as one who is subordinate to God and who operates only within the parameters that God sets for him. . . . [T]his basic notion that Satan is under divine control appears repeatedly. This motif may stand in a certain degree of tension with the conception of Satan as a hostile force, but it is a persistent theme in the biblical record. Satan is an enemy of God, but he is also a servant of God.[13]

A Christian's Defense

GOD'S PROTECTION[14]

The primary text that speaks of spiritual armor and weaponry is Ephesians 6:10–20, especially the whole armor of God (Gk. *panoplia*). Elsewhere, Paul also refers to armor of light (Rom. 13:12), weapons of righteousness (2 Cor. 6:7), and weapons of our warfare (2 Cor. 10:4).

---

13. Sydney H. T. Page, "Satan: God's Servant," *JETS* 30, no. 3 (2007): 465.

14. This section is adapted from John MacArthur, *Standing Strong: How to Resist the Enemy of Your Soul*, 3rd ed. (Colorado Springs: David C. Cook, 2012), 97–98, 117–18, 128–29, 140–42, 154–57, 180. Copyright © 2012 by John MacArthur. Used by permission of David C. Cook. Publisher permission required to reproduce. All rights reserved.

The Belt of Truth. In Paul's day, soldiers wore a tunic, a large square piece of material that had holes for the head and arms. It hung low and loose so that the soldier could cinch it around his waist with a belt. When he was ready to fight, he pulled the four corners of his tunic up through the belt, thus girding one's loins. It provided the soldier with the mobility and flexibility he needed for hand-to-hand combat.

It was common for a Roman soldier to wear a strap over his shoulder that connected to the front and back of the belt. He attached his sword to the strap along with decorations or medals from battle. After a Roman soldier put on his belt, attached the strap, and hooked on his sword, he was ready to fight.

In the spiritual realm, Christians are to gird their loins with "truth" (Eph. 6:14). That can refer to the content of truth (i.e., Scripture) or to an attitude of truthfulness, sincerity, honesty, and integrity. Since Paul referred to Scripture as a spiritual weapon in Ephesians 6:17, it means that here he was referring to a Christian's attitude. Believers who gird their loins with truth have a heart for the battle because of a commitment to Christ and his cause.

The Breastplate of Righteousness. Roman soldiers had different types of breastplates. Some were made of heavy linen strips that hung down very low. Pieces of metal or thin slices from the hooves and horns of an animal were hooked together and hung from the linen.

However, the most familiar type of breastplate was the molded metal chest plate that covered the vital areas of the torso from the base of the neck to the top of the thighs. The soldier needed to protect that area because much of the fighting was with a short sword (Gk. *machaira*) in hand-to-hand combat.

The breastplate covered two key areas: the heart and the vital organs, what the Jewish people referred to as "the bowels" (see Isa. 59:17; 1 Thess. 5:8). In Hebrew culture, the heart symbolically represented the mind or the thinking process (e.g., Prov. 23:7), while the bowels became a reference to the emotions because of the way they can affect one's intestinal organs. The mind and emotions encompass everything that causes a person to act.

God has provided the breastplate of righteousness (Eph. 6:14) to protect both the mind and emotions. What is this righteousness specifically? It is the practical, personal righteousness of a true believer that is born in him at regeneration and afterward strengthened by God the Spirit, so that a Christian becomes progressively more like Christ (2 Cor. 3:18; 2 Pet. 3:18).

Footwear of Readiness. In Paul's day, the normal footwear for the Roman soldier was a thick-soled, hobnailed semiboot. Thick leather straps secured it to the foot. Little pieces of metal that protruded like spikes from the bottom of the sole gave the soldier firmness of footing so that he could stand in the battle, hold his ground, and make quick moves without slipping, sliding, or falling.

The soldier's footwear provided not only sure footing but also protection for long marches covering tremendous amounts of terrain. In addition, the enemy commonly placed razor-sharp sticks in the ground for piercing the feet of the advancing soldiers. To protect themselves, soldiers wore boots with thick soles that couldn't be pierced. Even the best soldier is rendered ineffective if his foot has been injured.

In spiritual warfare, it's vital for the believer to be wearing the right kind of footwear. One can cinch up the waist with commitment and adorn the breastplate of holy living, but unless one has sure footing, there is a strong possibility of falling. So in Ephesians 6:15, Paul said that the feet are to be shod "with the readiness given by the gospel of peace."

Here, Paul is describing defensive armor, and when he writes of "readiness given by the gospel of peace," he is speaking of having embraced the gospel. If one is outfitted with the good news of peace, the spiritual combatant is protected and will be enabled to withstand the enemy's schemes (Eph. 6:11, 13).

The Shield of Faith. The Roman army used several kinds of shields. One was a small round shield that curled at the edges. A foot soldier would strap it to his forearm. It was light to allow the soldier greater mobility on the battlefield. In his other hand, he carried his sword so that the soldier could strike while he parried the blows of his opponent with his shield.

However, that is not the kind of shield Paul was referring to in Ephesians 6:16. Instead, he referred to a large, rectangular shield. This shield measured 4½ feet by 2½ feet. Made out of a thick plank of wood, it would be covered on the outside with either very thick metal or leather. The metal would deflect flaming arrows, while the leather would be treated to extinguish the fiery pitch on the arrows.

Spiritually speaking, when the flaming darts of the Evil One fly, a believer will be protected by raising the shield of salvific faith (Eph. 6:16; cf. Ps. 18:35). The shield will be so effective that the weapons of Satan will be extinguished, because well-equipped believers conquer overwhelmingly in the battle (Rom. 8:37).

The Helmet of Salvation. In Roman times, helmets were made out of two things: solid-cast metal or leather with patches of metal. The helmet protected the soldier's head from arrows, but its primary function was to ward off blows from a broadsword. This sword (Gk. *rhomphaia*) was 3 to 4 feet long and had a massive handle that was held with both hands like a baseball bat. The soldier was to lift it over his head and bring it down on his opponent's head. A helmet was necessary to deflect such a crushing blow to the skull.

In the spiritual realm, the believer must wear the helmet of salvation (Eph. 6:17). What does salvation here refer to? There are three possibilities: the past, present, or future aspects of salvation. Paul was not referring to the past aspect of salvation. He did not intend to say, "After girding one's loins with truth, donning the breastplate of righteousness, shodding one's feet with the gospel of peace, and taking up the shield of faith, one should—by the way—get saved." Paul assumes that the past act of salvation is already a reality. Instead, he is referring to the present and future aspects of our salvation. It is both the assurance of God's continuing work in the Christian life and the confidence in a full and final salvation to come. Paul elsewhere mentioned the helmet of salvation in 1 Thessalonians 5:8–9 (cf. Isa. 59:17).

The Sword of the Spirit. Paul wrote about "the sword of the Spirit" (Eph. 6:17). The Greek word (Gk. *machaira*) refers to a dagger anywhere from 6 to 18 inches long. It was carried in a sheath or scabbard at the soldier's side and could be used in hand-to-hand combat both defensively and offensively.

The sword of the Spirit, therefore, is not a broadsword (Gk. *rhomphaia*, see Rev. 1:16; 2:12, 16; 19:15, 21) that one just flails around, hoping to do some damage. It is incisive; it must hit a vulnerable spot, or it won't be effective. Elsewhere in Scripture, the Word of God is also referred to with this same Greek word (see Heb. 4:12).

The whole armor (Gk. *panoplia*) of God proves effective against the ploys of Satan. It is not optional but required. It is not partial but complete. It is not negotiable but commanded. With it, the believer will be strong (Eph. 6:10) and will be enabled to stand firm (Eph. 6:11, 13–14).

The Arsenal of Prayer. All six pieces of spiritual armor can be classified as primarily defensive in nature. Now Paul turns to the most effective offensive resource available—prayer (Eph. 6:18). He outlines six characteristics:

1. "At all times" speaks to frequency and duration.
2. "In the Spirit" refers to one's submission to the will of God's Spirit.
3. "All prayer and supplication" puts all varieties of prayer in play.
4. "Keep alert" demands constant focus on the situation at hand.
5. "All perseverance" is necessary in both positive and negative moments.
6. "All the saints" can include praying with regard to self and for other believers.

Prayer power represents the most effective weapon in the believer's spiritual armory and is to be employed as Paul instructed.

GOD'S PROVISIONS

The New Testament frequently reminds the reader that God has provided multiple means by which a Christian can be victorious over Satan in this life. The following ten provisions focus on the most important and encouraging truths found in the Bible to this end.

The Savior's Victory at Calvary. The ruler of this world will be cast out (John 12:31). Through his death, Christ will destroy the Devil, the one who has the power of death (Heb. 2:14). Believers have conquered the accuser of the brethren by the blood of the Lamb (Rev. 12:11).

The Overcomer's Promise. Believers will ultimately overcome the Evil One and his world system (1 John 2:13; 5:4–5).

Christ's Intercessory Prayer. Jesus, in his High Priestly role in the upper room, prayed that the Father would keep believers from the Evil One (John 17:15, 20; see 10:28–29).

Christ's Protection. All true believers will be protected by Christ so that the Evil One cannot do eternal harm to them (1 John 5:18).

The Spirit's Indwelling Power. Believers will overcome Satan because the power of the Holy Spirit within is greater than the power of the Devil without (1 John 4:4).

The Knowledge of Satan's Schemes. God has forewarned believers of Satan's evil plans in Scripture so that Christians can be prepared when the spiritual battle erupts (2 Cor. 2:11; 1 Pet. 5:8).

The Believer's Prayer. Christ's model prayer urged believers to pray, "Deliver us from the evil one" (Matt. 6:13). Paul commanded believers to be in constant prayer for victory over the spiritual forces of evil (Eph. 6:12, 18).

Biblical Instructions for Defeating Satan. First, submit yourselves to God (James 4:7a) and draw near to God, knowing that he will also draw near to you (James 4:8). Second, resist the Devil and he will flee (James 4:7b; 1 Pet. 5:9).

Shepherds Who Strengthen and Encourage the Church. Pastors are to establish and exhort the flock of God in the faith (1 Thess. 3:2), so that the tempter will fail with his temptations (1 Thess. 3:5).

Confidence That Christ Has Won the Ultimate Victory. At the end of Christ's millennial reign over earth, he will cast Satan into the lake of fire to be tormented for all eternity future (Rev. 20:10).

Satan's Judgments

From shortly after God declaring his creation "very good" (Gen. 1:31) until just before eternity future in the new heaven and new earth (Rev. 20:10), God has handed and will hand down multiple judgments on the rebellious Satan. The last one will be complete and final. God, who declared the end from the beginning (Isa. 46:10), has outlined the judicial history of Satan in Scripture.

SATAN'S ORIGINAL JUDGMENT

Satan was not originally created as the Evil One that he eventually chose to become. So when did the Devil first rebel against his holy Master? Genesis 1–3 does not recount the occasion but rather assumes it. Having declared the creation to be "very good" (Gen. 1:31), God subsequently chronicled a deceitful creature in Genesis 3 who set out to dupe the first humans so that they would serve his own purposes, not God's.

There is not one clear, direct passage in Scripture that explicitly reports this celestial treason. However, several places allude to it. First, Revelation 12:3–4 speaks of the red dragon, the ancient deceiver whose efforts were global (Rev. 12:9), who

Table 8.2 Serpent or Satan?

Genesis	Comment	Identification
3:1	The serpent is compared to the beasts of the field.	Serpent
3:1	Serpents cannot normally talk or know about God.	Satan
3:2	Serpents are not normally engaged in conversation with people.	Satan
3:4	Serpents do not normally reason.	Satan
3:13	Serpents do not normally deceive people verbally.	Satan
3:14	Satan does not crawl on his belly.	Serpent
3:15	It is difficult to determine the addressees.	Serpent/Satan

enlisted one-third of the heavenly host to join him in spiritual rebellion against God and to thus become unholy angels, or demons. There has not been and will not be another defection of angels beyond this one. Also, there will be redemption for none of the demons.

This brief statement in Revelation looks back to Ezekiel 28:11–19, which addresses the ancient king of Tyre and the satanic influence in his reign. Here it is difficult to clearly distinguish between the two, but it is rather obvious that both are in view.[15] Several facts should be inferred about Satan:

1. Satan is a created being (28:13).
2. Satan was created as a righteous angel (28:13–14).
3. Satan chose an unrighteous way of life (28:15).
4. Satan was subsequently dishonorably discharged by God from further heavenly, holy service on behalf of his Creator (28:16).

While referring to the future king of Babylon, Isaiah 14:4–21 seems also to allude to Satan in the same manner as Ezekiel. It is much like when Christ spoke about Peter and Satan in the same sentence (Matt. 16:23). God's judgment is rendered on the basis of Satan's five "I will" boasts (Isa. 14:13–14), which evidence his abominable pride. Paul likewise warns church leaders concerning Satan's original sin (1 Tim. 3:6–7). Though Satan and one-third of the angels in heaven were disqualified from the honorable role of serving God in heaven, they were not completely banned from a heavenly presence (cf. Job 1:6; 2:1).

SATAN'S EDENIC JUDGMENT

Was Eve speaking with a literal serpent or with Satan in Genesis 3:1–5? The brief analysis in table 8.2 sorts out the evidence. The New Testament (2 Cor. 11:3; Rev. 12:9; 20:2) reveals that the serpent is associated with Satan. From the analysis in table 8.2, it appears that the serpent is in view at times and Satan at others.

Apparently, this is a Satan-possessed creature similar to the description of Satan's entrance into Judas in Luke 22:3 and John 13:27. This same phenomenon would

---

15. For a more detailed discussion of Satan in Isa. 14:4–21, especially 14:12–14, and in Ezek. 28:1–19, especially 28:11–19, consult Dickason, *Angels: Elect and Evil*, 127–35.

certainly have been possible with the serpent. It is scripturally sound to maintain that nonrational beings are capable of speech when energized by a supernatural power. Balaam's donkey (Num. 22:28–30, 2 Pet. 2:16) is sufficient biblical evidence to establish the historical reality of this phenomenon. There seems to be no doubt that a real serpent is involved. Neither is there any question that Satan was directly involved.

So is God cursing the possessor, the one possessed, or both? To single out one or the other is difficult. It appears unreasonable that Satan would be left out of the curse since he was the instigator. Thus, it seems best to conclude that God is here addressing both the serpent and Satan.

After cursing the physical being, God turns to the spiritual being, Satan, and curses him.[16] God's message is a "first gospel" (or *protoevangelium*) and is prophetic of the struggle that began in the garden and its outcome between "your offspring"— Satan and unbelievers, who are called the Devil's children in John 8:44—and her offspring—Christ, a descendant of Eve, and those in him. In the midst of the curse passage, a message of hope shines forth: the woman's offspring called "he" is Christ, who will one day defeat the Serpent. Satan will only "bruise" Christ's heel (cause him to suffer), while Christ will bruise Satan's head (destroy him with a fatal blow). Paul, in a passage strongly reminiscent of Genesis 3, thus encouraged the believers in Rome that "the God of peace will soon crush Satan under your feet" (Rom. 16:20; cf. John 16:11). This *protoevangelium* in Genesis 3:15 anticipates Christ's redemptive victory on the cross over Satan and demons.

SATAN'S CALVARY JUDGMENT

During his ministry, Christ made statements concerning Satan's defeat and judgment that validated his victory cry on the cross, "It is finished" (John 12:31; 16:11; 19:30). Christ's power over demons certified his mastery of Satan (Matt. 12:22–29). Christ's authority, which he delegated to the disciples, reflected Satan's spiritual defeat (Matt. 10:1; Mark 3:13–15; Luke 9:1). New Testament statements concerning the salvation purchased by Christ's death, which had the power to deliver believers from the domain of Satan to God, reaffirmed Satan's failure (Acts 26:18; Col. 1:13; 2:15). Christ came to destroy the works of the Devil (1 John 3:8). A preview of what to expect occurred as the disciples were amazed at their power over demons (Luke 10:17); Christ responded, "I saw Satan fall like lightning from heaven," by which he meant that the power of the Devil was already diminished, as evidenced by their earthly victory over demons (Luke 10:18). Through his death on the cross, Christ destroyed the one who has the power of death, the Devil (Heb. 2:14).

The centerpiece of Satan's sentence will forever be the cross. While Satan would continue on earth long after Calvary, his attempts to spiritually murder the whole human race (e.g., by tempting Christ to avoid the cross, Matt. 16:21–23) had been thwarted by the Savior, and a redemptive remedy in Christ had been provided.

---

16. This paragraph is adapted from MacArthur, *MacArthur Study Bible: English Standard Version*, 22. Used by permission of Thomas Nelson.

SATAN'S TRIBULATIONAL JUDGMENT

Revelation 12:7–13 chronicles Satan and his angels' final physical banishment from the presence of God in heaven. They will have been defeated in heaven, and there will no longer be any place for them there (Rev. 12:8–9). This will occur midway through Daniel's seventieth week, or three and one-half years into the final seven-year week. From this point forward, Satan will no longer be able to accuse believers of sin in the presence of God (Rev. 12:12; cf. Isa. 24:21).

SATAN'S MILLENNIAL JUDGMENT

When Christ comes to claim his kingdom on earth (Rev. 19:11–21), Satan will be bound and imprisoned for one thousand years in the bottomless pit (Rev. 20:1–3). For a millennium, the earth will be free from Satan's roaming (see 1 Pet. 5:8). Christ will rule without any interference from the "ruler of this world" (John 12:31). Although the Bible does not say so explicitly, it may be assumed that all demons will be incarcerated with Satan during this time (Isa. 24:21–22).

SATAN'S ETERNAL JUDGMENT

In the end, Satan (Matt. 25:41; Rev. 20:10) and his evil angels (Matt. 25:41; 2 Pet. 2:4; Jude 6) will join the Antichrist and False Prophet, who will have already resided in the lake of fire for one thousand years (Rev. 19:20). In Matthew 8:29 (cf. Luke 8:31), when the demons inquired of Christ, "Have you come here to torment us before the time?" they most likely had the eternal judgment in mind. Shortly thereafter, all unbelievers throughout time will also arrive there as a result of the great white throne judgment (Matt. 25:41; Mark 9:48; Rev. 20:14–15).

Demons

Demons' Reality
Demons' Character
Demons' History
Demons' Power
Demons' Servant Role
A Christian's Defense
Demon Possession
Demons' Judgments

Demons' Reality

The factual reality of demons is made credible by the considerable number of times they are mentioned in the Bible (over one hundred times). Because the Bible serves as the Christian's only unassailable testimony to the very existence of demons, believers can confidently trust the truth it reports. The Bible's author, God Almighty, has been and will always be true (Pss. 12:6; 119:160) and trustworthy (Prov. 30:5; 2 Tim. 3:14–17).

BASIC FACTS

The evidence for the terms "demon," "spirit," and "unclean spirit" in the Old Testament is minimal compared to the New Testament. Of the 16 occurrences, 6 appear in 1 Samuel, 4 in Isaiah, 3 in the Psalms, and 1 each in Deuteronomy, Judges, and Zechariah. This amounts to 13 percent of the 120 total occurrences in the Bible.

The 104 other occasions, or 87 percent, occur in the New Testament. Demons appear in all four Gospels, which use the generic terms "demon," "spirit," "evil spirit," "unclean spirit," and "deceiving spirit" 83 times, with Luke providing the most mentions. Acts has 9 occurrences, the Epistles have 7, and Revelation has 5.

The overall biblical teaching on the topic of demons demonstrates God's desire to avoid the bizarre and unbelievable. It contains none of the exaggerated or spectacular ideas found in most literature outside the Bible.

BASIC CHARACTERISTICS

Demons display the three most basic qualities that define personhood. Their recognition of and conversations with Jesus illustrate their intellect (Luke 8:26–39), as do their capacity to know the truth about Christ (James 2:19) and their ability to author false doctrine (1 Tim. 4:1). Demons exhibit emotions when they shudder at the thought of Christ (James 2:19) or fear what Christ may do to them (Matt. 8:29; Mark 1:24; 5:7). By demanding of Christ, "If you cast us out, send us away into the herd of pigs," demons exercise their will (Matt. 8:31).

Four additional personal qualities complete this basic outline describing "unclean spirits." First, they are created *angels* in that they are Satan's angels (Matt. 25:41; Rev. 12:9). Since Christ created all things (Col. 1:16), demons are *created* angels (Neh. 9:6; Job 1:6; 2:1; 38:4–7).

Second, they are spirit beings. The Old Testament refers to them as spirit (Judg. 9:23; 1 Sam. 16:14–16, 23; 18:10; 19:9). The New Testament likewise refers to them as "spirits" (Matt. 8:16), "evil spirits" (Luke 7:21), and "unclean spirits" (Matt. 10:1).

Third, demons are described biblically as being mobile. As Satan roams the earth (1 Pet. 5:8), it can be expected that demons accompany him. They can reside in humans, be expelled, and later return (Matt. 12:43–45). Demons can also visit heaven, from which they are subsequently banished (Rev. 12:4, 9). And they carry out Satan's will on earth (Mark 1:34).

Finally, God will hold demons morally responsible for their evil deeds. They are judged both during earth's history (2 Pet. 2:4; Jude 6) and at the end of time (Matt. 25:41; Rev. 20:10).

BASIC CONTRASTS

The theology of demons presents a stark contrast to that of the Holy Spirit. Some of the most striking opposites are listed in table 8.3.

Table 8.3 Contrasting Demons and the Holy Spirit

Demons	The Holy Spirit		Demons	The Holy Spirit
unclean	holy		oppress	relieves
evil	righteous		enslave	liberates
deceiving	truthful		destructive	constructive
strong	strongest		enemies	friend
temporal	eternal		false	true
created	Creator		devious	honest
counterfeit	authentic			

Demons' Character

A survey of the Old and New Testament names and descriptive titles for demons will provide a general understanding of what they are like, to whom they owe their allegiance, and how and why they go about serving Satan.

The New Testament contains a wealth of information about "evil spirits." The Gospels and Revelation frequently discuss demons in Christ's lifetime and in the end times. On the other hand, the Old Testament only hints at the existence of demons. Taken together, though, the two Testaments deliver all that God intended Christians to know about these evil emissaries of Satan, who extend the power and reach of the Devil, who is not omnipresent like God.

OLD TESTAMENT

1. *Demon*: The Greek Old Testament (the Septuagint) uses the New Testament word for demon (*daimonion*) eight times to translate several different Hebrew words, since the Hebrew language did not have one word that uniformly referred to demons. The English translations vary but always refer to some form of demon activity or idolatrous worship, often pictured as spiritual immorality (Jer. 3:8–10; Ezek. 16:23–43; 23:22–30; cf. Rev. 17:1–5), which the Old Testament strictly condemns and prohibits (Lev. 17:7; 20:27; Deut. 18:10–12). These various translations include the following: "demons" (Deut. 32:17; Ps. 106:37); "burning incense" (Isa. 65:3 NASB); "destruction" (Ps. 91:6; cf. "Abaddon" and "Apollyon," Rev. 9:11); "fortune" (Isa. 65:11; cf. "cup" and "table" of "demons," 1 Cor. 10:21); "idols" (Ps. 96:5); and "wild goats" (Isa. 13:21; 34:14).

2. *Evil or harmful spirit* (Judg. 9:23; 1 Sam. 16:14–16, 23; 18:10; 19:9): This is also the major descriptive title used of demons in the New Testament, emphasizing their sinister character.

3. *Lying spirit* (1 Kings 22:22–23; 2 Chron. 18:22): The "lying spirit" (Satan; cf. "the father of lies," John 8:44) dispatches four hundred lying spirits (demons) to give a false message to the four hundred prophets of Ahab. What Satan, who is not omnipresent, could not do all at one time, he could accomplish by dispatching four hundred demons to impact four hundred false prophets.

4. *Prince of Greece, Prince of Persia* (Dan. 10:13, 20): This is a brief mention of some sort of celestial spiritual battle between Michael the chief holy angel

and the demonic rulers of Persia and Greece (Dan. 10:21; 11:2; Jude 9; Rev. 12:7). In context, it refers to Persia relinquishing its world rule to Greece in the future (Dan. 8:1–8, 20–22). It can be said that it appears the ruling world power has a demon for its advocate to battle Michael the defender of Israel (Dan. 10:21; 12:1). Nothing more can be understood or extrapolated from these few verses. There is no biblical basis for the erroneous teaching of modern-day territorial demons worldwide.

5. *Spirit of uncleanness* (Zech. 13:2): The Greek Old Testament (Septuagint) uses *akathartos* only once, while the New Testament uses the same term frequently to speak of demons. It appears to address the spiritual power (demons) behind the false prophets and idolaters. These appear to be the same unclean spirits and demonic spirits referred to in Revelation 16:13–14.

6. *Destroying angels* (Ps. 78:49): The phrase "A company of destroying angels" in Psalm 78:49 could possibly refer to demons. However, it seems more likely that the psalmist poetically personified God's wrath as angels or messengers.

NEW TESTAMENT

1. *Demon(s)* (Gk. *daimonion*, Matt. 7:22–Rev. 18:2): By far, this designation is the most common New Testament term for fallen angels, occurring sixty-three times. A few variations are also used but always with some direct reference to demons (Matt. 8:31; James 3:15). While the Old Testament can at times be vague with this word, the New Testament is unambiguously clear and consistent that it refers to evil spiritual beings.

2. *Angel* (Matt. 25:41; 2 Cor. 12:7; 2 Pet. 2:4; Jude 6: Rev. 12:7, 9): In all six instances of the New Testament calling demons "angels," they are understood as "messengers" associated with Satan and evil.

3. *Deceitful spirit(s)* (1 Tim. 4:1): These deceiving (Gk. *planos*) spirits will disseminate the false teachings or doctrines of demons.

4. *Evil spirit(s)* (Matt. 12:45; Luke 7:21; 8:2; 11:26; Acts 19:12, 13, 15–16): This title parallels the identical one in the Old Testament. Demons replicate the evil nature of Satan.

5. *Frog* (Rev. 16:13): Demons appear like frogs as they emerge from the satanic territory of Satan, the Antichrist, and the False Prophet at the conclusion of Daniel's seventieth week. Here they are also called "unclean spirits" and "spirits of demons."

6. *Host of heaven* (Isa. 24:21; 34:4): This term can be used for (1) the physical bodies in the sky (Ps. 33:6; Isa. 40:26), (2) holy angels (1 Kings 22:19; Neh. 9:6; Luke 2:13), and (3) evil angels (Deut. 4:19; 17:2–3; 2 Kings 17:16; 21:3, 5; 23:4–5). Because Isaiah writes that the "the LORD will punish the host of heaven" (Isa. 24:21) and that "all the host of heaven shall rot away" (34:4), this cannot refer to physical bodies or to holy angels. Therefore, it must refer to demons, who are the power behind idolatry and false worship.

7. *Locust* (Rev. 9:3): At the middle of Daniel's seventieth week, Satan ("a star from heaven") will release a portion of the demons (pictured as locusts), who have been incarcerated in the Abyss since the original moral fall (Rev. 12:4).

8. *Mute and deaf spirit* (Mark 9:25): When Jesus permanently casts a demon out of a boy, he refers to it as a "mute and deaf spirit" and also as an "unclean spirit."

9. *Spirit* (Matt. 8:16; 12:45; Mark 9:17, 20; Luke 9:39; 10:20; 11:26; Acts 16:16, 18; Rev. 16:14): This is the essential characteristic of all angels—both elect and evil.

10. *Spirit of divination* (Acts 16:16): A demon-inhabited fortune teller in Philippi is instantly relieved of her demon by Paul.

11. *Star* (Rev. 12:4): This generic term for all angels, both holy and evil, is used here in the context of Revelation 12 to describe one-third of all angels rejecting God and aligning themselves with Satan.

12. *Unclean spirit* (Matt. 10:1–Rev. 18:2): Twenty-three times demons are described as morally impure (Gk. *akathartos*). They are the opposite of angels who are holy.

Demons' History

CREATION

See "Satan's History" (p. 681).

FALL

See "Satan's History" (p. 681).

INTERMEDIATE JUDGMENTS

See "Satan's History" (p. 681), "Satan's Judgments" (p. 703), and "Demons' Judgments" (p. 719).

FALL TO TRIBULATION

Specific Encounters. God's revelation in the Bible is the only reliable information about Satan and demons. Little is said about demons in Scripture outside the Gospels. The biblical summaries in tables 8.4–8.8 focus on clear, historical accounts of human involvement with demons.[17]

General Descriptions. We can make numerous observations about demon activities in the Gospels and Acts. They are listed here in no special order of importance.

1. John the Baptist was accused of being demon possessed (Matt. 11:18; Luke 7:33).
2. Jesus was accused of being demon possessed (Matt. 9:34; 12:24; Mark 3:22, 30; Luke 11:15; John 7:20; 8:48–49; 10:20).
3. Names of Jesus used by demons:
   a. Son of God (Matt. 8:29; Mark 3:11; Luke 4:41)
   b. Jesus of Nazareth (Mark 1:24; Luke 4:34)
   c. Holy One of God (Mark 1:24; Luke 4:34)
   d. Jesus, Son of the Most High God (Mark 5:7; Luke 8:28)
4. Title for Paul and Silas used by demons: servant of the Most High God (Acts 16:17)

---

17. These charts are adapted from Richard Mayhue, *The Healing Promise: Is It Always God's Will to Heal?* (Fearn, Ross-shire, Scotland: Mentor, 2001), 144–45. Used by permission of Christian Focus.

Table 8.4 Old Testament Encounters with Demons

Encounter	Old Testament Passage
Abimelech and the men of Shechem	Judges 9:23–24, 56–57
Saul	1 Samuel 16:14–23
Saul	1 Samuel 18:10
Saul	1 Samuel 19:9
The prophets of Ahab	1 Kings 22:22–23; 2 Chron. 18:18–22

Table 8.5 Jesus's Encounters with Demons in the Gospels

Encounter	Matthew	Mark	Luke	John
Multitudes	4:24	1:39	—	—
Multitudes	8:16	1:29–34	4:38–41	—
Gadarene man	8:28–34	5:1–20	8:26–39	—
Dumb man	9:32–34	—	—	—
Blind and dumb man	12:22	—	—	—
Gentile girl	15:21–28	7:24–30	—	—
Epileptic	17:14–21	9:14–29	9:37–43	—
Man	—	1:23–28	4:33–37	—
Multitudes	—	3:11	—	—
Mary Magdalene	—	16:9	8:2	—
Multitudes	—	—	6:18	—
Multitudes	—	—	7:21	—
Man	—	—	11:14	—
Woman	—	—	13:10–17	—
Multitudes	—	—	13:32	—

Table 8.6 Others' Encounters with Demons in the Gospels

Encounter	Matthew	Mark	Luke	John
The Twelve	10:1, 8	6:7, 13	9:1	—
The Twelve	—	3:15	—	—
Unknown disciple	—	9:38	9:49	—
The Twelve	—	16:17	—	—
The Seventy-Two	—	—	10:17–20	—

Table 8.7 *Encounters with Demons in Acts**

Encounter	Acts
Multitudes	5:16
Multitudes	8:7
Paul and slave girl	16:16–18
Paul and multitudes	19:11–12
Sons of Sceva	19:13–17

*The Ananias and Sapphira incident (Acts 5:1–11) is not included because the phrase "why has Satan filled your heart to lie?" (5:3) speaks specifically of Satan rather than of being invaded by demons.

Table 8.8 *Encounters with Demons in the Epistles and Revelation*

Encounter	Epistles and Revelation
There are no specific encounters.*	

*The case of the unrepentant fornicator in 1 Corinthians 5:1–13 is omitted because (1) there is no evidence of demon involvement, and (2) there is a strong possibility that he was a counterfeit believer (cf. "so-called brother" [5:11 NASB] and "evil person" [5:13] as indicators).

5. Others, besides Christ, who cast out demons:
   a. The Twelve (Matt. 10:1–8; Mark 3:14–15; 6:7–13)
   b. Unknown person (Mark 9:38; Luke 9:49–50)
   c. The Seventy-Two (Luke 10:17–20)
   d. Peter and the apostles (Acts 5:16)
   e. Philip (Acts 8:7)
   f. Paul (Acts 16:16–18; 19:11–12)
6. Some falsely claimed to exorcise demons:
   a. Unknown people (Matt. 7:22)
   b. Sons of Sceva (Acts 19:13–16)
7. Physical symptoms of demon possession:
   a. Violence (Matt. 8:28; Acts 19:16)
   b. Mute (Matt. 9:32–33; Mark 9:17)
   c. Epilepsy (Matt. 17:15; Mark 9:18, 20)
   d. Crying out (Mark 1:23–26; 5:5)
   e. Superhuman strength (Mark 5:4)
   f. Masochistic (Mark 5:5)
   g. Naked (Mark 5:15)
   h. Physical impairment (Luke 13:10–13)
   i. Divination (Acts 16:16)
8. Concerns of demons:
   a. That Jesus would destroy them (Mark 1:24)
   b. That Jesus would torment them before the time (Matt. 8:29; Mark 5:7)
   c. That Jesus would send them out of the country (Mark 5:10)
   d. That they could remain embodied, even if in pigs (Matt. 8:31; Mark 5:12)
9. Multiple demons in one person:
   a. Many (Mark 5:9)

b. At least eight demons (Matt. 12:45)

c. Seven demons in Mary Magdalene (Luke 8:2)

10. Demons have names (e.g., "Legion," Mark 5:9).
11. Some demons only come out after prayer and fasting (Mark 9:14–29).
12. Demons can return after being evicted (Matt. 12:43–45; Luke 8:29).
13. Casting out demons is secondary to Christ's death and salvation (Luke 10:20).
14. The actual physical appearance of demons is never described in the Gospels, Acts, or the Epistles.

DANIEL'S SEVENTIETH WEEK

Revelation includes six descriptions of demon activity in the second half of Daniel's seventieth week:

1. Some of the demons originally locked in the Abyss are released (Rev. 9:1–3, 11).
2. Four special demons are released at the Euphrates River at the end (Rev. 9:13–15).
3. Idolatrous demon worship is promoted (Rev. 9:20).
4. Demons are permanently banished from heaven (Rev. 12:7–13).
5. Demons perform false signs (Rev. 16:13–14).
6. Demons inhabit Babylon (Rev. 18:2).

FINAL JUDGMENTS

It can surely be assumed that the three concluding judgments of Satan also include all the demons. This involves (1) the tribulation judgment (Rev. 12:7–13); (2) the millennial judgment (Rev. 20:7–9); and (3) the final judgment (Isa. 27:1; Rev. 20:10), whereby Satan and his angels find eternal residence in the lake of fire (Matt. 25:41; 2 Pet. 2:4; Jude 6; Rev. 20:10, 14–15). See "Satan's Judgments" (p. 703).

Demons' Power

Demons possess the great power of angels (Rom. 8:38; 1 Cor. 15:24), greater than humans but far less than their Creator. They have the power to carry out the following actions:

1. Indwell humans and animals (Mark 5:1–16)
2. Physically afflict people (Mark 9:17, 22)
3. Terrorize humans (1 Sam. 16:14–15; 18:10; 19:9; Acts 19:13–16; 2 Cor. 12:7)
4. Initiate false worship (1 Cor. 10:20–21)
5. Promote false doctrines (1 Tim. 4:1)
6. Perform false signs and wonders (2 Thess. 2:9; Rev. 16:13–14)
7. Deceive prophets (1 Kings 22:19–23)
8. Encourage idolatry (Deut. 32:17; Ps. 106:37)
9. Engineer death (Judg. 9:23, 56–57)

Demons work from a powerful heavenly hierarchy to execute their evil deeds. Words such as "angels," "authorities," "cosmic powers," "dominions," "powers," "rulers," and "thrones" can be used to describe the hierarchies of either holy or evil angels. In context, Romans 8:38; 1 Corinthians 15:24; Ephesians 2:2; 6:12; and Colossians 2:15 most likely refer to various ranks or levels among the evil angels, that is, the demon hierarchy. In context, Ephesians 1:21; Colossians 1:16; and 1 Peter 3:22 most likely refer to various ranks or levels in the holy angel hierarchy.

Scripture never elaborates on the specifics of these hierarchies to explain their order or function. Since Satan imitates and falsifies God's character and kingdom characteristics, it is most likely that there is both an authoritative functional hierarchy for holy angels who worship God and a parallel counterfeit hierarchy for evil angels who give their allegiance to Satan.

However strong demons might be, they also have serious weaknesses and vulnerabilities:

1. They unwittingly serve God's purposes (Judg. 9:23).
2. They were terrified of Christ and the gospel (Matt. 8:29; Mark 1:24; James 2:19).
3. They obeyed Christ (Matt. 8:32).
4. They obeyed the Twelve (Matt. 10:1–8) and the Seventy-Two (Luke 10:17–20).
5. They cannot separate believers in Christ from the love of God (Rom. 8:38).
6. They can be restrained by the Holy Spirit (2 Thess. 2:6; 1 John 4:4).
7. They have been judged already by God (2 Pet. 2:4; Jude 6) and will be again in the future (Rev. 20:10).

Demons' Servant Role

Refer to the discussion of "Satan's Servant Role" (p. 692), which comprehensively documents how God used Satan and demons to accomplish his divine purposes without violating his perfectly holy and righteous character.

A Christian's Defense

Consult the notes on "A Christian's Defense" against Satan (p. 699), which applies equally to demons.

Demon Possession

What does demon possession mean and involve? Can both Christians and non-Christians experience this phenomenon? Can it be internal and external in nature? What is the biblical remedy for demon possession? These important questions will be discussed and answered in what follows. The ultimate question to be resolved is, Can Christians be demonized—that is, indwelt spatially—leading to the need for a demon (or demons) to be cast out, such as observed in the Gospels and Acts?

One writer framed the issue as follows:

> Perhaps the most controversial question to be raised is, "Can a true believer be demonized?" Note that I am speaking not of demon possession, but of *demonization*. *Possession* implies ownership and total control. Christians, even disobedi-

ent ones, belong to God, not to Satan. Thus, Satan cannot control them totally. *Demonization* is a different matter, however. By demonization I mean that Satan, through his demons, exercises direct, partial control over an area or areas of the life of a Christian or non-Christian. Can that really happen to Christians?[18]

The discussion about what the Bible teaches will be undertaken along five lines of thinking—lexical, biblical, historical, theological, and practical. Only then can a conclusive and compelling biblical statement be made.

LEXICAL EVIDENCE

The New Testament uses four different phrases on 32 occasions to describe demon influence on humans in the Gospels and Acts:

1. one "having" a demon (Gk. *echō*, 16 times)
   a. Matthew 11:18
   b. Mark 3:30; 5:15; 7:25; 9:17
   c. Luke 4:33; 7:33; 8:27
   d. John 7:20; 8:48–49, 52; 10:20
   e. Acts 8:7; 16:16; 19:13
2. one who is "demonized" (Gk. *daimonizomai*, 13 times)
   a. Matthew 4:24; 8:16, 28, 33; 9:32; 12:22; 15:22
   b. Mark 1:32; 5:15–16, 18
   c. Luke 8:36
   d. John 10:21
3. one "with an unclean spirit" (Gk. *en*, 2 times): Mark 1:23; 5:2
4. one "afflicted" with an unclean spirit (Gk. *ochleomai*, 1 time): Acts 5:16

The first two uses (totaling 29 of 32 occurrences) refer to the same phenomenon. For example, Luke 8:27 (use 1) and 8:36 (use 2) both refer to the identical situation. In the same way, John 10:20 (use 1) and 10:21 (use 2) both refer to the same situation. And again, Mark 5:15 employs both use 1 and use 2 in the same verse, referring to the identical situation. Every major Greek New Testament lexicon defines *daimonizomai* as "to be possessed by a demon." The language of uses 3 and 4 imply what uses 1 and 2 explicitly mean.

The language used of demons "entering in," "going out," or being "cast out" is consistently employed in regard to demonized persons (Matt. 8:16, 32; 9:33; 12:22–24; Mark 1:34; 5:8, 13). If these terms mean anything, they suggest the idea of a demon actually taking up residence and powerful influence within the body of a demonized person. To understand the term "demonize" for anything else than someone who has a demon within is to misinterpret Scripture.

The term "demonized" in Scripture refers to "the invasion of a victim's body by a demon (or demons), in which the demon exercises living and dominant control over the victim, which the victim cannot successfully resist."[19] The elements of indwelling

---

18. Ed Murphy, *The Handbook for Spiritual Warfare* (Nashville: Thomas Nelson, 1992), ix.
19. Alex Konya, *Demons: A Biblically Based Perspective* (Schaumburg, IL: Regular Baptist, 1990), 21–22.

and the inability to resist the demon's will are what make demonization distinct from lesser forms of demonic influence. The New Testament uses this word only in the narrow sense of demon possession. Thus, other forms of external influence cannot properly be called "demon possession" or demonization. Rather, they can be referred to as demon oppression or demon harassment. Therefore, lexically speaking, in all thirty-two cases where the Gospels and Acts speak of people involved with demons, they refer to people within whom a demon or demons reside.

BIBLICAL ACCOUNTS

The Bible recounts 15 specific occasions where demons indwell humans:[20]

1. Old Testament (4 particular incidents):
   a. 1 Samuel 16:14–23: Saul
   b. 1 Samuel 18:10: Saul
   c. 1 Samuel 19:9: Saul
   d. 1 Kings 22:22–23: four hundred prophets of Ahab
2. Gospels (9 particular incidents):
   a. Matthew 8:28–34; Mark 5:1–17; Luke 8:26–37: Gadarene demoniac
   b. Matthew 9:32–34: demon-possessed man in Capernaum (dumb)
   c. Matthew 12:22–29: demon-possessed blind and dumb man
   d. Matthew 15:21–28; Mark 7:24–30: Syro-Phoenecian woman and daughter
   e. Matthew 17:14–20; Mark 9:14–29; Luke 9:37–43: coming off the Mount of Transfiguration
   f. Mark 1:21–28; Luke 4:31–37: man with demon in Capernaum synagogue
   g. Mark 16:9; Luke 8:2: Mary Magdalene
   h. Luke 11:14–26: dumb, demon-possessed man
   i. Luke 13:10–17: woman bent double
3. Acts (2 particular incidents):
   a. Acts 16:16–18: fortune teller in Philippi
   b. Acts 19:11–17: sons of Sceva
4. Epistles and Revelation (none)

Are there any clear biblical examples of true believers being indwelt by demons in the above Scripture passages? A review of the biblical data quickly eliminates 11 of the 15 possibilities—only Saul in the Old Testament (3 times) and the woman bent double in Luke 13:10–17 remain.

HISTORICAL ASPECTS

There are only four historical instances that can be biblically verified where the person with demon involvement might be a true believer. They are Saul in 1 Samuel 16; 18; and 19 and the woman afflicted for eighteen years in Luke 13.

Was Saul a true believer? For the sake of this discussion, it is assumed that he truly

---

20. See Dickason, *Angels: Elect and Evil.*

trusted in God's grace for salvation. As evidence, note the eight times Saul received the accolade "the LORD's anointed" (1 Sam. 24:6, 10; 26:9, 11, 16, 23; 2 Sam. 1:14, 16). Also, Samuel told Saul that in death the two of them would be together (1 Sam. 28:19).

Since Saul at least appears to have been a believer, it can be asked, was he indwelt by demons that needed to be cast out? The following language describes the way in which the "evil spirit" affected Saul:

1. "tormented him" (1 Sam. 16:14–15)
2. "upon you" (1 Sam. 16:16)
3. "upon Saul" (1 Sam. 16:23)
4. "upon Saul" (1 Sam. 18:10)
5. "upon Saul" (1 Sam. 19:9)

None of these phrases suggest that the evil or harmful spirit existed *within* Saul. In every instance, the text speaks about *external* torment. As a matter of fact, the Hebrew language has the perfect-tense word (*bo'*) that would certainly have been used if Saul had been indwelt. But it was not. However, this is the very word Ezekiel used when he said, "The Spirit entered into me" (Ezek. 2:2; 3:24), in a clear case of indwelling by the Holy Spirit.

With respect to the woman bent double in Luke 13:10–17, no one can question the fact that she suffered for eighteen years because of a spirit (Luke 13:11) identified as Satan (Luke 13:16). But was she a believer? Those who say yes do so because Christ referred to her as "a daughter of Abraham" (Luke 13:16). They suggest a parallel with Zacchaeus, who, on becoming a believer, was called "a son of Abraham" by Jesus. But a closer look at Luke 19:9 paints a different picture.

Salvation came *because* Zacchaeus was "a son of Abraham" and *because* "the Son of Man came to seek and to save the lost" (Luke 19:10). Jesus came to save his people (the Jews) from their sins (Matt. 1:21). Zacchaeus didn't become a "son of Abraham" as a result of salvation in the sense of Galatians 3:7, which says that "it is those of faith who are the sons of Abraham." Rather, he was a Jew—also known as a "son of Abraham"—and because Jesus came to save his people, he drew Zacchaeus to saving belief. Zacchaeus had always been a "son of Abraham"; only later did he believe in the Lord Jesus Christ for salvation.

Likewise, the woman in Luke 13, a daughter of Abraham, was an unbeliever who had been bound by a physical infirmity from Satan and possibly demons. She received release from her torment through the ministry of Jesus. She experienced resident evil not as a believer but as an unbeliever.

Thus, there is not one instance in Scripture where Satan or demons resided within a true believer and needed to be expelled.

THEOLOGICAL FACTORS

The New Testament Epistles never warn believers about the possibility of demon inhabitation, even though Satan and demons are discussed rather frequently. Nor do the New Testament Epistles ever instruct believers about how to cast out demons from either a believer or an unbeliever. It is biblically inconceivable that a true believer could be indwelt by demons when the Bible presents no clear historical example and gives no warnings or instructions for such a serious spiritual experience.

At least five other theological factors confirm this conclusion:

1. The thrust of 2 Corinthians 6:14–18 precludes thinking that the Holy Spirit and unclean spirits can cohabit in true believers—even temporarily.
2. Salvation, as described in Colossians 1:13, speaks of true "deliverance" from Satan and transference to the kingdom of Christ.
3. The following passages, when combined together, make a powerful statement that refutes the idea of demons indwelling Christians:
   a. Romans 8:37–39: We overwhelmingly conquer through Christ.
   b. 1 Corinthians 15:57: God gives us victory through our Lord Jesus Christ.
   c. 2 Corinthians 2:14: God always leads us in his triumph in Christ.
   d. 1 John 2:13–14: We have overcome the Evil One.
   e. 1 John 4:4: The greater power resides in us.
4. The sealing ministry of the Holy Spirit protects Christians against demon invasion (2 Cor. 1:21–22; Eph. 4:30).
5. The promise of 1 John 5:18 makes the idea of demon invasion an unbiblical concept and an impossibility for a true believer.

PRACTICAL CONCERNS

There can be no question that demons do at times reside within human beings. Otherwise, there would be no need to cast them out (Gk. *ekballō*). Scripture also affirms that when demons indwell human beings, they frequently debilitate the human host. Demonic residency has resulted in physical problems such as epilepsy (Matt. 17:14–18), blindness (Matt. 12:22), deafness (Mark 9:25), and the inability to speak (Matt. 9:32–33). When the demon is evicted, the physical problem also departs, and the person is healed.

Having understood these things, can true believers be indwelt by demons with a need for these demons to be evicted? After a complete study of the appropriate scriptures, the answer is no. Demonization (Gk. *daimonizomai*) refers only to unbelievers in whom a demon resides. The Bible concludes that the deliverance of a Christian from indwelling demons is an oxymoron.

The Bible stands supreme as the unique source of divine revelation about the spiritual world of Satan and demons. Clinical and counseling experiences will never be equal to Scripture and should never be used to draw conclusions that are not first clearly taught in the Word of God.

The Bible convincingly reveals that true believers cannot be inhabited by Satan or demons. However, they can be tormented, oppressed, and harassed externally, even to a severe degree like Saul (or centuries later, like Paul, who was allowed to endure a satanic thorn in the flesh, 2 Cor. 12:7). Should demons actually be found to indwell a person, this would be evidence that he or she lacks genuine salvation, no matter how strongly that person or a counselor or a pastor or even a demon argues otherwise. If one encounters a truly demonized person, then he must recognize the strength of the enemy, appeal to God in prayer (see Jude 9), and use the power of Scripture (Rom. 1:16)—especially the gospel—to deal with the situation.

Demons' Judgments

Earlier we discussed "Satan's Judgments" (see p. 703), and the treatment there of Satan's Edenic, Calvary, tribulational, millennial, and eternal judgments applies equally to demons. However, it would seem that the original judgment on demons had several variations. One portion of the entire group who initially rebelled with Satan (Rev. 12:4) was cast out of heaven and directly into the Abyss (2 Pet. 2:4; Jude 6; cf. Luke 8:31). Another part of the group who was cast out of heaven and directly into the Abyss will later be released in the middle of Daniel's seventieth week (Rev. 9:1–11). There seems also to be a special group of four demons bound at the Euphrates River who will be released at the end of Daniel's seventieth week (Rev. 9:13–15). Others who were originally cast down with Satan will accompany him throughout his time in heaven and on earth to do his treacherous bidding (Isa. 24:21; Rev. 12:7–9).

During Satan's millennial judgment/confinement, all demons will also be imprisoned with him. Finally, when Satan is released and then eternally judged, it appears certain that all demons will be with him then and forevermore (Isa. 24:22; Matt. 25:41; 2 Pet. 2:4; Jude 6; Rev. 20:10).

Angel of the Lord

Old Testament Appearances
Characteristics of Deity
Identification
New Testament Correlation

The Old Testament Hebrew word *mal'akh* and the New Testament Greek word *angelos* can both generally be translated "messenger," "envoy," or "ambassador" when referring to task or function. The messenger can be human in nature, such as the messengers of Jacob (Gen. 32:3, 6), the messengers of John the Baptist (Luke 7:24), or the messengers of Christ (Luke 9:52). Frequently, the messenger is a nonhuman, supernatural, created being, usually referred to as an "angel" (2 Chron. 32:21; Matt. 1:20, 24).

The phrase "angel of the LORD," appears only in the Old Testament, never the New Testament, and refers to a unique, one-of-a-kind envoy. Even "the angel of the Lord" in Matthew 1:24 indicates a created angelic being of no extraordinary significance since this text uses the definite article to point back to Matthew 1:20, which reads, "an angel of the Lord." In Acts 7:30–35, Stephen quotes Exodus 3:1–10, which refers to the historical appearance of the angel whom Isaiah identifies as "the angel of his presence" (Isa. 63:9).

This special person is mentioned in the Old Testament by multiple titles:

1. "the angel of the LORD" (Gen. 16:7)
2. "the angel of God" (Gen. 21:17)
3. "his angel" (Gen. 24:7, 40)
4. "my angel" (Ex. 23:23)
5. "the angel of his presence" (Isa. 63:9)
6. "the messenger of the covenant" (Mal. 3:1)

With these general observations serving as background, this ultimate question demands an answer: Who is the mystery angel of the Old Testament? At least four possible identities have been offered over the centuries: (1) an "angel" from heaven, possibly the archangel Michael; (2) Melchizedek; (3) the Lord (Yahweh) himself (a theophany); or (4) a christophany or *huiophany* (from Gk. *huios*, "son")—that is, a preincarnate appearance on earth by the Lord Jesus Christ. In order to determine which one of these possibilities is the correct identity, several lines of biblical evidence must be presented. After that, a conclusive identification will be offered.

Old Testament Appearances

The Hebrew noun for "angel"/"messenger" appears about 213 times in the Old Testament. In about 90 uses, mostly in the Historical Books, it refers to "the angel of the LORD." This phrase first occurs in Genesis 16:7 and continues to the final use in Malachi 3:1, appearing in sixteen of the thirty-nine Old Testament books. At other times, only "angel" is used, and then the identity is not quite as certain (Dan. 3:28; 6:22). Frequently, human messengers are in view (about 50 percent of the time). Table 8.9 provides a representative sample of "the angel of the LORD" encounters or mentions.

Characteristics of Deity

The "angel of the LORD" exhibits qualities that can only be associated with deity:

1. The "angel of the LORD" claims a divine nature (Ex. 3:2–5; Judg. 13:17–18).
2. The "angel of the LORD" displays divine attributes (Ex. 23:21; 33:14; Isa. 63:9).
3. Scripture equates the "angel of the LORD" with the Lord (Yahweh), even with God (Gen. 16:11–13; 22:9–18; 32:24–30; see Gen. 48:15–16; Ex. 3:2–6; 13:21–22 [compared with 14:19]; 32:34; 33:2; Num. 22:35 [compared with 23:5]; Judg. 6:11–16; 13:21–23; Hos. 12:4).
4. Yet the Lord (Yahweh) and the "angel of the LORD" are not the same person. For instance, the Lord sends the angel (Ex. 23:20–23). At other times, the "angel of the LORD" speaks to the Lord (Zech. 1:12), and the Lord answers the angel (Zech. 1:13).
5. The "angel of the LORD" is the chief protector of Israel (Ex. 14:19–20; 23:20–23; Josh. 5:13–15; Pss. 34:7; 35:5–6).
6. The "angel of the LORD" possesses the name of "the LORD" (Ex. 3:14; Judg. 13:17–18; see Isa. 9:6).
7. The "angel of the LORD" receives worship (Ex. 3:5; Josh. 5:15; Judg. 13:20).
8. The "angel of the LORD" forgives sin (Gen. 48:16; Ex. 23:21).

Table 8.9 *"The Angel of the* LORD*" in Scripture*

People	Passages
Hagar	Gen. 16:7–14; 21:17
Abraham	Gen. 22:11–18
Eliezer	Gen. 24:7, 40
Jacob	Gen. 31:11–13; 32:22–32 (see Gen. 48:15–16; Hos. 12:3–4)
Moses	Ex. 3:1–7 (see Acts 7:30–35); Ex. 12:23 ("the destroyer," cf. Heb. 11:28); Ex. 14:19–20 (see Num. 20:16); Ex. 23:20–23 (see Isa. 63:9)
Balaam	Num. 22:22–35
Joshua	Josh. 5:13–15 (see Ex. 3:5); Judg. 2:1–4
Gideon	Judg. 6:11–18
Manoah and his wife	Judg. 13:2–22
David	2 Sam. 24:16–17; 1 Chron. 21:15–18, 27
Elijah	1 Kings 19:4–8; 2 Kings 1:3–4, 15–16
Hezekiah	2 Kings 19:35 (see 2 Chron. 32:21; Isa. 37:36)
Shadrach, Meshach, and Abednego	Dan. 3:25, 28
Daniel	Dan. 6:22
Zechariah	Zech. 1:11–12; 3:1–10
Malachi	Mal. 3:1

Identification

The "angel of the LORD" has been identified by some as a special, created angel who is unnamed in the biblical record. In the writings of the apostolic fathers (ca. AD 150), the "angel of the LORD" is sometimes identified as Michael the archangel.[21] Later commentators occasionally followed suit. However, no created angel, even an archangel, ever possessed the traits of deity previously noted from the biblical record; thus, the angel view must be disqualified.

An infrequently encountered proposal suggests that the Old Testament "angel of the LORD" is the king of Salem, Melchizedek (Gen. 14:18), the mysterious high priest in whose order the Lord Jesus Christ is said to follow (Ps. 110:4; Heb. 5:6, 10; 6:20; 7:17). This idea presupposes that Melchizedek is the preincarnate Christ, which is easily dismissed because there is no substantial biblical evidence in support of this notion. Melchizedek, the historical king of Salem in the time of Abraham, could not have been Christ, who then later became a high priest after the order of himself.[22]

Another possibility might be that the "angel of the LORD" is a self-manifestation of the Lord (Yahweh) himself—that is, a true theophany.[23] While this approach recognizes the divine attributes of the angel, it does not account for the evidence of

---

21. *The Shepherd of Hermas* 3.8.3.
22. For a convincing refutation, see James A. Borland, *Christ in the Old Testament*, rev. ed. (Fearn, Ross-shire, Scotland: Christian Focus, 1999), 139–47.
23. Thomas E. McComiskey, "Angel of the Lord," in *Evangelical Dictionary of Theology*, ed. Walter A. Elwell (Grand Rapids, MI: Baker, 1984), 48.

at least two personages in many of the biblical accounts—the "angel of the LORD" and "the LORD"—which is in perfect harmony with the triune composition of the Godhead (God the Father, Eph. 1:3–6; God the Son, Eph. 1:7–12; and God the Holy Spirit, Eph. 1:13–14).

The only identification of the "angel of the LORD" that satisfies all the characteristics in the biblical record is the preincarnate appearance (a christophany or huiophany) of the second person of the triune Godhead, the eternal Son of God, the Lord Jesus Christ.[24] It is not surprising, then, that the earliest identifications of the "angel of the LORD" were that of a christophany.[25]

New Testament Correlation

The Old Testament "preincarnate Christ" view matches precisely with the New Testament explanation of God's eternal Son, the Lord Jesus Christ. First, by taking the name of "the LORD" (Gen. 16:11–13; 22:9–18), the "angel of the LORD" claims to be an eternal being. *Eternality* was the very assertion made by the Lord Jesus Christ (John 1:1; 8:58; 17:5).

Second, Christ claimed to be God, and Scripture states that he is indeed God (John 1:1; 5:18; 10:33; 2 Pet. 1:1; 1 John 5:20). This assertion harmonizes with the *deity* of the "angel of the LORD" (Ex. 3:2–6; Judg. 13:17–18).

Third, by claiming deity (Ex. 3:2–6; Judg. 13:17–18) and being an individual other than "the LORD" (Ex. 23:20–23; Isa. 6:1, 8 [with John 12:41–42]; Zech. 1:12–13), the "angel of the LORD" asserts that more than one person can be God. Only Christ, the second person of the triune Godhead, could make such a declaration, which corresponds perfectly with the *triunity* of God (Matt. 28:19; Mark 1:9–11; John 15:26; 2 Cor. 13:14).

Fourth, in his New Testament incarnation (as in his Old Testament preincarnate appearances), Christ fulfilled his *responsibility* to provide a revelation and explanation of God the Father that would otherwise have been beyond human comprehension (John 1:18; 10:30; 12:45; 14:7, 9; 2 Cor. 4:4; Col. 1:15, 19; 2:9; Heb. 1:3).

Thus, the attributes and activities of the Old Testament "angel of the LORD" compare perfectly with those of the New Testament incarnate Christ. In terms of Christ's eternality, deity, triunity, and responsibility, the biblical evidence overwhelmingly confirms that the "angel of the LORD" episodes in the Old Testament unquestionably involved the preincarnate Lord Jesus Christ.

Questions and Answers

What about Guardian Angels (Matt. 18:10)?
Should Angels Be Worshiped (Col. 2:18)?
Who Entertained Angels (Heb. 13:2)?

---

24. For the most compelling biblical presentation of this position, see C. Goodspeed, "The Angel of Jehovah," *BSac* 36, no. 144 (1879): 594–615.

25. For substantial documentation, see Günther Juncker, "Christ as Angel: The Reclamation of a Primitive Title," *TJ*, n.s., 15, no. 2 (1994): 221–50.

Some frequently asked questions were not answered in the previous discussions. The remaining significant inquiries are therefore included here.

What about Guardian Angels (Matt. 18:10)?

Humanistic and superstitious reasoning combined with sentimentalism have much to do with the idea of individual guardian angels. While the idea is said to be biblically based, a closer look at the supporting texts proves otherwise.

Jacob (Gen. 48:16) and the psalmist (Ps. 34:7) have been used to support the guardian angel idea. However, these passages speak about the "angel of the LORD" either indirectly (Jacob referring in Gen. 48:16 back to his encounter in Gen. 32:24–30) or directly (the psalmist commenting generally on multiple appearances in Israel's history from Genesis to Judges). Neither of these texts speak of personal guardian angels.

After Peter escaped incarceration by the aid of an angel (Acts 12:6–11), he went to the home of Mary, the mother of John Mark (12:12). The servant girl Rhoda reported to the prayer group that Peter was at the door, but they insisted, "It is his angel!" (12:13–15). There are two possible explanations for this response, neither of which involves a "guardian angel." First, they probably assumed that Peter had been beheaded like James (12:1–2) and that this was Peter's afterlife appearance form (in accord with Jewish superstition). Second, it is also possible that the use of the Greek word *angelos* here (12:15) refers to a human messenger reporting the death of Peter in spite of their prayers that the outcome would be otherwise.

The most likely biblical text to teach guardian angels is Matthew 18:10: "For I tell you that in heaven their angels always see the face of my Father who is in heaven." However, this suggests not that each believer has an individual guardian angel but rather that believers are collectively served by angels in general, often multiple angels aiding one person at the same time, as in the band of angels that carried Lazarus to heaven (Luke 16:22), the army of angels that fought for Israel (2 Kings 6:17), and the angels commanded by God to protect those who seek shelter in the shadow of the Almighty (Ps. 91:11).

How this works, for whom it works, and when it works, the Bible does not indicate specifically. However, while Scripture clearly says that angels are ministering spirits (Heb. 1:14), it does not say that there are individual guardian angels for each person alive in the world at one time.

Should Angels Be Worshiped (Col. 2:18)?

Angels are not to be worshiped (Col. 2:18); angels are to worship God (Heb. 1:6). One form of created being (humans) is not to worship other forms of God's creation (angels, animals, nature, the stars above). In Scripture, angels are always seen worshiping God, never approvingly being worshiped themselves (Isa. 6:1–4; Rev. 5:8–14).

Early in the history of Israel, the people were not only exhorted to worship God alone but were also prohibited from worshiping any object (Ex. 20:1–5; 34:14; Deut. 11:16; 30:17; Pss. 31:6; 97:7). The penalty for disobedience always proved severe (Ex. 32:1–10).

Christ was tempted by Satan (a created being) in the wilderness. Satan offered him all the kingdoms of the world and their glory if only the Savior would fall down and worship him. Christ immediately rejected the offer, quoting Deuteronomy 6:13. For good measure, Jesus replied to him, "Be gone, Satan!" (Matt. 4:10; Luke 4:8).

Later in the New Testament, people attempted to worship first Peter (Acts 10:25–26) and then Paul and Barnabas (Acts 14:9–15). In both cases, the ill-directed worship was summarily rejected. Near the end of John's life, he was so overwhelmed by angelic presence that he attempted to worship them on two separate occasions. In both cases, the angels rejected John's worship and redirected him to worship God (Rev. 19:9–10; 22:8–9).

Whether one looks to biblical precepts or biblical practices, angelic worship is forbidden as idolatry. God alone is to be worshiped.

Who Entertained Angels (Heb. 13:2)?[26]

The teaching in Hebrews 13:2 that "some have entertained angels unawares" is given not as the ultimate motivation for hospitality but rather to reveal that one never knows how far-reaching an act of kindness might be (cf. Matt. 25:40, 45). This is exactly what happened to Abraham and Sarah (Gen. 18:1–3), Lot (Gen. 19:1–2), Gideon (Judg. 6:11–24), and Manoah (Judg. 13:6–20). The writer of Hebrews is not suggesting that believers should expect angelic visitations. Rather, he is vividly implying that when one practices biblical hospitality (1 Tim. 3:2; Titus 1:8), one may at times experience unexpected blessing, as illustrated in the early portions of the Old Testament.

Into What Do Angels Long to Look (1 Pet. 1:12)?[27]

It is not that the angels have been uninvolved in God's plan of salvation. They announced Christ's birth (Luke 1:26–35; 2:10–14), ministered to him during his times of testing (Matt. 4:11; Luke 22:43), stood by the grave when he arose from the dead (Matt. 28:5–7; Mark 16:4–7; Luke 24:4–7), and attended his ascension into heaven (Acts 1:10–11).

---

26. This section is adapted from MacArthur, *MacArthur Study Bible: English Standard Version*, 1871. Used by permission of Thomas Nelson.

27. This section is adapted from John MacArthur, *1 Peter*, MNTC (Chicago: Moody Publishers, 2004), 58. Used by permission of Moody Publishers.

Since then, angels have rejoiced over sinners who repent (Luke 15:7, 10). The apostles became a spectacle to angels (1 Cor. 4:9). Angels are concerned over pastors who habitually sin (1 Tim. 5:21). They are ministering spirits sent out to serve on behalf of those who are to inherit salvation (Heb. 1:14). After death, believers will join the angels for heavenly worship (Rev. 5:11–14).

Angels are nearby enough to watch apostles, serve saints, worship with believers in heaven, and rejoice at an individual's salvation, but there is something additional on which they are intensely focused. Like Peter, John, and Mary, who stooped over to peer into the empty tomb (Luke 24:12; John 20:5, 11), or like a man looking intently into Scripture (James 1:25), angels strain to see the salvation fruit that is resulting from Christ's suffering on the cross, resurrection from the dead, and ascension into heaven.

Angels have a holy curiosity to understand the kind of mercy and grace they will never experience. The holy angels do not need to be saved, and the fallen angels cannot be saved. But the holy ones seek to understand salvation so that they might glorify God more fully, which is their primary reason for existence (Job 38:7; Ps. 148:2; Isa. 6:3; Luke 2:13–14; Heb. 1:6; Rev. 5:11–12; 7:11–12).

Do Churches Have Angels (Rev. 1:16, 20)?

The seven "stars" (Rev. 1:16) are the "messengers" of the seven churches (Rev. 1:20). Most English translations use "angel" instead of "messenger" to translate the Greek word *angelos*. However, here it is better to use the most general sense of this word, namely, "messenger," and let the context interpret its meaning.

Angelos can refer to good angels (Rev. 5:11) or evil angels (Matt. 25:41). Frequently in the New Testament, it is also used of human messengers (Matt. 11:10; Mark 1:2; Luke 7:24; James 2:25). "Star" in the Bible can refer to many things, such as an actual star (Rev. 6:13), demons (Rev. 9:1), humans (Rev. 12:1), Christ (Rev. 22:16), or angels (Job 38:7). It was common in ancient literature for "star" to represent an important person (Dan. 12:3). Society even has its own "stars" and "superstars" today.

With this in mind, there are three reasonable interpretations of "star." Some say that it refers to the "attitude" of the church. Others say that it refers to real angels. However, in this context the idea of a human being seems most satisfying.

First, "star" and "messenger" are used in both the Old Testament and the New Testament to refer to humans. Second, nowhere in the Bible are angels placed in a leadership position over the church. Third, well-established ecclesiology has concluded that Christ is not writing here to angels but to humans (Rev. 2:1, 8, 12, 18; 3:1, 7, 14). Finally, humans, not angels, are responsible to God for the conduct of the church (Heb. 13:17); angels are on the outside curiously looking in (1 Pet. 1:12).

The seven "messengers" actually represent the human leadership of the church, which comprises the elders and overseers. That they are in Christ's right hand represents Christ's power over his churches. It reminds leaders that they lead by Christ's authority, not their own.

How Will Christians Judge Angels (1 Cor. 6:3)?

The Greek verb *krinō* in 1 Corinthians 5:12, 13; 6:1, 2, and 3 primarily means to "judge," "decide," or "determine." So in what sense and for what angels will Christians bring judgment in the future?

Some have suggested that a Hebrew verb (*shaphat*) is translated *krinō* in the Septuagint with the alternative meaning of "rule over" (1 Sam. 8:20). Thus, it could possibly be used the same way in the New Testament, meaning that Christians are to rule over holy angels, since angels are servants of believers (Heb. 1:14). However, the context of 1 Corinthians 5:9–6:11 clearly conveys the idea of adjudication and cannot be used in the secondary sense of ruling.

Since *krinō* is employed here in a judicial sense, that raises some intermediate questions. First, in what way do holy angels need to be judged? Holy angels by their very nature do not need to be judged. Nor does Scripture give even the slightest indication by statement or example that they ever received or will receive judgment.

Second, how will Christians judge evil angels? They currently await the judgment of the great day (2 Pet. 2:4; Jude 6), which must coincide with the judgment of Satan when he will be thrown into the lake of fire (Rev. 20:10) and joined by his angels (Matt. 25:41). Since believers are promised that they will sit with Christ on his throne (Rev. 3:21) and have authority to judge (Rev. 20:4), then believers may judge evil angels with Christ in the judgment of the great day. It is to this event that Paul alludes in 1 Corinthians 6:3.

Do Isaiah 14 and Ezekiel 28 Refer to Satan?

Just as Scripture indirectly relates idols to demons (Deut. 32:17; Ps. 106:37–38) and an impetuous Peter to Satan (Matt. 16:23), so the king of Babylon (Isa. 14:4–21) and the king of Tyre (Ezek. 28:1–19) are indirectly related to Satan. Pagan kings who promoted false worship, even insisting that by nature they were actually deity, served as human surrogates for Satan. Such were these two kings.

Isaiah 14:12–14 provides a glimpse of Satan through the life of Babylon's king. It pictures one who would elevate himself to the level of God (Isa. 14:13–14) but who failed (Isa. 14:12) in his attempted self-exaltation. This was true of the Babylonian monarch in much the same manner as it replicated the earlier fall of the Evil One.

Ezekiel 28:2, 6, 12–17 also shows how the king of Tyre behaved in his reign similarly to Satan in the past. This ruler modeled Satan's previous attitudes and actions.

Therefore, one must be balanced when interpreting these two passages—careful not to ignore Satan, cautious not to treat the passages as though Satan were the exclusive subject, and prudent to understand that the primary or direct intent of the writers was to pronounce God's judgment on the actual kings while using Satan's background to illustrate the evilness of their rule. This approach would seem to be confirmed by the New Testament, which abundantly reveals truth about the Devil without directly quoting Isaiah 14 or Ezekiel 28.

Table 8.10 Man's Fallen Intellectual Capacity

"debased"	Rom. 1:28		"deluded"	Col. 2:4
"hardened"	2 Cor. 3:14		"deceived"	Col. 2:8
"blinded"	2 Cor. 4:4		"sensuous"	Col. 2:18
"futility"	Eph. 4:17		"depraved"	1 Tim. 6:5
"darkened"	Eph. 4:18		"corrupted"	2 Tim. 3:8
"hostile"	Col. 1:21		"defiled"	Titus 1:15

Does Satan Read Minds?[28]

Does the Devil have the power to know what individual people are thinking? The answer is no for the following reasons.

First, Satan is a created being (John 1:3; Col. 1:16). Therefore, he does not share with God the divine attribute of omniscience. Second, nowhere in Scripture is there even the slightest hint that the Evil One is all-knowing at all times, past, present, and future.

Third, Satan is the mediate, not immediate, cause of man's corrupted thinking. At the completion of creation, "God saw everything that he had made, and behold, it was very good" (Gen. 1:31). Adam and Eve were in righteous fellowship with God and had been given dominion over all of God's creation (Gen. 1:26–30). A life of earthly bliss described their potential future and that of their offspring before sin entered the picture.

Genesis 3:1–7 describes the far-reaching and devastating blow to the human mind that would affect every human being who lived thereafter. Without question, Satan waged war against God and the human race in this monumental passage, where the battlefield turns out to be Eve's mind. In the end, Eve exchanged the truth of God (Gen. 2:17) for the lie of Satan (Gen. 3:4–5), and the human mind has never been the same since.

Fourth, the extent of this mental corruption is illustrated by the many different negative New Testament words that describe the ruin of man's intellectual capacity as a result of original sin (see table 8.10).

As a result, God's two original created human beings, and every one of their offspring, experienced a brutal reversal in their relationship with God and his world:

1. They would concern themselves no longer with thoughts of God but with the thinking of men (Ps. 53:1; Rom. 1:25).
2. They would no longer have spiritual sight but would be blinded by Satan to the glory of God (2 Cor. 4:4).
3. They would no longer be wise but foolish (Ps. 14:1; Titus 3:3).
4. They would no longer be alive to God but would be dead in their sins (Rom. 8:5–11).

---

28. This section is adapted from Richard L. Mayhue, "Cultivating a Biblical Mind-Set," in *Think Biblically: Recovering a Christian Worldview*, ed. John MacArthur (Wheaton, IL: Crossway, 2003), 39–41. Used by permission of Crossway.

5. They would set their affections no longer on the things above but on the things of earth (Col. 3:2).
6. They would walk no longer in light but rather in darkness (John 12:35–36, 46).
7. They would live no longer in the realm of the Spirit but rather in the flesh (Rom. 8:1–5).
8. They would no longer possess eternal life but would face spiritual death—that is, eternal separation from God (2 Thess. 1:9).

So Satan can know the generally degenerate quality of a person's thinking as a result of his deceitful scheming in his garden confrontation with Eve, but he cannot know the specifics as a result of reading minds. Satan's two conversations with God and the encounter with Job (Job 1–2) illustrate this point. Satan pretended that he knew the details of Job's thinking, but subsequent events proved the Devil to be inept and unable to correctly know the particulars of Job's mind because he cannot read minds.

How Are Christ and Satan Related?

Christ created all things, and apart from him, nothing else has come into being (John 1:3, 10; 1 Cor. 8:6; Col. 1:16; Heb. 1:2). Satan is a created being and thus neither a peer nor a superior of Christ. Satan created nothing and is always an inferior being to the divine lordship and will of Jesus (1 John 3:8).

In Job 1:12 and 2:6, Satan had to submit to the will of God. In Matthew 4:10, Christ demanded that Satan depart from him. In the end, Christ will defeat Satan, judge him guilty of high crimes and treason, and sentence him to an eternity in the lake of fire (John 16:11; Rev. 20:9–10).

Christ is the Creator from whom Satan received life. Christ is the sovereign to whom Satan must submit. Christ is the Judge from whom the guilty-as-charged Satan will receive his final judgment and eternal sentence to hell.

Can Satan or Demons Perform Miracles?

Created beings such as Satan and demons do not have the miraculous power of omnipotent God. God has undeniably worked miracles through Christ (John 11:47–48) and the apostles (Acts 4:16) but never in like manner on behalf of Satan or demons.

One of Satan's chief strategies is to deceive (Rev. 12:9; 13:3, 12, 14; 19:20; 20:3, 8, 10), that is, to make a nonmiraculous act appear to be as powerful as an act by God. However, it is only an appearance, not a reality.

While Satan has powers beyond humans (Job 1:12; 2:6), they are limited by God. The magicians in Pharaoh's court matched in appearance the first three plagues from God (Ex. 7:11–12, 22; 8:7), but they could not continue from the fourth one on (Ex. 8:18–19); they admitted that their powers were far exceeded by God's omnipotence. Satan will empower false signs and wonders in the latter half of Daniel's seventieth week for the Antichrist (2 Thess. 2:9–10), the False Prophet (Rev. 13:13–14), and demons (Rev. 16:13–14).

Can Satan or demons heal like Jesus or the apostles? Neither Satan nor demons possess creative power and thus cannot heal miraculously as God heals. However, when demons depart from unbelievers (of their own volition), the illness could depart as well. This would give the appearance of the miraculous.

It seems that a negative answer to the question, can demons heal? was a self-evident truth to first-century Palestinians. Jesus had been accused of having a demon on at least six occasions: (1) Matthew 9:32–34; (2) Matthew 12:22–29; Mark 3:30; (3) Luke 11:14–26; (4) John 7:20; (5) John 8:48–49, 52; and (6) John 10:20–21. Those who best knew the fruit of Christ's ministry responded to this charge by saying, "A demon cannot open the eyes of the blind, can he?" (John 10:21 NASB). Thus, demons can possibly give the convincing appearance of healing, but they cannot heal miraculously in reality. They are deceiving spirits (1 Tim. 4:1) whose signs are not of God (Rev. 16:14).

Are Demons in the World Today?

Why do demons sometimes receive so much attention from the media? Are the reports biblically correct, or are they just the musings of uninformed people who see a demon behind every bush and under every rock? Has demon activity accelerated in the world? How can one know which concepts are biblically accurate and which are not?

This subject deserves a full-length book, but it will only be summarized here. Consider several preliminary, general observations:

1. We affirm the historical reality of Satan and demons, both in the past and in the present, as verified by the Bible.
2. We affirm that the Bible admonishes Christians to expect Satan and demons to operate now much as they did in both Old Testament and New Testament times (1 Pet. 5:6–11).
3. We affirm that the Bible teaches that, in living out the Christian life, one will experience real spiritual battle with Satan and his army of demons.
4. We affirm that Scripture alone, independent of personal experience or clinical data, will truthfully determine the reality of demonic experiences and provide an understanding of encounters with Satan and demons.
5. We affirm that instructions in the New Testament Epistles on how to conduct spiritual warfare were not limited to the first century (Eph. 6:10–20).

In Scripture, Satan and demons prominently involved themselves with spiritual darkness (Eph. 6:12), deception (2 Cor. 11:13–15), and death (John 8:44). They thrive in these kinds of environments. The United States has rapidly accelerated toward these conditions over the last decades, as witnessed by increases in false religion and idolatry, sexual immorality and perversions, drug use, occultic activity, interest in Satanism, godlessness, shamelessness over sin, lawlessness, devaluation of human life, and societal attempts to suppress biblical truth.

Not only is the world a setting where Satan and demons thrive, but also the Christian community has unwittingly set itself up for great deception. In the church, this normally finds two extremes—overemphasis or underemphasis on the spirit world.

Much of the Christian community today pays too little attention to scriptural teachings and warnings about Satan and demons. Because much demonic activity in the world occurs invisibly, people assume it doesn't exist. For some Christians, an ignorance of Scripture combined with an attitude of materialism produces an unhealthy indifference to the invisible war with darkness. For others, an unrealistic attitude of spiritual invincibility dominates. This leaves many Christians unwittingly ignorant, vulnerable, and unprepared for the current increase of spiritual warfare.

Can Christians Bind Satan?

Only a very few New Testament passages might help to answer this inquiry. Matthew 12:22–29; Mark 3:27; and Luke 11:14–23 spiritually match the strong man (Satan, Matt. 22:29) against the stronger man (Christ, Luke 11:22). This text has nothing to do with believers binding Satan, just Christ binding—that is, having the greater power over—Satan.

Matthew 16:16–19 (esp. 16:19) speaks metaphorically about the apostles forgiving or not forgiving sin using the terms "bind" for "prohibited"/"unforgiven" and "loose" for "permitted"/"forgiven." The ancient rabbis used these terms in exactly this manner in this context. The passage has everything to do with authority to deal with sin and nothing to do with Satan. John 20:23 makes the same point using the straightforward terms "forgive" and "withhold forgiveness." Matthew 18:15–18 should be understood similarly in the context of disciplining a sinning brother.

Revelation 20:1–3 speaks of Christ's millennial kingdom where at the outset Satan is bound physically and incarcerated by an angel from heaven for the entire one thousand years. This text is time specific and refers only to the angel of Revelation 20:1, Satan, and the one thousand years of Christ's future reign on earth.

This review of the very few Bible passages that might possibly relate to the question should cause one to conclude that none of them remotely deal with the question at hand. So the simple answer is no, Christians cannot bind Satan, because there is no biblical teaching that would lead to an affirmative response.

Who Are the "Sons of God" in Genesis 6:1–4?

Genesis 6:1–4 proves to be one of the most mysterious, elusive texts in the Bible and one of the most difficult to interpret. As such, one ought not to be overly dogmatic since it remains one of a handful of texts that has a wide range of divergent views, even among interpreters who generally agree on almost all other issues. Therefore, it is best not to make too much of any possible doctrinal or practical implications.

There are several reasons why such a difficult text is found so early in Scripture:

1. The only immediate biblical context is Genesis 1–5.
2. The details in the text are meager and obscure.
3. There are no explicit, clear texts relating to Genesis 6:1–4 in subsequent Old Testament and New Testament passages except Matthew 24:37–39 and Luke 17:26–27.

4. The setting is postfall and preflood, about which biblical facts are few and far between.

Yet the very tantalizing obscurity of this passage makes it fascinatingly attractive to inquiring students of Scripture.

A number of very important questions arise: Who are the "sons of God" (Gen. 6:2)? Who are the "Nephilim" (Gen. 6:4)? Are demons involved here?

Several assumptions will be made to accommodate this summary discussion:

1. Genesis 6:1–4 is not ancient mythology but rather true and accurate divinely revealed history.
2. This passage needs to be interpreted in the context of Genesis 1–5.
3. The Nephilim in Genesis 6:4 are not necessarily offspring from the sons of God and daughters of men. In fact, Nephilim also appear centuries later in a postflood exodus setting (Num. 13:33).
4. Demons cannot mate with humans directly, since reproduction is after one's own kind (Gen. 1:20–25). Additionally, spirit beings cannot reproduce, even among themselves (see Matt. 22:30; Mark 12:25).
5. While direct angelic-human reproduction is not realistic, one must consider the possibility of an indirect angelic-human relationship taking place between demon-possessed men and women.
6. Some have found supposed New Testament links to Genesis 6:1–4 in 1 Peter 3:19–20; 2 Peter 2:4; and Jude 6. While this is a possibility, there are other equally satisfactory interpretations of these New Testament texts that do not require a connection back to Genesis 6. Thus, whatever view one takes, it should not rely on these New Testament passages as primary proof of the relationship.

With these introductory thoughts as background, a brief explanation and evaluation of the three most common views follows. The reader can then decide which view seems to have the most support and fewest problems.

"SINFUL SETHITES" VIEW

John Murray and Gleason Archer have espoused this view.[29] They contend that the godly line of Seth sinfully deviated from God's plan and married the ungodly female offspring of Cain. Thus, the line of Seth was polluted by this unholy intermarriage, and this explains why Noah and his family (Sethites) were spared in the flood, while all others fell to God's universal judgment on the human race.

Here are the more attractive features of this view:

1. The equivalent of "sons of God" elsewhere in Scripture refers to godly men (Deut. 14:1; Ps. 73:15; Isa. 43:6; Hos. 1:10).
2. The basis of the flood judgment was human sin, not demonic sin (Gen. 6:5–7), which explains why God's Spirit would not abide in or contend with men forever (Gen. 6:3).

---

29. John Murray, *Principles of Conduct: Aspects of Biblical Ethics* (Grand Rapids, MI: Eerdmans, 1957), 243–49; Gleason Archer, *Encyclopedia of Bible Difficulties* (Grand Rapids, MI: Zondervan, 1982), 79–80.

3. The context of Genesis 1–5 correlates well with this view.
4. Marrying outside the faith would result in mixed marriages and contamination of the godly Sethite line, which explains the severity of the flood on the whole human race except for Noah's family.
5. "Sons of God" seems to refer to a godly line, and "daughters of men" seems to refer to a sinful line.
6. This view correlates well with the conditions existing in Noah's day as described in the Gospels (Matt. 24:37–39; Luke 17:26–27), which portray life as generally ignoring the holy things of God in order to pursue the mundane things of men like eating, drinking, and marrying.

Here are the more problematic features of this view:

1. "Men" does not correspond exactly with "sons of God."
2. There is no explicit indication that "daughters of men" is limited to the line of Cain.
3. There is no explicit indication that "sons of God" refers to the line of Seth.

"DEMON-POSSESSED MEN" VIEW

Duane Garrett and Willem VanGemeren have espoused this view.[30] They contend that demons (evil angels) took up bodily residence in men, who were then prompted to live ungodly, licentious lives with the women of the world. The moral pollution proved so great and so universal that God destroyed the entire human race except Noah and his family.

Here are the more attractive features of this view:

1. The exact phrase "sons of God" refers elsewhere in the Old Testament to angels (Job 1:6; 2:1; 38:7).
2. The view explains the alleged contrast between "sons of God" and "daughters of men."
3. This view is one of the most ancient of known Genesis 6:1–4 explanations.

Here are the more problematic features of this view:

1. This view seems to artificially introduce demons not otherwise found in the context of Genesis 1–5.
2. God's judgment was against not evil angels but humans, which explains why God's Spirit focused on humans, not demons.
3. The phrase "sons of God" never refers to demons.
4. Ancient tradition is not the equivalent of Scripture in historical accuracy.
5. "Angel" was a part of Moses's vocabulary (Gen. 19:1, 15; 28:12; 32:1), so it seems inexplicable that he would use "sons of God," especially when referring to evil angels.
6. This view does not correspond to the biblically explicit descriptions of conditions in Noah's day (Matt. 24:37–39; Luke 17:26–27), which do not mention demons.

---

30. Duane A. Garrett, *Angels and the New Spirituality* (Nashville: Broadman, 1995), 46–47; Willem VanGemeren, "The Sons of God in Genesis 6:1–4 (An Example of Evangelical Demythologization)," *WTJ* 43, no. 2 (1981): 320–48. See also MacArthur, *1 Peter*, 212–16.

"ROGUE RULERS" VIEW

Walter Kaiser and Meredith Kline have espoused this view.[31] They contend that "sons of God" was an ancient phrase used to describe rulers and their male offspring who were represented as having a direct connection with deity and who ravaged and abused the women of the day, which severely distorted God's holy design for marriage, even resulting in rampant polygamy.

Here are the more attractive features of this view:

1. "Sons of God" was used biblically of human rulers (Ps. 82:6; John 10:33–36).
2. This view fits the context of God's judgment on men, not on evil angels.
3. This view correlates with the general description of Noah's day as described in the Gospels (Matt. 24:37–39; Luke 17:26–27), where men seem to easily and sinfully ignore the more important demands of God.

Here are the more problematic features of this view:

1. This view assumes more detail than Genesis 6:1–4 offers.
2. Scripture does not describe kings as being associated with deity at this period of world history.

Prayer[32]

Dear Father, this is the great glory of the gospel:
    that through Your beloved Son's work on the cross
        You rescue us from the domain of darkness
            and translate us into His kingdom of heavenly light,
            making us fit to share in the inheritance of the saints.

One of the most striking examples of that in Your Word
    is the testimony of the apostle Paul,
    who became a powerful advocate of the faith
        he once tried to destroy.
All who believe can likewise testify
    that You have ransomed us from the bondage of sin,
    given us new life,
    and fully equipped us for Your service—
        even though like Saul of Tarsus,
        we were once blasphemers and disobedient.
We honor Your name because of Your transforming power in our lives.

---

31. Walter C. Kaiser Jr., *More Hard Sayings of the Old Testament* (Downers Grove, IL: InterVarsity Press, 1992), 33–38; Meredith Kline, "Divine Kingship and Genesis 6:1–4," *WTJ* 24, no. 2 (1962): 187–204.

32. This prayer is reproduced verbatim from John MacArthur, *At the Throne of Grace: A Book of Prayers* (Eugene, OR: Harvest House, 2011), 124–26. Used by permission of Harvest House.

You have put a new song in our mouths,
    a song of perpetual praise to You.

We thank You for the work of the indwelling Holy Spirit,
    who transforms lives from the inside out.
We rejoice in the assurance that our sins are forgiven.
We are profoundly aware of our eternal indebtedness to Christ,
    who paid an incomprehensible price to set us free.
And we know that we are now free indeed—
    free from enslavement to the law,
    and blessedly liberated from bondage to sin.
Enable us, we pray, to stand firm in that freedom.
Safeguard our hearts and seal our deliverance,
      so that we shall never again be subject to any yoke
        other than the easy yoke and light burden of Christ.

We know that apart from Your gracious empowerment,
    all our attempts at godly love and faithful service
      are utterly futile.
Apart from the Holy Spirit's enablement,
    we neither could nor would honor Jesus as Lord.
Apart from the intercessory work of Christ,
    we know that we would falter.
Apart from the grace You give us to persevere,
    we would surely fall away.
And apart from the purifying power of Your Word,
    we could never be fit for heaven.

We confess to our deep shame
    that our hearts are prone to coldness.
Our love for You is too shallow and too fickle
    to honor You in a worthy manner.
Our submission to Christ too often proves fragile and erratic.
Our walk is faltering and inconsistent.
We are too susceptible
    to the lure of the world,
    the lusts of our own flesh,
    and the wiles of the devil.

Grant us more grace
    to be diligent in our duties,
    faithful in our devotion to Christ,
    industrious in the work of the gospel,
    clear in our testimony to the world,
    steadfast in our defense of the truth,
    and untiring in our service to You.
May all our conduct be worthy of the gospel of Christ.
May every aspect of our lives bring honor to our Savior,
    our Lord Jesus Christ, in whose name we pray. Amen.

"A Mighty Fortress Is Our God"

A mighty fortress is our God,
A bulwark never failing;
Our helper He amid the flood
Of mortal ills prevailing.
For still our ancient foe
Doth seek to work us woe—
His craft and pow'r are great,
And armed with cruel hate,
On earth is not his equal.

Did we in our own strength confide,
Our striving would be losing,
Were not the right man on our side,
The man of God's own choosing.
Dost ask who that may be?
Christ Jesus, it is He—
Lord Sabaoth His Name,
From age to age the same,
And He must win the battle.

And tho' this world, with devils filled,
Should threaten to undo us,
We will not fear, for God hath willed
His truth to triumph thro' us.
The prince of darkness grim,
We tremble not for him—
His rage we can endure,
For lo, his doom is sure:
One little word shall fell him.

That word above all earthly pow'rs,
No thanks to them, abideth;
The Spirit and the gifts are ours
Thro' Him who with us sideth.
Let goods and kindred go,
This mortal life also—
The body they may kill;
God's truth abideth still:
His kingdom is forever.

~Martin Luther (1483–1546)

Bibliography

Primary Systematic Theologies

*Bancroft, Emery H. *Christian Theology: Systematic and Biblical*. 2nd ed. Grand Rapids, MI: Zondervan, 1976. 307–43.

Berkhof, Louis. *Systematic Theology*. 4th ed. Grand Rapids, MI: Eerdmans, 1939. 141–49.

Buswell, James Oliver, Jr. *A Systematic Theology of the Christian Religion*. 2 vols. Grand Rapids, MI: Zondervan, 1962–1963. 1:130–34.

Culver, Robert Duncan. *Systematic Theology: Biblical and Historical*. Fearn, Ross-shire, Scotland: Mentor, 2005. 176–90.

Dabney, Robert Lewis. *Systematic Theology*. 1871. Reprint, Edinburgh: Banner of Truth, 1985. 264–75.

Erickson, Millard J. *Christian Theology*. Grand Rapids, MI: Baker, 1986. 433–51.

*Grudem, Wayne. *Systematic Theology: An Introduction to Biblical Doctrine*. Grand Rapids, MI: Zondervan, 1994. 397–436.

Hodge, Charles. *Systematic Theology*. 3 vols. 1871–1873. Reprint, Grand Rapids, MI: Eerdmans, 1975. 1:637–48.

Reymond, Robert L. *A New Systematic Theology of the Christian Faith*. Nashville: Thomas Nelson, 1998. 658–63.

Strong, August Hopkins. *Systematic Theology: A Compendium Designed for the Use of Theological Students*. Rev. ed. New York: Revell, 1907. 443–64.

*Swindoll, Charles R., and Roy B. Zuck, eds. *Understanding Christian Theology*. Nashville: Thomas Nelson, 2003. 537–640.

Thiessen, Henry Clarence. *Introductory Lectures in Systematic Theology*. Grand Rapids, MI: Eerdmans, 1949. 190–212.

*Turretin, Francis. *Institutes of Elenctic Theology*. 3 vols. Edited by James T. Dennison Jr. Translated by George Musgrove Giger. 1679–1685. Reprint, Phillipsburg, NJ: P&R, 1992–1997. 1:539–67.

*Denotes most helpful.

Specific Works

*Borland, James A. *Christ in the Old Testament: Old Testament Appearances of Christ in Human Form*. Rev. ed. Fearn, Ross-shire, Scotland: Mentor, 1999.

Brooks, Thomas. *Precious Remedies against Satan's Devices*. 1652. Reprint, Carlisle, PA: Banner of Truth, 1984.

*Dickason, C. Fred. *Angels, Elect and Evil*. Chicago: Moody Press, 1975.

Joppie, A. S. *The Ministry of Angels*. Grand Rapids, MI: Baker, 1953.

*Konya, Alex. *Demons: A Biblically Based Perspective*. Schaumburg, IL: Regular Baptist Press, 1990.

Leahy, Frederick S. *Satan Cast Out: A Study in Biblical Demonology*. Carlisle, PA: Banner of Truth, 1975.

Lockyer, Herbert. *All the Angels in the Bible*. Peabody, MA: Hendrickson, 1995.

Lowe, Chuck. *Territorial Spirits and World Evangelization? A Biblical, Historical, and Missiological Critique of Strategic-Level Spiritual Warfare*. Fearn, Ross-shire, Scotland: Christian Focus, 1998.

*MacArthur, John. *How to Meet the Enemy*. Wheaton, IL: Victor, 1992.

*Mayhue, Richard. "Demons and Sickness." In *The Healing Promise: Is It Always God's Will to Heal?*, 129–39. Fearn, Ross-shire, Scotland: Mentor, 1997.

*———. "False Prophets and the Deceiving Spirit (1 Kings 22:19–23)." In *The Master's Perspective on Difficult Passages*, edited by Robert L. Thomas, 15–43. The Master's Perspective 1. Grand Rapids, MI: Kregel, 1998.

*———. *Unmasking Satan: Understanding Satan's Battle Plan and Biblical Strategies for Fighting Back*. 1988. Reprint, Grand Rapids, MI: Kregel, 2001.

Noll, Stephen F. *Angels of Light, Powers of Darkness: Thinking Biblically about Angels, Satan, and Principalities*. Downers Grove, IL: InterVarsity Press, 1998.

Page, Sydney H. T. *Powers of Evil: A Biblical Study of Satan and Demons*. Grand Rapids, MI: Baker, 1995.

Powlison, David. *Power Encounters: Reclaiming Spiritual Warfare*. Grand Rapids, MI: Baker, 1995.

Rhodes, Ron. *Angels among Us*. Eugene, OR: Harvest House, 1994.

Richards, Larry. *Every Good and Evil Angel in the Bible*. Nashville: Thomas Nelson, 1998.

Unger, Merrill F. *Biblical Demonology: A Study of Spiritual Forces at Work Today*. 1952. Reprint, Grand Rapids, MI: Kregel, 2012.

*Denotes most helpful.

"The Church's One Foundation"

The Church's one foundation
Is Jesus Christ, her Lord;
She is His new creation
By water and the Word:
From heav'n He came and sought her
To be His holy bride;
With His own blood He bought her,
And for her life He died.

Elect from every nation,
Yet one o'er all the earth,
Her charter of salvation
One Lord, one faith, one birth;
One holy name she blesses,
Partakes one holy food;
And to one hope she presses,
With ev'ry grace endued.

'Mid toil and tribulation
And tumult of her war,
She waits the consummation
Of peace forevermore;
Till with the vision glorious
Her longing eyes are blest,
And the great Church victorious
Shall be the Church at rest.

Yet she on earth has union
With God, the Three in One,
And mystic sweet communion
With those whose rest is won;
O happy ones and holy!
Lord, give us grace that we,
Like them, the meek and lowly,
On high may dwell with Thee.

~Samuel J. Stone (1839–1900)

9

The Church

Ecclesiology

The church is "the dearest place on earth." That eloquent description, articulated by renowned nineteenth-century preacher Charles Spurgeon, captures a proper Christian perspective regarding the church. For all who know and love the Lord Jesus Christ, no place in the world should be sweeter or more cherished than the church.

The church is precious for many reasons, first and foremost because the Lord Jesus died on her behalf (Eph. 5:25). Because the church is loved by Christ, it ought to be treasured by all who belong to him. As Spurgeon went on to explain,

Nothing in the world is dearer to God's heart than his church; therefore, being his, let us also belong to it, that by our prayers, our gifts, and our labours, we may support and strengthen it. If those who are Christ's refrained, even for a generation, from numbering themselves with his people, there would be no visible church, no ordinances maintained, and, I fear, very little preaching of the gospel.[1]

In light of its vital importance, believers have much to gain by carefully studying what God has revealed about the church in his Word.

Defining the Church

Throughout the New Testament, the church is primarily designated by the Greek word *ekklēsia*, a term meaning "those who are called out."[2] In the ancient world, the *ekklēsia* referred to a group of citizens who had been "called out" to administrate civic affairs or to defend the community in battle. Used in a general and nontechnical way, the term came to refer to any "assembly" or "congregation." It was in this sense that Stephen, in Acts 7:38, referred to "the congregation" of Israel as those called out from slavery in Egypt under the leadership of Moses (cf. Ex. 19:17). In Acts 19:32 and 41, Luke employed the term to refer to an angry mob that assembled in Ephesus after being incited by the silversmiths there.

Used in a specific New Testament sense, the church of God (Acts 20:28; 1 Cor. 1:2; 10:32; 11:16, 22; 15:9; 2 Cor. 1:1; Gal. 1:13; 1 Thess. 2:14; 2 Thess. 1:4; cf. Rom. 16:16) refers to the community of those who have been called out by God from their slavery to sin through faith in Jesus Christ (Rom. 1:7; 1 Cor. 1:2; Eph. 4:1; 1 Thess. 2:12; 2 Tim. 1:9; 1 Pet. 5:10; cf. Rom. 8:28). They are those whom he predestined in eternity past, called and justified in this present life, and promised to glorify in the future (Rom. 8:30; cf. Eph. 1:11). Consequently, the church is not the physical building where Christians meet, nor is it a religious institution, an ethical organization, or a sociopolitical association. Rather, the church is the assembly of the redeemed—those who have been called by God the Father to salvation as a gift to his Son (John 6:37; 10:29; 17:6, 9, 24). It is the corporate gathering of those who have been transferred from the domain of darkness into the kingdom of Christ (Col. 1:13) so that they are citizens of heaven and not of this world (Phil. 3:20; 1 Pet. 2:11).

The church was born on the day of Pentecost (Acts 2:1–21, 38–47), having been purchased by the crucified and risen Christ (Acts 20:28; cf. Col. 3:1–4), who ascended to the right hand of the Father, who "put all things under his feet and gave him as head over all things to the church" (Eph. 1:22). Following the coming of the Holy

---

1. Charles H. Spurgeon, "The Best Donation," sermon no. 2234, preached April 5, 1891, in *The Metropolitan Tabernacle Pulpit: Containing Sermons Preached and Revised* (Pasadena, TX: Pilgrim, 1975), 37:633, 635.
2. The English word *church* derives specifically from the Greek term *kuriakos*, referring to "those who belong to the Lord."

Spirit at Pentecost, the church steadily increased in numbers as the gospel was faithfully proclaimed throughout the world (Acts 2:41; 4:4; 5:14; 6:7; 9:31, 42; 11:21, 24; 14:1; 16:5). Souls were added to the church, one at a time, by the regenerating power of the Spirit as the Lord graciously drew individual sinners to himself (Acts 2:39). Thus, it was "the Lord [who] added to their number day by day those who were being saved" (2:47). On Paul's first missionary journey, the Gentiles responded to the preaching of the gospel by "rejoicing and glorifying the word of the Lord, and as many as were appointed to eternal life believed. And the word of the Lord was spreading throughout the whole region" (Acts 13:48–49). The power of the gospel message to convert people to Christ was found not in the preacher's ingenuity or persuasion (cf. 1 Cor. 2:4; 1 Thess. 1:5) but in the fact that God sovereignly called to himself a remnant, who would respond in saving faith. The advance of the gospel described in the book of Acts has continued throughout the centuries of church history, as the good news of salvation has been heralded by generations of faithful believers across the globe.

One day, the church age will reach its glorious fullness when Christ comes to rapture his own (1 Cor. 15:51–53; 1 Thess. 4:13–18). At that time,

> the Lord himself will descend from heaven with a cry of command, with the voice of an archangel, and with the sound of the trumpet of God. And the dead in Christ will rise first. Then [those believers] who are alive, who are left, will be caught up together with them in the clouds to meet the Lord in the air, and so [they] will always be with the Lord. (1 Thess. 4:16–17)

From that point forward, the church will be in the presence of her Savior for all eternity (cf. Rev. 22:3–5).

Throughout its history, the church has endured seasons of severe persecution from outside forces (John 15:18–25; 1 Pet. 1:6–7; 1 John 3:13), while also facing internal threats from false teachers (2 Pet. 2:1; Jude 3–4). In spite of such dangers, both from without and from within, the true church can never be defeated or extinguished. The Lord Jesus assured his disciples that he would build his church and that the gates of hades would not overcome it (Matt. 16:18). The "gates of hades" are a metaphor for death and, by extension, the power of Satan (Heb. 2:14). Christ's promise in Matthew 16:18 guarantees that the universal body of believers under his headship will have an enduring testimony that cannot be destroyed by this world, Satan, or even death (cf. 1 Cor. 15:54–57). No matter how legalistic or apostate its outward adherents may be, and no matter how decadent or hostile the rest of the world may become, Christ has promised that he will build his church. Though their outward circumstances may seem hopeless or impossible from a human perspective, God's people belong to a cause that cannot fail. As the architect, builder, owner, and Lord of his church, Christ comforts his followers with the truth that they are his personal possession (cf. Titus 2:14), the objects of his unfailing love and divine care (cf. Eph. 5:2, 25).

Christ's Design for His Church[3]

In Matthew 16:18, Jesus delivers seven hallmark principles for building his church. No one should launch out in starting a new church or take on the challenge of revitalizing a worn-out church until the defining truths of this scripture have gripped one's heart and mind.

A PERMANENT FOUNDATION

The initial characteristic involves a permanent foundation: "You are Peter, and *on this rock* I will build my church" (Matt. 16:18). Christ passionately pursued the lasting fruit of eternity. In his promise, he explicitly looked to an everlasting legacy. Jesus did not have in mind the temporary, the faddish, or the "here today, gone tomorrow." He pointed to the church as having a *forever* relevance.

The foundation was not Peter because Christ here distinguishes between a movable, detached boulder (the basic meaning of Cephas and Peter [Gk. *petros*]) and the unshakeable, immovable foundation suitable for the church. The word Christ used for "rock" (Gk. *petra*) means bedrock or mass of rock as used by the wise builder (Matt. 7:24–25).

What or who, then, is the rock? The Old Testament pictures God as the rock in whom believers find strength and refuge:

> There is none holy like the LORD;
> > There is none besides you;
> > There is no rock like our God. (1 Sam. 2:2)

> The LORD is my rock and my fortress and my deliverer,
> > My God, my rock, in whom I take refuge. (Ps. 18:2)

> For who is God, but the LORD?
> > And who is a rock, except our God? (Ps. 18:31)

Paul identified Christ as the rock in the wilderness (1 Cor. 10:4). Earlier in 1 Corinthians, the apostle wrote, "For no one can lay a foundation other than that which is laid, which is Jesus Christ" (3:11). Interestingly, one verse earlier Paul had claimed, "I laid a foundation" (1 Cor. 3:10). How did Paul "lay" Christ as the foundation? It had to be in his preaching of Christ (1 Cor. 2:1–2). Now, if Paul's testimony of Christ is the foundation that no one else can lay, then it seems best to understand the *bedrock foundation* of the church to be Peter's testimony of Christ: "You are the Christ, the Son of the living God" (Matt. 16:16). It was Peter's declaration that prompted Jesus's promise.

Since it is virtually impossible to separate the testimony of Christ from the reality of Christ, we can identify the "rock" as Christ himself in the fullness of his deity, his role as Redeemer, and his headship in the church. Christ alone is the rock of redemption on which the church is being built (Acts 4:11–12).

---

3. This section is adapted from Richard Mayhue, *What Would Jesus Say about Your Church* (Fearn, Ross-shire, Scotland: Christian Focus, 1995), 16–20. Used by permission of Christian Focus.

PERSONAL INVOLVEMENT

Second, Christ promised his personal involvement: "*I* will build my church" (Matt. 16:18). We have not been left to the task alone. Christ is with his people (Matt. 28:20) and in them (Col. 1:27). He is among his church constantly (Rev. 1:12–13, 20). Paul told the Corinthian church, "For we are God's fellow workers" (1 Cor. 3:9). What a privilege to be partners with Christ in building his church. How comforting to know that he built the church throughout its history and will continue to build it throughout its future. Christ's participation proves indispensable in raising up his church.

A POSITIVE EXPECTATION

"I *will* build my church" (Matt. 16:18). This is no idle dream about what might be. Christ's confident assertion guarantees that the church has a positive expectation. In times when the future of the church looks bleak and its condition uncertain, this powerful promise should lift believers' spirits. The church will be triumphant because Christ began building the church with the intention of completing her (Eph. 5:26–27).

A POWERFUL ADVANCE

Jesus claimed that his church would have a powerful advance: "I will *build* my church" (Matt. 16:18). The church experienced an explosive beginning with three thousand members being added the first day (Acts 2:41). "And the Lord added to their number day by day those who were being saved" (Acts 2:47).

What is contained in one mere sentence in Matthew 16 mushrooms into an expansive reality by the time of John's Revelation. Before the New Testament ended, churches had spread across the face of the Roman Empire. They included locations such as Antioch, Berea, Caesarea, Colossae, Corinth, Crete, Cyprus, Derbe, Ephesus, Galatia, Iconium, Joppa, Laodicea, Lystra, Pergamum, Philadelphia, Philippi, Sardis, Smyrna, Thessalonica, and Thyatira—reaching from Jerusalem to Rome. Christ's building efforts continue to this very hour, everywhere in the world, just as he intended (cf. Mark 16:15; Luke 24:47).

A PAID-IN-FULL OWNERSHIP

Christ bought the church with his own blood and therefore possesses the exclusive paid-in-full ownership of the church: "I will build *my* church" (Matt. 16:18; cf. Acts 20:28). Christ is Lord; we are his servants (2 Cor. 4:5). Paul writes to the believers in Rome, "All the churches of Christ greet you" (Rom. 16:16). Neither individually nor corporately do Christians have any ownership claim to the church. The church belongs uniquely to its Redeemer (1 Cor. 3:23; 6:19–20). Christ is Head of the church (Eph. 1:22; 5:23). The Chief Shepherd owns the flock that he leads (John 10:14–15).

A PEOPLE-CENTERED PRIORITY

For Christ, the church has a people-centered priority: "I will build my *church*" (Matt. 16:18). The church comprises an assembly of people who have believed in Jesus Christ for eternal life (Acts 4:32). Jesus uses living stones—individual people—to build his church (1 Pet. 2:5). The mandate of evangelization is to take the gospel to all the nations (Luke 24:47). The goal of edification is to present every believer complete in Christ (Col. 1:28).

The Greek word translated "church" literally means the congregation that has been called out. The New Testament pictures the church as made up of those who have been delivered out of the kingdom of darkness and transferred to the kingdom of Christ (Col. 1:13). The Thessalonians, for example, had turned from idols to serve a true and living God (1 Thess. 1:9). The church has been called into fellowship with Jesus Christ (1 Cor. 1:9). Christ has called his redeemed out of darkness into his marvelous light (1 Pet. 2:9).

A PROMISE OF SUCCESS

Jesus has promised success to the church: "I will build my church, and *the gates of hell shall not prevail against it*" (Matt. 16:18). How is this success to be understood? In the Old Testament, "gates of" is used with Sheol (Isa. 38:10) and death (Job 38:17; Pss. 9:13; 107:18), both referring to physical death. But as Jesus's promise makes clear, even the threat of death cannot overpower his church.

The writer of Hebrews encourages believers to know that through death Christ rendered powerless him who had the power of death, that is, the Devil (Heb. 2:14). Paul wrote this Christian victory song to the Corinthians:

> When the perishable puts on the imperishable, and the mortal puts on immortality, then shall come to pass the saying that is written:
>
> > "Death is swallowed up in victory."
> > "O death, where is your victory?
> >   O death, where is your sting?"
>
> The sting of death is sin, and the power of sin is the law. But thanks be to God, who gives us the victory through our Lord Jesus Christ. (1 Cor. 15:54–57; cf. John 11:25)

The Church and the Kingdom

During his earthly ministry, the Lord Jesus repeatedly demonstrated himself to be Israel's promised Messiah and King. Yet the nation refused to receive him (John 1:11; 5:43). Although the Jewish people had anticipated his arrival for centuries, longing for the times of messianic restoration and refreshment that were foretold by the prophets (Acts 3:19–26), they rejected their rightful King and the kingdom he offered (Acts 2:22–23). Consequently, Jesus said to the Jewish religious leaders of his day, "Therefore I tell you, the kingdom of God will be taken away from you and given to a people producing its fruits" (Matt. 21:43). Those words of rebuke underscored the divine judgment placed on Israel's hard-hearted leaders and the nation they represented.

Nonetheless, Israel's rejection did not undermine the gracious promises God made in the Old Testament. Those kingdom promises will one day be literally ful-filled when the Jewish people embrace their King in saving faith (Rom. 11:25–26). At the second coming of Christ, the nation will receive her Messiah (Zech. 12:10; 14:8–9), and his kingdom will be physically established on the earth for a thousand years (Rev. 20:1–6; cf. 2 Tim. 4:1). That reality is yet future. In the meantime, God is accomplishing his kingdom purposes through another people, as Christ's words in Matthew 21:43 make clear. That entity is the church (cf. Rom. 9:25–26; 1 Pet. 2:9).

The Old Testament prophets foretold details about both the Messiah's suffer-ing (Isa. 53:1–12) and his earthly kingdom (cf. Isa. 2:1–4; 9:6–7; Zech. 14:8–21). Yet they did not indicate that a prolonged period of time would transpire between those two realities. The notion of an intermediate period between Christ's first and second comings, during which Gentiles would be incorporated into the people of God alongside Jewish believers (Rom. 11:11–20), was a mystery not revealed until the New Testament (cf. Eph. 3:4–7).

Though the physical kingdom of Christ on earth awaits its future fulfillment, the Lord Jesus brought an internal, spiritual kingdom at his first coming (cf. Matt. 13:3–52; Luke 17:20–21). That kingdom can be defined as the realm of salvation. It is open only to those who have been regenerated by the Holy Spirit (John 3:3; cf. Matt. 13:11–16), having repented of their sin (Matt. 3:2; 4:17; cf. 5:3) and embraced the Lord Jesus in childlike faith (Matt. 19:13–14). It cannot be attained through self-righteousness or legalism (Matt. 5:20; 23:13) but is characterized by "righteousness and peace and joy in the Holy Spirit" (Rom. 14:17). The New Testament describes believers as those who have been delivered "from the domain of darkness and trans-ferred . . . to the kingdom of his beloved Son, in whom [they] have redemption, the forgiveness of sins" (Col. 1:13–14). In salvation, they become citizens of heaven (Phil. 3:20–21) and royal slaves in the service of their King (cf. Matt. 25:21, 23; 1 Thess. 2:12). The Lord Jesus reigns in the hearts of his people as they submit to his will and honor him with their lives (Titus 2:14). The magnificent reality of salvation is that, through faith, sinners may enter the kingdom of God where the triune God himself takes up residence in their hearts (John 14:17, 23).

The spiritual kingdom of Christ grows and advances through the preaching of the gospel (Mark 1:14–15; cf. Matt. 22:1–14; 2 Cor. 7:9–11), as children of darkness are transformed into children of light (Eph. 5:5, 8). The gospel proclaimed by the church is nothing less than "good news about the kingdom of God and the name of Jesus Christ" (Acts 8:12; cf. Matt. 4:23; 9:35; 13:19; 24:14). After preaching the gospel in a number of cities on their first missionary journey, Paul and Barnabas returned to strengthen "the souls of the disciples, encouraging them to continue in the faith, and saying that through many tribulations we must enter the kingdom of God" (Acts 14:22). On his third missionary journey, Paul "entered the synagogue [in Ephesus] and for three months spoke boldly, reasoning and persuading them about the kingdom of God" (Acts 19:8; cf. 20:25). The apostle later witnessed to a group of Jewish leaders who visited him in Rome, "testifying to the kingdom of God and trying to convince them about Jesus both from the Law of Moses and from the Prophets" (Acts 28:23; cf. 28:31). Accordingly, Paul described himself as a worker for God's kingdom (Col. 4:11), explaining that "the kingdom of God does not consist in talk but in power" (1 Cor. 4:20) and warning that "the unrighteous will not inherit the kingdom of God" (1 Cor. 6:9; cf. Gal. 5:21; Eph. 5:5).

As his spiritual kingdom, the church submits to Jesus Christ as her Head, Master, Lord, and King (Eph. 1:22; Col. 1:18). His law is her standard (cf. Gal. 6:2). His Word is her creed (cf. Col. 3:16). His will is her mandate (cf. Heb. 13:20–21). And his glory is her greatest ambition (cf. 2 Cor. 5:9). Thus, Peter could tell his Christian readers:

> You are a chosen race, a royal priesthood, a holy nation, a people for his own possession, that you may proclaim the excellencies of him who called you out of darkness into his marvelous light. Once you were not a people, but now you are God's people; once you had not received mercy, but now you have received mercy. (1 Pet. 2:9–10)

The Visible and Invisible Church

The New Testament recognizes that not everyone who externally associates with the church is a true believer (Matt. 13:24–30; Jude 4). Consequently, not all who are part of the visible church (the company of those who outwardly profess faith in Christ) are actually members of the invisible church (the community of those who truly possess saving faith in him). There are always false professors and hypocrites who associate themselves with the visible church. Jesus himself warned that many will claim to know him who in reality do not:

> Not everyone who says to me, "Lord, Lord," will enter the kingdom of heaven, but the one who does the will of my Father who is in heaven. On that day many will say to me, "Lord, Lord, did we not prophesy in your name, and cast out demons in your name, and do many mighty works in your name?" And then will I declare to them, "I never knew you; depart from me, you workers of lawlessness." (Matt. 7:21–23)

In light of Christ's sobering warning, those who profess faith in Christ ought to examine themselves to ensure that they are truly in the faith (2 Cor. 13:5; cf. 1 John 2:3–11).

The New Testament also warns about false teachers who deliberately seek to threaten the church from within (Matt. 7:15; Mark 13:22; 2 Pet. 2:1; 1 John 4:1; Jude 3–4). As Paul warned the Ephesian elders, "I know that after my departure fierce wolves will come in among you, not sparing the flock; and from among your own selves will arise men speaking twisted things, to draw away the disciples after them" (Acts 20:29–30). When local churches, or even entire denominations or so-called Christian movements, embrace false teaching—thereby abandoning the purity of the gospel (Gal. 1:6–9) and denying the authority of Jesus Christ (Titus 1:16; 2 Pet. 2:1; Jude 4)—they are rightly labeled "apostate," "heretical," and "false." Such churches are an abomination to the Lord (cf. Rev. 2:20–24; 3:1–4). By contrast, the true church exalts the lordship of Christ, submits to the authority of his Word, and upholds the truth of his gospel.

The Universal Church and Local Churches

The universal church includes all genuine Christians throughout the entirety of the church age. They are members of "the assembly of the firstborn who are enrolled in heaven" (Heb. 12:23), having been declared righteous because their sins have been washed away by the blood of Jesus Christ (Rev. 1:5). All true believers throughout church history—both those alive today and those already in heaven—make up the universal church.

The New Testament instructs those who are part of the universal church in every generation, scattered throughout the world, to meet together regularly in local assemblies. Such was clearly the pattern of the early church (cf. Acts 14:23, 27; 20:17, 28; 1 Cor. 11:18–20; Gal. 1:2; 1 Thess. 1:1). In keeping with that paradigm, the author of Hebrews offers this directive, "Let us consider how to stir up one another to love and good works, not neglecting to meet together, as is the habit of some, but encouraging one another, and all the more as you see the Day drawing near" (Heb. 10:24–25).

The local church is designed to equip believers by feeding them through the teaching of God's Word (Acts 2:42; 1 Tim. 4:13), leading them in corporate praise and worship (Eph. 5:18–20; Heb. 13:15), protecting them under the shepherding oversight of godly leaders (Acts 20:28; Heb. 13:7, 17; 1 Pet. 5:1–4), and providing them with opportunities to serve one another (1 Pet. 4:10–11). In accordance with God's design, active involvement in a local church is imperative for believers as they seek to live in a way that honors Jesus Christ. It is only through the ministry of the local church that Christians can receive the regular teaching, accountability, and encouragement necessary for them to stand firm in the faith they are called to proclaim. God has ordained the local church to provide the kind of environment where an uncompromising life can thrive as his people grow spiritually through the teaching of the Word (1 Pet. 2:2–3).

The Distinction between the Church and Israel[4]

In defining the church, it is necessary to understand the relationship between the New Testament church and Old Testament Israel. Proponents of replacement theology (also called supersessionism) insist that the church is the new Israel. According to this view, the blessings promised to the Jewish nation in the Old Testament have been entirely transferred to the church. But this position fails to recognize the distinction between the church and Israel that is maintained throughout the New Testament (cf. 1 Cor. 10:32). The New Testament presents the church as a new entity (Eph. 2:15), a mystery not fully revealed until this age (Eph. 3:1–6; 5:32; Col. 1:26–27).

---

4. For more on this topic, see Michael J. Vlach, *Has the Church Replaced Israel? A Theological Evaluation* (Nashville: B&H Academic, 2010). Also refer to chap. 10, "The Future."

This is consistent with Jesus's description of the church as a reality that, prior to his death and resurrection, was yet future (Matt. 16:18).

Of the more than two thousand uses of the term Israel in Scripture, more than seventy are found in the New Testament. Biblical commentators agree that most of these occurrences refer to ethnic Israel (either the nation as a whole or a group of Jewish people). However, some contend that on certain occasions the New Testament authors apply the name Israel to the church. Yet when the passages in question are studied carefully, it becomes evident that only ethnic Israelites are in view. Consequently, a compelling case can be made to demonstrate that, whenever the New Testament writers use the term Israel, they reserve it exclusively for national Israel.

Two New Testament passages, Romans 9:6 and Galatians 6:16, are the primary targets of debate regarding the meaning of the term Israel. In Romans 9:6, the apostle Paul explains that "not all who are descended from Israel belong to Israel." The context in Romans 9 indicates that Paul is speaking not about the entire church but about Jewish believers—a distinct remnant of ethnic Israelites within the larger unbelieving nation (cf. Rom. 11:5). That the apostle has Abraham's physical descendants in view is clear from Romans 9:3, where he directly states that he is speaking about his "kinsmen according to the flesh." Moreover, these verses occur within a broader section of Paul's argument in this epistle, in which he is asserting that God has not abandoned the nation of Israel in spite of her unbelief (Romans 9–11). In light of both the larger and narrower context, verse 6 can only refer to ethnic Israelites. They are "true Israel" in the sense that they are ethnic Israelites who have behaved as the genuine people of Yahweh by embracing their Messiah.

The other debated passage is Galatians 6:16. There Paul extends the following salutation to his readers: "And as for all who walk by this rule, peace and mercy be upon them, and upon the Israel of God." Some have suggested that "the Israel of God" in this passage refers to the church as a whole, but that interpretation is unconvincing. Both the grammar and context of the verse suggest that "the Israel of God" refers to Jewish Christians and not to the entire church. Grammatically, Paul is clearly referring to two distinct groups of people in this verse, with the pronoun "them" speaking of one group and "the Israel of God" speaking of a second.[5] A straightforward reading of the verse suggests that "them" refers to Gentile believers in the Galatian churches (cf. Acts 13:46–48) who submitted themselves to the apostolic instruction Paul had articulated in this epistle. In particular, they were not swayed by the false teaching of the Judaizers who insisted that Gentile Christians must be

---

5. Though advocates of replacement theology argue for an explicative use of *kai* in this verse (which would be translated "even"), such is very unlikely. As Robert Saucy explains, "This explicative sense is not common, especially in the writings of Paul. Therefore unless there are strong contextual grounds the usual copulative (i.e. 'and') should be retained." Robert L. Saucy, "Israel and the Church: A Case for Discontinuity," in *Continuity and Discontinuity: Perspectives on the Relationship between the Old and New Testaments: Essays in Honor of S. Lewis Johnson, Jr.*, ed. John S. Feinberg (Wheaton, IL: Crossway, 1988), 246. For a more detailed discussion of why the "Israel of God" in Gal. 6:16 can only refer to Jews, see Ernest DeWitt Burton, *Galatians*, ICC (Edinburgh: T&T Clark, 1920); Peter Richardson, *Israel in the Apostolic Church* SNTSMS 10 (Cambridge: Cambridge University Press, 1969); F. F. Bruce, *The Epistle to the Galatians*, NIGTC (Grand Rapids, MI: Eerdmans, 1982); S. Lewis Johnson Jr., "Paul and 'the Israel of God': An Exegetical and Eschatological Case-Study," in *Essays in Honor of J. Dwight Pentecost*, ed. Stanley D. Toussaint and Charles H. Dyer (Chicago: Moody Press, 1986); Hans Dieter Betz, *Galatians*, Hermeneia (Philadelphia: Fortress, 1979), 323.

circumcised (Gal. 6:12–15; cf. Acts 15:1; Gal. 2:3). If the first group refers to Gentile believers, it follows that the second group, having been distinguished from the first, refers to ethnic Jewish Christians. Because they had been circumcised in their hearts and not just physically (cf. Rom. 2:28–29), they were the true Israelites, the same group to whom Paul referred in Romans 9:6 (cf. Rom. 4:12; Phil. 3:3). Contextually, the apostle's commendation of Jewish Christians served as an important closing note at the end of this letter in which he pointedly denounced the Judaizers. Paul's strong refutation of the idea that the works of the Mosaic law were necessary for salvation may have led some to conclude that God had fully and finally done away with the Jewish nation (which was so closely associated with the observance of the law). The apostle's special note of greeting to Israelite believers illustrated the reality that such was not the case (cf. Rom. 11:1, 26).

Because the New Testament distinguishes between the church and Israel, it is necessary for believers to maintain that same distinction. Conflating the two can lead to significant hermeneutical and interpretive problems, in which promises and directives given specifically to the nation of Israel are spiritualized or allegorized and incorrectly applied to Gentile believers in the church. Though God is working through the international church in this present age (Gal. 3:28; Col. 3:11), and though the church shares in the blessings of the new covenant (Luke 22:20; 2 Cor. 3:3–8; Heb. 8:7–13; 9:15), in the future God will again turn his attention to the nation of Israel in fulfillment of his promises to them (Rom. 11:25–26; cf. Dan. 9:24–27).

Biblical Metaphors for the Church[6]

The New Testament uses many analogies to depict God's relationship to his people. He is their King; they are his subjects (Matt. 25:34; 1 Cor. 4:20; Phil. 3:20; Col. 1:13–14). He is the Creator; they are his creatures (2 Cor. 5:17; Eph. 2:10). He is the Shepherd; they are his sheep (John 10:3, 11, 14, 26; Heb. 13:20; 1 Pet. 2:25; 5:2–4). He is the Master; they are his slaves (Matt. 10:24–25; Rom. 14:4; Eph. 6:9; Col. 4:1; 2 Tim. 2:21; Jude 4). He is their Father (Matt. 6:9; Rom. 1:7); they are his adopted children (John 1:12; Rom. 8:16–17, 21; Phil. 2:15; 1 John 3:1–2; cf. Rom. 8:14, 19; 2 Cor. 6:18; Gal. 3:26; 4:6; Heb. 12:7) and the members of his household (Gal. 6:10; Eph. 2:19; 1 Tim. 3:15; 1 Pet. 4:17), to the point that the Lord Jesus "is not ashamed to call them brothers" (Heb. 2:11) and "God is not ashamed to be called their God" (Heb. 11:16).

The church is further described as the bride of Christ (2 Cor. 11:2; Eph. 5:23–32; Rev. 19:7–8; 21:9) and the body of Christ (Rom. 12:4–5; 1 Cor. 12:12, 27; Eph. 4:12, 25; 5:23, 30; Col. 1:24), of which he is the Head (Eph. 1:22–23; 4:15; Col. 1:18; 2:19). Both of these metaphors emphasize the spiritual union that exists between Christ and his own (cf. Gal. 2:20). Scripture speaks of believers being in Christ and of his being in them (John 17:23; cf. 2 Cor. 5:17; Col. 1:27). The Lord Jesus is more

---

6. This section is adapted from John MacArthur, *John 12–21*, MNTC (Chicago: Moody Publishers, 2008), 142. Used by permission of Moody Publishers.

than simply *with* his church; he is *in* his church, and his church is *in* him. The church is an organic whole, the living manifestation of Jesus Christ that pulses with the eternal life of God. The common denominator of all believers is that they possess divine life. Jesus said, "Because I live, you also will live" (John 14:19). The rest of the New Testament echoes that truth: "Whoever has the Son has life" (1 John 5:12), because "he who is joined to the Lord becomes one spirit with him" (1 Cor. 6:17).

The imagery of the body is unique in illustrating the relationship between Christ and the church.[7] God created the human body as a marvelously complex organism, with intricate and elaborate interrelatedness and harmony. As an interdependent and unified whole, it cannot function if divided into its parts. Likewise, the body of Christ is a unified whole. There are many religious organizations and functions, but only the church is the body of Christ, of which every true believer in Christ is a member. The Lord Jesus can be no more separated from his church than a head can be separated from its body. Conversely, those who are part of his church cannot be separated from him (John 10:28–29; Rom. 8:38–39) or each other (1 Cor. 12:12–27).

Another New Testament metaphor that illustrates the vital union that believers share with Christ is that of the vine and the branches (John 15:1–11; cf. Rom. 11:17). In the same way that a branch is wholly dependent on the vine for its life, nourishment, and growth, so believers depend fully on the Savior as the source of their spiritual vitality. A branch that is not connected to the vine cannot bear fruit. Likewise, apart from their union with Christ, believers are unable to bear spiritual fruit (John 15:4–10). It is only by abiding in him that Christians can exhibit fruits of repentance (Matt. 3:8) and the fruit of the Spirit (Gal. 5:22–24; Eph. 5:9).

The intimate fellowship that the church enjoys with God through Christ (John 17:21; 1 Cor. 1:9; 1 John 1:3; 2:24) is further illustrated by the New Testament's description of the church as the temple of God. In the Old Testament, the temple was the centerpiece of Israel's worship. It was the place where God's people went to worship him through the mediation of a priest. A veil separated the people from the Most Holy Place, in which the presence of God was manifested (Ex. 26:31–35). But the New Testament reveals that believers themselves are the temple of God and that every Christian has access to God through Christ (Heb. 4:14–16; 10:19–23). Having been built on the foundation of the Lord Jesus (1 Cor. 3:10–11; 1 Pet. 2:7), Christians are described as living stones who make up the temple of God (1 Pet. 2:4–8). They are also described as a kingdom of priests (1 Pet. 2:9–10; Rev. 1:6; 5:10). The apostle Paul uses temple imagery to depict believers both individually (1 Cor. 6:19–20) and corporately (1 Cor. 3:16–17; Eph. 2:21–22). Christ is the builder (Matt. 16:18); believers are the building (Eph. 2:20–22; cf. Heb. 3:3–6). The church, then, is a spiritual edifice (1 Pet. 2:5), the abode of the Holy Spirit (1 Cor. 3:16–17; 2 Cor. 6:16), the place where God's glory is manifested most clearly on earth, and the nucleus of

---

7. Some of the metaphors discussed here are also applied to Israel in the Old Testament. For example, the image of the vineyard, the flock, and the bride can be found in the Old Testament (e.g., Isa. 5:1–7; 40:11; Ezek. 16:32; Hos. 3:1–5). Other images, such as the kingdom, the family, and the temple are alluded to in the Old Testament. However, the metaphor of the body is unique to the church and has no Old Testament equivalent.

spiritual instruction and corporate worship for the redeemed. Unlike buildings made with stone, the church is a building made with living flesh. Believers are living stones in God's temple, offering spiritual sacrifices to him (cf. Rom. 12:1; Heb. 13:15–16).

Purposes of the Church

Exalting God
Edifying Believers
Evangelizing the Lost

When viewed from the standpoint of salvation history, the church exists to display the wisdom and mercy of God in this age (Eph. 3:10; cf. Rom. 9:23–24; 11:33; 1 Cor. 1:20–31) by proclaiming the gospel of Jesus Christ throughout the world (Matt. 28:19–20; Acts 1:8; 1 Pet. 2:9), so that sinners from every ethnic background (Rev. 5:9–10) might be rescued from the domain of darkness and ushered into the kingdom of God (Col. 1:12–13), and so that unbelieving Israel might be provoked to jealousy and repentance (Rom. 10:19; 11:11). Looking to the future, the New Testament also promises that the church will one day reign with Christ in glory (1 Cor. 6:2; cf. 2 Tim. 2:11–13; Rev. 20:4–6).

From the standpoint of how the church relates to its members, its purpose might be stated as follows: the church exists to glorify God (Eph. 1:5–6, 12–14; 3:20–21; 2 Thess. 1:12) by actively building its members up in the faith (Eph. 4:12–16), faithfully teaching the Word (2 Tim. 2:15; 3:16–17), regularly observing the ordinances (Luke 22:19; Acts 2:38–42), proactively fostering fellowship among believers (Acts 2:42–47; 1 John 1:3), and boldly communicating the truth of the gospel to the lost (Matt. 28:19–20). This purpose can be summarized under the following three headings.

Exalting God

Because God is zealous for his glory (Isa. 48:9–11; cf. Isa. 43:6–7; 49:3), his people should likewise be consumed with a desire to glorify and exalt him (1 Cor. 10:31; cf. 6:20). Consequently, a faithful church is God centered, not man centered. The church has been redeemed so that believers might glorify him both by serving one another (1 Pet. 4:11) and by proclaiming "the excellencies of him who called [them] out of darkness into his marvelous light" (1 Pet. 2:9).

One of the primary ways in which the church exalts God is through worship and praise. Whenever the church gathers, worship ought to be the ultimate priority (cf. John 4:23–24). Worship consists of ascribing the honor to God that he is due, declaring his glory both in words of praise (e.g., Pss. 29:2; 95:6; 99:5, 9; Heb. 12:28) and through acts of obedience (Rom. 12:1). True worship necessarily includes the exaltation of Jesus Christ, whom the Father has exalted by giving him a name that is above every name (Phil. 2:9; cf. Acts 5:31). Christ is "exalted above the heavens" (Heb. 7:26). For all eternity, the redeemed will praise his name (cf. Rev. 4:10; 5:12–13; 7:12; 14:7; 15:4). Meanwhile, the church is the one sphere on earth where Christ's name is truly and genuinely exalted.

Edifying Believers

In 1 Corinthians 14, Paul described a typical meeting in the early church with these words: "When you come together, each one has a hymn, a lesson, a revelation, a tongue, or an interpretation. Let all things be done for building up" (14:26). He similarly instructed the Thessalonian believers to "encourage one another and build one another up, just as you are doing" (1 Thess. 5:11). Such edification takes place through the ministry of the Word (Acts 20:32; 2 Tim. 3:15–17; 1 Pet. 2:2), the mentoring of godly leadership (Eph. 4:11–12), the selfless exercise of spiritual giftedness (1 Cor. 12:7; 1 Pet. 4:10), and the practice of the "one another" commands in the New Testament. A list of those commands includes the following:

1. Love one another (Rom. 12:10; 13:8; 1 Thess. 3:12; 4:9; 2 Thess. 1:3; 1 Pet. 1:22; 4:8; 1 John 3:11, 23; 4:7, 11–12; 2 John 5).
2. Live in harmony with one another (Rom. 12:16; 15:5; cf. Gal. 5:26; 1 Thess. 5:13).
3. Welcome one another (Rom. 15:7; cf. Rom. 16:16).
4. Admonish one another (Rom. 15:14; Col. 3:16).
5. Care for one another (1 Cor. 12:25).
6. Serve one another (Gal. 5:13; 1 Pet. 4:10).
7. Bear one another's burdens (Gal. 6:2).
8. Be patient with one another (Eph. 4:2; Col. 3:13).
9. Be kind to one another (Eph. 4:32).
10. Forgive one another (Eph. 4:32; Col. 3:13).
11. Sing praises with one another (Eph. 5:19; Col. 3:16).
12. Regard one another as more important than oneself (Phil. 2:3).
13. Speak truth to one another (Col. 3:9).
14. Encourage one another (1 Thess. 4:18; 5:11; Heb. 3:13; 10:25).
15. Seek good for one another (1 Thess. 5:15).
16. Stir up one another to love and good deeds (Heb. 10:24; cf. 1 Tim. 6:17–18).
17. Confess your sins to one another (James 5:16).
18. Pray for one another (James 5:16).
19. Be hospitable to one another (1 Pet. 4:9).
20. Be humble toward one another (1 Pet. 5:5).

The biblical context of these commands indicates that they are primarily intended to govern the believer's relationship to fellow Christians within the church. By putting these directives into practice, God's people fulfill the second Great Commandment, to love one's neighbor as oneself (Mark 12:31; cf. John 13:34; 15:12), thereby edifying the body of Christ (cf. Rom. 14:19; 15:2) and exemplifying the love of Christ to a watching world (John 13:35). This makes gospel transformation visible and verifiable, so that the message is proven to be as powerful as it claims.

Evangelizing the Lost

A church that is passionately pursuing the glory of God will likewise have a strong emphasis on evangelism, both locally and around the world. The church's evangelistic commission is articulated by Jesus himself in Matthew 28:18–20. There he instructed his followers with these words:

> All authority in heaven and on earth has been given to me. Go therefore and make disciples of all nations, baptizing them in the name of the Father and of the Son and of the Holy Spirit, teaching them to observe all that I have commanded you. And behold, I am with you always, to the end of the age.

The Great Commission indicates that true evangelism involves making disciples (and not merely convincing unbelievers to make decisions). As sinners respond in saving faith to the message of the gospel, they are to be initiated into the church through baptism and discipled by the church through sound teaching. The pattern of disciple making was established by Jesus himself, who sought to make disciples during his earthly ministry (Mark 1:16–22; 2:14; John 8:31). His example is to be continued by his people. True followers of Christ become "fishers of men" (Matt. 4:19), meaning that those who become his disciples are themselves to be disciple makers.

Believers in the early church were characterized by a passion to preach the gospel and make disciples (cf. Acts. 2:47; 14:21). Their zeal made their enemies take notice. The hostile Jewish leaders told Peter and the other apostles, "You have filled Jerusalem with your teaching" (Acts 5:28). Paul and his fellow missionaries were similarly accused of turning the world upside down (Acts 17:6). Their bold declaration of salvation through Jesus Christ reverberated throughout the known world (cf. Acts 1:8; 19:10). The church ought to be characterized by that same courageous zeal in every age.

Because they understand the hope of eternal salvation (Titus 1:2; cf. John 3:16; 11:25) and the converse reality of God's coming judgment (2 Cor. 5:11, 20; cf. 2 Pet. 3:11–15; Heb. 9:27), believers should be eager to proclaim the good news of salvation. Though the church will continue to exalt Christ and edify one another in heavenly glory, evangelism is something that can be done only in this life. The New Testament presents evangelism as the responsibility of church leaders (2 Tim. 4:5; cf. Eph. 4:11), Christian individuals (1 Pet. 3:15), and the church as a whole (1 Pet. 2:9). The salvation of sinners brings glory to God and instills his people with a contagious joy (cf. Luke 15:7, 10). Conversely, churches that ignore or devalue evangelism will experience stagnation and decline.

Spiritual Authority in the Church

Gifted Leaders
Elders
Deacons

Since the New Testament teaches that Jesus Christ is the Head of the church (Eph. 1:22; 4:15; 5:23; Col. 1:18; 2:19; cf. 1 Cor. 11:3), having had his sovereign lordship bestowed on him by his heavenly Father (Matt. 11:27; John 3:35; 5:22; Acts 2:36; Phil. 2:9–11), he is the church's supreme authority. As Jesus told his disciples when he commissioned them, "All authority in heaven and on earth has been given to me" (Matt. 28:18). The Old Testament similarly depicts the absolute authority of the promised Messiah (cf. Isa. 9:6–7). In Daniel 7:13–14, the prophet Daniel says of Christ,

> I saw in the night visions,
>
>> and behold, with the clouds of heaven
>>   there came one like a son of man,
>> and he came to the Ancient of Days
>>   and was presented before him.
>> And to him was given dominion
>>   and glory and a kingdom,
>> that all peoples, nations, and languages
>>   should serve him;
>> his dominion is an everlasting dominion,
>>   which shall not pass away,
>> and his kingdom one
>>   that shall not be destroyed. (cf. Matt. 24:30; 26:64)

The Lord Jesus repeatedly exhibited divine authority during his earthly ministry. He demonstrated his sovereign power over demons (Matt. 8:32; 12:22), disease (Matt. 4:23–24), sin (Matt. 9:6), and death (Mark 5:41–42; John 11:43–44), displaying his power over death especially in his crucifixion and resurrection (John 10:18). Having ascended to the Father's right hand, Christ—who created and sustains everything that exists (John 1:1–4; Col. 1:16–17; Heb. 1:3)—possesses the authority to rule heaven and earth (Eph. 1:20–21), to judge mankind (John 5:27–29; 17:2), to defeat Satan and his hosts (Rev. 19:20; 20:10), and to destroy death forever (1 Cor. 15:25–26). One day, all creation will recognize the supremacy of Jesus Christ, including those who presently reject him. As Paul told the Philippians, "God has highly exalted him and bestowed on him the name that is above every name, so that at the name of Jesus every knee should bow, in heaven and on earth and under the earth, and every tongue confess that Jesus Christ is Lord, to the glory of God the Father" (Phil. 2:9–11).

Submission to the sovereign lordship of Christ is not optional for believers. Rather, their highest calling and supreme obligation is to submit joyfully to his commands (e.g., John 14:15, 21, 23; 15:10; 1 John 5:3; 2 John 6). That submission is expressed both individually and corporately. Each believer's thoughts, attitudes, words, and actions ought to conform to the will of Christ as delineated in the Scriptures (Rom. 12:1–2; 1 Pet. 1:14–15). The same should be true of everything that happens in the corporate gathering of the church, as the congregation submits itself to the word of Christ (cf. Col. 3:16).

As the Head of the church, the Lord Jesus is not only her supreme authority but is also the source of her salvation. He is "the founder and perfecter of our faith" (Heb. 12:2), having purchased through his death "a people for his own possession who are zealous for good works" (Titus 2:14). Christ is the cornerstone on which the church is founded (1 Pet. 2:4–8). The church was established by him (Matt. 16:18) and is built on the apostolic witness to the truth about him (Eph. 2:20). Thus, the apostle Paul writes, "No one can lay a foundation other than that which is laid, which is Jesus Christ" (1 Cor. 3:11).

Gifted Leaders

The absolute rule of Christ as the Head of the church is administered through godly leaders whom he has given to lead his people (1 Thess. 5:12–13; Heb. 13:7, 17). In Ephesians 4:11, Paul says of the ascended Christ, "He gave the apostles, the prophets, the evangelists, the shepherds [pastors] and teachers" (cf. 1 Cor. 12:28). Two of the groups delineated in that verse were limited to the beginning of church history—namely, the apostles and the prophets, whose ministry played a unique foundational role in the establishment of the church.[8] Paul made that point earlier in Ephesians, when he explained that believers are part of God's household, having been "built on the foundation of the apostles and prophets, Christ Jesus himself being the cornerstone" (Eph. 2:20). By identifying the apostles and prophets with the foundation-laying stage of the church, Paul indicated that those offices were limited to the earliest stages of church history. The foundation of a building is laid once, at the beginning of construction. So also, the age of the apostles and prophets occurred at the outset of church history and has not been repeated since.

In keeping with their foundational role, the apostles and the prophets declared the revelation of God's Word (Eph. 3:5; cf. Acts 11:28; 21:10–11) and confirmed their message with miraculous signs (2 Cor. 12:12; cf. Acts 8:6–7; Heb. 2:3–4). Just as the superstructure of a building rests on its foundation, so all subsequent generations of the church have been built on the revelatory foundation laid by the apostles and prophets in the writing of the New Testament (cf. 2 Pet. 1:19–21). The other groups—evangelists and pastor-teachers—have continued to build on that foundation throughout church history by fervently proclaiming the gospel of grace and faithfully preaching the Word of truth (cf. 2 Tim. 4:1–5).

APOSTLES

The Greek word *apostolos*, translated "apostle," means "sent one" and applies to an ambassador, representative, or messenger. The term is sometimes used in the New Testament in a general sense to refer, for example, to the messengers of local churches (2 Cor. 8:23; Phil. 2:25). However, the primary New Testament use of the title applies to "apostles of Jesus Christ" (e.g., Gal. 1:1; 1 Pet. 1:1; Jude 17), those specific men whom Jesus personally selected to be his authorized representatives. That limited group included the Twelve (with Matthias replacing Judas Iscariot in Acts

---

8. For a discussion about the gift of apostleship in response to charismatic claims, see John MacArthur, *Strange Fire: The Danger of Offending the Holy Spirit with Counterfeit Worship* (Nashville: Thomas Nelson, 2013), 85–103. For a specific response to those who claim that Paul's statement in Eph. 4:11–13 implies that all five ministries listed there continue throughout church history, see *Strange Fire*, 100–102. For a survey of the church fathers' perspective on the uniqueness of apostleship, see *Strange Fire*, 96–99.

1:26) and Paul, who was commissioned by Christ to be an apostle to the Gentiles (Gal. 1:15–17; cf. 1 Cor. 15:7–9; 2 Cor. 11:5).

The apostles of Jesus Christ met three basic qualifications. First, they were chosen directly by the Lord Jesus (Mark 3:14; Luke 6:13; Acts 1:2, 24; Gal. 1:1). Second, they were able to perform the signs of an apostle, being authenticated by miraculous "signs and wonders and mighty works" (2 Cor. 12:12; cf. Matt. 10:1–2; Acts 1:5–8; 2:43; 4:33; 5:12; Heb. 2:3–4). Third, with their own eyes they were witnesses of the resurrected Christ (Acts 1:21–25; 10:39–41; 1 Cor. 9:1; 15:7–8). In 1 Corinthians 15:8, Paul explicitly states that he was the last person to have met this third qualification, indicating that there have been no genuine apostles since Paul. Moreover, Paul saw his apostleship as unique and extraordinary (1 Cor. 15:8–9); it was not a normative pattern for later generations of Christians to emulate. An honest assessment of modern claims to the office demonstrates conclusively that there are no apostles today and have not been in church history since the first century.

The New Testament apostles were Christ's authoritative revelatory agents. In the upper room, the Lord Jesus promised that, even after he was no longer physically present with them, he would continue to reveal his truth to them through the Holy Spirit (John 14:26; 15:26–27; 16:12–15). Accordingly, the early church recognized the apostles' teaching as having Christ's very authority. Because the apostolic writings were inspired, they were accorded the same weight as the Old Testament Scriptures (cf. Acts 2:42; 1 Cor. 14:37; 1 Thess. 2:13; 2 Tim. 3:16–17; 2 Pet. 3:16).

PROPHETS

The word translated "prophet," from the Greek *prophētēs*, means "one who speaks in the place of" or "a spokesman." New Testament prophets, then, were spokesmen for God, though second in rank to the apostles (1 Cor. 12:28). As in the Old Testament, prophets in the early church were primarily distinguished by their reception and delivery of new revelation from God (Acts 11:27–28), though sometimes they expounded on previously revealed truth (cf. Acts 13:1).

Due to the constant threat of false prophets (Matt. 7:15; Acts 20:29–31; Jude 3–4), the prophet's message was to be tested against truth that had been previously revealed (1 Cor. 14:29; 1 Thess. 5:20–22). The genuineness of a New Testament prophet's ministry, like that of his Old Testament counterparts, could be determined by his doctrinal accuracy (Deut. 13:1–5; Acts 20:29–30; 2 Pet. 2:1). Moreover, true prophets were characterized by both moral purity (Matt. 7:15–17; 2 Pet. 2:2–3; cf. Jer. 23:14–16) and revelatory accuracy (Deut. 18:20–22; Ezek. 13:3–9). Those who taught false doctrine, who lived in unrestrained lust and greed, or who delivered supposed revelation from God that was inaccurate and untrue, were to be disregarded by God's people as false prophets.[9]

When the canon of New Testament revelation was complete, the prophetic of-

---

9. For a longer discussion regarding the gift of prophecy in response to modern charismatic claims, see MacArthur, *Strange Fire*, 105–32.

fice was no longer necessary and passed off the scene (cf. Rev. 22:18–19). Like the apostles, prophets were given to lay the revelatory foundation for the church (Eph. 2:20). Once that foundation was established, the work of the apostles and prophets in the church age was completed. Nonetheless, the proclamation of the prophetic word (2 Pet. 1:19–21) continues through the faithful preaching of Scripture. In the future, after the church age ends, God will again raise up prophets to accomplish his revelatory purposes (cf. Rev. 11:3).

EVANGELISTS

Though all believers are commanded to take the good news of the gospel to the unconverted (Matt. 28:18–20; Acts 1:8), some are especially gifted as evangelists. Apart from Ephesians 4:11, the term "evangelist" occurs only twice in the New Testament. Philip is described as an evangelist in Acts 21:8 (cf. Acts 8:4–40), and Timothy is instructed to "do the work of an evangelist" in 2 Timothy 4:5. Nonetheless, evangelism is a significant New Testament theme. The Greek noun *euangelion* ("good news" or "gospel") is used more than seventy-five times, and the cognate verb *euangelizō* ("to declare the good news") occurs more than fifty times.

Evangelists are called to proclaim the good news of salvation through faith in Christ to the unbelieving world. The example of Philip demonstrates that early Christian evangelists sometimes preached the gospel to unreached people groups (like the Samaritans). In keeping with the Great Commission, their aim was to make disciples, incorporating them into the church through baptism and building them up in the faith through teaching (Matt. 28:18–20). The example of Timothy illustrates the close connection that ought to exist between the evangelist and the leadership of the local church.

Evangelists are uniquely gifted by God at reaching lost sinners with the saving truth of the gospel. Their ministry is one that every church ought to prioritize—both by encouraging evangelism in the local community and by supporting missionary work around the world.

PASTOR-TEACHERS

In Ephesians 4:11, the Greek word *poimēn* can be translated as either "pastor" or "shepherd." It describes the leadership, protection, and care that pastors exhibit toward the members of their flock. The Lord Jesus is the great Shepherd (Heb. 13:20–21; 1 Pet. 2:25); those whom he has given to the church as pastors are to be his undershepherds (1 Pet. 5:2). Their primary function is to feed the sheep (cf. John 21:15–17), a responsibility that they accomplish through teaching the Word (cf. 2 Tim. 3:16–17; 1 Pet. 2:2–3). Although teaching can be identified as its own ministry (1 Cor. 12:28), it is best to regard "shepherds and teachers" in Ephesians 4:11 as describing two facets of a single office of pastoral leadership. Other New Testament texts indicate that pastors are expected to be both shepherds (Acts 20:28; 1 Pet. 5:2) and teachers (1 Tim. 3:2; 5:17).

Like the apostles, pastors ought to devote themselves primarily "to prayer and to the ministry of the word" (Acts 6:4), as they make it their mission to proclaim Christ, "warning everyone and teaching everyone with all wisdom, that [they] may present everyone mature in Christ" (Col. 1:28). The diligent pastor-teacher is a "good servant of Christ Jesus" (1 Tim. 4:6), being approved as "a worker who has no need to be ashamed, rightly handling the word of truth" (2 Tim. 2:15; cf. 4:2), and struggling in prayer on behalf of his people (cf. Col. 4:12).

Though structure and administration have their place, true power in the church comes through prayer and the ministry of the Word. Consequently, the pastor-teacher is to prioritize prayer and preaching rather than becoming overly encumbered with the management of other administrative issues (cf. Acts 6:2, 4). The sheep are best served not through elaborate programs or slick presentations but through consistent, solid teaching. The image of a shepherd accentuates the spiritual care and biblical nourishment that pastors provide for their people as they lead them. A shepherd's heart is essential in those who would aspire to be pastors and teachers of God's people.

The New Testament uses two other terms to denote the office of the pastor. The first is "bishop" (from Gk. *episkopos*), which means "overseer" or "guardian." This word occurs five times in the New Testament (Acts 20:28; Phil. 1:1; 1 Tim. 3:2; Titus 1:7; 1 Pet. 2:25). In the secular Greek-speaking world, the term designated a delegate appointed by the emperor to provide leadership and political oversight to a municipality that had been newly founded or recently captured. Similarly, in the church, bishops operate under the authority of King Jesus as they lead in the church, albeit through humble service rather than authoritarian control (Mark 10:42–43). The spiritual overseer is responsible for both feeding (1 Tim. 3:2) and protecting the flock (Acts 20:28) under his charge.

The other term is "elder" (from Gk. *presbyteros*), which speaks to the seasoned spiritual maturity of those who lead in the church. In the New Testament, *presbyteros* can be used in a generic sense to refer to people of advanced age (Acts 2:17; cf. 1 Tim. 5:2). It can also refer to the first-century leaders of Israel (Matt. 15:2; 27:3, 41; Mark 7:3, 5; Luke 22:52; Acts 4:8). But in an ecclesiological context, the title designates a specific office of spiritual leadership within the church (e.g., Acts 11:30; 14:23; 15:2, 4, 6, 22; 16:4; 20:17; 21:18).

The New Testament concept of the office of elder is primarily drawn from Old Testament Judaism (cf. Ex. 12:21; 19:7; Num. 11:16; Deut. 27:1; 1 Sam. 11:3; 16:4). The elders of Israel were mature men who exhibited strong moral convictions, being characterized by truth, integrity, courage, and the fear of the Lord (Ex. 18:21–22; cf. Num. 11:16–17). Wise and discerning, they taught, interceded, and judged righteously and impartially (Deut. 1:13–17). The New Testament understanding of elders in the church includes those same attributes of personal strength, spiritual maturity, and moral integrity.

That the early church was led by elders is clearly demonstrated throughout the New Testament. For example, the Jerusalem church had elders (Acts 11:29–30), as did the churches that Paul planted on his missionary journeys (Acts 14:23; 20:17). The churches throughout Asia Minor to whom Peter addressed his epistles, were similarly led by elders. Thus, Peter could write, "I exhort the elders among you, as a fellow elder . . . : shepherd the flock of God that is among you" (1 Pet. 5:1–2). The book of Revelation further indicates that twenty-four elders will represent the redeemed in eternity future (e.g., Rev. 4:4, 10; 5:5–6, 8, 11, 14; 7:11).

Textual evidence indicates that all three New Testament terms ("pastor," "bishop," and "elder") refer to the same office of church leadership. A comparison of 1 Timothy 3:1–7 and Titus 1:6–9 demonstrates that the qualifications for a bishop and an elder are the same, suggesting that the two offices are identical. In Titus 1:5–7, Paul even uses both titles to refer to the same person. All three terms are found together in 1 Peter 5:1–2:

> So I exhort the elders [plural of *presbyteros*] among you, as a fellow elder and a witness of the sufferings of Christ, as well as a partaker in the glory that is going to be revealed: shepherd [Gk. *poimainō*] the flock of God that is among you, exercising oversight [Gk. *episkopeō*], not under compulsion, but willingly, as God would have you; not for shameful gain, but eagerly.

Acts 20 also illustrates the interchangeable nature of these three terms. After assembling the elders (plural of *presbyteros*, 20:17) of the Ephesian church together, Paul warns them with these words: "Pay careful attention to yourselves and to all the flock, in which the Holy Spirit has made you overseers [plural of *episkopos*], to care for [*poimainō*] the church of God, which he obtained with his own blood" (20:28).

Though all three terms are synonymous, each has a unique emphasis within the biblical context: "elder" emphasizes a man's maturity and personal character; "bishop" speaks to his leadership role as protector of the flock; and "pastor" emphasizes his sincere care for the people whom he serves. Regrettably, throughout church history, some of these titles (such as *bishop* and even *pastor*) have been abused by unbiblical ecclesiastical hierarchies and power-hungry spiritual leaders. As a result, the title *elder* may be preferable in some contexts, because it does not generally carry the cultural connotations that have sometimes been imposed on the other two titles. We will explore the office of elder in more detail in the following section.

Elders

By God's design, churches depend on faithful leadership in order to be strong, healthy, productive, and fruitful. Scripture teaches that God has given elders to each local congregation in order to oversee and lead his people. As those tasked with feeding and protecting the flock, elders will one day give an account before the Lord for the souls under their spiritual care. In fact, spiritual authority, unlike worldly leadership, is characterized by Christlike humility and a desire to serve (Mark 10:43–45). Any who wish to lead in the church must demonstrate personal holiness, doctrinal purity, self-sacrifice, spiritual discipline, and Christ-centered devotion. The office of elder entails a responsibility that must not be taken lightly (cf. Luke 12:48), as highlighted in the sober warning of James 3:1: "Not many of you should become teachers, my brothers, for you know that we who teach will be judged with greater strictness."

RESPONSIBILITIES

In 1 Timothy 3:5, Paul indicates that one of the responsibilities of an *episkopos* is to "care for God's church." As part of that general responsibility, elders hold authority delegated to them from Christ the Head to provide leadership and give oversight to local church affairs. Paul writes, "Let the elders who rule well be considered worthy of double honor, especially those who labor in preaching and teaching" (1 Tim. 5:17). The term translated "rule" (Gk. *proistēmi*) is applied to elders several times throughout the New Testament (Rom. 12:8; 1 Thess. 5:12; 1 Tim. 3:4–5, 12; 5:17). It designates the position of oversight that is entrusted to them by Christ himself, signifying that there is no earthly authority in the local church higher than theirs.

Yet their authority is not coerced by force or intimidation; rather, it is an authority built on precept and example to which the church gladly submits (cf. Heb. 13:17). Though elders are called to lead the local church, it is important to emphasize that the congregation does not belong to them. It is not their flock. Rather, the members of the church constitute the "flock of God" (1 Pet. 5:2), which he bought (Acts 20:28) and for which the elders serve as caretakers and stewards.

As noted above, the God-given responsibility of preaching and teaching lies with the elders (1 Tim. 5:17). That is why elders must be "able to teach" (1 Tim. 3:2), exhibiting an aptitude to instruct in sound doctrine and refute error and falsehood (Titus 1:9). Such teaching necessarily involves the careful exposition of the Scriptures (1 Tim. 4:13; 2 Tim. 2:15; cf. Neh. 8:8) and is the primary means by which the flock is spiritually fed and nourished (1 Pet. 2:2; cf. Ps. 1:2–3; Heb. 5:12–13). As Paul reminded Timothy, "All Scripture is breathed out by God and profitable for teaching, for reproof, for correction, and for training in righteousness, that the man of God may be complete, equipped for every good work" (2 Tim. 3:16–17). Accordingly, Timothy was to "preach the word; be ready in season and out of season; reprove, rebuke, and exhort, with complete patience and teaching" (2 Tim. 4:2).

Beyond teaching, elders are also responsible to determine church polity (cf. Acts 15:22), ordain other elders (1 Tim. 4:14), set an example for the sheep to follow (1 Pet. 5:1–3; Heb. 13:7), protect the flock from doctrinal error (Acts 20:28–30), and pray for the members of the church (James 5:14). By God's design, elders play a central role in the health and function of the church.

Revelation 2–3 contains Christ's letters to the seven churches of Asia Minor.[10] They are the only scriptural accounts of Christ directly critiquing his local churches. In them, he commends what is right and condemns what is wrong. Christ's remarks stand as profoundly important for every generation to be reminded of Christ's will for his church, both positive and negative.

God's Word has preserved those qualities that he commends and condemns.

---

10. Adapted from Mayhue, *What Would Jesus Say about Your Church?*, 213–16. Used by permission of Christian Focus.

Taken together, they serve as a "plumb line" of the perfect standards that Christ has set down for the church against which to compare the current reality in the church. It is the responsibility of every elder (and a commendable practice even for every Christian) to contemplate this one overarching question: If Jesus Christ were to write my church a letter, like he wrote in Scripture, what would he say? What would he commend? What would he condemn? The elders must guide the church in pursuing what Jesus commends and eschewing what he condemns.

The Lord commended these features:

- Good deeds
- Hard work
- Endurance
- Discernment
- Suffering
- Faithfulness to the end
- Holding fast to Christ's name
- Not denying the faith
- Love
- Faith
- Service
- Righteous living
- Keeping Christ's Word
- Submission
- Repentance
- Patience
- Accepting God's Word
- Standing firm
- Pleasing God
- Loving the brethren
- Prayer
- Evangelistic fervor
- Baptismal emphasis
- Strong teaching/preaching
- Spiritual leadership
- Dependence on God
- Joyful attitudes
- Generosity
- Boldness
- Growth
- Ministry of the Holy Spirit
- Discipleship
- Sacrifice
- Spiritual priorities
- Spiritual potential
- Submission to God's sovereignty
- True worship

By contrast, the Lord condemned the following characteristics:

- Lost love
- Absence of first deeds
- Compromise
- Tolerating sin
- Immorality
- Idolatry
- Deadness
- Incomplete deeds
- Lukewarmness
- Hypocrisy
- False teaching
- Undisciplined living
- Disunity
- Sin
- Arrogant divisions
- Prolonged spiritual immaturity
- Suing one another
- Abusing Christian liberty
- Profaning the Lord's Supper
- Misappropriating spiritual gifts
- Unwillingness to forgive
- Slow to give
- Critical of leadership

QUALIFICATIONS

The apostle Paul delineates the qualifications for elders in 1 Timothy 3:1–7 and Titus 1:6–9. In both places, the overarching standard for an elder is that he must be "above reproach," meaning that he is a man of impeccable spiritual and moral character. Aside from the ability to teach, the qualities Paul outlines only amplify the fundamental principle that elders are to be men whose lives are characteristically free from any corruption or stain that might bring reproach on the gospel.

In every sphere of life—marriage, family, community, and church—the elder must be above reproach. He must be "the husband of one wife" (1 Tim. 3:2), which could be literally translated "a one-woman man." This qualification is far more than merely a prohibition of polygamy. It speaks of the man's moral integrity and sexual fidelity in his role as a husband; he is fully devoted to the one wife whom God has given him. If he is not married, his life ought to be an example of moral purity, free from fornication or a reputation for flirtatious behavior.

Elders are also to be "sober-minded" and "self-controlled" (1 Tim. 3:2). Their thoughts ought to be characterized by wisdom and maturity, while their actions exhibit both temperance and moderation. An elder ought to conduct himself in a "respectable" manner toward those who know him (1 Tim. 3:2), in keeping with his role as one of the representative leaders of Christ's church. At the same time, he is to be "hospitable" toward others in the church, including those who do not know him (1 Tim. 3:2). The word "hospitable" speaks of "the love of strangers," indicating that an elder is welcoming and friendly to all.

In 1 Timothy 3:3, Paul continues by listing several negative qualities that must be absent from the life of an elder: "not a drunkard, not violent but gentle, not quarrelsome, not a lover of money." As a servant of Christ, an elder must not be controlled by sinful addictions (e.g., drunkenness, Eph. 5:18), reckless passions (e.g., anger and belligerence, Eph. 4:26–27), or financial ambitions (e.g., the love of money, 1 Tim. 6:9–10). Those enslaved to their own lusts (2 Pet. 2:19) show themselves to be unworthy of spiritual leadership in the church.

First Timothy 3:4 explains further that an elder "must manage his own household well, with all dignity keeping his children submissive." The first sphere in which a potential elder must demonstrate irreproachable behavior is in his home, in the presence of those who know him most intimately. His skill in managing his family establishes a precedent regarding his ability to shepherd the church, "for if someone does not know how to manage his own household, how will he care for God's church?" (1 Tim. 3:5).

In light of this high standard, it is understandable that an elder should not be a recent convert (1 Tim. 3:6). Many years are usually needed for a man to reach the level of personal and spiritual maturity required of an elder. Moreover, there must be adequate time for others to observe his life and affirm his qualifications. As Paul warned Timothy, those elevated to the position of elder prematurely are highly susceptible to the sin of pride.

First Timothy 3:7 goes on to state, "He must be well thought of by outsiders, so that he may not fall into disgrace, into a snare of the devil." Beyond his family and the local congregation of believers, an elder must also have an excellent reputation

Table 9.1 Lists of Elder Qualifications

1 Timothy 3:2–7	Titus 1:6–9
Above reproach (3:2)	Above reproach (1:6)
Husband of one wife (3:2)	Husband of one wife (1:6)
Sober-minded (3:2)	
Self-controlled (3:2)	Self-controlled and disciplined (1:8)
Respectable (3:2)	
Hospitable (3:2)	Hospitable (1:8)
Able to teach (3:2)	Holding firm to the Word, able to give instruction in sound doctrine, and to rebuke those who contradict it (1:9)
Not a drunkard (3:3)	Not a drunkard (1:7)
Not violent but gentle (3:3)	Not violent (1:7)
Not quarrelsome (3:3)	Not quick-tempered (1:7)
Not a lover of money (3:3)	Not greedy for gain (1:7)
Skilled manager of his household (3:4)	Above reproach as God's steward (1:7)
Keeping his children submissive with all dignity (3:4)	Having faithful children not open to the charge of debauchery or insubordination (1:6)
Not a recent convert lest he become conceited (3:6)	Not arrogant (1:7)
Well thought of by outsiders (3:7)	
	A lover of good (1:8)
	Upright (1:8)
	Holy (1:8)

with those outside the church. In both his business and social engagements with unbelievers, he is called to be above reproach.

The apostle Paul reiterates a similar list of qualifications in Titus 1:6–9. As in 1 Timothy 3, an elder is to be the husband of one wife. Additionally, Paul explains that his children should be "believers and not open to the charge of debauchery or insubordination" (Titus 1:6). Because the behavior of an elder's children reflects on his spiritual leadership in the home, they must not be characterized by dissipation or rebellion.

"As God's steward," an elder "must be above reproach"; he is not to be "arrogant," "quick-tempered," "a drunkard," "violent," or "greedy for gain" (Titus 1:7). Conversely, he must be "hospitable, a lover of good, self-controlled, upright, holy, and disciplined" (Titus 1:8). Added to that, he ought to be a skillful student of God's Word, being "able to give instruction in sound doctrine" while also rebuking "those who contradict it" (Titus 1:9). A comparison of the two lists demonstrates their consistent parallels (see table 9.1).

It should be noted that the New Testament makes no provision for women to serve as elders or pastors. As Paul explains in 1 Timothy 2:11–12, "Let a woman learn quietly with all submissiveness. I do not permit a woman to teach or to exercise authority over a man; rather, she is to remain quiet." The verb "to teach" in 1 Timothy 2:12 could be better translated as "to be a teacher." It indicates that women are not to hold teaching positions over men in the church, thus excluding them from the office of elder (since teaching the congregation is one of the elders' primary responsibilities). Thus, the biblical pattern is that only men may serve as elders and pastors. That stipulation is not born out of first-century cultural bias or Pauline prejudice. Rather, it is grounded in both the created order and the events of the fall. As Paul explains, "For Adam was formed first, then Eve; and Adam was not deceived, but the woman was deceived and became a transgressor" (1 Tim. 2:13–14).

The teaching in 1 Timothy 2 shows that women in the church are not permitted to hold the office of pastor or teacher (cf. Acts 13:1; 1 Cor. 12:28; Eph. 4:11). However, this would not preclude a woman from teaching in other appropriate contexts, such as teaching other women (Titus 2:3–4) or teaching children (2 Tim. 1:5; 3:14–15). The Bible clearly indicates that women are spiritual equals with men and that the ministry of women is essential to the body of Christ. Nonetheless, by God's design, women are excluded from leadership over men in the church.

ORDINATION

In the New Testament, elders were uniquely set apart for their office. The Greek word *kathistēmi*, meaning "to ordain," was normally used to describe the appointment of elders. The ordination process signifies a divine calling and setting aside to spiritual leadership that is officially recognized by the church.

Paul offers important details about the ordination process when he tells Timothy, "Do not neglect the gift you have, which was given you by prophecy when the council of elders laid their hands on you" (1 Tim. 4:14). The practice of laying hands on a man being ordained finds its roots in the Old Testament sacrificial system. When the Israelites brought sacrifices to be offered to the Lord, they would place their hands on the sacrifice in order to identify themselves with it (Lev. 1:4; 3:2–13; 4:4–33; 8:14, 18, 22; 16:21). Ordination in the New Testament similarly pictures the solidarity between the elders and the man being ordained.

In the Old Testament, the laying on of hands was also used to symbolize a transference of authority (Num. 27:18–23; Deut. 34:9) or to convey a blessing given from one party to another (Gen. 48:13–20; 2 Kings 13:16; Job 9:33; Ps. 139:5). Authority and blessing are also both reflected in New Testament ordination, as the leadership of the church affirms the newly ordained elder in his duties.

The solidarity represented by ordination necessitates that it not be performed rashly. As Paul warned Timothy, "Do not be hasty in the laying on of hands, nor take part in the sins of others; keep yourself pure" (1 Tim. 5:22). In light of that admonition, men being considered for ordination must be adequately tested, demonstrating that they are qualified to serve in pastoral ministry. They must be above reproach, morally pure, doctrinally sound, and capable leaders and teachers. As current church leaders look to the next generation, they should seek to raise up younger men who can begin prayerfully preparing themselves to become elders in the future (cf. 2 Tim. 2:2).

According to the New Testament pattern, the ordination process was overseen and administered by the recognized leadership of the church. For example, in Acts 14:23, it was Paul and Barnabas who "appointed elders in every church." In Titus 1:5, Paul instructed Titus to "appoint elders in every town." First Timothy 4:14 indicates that the elders themselves were to ordain other elders. Whether the appointment was made by an apostle, an apostolic delegate, or a team of local church elders, the basic principle is clear: the ordination of new elders is the responsibility of those who currently serve as part of the church's recognized spiritual leadership.

Those who assert that it is the congregation's responsibility to select and approve new elders often appeal to Acts 6:2–6 to support that notion. There Luke writes,

> And the twelve summoned the full number of the disciples and said, "It is not right that we should give up preaching the word of God to serve tables. Therefore, brothers, pick out from among you seven men of good repute, full of the Spirit and of wisdom, whom we will appoint to this duty. But we will devote ourselves to prayer and to the ministry of the word." And what they said pleased the whole gathering, and they chose Stephen, a man full of faith and of the Holy Spirit, and Philip, and Prochorus, and Nicanor, and Timon, and Parmenas, and Nicolaus, a proselyte of Antioch. These they set before the apostles, and they prayed and laid their hands on them.

At least two observations from this text need to be considered. First, the seven men who were chosen are not called elders. They were chosen to serve tables, not to lead the church. (In church history, these men were more closely associated with the role of deacon.) Second, the congregation brought these men to the apostles for approval, not vice versa. The apostles not only initiated the process (Acts 6:3), they were also the ones who ultimately appointed these men to minister (Acts 6:6). The final responsibility rested with the leaders of the church and not the congregation. Though there are no apostles in the church today, the pattern established in Scripture still holds: new leaders in the church ought to be ordained by other recognized leaders.

In identifying future elders, the starting point is a God-given desire in the heart of the individual. Paul explains, "If anyone aspires to the office of overseer, he desires a noble task" (1 Tim. 3:1). Stated negatively, those who do not desire the office of elder are not qualified to hold it. Potential elders should not be coerced or manipulated into pursuing the office, since serving in that capacity begins with a humble and heartfelt willingness to lead. As Peter reminded the fellow elders to whom he wrote, "Shepherd the flock of God that is among you, exercising oversight, not under compulsion, but willingly, as God would have you" (1 Pet. 5:2).

Before the ordination can be completed, the elders must prayerfully seek the Lord's will with regard to the appointment. The biblical precedent for this is found in Acts 14:23: "When they had appointed elders for them in every church, with prayer and fasting they committed them to the Lord in whom they had believed." Because they understood what was at stake, Paul and Barnabas diligently sought the Lord in prayer as part of the ordination process (cf. Acts 13:2). Appointing elders in an attitude of prayer rightly recognizes that God is ultimately the One who gifts, calls, and commissions men to spiritual leadership. As Paul exhorted the Ephesian elders, "Pay careful attention to yourselves and to all the flock, in which the Holy Spirit has made you overseers, to care for the church of God" (Acts 20:28). Because it is the highest calling from God in the life of a local church, spiritual leadership must not be taken lightly or sought superficially. Selections and appointments ought to be made in the context of careful consideration and prayerful wisdom (cf. James 1:5).

In summary, the elders constitute a group of mature and godly men who desire to lead and feed God's flock. They have been specially called and commissioned to the ministry by the Lord himself. Having aspired to the office and having met the necessary biblical qualifications, they are prayerfully appointed by other elders whom they subsequently partner with as spiritual leaders in the church.

SUPPORT

The New Testament indicates that it is appropriate for elders to be compensated financially by the church for their ministry labors. Paul articulates this principle when he writes, "Let the elders who rule well be considered worthy of double honor, especially those who labor in preaching and teaching. For the Scripture says, 'You shall not muzzle an ox when it treads out the grain' and, 'The laborer deserves his wages'" (1 Tim. 5:17–18). The word translated "honor" in 5:17 (from Gk. *timē*) refers to remuneration, as the biblical allusions in 5:18 make clear.

The apostle expands on this theme in 1 Corinthians 9:4–9:

> Do we not have the right to eat and drink? Do we not have the right to take along a believing wife, as do the other apostles and the brothers of the Lord and Cephas? Or is it only Barnabas and I who have no right to refrain from working for a living? Who serves as a soldier at his own expense? Who plants a vineyard without eating any of its fruit? Or who tends a flock without getting some of the milk?
>
> Do I say these things on human authority? Does not the Law say the same? For it is written in the Law of Moses, "You shall not muzzle an ox when it treads out the grain." Is it for oxen that God is concerned?

A soldier is paid by his nation; a farmer enjoys a portion of his own harvest; a shepherd receives milk from his flock; and even an ox is allowed to eat while treading out the grain. Drawing a parallel to pastoral ministry, Paul contends that it is acceptable for pastors to be supported by the congregation to whom they minister. The apostle continues to make this point in verse 13: "Do you not know that those who are employed in the temple service get their food from the temple, and those who serve at the altar share in the sacrificial offerings?" If Old Testament priests were permitted to live off the offerings brought by the people, then it is also permissible for new covenant ministers to be supported by those in the church.

Yet as Paul implies in verse 6, this kind of subsidy is a right, not a mandate. As an apostle and a minister of the gospel, he clearly had a right to receive financial support from the church. However, Paul decided not to exercise this right for himself, choosing instead to work as a tentmaker (Acts 18:3) so that he might proclaim the gospel without adding any financial burden to the church (1 Cor. 9:18; cf. 1 Thess. 2:9).

Within a group of elders, it is likely that some will be supported by the church while others will earn a living through other means. Both situations are biblically permissible, and neither affects a man's qualification for pastoral leadership. Often, elders who are paid by the church are referred to as *clergy* (or *staff elders*), while elders who support themselves outside the church are called *lay elders*. While such designations can be useful in certain situations, it is important to understand that no such distinction is found in Scripture. The Bible makes no qualitative difference between a lay pastor and a staff pastor. Every elder is responsible to provide leadership, care, oversight, protection, sound teaching, and a godly example to the flock. As those who have been set apart by God and ordained by the church, they are all called to the same standard of accountability before the Lord, whether or not they receive financial remuneration from the church.

PLURALITY

Scripture presents pastoral ministry as a team effort, involving a plurality of elders in each local congregation. The word *presbyteros* almost always occurs in the plural when used in the New Testament (e.g., Acts 11:30; 14:23; 15:2; 20:17; Titus 1:5; James 5:14). The few exceptions occur when a biblical author applies the term to himself (e.g., 1 Pet. 5:1; 2 John 1; 3 John 1) or when an individual elder is being singled out from the larger group (1 Tim. 5:19). The clear norm was that first-century churches were governed by multiple elders. Consequently, Paul can address the believers in Philippi by greeting "all the saints in Christ Jesus who are at Philippi, with the overseers [plural of *episkopos*] and deacons" (Phil. 1:1). Significantly, the New Testament never mentions a one-pastor congregation.[11]

A church that is governed by a plurality of godly elders enjoys all the divinely intended benefits, including their combined knowledge, wisdom, and experience. Such not only provides a wealth of counsel for shepherding the flock (Prov. 11:14; 15:22), it also safeguards the congregation from the self-serving preferences of a single individual.

In leading the local congregation, elders ought to operate on the principle of unanimity with their fellow elders. That kind of unity reflects the fact that they all have the mind of Christ and are guided by the same Spirit (1 Cor. 1:10; Eph. 4:3; Phil. 1:27; 2:2). On those occasions when they disagree over a decision, the elders should wait and seek God's will through additional prayer and study until they are able to reach a consensus. In this way, the leadership team will not only display a unified

---

11. Some appeal to Revelation 1–3 to support an only-one-pastor model, arguing that "the angels [lit., 'messengers'] of the seven churches" (1:20) refer to the singular pastors of each church. However, the text does not state how many elders were operating in each assembly. Given the New Testament pattern, which clearly depicts a plurality of godly leaders in every local congregation (cf. Acts 14:23; Titus 1:5), it is likely that these messengers were key leaders who represented a group of elders in each church.

front but also model the harmony that ought to characterize the entire congregation (cf. Rom. 15:5; 2 Cor. 13:11; 1 Pet. 3:8).

Obviously, there will be diversity within the elder team—as each elder employs his unique giftedness for the benefit of all. The variety of gifts and skills serves to strengthen the church's leadership, which in turn builds up the entire congregation. Some of the elders may be particularly gifted as counselors, others as preachers, and others as administrators. Some may minister in a highly visible role, while others serve behind the scenes. Both the diversity and the unity reflected within the group of elders illustrate the way the body of Christ as a whole ought to function (cf. 1 Cor. 12:4–28).

Within each group of spiritual leaders, some will be given a more visible or vocal role of leadership. The New Testament bears this out. Among the apostles, Peter emerged as the spokesman for the entire group (cf. Matt. 15:15; 16:16–17; Mark 11:21; Luke 12:41; John 6:68). That pattern continued after the birth of the church on the day of Pentecost. In the first few chapters of Acts, Peter and John often ministered together—yet the biblical narrative implies that only Peter preached any sermons (Acts 2:14–40; 3:12–26; 4:8–12; 5:29–32). At the Jerusalem Council in Acts 15, James the brother of Jesus is seen functioning as the spokesman for the Jerusalem church (Acts 15:13–21), though Peter also spoke on that occasion (Acts 15:7–11). On his missionary journeys, the apostle Paul was the primary speaker for the group of men with whom he traveled (cf. Acts 14:12). Though their role may have been more visible, these leaders among leaders were not spiritually superior to their ministry coworkers (cf. 1 Pet. 5:1). Their office, honor, privileges, and responsibilities were equal, even if their role was unique.

The biblical precedent is clear. Though the specific roles of each leader will differ according to his giftedness, church ministry is a team effort. The apostle Paul was quick to commend his colaborers in the gospel. Some served alongside him as preachers and evangelists. Others supported the ministry in less visible ways. All their contributions were vital, because their unique roles of leadership contributed to the overall strength of the ministry. Moreover, it mitigated against the self-styled, despotic leadership of egomaniacs like Diotrephes who always put themselves first (3 John 9).

CHURCH GOVERNMENT

As shepherds of the flock, elders are to lead both by giving direction and by personal example, and they are to feed by teaching God's Word and by protecting the people from error. Because they operate under the authority of Christ, the Chief Shepherd, they represent the highest level of spiritual authority within the local church and are answerable to him (1 Pet. 5:2–4). Consequently, each local assembly ought to be governed by its own elders (cf. Titus 1:5), without coercion from external hierarchies or parachurch organizations. Churches are free to cooperate with other churches but should do so at the discretion of the elders in keeping with biblical principles. As the God-ordained leaders of the church, the elders ought to determine matters of policy, membership, and discipline as they prayerfully look for guidance from the Scriptures (cf. Acts 15:19–31; 20:28; 1 Cor. 5:4–7, 13; 1 Pet. 5:1–4).

Democratic political values often prompt modern churchgoers to be suspicious of elder rule, opting instead for a congregational form of church government. But this runs contrary to the clear New Testament paradigm for spiritual leadership within the church, which calls for elders to take the primary responsibility for serving and leading God's people.

Historically, various forms of church government include the episcopal, presbyterian, and congregational forms.[12] An episcopal form of church government places primary leadership responsibility with the *episkopos*, or "bishop." Variations of this ecclesiastical structure are found in Methodism, Anglicanism, and Roman Catholicism, and can involve multiple levels of hierarchy (e.g., priests, bishops, archbishops). Though prominent throughout much of church history, this system has at least two significant weaknesses. First, it creates a positional distinction between the *episkopos* ("bishop") and the *presbyteros* ("elder") not found in the New Testament. Consequently, a biblical case for this form of church government cannot successfully be made. Second, this form of church government is especially vulnerable to corruption due to its hierarchical structure of ecclesiastical leadership, which can wrongly put the focus on titles and positions of authority rather than on the spiritual qualifications for pastoral ministry. Such corruption is nowhere more apparent than in Roman Catholicism with its history of papal corruption, doctrinal deviation, and spiritual abuses.[13]

The presbyterian form of church government focuses on the role of the *presbyteros*, or "elder," noting that the terms "bishop" and "elder" are interchangeable in the New Testament (cf. 1 Tim. 3:1–2; Titus 1:7). This approach is primarily found within Presbyterian and Reformed denominations. The emphasis on elder rule is clearly affirmed in the New Testament (1 Thess. 5:12; Heb. 13:17). However, the extrabiblical hierarchical structures historically associated with this form of church government (e.g., local church sessions, regional presbyteries, larger synods, general assemblies) have neither New Testament precedent nor support.

Congregational forms of church government emphasize the individual authority of each local congregation. Denominational groups such as Baptists, Congregationalists, and many Lutherans are characterized by variations of congregationalism. On the one hand, congregationalism emphasizes the autonomy of each local church, noting that the New Testament portrays such a picture of the first-century church. Thus, a congregational form of church government rightly rejects the ecclesiastical hierarchy represented by the other two systems. On the other hand, many forms of congregationalism also insist on a democratic approach to leadership, in which all church members (rather than just the elders) are involved in church decision making.

---

12. For a more detailed discussion of these forms of church government, see the helpful survey in Millard J. Erickson, *Christian Theology*, 2nd ed. (Grand Rapids, MI: Baker, 2001), 1080–93.
13. Cf. William Webster, *The Church of Rome at the Bar of History* (Carlisle, PA: Banner of Truth, 1997); E. R. Chamberlin, *The Bad Popes* (Stroud, UK: Sutton, 2003).

Though popular in the American church, where democratic values are reflected in secular politics, that kind of congregational rule ignores the prerogative and responsibility that the New Testament gives to elders to lead and shepherd the flock.

AUTHORITY

On account of both their position of leadership and their responsibility for the flock, elders ought to be treated with great respect. As Paul told the believers in Thessalonica: "We ask you, brothers, to respect those who labor among you and are over you in the Lord and admonish you, and to esteem them very highly in love because of their work" (1 Thess. 5:12–13). The members of the church are to hold their leaders in high esteem because of their God-given calling.

Not only are believers to esteem their leaders, they are also to emulate them. The author of Hebrews writes, "Remember your leaders, those who spoke to you the word of God. Consider the outcome of their way of life, and imitate their faith" (Heb. 13:7). Church members are instructed to follow the godly example of their spiritual leaders, as the elders model what it means to live in a Christ-honoring way (cf. 1 Cor. 4:16; 11:1).

The church's attitude toward its leadership is further spelled out in Hebrews 13:17: "Obey your leaders and submit to them, for they are keeping watch over your souls, as those who will have to give an account. Let them do this with joy and not with groaning, for that would be of no advantage to you." The congregation is to submit to the leadership of the elders, recognizing that the elders are accountable to the Lord for those under their spiritual care. When church members respond to their leaders with an attitude of eager willingness and heartfelt thanks, the elders' responsibility to lead transforms from a drudgery into a great delight.

Though elders are to be respected, they are not above God's law. Credible accusations of sin against an elder should not be ignored or treated lightly. First Timothy 5:19–21 states,

> Do not admit a charge against an elder except on the evidence of two or three witnesses. As for those who persist in sin, rebuke them in the presence of all, so that the rest may stand in fear. In the presence of God and of Christ Jesus and of the elect angels I charge you to keep these rules without prejudging, doing nothing from partiality.

When elders sin, they are subject to the same process of church discipline as any other member of the church (cf. Matt. 18:15–17). Their leadership role does not exempt them from the same standard of holiness to which all believers are held. If anything, their accountability to that standard is higher, not lower, due to the visible nature of their leadership role. When a church willfully ignores sin in the lives of its leaders, its testimony before the watching world suffers accordingly. Additionally, the purity of the people is negatively affected, as they begin to emulate the lax attitude toward sin that they observe in their leadership (cf. Luke 6:40). A church's disobedience in this regard will invite the chastising judgment of God, rather than his blessing (cf. Heb. 12:3–11; Rev. 2:20–23; 3:19).

Deacons

In defining the office of deacon, the New Testament puts primary weight on a person's moral character. That is why Scripture reveals more about the spiritual qualifications for deacons than it does about the specific nature of their role in the local church. Biblically speaking, the emphasis is not on organizational structure but on the moral integrity, spiritual maturity, and doctrinal purity of those who serve in an official capacity.

The Greek words *diakonos* ("servant"), *diakonia* ("service"), and *diakoneō* ("to serve") are all used to describe the ministry of a deacon. Initially, this word group may have specifically applied to serving food and waiting tables (cf. Luke 4:39; 10:40; 17:8; 22:27; John 2:5, 9; 12:2; Acts 6:2), but it came to include any service or ministry that might be performed to meet the needs of other people (cf. John 12:26; Rom. 13:3–4). These words were also used to describe spiritual service to the Lord on the part of a believer, including acts of obedience or acts of service on behalf of the church (cf. Acts 20:19; Rom. 12:6–7; 15:25; 1 Cor. 12:5; 16:15; 2 Cor. 4:1; 8:3–4; 9:1; Rev. 2:19).

OFFICE

Beyond these general descriptions of service, 1 Timothy 3:8–13 uses the word "deacon" to also refer to a specific office within the church. There the apostle Paul writes,

> Deacons likewise must be dignified, not double-tongued, not addicted to much wine, not greedy for dishonest gain. They must hold the mystery of the faith with a clear conscience. And let them also be tested first; then let them serve as deacons if they prove themselves blameless. Their wives [lit., "women"] likewise must be dignified, not slanderers, but sober-minded, faithful in all things. Let deacons each be the husband of one wife, managing their children and their own households well. For those who serve well as deacons gain a good standing for themselves and also great confidence in the faith that is in Christ Jesus.

The word "likewise" in verse 8 points back to verse 1, where Paul introduces the qualifications for "the office of overseer." The implication is that the deacons described in verses 8–13 occupy a recognized office in the church, just as the elders do. As the elders lead the church, they are assisted in their ministry by the deacons.

In listing the qualifications for deacons, Paul emphasizes the personal character and spiritual maturity of the individual. Deacons must be "dignified," honorable in behavior and respectable in reputation. Because they are consistent and truthful in their speech, they are "not double-tongued," meaning that they do not insist one thing to be true to one person and something different to someone else. They are not "addicted to much wine" but are known for being sober-minded and Spirit-filled (cf. Eph. 5:18). A deacon must not be "greedy for dishonest gain" or motivated by the love of money (1 Tim. 6:9–10), especially since his service in the church might involve handling funds. Throughout church history, deacons have often been entrusted with collecting the offering. That kind of financial stewardship requires total trustworthiness.

Deacons ought to be theologically grounded in their doctrinal convictions. As Paul explains, "They must hold the mystery of the faith with a clear conscience" (1 Tim. 3:9). They not only embrace sound doctrine ("the mystery of the faith") but also apply it consistently in their actions, which is why their consciences are clear. A track record of faithfulness should be evident in their lives. Thus, they should "be tested first; then let them serve as deacons if they prove themselves blameless" (1 Tim. 3:10). In the same way that elders are to be above reproach, so also deacons must demonstrate a consistent pattern of life that is irreproachable. Such is in keeping with their official capacity of visible service within the church of Jesus Christ.

According to 1 Timothy 3:12, deacons must "be the husband of one wife." As with elders, this is not merely a prohibition of polygamy. Instead, it speaks to the sexual purity and moral integrity that ought to be true of every deacon. It is not simply that he has one wife but that he is absolutely faithful to that one woman. His marital life is characterized by total consecration and pure devotion to her. The consistency of his Christian walk is also evidenced in his role as a father, since deacons must manage "their children and their own households well" (1 Tim. 3:12). By leading his family well, he demonstrates that he is also capable of serving in key roles of responsibility within the church (cf. 1 Tim. 3:5).

The office of elder is primarily one of spiritual oversight—leading and feeding the flock. The office of deacon is primarily one of spiritual service—assisting the elders in meeting the needs of church members. Though the two offices differ, the qualifications for both clearly overlap. In reality, the qualifications outlined for deacons in 1 Timothy 3:8–13 encompass spiritual goals that all believers should pursue. Whether or not they are officially recognized as holding the office of deacon, they are called to be faithful servants of the Lord Jesus Christ (cf. Matt. 25:23). In that sense, all should aspire to wholeheartedly serve their Master by serving his people in the church. The promise that Paul articulates for deacons in this passage certainly applies to all who serve the Lord faithfully: "Those who serve well as deacons gain a good standing for themselves and also great confidence in the faith that is in Christ Jesus" (1 Tim. 3:13).

DEACONESSES

First Timothy 3:11 indicates that the office of deacon was available not only to men but also to women (i.e., deaconesses). There Paul writes, "Women must likewise be dignified, not malicious gossips, but temperate, faithful in all things" (NASB). Some interpret this verse as referring to the wives of deacons, but such is unlikely for at least three reasons. First, though some English translations insert it, Paul does not place a possessive pronoun ("their") before the word "women" (or "wives"). Consequently, the grammar suggests that the women addressed in 3:11 are relationally distinct from the men addressed in the previous verses.

Second, the apostle does not address the wives of elders in this same context (3:2–7). If Paul's intention was to elaborate on the behavior of a deacon's wife, it seems strange that he neglected to address the wives of elders along similar lines. However, if the women addressed in 3:11 are deaconesses, and not the wives of deacons, then Paul's pattern makes perfect sense. The apostle did not need to address women in his articulation of elder qualifications for the simple fact that there are no female elders. However, he did address women in 3:11 because there are female deacons.

Third, the description of Phoebe in Romans 16:1 provides a likely example of a woman who served as a deaconess. There Paul writes, "I commend to you our sister Phoebe, a servant [a form of *diakonos*] of the church at Cenchreae." It appears that Phoebe served in some recognized capacity within her local congregation, prompting Paul to draw attention to her. If so, she is likely a New Testament example of a deaconess. Like their male counterparts, deaconesses are to be above reproach in all their behavior (a point implied by Paul's use of the term "likewise" in 1 Tim. 3:11). Specifically, they "must be dignified, not slanderers, but sober-minded, faithful in all things."

ACTS 6 AND DEACONS

Throughout church history, many have understood Acts 6:1–6 as a New Testament example of deacons. In that passage, Luke writes,

> Now in these days when the disciples were increasing in number, a complaint by the Hellenists arose against the Hebrews because their widows were being neglected in the daily distribution [*diakonia*]. And the twelve summoned the full number of the disciples and said, "It is not right that we should give up preaching the word of God to serve [a form of *diakoneō*] tables. Therefore, brothers, pick out from among you seven men of good repute, full of the Spirit and of wisdom, whom we will appoint to this duty. But we will devote ourselves to prayer and to the ministry [*diakonia*] of the word." And what they said pleased the whole gathering, and they chose Stephen, a man full of faith and of the Holy Spirit, and Philip, and Prochorus, and Nicanor, and Timon, and Parmenas, and Nicolaus, a proselyte of Antioch. These they set before the apostles, and they prayed and laid their hands on them.

Those who interpret this passage as referring to deacons note that the Greek terms *diakonia* and *diakoneō* are both used. However, the use of those terms is inconclusive in this context, since *diakonia* is also applied to the ministry of the apostles in 6:4. So should the seven men listed in Acts 6:5 be regarded as the church's first deacons?

In answering that question, it is important to note that the New Testament never specifically refers to them as "deacons." Though Stephen and Philip are both mentioned later in Acts (6:8–15; 7:1–60; 8:5–12, 26–40), neither are called deacons. They are seen preaching and evangelizing, not waiting tables, suggesting that they administered

Table 9.2 Qualifications for Elders and Deacons

Elders	Deacons
Above reproach (1 Tim. 3:2; Titus 1:6)	Proven blameless (1 Tim. 3:10)
Husband of one wife (1 Tim. 3:2; Titus 1:6)	Husband of one wife (1 Tim. 3:12)
Sober-minded (1 Tim. 3:2)	Sober-minded [deaconesses] (1 Tim. 3:11)
Self-controlled and disciplined (1 Tim. 3:2; Titus 1:8)	
Respectable (1 Tim. 3:2)	Dignified (1 Tim. 3:8)
Hospitable (1 Tim. 3:2; Titus 1:8)	
Holding firm to the Word (Titus 1:9)	Holding the mystery of the faith with a clear conscience (1 Tim. 3:9)
Able to teach (1 Tim. 3:2); able to give instruction in sound doctrine and to rebuke those who contradict it (Titus 1:9)	
Not a drunkard (1 Tim. 3:3; Titus 1:7)	Not addicted to much wine (1 Tim. 3:8)
Not violent but gentle (1 Tim. 3:3; Titus 1:7)	
Not quarrelsome or quick-tempered (1 Tim. 3:3; Titus 1:7)	
Not a lover of money or greedy for gain (1 Tim. 3:3; Titus 1:7)	Not greedy for dishonest gain (1 Tim. 3:8)
Skilled manager of his household (1 Tim. 3:4)	Manages household well (1 Tim. 3:12)
Keeping his children submissive with all dignity (1 Tim. 3:4); having faithful children not open to the charge of debauchery or insubordination (Titus 1:6)	Manages children well (1 Tim. 3:12)
Above reproach as God's steward (Titus 1:7)	Faithful in all things [deaconesses] (1 Tim. 3:11)
Not a recent convert lest he become conceited (1 Tim. 3:6); not arrogant (Titus 1:7)	Must first be tested before serving (1 Tim. 3:10)
Well thought of by outsiders (1 Tim. 3:7)	(Implied in 1 Tim. 3:8)
A lover of good (Titus 1:8)	
Upright (Titus 1:8)	(Implied in 1 Tim. 3:10)
Holy (Titus 1:8)	(Implied in 1 Tim. 3:10)
	Not double-tongued (1 Tim. 3:8)
	Not a slanderer [deaconesses] (1 Tim. 3:11)

food distribution in Jerusalem only temporarily. Thus, it seems best to conclude that the situation in Acts 6:1–6 involved a temporary dilemma in the early church and that these seven men were selected to resolve a one-time crisis (rather than being appointed to a permanent office).[14] Accordingly, the terms *diakonia* and *diakoneō* in Acts 6 should be interpreted in the general sense of "service" and "to serve."

---

14. It might also be noted that some years later, when a famine occurred in Judea and the Jerusalem church received aid from the church in Antioch, the distribution of food came under the care of the elders, with no mention of deacons (Acts 11:29–30). The fact that the men chosen in Acts 6 are not mentioned in Acts 11 further supports the conclusion that their role was temporary.

While the seven men in Acts 6 cannot be classified as deacons in an official sense, they do anticipate the office of deacon in three important ways. First, these seven men helped the apostles accomplish an administrative task in much the same way that deacons ought to assist elders in a local church, so that the elders can remain focused on their primary spiritual responsibilities of teaching and prayer (cf. Acts 6:4). Second, the prerequisite qualifications for their service were related to their spiritual character. Much like Paul's list of qualifications in 1 Timothy 3:8–13, the emphasis in Acts 6:3 is on the moral virtue of these men: they had to be "of good repute, full of the Spirit and of wisdom." Third, these qualifications suggest that their role encompassed more than just organizing and implementing the distribution of food. They were tasked with resolving a conflict, one in which they undoubtedly provided much biblical counsel as they addressed the grievances of those who had been neglected. In providing physical care to the members of the congregation, their role also entailed a sensitivity to the spiritual state of the individuals to whom they ministered. Such should also characterize anyone who occupies the office of deacon.

QUALIFICATIONS

In terms of spiritual qualifications, the primary difference between deacons and elders is that elders must possess the ability to teach (1 Tim. 3:2), while the office of deacon has no such prerequisite. Nonetheless, deacons contribute to the teaching ministry of the elders by assisting them with other tasks, thereby freeing up the elders for the ministry of the Word. Comparing the qualifications for each office from 1 Timothy 3 and Titus 1 demonstrates the close parallels between the two (see table 9.2).

Though deacons share the same spiritual qualifications as elders, they do not perform the same role in the church. Deacons care for the flock under the oversight of the elders by organizing and executing administrative tasks and other service-oriented ministries. Their faithful service exemplifies the kind of spiritual greatness that Jesus commended when he told his disciples: "Whoever would be great among you must be your servant, and whoever would be first among you must be your slave, even as the Son of Man came not to be served but to serve, and to give his life as a ransom for many" (Matt. 20:26–28). The deacon's role is one of selfless service on behalf of others—a role that Christ himself modeled perfectly (Phil. 2:3–7). The reward for such service does not consist of temporal riches or worldly fame; rather, it is measured in terms of the eternal blessings that await those who faithfully serve their heavenly Master (1 Tim. 3:13; cf. Matt. 25:21, 23).

Biblical Dynamics of Church Life

Devoted to Christ
Devoted to Scripture
Devoted to One Another
Devoted to the Lord's Table
Devoted to Prayer
Results of Devotion

One of the most defining depictions of the early church is found in Acts 2:41–47. As Luke describes the Jerusalem church in its infancy, he delineates a number of key distinctives that characterized the devotion of that remarkable congregation. At least five marks of that faithful church establish an important precedent that churches today should seek to emulate. These marks will be developed in greater detail in the section "Means of Grace within the Church" (p. 780).

Devoted to Christ

According to Acts 2:41, about three thousand people responded in saving faith to Peter's evangelistic sermon preached on the day of Pentecost (Acts 2:14–40). They were baptized and incorporated into the church, and they demonstrated the genuineness of their profession of faith in their continual devotion to Christ. In Acts 2:42, the Greek verb translated "devoted" (a form of *proskartereō*) carries the idea of steadfast dedication and persevering affection. In the face of ridicule, rejection, and persecution, these believers displayed a courageous love for the Lord Jesus and his church. They exhibited the abiding commitment to Christ that characterizes genuine believers (John 15:1–4; cf. Matt. 13:3–9, 21; 1 John 2:19), showing themselves to truly be his disciples (John 8:31).

It is important, even if seemingly obvious, to note that the first church was composed of saved individuals. Too many modern churches are dominated by unbelievers. Some even focus more attention on appealing to unbelievers than on caring for the redeemed. But that does not fit the biblical model. Churches that are courageously devoted to the Lord Jesus will be characterized by purity in both life and doctrine (cf. 1 Tim. 4:16), often causing the world to resist or avoid them (cf. Acts 5:13–14). Their priority will be to honor Christ, the Head of the church, by equipping their members both to do the work of the ministry (Eph. 4:12) and to evangelize the lost as they go throughout their daily lives (Matt. 28:19).

Unbelievers are obviously welcome to attend church services, being exposed to God-honoring praise and biblical preaching in the hopes that they will be convicted and repent (1 Cor. 14:24–25). But the purpose of a church service is to edify and equip the saints as they join together in corporate worship through congregational singing, prayer, the teaching of God's Word, and the observance of the ordinances. Moreover, any form of membership or service in the church is restricted to believers. Those who are not part of the invisible, universal church can have no legitimate role of leadership or service in the visible, local church (2 Cor. 6:14–15).

The New Testament commends churches that demonstrate a Christ-centered commitment to both moral and doctrinal purity. Consider Paul's approbation of the Thessalonian church:

> We give thanks to God always for all of you, constantly mentioning you in our prayers, remembering before our God and Father your work of faith and labor of love and steadfastness of hope in our Lord Jesus Christ. For we know, brothers loved by God, that he has chosen you, because our gospel came to you not

only in word, but also in power and in the Holy Spirit and with full conviction. You know what kind of men we proved to be among you for your sake. And you became imitators of us and of the Lord, for you received the word in much affliction, with the joy of the Holy Spirit, so that you became an example to all the believers in Macedonia and in Achaia. For not only has the word of the Lord sounded forth from you in Macedonia and Achaia, but your faith in God has gone forth everywhere, so that we need not say anything. For they themselves report concerning us the kind of reception we had among you, and how you turned to God from idols to serve the living and true God, and to wait for his Son from heaven, whom he raised from the dead, Jesus who delivers us from the wrath to come. (1 Thess. 1:2–10)

The Thessalonian church was characterized by genuine faith, sacrificial love, and steadfast hope. When they heard the good news of salvation preached, they believed, courageously enduring for Christ's sake in the face of persecution so that the example of their faithfulness encouraged other believers and sounded forth a powerful testimony for the gospel. It was clearly a congregation defined by devotion to Christ.

The same cannot be said about the churches at Pergamum and Sardis, which were so dominated by the influence of unbelievers that the Lord severely rebuked them (Rev. 2:14–16; 3:1–3). Their accommodation with the world allowed idolatry, immorality, and hypocrisy to run rampant. Christ's stern warning to those congregations underscores his concern for the purity of any church in any age.

Though the church should demonstrate love and compassion toward unbelievers, it must never embrace them as part of the fellowship until they repent and believe the gospel. By God's design, the church is an assembly of redeemed worshipers who together are growing in Christlike holiness. Those who would attempt to turn it into something else, even in the name of evangelism, do so in contradiction to what the Scriptures teach.

Devoted to Scripture

In Acts 2:42, Luke explains that the believers in the Jerusalem church "devoted themselves to the apostles' teaching." The content of that instruction included expositions of the Old Testament Scriptures (Acts 6:4; cf. Luke 24:44–49), teachings from the life and ministry of Jesus (John 14:26; 1 Cor. 11:23–26), and new revelation given by the Holy Spirit to the apostles (John 16:12–15). The apostles' teaching, which is now recorded in the New Testament Scriptures, is to be the focus of every church's preaching and teaching ministry.

A commitment to the apostles' teaching is essential to the spiritual development and well-being of all believers. Exposure to God's Word renews the mind (cf. Rom. 12:2) through the illuminating power of the Holy Spirit (1 Cor. 2:10–16) and produces spiritual growth (1 Tim. 4:6; 1 Pet. 2:2). That is why the New Testament emphasizes the importance of reading and teaching the Scriptures (1 Tim. 4:13), charging pastors to preach the Word faithfully and without compromise (2 Tim. 4:1–2). As Paul instructed the members of the Colossian church: "Let the word of

Christ dwell in you richly, teaching and admonishing one another in all wisdom, singing psalms and hymns and spiritual songs, with thankfulness in your hearts to God" (Col. 3:16).

Churches that neglect the preaching of God's Word leave their people spiritually malnourished (cf. Hos. 4:6) and susceptible to both temptation and error because they are ill-equipped to use the "sword of the Spirit" (Eph. 6:17). Conversely, those who faithfully proclaim what Scripture teaches firmly establish their congregations in the truth (cf. Ps. 1:1–3; 1 John 2:12–14).

Devoted to One Another

The account in Acts 2 continues by explaining that the members of the early church were also devoted to "the fellowship" (Acts 2:42). These early Christians were distinguished by a consistent devotion and sacrificial commitment to their fellow members of the body of Christ. The term "fellowship" (Gk. *koinōnia*) refers to "sharing" or "partnership." Every believer is in permanent fellowship with the Lord Jesus Christ through faith in him (John 17:21; 1 Cor. 1:9). As a result, believers are also in fellowship with one another (1 John 1:3). They demonstrate that fellowship through a loving commitment to serve fellow believers and encourage them to love and good deeds. A person also exhibits that fellowship in a desire to be an active member of the local body of believers. Thus the author of Hebrews writes, "Let us consider how to stir up one another to love and good works, not neglecting to meet together, as is the habit of some, but encouraging one another, and all the more as you see the Day drawing near" (Heb. 10:24–25). As these words indicate, the Christian life is not to be lived in isolation but in constant communion with Christ and his people. In the same way that every member of a local church should be part of the universal church, so every member of the universal church ought to be a faithful, participating member in a local congregation.

Devoted to the Lord's Table

According to Acts 2:42, the first church was also devoted "to the breaking of bread," a reference to the celebration of the Lord's Supper. Jesus himself commanded his followers to commemorate his death on a consistent basis (1 Cor. 11:24–29), continually reminding themselves of the salvation provided through his once-for-all sacrifice (cf. Heb. 9:26, 28; 1 Pet. 3:18). Communion symbolizes the believer's union with Christ (cf. Rom. 6:5) and the unity that believers share with one another (cf. Eph. 4:5). As Paul explained in 1 Corinthians 10:16–17, "The cup of blessing that we bless, is it not a participation in the blood of Christ? The bread that we break, is it not a participation in the body of Christ? Because there is one bread, we who are many are one body, for we all partake of the one bread."

Celebrating the Lord's Table also causes believers to examine their hearts, confessing and repenting of any known sin. In that way, it operates as a purifying influence in the church, as believers reflect on the cross and forsake their sin. Those who participate in the Lord's Supper in an unworthy manner invite the Lord's chastising judgment (1 Cor. 11:27–32).

Devoted to Prayer

Finally, Acts 2:42 explains that the early church was also devoted to "prayers." Recognizing the necessity of divine wisdom and assistance (cf. John 14:13–14; James 1:5), these believers were characterized by a relentless commitment to corporate prayer (cf. Acts 1:14, 24; 4:24–31). That same priority ought to mark the church today, as believers rely on the providential care and sovereign power of God. Congregations that fail to commune with the Lord through prayer will inevitably be characterized by spiritual weakness and apathy. By contrast, the New Testament repeatedly calls believers to pray fervently and continually (Luke 18:1; Rom. 12:12; Eph. 6:18; Col. 4:2; 1 Thess. 5:17).

Results of Devotion

The church of Acts 2:42 understood the vital importance of pursuing the right priorities. They were devoted to Christ, his Word, his people, the commemoration of his death, and the practice of prayer. Those unique expressions of the life of that first church ought to be the hallmarks of every church. They are representative of the means by which God shapes and grows the church into what he wants it to be.

In Acts 2:43–47, Luke details the results that flowed out of the devotion exhibited by these first-century believers. He writes,

> And awe came upon every soul, and many wonders and signs were being done through the apostles. And all who believed were together and had all things in common. And they were selling their possessions and belongings and distributing the proceeds to all, as any had need. And day by day, attending the temple together and breaking bread in their homes, they received their food with glad and generous hearts, praising God and having favor with all the people. And the Lord added to their number day by day those who were being saved.

As God worked through this community of believers, they experienced a sense of holy awe as they witnessed the miraculous signs being performed by the apostles (Acts 2:43). Their congregation was also characterized by sacrificial sharing and selfless generosity (Acts 2:44–45). It should be noted that, although they were eager to sell their belongings to meet the needs of others, the early church did not practice communism or communalism. The imperfect tense of the verbs "selling" and "distributing" indicates that these were ongoing actions, meaning that believers sold personal belongings as individual needs arose in response to the Spirit's prompting (cf. 1 Cor. 16:1–2). Furthermore, Acts 2:46 makes it clear that these believers retained ownership of their homes. And the later narrative in Acts reveals that personal property was sold only on a voluntary basis (Acts 5:4; cf. 2 Cor. 8:13–14). Of course, the fact that they were willing to part with their material possessions for the sake of serving others (Acts 4:34–36) demonstrates the genuineness of their love for one another.

This early congregation also experienced supernatural joy (Acts 2:46). The generosity of their heartfelt love for one another produced an uncontainable gladness that erupted in praise to God (Acts 2:47). It also expanded their witness to the unbelievers around them, who responded favorably to the irrefutable transformation and selfless virtues they observed in the lives of these believers. As a result, many more came to embrace the Lord Jesus in saving faith, as God used the testimony of this faithful church to draw unbelieving sinners to himself (Acts 2:47). Unbelievers were continually being saved as they watched how these early followers of Jesus exhibited a joyful and Spirit-filled unity. The ultimate impact of the early church's spiritual pursuits and Christlike character was effective evangelism.

A healthy church in any age will be characterized by the same spiritual pursuits as the church depicted in Acts 2:42–47. As believers devote themselves to the right priorities, the Spirit will produce Christlike character within them (cf. Rom. 5:4; 2 Cor. 3:18). That in turn will provide a compelling testimony to the world of the transforming power of the gospel—a witness that God can use to reach many unbelievers with the truth of salvation.

Means of Grace within the Church[15]

> God's Word
> Baptism
> The Lord's Table
> Prayer
> Worship
> Fellowship
> Church Discipline

As illustrated by the Jerusalem church in Acts 2, God uses various means to bring blessing, strengthen faith, and cultivate spiritual growth in the lives of his people. Historically, these have been called "means of grace."[16] They are the instruments through which God's Spirit graciously grows believers in Christlikeness as he fortifies them in the faith and conforms them into the image of the Son (2 Cor. 3:17–18). Though some limit these means of grace to the preaching of the Word and the observance of the ordinances (baptism and the Lord's Supper), the New Testament teaches that

---

15. For further discussion concerning the means of grace as they relate to the believer's sanctification, see "The Character of Progressive Sanctification," in chap. 7 (p. 638).

16. "Means of grace" should not be confused with the "sacraments" of Roman Catholicism. According to Roman Catholic theology, the sacraments include baptism, confirmation, the Eucharist, acts of penance, extreme unction (or "last rights"), ordination to the priesthood ("holy orders"), and marriage. As Wayne Grudem rightly points out: "There is not only a difference in the lists given by Catholics and Protestants; there is also a difference in fundamental meaning. Catholics view these as 'means of salvation' that make people more fit to receive justification from God. But in the Protestant view, the means of grace are simply means of additional blessing within the Christian life, and do not add to our fitness to receive justification from God. Catholics teach that the means of grace impart grace whether or not there is subjective faith on the part of the minister or the recipient, while Protestants hold that God only imparts grace when there is faith on the part of the persons receiving these means. And while the Roman Catholic Church firmly restricts the administration of the sacraments to the clergy, our list of means of grace includes many activities that are carried out by all believers." Wayne Grudem, *Systematic Theology: An Introduction to Biblical Doctrine* (Grand Rapids, MI: Zondervan, 1994), 951–52.

God also promotes the spiritual welfare of his people through other means as well—including prayer, worship, fellowship, and the process of church discipline. In that sense, all of these might rightly be considered means of grace and spiritual blessing.[17]

God's Word

The primary means the Spirit of God uses to grow believers in sanctification is his Word. As Peter explains to his readers, "Therefore, putting aside all malice and all deceit and hypocrisy and envy and all slander, like newborn babies, long for the pure milk of the word, so that by it you may grow in respect to salvation, if you have tasted the kindness of the Lord" (1 Pet. 2:1–3 NASB). The relationship between the believer's sanctification and the Scriptures is underscored by the Lord Jesus in his High Priestly Prayer; speaking of believers he said to the Father, "Sanctify them in the truth; your word is truth" (John 17:17). A comparison of the parallel passages in Ephesians 5:18–6:9 and Colossians 3:16–4:1 reveals that to "be filled with the Spirit" (Eph. 5:18) is to "let the word of Christ dwell in you richly" (Col. 3:16). Putting these two passages together, it becomes clear that as believers saturate their minds with the Word of God, they come under the Spirit's control (cf. Rom. 8:14; Gal. 5:16–18), thereby producing the fruit of the Spirit (Gal. 5:22–23). The Scripture is a key part of the Spirit's armor against sin and temptation (Eph. 6:17; cf. Matt. 4:4, 7, 10).

The Holy Spirit inspired the Scriptures through the superintendence of the human authors (2 Pet. 1:21; cf. 1 Sam. 19:20; 2 Sam. 23:2; Isa. 59:21; Ezek. 11:5, 24; Mark 12:36; John 14:17, 26; 16:13–15; Acts 1:16; 1 Pet. 1:11). And he continues to illumine the Scriptures in the hearts and minds of believers, enabling them to understand and obey what he has revealed (1 Cor. 2:14–16; cf. Ps. 119:18; 2 Cor. 4:6; 1 John 2:27). The Spirit not only inspired and illumines Scripture, he also animates it. He energizes the preaching of the gospel (1 Pet. 1:12) so that his Word convicts the hearts and minds of sinners (Heb. 4:12), bringing regeneration to the unconverted (cf. Eph. 5:26; Titus 3:5; James 1:18). Paul reiterated this truth when he told the Thessalonian believers, "Our gospel came to you not only in word, but also in power and in the Holy Spirit and with full conviction" (1 Thess. 1:5). He similarly told the Corinthians, "My speech and my message were not in plausible words of wisdom, but in demonstration of the Spirit and of power, so that your faith might not rest in the wisdom of men but in the power of God" (1 Cor. 2:4–5). The sovereign power of the Holy Spirit is further illustrated in the divine promise of Isaiah 55:11: "So shall my word be that goes out from my mouth; it shall not return to me empty, but it shall accomplish that which I purpose, and shall succeed in the thing for which I sent it."

Both the evangelization of unbelievers (Rom. 10:14–15) and the edification of the saints (Acts 20:32) depend on the faithful proclamation of the Spirit-empowered Scriptures. The apostle Paul summarized the vital necessity of Scripture when he told Timothy, "All Scripture is breathed out by God and profitable for teaching, for reproof, for correction, and for training in righteousness, that the man of God may

---

17. For a similar list of the "means of grace," see Grudem, *Systematic Theology*, 951.

be complete, equipped for every good work" (2 Tim. 3:16–17). All that believers need to walk in righteousness and sanctification is found on the pages of God's Word. The knowledge of God revealed in Scripture is all they require for life and godliness (2 Pet. 1:3). Consequently, believers hunger for God's Word because they recognize that it feeds their souls (Job 23:12; 1 Pet. 2:2).

It is essential for churches to prioritize the vital ministry of the Word—just as the apostles themselves did (Acts 6:4). This ministry is primarily accomplished through reading, preaching, and teaching the Scriptures. As Paul instructed Timothy, "Until I come, devote yourself to the public reading of Scripture, to exhortation, to teaching" (1 Tim. 4:13). God-honoring preaching begins with careful study of the Word, so that the preacher interprets the text accurately. Such is the duty of a faithful work-man, that he rightly handle the Word of truth (2 Tim. 2:15). Having studied the text carefully, the preacher must proclaim it completely, clearly, and courageously to the congregation. The apostle Paul, after highlighting the sufficiency of Scripture in 2 Timothy 3:16–17, immediately challenged his spiritual protégé with these words: "I charge you in the presence of God and of Christ Jesus, who is to judge the living and the dead, and by his appearing and his kingdom: preach the word; be ready in season and out of season; reprove, rebuke, and exhort, with complete patience and teaching" (2 Tim. 4:1–2). No matter the consequences or the tide of popular opin-ion, Timothy was to proclaim the whole truth of Scripture without compromise or capitulation. Pastors and elders in today's church share that same divine mandate; they too are accountable to God himself for faithfully fulfilling that primary respon-sibility (cf. James 3:1).

Baptism

By both example and instruction, the Lord Jesus gave the church two ordinances that they are to observe: baptism (Matt. 3:13–17; 28:19) and the celebration of the Lord's Supper (Luke 22:19–20). The word *baptize* (from Gk. *baptizō*) means "to immerse" or "to dip." When used literally, the term refers to actions like the dipping of fabric into dye or the immersion of a person in water. But it is also used figuratively in the New Testament to emphasize the close identity and solidarity between two people. For example, in 1 Corinthians 10:2, Paul explains that Old Testament Israel was baptized into Moses. That figurative use of the word underscored the solidarity of the Israelites with their God-ordained spokesman and leader.

SPIRIT BAPTISM

In an infinitely more profound way, the New Testament teaches that all believers are immersed into Christ Jesus at the moment of conversion (Rom. 6:3; cf. Matt. 3:11). They are baptized by Christ with his Holy Spirit. Through this Spirit baptism (which is entirely God's work), believers are united with Christ (1 Cor. 6:17; 2 Cor. 5:17; Gal. 3:27) and placed into his body, the church (1 Cor. 12:13). It is this spiritual reality that Peter speaks of when he writes, "Baptism, which corresponds to this, now saves you, not as a removal of dirt from the body but as an appeal to God for a good conscience, through the resurrection of Jesus Christ" (1 Pet. 3:21). As this verse makes clear, it is not the external action of water that saves (the "removal of dirt from the body") but the internal reality of "an appeal to God for a good conscience," which is possible only through faith in the death and "resurrection of Jesus Christ" (cf. Rom. 10:9–10; Heb. 9:14; 10:22).

Spirit baptism occurs only once, at the moment of salvation, and should not be sought as a secondary, postconversion experience. That singular Spirit baptism occurs at conversion, when the believer is born again and placed into the sphere of the Spirit's sanctifying power and indwelling presence. In 1 Corinthians 12:13, Paul writes, "For in one Spirit we were all baptized into one body—Jews or Greeks, slaves or free—and all were made to drink of one Spirit." Here, Paul emphasizes the unity and equality that believers possess because they have all been incorporated by Christ into the church through his Spirit. Those today who insist that Spirit baptism is a secondary experience, one that separates the spiritual elite from ordinary Christians, turn that verse on its head. Contrary to such misguided notions, the New Testament Epistles clearly teach that all believers receive the Holy Spirit in his fullness at the moment of salvation (cf. Rom. 6:3, 5; Gal. 3:27; Eph. 2:18).

Some look to the book of Acts to defend their view that believers ought to seek a baptism of the Holy Spirit after conversion. However, such efforts fail to account for the transitional nature of what was happening in Acts. In commenting on 1 Corinthians 12:13, MacArthur explains that

> Scripture contains no command, suggestion, or method for believers to seek or receive the baptism of the Spirit. You do not seek or ask for that which you already possess. . . . [The] special transitional events [in Acts of those waiting to receive Spirit baptism] did not represent the norm, as our present text makes clear, but were given to indicate to all that the Body was one (Acts 11:15–17).[18]

BAPTISM A SYMBOL FOR BELIEVERS

In order to symbolize that internal reality of salvation, the New Testament calls believers to be baptized in water as a public testimony to their faith in and solidarity with the Lord Jesus. Water baptism, then, is the outward, postconversion demonstration of an inward reality that has already occurred at conversion. The baptism of John the Baptist symbolized repentance from sin and turning to God (Matt. 3:6; cf. Acts 19:4–5). In Christ, baptism not only signifies a turning away from sin but also serves as a public affirmation of one's identification and union with him in his death, burial, and resurrection.

Scripture presents baptism as the first step of obedience for believers after they have embraced the Lord Jesus in saving faith. Though not salvific, baptism is commanded by Christ himself (Matt. 28:19). Those unwilling to confess their Lord and Savior

---

18. John MacArthur, *1 Corinthians*, MNTC (Chicago: Moody Press, 1984), comment on 1 Cor. 12:13.

publicly through baptism are living in disobedience and thus call into question the genuineness of their faith because they are unwilling to obey (cf. Matt. 10:32–33).

The proper mode of baptism is by immersion, as indicated by the Greek word *baptizō*. Immersion also serves as a symbol of one's burial and resurrection, signifying the spiritual reality that believers have died to sin and risen with Christ (cf. Rom. 6:4, 10).

Though pervasive throughout church history, the practice of infant baptism lacks clear New Testament support, since saving faith precedes baptism and not vice versa. In Scripture, only believers are said to be baptized.[19] The New Testament definition of baptism, in fact, requires that the inner realities of repentance and faith precede the external symbol. In Acts 2:38, only those who believed and repented were called to be baptized. According to Colossians 2:12, those who have been baptized into Christ (a spiritual reality represented by water baptism) have been "raised with him through faith." First Peter 3:21 explains that baptism symbolizes "an appeal to God for a good conscience." Yet none of these realities—repentance, faith, or a conscious appeal to God for a good conscience—can be exhibited by an infant.[20] Hence, the practice of infant baptism (or paedobaptism) should be rejected. Believer's baptism (or credobaptism) appears to have been the prevailing practice of the early church until at least the third century, when explicit attestations of paedobaptism appear more frequently in extant Christian literature.[21]

BAPTISM AND SALVATION

Importantly, water baptism plays no part in the work of salvation. Rather, it is only a symbol of the believer's union with Christ and of Spirit baptism. The thief on the cross provides an unmistakable example of one who was saved without being baptized (Luke 23:40–43). Similarly, Cornelius was clearly saved and received the Holy Spirit before being baptized in water (Acts 10:44–48). The apostle Paul could tell the Corinthians, "I thank God that I baptized none of you except Crispus and Gaius, so that no one may say that you were baptized in my name. . . . For Christ did not send me to baptize but to preach the gospel, and not with words of eloquent wisdom, lest the cross of Christ be emptied of its power" (1 Cor. 1:14–17). Certainly, Paul would never have made such a statement if water baptism were necessary for salvation. This conclusion is confirmed by the apostle's delineation of the gospel later in that same epistle, where he makes no mention of baptism (1 Cor. 15:1–4).

In addition, though it is not likely part of Mark's original Gospel, Mark 16:16

---

19. Arguments for infant baptism from the "household" passages in Acts 10:34–48; 11:14; 16:11–15; and 1 Cor. 1:4–16 are unconvincing. Not only are no infants or children mentioned (making this an argument from silence), but it is clear that in each case the recipients of baptism first heard the gospel and believed.

20. For further explanation of these and similar texts, see the concise response to paedobaptism in John Piper, *Brothers, We Are Not Professionals*, exp. ed. (Nashville: B&H, 2013), 154–62. As Piper points out, circumcision was a sign of the old covenant, which was entered into through physical birth. But water baptism is a sign of the new covenant, which is entered into through spiritual birth. Consequently, baptism should be administered only to those who have first experienced spiritual birth.

21. For a detailed discussion of this point, see Everett Ferguson, *Baptism in the Early Church: History, Theology, and Liturgy in the First Five Centuries* (Grand Rapids, MI: Eerdmans, 2009). See also Hendrick Stander and Johannes Louw, *Baptism in the Early Church*, rev. ed. (Leeds: Carey, 2004).

records that Jesus told his disciples, "Whoever believes and is baptized will be saved, but whoever does not believe will be condemned." Putting aside questions regarding the text's authenticity,[22] it is apparent that the first half of that verse emphasizes the close connection between saving faith and the believer's subsequent identification with Christ in the waters of baptism. However, as the second half of the verse makes clear, sinners are condemned for unbelief, not for failing to be baptized. The rest of Scripture repeatedly indicates that divine forgiveness is granted on the basis of God's grace received through a repentant faith alone (Acts 3:19; 5:31; 26:20; Rom. 3:28; 4:4–5; Eph. 2:8–9), thereby excluding the subsequent act of water baptism as a necessary prerequisite for salvation.

In spite of Scripture's clarity regarding what is necessary for salvation (Acts 16:30–31), some mistakenly insist that the symbol of water baptism is actually the means of salvation rather than an outward demonstration of it. By confusing the symbol of water baptism with the reality of God's grace in salvation, they eliminate the reality by adding works to the gospel (cf. Rom. 11:6).

Those who teach that baptism produces salvation (a view known as "baptismal regeneration") often point to Peter's words on the day of Pentecost.[23] There he told his audience, "Repent and be baptized every one of you in the name of Jesus Christ for the forgiveness of your sins, and you will receive the gift of the Holy Spirit" (Acts 2:38). But to conclude that Peter was making salvation contingent on baptism not only runs contrary to the overall teaching of Scripture, in which salvation is solely by faith (cf. John 1:12; 3:16; Acts 16:31; Rom. 3:21–30; 4:5; 10:9–10; Gal. 2:16; Phil. 3:9), but also ignores the immediate context of Peter's sermon. The Jewish audience to whom Peter spoke risked public ridicule and rejection if they identified themselves with Christ (cf. John 9:22; 12:42–43). Peter therefore challenged them to demonstrate the genuineness of their repentance by publicly identifying with the Lord Jesus through baptism. In a similar way, Jesus called the rich young ruler to demonstrate the sincerity of his repentance by giving away his wealth (Luke 18:18–27). Yet no one would conclude from that text that voluntary poverty is necessary for salvation. God's grace is not preconditioned on either water or wealth. But true repentance will always evidence itself in obedience to the Lord's will.

Lexically, the Greek preposition *eis* ("for") can mean "for the purpose of," but it can also mean "because of" or "on the occasion of."[24] An example of that second meaning is found in Matthew 12:41, where Jesus explains that the Ninevites repented

---

22. For further discussion about the authenticity of Mark 16:9–20, see John MacArthur, *Mark 9–16*, MNTC (Chicago: Moody Publishers, 2015), 407–18.

23. Another popular proof text for baptismal regeneration is Acts 22:16. However, such an interpretation contradicts Paul's clear teaching regarding the gospel of grace through faith throughout his epistles (cf. Rom. 3:22, 24–26, 28, 30; 4:5; 10:9–10; Gal. 2:16; Eph. 2:8–9; Phil. 3:9; Titus 3:4–7), while also ignoring the grammar of the verse: "The phrase 'wash away your sins' must be connected with 'calling on His name,' since connecting it with 'be baptized' leaves the participle *epikalesamenos* ('calling') without an antecedent. Paul's sins were washed away not by baptism but by calling on the name of the Lord (cf. Rom. 10:13). A literal translation of the verse says, 'Arise, get yourself baptized and your sins washed away, having called on His name.' Both imperatives reflect the reality that Paul had already called on the Lord's name, which is the act that saves. Baptism and the washing away of sins follow." John MacArthur, *Acts 13–28*, MNTC (Chicago: Moody Press, 1996), 269. Biblical quotations set in bold in the original are set within quotation marks in this quote.

24. A. T. Robertson, *Word Pictures in the New Testament* (1930; repr., Grand Rapids, MI: Baker, 1982), 3:35–36; H. E. Dana and J. R. Mantey, *A Manual Grammar of the Greek New Testament* (Toronto: Macmillan, 1957), 104.

because of Jonah's preaching. Thus, when Peter said, "Be baptized . . . for [*eis*] the forgiveness of your sins," the word "for" should rightly be translated "because of." Peter was calling for water baptism to be performed "because of" the remission of sins, not in order to produce it. As the rest of Acts makes clear, baptism follows forgiveness and not vice versa (cf. Acts 8:12, 34–39; 10:34–48; 16:31–33). Every believer enjoys the complete remission of sins from the moment of conversion (cf. Matt. 26:28; Luke 24:47; Eph. 1:7; Col. 2:13; 1 John 2:12). Water baptism is merely an external demonstration of what has already occurred in the heart through the regenerating power of the Holy Spirit.

Though baptism does not produce salvation, it is closely associated with it (cf. Eph. 4:5). In the book of Acts, those who believed were baptized immediately (Acts 2:41; 8:38; 9:18; 10:48; 18:8; 19:1–5), indicating that it should closely follow a genuine profession of faith.[25] Believers are to be baptized "in the name of the Father and of the Son and of the Holy Spirit" (Matt. 28:19). Such is not a sacramental formula but rather a comprehensive acknowledgment of the union believers have with the triune God through faith in Christ.

The Lord's Table

A second ordinance that must be observed by the church is the Lord's Table (or the Lord's Supper). Unlike baptism, which is observed once following conversion, the Lord's Supper is to be celebrated repeatedly throughout the Christian life.

BACKGROUND AND PRACTICE

On the night before his death, the Lord Jesus celebrated a final Passover meal with his disciples, transforming it into a celebration of infinitely greater importance. Whereas the Passover commemorated Israel's deliverance from slavery in Egypt (Ex. 12:1–14), the Lord's Supper points to the ultimate deliverance of God's people from slavery to sin and death. The Passover looked back to the temporary rescue from physical bondage; the Lord's Supper commemorates the eternal and spiritual deliverance provided through the new covenant. The lambs slaughtered during the Passover merely foreshadowed the sacrifice of the spotless Lamb of God who died on a cross to redeem sinners once for all (1 Pet. 1:18–19; cf. Heb. 9:25–26).

The observance of Communion was practiced by the church from its inception on the day of Pentecost (Acts 2:42). The early church also developed congregational meals that came to be known as love feasts (Jude 12), which were usually concluded with a celebration of the Lord's Supper. These meals were designed to foster fellowship and mutual care among the members of the church. But some used these meals as an opportunity to show partiality and engage in drunkenness (1 Cor. 11:18, 21; cf. 2 Pet. 2:13). When they connected such behavior to the Lord's Supper, they desecrated the holy ordinance. It is in that context that Paul offered this stern warning:

---

25. It may be difficult to determine the genuineness of a young child's profession of faith. In such cases, it is often wise to postpone baptism until a time when it is clear that the child adequately understands faith, repentance, and the truths of the gospel.

Whoever, therefore, eats the bread or drinks the cup of the Lord in an unworthy manner will be guilty concerning the body and blood of the Lord. Let a person examine himself, then, and so eat of the bread and drink of the cup. For anyone who eats and drinks without discerning the body eats and drinks judgment on himself. That is why many of you are weak and ill, and some have died. But if we judged ourselves truly, we would not be judged. But when we are judged by the Lord, we are disciplined so that we may not be condemned along with the world. (1 Cor. 11:27–32)

Though believers ought to pursue holiness at all times (1 Pet. 1:15–17), the celebration of the Lord's Supper is an occasion when they ought to carefully examine their hearts, confessing and repenting from any known sin before the Lord. Those who participate in Communion without repenting of known sin profane the celebration and invite the chastisement of God.

Earlier in 1 Corinthians 11, Paul offers an explanation of the ordinance itself. He writes,

For I received from the Lord what I also delivered to you, that the Lord Jesus on the night when he was betrayed took bread, and when he had given thanks, he broke it, and said, "This is my body which is for you. Do this in remembrance of me." In the same way also he took the cup, after supper, saying, "This cup is the new covenant in my blood. Do this, as often as you drink it, in remembrance of me." For as often as you eat this bread and drink the cup, you proclaim the Lord's death until he comes. (1 Cor. 11:23–26)

Because 1 Corinthians might have been written before the four Gospels, these words from Paul may represent the earliest written record of the Lord's final Passover meal.

During a traditional Passover meal, four cups of wine would be passed around the table. After drinking the first cup, bitter herbs would be dipped in a fruit sauce and eaten while a message was given explaining the meaning of Passover. Then the first part of the Hallel (consisting of Psalms 113–118) would be sung (Hallel is Hebrew for "praise"). After the second cup had been passed, unleavened bread would be broken and passed. It would have been at this point that Jesus "took bread, and when he had given thanks, he broke it and gave it to them, saying, 'This is my body, which is given for you. Do this in remembrance of me'" (Luke 22:19). The Greek verb translated "had given thanks" is the participial form of *eucharisteō*, which is transliterated into English as "Eucharist," a name that has historically been used to designate the celebration of Communion.

Following the breaking of the bread during the Passover, the roasted lamb would be eaten. After prayer, the third cup was passed and the rest of the Hallel was sung. It was the third cup that Jesus transformed into the cup of Communion. Luke writes, "And likewise [Jesus took] the cup after they had eaten, saying, 'This cup that is poured out for you is the new covenant in my blood'" (Luke 22:20). The fourth and final cup of Passover, which looked forward to the coming kingdom, was passed just before leaving.

VIEWS ON THE MEANING OF COMMUNION

Jesus's repeated instruction, "Do this in remembrance of me," indicates that the celebration of the Lord's Supper is not optional. Every believer should observe it routinely, and prolonged failure to do so constitutes a sin. Jesus instituted his Supper as a perpetual memorial for his followers so that they might repeatedly reflect on the eternal significance of his death. Moreover, when believers celebrate the Lord's Supper, they commune with the risen Christ who indwells them and is spiritually present with his people (1 Cor. 10:16). Though some insist that the bread and the cup are transformed into the actual body and blood of Jesus, being again offered as a sacrifice, such a notion severely stretches the words of Christ beyond their intended meaning. The bread and cup are symbols, chosen by the Lord himself to signify and memorialize his atoning death. To celebrate Communion is not to offer a new sacrifice and thus confuse the atonement; rather, it is to rejoice in the once-for-all sacrifice of the Lord Jesus (cf. Rom. 6:10; Heb. 9:26–28; 1 Pet. 3:18).

Throughout church history, four major views of the Lord's Table might be delineated: the Roman Catholic view of transubstantiation; the Lutheran view of consubstantiation, or real presence; the Reformed view emphasizing Christ's spiritual presence; and the Zwinglian view of a memorial celebration.[26] The Catholic view purports that the substance of the elements is transformed into the physical body and blood of Christ at the moment of the priest's blessing. Consequently, the Catholic celebration of the Eucharist is regarded as an actual sacrifice. But this view of Communion must be rejected for at least two reasons. First, it fails to recognize the symbolic significance of Christ's statements "This is my body" and "This is my blood" (Matt. 26:26–28). When Jesus said, "I am the bread of life," in John 6:35 (a verse Roman Catholics often use to support their understanding of the Eucharist), his statement ought to be interpreted in the same way as his other "I am" statements, such as "I am the light of the world" (John 8:12), "I am the door" (John 10:9), "I am the good shepherd" (John 10:11), and "I am the vine" (John 15:1). These metaphorical expressions illustrate the truth of the gospel in profound ways, but they are not to be understood in woodenly literalistic terms. Second, by viewing the Eucharist as a repeated or ongoing sacrifice, the Catholic view undermines the reality that Christ's death on the cross was a once-for-all sacrifice (Rom. 6:10; Heb. 9:28; 10:10; 1 Pet. 3:18), fully completed at Calvary (John 19:30).[27]

Though Martin Luther rejected the Roman Catholic notion of transubstantiation and the idea that the Eucharist was a propitiatory sacrifice, he nonetheless maintained that Christ's body and blood are really present "in, with, and under" the Communion elements. This view, referred to as consubstantiation or real presence, represents a softening of the Roman Catholic position. Though more preferable than the Catholic view for obvious reasons, Luther's insistence on the "real presence" of Christ continued to ignore the symbolic nature of Jesus's statements.

Other Reformers such as Ulrich Zwingli and John Calvin distanced themselves from

---

26. For a more detailed survey of this history, see Erickson, *Christian Theology*, 1123–28.
27. For more on this point, see "The Perfect Sufficiency of the Atonement," in chap. 7 (p. 539).

the Roman Catholic position further than Luther did. For Zwingli, the Lord's Table was primarily a memorial celebration that commemorated the work of Christ on the cross. That Jesus intended this celebration to serve as a memorial is clear from his instruction, "Do this in *remembrance* of me" (1 Cor. 11:24–25). Beyond influencing the Reformed tradition, Zwingli's position was adopted by a number of Anabaptist groups. John Calvin taught that, although Christ is not physically present in the celebration of Communion, he is nonetheless spiritually present. Though Calvin stressed this point more than Zwingli did, his views did not necessarily exclude those of Zwingli. Accordingly, when Calvin met with Heinrich Bullinger (Zwingli's successor in Zurich) in 1549, the two agreed that their views regarding the nature of Communion were generally compatible.

On the one hand, it is not wrong to speak of the Lord Jesus being spiritually present with his people when they celebrate Communion, since he is spiritually present with believers all the time (Matt. 28:20; Heb. 13:5). On the other hand, the language of *spiritual presence* can be potentially confusing and unhelpful—perhaps causing some to think in terms of mystical encounters, ecstatic experiences, or the real presence in a Lutheran or even Roman Catholic way. When all the biblical texts are considered, the Lord's Table is best understood as a memorial celebration that strengthens believers in their walk with Christ because it (1) commemorates Jesus's substitutionary sacrifice (symbolized by the elements of the bread and the cup); (2) reminds believers of the historical truths of the gospel, including Christ's incarnation, death, resurrection, and ascension; (3) prompts believers to repent of any known sin; (4) causes them to rejoice in their redemption from sin and in their saving union with Christ; (5) motivates them to continue walking in loving obedience to the Lord; and (6) reminds them to hope in his imminent return.

ANTICIPATION

Communion not only prompts believers to look back in remembrance, it also reminds them to look forward in anticipation. So Paul states, "As often as you eat this bread and drink the cup, you proclaim the Lord's death until he comes" (1 Cor. 11:26). The Lord's Supper reminds believers that, although Jesus died, he did not remain in the grave. Having risen and ascended to the Father's right hand, he is coming again. As he promised his disciples on the night before his death, "If I go and prepare a place for you, I will come again and will take you to myself, that where I am you may be also" (John 14:3). That same night, he also said, "Truly, I say to you, I will not drink again of the fruit of the vine until that day when I drink it new in the kingdom of God" (Mark 14:25). Celebrating the Lord's Supper anticipates the hope of Jesus's return, the joys of heaven, and the future glories of the marriage supper of the Lamb (Rev. 19:9).

Prayer[28]

Though often neglected in many churches, prayer (both corporate and private) is a vital means of grace that God uses to grow his people in holiness (cf. Heb. 4:16). In

---

28. This section is adapted from John MacArthur, *1 and 2 Thessalonians*, MNTC (Chicago: Moody Publishers, 2002), 186–88. Used by permission of Moody Publishers.

1 Thessalonians 5:17, Paul instructed the church in Thessalonica to "pray without ceasing." That imperative designates the heart attitude that ought to characterize every congregation. The command "pray" (from Gk. *proseuchomai*; cf. Matt. 6:5–6; Mark 11:24; Luke 5:16; 11:1–2; Acts 10:9; Rom. 8:26; 1 Cor. 14:13–15; Eph. 6:18; Col. 1:9; 2 Thess. 3:1; James 5:13–14, 16) includes all facets of prayer: dependence, adoration, confession, intercession, thanksgiving, and supplication. The phrase "without ceasing" refers to a constant way of life that is characterized by a prayerful attitude, not an endless string of utterances (cf. Matt. 6:7).

The perfect example of this kind of prayer was the Lord Jesus himself, whose fervent prayer life is depicted in the four Gospels (Matt. 14:23; 26:38–46; Mark 1:35; 6:46; Luke 9:18, 28–29; 22:41, 44; John 6:15; 8:1–2; 17:1–26). Jesus also taught his disciples how to pray (Matt. 6:5–14; Luke 11:2–4) and illustrated the importance of persistent prayer in his parables (Luke 11:5–10; 18:1–8). This heartfelt commitment to prayer was exemplified by the early church (Acts 2:42; cf. 1:14; 4:23–31; 12:11–16), including the apostles, who prioritized it alongside the ministry of the Word (Acts 6:4). Paul's ministry was similarly characterized by a constant attitude of prayerfulness (cf. Rom. 12:12; Eph. 6:18–19; Phil. 4:6; Col. 4:2; 2 Thess. 3:1; 1 Tim. 2:8).

God-honoring prayer is motivated by a number of factors, including a yearning to fellowship with the Lord and bring glory to him (Pss. 27:4; 42:1–2; 63:1–2; 84:1–2; cf. John 14:13–14), a dependence on God for his provision (Matt. 6:11; cf. Luke 11:9–13; 1 John 5:14–15), a need for heavenly wisdom in the midst of trials (James 1:5; cf. Matt. 6:13; 1 Cor. 10:13), a plea for deliverance in the face of trouble (cf. Ps. 20:1; Jonah 2:1–2), a longing to find relief from anxiety and fear (Phil. 4:6–7; cf. Ps. 4:1), a desire to express thanksgiving to God for his goodness (Ps. 44:1–4; Phil. 1:3–5), a need to confess sin (Ps. 32:5; Prov. 28:13; 1 John 1:9), a yearning to see the salvation of unbelievers (1 Tim. 2:1–4; cf. Matt. 9:37–38; Rom. 10:1), and a desire for spiritual growth both for oneself and for other Christians. The apostle Paul's desire to see believers grow in Christlikeness was a primary motivation in his prayer life. As he explained,

> For this reason I bow my knees before the Father, from whom every family in heaven and on earth is named, that according to the riches of his glory he may grant you to be strengthened with power through his Spirit in your inner being, so that Christ may dwell in your hearts through faith—that you, being rooted and grounded in love, may have strength to comprehend with all the saints what is the breadth and length and height and depth, and to know the love of Christ that surpasses knowledge, that you may be filled with all the fullness of God. (Eph. 3:14–19; cf. 1:15–19; Col. 1:9–12)

Worship

Worship is the theme of salvation history, the supreme purpose for which believers were redeemed (John 4:23), and the occupation with which they will be eternally enthralled (Rev. 22:3–4; cf. 19:1–6). To worship the Lord is to ascribe to him the honor, glory, adoration, praise, reverence, and devotion that is due him, both for his greatness and for his goodness. As the sovereign Creator of the universe, the triune God alone—Father, Son, and Holy Spirit—is worthy of worship (cf. Isa. 42:8; 48:11; Matt. 4:10; Rev. 14:7). The veneration or worship of angels, saints, or other supposed deities constitutes idolatry, and is strictly prohibited in Scripture (Ex. 20:3–5; cf. Col. 2:18; Rev. 19:10; 22:9). It is the inexcusable refusal to worship the true God that brings his judgment on the unregenerate world (Rom. 1:18–32).

True worship must begin in the heart and mind of the worshiper. Hence, it cannot be equated with elaborate services, ornate buildings, eloquent prayers, or beautiful music. Those things may be outward expressions of genuine worship, but God accepts only that which flows from sincere devotion to him. Though many associate a church's worship with its music program, music is only one avenue through which worship can be expressed. Forms of worship can include prayer, expressions of praise and thanksgiving (Heb. 13:15), and serving others for the sake of Christ (Heb. 13:16; cf. Phil. 4:18). During the worship service itself, the congregation joins in corporate worship by praising God through song, beseeching him in prayer, and listening to the reading and preaching of his Word. Contributing financially to the church through giving is also an expression of worship when done from a heart of joy. As Paul told the Corinthians,

> Whoever sows sparingly will also reap sparingly, and whoever sows bountifully will also reap bountifully. Each one must give as he has decided in his heart, not reluctantly or under compulsion, for God loves a cheerful giver. And God is able to make all grace abound to you, so that having all sufficiency in all things at all times, you may abound in every good work. . . . You will be enriched in every way to be generous in every way, which through us will produce thanksgiving to God. For the ministry of this service is not only supplying the needs of the saints but is also overflowing in many thanksgivings to God. By their approval of this service, they will glorify God because of your submission that comes from your confession of the gospel of Christ, and the generosity of your contribution for them and for all others, while they long for you and pray for you, because of the surpassing grace of God upon you. Thanks be to God for his inexpressible gift! (2 Cor. 9:6–15)

For believers, the supreme act of worship is to offer all of themselves as a living sacrifice to the Lord (cf. Matt. 22:37). Paul thus exhorted the Romans with these words:

> I appeal to you therefore, brothers, by the mercies of God, to present your bodies as a living sacrifice, holy and acceptable to God, which is your spiritual worship. Do not be conformed to this world, but be transformed by the renewal of your mind, that by testing you may discern what is the will of God, what is good and acceptable and perfect. (Rom. 12:1–2)

Worship, then, encompasses much more than the singing portion of a church service; it is a way of thinking and living for God's honor and glory.

While worship may be passionate, it must always be grounded in truth. As Jesus explained, "The hour is coming, and is now here, when the true worshipers will worship the Father in spirit and truth, for the Father is seeking such people to worship him. God is spirit, and those who worship him must worship in spirit and truth" (John 4:23–24; cf. Phil. 3:3). Many in the church today confuse emotionalism for worship. But emotional experiences that are not governed by theological truth do not honor the Lord. Genuine worship engages the mind; it does not bypass it (cf. 1 Cor. 14:15, 19). Moreover, God-honoring expressions of worship are characterized by decency and orderliness (1 Cor. 14:40). Churches should not promote mindless, chaotic, or worldly practices in the name of worship. Such practices undermine rather than foster the kind of worship that honors God.

Fellowship

As noted above, the word *fellowship* comes from the Greek term *koinōnia*, meaning "partnership" or "sharing." The basis for fellowship is salvation. Because believers are in fellowship with the Lord Jesus, they are also in fellowship with one another. As the apostle John explains, "That which we have seen and heard we proclaim also to you, so that you too may have fellowship with us; and indeed our fellowship is with the Father and with his Son Jesus Christ" (1 John 1:3; cf. 1 Cor. 6:17). The practice of fellowship (i.e., what believers do) is premised on their position of fellowship in Christ (i.e., who believers are in him). Because they are united to the Lord Jesus in faith, they are united to one another in love (cf. John 13:35; 17:21).

The practice of fellowship consists of sacrificial service toward other members of the body of Christ (Phil. 2:1–4; cf. Acts 4:32–37). Using the metaphor of a human body, the apostle Paul explains how each church member ought to contribute to the life of the whole:

> For just as the body is one and has many members, and all the members of the body, though many, are one body, so it is with Christ. For in one Spirit we were all baptized into one body—Jews or Greeks, slaves or free—and all were made to drink of one Spirit.
>
> For the body does not consist of one member but of many. If the foot should say, "Because I am not a hand, I do not belong to the body," that would not make it any less a part of the body. And if the ear should say, "Because I am not an eye, I do not belong to the body," that would not make it any less a part of the body. If the whole body were an eye, where would be the sense of hearing? If the whole body were an ear, where would be the sense of smell? But as it is, God arranged the members in the body, each one of them, as he chose. If all were a single member, where would the body be? As it is, there are many parts, yet one body.
>
> The eye cannot say to the hand, "I have no need of you," nor again the head to the feet, "I have no need of you." On the contrary, the parts of the body that seem to be weaker are indispensable, and on those parts of the body that we think less honorable we bestow the greater honor, and our unpresentable parts are treated with greater modesty, which our more presentable parts do not require. But God

has so composed the body, giving greater honor to the part that lacked it, that there may be no division in the body, but that the members may have the same care for one another. If one member suffers, all suffer together; if one member is honored, all rejoice together.

Now you are the body of Christ and individually members of it. (1 Cor. 12:12–27)

This is a magnificent metaphor illustrating the common life that believers share under their Head, the Lord Jesus. It is this kind of unity, commonality, and togetherness that ought to characterize the fellowship in every church (Rom. 12:16). Expressions of fellowship include discipleship (Matt. 28:19–20; 2 Tim. 2:2), mutual accountability (Gal. 6:1–2; Heb. 10:24–25), and joyful service (1 Cor. 15:58; Eph. 4:12; Rev. 22:12). The "one another" commands of the New Testament (listed above on p. 752) further elaborate on how fellowship should be expressed within the congregation (cf. Rom. 12:10, 16; 13:8; 15:5, 7, 14; 16:16; 1 Cor. 12:25; Gal. 5:13, 26; 6:2; Eph. 4:2, 32; 5:19; Phil. 2:3; Col. 3:9, 13, 16; 1 Thess. 3:12; 4:9, 18; 5:11, 13, 15; 2 Thess. 1:3; Heb. 3:13; 10:24–25; James 5:16; 1 Pet. 1:22; 4:8–10; 5:5; 1 John 3:11, 23; 4:7, 11–12; 2 John 5).

The fellowship of believers not only provides a context for Christian service, it also offers spiritual protection to its members. The Christian life is meant to be lived not in isolation but in community with other believers as they "stir up one another to love and good works" (Heb. 10:24). Like sheep who get separated from the rest of the flock, Christians who isolate themselves from the church become easier prey to temptation and sin. Consequently, the New Testament instructs believers to regularly attend and participate in the local church (Heb. 10:25).

Church Discipline

Though the word *discipline* carries negative connotations, the practice of church discipline ought to be motivated by a positive, loving desire both to preserve the purity of the church (2 Cor. 7:1; cf. Acts 5:11; 1 Cor. 5:1–13; 2 Thess. 3:6–15; 1 Tim. 1:19–20; Titus 1:10–16) and to restore sinning brothers and sisters to the fellowship (cf. Luke 15:3–8; Jude 23). Church discipline should never be motivated out of self-righteous pride, political agendas, a desire to exercise power in an unbiblical way, or an intent to embarrass people. Rather, it should be overseen by the elders who, as shepherds of the flock, sincerely long to see wandering sheep repent, return, and be restored (cf. Gal. 6:1).

The process of church discipline is outlined by the Lord Jesus in Matthew 18:15–17:

If your brother sins against you, go and tell him his fault, between you and him alone. If he listens to you, you have gained your brother. But if he does not listen, take one or two others along with you, that every charge may be established by the evidence of two or three witnesses. If he refuses to listen to them, tell it to the church. And if he refuses to listen even to the church, let him be to you as a Gentile and a tax collector.

This passage delineates a four-step process for how churches are to deal with sin among their members. First, believers are to address sin on an individual level, approaching the offending party with a spirit of gentleness and humility. If the sinning brother responds to that private confrontation in repentance, the church discipline process comes to an end. He is forgiven and restored (Matt. 18:15). But if he refuses to repent, the process moves to a second step, in which one or two more believers join in confronting the sinning brother. These witnesses (cf. Num. 35:30; Deut. 17:6; 19:15; John 8:17; 2 Cor. 13:1; 1 Tim. 5:19; Heb. 10:28) primarily confirm that the sin was committed, and they also observe how the offending party responds after being confronted a second time (Matt. 18:16). It is hoped that the added weight of their rebuke will be enough to prompt a change of heart in the sinning brother.

Should he still refuse to repent after being given adequate time, the process moves to a third step. In light of the sinning brother's persistent hardheartedness, the witnesses are to bring the matter to the church (Matt. 18:17) by notifying the elders, who in turn communicate it to the congregation. Because of the public nature of this step, the elders must perform due diligence to confirm the facts of the situation—that the church member has sinned, has been confronted, and has refused to repent—before announcing it to the entire congregation. The purpose of alerting the church is twofold: to remind other members of the seriousness of sin (cf. 1 Tim. 5:20) and to encourage them to confront the sinning brother in the hopes that he will repent and be restored.

If the confronted brother still refuses to repent, the final step of church discipline is to formally separate and to ostracize him from the fellowship. The unrepentant person is no longer to be treated as a brother but as "a Gentile and a tax-collector" (Matt. 18:17)—meaning as an outsider to whom the benefits and blessings of church membership are no longer extended. The motivation is not to punish the person but to see him yet come to his senses and repent (cf. 2 Thess. 3:11–15). Consequently, the only contact with such individuals should be for the purpose of admonishing them and calling them to repentance. In the early church, believers were not even to share a meal with those who persisted in unrepentant sin (1 Cor. 5:11; cf. 2 Thess. 3:6, 14). Putting them out of the church protects the purity of the remaining members (1 Cor. 5:6) and safeguards the congregation's testimony in the eyes of the world.

The authority to practice church discipline in this manner comes from the Lord Jesus himself. Immediately after outlining the discipline process, Jesus explained,

> Truly, I say to you, whatever you bind on earth shall be bound in heaven, and whatever you loose on earth shall be loosed in heaven. Again I say to you, if two of you agree on earth about anything they ask, it will be done for them by my Father in heaven. For where two or three are gathered in my name, there am I among them. (Matt. 18:18–20)

The phrases "bound in heaven" and "loosed in heaven" were rabbinical expressions that spoke, respectively, of actions either forbidden or permitted in light of God's truth. In this context, the Lord's meaning is clear. When the church follows the biblical procedure for church discipline, its verdict stands in harmony with God's revealed will. Consequently, churches that excommunicate unrepentant members after following the proper process for discipline can rest in knowing that their actions meet with God's authoritative approval. Church discipline is therefore an earthly expression of heaven's holiness.

Unity and Purity

The New Testament emphasis on fellowship underscores the biblical call to pursue love and spiritual unity in the church. As Jesus told his disciples, "A new commandment I give to you, that you love one another: just as I have loved you, you also are to love one another. By this all people will know that you are my disciples, if you have love for one another" (John 13:34–35). At the same time, the Lord's instructions for church discipline in Matthew 18:15–20 remind believers that he desires his church to be pure, both in doctrine and in practice. Both of these qualities, unity and purity, must be maintained as believers consider how to relate to other professing Christians.

On the one hand, the New Testament repeatedly calls believers to live in harmony with one another (Rom. 12:16; 15:5; Col. 3:14). They are to "have unity of mind" (1 Pet. 3:8) as they eagerly seek "to maintain the unity of the Spirit in the bond of peace" (Eph. 4:3). Believers are commanded to love one another (Rom. 12:10; 13:8; 1 Thess. 3:12; 4:9; 2 Thess. 1:3; 1 Pet. 1:22; 4:8; 1 John 3:11, 23; 4:7, 11–12; 2 John 5), following the selfless and sacrificial example of Christ by showing preference to others (Phil. 2:5). Thus Paul told the Philippians,

> If there is any encouragement in Christ, any comfort from love, any participation in the Spirit, any affection and sympathy, complete my joy by being of the same mind, having the same love, being in full accord and of one mind. Do nothing from selfish ambition or conceit, but in humility count others more significant than yourselves. Let each of you look not only to his own interests, but also to the interests of others. (Phil. 2:1–4)

Those who cause divisions in the church are to be confronted (cf. Rom. 16:17; 1 Cor. 1:10) and disciplined if they do not repent (Titus 3:10–11; cf. James 3:14–18).

On the other hand, the New Testament also instructs believers to guard the truth (1 Tim. 6:20; 2 Tim. 1:14), to contend earnestly for the purity of the faith (Jude 3), and to watch their life and doctrine closely (1 Tim. 4:16). Scripture repeatedly warns Christians to be on the alert against sin (Eph. 6:10–18; 1 Pet. 5:8; 1 John 2:15–17) and error (2 Tim. 3:1–9; 2 Pet. 2:1–2; 1 John 4:1–3). They are not to associate with immoral people (1 Cor. 5:9; Eph. 5:11; 2 Thess. 3:6, 14) or those who propagate error (2 John 10; cf. Gal. 1:8–9; Titus 3:10). In fact, the New Testament reserves its harshest condemnations for false teachers who would seek to undermine sound doctrine and promote immoral behavior (cf. 2 Pet. 2:1–3). Such purveyors of error are variously condemned as "ravenous wolves" (Matt. 7:15; Acts 20:29), "dogs" who return to their own vomit (2 Pet. 2:22; cf. Phil. 3:2), "blots and blemishes" (2 Pet. 2:13), "accursed children" (2 Pet. 2:14), "slaves of corruption" (2 Pet. 2:19), pigs that return "to wallow in the mire" (2 Pet. 2:22), "unreasoning animals" (Jude 10; cf. 2 Pet. 2:12), "hidden reefs" (Jude 12), "waterless clouds" (Jude 12; cf. 2 Pet. 2:17), "fruitless trees" (Jude 12), "wild waves of the sea" that "[cast] up the foam of their own shame" (Jude 13), and "loud-mouthed boasters" (Jude 16).

By contrast, the church ought to be a place where righteousness and truth are championed and never compromised. Thus Paul describes "the church of the living God" as "a pillar and buttress of the truth" (1 Tim. 3:15). Its leaders are "to give instruction in sound doctrine and also to rebuke those who contradict it" (Titus 1:9). And in the face of falsehood, believers are to use the truth to "destroy arguments and every lofty opinion raised against the knowledge of God, and take every thought captive to obey Christ" (2 Cor. 10:5).

When biblical calls for unity are considered alongside commands for purity and truth, it becomes clear that the unity described in Scripture is not a superficial unity that turns a blind eye to fundamental doctrinal or moral issues. Rather, true unity is grounded in a shared commitment to the lordship of Christ and the truth of his gospel. The New Testament rejects any so-called unity that dilutes doctrinal or moral purity. When believers separate from apostates and false teachers, they are not being divisive; they are following a divine mandate. As Paul explained to the Corinthians,

> Do not be unequally yoked with unbelievers. For what partnership has righteousness with lawlessness? Or what fellowship has light with darkness? What accord has Christ with Belial? Or what portion does a believer share with an unbeliever? What agreement has the temple of God with idols? For we are the temple of the living God; as God said,
>
> > "I will make my dwelling among them and walk among them,
> >   and I will be their God,
> >   and they shall be my people.
> > Therefore go out from their midst,
> >   and be separate from them, says the Lord,
> > and touch no unclean thing;
> >   then I will welcome you,
> > and I will be a father to you,
> >   and you shall be sons and daughters to me,
> > says the Lord Almighty." (2 Cor. 6:14–18)

Given the modern climate of ecumenism and political correctness, church leaders face the temptation to ignore fundamental doctrinal deviations and moral perversions for the sake of "unity" and "love." Yet Christ-honoring love "does not rejoice at wrongdoing, but rejoices with the truth" (1 Cor.13:6), and true unity is grounded in sound doctrine (cf. 1 Tim. 6:3–4; 2 Tim. 4:3–4). At a local-church level, this commitment to purity is primarily evidenced through the faithful preaching of the Word (where sin is addressed and confronted) and through the practice of church discipline (cf. Matt. 18:15–20; 2 Thess. 3:6, 14). Outside a local church context, church leaders should recognize that they cannot partner with organizations or institutions that have abandoned their commitment to sound doctrine or to biblical standards of morality. Though believers can certainly link arms in ministry with fellow Christians who uphold and exemplify the purity of the gospel, they should not partner with groups or individuals who undermine gospel truth in any way.

Church Membership[29]

The Definition
The Biblical Basis

In a day when commitment is a rare commodity, it should come as no surprise that so many believers make church membership such a low priority. Sadly, it is not uncommon for Christians to move from church to church, never submitting themselves to the loving oversight of elders and never committing themselves to a group of fellow believers.

To neglect—or refuse—to join a church as a formal member, however, reflects a misunderstanding of the believer's responsibility to the body of Christ. And it also cuts one off from the many blessings and opportunities that flow from this commitment. It is essential for every Christian to understand what church membership is and why it matters.

The Definition

When an individual is saved, he becomes a member of the body of Christ (1 Cor. 12:13). Because he is united to Christ and the other members of the body in this way, he is therefore qualified to become a member of a local expression of that body.

To become a member of a church is to formally commit oneself to an identifiable, local body of believers who have joined together for specific, divinely ordained purposes. These purposes include receiving instruction from God's Word (1 Tim. 4:13; 2 Tim. 4:2), serving and edifying one another through the proper use of spiritual gifts (Rom. 12:3–8; 1 Cor. 12:4–31; 1 Pet. 4:10–11), participating in the ordinances (Luke 22:19; Acts 2:38–42), and proclaiming the gospel to those who are lost (Matt. 28:18–20). In addition, when one becomes a member of a church, he submits himself to the care and the authority of the biblically qualified elders whom God has placed in that assembly.

The Biblical Basis

Although Scripture does not contain an explicit command to formally join a local church, the biblical foundation for church membership permeates the New Testament. This biblical basis can be seen most clearly in (1) the example of the early church, (2) the existence of church government, (3) the exercise of church discipline, and (4) the exhortation to mutual edification.

---

29. This section is adapted from Grace Community Church, "Church Membership: A Grace Community Church Distinctive" (Sun Valley, CA: Grace Community Church, 2002). Used by permission of Grace Community Church.

THE EXAMPLE OF THE EARLY CHURCH

In the early church, coming to Christ meant coming to the church. The idea of experiencing salvation without belonging to a local church is foreign to the New Testament. When individuals repented and believed in Christ, they were baptized and brought into the church (Acts 2:41, 47; 5:14; 16:5). More than simply living out a private commitment to Christ, this meant formally joining together with other believers in a local assembly and devoting themselves to the apostles' teaching, fellowship, the breaking of bread, and prayer (Acts 2:42).

The Epistles of the New Testament were written to churches. In the case of the few written to individuals—1 and 2 Timothy, Titus, and Philemon—these men were leaders in churches. As the New Testament Epistles themselves demonstrate, the Lord assumed that believers would be committed to a local assembly. The New Testament also bears evidence that just as there was a list of widows eligible for financial support (1 Tim. 5:9), there may also have been a list of members that grew longer as people were saved (cf. Acts 2:41, 47; 5:14; 16:5). In fact, when a believer moved to another city, his church often wrote a letter of commendation to his new church (Acts 18:27; Rom. 16:1; Col. 4:10; cf. 2 Cor. 3:1–2). Such letters would be impossible to write if these believers were not known by and accountable to their spiritual leaders.

In the book of Acts, much of the terminology fits only with the concept of formal church membership. Phrases such as "the whole congregation" (Acts 6:5 NASB), "the church in Jerusalem" (Acts 8:1), "the disciples" in Jerusalem (Acts 9:26), "in every church" (Acts 14:23), "the whole church" (Acts 15:22), and "the elders of the church" in Ephesus (Acts 20:17) all suggest recognizable church membership with well-defined boundaries (see also 1 Cor. 5:4; 14:23; Heb. 10:25), because unless one knows who the members of the church are, one cannot say whether the "whole church" is present. In other words, knowing that the "whole church" has gathered implies that the leadership is aware of everyone who belongs to that local congregation, which, in turn, implies recognized membership.

THE EXISTENCE OF CHURCH GOVERNMENT

The New Testament displays a consistent pattern of a plurality of elders overseeing each local body of believers. The specific duties given to these elders presuppose a clearly defined group of church members under their care.

Among other things, these godly men are responsible to shepherd God's people (Acts 20:28; 1 Pet. 5:2), to labor diligently among them (1 Thess. 5:12), to have charge over them (1 Thess. 5:12; 1 Tim. 5:17), and to keep watch over their souls (Heb. 13:17). Scripture teaches that the elders will give an account to God for the individuals allotted to their charge (Heb. 13:17; 1 Pet. 5:3–4).

Those responsibilities require that there be a distinguishable, mutually understood membership in the local church. Elders can shepherd their people, provide oversight for them, and give an account to God for their spiritual well-being only if they know who is part of the flock and who is not. The elders of a church are not responsible for the spiritual well-being of every individual who visits the church or those who attend sporadically. Rather, they are primarily responsible to shepherd those who have submitted themselves to the care and authority of the elders, and this is done through church membership.

Conversely, Scripture teaches that believers are to submit to their elders. Hebrews 13:17 says, "Obey your leaders, and submit to them." The question for each believer is, "Who are your leaders?" The one who has refused to join a local church and entrust himself to the care and authority of the elders has no leaders. For that person, obedience to Hebrews 13:17 is impossible. To put it simply, this verse implies that every believer knows to whom he must submit, which in turn assumes a clearly defined church membership.

THE EXERCISE OF CHURCH DISCIPLINE

As noted above, Matthew 18:15–17 outlines how the church is to seek the restoration of a believer who has fallen into sin—a four-step process commonly known as church discipline.[30] The exercise of church discipline according to Matthew 18 and other passages (1 Cor. 5:1–13; 1 Tim. 5:20; Titus 3:10–11) presupposes that the elders of a church know who their members are. Without any kind of formal relationship between the congregation and its leaders, there would be no basis for the spiritual accountability that the New Testament requires. Further, when disciplined, unrepentant individuals are to be excluded precisely from *membership* in the church.

THE EXHORTATION TO MUTUAL EDIFICATION

The New Testament teaches that the church is the body of Christ, and that God has called every member to a life devoted to the growth of the body. In other words, Scripture exhorts all believers to edify the other members by practicing the "one another" commands of the New Testament (e.g., Heb. 10:24–25) and exercising their spiritual gifts (Rom. 12:6–8; 1 Cor. 12:4–7; 1 Pet. 4:10–11). Mutual edification can only take place in the context of the corporate body of Christ. Exhortations to this kind of ministry presuppose that believers have committed themselves to other believers in a specific local assembly. Church membership is simply the formal way to make that commitment.

Living out a commitment to a local church involves many responsibilities: exemplifying a godly lifestyle in the community, exercising one's spiritual gifts in diligent service, contributing financially to the work of the ministry, giving and receiving admonition with meekness and in love, and faithfully participating in corporate worship. Much is expected because much is at stake, for only when every believer is faithful to this kind of commitment is the church able to live up to her calling as Christ's representative on earth.

---

30. For more, see "Church Discipline" (p. 793).

Spiritual Gifts within the Church

Categorizing Gifts
Surveying Gifts
Using Gifts

Few areas of doctrine are more controversial or confused in the church today than spiritual gifts. Such was also true in the first century, at least in Corinth, which explains why the apostle Paul addressed the issue so thoroughly in 1 Corinthians 12–14.[31] Though they can be and are abused and even counterfeited, spiritual gifts (Gk. *charismata*, or "gifts of grace") play a vital role in the body of Christ. Since each member uniquely contributes to the edification of the whole, it is critical to understand what God's Word teaches about the nature and exercise of spiritual gifts.

Not only has Christ endowed his church with gifted men to equip the saints (Eph. 4:11–12), but his Spirit also bestows all believers with spiritual abilities to build up one another in the church (Rom. 12:5–8; 1 Cor. 12:4–31; 1 Pet. 4:10–11). The triune God is the source of these gifts. As Paul explains in 1 Corinthians 12:4–6, they are given by the "same Spirit," the "same Lord," and the "same God."

As all believers without exception are baptized with the Spirit at the moment of conversion (1 Cor. 12:13), they all without exception receive supernatural endowments for service within the church according to the Spirit's sovereign prerogative (1 Cor. 12:4, 6–11). These spiritual gifts are not limited to only a select group of Christians. Since all believers are supernaturally gifted, they are all obligated to exercise their giftedness in ministry to others.

As spiritual gifts uniquely equip each believer to minister to the corporate body of Christ, the resulting way in which those in the church edify each other testifies effectively to God's power before a watching world. When believers exercise their giftedness, they also exhibit Christlike behavior. As God incarnate, the Lord Jesus possessed these qualities in perfect completeness. Believers put him on display as they employ these gifts for the sake of his body, the church, through the power of his Spirit.

The primary Greek word associated with spiritual gifts is *charisma*, meaning "gift of grace." It is almost always used in the New Testament to designate a gift that has been freely bestowed by God, including the gift of salvation (Rom. 5:15–16; 6:23), the undeserved blessings of God (Rom. 1:11; 11:29), and divine enablements for ministry (Rom. 12:6; 1 Pet. 4:10). Because God bestows them on believers by his grace (1 Cor. 12:4, 7, 11, 18), these enablements cannot be earned, learned, or manufactured. They are given as "grace gifts" according to his divine will, so that believers should be grateful for whatever gift they have received.

Another important Greek term, *pneumatikos* ("pertaining to the Spirit"), is found in 1 Corinthians 12:1. Literally meaning "spirituals" or "spiritualities," this word refers to that which has spiritual characteristics or is under spiritual control. Though it can apply to either persons or things, the context in 1 Corinthians 12:1

---

31. For a cessationist interpretation of 1 Corinthians 12–14, see Robert L. Thomas, *Understanding Spiritual Gifts: A Verse-by-Verse Study of 1 Corinthians 12–14*, 2nd ed. (Grand Rapids, MI: Kregel, 1999). See also MacArthur, *1 Corinthians*.

indicates that it refers there to spiritual things—namely, to the gifts of grace that the Holy Spirit bestows on believers (cf. 1 Cor. 12:4, 9, 28, 30–31; 14:1). With the exception of Ephesians 6:12, where it speaks of hostile spiritual forces, this term is always used in the New Testament to refer to that which relates to the Holy Spirit. When applied to spiritual gifts, it designates the fact that those abilities bestowed by the Spirit are to be used under his control for the glory of Christ.

Unlike natural abilities or talents, which can be exhibited by believers and unbelievers alike, spiritual gifts are only received at the moment of salvation. The Holy Spirit supernaturally endows them on believers so that they can effectively minister to one another through his divine enablement.

Believers are each uniquely gifted so that the diversity of their giftedness covers everything necessary to contribute to the unity of the body. As Paul explains in 1 Corinthians 12:7–27, the body would not function properly if every member had the same function. The Holy Spirit endows believers with a variety of gifts so that as each member exercises his or her gift, the entire body works together productively. Believers are to faithfully steward the gifts they receive (1 Pet. 4:10), employing their unique giftedness to glorify God and edify their fellow believers. As they do so, the body is shaped into the image of the Head, the Lord Jesus Christ (cf. Eph. 4:11–13).

Spiritual gifts are not signs of prestige or privilege, nor should they produce spiritual pride. Rather, they are given for believers to serve with a spirit of selflessness (Phil. 2:2–4) and humility (Rom. 12:3). The exercise of spiritual gifts should not cause disruption or division within the church (1 Cor. 14:40).

The purpose of spiritual gifts is not self-edification but the edification of others (1 Pet. 4:10; cf. Eph. 4:11–12). Paul explicitly states that they are given "for the common good" (1 Cor. 12:7). Accordingly, God intends believers to use their spiritual gifts in relationship to other believers—not by oneself in private.[32] To be sure, believers are personally blessed as they use their giftedness to serve others, but that blessing is a byproduct and not the purpose of employing their gifts.

To use one's gift to edify oneself clearly runs contrary to Paul's entire point in 1 Corinthians 12–14, where he repeatedly emphasizes the priority of love for others as essential to the proper exercise of spiritual gifts (1 Cor. 12:7–10; 13:1–7; 14:12, 26). Using extreme examples to make his point, Paul writes,

> If I speak in the tongues of men and of angels, but have not love, I am a noisy gong or a clanging cymbal. And if I have prophetic powers, and understand all mysteries and all knowledge, and if I have all faith, so as to remove mountains,

---

32. Some might object by pointing to 1 Cor. 14:4, where Paul wrote, "The one who speaks in a tongue builds up himself, but the one who prophesies builds up the church." But that verse does not validate self-edification as a legitimate end in itself. If it did, it would run contrary to Paul's instruction throughout the entirety of chapters 12–14. In actuality, Paul is making the exact opposite point. He is demonstrating the superiority of prophecy over tongues, because prophecy edified other people immediately without first needing to be interpreted (1 Cor. 14:5). That is why the apostle insisted on the translation of the foreign languages that were spoken (14:27–28), so that the gift of tongues could fulfill its purpose of edifying others (12:7). He is saying, "The one who speaks in a tongue [without an interpreter] builds up [only] himself, [which is undesirable and contrary to the purpose of spiritual gifts], but the one who prophesies builds up the church. . . . [Therefore,] the one who prophesies is greater than the one who speaks in tongues, unless someone interprets, so that the church may be built up."

but have not love, I am nothing. If I give away all I have, and if I deliver up my body to be burned, but have not love, I gain nothing. (1 Cor. 13:1–3)

As these words demonstrate, the loveless exercise of any gift (no matter how elevated or extreme) nullifies its spiritual value. But when spiritual gifts are employed properly, out of a loving desire to edify fellow believers, the church is built up, Christ is manifested, and God is glorified (cf. 1 Cor. 12:4–27).

Categorizing Gifts

The New Testament provides a few lists of spiritual gifts (Rom. 12:6–8; 1 Cor. 12:8–10, 28–30; cf. 1 Cor. 13:1–3, 8–9; Eph. 4:11; 1 Pet. 4:10–11). Because these lists are not identical (see table 9.3 [p. 807]), it is best to interpret them as representative compilations (rather than exhaustive lists) of the ways in which the Lord empowers his people for ministry. The apostle Peter says that each believer has received "a gift" (1 Pet. 4:10), but that single divine enablement can be a combination of spiritual abilities, such as those listed in Romans 12 and 1 Corinthians 12. Peter also divides them into the general categories of speaking gifts and serving gifts (1 Pet. 4:11).

Due to the unique manner in which the Holy Spirit endows each believer for spiritual service, it can be counterproductive to categorize spiritual gifts too narrowly or too rigidly. For example, taking a written test to ascertain one's giftedness (based on such categorizations) is often unhelpful, since each believer receives a unique blending of abilities from the Holy Spirit that constitute his gift. The best way to discover one's spiritual giftedness is by engaging in ministry according to one's God-given desires, opportunities to serve, and the response of those served. As believers minister to one another, their areas of giftedness gradually become apparent both to them and to others.

In a broad sense, the gifts might be categorized under two major headings: the temporary, miraculous gifts and the permanent, ministering gifts. The miraculous gifts include the apostolic sign gifts (Heb. 2:3–4; cf. 2 Cor. 12:12) and the revelatory gifts, through which God gave new revelation to his church. These gifts were limited to the apostolic age of the church (see discussion below). The ministering gifts, including both speaking gifts and serving gifts (1 Pet. 4:10–11), continue to be bestowed by the Holy Spirit in his church for the purpose of edification, growth, and witness.

MIRACULOUS GIFTS

At critical times throughout redemption history, God authenticated his messengers by empowering them to perform miraculous signs. During the exodus from Egypt and the establishment of the nation of Israel, God validated the roles of Moses and Joshua through supernatural deeds that he accomplished through them (Ex. 4:3–4, 30; 7:10, 12; 17:5–6; Num. 16:46–50; Josh. 10:12–14). In the face of Israel's apostasy centuries later, the ministries of Elijah and Elisha were similarly authenticated by signs and wonders (1 Kings 17:9–24; 18:41–45; 2 Kings 1:10–12; 2:8, 14; 4:1–7, 18–41; 5:1–19; 6:6, 17).

In the New Testament, the ministry of Jesus Christ was also confirmed by miracles and healings (John 2:11, 23; 3:2; 4:54; 6:2, 14; 7:31; 10:37–38; 12:37; 20:30). Thus, Jesus could tell the unbelieving religious leaders, "The works that I do in my Father's name bear witness about me" (John 10:25; cf. 5:36; 10:38; 14:11). Later, Peter reminded the crowds at Pentecost that Jesus was "a man attested to you by God with mighty works and wonders and signs that God did through him in your midst, as you yourselves know" (Acts 2:22). The signs and wonders Jesus did proved that he was who he claimed to be.

The birth of the church was also marked by miraculous signs—including the ability of the disciples to speak fluently in foreign languages (Acts 2:4–11). During Jesus's ministry, he had given his disciples power to heal and cast out demons (Matt. 10:1, 8; Mark 6:12–13). After his ascension, the apostles continued to exhibit that supernatural power (Mark 16:20; Acts 2:43; 4:30; 5:12; 6:8; 8:6, 13; 14:3; 15:12). The message they proclaimed was validated through the signs and wonders they performed.

During the apostolic era, God gave many believers extraordinary gifts to demonstrate that he was working through the newly established church. Gentile converts (like Cornelius in Acts 10:46) received the same gift of languages that the apostles had exhibited on the day of Pentecost (Acts 11:17). That supernatural ability served as a sign to unbelievers (and especially unbelieving Israel) that the gospel is true (1 Cor. 14:22; cf. Isa. 28:11) and that its truth is to be proclaimed throughout the entire world (cf. Matt. 28:18–20; Acts 1:8). Others, such as Stephen and Philip, exhibited the ability to perform miracles and healings (Acts 6:8; 8:5–7), publicly confirming the legitimacy of their evangelistic ministries.

Such extraordinary gifts were necessary to validate that the church was a true work of God and to authenticate the apostles as his chosen messengers. Signs and wonders demonstrated that God himself affirmed the gospel they proclaimed. As the author of Hebrews explains with reference to the gospel, "It was declared at first by the Lord, and it was attested to us by those who heard, while God also bore witness by signs and wonders and various miracles and by gifts of the Holy Spirit distributed according to his will" (Heb. 2:3–4). The apostle Paul similarly explains that his evangelistic ministry to the Gentiles was validated by "the power of signs and wonders" (Rom. 15:19). As he told the Corinthians, "The signs of a true apostle were performed among you with utmost patience, with signs and wonders and mighty works" (2 Cor. 12:12).

This level of miraculous authentication was necessary at a time when the church was still being established and the canon of Scripture was not yet complete. As those who received divine revelation through the Holy Spirit (John 14:26; 16:12–15; cf. 1 Thess. 2:13; 2 Pet. 3:15–16), the apostles and prophets were laying the doctrinal foundation for the church (Eph. 2:20; cf. Acts 2:42). Revelatory gifts were obviously needed in order to complete that task, and sign gifts were also necessary to authenticate their claim to be God's spokesmen (cf. 2 Cor. 12:12). Once the apostolic age ended and the New Testament canon was complete, the gifts uniquely associated with the offices of apostle and prophet were no longer needed and passed away. Now, the completed canon of the sufficient Scripture stands as its own self-authentication, being the full revelation of the mind and will of God.

THE TEMPORARY NATURE OF MIRACULOUS GIFTS[33]

Cessationism is the view that the sign gifts (e.g., the performing of miracles, gifts of healing, speaking in tongues) and the revelatory gifts (i.e., the reception and proclamation of new revelation from God) passed away when the foundation stage of the church ended. Those kinds of miraculous phenomena did not continue beyond the apostolic era and thus have not been given to believers since. Miraculous gifts will not return until the tribulation period, after the church has been raptured and during the ministry of the two witnesses (cf. Rev. 11:3–11). In contrast to cessationism, the *charismatic* or *continuationist* position asserts that the miraculous and revelatory gifts are still in operation today.

One approach to defending the cessationist position begins with recognizing that there are no apostles in the church today[34]—a fact ubiquitously affirmed throughout church history and acknowledged by many modern noncessationists. As noted above, no one today can meet the qualifications necessary for apostleship (which include seeing the risen Christ with one's own physical eyes; cf. Acts 1:22; 9:1–9). Paul explicitly states that the resurrected Jesus appeared "last of all" to him (1 Cor. 15:8). Hence, there were no apostles after Paul.

That there have been no apostles since the first century is significant for at least three reasons: (1) it demonstrates that God did not intend everything that characterized the early church to be normative for the rest of church history; (2) it shows that at least one significant ministry function listed in 1 Corinthians 12:28–30 has ceased; and (3) it verifies that the canon of Scripture is in fact closed, since an apostle must authorize a book for it to be recognized as canonical.

The cessation of apostleship is also significant because of its close connection with the New Testament office of prophet. In Ephesians 2:20, Paul links these two offices together, explaining that the church was "built on the foundation of the apostles and prophets," with Jesus Christ being the cornerstone. (That Paul has New Testament prophets in view is clear from his subsequent references to them in Eph. 3:5 and 4:11.) Before the canon of Scripture was complete, the doctrinal foundation of the church—consisting of divine revelation delivered through the apostles and prophets—was still being established. But once that foundation was laid with the

---

33. This section is adapted from MacArthur's comments in this interview with Tim Challies, "John MacArthur Answers His Critics," *Challies.com: Informing the Reforming* (blog), November 4, 2013, http://www.challies.com/interviews/john -macarthur-answers-his-critics. Used by permission of Tim Challies.

34. For example, this is the approach taken by Samuel E. Waldron, *To Be Continued? Are the Miraculous Gifts for Today?* (Merrick, NY: Calvary Press, 2005). See also Thomas R. Edgar, *Satisfied by the Promise of the Spirit* (Grand Rapids, MI: Kregel, 1996), 52–88; MacArthur, *Strange Fire*, 85–103.

completion of the New Testament, the purpose for those offices was fulfilled, and they passed away. To follow Paul's metaphor, the foundation is not rebuilt at every phase of construction; it is laid only once at the beginning of the construction process.

The apostolic age came to its end when John, the last surviving apostle, died. Significantly, John was also the last canonical prophet (cf. Rev. 1:3; 22:18–19), with the book of Revelation completing the New Testament Scriptures. Consequently, the revelatory role of New Testament prophets, like that of the apostles, was fulfilled, and the gifts associated with that role were no longer needed.

God's completed revelation in his written Word is so powerful and glorious that it no longer needs miraculous confirmation. As Peter explains, the prophetic word is even *more sure* than the most extraordinary of eyewitness experiences (2 Pet. 1:16–21). In the all-sufficient Scriptures, God's truth is self-attesting and self-evident, as the illuminating power of the Holy Spirit confirms (Heb. 4:12). Consequently, the signs and wonders of the apostolic age are no longer necessary. The Bible is all that is needed to validate the message of those who claim to be God's spokesmen.

The cessationist position is further confirmed by comparing modern "charismatic gifts" with the realities described in the New Testament. Scripture provides a clear picture of the miraculous sign and revelatory gifts, but when modern charismatic phenomena are measured against that biblical standard, they fall far short. Though charismatics use biblical terminology to describe their experiences, nothing about modern "miraculous gifts" matches the biblical reality.

For example, God's Word explicitly says that true prophets must adhere to a standard of 100 percent accuracy (Deut. 18:20–22), and nothing in the New Testament exempts them from that standard. The book of Acts depicts the gift of tongues as producing real human languages (Acts 2:6–11), and nothing in 1 Corinthians necessitates that they be redefined as something else. The New Testament further describes the miraculous healings of Jesus and the apostles (including the healing of organic diseases like paralysis, blindness, and leprosy) as being immediate, complete, and undeniable (e.g., Mark 1:42; 10:52). These and many other Scripture passages demonstrate the truly extraordinary quality of the biblical gifts. (See further discussion about these gifts below.)

By comparison, the modern counterfeits of the charismatic movement simply do not match up to their biblical counterparts. Modern "prophetic revelation" is fallible and full of errors. Modern "tongues" consists of unintelligible speech that does not conform to any human language. Modern "gifts of healing" do not compare to the miracles performed by Jesus and the apostles. Incredibly, many continuationist scholars acknowledge this discontinuity, arguing for a lesser quality or lower category of gifts in which to place these modern charismatic expressions. Such admissions, however, provide a tacit acknowledgment that the true sign gifts (as depicted in Scripture) have not continued.[35]

---

35. Some commentators appeal to 1 Cor. 13:10 to support their position either for or against cessationism. But doing so stretches the point of that text beyond what Paul intended. While the meaning of the Greek word translated "perfect" (*teleion*) has been widely debated by commentators, "of the possible interpretations, the believer's entrance into the Lord's presence best fits Paul's use of the 'perfect' in 1 Corinthians 13:10." Accordingly, it is important to note that Paul's purpose in this chapter was not to identify how long the spiritual gifts would continue into later centuries of church history, as that

The fact is that modern charismatic experiences do not match what the Bible describes as the miraculous and revelatory gifts of the New Testament period. There is nothing extraordinary about fallible prophecy, irrational tongues, or the counterfeit miracles performed by modern faith healers. What a contrast they are to the genuine gifts recorded on the pages of Scripture, which produced wonder, awe, and worship in the hearts of those who witnessed them (cf. Mark 1:27; 2:12; Luke 4:36; 8:56; Acts 2:7, 12; 8:13; 10:45). Cessationism, then, is motivated by a concern to honor the Holy Spirit by safeguarding a true understanding of his miraculous work as portrayed in Scripture.

MINISTERING GIFTS

Though the sign gifts and revelatory gifts were limited to the foundational age of the church, the Holy Spirit continues to endow believers for edification in the church through what might be called his *permanent, ministering gifts*. These include both speaking gifts and serving gifts. Thus Peter explained in 1 Peter 4:10–11,

> As each has received a gift, use it to serve one another, as good stewards of God's varied grace: whoever speaks, as one who speaks oracles of God; whoever serves, as one who serves by the strength that God supplies—in order that in everything God may be glorified through Jesus Christ. To him belong glory and dominion forever and ever. Amen.

Speaking gifts proclaim the truth of Scripture through preaching, teaching, encouraging, exhorting, and so on. Serving gifts minister to others in a Christlike way through acts like helping, giving, administrating, and showing mercy.

Surveying Gifts

Within the broad categories noted above, the New Testament identifies a number of specific spiritual gifts. The three primary lists, from Romans 12:6–8 and 1 Corinthians 12:8–10 and 12:28–30, are compared in table 9.3. Combining the gifts in these three passages produces the "master list" of representative spiritual gifts in table 9.4. With these gifts delineated in these two tables, it is now possible to consider how each of them operates.

APOSTLESHIP

The Greek term *apostolos* refers to an ambassador, an emissary, or someone sent on a mission. Though it is sometimes used in the New Testament in a general sense

---

would have been essentially meaningless to the original readers of this letter. Rather, he was making a point that specifically pertained to his first-century audience: when you Corinthian believers enter the glorified perfection of eternity in heaven, the spiritual gifts you now prize so highly will no longer be necessary (since the partial revelation they provide will be made complete). But love has eternal value, so pursue love because it is superior to any gift (v. 13). . . . To determine the point in church history when the miraculous and revelatory gifts would pass away we must look elsewhere than 1 Corinthians 13:10, to places like Ephesians 2:20 where Paul indicated that the prophetic offices were only for the foundational age of the church. Nonetheless, Paul's broader principle, that love is superior to spiritual giftedness, still applies to modern believers as we also look forward to our heavenly glorification." MacArthur, *Strange Fire*, 148–49. Cf. Edgar, *Satisfied by the Promise of the Spirit*, 246.

Table 9.3 Three Primary Lists of Spiritual Gifts

Romans 12:6–8	1 Corinthians 12:8–10	1 Corinthians 12:28–30
Prophecy	Utterance of wisdom	Apostleship (apostles)
Service	Utterance of knowledge	Prophecy (prophets)
Teaching	Faith	Teaching (teachers)
Exhortation	Gifts of healing	Working of miracles
Giving (contributing)	Working of miracles	Gifts of healing
Leading	Prophecy	Helping
Acts of mercy	Distinguishing between spirits	Administrating
	Speaking in tongues	Speaking in tongues
	Interpreting tongues	Interpreting tongues

Table 9.4 Master List of Representative Spiritual Gifts

Category		Spiritual Gift	Passages
Miraculous gifts	Sign gifts and revelatory gifts	Apostleship	1 Cor. 12:28–29; cf. Eph. 4:11
		Working of miracles	1 Cor. 12:10, 28–29
		Gifts of healing	1 Cor. 12:9, 28, 30
		Speaking in tongues	1 Cor. 12:10, 28, 30; cf. 1 Cor. 13:1; 14:22
		Prophecy	1 Cor. 12:10, 28–29; cf. Eph. 4:11
		Words of wisdom	1 Cor. 12:8; cf. 13:2
		Words of knowledge	1 Cor. 12:8; cf. 13:2
		Interpreting tongues	1 Cor. 12:10, 28, 30; cf. 14:6–18
		Distinguishing between spirits	1 Cor. 12:10
Ministering gifts	Speaking gifts and serving gifts	Preaching*	Rom. 12:6; cf. 1 Tim. 4:13–14; 1 Pet. 4:11
		Teaching	Rom. 12:7; 1 Cor. 12:28–29
		Exhortation	Rom. 12:8
		Service and helping	Rom. 12:7; 1 Cor. 12:28; 1 Pet. 4:11
		Leading and administrating	Rom. 12:8; 1 Cor. 12:28
		Giving	Rom. 12:8; cf. 1 Cor. 13:3
		Showing mercy	Rom. 12:8
		Faith	1 Cor. 12:9; cf. 13:2
		Spiritual discernment	1 Cor. 12:10
		Evangelism	Eph. 4:11
		Shepherding and teaching	Eph. 4:11

*Preaching is similar to the nonrevelatory exercise of the gift of prophecy.

to designate "apostles of the churches" (2 Cor. 8:23; cf. Phil. 2:25), it is primarily used to refer to a specific group of "apostles of Jesus Christ." As explained earlier, the title "apostle of Jesus Christ" (cf. 1 Cor. 1:1; 1 Pet. 1:1) refers specifically to the twelve disciples (with Matthias having replaced Judas, Acts 1:26) and Paul, who was specially chosen as the apostle to the Gentiles (Gal. 1:15–17; cf. 1 Cor. 15:7–9). These men were selected by the Lord (cf. Mark 3:13; Acts 26:16) and were eyewitnesses of the resurrected Christ (Acts 1:22; 9:1–9), a necessary prerequisite for being an apostle. Because Paul states that the resurrected Jesus appeared to him "last of all" (1 Cor. 15:8), there were no apostles after him.

The apostles of Jesus Christ had three primary responsibilities. First, they were used by the Lord to lay the doctrinal foundation of the church (Eph. 2:20). Second, they were appointed to receive, preach, and write divine revelation (cf. Acts 2:42; 6:4; Eph. 3:5). Third, they were called to confirm that divine Word through "signs and wonders and mighty works" (2 Cor. 12:12; cf. Heb. 2:3–4). When John, the last surviving apostle, died and the apostolic age came to an end, the apostles did not appoint new apostles to lead the church. Instead, they appointed elders (Titus 1:5; cf. 2 Tim. 2:2). The record of church history demonstrates that those who came after the apostles did not consider themselves apostles. Rather, they regarded the apostles and the apostolic age as unique and unrepeatable.

The New Testament identifies apostleship as both an office and a gift. Ephesians 4:11 refers to apostles (along with prophets, evangelists, pastor-teachers) as gifts given by Jesus Christ to the church, and 1 Corinthians 12 includes "apostles" in the list of charismatic gifts delineated in that chapter (1 Cor. 12:4–5, 28–31). Paul's inclusion of apostleship in 1 Corinthians 12 is significant because it demonstrates that not everything included in that passage has continued throughout church history to the present.

WORKING OF MIRACLES

Among the signs that validated the ministry of the apostles was the "working of miracles" (1 Cor. 12:10, 28–29). A *miracle* might be broadly defined as an extraordinary work of God in which he suspends or overrides the normal courses of nature so that the result cannot be explained by any natural cause. Miracles are distinct from acts of providence, in which God works through natural means to accomplish his sovereign purposes. More specifically, the working of miracles was a gift that involved human agency. Those bestowed with this gift were empowered by God to perform supernatural signs and wonders. The working of miracles validated them as spokesmen for God (cf. Acts 2:22; 14:3; 2 Cor. 12:12; Heb. 2:3–4).

Throughout his earthly ministry, the Lord Jesus performed miracles to manifest his glory (John 2:11) and authenticate his message (John 5:36; 10:38; 14:11). Jesus's miracles demonstrated his power over nature (e.g., turning water into wine, creating food, calming the wind and waves), demons, disease, and death. The New Testament does not record any of the apostles performing miracles over nature, but they did exhibit power over demons, disease, and death (cf. Acts 9:41–42; 20:7–12).

It is in that first sense, authority over demons, that the word "miracles" is being used in 1 Corinthians 12:10, 28–29. The Greek word for "miracle" (*dynamis*) means "power" and is frequently connected in the Gospels with the casting out of demons (e.g., Luke 4:36; 6:18–19). Jesus gave his disciples power over demons (Luke 9:1; 10:17–19), and the apostles continued to demonstrate that authority after Pentecost (e.g., Acts 13:6–12; 16:16–18). Other early evangelists, like Philip and Stephen, were also given this Spirit-endowed ability to authenticate their message (Acts 6:8; 8:7).

Again, this miraculous power was a sign that validated the preaching of the gospel during the apostolic age only. The New Testament even sternly warns those who might pretend to have such authority (cf. Acts 19:14–16; Jude 8–10). Thus, this power is clearly not an ability given to believers in the church since the days of the apostles.

GIFTS OF HEALING

If the working of miracles relates to divinely granted authority over demons, the term "gifts of healing" (1 Cor. 12:9, 28) refers to supernatural power over disease. Miraculous healing was displayed in the ministries of Christ (Matt. 8:16–17), the apostles (Matt. 10:1), the seventy-two (Luke 10:1, 9), and some apostolic associates (Acts 8:5–7). The New Testament record of the healings performed by these individuals demonstrates that they were immediate, undeniable, and always complete (cf. Matt. 8:2–3; 9:1–8; 20:29–34; 21:14; Mark 1:42; 8:22–26; 10:52; Luke 17:11–21; John 5:1–9; Acts 3:8; 14:8–18). A comparison with the supposed healings performed by modern "faith healers" reveals that the contemporary counterfeit cannot measure up to the biblical reality.[36] Jesus and the apostles, for the duration of their ministries, banished sickness and disease from the locations in which they preached, an accomplishment no modern "healer" could ever claim.

Miraculous healings served to authenticate God's messenger (cf. John 10:38; Acts 2:22; Rom. 15:18–19; 2 Cor. 12:12; Heb. 2:3–4), not merely to restore the sick to physical health. That explains why Paul did not heal himself (cf. Gal. 4:13) or some of his closest friends (Phil. 2:27; 1 Tim. 5:23; 2 Tim. 4:20). When Paul healed the lame man in Lystra (Acts 14:9–10) or when Peter raised Tabitha from the dead (Acts 9:41), it was so that people would hear and believe the gospel (cf. Acts 9:42).

As one of the extraordinary apostolic gifts, miraculous healing ceased when the apostolic age came to an end. Though believers no longer possess such supernatural abilities, they do have the right to ask God to heal them, knowing that he hears and answers the prayers of his people (James 5:13–16; cf. Luke 18:1–6; 1 John 5:14–15). In response to their prayers, the Lord may choose to heal an illness providentially, though he is not obligated to do so.

Believers can and should rejoice when God heals someone in response to answered prayer. However, it is important to note that such answers to prayer are not the same as the gifts of healing exemplified in the New Testament ministries of Christ and the

---

36. For more on this point, see MacArthur, *Strange Fire*, 155–76. See also Richard Mayhue, *The Healing Promise: Is It Always God's Will to Heal?* (Fearn, Ross-Shire, Scotland: Mentor, 1997).

apostles. That no one today possesses such a gift is evident from the fact that no one can heal like Jesus and the apostles did—being able to immediately and permanently restore the sick and injured to full health with nothing but a word or a touch.

SPEAKING IN AND INTERPRETING TONGUES[37]

The Greek word for "tongues" (*glōssa*) is best translated "languages." The exercise of this gift is most clearly seen on the day of Pentecost, described by Luke in Acts 2:4–11. There the apostles, along with some of the 120 who were gathered in the upper room (Acts 1:15), began speaking fluently in foreign languages and dialects that they did not know.

This sign to the unbelieving Jewish crowds at Pentecost (cf. 1 Cor. 14:22) not only caught the people's attention (Acts 2:12) but also illustrated the reality that the gospel was to be preached throughout the entire world (cf. Acts 1:8). Accordingly, the gift of tongues consisted of the supernatural ability for someone to speak fluently in a foreign language that person had never before studied or spoken. It was obviously a supernatural gift, especially useful in the cause of evangelism, as unbelievers heard God being praised in their own language (Acts 2:8). When used in the church, the foreign language required translation so that those in the congregation who did not know that language could be edified (1 Cor. 14:5–17, 27–28). Though many today claim to speak in tongues, it is clear that no one today possesses an ability like that demonstrated by the apostles on the day of Pentecost.

Some recent commentators have attempted to distance the gift of languages depicted in Acts 2 (which clearly consisted of actual foreign languages) from the gift of languages described in 1 Corinthians 12–14, in an effort to make room for the unintelligible utterances that characterize modern *glossolalia* (or tongues speech). However, the exegetical evidence indicates that the tongues speech depicted in 1 Corinthians consisted of the same basic phenomenon as that found in Acts 2. In both places, the genuine gift of tongues resulted in the supernatural ability to speak human foreign languages.[38] As MacArthur notes,

> In defending nonsensical speech, most charismatics retreat to the book of 1 Corinthians—contending that the gift [of tongues] described in 1 Corinthians 12–14 is categorically different from that of Acts. But once again, this assertion is not permitted by the text. A simple word study effectively makes that point, since both passages utilize the same terminology to describe the miraculous gift. In Acts, Luke uses *laleo* ("to speak") in combination with *glōssa* ("tongues") four different times (Acts 2:4, 11; 10:46; 19:6). In 1 Corinthians 12–14, Paul uses forms of that same combination thirteen times (1 Cor. 12:30; 13:1; 14:2, 4, 5 [2x], 6, 13, 18, 19, 21, 27, 39).

---

37. This section is adapted from Nathan A. Busenitz, "Are Tongues Real Foreign Languages? A Response to Four Continuationist Arguments," *MSJ* 25, no. 2 (2014): 63–84. Used by permission of *MSJ*.

38. It should be noted that Paul's mention of the "tongues of angels" in 1 Cor. 13:1 is a hyperbolic expression, made clear by the other extreme examples he uses in verses 2–3. The apostle's point is that if someone were to speak in human foreign languages (the "tongues of men") or even in the languages of angels (a hypothetical scenario designed to make a rhetorical point), it would still be meaningless if love were absent.

These linguistic parallels carry added significance when we consider that Luke was Paul's traveling companion and close associate, even writing under Paul's apostolic authority. Because he penned the book of Acts around AD 60, roughly five years *after* Paul wrote his first epistle to the Corinthians, Luke would have been well aware of their confusion regarding the gift of languages. Certainly, Luke would not have wanted to add to that confusion. Thus, he would not have used the exact same terminology in Acts as Paul did in 1 Corinthians unless what had happened at Pentecost was identical to the authentic gift Paul described in his epistle.

The fact that Paul noted "various kinds of tongues" in 1 Corinthians 12:10 does not imply that some are real languages and others are merely gibberish. Rather, the Greek word for "kinds" is *genos*, from which we derive the word "genus." *Genos* refers to a family, group, race, or nation. Linguists often refer to language "families" or "groups," and that is precisely Paul's point: there are various families of languages in the world, and this gift enabled some believers to speak in a variety of them. In Acts 2, Luke emphasized that same idea in verses 9–11, where he explained that the languages that were spoken came from at least sixteen different regions.

Of course, other parallels between Acts and 1 Corinthians 12–14 can also be established. In both places, the Source of the gift is the same—the Holy Spirit (Acts 2:4, 18; 10:44–46; 19:6; 1 Cor. 12:1, 7, 11, et al.). In both places, the reception of the gift is not limited to the apostles, but also involved lay people in the church (cf. Acts 1:15; 10:46; 19:6; 1 Cor. 12:30; 14:18). In both places, the gift is described as a speaking gift (Acts 2:4, 9–11; 1 Cor. 12:30; 14:2, 5). In both places, the resulting message can be translated and thereby understood, either by those who already know the language (as on the day of Pentecost—Acts 2:9–11) or by someone gifted with the ability to translate (1 Cor. 12:10; 14:5, 13).

In both places, the gift served as a miraculous sign for unbelieving Jews (Acts 2:5, 12, 14, 19; 1 Cor. 14:21–22; cf. Isa. 28:11–12). In both places, the gift of languages was closely associated with the gift of prophecy (Acts 2:16–18; 19:6; 1 Cor. 14). And in both places, unbelievers who did not understand what was being spoken responded with mockery and derision (Acts 2:13; 1 Cor. 14:23). Given so many parallels, it is exegetically impossible to claim that the phenomenon described in 1 Corinthians was inherently different from that of Acts 2. Since the gift of tongues consisted of authentic foreign languages on the Day of Pentecost, then the same was true for the believers in Corinth.[39]

Because of its dramatic nature, along with the fact that it was the gift first exercised by the apostles on the day of Pentecost, the Corinthians prized this gift above all others. But as Paul points out in 1 Corinthians 14:6–19, an untranslated message spoken in a foreign language does not edify the other members of the congregation because they do not understand what is being said.

That is why the person speaking in a foreign language had to have his message interpreted (translated)—so that the hearers could be edified. The gift of interpreting tongues, then, was the ability to translate a message spoken in a foreign language into the language of the audience, so they could understand and be edified. All spiritual

---

39. MacArthur, *Strange Fire*, 140–41. Note the entire discussion regarding the gift of tongues from 133–54.

gifts are to be exercised out of love and for the purpose of mutual edification, so such an interpretation was required (1 Cor. 14:26–27). If there was no interpreter, the speaker was instructed to keep his message to himself (1 Cor. 14:28).

PROPHECY AND PREACHING

In both 1 Corinthians 12:28 and Ephesians 4:11, Paul lists "prophets" immediately after "apostles." Like apostleship, prophecy encompassed both an office and a gift. Because they were given divine revelation, the New Testament prophets assisted the apostles in laying the doctrinal foundation of the church (Eph. 2:20).

As with prophets in the Old Testament, New Testament prophets were held to the highest standards of revelatory accuracy (cf. Deut. 18:20–22; Ezek. 13:3–9), doctrinal purity (cf. Deut. 13:1–5; 2 Pet. 2:1), and moral integrity (cf. Jer. 23:14–16; 2 Pet. 2:2–3).[40] This was especially important because of the continual threat that false prophets posed to the early church (cf. Matt. 7:15; 24:11; 2 Tim. 4:3–4; 2 Pet. 2:1–3; 1 John 4:1; Jude 4), which explains why prophecies needed to be tested for doctrinal orthodoxy (cf. 1 Cor. 14:29; 1 Thess. 5:20–22; 1 John 4:1–6). According to Romans 12:6, the content of prophecy was to be measured against "our faith" (or literally, "the faith"), meaning that it was to be evaluated against the body of Christian truth that God the Holy Spirit had previously revealed (cf. 1 Tim. 3:9; 4:1, 6; Jude 3, 20).

On the one hand, the gift of prophecy involved the reception and declaration of new revelation from God (cf. Acts 11:27–28; 1 Tim. 4:14; 2 Pet. 1:21), which was sometimes predictive in nature (cf. Acts 11:27–28; 21:10–11). On the other hand, this gift also included publicly proclaiming and reiterating that which had previously been revealed—a role implied by the connection of prophets with teachers in Acts 13:1 (cf. Acts 15:32). Thus, the gift of prophecy was exercised through the proclamation of divinely revealed truth, whether new or old (cf. Rom. 12:6). Such is conveyed by the Greek verb *prophēteuō* ("to prophesy"), which literally means "to proclaim" or "to speak forth." Those who prophesied or preached on God's behalf declared the truth of his Word, speaking "to people for their upbuilding and encouragement and consolation" (1 Cor. 14:3). Like all other gifts, prophecy was to be exercised in love (cf. Eph. 4:15).

Though the Corinthians elevated the gift of languages above the gift of prophecy, Paul explains that prophecy is actually superior because it does not require translation in order to expose people to God's truth (1 Cor. 14:1–5). As with apostleship, the office of prophet passed off the scene shortly after the canon of the New Testament was complete (cf. Rev. 22:18–19) and the doctrinal foundation of the church was established (Eph. 2:20). Old Testament prophets disappeared after the Old Testament

---

40. Regarding New Testament prophets, it is important to recognize that "the New Testament uses identical terminology to describe both Old and New Testament prophets. In the book of Acts, Old Testament prophets are mentioned in Acts 2:16; 3:24–25; 10:43; 13:27, 40; 15:15; 24:14; 26:22, 27; and 28:23. References to New Testament prophets are interspersed using the same vocabulary without any distinction, comment, or caveat (cf. Acts 2:17–18; 7:37; 11:27–28; 13:1; 15:32; 21:9–11)." MacArthur, *Strange Fire*, 119.

canon was completed; so also New Testament prophets were no longer needed after the New Testament was finished.

However, there is a sense in which prophecy has continued in church history through the preaching of Scripture, the prophetic Word (Rom. 12:6; 2 Pet. 1:19). Ever since the closing of the canon, God has ceased his revelatory work in the church. Nonetheless, those who faithfully proclaim the truth of God's Word fulfill a role that exhibits a prophetic character. As Paul reminded Timothy,

> All Scripture is breathed out by God and profitable for teaching, for reproof, for correction, and for training in righteousness, that the man of God may be complete, equipped for every good work.
>
> I charge you in the presence of God and of Christ Jesus, who is to judge the living and the dead, and by his appearing and his kingdom: preach the word; be ready in season and out of season; reprove, rebuke, and exhort, with complete patience and teaching. (2 Tim. 3:16–4:2)

WORDS OF WISDOM AND KNOWLEDGE

Only a little detail is given about the "utterance of wisdom" and the "utterance of knowledge" (1 Cor. 12:8), but clearly they involved an individual receiving and declaring revelation from God. It seems that those who were given a "word of wisdom" were able to rightly understand divinely revealed truth and articulate the proper application of it for everyday life (cf. Matt. 13:54; Mark 6:2; Acts 6:10; James 1:5; 3:17; 2 Pet. 3:15). Those who communicated a "word of knowledge" provided insight into the profound truths of God's Word (cf. Eph. 3:3; Col. 1:26; 2:2).

In 1 Corinthians 13:2, the apostle seems to reference these gifts when he writes, "If I . . . understand all mysteries and all knowledge. . . ." Accordingly, those gifted with knowledge and wisdom had the ability to grasp the mysteries of divine revelation while also understanding how to apply such truth at a practical level. Knowledge centered on comprehending the truth, while wisdom explained how to act on it.

Any revelatory aspect associated with these gifts ceased with the completion of the New Testament canon and the end of the apostolic age. Nonetheless, God still gives some of his children a heightened ability to understand and articulate the truth of his Word. Those who have this gift today are specially equipped to uncover the truths of Scripture so as to help others understand and apply them.

DISTINGUISHING BETWEEN SPIRITS

With this gift, God divinely enables someone to discern true from false statements made by people deceptively claiming that their words were prophetic revelations from God (1 Cor. 12:10). The exercise of this gift is illustrated by both Peter, when he recognized the spiritual duplicity of Ananias (Acts 5:3), and Paul, who perceived that a slave girl was possessed by an evil spirit (Acts 16:16–18). This represents the temporary, miraculous aspect of the gift. Since the completion of the New Testament canon, the operation of this gift has primarily involved the ability to identify false-hood by comparing it to biblical truth (cf. Acts 17:11; 1 Thess. 5:20–22).

TEACHING

Another group that Paul identifies in 1 Corinthians 12:28 is that of "teachers" (cf. Rom. 12:7; Eph. 4:11). Like apostleship and prophecy, teaching can refer to both an office and a gift. The gift of teaching involves the Spirit-endowed ability to interpret and articulate the truth of God's Word clearly and accurately so that others can understand and learn (cf. Acts 18:24–25; 2 Tim. 2:2). Although this gift is a neces-sary qualification for elders (1 Tim. 3:2; Titus 1:9; cf. 1 Tim. 4:16), it is not reserved exclusively for pastors.

The apostolic church was characterized by the regular teaching of God's Word (Acts 2:42; 15:35; 18:24–25; 2 Tim. 1:11). Such should characterize every church, since teaching is a necessary part of disciple making. As Jesus instructed his follow-ers, "Go therefore and make disciples of all nations, . . . teaching them to observe all that I have commanded you" (Matt. 28:19–20). Recognizing the vital importance of this spiritual work, Paul charged Timothy with these words: "What you have heard from me in the presence of many witnesses entrust to faithful men who will be able to teach others also" (2 Tim. 2:2). Faithful church leaders are those who rightly di-vide the Word of God (2 Tim. 2:15) and impart its truth to the congregation. Many lay people are also given this enablement to place sound instruction throughout the fellowship of the church.

EXHORTATION

The Greek words *parakaleō* ("exhorts") and *paraklēsis* ("exhortation") in Romans 12:8 are both compounds of *para* ("alongside") and *kaleō* ("to call"). These same words are joined together to constitute the title *paraklētos* ("paraclete," "advocate," "comforter," "helper"), used in reference to both the Lord Jesus (1 John 2:1) and the Holy Spirit (John 14:16, 26; 15:26; 16:7). The gift of exhortation, then, involves coming alongside fellow believers to help and encourage them in the way of godliness (cf. Heb. 10:24–25). Depending on the situation, it may manifest itself by admonish-ing those caught in sin, correcting those tempted by error, comforting the hurting, or strengthening the weak. Exhortation is needed in a variety of ministry contexts and may look different in each. As Paul told the Thessalonians, "We urge you, brothers, admonish the idle, encourage the fainthearted, help the weak, be patient with them all" (1 Thess. 5:14; cf. 2 Cor. 1:3–5; 2 Tim. 3:16–17; 4:2).

Paul and Barnabas exemplified the ministry of exhortation on their first mis-sionary journey. After preaching the gospel in the cities of southern Galatia, "they returned to Lystra and to Iconium and to Antioch, strengthening the souls of the disciples, encouraging them to continue in the faith, and saying that through many tribulations we must enter the kingdom of God" (Acts 14:21–22). Those with the gift of exhortation ought to make sure they exhort in love (Eph. 4:15). They also ought to encourage from the Scriptures, recognizing that God's Word is "profitable for teaching, for reproof, for correction, and for training in righteousness" (2 Tim. 3:16). Whereas preaching declares the truth of God's Word and teaching explains it, exhortation calls fellow Christians to be doers of the Word and not just hearers (James 1:22).

SERVICE AND HELPING

The gift of "service" (Rom. 12:7) and the gift of "helping" (1 Cor. 12:28) are virtually synonymous. "Service" is derived from the same Greek word translated "deacon" (*diakonia*). It is a broad term that can refer to any kind of practical assistance or help (cf. Acts 20:35). "Helping" (from Gk. *antilēmpsis*) is a similarly broad term, referring to any kind of service or assistance rendered on behalf of others. Often these acts of service involve completing mundane and unglamorous tasks. Yet they are essential to the life and ongoing effectiveness of the church. By gladly performing such tasks, those helpers gifted in areas of service free up those gifted in other areas to do what the Spirit has specially equipped them to do. This principle is illustrated by the seven men chosen to administrate food for the widows so that the apostles could focus on prayer and the ministry of the Word (Acts 6:3–4).

In his letter to the Philippians, Paul describes Epaphroditus as his "fellow worker and fellow soldier, and your messenger and minister to my need, . . . [who] nearly died for the work of Christ, risking his life to complete what was lacking in your service to me" (Phil. 2:25–30). Clearly, part of Epaphroditus's spiritual gifting included a supernatural desire and ability to help and to serve. His faithfulness to the Lord expressed itself in sacrificial service to Paul. Though not featured publicly, those who selflessly serve in the church, behind the scenes, will one day be rewarded openly by the Lord (cf. Col. 3:22–24).

LEADING AND ADMINISTRATING

Those with the gift of leading (Rom. 12:8) or "administrating" (1 Cor. 12:28) are responsible to guide the congregation, both spiritually and in everyday decision making. The phrase "the one who leads" translates the participial form of the Greek term *proistēmi* ("to stand before"). It is used in the New Testament to describe headship in both the home (1 Tim. 3:4–5, 12) and the church (1 Tim. 5:17). "Administrating" is from the Greek word *kybernēsis*, meaning "to guide." Acts 27:11 and Revelation 18:17 use that same term to refer to a pilot who steers a ship. Such illustrates the way in which gifted leaders help others navigate through life and ministry by guiding them with wisdom and good counsel (cf. Prov. 12:5; Ezek. 27:8, where the same Greek term is used in the Septuagint). Though this gift is not limited to a particular office, the gift of leadership in the church clearly belongs to the pastors and elders whom God has ordained to shepherd the flock. They feed and lead the flock of God.

Romans 12:8 indicates that those with this enablement ought to lead with "zeal." That term (from Gk. *spoudē*) can also be translated "diligence." Rather than exhibiting laziness or apathy, effective spiritual leadership is characterized by earnestness and eagerness. At the same time, spiritual leadership should also be marked by humility and selflessness (cf. Mark 10:42–45). The apostle Peter emphasized that truth when he charged his fellow elders,

> Shepherd the flock of God that is among you, exercising oversight, not under compulsion, but willingly, as God would have you; not for shameful gain, but eagerly; not domineering over those in your charge, but being examples to the flock. And when the chief Shepherd appears, you will receive the unfading crown of glory. (1 Pet. 5:2–4)

GIVING

In Romans 12:8, Paul describes the gift of giving with these words: "the one who contributes, in generosity." The Greek word translated "contributes" is a form of the verb *metadidōmi*, which could also be rendered "gives" or "shares." It speaks of sacrificial generosity in giving for the sake of meeting another's needs (cf. 2 Cor. 8:2–5). Although every believer is called to share and to give (Eph. 4:28; cf. Luke 3:11), those with the gift of giving are particularly equipped with the strong desire and eagerness to contribute sacrificially to others. Consequently, they experience the full measure of knowing that "God loves a cheerful giver" (2 Cor. 9:7).

The term "generosity" comes from the Greek word *haplotēs* and speaks of a sincere liberality. Such giving is fueled not by an ulterior motive but out of genuine love for others and, ultimately, the Lord. It is not hypocritical, like the pompous generosity of the Pharisees (Matt. 6:2) or the deceitful scheming of Ananias and Sapphira (Acts 5:1–11). A genuine desire to give and to share was a hallmark of the early church (Acts 2:44–45). That attitude still characterizes those with this gift.

SHOWING MERCY

The list of gifts in Romans 12 concludes with these words: "the one who does acts of mercy, with cheerfulness" (12:8). The Greek verb *eleeō* ("does acts of mercy") conveys both an attitude of sympathy toward those who are hurting and an ability to comfort and encourage them effectively. Those gifted with mercy are supernaturally sensitive to sorrow and suffering and are specially equipped by the Holy Spirit to comfort and console the downcast. The gift of mercy goes beyond simply feeling sorry for people; it springs into action by finding ways to lift up others. Such giftedness often manifests itself through acts of kindness to the homeless, the elderly, the sick, the handicapped, the suffering, and the sorrowing.

Those who exercise this gift do not consider it a drudgery or a mere duty. Rather, it is their great delight, as they reach out with cheerfulness in the name of the God of mercy and grace (cf. 1 Pet. 5:10). The Lord Jesus consistently exhibited this quality during his earthly ministry, graciously responding with compassion toward the suffering and needy people who came to him (cf. Luke 4:18–19). Those who show mercy and kindness to others follow in the footsteps of his supreme example.

FAITH

The gift of faith, delineated by Paul in 1 Corinthians 12:9, refers to an extraordinary ability to trust God in the face of difficulty and hardship. The "faith" of which Paul speaks is not saving faith but rather unwavering confidence in the power and promises of God. Those with the gift of faith are characterized by persistent prayer, confident in knowing that God hears the pleas of his people (cf. James 5:16–18). They resonate with the truth of Jesus's words, "For truly, I say to you, if you have faith like a grain of mustard seed, you will say to this mountain, 'Move from here to there,' and it will move, and nothing will be impossible for you" (Matt. 17:20; cf. 1 Cor. 13:2).

The entire congregation is strengthened when those with this gift exercise faith in the midst of trials and tribulations. This quality of unwavering confidence in God's promises marked the Old Testament saints listed in Hebrews 11. Through their example of faith, setting their eyes on Christ, they have provided "so great a cloud of witnesses" for later generations of believers to follow (Heb. 12:1–2). Similarly, throughout church history, countless believers with this gift have responded to difficulties, dangers, and even death with unflinching resolve and trust in God. From humble laymen and laywomen who were strong in faith to dedicated missionaries and noble martyrs, the testimonies of the faithful have continued to embolden subsequent generations of Christians throughout the centuries.

SPIRITUAL DISCERNMENT

The "ability to distinguish between spirits" (1 Cor. 12:10) refers to the permanent gift of spiritual discernment—the Spirit-empowered capacity to identify forms of doctrinal error and religious deception. As "the father of lies" (John 8:44), Satan continually seeks to counterfeit the true work of God by disguising himself as "an angel of light" (2 Cor. 11:14). He does this primarily through false teachers, who dispense the "teachings of demons" (1 Tim. 4:1). That is why the apostle John warned his readers, "Beloved, do not believe every spirit, but test the spirits to see whether they are from God, for many false prophets have gone out into the world" (1 John 4:1).

EVANGELISM

The office or gift of evangelist, referenced third in Ephesians 4:11, involves the divine enablement to explain, exhort, and apply the gospel to non-Christians. Paul employed the Greek verb *euangelizō* ("to preach the gospel") twenty-one times in his letters. He urged Timothy to "do the work of an evangelist" (2 Tim. 4:5) both in general and at Ephesus in particular (cf. Philip of Caesarea in Acts 21:8). Thus, the evangelist appears to be primarily a church planter whose duty it is to establish new churches through gospel preaching. Once a congregation is birthed, the church would then be led by a shepherd-teacher, while the evangelist would move on to a new work in a fresh location.

SHEPHERDING AND TEACHING

This office or gift, referenced fourth in Ephesians 4:11, involves the divine enablement to pastor by leading, feeding, protecting, and otherwise caring for believers in local churches. For example, the content of Paul's letter to Titus describes the kind of instructions one would expect him to receive in order to be a fruitful shepherd-teacher. Since Titus is the only Pauline epistle that does not contain the Greek verb *euangelizō* or its cognate noun *euangelion* ("gospel"), one can assume that the letter's content refers to the work of growing and maturing a local church after it has first been well established by an evangelist.

Using Gifts

A survey of the spiritual gifts listed throughout the New Testament highlights the diversity of Spirit-endowed abilities that God has given to believers in order to build up one another in the body of Christ (cf. 1 Cor. 12:4–29). While believers ought to consider the ways in which God has gifted them for service, they should focus not ultimately on their gifts but on the Giver. As they edify other believers by exercising their giftedness, they simultaneously bring honor to the Lord of the church. In this way, they become living sacrifices of worship that are holy and acceptable to God (Rom. 12:1). To reiterate the words of Peter,

> As each has received a gift, use it to serve one another, as good stewards of God's varied grace: whoever speaks, as one who speaks oracles of God; whoever serves, as one who serves by the strength that God supplies—in order that in everything God may be glorified through Jesus Christ. To him belong glory and dominion forever and ever. Amen. (1 Pet. 4:10–11)

In summary, it seems that the categories of nonmiraculous ministering gifts are very general and broad. The New Testament does not define them in any narrow sense, leading to the understanding that the Holy Spirit applies these abilities in a unique way in the life of every believer.

Since Peter says that each believer has received "a gift," it is fair to surmise that the gift each one receives is a combination or blending of the abilities and enablements needed to serve the body of Christ effectively. This giftedness is specially designed by God to equip each believer for ministry in the church. Like a skilled painter using a palette of colors, the Holy Spirit uniquely blends these gifts in each believer. For this reason, it is unhelpful to overdefine one's giftedness. What is useful is to serve with an open heart and an open hand, rejoicing in all the ways the Lord uses believers to make his image glorious in the church.

A Foretaste of Heaven

In concluding a discussion on the church, it is fitting to remember that the church provides believers with a foretaste of heaven. Though imperfect, the church represents the one place where the activities of heaven are reflected on earth.

The church resembles heaven in a number of important ways. In the church, God's people desire to submit to his moral will as expressed in his Word (Matt. 6:10). They seek to obey him out of their love and devotion to him (John 14:15; 1 John 2:3). In heaven, believers will serve him perfectly (Rev. 22:3–5), and that future hope motivates their pursuit of holiness in this life (1 John 3:2–3).

In the church, believers offer continual adoration to God as a sacrifice of praise (Heb. 13:15). Such expressions of worship characterize the life of heaven. The apostle John provides a glimpse of heaven's perpetual worship in Revelation 4:8–11:

> And the four living creatures, each of them with six wings, are full of eyes all around and within, and day and night they never cease to say,
>
> > "Holy, holy, holy, is the Lord God Almighty,
> > who was and is and is to come!"
>
> And whenever the living creatures give glory and honor and thanks to him who is seated on the throne, who lives forever and ever, the twenty-four elders fall down before him who is seated on the throne and worship him who lives forever and ever. They cast their crowns before the throne, saying,
>
> > "Worthy are you, our Lord and God,
> > to receive glory and honor and power,
> > for you created all things,
> > and by your will they existed and were created."

For all eternity, believers will exalt the Lord Jesus for his work of redemption (Rev. 5:11–14; cf. Phil. 2:9–11). The worship that echoes through the halls of Christ-exalting churches here on earth will continue to reverberate without end throughout the halls of heaven.

In the church, though its members are not yet perfected, one begins to glimpse the holiness and purity that characterizes heaven. The absolute holiness of heaven is underscored in Revelation 21:8 and 22:14–15, which explain that the eternal glory of the new earth will be free from immorality, idolatry, and any form of impurity. The church reflects this holiness when its members walk in righteousness (Eph. 4:1; Phil. 1:27; Col. 1:10; 1 Pet. 1:16; cf. Ps. 15:2) and when they are faithful to discipline those who persist in unrepentant sin (Matt. 18:15–20; 1 Cor. 5:13).

In the church, God's people also enjoy rich fellowship with one another. That fellowship is a foretaste of the perfect communion they will one day share with all the saints and with their Savior, the Lord Jesus (cf. 1 John 1:3; 3:2). When believers gather in the church, they are reminded that they are citizens of heaven (Phil. 3:20–21) and that this world is not their home (cf. 1 John 2:15–17). They are part of the fellowship of the saints, belonging to "the assembly of the firstborn who are enrolled in heaven" (Heb. 12:23).

Submission to God's will, Christ-centered worship, the pursuit of holiness, and fellowship with other believers—these are just some of the ways that the church on earth foreshadows the glories of heaven. Such anticipations should cause believers to grow both in their love for the church and in their longing for heaven. As the apostle Paul explained to the Corinthians, "For now we see in a mirror dimly, but then face to face. Now I know in part; then I shall know fully, even as I have been fully known" (1 Cor. 13:12). In light of that kind of heavenly perspective, what a joy it is for believers to be part of the company of the redeemed, eagerly "waiting for our blessed hope, the appearing of the glory of our great God and Savior Jesus Christ, who gave himself for us to redeem us from all lawlessness and to purify for himself a people for his own possession who are zealous for good works" (Titus 2:13–14).

Prayer[41]

Our Father, thank You that You have
    designed a plan of redemption
    that rescues the unworthy and the guilty from their plight
        and places them into Your kingdom.
That kingdom exists not only as a heavenly, eternal realm;
    it also has a vital presence now on this earth.
We rejoice that You design to build Your kingdom
    through Your Body, the church,
        every member having an important part to play.

Thinking of the apostle Paul, we recognize the unique gifts and abilities
    he was given to advance Your kingdom,
        yet we are greatly encouraged to realize
            that the Holy Scriptures honor by name
                those who helped him.
You surrounded Paul with people we would not know
    had he not named those who prayed for him,
    encouraged him, and assisted him in Your great work.

Thank You, Lord, for such an example
    of the Body of Christ working together.
We are reminded that You not only save sinners;
    You also bring them together in one Body
        under the power of Your Spirit
            to accomplish Your glorious purposes.
Your grace is abundant in every way.
We bless You for the gospel and all that it brings:
    salvation,
    liberation,
    healing,

----

41. This prayer is reproduced verbatim from John MacArthur, *At the Throne of Grace: A Book of Prayers* (Eugene, OR: Harvest House, 2011), 226–28. Used by permission of Harvest House.

wholeness,
   and hope.
Thank You that You enjoy us and blend us together
   in this wonderful entity called the Body of Christ.

We confess there are times
   when we are not useful as we should be—
   and sometimes we are even a hindrance to Your work.
We grieve the Holy Spirit. We seek the pleasures of the world.
We live without heed to our duties. We trifle with things that are evil.

We confess, moreover, that we are at times
   unloving, uncaring, proud, selfish, impatient, too earthly minded,
   and too apathetic about the things that really matter.
How desperately we need to come before You
   to be washed and forgiven all such things.
May we mortify our sins at their first appearance
   and never let them linger!
Our heartfelt desire is to manifest Christ in His great glory.
We are the Body of which He is Head.
May we honor Him accordingly in everything we do and teach.

In all the ways we have offended You, Lord,
   we humbly ask for Your pardon.
How grateful we are that You are willing to forgive repentant sinners
   and restore us for useful service!
Our earnest desire is to be suitable instruments in Your hands.
May we be faithful in Your service.
Enlarge our capacity for gospel work,
   and intensify the reflection of Your glory on our faces.

You, Lord, are everything we need;
   may we desire nothing more.
You are our stronghold and our Deliverer.
You are our strength and our hope.
You are our Guide and our Keeper.
You are the one true God, and the Rock of our salvation.
All Your grace abounds to us;
   we always have full sufficiency in everything.
Indeed, we have an abundance for every good deed.
May we not squander such exquisite blessings.

Cleanse us, so that we might more clearly reflect
   the glory of Christ.
Help us, even now, to give more perfect expression
   to the praise that will occupy our hearts throughout all eternity.
As always, we bring all these petitions in His blessed name.
May they be heard and answered
   as they are consistent with Your will. Amen.

"Stand Up, Stand Up for Jesus"

Stand up, stand up for Jesus, ye soldiers of the cross;
Lift high His royal banner, it must not suffer loss.
From vict'ry unto vict'ry, His army shall He lead,
Till every foe is vanquished and Christ is Lord indeed.

Stand up, stand up for Jesus, the trumpet call obey;
Forth to the mighty conflict, in this His glorious day.
Ye that are men, now serve Him against unnumbered foes;
Let courage rise with danger and strength to strength oppose.

Stand up, stand up for Jesus, stand in His strength alone;
The arm of flesh will fail you, ye dare not trust your own.
Put on the gospel armor, each piece put on with prayer;
Where duty calls, or danger, be never wanting there.

Stand up, stand up for Jesus, the strife will not be long;
This day the noise of battle, the next the victor's song;
To him who overcometh a crown of life shall be;
He, with the King of glory, shall reign eternally.

~George Duffield Jr. (1818–1888)

Bibliography

Primary Systematic Theologies

Bancroft, Emery H. *Christian Theology: Systematic and Biblical.* 2nd ed. Grand Rapids, MI: Zondervan, 1976. 281–306.

Berkhof, Louis. *Systematic Theology.* 4th ed. Grand Rapids, MI: Eerdmans, 1939. 555–658.

Buswell, James Oliver, Jr. *A Systematic Theology of the Christian Religion.* 2 vols. Grand Rapids, MI: Zondervan, 1962–1963. 2:216–80.

Culver, Robert Duncan. *Systematic Theology: Biblical and Historical.* Fearn, Ross-shire, Scotland: Mentor, 2005. 799–1006.

Dabney, Robert Lewis. *Systematic Theology.* 1871. Reprint, Edinburgh: Banner of Truth, 1985. 758–817.

Erickson, Millard J. *Christian Theology.* Grand Rapids, MI: Baker, 1986. 1025–146.

Grudem, Wayne. *Systematic Theology: An Introduction to Biblical Doctrine.* Grand Rapids, MI: Zondervan, 1994. 853–1088.

Hodge, Charles. *Systematic Theology.* 3 vols. 1871–1873. Reprint, Grand Rapids, MI: Eerdmans, 1975. 3:466–709.

Lewis, Gordon R., and Bruce A. Demarest. *Integrative Theology.* 3 vols. Grand Rapids, MI: Zondervan, 1987–1994. 3:241–363.

Reymond, Robert L. *A New Systematic Theology of the Christian Faith.* Nashville: Thomas Nelson, 1998. 805–976.

Strong, August Hopkins. *Systematic Theology: A Compendium Designed for the Use of Theological Students*. Rev. ed. New York: Revell, 1907. 887–980.

*Swindoll, Charles R., and Roy B. Zuck, eds. *Understanding Christian Theology*. Nashville: Thomas Nelson, 2003. 1077–242.

*Thiessen, Henry Clarence. *Introductory Lectures in Systematic Theology*. Grand Rapids, MI: Eerdmans, 1949. 403–37.

Turretin, Francis. *Institutes of Elenctic Theology*. 3 vols. Edited by James T. Dennison Jr. Translated by George Musgrove Giger. 1679–1685. Reprint, Phillipsburg, NJ: P&R, 1992–1997. 3:1–560.

*Denotes most helpful.

Specific Works

Adams, Jay. *Handbook of Church Discipline: A Right and Privilege of Every Church Member*. Grand Rapids, MI: Zondervan, 1984.

Amandus, Dave, ed. *Fundamentals of the Faith: 13 Lessons to Grow in the Grace and Knowledge of Jesus Christ*. Chicago: Moody Publishers, 2009.

Dever, Mark. *The Church: The Gospel Made Visible*. Nashville: B&H Academic, 2012.

———. *Nine Marks of a Healthy Church*. 3rd ed. Wheaton, IL: Crossway, 2013.

Dever, Mark, and Paul Alexander. *The Deliberate Church: Building Your Ministry on the Gospel*. Wheaton, IL: Crossway, 2005.

DeYoung, Kevin, and Ted Kluck. *Why We Love the Church: In Praise of Institutions and Organized Religion*. Chicago: Moody Publishers, 2009.

Duncan, Ligon, and Susan Hunt. *Women's Ministry in the Local Church*. Wheaton, IL: Crossway, 2006.

Edgar, Thomas R. *Satisfied by the Promise of the Spirit: Affirming the Fullness of God's Provision for Spiritual Living*. Grand Rapids, MI: Kregel, 1996.

Gilley, Gary E. *This Little Church Went to Market: Is the Modern Church Reaching Out or Selling Out?* Rev. ed. Darlington, UK: Evangelical Press, 2005.

Gordon, T. David. *Why Johnny Can't Preach: The Media Have Shaped the Messengers*. Phillipsburg, NJ: P&R, 2009.

Grudem, Wayne, and Dennis Rainey, eds. *Pastoral Leadership for Manhood and Womanhood*. Foundations for the Family. Wheaton, IL: Crossway, 2003.

Hughes, R. Kent, and Douglas Sean O'Donnell. *The Pastor's Book: A Comprehensive and Practical Guide to Pastoral Ministry*. Wheaton, IL: Crossway, 2015.

*Jefferson, Charles. *The Minister as Shepherd: The Privileges and Responsibilities of Pastoral Leadership*. 1912. Reprint, Charleston, SC: BiblioLife, 2006.

Lawson, Steven J. *Famine in the Land: A Passionate Call for Expository Preaching*. Chicago: Moody Publishers, 2003.

———. *The Kind of Preaching God Blesses*. Eugene, OR: Harvest House, 2013.

Leeman, Jonathan. *Church Discipline: How the Church Protects the Name of Jesus*. 9Marks: Building Healthy Churches. Wheaton, IL: Crossway, 2012.

———. *Church Membership: How the World Knows Who Represents Jesus*. 9Marks: Building Healthy Churches. Wheaton, IL: Crossway, 2012.

Lloyd-Jones, D. Martyn. *Preaching and Preachers*. Edited by Kevin DeYoung. 40th anniversary ed. Grand Rapids, MI: Zondervan, 2012.

MacArthur, John. *1 Timothy*. MacArthur New Testament Commentary. Chicago: Moody Publishers, 1995.

———. *2 Timothy*. MacArthur New Testament Commentary. Chicago: Moody Publishers, 1995.

———. *Ashamed of the Gospel: When the Church Becomes Like the World*. 3rd ed. Wheaton, IL: Crossway, 2010.

*———, ed. *Evangelism: How to Share the Gospel Faithfully*. The John MacArthur Pastor's Library. Nashville: Thomas Nelson, 2011.

*———. *The Master's Plan for the Church*. Rev. ed. Chicago: Moody Publishers, 2008.

*———, ed. *Pastoral Ministry: How to Shepherd Biblically*. The John MacArthur Pastor's Library. Nashville: Thomas Nelson, 2005.

*———, ed. *Preaching: How to Preach Biblically*. The John MacArthur Pastor's Library. Nashville: Thomas Nelson, 2005.

———. *Reckless Faith: When the Church Loses Its Will to Discern*. Wheaton, IL: Crossway, 1994.

*———. *Strange Fire: The Danger of Offending the Holy Spirit with Counterfeit Worship*. Nashville: Thomas Nelson, 2013.

———. *Titus*. MacArthur New Testament Commentary. Chicago: Moody Press, 1996.

———. *Welcome to the Family: What to Expect Now That You're a Christian*. Nashville: Thomas Nelson, 2004.

*———. *Worship: The Ultimate Priority*. Chicago: Moody Publishers, 2012.

*MacArthur, John, and Wayne A. Mack, eds. *Counseling: How to Counsel Biblically*. The John MacArthur Pastor's Library. Nashville: Thomas Nelson, 2005.

Marshall, Colin, and Tony Payne. *The Trellis and the Vine*. Kingsford, NSW, Australia: Matthias Media, 2009.

*Mayhue, Richard. *The Healing Promise: Is It Always God's Will to Heal?* Fearn, Ross-shire, Scotland: Mentor, 1997.

———. *What Would Jesus Say about Your Church?* Fearn, Ross-shire, Scotland: Christian Focus, 1995.

Mohler, R. Albert, Jr. *He Is Not Silent: Preaching in a Postmodern World*. Chicago: Moody Publishers, 2008.

Montoya, Alex. *Preaching with Passion*. Grand Rapids, MI: Kregel, 2007.

Piper, John. *Brothers, We Are Not Professionals*. Expanded edition. Nashville: B&H, 2013.

Piper, John, and Wayne Grudem, eds. *Recovering Biblical Manhood and Womanhood: A Response to Evangelical Feminism*. Wheaton, IL: Crossway, 2012.

*Radmacher, Earl D. *What the Church Is All About: A Biblical and Historical Study*. Chicago: Moody Press, 1978.

*Saucy, Robert L. *The Church in God's Program*. Chicago: Moody Press, 1972.

Schreiner, Thomas R., and Matthew R. Crawford, eds. *The Lord's Supper: Remembering and Proclaiming Christ until He Comes*. NAC Studies in Bible and Theology 10. Nashville: B&H Academic, 2011.

Schreiner, Thomas R., and Shawn D. Wright, eds. *Believer's Baptism: Sign of the New Covenant in Christ*. NAC Studies in Bible and Theology 2. Nashville: B&H Academic, 2007.

Spurgeon, Charles H. *Lectures to My Students*. 1875. Reprint, Peabody, MA: Hendrickson, 2010.

*Strauch, Alexander. *Biblical Eldership: An Urgent Call to Restore Biblical Church Leadership*. Rev. ed. Littleton, CO: Lewis and Roth, 1995.

———. *Meetings That Work: A Guide to Effective Elders' Meetings*. Littleton, CO: Lewis and Roth, 2001.

———. *The New Testament Deacon: Minister of Mercy*. Littleton, CO: Lewis and Roth, 1992.

Thomas, Robert L. *Understanding Spiritual Gifts: A Verse-by-Verse Study of 1 Corinthians 12–14*. Rev. ed. Grand Rapids, MI: Kregel, 1998.

Waldron, Samuel E. *To Be Continued? Are the Miraculous Gifts for Today?* Merrick, NY: Calvary Press, 2005.

Wright, David F. *Baptism: Three Views*. Downers Grove, IL: IVP Academic, 2009.

*Denotes most helpful.

"Hallelujah, What a Savior!"

"Man of Sorrows!" what a name
For the Son of God, who came
Ruined sinners to reclaim!
Hallelujah, what a Savior!

Bearing shame and scoffing rude,
In my place condemned He stood—
Sealed my pardon with His blood:
Hallelujah, what a Savior!

Guilty, vile and helpless we,
Spotless Lamb of God was He;
Full atonement! can it be?
Hallelujah, what a Savior!

Lifted up was He to die,
"It is finished!" was His cry;
Now in heav'n exalted high:
Hallelujah, what a Savior!

When He comes, our glorious King,
All His ransomed home to bring,
Then anew this song we'll sing:
Hallelujah, what a Savior!

~Philip P. Bliss (1838–1876)

10

The Future

Eschatology

Major Subjects Covered in Chapter 10

Introduction to Eschatology

Personal Eschatology

Cosmic Eschatology

Theologies often minimize the discussion of future events, especially as they relate to Old Testament promises for national Israel. Because end-time events serve as the culmination of God's redemptive purposes, this chapter aims to summarize all that God has revealed about both personal and prophetic eschatology.

Introduction to Eschatology

Eschatology Defined
Eschatology in God's Plans
Eschatological Models
Eschatology and Bible Interpretation
Eschatology and Jesus Christ

Eschatology Defined

Who doesn't like a thrilling conclusion to a great story? As the tale continues and the plot builds, one wonders, how is this going to end? What surprises and twists lie ahead? Will good win over evil? The Bible presents the greatest story ever told. There is a dramatic start—"In the beginning, God created the heavens and the earth"

(Gen. 1:1). It has exciting characters—Adam, Eve, Abraham, Moses, David, the apostles, the Antichrist, and others. There is the ultimate good-versus-evil storyline—the great cosmic battle between God and Satan. It has a hero—Jesus—who arises from humble beginnings to pull off the greatest rescue mission in history. Then there is the church, which carries on the message of Jesus amid persecution from Satan and the world. But what comes next?

History has experienced three of the four major parts in the Bible's storyline—creation, fall, and redemption. The last to come is *restoration*, which involves the defeat of evil and the establishment of God's kingdom on earth. How could any Christian not be excited about the future? Yet Christians are sometimes reluctant to study what the Bible says about events to come. Perhaps they think that end-time issues are secondary in importance or too hard to understand. Actually, approximately one-quarter of the Bible was prophecy at the time it was written. But the end matters most. It is the purpose for everything!

The Bible presents the glorious end to come as the source of ultimate hope and encouragement for the Christian. After telling the Corinthians about the coming resurrection and the transformation of the body, Paul stated, "Therefore, my beloved brothers, be steadfast, immovable, always abounding in the work of the Lord, knowing that in the Lord your labor is not in vain" (1 Cor. 15:58). Also, the more a Christian lives in light of Jesus's coming, the more his godliness should increase. As John promised, "We know that when he [Jesus] appears we shall be like him, because we shall see him as he is. And everyone who thus hopes in him purifies himself as he is pure" (1 John 3:2–3). The Christian can also rejoice that the difficulties of this life will one day end. Death will be defeated (1 Cor. 15:54–55). Reunion with departed loved ones will take place (1 Thess. 4:17). We will see God's face (Rev. 22:3–4).

Yet the story will not end well for everyone. End-time events serve as a warning for those who have not yet trusted in Jesus for salvation. Judgment is coming. Nonbelievers should "flee from the wrath to come" (Luke 3:7) by trusting in Jesus. Non-Christians should repent so they are not suddenly overcome by the day of the Lord (1 Thess. 5:2–3). Those who refuse God's salvation plan will be cut off from the glories of the kingdom and banished from God's presence forever (2 Thess. 1:9; Rev. 21:8). So, then, the study of eschatology involves tracking what God is doing in history on a grand cosmic level, yet it is intensely practical since it involves one's destiny. Much is at stake! The end of the story is the whole point of the story!

In the broad study of Christian beliefs, eschatology is the final category of doctrine. Some mistakenly think that *last* means *least* in importance. On the contrary, eschatology reveals events to come that are associated with the final "restoration of all things" (Acts 3:21 NASB). The term *eschatology* comes from the Greek word *eschatos*, which means "last," "end," or "final." Thus, eschatology involves the study of last things. In the context of Christian doctrine, eschatology is the study of the end times and the events associated with the return of Jesus, including the tribulation, resurrections, judgments, and the kingdom.

Future events are linked to the character of God. Humans attempt to predict things accurately based on past patterns, but their predictions are often wrong. Even with advances in technology, people lack the ability to affect the future and the knowledge to understand it. God, on the other hand, is all-powerful and all-knowing. Since God is sovereign, he is in direct control of every detail in the universe. And since God is omniscient (all-knowing), he knows and secures exactly what he wills to occur. Such truths are comforting to Christians, since they know that God's purposes will be accomplished. Righteousness will prevail. Evil will be defeated. The Bible presents God as fully in control of the beginning and the end. As God himself says, "I am God, and there is no other; I am God, and there is none like me, declaring the end from the beginning and from ancient times things not yet done, saying, 'My counsel shall stand, and I will accomplish all my purpose'" (Isa. 46:9–10).

Two primary categories of eschatology exist—personal and cosmic. Personal eschatology addresses the future of the human person and matters such as death, the intermediate state, resurrection, judgment, and where a person will reside eternally. It answers the question, what is a person's destiny? Cosmic or prophetic eschatology addresses broader issues such as the biblical covenants, the rapture, the tribulation period, the second coming of Jesus, the millennium, and the eternal state. Whereas personal eschatology focuses more narrowly on the destiny of individual human beings, cosmic eschatology addresses broader issues and how God will deal with his creation as a whole, whether in heaven or on earth.

Eschatology in God's Plans

The Bible's storyline has a historical flow. There is a beginning, a middle, and an end or culmination. In the beginning God creates a wonderful universe. Then there is a dark turn as a deceiving, tempting force (Satan) arrives in the form of a serpent. God's image bearers fall for Satan's lie and sin against their Creator, which brings sin, death, and curses into the world. Then God implements a plan through promises and covenants by which he intends to restore the creation, including mankind, through an ultimate man and Savior—Jesus Christ (Gen. 3:15; 12:2–3). After many centuries this promised Savior and King arrives. Jesus comes to his people, but they reject him (John 1:11). The violent death he willingly suffers provides atonement as the foundation for the reconciliation of all things (Col. 1:20). He then returns to heaven, and from there he pours out the Holy Spirit on believers and builds his church.

In the future, this King will unleash divine wrath on the world in preparation for his personal and bodily return to earth (Rev. 19:11–16). When he comes again, he will resurrect dead saints and reward his followers with a kingdom reign on the earth for a thousand years (Rev. 20:4). After this successful reign, Satan and all evildoers will finally be judged and sentenced to the everlasting lake of fire (Rev. 20:11–15). Then a perfect eternal state in a new heaven and new earth will commence (Rev. 21:1–22:5). God's redeemed and glorified saints will serve him and will reign forever

(Rev. 22:5). Eschatology focuses particularly on "the end or culmination" and what events will occur around it.

Eschatological Models

Differing views of eschatology often result from contrasting assumptions regarding God's purposes. Prior beliefs about how God works can influence how one approaches prophetic texts and the Bible's storyline. Wrong assumptions distort what God has revealed. The Christian must make sure his understanding of God's purposes stems from the Bible and not from other worldviews or philosophies.

There are two models or approaches for viewing God's purposes—the spiritual vision model and the new creation model.[1] These models function as overall approaches for viewing God's purposes.

SPIRITUAL VISION MODEL

The spiritual vision model elevates "spiritual" realities over physical matters. In this view, a stark dualism exists between the spiritual and the material with the spiritual valued more than the physical. Material realities are perceived as bad, inferior, or evil. The spiritual vision model adopts the worldview of the Greek philosopher Plato (ca. 428–348 BC) and the philosophies stemming from his views. Plato taught the superiority of the spiritual over the material. Religious variations of Platonism often present the soul's escape from the body to a purely spiritual existence as the highest ideal and goal. Gnosticism, which was a major threat to the early church, was one form of Platonism. Gnosticism disparaged the goodness of the material world.

While most early Christians were neither Platonists nor Gnostics, Plato's ideas often infiltrated the early church. Origen (ca. AD 184–ca. 254) came close to denying bodily resurrection. The influential theologian Augustine (AD 354–430) believed that the idea of an earthly kingdom of Jesus was carnal and opted for the view that the kingdom of God is a spiritual entity, the church. His spiritual view of God's kingdom, as explained in his work *The City of God*, came to be known as *amillennialism*. These two influential theologians downplayed the physical aspects of Bible prophecy and elevated the spiritual. The Roman Catholic Church of the Middle Ages, which embraced Augustine's amillennial perspective, also operated according to overspiritualized assumptions about God's kingdom.

The unbiblical mixture of Plato's ideas with Christianity has been called "Christoplatonism."[2] Such an approach to God's purposes can be seen in statements like "God is interested in saving the soul, not the body," or "God's kingdom is spiritual, not physical," or "A Christian's eternal destiny is heaven, not earth." Spiritual-vision-model thinking can also be spotted in beliefs that physical, land, and national promises to Israel in the Old Testament must be fulfilled spiritually in the church or be absorbed into the person of Christ. It is evident when people think

---

1. For more on the concepts of the spiritual vision model and the new creation model, see Craig A. Blaising, "Premillennialism," in *Three Views on the Millennium and Beyond*, ed. Darrell L. Bock (Grand Rapids, MI: Zondervan, 1999), 160–81.
2. Randy C. Alcorn, *Heaven* (Wheaton, IL: Tyndale, 2004), 475.

their eternal destiny is a bodiless existence in the sky or sitting on a cloud all day with nothing to do. To use a cultural example, Gary Larson's famous cartoon strip *The Far Side* once showed a man in heaven on a cloud with wings on his back and a halo on his head. Obviously bored out of his mind, the man said to himself, "Wish I'd brought a magazine." The message—the future in heaven is terminally boring.

For much of church history the church adopted spiritualized views of the future. Existence in heaven was regarded as an escape from the carnal physical world. Even today many think that man's final destiny will be a static spiritual existence in the sky apart from any physicality. But there is a better way—the biblical way.

NEW CREATION MODEL

The new creation model, on the other hand, affirms the goodness of all of God's creation, including its material elements. Paul declared, "For by him [Jesus] all things were created, in heaven and on earth, visible and invisible" (Col. 1:16). The creation is composed of both spiritual and material realities, and both matter to God. Both were negatively affected by sin and the fall of man, and both will eventually be restored by God. Peter spoke of the coming "restoration of all things" in Acts 3:21 (NASB). A new creation approach does not deny the importance of spiritual truths and realities; it affirms them. But it opposes efforts to spiritualize physical realities or treat them as inferior. Spiritual and physical blessings come together.

Passages like Isaiah 11; 25; 65; 66; Romans 8; and Revelation 21 affirm that God's future plans involve material realities. They speak of a regenerated earth and tangible matters such as nations, kings, economics, agriculture, the animal kingdom, and sociopolitical issues. These matters are not erased with Christ's kingdom but restored. When discussing the glories of the coming new earth, God declares, "Behold, I am making all things new" (Rev. 21:5). Negative consequences that resulted because of sin such as death, decay, and the curse will be removed, but the basics of the creation environment will be redeemed. The final destiny of God's people is not an ethereal spiritual presence in the sky but a tangible existence on a new earth.

The new creation model also affirms the continuing importance of both individuals and national entities. God pursues the salvation of individual human beings, and he also judges and blesses nations as national entities. The nation of Israel is the clearest example (Matt. 19:28; Acts 1:6). Also, the table of nations in Genesis 10–11 shows that God is sovereign over and concerned for all people groups. The Abrahamic covenant reveals that God's purposes extend to involve blessing all nations (Gen. 12:3; 22:18).

The Bible also teaches that God will use Israel as a means of blessing the nations (Gen. 12:2–3). Israel was the vessel through whom Jesus the Messiah came and is the center of the Messiah's kingdom, in which Israel will lead in both service and function (Isa. 2:2–4; Acts 3:25; Rom. 11:11–12, 15). Isaiah 19:16–25 tells of the day when Egypt and Assyria will become the people of God alongside Israel, who is also God's people. Nations with their kings even exist on the new earth (Rev. 21:24, 26).

Thus, God's plans involve nations, including Israel. Jesus brings harmony among Jews and Gentiles, but he does not erase ethnicities (Eph. 2:11–22; 3:6). One should thus avoid "nation bias" in determining which prophetic references to Israel or other nations should be spiritualized for this church age.

The new creation model also connects eschatology and protology. *Eschatology* is about "last things" while *protology* concerns "first things." If one grasps God's original purposes for man and the creation, then one is in a better position to grasp what is still to come. God created a tangible world in six days and then deemed it "very good" (Gen. 1:31). The goodness of all parts of God's creation refutes Eastern religions such as Hinduism and Buddhism that view the physical world as illusion (*maya*) and as something that must be overcome for enlightenment. This thinking also counters all forms of Platonism and their negative views of the material realm. While the universe consists of material and immaterial realities (Col. 1:16), there is no essential dualism in which spirit is viewed as inherently superior to the physical. Man himself is a complex unity of body and soul, material and immaterial. God made man as a physical entity to live on a physical earth. Thus, God's purposes include the physical realm.

That God's kingdom purposes are related to this earth is seen in the commands given to Adam in Genesis 1:26–28, where Adam is told to "have dominion over," "subdue," and "fill" the earth. God created the world and then designated man as a mediator to rule over it for God's glory. Adam failed this command and did not fulfill God's intent for mankind. Man was subject to death, and the ground was cursed and subjected to futility (Gen. 3:17–19; Rom. 8:20). Today, humanity is characterized by sin, and the creation works against man. But God's plan is to restore and regenerate this earth (Matt. 19:28; Acts 3:21).

Eschatology and Bible Interpretation

Using correct interpretative principles is critical for understanding Bible prophecy and eschatology. This involves a consistent use of grammatical-historical interpretation to all areas of the Bible, including its prophetic sections. This approach seeks to understand the original meaning of the Bible writers and what the original readers would have understood. It views Bible texts as having a single meaning, not multiple, hidden, or allegorical meanings. Fortunately, most Bible-believing Christians use grammatical-historical interpretation for most passages of Scripture. But unfortunately, there is a long history of unwarranted abandonment of grammatical-historical interpretation when it comes to eschatological sections. A spiritual approach to prophecy has often led to beliefs that the church is the new Israel or that land promises in the Old Testament are only about spiritual blessings for the church.

For example, Isaiah 2:2–4 speaks of a coming era when people from the nations will make their way to the city of Jerusalem to learn about God. During this time there will be no war, only peace, as the Lord reigns over the earth. This era of international harmony among nations has not yet occurred, but some spiritualize this passage, viewing it as being fulfilled in this age when people from different countries believe the gospel and join the church. But the church is not in view in this passage. To use another example, Revelation 7:4–8 speaks of 144,000 Jewish people, consisting of twelve thousand from each of the twelve tribes of Israel. This group is contrasted with a large group of saved Gentiles "from every nation, from all tribes and peoples and languages." The group in Revelation 7:4–8 is clearly Jewish, but some take this as describing the church, not Israel. This approach does not fit with grammatical-historical hermeneutics since there are no contextual reasons to take this passage as referring to anything other than representatives of ethnic Israel.

Abandoning grammatical-historical interpretation also leads to discarding what the Bible says about the coming millennial kingdom of Jesus. Even those who deny a future earthly kingdom of Jesus admit that a literal approach to Old Testament prophecy must lead to a coming, literal, earthly kingdom. For instance, O. T. Allis conceded that "the Old Testament prophecies if literally interpreted cannot be regarded as having been fulfilled or as being capable of fulfillment in this age."[3] And Floyd E. Hamilton acknowledged, "Now we must frankly admit that a literal interpretation of the Old Testament prophecies gives us just such a picture of an earthly reign of the Messiah as the premillennialist pictures."[4]

The grammatical-historical approach to interpretation fits with normal means of communication. It also has support from the fact that many prophecies concerning Jesus's first coming were fulfilled in a normal, literal sense. Jesus came from a virgin (Isa. 7:14), was born in Bethlehem (Mic. 5:2), and died an awful death on behalf of his people (Isaiah 53). If prophecies of Jesus's first coming were fulfilled literally, so too will prophecies concerning his second coming.

Eschatology and Jesus Christ

Jesus is the center of God's kingdom program. He is the ultimate King. Both the King (Jesus) and the realm of his kingdom are the subject of many Old Testament prophecies. The first verse of the New Testament declares, "The book of the genealogy of Jesus Christ, the son of David, the son of Abraham" (Matt. 1:1). Not only is Jesus the rightful descendant of David and Abraham, but he is also qualified to fulfill the Davidic and Abrahamic covenants. All the prophecies and covenants of the Bible find their fulfillment in Jesus. So Paul declared, "For all the promises of God find their Yes in him" (2 Cor. 1:20).

Yet Christians are often confused about Jesus's role in fulfilling Old Testament promises. Some believe that promises concerning Israel and Israel's land in the Old Testament are fulfilled or absorbed into Jesus in such a way that one should not expect a future literal fulfillment of these matters. Allegedly, since Jesus is the ultimate or true Israelite who replaced Israel, no theological significance exists for the nation

---

3. O. T. Allis, *Prophecy and the Church: An Examination of the Claim of Dispensationalists That the Christian Church Is a Mystery Parenthesis Which Interrupts the Fulfilment to Israel of the Kingdom Prophecies of the Old Testament* (1945; repr., Nutley, NJ: Presbyterian and Reformed, 1977), 238.

4. Floyd E. Hamilton, *The Basis of the Millennial Faith* (Grand Rapids, MI: Eerdmans, 1942), 38.

of Israel anymore. But this is the wrong approach. Jesus is the focal point of God's purposes, and through him all promises, prophecies, and covenants will be fulfilled. This occurs through the literal fulfillment of what was promised. The specific details of the Old Testament promises and prophecies matter and must be fulfilled as predicted.

When addressing the misperception that he was doing away with the Hebrew Scriptures, Jesus said,

> Do not think that I have come to abolish the Law or the Prophets; I have not come to abolish them but to fulfill them. For truly, I say to you, until heaven and earth pass away, not an iota, not a dot, will pass from the Law until all is accomplished. (Matt. 5:17–18)

When Jesus referred to "the Law or the Prophets," he meant the Hebrew Scriptures as a whole, including its prophecies. "All" in the Old Testament had to be "accomplished." This included every "iota" and "dot" in the alphabet. In other words—everything. Whatever the Hebrew Scriptures predicted had to happen just as predicted.

That Jesus expected a literal fulfillment of Old Testament prophecies is seen in the prophetic section of Matthew 24–25. Jesus said, "So when you see the abomination of desolation spoken of by the prophet Daniel, standing in the holy place . . ." (Matt. 24:15), and then explained how this terrible event meant that the people living in Judea would have to flee from persecution (Matt. 24:16–21). Here Jesus relied on a literal and contextual understanding of Daniel 9:27, which speaks of a coming desolation of the Jewish temple by an evil prince. Jesus did not spiritualize this Old Testament text or say that its details did not matter anymore or that the details were absorbed into him. Instead, he expected a literal fulfillment of this event. Also, Jesus said that the cosmic signs predicted in Isaiah 13:10 would occur (Matt. 24:29). He further relied on Daniel 7:13 to say that the Son of Man would come on the clouds of glory (Matt. 24:30). Repeatedly, Jesus viewed the details of Old Testament prophecies as needing to be fulfilled just as the Old Testament stated. If Jesus viewed the details of Old Testament prophecies as still needing fulfillment, so should Christians.

Like Jesus, the New Testament writers also viewed Old Testament prophecies as requiring exact fulfillment after Jesus's first coming. Both Paul and Peter said that the day of the Lord still needed to occur (1 Thess. 5:2; 2 Pet. 3:10). In line with Daniel 9:27, Paul expected a coming Antichrist figure, a "man of lawlessness," who would enter the Jewish temple exalting himself and declaring himself to be God (2 Thess. 2:3–4). Paul also declared a coming salvation for the nation of Israel in connection with new covenant promises for the nation (Rom. 11:26–27). The New Testament does not transcend or alter the Old Testament prophetic expectation but sees the Old Testament prophecies as needing to be fulfilled over the course of the two comings of Jesus.

The Old Testament predicted a Messiah who would reign over a worldwide kingdom (Zech. 14:9) but would also suffer for the sins of his people (Isaiah 53).

Yet there was little in the Old Testament to indicate two comings of this Messiah. The truth of two distinct arrivals of the Messiah was revealed in the New Testament.

Both John the Baptist and Jesus proclaimed that Jesus was the King and that the kingdom of heaven was near (Matt. 3:2; 4:17). Jesus's healings, exorcisms, words, and natural miracles verified this claim. But Jesus experienced opposition from the people of Israel. The cities were not believing in him (Matt. 11:20–24), and Israel's religious leaders committed blasphemy by saying that Jesus was working with Satan (Matt. 12:22–32). Soon after, Jesus started speaking in parables to hide truth from those who refused to believe and to give truth to those who had faith (Matt. 13:10–17). As the Gospels unfold, it becomes clearer that two comings of Jesus will be necessary. In Luke 19:11–27, Jesus likened himself to a nobleman who traveled to a faraway country to receive a kingdom and then returned to rule. Jesus needed to go away for a time before his kingdom reign would take place. Just before his death, Jesus said, "It is to your advantage that I go away, for if I do not go away, the Helper will not come to you" (John 16:7).

Understanding the two comings of Jesus is important for grasping the fulfillment of Bible prophecy. Two comings means that the fulfillment of prophecies related to him also occurs in stages. Some prophecies were fulfilled with Jesus's first coming, while others await his return. For example, in Acts 3:18, Peter told the people in Jerusalem, "But what God foretold by the mouth of all the prophets, that his Christ would suffer, he thus fulfilled." This shows that prophecies of Jesus's suffering and atonement were fulfilled at his first coming. Yet Peter went on to say that heaven must receive Jesus for a while "until the time for restoring all the things about which God spoke by the mouth of his holy prophets long ago" (Acts 3:21). The "restoring" of "all things" that the prophets predicted was still future and would occur when the Father sent Jesus, the Christ appointed for them (Acts 3:20).

Comprehending eschatology also involves discerning which details of prophecy were fulfilled with Jesus's first coming and which await his second coming. If one sees too much fulfillment with Jesus's first coming, one will miss significant matters that still need to occur at Jesus's return. On the other hand, if one places too much significance on the second coming of Jesus, one could miss significant fulfillment that occurred with Jesus's first advent.

In sum, prophecies related to the person of Jesus and his identity as the Messiah and suffering servant of the Lord were fulfilled with his first coming. Also, prophecies related to Jesus's work on the cross as atonement for sin were fulfilled. In addition, the inauguration of the new covenant by Jesus with his death is a major fulfillment of Old Testament prophecy. Yet much still needs to occur. Prophecies related to Daniel's seventieth week, the day of the Lord, the salvation of Israel, the Antichrist, the millennium, and other events await the time of Jesus's second coming.

Personal Eschatology

Death
The Intermediate State
Resurrection

Hell

Heaven

What happens when one dies? The answer to this question is related to personal eschatology. Since the Bible teaches about the important destinies for both unbelievers and believers, this part looks at personal eschatology from the standpoint of these two groups.

Death

Death is an unpleasant topic, but Scripture teaches what most intuitively know—death is the destiny of human beings. While all recognize the blunt reality of death, the Bible alone reveals its origin, its significance, and what must happen for it to be defeated. Death is not nonexistence. The primary meaning of death is separation. Thus Genesis 35:18 says of Rachel, "Her soul was departing (for she was dying)." After death, her soul went on living, though it was separated from her body.

The Bible speaks of three types of death. First, *physical death* involves the cessation of bodily life. When key organs such as the brain and heart cease to function, physical death occurs. At this point, a separation transpires between a person's body and his soul/spirit. James declared, "The body apart from the spirit is dead" (James 2:26). In regard to physical death, Ecclesiastes 12:7 explains, "The dust [body] returns to the earth as it was, and the spirit returns to God who gave it."

Second, *spiritual death* involves alienation from God. A person can be physically alive yet spiritually dead. In fact, all people are conceived and born into a state of spiritual separation from God (Ps. 51:5). This occurs because of imputed sin from Adam and an inherited sin nature from our ancestors. Paul addressed spiritual death when he told the Ephesians, "You were dead in your trespasses and sins" (Eph. 2:1 NASB). Speaking of their previous condition before Christ, Paul noted that the Ephesians were physically alive but spiritually separated from God.

Third, *eternal death* is punishment and banishment from God for eternity. This happens to those who physically die while spiritually dead. The unrepentant will experience eternal, conscious separation from God's presence to bless (2 Thess. 1:9). The lake of fire is their destiny (Rev. 21:8). Not everyone, though, will experience eternal death; those who believe in Jesus will evade it.

Scripture teaches other important truths about death. First, sin is the cause of death. Contrary to the secular worldview, death is not the result of natural processes stemming from a random and chance universe. Death happens because the first man, Adam, sinned against the Creator. Adam was told that he would die if he ate from the tree of the knowledge of good and evil (Gen. 2:15–17), and Romans 5:12 explains that "sin came into the world through one man [Adam], and death through sin." At its core, death is a spiritual matter with wide-ranging and far-reaching consequences.

Second, death is real, not an illusion. There is an actual separation of the body from the soul. Although Christians recognize this truth, some cults and quasi-Christian sects have denied the reality of sickness and death.

Third, death is unnatural. God did not create man to die, and death was not an original part of the creation (Genesis 1–2). That is why mourning and tears are often associated with death in the Bible (Gen. 50:1, 3). Jesus wept for Lazarus with real tears (John 11:35). Death is a disruption to life. It should never be glamorized or downplayed. In this fallen world, death may seem natural since it is all around us. But God did not create man to die, and a day is coming when death will be defeated. Death will not be present in the new heaven and new earth (Revelation 21–22; esp. 21:4). Death, therefore, is an intrusion in God's universe, an enemy that needs to be conquered. In regard to Jesus's coming kingdom reign, Paul thus declared, "The last enemy to be destroyed is death" (1 Cor. 15:26). The apostle John likewise revealed that "death" will be "thrown into the lake of fire" (Rev. 20:14). Death is headed for defeat because of Jesus. The believer can rejoice with Paul in saying,

> "Death is swallowed up in victory."
> "O death, where is your victory?
> O death, where is your sting?" (1 Cor. 15:54–55)

Fourth, in this age death is an inescapable reality that ushers one into accountability before the Creator.[5] Hebrews 9:27 declares, "It is appointed for man to die once, and after that comes judgment." Death is not a guaranteed transition to a peaceful non-existence or nirvana. Nor is heaven the default destiny for all who die. For unbelievers, death is a fearsome thing, and its proximity should cause all to repent. In the parable of the rich fool, Jesus told of a rich man who greedily kept acquiring barns, grain, and goods with no thought of using his wealth for God. Then one day, "God said to him, 'Fool! This night your soul is required of you, and the things you have prepared, whose will they be?'" (Luke 12:20). Unexpectedly, the rich fool would be facing God.

Fifth, death is a transition from one state of existence to another. It is not a transfer from existence to nonexistence. Believers will transition to the intermediate heaven where God, the resurrected Jesus, angels, and previously deceased believers reside (Rev. 6:9–11). The nonbeliever will transition to hades, a temporary place of punishment for the wicked (Luke 16:19–31). What the intermediate heaven and hades are like will be further discussed below.

DEATH AND THE UNBELIEVER

Death is a source of fear only for those who do not know God. For the unbeliever, death not only brings an end to one's current, physical life, but it also takes a person into direct accountability with God for a life lived apart from him (Heb. 9:27). Jesus warned that people should fear God "who can destroy both soul and body in hell" (Matt. 10:28).

While alive, all people, including nonbelievers, experience God's common grace in blessings such as food, air, sunshine, and relationships. Paul alludes to this when he

---

5. The exceptions to this will be believers who are living at the time of the rapture (1 Thess. 4:13–18) and those alive at the time of Jesus's second coming to earth (Matt. 25:31–46).

asks, "Do you think lightly of the riches of His kindness and tolerance and patience, not knowing that the kindness of God leads you to repentance?" (Rom. 2:4 NASB). Yet Paul also warns of rejecting God's kindness: "But because of your stubbornness and unrepentant heart you are storing up wrath for yourself in the day of wrath and revelation of the righteous judgment of God" (Rom. 2:5 NASB). Experiencing God's blessings without giving him honor increases wrath for a person. Also, those who die in unbelief will experience eternal death with no chance of reprieve or escape. While sentencing to the lake of fire will not come until the final judgment, the destiny of the unsaved is sealed at the point of death. There is no postmortem second chance. Proverbs 11:7 sums up what death means for the wicked: "When the wicked dies, his hope will perish."

DEATH AND THE BELIEVER

Believers in Christ are not spared from the consequences of physical death. Even for the Christian, death may be sudden, the result of a tragic accident, or the end of a long painful illness. On the one hand, Christians are a new creation (2 Cor. 5:17) and have experienced inner renewal through the work of the Holy Spirit, but on the other hand, their physical bodies still decay. As Paul stated, "Though our outer self is wasting away, our inner self is being renewed day by day" (2 Cor. 4:16). For reasons known only to him, God has determined that the removal of death awaits the future (Isa. 25:8). So how does death relate to the believer in Christ?

Death is a result of sin, but the Christian is forgiven of all sins: "There is . . . no condemnation for those who are in Christ Jesus" (Rom. 8:1). Therefore, death is not a punishment for the Christian like it is for the nonbeliever. Instead, physical death occurs because we live in a fallen world still awaiting the restoration of all things (Acts 3:21). The process of decay and death reminds Christians of their frailty and total reliance on God. Suffering and death also help Christians identify with and grow closer to Jesus, which is why Paul said that he desired to "know him [Jesus] and the power of his resurrection" and to "share his sufferings, becoming like him in his death" (Phil. 3:10).

While on the road to physical death, the Christian does not have to fear death, for Christ has conquered it (Rev. 1:18). Jesus, through his sacrificial death, is able to "deliver all those who through fear of death were subject to lifelong slavery" (Heb. 2:14–15). Paul said, "For I am sure that neither death nor life . . . will be able to separate us from the love of God in Christ Jesus our Lord" (Rom. 8:38–39). In fact, Paul viewed the options of continuing his present ministry on earth or departing to be with Christ as a difficult choice: "If I am to live in the flesh, that means fruitful labor for me. Yet which I shall choose I cannot tell. I am hard pressed between the two. My desire is to depart and be with Christ, for that is far better. But to remain in the flesh is more necessary on your account" (Phil. 1:22–24). Paul knew God wanted him to remain on earth and serve others, yet he desired to be present with Christ in heaven. He did not loathe death because it meant being immediately with Jesus.

Paul told the Corinthians, "Yes, we are of good courage, and we would rather be away from the body and at home with the Lord" (2 Cor. 5:8). Again, Paul viewed departure from the body (physical death) as preferable since he would be with Jesus. In addition to being an encouragement for the believer, these verses refute the unbiblical concept of soul sleep, in which physical death means nonexistence until the resurrection. The believer is never separated from Christ.

Death is indeed a fearful enemy that needs to be conquered. Yet because of Jesus's death, the power of sin and death are broken for the Christian. The final removal of death awaits the return of Jesus, yet Christians in this fallen world know that physical death is not the end. It ushers the Christian immediately and eternally into the presence of Jesus. The stark contrast between death for unbelievers and believers is summarized in Proverbs 14:32: "The wicked is overthrown through his evildoing, but the righteous finds refuge in his death."

The Intermediate State

The intermediate state refers to the conscious existence of people between physical death and the resurrection of the body. It applies to both believers and unbelievers, although the destinies of these two groups are different. Since the focus of the New Testament is on the imminent return of Jesus and the kingdom of God on earth (Isaiah 11; 65:17–25; Revelation 20–22), scriptural data concerning the intermediate state is brief. Yet enough information exists for one to have real knowledge on this topic.

THE INTERMEDIATE STATE OF THE UNBELIEVER

The intermediate state of unbelievers involves conscious torment in a place called *hades*, from *hadēs*, the Greek term for the abode of the dead.[6] In the Septuagint, it was used to translate the Hebrew word *sheol*, which referred to the realm of the dead in general, without necessarily distinguishing between righteous and unrighteous souls. But in the New Testament, hades refers to the place of the wicked prior to the final judgment in the lake of fire (Rev. 20:13). Hades, therefore, serves to describe a temporary place of conscious torment for the wicked.

The most explicit discussion of hades is found in Luke 16:19–31, the account of the rich man and Lazarus. The rich man, who was clothed in luxury, had little concern for the poor beggar Lazarus. When the rich man died, his body was buried (16:22); yet his immaterial part was relocated to hades, where he was "in torment" (16:23). He called out to Abraham for mercy, saying, "I am in anguish in this flame" (16:24). The rich man was in agony. He also had memory, not only recalling Abraham and Lazarus but also desiring to help his five living brothers. He was aware that his presence in hades was deserved. Abraham also appealed to the rich man's memory: "Child, remember that you in your lifetime received your good things, and

---

6. This paragraph is adapted from John MacArthur, ed., *The MacArthur Study Bible: English Standard Version* (Wheaton, IL: Crossway, 2010), 1510. Charts and notes from *The MacArthur Study Bible: English Standard Version* originate with *The MacArthur Study Bible*, copyright © 1997 by Thomas Nelson. Used by permission of Thomas Nelson. www.thomas nelson.com.

Lazarus . . . bad things" (16:25). All these details reveal a place of torment with self-consciousness and memory.

How literally should this account be understood, and what truths about the intermediate state can be gleaned from it? Is this parable describing a real or fictional account? The mention of names (Lazarus and Abraham) cannot be made to indicate an actual account of real people. Although it is a parable, the Lord designed it to explain actual postdeath circumstances.

THE INTERMEDIATE STATE OF THE BELIEVER

The intermediate destiny of the believer differs drastically from that of the unbeliever. It involves a conscious, peaceful existence in heaven with Jesus between physical death and the resurrection of the body. The believer's soul is translated immediately to the presence of Jesus in heaven upon physical death (2 Cor. 5:8; Phil. 1:22–24). As Stephen was being stoned, he cried out to Jesus, whom he saw in heaven, "Lord Jesus, receive my spirit" (Acts 7:59). To the repentant thief on the cross, Jesus promised, "Truly, I say to you, today you will be with me in Paradise" (Luke 23:43).

When death occurs, the body is buried while the soul is taken immediately to heaven. Paul said that being with the Lord Jesus in this state is "far better" (Phil. 1:23) than physical life in a fallen world (2 Cor. 5:8). Yet he also stated that the intermediate condition is comparable to being "naked" (2 Cor. 5:3), since humans were not created to be disembodied. Humans are most whole when clothed with a physical body. It is the glorification of the resurrected body for which Paul longs most (2 Cor. 5:1–2). For the Christian, resurrection is better than the intermediate state, which is better than life in this fallen world.

The intermediate state also means rest from the toils of this life. In Revelation 14:13, John states, "And I heard a voice from heaven saying, 'Write this: Blessed are the dead who die in the Lord from now on.' 'Blessed indeed,' says the Spirit, 'that they may rest from their labors, for their deeds follow them!'" Revelation 6:9–11 offers the most detailed information concerning the intermediate state. The apostle John witnesses a scene where souls appear in heaven under an altar. These are those "who had been slain for the word of God and for the witness they had borne" (6:9). They are Christian martyrs whose souls now appear in heaven. Verses 10–11 state,

> They cried out with a loud voice, "O Sovereign Lord, holy and true, how long before you will judge and avenge our blood on those who dwell on the earth?" Then they were each given a white robe and told to rest a little longer, until the number of their fellow servants and their brothers should be complete, who were to be killed as they themselves had been.

Several truths about the intermediate state of believers can be gleaned here. First, while in heaven, these saints have keen self-awareness and knowledge of others and of world circumstances. They know they were killed for their testimony for Jesus, and they want judgment on earth for their murderers. These saints remember past experiences and have hope for the future. Second, they are mindful of the distinction between heaven and earth. Even after arriving in heaven, they do not forget about earth altogether or act as if heaven is all that matters. Third, heaven is not their final destiny. Even in heaven, the saints long for justice on the earth, a justice that will come with the return of Jesus and the saints in Revelation 19:11–21. The intermediate heaven is not their final home. The truth of Revelation 5:10 applies to these saints: "They shall reign on the earth."

Fourth, the martyred saints in heaven appear to have some body-like form. They can be seen by John ("I saw . . . the souls," Rev. 6:9). They have an audible element in that they can speak and be heard ("They cried out with a loud voice," 6:10). Also, they can wear clothing ("They were each given a white robe," 6:11). And they operate within the confines of time ("They were . . . told to rest a little longer," 6:11). It is plain, then, that intermediate-state saints in heaven have a real existence. However, this is not bodily existence; physical death has occurred, and their bodies remain in the ground awaiting resurrection. Plus, the resurrection of the body is still future. Yet a real and localized presence of believers in heaven appears to be the reality.

SIGNIFICANCE OF THE INTERMEDIATE STATE

What role does the intermediate state play in God's broader cosmic plans? The souls of unbelievers are in hades. The souls of departed saints and the resurrected Jesus are in heaven. So the intermediate state is vitally important in God's plans. Yet one should avoid extremes concerning the intermediate state's significance.

One extreme downplays the significance or even existence of the intermediate state. Some teach that there is no intermediate-state existence for believers or unbelievers, opting for what is called *soul sleep*. In this view, when a person dies, he or she ceases to exist until Jesus returns and his or her body is resurrected. Then the person is brought to life. But multiple passages, including those discussed above, describe conscious existence for people between physical death and the resurrection of the body.

On the other extreme, the intermediate state can be overemphasized in two ways. The first occurs when the intermediate heaven is viewed as the final state of believers. When Christians think that their eternal destiny is the present heaven, not the new heaven and new earth (Rev. 21:1), they are overemphasizing the present heaven. Some popular hymns such as "I'll Fly Away"—with lyrics like "to a land where joy will never end, I'll fly away"—might give the impression that the destiny of the Christian is "out there" forever, and that the "land" God promises is heaven. But the intermediate heaven is not the ultimate destiny of believers—the new earth is. So Peter declared, "But according to his promise we are waiting for new heavens and a new earth in which righteousness dwells" (2 Pet. 3:13).

A second erroneous perspective is viewing the intermediate state as the millennial reign of Jesus and the saints in heaven in this era. This is held by some amillennialists.[7]

---

7. One example is the amillennialist Sam Storms, who says, "I am now persuaded that Revelation 20:4–6 is concerned exclusively with *the experience of the martyrs in the intermediate state*." Sam Storms, *Kingdom Come: The Amillennial Alternative* (Fearn, Ross-Shire, Scotland: Mentor, 2013), 451. Italics original. He also says, "In Revelation 20 he [John] . . . describes the intermediate state as souls *living and reigning with Christ*." *Kingdom Come*, 461. Italics original.

But the Bible does not present the millennial reign of Jesus and the saints as occurring in heaven. Instead, it will be fulfilled on earth, from and over the realm where God originally tasked man to rule (Gen. 1:26–28). The reign of Jesus and the saints is needed on earth, not in heaven, which already possesses the universal kingdom reign of God. The martyred saints who appear in heaven in Revelation 6:9–11 are pictured as longing for justice on the earth. They are not reigning yet but are waiting to reign, a waiting that will be satisfied with the resurrection and reign of the saints after the return of Jesus (Rev. 20:4). In sum, the millennial reign of Jesus and the saints is not a hidden reign from heaven but a visible, tangible reign in the realm where God created mankind to rule—the earth.

The intermediate state is for deceased believers in heaven or unbelievers in hades during this age before the second coming of Jesus and the resurrection of the body. But it is not the final state or destiny for human beings.

Resurrection

God created human beings as a complex unity of body and soul. In this age physical death results in the separation of a person's body from his or her soul. But this state does not last forever. Everyone is destined for a resurrection of the body fitted for his or her eternal destiny.

Since most people die physically before the return of Jesus, the resurrection is often referred to as a coming out of the grave. For instance, Daniel stated that after a specific "time of trouble," "many of those who sleep in the dust of the earth shall awake, some to everlasting life, and some to shame and everlasting contempt" (Dan. 12:1–2). Those who have died and been buried will one day be "awake." This is a physical resurrection of the body. This same truth is affirmed by Jesus in John 5:28–29:

> Do not marvel at this, for an hour is coming when all who are in the tombs will hear his voice and come out, those who have done good to the resurrection of life, and those who have done evil to the resurrection of judgment.

In a later section, we will discuss the timing and stages of God's resurrection program, but here the focus is on what resurrection means for both believers and unbelievers. Resurrection occurs for both groups, but not all awake to the same destiny. Since Scripture gives more details on the resurrection of believers, we will begin our discussion there.

RESURRECTION OF THE BELIEVER

Believers in God are destined for the resurrection of the body. One of the earliest biblical figures, Job, expressed confidence in resurrection:

> For I know that my Redeemer lives,
>   and at the last he will stand upon the earth.
> And after my skin has been thus destroyed,
>   yet in my flesh I shall see God. (Job 19:25–26)

Job knew his "skin" would be "destroyed" (physical death) but that this was not the end. His "Redeemer" would stand on the earth, and in the end Job would, in his "flesh," "see God." Physical resurrection is real and occurs because of the Redeemer. Isaiah also declared the resurrection of the body for the saved:

> Your dead shall live; their bodies shall rise.
>   You who dwell in the dust, awake and sing for joy!
> For your dew is a dew of light,
>   and the earth will give birth to the dead. (Isa. 26:19)

The most extended discussion of the nature of the resurrection body for believers is found in 1 Corinthians 15:35–49. Paul addressed the questions "How are the dead raised?" and "With what kind of body do they come?" (15:35). He then contrasted the flawed, mortal bodies we now have with the glorified bodies we will receive in the coming age. Glorified bodies will be imperishable. They do not decay or die like our present perishable bodies (15:42). Our future bodies will not be tainted with the shame of sin. They will be powerful, not weak (15:43). They will be spiritual bodies, not natural bodies (15:44). Jesus is the prototype of glorified bodies, while our natural bodies take after Adam (15:45–46).

The mention of "spiritual" bodies does not mean immaterial or ghostlike. They are spiritual because their source is God, by means of resurrection and glorification. Paul taught that glorified bodies were physical bodies when he said, "We wait eagerly for . . . the redemption of our bodies" (Rom. 8:23). He also stated that when Jesus comes, he "will transform our lowly body to be like his glorious body" (Phil. 3:21). Just as Jesus had a tangible, physical existence when he rose from the dead, so too will Jesus's followers. After all, Jesus is the "firstfruits" of those who die in him (1 Cor. 15:20). Glorified bodies are required to enter God's eternal kingdom (1 Cor. 15:50).

Resurrection involves the body coming to life and reuniting with the soul. When discussing the rapture of the church in 1 Thessalonians 4:13–18, Paul said, "God will bring with him those who have fallen asleep" (1 Thess. 4:14), referring to the souls of deceased Christians in heaven. So at the rapture God will bring the souls of departed Christians and join them with their resurrected bodies (1 Thess. 4:16).

Since the final destiny of believers is the new earth, resurrected bodies are suited perfectly for everlasting life on the new earth. The new earth will no longer experience curse, decay, or death. And those alive on it will not experience these either. The believer has much to look forward to.

RESURRECTION OF THE UNBELIEVER

Scripture gives fewer details concerning the nature of the resurrection body of the lost, but some conclusions are possible. Daniel 12:2 says that the unsaved "awake" to "shame and everlasting contempt." Unbelievers experience a tangible bodily resurrection. As we saw in Daniel 12:2 and John 5:28–29, they come out of the grave. So the body that died and was buried is the body that comes out of the grave. It is resurrected, but the person is the same. So there is a one-to-one correspondence.

Second, the resurrection body of the unsaved is suited to experience the lake of fire. Just as believers will receive a body to live on the new earth (Rev. 21:1–22:5), which is a real place, nonbelievers will receive a body fit to experience the lake of fire, which also is an actual place. Revelation 20:15 states, "And if anyone's name was not found written in the book of life, he was thrown into the lake of fire." Such a parallel between believers and unbelievers is explained in Isaiah 66:22–24, which first describes conditions of the new earth for believers (66:22–23) and then describes conditions for the unsaved (66:24): "And they shall go out and look on the dead bodies of the men who have rebelled against me. For their worm shall not die, their fire shall not be quenched, and they shall be an abhorrence to all flesh." This indicates a tangible existence for the lost.

Both Revelation 20:15 and Isaiah 66:24 reveal the awful destiny of the unrepentant. These texts depict unending fiery judgment. The apostle John revealed that unbelievers "will drink the wine of God's wrath, poured full strength into the cup of his anger, and he will be tormented with fire and sulfur in the presence of the holy angels and in the presence of the Lamb. And the smoke of their torment goes up forever and ever, and they have no rest, day or night" (Rev. 14:10–11). This reveals a miserable existence: eternal conscious torment characterized by no rest for those who abide there.

Hell

The Bible presents the eternal reality of hell. Hell is a real place of fiery torment for the unrepentant that lasts forever. Of the twelve references to "hell" in the Bible, the vast majority come from Jesus's own mouth.[8] The following is a sample of Jesus's words on this topic.

> And whoever says, "You fool!" will be liable to the hell of fire. (Matt. 5:22)

> And do not fear those who kill the body but cannot kill the soul. Rather fear him who can destroy both soul and body in hell. (Matt. 10:28)

> You serpents, you brood of vipers, how are you to escape being sentenced to hell? (Matt. 23:33)

> And if your hand causes you to sin, cut it off. It is better for you to enter life crippled than with two hands to go to hell, to the unquenchable fire. (Mark 9:43)

The Greek term translated "hell" in the above passages is *gehenna*, which occurs twelve times in the New Testament and relates to the Valley of Hinnom on the south and east sides of Jerusalem. In this place children were sacrificed in fire to the god Molech (2 Kings 23:10; Jer. 7:31–32). Some hold that the Valley of Hinnom was also the place where dead bodies of criminals and animals were burned.[9] This awful

---

8. For a more thorough treatment of hell, see the following articles from *Master's Seminary Journal* 9, no. 2 (1998): Richard L. Mayhue, "Hell: Never, Forever, or Just for a While?," 129–45; Robert L. Thomas, "Jesus' View of Eternal Punishment," 147–67; James E. Rosscup, "Paul's Concept of Eternal Punishment," 169–89; Trevor Craigen, "Eternal Punishment in John's Revelation," 191–201; Larry Dean Pettegrew, "A Kinder, Gentler Theology of Hell?," 203–17.

9. See Paul Enns, *The Moody Handbook of Theology* (Chicago: Moody Press, 1989), 375.

place of fiery doom was used by Jesus and New Testament writers to symbolize the future place of punishment for the wicked. These references show that hell is real. People should strive to avoid this dreadful place. Other passages, while not using the term "hell," further describe the eternal fire awaiting the wicked:

> Then he [Jesus] will say to those on his left, "Depart from me, you cursed, into the eternal fire prepared for the devil and his angels." (Matt. 25:41)

> If anyone worships the beast and its image and receives a mark on his forehead or on his hand, he also will drink the wine of God's wrath, poured full strength into the cup of his anger, and he will be tormented with fire and sulfur in the presence of the holy angels and in the presence of the Lamb. And the smoke of their torment goes up forever and ever, and they have no rest, day or night. (Rev. 14:9–11)

> And if anyone's name was not found written in the book of life, he was thrown into the lake of fire. (Rev. 20:15)

The fiery torment of hell is unending. Also, hell is not merely a "state of mind" or some sort of spiritual existence. The language used cannot be attributed to metaphor alone.

Hell is associated with three everlasting negative consequences: (1) punishment, (2) destruction, and (3) banishment. Not one of these concepts explains all of what hell is, but together they offer a multidimensional understanding of why hell is so terrible. First, the wicked are punished and receive retribution for their deeds (Luke 12:47–48). God's punishment is not a vindictive but a righteous retribution for wrongs committed. Second, hell involves destruction (2 Thess. 1:9), which entails the concepts of ruin and waste. Those who die in unbelief have squandered opportunities to live a life that mattered for God. They are enemies of God, and loss and ruin are their fate (Matt. 7:19). Third, hell includes banishment. Not only are the wicked punished and not only do they suffer ruin, but they are also banished from the blessings of the kingdom of God and are denied access to the glories of the new earth. God as King has removed them with no hope of entering his presence (Rev. 22:14–15).

SHEOL

Other terms in the Bible are connected with hell. The Hebrew term *sheol* is found sixty-five times in the Old Testament. Depending on the context, the term is translated as "grave," "pit," or "hell." In general, sheol refers to the abode of the dead. Psalm 88:3 states, "For my soul is full of troubles, and my life draws near to Sheol." Being in sheol means one is cut off from the living with no access to matters on earth. Yet sheol does not mean escape from God's presence. As Psalm 139:8 declares, "If I make my bed in Sheol, you are there!"

TARTARUS

Another reference to hell is found in 2 Peter 2:4: "For if God did not spare angels when they sinned, but cast them into hell and committed them to chains of gloomy darkness to be kept until the judgment . . ." The Greek term for "cast them into hell" here is not *gehenna* or *hadēs*. It is *tartaroō*, from which we get *tartarus*, the only time this term is used in the New Testament. In Greek mythology, tartarus was a subterranean realm, even lower than hades, where the wicked were punished. According to Roman mythology, tartarus was the place where the enemies of the gods were banished. The Jews eventually came to use this term to describe the place where fallen angels were sent. It was the lowest hell, the deepest pit, and the most terrible place of torture. According to 2 Peter 2:4, angels were sent to tartarus when they sinned. This could refer to the angels ("sons of God") in Genesis who sinned by trying to pervert the human race by cohabitating with the daughters of men (Gen. 6:2).

ABYSS

While not identified as "hell," another term used for confinement in the Bible is *Abyss* (Gk. *abyssos*). The Abyss is a prison for fallen angels that halts them from having any access to or influence on the earth. As Jesus was about to cast out many demons from a man, Luke 8:31 reports that the demons "begged him not to command them to depart into the abyss." The demons feared the Abyss since it would mean the total cessation of their activities on earth. In Revelation 9, demon-like creatures are released from the Abyss to inflict damage on the people of the earth (Rev. 9:1–2). It is their release from the Abyss that allows these creatures to harm people, since they cannot touch people on the earth while in the Abyss.

The Abyss is mentioned again in Revelation 20:1–3. It is a "pit" into which Satan will be thrown after the second coming of Jesus. Once Satan is incarcerated, the Abyss will be "shut" and "sealed . . . over him" so that Satan cannot deceive the nations for a thousand years (Rev. 20:3). The Abyss functions as a prison to hold the person of Satan. As a result, Satan himself and his deceiving activities will totally cease on the earth, since captivity in the Abyss absolutely removes his influence on the earth. Once the thousand years are completed, Satan will be released from the Abyss to deceive the nations one more time, but he will immediately be destroyed and sent to the lake of fire forever (Rev. 20:7–10).

DEVIANT VIEWS OF HELL

A real, torturous, and unending hell for the lost is so horrible to contemplate that many refuse to believe it. Some have offered alternatives to the biblical doctrine of hell. The following are distortions of this reality.

Universalism. Increasingly popular is the notion that all people will end up in heaven and that no one will be lost in hell forever. This view is called *universalism* since it affirms that all people will be saved. Universalism can take several forms. First, some believe that the atoning work of Christ will be applied to all people whether they believe or not. So all people will enter the presence of God. Second, others hold that people who die in unbelief or having never heard of Jesus will be given a postmortem opportunity to believe in Jesus, to which all will respond positively. A third form of universalism asserts that people will be punished for a while in hell but will eventually be welcomed into heaven.

Universalism is contradicted by multiple statements in Scripture that not all are saved and that some will experience eternal punishment (Matt. 25:41, 46; Rev. 20:11–15). When discussing the glories of the new earth (Rev. 21:1–7), John made it clear that not all would experience this place: "But as for the cowardly, the faithless, the detestable, as for murderers, the sexually immoral, sorcerers, idolaters, and all liars, their portion will be in the lake that burns with fire and sulfur, which is the second death" (Rev. 21:8). Contrary to universalism, the story does not end well for everyone. Belief in Christ is a prerequisite for those who will enter glory (John 3:36). Those who do not believe are set to face judgment for their sins forever.

Annihilationism. Another distortion of the doctrine of hell is annihilationism, the idea that the wicked will cease to exist. This could occur at physical death, in a coming judgment, or after a finite period of punishment in hell. Allegedly, the wicked will reach a point when they no longer exist. How do annihilationists respond to the Bible's descriptions of hell being "forever" or "eternal"? For them, it is not that a person exists in hell forever but that the consequence of being eliminated lasts forever. Eternal ruin refers to being taken out of existence as a perpetual punishment. Annihilationism is sometimes linked with belief in conditional immortality.

From this perspective, humanity does not possess inherent immortality. Death means a person no longer exists. Only those who believe in Jesus are granted immortality as a gift from God, while the wicked are not allowed to continue their existence. But biblical language such as "eternal fire" (Matt. 25:41), "smoke of their torment goes up forever and ever" (Rev. 14:11), and "they have no rest, day or night" (Rev. 14:11), reveals unending torment rather than cessation. Having no rest indicates self-consciousness. Plus, eternal life and eternal punishment parallel each other. Jesus stated, "And these [the wicked] will go away into eternal punishment, but the righteous into eternal life" (Matt. 25:46). Just as eternal life for the believer is unending, so too is eternal punishment for the unbeliever. Annihilationism also fails to do justice to how serious sin is, since sin is an infinite offense against an infinitely holy God, thus demanding an infinite punishment. It is an eternal matter that cannot be overcome by a temporary penalty. If it could, sin against God would be a finite matter. Yet a finite punishment for sin would indicate finitude in the holiness of God. It is precisely because God is infinitely holy that even a single offense against his holiness requires infinite punishment. The eternality of hell therefore cannot be rejected without undermining the holiness of God.

Spiritual Punishment. Some hold that the lost will experience eternal, conscious punishment but that this punishment is not a physical punishment in a literal place of fire. For them, fire is not literal but rather represents alienation from God. Hell is primarily about spiritual separation from God, not physical anguish in a tangible lake of fire.

This view, however, does not adequately account for the reality that both the righteous and the wicked rise bodily from the dead and are granted bodies suited to their eternal destinies. If the lake of fire is just metaphorical for a nonliteral state of existence, does this mean the new earth is only metaphorical and just a spiritual state of existence for believers? It is best to understand that both the righteous and the wicked receive bodies that fit them for their eternal destinies—whether on a tangible new earth or in a real lake of fire.

Negative Conditions in This Life. Some relegate hell to a figure of speech or metaphor for difficulties in this life. Statements such as "My life is a living hell" reflect this thinking. Such a perspective trivializes what hell really is and can lead people to think that this life is the worst that things can be. While many dreadful things can occur in this fallen world, our experiences are mixed with God's common goodness such as love, personal relationships, food, rain, and sunshine. In hell, though, God's common goodness and grace are removed, and the lost must face the undiluted wrath of God. Hell is exceedingly more than a metaphor for tough times in this life, so to confuse the two is dangerous.

Heaven[10]

The term "heaven" is used approximately six hundred times in the Bible. The Hebrew term often translated "heaven" (*shamayim*) literally means "the heights." The Greek term (*ouranos*) refers to that which is raised up or lofty. The Bible uses these terms to refer to three different places—the atmospheric heaven, the planetary heaven, and the third heaven.

THE ATMOSPHERIC HEAVEN

The atmospheric, or first, heaven is the sky or troposphere—the region of the breathable atmosphere that covers the earth. Genesis 7:11–12 refers to this: "And the windows of the heavens were opened. And rain fell upon the earth forty days and forty nights." Here "heavens" refers to the blanket of atmosphere around the world, which is where the hydrological cycle occurs. Psalm 147:8 declares that God "covers the heavens with clouds." God uses the atmospheric heaven to provide good things to all people: "He did good by giving you rains from heaven and fruitful seasons, satisfying your hearts with food and gladness" (Acts 14:17).

THE PLANETARY HEAVEN

The planetary, or second, heaven is where the sun, moon, planets, and stars exist. This understanding of heaven is referred to in Genesis 1:14–17:

> And God said, "Let there be lights in the expanse of the heavens to separate the day from the night. And let them be for signs and for seasons, and for days and

10. This section is adapted from John MacArthur, *The Glory of Heaven: The Truth about Heaven, Angels, and Eternal Life* (Wheaton, IL: Crossway, 1996), 55–56. Used by permission of Crossway, a publishing ministry of Good News Publishers, Wheaton, IL 60187, www.crossway.org.

years, and let them be lights in the expanse of the heavens to give light upon the earth." And it was so. And God made the two great lights—the greater light to rule the day and the lesser light to rule the night—and the stars. And God set them in the expanse of the heavens to give light on the earth.

The planetary or stellar heaven serves several purposes. The lights in this heaven separate day and night and exist for signs and seasons. The feasts of Israel would later be tied to the planetary heaven (Num. 10:10; 28:14). The planetary heaven also reveals the glory of God (Ps. 19:1–4). In addition, the cosmic bodies of the planetary heaven testify to the enduring commitment of God to the nation of Israel. Thus, immediately after mentioning the sun, moon, and stars in Jeremiah 31:35, God declares, "If the heavens above can be measured, and the foundations of the earth below can be explored, then I will cast off all the offspring of Israel for all that they have done, declares the LORD" (31:37). The planetary heaven will play a major role in the coming tribulation period, as Matthew 24:29 states, "Immediately after the tribulation of those days the sun will be darkened, and the moon will not give its light, and the stars will fall from heaven, and the powers of the heavens will be shaken." The shaking of the planetary heaven during the tribulation period reveals that God's wrath has come on the unbelieving world of that time (Rev. 6:12–17).

THE THIRD HEAVEN

The third heaven is the dwelling place of God, the holy angels, and deceased saints. Paul referred to this third heaven in 2 Corinthians 12:2–4:

> I know a man in Christ [Paul] who fourteen years ago was caught up to the third heaven—whether in the body or out of the body I do not know, God knows. And I know that this man was caught up into paradise—whether in the body or out of the body I do not know, God knows—and he heard things that cannot be told, which man may not utter.

To affirm that God dwells in the third heaven does not mean God is contained there. First Kings 8:27 declares, "Behold, heaven and the highest heaven cannot contain you." God is omnipresent, and his presence extends to every realm. But the third heaven is uniquely God's home. It is the command post and center of operation for his universal kingdom, from which he rules over everything in the universe (Ps. 103:19). God's throne resides in heaven, and it is there that he is worshiped (Revelation 4). This third heaven is also the place from which the New Jerusalem will descend to earth after the millennium. In his vision, the apostle John saw "the holy city Jerusalem coming down out of heaven from God" (Rev. 21:10; cf. 3:12).

Concerning its inhabitants, God the Father is the center of the third heaven. Jesus said that we should pray, "Our Father in heaven, hallowed be your name" (Matt. 6:9). He also instructed his people to pray for God's will to be done on earth as it currently is in heaven (Matt. 6:10). In Revelation 4:2, John saw that "a throne stood in heaven, with one seated on the throne," and with those around the throne continually saying, "Holy, holy, holy, is the Lord God Almighty" (Rev. 4:8). Psalm 2:4 states that God the Father "sits in the heavens" and "laughs" at the rebellious nations on earth who challenge his authority.

The resurrected Jesus is also in the third heaven. At Jesus's ascension, two angels declared, "Men of Galilee, why do you stand looking into heaven? This Jesus, who was taken up from you into heaven, will come in the same way as you saw him go into heaven" (Acts 1:11). While being stoned, Stephen cried out, "Behold, I see the heavens opened, and the Son of Man standing at the right hand of God" (Acts 7:56). Jesus's presence in heaven is linked with Psalm 110:1–2 and its prediction that the Messiah would have a time at God's right hand before reigning from Jerusalem (cf. Heb. 8:1). Hebrews 9:24 states that Christ with his priestly ministry has entered into heaven on our behalf.

Deceased brothers and sisters in Christ are also in the third heaven. Hebrews 12:23 speaks of "the general assembly and church of the firstborn who are enrolled in heaven" (NASB). As for living saints, their "names are written in heaven" (Luke 10:20), and their "citizenship is in heaven" (Phil. 3:20). Also, their reward is in heaven (Matt. 5:12).

As glorious as the present third heaven is, it is not the final domain of God and his saints. Second Peter 3:13 declares, "But according to his promise we are waiting for new heavens and a new earth in which righteousness dwells." Revelation 21:1–2 reveals that the New Jerusalem will come down from heaven upon the new earth. There God will dwell with his people (Rev. 21:3). He will wipe away their tears and remove all negative remnants of the previously cursed world (Rev. 21:3–7). Thus, in the fullest way heaven will come to earth. There will be no sickness, no hunger, no trouble, and no tragedy, just absolute joy and eternal blessings.

Cosmic Eschatology

The Kingdom of God
Futuristic Premillennialism
Israel and the Church
Resurrection Order
Future Judgments
Covenants
Timing of Bible Prophecy Fulfillment
Millennial Views
Daniel's "Seventy Weeks" Prophecy
Events to Come

The Kingdom of God[11]

While many important themes reside in the Bible, the kingdom of God seems to be the central theme that ties them all together. As we have already argued in chapter 1,

---

11. This section is adapted from Richard L. Mayhue, "The Kingdom of God: An Introduction," *MSJ* 23, no. 2 (2012): 167–71; William D. Barrick, "The Kingdom of God in the Old Testament," *MSJ* 23, no. 2 (2012): 173–92; F. David Farnell, "The Kingdom of God in the New Testament," *MSJ* 23, no. 2 (2012): 193–208. Used by permission of *MSJ*. For a

the kingdom of God should be considered the grand, overarching theme of Scripture, encompassing all the other major themes in the Bible.[12] Here we want to expound on that idea by looking in more detail at what both the Old and New Testaments teach us about the kingdom of God. Before we get into each of these topics, let us first consider the multifaceted nature of God's kingdom through the following contrasts found in Scripture's descriptions of the kingdom:[13]

1. Certain passages present the kingdom as something that has always existed (Pss. 10:16; 145:11–13), yet elsewhere the kingdom has a definite historical beginning (Dan. 2:44).
2. The kingdom is described as universal in scope (Ps. 103:19) but is also revealed as a local rule on earth (Isa. 24:23).
3. Sometimes the kingdom is pictured as the direct rule of God (Pss. 22:28; 59:13); at other times, it is presented as the rule of God through a mediator (Ps. 2:4–6; Dan. 4:17, 25).
4. The Bible in some places describes the kingdom as entirely future (Zech. 14:9; Matt. 6:10), while in other places, the kingdom is portrayed as a current reality (Ps. 29:10; Dan. 4:3).
5. On the one hand, the kingdom of God is set forth as God's sovereign, unconditional rule (Dan. 4:3, 34–35); on the other hand, it appears to be based on a covenant between God and man (Ps. 89:27–29).
6. God's kingdom is said to be everlasting (Dan. 4:3), but God will bring an end to part of his kingdom (Hos. 1:4).
7. The kingdom is not eating and drinking (Rom. 14:17), nor can it be inherited by flesh and blood (1 Cor. 15:50), yet the kingdom is also spoken of in earthly, tangible senses (Pss. 2:4–6; 89:27–29).
8. The kingdom is among the Jews (Luke 17:21), yet Jesus also told his disciples to pray that it would come (Matt. 6:10).
9. Paul preached "the kingdom of God" (Acts 28:31), yet Christians are now in "the church age" (Acts 2).
10. Children of the kingdom can be cast into hell (Matt. 8:12), yet only the righteous shall inherit the kingdom (1 Cor. 6:9–10).
11. The earthly domain has been temporarily handed over to Satan (Luke 4:6), yet all the earth is the Lord's (Ps. 24:1).
12. The kingdom is for Israel (2 Sam. 7:11–13), yet Christ also gave it to the nations (Matt. 21:43).

KINGDOM IN THE OLD TESTAMENT

God's kingdom program started in Genesis 1 when the King of the universe created the world in six days. There is a King—God. And there is the realm of the King—earth. Man, created as God's image bearer on the sixth day, was tasked with a kingdom

---

more comprehensive study of this topic, see these three articles and the following articles from the same journal issue (*MSJ* 23, no. 2 [2012]): Keith Essex, "The Mediatorial Kingdom and Salvation," 209–23; Michael J. Vlach, "The Kingdom of God and the Millennium," 225–54; Nathan Busenitz, "The Kingdom of God and the Eternal State," 255–74; Dennis M. Swanson, "Bibliography of Works on the Kingdom of God," 275–81.

12. See "What Is the Overarching and Unifying Theme of Scripture?" (p. 42).

13. The initial five contrasts were put forth by Alva J. McClain, *The Greatness of the Kingdom: An Inductive Study of the Kingdom of God* (Chicago: Moody Press, 1959), 19–20.

command—fill, rule, and subdue the earth for God's glory (Gen. 1:26–28). The word "rule" (Heb. *radah*) is a kingly term used later of Messiah's future reign in Psalm 110:2 (NASB): "The LORD will stretch forth Your strong scepter from Zion, saying, 'Rule [*radah*] in the midst of Your enemies.'"

But man failed his kingdom task when Adam sinned against God (Genesis 3). The fall interrupted God's creation command for mankind. Tragically, the fulfillment of humanity's promised potential could no longer reach its fullest expression because of man's fallen nature. Any exercise of that original dominion has proven to be incomplete and imperfect. The psalmist referred to that high and lofty role in Psalm 8:3–9, which reaffirmed man's right "to rule over the works of God's hands," including the sheep, oxen, beasts of the field, birds of the heavens, and fish of the sea. The psalmist presented the ideal for mankind, not the current reality—the designed future of kingdom rule, not the diminished past and present. Of course, the Messiah, as the "Son of Man," would fulfill mankind's role as the human race's only perfect representative (cf. Heb. 2:5–14). He would rule over the earth and succeed as the last Adam in the realm where the first Adam failed (cf. 1 Cor. 15:20–28, 45).

The means for restoring God's mediatorial kingdom on earth would come through four eternal and unconditional biblical covenants—the Noahic, Abrahamic, Davidic, and new covenants. Together, these covenants have revealed both the kings and King (Jesus) of God's kingdom plans and the details of this kingdom. The Noahic covenant promised stability of nature so God's kingdom purposes could play out in history (Gen. 8:21–22). The Abrahamic covenant guaranteed a seed line involving Abraham and the developing people of Israel, which would be the vehicle and means for blessing the people groups of the world (Gen. 12:2–3). This covenant also promised a land for Israel (Gen. 12:6–7) that would serve as the basis for God's earthly kingdom rule and as a microcosm of what God would do for all nations (Isa. 2:2–4; 27:6). The Davidic covenant directly discussed the role of David and his descendants in establishing God's kingdom on earth, which would bless both Israel and the Gentiles (2 Sam. 7:12–19). The new covenant revealed God's plans to enable his people to love and serve him through a new heart and the indwelling Holy Spirit (Jer. 31:31–34; Ezek. 36:26–27).

A kingdom of God on earth was established with the deliverance of the Israelites from Egypt, the giving of the Mosaic covenant, and the possession of the land of Canaan. On Mount Sinai God told the people of Israel, "You shall be to me a kingdom of priests and a holy nation" (Ex. 19:6). Eventually, Israel received monarchs in the form of Saul, David, and Solomon. David was the one through whom the Davidic covenant was given (2 Sam. 7:12–16). The high point of Israel's kingdom occurred during the reign of Solomon in 1 Kings 8–10, when the descendants and land of Israel were large and prosperous and when Gentile leaders were seeking the wisdom of Israel's king (1 Kings 10:23–25). But Israel's condition deteriorated from there. From the time of 1 Kings 11 onward, Solomon committed idolatry, and Israel marched along in disobedience to God. The promised curses of the Mosaic covenant unfolded. Israel was divided into two kingdoms with both headed toward captivity and dispersion. The ten tribes of Israel were conquered by Assyria in 722 BC, and Judah was conquered by Babylon and the temple destroyed in 586 BC.

In the declining and then captive kingdom of Israel, the prophets took center stage as God's spokesmen. They rebuked both Israel's leaders and the people for turning from God and breaking the Mosaic covenant. Yet they also foretold of a kingdom under the Messiah in the latter days (Isa. 2:2–4). This kingdom would involve a restoration of the Davidic kingdom under the Messiah in Israel and blessings for the nations under Israel's king (cf. Amos 9:11–12). The restored kingdom would have spiritual requirements since faith and a willing heart to serve God were necessary to enter it, yet this kingdom would include physical and material prosperity for Israel and the nations. This hope went unrealized at the end of the Old Testament era. While segments of the people of Israel would return to their land and eventually rebuild the temple, they remained under the rule and direction of Gentile powers (cf. Daniel 2; 7). Only the Messiah could bring the needed spiritual and national deliverance.

KINGDOM IN THE NEW TESTAMENT

At the beginning of the New Testament era, there was great anticipation concerning the Messiah and the kingdom of God. The angel Gabriel informed Mary that she would have a Son who would be great and sit on the throne of his father David. He would rule over Israel forever (Luke 1:32–33). Zechariah prophesied that God was remembering the Abrahamic covenant and would deliver Israel from her enemies (Luke 1:72–74). He also declared, repeating the angel of the Lord's message, that the child his wife Elizabeth was to bear would be the forerunner to the Messiah to prepare for his coming (Luke 1:16–17). In Jerusalem, the righteous Simeon was "waiting for the consolation of Israel" as the Holy Spirit was upon him (Luke 2:25). The prophetess Anna was one of several "who were waiting for the redemption of Jerusalem" (Luke 2:38). Messianic kingdom expectations were high, and this hope would not go unfulfilled.

The expectation of the promised Davidic King was fulfilled in Jesus. The first verse of the New Testament declares, "The book of the genealogy of Jesus Christ, the son of David, the son of Abraham" (Matt. 1:1). Both Jesus and his forerunner, John the Baptist, proclaimed the same message—"Repent, for the kingdom of heaven is at hand" (Matt. 3:2; 4:17). Since no definition or redefinition of the kingdom was offered, the kingdom they preached was the same as the kingdom proclaimed by the Old Testament prophets, namely, an earthly kingdom under the Messiah with a restored Israel and blessings for the nations (Matt. 19:28). Repentance was the condition for entering this kingdom.

Jesus explained what he expected from those who would enter his kingdom (Matthew 5–7). He also performed miracles to prove his credentials as King. His miracles in nature, physical healings, exorcisms, and raising of the dead fulfilled Old Testament prophecy and showed that the kingdom had come upon the people (Isaiah 35;

Matt. 11:2–5; 12:28). The kingdom message at this time was solely directed to the people of Israel (Matt. 10:5–7). Yet the people of Israel did not repent. The cities of Israel rejected the kingdom message (Matt. 11:20–24), and the leaders committed blasphemy against the Holy Spirit by attributing Jesus's miracles to the power of Satan (Matt. 12:22–32). This was a wholesale national rejection by Israel of her Messiah, an act that would bring judgment on Israel in the form of the AD 70 destruction of Jerusalem (Matt. 23:37–39; Luke 19:41–44). In response, Jesus began to speak of the kingdom as coming in the future after his return to heaven (Luke 19:11) and after the events of the tribulation period (Luke 21:31).

Jesus spoke of the "secrets of the kingdom of heaven" in the form of parables (Matt. 13:11). These parables revealed new truths concerning the kingdom program between Jesus's first and second comings. The Old Testament did not explicitly teach two comings of the Messiah with a significant gap between them. This was new in revealed truth. Although the kingdom itself would not be established until Jesus's return, several truths related to the kingdom would begin to exist in the church age. The parable of the sower revealed that the gospel of the kingdom would be preached and would receive various responses (Matt. 13:3–9, 18–23). The parable of the wheat and tares showed that the sons of the kingdom and the sons of the Devil would coexist in this age and would only be separated when Jesus returned at the end of the age with his angels (Matt. 13:24–30, 36–43). The parables of the mustard seed and leaven showed that the kingdom, through its message and children, would start small but grow to be large (Matt. 13:31–33).

In the latter part of Jesus's ministry, his message focused mostly on his coming sacrificial death (Matt. 16:21). Yet he still predicted the kingdom's coming: "Truly, I say to you, in the new world, when the Son of Man will sit on his glorious throne, you who have followed me will also sit on twelve thrones, judging the twelve tribes of Israel" (Matt. 19:28). Here Jesus foretold of sitting on the glorious Davidic throne and of his disciples ruling with him over a restored and united national Israel at the time of cosmic renewal, which is clearly future. Also, in reference to his second coming, Jesus stated, "When the Son of Man comes in his glory, and all the angels with him, then he will sit on his glorious throne" (Matt. 25:31). Jesus thus made it clear that his earthly reign from David's throne would occur at the time of his return with his angels.

With his death, resurrection, and ascension, Jesus has been exalted as Messiah to the right hand of God the Father, where Jesus possesses all authority in heaven and earth (Matt. 28:18; Eph. 1:20–22). Yet the actual exercise of his kingdom authority on earth awaits the future. The writer of Hebrews thus says, "He [Jesus] sat down at the right hand of God, waiting from that time until his enemies should be made a footstool for his feet" (Heb. 10:12–13). Jesus's session at the right hand of the Father will then lead to a reign over the earth from Jerusalem (Ps. 110:1–2). On the day of his ascension, Jesus's apostles asked if at that time the kingdom would be restored to Israel (Acts 1:6). Jesus said that the timing of this event was known only to the

Father and that the disciples were to focus on gospel proclamation to the ends of the earth (Acts 1:7–8).

The New Testament Epistles reveal that salvific benefits of the kingdom apply to believers in this church age. Christians experience the new covenant spiritual blessings of a new heart and the indwelling Holy Spirit (2 Cor. 3:6). They are positionally transferred into the kingdom of God's Son (Col. 1:13) and experience kingdom righteousness in their lives (Rom. 14:17). Yet the earthly kingdom *reign* of Jesus and his saints is presented as future. Paul explained that faithful endurance by Christians now will lead to a future "reign" in Jesus's kingdom—"If we endure, we will also reign with Him" (2 Tim. 2:12). This present age is characterized by trials, but for those who endure, the kingdom is their reward. Paul thus charged the Thessalonians "to walk in a manner worthy of God, who calls you into his own kingdom and glory" (1 Thess. 2:12). Near the end of his life Paul declared, "The Lord will rescue me from every evil deed and bring me safely into his heavenly kingdom" (2 Tim. 4:18). Peter told his readers to make certain their calling and election: "For in this way there will be richly provided for you an entrance into the eternal kingdom of our Lord and Savior Jesus Christ" (2 Pet. 1:10–11). The kingdom, therefore, is presented in the Epistles as a future reward for those who endure and persevere for God during this present age of trials and persecutions.

In the book of Revelation, Jesus is presented as the "the ruler of kings on earth" (Rev. 1:5), a rule that will be actualized with his second coming to earth and his reign as described in Revelation 19:11–20:6. The churches of Revelation 2–3 are exhorted to stand firm for Jesus in this present age knowing that a kingdom reward will follow. For those who persevere, Jesus "will give authority over the nations" (2:26). They will also sit with Jesus on his throne (3:21). Revelation 5:9–10 says that those who have been purchased with Jesus's blood and form the nucleus of God's kingdom will reign over the earth: "And you have made them a kingdom and priests to our God, and they shall reign on the earth."

With his return to earth, Jesus will rule the nations (19:11–15). He will destroy his enemies and establish his millennial reign on the earth (19:17–20:6). This will involve the binding of Satan in the Abyss (20:1–3) and the resurrection of martyred saints, who will then begin to rule over the earth (20:4). The end of the millennium will culminate in a dramatic act of judgment as God will destroy the recently released Satan and those from the nations who launch an attack against the beloved city of Jerusalem (20:7–10). This millennial reign of Jesus will then lead to the eternal kingdom described in Revelation 21:1–22:5, where the full presence of God will be manifest in the New Jerusalem. The Father and the Son will be on the throne, and God's people will reign forever and ever (22:1–5).

More about the kingdom will be discussed below in portions about the millennium and the eternal state. In summary, the kingdom of God can be explained in this manner: the divine, eternal triune God literally created a kingdom and two kingdom citizens who were to have dominion over it. But an enemy usurped their rightful allegiance to the King and captured the original kingdom citizens. God intervened with consequential curses that exist to this day. Ever since, God has been redeeming sinful, rebellious people to be restored as qualified kingdom citizens, both now in a spiritual sense and later in a kingdom-on-earth sense. Finally, the enemy will be vanquished forever, as will sin. Thus, Revelation 21–22 describes the final and eternal expression of the kingdom of God, in which the eternal triune God will restore the kingdom to its original purity, removing the curse and establishing the new heaven and the new earth as the everlasting abode of God and his people.

Futuristic Premillennialism[14]

Many different approaches to cosmic eschatology have been offered. The one we believe to be most faithful to Scripture is futuristic premillennialism. As a refinement of dispensational premillennialism, futuristic premillennialism affirms a futuristic view of Daniel's seventieth week (Dan. 9:27), which includes the events of Matthew 24 and the judgments of seals, trumpets, and bowls described in Revelation 6–18. Not only is the millennial kingdom of Revelation 20 future, so too is the tribulation period that precedes the millennium. This futuristic understanding of Daniel's seventieth week contrasts with other eschatological approaches, such as amillennialism and postmillennialism, which place Daniel's seventieth week and the tribulation period in this present age.

Futuristic premillennialism is based on three main beliefs. First, it accords with the consistent use of the grammatical-historical method of interpretation to all areas of the Bible, including its prophetic and eschatological passages. This means prophetic passages must be understood according to their normal and natural sense. This approach takes into account the various genres found in the Bible and the use of symbols that convey literal truths. As a result, futuristic premillennialism expects a literal fulfillment of all physical, national, land, and spiritual blessings in the Bible, including those to Israel and the nations.

Second, futuristic premillennialism maintains the biblical distinction between Israel and the church and understands that the Bible does not confuse the two. The identity of Israel in the Bible always includes physical descendants of Abraham, Isaac, and Jacob. In fact, all seventy-seven uses of Israel in the New Testament refer to ethnic Israel. Sometimes the term Israel is used of believing Jews only (Rom. 9:6; Gal. 6:16), but it is never used to speak of a spiritual community regardless of ethnicity. Also, the church is never called Israel. For example, in the book of Acts, Luke refers to the church nineteen times and to Israel twenty times, but he never calls the church Israel. This compellingly demonstrates God's intention in keeping these identities distinct.

Futuristic premillennialism rejects all forms of replacement theology or supersessionism, in which the church is viewed as the replacement or fulfillment of promises to national Israel in such a way that removes the theological significance of Israel in God's plans. It affirms the great importance of the church in God's kingdom purposes

---

14. For a significantly expanded treatment, see John MacArthur and Richard Mayhue, gen. eds., *Christ's Prophetic Plans: A Futuristic Premillenial Primer* (Chicago: Moody Publishers, 2012).

but looks forward to a future fulfillment of God's covenant promises to Israel and the nations in a future millennial kingdom. Israel will be both saved and restored, and it will have a role of leadership toward the nations. Futuristic premillennialism understands that the identity of Israel does not expand to include Gentiles. Instead, "the people of God" expands to include Gentiles alongside believing Israel (Isa. 19:24–25). Futuristic premillennialism also affirms that the fulfillment of God's promises occurs in stages. What was not fulfilled with Jesus's first coming must be fulfilled with events leading up to and including his second coming.

Third, futuristic premillennialism recognizes that Scripture presents a coming fulfillment of Daniel's seventieth week that is a seven-year period of tribulation and that comes before Jesus's earthly millennial kingdom (Dan. 9:27). While the church faces tribulation generally in this age, a future special period of tribulation will involve God's unique and catastrophic judgments and wrath on the entire earth (Revelation 6–19). This tribulation includes the judgments of seals, trumpets, and bowls described in Revelation 6–16. This coming tribulation culminates in the return of Jesus and the establishment of his thousand-year kingdom on earth. Futuristic premillennialism contrasts with theological beliefs that often view this present age between the two comings of Jesus as both the predicted tribulation period and the kingdom of Jesus. For futuristic premillennialism, the tribulation of Revelation 6–18 precedes the coming of Christ, the establishment of his kingdom (Revelation 19–20), and the eternal state (Revelation 21–22).

Israel and the Church

Understanding eschatology requires knowing how God works through both Israel and the church.

ISRAEL

Israel is the nation and people that stem from the line of Abraham, Isaac, and Jacob. The story of Israel begins in Genesis 12 with the calling of Abraham (then known as Abram). The backdrop is Genesis 10–11, which describes the Tower of Babel event and the spreading of people groups and nations throughout the world. Yet the nations remain sinful with no hope apart from God's intervention. Genesis 12:2–3 reveals that Abraham and the "great nation" to come from him will be the vehicle for blessing the nations of the earth (cf. 22:18).

Israel will be a blessing to the nations in two main ways. First, Israel will be the vessel through which the Savior (Messiah) will come. After the fall, God promised that a specific "he" from the offspring of the woman would arrive and reverse the curse and defeat the power behind the Serpent, that is, Satan (Gen. 3:15). This is fulfilled in Jesus, the ultimate offspring (Gal. 3:16). A messianic hope is found in Genesis 49:8–12, where Jacob said that from his son Judah would eventually come a king who would bless the world. He would be the one called "Shiloh" or "the one to whom it [a kingly reign] belongs," and to him would be the "obedience of the peoples" (Gen. 49:10). So from Israel will come a Savior who will also be King of the world.

Second, Israel is destined to fulfill a role of service and leadership to the other nations of the world. Since God has planned a successful kingdom reign on earth (Isa. 52:13), God will use Israel as a nation, under her Messiah, to carry out a representative role to the nations (Isa. 2:2–4). Israel is a means for global blessings. Israel as a nation/people and Israel's land are intended to function as microcosms of what God will do for all nations. Israel will also be a platform for the blessings of the nations. As God blesses Israel in the Land of Promise, God will bless other nations and their lands. As Isaiah 27:6 predicts, "In days to come Jacob shall take root, Israel shall blossom and put forth shoots and fill the whole world with fruit."

To understand Israel's future role as a nation, one must grasp Israel's past. We have seen aspects of this history in our discussion of the kingdom of God, but it bears recounting the story particularly from the viewpoint of Israel. With the exodus from Egypt, the growing people of Israel were freed from slavery to pursue their destiny to become a "kingdom of priests and a holy nation" (Ex. 19:6). A priest is one who represents others to God, and Israel was called by God as a holy nation to represent the nations before God. Deuteronomy 4:5–6 promised that if Israel obeyed God's commandments, then the peoples of the earth would "hear all these statutes" and say, "Surely this great nation is a wise and understanding people." Israel's obedience was meant to serve as a witness to the nations, who would thus be drawn to Israel's God.

They seemed to be achieving their purpose during the high point of Israel's kingdom under Solomon (1 Kings 8–10). The descendants of Israel were many, and the boundaries of Israel's land were large. During this time foreign leaders and nations, illustrated by the queen of Sheba, were seeking the wisdom of Israel's king—Solomon (1 Kings 10:1–10, 24). The promise that the nations of the earth would be blessed through Abraham's descendants (Gen. 22:18) appeared on the brink of fulfillment. But Solomon's idolatry (1 Kings 11) halted this progress and put Israel on a trajectory toward disobedience and dispersion. Instead of being a holy nation that positively attracted the nations to God, Israel worshiped the gods of the nations and was soon taken captive by the nations. After Solomon, the kingdom was divided, and eventually both the northern tribes of Israel and the southern tribes of Judah were led into captivity. Some Jews would return to the land but always under the authority of Gentile powers and never with the freedom and grandeur that occurred in the early years of Solomon's reign.

After the monarchy ended in Israel, the prophets became the central players. Their messages focused on three key areas: (1) rebuke to Israel for breaking the Mosaic covenant (e.g., Ezekiel 1–24; Micah 1–3); (2) warnings and predictions for the nations (e.g., Isaiah 13–23; Ezekiel 25–32); and (3) promises of a glorious kingdom in which Israel would be restored under her Messiah and the nations of the earth would be blessed (e.g., Isa. 2:2–4; 19:24–25; Amos 9:11–15).

When Jesus appeared, he arrived as the offspring of Abraham and David (Matt.

1:1) who presented the kingdom of heaven that the Old Testament prophets predicted (Matt. 4:17). Yet the cities of Israel rejected the King and his kingdom (Matt. 11:20–24), and the leaders of Israel rejected Jesus by attributing his works to Satan (Matt. 12:24). This escalated Israel's sin of unbelief. The consequence for this rejection of Israel's Messiah was the dispersion and destruction of Israel's temple in AD 70, something predicted by Daniel (Dan. 9:26) and Jesus (Matt. 23:38; Luke 19:41–44; 21:20–24). Since the destruction of Jerusalem in AD 70, Israel has continued to experience the "times of the Gentiles" (Luke 21:24), during which Israel has been oppressed by Gentile powers.

So how does Israel relate to eschatology? The first purpose of Israel—to be a vehicle for the Savior and Messiah—has been fulfilled. Jesus, the ultimate Israelite (Isa. 49:3; Gal. 4:4–5) and offspring of Abraham (Gal. 3:16), arrived bringing forgiveness and salvation to all who believe in him, regardless of nationality. Forgiveness of sins and the indwelling Holy Spirit have been given to both believing Jews and Gentiles in this age between Jesus's two comings. Yet Israel's role in leading and serving other nations awaits fulfillment (Isa. 2:2–4). The picture of Israel that the prophets offered as a prominent nation in an earthly reign of the Messiah is yet future (see Isaiah 60). In Matthew 19:28, Jesus said that during the coming time of cosmic renewal ("the new world"), he would "sit on his glorious throne" and the apostles would "also sit on twelve thrones, judging the twelve tribes of Israel." This word speaks of a restored and unified nation of Israel. Also, after forty days of instruction about the kingdom from the risen Jesus, the apostles asked him, "Lord, will you at this time restore the kingdom to Israel?" (Acts 1:3, 6). Jesus assumed the correctness of their belief in a restoration of the kingdom to Israel but told them that the timing of this event was known only by the Father (Acts 1:7). This statement also affirms a restored kingdom to Israel.

Paul declared a future salvation of Israel when he stated, "All Israel will be saved" (Rom. 11:26). This salvation of Israel will bring even greater blessings for the world. In Romans 11:12, Paul stated, "Now if their [Israel's] trespass means riches for the world, and if their failure means riches for the Gentiles, how much more will their full inclusion mean!" He then said, "For if their rejection means the reconciliation of the world, what will their acceptance mean but life from the dead?" (11:15). In Romans 11, Paul addressed the unbelieving people of Israel in the church age. While a remnant of believing Jewish people exists, the people as a whole reside in unbelief. But when Israel is saved, blessings to the world will be even greater than they are now. Then the world will see the cosmic renewal that the Old Testament prophets foretold (Isaiah 11; 65:17–25).

Yet the road to this glorious future for Israel will not be straight and level. Israel is currently experiencing a temporary hardening and facing the consequences for rejecting the Messiah. Jesus declared that Israel missed its time of "visitation," and in so doing they experienced the judgment of the destruction of Jerusalem in AD 70 and are currently experiencing the "times of the Gentiles" (Luke 19:41–44; 21:20–24).

Yet in this age, there is a remnant of believing Jews (Rom. 11:5), whom Paul calls the "Israel of God" (Gal. 6:16). This elect and faithful remnant serves as a reminder of a coming salvation of "all Israel" in accord with Old Testament prophecies (Rom. 11:26–27). Zechariah foretold that a day is coming when God will "pour out" a "spirit of grace" on the people of Israel so that they will "look on . . . him whom they have pierced" and "they shall mourn for him" (Zech. 12:10). This speaks of the national salvation and restoration of Israel and of their entrance into new covenant blessings.

In the future, there will be a seven-year period (Dan. 9:27) during which God's plan to restore Israel will resume. The last half of this period will include unprecedented persecution and the wrath of Antichrist, who will commit an abominable act in the Jerusalem temple (Matt. 24:15; 2 Thess. 2:3–4). Jeremiah says that this will be a unique period, "a time of distress for Jacob," but that "he shall be saved out of it" (Jer. 30:7). The nations will come against Jerusalem for her destruction, but the returning Lord Jesus will rescue the inhabitants of Jerusalem and establish his kingdom on the earth (Zech. 14:1–9). The nations will then stream to Jerusalem and experience the blessings of royal judgments by the Messiah who reigns from Jerusalem (Isa. 2:2–4; 9:7).

God will fulfill all promises and biblical covenants with Israel just as he said. He will do so not because Israel is so great but because God is impeccably true to his name and his promises to the patriarchs of Israel (Deut. 7:6–9). As Paul stated emphatically in Romans 11:1: "I ask, then, has God rejected his people? By no means!" He then linked Israel's salvation with God's electing purposes: "But as regards election, they are beloved for the sake of their forefathers. For the gifts and the calling of God are irrevocable" (Rom. 11:28–29). Israel, therefore, is essential to God's purposes and may not be dismissed without denigrating the faithfulness of God to his promises.

CHURCH

The church was not explicitly predicted in the Old Testament, but it is a major phase of God's kingdom program and is connected to the covenants of promise (i.e., Abrahamic, Davidic, and new covenants). The greater, ultimate Son of David (Jesus) arrived bringing salvation to all who believe in him. In Galatians 3, Paul stated that Gentile Christians are connected to the Abrahamic promises of Genesis 12:3 and 22:18, which declared that God's blessings would one day go to Gentiles. Members of the church are spiritual sons of Abraham and are related to the Abrahamic covenant (Gal. 3:7–9, 29). Jesus's death brought an inauguration of the new covenant, and those who trust in Jesus benefit from the new covenant. This includes the new covenant promise of the indwelling Holy Spirit, who enables Christians to obey God as they should (Acts 2:4, 17; Rom. 8:3–4). Christians are also proclaimers of this covenant (2 Cor. 3:6; cf. Heb. 8:8–13). And Jew-Gentile spiritual unity under Israel's Messiah is already occurring (Acts 15:14–18; Eph. 2:11–22; 3:6). So while the Old Testament did not predict the church with its structure and mission for this age, the church is connected to promises relating to salvation, the indwelling ministry of the Holy Spirit, and redemptive unity among Jews and Gentiles.

The church has a unique mission before Jesus returns to rule the nations. It is the vehicle for kingdom proclamation while Israel is undergoing a temporary hardening (Rom. 11:11). It is called to take the gospel and the message of the kingdom to the nations. This is its Great Commission (Matt. 28:19–20). Those who believe in Jesus become "sons of the kingdom" (Matt. 13:38) and are to evidence kingdom righteousness in their lives (Matthew 5–7).

The church is a persecuted minority in this age. It faces persecution from Satan and those who do his bidding. God's teaching about what is to come motivates the church that operates in this present evil age with the promise of reward (Gal. 1:4). Endurance in this age will lead to a kingdom reign in the future. Paul stated, "If we endure, we will also reign with him" (2 Tim. 2:12). John promised the church in Thyatira, "The one who conquers and who keeps my works until the end, to him I will give authority over the nations, and he will rule them with a rod of iron" (Rev. 2:26–27). Those who persevere in doing what Jesus wants will share Jesus's rule over the nations when he comes again. Jesus also promised, "The one who conquers, I will grant him to sit with me on my throne" (Rev. 3:21). The church faces difficulties and troubles in this age between Jesus's two comings, but Jesus will reward the church with positions of authority in his kingdom rule over the nations. Radical commitment to Jesus now leads to incredible reward in the future.

Yet the church is not the final phase of God's kingdom program before the eternal state. Much still needs to be fulfilled, including an international reign of the Messiah on and over the earth. Israel has not yet been saved and restored as a nation. The nations as national entities are not serving God (Isa. 19:24–25), nor are they experiencing international harmony and the removal of war (Isa. 2:2–4). The renewal of the planet (Matt. 19:28; Rom. 8:19–23) and harmony in the animal kingdom (Isa. 11:6–9) must still happen. Satan still actively deceives the world and persecutes the saints of God (Revelation 12–13). Creation as a whole still works against man as it remains under the curse (Gen. 3:17). Earthquakes, tornadoes, snakebites, malaria, infant mortality, and many other negative experiences remind everyone that creation is not subdued. Humanity, while still required to rule the earth for God (Ps. 8:6), is not yet ruling the earth in a successful way for the glory of God (Gen. 1:26–28; Heb. 2:5–8). These conditions do not fit the kingdom characteristics predicted by the prophets. There must be a successful reign of Jesus the Messiah and his saints on this earth before Jesus hands the kingdom over to the Father and the eternal state begins (1 Cor. 15:24–28). While Christians celebrate many spiritual blessings already, there is still much more to come.

Understanding that the church is not the final phase of God's kingdom program is necessary for avoiding wrong views of eschatology. Some eschatological positions have viewed this age as the primary fulfillment of Jesus's kingdom reign and have claimed that the church is the fulfillment or replacement of Israel. Many Old Testament prophecies have been spiritualized to fit this current age, when in reality they describe coming kingdom conditions on the earth. Currently, the church is a strategic instrument of God's kingdom purposes in this age, tasked with taking the gospel to the nations. Members of the church, both living and dead, are destined for the rapture event of 1 Thessalonians 4:14–17, in which Jesus will snatch all Christians into the air to be with him to avoid the wrath of God in the coming day of the Lord (1 Thess. 1:10). When Jesus comes to earth, the church will return with him and participate in Jesus's millennial kingdom reign by ruling the nations (Rev. 2:26–27). In sum, the church is experiencing many great blessings, yet it looks forward to ruling with Jesus in his coming millennial kingdom.

Resurrection Order

What resurrection means for individuals has been discussed above. Here we discuss God's resurrection plans more broadly concerning the timing and subjects of the various resurrections of Scripture. Passages such as Daniel 12:2; John 5:28–29; and Romans 2:5–8 explicitly state that there will be a resurrection of the righteous and the wicked. But does this mean that the resurrection of both groups occurs at the same time? Some think that it does, but we believe that it does not. The resurrection program occurs in stages. Just as there are phases to other aspects of God's program such as covenants, kingdom, salvation, and the day of the Lord, the judgments of Scripture occur in phases as well.

Two passages explicitly reveal an order in the resurrection program. First, Paul mentions three phases in 1 Corinthians 15:22–24: "For as in Adam all die, so also in Christ all will be made alive. But each in his own order: Christ the first fruits, after that those who are Christ's at His coming, then comes the end, when He hands over the kingdom to the God and Father, when He has abolished all rule and all authority and power" (NASB). The "order" of the resurrection phases is as follows:

Phase 1: Christ the firstfruits
Phase 2: After that those who are Christ's at his coming
Phase 3: Then comes the end

Second, the apostle John tells of two resurrections separated by a thousand years. In Revelation 20:4–5, he writes concerning certain martyrs, "They came to life and reigned with Christ for a thousand years. The rest of the dead did not come to life until the thousand years were completed" (NASB). Note that there is one group that comes to life (i.e., is resurrected) and reigns with Christ for a thousand years, and then there is another group called "the rest of the dead," who are not resurrected until the thousand years runs its course. This shows two resurrections separated by a thousand years. So, then, two Bible passages explicitly teach stages in the resurrection program. When viewed together, they describe four phases of resurrection activity.

In regard to 1 Corinthians 15:20–24, Jesus Christ's resurrection around AD 30 was the first phase of the resurrection program, the "firstfruits" of what is to come. His bodily resurrection serves as the template and guarantee for the resurrection of all who believe in him.

The second phase of the resurrection—"those who are Christ's at His coming"—involves those who are raised in connection with the second coming of Jesus. This includes resurrected church saints, both dead and alive, at the rapture as described in 1 Thessalonians 4:14–17. At the rapture, the dead in Christ will rise first, and then living saints will be "caught up" to meet Jesus in the air.

While not occurring at the time of the rapture, this third phase includes resurrected Old Testament saints (Dan. 12:2) and martyred saints during the tribulation period (Rev. 20:4). They experience resurrection as a result of Jesus's coming to earth. Revelation 6:9–11 tells of martyrs who gave their lives because of their testimony for Jesus. These souls in heaven call out for the avenging of their blood on earth but are told to wait a little while. Revelation 20:4 is the fulfillment of their expectation: "They came to life and reigned with Christ for a thousand years."

The fourth phase of the resurrection is what Paul calls "the end" and occurs after the millennial reign of Jesus. According to Revelation 20:5, this involves "the rest of the dead," who in this context are unbelievers, those destined for the great white throne judgment of Revelation 20:11–15. So unbelievers are present at the resurrection after the thousand-year reign of Christ.

But do any believers experience resurrection at this fourth stage of the resurrection program? This is more difficult to answer, but they might for the following reason. Nonglorified saints will enter the millennial kingdom as a result of being saved during the seven-year tribulation period. These are nonglorified saints who bore children with nonglorified bodies during the millennial kingdom (Isa. 65:20, 23). However, since 1 Corinthians 15:50 states that nonglorified bodies cannot enter God's eternal kingdom, these saints must receive glorified bodies at some point. It is likely that these nonglorified saints will receive resurrection bodies immediately at death or at the end of the millennium.

Bringing all this together, five conclusions can be offered concerning the order of resurrections:

1. The Bible speaks of the resurrection of the redeemed as "the first resurrection" (Rev. 20:5), the "resurrection of life" (John 5:29), "eternal life" (Rom. 2:7), or "everlasting life" (Dan. 12:2).
2. This "first resurrection" of the redeemed occurs in three phases: (a) Christ the firstfruits (1 Cor. 15:23); (b) church saints (1 Cor. 15:23, 50–58; 1 Thess. 4:13–18); (c) Old Testament saints (Ezek. 37:12–14; Dan. 12:2) and tribulation saints (Rev. 20:4).
3. The Bible does not use the term "second resurrection" but refers to the resurrection of the unredeemed as "a resurrection of judgment" (John 5:29) or "the second death" (Rev. 20:6, 14; 21:8).
4. The Bible gives no warrant to conclude that only one general resurrection of the righteous will occur at the end.
5. Thus, there are four recognized times of resurrection in Scripture: (a) Christ's resurrection (1 Cor. 15:23); (b) church saints' resurrection (1 Cor. 15:23, 50–58; 1 Thess. 4:13–18); (c) the resurrection of Old Testament saints (Ezek.

37:12–14; Dan. 12:2) and tribulation saints (Rev. 20:4); and (d) the resurrection of the unredeemed of all time (Rev. 20:5).

Future Judgments

The Bible clearly teaches that all people will face a judgment day before God when his judgment will be all that matters. A day of reckoning is coming when all will stand before the Creator to account for every thought and deed.

God is the sovereign, holy, and righteous Creator of the universe. Man is his creation, a volitional being who is obligated to serve God and live in conformity to his righteous laws and commands. Man is not an autonomous being. Everything he is and does must be measured against his Creator. Because God is perfectly holy, he cannot allow sin to go unpunished. Judgment, therefore, is a divine necessity. Moral creatures must stand before God someday to account for their deeds and motives: "And no creature is hidden from his sight, but all are naked and exposed to the eyes of him to whom we must give account" (Heb. 4:13).

As with other aspects of eschatology, God's judgments are multifaceted, occurring in stages. Some judgments of God such as the global flood judgment, his judgment on Sodom and Gomorrah, and past historical judgments on Israel and Judah have already occurred. Judgments described in Romans 1:18–32 have gone on throughout all human history as God's wrath has fallen on corrupt societies. Plus, there is a sense in which the wrath of God already remains on the unbeliever (John 3:36). The focus of this section, however, is on future judgments.

THE JUDGMENT SEAT OF CHRIST

All Christians are headed for a day of judgment before Jesus Christ. Scripture explicitly mentions the judgment seat of Christ in two places; in each, Paul is addressing Christians:

> For we must all appear before the judgment seat of Christ, so that each one may receive what is due for what he has done in the body, whether good or evil. (2 Cor. 5:10)

> Why do you pass judgment on your brother? Or you, why do you despise your brother? For we will all stand before the judgment seat of God. (Rom. 14:10)

In both cases, the Greek word for "judgment" is *bēma*. In ancient times, a *bēma* was a raised platform or step used in athletic or political arenas.[15] Rulers or judges would ascend the *bēma* to render decisions in legal cases. Pilate judged Jesus from his *bēma* seat (Matt. 27:19; John 19:13). In athletic events, an authority figure would be elevated to a *bēma* to judge the competition and award the winners.

Scripture reveals several truths about the judgment seat of Christ. First, Jesus is the Judge who presides over this *bēma* judgment. Second Corinthians 5:10 states that this is a judgment seat "of Christ." Also, since the Father has granted all judg-

---

15. Consult Samuel L. Hoyt, *The Judgment Seat of Christ: A Biblical and Theological Study*, rev. ed. (Duluth, MN: Grace Gospel, 2015).

ment to the Son (John 5:22, 27), little doubt exists that the "judgment seat of God" in Romans 14:10 also involves Jesus.

Second, the subjects of this judgment are Christians. In both 2 Corinthians 5:10 and Romans 14:10, Paul addresses Christians in Rome and Corinth. There will be other judgments, including the great white throne judgment for unbelievers at a later time (Rev. 20:11–15), but the judgment here is for Christians. In 1 Corinthians 3:11–15, Paul speaks of a judgment for Christians who have Jesus Christ as their foundation.

This judgment results in rewards for what a Christian has done with his or her life—for deeds good or bad (2 Cor. 5:10). This is a whole-life evaluation. The "good" refers to those works done in the power of the Holy Spirit that bring glory to God. The "bad"' refers to worthless deeds that do not bring God honor, works done in the flesh (Gal. 5:19–21). This evaluation of good and bad deeds is further explained in 1 Corinthians 3:12–15:

> Now if anyone builds on the foundation with gold, silver, precious stones, wood, hay, straw—each one's work will become manifest, for the Day will disclose it, because it will be revealed by fire, and the fire will test what sort of work each one has done. If the work that anyone has built on the foundation survives, he will receive a reward. If anyone's work is burned up, he will suffer loss, though he himself will be saved, but only as through fire.

The "gold, silver, [and] precious stones" here are the "good" of 2 Corinthians 5:10. Likewise, the "wood, hay, [and] straw" represent the "bad." The Lord Jesus with his judgment of fire "will test what sort of work each one has done" (1 Cor. 3:13). Good works will lead to a reward (1 Cor. 3:14), but bad works will be burned up in the fire. They cannot lead to reward. In fact, bad or worthless deeds are linked with suffering "loss" (1 Cor. 3:15). What is this loss? It cannot be a loss of salvation since Paul says, "though he himself will be saved" (1 Cor. 3:15). Nor can it be a punitive loss coming from judgment for sin. The Christian is under no condemnation for sin since Jesus has atoned for his sins (Rom. 8:1). The "loss" could be the realization and awareness of lost opportunities for Christ and a deep remorse for wasting valuable opportunities to bring God glory and to gain greater eternal reward. Still, the Christian's appearance before Jesus is a joyous event. Paul told the Corinthians to "wait for the revealing of our Lord Jesus Christ, who will sustain you to the end, guiltless in the day of our Lord Jesus Christ" (1 Cor. 1:7–8). Yet the Christian should strive to avoid a sense of shame and loss. John warned about this when he said, "And now, little children, abide in him, so that when he appears we may have confidence and not shrink from him in shame at his coming" (1 John 2:28).

The judgment seat of Christ does not stop with an evaluation of deeds; rather, it goes deeper to motives. First Corinthians 4:5 says that the Lord "will bring to light the things now hidden in darkness and will disclose the purposes of the heart. Then each one will receive his commendation from God." Thus, the judgment before Jesus is so penetrating that motives behind deeds are evaluated as well. Not only does what we do matter, but so does why we do what we do.

The *bēma* of Jesus also has corporate implications for the church. The resurrected and rewarded church will return victoriously with Jesus at his second coming to earth (Rev. 19:14). The church will also be granted the right to share in Jesus's Davidic throne reign (Rev. 3:21) and to rule the nations with him (Rev. 2:26–27). Thus, faithful service in this age affects a Christian's position in the coming kingdom of Jesus. Not all Christians will receive equal reward and authority; according to Luke 19:11–27, some will be granted more ruling authority than others.

JUDGMENT OF ISRAEL

Jesus will return to earth and set up his kingdom (Zech. 14:4, 9), yet since only those who are redeemed can enter the kingdom (John 3:3), there must be judgments to determine who will enter. One of these judgments involves Jews living at the time of Jesus's return. Ezekiel 20:33–38 explicitly explains this event:

> As I live, declares the Lord God, surely with a mighty hand and an outstretched arm and with wrath poured out I will be king over you. I will bring you out from the peoples and gather you out of the countries where you are scattered, with a mighty hand and an outstretched arm, and with wrath poured out. And I will bring you into the wilderness of the peoples, and there I will enter into judgment with you face to face. As I entered into judgment with your fathers in the wilderness of the land of Egypt, so I will enter into judgment with you, declares the Lord God. I will make you pass under the rod, and I will bring you into the bond of the covenant. I will purge out the rebels from among you, and those who transgress against me. I will bring them out of the land where they sojourn, but they shall not enter the land of Israel. Then you will know that I am the Lord.

This coming judgment of Israel will be a mighty act of God. With "wrath poured out," God will "be king" over Israel (Ezek. 20:33). He will gather Jews from the "countries" where they were scattered (Ezek. 20:34). The setting for this judgment scene will be "the wilderness of the peoples," and it will be an actual face-to-face meeting that parallels God's meeting with Israel in the wilderness of Egypt (Ezek. 20:35–36). Israel will pass under the Lord's kingly and shepherd-like rod to enter the "bond of the covenant" (Ezek. 20:37). This refers not to the Mosaic covenant but to national Israel's entrance into the blessings of the new covenant. Paul speaks of this in Romans 11:26–27, where the salvation of "all Israel" is linked with the new covenant passages of Isaiah 59:20–21 and Jeremiah 31:31–34. The new covenant was inaugurated with Jesus's death (Luke 22:20), and some of its spiritual blessings are experienced in this present age, but Israel will come into the covenant as Jesus establishes his kingdom on earth. Yet not all Israelites will enter this kingdom. The Lord says, "I will purge out the rebels from among you" (Ezek. 20:38a). Even for Israel, spiritual birth is the prerequisite for entering the kingdom of God. The wicked will not enter the kingdom. Though they have been gathered from the nations for this judgment, "they shall not enter the land of Israel" (Ezek. 20:38b).

This judgment of Israel could occur during the coming tribulation period or at a specific judgment setting immediately after Jesus's return to earth. The judgment of Israel at Jesus's return may also be in view in the parables of the ten virgins (Matt. 25:1–13) and the talents (Matt. 25:14–30). In these parables, the coming of Jesus finds people who are both foolish and wise concerning his return. The application of these parables certainly goes beyond Israel to all who await Jesus's return, but the Jewish context of Matthew 24–25 makes application of these parables to Israel likely, especially since the sheep-goat judgment described in Matthew 25:31–46 focuses specifically on Gentile nations.

JUDGMENT OF THE NATIONS

The return of Jesus to earth also results in a judgment of living Gentiles. Two passages directly address this: Joel 3:1–16 and Matthew 25:31–46. First, the prophet Joel predicted,

> For behold, in those days and at that time, when I restore the fortunes of Judah and Jerusalem, I will gather all the nations and bring them down to the Valley of Jehoshaphat. And I will enter into judgment with them there, on behalf of my people and my heritage Israel. (Joel 3:1–2a)

The context of this passage is the day-of-the-Lord judgments of Joel 2, which involve the salvation and blessing of Israel. At this "time" when God restores Israel, he will "gather all the nations" and judge them on behalf of Israel. The Gentile nations will be judged for scattering the Jewish people and dividing up Israel's land, as well as for other atrocities (Joel 3:2b–3). The place of this judgment is specific—"the Valley of Jehoshaphat." From there God will "judge all the surrounding nations" (Joel 3:12). In sum, Joel 3 reveals that God will judge the nations that harmed Israel.

Next, Matthew 25:31–46 also describes a general judgment of Gentile nations:

> When the Son of Man comes in his glory, and all the angels with him, then he will sit on his glorious throne. Before him will be gathered all the nations, and he will separate people one from another as a shepherd separates the sheep from the goats. (Matt. 25:31–32)

This judgment of Gentiles is often referred to as *the sheep-goat judgment* since believers are likened to "sheep" and the wicked to "goats." The purpose of this judgment is to determine who is qualified to enter Jesus's earthly kingdom and who is not. The righteous sheep enter Jesus's kingdom while the wicked are excluded from it and slain.

The basis of this judgment is how the Gentile peoples treated others. Those who treated "the least of these" (Matt. 25:40, 45) with kindness and mercy were really treating Jesus in that way, even though they were unaware of it. Likewise, mistreatment or neglect of others showed contempt for Jesus. This judgment, which is based on acts of compassion, does not indicate that salvation is based on works but rather makes clear that works accurately reveal character (see Rom. 2:5–11). Faith, or the lack of it, is evidenced by works.

While the treatment of the group called "the least of these" has implications for all people, this passage may also have the treatment of the Jewish people in view. Joel 3, which is the background for the judgment of Matthew 25:31–46, declares that the judgment of the nations was on behalf of Israel and reflected how the Gentile nations treated Israel. This may be the case in Matthew 25 as well, especially since persecution of Jews is described in Matthew 24:15–28.

Matthew 25 makes no mention of a resurrection from the dead for those experiencing this judgment. This judgment, therefore, is for Gentiles alive at the time of Jesus's return. Also, it makes no mention of glorification. The "sheep" enter the earthly kingdom of Jesus in their mortal bodies, while the "goats" are executed and enter eternal fire (Matt. 25:41, 46).

JUDGMENT OF SATAN AND DEMONS

For more on the judgment of Satan and demons in history, refer to the discussion of "Satan's Judgments" (p. 703) and "Demons' Judgments" (p. 719) in chapter 8. In this section the focus is only on future judgments for Satan and all his demons.

Satan and his demons suffered original judgment when Satan sinned against God in heaven (Rev. 12:1–4). They also experienced a Calvary judgment where their power was defeated by Jesus at the cross (Col. 2:14–15). Yet three future judgments for Satan and the demons await—tribulational, millennial, and eternal judgments.

Revelation 12:7–13 tells of a tribulational judgment when Satan and his demons will be thrown from heaven to earth. At this point, Satan's access to heaven will be forever removed, and he will turn his attention to persecuting Israel on earth. This will happen around the midpoint of Daniel's seventieth week (Dan. 9:27) since this event is linked with the period called "a time, and times, and half a time" (Rev. 12:14), which is three and one-half years. From this point onward, Satan will no longer be able to accuse believers of sin in the presence of God (Rev. 12:10–11).

Satan is currently active, opposing God's plans, deceiving the nations, and persecuting the saints of God. But Revelation 20:1–3 chronicles a coming millennial judgment, after Jesus's return to earth (Rev. 19:11–21), when Satan will be seized, bound, and thrown into a pit. This pit is not the lake of fire but a spiritual prison that will completely remove Satan's access to the earth and his ability to deceive. It is probable that all demons will be incarcerated with Satan during this time, while Jesus and his saints will rule the earth for a thousand years with no interference from Satan and his corrupt fallen angels (Rev. 20:4).

The final judgment of Satan and the demons will take place in the eternal judgment after the millennium (Rev. 20:7–10). The forces of hell will be released for one final yet doomed rebellion. Satan, demons, and a foolish Christ-rejecting multitude from the nations will attempt to attack the beloved city of Jerusalem, but fire from heaven will instantly consume them in judgment. At that time, Satan and all demons (Matt. 25:41; 2 Pet. 2:4; Jude 6) will join the Antichrist and the false prophet in the lake of fire (Rev. 20:10). This is the final judgment of Satan and his demons, when they will forever be removed from opposing God's kingdom and God's people.

THE GREAT WHITE THRONE JUDGMENT

All unbelievers are ultimately destined for the great white throne judgment. This terrifying event is described in Revelation 20:11–15:

> Then I saw a great white throne and him who was seated on it. From his presence earth and sky fled away, and no place was found for them. And I saw the dead, great and small, standing before the throne, and books were opened. Then another book was opened, which is the book of life. And the dead were judged by what was written in the books, according to what they had done. And the sea gave up the dead who were in it, Death and Hades gave up the dead who were in them, and they were judged, each one of them, according to what they had done. Then Death and Hades were thrown into the lake of fire. This is the second death, the lake of fire. And if anyone's name was not found written in the book of life, he was thrown into the lake of fire.

This final sentencing of the lost is the most serious, sobering, and tragic passage in the Bible. This is the last courtroom scene in history.

The timing of this great white throne judgment takes place after the thousand-year reign of Christ and his saints (Rev. 20:4–7). The One present on the throne is none other than God Almighty (Rev. 4:2–11), which must certainly refer to Jesus since all judgment has been granted to him (John 5:22, 26–27).

The purpose of this judgment is to declare who will be sent to the lake of fire (Rev. 20:15), which is also referred to as "the second death" (Rev. 20:6). The subjects of the great white throne judgment are unbelievers, whose bodies are raised from "Death and Hades" for this judgment (Rev. 20:13).

The basis of the great white throne judgment is works (Rev. 20:13), and the evidence for this judgment is contained in books that reveal the character and deeds of every person. The reference to "books were opened" may include records of the deeds of those before the throne. Then "another book" identified as "the book of life" is opened. This book lists those who have been saved by Jesus. The book of life is a testimony against the unsaved, whose names are not in it. These are "thrown into the lake of fire," which is the final destiny of the lost.

ARE THE SHEEP-GOAT JUDGMENT AND THE GREAT
WHITE THRONE JUDGMENT THE SAME?[16]

Some theologians view the sheep-goat judgment of Matthew 25:31–46 and the great white throne judgment of Revelation 20:11–15 as the same event. They suggest that both describe a judgment scene and a fiery destiny for the wicked. But a close examination reveals that these two judgments cannot be the same. First, the *timing* of the sheep-goat judgment occurs in close proximity to Jesus's second coming (see Matt. 25:31–32). Jesus comes in glory with his angels and sits on his glorious

---

16. This section is adapted from Michael Vlach, "Why the Sheep/Goat Judgment and Great White Throne Judgment Are Not the Same Event," *Mike Vlach* (blog), July 23, 2011, http://mikevlach.blogspot.com/2011/06/why-sheepgoat-judgment -and-great-while.html. Used by permission of the author.

throne (i.e., his Davidic throne), and then all the nations are gathered before him for judgment. So the sheep-goat judgment is closely connected to Jesus's second coming. On the other hand, the great white throne judgment occurs after the thousand-year reign of Jesus and his saints (Rev. 20:4–7). Subsequent to the thousand years (Rev. 20:7), the great white throne judgment takes place (Rev. 20:11–15). This point alone shows that these judgments are distinct. One judgment occurs at the beginning of Jesus's kingdom reign, while the other occurs after the millennium in the transition to the eternal state. Also, the resurrections, separated by a thousand years (see Rev. 20:4–5), strongly suggest that these are two distinct judgments.

In addition to timing, differences exist in the details of these judgments. The *purpose* of the sheep-goat judgment is to see who will inherit the kingdom (Matt. 25:34) and who will not (Matt. 25:41). The purpose of the great white throne judgment is to see who will be sent to the lake of fire (Rev. 20:15). Their purposes are different, and no hope is offered at the great white throne.

Also, the *subjects* of the sheep-goat judgment are both believers and nonbelievers—sheep and goats (Matt. 25:32). But the subjects of the great white throne are only unbelievers. While Revelation 20:11–15 does not exclude believers being present as spectators at this judgment, it does not mention them. The subjects of the sheep-goat judgment are those alive at the time of the second coming of Jesus, but the great white throne judgment involves the resurrection of the lost (Rev. 20:13). The sea and hades give up their dead for this judgment. These differences indicate that the two judgments are each unique and occur at separate times.

Covenants[17]

Covenants are central to God's plans and constitute the vehicles through which God's kingdom purposes unfold. A covenant is a formal agreement or treaty between two parties with obligations and regulations. The vast majority of covenants in the Bible (1) are unconditional or nonnullifiable in that once the covenant is ratified, the covenant must be fulfilled, and (2) are referred to as everlasting. The unconditional covenants include the Noahic, Abrahamic, priestly, Davidic, and new covenants. The one conditional and temporary covenant is the Mosaic covenant. These are biblical covenants since they are explicitly found in Scripture. God's covenant plans can be understood through the study of these biblical covenants.

Some theologians assert that the biblical covenants should be understood through theologically derived covenants. Covenant theology affirms three such covenants: (1) the covenant of works, (2) the covenant of grace, and (3) the covenant of redemption. While there may be certain truths associated with these theological covenants, such as God having a salvation plan from eternity and God working with his people on the basis of grace after the fall of Adam, these are not actual covenants found in the Bible. Their inclusion in discussions of God's covenant program involves saying more than Scripture has explicitly said and can lead to confusion and wrong views.

---

17. For a more detailed discussion of covenants, consult the articles in *MSJ* 10, no. 2 (1999): 173–280.

Theologically derived covenants imposed on the biblical covenants can alter God's intended revelation. Covenant theology, for example, has often used the extrabiblical covenant of grace idea to deny the biblical distinction between Israel and the church. Supposedly, if all people are saved by grace though faith alone, then there can be no distinctions between Israel and the church. But this does not follow. The affirmation of this covenant of grace has often led to the false position of replacement theology or supersessionism in which the church is viewed as the replacement or fulfillment of Israel in such a way that God no longer is working with Israel as a nation. But while the saints of every age are saved by grace alone through faith alone, there are distinctions in the people of God.

Futuristic premillennialism, on the other hand, asserts that God's covenant plans should be anchored in a proper understanding of the biblical covenants and how they unfold in salvation history. Introducing theological covenants is not necessary since God's covenant program can be understood through the biblical covenants. This approach allows one to grasp truths such as salvation by grace alone through faith alone for all peoples who believe, while understanding that discontinuities also exist in regard to identity, structure, and function for Israel, the nations, and the church.

THE NOAHIC COVENANT

Man was created with an immediate obligation to worship and serve God his Creator (Genesis 1–2). So man has possessed inherent obligations to God from the beginning. Yet the first occurrence of the word "covenant" (*berit*) is found in a postfall context in Genesis 6:18, where God says to Noah, "But I will establish my covenant with you." Thus, the first biblical covenant is the Noahic covenant, which is also called an "everlasting covenant" in Genesis 9:16.

The establishing or confirming of the Noahic covenant is mentioned in Genesis 6:18; 9:9, 11, 12, 13, 15, 16, 17. The substance of the covenant is found in Genesis 8:20–9:17. The context of the Noahic covenant is (1) creation (Genesis 1–2); (2) man's sinfulness (Gen. 6:5–13); (3) Noah finding favor with God (Gen. 6:8); and (4) the sacrifices of Noah (Gen. 8:20–21).

The Noahic covenant makes several provisions for humanity. First, God commits to provide stability of nature: "While the earth remains, seedtime and harvest, cold and heat, summer and winter, day and night, shall not cease" (Gen. 8:22). This promise is assuring since it guarantees the stability of nature so that mankind can function without the threat of global catastrophe. As long as "the earth remains," humans can count on the cycle of seasons. Not only is this a blessing to all creation, both animate and inanimate, but it also allows for God's kingdom plans to unfold in history. Thus, the Noahic covenant functions as the platform on which God's kingdom and salvation plans play out. It is also the basis for the fulfillment of the other biblical covenants.

Second, Noah is told to multiply and fill the earth (Gen. 9:1, 7), a reissuing of the command first given to Adam (Gen. 1:28). Immediately after the global flood, Noah and his sons functioned much like Adam did as the initial representative of humanity tasked with procreation. Third, God causes animals, birds, and fish to fear man (Gen. 9:2). Fourth, animals become food for man just like the plants were at creation, although humans are not to eat meat with blood in it (Gen. 9:3–4). Fifth, man's life is sacred; neither man nor animal is to kill a human being (Gen. 9:5). This affirms the dignity of man as God's image bearer even after the fall of mankind. Sixth, capital punishment is instated as the punishment for those who murder an image bearer of God (Gen. 9:6). Seventh, God promises never to destroy the world by water again (Gen. 9:15).

The Noahic covenant is an unconditional and eternal covenant still in effect today. Man continues to experience stability of nature for the outworking of God's purposes and of man's relationship to other people and animals.

THE ABRAHAMIC COVENANT

The Noahic covenant is the initial platform for God's purposes, yet the Abrahamic covenant details how God plans to save people and restore all things. This restoration will occur through three great promises: (1) land for Abraham, (2) a great number of descendants of Abraham, and (3) universal blessings for the nations.

This Abrahamic covenant is also the basis for the other covenants that God will institute. The initial and foundational promises of the Abrahamic covenant are found in Genesis 12:1–3:

> Now the LORD said to Abram, "Go from your country and your kindred and your father's house to the land that I will show you. And I will make of you a great nation, and I will bless you and make your name great, so that you will be a blessing. I will bless those who bless you, and him who dishonors you I will curse, and in you all the families of the earth shall be blessed."

Several promises are contained here. First, God promises to make Abraham a "great nation." This nation will become Israel, composed of descendants from Abraham, Isaac, and Jacob. Second, God promises Abraham that he will be blessed and his name made great. Third, Abraham will be a blessing for others. Fourth, God will treat others based on how they treat Abraham, whether for blessing or curse. Fifth, Abraham and the nation to come from him will be a blessing to "all the families of the earth." Thus, Abraham and Israel will be used by God as a means for bringing blessings to Gentiles. With the Abrahamic covenant, God's plans include both Israel and Gentiles.

Other chapters expand on the Abrahamic promises. Genesis 12:6–7 promises land to Abraham's descendants, and Genesis 13:14–17 promises this land to them "forever." In Genesis 15, God commits to protect and reward Abraham (15:1). Abraham's descendants will be as numerous as the stars (Gen. 15:5). The unilateral ratification of the covenant takes place in Genesis 15:7–17, where God passes through bloody animal pieces to signify that he unconditionally obligates himself to fulfill this covenant. The specific dimensions of the land promise are given by God in Genesis 15:18–21—from the river of Egypt to the river Euphrates (Gen. 15:18).

Genesis 17 offers even more details. God will multiply Abraham's descendants (Gen. 17:2), and Abraham will be a father of many nations (Gen. 17:5). Kings will come from Abraham (Gen. 17:6), in anticipation of the coming Davidic covenant, which highlights the importance of the kingly line in God's program (2 Sam. 7:12–16). The Abrahamic covenant is viewed as "everlasting" (Gen. 17:7). All the land of Canaan is promised to Abraham (Gen. 17:8). Circumcision is the sign of the covenant (Gen. 17:10–14). In Genesis 22:15–18, God reaffirms his covenant with Abraham by declaring that Abraham's descendants will be innumerable (Gen. 22:17) and that the nations of the earth will be blessed through his seed (Gen. 22:18).

With the Abrahamic covenant, God obligates himself to bring blessings to three parties. He gives some promises to Abraham, some to the nation of Israel, and others to the families of the earth. Abraham will be personally blessed as God will make his name great and make him the father of many nations. Israel will be blessed as it becomes a nation that inherits a land forever and experiences peace from her enemies. Gentile peoples will also be blessed as God brings them into his covenant and blesses them as the people of God alongside Israel.

Importantly, while the covenants primarily focus on Israel, they are not restricted to Israel nor seen as applying only to Israel. As Genesis 12:3 and 22:18 reveal, it was God's intent to include Gentiles in the covenant promises. Paul affirms this in Galatians 3:7–9, where he links Gentile salvation in the church to what God promised Abraham in Genesis 12:3 and 22:18 concerning blessings to Gentiles. Paul also draws on the significance of the Abrahamic covenant in Romans 4. In addition to revealing Abraham as the primary example of imputed righteousness through faith alone (cf. Rom. 4:3 with Gen. 15:6), Paul says that the timing of Abraham's faith is important. Abraham was counted as righteous before he was circumcised so that Abraham could be the father of two groups—Gentiles who are saved by faith and Jews who believe (see Rom. 4:10–12). Believing Gentiles and Jews retain their ethnic identities, but both are united to Abraham through faith and are identified as descendants of Abraham (see Gal. 3:29). The Abrahamic covenant, therefore, affirms that all kinds of people will be saved by grace through faith like Abraham but that Jews and Gentiles will retain their ethnic identities within the people of God.

In Matthew 1:1, Jesus is declared "the son of Abraham." Mary stated that God was bringing help to "his servant Israel, in remembrance of his mercy, as he spoke to our fathers, to Abraham and to his offspring forever" (Luke 1:54–55). As he was "filled with the Holy Spirit," John the Baptist's father, Zechariah, prophesied that God was remembering "his holy covenant, the oath that he swore to our father Abraham, to grant us that we, being delivered from the hand of our enemies, might serve him without fear" (Luke 1:67, 72–74). Both Mary and Zechariah expressed hope that God would save Israel and deliver Israel from her enemies. These truths concerning national salvation and deliverance for the nation of Israel do not need to be spiritualized as referring to the church today. Instead, they will be fulfilled by Jesus at his second coming (see Zechariah 14; Rom. 11:26).

THE MOSAIC COVENANT

The Mosaic covenant is the law God gave Israel through Moses to govern the life and conduct of Israel in the Promised Land of Canaan (Ex. 19:5–6). This Mosaic covenant, given to Israel after the exodus from Egypt, included commandments (Ex. 20:1–17) along with rules governing Israel's social life (Ex. 21–23) and worship system (Ex. 25–31). Together, the Mosaic covenant consisted of 613 commandments, of which the Ten Commandments are a summation (Ex. 20:1–17). The Sabbath was the sign of this covenant (Ex. 31:16–17).

This covenant was bilateral, conditional, and nullifiable, being contingent on Israel's obedience to God. Adherence to the Mosaic covenant was the means through which Israel could stay connected to the blessings of the Abrahamic covenant. Keeping the Mosaic covenant out of love to God would lead to spiritual and material prosperity, but disobedience would result in judgment, including removal from the land and dispersion throughout the nations (Deuteronomy 28–29).

The Mosaic covenant was a gracious covenant. It was not a means of salvation but the God-intended way for Israel to show its love and commitment to God. Though Israel promised to obey (Ex. 24:1–8), the biblical record demonstrates that Israel disobeyed God and faced curses for breaking the covenant. In addition to continually violating the law, Israel perverted the law in two main ways. First, many Jews wrongly twisted the covenant to become a means of works-righteousness salvation (Rom. 9:30–32). Second, many emphasized the external rituals of the covenant at the expense of the heart of love (Mic. 6:6–8).

The Mosaic covenant was holy, righteous, and good (Rom. 7:12). So the problem arising with the covenant was within the hearts of people, not in the covenant itself. The Mosaic covenant also revealed the people's sinfulness:

> For by works of the law no human being will be justified in his sight, since through the law comes knowledge of sin. (Rom. 3:20)

> Now the law came in to increase the trespass, but where sin increased, grace abounded all the more. (Rom. 5:20)

> Why then the law? It was added because of transgressions, until the offspring should come to whom the promise had been made. (Gal. 3:19)

Since Israel failed and broke the Mosaic covenant, God promised that it would be superseded by a better, new covenant. As Jeremiah 31:31–32 proclaims,

> Behold, the days are coming, declares the LORD, when I will make a new covenant with the house of Israel and the house of Judah, not like the covenant that I made with their fathers on the day when I took them by the hand to bring them out of the land of Egypt, my covenant that they broke, though I was their husband, declares the LORD.

The end of the Mosaic covenant as a rule of life occurred with the death of Jesus because he fulfilled the demands of the covenant and established the new covenant with his blood (Luke 22:20). Paul explained, "For Christ is the end of the law for righteousness to everyone who believes" (Rom. 10:4). He also said that Christ became our peace "by abolishing the law of commandments expressed in ordinances" (Eph. 2:14–15). The writer of Hebrews similarly stated, "In speaking of a new covenant, he makes the first one [the Mosaic covenant] obsolete. And what is becoming obsolete and growing old is ready to vanish away" (Heb. 8:13).

Since the Mosaic covenant was given to Israel alone (Ex. 19:3; 34:27) and since Christ brought an end to the covenant with his death (Eph. 2:14–15), Christians are not under the Mosaic covenant and its laws:

> For sin will have no dominion over you, since you are not under law but under grace. (Rom. 6:14)

> What then? Are we to sin because we are not under law but under grace? By no means! (Rom. 6:15)

> But if you are led by the Spirit, you are not under the law. (Gal. 5:18)

That Christians are not under the Mosaic law does not mean they are free to sin. They are joined to Christ and are under the new covenant. So in 1 Corinthians 9:20–21, Paul declared that he was now under the law of Christ, not the law of Moses:

> To those under the law I became as one under the law (though not being myself under the law) that I might win those under the law. To those outside the law I became as one outside the law (not being outside the law of God but under the law of Christ) that I might win those outside the law.

Paul also stated, "But now we [Christians] are released from the law, having died to that which held us captive, so that we serve in the new way of the Spirit and not in the old way of the written code" (Rom. 7:6). The Christian is released from the Mosaic law to serve in the new way of the Holy Spirit. The Christian, therefore, is not lawless but is under a better law—the law of Christ and the new covenant. Only this time, the Spirit enables the person to obey God willingly.

That Christians are not under the Mosaic covenant is evident since penalties for breaking this covenant are no longer enforced. For example, sexual immorality was a capital offense under the Mosaic code (Lev. 20:10–16), yet for an incest case in 1 Corinthians 5, Paul charged the church not to execute this person but to "purge the evil person from among you" (1 Cor. 5:13).

Nevertheless, this is not to say that the Mosaic covenant is not relevant today, for it most certainly is. "All Scripture is breathed out by God and profitable for teaching, for reproof, for correction, and for training in righteousness" (2 Tim. 3:16). The Mosaic covenant reveals unchanging attributes of and truths about God's character, which is the basis of his required principles for life. Paul sometimes quotes Mosaic legislation as wisdom for right living (Eph. 6:1–2). Plus, God's moral commands in the Old Testament show great continuity with what God expects from believers in this age. Nine of the original Ten Commandments are picked up and reapplied as part of the law of Christ in the New Testament—the one exception being the Sabbath command. The Israelites' varied responses to the Mosaic law also offer examples that motivate believers to pursue godly living. Concerning the Israelites in the wilderness, Paul exhorted, "Now these things took place as examples for us, that we might not desire evil as they did" (1 Cor. 10:6). He also declared, "For whatever was written in former days was written for our instruction, that through endurance and through the encouragement of the Scriptures we might have hope" (Rom. 15:4).

THE PRIESTLY COVENANT[18]

With the priestly covenant of Numbers 25, God promised a perpetual priesthood in the line of Phinehas that would continue all the way through the Lord's earthly millennial temple. At a time when the Lord was dealing with many in Israel who had joined themselves to Baal of Peor, Phinehas, a priest, took a spear and pierced an Israelite man and a Midianite woman who had committed immorality in a tent before the congregation of Israel. The Lord honored Phinehas with a covenant of peace that involved a perpetual priesthood for him and his descendants:

> Then the LORD spoke to Moses, saying, "Phinehas the son of Eleazar, the son of Aaron the priest, has turned away My wrath from the sons of Israel in that he was jealous with My jealousy among them, so that I did not destroy the sons of Israel in My jealousy. Therefore say, 'Behold, I give him My covenant of peace; and it shall be for him and his descendants after him, a covenant of a perpetual priesthood, because he was jealous for his God and made atonement for the sons of Israel.'" (Num. 25:10–13 NASB)

This covenant given to Phinehas also included his descendants (Num. 25:13). God promised Phinehas and his offspring a perpetual priesthood, highlighting its enduring nature. The genealogical line of Phinehas will continue into the millennial kingdom through Zadok (1 Chron. 6:50–53). Ezekiel indicates that the only priests who will be permitted to minister in the millennial temple will be those of the line of Zadok (Ezek. 44:15; 48:11). Non-Zadokian priests will be prohibited from the priestly office because of past idolatrous activity (Ezek. 44:10).

The perpetual nature of the priestly covenant suggests that it stands as a separate covenant and not as part of the Mosaic covenant, which is temporary. First, the terminology employed is similar to the covenants made with Noah, Abraham, David, and the new covenant. Second, that it remains when the Mosaic covenant was rendered obsolete speaks even louder for its standing as a separate covenant. The Mosaic covenant was abrogated by the new covenant, but the promise given to Phinehas continues into the millennium. Third, the language of Jeremiah 33:20–21 places its permanence alongside the Davidic covenant, contending that it remains in force as long as the cycle of day and night remains: "Thus says the LORD, 'If you

---

18. This section is adapted from Irvin A. Busenitz, "Introduction to the Biblical Covenants: The Noahic Covenant and the Priestly Covenant," *MSJ* 10, no. 2 (1999): 173–89. Used by permission of *MSJ*.

can break My covenant for the day, and My covenant for the night, so that day and night will not be at their appointed time, then My covenant may also be broken with David My servant so that he will not have a son to reign on his throne, and with the Levitical priests, My ministers" (NASB).

THE DAVIDIC COVENANT

The Davidic covenant is the next unconditional covenant of promise. The context for it was David's desire to build a suitable dwelling place for God's presence. God would not allow David to build a house for God since he was a man of war, but God promised the perpetuity of David's descendants on the throne in Israel. While several passages reveal truths concerning this covenant, the heart of the Davidic covenant is found in 2 Samuel 7:12–16:

> When your days are fulfilled and you lie down with your fathers, I will raise up your offspring after you, who shall come from your body, and I will establish his kingdom. He shall build a house for my name, and I will establish the throne of his kingdom forever. I will be to him a father, and he shall be to me a son. When he commits iniquity, I will discipline him with the rod of men, with the stripes of the sons of men, but my steadfast love will not depart from him, as I took it from Saul, whom I put away from before you. And your house and your kingdom shall be made sure forever before me. Your throne shall be established forever.

This passage outlines several provisions in the Davidic covenant. David's name will be made great (7:9). A home will be provided for Israel (7:10). Israel will be given undisturbed rest from all enemies (7:10–11). A house or dynasty in the line of David will endure (7:11). A coming son will establish this kingdom (7:12). Solomon will build the temple (7:13). Solomon's kingdom will be established forever (7:13). God will be a father to Solomon, and when Solomon disobeys, God will not take the kingdom from him as he did with Saul (7:14–15). David's dynasty and kingdom will endure forever, and the throne of David will be established forever (7:16).

In 2 Samuel 7:18–29, David offers a prayer of gratitude to the Lord. This covenant God is making with him is "instruction for mankind" (7:19). The word for "instruction" is *torah* ("law"), and the phrase could be rendered "law for mankind." This means the Davidic covenant will positively impact Gentiles, and it reaffirms the promise of the Abrahamic covenant that God's blessings will include Gentiles (see Gen. 12:3; 22:18). The Davidic covenant also pushes God's covenant plans forward by focusing on the royal descendants who are coming from the broader category of Abraham's national descendants via Isaac and Jacob. While 2 Samuel 7 does not mention the term *covenant*, the word is found in Psalm 89:3–4: You have said, "I have made a covenant with my chosen one; I have sworn to David my servant: I will establish your offspring forever, and build your throne for all generations."

As the New Testament era arrives, Jesus is manifested as the ultimate Son of David. The Gospels begin, "The book of the genealogy of Jesus Christ, the son of David" (Matt. 1:1). Jesus was recognized as the Son of David throughout his earthly ministry (see Matt. 9:27; 15:22; 21:15). The early church believed that the crucified and risen Jesus was the fulfillment of the promised seed of David and that because of this, he had to be resurrected from the dead (see Acts 2:30–36; 13:34–37). In Revelation, John identified Jesus as "the one who has the key of David" (Rev. 3:7), and Jesus referred to himself as both "the root and the descendant of David" (Rev. 22:16).

The Davidic covenant contains promises that were fulfilled with Jesus's first coming, while other promises await fulfillment at his second coming. Jesus's manifestation as King in the line of David is a first-coming fulfillment. Those who believe in him are positionally transferred to the kingdom (Col. 1:13). The spreading of messianic salvation to Gentiles is also a fulfillment of the Davidic covenant (Acts 15:14–18). But Jesus's ultimate assumption of the throne of David and his kingdom reign await his second coming in glory (Matt. 25:31), when the earth will be renewed and he and the apostles will rule over a united and restored nation of Israel (Matt. 19:28).

THE NEW COVENANT

The Abrahamic covenant promised Abraham many descendants and a great nation that would come from him. He and this nation would mediate blessings to the world (Gen. 12:2–3). Then the Davidic covenant promised a kingly line from David that would rule Israel (2 Sam. 7:12–16) and ultimately the earth (Zech. 14:9; Matt. 25:31–34). But the hearts of the people still needed to be changed. What good would descendants, land, and a king be without people who loved God and desired to obey him? This is where the new covenant is significant. The new covenant is an unconditional and eternal covenant whereby God enables and empowers his people to serve him willingly and to remain in his blessings. The foundational passage that describes this covenant is Jeremiah 31:31–34:

> Behold, the days are coming, declares the LORD, when I will make a new covenant with the house of Israel and the house of Judah, not like the covenant that I made with their fathers on the day when I took them by the hand to bring them out of the land of Egypt, my covenant that they broke, though I was their husband, declares the LORD. For this is the covenant that I will make with the house of Israel after those days, declares the LORD: I will put my law within them, and I will write it on their hearts. And I will be their God, and they shall be my people. And no longer shall each one teach his neighbor and each his brother, saying, "Know the LORD," for they shall all know me, from the least of them to the greatest, declares the LORD. For I will forgive their iniquity, and I will remember their sin no more.

The historical context of this promise was a time of apostasy in Judah. Jeremiah the prophet warned Judah that God's judgment was coming on the people because they had failed to keep the Mosaic covenant. The recipient of the new covenant was Israel, although all the unconditional covenants (Abrahamic, Davidic, new) were intended to eventually extend to Gentiles as well (Gen. 12:3; 2 Sam. 7:19; Isa. 52:15). God desired Israel to be the vehicle for God's covenant plans, but as Israel was blessed, so too were Gentiles to be blessed. God contrasted the new covenant with the Mosaic covenant in that the new covenant was "not like the covenant" God made at the time of the exodus (Jer. 31:32). The Mosaic covenant was a conditional and nullifiable covenant that Israel constantly broke. God was faithful to the covenant, but Israel was not. The substance of the new covenant was that God would put his law within his people and "write it on their hearts" (Jer. 31:33). They would be God's people and would wholeheartedly obey his law. They no longer needed to be compelled by an external threat. Obedience would be internal, and all who participated in this covenant would know God and obey him.

A new heart is the center of the new covenant. While the Mosaic law was "holy," "righteous," and "good" (Rom. 7:12), it did not enable people to obey. Yet the new covenant enables God's people to lovingly serve him. Ezekiel 36:26–27 includes the indwelling Holy Spirit as part of this covenant, whose redemptive features became effective in AD 30:

> And I will give you a new heart, and a new spirit I will put within you. And I will remove the heart of stone from your flesh and give you a heart of flesh. And I will put my Spirit within you, and cause you to walk in my statutes and be careful to obey my rules.

As God places the Holy Spirit within his people, God will cause them to "walk" in his "statutes" and "obey" his "rules."

Other passages also teach about the new covenant. Deuteronomy 30:1–6 predicted a regathering and restoration of Israel with a new heart to obey God as the basis for material and land blessings. Ezekiel 16:53–63 links the new covenant with national forgiveness for Israel. Ezekiel 37:21–28 reveals that God will gather, unify, and restore the nation of Israel under the ultimate David who will be king over Israel, which will then live in peace and prosper. According to Isaiah 32:15–20, the Holy Spirit will be poured out on Israel, and there will be justice, prosperity, and peace under the Davidic king (Isa. 32:1). These texts reveal the important connection between the Davidic covenant and the new covenant. New covenant blessings are bestowed in relation to the ultimate Davidic King, the Messiah. As Isaiah 59:20–21 shows, when the Redeemer comes to Zion, God will place his Holy Spirit on Israel. Paul quotes this text in his discussion of the coming salvation of Israel in Romans 11:26–27.

The various new covenant passages reveal both spiritual and physical blessings. A new heart, the indwelling Holy Spirit, and forgiveness of sins are the spiritual blessings at the center of the covenant. Yet there also are national and material blessings, such as a united and restored Israel in the Land of Promise, the rebuilding of Jerusalem, and material prosperity for Israel (Isa. 61:8; Jer. 32:41; Ezek. 34:25–27). The spiritual, physical, and national promises are all important, and all need to be fulfilled.

The new covenant is based unconditionally on the "I will" of God (Jer. 31:31–34; Ezek. 16:60–62). Also, on multiple occasions the covenant is called eternal (Isa. 24:5; 61:8; Jer. 31:36, 40; 32:40; 50:5; Ezek. 37:26). It is as certain as it is everlasting.

The New Testament presents Jesus as the Son of David who is the Mediator of the new covenant and the One who brings new covenant blessings. John the Baptist declared that the Messiah "will baptize you with the Holy Spirit and fire" (Matt. 3:11). Since the ministry of the Holy Spirit was closely linked with the new covenant, John declared that Jesus was the One who would bring the new covenant to believers. At the Last Supper Jesus explicitly linked his death with the new covenant: "This cup that is poured out for you is the new covenant in my blood" (Luke 22:20). Paul mentioned this event in 1 Corinthians 11:25: "In the same way also he took the cup, after supper, saying, 'This cup is the new covenant in my blood. Do this, as often as you drink it, in remembrance of me.'" Jesus ratified the new covenant with his sacrificial death and his identity as the suffering servant of the Lord (Isa. 53:3–6).

The new covenant is in effect in this church age. Those who trust in Jesus the Messiah are indwelt with the Holy Spirit and participate in the full promises of the new covenant. Those who proclaim the gospel in this age are presenting the new covenant. Paul said that God "has made us sufficient to be ministers of a new covenant, not of the letter but of the Spirit" (2 Cor. 3:6). Quoting the new covenant passage of Jeremiah 31:31–34 in Hebrews 8:8–12, the writer of Hebrews explains that the new covenant is superior to the old covenant, which is becoming "obsolete" (Heb. 8:13). Hebrews 9:15 and 12:24 both affirm that Jesus is "the mediator of a new covenant." Yet while spiritual blessings of the new covenant are in effect for the church, national and physical promises of the new covenant regarding Israel still need to be fulfilled. The Lord thus declared, "Behold, the days are coming" (Jer. 31:27, 31, 38) when Israel will receive the salvation promised in the new covenant. This will occur when Jesus returns.

Timing of Bible Prophecy Fulfillment

A study of eschatology involves understanding when various prophecies are fulfilled. Some were fulfilled in Old Testament times, others were fulfilled with the first coming of Jesus, and others await fulfillment at Jesus's second coming. But when it comes to major prophetic sections such as Daniel 9:24–27; Matthew 24–25; Luke 21; 2 Thessalonians 2; and Revelation 6–20, there is disagreement among Christian theologians. Some hold to past fulfillment of these passages, some to present fulfillment, and others to future fulfillment. Also, some assert that timing is not even an issue in these passages. The four views concerning the timing of key prophetic sections are preterism, historicism, idealism, and futurism. The position affirmed here is futurism, but it is helpful to summarize all four views.

PRETERISM

The word *preterism* is based on the Latin term *preter*, which means "past." Preterism asserts that most or all eschatological passages describing a tribulation and the return of Jesus were fulfilled with first-century events surrounding the AD 70 destruction of Jerusalem.[19]

The preterist understanding relies heavily on timing indicators in the New Tes-

---

19. For more on preterism, consult Richard L. Mayhue, "Jesus: A Preterist or Futurist?," *MSJ* 14, no. 1 (2003): 9–22.

tament such as "near," "soon," "quickly," and "this generation." Much emphasis is given to Jesus's words in Matthew 24:34: "This generation will not pass away until all these things take place." Preterists understand "this generation" to refer to those alive at the time of Jesus's words. Thus, most or all of the events described in Matthew 24 needed to happen in the first century, and the same is true of other statements identifying Jesus's coming as "near" or appearing "quickly" (James 5:8; Rev. 1:1, 3; 2:16; 22:10, 20). The preterist view holds that the tribulation period occurred during the siege of Jerusalem in the late 60s and that Jesus came in the form of the Roman armies in AD 70 to destroy Jerusalem and the temple and bring an end to the Jewish age.

Two main forms of preterism exist. First, full or consistent preterism asserts that all Bible prophecy concerning Jesus's second coming was fulfilled with the events surrounding AD 70. This includes the second coming of Jesus, the resurrection, and the eternal state. Thus, we should expect no future coming of Jesus because Jesus already came in AD 70. We are currently, therefore, in the new heaven and new earth of Revelation 21–22. Second, partial or moderate preterism affirms that much of the Olivet Discourse and Revelation were fulfilled in events surrounding the AD 70 destruction of Jerusalem but that a few passages such as Acts 1:9–11; 1 Corinthians 15:51–53; and 1 Thessalonians 4:16–17 teach a future bodily return of Jesus Christ. Some partial preterists assert that a major part of the Olivet Discourse, Matthew 25:32–46, which describes the judgment of the nations, awaits future fulfillment.

Preterism has features that disqualify it from being true. First, it is tied to an unlikely date for the writing of Revelation. Since preterists believe that Revelation is predictive prophecy concerning events leading up to the destruction of Jerusalem in AD 70, the book of Revelation absolutely had to be written before AD 67. But the consensus view from church history is that Revelation was written in the reign of Domitian around AD 95. For instance, Irenaeus wrote (ca. AD 180) that Revelation was penned near the end of Domitian's reign. If Revelation were written after AD 67, which is highly likely, all forms of preterism collapse.

Second, the preterist understanding of timing indicators such as "this generation," "near," and "quickly" is questionable. These do not demand that Jesus had to return in a few years or decades. On two occasions, Jesus stated that only the Father knew when prophetic events would be fulfilled. Jesus said, "But concerning that day and hour no one knows, not even the angels of heaven, nor the Son, but the Father only" (Matt. 24:36). Also, when asked about the timing of the restoration of national Israel, Jesus stated, "It is not for you to know times or seasons that the Father has fixed by his own authority" (Acts 1:7).

When Jesus declared that "this generation will not pass away until all these things take place," he was not saying that the prophetic events of Matthew 24–25 had to occur within a few years or decades. He was projecting into the future within a prophetic context. The generation of people living when the future eschatological events of Matthew 24 began to occur, whenever that would take place, would be the ones to witness the second coming of Jesus to earth. When this will happen is unknown, but when the events of Matthew 24 unfold, the return of Jesus will occur soon thereafter.

Also, the terms "near" and "soon" do not mean "in a few years" but rather convey the idea of imminence. Since no one but God knows when the tribulation period will occur, every generation should live with the imminent expectation that these events could break forth at any moment. Imminence does not demand that events must happen within a short period of time but cautions that they could occur at any time. That is why these warnings of the nearness of Jesus's coming can apply to any group of Christians in history—first century, twenty-first century, or any century.

Third, the events predicted in Jesus's Olivet Discourse and Revelation simply did not happen in the first century. Jesus predicted that "many" would come claiming, "I am the Christ" (Matt. 24:5), but the first century did not witness many claiming to be the Messiah. The gospel was not proclaimed to the whole world before AD 70 (Matt. 24:14). The cosmic signs concerning the darkening of the sun, the moon not giving its light, and the stars falling from heaven have not occurred (Matt. 24:29). Jesus has not returned on the clouds of heaven in power and great glory (Matt. 24:30). Nor has he come in glory with all his angels to sit on the Davidic throne (Matt. 25:31). The nations have not been gathered before Jesus for judgment with the righteous entering Jesus's kingdom and the wicked being thrown into eternal fire (Matt. 25:32–46). We have not seen the worldwide judgments of the seals, trumpets, and bowls of Revelation 6–18. Therefore, preterism cannot be true.

HISTORICISM

Historicism asserts that the prophesied events of the Olivet Discourse and the book of Revelation describe history as it has unfolded over the centuries since the first coming of Christ. Events such as earthquakes, persecutions, wars, and false prophets that occur in this age are often viewed as fulfillments of Bible prophecy. Prophecies in Revelation about the dragon, beast, false prophet, and whore of Babylon refer to Satan working through the Roman Empire and the Roman Catholic Church, including the papacy. During the time of the Reformation, some like Martin Luther believed that the pope and the papacy were the predicted Antichrist. While historicism can be found throughout much of church history, it was popular from the sixteenth through the nineteenth centuries but has waned considerably in the last century, despite some remaining advocates.

IDEALISM

Unlike preterism, historicism, and futurism, the position of idealism does not stress a past, present, or future fulfillment of biblical prophecy. Instead, it ignores historical realities and views these prophetic passages as teaching timeless truths and principles for Christians of all generations. All Christians should endure trials and difficulties knowing they will be rewarded by God, who is in control of all things. There is a real battle between good and evil, but good will win in the end. Idealists hold that prophetic truths are not just for first-century Christians (i.e., preterists) or the last generation of Christians (futurists) but for all Christians of all ages.

The appeal of idealism is that it makes the book of Revelation relevant to all generations of Christians. Yet futurism can make the same claim, although with a different emphasis. Plus, idealism does not do justice to the fact that Jesus says that the book of Revelation relates to the past, present, and future: "Therefore write the things which you have seen, and the things which are, and the things which will take place after these things" (Rev. 1:19 NASB). Idealism fails in that Revelation is speaking of actual historical events with time frames such as 42 months and 1,260 days that cannot be reinterpreted to mean general truths for believers of all ages. These are actual events that must occur in history.

FUTURISM

Futurism asserts that prophecies concerning the tribulation, the rise of the Antichrist, the salvation of Israel, the return of Jesus, the millennium, and the eternal state await future fulfillment. The events of Daniel 9:24–27; Matthew 24–25; and Revelation 6–20 will be fulfilled in a future era. Futurism does not assert that all prophecies in the Bible are still future, because many have already been fulfilled, but it affirms that there are major prophecies that still need to happen, just as others happened in the past.

The case for futurism is strong. First, many prophetic events have simply not yet happened. In 2 Thessalonians 2, Paul predicted a coming man of lawlessness who would go into the temple of God declaring himself to be God, thus drawing the wrath of the returning Son of God, who would destroy this evil person (2 Thess. 2:3–4, 8). This event has not yet occurred in history. In 2 Peter 3, Peter told of a coming day of the Lord in which the earth would be purged with fire. Revelation 6–19 details global judgments on the earth that have not happened yet. Also, the return of Jesus remains future.

Futurism holds that the seventieth week of Daniel (Dan. 9:27) and the events it describes are still future. Futurists also realize that major areas of fulfillment coincide with both comings of Jesus. Just as Jesus's first coming brought many areas of Old Testament prophecy to fulfillment, so too will the second coming of Jesus (Acts 3:18–21). Critics sometimes claim that if the book of Revelation refers to events that would not happen for thousands of years, it was irrelevant to John's original audience. This is inaccurate. The events presented in Revelation are linked with imminence, which means that they could break onto the scene at any moment and that Christians must be spiritually ready. With the perspective of hindsight, we know now that these events did not occur for the original readers of Revelation, but that does not mean the warnings of Revelation were irrelevant to the original audience. The warnings and descriptions are relevant for all generations, including our own, even if the Lord should delay his coming.

Futurism coincides with the favored view that the apostle John wrote the book of Revelation in the AD 90s, well after the destruction of Jerusalem in AD 70. This means that from his standpoint in history, the tribulation he wrote about could not have been fulfilled in AD 70 but must be fulfilled in the future.

Millennial Views

The millennium is one of the most debated issues in eschatology. The debate centers on the meaning of the "thousand years" mentioned six times in Revelation 20:1–7. This "thousand years" refers to the kingdom reign of Jesus with his saints. During this time, Satan is bound (Rev. 20:1–3), and resurrected saints reign with Jesus for a thousand years (Rev. 20:4). After a thousand years, Satan is released and leads a rebellion against Jerusalem but is immediately destroyed (Rev. 20:7–10). This period is called a "millennium," from the Latin terms *mille*, meaning "thousand," and *annum*, "year." The millennium is a thousand-year period. In spite of the clarity of the text, a long-running debate has transpired concerning how to understand the thousand years of Revelation 20:1–7. Three primary views have emerged: amillennialism, postmillennialism, and premillennialism.

AMILLENNIALISM

Amillennialism asserts that the millennium of Revelation 20 is being fulfilled spiritually in this present age between the two comings of Jesus and has nothing to do with an actual thousand years. The term *amillennialism* is somewhat misleading. The prefix *a* means "no." But those who hold to amillennialism are not saying that there is no millennium. Instead, they claim that the millennial reign of Jesus and the saints is being realized now. Thus, the millennium is currently occurring. Some amillennialists believe that the millennium is being fulfilled from heaven as Jesus and perfected saints rule from heaven. Others believe that the kingdom reign involves the church on earth or the rule of God over the lives of believers. Some combine these two ideas.

In order to teach that the millennium is present and spiritual, amillennialism has to rely heavily on a recapitulation view of Revelation. In this approach, Revelation does not present events sequentially but rather captures events between the two comings of Jesus from multiple angles (perhaps as many as seven) that describe the same period of time. This recapitulation understanding allows the amillennialist to view the second coming of Revelation 19 as occurring at the end of the thousand years mentioned in Revelation 20 and not before. So Revelation 20 does not follow Revelation 19 chronologically but takes the reader back to the beginning of the age between Jesus's two comings, a time that includes the binding of Satan (Rev. 20:1–3) and the reign of the saints (Rev. 20:4). For amillennialists, Satan is bound in this age in the sense that he was defeated at the cross by Christ and is unable to stop the spread of the gospel to the nations. And the saints of God are currently reigning with Jesus. When this era of the millennial kingdom runs its course, then Jesus will return from heaven. At that time, there will be one general resurrection and judgment of the righteous and the wicked, and then the eternal state will commence. Important to amillennialism is that both tribulation and Christ's millennial kingdom reign run concurrently in this age. These are present, not future, events.

Premillennialism, not amillennialism, was the predominant view in the first two hundred years of church history. However, the early church did evidence hints of what would later become amillennialism. For example, Origen (ca. AD 184–ca. 254) popularized the allegorical approach to interpreting Scripture and in doing so laid a hermeneutical basis for the view that the promised kingdom of Christ was spiritual and not earthly in nature. Eusebius (ca. AD 260–ca. 340), an associate of the emperor Constantine, viewed Constantine's reign as the messianic banquet, and he held to anti-premillennial views. Tyconius (d. ca. AD 390), an African Donatist of the fourth century, was one of the earliest theologians to challenge premillennialism. He rejected the eschatological and futuristic view of Revelation 20 and viewed the first resurrection of Revelation 20:4 as a spiritual resurrection, which he identified with the new birth. Augustine (AD 354–430), who is often referred to as the "father of amillennialism," popularized the views of Tyconius. He abandoned premillennialism because of what he considered to be the excesses and carnalities of this view. Augustine was the first to identify the church in its visible form with the kingdom of God. For him, the millennial rule of Christ was taking place in and through the church. His book *City of God* was significant in promoting amillennialism, which soon became the prevailing doctrine of the Roman Catholic Church, survived the Reformation, and is still held by many today.

Amillennialism has problems that disqualify it. First, it is an overspiritualized position and does not adhere to a consistent use of grammatical-historical interpretation. Without exegetical warrant, it transforms physical and national promises to Israel into spiritual promises for the church and holds that the church has become the new or true Israel. Also, amillennialism does not fit the Bible's storyline or do justice to what the Scripture says about Jesus's kingdom. The rule of the last Adam—Jesus (1 Cor. 15:45)—must occur from the same realm over which the first Adam was tasked to rule but failed. God's plan is for man to reign successfully over the earth (Gen. 1:26–28), which is dramatically improved due to the Messiah's presence (Isaiah 11). Yet amillennialism offers a spiritual kingdom from heaven with little or no influence on the earth. It posits a millennial kingdom of Jesus with no change on earth and where the enemies of God run rampant in rebellion. This is refuted by Revelation 5:10, which says that the reign of Jesus and the saints will be "on the earth" with God's enemies defeated (Rev. 19:20–20:3). Jesus's kingdom will not be a hidden kingdom. When it is in operation, all will know about it and submit to it (Zech. 14:9).

Second, amillennialism's separation of Revelation 20 from the second-coming events of Revelation 19 is unwarranted. Revelation 19 describes the return of Jesus with the defeat of his enemies, including the kings of the earth, the beast, and the false prophet. Then Revelation 20 describes the incarceration of God's greatest enemy—Satan. All three enemies are engaged at this time. Also, it is best to view Revelation 20:1–3 as the imprisonment of Satan at the second coming of Jesus. The language of binding, sealing, and shutting in the Abyss indicates a personal imprisonment and a complete cessation of Satan's activities. The amillennial scenario oddly holds that Revelation 20 takes the reader back to the first coming of Christ and allows Satan to be very active except for one activity—deceiving the nations. And even on this point there is a problem since Revelation 12 and 13 state that Satan is indeed deceiving the nations of the earth between the two comings of Jesus. It is odd to posit a scenario in which the kings of the earth, the beast, and the false prophet are judged at the return of Jesus, but Satan's imprisonment is separated from the judgment of these other groups. It is better to view all these groups, including Satan, as being judged at the return of Jesus.

Third, the amillennial claim based on Revelation 20:4 that the saints are reigning in this age is also inaccurate. Revelation 20:4 describes the victorious reign of the martyrs on earth (Rev. 5:10) who were killed for their testimony for Jesus, according to Revelation 6:9–11. The Scripture consistently presents the church as persevering under trials and persecution from wicked people and Satan in this age (Revelation 2–3). The church is not reigning now, but the church is promised positions of reigning in the future if it remains faithful in this age (Rev. 2:26–27; 3:21).

Fourth, amillennialism makes an unnatural distinction between the first resurrection and the second resurrection of Revelation 20:4–5. Amillennialists claim that the first resurrection is a spiritual resurrection to salvation or regeneration, while the second resurrection is a bodily resurrection. Yet the Greek term for "came to life" (*ezēsan*) is the same in both cases. It is difficult to argue persuasively that this term refers to spiritual resurrection in 20:4 when it clearly means bodily resurrection in 20:5. The better answer is that both uses of *ezēsan* refer to physical resurrection. Since this is the case, amillennialism cannot be correct because no bodily resurrection has ever occurred (except for Jesus's), and thus these must both be future from our standpoint in history.

POSTMILLENNIALISM

Postmillennialism also claims that the millennium of Revelation 20 (which is not viewed to mean "one thousand") occurs between the two comings of Jesus. Through the reign of Jesus from heaven and the Holy Spirit–blessed gospel, the kingdom of God will start small but will increasingly grow, spread, and become the dominant influence in the world. Not only will most people be saved, but also all areas of society will be transformed. The world will experience a golden era of peace, prosperity, and blessing. After a long period of a largely Christianized world, this millennial kingdom will then lead to the return of Jesus from heaven. At that time, Jesus will resurrect and judge all humanity, including the righteous and the wicked.

Postmillennialism interprets Revelation 20:1–6, with the binding of Satan and the reign of the saints, as occurring in this present age. But unlike amillennialism, the postmillennial view is optimistic in that it sees this millennium eventually transforming the world for Christ. The kingdom that begins as a spiritual-redemptive reality eventually permeates the creation, bringing it into conformity to God's righteous standards. Only after this golden era of peace and prosperity will Jesus return.

Postmillennialists offer several lines of support from Scripture. They use psalms and prophecies from the Old Testament that describe prosperous and peaceful conditions on earth as evidence for a millennium before the return of Jesus (e.g., Psalm 72; Isa. 65:17–25). The Great Commission (Matt. 28:19–20) is understood as the vehicle for the transformation of the nations. In addition, the parables of the mustard seed and leaven (Matt. 13:31–33) show a gradual yet large growth of the kingdom after a small beginning.

Several major problems disqualify the postmillennial position. It rightly asserts that the millennial kingdom of Jesus results in a transformation of all aspects of creation and involves more than personal salvation. In this sense, it is better than amillennialism, which views the kingdom of Jesus as having little or no impact on the earth. Its major flaw, though, is its assertion that Jesus's millennial kingdom and the transformation of all aspects of society occur before Jesus's second coming. There simply is no biblical evidence that the world will be Christianized before the second coming of Jesus. Both premillennialism and amillennialism rightly assert that this present age before Jesus's return will witness a worsening of conditions on earth. Far from teaching that the world is heading for a Christian golden age before Jesus's coming, the Bible presents deteriorating conditions. This is seen in the divine judgments and persecution from Satan in Revelation 6–18. Also, Paul wrote, "But understand this, that in the last days there will come times of difficulty" (2 Tim. 3:1). He also noted that Christians will continue to be persecuted and that "evil people and impostors will go on from bad to worse" (2 Tim. 3:12–13). Jesus expected bad conditions in the future when he asked, "When the Son of Man comes, will he find faith on earth?" (Luke 18:8). The biblical evidence that the world will get worse before the return of Christ is significant.

Postmillennialists often quote Old Testament texts that speak of the earth being transformed as evidence for their view, but premillennialists also claim the same passages. The issue is not *whether* the Messiah's kingdom will transform everything—it will. The main issue is *when* these conditions will occur. What is lacking from postmillennialism is evidence that the earth will be transformed before the return of Jesus and without the physical presence of the Messiah on earth. Passages like Psalm 72; Isaiah 11; and Zechariah 14 certainly speak of earthly blessings, but these occur with the presence of the Messiah on earth. The Scripture does not teach that world conditions will improve greatly without the Messiah reigning on the earth.

Another major problem facing postmillennialism is that nearly two thousand years of church history have not produced anything close to the Christian golden age that the postmillennial view says will occur. While Scripture, not experience, is the basis for evaluating any theological view, the world is not becoming more Christian. Conditions continue to worsen, not improve. Even areas once permeated by the gospel, such as major parts of Europe during the Reformation or the American

Northeast in the time of the Great Awakening, are now secular in their worldview. Overall, both in the United States and in the world, the influence of Christianity is diminished. Non-Christian worldviews and philosophies such as Islam and secularism are increasing dramatically. While advances in technology have made the world more bearable and convenient at times, such advances have also brought greater chances for calamity. Weapons of mass destruction are one such example.

Postmillennialism suffers from many of the same issues that debilitate amillennialism. It too is dependent on the unlikely view that the events of Revelation 20 precede the second-coming events of Revelation 19. Postmillennialism also struggles in its understanding that Satan is bound in this present age. It wrongly affirms that the reign of the saints described in Revelation 20:4 is occurring today. These structural problems make postmillennialism unsustainable.

PREMILLENNIALISM

Premillennialism follows the clear sequential chronology of John's apocalypse and asserts that the kingdom of Revelation 20:1–7 occurs on earth after the second coming of Jesus described in Revelation 19:11–21 but before the eternal state of Revelation 21:1–22:5. The reason this view is called premillennialism is because Jesus returns before (*pre-*) the millennium. The millennium, therefore, is future and earthly. It is future in that the millennium is not occurring in this present age, and it is earthly in that the millennium is a kingdom reign on the earth. The millennium is sometimes referred to as an intermediate kingdom since it comes between this present age and the eternal state (Rev. 21:1–22:5). Most premillennialists believe that this intermediate kingdom lasts for a literal "thousand years." What unites all premillennialists is the belief that there will be a kingdom of Jesus on earth with his saints after this present age but before the eternal state.

Premillennialism also teaches that a thousand years separate the first and second resurrections of Revelation 20:5. Revelation 20:4 states that martyrs for Christ "came to life and reigned with Christ for a thousand years," but Revelation 20:5 then declares, "The rest of the dead did not come to life until the thousand years were ended." Premillennialism holds that these two resurrections are bodily resurrections from the dead that are separated by a thousand-year period. The order is (1) a bodily resurrection of the saints; (2) a thousand-year period; and (3) a bodily resurrection of the lost.

Biblical Support for Premillennialism. Premillennialism has the backing of Scripture. First, it offers the clearest understanding of Revelation 19:11–21:8, which includes a sequence of events with a chronological time marker—*kai eidon* (Gk. "then I saw" in Rev. 19:11, 17, 19; 20:1, 4, 11, 12; 21:1). These markers indicate a progression of events beginning with a tribulation period and followed by the second coming of Jesus, a thousand-year reign of Jesus, and finally, the eternal state.

Second, the binding of Satan described in Revelation 20:1–3 must be a future reality and not a present one.[20] The language of 20:1–3 indicates a dramatic incarceration of the person Satan in a specific location—the Abyss. Much more than a curtailing of Satan's deceptive activities, this is the incarceration of Satan himself. The binding of Satan is not occurring today. In fact, Satan's ability to deceive the world is evident in this present age. Paul states that "the god of this world [Satan] has blinded the minds of the unbelievers, to keep them from seeing the light of the gospel of the glory of Christ" (2 Cor. 4:4). Peter warns, "Be sober-minded; be watchful. Your adversary the devil prowls around like a roaring lion, seeking someone to devour" (1 Pet. 5:8). John declares, "The whole world lies in the power of the evil one" (1 John 5:19). These passages, written by three apostles after the death, resurrection, and ascension of Jesus, reveal that Satan is actively involved in worldwide deception. Plus, Revelation 12:9 states that before Jesus returns, Satan will be actively deceiving the nations with much success: "And the great dragon was thrown down, that ancient serpent, who is called the devil and Satan, the deceiver of the whole world."

Third, the reign of the saints mentioned in Revelation 20:4 best fits with a future kingdom reign after Jesus's second coming. This passage says that the martyred saints "came to life," which refers to physical resurrection. These saints first appeared in Revelation 6:9–11 as those who were killed for their testimony for Jesus. Coming to life means the resurrection of the body for these faithful saints, and since physical resurrection has not yet occurred, "came to life" in Revelation 20:4 refers to resurrection after the return of Jesus. Also, Revelation 5:10 affirms the coming reign of the saints on earth—"they shall reign on the earth." However, the experience of the church in this age is persecution, not reigning (Revelation 2–3). Reigning is held out as a motivation for those who endure until Jesus returns (Rev. 2:26–27).

Fourth, several Old Testament passages point to an intermediate kingdom that is far better than this present age but not yet perfect like the final eternal state. For example, Isaiah 65:17–25 predicts a time of incomparable prosperity, peace, and harmony of creation, yet a time when the possibility of death still remains. Isaiah 65:20 states, "No more shall there be in it an infant who lives but a few days, or an old man who does not fill out his days, for the young man shall die a hundred years old, and the sinner a hundred years old shall be accursed." The reason why Isaiah 65:20 points toward a coming earthly kingdom is that the conditions described here do not fit this present age when lifespans are around eighty years. Nor do they fit the coming eternal state, when sin will not exist and no one will die. But they do fit an intermediate kingdom, like that described in Revelation 20. Some have speculated that Isaiah may be using "ideal language" to indicate long life without death actually occurring, but this is unlikely. In Isaiah 25:8, the prophet explicitly predicts the eradication of death ("He will swallow up death forever"), showing that Isaiah knew how to state that death would be totally removed.

Zechariah 14 also depicts conditions consistent with a future millennial kingdom.

---

20. This paragraph is adapted from Michael J. Vlach, "The Kingdom of God and the Millennium," *MSJ* 23, no. 2 (2012): 246–49. Used by permission of *MSJ*.

The opening verses describe a great siege of Jerusalem by the nations of the earth (Zech. 14:1–2). But this is followed by the Lord fighting on behalf of Jerusalem, which leads to the Lord's feet touching down on the Mount of Olives (Zech. 14:4). After this the Lord will reign over the earth: "And the LORD will be king over all the earth. On that day the LORD will be one and his name one" (Zech. 14:9). Yet during this time of the Lord's reign on the earth, nations can still sin and suffer the consequences. Such a scenario is described in Zechariah 14:16–19:

> Then everyone who survives of all the nations that have come against Jerusalem shall go up year after year to worship the King, the LORD of hosts, and to keep the Feast of Booths. And if any of the families of the earth do not go up to Jerusalem to worship the King, the LORD of hosts, there will be no rain on them. And if the family of Egypt does not go up and present themselves, then on them there shall be no rain; there shall be the plague with which the LORD afflicts the nations that do not go up to keep the Feast of Booths. This shall be the punishment to Egypt and the punishment to all the nations that do not go up to keep the Feast of Booths.

This passage describes a period when the nations will be required to go up to Jerusalem. Those who do not, like Egypt, will face the prospect of "no rain," "plague," and "punishment." Such conditions in which the nations of the earth travel to Jerusalem with the possibility of punishment for disobedience does not fit this present age or the coming eternal state. These conditions are not fulfilled today since no nation on earth serves the Lord or even attempts to make pilgrimages to Jerusalem. Nor will these conditions be true of the eternal state in which no sin or consequences for sin are possible. Yet the events of Zechariah 14 fit well with an earthly kingdom.

An Old Testament backdrop for an intermediate kingdom is also found in Isaiah 24. The first twenty verses of Isaiah 24 describe global judgments on the earth for transgressing God's laws (Isa. 24:5). Then a two-stage judgment of God's enemies is mentioned in 24:21–23: "On that day the LORD will punish the host of heaven, in heaven, and the kings of the earth, on the earth. They will be gathered together as prisoners in a pit; they will be shut up in a prison, and after many days they will be punished. Then the moon will be confounded." Both evil spiritual forces ("the host of heaven") and evil human forces ("kings of the earth") will be judged. There will also be an incarceration. They will be "gathered together as prisoners in a pit," and "shut up in prison." But then we are told, "After many days they will be punished." The order of events here is imprisonment for many days and then punishment. The "after many days" phrase coincides well with the concept of an intermediate kingdom of a thousand years in Revelation 20, which says that Satan will be bound in the Abyss for a thousand years, then released for a short time, and finally, sentenced to the lake of fire (Rev. 20:1–3, 7).

A fifth reason for premillennialism is that this view best fits the Bible's redemptive storyline. God created the first Adam to rule from and over the earth. Adam failed, but Christians now look to the last Adam (1 Cor. 15:45) to succeed where the first Adam failed. Man's task from Genesis 1:26–28 was to rule from the earth and over the earth. In the premillennial scenario, this is exactly what Jesus does. He successfully rules from earth over the earth with an extended reign that is recognized by all. When Jesus does this, he then hands the kingdom over to God the Father so that the eternal kingdom can commence (1 Cor. 15:24, 28). Those who belong to Jesus are also destined for a kingdom reign on the earth. Persecution on earth is the norm for the saints in this age, but a time is coming when the saints will rule in the realm where they are currently persecuted (Dan. 7:26–27; Rev. 2:26–27; 5:10).

Two Forms of Premillennialism. Two forms of premillennialism exist: futuristic premillennialism (cf. "Futurism," p. 883) and historic premillennialism.

Futuristic premillennialism. First, futuristic premillennialism holds that Daniel's seventieth week and the seal, trumpet, and bowl judgments of Revelation 6–18 are future from the present standpoint in history. So not only is the millennial kingdom future, but the special tribulation period with its divine judgments is also future. This explains why futuristic premillennialism is "futuristic."

Futuristic premillennialism also holds that the nation of Israel will have an important identity and role in the coming tribulation period and millennial kingdom. Old Testament and New Testament prophecies concerning Israel and Israel's role in the future must be fulfilled literally with the nation of Israel. Thus, futuristic premillennialism rejects all forms of replacement theology or supersessionism that see the church as the replacement or fulfillment of Israel in any way that denies the future theological significance of God's promises to Israel as a nation. Not only does God have a plan for individuals and the church, he also has a plan for the nations of the earth, and Israel has a role of leadership and service to the nations in Jesus's kingdom (Isa. 2:2–4). The millennium will be a time when all aspects of the covenants and promises made to Israel will be fulfilled for Israel.

Historic premillennialism. A second form of premillennialism is historic premillennialism. This view has roots in the early church, but its most significant representative in modern times was George Eldon Ladd (1911–1982), whose kingdom views have many followers today.[21]

Like futuristic premillennialism, historic premillennialism sees the millennial kingdom of Revelation 20 as future and earthly but differs with futuristic premillennialism on four areas. First, historic premillennialists sometimes view Daniel's seventieth week and the judgments of Revelation 6–18 as occurring throughout this present age. Many historic premillennialists also believe that the Davidic reign of Jesus is occurring in an "already" sense in this age. Thus, they uphold a current presence of both the tribulation period and Jesus's Davidic reign.

Second, while affirming a future salvation of Israel, some historic premillennialists see Israel as being incorporated into the church with little or no unique role for the nation of Israel in the future earthly kingdom. Thus, while holding to a salvation of

---

21. Not all who identify with historic premillennialism embrace George Ladd's views. Some see a future role for Israel and do not believe that the New Testament reinterprets the Old Testament. Yet most academic adherents of historic premillennialism in the last half century have identified with many of Ladd's views best presented in his work *The Presence of the Future: The Eschatology of Biblical Realism* (Grand Rapids, MI: Eerdmans, 1974).

ethnic Israel in the last days, historic premillennialists (in the tradition of Ladd) often hold to a form of replacement theology, believing that the church is the replacement for and receives the fulfillment of promises made to Israel. Whatever role Israel has in God's future purposes, there is no role for Israel apart from the church.

Third, historic premillennialism in the tradition of Ladd believes that the New Testament sometimes reinterprets the Old Testament and that physical promises made to Israel can be changed to spiritual blessings for the church. As Ladd stated,

> The Old Testament must be interpreted by the New Testament. In principle it is quite possible that the prophecies addressed originally to literal Israel describing physical blessings have their fulfillment exclusively in the spiritual blessings enjoyed by the church. It is also possible that the Old Testament expectation of a kingdom on earth could be reinterpreted by the New Testament altogether of blessings in the spiritual realm.[22]

Ladd even escalated the concept of "reinterpretation" to "radical reinterpretation." In regard to Peter's understanding of Jesus's ascension in Acts 2, Ladd said, "This involves a rather radical reinterpretation of the Old Testament prophecies, but no more so than the entire reinterpretation of God's redemptive plan by the early church."[23] This language of "radical reinterpretation" is strongly rejected by futuristic premillennialists, since there is no reason to reinterpret previously inspired revelation.

Fourth, historic premillennialists believe that the church goes through the tribulation and is not raptured prior to it. Thus, they affirm a posttribulational view of the rapture.

Historic premillennialism is to be commended for affirming a future millennial kingdom and the salvation of ethnic Jews in the end times. But it errs in taking a "historic" understanding of Daniel's seventieth week and the Davidic reign of Jesus. These events are future from our current perspective. Also, it errs in confusing Israel and the church and not seeing theological significance for the nation of Israel in the future (Matt. 19:28; Acts 1:6). Most troubling, though, is the belief that the New Testament at times "reinterprets" the Old Testament and spiritualizes physical and national promises to the church. Historic premillennialism also errs in seeing the church as going through Daniel's seventieth week. For these reasons futuristic premillennialism is the strongly preferred view.

Daniel's "Seventy Weeks" Prophecy

Daniel 9:24–27 with its "seventy weeks" prophecy is one of the most important prophetic passages in the Bible. This text has often been referred to as the "backbone of Bible prophecy" and rightfully so, since several New Testament prophetic passages rely heavily on its contents (Matt. 24:15; 2 Thessalonians 2; Revelation 11–13). Jesus, Paul, and John all refer to this section. A proper understanding of Bible prophecy hinges on rightly interpreting this text:

---

22. George Eldon Ladd, "Revelation 20 and the Millennium," *RevExp* 57, no. 2 (1960): 167.
23. George Eldon Ladd, *A Theology of the New Testament*, rev. ed. (Grand Rapids, MI: Eerdmans, 1994), 373.

Seventy weeks are decreed about your people and your holy city, to finish the transgression, to put an end to sin, and to atone for iniquity, to bring in everlasting righteousness, to seal both vision and prophet, and to anoint a most holy place. Know therefore and understand that from the going out of the word to restore and build Jerusalem to the coming of an anointed one, a prince, there shall be seven weeks. Then for sixty-two weeks it shall be built again with squares and moat, but in a troubled time. And after the sixty-two weeks, an anointed one shall be cut off and shall have nothing. And the people of the prince who is to come shall destroy the city and the sanctuary. Its end shall come with a flood, and to the end there shall be war. Desolations are decreed. And he shall make a strong covenant with many for one week, and for half of the week he shall put an end to sacrifice and offering. And on the wing of abominations shall come one who makes desolate, until the decreed end is poured out on the desolator.

DEFINING THE "SEVENTY WEEKS"

The context of this passage is Daniel's awareness of Jeremiah's prophecy that Jerusalem's desolation at the hands of the Babylonians would end after seventy years (Dan. 9:2; cf. Jer. 25:12; 29:10). Leviticus 25 mandated that every seventh year the people of Israel needed to give the land a rest. But on seventy occasions Israel failed to observe a Sabbath rest for the land. The seventy-year Babylonian captivity was God's way of giving the land the rest he wanted it to have. As Daniel contemplated Jeremiah's prophecy, he prayed on behalf of his sinful people, Israel (Dan. 9:3–19). The angel Gabriel then came to Daniel and relayed a vision concerning Israel's future.

The "seventy weeks" of Daniel 9:24 is at the heart of this prophecy and concerns Daniel's "people" and the "holy city." Daniel's "people" must be Israel since the Babylonian captivity affected the people of Israel and Daniel's prayer was on behalf of Israel. The "holy city" must refer to Jerusalem since Jeremiah's prophecy concerned "the end of the desolations of Jerusalem" (Dan. 9:2). To interpret Israel and Jerusalem as anything else does injustice to the context.

But what are the "seventy weeks" to which Gabriel refers? In Hebrew, "seventy weeks" literally means "seventy sevens." Seventy sevens (or seventy times seven) equals 490. But 490 what? Days? Months? Years? The context indicates that 490 years are in view since Sabbath-year violations were the reason for Israel's expulsion and the ensuing seventy-year Babylonian captivity. (The ancients' year consisted of 360 days.) Also, a period of 490 days or 490 months would be far too short for the fulfillment of the six predictions in 9:24.

This 490-year period of Daniel 9:24 will yield six results: it will (1) "finish the transgression," (2) "put an end to sin," (3) "atone for iniquity," (4) "bring in everlasting righteousness," (5) "seal both vision and prophecy," and (6) "anoint the most holy place" (NASB). The first three effects focus on defeating sin in Israel. The final three focus on positive developments regarding the kingdom—the bringing in of righteousness with Messiah's kingdom, fulfillment of all prophecies in Scripture, and anointing the temple in Jerusalem. The basis for the first three was accomplished with Jesus's first coming and death, although their application to Israel as a nation is still future. The final three await fulfillment at the second coming of Jesus. At this point in history, everlasting righteousness has not been brought in, all prophecies in Scripture have not yet been fulfilled, and the temple in Jerusalem has not been anointed. But these will occur when Jesus establishes his millennial kingdom.

The seventy weeks (490 years) begin with "the going out of the word to restore and build Jerusalem" (Dan. 9:25). This restoration was likely fulfilled in ca. 445 BC, when King Artaxerxes decreed that the Jews could return and rebuild Jerusalem (Neh. 2:1–8). Next, the "seven weeks" or forty-nine years can refer to the closing of Nehemiah's career in the rebuilding of "squares and moat," as well as to the end of the ministry of Malachi and the close of the Old Testament. After these forty-nine years, another "sixty-two" more weeks or 434 years (sixty-two times seven) is added to the timeline. Put together, this 483 years following Artaxerxes's decree in ca. 445 BC culminates in Jesus's entry into Jerusalem in March AD 30.

Daniel 9:26 declares that "after" sixty-two weeks, which is really sixty-nine weeks (seven plus sixty-two), the "anointed one shall be cut off and shall have nothing." Days after entering Jerusalem, Jesus is crucified. That the Messiah "has nothing" is shocking. The Messiah of Israel comes, is killed, and dies with nothing. No kingdom and no everlasting righteousness occur. The rest of verse 26 describes other events "after" the first sixty-nine weeks: "And the people of the prince who is to come shall destroy the city and the sanctuary. Its end shall come with a flood, and to the end there shall be war. Desolations are decreed." This statement predicts the destruction of Jerusalem and the Jewish temple with the Roman invasion of Jerusalem in AD 70 (Luke 21:20–24).

The "people" in Daniel 9:26 refers to the Romans since they were the ones who destroyed Jerusalem in AD 70. From this "people" a "prince who is to come" will someday arrive. This is the evil Antichrist figure who will arise sometime after the destruction of the city and the sanctuary. That this is an evil person and not Jesus the Messiah is affirmed by the descriptions in Daniel 9:27, in which he commits an abominable act in the temple and is destroyed for his desolations. Also, he will make a covenant with the people of Israel for one week (seven years), something Jesus never did. So the context points to the evil Antichrist figure, who is also identified as the "little horn" in Daniel 7:8 and the willful king of Daniel 11:36. The statements "There shall be war" and "Desolations are decreed" (Dan. 9:26) reveal that Jerusalem's trials and woes will continue even after the destruction of Jerusalem. That has certainly been the case, as Israel's tumultuous history since AD 70 shows. Jesus himself predicted that the "times of the Gentiles" would continue even after the destruction of Jerusalem in AD 70 (Luke 21:24).

Daniel 9:27 goes on to say that the evil prince from the Romans "shall make a strong covenant with many for one week." The "many" refers to the people of Israel, and the "one week" is a seven-year period. Just as the first sixty-nine weeks were literal, so too must the last week of seven years be literal. To make the final week anything other than a seven-year period is to violate the context. That this covenant is future from our standpoint is verified by the fact that no seven-year covenant between a leader from the Roman Empire and the Jewish people has ever happened in history.

At "half of the week" (three and one-half years), this leader breaks the covenant with Israel. He "shall put an end to sacrifice and offering." In other words, he halts the Jewish worship system. This happens "on the wing of abominations" by the "one who makes desolate." This desolator sets up an abomination in an area of the temple. Jesus picks up this wording when he states, "So when you see the abomination of desolation spoken of by the prophet Daniel, standing in the holy place" (Matt. 24:15).

Yet this desolator is headed for destruction. He does his "abominations" only "until the decreed end is poured out on the desolator" (Dan. 9:27). God's wrath will be visited on this evil prince. Paul draws on Daniel 9:27 when he refers to a coming "man of lawlessness" (2 Thess. 2:3) whom Jesus will slay with his coming: "And then the lawless one will be revealed, whom the Lord Jesus will kill with the breath of his mouth and bring to nothing by the appearance of his coming" (2 Thess. 2:8).

GAP BETWEEN THE SIXTY-NINTH AND SEVENTIETH WEEKS

Many interpreters agree that the sixty-nine weeks (483 years of 360 days each) of Daniel's prophecy were fulfilled with Jesus's first coming and his death around AD 30. But some disagree about whether the final week of years, a seven-year period, was fulfilled immediately after the first sixty-nine weeks expired or whether there is a gap of time between the end of the sixty-ninth weeks and the beginning of the seventieth week. In other words, did Daniel's seventieth week expire in the late 30s—that is, in the seven years following the end of the sixty-ninth week around AD 30—or will Daniel's seventieth week be fulfilled in the future? The correct view is the latter.

Opponents of a gap often ask, where in Daniel 9:24–27 do we see any evidence of a large gap between the sixty-ninth and seventieth weeks? For them, the seventieth week runs immediately after the sixty-ninth week. However, evidence for a gap between the sixty-ninth and seventieth weeks is strong. The following reasons explain why there is a gap.

1. A gap exists between the first and second comings of Jesus. Bible prophecy is best grasped in the context of the two comings of Jesus. A significant gap of time exists between the first coming and second coming of Jesus. Since this is the case, it is reasonable to expect a gap in the fulfillment of prophecies about Jesus. For example, Zechariah 9:9 predicted that the Messiah would come to Jerusalem lowly on a donkey. This was fulfilled with Jesus's triumphal entry into Jerusalem (Matt. 21:1–8). But Zechariah 9:10 also declared a worldwide reign of the Messiah on the earth: "He shall speak peace to the nations; his rule shall be from sea to sea, and from the River to the ends of the earth." This verse will be fulfilled with Jesus's second coming, and it certainly did not immediately follow his entry into Jerusalem on a donkey in the first century. So a gap separates verse 9 from verse 10. Gaps of time in prophetic passages such as Zechariah 9:9–10 indicate that a gap could be present in Daniel 9:24–27. Such is to be expected with two comings of Jesus.

2. *Daniel 9:26 states that the Messiah will be cut off "after" the sixty-nine weeks.* Daniel's use of the word "after" reveals a gap. Daniel 9:26 reads, "Then after the sixty-two weeks the Messiah will be cut off and have nothing." The Messiah is not cut off at the "end" of the sixty-nine weeks or at the "beginning" of the seventieth week. Instead, he is cut off "after" the sixty-nine weeks. So within the text, a term indicates a gap between the sixty-ninth and seventieth weeks.

3. *The destruction of Jerusalem predicted in Daniel 9:26 occurred decades after the culmination of the sixty-ninth week.* Daniel 9:26 states that "after the sixty-two weeks," the coming prince "will destroy the city and the sanctuary"—a reference to Jerusalem and the temple. This destruction took place in AD 70. If the entire seventy-week prophecy continued with no gap, the seventieth week would have expired in the AD 30s. But Jerusalem and the temple were not destroyed then. Since Jerusalem and the temple were destroyed nearly four decades after the end of the sixty-ninth week, a gap between the sixty-ninth week and seventieth week is necessary to include the AD 70 destruction.

4. *The six predictions of Daniel 9:24 have not yet all been fulfilled.* In Daniel 9:24, Daniel mentions six important predictions that will result from the seventy-weeks decree: (1) "to finish the transgression," (2) "to make an end of sin," (3) "to make atonement for iniquity," (4) "to bring in everlasting righteousness," (5) "to seal up vision and prophecy," and (6) "to anoint the most holy place" (NASB). If one holds that the seventy weeks expired in the first century, then all six predictions should have been completely fulfilled in the 30s. But they were not. The basis for the first three occurred with Jesus's first coming. Yet Israel's sin against God has not yet been reversed. So even while Jesus's death has already atoned for sin, Israel has not yet experienced this benefit. The salvation of Israel is still to come (see Zech. 12:10; Rom. 11:26). Then there are other matters that have not yet occurred. Everlasting righteousness has not been established. Not all prophecies have been fulfilled. The anointing of the temple in Messiah's kingdom has not yet taken place. Since several predictions of Daniel 9:24 have yet to occur, these must be fulfilled in the future.

5. *What is described for the seventieth week of Daniel 9:27 has not yet been fulfilled.* The lack of fulfillment of Daniel 9:27 at this point in history is evidence that Daniel's seventieth week will be fulfilled at a future time. A coming evil prince from the Roman Empire has not made a seven-year covenant with the Jewish people. No violation of a seven-year covenant has occurred after three and one-half years. No Antichrist figure has committed abominations in the temple. Nor has the one doing this been destroyed. These events were not completed in the AD 30s and thus await future fulfillment.

6. *Jesus refers to the abomination of desolation of Daniel 9:27 as future after his first coming.* In Matthew 24–25, Jesus predicted events to come. With Matthew 24:15, Jesus declared, "So when you see the abomination of desolation spoken of by the prophet Daniel, standing in the holy place (let the reader understand) . . ." This is the same event predicted in Daniel 9:27: "On the wing of abominations shall come

one who makes desolate." This event, though, was future from Jesus's standpoint and was not fulfilled in the 30s.

7. *In the AD 50s Paul spoke of the events of Daniel 9:27 as future.* In 2 Thessalonians 2, Paul writes about a "man of lawlessness" being revealed who enters a temple and declares himself to be God (2 Thess. 2:3–4). He also speaks of this wicked man as facing the wrath of the Lord Jesus, who slays him at his return: "And then the lawless one will be revealed, whom the Lord Jesus will kill with the breath of his mouth and bring to nothing by the appearance of his coming" (2 Thess. 2:8). Paul relies on Daniel 9:27 to establish that there will be a coming abomination of desolation by a wicked person and that this person will be destroyed by God. That Paul is predicting these events in the 50s shows that these events are future from his standpoint and were not fulfilled in the 30s. Paul's inspired commentary of Daniel 9:27 shows that the events of Daniel's seventieth week are set in the future.

8. *Revelation places the time frame of Daniel 9:27 in the future.* Daniel 9:27 tells of a seven-year period in which a coming prince will make a covenant with the "many" for one week (seven years). But in the middle of this week, at the three-and-one-half-year mark, he will break this covenant. Writing in the AD 90s, the apostle John referred to a coming three-and-one-half-year period on multiple occasions. In Revelation 11:2, he says that the "holy city" [Jerusalem] will be trampled for "forty-two months." "Forty-two months" is three and one-half years. And since Daniel 9:27 also speaks of an "abomination" event in Jerusalem, John is clearly connecting his statement with Daniel 9:27. Since John is writing several decades after the AD 30s, he must view the last half of the seventieth week of Daniel as being future from his vantage point. And if so, there must be a gap between the sixty-ninth and seventieth weeks. John also predicts the nation of Israel fleeing to the wilderness for "1,260 days" (Rev. 12:6). This time frame is equal to three and one-half years. In Revelation 13:5, John describes an evil "beast" who speaks arrogantly and blasphemes for "forty-two months." This parallels Daniel 9:27 and the association of an evil figure with a three-and-one-half-year period. In sum, since John refers to the time frame and events of Daniel 9:27 as needing to be fulfilled in the future, this shows that the events of this period must be future.

Events to Come

Several prophetic events await future fulfillment. These include the rapture, the tribulation period, the coming of the Antichrist, the day of the Lord, the second coming of Jesus, the millennium, Satan's final revolt, and the eternal state.

THE RAPTURE[24]

The rapture is one of the most recognizable events of eschatology. Popular books and movies have made the rapture a topic of discussion for many. Some fixate on

---

24. This section is adapted from Richard L. Mayhue, "Why a Pretribulational Rapture?," *MSJ* 13, no. 2 (2002): 241–53. Used by permission of *MSJ*.

this issue, and others ignore it or treat it with scorn. But what is the biblical view of the rapture?

The English word *rapture* comes from the Latin term *raptura*, which in Latin Bibles translates the Greek word *harpazō*. This Greek word means "to suddenly remove" or "to snatch away." The New Testament uses it in reference to stealing or plundering (Matt. 11:12; 12:29; 13:19; John 10:12, 28, 29) and removing (John 6:15; Acts 8:39; 23:10; Jude 23). A third use focuses on being caught up to heaven, as visible in Paul's third-heaven experience (2 Cor. 12:2–4) and Christ's ascension (Rev. 12:5). *Harpazō* also describes God's sudden taking of the church from earth to heaven as the first part of Christ's second coming (1 Thess. 4:17). However, this word contains no hint of the rapture's time in relation to Daniel's seventieth week. The timing of the rapture must be determined by other factors.

First Thessalonians 4:16–17 tells of a rapture that is eschatological in nature. Here, *harpazō* is translated "caught up":

> For the Lord Himself will descend from heaven with a shout, with the voice of the archangel and with the trumpet of God, and the dead in Christ will rise first. Then we who are alive and remain will be caught up together with them in the clouds to meet the Lord in the air, and so we shall always be with the Lord (NASB).

While not employing *harpazō*, 1 Corinthians 15:51–52 refers to the same eschatological event as 1 Thessalonians 4:16–17:

> Behold, I tell you a mystery; we will not all sleep, but we will all be changed, in a moment, in the twinkling of an eye, at the last trumpet; for the trumpet will sound, and the dead will be raised imperishable, and we will be changed (NASB).

Thus, Scripture points to an eschatological rapture, even though neither of these foundational texts contains any explicit time indicators.

Views on the Timing of the Rapture. The passages cited above mention a snatching away and transforming of Christians, but they do not state when this event occurs. Four views on the timing of the rapture exist. These views address when the rapture will happen in relation to the coming seventieth week of Daniel.

First, the pretribulational rapture view asserts that the church will be raptured before Daniel's seventieth week. Since the entire period of tribulation is the "wrath of God," the church must be rescued prior to the tribulation to fulfill God's promise that the church will escape the wrath of God (1 Thess. 1:9–10; Rev. 3:10). The pretribulational rapture functions as a rescue mission by which Jesus delivers his church from the divine wrath of the tribulation.

Second, the midtribulational rapture view argues that the church will be raptured at the midpoint of Daniel's seventieth week. The church goes through the first half of the tribulation but then is raptured at the midpoint to avoid the most severe wrath of God that characterizes the latter period of Daniel's seventieth week. The midtribulational perspective arbitrarily does not see the first half of the tribulation as divine wrath; it maintains that the wrath of man and Satan is occurring but not the wrath of God.

Third, the prewrath rapture view teaches that the rapture will occur somewhere in the latter part of the tribulation and removes the church from the trumpet and bowl judgments, which it defines as the wrath of God. The rapture occurs after the midpoint of the tribulation but before Jesus's second coming to earth.

Fourth, the posttribulational rapture view asserts that the rapture occurs at the time of the second coming and is the initial phase of Jesus's bodily return. The church, which goes through the tribulation period, is snatched into the air to meet the returning Jesus, who then descends to earth with his people. The posttribulational scenario is like subjects of a king rushing out of a city to greet the returning and victorious king and then immediately returning to the city. This is the only rapture view that has the church going through the entire tribulation period.

Evidence for Pretribulationism. Pretribulationism has the most biblical support, and we believe that it is the correct view for several reasons. First, Jesus declares that the church will be removed prior to the hour of trial that is coming on the entire earth: "Because you have kept my word about patient endurance, I will keep you from the hour of trial that is coming on the whole world, to try those who dwell on the earth" (Rev. 3:10). Jesus promises a reward for "patient endurance." This reward is that one is kept from a unique period—"the hour of trial that is coming on the whole world." This helps answer the why of the rapture. The rapture is a promise or reward to the church for enduring patiently during suffering. The church that endures the trials of this present age will be kept from the special hour of testing for the people of the earth.

Does the phrase "keep you from" (Gk. *tēreō ek*) in Revelation 3:10 mean "a continuing safe state outside of" or "a safe emergence from within"? The former would be consistent with a pretribulational rapture, the latter with a posttribulational rapture. The Greek preposition *ek* sometimes carries the idea of emergence, but this is not always so. Two notable examples are found in 2 Corinthians 1:10 and 1 Thessalonians 1:10. In the 2 Corinthians passage, Paul rehearses how God rescued him from death. Here Paul did not emerge from a state of death but was rescued from potential danger. Even more convincing is 1 Thessalonians 1:10, where Paul states that Jesus will rescue believers out of the wrath to come. The idea is not emergence after going through something but rather protection from entering it.

Also, if Revelation 3:10 refers to divine protection within the hour of trial, then what about those who died for Jesus during this time? Were they not protected? The widespread martyrdom of saints during the tribulation demands that the promise means "keeping out of " the hour of testing, not "keeping within."

Second, the church goes unmentioned in Revelation 6–18. The common New Testament term for "church" is *ekklēsia*. It is used nineteen times in Revelation 1–3 in relation to the historical church of the first century. However, "church" appears only once more in Revelation, in the epilogue of the book (Rev. 22:16). Nowhere in Revelation 6–18 is the "church" mentioned. Why is this significant? It is unlikely that John would shift from detailed instructions for the church in Revelation 1–3 to absolute silence about the church for thirteen chapters if the church continued into the tribulation. If the church will experience the tribulation, surely the most detailed study of tribulation events would include the church's role in this period. But it does not. A pretribulational rapture best explains the total absence of the "church" on earth during the events of Revelation 6–18.

Third, the rapture is rendered inconsequential if the church goes through the tribulation. If God miraculously preserves the church through the tribulation, why have a rapture at all? If it is to avoid the wrath of God at Armageddon, then why would God not continue to protect the saints on earth (as postulated by posttribulationism) as he protected the church in the events leading up to Armageddon or as God protected Israel from the plagues in Egypt (Ex. 8:22; 9:4, 26; 10:23; 11:7)?

Also, if the rapture occurs in connection with a posttribulational coming, the subsequent separation of the sheep from the goats in Matthew 25:31–46 would be redundant. Separation would have already taken place at the rapture with no need of another. Plus, if all tribulation believers are raptured and glorified just prior to the millennial kingdom, what people will populate the kingdom? Every believer would have a glorified body at that time, while the Scripture indicates that living unbelievers will be judged at the end of the tribulation and removed from the earth (Matt. 13:41–42; 25:41). These realities do not correlate with the Bible's teaching that children will be born to believers during the millennium and that these children will be capable of sin and rebellion (Isa. 65:20; cf. Rev. 20:7–10), which would not be possible if all believers on earth had been glorified through a posttribulational rapture.

In addition, the posttribulational paradigm of the church being raptured and then immediately brought back to earth leaves no time for the *bēma* judgment of Christ (1 Cor. 3:10–15; 2 Cor. 5:10) or for the marriage supper (Rev. 19:6–10). Thus, the timing of a posttribulational rapture does not make sense chronologically. It is incongruous with the sheep-goat nation judgment and two critical end-time events. A pretribulational rapture avoids these difficulties.

Fourth, the Epistles contain no preparatory warnings of an impending tribulation for church-age believers. God's instructions to the church in the Epistles contain a variety of warnings, but believers are not warned to prepare for entering and enduring the tribulation. The New Testament warns vigorously about coming error and false prophets (Acts 20:29–30; 2 Pet. 2:1; 1 John 4:1–3; Jude 4). It warns against ungodly living (Eph. 4:25–5:7; 1 Thess. 4:3–8; Heb. 12:1). The New Testament admonishes believers to endure in the midst of present tribulation (1 Thess. 2:13–14; 2 Thess. 1:4). However, there is silence concerning preparing the church for the global and catastrophic tribulation described in Revelation 6–18. It is difficult to view the Scripture as being silent on such a traumatic event for the church if the church is to endure this period. If the church experienced any of the tribulation period, one would expect the Epistles to teach the church's existence, purpose, and conduct in it.

Yet there is no teaching on this matter. Only a pretribulational rapture satisfactorily explains this lack of instruction for the church.

Fifth, 1 Thessalonians 4:13–18 demands a pretribulational rapture. Suppose that some other rapture view is true. What then would we expect to find in 1 Thessalonians 4? The reverse of the concerns reflected there. To begin, we would expect the Thessalonians to be rejoicing that their loved ones are home with the Lord and will not endure the horrors of the tribulation. But instead, we discover that the Thessalonians are actually grieving because they fear their loved ones will miss the rapture. Only a pretribulational rapture accounts for this grief. Also, we would expect the Thessalonians to be grieving over their own impending trial rather than over their loved ones who escaped it. Furthermore, we would expect them to be inquisitive about their own future. But the Thessalonians have no fears or questions about the coming tribulation. We would expect Paul to have provided instructions and exhortation for such a supreme test. But we find no indication of any impending tribulation.

Sixth, the close parallels between John 14:1–3 and 1 Thessalonians 4:13–18, two texts referring to Christ's second coming, fit with a pretribulational rapture:

1. The promise of presence with Christ:

   "Where I am, there you may be also." (John 14:3 NASB)

   "So we shall always be with the Lord." (1 Thess. 4:17 NASB)

2. The promise of comfort:

   "Do not let your heart be troubled." (John 14:1 NASB)

   "Therefore comfort one another with these words." (1 Thess. 4:18 NASB)

Jesus instructed the disciples that he was going to his Father's house (heaven) to prepare a place for them. He promised them that he would return and receive them so that they could be with him wherever he was (John 14:1–3). The phrase "where I am," while implying continued presence in general, here means presence in heaven in particular. Our Lord told the Pharisees in John 7:34, "Where I am you cannot come." He was not talking about his present abode on earth but his resurrected presence at the right hand of the Father. In John 14:3, "where I am" must mean "in heaven," or the intent would not make sense.

A posttribulational rapture demands that the saints meet Christ in the air and immediately descend to earth without experiencing what our Lord promised in John 14. Since John 14 refers to the rapture and makes no reference to judgment, then only a pretribulational rapture satisfies the language of John 14:1–3 and allows raptured saints to dwell for a meaningful time with Christ in his Father's house.

Seventh, events at Christ's return to earth after the tribulation differ from the rapture. If one compares what happens at the rapture in 1 Thessalonians 4:13–18 and 1 Corinthians 15:50–58 with what happens in the final events of Christ's second coming in Matthew 24–25, at least eight significant contrasts or differences can be observed, which demand that the rapture and Christ's second coming occur at different times:

1. At the rapture, Christ comes in the air and returns to heaven (1 Thess. 4:17), while at the final event of the second coming, Christ comes to earth to dwell and reign (Matt. 25:31–32).
2. At the rapture, Christ gathers his own (1 Thess. 4:16–17), while at the second coming, angels gather the elect (Matt. 24:31).
3. At the rapture, Christ comes to reward (1 Thess. 4:17), while at the second coming, Christ comes to judge (Matt. 25:31–46).
4. At the rapture, resurrection is prominent in Jesus's coming (1 Thess. 4:15–16), while at the second coming, no resurrection is mentioned with Christ's descent.
5. At the rapture, believers depart from the earth (1 Thess. 4:15–17), while at the second coming, unbelievers are taken away from the earth (Matt. 24:37–41).
6. At the rapture, unbelievers remain on the earth (implied), while at the second coming, believers remain on the earth (Matt. 25:34).
7. At the rapture, there is no mention of Christ's kingdom on earth, while at the second coming, Christ's kingdom on earth is established (Matt. 25:31, 34).
8. At the rapture, believers will receive glorified bodies (cf. 1 Cor. 15:51–57), while at the second coming, no one who is alive receives glorified bodies.

Additionally, several of Christ's parables in Matthew 13 confirm differences between the rapture and Christ's second coming to earth. In the parable of the wheat and the tares, the tares (unbelievers) are taken out from among the wheat (believers) at the climax of the second coming (Matt. 13:30, 40), while believers are removed from among unbelievers at the rapture (1 Thess. 4:15–17). In the parable of the dragnet, the bad fish (unbelievers) are taken out from among the good fish (believers) at the culmination of Christ's second coming (Matt. 13:48–50), while believers are removed from among unbelievers at the rapture (1 Thess. 4:15–17). Finally, there is no mention of the rapture in the detailed second-coming texts Matthew 24 and Revelation 19.

THE TRIBULATION PERIOD

Jesus promised his followers that they would experience tribulation in the world (John 16:33). This has indeed happened as many Christians have suffered and died for the cause of Christ. Yet Jesus also predicted a unique time that would be the most severe and difficult in human history: "For then there will be great tribulation, such as has not been from the beginning of the world until now, no, and never will be" (Matt. 24:21). This unique time is called the tribulation or tribulation period, based on Jesus's use of this term in Matthew 24:9, 21. The tribulation is a period of divine judgments before the return of Jesus Christ and the establishment of his kingdom on earth. This period will last seven years, based on the future seventieth week of Daniel, which is seven years in length (Dan. 9:27).

The Bible reveals more about the coming tribulation than any other prophetic event still to come. The Old Testament predicts a time of tribulation for Israel in connection with Israel's regathering from the nations. In Deuteronomy 4:30, God tells Israel, "When you are in tribulation, and all these things come upon you in the latter days, you will return to the LORD your God and obey his voice." Jeremiah predicts a "time of distress for Jacob" (Jer. 30:7). Zephaniah foretells of "a day of distress and anguish" (Zeph. 1:15). Isaiah calls this "a day of vengeance, a year of recompense for the cause of Zion" (Isa. 34:8).

Matthew 24–25 (along with Mark 13; Luke 21) and Revelation 6–19 offer the most detailed information concerning the tribulation period in the New Testament. Jesus speaks of "birth pains" such as wars, rumors of wars, famines, and earthquakes in various places (Matt. 24:4–8). Persecution of Jesus's followers will be intense (Matt. 24:9). Apostasy and betrayal will occur (Matt. 24:10). Many false prophets will arise (Matt. 24:11), and lawlessness will increase (Matt. 24:12). Yet in the midst of this terrible period, the gospel of the kingdom will be proclaimed to the whole world (Matt. 24:14), and both Jews and Gentiles will be saved (Rev. 7:4–9).

Strategic to this period is the fulfillment of the "abomination of desolation," an event first spoken of by Daniel (Dan. 9:27). From Daniel's chronology, this distinguishing event occurs at the midpoint of the tribulation, or at the three-and-one-half-year mark, and it describes the Antichrist's breaking of his covenant with Israel in which he tries to stop the Jewish worship system in the temple. Paul notes that this "man of lawlessness" enters the temple declaring himself to be God (2 Thess. 2:3–4). This event launches a severe persecution in Israel, which is why Jesus warns the residents of Judea to flee with no thought of returning for any item (Matt. 24:16–20). The end of this period brings cosmic signs: "Immediately after the tribulation of those days the sun will be darkened, and the moon will not give its light, and the stars will fall from heaven" (Matt. 24:29). Jesus returns to earth in power and glory (Matt. 24:30) and gathers his elect (Matt. 24:31). The return of Jesus in glory with his angels leads to a judgment of nations to see who will enter his kingdom (Matt. 25:31–46).

Revelation 6–19 details the judgments that occur during the tribulation in the form of seals, trumpets, and bowls. These massive judgments are predominately sequential and reveal escalating judgments from God against an unbelieving world and the kingdom of the Antichrist. Since Jesus is the One who opens the seal judgments, all subsequent judgments are the wrath of God and Jesus (Rev. 6:1). The six seals include (1) the arrival of Antichrist, (2) war, (3) famine, (4) death, (5) martyrdom, and (6) earthquake (Rev. 6:2–12). These correspond closely with the conditions of "birth pains" found in Matthew 24:4–7. At the time of the sixth seal (earthquake), the people on earth realize they are facing the great wrath of God and the Lamb (Rev. 6:16–17). The wrath of God does not begin at this point since it already started with the first seal, but at this time the earth dwellers realize with certainty that it is God's wrath they are experiencing.

Next, the seventh seal brings the second wave of judgments—the seven trumpets:

1. First trumpet: One-third of the earth, trees, and grass are burned up (Rev. 8:7).
2. Second trumpet: One-third of the sea creatures die, and the ships are destroyed (8:8–9).

3. Third trumpet: One-third of the waters are polluted, and many die (8:10–11).
4. Fourth trumpet: One-third of the sun, moon, and stars are darkened (8:12).
5. Fifth trumpet: Locusts/demons are released to torment people (9:1–11).
6. Sixth trumpet: Four bound demons are released to kill one-third of humanity (9:13–19).
7. Seventh trumpet: Christ's kingdom reign is proclaimed (11:15–18).

The final cluster of judgments are the bowl judgments. These come later in the tribulation period in rapid succession and are extremely severe:

1. First bowl: Painful sores come on people (Rev. 16:2).
2. Second bowl: The sea becomes like blood, and everything in the sea dies (16:3).
3. Third bowl: The rivers and springs of water are turned to blood (16:4–7).
4. Fourth bowl: The sun scorches people with fire and heat (16:8–9).
5. Fifth bowl: Darkness and intense pain afflict humanity (16:10–11).
6. Sixth bowl: The Euphrates River is dried up to prepare the way for kings from the East (16:12–16).
7. Seventh bowl: Severe earthquakes split the great city into three parts, cities fall, and severe hail drops from heaven (16:17–21).

The purpose of the tribulation is twofold. First, God will use the tribulation to save Israel. This involves the completion of the purposes of Daniel 9:24, such as dealing finally with Israel's sin, bringing in everlasting righteousness, and anointing the temple. Also, Jeremiah 30:7 says that this will be "a time of distress for Jacob [Israel]," yet Israel "will be saved from it." Israel enters the tribulation making a covenant with the Antichrist but ends this period by calling on her Messiah.

Second, God will use the tribulation to judge the unbelieving world. Revelation 3:10 refers to the tribulation as "the hour of trial that is coming on the whole world, to try those who dwell on the earth." Isaiah 24 describes this as a time of global judgment in which "the Lord will empty the earth and make it desolate" and "will twist its surface and scatter its inhabitants" (Isa. 24:1). The reason is because of man's sinfulness: "For they have transgressed the laws, violated the statutes, broken the everlasting covenant" (Isa. 24:5). Thus, the tribulation is a time of intense global wrath from God on a sinful, rebellious world.

THE ANTICHRIST

The Bible predicts a coming Antichrist, a representative of Satan who is the embodiment of evil. The term *antichrist* (Gk. *antichristos*) is found in 1 John 2:18: "Children, it is the last hour, and as you have heard that antichrist is coming, so now many antichrists have come." John refers to a specific Antichrist to come, yet he also mentions "antichrists" that have already arrived. These are not *the* Antichrist, but they function in the spirit of antichrist, opposing who Jesus is and what he stands for. We can expect many who possess the antichrist spirit while knowing that a personal Antichrist is also still coming.

The prefix *anti-* can mean "against" or "instead of." So is the coming Antichrist openly "against" Jesus, or is he a counterfeit pretending to be a messiah figure? Both concepts could be true. He is a counterfeit to the Messiah in that he will make a deceptive treaty with the people of Israel (Dan. 9:27) and pretend to be their savior. Yet he is against Jesus by opposing Jesus and his saints. He also will persecute Israel at the midpoint of Daniel's seventieth week. In sum, he is both a counterfeit and one who opposes Christ.

Daniel offers the most detailed information about the Antichrist in the Old Testament. This evil person is the blasphemous political ruler, the "little horn" who speaks great and boastful words and wages war against the saints of God (Dan. 7:8, 21). He is the wicked "prince" who arises from the Romans (Dan. 9:26). This prince makes a covenant with the Jewish people for seven years but breaks this covenant at the midpoint, stopping the Jewish sacrificial system and desolating the temple (Dan. 9:27). In Daniel 11:36–45, he is the willful king who exalts himself, speaks against God, rejects any rival gods, and trusts in his military might.

The apostle Paul refers to the Antichrist as the "man of lawlessness" (2 Thess. 2:3). Relying on Daniel 9:26–27 and 11:36–45, Paul reveals that this evil man arrives in connection with the day of the Lord (2 Thess. 2:1–2). This person "opposes and exalts himself against every so-called god or object of worship, so that he takes his seat in the temple of God, proclaiming himself to be God" (2 Thess. 2:4). His presence in God's temple is associated with the desolation of the temple that Daniel 9:27 predicted. Jesus refers to this event as "the abomination of desolation spoken of by the prophet Daniel, standing in the holy place" (Matt. 24:15). This horrible event of desolation leads to intense persecution in Judea, which Jesus warns about in Matthew 24:16–22.

The most detailed discussion of the Antichrist was revealed to the apostle John and recorded in Revelation 13. John refers to this individual as a "beast." This beast comes from the nations and is empowered by Satan (Rev. 13:1–2). He recovers from a mortal wound with some kind of resurrection that causes the world to marvel at him (Rev. 13:3). He blasphemes God (Rev. 13:5–6), wages war on the saints, and exercises authority over the earth (Rev. 13:7–8). He attempts to establish a permanent kingdom on earth for Satan.

Debate exists as to whether the Antichrist will be a Jew or a Gentile. Possible evidence for being a Jew is found in Daniel 11:37, which says that he will "pay no attention to the gods of his fathers." Some translations such as the King James Version set "God" in the singular. If this is the case, then he is rejecting the God of the Jewish patriarchs. Most translations, however, render this as "gods," making it likely that Gentile gods are in view. This latter view is the more probable case. So the Antichrist arises from European nations (Dan. 7:7–8, 23–25; cf. Rev. 13:1). Also, since he is the prince who comes from the people who destroyed Jerusalem and the temple in AD 70 (Dan. 9:26), he must come from the Roman Empire, for the Romans were the ones who destroyed Jerusalem and the temple. Also, Daniel's prediction concerning Antiochus IV Epiphanes (215–164 BC) in Daniel 8:9–14, 23–25 supports the view that the Antichrist will be a Gentile. Antiochus was a Syrian who desecrated the Jewish temple around 167 BC by instituting Zeus worship in Jerusalem and having a pig slaughtered in the temple. This desolating act seems to prefigure what the Antichrist of Daniel 9:27 will do. Since Antiochus was a Gentile, the Antichrist will probably be a Gentile as well.

While a frightening and powerful figure, the Antichrist has a brief career and is destroyed. Paul says that Jesus "will kill [the man of lawlessness] with the breath of his mouth and bring [him] to nothing by the appearance of his coming" (2 Thess. 2:8). Daniel says that a "decreed end is poured out on the desolator" (Dan. 9:27) and that "he shall come to his end, with none to help him" (Dan. 11:45). This "beast" is thrown into the lake of fire at Jesus's return, where his fate is sealed forever (Rev. 19:20).

THE DAY OF THE LORD[25]

The biblical phrase "the day of the Lord" stands as a key term in understanding God's revelation about the future. The New Testament writers' use of "the day of the Lord" rested on their understanding of the Old Testament Prophets. A survey of the Old Testament indicates that the prophets used it when speaking of both near-historical events and far-future eschatological events involving God's wrath. The New Testament writers picked up on the eschatological use and applied "the day of the Lord" both to the judgment that will climax the tribulation period and to the judgment that will usher in the new earth.

The specific phrase "the day of the Lord" or a close variant appears nineteen times in the Old Testament (Obad. 15; Joel 1:15; 2:1, 11, 31; 3:14; Amos 5:18 [2×], 20; Isa. 2:12; 13:6, 9; Zeph. 1:7, 14 [2×]; Ezek. 13:5; 30:3; Zech. 14:1; Mal. 4:5). "The day of the Lord" appears in four uncontested New Testament passages—Acts 2:20; 1 Thessalonians 5:2; 2 Thessalonians 2:2; and 2 Peter 3:10. Four times this period is referred to as the "day of vengeance" (Isa. 34:8; 61:2; 63:4; Jer. 46:10). The New Testament calls it a "day of wrath" (Rom. 2:5), a "day of visitation" (1 Pet. 2:12), and the "great day of God the Almighty" (Rev. 16:14).

Ever since the fall of man in Genesis 3, mankind has been in rebellion against its Creator, but a time is coming when God will judge the entire world with calamitous wrath to prepare for the establishment of his kingdom. The day of man will give way to the day of the Lord. That final day of the Lord is the time of ultimate divine wrath against sinners for their rebellion against God.

The Old Testament prophets wrote much more about the day of the Lord and provided the foundation for the New Testament references, using the phrase in reference to both near-historical fulfillment and far-future eschatological events. For example, Joel 1:15 refers to a historical day of the Lord involving a severe locust plague within Israel as described in Joel 1. Yet the day of the Lord in Joel 2 and 3 refers to a future

---

25. This section is adapted from Richard L. Mayhue, "The Bible's Watchword: Day of the Lord," *MSJ* 22, no. 1 (2011): 65–88. Used by permission of *MSJ*. For a fuller discussion of the topic, see the article.

day of the Lord in which Israel is restored and blessed and the Gentile nations are judged based on how they treated God's people Israel. The historical day of the Lord serves as a harbinger for a greater day of the Lord to come.

The New Testament writers picked up on the eschatological usage and applied the phrase both to the judgment that will climax the tribulation period and the judgment that will usher in the new earth. The day of the Lord occurs through providential means (Ezek. 30:3) or directly at the hand of God (2 Pet. 3:10). At times, the near fulfillment (Joel 1:15) prefigures the far fulfillment (Joel 3:14). Two periods of the day of the Lord are yet to be fulfilled on earth: (1) the judgment that climaxes the tribulation period (2 Thess. 2:2; Rev. 16–18) and (2) the consummating judgment of this earth after the millennium that ushers in the new earth (2 Pet. 3:10–13; Rev. 20:7–21:1).

In sum, the day of the Lord can be summarized in six assertions:

1. The day of the Lord involves judgment only, not judgment and blessing.
2. The day of the Lord occurs twice in God's prophetic plan, not once.
3. The day of the Lord occurs at the end of the tribulation period, not throughout its duration.
4. The day of the Lord occurs again at the end of the millennium, not throughout its duration.
5. The day of the Lord as defined here does not necessarily prove pretribulationism, but it certainly and easily allows for it.
6. The day of the Lord supports futuristic premillennialism.

THE SECOND COMING OF JESUS

The focal point of prophetic events still to come is the second coming of Jesus Christ. While specific language of "second coming" is rare in Scripture, the concept is well established (Matt. 25:31; John 14:3; Acts 1:11). Belief in the return of Jesus is an indispensable doctrine of orthodox Christianity. The New Testament declares the necessity of a second coming of Jesus. The word "second" is used in Hebrews 9:28: "So Christ, having been offered once to bear the sins of many, will appear a second time, not to deal with sin but to save those who are eagerly waiting for him." The second coming of Jesus will put an end to the present age and to Daniel's seventieth week, which features a Satan-inspired global reign of the Antichrist. The second coming is also the starting point for the millennial reign of Jesus on the earth. The return of Jesus functions as an important transition point from this present evil age to the righteous kingdom of Jesus.

The Old Testament did not explicitly reveal two comings of the Messiah separated by a considerable period of time. It predicted both a suffering servant and a reigning king but did not explain that these roles would be fulfilled over two comings. Evidence for a gap could exist in Psalm 110, which states that David's Lord, the Messiah, will have a session at the right hand of God "until" the Messiah reigns over his enemies from Jerusalem (Ps. 110:1–2). Yet Scripture gives no indication that Old Testament saints or even Jesus's disciples before the cross expected a separation between Jesus's first and second comings. With the testimony of progressive revelation and the hindsight of history, we can look at the Old Testament and see that kingdom passages still need to be fulfilled at the second coming of Jesus.

Zechariah 14 addresses the second coming. The context is a siege of Jerusalem that leads to the return of the Lord: "Then the Lord will go out and fight against those nations as when he fights on a day of battle. On that day his feet shall stand on the Mount of Olives that lies before Jerusalem on the east" (Zech. 14:3–4). Since this prophecy did not occur with Jesus's first coming, this must refer to the event of his second coming. Jesus ascended from the Mount of Olives (Acts 1:12) and will return to the same spot at his return.

The second coming is detailed in several New Testament sections. Jesus discussed his return to earth in his Olivet Discourse (Matthew 24–25; Mark 13; Luke 21). His disciples asked him, "What will be the sign of your coming?" (Matt. 24:3). Jesus detailed several events but then declared, "Immediately after the tribulation of those days," the tribes of the earth "will see the Son of Man coming on the clouds of heaven with power and great glory" (Matt. 24:29–30). He also said, "When the Son of Man comes in his glory, and all the angels with him, then he will sit on his glorious throne" (Matt. 25:31). In Luke's Gospel, Jesus explained that after cosmic signs, "they will see the Son of Man coming in a cloud with power and great glory" (Luke 21:27). At his religious trial, Jesus told the high priest Caiaphas, "But I tell you, from now on you will see the Son of Man seated at the right hand of Power and coming on the clouds of heaven" (Matt. 26:64). Another key second coming passage is Acts 1:9–11:

> And when he had said these things, as they were looking on, he was lifted up, and a cloud took him out of their sight. And while they were gazing into heaven as he went, behold, two men stood by them in white robes, and said, "Men of Galilee, why do you stand looking into heaven? This Jesus, who was taken up from you into heaven, will come in the same way as you saw him go into heaven."

The same Jesus who was bodily among his disciples for forty days after his resurrection was taken to heaven. Yet he will return in the same manner as he left. Peter's sermon in Acts 3 reveals the significance of the two comings of Jesus and is one of the clearest passages that discusses both comings. Peter stated, "But what God foretold by the mouth of all the prophets, that his Christ would suffer, he thus fulfilled" (Acts 3:18). So Jesus "fulfilled" what the Old Testament prophets predicted concerning his suffering. Then Peter referred to the second coming and kingdom in Acts 3:19–21:

> Repent therefore, and turn back, that your sins may be blotted out, that times of refreshing may come from the presence of the Lord, and that he may send the Christ appointed for you, Jesus, whom heaven must receive until the time for restoring all the things about which God spoke by the mouth of his holy prophets long ago.

This passage reveals the necessity of a future sending of Christ and the restoration of all things that is connected with the message of the "holy prophets," who are the

Old Testament prophets. Thus, while many Old Testament passages apply to the second coming of Jesus, the doctrine of a second coming is primarily a matter of New Testament revelation.

The second coming of Jesus happens in two phases. Jesus will descend from heaven to snatch or rapture his church into the air to be with him in heaven for the duration of the seven-year tribulation. The purpose of this coming is a rescue mission to keep the church from experiencing the divine wrath of this period. A second phase is the personal and bodily return of Jesus to earth to establish his kingdom on earth.

THE MILLENNIUM

The millennium is the coming thousand-year reign of Jesus and his saints on the earth after this present age and before the eternal state. It occurs soon after Daniel's seventieth week and the return of Jesus, and it is the time when mankind, through the last Adam, Jesus, fulfills the mandate to rule and subdue the earth successfully on God's behalf (Gen. 1:26–28). Jesus the Messiah also fulfills the promise that an ultimate Son of David will rule from David's throne over Israel (Luke 1:32–33) and the entire earth (Zech. 14:9). Jesus's enemies who opposed him during the tribulation are defeated (Rev. 19:20–21). Satan is bound (Rev. 20:1–3). Deceased Old Testament saints and martyrs from the tribulation period come to life and reign with Christ (Dan. 12:2; Rev. 20:4). Jesus rules and shares his kingdom reign with the church of the current age, which remained faithful during persecution (Rev. 2:26–27; 3:21; 5:10).

The millennial kingdom is a time of creation renewal, prosperity, righteousness, peace, and international harmony on the earth (Matt. 19:28; Isa. 2:2–4; 11; 65:17–25). It is also the period when all covenant promises, both spiritual and physical, come to complete fulfillment for both Israel and the nations. Israel is saved and restored, and she fulfills her role of leadership and service to the nations, functioning out of the capital city of Jerusalem (Isa. 2:2–4). Nations, who have also become the people of God, experience spiritual and physical blessings alongside Israel (Isa. 19:16–25; 27:6). While the eternal state will certainly exhibit these characteristics perfectly, these matters need to first be fulfilled under the mediatorial rulership of man with the ultimate man, Jesus. When the last Adam completes his mission, then Jesus will hand the kingdom over to God the Father, and the eternal kingdom of the Father will commence (1 Cor. 15:24–28).

The millennium must also come for a Christ-centered reason. There must be a sustained, recognized, and visible reign of Jesus in the realm (the earth) where Jesus experienced rejection at his first coming. At his first coming, Jesus came unto his own, but they did not receive him (John 1:11). He was rejected and killed. The Jesus who stood bound before men at his passion will return in glory on the clouds of heaven to reign over the earth (Matt. 26:63–66). The millennial kingdom spotlights the recognition of Jesus as King. He will reign in glory for an extended period before he hands his kingdom over to the Father in triumph and the eternal state begins (1 Cor. 15:24–28). This is also the time when the saints of God are vindicated and reigning in the realm where they experienced persecution from Satan and the world (Rev. 6:9–11; 20:4).

This millennium is sometimes referred to as an intermediate kingdom since it comes after this present age yet before the eternal state. It is dramatically better than this present age but is not yet perfect like the coming eternal state. For example, infant mortality is nonexistent and lifespans are greatly expanded, but the possibility for death still exists. A person who dies at the age of one hundred will be thought accursed (Isa. 65:20). Also, unlike today or the coming eternal state, the millennium features nations who serve God yet have inhabitants who are still capable of sinning and receiving punishment (Zech. 14:16–19).

SATAN'S FINAL REVOLT

At the end of the millennium, Satan is released from his incarceration in the Abyss and leads an intentional revolt against the holy city of Jerusalem. Those involved in this rebellion are immediately destroyed with fire from heaven, and Satan is sent to the lake of fire forever (Rev. 20:7–10). The nucleus for this rebellion comes from those born during the millennial kingdom who do not trust in Christ as their Savior. When given the opportunity to join forces with the recently released Satan, they gladly do so. This event indicates not God's weakness but rather an opportunity for a devastating show of divine force against his enemies. While the participants are expecting a war, the result is more like an execution as they are immediately vanquished.

This rebellion highlights two important truths. First, the presence of unbelievers in the millennium while Satan is bound in the Abyss shows that man's primary problem is a wicked heart, whether Satan is present or not. Even under ideal conditions with Jesus physically present on the earth, some choose to rebel in sin. Second, the rebellion offers a display of God's power against evil before the great white throne judgment takes place (Rev. 20:11–15) and the eternal state begins (Rev. 21:1–22:5). This is a dramatic display of kingdom power over the final rebellion against God in human history.

THE ETERNAL STATE

The new heaven and new earth are the final destiny of redeemed humanity. The millennium is past. The great white throne judgment has occurred. Satan and all unbelievers have been cast into the lake of fire forever. A glorious destiny awaits God's saints when they will live on a new earth with direct access to God, who will then live among them. This is what John the apostle explains: "Then I saw a new heaven and a new earth, for the first heaven and the first earth had passed away" (Rev. 21:1).

This "new heaven" and "new earth" language occurs three other times in the Bible: Isaiah 65:17; Isaiah 66:22; and 2 Peter 3:13. The latter reference reveals that this new heaven and new earth are what believers are ultimately anticipating: "But according to his promise we are waiting for new heavens and a new earth in which righteousness dwells" (2 Pet. 3:13). Hebrews 12:26–27 also alludes to eternity future. So the believer's ultimate hope and destination is not the current heaven but the new earth.

The most extended discussion of the new heaven and new earth, often called the eternal state, is found in Revelation 21:1–22:5. John's language indicates that the "new heaven" and "new earth" have similarities with and differences from the present heaven and earth. Even though it is "new," there is still a heaven (or sky) and an earth where people will dwell. Yet it is contrasted with the present heaven and earth in that the older heaven and earth have "passed away."

The New Earth: Entirely New or Restored? Will this new heaven and new earth be entirely new, another out-of-nothing creation of God, after the first heaven and earth are annihilated? Or are the new heaven and new earth a restoration and renewal of the present planet? The biblical language describing the destruction of the old order argues in favor of a completely new planet, because the old has been put out of existence. John writes that the first heaven and earth "passed away" (Rev. 21:1). Then there is the strong wording of fiery destruction in 2 Peter 3:

> The heavens and earth that now exist are stored up for fire. (3:7)

> But the day of the Lord will come like a thief, and then the heavens will pass away with a roar, and the heavenly bodies will be burned up and dissolved, and the earth and the works that are done on it will be exposed. (3:10)

> Since all these things are thus to be dissolved . . . (3:11)

> The heavens will be set on fire and dissolved, and the heavenly bodies will melt as they burn! (3:12)

In further support of the annihilation of the present universe is Jesus's statement, "Heaven and earth will pass away, but my words will not pass away" (Matt. 24:35). Psalm 102 declares that the earth and the heavens "will perish" and "wear out like a garment" (Ps. 102:25–26). Isaiah 24:20 states, "The earth staggers like a drunken man; it sways like a hut . . . and it falls, and will not rise again." In his first epistle, John writes, "The world is passing away" (1 John 2:17).

On the other hand, arguments for the renewal of this earth include the following. First, Paul teaches that the creation is longing for glorification, not annihilation. He states that "the creation waits with eager longing for the revealing of the sons of God" (Rom. 8:19) and that the creation was subjected to futility but "in hope" (Rom. 8:20). He then says, "The creation itself will be set free from its bondage to corruption and obtain the freedom of the glory of the children of God" (Rom. 8:21). This picture portrays the creation as anticipating glorification, not annihilation.

Second, the creation's anticipation for glorification is linked with the glorification of God's people (Rom. 8:23). A parallel exists. Believers are not annihilated but resurrected. Like Jesus, who rose bodily from the grave, there is a one-to-one correspondence between believers now and who they will be in the future. If the destiny of the earth parallels that of believing mankind, then the creation that exists now will also exist in the future, albeit in a glorified form. Just as creation suffered when man fell because of sin, so too the creation will be restored when God's people are given glorified bodies.

Third, the Bible uses renewal language to describe the earth. Jesus predicted a coming "regeneration" of the cosmos (Matt. 19:28 NASB). Peter foretold a coming restoration of all things (Acts 3:21). Everything in heaven and earth is being reconciled to Jesus because of the blood of Jesus's cross (Col. 1:20). This terminology indicates that the universe is heading for a renewal in which the marred earth is fixed and made better than ever. A renewal view asserts that God, not Satan, achieves the final victory over God's "very good" creation (Gen. 1:31).

What about the destruction language of 2 Peter 3? Those who hold a renewal view reason that destruction does not mean annihilation. The same passage speaks of the world being destroyed by water at the time of Noah (2 Pet. 3:6), but the world was not annihilated with the flood. Also, the best rendering of 2 Peter 3:10 is not that the earth is "burned up," as some translations state, but that "the earth . . . will be exposed." The idea is that of being "found" or "manifested," much like metal that goes through a refiner's fire is not annihilated but purified (Mal. 3:2–3).

Life on the New Earth. Whether the new earth will be an entirely new planet or a renovated planet, the new earth will be a tangible place where believers in actual physical bodies will dwell. God made man as a complex unity of body and soul to live in a physical environment, and man's destiny on the new earth will include residing on a physical planet.

Altogether, there are ten features that make the new earth new and highlight the glory of the coming eternal state. John summarizes these characteristics in Revelation 21:1–22:5.

1. New heaven and earth (21:1)
2. New Jerusalem (21:2, 9–21)
3. New people of God (21:3)
4. New compassion (21:4)
5. New order (21:5–8)
6. New temple (21:22)
7. New light (21:23)
8. New population (21:24–27)
9. New life (22:1–2)
10. New glory (22:3–5)

The Bible speaks of a New Jerusalem that will be the capital city of the new earth. John says, "And I saw the holy city, new Jerusalem, coming down out of heaven from God, prepared as a bride adorned for her husband" (Rev. 21:2). This is a real city where God will dwell among his people (21:3). The city has "a great, high wall, with twelve gates" (21:12). It is laid out as a square that is approximately 1,400 miles long and wide (21:16). These dimensions ought to be understood literally since "human measurement" is mentioned (21:17). The wall of the city is made of jasper and the city is "pure gold, like clear glass" (21:18). The foundations of the wall of the city "were adorned with every kind of jewel" (21:19). The size, beauty, and grandeur of this city are hard to grasp, but this does not detract from the real nature of this city.

No temple exists in the New Jerusalem. Both God and Jesus function as its temple (21:22). Since the glory of God illumines the city, no need exists for the light of the sun or moon to shine on it (21:23). The nations and kings of the earth will be drawn to the city because of its light and "will bring their glory into it" (21:24, 26). The presence of nations and world leaders shows that literal nations exist on the new earth and that activity takes place outside the New Jerusalem. While there is one people of God in regard to salvation, the presence of nations reveals ethnic and national diversity on the new earth. The best cultural contributions of these nations are brought to the New Jerusalem. These nations act in complete harmony since the leaves of the tree of life, which appears for the first time since the fall of man in Genesis 3, function "for the healing of the nations" (Rev. 22:2). Access to the city is always open as "its gates will never be shut" and no night will ever exist there (21:25). From the throne of God and Jesus the Lamb flows the "river of the water of life" (22:1). The tree of life, last seen in Genesis 3:24, is present again. It bears "twelve kinds of fruit, yielding its fruit each month" (Rev. 22:2). The mention of "each month" indicates that time exists on the new earth.

Yet for all the beauty of this city, the best part is the presence of God and the Lamb, who are on the throne (21:3; 22:3). God's servants will worship him and "will see his face" with eternal, unbroken fellowship (22:3–4). No barrier will remain between God and his people. The final depiction of the New Jerusalem reveals that the saints "will reign forever and ever" (22:5). Genesis 1:26–28 revealed that God created man to rule and subdue the earth, and the last verse describing the new earth explains that God's people will be reigning. Then there will be no deception of Satan (Genesis 3) and no potential for sin. Everyone here has been washed in the blood of the Lamb and will serve the Creator willingly. The wicked will never enter this city (Rev. 21:27), and the story ends well for the people of God.

This destiny for which believers are headed is no fairy tale and will be as real as the current planet that humanity now inhabits. The new heaven and new earth will give perspective as to why Christians exist and serve God in this present age. This present fallen world will not exist forever. Sin, the curse, and death will be forever removed (Rev. 22:3). Man will be fully restored in his previously marred relationships with God, people, and creation. This picture expresses the ultimate hope of eschatology. This is the actual, thrilling conclusion to a really great story. So our heartfelt response to the end of the story that we eagerly anticipate and vigorously strive for should be that of the apostle John, "Come, Lord Jesus!" (Rev. 22:20).

Prayer[26]

Father, we thank You for the truth revealed in Your written Word,
    which testifies to us about Your Son,
        the Lord Jesus Christ.
We thank You also for the testimony of the Holy Spirit,
    who attested to Christ with many miracles and wonders
        at the dawn of the gospel era.
We thank You as well for the audible testimony You gave
    at the time of Jesus' water baptism:
    "This is My beloved Son, in whom I am well pleased."
And above all, we thank You for the blood of Christ,
    the ultimate proof that Christ always does
        the things that are pleasing to You.
That precious blood is a most satisfactory sacrifice
    for all the sins of all who would ever believe
        these testimonies about Christ.
We affirm that all these impeccable testimonies are true,
    and we confess that Christ is indeed
        the Son of God and the only Savior—
        and that by believing in Him we have eternal life.

We thank You, O God, that You granted us
    this eternal life through Your mercy.
One of the fruits of that gift for us is eternal joy.
What amazing love that You sent Your Son to
    sorrow, suffer, and die that we might know *joy*!
How can we thank You enough?

You have commanded us to rejoice always and in every circumstance—
    even our trials are an occasion for rejoicing.
Joy is such a delightful duty,
    and yet we humbly confess that because we are weak and sinful,
    grumbling and complaining sometimes seem to come more naturally
        as a response to the issues of life.
Forgive us for such a bleak and ungrateful response
    to the grace You show us each day,
    and help us even now to be glad participants in heaven's joy.

By making joy both a privilege and a duty in our daily lives,
    and by preparing us for an even greater eternal joy,
    You show Yourself to be a God of gladness and cheer.
Though sorrow is an inevitable part of the human experience
    because of our sin,
    You meet our sorrow with countless reasons
        to be grateful and glad,
        full of hope and full of rejoicing.

---

26. This prayer is reproduced verbatim from John MacArthur, *At the Throne of Grace: A Book of Prayers* (Eugene, OR: Harvest House, 2011), 80–82. Used by permission of Harvest House.

Our weeping may endure for a night,
    but joy will come in the morning.

Your mercies, likewise, are new every morning.
How gracious and merciful You are
    to those who are sinful and once Your enemies!
We are utterly unworthy,
    but still You chose to bless us with so great a salvation.
You have turned our mourning into dancing;
    You loosed our sackcloth and clothed us with gladness.
Even in our sorrow we find our way to joy by thinking of
        Your love,
        Your forgiveness,
        Your tender mercies,
        Your sympathy for our weaknesses,
    and the hope of eternity in Your presence.

We look forward with glad expectation
    to that perfect, endless joy that will be ours
        when we meet You face-to-face.

Fill our hearts even now with heaven, dearest Lord.
May we live free of the failures
    that mar our lives and spoil all earthly joy.
Lord, lead us out of those things
    into the place of obedience and faithfulness.
We thank You for the promises of
    Your power and Your care.
In the name of Christ our Savior we pray. Amen.

"It Is Well with My Soul"

When peace like a river attendeth my way,
When sorrows like sea billows roll;
Whatever my lot, Thou has taught me to say,
"It is well, it is well with my soul."

Refrain:
It is well with my soul,
It is well with my soul,
It is well, it is well with my soul.

Tho' Satan should buffet, tho' trials should come,
Let this blest assurance control,
That Christ has regarded my helpless estate,
And hath shed His own blood for my soul.

My sin—O the bliss of this glorious tho't—
My sin—not in part but the whole,

Is nailed to the cross, and I bear it no more,
Praise the Lord, praise the Lord, O my soul!

And, Lord, haste the day when the faith shall be sight,
The clouds be rolled back as a scroll,
The trump shall resound and the Lord shall descend,
"Even so"—it is well with my soul.

~Horatio G. Spafford (1828–1888)

Bibliography
Primary Systematic Theologies

Bancroft, Emery H. *Christian Theology: Systematic and Biblical*. 2nd ed. Grand Rapids, MI: Zondervan, 1976. 345–410.

Berkhof, Louis. *Systematic Theology*. 4th ed. Grand Rapids, MI: Eerdmans, 1939. 661–738.

Buswell, James Oliver, Jr. *A Systematic Theology of the Christian Religion*. 2 vols. Grand Rapids, MI: Zondervan, 1962–1963. 2:281–553.

Culver, Robert Duncan. *Systematic Theology: Biblical and Historical*. Fearn, Ross-shire, Scotland: Mentor, 2005. 1008–156.

Dabney, Robert Lewis. *Systematic Theology*. 1871. Reprint, Edinburgh: Banner of Truth, 1985. 817–62.

Erickson, Millard J. *Christian Theology*. Grand Rapids, MI: Baker, 1986. 1149–241.

Grudem, Wayne. *Systematic Theology: An Introduction to Biblical Doctrine*. Grand Rapids, MI: Zondervan, 1994. 1091–167.

Hodge, Charles. *Systematic Theology*. 3 vols. 1871–1873. Reprint, Grand Rapids, MI: Eerdmans, 1975. 3:713–880.

Lewis, Gordon R., and Bruce A. Demarest. *Integrative Theology*. 3 vols. Grand Rapids, MI: Zondervan, 1987–1994. 3:369–499.

Reymond, Robert L. *A New Systematic Theology of the Christian Faith*. Nashville: Thomas Nelson, 1998. 979–1093.

Shedd, William G. T. *Dogmatic Theology*. 3 vols. 1889. Reprint, Minneapolis: Klock & Klock, 1979. 2B:591–754; 3:471–528.

Strong, August Hopkins. *Systematic Theology: A Compendium Designed for the Use of Theological Students*. Rev. ed. New York: Revell, 1907. 981–1056.

*Swindoll, Charles R., and Roy B. Zuck, eds. *Understanding Christian Theology*. Nashville: Thomas Nelson, 2003. 1243–371.

*Thiessen, Henry Clarence. *Introductory Lectures in Systematic Theology*. Grand Rapids, MI: Eerdmans, 1949. 441–518.

Turretin, Francis. *Institutes of Elenctic Theology*. 3 vols. Edited by James T. Dennison Jr. Translated by George Musgrove Giger. 1679–1685. Reprint, Phillipsburg, NJ: P&R, 1992–1997. 3:561–637.

*Denotes most helpful.

Specific Works

Benware, Paul N. *Understanding End Times Prophecy: A Comprehensive Approach.* Rev. ed. Chicago: Moody Press, 2006.

Diprose, Ronald E. *Israel in the Development of Christian Thought.* Rome: Istituto Biblico Evangelico Italiano, 2000.

Erdmann, Martin. *The Millennial Controversy in the Early Church.* Eugene, OR: Wipf & Stock, 2005.

*Feinberg, Charles L. *Millennialism: The Two Major Views: The Premillennial and Amillennial Systems of Biblical Interpretation Analyzed and Compared.* 3rd ed. 1980. Reprint, Winona Lake, IN: BMH, 2006.

Fruchtenbaum, Arnold G. *Israelology: The Missing Link in Systematic Theology.* Rev. ed. Tustin, CA: Ariel Ministries, 2001.

*Horner, Barry E. *Future Israel: Why Christian Anti-Judaism Must Be Challenged.* NAC Studies in Bible and Theology 3. Nashville: B&H, 2007.

House, H. Wayne, ed. *Israel: The Land and the People: An Evangelical Affirmation of God's Promises.* Grand Rapids, MI: Kregel, 1998.

*Ice, Thomas, and Timothy J. Demy, eds. *When the Trumpet Sounds.* Eugene, OR: Harvest House, 1995.

LaHaye, Tim, and Ed Hindson, eds. *The Popular Encyclopedia of Bible Prophecy.* Eugene, OR: Harvest House, 2004.

Larsen, David L. *Jews, Gentiles, and the Church: A New Perspective on History and Prophecy.* Grand Rapids, MI: Discovery House, 1995.

MacArthur, John. *The Glory of Heaven: The Truth about Heaven, Angels, and Eternal Life.* 2nd ed. Wheaton, IL: Crossway, 2013.

———. *Matthew 24–28.* Chicago: Moody Press, 1989.

*———. *The Second Coming: Signs of Christ's Return and the End of the Age.* Wheaton, IL: Crossway, 1999.

*MacArthur, John, and Richard Mayhue. *Christ's Prophetic Plans: A Futuristic Premillennial Primer.* Chicago: Moody Publishers, 2012.

Mayhue, Richard L. *1 & 2 Thessalonians: Triumphs and Trials of a Consecrated Church.* Fearn, Ross-Shire, Scotland: Christian Focus, 2005.

———. *Snatched before the Storm! A Case for Pretribulationism.* The Woodlands, TX: Kress Christian Publications, 2008.

*McClain, Alva J. *The Greatness of the Kingdom: An Inductive Study of the Kingdom of God.* 1959. Reprint, Winona Lake, IN: BMH, 2007.

Pentecost, J. Dwight. *Things to Come: A Study in Biblical Eschatology.* Grand Rapids, MI: Zondervan, 1964.

*Peterson, Robert A. *Hell on Trial: The Case for Eternal Punishment.* Phillipsburg, NJ: P&R, 1995.

Saucy, Robert L. *The Case for Progressive Dispensationalism: The Interface between Dispensational and Non-Dispensational Theology.* Grand Rapids, MI: Zondervan, 1993.

*Showers, Renald E. *There Really Is a Difference: A Comparison of Covenant and Dispensational Theology.* Bellmawr, NJ: Friends of Israel Gospel Ministry, 1990.

Thomas, Robert L. *Revelation 1–7: An Exegetical Commentary.* Chicago: Moody Press, 1992.

———. *Revelation 8–22: An Exegetical Commentary.* Chicago: Moody Press, 1995.

*Vlach, Michael J. *Has the Church Replaced Israel? A Theological Evaluation*. Nashville: B&H Academic, 2010.

Walvoord, John F. *Daniel*. Revised and edited by Charles H. Dyer and Philip E. Rawley. The John Walvoord Prophecy Commentaries. Chicago: Moody Publishers, 2012.

*Denotes most helpful.

Appendix

The Progress of Revelation[1]

Old Testament		
BOOK	**APPROXIMATE WRITING DATE**	**AUTHOR**
Job	Unknown	Unknown
Genesis	1445–1405 BC	Moses
Exodus	1445–1405 BC	Moses
Leviticus	1445–1405 BC	Moses
Numbers	1445–1405 BC	Moses
Deuteronomy	1445–1405 BC	Moses
Psalms	1410–450 BC	Multiple authors
Joshua	1405–1385 BC	Joshua
Judges	ca. 1043 BC	Samuel
Ruth	ca. 1030–1010 BC	Samuel (?)
Song of Solomon	971–965 BC	Solomon
Proverbs	971–686 BC	Solomon primarily
Ecclesiastes	940–931 BC	Solomon
1 Samuel	931–722 BC	Unknown
2 Samuel	931–722 BC	Unknown
Obadiah	850–840 BC	Obadiah
Joel	835–796 BC	Joel
Jonah	ca. 775 BC	Jonah
Amos	ca. 750 BC	Amos
Hosea	750–710 BC	Hosea
Micah	735–710 BC	Micah
Isaiah	700–681 BC	Isaiah

1. These charts are adapted from John MacArthur, ed., *The MacArthur Study Bible: English Standard Version* (Wheaton, IL: Crossway, 2010), xxiv–xxv, originally appearing in *The MacArthur Study Bible*, copyright © 1997 by Thomas Nelson. Used by permission of Thomas Nelson. www.thomasnelson.com.

Old Testament

BOOK	APPROXIMATE WRITING DATE	AUTHOR
Nahum	ca. 650 BC	Nahum
Zephaniah	635–625 BC	Zephaniah
Habakkuk	615–605 BC	Habakkuk
Ezekiel	590–570 BC	Ezekiel
Lamentations	586 BC	Jeremiah
Jeremiah	586–570 BC	Jeremiah
1 Kings	561–538 BC	Unknown
2 Kings	561–538 BC	Unknown
Daniel	536–530 BC	Daniel
Haggai	ca. 520 BC	Haggai
Zechariah	480–470 BC	Zechariah
Ezra	457–444 BC	Ezra
1 Chronicles	450–430 BC	Ezra (?)
2 Chronicles	450–430 BC	Ezra (?)
Esther	450–331 BC	Unknown
Malachi	433–424 BC	Malachi
Nehemiah	424–400 BC	Ezra

New Testament

BOOK	APPROXIMATE WRITING DATE	AUTHOR
James	AD 44–49	James
Galatians	AD 49–50	Paul
Matthew	AD 50–60	Matthew
Mark	AD 50–60	Mark
1 Thessalonians	AD 51	Paul
2 Thessalonians	AD 51–52	Paul
1 Corinthians	AD 55	Paul
2 Corinthians	AD 55–56	Paul
Romans	AD 56	Paul
Luke	AD 60–61	Luke
Ephesians	AD 60–62	Paul
Philippians	AD 60–62	Paul
Colossians	AD 60–62	Paul
Philemon	AD 60–62	Paul
Acts	AD 62	Luke
1 Timothy	AD 62–64	Paul
Titus	AD 62–64	Paul
1 Peter	AD 64–65	Peter

New Testament		
BOOK	APPROXIMATE WRITING DATE	AUTHOR
2 Timothy	AD 66–67	Paul
2 Peter	AD 67–68	Peter
Hebrews	AD 67–69	Unknown
Jude	AD 68–70	Jude
John	AD 80–90	John
1 John	AD 90–95	John
2 John	AD 90–95	John
3 John	AD 90–95	John
Revelation	AD 94–96	John

Basic Glossary[1]

Abrahamic covenant. The covenant God made with Abraham in Genesis 12.

Adam, last or second. A reference in 1 Corinthians 15 and Romans 5 to Jesus Christ, contrasting him with Adam (the first Adam).

adonai. A Hebrew name for God, meaning basically "Lord."

adoption. That part of salvation in which God receives the estranged sinner back into the relationship and benefits of being his child. The term connotes positive favor, as contrasted with mere forgiveness and remission of sins.

Adoptionism. A type of Christology according to which Jesus, a human being, was chosen by God to be elevated to divine sonship.

advent. The coming of Christ. The first advent refers to his initial coming in the incarnation. The second advent is the future second coming.

allegorical interpretation. A method of biblical interpretation that attempts to find a deeper meaning than the literal.

amillennialism. The view that there will be no period of earthly reign of Christ either before or after his second coming. The thousand years of Revelation 20:1–7 are regarded as symbolic, either of the completeness of Christ's reign or of believers' bliss in heaven.

analogia scriptura. The belief that, Scripture being a unity, the meaning of one passage is illuminated by a study of other portions.

angelology. The study or doctrine of angels.

angelophanies. The assuming of visible form by angels for special occasions.

angels, fallen. Angels who disobeyed God, fell from their place of service to God, and now serve Satan, the chief of such fallen angels, that is, demons.

angels, holy. Those angels who have not fallen from their position of obedience.

annihilationism. The belief that at least some humans will permanently cease to exist at death or some point thereafter.

anthropocentrism. The view that humans and human values rather than God and his values are the central fact of the universe.

anthropology. The study of human nature and culture. Theological anthropology is a theological interpretation of humanity.

---

1. This glossary is drawn with minor revisions from Millard J. Erickson, *The Concise Dictionary of Christian Theology*, rev. ed. (Wheaton, IL: Crossway, 2001). Used by permission of Crossway, a publishing ministry of Good News Publishers, Wheaton, IL 60187, www.crossway.org.

anthropomorphism. Conceiving of God as having human characteristics or existing in human form.

anthropopathism. Conceiving of God as having human emotions.

Antichrist. An opponent and impersonator of Christ. From 1 John 2:18, 22; and 4:3, Antichrist appears to be a spirit present throughout the age of the church. Some have sought to identify specific persons or offices as the Antichrist. The Reformers and others identified him with the papacy. It appears that there is a spirit or principle of rebellion at work in the world that will come to completion in personal form in the last days.

antinomianism. An opposition to law; specifically, a rejection of the idea that the Christian's life need be governed by laws or rules.

antitype. New Testament realities of which certain Old Testament persons, objects, or practices are types or figures.

Apollinarianism. A fourth-century interpretation of the person of Christ: the divine Christ did not take on a complete human nature, but only its flesh; his human soul (rationality or *nous*) was replaced by the Logos or Word.

apostasy. A "falling away," usually a deliberate and total abandonment of the faith previously held.

archangels. Chief angels. The only one named in Scripture is Michael (Jude 9). The only other reference to "archangel" (1 Thess. 4:16) does not give a name. The other angel named in Scripture, Gabriel (Dan. 8:16; 9:21; Luke 1:19, 26), is not identified as an archangel.

Arianism. A view of the person of Christ according to which he is the highest of the created beings and is thus appropriately referred to as god but not *the* God.

Arminianism. A view that contradicts the Calvinist understanding of predestination. Arminianism holds that God's decision to give salvation to certain persons and not to others is based on his foreknowledge of who will believe. It also includes the idea that genuinely regenerate people can lose their salvation, and that some actually do. Arminianism often has a less serious view of human depravity than does Calvinism.

ascension of Christ. Jesus's bodily departure from the earth and return to heaven on the fortieth day after his resurrection (Luke 24:51; Acts 1:9).

aseity. A reference to the fact that the basis of God's life is within himself and is not caused by anything external.

assurance (of salvation). The divinely given confidence of the believer that he or she is truly saved.

atheism. The belief that there is no God.

atonement. The aspect of the work of Christ, and particularly his death, that secures the restoration of fellowship between individual believers and God.

Atonement, Day of. The day on which the Old Testament priest made atonement for all the sins of the people (Lev. 16).

atonement, example theory of. The incomplete view of the atonement that the effect of the atonement was through the example Jesus gave us of dedication to the Father, which we then should emulate.

atonement, governmental theory of the. The incomplete view of the atonement that the major effect of the death of Christ was to demonstrate the holiness of God's law and the seriousness of transgressing it.

atonement, limited. The interpretation of the atonement that says Christ died for only the elect. It is also referred to as particular redemption.

atonement, moral-influence theory of the. The incomplete view of the atonement that the effect of Christ's death was to demonstrate to us the love of God and thus to induce us to respond to God's offer of salvation.

atonement, penal-substitution theory of the. The view of the atonement that Christ's death is a sacrifice offered in payment of the penalty for our sins. It is accepted by God the Father as satisfaction in place of the penalty due to believers in Christ.

atonement, ransom theory of the. The erroneous view of the atonement that the blood of Christ was a ransom paid to Satan to deliver humans from his control.

atonement, satisfaction theory of the. The incomplete view of the atonement that Christ's death was a sacrifice to God to satisfy his wounded honor resulting from the wrong that humans have done against him.

atonement, unlimited. The doctrine that Christ died for all persons, whether elect or not.

atonement, vicarious. The view that the atoning death of Christ was on behalf of sinners.

attributes of God. The characteristics or qualities of God that constitute him as what he is. They should not be thought of as something attributed to or predicated of him, as if something could be added to his nature. Rather, they are inseparable from his being.

attributes of God, communicable. Attributes of God for which corresponding characteristics can be found in human nature.

attributes of God, incommunicable. Attributes of God for which no corresponding characteristics can be found in human nature.

baptism, believers'. Baptism in which a credible profession of faith is first required. This is sometimes referred to as credobaptism.

baptism, infant. The practice of baptizing infants.

baptism with the Holy Spirit. The act of Jesus Christ, from Pentecost on, of placing every true believer with the Holy Spirit into the church at the moment of salvation (1 Cor. 12:13).

Bible, authority of the. The teaching that since God, the supreme authority, has given us the Bible by divine inspiration, it has derivatively the right to prescribe the belief and actions of Christians.

Bible, canon of the. The collection of books accepted by the church as authoritative.

Bible, inspiration of the. The act of the Holy Spirit upon biblical writers that ensured that what they wrote preserved divine revelation faithfully and made the Bible effectively the Word of God.

biblical theology. Organization of theological teachings in terms of the portions of the Bible where they occur rather than by topic. Biblical theology makes no attempt to restate the biblical expressions in a contemporary form.

biblicism. A very strong and even unquestioning commitment to the authority of the Bible.

bibliology. The doctrine of Scripture.

blasphemy. Irreverent and insulting or slanderous expressions against God.

bride of Christ. A term for the church.

call, calling. God's summons of humans to salvation or to special positions of service.

Calvinism. The thought of John Calvin. The term is applied particularly to the doctrine of predestination, according to which God sovereignly chooses some to salvation not because of any merit or even foreseen faith but simply by his free will and unmerited grace.

canon. The collection of books accepted by the church as authoritative.

canonization. The process of recognizing the canon of Scripture.

Christ. Literally, "the anointed one," the title designating Jesus as the Messiah.

Christ, deity of. The idea that Christ is God as is the Father.

Christ, humanity of. The idea that Jesus was as fully human as we are, except that he was without a sinful nature and actual sin.

Christ, impeccability of. The idea that Christ was unable to sin.

Christ, preexistence of. The concept that the person who was born at Bethlehem as Jesus of Nazareth was the preexistent second person of the Trinity.

Christ, two natures of. The doctrine that Jesus was in one person both divine and human.

Christ, vicarious death of. The doctrine that Christ's death had a value on behalf of true believers.

Christ as king. A reference to one of the three offices of Jesus Christ; his ruling power.

Christ as priest. A reference to one of the three offices of Jesus Christ; his atoning and intercessory work.

Christ as prophet. A reference to one of the three offices of Jesus Christ; his work of revelation.

Christ as substitute. The idea that Christ's death was in the place of those who would believe in him.

Christian doctrines. Christianity's teachings about the nature of God, his work, and his relationship to his creation.

Christological. Pertaining to the Christ, or more specifically the doctrine of Christ.

Christology. The doctrinal study of the person and work of Christ.

church, the. Those who are true believers in Christ. The term is used in the New Testament both in a universal sense (all such believers) and in a local sense (a particular group of believers gathered in one place).

church discipline. The church's active guidance of the conduct of its members. The term frequently carries several connotations—namely, either instruction aimed at correction or even excommunication.

church fathers. The church leaders of the period immediately following the beginning of the New Testament era.

common grace. Kindness extended to all persons through God's general providence; for example, his provision of sunshine and rain for everyone.

compatibilistic freedom. The idea that human freedom is not inconsistent with God's sovereign determination of all events, including human thoughts, choices, and actions.

conditional immortality. A variety of annihilationism according to which immortality is a special gift to believers; unbelievers simply pass out of existence at death.

conscience. The sense of being obligated to do the right and avoid the wrong; in some views, a virtual faculty of human nature.

cosmological argument for God. An argument for the existence of God: since every existent thing in the universe must have a cause, there must be a God.

creatio ex nihilo. Literally, "creation out of nothing," the idea that God created without the use of previously existing materials.

crucified with Christ. A reference to the believer's identification with Christ in his death (Gal. 2:20).

Davidic covenant. The covenant in which God granted the kingdom to David and his descendants forever (2 Samuel 7; cf. 2 Chron. 13:5).

death, first. Physical death.

death, second. The final state of those who die apart from the salvation offered by God. The term is found in Revelation 2:11; 20:6, 14; and 21:8.

decree of God. The decision of God that, made in eternity, renders certain all that occurs within time.

decretive will of God. God's decisions that actually bring to pass every event that occurs.

deism. Belief in a God who created but has no continuing involvement with the world and events within it.

demon possession. A condition of being inhabited and dominated by demons.

demons. Fallen angels who now work evil under the leadership of their chief, Satan.

depravity, total. The idea that sinfulness affects the whole of one's nature and colors all that one does; it does not necessarily mean that one is as sinful as one can possibly be.

dichotomism. A view of human nature that regards it as consisting of two components, usually a material and a spiritual element (i.e., body and soul).

Docetism. The belief that the humanity of Jesus was not genuine—he merely seemed to be human.

earth, new. The completely redeemed universe of the future; it is referred to as "new heavens and a new earth" (2 Pet. 3:13).

Ebionism. An early Christological heresy that thought of Jesus as human but not divine.

ecclesiology. A doctrinal study of the church.

edification. Literally "building up"; the strengthening of the spiritual life of Christians and congregations.

effectual calling. God's irresistible, saving grace working upon the elect so that they respond in faith.

efficacious grace. A reference to the fact that those whom God has chosen for eternal life will unfailingly come to belief and salvation.

elder. A leader in the synagogue, in the early church, or in a local congregation of some denominations today. The qualifications for the office are stated in 1 Timothy 3:1–7 and Titus 1:5–9.

elect. Those specially chosen by God. The term can refer either to the nation Israel or to individuals designated for salvation or for special positions of service.

election. God's decision in choosing a special group or certain persons for salvation or service. The term is used especially of the predestination of the individual recipients of salvation.

elohim. A very common Hebrew name for deity, generic in nature, so that it is applied both to heathen gods and to the true God of the Israelites.

el shaddai. A Hebrew name for God that emphasizes his power.

Emmanuel. A name for Jesus that means "God with us" (also "Immanuel").

endurance. The ability of the Christian, by God's gracious enabling, to persevere through trials, temptations, and afflictions.

eschatology. The study of the last things or of the future generally.

eternal death. The finalization of spiritual death; the permanent separation of the sinner from God.

eternal destiny. The future state of the person, whether in heaven or hell, with God or apart from him.

eternal generation. The eternal, necessary, and self-differentiating act of God the Father by which he generates the personal subsistence of the Son and thereby communicates to the Son the entire divine essence.

eternal life. The spiritual life given to the believer; it surpasses natural life in quality and also extends beyond this life to eternity.

eternal punishment. The endless nature of the punishment that unredeemed sinners will experience beyond this life.

eternal security of the believer. The doctrine that truly regenerate believers will never lose their salvation but will persevere in faith by the grace of God.

Eutychianism. The teaching that Jesus had only one nature.

evil angels. Angels who rebelled against God and thus fell. Under their leader, Satan, they now engage in opposing God's work. They are also known as demons.

Evil One, the. Satan.

evil spirits. Demons.

evolution. The process of development from one form into another; in particular, the biological theory that all living forms have developed from simpler forms by a series of gradual steps.

exegesis. The obtaining of the meaning of a passage by drawing the meaning out from, rather than reading it into, the text.

exposition. Interpretation, explanation, and clarification of a biblical passage.

extrabiblical. Pertaining to material not found in the Bible.

fall. Adam and Eve's initial sin of disobedience as a result of which they lost their standing of favor with God (Genesis 3).

fall, literal view of the. Belief that the fall was an actual space-time event that happened to two historical persons.

fiat creationism. The belief that God created by a direct act. It frequently also includes the ideas that creation took place in a brief period of time and that there has been no natural development of intermediate forms.

filling of the Holy Spirit. The Holy Spirit's control of the total life of the Christian. The filling of the Holy Spirit can be repeated and frequently needs to be. It is to be distinguished from the baptism of the Holy Spirit, which occurs once at the time of regeneration.

final state. The state of the individual following the resurrection, whether in heaven or hell.

first death. Physical death.

flesh. Human nature. In the Bible the term has both a literal and figurative meaning: it is used of the physical nature and also of the sinful nature of human beings.

fruit of the Spirit. A group of spiritual virtues referred to by Paul in Galatians 5:22–23; for example, love, joy, and peace.

functional subordination. The idea that the incarnate Christ, the second person of the Trinity, while not ceasing to be equal with the Father in what he was, made himself subject to the Father in what he did.

futuristic. Pertaining to the future.

gehenna. Transliteration of the Hebrew for the Valley of Hinnom (2 Kings 23:10). It came to represent the final spiritual state of the ungodly (Matt. 10:28; Mark 9:43).

glorification. The final step in the process of salvation; it involves the completion of sanctification and the removal of all spiritual defects.

glorified body. The resurrection or perfected body of the future.

Gnosticism. A movement in early Christianity, beginning already in the first century, that (1) emphasized a special higher truth that only the more enlightened receive from God, (2) taught that matter is evil, and (3) denied the humanity of Jesus.

God, aseity of. A reference to the fact that the basis of God's life is within himself and is not caused by anything external.

God, eternity of. The fact that God has no beginning and will have no end. He always has been and always will be.

God, glory of. The splendor, greatness, and magnificence of God.

God, grace of. God's dealing with his people not on the basis of what they deserve but simply in terms of his goodness and generosity relating to their needs.

God, holiness of. God's separateness from all else and particularly from all evil.

God, immanence of. God's presence and activity within the created world of nature.

God, immutability of. The doctrine that God is unchanging. In some Greek thought this teaching became virtually a static view of God. Properly understood, however, it is simply an emphasis on the unchanging character and dependability of God.

God, incomprehensibility of. A reference to the fact that the greatness of God results in our never being able to fully and exhaustively understand him.

God, oneness of. The fact that God, although three persons, is yet one in essence.

God, perfection of. The absolute completeness and fullness of God. He does not lack anything or have any moral imperfection.

God, self-existence of. That attribute of God whereby he exists simply of himself without the need of any external force or cause.

God, sovereignty of. God's supremacy and meticulous control over all that occurs.

God, transcendence of. God's separation from and superiority to the creation and history.

God, unity of. A reference to the fact that God is one God, not many, nor is composed of parts but is simple and uncompounded.

God, wrath of. God's displeasure with evil; it is expressed in judgment and punishment.

God-breathed. A reference to the divine inspiration of the Bible (2 Tim. 3:16).

Godhead. The triune God—Father, Son, and Holy Spirit.

godliness. Likeness to God in moral and spiritual character.

God-man. The incarnate second person of the Trinity, Jesus Christ.

gospel. The message of salvation offered by God to all who believe; also, when capitalized, one of the first four books of the New Testament, which recount the life and teachings of Jesus.

gospel of Christ. A Pauline term for the message of salvation (Rom. 15:19; 1 Cor. 9:12; 2 Cor. 2:12; 9:13; 10:14; Gal. 1:7; Phil. 1:27; 1 Thess. 3:2).

grace, common. Grace extended to all persons through God's general providence; for example, his provision of sunshine and rain for everyone.

grace, efficacious. A reference to the fact that those whom God has chosen for eternal life will unfailingly come to belief and salvation.

grace, means of. Channels by which God conveys his blessings to humans.

grammatical-historical exegesis. Interpretation of the Bible that emphasizes that a passage must be explained in the light of its syntax, context, and historical setting.

hamartiology. A study of sin.

head. The part of the body that is most prominent and exercises control over the rest. Hence Christ is spoken of as the head of the church and of all things (Eph. 1:10, 22–23).

heaven. The future abode of believers. A place of complete happiness and joy, it is distinguished especially by the presence of God.

hell. The place of future punishment of wicked or unbelieving persons; it is a place of great anguish from which God is absent to bless and present only to bring judgment.

heresy. A belief or teaching that contradicts Scripture and Christian theology.

hermeneutics. The science of interpretation of the Scripture.

historical theology. Study of the chronological development of theological thought; in the case of Christianity, the study of the development of Christian theology from biblical times to the present.

Holy Spirit. The third person of the Trinity, fully divine and fully personal.

homiletics. The science and art of the preparation and delivery of sermons.

homoousios. A term used by orthodox Christians, particularly Athanasius and his followers, to insist that Jesus is of the very same nature as the Father.

hypostasis. From a Greek word for "substance" or "nature," the real or essential nature of something as distinguished from its attributes. In Christian thought the term is used in reference to any one of the three distinct persons in the Trinity, and especially Christ, the second person of the Trinity, in his divine and human natures.

hypostatic union. The union of Jesus's divine and human natures in one person, without confusion, without change, without division, and without separation.

illumination. The work of the Holy Spirit giving understanding when the Scripture is heard or read.

image of God. That which distinguishes human beings from the rest of God's creatures: the human is created in God's own image (Gen. 1:26).

imago dei. Latin term for "image of God."

immanence. God's presence and activity within the creation and human history.

imminence. The condition of something that could happen at any time or is about to happen. When applied to the second coming, the term means that Christ could return at any time.

immutability of God. The doctrine that God is unchanging. In some Greek thought this teaching became virtually a static view of God. Properly understood, however, it is simply an emphasis upon the unchanging character and dependability of God.

imputation. The judicial reckoning or forensic transfer of one person's sin or righteousness to another.

imputation, doctrine of. Either the justification of believers on the basis of Christ's righteousness or the condemnation of unbelievers on the basis of Adam's sin.

imputation of Christ's righteousness. God's act of crediting the righteousness of Christ to sinners who trust in him for salvation.

incarnate Christ. The state of Christ since the time of his becoming a human being.

indwelling. The presence of the Holy Spirit within the life of the believer.

inerrancy. The view that the Bible is completely true and truthful in all that it teaches.

infallibility. A reference to the doctrine that the Bible is unfailing in its purpose.

infant baptism. The practice of baptizing infants.

infralapsarianism. A form of Calvinism that teaches that the decree of the fall logically preceded that of election. The order of God's decrees, then, is (1) to create human beings; (2) to permit the fall; (3) to save some and condemn others; and (4) to provide salvation only for the elect.

inscripturation. God's preserving his revelation in writing through the process of inspiration by the Holy Spirit.

inspiration. The act of the Holy Spirit upon the biblical writers that ensured that what they wrote was the Word of God.

inspiration, plenary. The view that all Scripture, not simply certain books or certain portions of books or certain types of material, is inspired.

inspiration, verbal theory of. The doctrine that the Holy Spirit so guided the biblical writer that even the individual words and details are what God intended to be written.

intercession of Christ. A reference to the doctrine that Christ's current ministry on behalf of believers includes mediating for them before the Father (Rom. 8:34; Heb. 7:25).

intercessory work of the Holy Spirit. The concept that the Holy Spirit intercedes for us when we do not know how to pray (Rom. 8:26–27).

intermediate state. The condition of persons between the time of their death and the resurrection.

irresistible grace. The grace of God in the act of regeneration by which God efficaciously opens blind eyes to the glory of Christ and communicates spiritual life to the sinner's dead heart. The doctrine is sometimes also referred to as efficacious grace.

Jerusalem, New. In Revelation 3:12 and 21:2, a reference to the ultimate state of the church.

Jesus Christ. A compound name for the incarnate second person of the Trinity: *Jesus* refers to the man from Nazareth, and *Christ* is Greek for "Messiah," which means "anointed." In Acts 5:42, he is referred to as Jesus the Christ; apparently this was abbreviated to the form *Jesus Christ*.

Jesus of Nazareth. The name given to the child born to the Virgin Mary, who had conceived under the influence of the Holy Spirit.

judgment seat. The platform on which a civil magistrate sits during judicial proceedings. The term is used of the final judgment of true believers to be rendered by Jesus Christ.

justification by faith. Declaration that the person has been restored to a state of righteousness through belief and trust in the work of Christ rather than on the basis of one's own accomplishment.

kenosis. Christ's making himself of no effect by taking upon himself a human nature (Phil. 2:7), thus becoming functionally subordinate to the Father, veiling though not divesting himself of his divine attributes.

kingdom of God. The reign of God, whether internally within the hearts of humans or externally on earth.

lake of fire. The place of eternal punishment for the wicked. It is mentioned six times in the book of Revelation (19:20; 20:10; 20:14 [2×]; 20:15; 21:18), being also referred to as "the fiery lake" and "the lake of burning sulphur."

Lamb of God, the. A reference by John the Baptist to Christ as the one who takes away the sin of the world by bearing sin's punishment in his own person (John 1:29, 36; 1 Cor. 5:7; 1 Pet. 1:18–19).

lay elders. Officers who hold positions of leadership in the church but are not formally ordained ministers.

liberalism. Any movement that is open to redefining or changing the traditional doctrines and practices of Christianity.

limited atonement. A reference to the view that Christ's atoning death was only for the elect.

literalism. Biblical translation or interpretation that takes the meaning of language in its plainest, most obvious, and often most concrete sense.

Lord's Day. The first day of the week; Sunday.

lordship of Christ. Jesus Christ's authority and rule over all things, especially as reflected in the life of the Christian.

lordship salvation. The teaching that saving faith is characterized by repentance of sin and acceptance of Jesus Christ as Lord as well as Savior.

man, natural. The human in the unredeemed condition, outside salvation in Jesus Christ.

man, new. A term used by Paul of the regenerate human being (Eph. 4:22–24; Col. 3:9–10).

man, old. A term used by Paul of the unregenerate human being or the human apart from salvation in Christ (Rom. 6:6; Eph. 4:22–24; Col. 3:9–10); it contrasts with the new man.

man of sin. A translation sometimes given of Paul's reference in 2 Thessalonians 2:3 to the Antichrist. "Man of lawlessness" is a better translation.

mediator. One who goes between two parties in an attempt to reconcile them. Jesus Christ is the only saving Mediator between God and the human race.

millennial kingdom. In premillennialism, the kingdom to be set up by Christ on earth during the thousand years following his second coming.

millennium, the. The period of a thousand years of Christ's reign on earth.

Modalism. The view that the three members of the Trinity are different modes of God's activity rather than distinct persons.

Monarchianism. An approach that stressed the unity of God, particularly a movement in the second and third centuries. It took two forms: Dynamic Monarchianism and Modalistic Monarchianism.

Monarchianism, Dynamic. A view that Jesus was not of the essence of God but that God was at work in him.

Monarchianism, Modalistic. A movement that interpreted the Trinity as successive revelations of God—first as Father, then as Son, and finally as Holy Spirit. It began in the third century.

monergism. The view that regeneration is accomplished exclusively by the working of God.

monism. A philosophy or theology that explains everything in terms of one principle; a view that reality is of only one type.

moral argument for God. A proof for the existence of God: God is needed as an explanation for moral values and the moral impulse.

Mosaic covenant. The body of laws given by God through Moses.

mystery. That which is unknown or not fully comprehended. Paul declares that God has revealed his mysteries so that they are no longer uncomprehended (e.g., Eph. 1:9; 3:3).

natural theology. Theology developed apart from the special revelation in Scripture; it attempts to demonstrate certain elements of theology from experience and reason alone.

Nestorianism. A heretical view in effect dividing Christ into two persons, divine and human.

new birth. Regeneration; God's giving new life to the believer.

new body. The body that will be received in the resurrection.

new covenant. The Christian dispensation and the economy introduced by Christ and the apostles. In some cases, the new covenant is a synonym for the gospel of Christ.

new creation. A reference to the regeneration that takes place in the believer and also to the future remaking and restoring of the entire creation.

new earth. That which together with the new heaven will be brought to pass in the future by the work of God (Rev. 21:1).

new man. The regenerate person or believer.

offices of Christ. The roles or functions of Christ, traditionally prophet, priest, and king.

old man. The person prior to new birth.

omnipotence of God. God's ability to do all things that are proper objects of power.

omnipresence of God. A reference to the fact that God is everywhere present and has access to all portions of reality.

omniscience of God. God's knowing all things that are proper objects of knowledge, including all future events.

oneness of God. The fact that God, although three persons, is yet one in essence.

ontological argument for God. An argument drawing on pure logical thought rather than sensory observation of the physical universe to prove the existence of God. A usual form is that God is the greatest of all conceivable beings. Such a being must exist because if he did not, one could still conceive of a greater being—namely, an identical being that also has the attribute of existence. Anselm and René Descartes are two of the most famous proponents of the ontological argument.

open theism. Rejecting the classical view of God's immutability and omniscience, this theology holds that God grows, discovers things he did not know, and changes his mind. God has taken the risk of creating humans, whose actions he cannot necessarily foreknow.

order of salvation *(ordo salutis)*. The traditional sequence of discussions of the different aspects of salvation; for example, regeneration, conversion, justification, sanctification.

original sin. The effect of the sin of Adam on those united to him. Affecting our behavior independent of and prior to any action of our own, original sin speaks of both imputed guilt and the inherited corruption of Adam's sin to all human persons apart from Jesus.

ousia. A word for being, referring especially to the undivided nature of God.

overseer. A literal translation of the Greek word for "bishop"—one who is given responsibility to supervise the work of the church.

paedobaptism. The practice of baptizing infants.

pantheism. The belief that everything is divine, eliminating the distinction between creature and Creator.

Paraclete. A Greek term used to refer to the Holy Spirit (John 14:16, 26; 15:26; 16:7). It is usually translated "Counselor" or "Comforter."

Patripassianism. The idea that the Son was actually God the Father manifested in a different form and that, therefore, the Father suffered and died on the cross in the person of the Son.

Pelagianism. The heretical theology stemming from the thought of Pelagius, which emphasizes human ability and free will rather than depravity and sinfulness. In the view of most Pelagians, it is possible to live without sin. The effect of Adam's sin on his descendants was simply that of a bad example.

perfectionism. The unbiblical view that it is possible to attain a state in which the believer no longer sins in this life.

perfection of God. The absolute completeness and fullness of God. He does not lack anything or have any moral imperfection.

perfections, absolute. Those attributes of God that are independent of his relationship to created objects and persons.

perishable body. The physical nature of humans that is subject to death and decay.

perseverance. The teaching that those who are genuine believers will endure in the faith to the end.

personal salvation. Salvation regarded in terms of the individual's relationship to God rather than in terms of changing the structures of society.

pneumatology. A study of the Holy Spirit.

polytheism. Belief in more than one God.

postmillennialism. The eschatological approach that believes Christ will return following the thousand-year reign. This means he will reign without being physically present.

predestination. Generally, God's eternal, uninfluenced determination of all things; specifically, God's eternal choice of those who will be saved and those who will be passed over and condemned for their sin.

preexistence. A state of existence before this life. Classical Christianity uses the term for the preincarnate second person of the Trinity, who became incarnate as Jesus of Nazareth.

premillennialism. The belief that Christ will return and then set up his earthly reign for a period of one thousand years.

preservation. That aspect of divine providence that pertains to God's maintaining in existence all that he has created.

preterist view. An interpretation of eschatology and particularly the book of Revelation that holds that the events referred to had already taken place or were taking place at the time of writing.

procession of the Spirit. The eternal, necessary, and self-differentiating act of the Father and the Son by which they spirate the personal subsistence of the Spirit and thereby communicate to him the entire divine essence. The Eastern Orthodox Church, objecting to a phrase in the Western version of the Nicene Creed that says the Holy Spirit proceeds from the Father and the Son (*filioque*), separated from the Western church.

prolegomena. A study of introductory theological matters.

prophecy. Generally, the authoritative declaration or speaking forth on behalf of God, akin to preaching; more specifically, the infallible declaration of divine revelation, often but not restricted to predicting what will come to pass.

propitiation. A reference to the idea that Christ's atonement satisfies the wrath of God.

providence, divine. God's care for the creation, involving his preserving its existence and meticulously guiding it to his intended ends.

rapture, midtribulational view of the. The idea that the church will go through half of the tribulation and then be raptured by Christ.

rapture, posttribulational view of the. The doctrine that the church will go through the great tribulation and then will be caught up to meet Christ.

rapture, pretribulational view of the. The idea that Christ will remove the church from the world prior to Daniel's seventieth week.

Reformed theology. Theology that emphasizes the sovereignty of God, especially with respect to the matter of salvation, that is particularly associated with a theological tradition stemming from the Reformation of the sixteenth century, and that is sometimes referred to as encompassing the doctrines of grace.

regeneration. The work of the Holy Spirit in creating a new life in the sinful person, by which act he repents and comes to believe in Christ.

repentance. Godly sorrow for one's sin and a resolve to turn from it.

resurrection of Christ. The historical event and doctrine of Christ's coming back to life on the Sunday following his crucifixion.

revelation. The making known of what is unknown; the unveiling of what is veiled.

revelation, general. Revelation that is available to all persons at all times, particularly through the physical universe.

revelation, progressive. A reference to the doctrine that later revelation is built on earlier revelation. Thus it contains truths that were not previously known.

revelation, special. God's manifestation of himself at particular times and places through particular events—for example, the exodus and Isaiah's vision in chapter 6; also, the Scriptures.

righteousness. The state of being just or morally pure, whether in one's own strength or on the basis of imputed virtue.

Sabellianism. A view deriving from the thought of Sabellius, which was essentially a Modalistic Monarchianism: God is one being, one person, who successively takes on three different forms or manifestations.

salvation. The divine act of delivering a believer from the power and curse of sin and then restoring that individual to the fellowship with God for which humans were originally intended.

salvation by grace. Salvation understood as a free gift undeserved by the recipient.

sanctification. A reference to initial salvation, then to progressively growing in Christlikeness, and ultimately to final sanctification or glorification.

Satan. The devil, a high angelic creature who rebelled against God and therefore was cast out of heaven. He became the leader of the opposition to God and the heavenly forces.

Scripture. Literally, "writing"; the canonical books of the Old and New Testaments.

Scripture, authority of. The right of the Scripture, as God's message to us, to prescribe faith and practice for Christian believers.

second death. The final state of those who die apart from the salvation offered by God. The term is found in Revelation 2:11; 20:6, 14; and 21:8.

security of the believer. The view that Christians are kept by the power of God unto final salvation. The doctrine is also referred to as "perseverance of the saints."

Serpent. The being that tempted Eve in the garden of Eden. This is generally thought of as an appearance of Satan, the term being used of him elsewhere in Scripture (Rev. 20:2).

sin, Adam's. The initial sin of Adam in the garden of Eden. Constituting the fall, it has had far-reaching consequences for the human race.

sin, mortal. Sin that causes spiritual death. In Roman Catholic theology, mortal sin extinguishes the life of God in the soul, while venial sin merely weakens that life. With mortal sin there is a deliberate and intentional determination to resist God in everything one does, but with venial sin there is a tension between the wrongful action and the person committing it.

sin, universality of. A reference to the fact that all persons are sinners and that sin is found in all cultures, races, and social classes.

sin, unpardonable. Blasphemy against the Holy Spirit, a sin that Jesus declared "eternal," as contrasted with sins that can be forgiven (Matt. 12:31–32; Mark 3:28–29; Luke 12:10). Jesus made this statement after the Pharisees had attributed to Beelzebul the work that Jesus had done by the power of the Holy Spirit.

sin, venial. In the Roman Catholic system, a sin that does not cause spiritual death. Venial sin is chosen but not with the purpose of resisting God in everything that one does.

Socinianism. A heretical system of doctrine deriving from the thought of Faustus Socinus that emphasized morality; denied the deity of Christ, predestination, divine foreknowledge, and original sin; and regarded the atonement of Christ as an example rather than as satisfaction paid to the Father.

solidarity of the human race. A reference to the idea that all humans are descended from the same ancestors and therefore are affected by the actions of Adam, particularly the first sin in the garden of Eden.

soteriology. The study of salvation.

soul, creationist view of the origin of the. The belief that God directly and specially creates each individual soul at birth; in other words, the soul is not transmitted from the parents.

soul, traducianist view of the origin of the. The belief that the soul together with the body is propagated at conception by the parents.

sovereignty of God. God's absolute rule and authority over all things.

sovereign will. A reference to the fact that God's choices and decisions are in no way constrained by factors outside himself; also, God's right to choose without being answerable to anyone or anything outside himself.

spiration. Literally, "breathing," a term often used in reference to the idea found in 2 Timothy 3:16 that the Scriptures are God-breathed.

Spirit, sealed with the. A reference to God's work of marking the believer with the Holy Spirit (Eph. 1:13).

Spirit-filled. Pertaining to believers so controlled by the Holy Spirit that all of their life is spiritual in nature.

Spirit of God. In the Old Testament, an expression frequently thought of as referring to the Holy Spirit and so identified by Peter in his quotation of Joel 2:29 (see Acts 2:18).

spiritual death. Separation from God.

spirituality. Deep commitment and likeness to God as a result of the regenerating work and sanctifying influence of the Holy Spirit.

spiritually dead. The state of unbelievers. Because of sin's effect they are unresponsive to spiritual matters (1 Cor. 2:14) and totally unable to please God (Rom. 8:7–8).

spiritual warfare. The Christian's struggle against otherworldly forces (Eph. 6:10–17).

spotless Lamb of God. Jesus the perfect sacrifice.

substitution. The act of taking the place of another.

substitutionary death. A reference to the idea that Jesus's death was in the place of the elect.

supralapsarianism. The view that the decrees of God occurred (logically) in the following order: (1) to save some humans and condemn others; (2) to create both the elect and the reprobate; (3) to permit the fall of all humans; (4) to provide salvation only for the elect.

synergism. The idea that the human works together with God in certain aspects of salvation—especially in regeneration, which is said to be a cooperative effort of divine aid and human faith.

systematic theology. The discipline that attempts to arrange the doctrinal content of Scripture in a coherent fashion.

teleological argument for God. An argument for the existence of God: the order of the universe must be the work of a supreme designer.

theism. Belief in a personal God.

theocentric. Pertaining to something that focuses on God as the highest value.

theodicy. An attempt to show that God is not the chargeable or blameworthy cause of evil.

theology proper. Study of the doctrine of God.

theophany. A visible appearance or manifestation of God, particularly in the Old Testament.

total depravity. A reference to the belief that humans begin life with all aspects of their nature corrupted by the effects of sin; thus, all their actions will lack totally pure motives. This does not mean, however, that they are as wicked as they can possibly be.

traducianism. The belief that the human soul is received by transmission from one's parents.

transcendence of God. God's otherness or separateness from the creation and the human race.

trichotomism. The view that human nature is made up of three parts, usually identified as body, soul, and spirit.

Trinity. A reference to the doctrine that God is one and yet exists eternally in three persons—Father, Son, and Holy Spirit.

type. An actual historical event or person that in some ways symbolizes or anticipates a later occurrence; particularly, an Old Testament foreshadowing of a New Testament event.

unbeliever. From the Christian perspective, a non-Christian or unregenerate person.

unconditional covenant of God. An agreement with humanity that God will fulfill simply because he has promised to do so. It contrasts with a conditional covenant, fulfillment of which is dependent on some action or response by humans.

unconditional election. A reference to the Calvinistic view that God's choice of certain persons to salvation is not dependent on any foreseen virtue or faith on their part.

union with Christ. A basic dimension of the doctrine of salvation: by being identified with Christ in his atoning death as well as in his resurrection power, believers are credited with his righteousness and share in his holiness.

Unitarianism. Belief in God as one person alone.

universalism. The unbiblical belief that in the end all humans will be saved and restored to God.

unrighteous. Those who have not been justified and forgiven.

unsaved. Those who are still in their sins and therefore separated from God.

verbal inspiration. A reference to the doctrine that the Holy Spirit so guided the writers of Scripture that even their choice of individual words conformed to God's intention.

virgin birth. A reference to the teaching that the conception of Jesus took place by a miraculous work of the Holy Spirit without Mary's having had any sexual relationship with a male.

Word of God. The message that came from God. New Testament writers and Jesus refer to the Old Testament as the Word of God (see John 10:35). The Bible in its entirety is today spoken of as the Word of God.

work of Christ. The ministry of Christ, particularly his redemptive life and death.

worldview. A broad conceptual synthesis that forms one's perspective on the whole of reality.

worship. Offering of homage, honor, and praise to God.

wrath of God. God's opposition to and hatred of evil, together with his intention to punish it.

Yahweh. Transliteration of the major Hebrew name for God.

General Bibliography

Primary Systematic Theologies

Bancroft, Emery H. *Christian Theology: Systematic and Biblical*. 2nd ed. Grand Rapids, MI: Zondervan, 1976.

Berkhof, Louis. *Systematic Theology*. 4th ed. Grand Rapids, MI: Eerdmans, 1939.

Buswell, James Oliver, Jr. *A Systematic Theology of the Christian Religion*. 2 vols. Grand Rapids, MI: Zondervan, 1962–1963.

Culver, Robert Duncan. *Systematic Theology: Biblical and Historical*. Fearn, Ross-shire, Scotland: Mentor, 2005.

Dabney, Robert Lewis. *Systematic Theology*. 1871. Reprint, Edinburgh: Banner of Truth, 1985.

Erickson, Millard J. *Christian Theology*. Grand Rapids, MI: Baker, 1986.

Grudem, Wayne. *Systematic Theology: An Introduction to Biblical Doctrine*. Grand Rapids, MI: Zondervan, 1994.

Hodge, Charles. *Systematic Theology*. 3 vols. 1871–1873. Reprint, Grand Rapids, MI: Eerdmans, 1975.

Lewis, Gordon R., and Bruce A. Demarest. *Integrative Theology*. 3 vols. Grand Rapids, MI: Zondervan, 1987–1994.

Reymond, Robert L. *A New Systematic Theology of the Christian Faith*. Nashville: Thomas Nelson, 1998.

Shedd, William G. T. *Dogmatic Theology*. 3 vols. 1889. Reprint, Minneapolis: Klock & Klock, 1979.

Strong, August Hopkins. *Systematic Theology: A Compendium Designed for the Use of Theological Students*. Rev. ed. New York: Revell, 1907.

Swindoll, Charles R., and Roy B. Zuck, eds. *Understanding Christian Theology*. Nashville: Thomas Nelson, 2003.

Thiessen, Henry Clarence. *Introductory Lectures in Systematic Theology*. Grand Rapids, MI: Eerdmans, 1949.

Turretin, Francis. *Institutes of Elenctic Theology*. 3 vols. Edited by James T. Dennison Jr. Translated by George Musgrove Giger. 1679–1685. Reprint, Phillipsburg, NJ: P&R, 1992–1997.

Biblical Theologies

Whole Canon

Kaiser, Walter C., Jr. *Toward an Exegetical Theology: Biblical Exegesis for Preaching and Teaching*. Grand Rapids, MI: Baker, 1981.

Schreiner, Thomas R. *The King in His Beauty: A Biblical Theology of the Old and New Testaments*. Grand Rapids, MI: Baker Academic, 2013.

Vos, Geerhardus. *Biblical Theology: Old and New Testaments*. Grand Rapids, MI: Eerdmans, 1948.

Old Testament

Kaiser, Walter C., Jr. *Toward an Old Testament Theology*. Grand Rapids, MI: Zondervan, 1978.

Merrill, Eugene H. *Everlasting Dominion: A Theology of the Old Testament*. Nashville: Broadman & Holman, 2006.

Payne, J. Barton. *The Theology of the Older Testament*. Grand Rapids, MI: Zondervan, 1962.

Zuck, Roy B., ed. *A Biblical Theology of the Old Testament*. Chicago: Moody Press, 1991.

New Testament

Guthrie, Donald. *New Testament Theology*. Downers Grove, IL: InterVarsity Press, 1981.

Ladd, George Eldon. *A Theology of the New Testament*. 2nd ed. Grand Rapids, MI: Eerdmans, 1993.

Schreiner, Thomas R. *New Testament Theology: Magnifying God in Christ*. Grand Rapids, MI: Baker Academic, 2008.

Zuck, Roy B., ed. *A Biblical Theology of the New Testament*. Chicago: Moody Press, 1994.

Histories of Doctrine

Allison, Gregg R. *Historical Theology: An Introduction to Christian Doctrine*. Grand Rapids, MI: Zondervan, 2011.

Berkhof, Louis. *The History of Christian Doctrines*. 1937. Reprint, Grand Rapids, MI: Baker, 1975.

Bray, Gerald. *God Has Spoken: A History of Christian Theology*. Wheaton, IL: Crossway, 2014.

González, Justo L. *A History of Christian Thought*. Rev. ed. 3 vols. Nashville: Abingdon, 1987.

Hannah, John D. *Our Legacy: The History of Christian Doctrine*. Colorado Springs: NavPress, 2001.

Heine, Ronald E. *Classical Christian Doctrine: Introducing the Essentials of the Ancient Faith*. Grand Rapids, MI: Baker Academic, 2013.

Kelly, J. N. D. *Early Christian Doctrines*. 5th ed. London: Continuum, 2000.

Pelikan, Jaroslav. *The Christian Tradition: A History of the Development of Doctrine*. 5 vols. Chicago: University of Chicago Press, 1971–1989.

Schaff, Philip. *The Creeds of Christendom*. 3 vols. New York: Harper & Brothers, 1877.

Shedd, William G. T. *A History of Christian Doctrine*. 2 vols. New York: Charles Scribner, 1863.

Handbooks of Theology

Boice, James Montgomery. *Foundations of the Christian Faith: A Comprehensive and Readable Theology*. Rev. ed. Downers Grove, IL: InterVarsity Press, 1986.

Chafer, Lewis Sperry. *Major Bible Themes: 52 Vital Doctrines of the Scripture Simplified and Explained*. Revised by John F. Walvoord. Grand Rapids, MI: Zondervan, 1974.

Enns, Paul. *The Moody Handbook of Theology*. Chicago: Moody Press, 1989.

Evans, William. *The Great Doctrines of the Bible*. Revised by S. Maxwell Coder. Chicago: Moody Press, 1974.

Lightner, Robert P. *Handbook of Evangelical Theology: A Historical, Biblical, and Contemporary Survey and Review*. Grand Rapids, MI: Kregel, 1995.

Milne, Bruce. *Know the Truth: A Handbook of Christian Belief*. 3rd ed. Downers Grove, IL: InterVarsity Press, 2009.

Packer. J. I. *Concise Theology: A Guide to Historic Christian Beliefs*. Wheaton, IL: Tyndale, 1993.

Watson, Thomas. *A Body of Divinity*. 1692. Reprint, Edinburgh: Banner of Truth, 1965.

Theological Dictionaries

Bercot, David W., ed. *A Dictionary of Early Christian Beliefs: A Reference Guide to More Than 700 Topics Discussed by the Early Church Fathers*. Peabody, MA: Hendrickson, 1998.

Cairns, Alan. *Dictionary of Theological Terms: A Ready Reference of over 800 Theological and Doctrinal Terms*. 3rd ed. Greenville, SC: Ambassador-Emerald International, 2002.

Elwell, Walter A., ed. *Evangelical Dictionary of Theology*. 2nd ed. Grand Rapids, MI: Baker, 2001.

Erickson, Millard J. *The Concise Dictionary of Christian Theology*. Rev. ed. Wheaton, IL: Crossway, 2001.

Holloman, Henry W. *Kregel Dictionary of the Bible and Theology: Over 500 Key Theological Words and Concepts Defined and Cross-Referenced*. Grand Rapids, MI: Kregel Academic & Professional, 2005.

Huey, F. B., Jr., and Bruce Corley, eds. *A Student's Dictionary for Biblical and Theological Studies*. Grand Rapids, MI: Zondervan, 1983.

Other Theologies

Akin, Daniel L., ed. *A Theology for the Church*. Nashville: B&H Academic, 2007.

Ames, William. *The Marrow of Theology*. Translated and edited by John D. Eusden. 1629. Reprint, Grand Rapids, MI: Baker, 1997.

Boyce, James P. *Abstract of Systematic Theology*. 1887. Reprint, Hanford, CA: den Dulk Christian Foundation, n.d.

Chafer, Lewis Sperry. *Systematic Theology*. Edited by John F. Walvoord. 4 vols. Grand Rapids, MI: Kregel, 1993.

Dagg, J. L. *Manual of Theology*. 1857. Reprint, Harrisonburg, VA: Sprinkle, 2009.

Dick, John. *Lectures on Theology*. Cincinnati, OH: Applegate, 1856.

Frame, John M. *Systematic Theology: Introduction to Christian Belief*. Phillipsburg, NJ: P&R, 2013.

Gill, John. *A Body of Doctrinal Divinity*. 1769. Reprint, Paris, AR: Baptist Standard Bearer, 1984.

Kuyper, Abraham. *Encyclopedia of Sacred Theology: Its Principles*. New York: C. Scribner's Sons, 1898.

McCune, Rolland. *A Systematic Theology of Biblical Christianity*. 3 vols. Allen Park, MI: Detroit Baptist Theological Seminary, 2009–2010.

Ussher, James. *A Body of Divinity, or, The Sum and Substance of Christian Religion*. 3rd ed. London: Thomas Downes and George Badger, 1649.

About the General Editors

John MacArthur, DD, LittD

Dr. John MacArthur is senior pastor of Grace Community Church in Sun Valley, California (1969–present), and president of the Master's University and Seminary, as well as an author, conference speaker, and featured teacher with the Grace to You media ministry. In 1985, he became president of the Master's College (formerly Los Angeles Baptist College), now an accredited, four-year liberal arts Christian university in Santa Clarita, California. In 1986, John founded the Master's Seminary, a graduate school dedicated to training men for full-time pastoral roles and missionary work.

Since completing his first best-selling book, *The Gospel according to Jesus*, in 1988, Dr. MacArthur has written nearly four hundred books and study guides, including *Ashamed of the Gospel*, *The Jesus You Can't Ignore*, *The Murder of Jesus*, *One Perfect Life*, *Our Sufficiency in Christ*, *Slave*, *Strange Fire*, *A Tale of Two Sons*, *The Truth War*, and *Twelve Ordinary Men*. John's titles have been translated into more than two dozen languages. The *MacArthur Study Bible*, the cornerstone resource of his ministry, is available in Arabic, Chinese, English (ESV, NASB, NIV, and NKJV), French, German, Italian, Portuguese, Russian, and Spanish. The thirty-three-volume *MacArthur New Testament Commentary* series was completed in 2015.

If you wish to know more about Dr. MacArthur's ministry, consult Iain H. Murray, *John MacArthur: Servant of the Word and Flock* (Edinburgh: Banner of Truth, 2011), and *The Master's Seminary Journal* 22, no.1 (2011), a festschrift in honor of Dr. John MacArthur.

Richard Mayhue, ThD

From 1980 to 1984, Dr. Richard Mayhue was a member of the pastoral staff at Grace Community Church, where he served as an associate to Dr. MacArthur in a teaching ministry and as director for the well-known Shepherds' Conference. From 1984 to 1989, he pastored the historic Grace Brethren Church of Long Beach, California. Dr. Mayhue joined the faculty of the Master's Seminary in 1989 and was appointed dean of the seminary the following year (1990–2014). Dr. Mayhue also served as provost of the Master's College from 2000 to 2008. He has authored, contributed to, or edited over thirty books, including *1 & 2 Thessalonians*, *Bible Boot Camp*, *Christ's Prophetic Plans*, *The Healing Promise*, *How to Interpret the Bible for Yourself*,

Practicing Proverbs, Seeking God, Unmasking Satan, and *What Would Jesus Say about Your Church?,* as well as numerous journal articles.

In 2016, Dr. Mayhue completed over forty years in pastoral and seminary ministry and retired as executive vice president, dean, and research professor of theology emeritus at the Master's Seminary. If you wish to know more about Dr. Mayhue's ministry, see *The Master's Seminary Journal* 25, no. 2 (2014), a tribute to Dr. Richard Mayhue, and consult his personal website, RichardMayhue.net.

Final Hymn of Reflection

Be Thou My Vision

Be Thou my Vision, O Lord of my heart;
Naught be all else to me, save that Thou art—
Thou my best thought, by day or by night,
Waking or sleeping, Thy presence my light.

Be Thou my Wisdom, and Thou my true Word;
I ever with Thee and Thou with me, Lord;
Thou my great Father, I Thy true son,
Thou in me dwelling, and I with Thee one.

Riches I heed not, nor man's empty praise,
Thou mine inheritance, now and always;
Thou and Thou only, first in my heart,
High King of heaven, my Treasure Thou art.

High King of heaven, my victory won,
May I reach heaven's joys, O bright heaven's Sun!
Heart of my own heart, whatever befall,
Still be my Vision, O Ruler of all.

~ancient Irish hymn
translated by Mary E. Byrne (1880–1931)
versified by Eleanor H. Hull (1860–1935)

General Index

Scripture Index